9781644134559

I0824616

MISSALE VETUSTUM (1962)

"One with herself inwardly..."

Peter Seewald: "The reauthorization of the 1962 Missal is often interpreted primarily as a concession to the Society of Saint Pius X."

Pope Emeritus Benedict XVI: "That is just absolutely false! **It was important for me that the Church is one with herself inwardly, with her own past;** that what was previously holy to her is not somehow wrong now."

— *Pope Benedict XVI "In His Own Words"* (2016)

"Continuity with the Church..."

(2003) *Josef Cardinal Ratzinger:* "I think it's important to [...] **demonstrate the continuity of the Church.** We are today not another Church as 500 years ago; it's always the same Church. And what is at one time holy for the Church is always holy for the Church, and is not in another time an impossible thing."

"Holiest & Highest Possession..."

Josef Cardinal Ratzinger: "A community is calling its very being into question when it suddenly declares that what until now was **its holiest and highest possession** is strictly forbidden and when it makes the longing for it seem downright indecent. Can it be trusted any more about anything else? Won't it proscribe tomorrow what it prescribes today?"

— Peter Seewald • *"Salt of the Earth"* (1996)

HE WHO DOES GOD'S WORK DOES NOT DO SO IN VAIN.

Saint Edmund Campion MISSAL

FOR THE TRADITIONAL LATIN MASS

THIS THIRD EDITION of the *Saint Edmund Campion Missal* contains everything needed to assist at Sundays and Holy Days in the Classical Roman Rite (*Missale Vetustum*), which Pope Benedict XVI called the "Extraordinary Form." It also contains the *ad libitum* prefaces (added by Pope Francis on 2/22/2020) with elegant new English translations. For the first time in history, the ancient Offertory and Communion verses have been included. These verses form an important part of our patrimony and were praised by Pope Pius XII. No effort has been spared to make this new edition slim and convenient for the faithful, both young and old. The vernacular fonts are quite large, yet space was still found for the beautiful artwork and color images of the priest from the first edition, including a brand new alphabet of initial letters. Copious explanations (printed in an unobtrusive font), manuscript evidence, and extraordinary hymns—in both Latin and English—were included. In particular, exhaustive comparisons between the Holy Weeks (1950 + 1962) will be appreciated. In addition to the 1962 version of Holy Week, the full 1950 version is also provided, translated by Monsignor Knox. Permission to use the 1950 version was first given by the Vatican in 2018. As of 16 July 2021, this permission may be sought from the local ordinary.

MASS ORDINARY • Two versions are provided. **Version 1** is by Father Lasance, presented "simply" (no images, no artwork, no commentary) for those already familiar with the *Missale Vetustum*. **Version 2** uses a rare translation by Monsignor Ronald Knox, with IMPRIMATUR (11/24/1950) from the Roman Catholic Archdiocese of Westminster. Pictures of the priest, commentary, sacred artwork, and ancient manuscripts (reproduced in full color) adorn this version. According to Archbishop Fulton J. Sheen, the Bible translation by Monsignor Knox is greater than any other. ✠

Third Edition (*Sophia Institute Press*, 2022)

NOMENCLATURE • Father Fortescue has written: "Like all other liturgical functions, like offices and ranks in the Church, indeed like everything else in the world, the religious service that we call the Mass existed long before it had a special technical name." It seems useful to list some of the names, although each has its own advantages and disadvantages: *1962 Missal; Traditional Latin Mass; Missale Vetustum; Tridentine Mass; Usus Antiquior; Mass of the Ages; Missal of Pius V; Missale Antiquius; Ordo Antiquus; Missale Pristinum; Classical Roman Rite; Extraordinary Form.*

ABBREVIATIONS • For the last 1,400 years, Catholics have used abbreviations in their religious books for a variety of reasons. We have adopted simple abbreviations, for two reasons: (1) to begin to familiarize Catholics with this tradition; (2) to assure gorgeous, even spacing for the eye and eliminate ugly white gaps.

This *Pontificale* (circa 1872AD) shows **"Dómine"** and **"tuam"** how they are usually abbreviated:

℟. Leváte.
Fac nos, quǽsumus Dñe, Sanctórum tuórum tibi

℟. Leváte.
Domum tuã, quǽsumus Dómine, cleménter ingrédere:

This page from the Knox *Holy Week Book* shows **"Exémplum"** abbreviated:

et Magíster: et vos debétis alter altérius laváre pedes. Exémplũ enim dedi vobis, ut, quemádmodum ego feci

and you are right, it is what I am. Why then, if I have washed your feet, I who am the Master and the Lord,

The following is from approximately 1750AD. The word **"supérnum"** is abbreviated as *supernũ*:

We have not used any extreme abbreviations. Early manuscripts, such as 121Einsie|961 (created circa 961AD) printed vowels only. On the right is Psalm 24 (INTROIT, *3rd Sunday after Pentecost*): "Ad te, Dómine, levávi ánimam … etc."

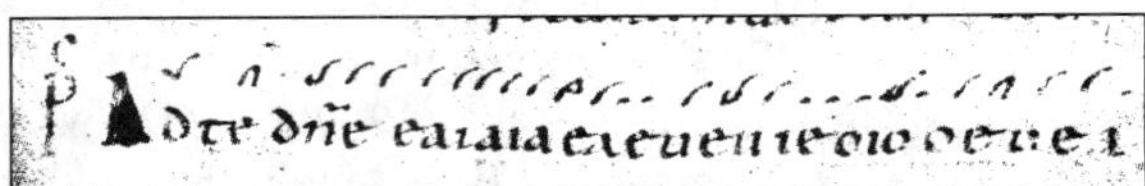

SAINT EDMUND CAMPION MISSAL, Third Edition

liturgy.sophiainstitute.com

Published with Ecclesiastical permission.

Printed in India

The translations by Monsignor Ronald Knox bear an IMPRIMATUR (24 November 1950) from the Roman Catholic Archdiocese of Westminster. They were published by *Burns Oates & Washbourne Ltd*. The passages from Sacred Scripture are similar but not identical to the famous "Knox Bible." Monsignor Knox, a brilliant theologian and polymath, was commissioned by the bishops of England and Wales to translate the entire Bible into English—both the Old and the New Testaments—during the 1940s. The splendid image of the Patron Saints of North America on page 640 was commissioned from artist Matthew Alderman (matthewalderman.com). This book was made possible by the generosity of John & Kathleen; please offer prayers for them if this book assists your spiritual life.

Foreword to the Third Edition

THIS BOOK owes much to many men, but to none more than Edmund Campion (1540-1581) and Ronald Knox (1888-1957). Though four centuries of time separate the two, they are not, speaking fundamentally and in the profoundest sense, divided from each other: for elements both natural and supernatural unite them. Both are sons of England; both possessed a brilliant mind and excelled in their academic careers; both were seekers after truth, so much so that, for the sake of conscience, they turned from bright prospects of social acclaim and worldly happiness to a course that they knew would bring them to public disgrace and earthly suffering. Both died, one might also note, in the reign of a Queen Elizabeth, even if only one of them died horribly and in disgrace at the queen's behest. Each of these men welcomed the kindly light of faith into their souls, a light that transfigured their inner lives, allowing them to see all things anew and to say with Paul: "For love of him I have lost everything, treat everything else as refuse, if I may have Christ to my credit" (Phil 3:8). They looked beyond this world, the fashion of which passes away (cf. I Cor 7:31), to a world without end and glory everlasting.

* * *

WHEN Edmund Campion was 13 years old, Mary Tudor (daughter of Henry VIII and Catherine of Aragon) who, unlike Edward VI, her half-brother and predecessor on the English throne, was a Catholic, deposed the novendial pretender Lady Jane Grey and restored her kingdom to spiritual communion with Rome. Five years later, however, Mary's half-sister Elizabeth I succeeded her and once more sundered the nation from Catholic unity, claiming headship of the Church in England like her father before her. As her long rule went on, Elizabeth acted with greater and greater severity against those of her subjects who professed that the Pope, and not she, was the visible head of the Church. Most people conformed, outwardly at least, with the reversion to Protestantism. In 1564 Edmund Campion, then 24 years of age, took his Master's degree at Oxford and was ordained deacon in an Anglican ceremony. All may have seemed well with him, but an interior struggle was underway. The truth of the Catholic claims had laid hold on him. His inner turmoil was over in 1571 when, having made his way to the English seminary at Douai, a formal reconciliation to the Church took place and he began formation for the Catholic priesthood. He was now 31. In the same year it became a crime of high treason in England to be received into the Catholic Church, or to receive another (13 Eliz c2): the punishment was death by drawing, hanging and quartering.

The year 1573 saw Campion in Rome, where he entered a religious order, the Jesuits, or Society of Jesus, then only a few decades old. Five years later he became a priest. In 1580 the Jesuits inaugurated a mission to England, and Father Campion, 40 years of age and two years ordained, received his obedience to this enterprise. In his brief time on the mission, which ended with his capture, trial and execution, Campion found himself, again like Paul, in danger from his own people, facing "danger in cities; danger in the wilderness … danger among false brethren," dealing with "toil and weariness … sleepless, hungry and thirsty" (II Cor 11:26-27). Under such conditions he and his confreres served the Good Shepherd and the scattered flock.

One would hardly expect Campion to have produced literature under such circumstances, yet flashes of his art and learning did appear. An example is the document nicknamed Campion's Brag, where he explained his aims: "Of free cost to preach the Gospel, to minister the Sacraments, to instruct the simple, to reforme sinners, to confute errors—in brief, to crie alarme spiritual against foul vice and proud ignorance, wherewith many my dear Countrymen are abused." Here too one encounters this memorable and stirring passage: "Many innocent hands are lifted up to Heaven for you daily by those English students, whose posteritie shall never die, which beyond seas, gathering virtue and sufficient knowledge for the purpose, are determined never to give you over, but either to win you Heaven, or to die upon your pikes."

There is also Campion's declaration on behalf of his order: "We have made a league—all the Jesuits in the world, whose succession and multitude must overreach all the practices of England—cheerfully to carry the cross you shall lay upon us, and never to despair your recovery, while we have a man left to enjoy your Tyburn, or to be racked with your torments, or consumed with your prisons. The expense is reckoned, the enterprise is begun; it is of God, it cannot be withstood. So the Faith was planted: so it must be restored." These are but glimpses of Campion's ability, glimpses of what he might have achieved as a man of letters: but it was the blood he was ready to pour forth, not the ink, that gave most glory to God, bringing souls to their salvation and himself to high sanctity. It was perseverance and fortitude, not style or wit, that made him worthy of the altars.

When Campion's martyrdom occurred John Donne (1572-1631) was nine years old. His life and career present a stark contrast to Campion's. Although his family was Catholic on both sides, the allure of the world and human respect proved too much for him. He defected from the faith of his fathers. Having passed a riotous youth, Donne attained a certain gravity. His anti-Catholic, and especially anti-Jesuit, tracts, such as *Pseudo-Martyr* (1610) and *Ignatius His Conclave* (1611), gained him favorable attention. In 1615 he took Anglican orders. In 1621, at the age of 49, he obtained his richest reward and highest post as Dean of Saint Paul's in London.

After Campion the massacre of Catholics continued for another hundred years. The last martyr of Tyburn was Oliver Plunkett (d. 1681), Archbishop of Armagh and Primate of All Ireland, who like Campion underwent a show trial and suffered the penalty of high treason, a victim of the Popish Plot, a false conspiracy against Charles II fabricated by Anglican clergyman Titus Oates.

* * *

RONALD KNOX, as already noted, died in the reign of Elizabeth II. He was born in that of Queen Victoria and was 12 years old when she died, the Victorian era yielding to the Edwardian. Knox's father was an Anglican bishop, first suffragan of Coventry, then ordinary of Manchester. His parentage being so, it is not surprising that he added to his scholarly pursuits and achievements an interest in religion. The Anglo-Catholic movement was burgeoning as Knox grew up, and he happily embraced it. In company with many others he conceived a desire and an ambition to nurture in England a religious life like that one might observe on the Continent. He admired such writers as Robert Hugh Benson (1871-1914), who succumbed to "Roman fever" in 1903 and whose own father was an Anglican bishop, and G.K. Chesterton (1874-1936), whom Knox, strange though it may seem, actually preceded into the Church.

In 1912 Knox received Anglican presbyteral ordination and appointment as chaplain of Trinity College, Oxford. As had been the case with Campion, one might have supposed that Knox was content: yet the seeds of spiritual trouble were soon to germinate for him as well as for others. Knox had made his pre-ordination retreat at the Anglican monastery on Caldey Island. In the following year, 1913, all but a few of this community became Catholics, which naturally caused great consternation among Anglicans generally, and Anglo-Catholics in particular. Then war broke out, that known at first as the Great War and afterwards as World War I. Knox found his interior peace shattered as friends of his, facing the prospect of death in combat, converted to Catholicism. He also found it impossible to maintain in the face of the evidence that the duties of an Anglican padre were identical to those of Catholic military chaplains.

In 1917 Knox entered the Church. He became a priest a mere two years later, ordained "on his own patrimony," a rare situation that allowed him greater freedom in ministry than was usual, but which also obliged him to support himself financially. Besides any other purpose, therefore, his writing served an important practical need. His residence before and after ordination was Saint Edmund's, Ware, which was both a seminary and a school (Cardinal Bourne had considered sending Knox to the United States): thus he both studied and taught there. The pandemic of 1918 (the "Spanish Flu") was raging when he arrived: there was illness in three-quarters of the college. Knox remained at Saint Edmund's until 1926, when he became the Catholic chaplain to undergraduates at Oxford. At Saint Edmund's he had learned the ways of the British Catholic clergy and, through weekend preaching engagements, he became acquainted with the laity too. He returned to Oxford no longer part of the Establishment but a true priest, on the fringe of the university but in the heart of the Church. In 1936 he received an ecclesiastical honor, appointment as a "domestic prelate," thus becoming Monsignor Knox (in 1951 he would rise in the ranks of *monsignori* as a "pronotory apostolic ad instar").

As his chaplaincy ended Knox turned to a task that was herculean indeed, but one for which, with his natural gifts and the talents he had nurtured, he was uniquely fitted. It was the single-handed translation of the Bible into English from the Latin Vulgate. Few then and fewer now are those who could attempt this feat, let alone achieve it. Achieve it he did, and the Catholic hierarchy of England and Wales, along with that of Scotland, duly authorized it. Another labor of Knox's love was *Enthusiasm*, a book published in 1950 after decades of research and reflection. It deals with the aberrations in Christian thought and behavior that can occur, and have occurred, when, claiming to have the Lord for their teacher (cf. Jn 6:45), proponents of private interpretation despise the authority of the Church and claimants to private revelation dismiss her governance.

A figure to whom one may compare Knox is Evelyn Underhill (1875-1941), a writer religiously engaged as he was, author of *Mysticism* (1911) and other related works. Drawn like Knox to Catholicity, she nonetheless baulked at entering the Church, not only on account of her husband's disapproval but also, it has been said, due to her own disapproval of Pope Pius X's condemnation (in 1907) of the heresy of Modernism.

* * *

SINCE THIS MISSAL draws so deeply from the fount of Knox's translations, it seems apt to say something of their nature. Steeped as he was in the authors of classical Greek and Rome, then in the later writers of the Church, distinguished as he was for both prose and verse (and not merely in English) and there being as yet no strong impulse in the Church to celebrate the sacred Liturgy in vernacular languages, Knox regarded translation differently than some do today. Now that vernacular texts often replace the original, rather than simply complementing the Latin, great contention has arisen over the best way to translate. Some favor the method known as "formal equivalence" while others opt for "dynamic equivalence." Having in mind not a replacement but a complement, Knox (following Belloc) preferred the dynamic approach, which he termed "literary," as opposed to "literal."

Since this missal provides the original Latin texts, it may freely set beside them a dynamic, or literary, English version. We may then rejoice in Knox's skillful and sensitive wording, the work of a master that is worthy to stand with the beautiful model it portrays. We do well to remember Knox's own comment: "The translator … must never be frightened of the word 'paraphrase'; it is a bogey of the half-educated."

The pygmy that stands on the shoulders of a giant may well harbor a sense of superiority should he forget or ignore his position. Making use of this book, let us remember those who have had charge of us, and preached God's word to us (cf. Heb 13:6), our forebears in faith, its champions, especially Edmund Campion and Ronald Knox. Let us join with them in prayer. Let us look to their example: and let us follow it.

Rev'd Dominic Popplewell, FSSP
In Festo Annuntiationis beatae Mariae virginis
25 March 2022

SOLEMN FEASTS

GREGORIAN CHANT HYMNS

HOLY WEEK & MORE

HEBDOMADA MAJOR

FUNERALS, WEDDINGS, AND CONFIRMATION

THE HOLY MASS

HYMNS

From the Saint Jean de Brébeuf Hymnal (2018) Used with permission.

EXPLANATIONS

ABOUT THIS MISSAL

TO CREATE a hand-missal for congregations, containing precisely what is needed ***and nothing else*** : this was our endeavor. Realizing how odious it is for the faithful (especially parents of small children) to hold excessively bulky tomes, our editorial team diligently sought to avoid a common pitfall: viz. the inclusion of items extraneous to a hand-missal. Congregations should be given everything in one place, not "bits and pieces" taken from a myriad of sources. Moreover, we have meticulously formatted each page (assuring an "evenness" for praying eyes) and purposefully constructed a "visual hierarchy" which places each feast's Gospel reading as the center-piece.

Splendid resources are available today, which—were they to be combined into one book—would produce 2,000 pages of something far too heavy to hold comfortably. For parochial choirs, we recommend the *Saint Antoine Daniel Kyriale* (2019). For parishes which sing the Divine Office, we recommend Albert Bloomfield's *Tenebrae* (2014) and *Vespers with Gregorian Chant* (2015). For congregations which participate in the ORDINARIUM MISSAE, experience shows the best method is to "pick up" the melodies by ear. For parishes seeking an authentically Catholic HYMN BOOK—one that does not mimic protestant models—the best choice is the *Saint Jean de Brébeuf Hymnal* (2018), and that resplendent hymnal contains ***three versions*** of the Stations of the Cross: (a) by Fulton J. Sheen; (b) by Josef Ratzinger; (c) by Alphonsus Liguori.

It will still be necessary, of course, for priests, musicians, and servers to seek out the normal resources. Our hand-missal will not substitute for those. At the same time, we believe this third edition—especially due to its ***copious explanations*** of the 1950 Holy Week—will be welcomed as a handy "guide to ceremonies." Where education and beauty conflict, we chose education.[1]

THREE IMPORTANT WORDS • For the *Missale Vetustum*, the Gospel reading almost always begins with the words IN ILLO TEMPORE ("at that time"). For the human mind, ***the first words*** of a sentence, paragraph, or poem are pivotal. It would not be wise—from the standpoint of typography—to have every Gospel reading begin with the same three words. Such a course of action would not help those struggling to locate the correct page; nor would it imprint upon the human mind what must be emphasized. For this reason, we have included those three words—*In illo témpore*—in the Latin, but not in the English. (There are exceptions, such as the Octave Day of Christmas.) When it comes to a priest reading the Gospel to his congregation in English, it will not be difficult to add those three words—if desired—since they are included in the Latin.

1 This explains why we chose "in line" references, rather than endnotes (dreaded by readers everywhere owing to their inconvenience). We have accented all capital letters—for the benefit of a generation rediscovering Latin after having been unjustly deprived of their birthright. Formerly, the convention for ante-penult accents was to omit them for capital letters—assuming readers would know this—but the result in our age has often been painful; e.g. a recent publication (by a worldwide organization) has each office beginning with "Apéri, [sic] Dómine, os meum"—whereas the correct pronunciation is ***áperi***, not ***apéri***. Because of the current plague of disinformation, we have attempted to cite every source. In a few cases, we have not done so (as it would have encumbered the text), but in those instances the citations are extremely well-known and will not cause great difficulty. Our inclusion of a citation does not *ipso facto* mean we consider it "definitive"—sometimes, we merely wished to document what an authority has said.

RUBRICAL NOTES • Our rubrical treatment has, by design, a certain inconsistency. When it comes to rubrics providing virtually nothing of value to the congregation—such as instructing the Deacon to stand on the left side, or instructing the Master of Ceremonies to fetch the biretta, or instructing the Altar boy to light a candle—we have omitted such items. ***Where it seemed appropriate,*** we "supplement" the rubrics with helpful details from authors like Father Fortescue; yet we normally include the original Latin, as well. When it comes to the 1950 version of Holy Week, we provide abundant rubrical notes, since many are currently unfamiliar with those rites. We strongly believe in "padding" liturgical books; i.e. expanding or limiting the amount of rubrical notes depending upon how unfamiliar (or how important) certain ceremonies are.

ENGLISH TRANSLATIONS • Generally speaking, our hand-missal uses translations by Father Francis Xavier Lasance (d. 1946), who followed the normal procedure of his day: original translations for orations; Douay-Rheims-Challoner (DRCH) for the Gospels; traditional version of the *Ordo Missae*. Obviously, we could not use Father Lasance for liturgical items added after his death, such as the feast of the Assumption (1950) or the concluding prayers of Good Friday (1955). The translations by Lasance are quite literal, which some Catholics appreciate. On the other hand, the English language changes over the course of the centuries, and a good example is Father Lasance's use of *heap* : "We heap Thine altars with gifts, O Lord, celebrating...etc." Such usage was common in olden times; e.g. Sir William Kirkham Blount: "to expiate the sins of men and heap upon them his Grace." In an effort to be literal, Father Lasance sometimes allowed phrases not particularly beautiful: e.g. "Before I formed thee in the bowels of thy mother, I knew thee..." We consider a literal translation preferable to the colloquial and "trendy" translations popular after Vatican II.

TREASURE FROM 1950 • We provide two versions of Holy Week: 1950 and 1962. The 1950 translation is by Monsignor Ronald Knox,[2] with IMPRIMATUR (24 November 1950) by the Archdiocese of Westminster. We believe our third edition is justified ***if for no other reason*** than making this magnificent translation better known. Consider a few excepts from the Good Friday "Reproaches" as translated by Knox:

℣. Through the sea I opened a passage for thee, and should a lance open my side?

℣. With water from the rock thy sore need I met; thou mine with vinegar and gall.

℣. A royal sceptre my gift was to thee; thine to me, a crown of thorns.

℣. High above earth I exalted thee; and thou me, but gibbeted on a Cross.

ARCHBISHOP SHEEN • Fulton J. Sheen, in his famous *Life of Christ* (1958), declared as follows: "Of the many translations of Scripture, we have chosen the Knox translation as the best, using the Rheims Douay version only in a very few texts."

2 The reader will notice that Monsignor Knox—like Father Fortescue and many others—does not capitalize pronouns referring to God. As a matter of principle, we never modify the originals; and we hope the charitable reader will accept this choice.

ASSIGNING DATES TO MANUSCRIPTS

CHARLEMAGNE began his rule in 768AD and continued expanding his empire until his death in 814AD. His rule—and that of his family—brought great stability. As a consequence of his vast conquests, he was recognized as the first (western) emperor to rule since the fall of the Roman Empire three centuries earlier. Charlemagne was a great promoter of learning, and he summoned to his court important scholars such as PAUL THE DEACON (from Monte Cassino), ALCUIN OF YORK (from England), and ABBAT EINHARD (from the German-speaking section of the Frankish Kingdom). Charlemagne attempted to learn how to write—even practicing the formation of letters in his bed in old age—but never succeeded, and whether he could read is not known. Regardless, under Charlemagne great advances were made in literacy, including "Carolingian minuscule."

STABILITY IS KEY • It is incorrect to assert—as some irresponsible scholars have—that the Carolingian era "created" or "invented" the repertoire of plainsong. A more accurate statement is that, ***owing to the stability*** Charlemagne and his family provided, manuscripts produced in the Carolingian era had a better chance to survive. Incidentally, this is not just the case with liturgical manuscripts; the Carolingian era witnessed a movement to write down (i.e. preserve) knowledge, whether medicinal, botanical, geographical, astronomical, theological, liturgical, etc. One of the wonders of the world is the way that Catholic musicians carefully preserved thousands of ancient chants by means of an adiastematic notation which had no value whatsoever unless the scribe (or singer) already had the melody fully memorized.

WHAT WE CANNOT KNOW • A serious error (made by more than one scholar) is to assume that if a particular manuscript is found in a particular location, that means it was created there a millennium earlier. In reality, we may never know where many liturgical manuscripts originated. ***Many things might occur*** over a millennium: wars take place; cities are destroyed; buildings catch fire; old monasteries die out; new monasteries arise; and so forth. Scholars, of course, will never stop producing conjecture as to where a particular manuscript may have been created. Sometimes scholars examine "local feasts," basing a hypothesis on those. Others attempt to identify which king might be depicted in the illustrations, and then—based on that—guess whether the manuscript may have been created during his reign. A sensible person recognizes the limitations of such speculation. Moreover, the difficulties are multiplied when we realize many manuscripts consist of several books which were combined at a later date. Furthermore, manuscripts from this era could require decades (and several lifetimes) to complete.

WHAT WE CAN INDEED KNOW • The reason ancient Catholic manuscripts possess such tremendous value is because they ***correspond to one another***. Even today, scholars cannot begin to explain the astonishing correlation between manuscripts, and all this was done in an age before telephones, radio, automobiles, trains, or airplanes. When it comes to the antiquity of manuscripts—that is to say, in what century they were created—scholars have attained a fair amount of success thanks to the science of PALEOGRAPHY, which can assign a date (with reasonable certitude) based on handwriting comparison.

APPROXIMATE DATES • For the aforementioned reasons, it is not possible—and may never be possible—to know the provenance of a manuscript, or exact date it was created. The dates we have assigned are therefore ***approximations only***.

Manuscripts Cited

The system of nomenclature for ancient liturgical manuscripts is thorny. Scholars often refer to them according to the number assigned by the library in which they are currently kept and/or by the town name of the monastery with which they are associated. Problems begin when the library assigns a new number, or when the manuscript is moved to a different library, or when scholars reach a different conclusion about where the MS may have come from. Manuscripts are often "compilations" containing different books—*sometimes from different centuries!*—bound together at a later date. It is grave error to assume ***ipso facto*** that a particular MS was created near the place where it currently resides; e.g. a book from Ireland may end up in a monastery in Italy.

We have included various names by which these MSS are designated—although many are nothing more than abbreviations of library names—in an effort to demystify the nomenclature.

Please Note: Manuscripts cited in the **color section** (pages 201-280) are not included below, but we trust they are self-explanatory. For assistance, please contact the publisher.

Blandin10144|768 • Approximately 768AD — This is one of the manuscripts included in René-Jean Hesbert's famous *Antiphonale Missarum Sextuplex* (1967). It is currently kept in Brussels, at the Royal Library of Belgium. It has been associated with the abbey of Mont-Blandin, where it was kept at least until 1566AD. For a long time, it was believed this MS had disappeared during the total destruction of the abbey in 1578AD. *Other names include:* Brussels 10127-10144 ✠ Bibliothèque royale de Belgique Ms. 10127-10144 ✠ Codex lat 10127-10144 ✠ L'Antiphonaire Du Mont-Blandin ✠ Mont Blandin Antiphonal.

12050corbie|853 • Approximately 853AD — It is associated with Corbie Abbey, which was a Benedictine monastery (about 23 minutes east of Amiens) dedicated to Saint Peter and founded by Balthild, the widow of Clovis II. It is one of the manuscripts included in René-Jean Hesbert's *Antiphonale Missarum Sextuplex* (1967). Some people believe Rodradus (a priest) copied this manuscript for Bishop Hilmerad of Amiens, who ordained him to the priesthood. *Other names include:* Corbiensis ✠ Paris, Bibliotheque Nationale, lat. 12050 ✠ Antiphonal of Corbie ✠ Saint-Pierre de Corbie.

17436compiegne|862 • Approximately 862AD — Compiègne is about 500 miles north of Albi, France, and approximately 55 miles north of Paris. It is one of the manuscripts included in René-Jean Hesbert's *Antiphonale Missarum Sextuplex* (1967). "It is written in an early, non-diastematic type of Aquitanian neumes, which may be compared with the later, diastematic type shown in Albi|1047" {Apel p123}. *Other names include:* MsLat17436 ✠ Antiphonary of Charles the Bald ✠ Antiphonal of Compiègne ✠ Paris, BibL nat lat. 17436.

Bamberg6lit|905 • Approximately 905AD — The city of Bamberg is just north of Nuremberg. *Other names include:* Bamberg, Staatsbibliothek Lit. 6 ✠ Bamberg 6.

239Laon|927 • Approximately 927AD — Considered an excellent example of the Metz or Lorraine notation; some scholars also speak of "Laon" notation {Hiley p361}. Rebecca Maloy calls this "La 239." *Other names include:* F-LA:Ms0239 ✠ Graduel de Laon Ms 239.

381sanGall|928 • Approximately 928AD — *Saint Gall Manuscript 381* • This manuscript is easy to identify, because authors normally include the number "381." For example, Anton Stingl calls this SG381. (This holds true for most of the Saint Gall books.) Dr. Peter Wagner wrote in 1907: "This manuscript contains, among other things, the complete Introit and Communion verses of the liturgical year, expressed in neums; some years ago, I copied in full this precious memorial."

342sanGall|933 • Approximately 933AD — Considered "the earliest complete extant gradual of Saint Gall." *Other names include:* F-AN:Ms0091 ✠ CH-SGs: Cod 0342 ✠ Cod. Sang. 342.

91angers|944 • Approximately 944AD — Dom Jausions copied this gradual and the copy is at Solesmes; indeed, the Bibliothèque d'Angers was one of the first libraries Dom Jausions went to when he and and Dom Pothier began copying manuscripts. *Other names include:* F-AN:Ms0091.

47chartres|957 • Approximately 957AD — Speaking about sequences, David Hiley mentions this MS: "In some early sources the melodies alone are copied, without texts, for example in Chartres, Bibliothèque Municipale 47." Rebecca Maloy calls this "Cha 47." *Other names include:* Manuscrit 47 de Chartres ✠ F-CHRm:Ms0047.40 ✠ Antiphonaire de saint Grégoire.

121einsie|961 • Approximately 961AD — The second part of this codex contains a "Libyer Ymnorum," the Sequences of Notker of Saint Gall. It may have been written in Einsiedeln itself (Switzerland), possibly for the third Abbat, Gregor the Englishman. It has the ADDITAMENTA containing "extra" Communion verses. Anton Stingl calls this manuscript "E." Rebecca Maloy calls this "Ei 121." *Other names include:* CH-E-121 ✠ Einsiedeln Codex 121; Graduale, Notkeri Sequentiæ.

Renaud|965 • Approximately 965AD — Mont-Renaud is near the city of Noyon in North France. This manuscript has the same handwriting as "British Library Egerton MS 857 Roman Gradual." *Other names include:* F-Col_part:Mont-Renaud ✠ Antiphonary of Mont Renaud.

9448prum|983 • Approximately 983AD — Sometimes called *Graduel de l'abbaye de Prüm.*

StDenisMissal|988 • Approximately 988AD — *Other names include:* Missel de Saint-Denis Ms 118 ✠ Bibliothèque nationale de France. Département des Manuscrits. Latin 9436 ✠ S. Gregorii magni liber Sacramentorum ✠ F-LA:Ms 0118 ✠ Graduel, sacramentaire, lectionnaire de Saint-Denis.

GradualDenis|1020 • Approximately 1020AD — The Basilica of Saint-Denis was a large medieval abbey church—currently it is a cathedral in the city of Saint-Denis, a northern suburb of Paris. *Other names include:* Graduel à l'usage de l'abbaye de Saint-Denis ✠ Antiphonary (Saint-Denis).

Montpellier H. 159 (1021) • Approximately 1021AD — This is the famous bi-lingual manuscript which allowed scholars to decipher the early neumes; it is considered to be the "Rosetta Stone" of Gregorian Chant. A wonderful transcription of this MS was made by Finn Egeland Hansen in 1974. *Other names include:* Tonary of Saint Bénigne of Dijon ✠ Faculty of Medicine manuscript.

123angelica|1023 • Approximately 1023AD — Gradual 123 of the Biblioteca Angelica in Rome. Anton Stingl calls this "An." Rebecca Maloy calls this "RoA 123." Associated with Bologna. *Other names include:* Graduel et Tropaire de Bologne.

Helmst|1026 • Approximately 1026AD — This MS is remarkable when it comes to the "extra" Communion verses, since it has a great variety and its condition is pristine. Anton Stingl calls this "MiW." *Other names include:* Cod. Guelf. 1008 Helmst.

9434Tours|1028 • Approximately 1028AD — Many communion antiphons in this MS appear to have a "Gloria Patri" (sometimes without neumes above), and some also contain the ancient Communion-verses—cf. the Last Sunday after Pentecost. *Other names include:* Missel de Saint-Martin de Tours ✠ Paris, Bibliothèque nationale de France lat 9434 ✠ St-Martin de Tours 9434.

382sanGall|1030 • Approximately 1030AD — Speaking of this manuscript, Dr. Wagner wrote: "Not infrequently we find the *Gloria* and *Credo* written in Greek (usually written in Latin character) ... the scribes seldom knew Greek, and so these renderings of Greek texts in Latin characters teem with mistakes of every kind." {Wagner p46}. Some authors refer to it as a "Tropary, Versicularium, and Sequentiary." *Other names include:* Le Codex 382 de la Bibliotheque de Saint-Gall.

75cambrai|1031 • Approximately 1031AD — David Hiley mentions how this manuscript contains a "Missa Græca," which is evidence of a lively interest in Greek learning, typical particularly of northern French centers in the second part of the 9th century {Hiley p528}. *Other names include:* Cambrai, Bibliothèque municipale 75.

Narbonne|1033 • Approximately 1033AD — Narbonne is Southeast of Toulouse and Albi.*Other names include:* F-Pn:MsLat00780 ✠ Paris 780 ✠ Graduel A l'usage de Narbonne ✠ Paris, Bibliothèque Nationale, lat. 780 Graduale Narbonense.

339sanGall|1039 • Approximately 1039AD — As with so many of the Saint Gall MSS, this specimen is pristine and easy to read. A very real danger (which must be guarded against) is to regard this manuscript as more "important" or more "representative" than others just because it is easy to read; numerous scholars have fallen prey to this lethal trap. Perhaps owing to how easy it is to read, it was published in the first volume of the *Paléographie musicale*. Some believe this MS was copied by a monk named Hartker. Rebecca Maloy calls this "SG 339." *Other names include:* Antiphonale missarum sancti Gregorii ✠ PalMus 1 (Solesmes, 1889) ✠ St Gall, Stiftsbibliothek 339 ✠ Cod. 339 of St. Gall ✠ Le Codex 339 de la Bibliotheque de Saint-Gall.

Yrieix|1040 • Approximately 1040AD — Saint Aredius (d. 591) is also known as SAINT YRIEIX; and Saint-Yrieix is the monastery for which it was compiled. Dom Mocquereau published it in 1889. Rebecca Maloy calls this "Pa 903." Anton Stingl calls this "Y." Willi Apel calls this "the 11th Century Gradual of Saint Yrieix." *Other names include:* Graduale, Troparium et Prosarium ad usum Sancti Aredii ✠ Graduel De Saint-Yrieix ✠ F-Pn:MsLat00903.

Albi|1047 • Approximately 1047AD — Associated with Albi, a city in Southern France, not too far from Montpellier. This manuscript may have been copied at St. Michel-de-Gaillac. The notation and letters are virtually identical to 4951STEVEN|1128. Anton Stingl calls this "A." Rebecca Maloy calls this "Pa 776." *Other names include:* F-Pn776 ✠ F-Pnm lat. 776 ✠ Graduale Albiense.

376sanGall|1052 • Approximately 1052AD — *Saint Gall Manuscript 376* • Like so many manuscripts at the library of Saint Gall, this manuscript is incredibly clean, beautiful, and legible. *Other names include:* St Gall, Stiftsbibliothek 376 ✠ Sankt-Gallen, Stiftsbibliothek 376.

857noyon|1057 • Approximately 1057AD — A truly beautiful manuscript whose current location is the British Library in London. "Its contents are the same as in St. Gall 339, but without the Offertory verses" {Apel p122}. *Other names include:* Egerton 857.

Rome|1071 • Approximately 933AD — This Gradual was produced in 1071AD by the archpresbyter of the Church of Santa Cecilia in Trastevere; i.e. it is a manuscript written *for and at* the Basilica Santa Cecilia. "Trastevere" refers to the city of Rome. Rebecca Maloy calls this "Bod 74." *Other names include:* CB 74 ✠ Bibliotheca Bodmeriana Codex 74 ✠ Saint Cecilia Gradual ✠ CH-Cobodmer:C0074 ✠ Bibliotheca Bodmeriana C 74 ✠ Das Graduale von Santa Cecilia in Trastevere ✠ Cod. Bodmer 74.

StMaur|1079 • Approximately 1079AD — This is a particularly beautiful manuscript which has been associated with Abbaye Saint-Maur-des-Fossés, located 7.3 miles from the center of Paris. It is currently held at the Bibliothèque nationale de France. *Other names include:* Ms Latin 12584.

5319vaticanus|1105 • Approximately 1033AD — This is considered to be one of the four sources of Old Roman Chant. "The notation is an example of the Beneventan neumes" {Apel p123}. Rebecca Maloy calls this "Vat 5319." *Other names include:* Manuscript-Vat.lat.5319 ✠ Vaticanus latinus 5319 ✠ Rome, Vatican Library, lat. 5319 ✠ Rome, Biblioteca Apostolica Vaticana, Vat. lat. 5319.

4951steven|1128 • Approximately 1128AD — Associated with Saint Stephen ("Étienne") of Toulouse. Toulouse is very close to Albi; and the notation and letters in this MS are virtually identical to ALBI|1047. Rebecca Maloy calls this "Lo 4951." Stanbrook Abbey calls this "Harleian No. 4951." *Other names include:* Gradual of Saint-Etienne of Toulouse ✠ Harley 4951.

Thomas391|1291 • Approximately 1291AD — It was formerly known as "371" but currently as "391." Regarding its "extra" Communion verses, Dr. Peter Wagner wrote: "As with the other chants, so with the Communion: the original form was preserved longest in Germany. The library of the church of S. Thomas at Leipzig contains a MS from the 1200s which gives the Communion-verses for all the days of the Church's year. At that time they were still sung in some parts of Germany, like the Introit-verses and those of the Offertory." *Other names include:* Codex 371 of the St. Thomas Archives, Leipzig ✠ S. Thomas at Leipzig 371 ✠ Leipzig 371 or Leipzig 391 ✠ Cantus: D-LEu : Ms Thomas 391.

OFFERTORY VERSES

READERS WILL NOTICE HOW this third edition of the *Campion Missal* contains the ancient Offertory verses. These "extra" verses—unlike the Communion verses—are relatively stable; i.e. all the ancient manuscripts generally contain the same texts and melodies. (This is not to say that no variation whatsoever exists, especially vis-à-vis how many verses are included in the ancient sources.) These ancient verses are part of the patrimony of the Roman Rite, yet optional according to the 1962 rubrics; therefore, we print these "extra" verses in italics. It goes without saying that modern feasts—such as the feast of *Christ the King*, composed in 1925—do not have these ancient Offertory verses.

POPE PIUS XII • Under Pope Pius XII, the Sacred Congregation of Rites issued *De Musica Sacra* (3 September 1958), which says in paragraph 27(b):

27b Following the Offertory antiphon, it is permitted to sing in the ancient Gregorian modes the verses which were once sung after the antiphon. If the Offertory antiphon is taken from a psalm, **the other verses** (of the same psalm) **may be sung.** In such cases, the antiphon may be repeated after every one or two verses of the psalm and, when the Offertory of the Mass is completed, the psalm should be concluded with the *Gloria Patri* and the antiphon repeated. If the antiphon is not taken from a psalm, any psalm suited to the feast may be used.

27b Post antiphonã ad Offertoriũ canere licet antiquos gregorianos modulos illorũ versuũ, qui olĩ post antiphonã decantabantur. Si vero antiphona ad Offertoriũ a quodã psalmo desumpta sit, licet alios eiusdem psalmi versus decantare; quo in casu, post singulos vel binos versus psalmi, repeti potest antiphona, et, Offertorio expleto, psalmus clauditur cum *Glõ Pã*, et repetitur antiphona. Si vero antiphona e psalmo non sit desumpta, seligi potest alius psalmus solemnitati congruens.

THEY BEGIN TO VANISH • Willi Apel has written: "It was not until the 12th century that the Offertories lost their verses—the only exception being the *Missa Pro Defunctis*, which to the present day has retained one verse: *Hóstias et preces*." Father Fortescue, citing *Rationale IV* §26, reminds us that Bishop Durandus (d. 1296AD) "notes with disapproval that in his time the verses of the psalm are left out." Dr. Peter Wagner gives an excellent summary {Wagner p98} vis-à-vis when the "extra" verses began to vanish:

> There are manuscripts as early as circa 1050AD which do not mark the Offertory-verses: from this we must conclude that this was when the offering of the people fell into disuse. The Offertory-verses are wanting in most manuscripts after the 1100s, but they were still sung in German Churches during the 1200s, on some feasts even in the 1400s and 1500s, especially on Christmas day. (Two manuscripts from the 1200s—in the City Library of Trier—still have all the verses.) Durandus of Mende considers the reason for the omission of the verses to be the need of greater brevity, and the endeavor to make both clergy and people devote themselves more to the prayers. **Ralph of Tongres gives the important information that, since their omission, the Offertory itself was performed more slowly.** [*We have placed this last sentence in bold, owing to its importance.*]

It will be noticed that Dr. Wagner subscribes to a belief—very common in his day—which posits that the Offertory-verses disappeared when congregations ceased bringing "gifts" to the Altar. Some believe this procession may have included other items, such as alms for the poor and even animals (in days which pre-dated standard currency). If there ever was such a procession, very little is known about it; cf. Adrian Fortescue's *A Study of the Roman Liturgy* (London: Longmans and Green, 1912) pages 299-300.

UNHAPPY COINCIDENCE • The disappearance of the "extra" verses coincides (roughly speaking) with the invention of "staff notation"—i.e. the ability to notate pitches with precision. Its predecessor, the old "adiastematic" notation, was only useful to those who already knew the melody by heart. As a result, we cannot know how certain Offertory-verses sounded—because the "extra" verses were dying out just as staff notation was becoming popular. An example would be the Offertory for the feast of Saint Thomas (21 December): IN OMNEM TERRAM. Typical sources—such as Montpellier H. 159—contain only the first verse: *Caeli enárrant glóriam* (Ps 18:2). But there are two additional verses found in "heightened neume" manuscripts such as STDENISMISSAL|988 (folio 110r), ALBI|1047 (folio 9r), 4951STEVEN|1128 (folio 126r), and YRIEIX|1040 (folio 28r). The "heightened neume" manuscripts—while certainly more useful than fully adiastematic manuscripts (a.k.a. "in campo aperto")—are insufficient to decipher the exact pitches.

NOTABLE CHARACTERISTICS • Below are important things to know vis-à-vis these "extra" Offertory verses:

(1) Very Ancient • The early manuscripts meticulously preserve these "extra" verses, and this is quite remarkable since many are of astonishing length, e.g. *Precátus est Móyses* on the 12th Sunday after Pentecost. That means they take up enormous amounts of space in the ancient manuscripts.

(2) Intricacy & Text Painting • The "extra" verses are of stupendous difficulty, with difficult leaps and a wide tessitura. Moreover, their emphasis on "text painting" is stark; e.g. the way Moses is made to "stutter" when he prays; cf. the words *orávit Móyses Dóminum* on the 18th Sunday after Pentecost.

(3) Random Repeats • These "extra" verses exhibit special traits, such as erratically repeating sections {Wagner p95}. For example, examine the words *ut vídeat bona* on the 21st Sunday after Pentecost, or the words *fecit Sálomon solemnitátem in témpore illo* on the feast of 9 November. Sometimes when there is a "repeat" the musical notes are identical—but sometimes the musical notes are completely different; e.g. the famous *Jubiláte Deo* offertories which occur on the 1st and 2nd Sundays after Epiphany. [*Both begin with the same two words—"Jubiláte Deo"—but they are completely different.*]

(4) Structure • In spite of what was stated in *De Musica Sacra* (see above), the basic structure of the Offertory is not akin to the Introit—and none that we are aware of indicate the *Glória Patri*. Dr. Peter Wagner suggests that structure of the Offertory is better compared to a Responsory. Most of the manuscripts have the "repeat" starting from the middle of the antiphon—not its beginning—but as Willi Apel notes, there are sometimes "divergent indications for the repeat of the Antiphon." The Offertory for the *Nativity of St John the Baptist* (24 June) demonstrates the most typical structure:

OFFERTORY • NATIVITY OF SAINT JOHN THE BAPTIST:

Justus ut palma florébit : * sicut cedrus, quæ in Líbano est, multiplicábitur.

℣. Bonum est confitéri Dómino: et psállere nómini tuo Altíssime.
* *sicut cedrus, quæ in Líbano est, multiplicábitur.*

℣. Ad annuntiándum mane misericórdiam tuam: et veritátem tuam per noctem.
* *sicut cedrus, quæ in Líbano est, multiplicábitur.*

℣. Plantátus in domo Dómini, in átriis domus Dei nostri florébit.
* *sicut cedrus, quæ in Líbano est, multiplicábitur.*

BIBLICAL CITATIONS • When it comes to the Offertory, we do not give Biblical citations for the "extra" verses (printed in italic fonts). We only provide the Biblical citation for the mandatory part, called ANTIPHONA AD OFFERTORIUM by the 1962 Missal. We made this choice because most of the "extra" verses do not come ***directly*** from Sacred Scripture—at least not in a way easy to indicate. Many Offertories "combine" different sections of Bible verses; for example, cf. the 3rd, 4th, 6th, 8th, and 10th Sundays after Pentecost. Others draw from various sections of the Bible; e.g. Low Sunday, which mixes the Gospel of Saint Luke with that of Saint Matthew, or the 22nd Sunday after Pentecost, which mixes the book of Esther with Jeremias.

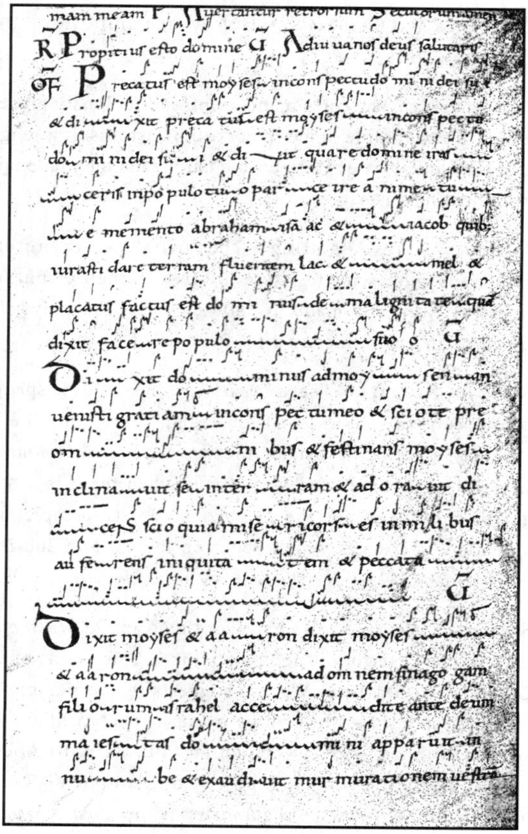

A. D. 1079

This image shows the Offertory for the 12th Sunday after Pentecost, from StMaur|1079, a manuscript created circa 1079AD (f. 151v).

These melodies were preserved with great care, and—although the black and white reproduction does not show it—were quite colorful and sumptuous.

The squiggly lines that resemble waves show the melismata. This type of manuscript is called a "heightened neume" manuscript because it uses the (relative) height of the notes to give an idea of melodic contour.

COMMUNION VERSES

NOT ONLY does this third edition of *Saint Edmund Campion Missal* contain the ancient Offertory-verses, it also includes the "extra" verses for Communion. In the past—when speaking of these ancient verses—some publications have cited only a handful of manuscripts. As a matter of fact, these "extra" verses can be found in numerous manuscripts, and are without question part of the Roman Rite's patrimony. To highlight this reality, we have attempted to draw from a large number of MSS, meticulously citing our sources each time. The CANTUS database was quite helpful, but occasionally we chose manuscripts not yet catalogued by the CANTUS database—again, to highlight the richness of the tradition.

NOT AS STABLE • The Communion-verses are not as stable as the Offertory-verses; i.e. when a communion antiphon does not come from a psalm, different manuscripts provide sundry options. ***It is a grave error*** to deem certain MSS as "better" than others simply because they are cleaner, more colorful, or more easy to access—and this has constituted a fatal flaw in several recent studies on the Communion-verses. Because the "extra" verses are always optional, we have printed them in the italic font.

NOT A COINCIDENCE • It was no coincidence that these "extra" verses were promoted by Church authorities ***at the precise moment*** Church authorities were encouraging priests to distribute Communion at the "proper" time—cf. *Code of Rubrics* (1961) §502—instead of distributing Communion before Mass or after Mass. To encourage the faithful to receive Holy Communion during Mass (rather than outside of Mass), the laws of Eucharistic fasting were loosened under Pope Pius XII: first with *Christus Dominus* (6 January 1953), then with *Sacram Communionem* (19 March 1957). On 3 September 1958, the Vatican issued *De Musica Sacra*, which says in paragraph 27(c):

27c Si autem fideles communicandi sint, cantus eiusdẽ antiphonae inchoetur dum sacerdos sacram Communionem distribuit. Si eadem antiphona ad Communionem e quodam psalmo desumpta sit, licet alios eiusdẽ psalmi versus decantare; quo in casu, post singulos vel binos versus, repeti potest antiphona, et, Communione expleta, psalmus clauditur cum *Gloria Patri*, et repetitur antiphona. Si vero antiphona non sit de psalmo, seligi potest psalmus solemnitati et actioni liturgicae congruens.

27c If the faithful are to communicate, the communion antiphon is sung when the priest distributes Holy Communion. If this Communion antiphon has been taken from a psalm, **the other verses** (of the same psalm) **may be sung,** in which case the antiphon may be repeated after every one or two verses and—the Communion over—the psalm should be concluded with the *Glória Patri* and the repeated antiphon. But if the antiphon be not from a psalm, a psalm fitting to the solemnity of the liturgical action may be chosen.

MODERN EDITIONS • The ancient Communion-verses can be found in many modern publications. But do all contain the same verses for the same antiphon? In cases where the antiphon comes from a psalm, all publications usually have the same verses. When the antiphon does not come from a psalm, different editors choose different solutions. Examples of modern editions which include the "extra" verses are: *Mass and Vespers* (Desclée, 1957); *Versus Psalmorum et Canticorum* (Desclée, 1962); *Ordo Cantus Missae* (Libreria Editrice Vaticana, 1970); *Graduale Romanum* (Solesmes Abbey, 1973); *Com-*

munion Antiphons with Psalms (Church Music Association of America, 2008); *Versus Ad Communionem* (Anton Stingl, 2017); and *Ad Communionem* (Kyle Lartigue, 2017).

<u>ONLY HALF THE ANTIPHON</u> • Fulton J. Sheen said in 1940: "It is a long established principle of the Church never to completely drop from her public worship any ceremony, object, or prayer which once occupied a place in that worship." We see this clearly in the *Requiem* Communion, which still has its verse and repeats only the <u>second half</u> of the antiphon: "Cum sanctis tuis in ætérnum, quia pius es" {Wagner p105}. [Note: In spite of what some have claimed {Stingl pXI}, this practice is <u>not</u> called "repetendum," as we shall discuss below.) Consider the following example—page 420 of 121EINSIE|961 (from approximately 961AD)—which shows *Passer Invénit* from the 3rd Sunday of Lent:

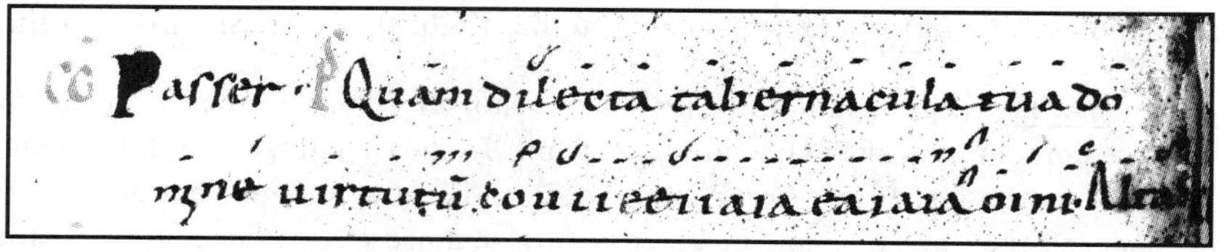

After the *Passer* communion antiphon—which is Psalm 83 (verses 4-5)—we can clearly observe the "extra" verse, which is none other than Psalm 83 (verse 2): *Quam dilécta*...etc. At the end, one can see the word "Altária" with neumes over it. That means only the <u>second half</u> of the antiphon is repeated, starting at the word "Altária"—and the reader can verify this:

This technique—viz. repeating only the <u>second half</u> of the antiphon—was also common for the INTROIT, at least until the time of Durandus {Wagner p59}.

<u>A SMALL DIGRESSION</u> • The excerpt from 121EINSIE|961 demonstrates a very common way of notating psalms—***by vowels only***. That is to say, in an effort to make the words fit, the scribe eliminated all the consonants, leaving only the vowels:

co u í i e é i i á i a e a i á i a ó i ni

...and since the singers had the psalter committed to memory, they could easily sing:

concupíscit et déficit ánima mea in átria Dómini

VERSUS AD REPETENDUM • A mysterious concept associated with the Communion-verses is the *Versus ad Repetendum*. Much is still unknown—Father Jungmann calls it "a riddle"—but certain manuscripts clearly do indicate a *Repetendum*, and the general scholarly consensus says this mysterious verse was inserted ***after the doxology,*** but before the final statement of the antiphon {Wagner p105; McFarland p45; Dyer p565; Hiley p497; Apel p191; Jungmann p395}. Since we examined the communion antiphon for the 3rd Sunday of Lent (see above), let us continue with that example—below is how a *Repetendum* appears in StDenisMissal|988, a manuscript created circa 988AD:

We see indicated the Communion (*Passer Invénit Sibi Domum*...etc.) followed by verse 2 of Psalm 83 ("Quam diléctа") and then we observe the *Repetendum* —"Etenim benedictionem dabit legislator..."—which is verse 8 of the same psalm. Dr. Ruth Steiner, along with many other scholars, expresses curiosity as to how the *Repetendum* is determined: "A number of manuscripts give supplementary verses, sometimes explicitly called *Versus ad Repetendum*, for introits, and also for communions; but the sources frequently disagree as to the choice of the verse" {McFarland p47}.

BEGAN TO DIE AWAY • Until the time of Pope Pius XII, the Communion-verses had not been a part of the liturgy for more than 800 years. When exactly did they disappear, and for what reason? It will be remembered that "general Communion" (i.e. reception by the congregation) sharply declined to such a point that the Lateran Council of 1215AD had to order Catholics to receive Communion at least once a year {Giampietro p67}. The many reasons why general Communion waned are described ably in Father Jungmann's *Missarum Sollemnia* (Benziger Brothers, 1950) pages 359-367. Dr. Wagner connects the loss of the Communion-verses with the decline of general Communion {Wagner p105}:

> The practice of general communion at the Masses of solemn days must have gone out from the 11th century onward, **as from that time the manuscripts begin to leave out the verses.** Those of the 12th century very seldom have them. As with the other chants, so with the Communion—the original form was preserved longest in Germany: the library of the church of S. Thomas at Leipzig contains a manuscript of the 13th century, which gives the Communion-verses for all the days of the Church's year. At that time they were still sung in some parts of Germany, like the Introit-verses and those of the Offertory. From the 14th century onwards they disappeared everywhere.

Father Jungmann agrees, suggesting that once Sunday Communion "slowed down, the grounds for a Communion song also crumbled" {Jungmann p396}. Father Jungmann also agrees—generally speaking—with Dr. Wagner's timetable: "The psalm begins to be missed in the manuscripts during the 10th century, and by the 12th century it is found only very seldom. [...] Bernold of Constance (d. 1100AD) still mentions the addition of the psalm with the *Gloria Patri* but with the quiet limitation, *si necesse fuerit*."

NON-PSALTER ANTIPHONS • Difficulties normally do not arise when the antiphon comes from a psalm; but how did the ancient Catholics determine the "extra" verses when the antiphon was not from a psalm? A quote by Dr. Peter Wagner is an excellent place to start. (It should be noted that this is merely an excerpt—but in the full text, he provides examples of each scenario.) Dr. Wagner explains {Wagner p104} :

> As to the relation of the Communion-verse to the antiphon, when taken from a psalm, the same rules hold good as at the Introit; *viz.* if the Communion is the **beginning** of a psalm, the first verse of the Communion is the one immediately or almost immediately following. If the antiphon is taken from the **middle** of the psalm, the first Communion-verse is the first verse of the psalm. But if the antiphon be not from a psalm, *its verses are from the same psalm as those of the Introit.* Many manuscripts simply give a reference to this: the expression **"psalmus ut supra"** is found in this case.

Father Jungmann agrees, writing on page 395 (*Missarum Sollemnia*, Volume II) :

> The oldest manuscripts of the Mass song-book, which belong to the 8th or 9th century, give us the same picture for the communion as for the introit: the antiphon [...] is intoned; thereupon follow the initial words of the psalm, or else, in those many cases in which the introit psalm is simply to be repeated, the remark: **"Psalm. ut supra."**

Therefore, one solution to non-psalm antiphons is to "duplicate" the Introit verses, and this creates symmetry between the first and last members of the *Propria Missae*. For an example, cf. 239LAON|927 for the Second Sunday of Advent (a non-psalm antiphon).

MORE ON "UT SUPRA" • The expression **"psalmus ut supra"** is not utilized solely for non-psalm antiphons. Consider *Unam pétii*—communion antiphon for the 5th Sunday after Pentecost—which is the fourth verse of Psalm 26. Examining 239LAON|927 (a very important MS created approximately 927AD), we see **"Psl Ut sup"** which steers the singer back to the Introit verses. This particular example is quite a happy one, since the Introit verses are, in fact, the beginning of Psalm 26:

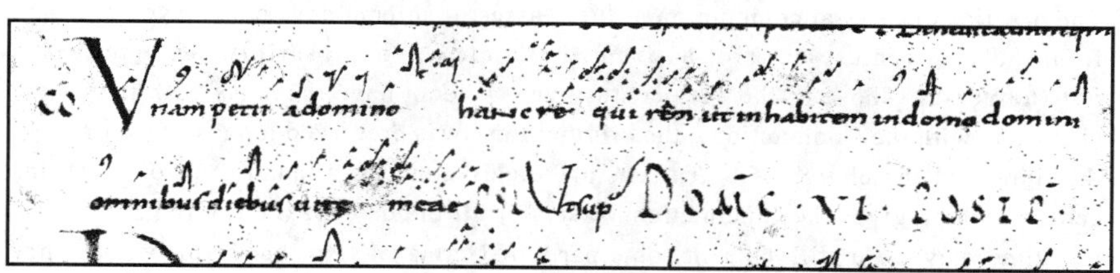

PSALM 33 • When it comes to non-psalm antiphons, more options are available than simply "doubling" the Introit verses. One may always choose **Psalm 33** which for "almost all Eastern and Western liturgies" constituted "the unvarying Communion-chant which in all Masses accompanied the administration of the Holy Eucharist" {Wagner p103}. Indeed, "we meet with **Psalm 33** as a Communion song almost everywhere in ancient Christendom" {Jungmann p392}. David Hiley reminds us:

> The singing of a chant at the [...] distribution of Communion, is attested at an early date. The singing of **Psalm 33** during the distribution is recorded both by Cyril, bishop of Jerusalem (349-387), and in the 'Apostolic Constitutions' (later 4th century). Verse 9 of the psalm—"O taste and see that the Lord is good"—no doubt inspired this choice.

Still More Options • In a very important publication by Solesmes Abbey—"Mass and Vespers" (1957)—we read the following on page 1,997 :

> The Church's new legislation concerning the Eucharistic fast makes it possible for many of the faithful to communicate at a sung Mass. The singing of the Communion Antiphon alone—which sufficed at sung Mass when Holy Communion was not given—is insufficient under the new conditions, which moreover are merely a return to ancient usage. Therefore it seems opportune to add here the Psalms which normally should accompany the Communion Antiphon proper to the day. When the Antiphon is itself taken from a Psalm, the choice of a Psalm is not in doubt. When this is not the case, the ancient rule was to make use of the Psalm of the Introit.

Yet for many of the non-psalm antiphons, the truth is more complicated; viz. the ancient manuscripts often select what might be called "surprising" verses; either from the New Testament or from the Psalter. Consider the communion antiphon **(Luke 15:10)** for the 3rd Sunday after Pentecost. Some MSS use various Old Testament options: Psalm 16; Psalm 31; Psalm 96; Psalm 129; and so on. A very important MS—viz. Bamberg6lit|905 from approximately 905ad—instructs the singer to use the Introit verses.

But a number of manuscripts take the "extra" verses from the Gospel of Saint Luke, as we can see in 4951steven|1128, a manuscript created circa 1128ad :

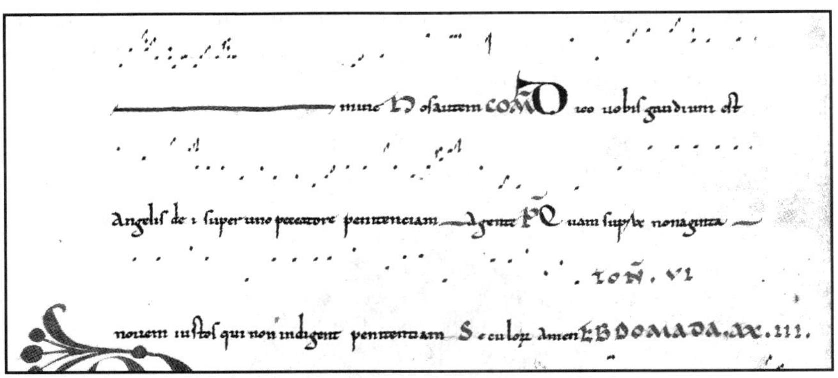

We observe the antiphon itself (Luke 15:10) *Dico vobis: gáudium est ángelis Dei super uno peccatóre pœniténtiam agénte* — "I say to you: there is joy before the angels of God upon one sinner doing penance." Then we see the psalm verse: *Quam super nonagínta novem justis, qui non índigent pœniténtia* — "than over ninety-nine righteous who are not in need of penance." The ancient MS chose a verse from earlier (Luke 15:7) in a truly ingenious way.

FLEXIBILITY AND FREEDOM • It would be false to claim that all Catholics—in every locality—for the last 2,000 years have sung the communion antiphon the same way. To demonstrate the variety, consider *Diffúsa Est Grátia* as found in ALBI | 1047, a manuscript created circa 1047AD :

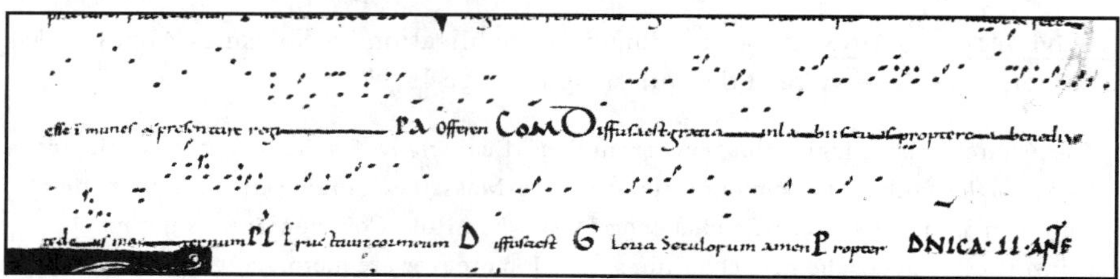

This ancient MS indicates the following performance instructions: first, the full antiphon is sung; then verses from Psalm 44 ("Eructávit cor meum"); second, the full antiphon; third, the doxology ("Glória Patri"); fourth, the second half of the antiphon.

GREATER THAN ANY OTHER ART • For this third edition of the *Campion Missal*, we have attempted to provide a "sampling" from the riches of our Catholic musical heritage, which the Second Vatican Council declared to be ***"a treasure of inestimable value, greater even than that of any other art"*** (SC §112). Of course each choirmaster will ultimately decide which Communion-verses will be used—or whether they will be used at all, since they are encouraged (but not required) by the current rubrics.

PRACTICAL CONSIDERATIONS • Any number of options may be used. Some parishes may use plainsong for weekday Masses, but a choral setting of the communion antiphon for the Sunday high Mass. Others may have the congregation join in singing Psalm 33; still others may decide to sing only the verse provided by our book. A wonderful goal would be to familiarize 100% of Catholic congregations with the entire psalter as was the case in former ages; but this will take time. Until such a goal is reached, congregations can—at a minimum—pray the communion antiphon along with its ancient verse, and begin to understand it not as a "sentence chosen at random," but rather as part of a magnificent tapestry stretching back the early Church.

Ancient liturgical books frequently begin, not with the season of Advent, but with the feast of Christmas—the anniversary of Christ's birth—which seems only natural. Toward the "end" of the book (or liturgical year) the readings tended to focus on the end of the world and the Second Coming—again, a very natural thing. This helps explain why Advent has three themes: (1) preparation to celebrate the feast of our Lord's advent into the world; (2) a focus on Christ's advent to each Catholic "individually" in Holy Communion and through Grace; and (3) a focus on the Redeemer's final advent as judge: both at a man's death and at the end of the world. Prior to 1962, Deacon and Subdeacon wore folded chasubles during Advent (but not on the vigil of Christmas).

I Classis.

—First Sunday of Advent—

DOMINICA PRIMA ADVENTUS *Station at Saint Mary Major*

INTROIT. *Ps 24: 1-3*

Ad te levávi ánimam meam: Deus meus, in te confído, non erubéscam: neque irrídeant me inimíci mei: étenim univérsi, qui te exspéctant, non confundéntur. ℣. Vias tuas, Dómine, demónstra mihi: et sémitas tuas édoce me. ℣. Glória Patri.

TO THEE, O Lord, have I lifted up my soul: in Thee, O my God, I put my trust; let me not be ashamed. Neither let my enemies laugh at me; for none of them that wait on Thee shall be confounded. (Ps 24: 4) Show, O Lord, Thy ways to me, and teach me Thy paths. ℣. Glory.

COLLECT.

Excita, quǽsumus, Dómine, poténtiam tuam, et veni: ut ab imminéntibus peccatórum nostrórum perículis, te mereámur protegénte éripi, te liberánte salvári. Qui vivis.

Bestir, O Lord, Thy might, we pray Thee, and come; That, defended by Thee, we may deserve rescue from approaching dangers brought on by our sins, and being set free by Thee, obtain our salvation. Who livest.

EPISTLE. *Rom 13: 11-14*

Fratres: Sciéntes, quia hora est jam nos de somno súrgere. Nunc enim própior est nostra salus, quam cum credídimus. Nox præcéssit, dies autem appropinquávit. Abjiciámus ergo ópera tenebrárum, et induámur arma lucis. Sicut in die honéste ambulémus: non in comessatiónibus et ebrietátibus, non in cubílibus et impudicítiis, non in contentióne et æmulatióne: sed induímini Dóminum Jesum Christum.

BRETHREN, knowing the time, that it is now the hour for us to rise from sleep; for now our salvation is nearer than when we believed. The night is past, and the day is at hand; let us therefore cast off the works of darkness, and put on the armor of light. Let us walk honestly as in the day; not in rioting and drunkenness, not in chambering and impurities, not in contention and envy; but put ye on the Lord Jesus Christ.

GRADUAL & ALLELUIA. *Ps 24: 3-4 & Ps 84: 8*

Univérsi, qui te exspéctant, non confundéntur, Dñe. ℣. Vias tuas, Dñe, notas fac mihi: et sémitas tuas édoce me.

Allelúja, allelúja. ℣. Osténde nobis, Dómine, misericórdiam tuam: et salutáre tuum da nobis. Allelúja.

NONE OF THEM that wait on Thee shall be confounded. ℣. Show, O Lord, Thy ways to me, and teach me Thy paths.

Alleluia, alleluia. ℣. Show us, O Lord, Thy mercy: and grant us Thy salvation. Alleluia.

GOSPEL. *Luke 21: 25-33*

At that time, Jesus said to His disciples: **THERE SHALL BE SIGNS** in the sun, and in the moon, and in the stars: and upon the earth distress of nations, by reason of the confusion of the roaring of the sea and of the waves, men withering away for fear and expectation of what shall come upon the whole world. For the powers of heaven shall be moved; and then they shall see the Son of man coming in a cloud with great power and majesty. But when these things begin to come to pass, look up and lift up your heads, because your redemption is at hand. And He spoke to them a similitude: See the fig-tree, and all the trees: when they now shoot forth their fruit, you know that summer is nigh; so you also, when you shall see these things come to pass, know that the kingdom of God is at hand. Amen I say to you, this generation shall not pass away, till all things be fulfilled. Heaven and earth shall pass away, but My words shall not pass away. CREDO.

In illo témpore: Dixit Jesus discípulis suis: Erunt signa in sole et luna et stellis, et in terris pressúra géntium præ confusióne sónitus maris et flúctuum: arescéntibus homínibus præ timóre et exspectatióne, quæ supervénient univérso orbi: nam virtútes cælórum movebúntur. Et tunc vidébunt Fílium hóminis veniéntem in nube cum potestáte magna et majestáte. His autem fíeri incipiéntibus, respícite et leváte cápita vestra: quóniam appropínquat redémptio vestra. Et dixit illis similitúdinem: Vidéte ficúlneam et omnes árbores: cum prodúcunt jam ex se fructum, scitis, quóniam prope est æstas. Ita et vos, cum vidéritis hæc fíeri, scitóte, quóniam prope est regnum Dei. Amen, dico vobis, quia non præteríbit generátio hæc, donec ómnia fiant. Cælum et terra transíbunt: verba autem mea non transíbunt.

OFFERTORY. *Ps 24: 1-3*

TO THEE, O Lord, have I lifted up my soul: in Thee, O my God, I put my trust; let me not be ashamed: neither let my enemies laugh at me: for none of them that wait on Thee shall be confounded. ℣. *Direct me in Thy truth, and teach me; for Thou art God my Savior; and on Thee have I waited all the day long.* ℣. *Look Thou upon me, and have mercy on me, O Lord; Keep Thou my soul, and deliver me: I shall not be confounded, for I have hoped in Thee.*

Ad te, Dómine, levávi ánimam meam: Deus meus, in te confído, non erubéscam: neque irrídeant me inimíci mei: étenim univérsi, qui te exspéctant, non confundéntur. ℣. *Dírige me in veritáte tua et doce me, quia tu es Deus salutáris meus: et te sustínui tota die.* ℣. *Réspice in me et miserére mei, Dómine, custódi ánimam meam et éripe me, non confúndar, quóniam invocávi te.*

This Offertory is identical to the Tenth Sunday after Pentecost. Regarding the Offertory on the First Sunday of Advent, the 1962 Missal omits the word "Dómine" (although the ancient Gradual includes it) printing instead: *Ad te levávi ánimam meam.* Yet for the Offertory on the Tenth Sunday after Pentecost, the 1962 Missal includes the word "Dómine," printing: *Ad te, Dómine, levávi ánimam meam.* It would appear some unknown hand felt uncomfortable—since the Introit on the First Sunday of Advent does not include the word "Dómine"—and tried to rectify a perceived error. The ancient Gradual does not include "Dómine" for the Introit.

SECRET.

Cleansing us by their mighty power, may these Holy Mysteries, O Lord, make us come more pure before Thee who art their author. Though our Lord.

Hæc sacra nos, Dómine, poténti virtúte mundátos ad suum fáciant purióres veníre princípium. Per Dóminum.

COMMUNION. *Ps 84: 13*

THE Lord will give goodness: and our earth shall yield her fruit. ℣. *What blessings, Lord, Thou hast granted to this land of Thine, restoring Jacob's fortunes.*

—BAMBERG6LIT|905 • Circa 905AD

Dóminus dabit benignitátem: et terra nostra dabit fructum suum. (Ps 84: 1) ℣. *Benedixísti, Dómine, terram tuam: avertísti captivitátem Jacob.*

POSTCOMMUNION.

Suscipiámus, Dómine, misericórdiam tuam in médio templi tui: ut reparatiónis nostræ ventúra sollémnia cóngruis honóribus præcedámus. Per Dóminum.

May we receive Thy mercy, O Lord, in the midst of Thy temple, that with due reverence we may prepare for the coming festival of our redemption. Through our Lord.

REGARDING THE COMMUNION ANTIPHON • It will be noticed that a single manuscript citation has been provided for the communion antiphon, indicating the source of the "extra" verses as well as their provenance. A large number of manuscript sources could have been listed—and not all indicate the same "extra" verses (or even the same psalm). In particular, HELMST|1026 tends to indicate verses which do not correspond to the other manuscripts—at least those which have survived long enough for us to consult. Rather than cluttering the text, the editors hope one manuscript citation for each feast will suffice.

I Classis.

—*Second Sunday of Advent*—

DOMINICA SECUNDA ADVENTUS *Station at the Holy Cross in Jerusalem*

INTROIT. *Is 30: 30*

Pópulus Sion, ecce, Dóminus véniet ad salvándas gentes: et audítam fáciet Dóminus glóriam vocis suæ in lætítia cordis vestri. ℣. Qui regis Ísraël, inténde: qui dedúcis, velut ovem, Joseph. ℣. Glória Patri.

PEOPLE OF SION, behold, the Lord shall come to save the nations; and the Lord shall make the glory of His voice to be heard in the joy of your heart. (Ps 79: 2) Give ear, O Thou that rulest Israel: Thou that leadest Joseph like a sheep. ℣. Glory.

COLLECT.

Excita, Dómine, corda nostra ad præparándas Unigéniti tui vias: ut, per ejus advéntum, purificátis tibi méntibus servíre mereámur: Qui tecum.

Stir up our hearts, O Lord, to prepare the ways of Thine only-begotten Son, that through His coming we may be worthy to serve Thee with purified minds. Who livest.

EPISTLE. *Rom 15: 4–13*

Fratres: Quæcúmque scripta sunt, ad nostram doctrínam scripta sunt: ut per patiéntiam et consolatiónem Scripturárum spem habeámus. Deus autem patiéntiæ et solácii det vobis idípsum sápere in altérutrum secúndum Jesum Christum: ut unánimes, uno ore honorificétis Deum et Patrem Dómini nostri Jesu Christi. Propter quod suscípite ínvicem, sicut et Christus suscépit vos in honórem Dei. Dico enim Christum Jesum minístrum fuísse circumcisiónis propter veritátem Dei, ad confirmándas promissiónes patrum: gentes autem super miseri-

BRETHREN, what things so ever were written, were written for our learning; that through patience and the comfort of the Scriptures we might have hope. Now the God of patience and of comfort grant you to be of one mind one toward another, according to Jesus Christ: that with one mind, and with one mouth, you may glorify God and the Father of our Lord Jesus Christ. Wherefore receive one another; as Christ also hath received you, unto the honor of God. For I say that Christ Jesus was minister of the circumcision for the truth of God, to confirm the promises made unto the fathers. But that the Gentiles are to glorify God for His mercy, as it is written: Therefore will I confess to Thee, O Lord, among the Gentiles, and will sing to Thy name. And again He saith: Rejoice, ye Gentiles, with His people. And again: Praise the Lord, all ye Gentiles; and magnify Him, all ye people. And again, Isaias saith: There shall be a root of Jesse; and He that shall rise up to rule the Gentiles, in Him the Gentiles shall hope. Now the God of hope fill you with all joy and peace in believing; that you may abound in hope, and in the power of the Holy Ghost.

córdia honoráre Deum, sicut scriptum est: Proptérea confitébor tibi in géntibus, Dómine, et nómini tuo cantábo. Et íterum dicit: Lætámini, gentes, cum plebe ejus. Et iterum: Laudáte, omnes gentes, Dóminum: et magnificáte eum, omnes pópuli. Et rursus Isaías ait: Erit radix Jesse, et qui exsúrget régere gentes, in eum gentes sperábunt. Deus autem spei répleat vos omni gáudio et pace in credéndo: ut abundétis in spe et virtúte Spíritus Sancti.

GRADUAL & ALLELUIA. *Ps 49: 2–3, 5 & Ps 121: 1*

OUT OF SION the loveliness of His beauty: God shall come manifestly. ℣. Gather ye together His saints to Him; who have set His covenant before sacrifices. | Alleluia, alleluia. ℣. I rejoiced at the things that were said to me: we shall go into the house of the Lord. Alleluia.

Ex Sion spécies decóris ejus: Deus maniféste véniet. ℣. Congregáte illi sanctos ejus, qui ordinavérunt testaméntum ejus super sacrifícia.

Allelúja, allelúja. ℣. Lætátus sum in his, quæ dicta sunt mihi: in domum Dómini íbimus. Allelúja.

GOSPEL. *Matt. 11: 2-10*

WHEN JOHN had heard in prison the works of Christ: sending two of his disciples, he said to Him: Art Thou He that art to come, or do we look for another? and Jesus making answer, said to them, Go and relate to John what you have heard and seen. The blind see, the lame walk, the lepers are cleansed, the deaf hear, the dead rise again, the poor have the gospel preached to them; and blessed is he that shall not be scandalized in Me. And when they went their way, Jesus began to say to the multitudes concerning John, What went you out into the desert to see? a reed shaken with the wind? But what went you out to see? a man clothed in soft garments? Behold they that are clothed in soft garments are in the houses of kings. But what went you out to see? a prophet? yea, * I tell you, and more than a prophet. For this is He of whom it is written, Behold I send My angel before Thy face, who shall prepare Thy way before Thee. CREDO.

In illo tempore: Cum audísset Joánnes in vínculis ópera Christi, mittens duos de discípulis suis, ait illi: Tu es, qui ventúrus es, an álium exspectámus? Et respóndens Jesus, ait illis: Eúntes renuntiáte Joánni, quæ audístis et vidístis. Cæci vident, claudi ámbulant, leprósi mundántur, surdi áudiunt, mórtui resúrgunt, páuperes evangelizántur: et beátus est, qui non fúerit scandalizátus in me. Illis autem abeúntibus, cœpit Jesus dícere ad turbas de Joánne: Quid exístis in desértum vidére? arúndinem vento agitátam? Sed quid exístis vidére? hóminem móllibus vestítum? Ecce, qui móllibus vestiúntur, in dómibus regum sunt. Sed quid exístis vidére? Prophétam? Etiam dico vobis, et plus quam Prophétam. Hic est enim, de quo scriptum est: Ecce, ego mitto Ángelum meum ante fáciem tuam, qui præparábit viam tuam ante te.

* *Note: The word "yea" is pronounced as "yay." The word means "yes," whereas "nay" means "no" in English.*

OFFERTORY. *Ps 84: 7-8*

Deus, tu convérsus vivificábis nos, et plebs tua lætábitur in te: osténde nobis, Dómine, misericórdiam tuam, et salutáre tuum da nobis. ℣. *Benedixísti, Dñe, terrã tuã: avertísti captivitátem Jacob: remisísti iniquitátem plebis tuæ.* ℣. *Misericórdia et véritas obviavérunt sibi: véritas de terra orta est et justítia de cælo prospéxit.*

O GOD, TURNING, Thou wilt bring us life; and Thy people shall rejoice in Thee: show us, O Lord, Thy mercy, and grant us Thy salvation. ℣. *Lord, Thou hast blessed Thy land: Thou hast turned away the captivity of Jacob: Thou hast forgiven the iniquity of thy people.* ℣. *Mercy and truth have met each other: Truth is sprung out of the earth: and justice hath looked down from heaven.*

SECRET.

Placáre, quǽsumus, Dómine, humilitátis nostræ précibus et hóstiis: et, ubi nulla súppetunt suffrágia meritórũ, tuis nobis succúrre præsídiis. Per Dñm.

Be appeased, we beseech Thee, O Lord, by the prayers and offerings of our lowliness, and where no support of merits is at hand, do Thou hasten to us with Thine aid. Through our Lord.

COMMUNION. *Bar 5: 5; 4: 36*

Jerúsalem, surge et sta in excélso, et vide jucunditátem, quæ véniet tibi a Deo tuo. (Ps 147:1) ℣. *Lauda, Jerúsalem, Dóminum; lauda Deum tuum, Sion.* —RENAUD|965 • Circa 965AD

ARISE, O Jerusalem, and stand on high: and behold the joy that cometh to thee from thy God. ℣. *Praise the Lord, O Jerusalem: praise thy God, O Sion.*

POSTCOMMUNION.

Repléti cibo spirituális alimóniæ, súpplices te, Dómine, deprecámur: ut, hujus participatióne mystérii, dóceas nos terréna despícere et amáre cæléstia. Per Dóminum.

Filled with the food of spiritual nourishing, we humbly beseech Thee, O Lord, that by our partaking of this mystery Thou wouldst teach us to condemn earthly and love heavenly things. Through our Lord.

I Classis.

—*Third Sunday of Advent*—

DOMINICA TERTIA ADVENTUS *Station at St. Peter's*

INTROIT. *Philip 4: 4-6*

Gaudéte in Dómino semper: íterum dico, gaudéte. Modéstia vestra nota sit ómnibus homínibus: Dóminus enim prope est. Nihil sollíciti sitis: sed in omni oratióne petitiónes vestræ innotéscant apud Deum. ℣. Benedixísti, Dómine, terram tuam: avertísti captivitátem Jacob. ℣. Glória Patri.

REJOICE in the Lord always; again I say, rejoice. Let your modesty be known to all men: for the Lord is nigh. Be nothing solicitous; but in everything by prayer let your requests be made known to God. (Ps 84: 2) Lord, Thou hast blest Thy land; Thou hast turned away the captivity of Jacob. ℣. Glory.

COLLECT.

Incline Thine ear to our prayers, O Lord, we beseech Thee; and make bright the darkness of our minds by the grace of Thy visitation. Who livest.

Aurem tuam, quǽsumus, Dómine, précibus nostris accómmoda: et mentis nostræ ténebras, grátia tuæ visitatiónis illústra: Qui vivis.

EPISTLE. *Philip 4: 4-7*

BRETHREN, Rejoice in the Lord always: again I say, rejoice. Let your modesty be known to all men. The Lord is nigh. Be nothing solicitous; but in everything by prayer and supplication with thanksgiving let your requests be made known to God. And the peace of God, which surpasseth all understanding, keep your hearts and minds in Christ Jesus our Lord.

Fratres: Gaudéte in Dómino semper: íterum dico, gaudéte. Modéstia vestra nota sit ómnibus homínibus: Dóminus prope est. Nihil sollíciti sitis: sed in omni oratióne et obsecratióne, cum gratiárum actióne, petitiónes vestræ innotéscant apud Deum. Et pax Dei, quæ exsúperat omnem sensum, custódiat corda vestra et intellegéntias vestras, in Christo Jesu, Dómino nostro.

GRADUAL & ALLELUIA. *Ps 79: 2-3 & Ps 79: 2*

THOU O Lord, that sittest upon the cherubim, stir up Thy might, and come. ℣. Give ear, O Thou that rulest Israel: Thou that leadest Joseph like a sheep.
Alleluia, alleluia. ℣. Stir up Thy might, O Lord, and come: that Thou mayest save us. Alleluia.

Qui sedes, Dómine, super Chérubim, éxcita poténtiam tuam, et veni. ℣. Qui regis Israël, inténde: qui dedúcis, velut ovem, Joseph.
Allelúja, allelúja. ℣. Excita, Dómine, poténtiam tuam, et veni, ut salvos fácias nos. Allelúja.

GOSPEL. *John 1: 19-28*

THE JEWS SENT from Jerusalem priests and Levites to John, to ask him, Who art thou? And he confessed, and did not deny; and he confessed, I am not the Christ. And they asked him, What then? Art thou Elias? And he said, I am not. Art thou the prophet? And he answered, No. They said therefore unto him, Who art thou that we may give an answer to them that sent us? What sayest thou of thyself? He said, I am the voice of one crying in the wilderness, Make straight the way of the Lord, as said the prophet Isaias. And they that were sent were of the pharisees. And they asked him, and said to him, Why, then, dost thou baptize, if thou be not Christ, nor Elias, nor the prophet? John answered them, saying, I baptize with water; but there hath stood one in the midst of you, Whom you know not; the same is He

In illo tempore: Misérunt Judǽi ab Jerosólymis sacerdótes et levítas ad Joánnem, ut interrogárent eum: Tu quis es? Et conféssus est, et non negávit: et conféssus est: Quia non sum ego Christus. Et interrogavérunt eũ: Quid ergo? Elías es tu? Et dixit: Non sum. Prophéta es tu? Et respóndit: Non. Dixérunt ergo ei: Quis es, ut respónsum demus his, qui misérunt nos? Quid dicis de te ipso? Ait: Ego vox clamántis in desérto: Dirígite viam Dómini, sicut dixit Isaías Prophéta. Et qui missi fúerant, erant ex pharisǽis. Et interrogavérunt eum, et dixérunt ei: Quid ergo baptízas, si tu non es Christus, neque Elías, neque Prophéta? Respóndit eis Joánnes, dicens: Ego baptízo in aqua: médius autem vestrum stetit, quem vos nescítis. Ipse est, qui post me ventúrus est, qui ante me factus est: cujus ego non sum dignus ut solvam ejus corrígiam calceaménti. Hæc in Bethánia facta sunt trans Jordánem, ubi erat Joánnes baptízans.

that shall come after me, Who is preferred before me, the latchet of Whose shoe I am not worthy to loose. These things were done in Bethania beyond the Jordan, where John was baptizing. CREDO.

OFFERTORY. *Ps 84: 2*

Benedixísti, Dómine, terram tuam: avertísti captivitátem Jacob: remisísti iniquitátem plebis tuæ. ℣. *Operuísti ómnia peccáta eórum: mitigásti omnem iram tuam.* ℣. *Osténde nobis Dómine misericórdiam tuam et salutáre tuum da nobis.*

LORD, Thou hast blest Thy land: Thou hast turned away the captivity of Jacob: thou hast forgiven the iniquity of Thy people. ℣. *Thou hast covered all their sins: Thou hast mitigated all Thy anger.* ℣. *Show us, O Lord, Thy mercy: and grant us Thy salvation.*

SECRET.

Devotiónis nostræ tibi, quǽsumus, Dómine, hóstia júgiter immolétur: quæ et sacri péragat instirúta mystérii, et salutáre tuum in nobis mirabíliter operétur. Per Dóminum.

May the sacrifice of our devotion, we beseech Thee, O Lord, be continually offered to Thee, both to carry out Thy designs in this holy Mystery and wonderfully to work in us Thy salvation. Through our Lord.

COMMUNION. *Is 35: 4*

Dícite: pusillánimes, confortámini et nolíte timére: ecce, Deus noster véniet et salvábit nos. (Ps 84: 2) ℣. *Benedixísti, Dómine, terram tuam; avertísti captivitátem Jacob.*
—COMPIEGNE|862 • Circa 862AD

SAY to the faint-hearted: Take courage, and fear not: behold our God will come and will save us. ℣. *What blessings, Lord, Thou hast granted to this land of Thine, restoring Jacob's fortunes.*

POSTCOMMUNION.

Implorámus, Dómine, cleméntiam tuam: ut hæc divína subsídia, a vítiis expiátos, ad festa ventúra nos prǽparent. Per Dóminum.

We implore Thy clemency, O Lord, that cleansed from our sins, these divine aids may prepare us for the coming festival. Through our Lord.

This Sunday's communion antiphon does not come from a psalm; it comes from the Book of Isaias. When the communion antiphon does not come from a psalm, the singers had multifarious options for the "extra" verses. A very common practice was to take additional verses from the Introit, as was done in COMPIEGNE|862 for the Third Sunday of Advent. Another common practice was to take the "extra" verses from Psalm 33, "the unvarying Communion-chant which in all Masses accompanied the administration of the Holy Eucharist" for the earliest Catholic liturgies {Wagner p103}. However, additional options were also available; for instance, other ancient manuscripts chose Psalm 49 or Psalm 95 for this particular communion antiphon.

—*Fourth Sunday of Advent*— *I Classis.*

DOMINICA QUARTA ADVENTUS *Station at the Church of the Twelve Holy Apostles*

INTROIT. *Is 45: 8*

DROP DOWN DEW, ye heavens, from above, and let the clouds rain the just; let the earth be opened and bud forth a Savior. (Ps 18: 2) The heavens show forth the glory of God, and the firmament declareth the work of His Hands. ℣. Glory.

Roráte, cæli, désuper, et nubes pluant justum: aperiátur terra, et gérminet Salvatórem. ℣. Cæli enárrant glóriam Dei: et ópera mánuum ejus annúntiat firmaméntum. ℣. Glória Patri.

COLLECT.

Bestir, O Lord, Thy might, we beseech thee, and come; and with great power come to our aid, that, by the help of Thy grace, that which is hindered by our sins may be hastened by Thy merciful forgiveness. Who livest.

Éxcita, quǽsumus, Dómine, poténtiam tuam, et veni: et magna nobis virtúte succúrre; ut per auxílium grátiæ tuæ, quod nostra peccáta præpédiunt, indulgéntiæ tuæ propitiatiónis accéleret: Qui vivis.

EPISTLE. *I Cor 4: 1-5*

BRETHREN, let a man so account of us as of the ministers of Christ, and the dispensers of the mysteries of God. Here now it is required among the dispensers, that a man be found faithful. But to me it is a very small thing to be judged by you, or by man's day: but neither do I judge my own self. For I am not conscious to myself of any thing, yet am I not hereby justified: but He that judgeth me is the Lord. Therefore judge not before the time, until the Lord come; Who both will bring to light the hidden things of darkness, and will make manifest the counsels of the hearts: and then shall every man have praise from God.

Fratres: Sic nos exístimet homo ut minístros Christi, et dispensatóres mysteriórum Dei. Hic jam quǽritur inter dispensatóres, ut fidélis quis inveniátur. Mihi autem pro mínimo est, ut a vobis júdicer aut ab humáno die: sed neque meípsum júdico. Nihil enim mihi cónscius sum: sed non in hoc justificátus sum: qui autem júdicat me, Dóminus est. Itaque nolíte ante tempus judicáre, quoadúsque véniat Dóminus: qui et illuminábit abscóndita tenebrárum, et manifestábit consília córdium: et tunc laus erit unicuíque a Deo.

GRADUAL & ALLELUIA. *Ps 144: 18, 21 & Trad.*

THE LORD is nigh unto all them that call upon Him, to all that call upon Him in truth. ℣. My mouth shall speak the praise of the Lord; and let all flesh bless His holy name.

Alleluia, alleluia. ℣. Come, O Lord, and do not delay; forgive the sins of Thy people Israel. Alleluia.

Prope est Dóminus ómnibus invocántibus eum: ómnibus, qui ínvocant eum in veritáte. ℣. Laudem Dómini loquétur os meum: et benedícat omnis caro nomen sanctum ejus.

Allelúja, allelúja. ℣. Veni, Dómine, et noli tardáre: reláxa facínora plebis tuæ Israël. Allelúja.

GOSPEL. *Luke 3: 1-6*

Anno quintodécimo impérii Tibérii Cǽsaris, procuránte Póntio Piláto Judǽam, tetrárcha autem Galilǽæ Heróde, Philíppo autem fratre ejus tetrárcha Iturǽæ et Trachonítidis regiónis, et Lysánia Abilínæ tetrárcha, sub princípibus sacerdótum Anna et Cáipha: factum est verbum Dómini super Joánnem, Zacharíæ filium, in desérto.

IN THE FIFTEENTH year of the reign of Tiberius Cæsar, Pontius Pilate being governor of Judea, and Herod being tetrarch of Galilee, and Philip his brother tetrarch of Iturea and the country of Trachonitis, and Lysanias tetrarch of Abilina, under the high priests Annas and Caiphas; the word of the Lord came to John the son of Zachary, in the desert.

Et venit in omnem regiónem Jordánis, prædicans baptísmum pæniténtiæ in remissiónem peccatórum, sicut scriptum est in libro sermónum Isaíæ Prophétæ: Vox clamántis in desérto: Paráte viam Dómini: rectas fácite sémitas ejus: omnis vallis implébitur: et omnis mons et collis humiliábitur: et erunt prava in diréta, et áspera in vias planas: et vidébit omnis caro salutáre Dei.

And he came into all the country about the Jordan, preaching the baptism of penance for the remission of sins; as it is written in the book of the sayings of Isaias the prophet: A voice of one crying in the wilderness: Prepare ye the way of the Lord, make straight His paths. Every valley shall be filled; and every mountain and hill shall be brought low: the crooked shall be made straight, and the rough ways plain: and all flesh shall see the salvation of God. CREDO.

OFFERTORY. *Luke 1: 28*

Ave, María, grátia plena; Dóminus tecum: benedícta tu in muliéribus, et benedíctus fructus ventris tui. ℣. *Quómodo in me fiet hoc, quæ virum non cognósco? Spíritus Dómini supervéniet in te et virtus Altíssimi obumbrábit tibi.* ℣. *Ideóque, quod nascétur ex te Sanctum, vocábitur Fílius Dei.*

HAIL, MARY, full of grace; the Lord is with thee: blessed art thou among women, and blessed is the fruit of thy womb. ℣. *How shall this be done, because I know not man? The Holy Ghost shall come upon thee, and the power of the most High shall overshadow thee.* ℣. *Thus this holy offspring of thine shall be called the Son of God.*

Identical to the Offertory for the Immaculate Conception, except that the Offertory for the Immaculate Conception removes: ET BENEDICTUS FRUCTUS VENTRIS TUI *("and blessèd is the fruit of thy womb.")*

SECRET.

Sacrifíciis præséntibus, quǽsumus, Dómine, placátus inténde: ut et devotióni nostræ profíciant et salúti. Per Dóminum.

Look with favor, we beseech Thee, O Lord upon these offerings here before Thee, that they may profit both for our devotion and for our salvation. Through our Lord.

COMMUNION. *Is 7: 14 with Is 7: 15*

Identical to the Annunciation:

Ecce Virgo concípiet et páriet fílium: et vocábitur nomen ejus Emmánuel. (Ps 18: 6-7) ℣. *Exsultávit ut gigas ad curréndam viam; a summo cælo egréssio ejus.* —121EINSIE|961 • Circa 961AD

BEHOLD a virgin shall conceive, and bring forth a Son, and His name shall be called Emmanuel. ℣. *He exults like some great runner who sees the track before Him; here, at one end of heaven, is its starting-place.*

POSTCOMMUNION.

Having received Thy gifts, O Lord, we pray that the saving effect of the mystery may increase as we frequent it. Through our Lord.

Sumptis munéribus, quǽsumus, Dómine: ut, cum frequentatióne mystérii, crescat nostræ salútis efféctus. Per Dóminum.

—*Vigil of Christmas*— *I Classis.*

IN VIGILIA NATIVITATIS DOMINI *Station at Saint Mary Major*

INTROIT. *Ex 16: 6-7*

THIS DAY YOU SHALL KNOW that the Lord will come, and save us: and in the morning you shall see His glory. (Ps 23: 1) The earth is the Lord's and the fulness thereof, the world, and all they that dwell therein. ℣. Glory.

Hódie sciétis, quia véniet Dóminus et salvábit nos: et mane vidébitis glóriam ejus. ℣. Dómini est terra, et plenitúdo ejus: orbis terrárum, et univérsi, qui hábitant in eo. ℣. Glória Patri.

COLLECT.

O God, Who dost gladden us year by year with the expectation of our redemption, grant that we, who now with joy receive Thine only begotten Son as our Redeemer, may behold Him also without fear, when He cometh as our judge, our Lord Jesus Christ. Who with Thee.

Deus, qui nos redemptiónis nostræ ánnua exspectatióne lætíficas: præsta; ut Unigénitum tuum, quem Redemptórem læti suscípimus, veniéntem quoque Júdicem secúri videámus, Dóminum nostrum Jesum Christum, Fílium tuum: Qui tecum.

EPISTLE. *Rom 1: 1-6*

PAUL, A SERVANT of Jesus Christ, called to be an apostle, separated unto the gospel of God, which He had promised before by His prophets in the Holy Scriptures, concerning His Son, Who was made to Him of the seed of David according to the flesh, Who was predestinated the Son of God in power, according to the spirit of sanctification, by the resurrection of our Lord Jesus Christ from the dead: by Whom we have received grace and apostleship for obedience to the faith, in all nations, for His name, among whom are you also the called of Jesus Christ.

Paulus, servus Jesu Christi, vocátus Apóstolus, segregátus in Evangélium Dei, quod ante promíserat per Prophétas suos in Scriptúris sanctis de Fílio suo, qui factus est ei ex sémine David secúndum carnem: qui prædestinátus est Fílius Dei in virtúte secúndum spíritum sanctificatiónis ex resurrectióne mortuórum Jesu Christi, Dómini nostri: per quem accépimus grátiam, et apostolátum ad obediéndum fídei in ómnibus géntibus pro nómine ejus, in quibus estis et vos vocáti Jesu Christi, Dómini nostri.

GRADUAL. *Ex 16: 6-7 & Ps 79: 2-3*

THIS DAY you shall know that the Lord will come, and save us; and in the morning you shall see His glory. ℣. Give ear, O Thou that rulest Israel: Thou that leadest Joseph like a sheep; Thou that sittest upon the cherubim, appear before Ephraim, Benjamin, and Manasses.

Hódie sciétis, quia véniet Dóminus et salvábit nos: et mane vidébitis glóriam ejus. ℣. Qui regis Ísraël, inténde: qui dedúcis, velut ovem, Joseph: qui sedes super Chérubim, appáre coram Éphraïm, Bénjamin, et Manásse.

ALLELUIA. *The following is added if this vigil falls on a Sunday.*

Allelúja, allelúja. ℣. Crástina die delébitur iníquitas terræ: et regnábit super nos Salvátor mundi. Allelúja.

Alleluia, alleluia. ℣. Tomorrow shall the iniquity of earth be wiped out; and the Savior of the world shall reign over us. Alleluia.

GOSPEL. *Matt 1: 18-21*

Cum esset desponsáta Mater Jesu Maria Joseph, ántequam conveníren, invénta est in útero habens de Spíritu Sancto. Joseph autem, vir ejus, cum esset justus et nollet eam tradúcere, vóluit occúlte dimíttere eam. Hæc autem eo cogitánte, ecce, Ángelus Dómini appáruit in somnis ei, dicens: Joseph, fili David, noli timére accípere Maríam cónjugẽ tuam: quod enim in ea natum est, de Spíritu Sancto est. Páriet autem fílium, et vocábis nomen ejus Jesum: ipse enim salvum fáciet pópulum suum a peccátis eórum.

WHEN MARY, the mother of Jesus, was espoused to Joseph, before they came together, she was found with child, of the Holy Ghost. Whereupon Joseph her husband, being a just man, and not willing publicly to expose her, was minded to put her away privately. But while he thought on these things, behold the angel of the Lord appeared to him in his sleep, saying: Joseph, son of David, fear not to take unto thee Mary thy wife, for that which is conceived in her is of the Holy Ghost. And she shall bring forth a son; and thou shalt call His name Jesus. For He shall save His people from their sins.

1962 • If this feast falls on a Sunday, the "Credo" is said. | *Si venerit in dominica, dicitur "Credo."*

OFFERTORY. *Ps 23: 7*

Tóllite portas, príncipes, vestras: et elevámini, portæ æternáles, et introíbit Rex glóriæ. ℣. *Dómini est terra et plenitúdo ejus: orbis terrárum et univérsi, qui hábitant in eo.* ℣. *Ipse super mária fundávit eum et super flúmina præparávit eum.*

LIFT UP your gates, O ye princes, and be ye lifted up, O eternal gates: and the King of glory shall enter in. ℣. *The earth is the Lord's and the fullness thereof: the world, and all they that dwell therein.* ℣. *For He hath founded it upon the seas; and hath prepared it upon the rivers.*

SECRET.

Da nobis, quǽsumus, omnípotens Deus: ut, sicut adoránda Fílii tui natalítia prævenímus, sic ejus múnera capiámus sempitérna gaudéntes: Qui tecũ.

Grant us, we beseech Thee, O almighty God, that, as in anticipation we come to celebrate the adorable birthday of Thy Son, so we may joyously lay hold upon His everlasting rewards. Who with Thee.

COMMUNION. *Is 40: 5*

Revelábitur glória Dómini: et vidébit omnis caro salutáre Dei nostri. (Ps 97: 5) ℣. *Psállite Dómino in cíthara; in cíthara et voce psalmi.*

—StDenisMissal|988 • Circa 988AD

THE GLORY of the Lord shall be revealed; and all flesh shall see the salvation of our God. ℣. *Sing praise to the Lord on the harp; on the harp, and with the voice of a psalm.*

I WILL PUT THIS FLEECE OF WOOL ON THE FLOOR: IF THERE BE DEW ON THE FLEECE ONLY, AND IT BE DRY ... (Judges 6 : 37)

SI ROS IN SOLO VELLERE FUERIT ET IN OMNI TERRA • JUDGES 6:37

YOU SHALL FIND THE INFANT WRAPPED IN SWADDLING CLOTHES, AND LAID IN A MANGER.

FACIAMUS HOMINEM AD IMAGINEM ET SIMILIT. • GENESIS 1:26

LET US MAKE MAN TO OUR IMAGE AND LIKENESS: AND LET HIM HAVE DOMINION OVER THE FISHES OF THE SEA ... (Gen 1:26)

POSTCOMMUNION.

Da nobis, quǽsumus, Dómine: unigéniti Fílii tui recensíta nativitáte respiráre; cujus cæléstí mystério páscimur et potámur. Per eúmdem Dóminum.

Grant us, we beseech Thee, O Lord, that we may begin a new life with this festival of the Nativity of Thine only begotten Son, Who, in these mysteries, feeds us with the meat and drink of that life which is eternal. Through the same.

I Classis.

—Christmas Midnight Mass—

IN NAVITATE DOMINI AD PRIMAM MISSAM IN NOCTE *Station at Saint Mary at the Crib*

INTROIT. *Ps 2: 7*

Dóminus dixit ad me: Fílius meus es tu, ego hódie génui te. ℣. Quare fremuérunt gentes: et pópuli meditáti sunt inánia? ℣. Glória Patri.

THE LORD HATH said to Me: Thou art My Son, this day have I begotten Thee. (Ps 2: 1) Why have the Gentiles raged, and the people devised vain things? ℣. Glory.

COLLECT.

Deus, qui hanc sacratíssimam noctem veri lúminis fecísti illustratióne claréscere: da, quǽsumus; ut, cujus lucis mystéria in terra cognóvimus, ejus quoque gáudiis in cælo perfruámur: Qui tecum.

O God, Who has brightened this most holy night with the shining of the true light, grant, we beseech Thee, that we may enjoy in heaven the delights of Him whose mystical light we have known on earth. Who with Thee.

EPISTLE. *Titus 2: 11-15*

Caríssime: Appáruit grátia Dei Salvatóris nostri ómnibus homínibus, erúdiens nos, ut, abnegántes impietátem et sæculária desidéria, sóbrie et juste et pie vivámus in hoc sǽculo, exspectántes beátam spem et advéntum glóriæ magni Dei et Salvatóris nostri Jesu Christi: qui dedit semetípsum pro nobis: ut nos redímeret ab omni iniquitáte, et mundáret sibi pópulum acceptábilem, sectatórem bonórum óperum. Hæc lóquere et exhortáre: in Christo Jesu, Dómino nostro.

DEARLY BELOVED, the grace of God our Savior hath appeared to all men, instructing us, that, denying ungodliness and worldly desires, we should live soberly, and justly, and godly in this world, looking for the blessed hope and coming of the glory of the great God and our Savior Jesus Christ, Who gave Himself for us, that He might redeem us from all iniquity, and might cleanse to Himself a people acceptable, a pursuer of good works. These things speak, and exhort: In Christ Jesus our Lord.

GRADUAL & ALLELUIA. *Ps 109: 3, 1 & Ps 2: 7*

Tecum princípium in die virtútis tuæ: in splendóribus Sanctórum, ex útero ante lucíferum génui te. ℣. Dixit Dóminus Dómino meo: Sede a dextris meis: donec ponam inimícos tuos, scabéllum pedum tuórum.

WITH THEE is the principality in the day of Thy strength in the brightness of the saints, from the womb before the day-star I begot Thee. ℣. The Lord said to my Lord: Sit Thou at My right hand, until I make Thy enemies Thy footstool.

Alleluia, alleluia. ℣. The Lord hath said to Me: Thou art My Son, this day have I begotten Thee. Alleluia.

Allelúja, allelúja. ℣. Dóminus dixit ad me: Fílius meus es tu, ego hódie génui te. Allelúja.

GOSPEL. *Luke 2: 1-14*

A DECREE WENT OUT from Caesar Augustus, that the whole world should be enrolled. This enrolling was first made by Cyrinus, the governor of Syria. And all went to be enrolled, every one into his own city. And Joseph also went up from Galilee out of the city of Nazareth, into Judea to the city of David, which is called Bethlehem, because he was of the house and family of David, to be enrolled with Mary his espoused wife, who was with child. And it came to pass that when they were there, her days were accomplished, that she should be delivered. And she brought forth her firstborn Son, and wrapped Him up in swaddling clothes, and laid Him in a manger, because there was no room for them in the inn. And there were in the same country shepherds watching, and keeping the night watches over their flock.

In illo témpore: Éxiit edíctum a Cǽsare Augústo, ut describerétur univérsus orbis. Hæc descríptio prima facta est a prǽside Sýriæ Cyríno: et ibant omnes ut profiteréntur sínguli in suam civitátem. Ascéndit autem et Joseph a Galilǽa de civitáte Názareth, in Judǽam in civitátem David, quæ vocátur Béthlehem: eo quod esset de domo et fámilia David, ut profiterétur cũ María desponsáta sibi uxóre prægnánte. Factum est autem, cum essent ibi, impléti sunt dies, ut páreret. Et péperit fílium suum primogénitum, et pannis eum invólvit, et reclinávit eum in præsépio: quia non erat eis locus in diversório. Et pastóres erant in regióne eádem vigilántes, et custodiéntes vigílias noctis super gregem suum.

And behold an angel of the Lord stood by them, and the brightness of God shone round about them, and they feared with a great fear. And the angel said to them: Fear not; for behold I bring you good tidings of great joy, that shall be to all the people; for this day is born to you a Savior, Who is Christ the Lord, in the city of David. And this shall be a sign unto you: You shall find the infant wrapped in swaddling clothes, and laid in a manger. And suddenly there was with the angel a multitude of the heavenly army, praising God, and saying: Glory to God in the highest; and on earth peace to men of good will. CREDO.

Et ecce, Ángelus Dómini stetit juxta illos, et cláritas Dei circumfúlsit illos, et timuérunt timóre magno. Et dixit illis Ángelus: Nolíte timére: ecce enim, evangelízo vobis gáudiũ magnũ, quod erit omni pópulo: quia natus est vobis hódie Salvátor, qui est Christus Dóminus, in civitáte David. Et hoc vobis signum: Inveniétis infántem pannis involútum, et pósitum in præsépio. Et súbito facta est cum Ángelo multitúdo milítiæ cæléstis, laudántium Deum et dicéntium: Glória in altíssimis Deo, et in terra pax homínibus bonæ voluntátis.

OFFERTORY. *Ps 95: 11, 13*

LET THE HEAVENS rejoice, and let the earth be glad before the face of the Lord, because He cometh. ℣. *Sing ye to the Lord a new canticle: sing to the Lord, all the earth.* ℣. *Sing to the Lord, and bless his name; never cease to bear record of his power to save.*

Lætántur cæli et exsúltet terra ante fáciem Dómini: quóniam venit. ℣. *Cantáte Dómino cánticum novum, cantáte Dómino omnis terra.* ℣. *Cantáte Dómino: benedícite nomen ejus: bene nuntiáte de die in diem salutáre ejus.*

SECRET.

Accépta tibi sit, Dómine, quǽsumus, hodiérnæ festivitátis oblátio: ut, tua gratia largiénte, per hæc sacrosáncta commércia, in illíus inveniámur forma, in quo tecum est nostra substántia: Qui tecum.

May the oblation of this day's festivity, we pray Thee, O Lord, find acceptance with Thee; that, by the bounty of Thy grace, we may, through this sacred intercourse, be found made like unto Him in Whom our substance is united with Thee. Who with Thee.

The Preface of the Nativity (page 189) follows the Secret.

COMMUNION. *Ps 109: 3*

In splendóribus Sanctórum, ex útero ante lucíferum génui te. (Ps 109: 1) ℣. *Dixit Dóminus Dómino meo: Sede a dextris meis.* —StDenisMissal|988 • Circa 988AD

IN THE BRIGHTNESS of the saints, from the womb before the day-star I begot Thee. ℣. *To the Master I serve the Lord's promise was given, Sit here at my right hand.*

POSTCOMMUNION.

Da nobis, quǽsumus, Dómine, Deus noster: ut, qui Nativitátem Dómini nostri Jesu Christi mystériis nos frequentáre gaudémus; dignis conversatiónibus ad ejus mereámur perveníre consórtium: Qui tecum.

Grant, we beseech Thee, O Lord our God, that we, who rejoice to celebrate with these mysteries the nativity of our Lord Jesus Christ, may deserve by worthy living to attain His companionship. Who with Thee.

I Classis.

—Christmas Mass at Dawn—

IN NAVITATE DOMINI AD SECUNDAM MISSAM IN AURORA *Station at Saint Anastasia*

INTROIT. *Is 9: 2, 6*

Lux fulgébit hódie super nos: quia natus est nobis Dóminus: et vocábitur Admirábilis, Deus, Princeps pacis, Pater futúri sǽculi: cujus regni non erit finis. ℣. Dóminus regnávit, decórem indútus est: indútus est Dóminus fortitúdinem, et præcínxit se. ℣. Glória Patri.

A LIGHT SHALL SHINE UPON US this day: for the Lord is born to us: and He shall be called wonderful, God, the prince of peace, the Father of the world to come: of Whose reign there shall be no end. (Ps 92: 1) The Lord hath reigned, He is clothed with beauty: the Lord is clothed with strength, and hath girded Himself. ℣. Glory.

COLLECT.

Da nobis, quǽsumus, omnípotens Deus: ut, qui nova incarnáti Verbi tui luce perfúndimur; hoc in nostro resplén-deat ópere, quod per fidem fulget in mente. Per eúmdem.

Grant, we beseech thee, O Almighty God, that we who are filled with the new light of Thine Incarnate Word, may show forth in our deeds that which by faith shineth in our minds. Through the same.

COLLECT. *Commemoration of St. Anastasia.*

Grant, we beseech Thee, O almighty God, that we who honor the solemnity of Thy blessed martyr Anastasia may experience the effect of her intercession with Thee. Through Our Lord.

Da, quæsumus, omnípotens Deus: ut, qui beátæ Anastásiæ Mártyris tuæ solémnia cólimus; ejus apud te patrocínia sentiámus. Per Dóminum.

According to Father Johann Peter Kirsch, Christmas (on 25 December) was not among the earliest festivals of the Church. The feast of Saint Anastasia was celebrated on 25 December, but when Christmas eclipsed it—perhaps in the fourth century—this martyr was not forgotten; she is commemorated.

EPISTLE. *Titus 3: 4-7*

DEARLY BELOVED, The goodness and kindness of God our Savior hath appeared: not by the works of justice, which we have done, but according to His mercy He saved us by the laver of regeneration, and renovation of the Holy Ghost, Whom He hath poured forth upon us abundantly through Jesus Christ our Savior: that, being justified by His grace, we may be heirs according to hope of life everlasting: in Christ Jesus our Lord.

Caríssime: Appáruit benígnitas et humánitas Salvatóris nostri Dei: non ex opéribus justítiæ, quæ fécimus nos, sed secúndum suam misericórdiam salvos nos fecit per lavácrum regeneratiónis et renovatiónis Spíritus Sancti, quem effúdit in nos abúnde per Jesum Christum, Salvatórem nostrum: ut, justificáti grátia ipsíus, herédes simus secúndum spem vitæ ætérnæ: in Christo Jesu, Dómino nostro.

GRADUAL & ALLELUIA. *Ps 117: 26-27, 23 & Ps 92: 1*

BLESSED is He that cometh in the Name of the Lord: the Lord is God, and He hath shone upon us. ℣. This is the Lord's doing: and it is wonderful in our eyes. | Alleluia, alleluia. ℣. The Lord hath reigned, He is clothed with beauty: the Lord is clothed with strength, and hath girded Himself with power. Alleluia.

Benedíctus, qui venit in nómine Dómini: Deus Dóminus, et illúxit nobis. ℣. A Dómino factum est istud: et est mirábile in óculis nostris.

Allelúja, allelúja. ℣. Dóminus regnávit, decórem índuit: índuit Dóminus fortitúdinem, et præcínxit se virtúte. Allelúja.

GOSPEL. *Luke 2: 15-20*

THE SHEPHERDS SAID one to another: Let us go over to Bethlehem, and let us see this word that is come to pass, which the Lord hath showed to us. And they came with haste; and they found Mary and Joseph, and the Infant lying in the manger. And seeing, they understood of the word that had been spoken to them concerning this child. And all that heard wondered: and at those things that were told them by the shepherds. But Mary kept all these words, pondering them in her heart. And the shepherds returned, glorifying and praising God, for all the things they had heard and seen, as it was told unto them. CREDO.

In illo témpore: Pastóres loquebántur ad ínvicem: Transeámus usque Béthlehem, et videámus hoc verbum, quod factum est, quod Dóminus osténdit nobis. Et venérunt festinántes: et invenérunt Maríam et Joseph, et Infántem pósitum in præsépio. Vidéntes autem cognovérunt de verbo, quod dictum erat illis de Púero hoc. Et omnes, qui audiérunt, miráti sunt: et de his, quæ dicta erant a pastóribus ad ipsos. María autem conservábat ómnia verba hæc, cónferens in corde suo. Et revérsi sunt pastóres, glorificántes et laudántes Deum in ómnibus, quæ audíerant et víderant, sicut dictum est ad illos.

OFFERTORY. *Ps 92: 1-2*

Deus enim firmávit orbem terræ, qui non commovébitur: paráta sedes tua, Deus, ex tunc, a sæculo tu es. ℣. *Dóminus regnávit, decórem índuit: índuit Dóminus fortitúdinem et præcínxit se virtúte.* ℣. *Mirábilis in excélsis Dóminus: testimónia tua credibília facta sunt nimis: domum tuam decent Sancta, Dómine, in longitúdinem diérum.*

** The word "ENIM" does not occur in the 1962 Missal but is in the Roman Gradual.*

GOD HATH established the world, which shall not be moved: Thy throne, O God, is prepared from of old; Thou art from everlasting. ℣. *The Lord hath reigned, He is clothed with beauty: the Lord is clothed with strength, and hath girded Himself.* ℣. *Wonderful is the Lord on High: How faithful, O Lord, are Thy promises! Holy is Thy house, and must needs be holy until the end of time.*

SECRET.

Múnera nostra, quǽsumus, Dómine, Nativitátis hodiérnæ mystériis apta provéniant, et pacem nobis semper infúndant: ut, sicut homo génitus idem refúlsit et Deus, sic nobis hæc terréna substántia cónferat, quod divínum est. Per eúmdem.

May our gifts, we pray Thee, O Lord, come forth agreeable to the mysteries of this day's nativity, and may they shower upon us peace; that as He who was begotten as man shone forth also as God, so also may this earthly substance bring us that which is divine. Through the same.

SECRET. *Commemoration of St. Anastasia.*

Áccipe, quǽsumus, Dómine, múnera dignánter obláta: et, beátæ Anastásiæ Mártyris tuæ suffragántibus méritis, ad nostræ salútis auxílium proveníre concéde. Per Dóminum.

Accept, we pray Thee, O Lord, the gifts duly offered to Thee, and, by the interceding merits of blessed Anastasia, Thy martyr, grant them to be profitable for the furtherance of our salvation. Through our Lord.

The Preface of the Nativity (page 189) follows the Secret.

COMMUNION. *Zach 9: 9*

Exsúlta, fília Sion, lauda, fília Jerúsalem: ecce, Rex tuus venit sanctus et Salvátor mundi. (Ps 147: 1) ℣. *Lauda, Jerúsalem, Dóminum; lauda Deum tuum, Sion.*

—GRADUALDENIS|1020 • Circa 1020AD

REJOICE GREATLY, O daughter of Sion, shout for joy, O daughter of Jerusalem behold Thy King comes, holy, the Savior of the world. ℣. *Praise the Lord, Jerusalem; Sion, exalt thy God!*

POSTCOMMUNION.

Hujus nos, Dómine, sacraménti semper nóvitas natális instáuret: cujus Natívitas singuláris humánam répulit vetustátem. Per eúmdem.

May the Christmas renewal of this sacrament ever restore us, O Lord, Whose miraculous birth did put away the ancient things of mankind. Through the same.

POSTCOMMUNION. *Commemoration of St. Anastasia.*

Satiásti, Dómine, famíliam tuã munéribus sacris: ejus, quǽsumus, semper interventióne nos réfove, cujus solémnia celebrámus. Per Dóminum.

Thou hast filled Thy household, O Lord, with sacred gifts; ever cherish us by the intercession of her whose feast we celebrate. Through our Lord.

Christmas is the only feast given three Masses according to the 1962 calendar: "Ad Primam Missam" in nocte; "Ad Secundam Missam" in aurora; and "Ad Tertiam Missam" in die nativitatis Domini. However, Ildefonsus—a Spanish bishop writing in 845AD—alludes to triple Masses celebrated on Christmas, Easter Sunday, Pentecost Sunday, and the Transfiguration.

—*Christmas Daytime Mass*— *I Classis.*

IN NAVITATE DOMINI AD TERTIAM MISSAM IN DIE *Station at Saint Mary Major*

INTROIT. *Is 9: 6*

A CHILD IS BORN TO US, and a Son is given to us: whose government is upon His shoulder: and His name shall be called, the Angel of great counsel. (Ps 97: 1) Sing ye to the Lord a new canticle: because He hath done wonderful things. ℣. Glory.

Puer natus est nobis, et fílius datus est nobis: cujus impérium super húmerum ejus: et vocábitur nomen ejus magni consílii Ángelus. ℣. Cantáte Dómino cánticum novum, quia mirabília fecit. ℣. Glória Patri.

COLLECT.

Grant, we beseech Thee, almighty God, that the new birth in the flesh of Thine only-begotten Son may set us free, whom the old bondage doth hold under the yoke of sin. Through the same.

Concéde, quǽsumus, omnípotens Deus: ut nos Unigéniti tui nova per carnem Nativitas líberet; quos sub peccáti jugo vetústa sérvitus tenet. Per eúmdem.

EPISTLE. *Heb 1: 1-12*

GOD, Who diversely and many ways spoke in times past to the fathers by the prophets, last of all, in these days hath spoken to us, by His Son, Whom He hath appointed heir of all things, by Whom also He made the world. Who being the brightness of His glory, and the figure of His substance, and upholding all things by the word of His power, making purgation of sins, sitteth on the right hand of the majesty on high; being made so much better than the angels, as He hath inherited a more excellent name than they.

Multifáriam, multísque modis olim Deus loquens pátribus in Prophétis: novíssime diébus istis locútus est nobis in Fílio, quem constítuit herédem universórum, per quem fecit et sǽcula: qui cum sit splendor glóriæ, et figúra substántiæ ejus, portánsque ómnia verbo virtútis suæ, purgatiónem peccatórum fáciens, sedet ad déxteram majestátis in excélsis: tanto mélior Ángelis effectus, quanto differéntius præ illis nomen hereditávit.

For to which of the angels hath He said at any time: Thou art My Son, today have I begotten Thee? And again: I will be to Him a father, and He shall be to Me a son? And again, when He bringeth in the first-begotten into the world, He saith, And let all the angels of God adore Him. And to the angels indeed He saith, He that maketh His angels spirits, and His ministers a flame of fire. But to the Son: Thy throne,

Cui enim dixit aliquándo Angelórum: Fílius meus es tu, ego hódie génui te? Et rursum: Ego ero illi in patrem, et ipse erit mihi in fílium? Et cum íterum introdúcit Primogénitum in orbem terræ, dicit: Et adórent eum omnes Ángeli Dei. Et ad Ángelos quidẽ dicit: Qui facit Ángelos suos spíritus, et minístros suos flammam ignis. Ad Fílium autem: Thronus tuus, Deus, in sǽculum sǽculi: virga æquitátis, virga

QUEM EDITUM EX VIRGINE PAVESCIT OMNIS ANIMA: PER QUEM ET NOS RESURGERE, DEVOTA MENTE CREDIMUS. (5th cent.)

BEATUS AUCTOR SAECULI SERVILE CORPUS INDUIT: UT CARNE CARNEM LIBERANS NON PERDERET QUOS CONDIDIT.

FENO IACERE PERTULIT PRAESEPE NON ABHORRUIT: PARVOQUE LACTE PASTUS EST PER QUEM NEC ALES ESURIT.

HE SUBMITTED TO LYING IN HAY, DID NOT RECOIL FROM THE MANGER: AND HE BY WHOM NO BIRD GOES HUNGRY WAS FED WITH A LITTLE MILK.

O God, is for ever and ever; a scepter of justice is the scepter of Thy kingdom. Thou hast loved justice, and hated iniquity; therefore God, Thy God, hath anointed Thee with the oil of gladness above Thy fellows. And: Thou in the beginning, O Lord, didst found the earth; and the works of Thy hands are the heavens. They shall perish, but Thou shalt continue; and they shall all grow old as a garment; and as a vesture shalt Thou change them, and they shall be changed; but Thou art the self-same, and Thy years shall not fail.

regni tui. Dilexísti justítiam et odísti iniquitátem: proptérea unxit te Deus, Deus tuus, óleo exsultatiónis præ partícipibus tuis. Et: Tu in princípio, Dómine, terram fundásti: et ópera mánuum tuárũ sunt cæli. Ipsi períbunt, tu autem permanébis; et omnes ut vestiméntum veteráscent: et velut amíctum mutábis eos, et mutabúntur: tu autem idem ipse es, et anni tui non defícient.

GRADUAL & ALLELUIA. *Ps 97: 3, 2 & Trad.*

ALL THE ENDS OF THE EARTH have seen the salvation of our God: sing joyfully to God all the earth. ℣. The Lord hath made known His salvation; He hath revealed His justice in the sight of the Gentiles. Alleluia, alleluia. ℣. A hallowed day hath dawned for us: come ye Gentiles, and adore the Lord; for this day a great light hath descended upon the earth. Alleluia.

Vidérunt omnes fines terræ salutáre Dei nostri: jubiláte Deo, omnis terra. ℣. Notum fecit Dóminus salutáre suum: ante conspéctum géntium revelávit justítiam suam.
Allelúja, allelúja. ℣. Dies sanctificátus illúxit nobis: veníte, gentes, et adoráte Dóminum: quia hódie descéndit lux magna super terram. Allelúja.

GOSPEL. *John 1: 1-14*

IN THE BEGINNING was the Word, and the Word was with God, and the Word was God. The same was in the beginning with God. All things were made by Him, and without Him was made nothing that was made. In Him was life, and the life was the light of men: and the light shineth in darkness, and the darkness did not comprehend it. There was a man sent from God, whose name was John. This man came for a witness to give testimony of the light, that all men might believe through him. He was not the light, but was to give testimony of the light. That was the true light which enlighteneth every man that cometh into this world. He was in the world, and the world was made by Him, and the world knew Him not. He came unto His own, and His own received Him not. But as many as received Him, to them He gave power to become the sons of God: to them that believe in His name: who are born, not of blood, nor of the will of the Flesh, nor of the will of man, but of God. (*genuflect*) AND THE WORD WAS MADE FLESH, and dwelt among us: and we saw His glory, the glory as of the only begotten of the Father, full of grace and truth. CREDO.

In princípio erat Verbum, et Verbum erat apud Deum, et Deus erat Verbum. Hoc erat in princípio apud Deum. Omnia per ipsum facta sunt: et sine ipso factum est nihil, quod factum est: in ipso vita erat, et vita erat lux hóminum: et lux in ténebris lucet, et ténebræ eam non comprehendérunt. Fuit homo missus a Deo, cui nomen erat Joánnes. Hic venit in testimónium, ut testimóniũ perhibéret de lúmine, ut omnes créderent per illum. Non erat ille lux, sed ut testimónium perhibéret de lúmine. Erat lux vera, quæ illúminat omnem hóminem veniéntem in hunc mundum. In mundo erat, et mundus per ipsum factus est, et mundus eum non cognóvit. In própria venit, et sui eum non recepérunt. Quotquot autem recepérunt eum, dedit eis potestátem fílios Dei fíeri, his, qui credunt in nómine ejus: qui non ex sanguínibus, neque ex voluntáte carnis, neque ex voluntáte viri, sed ex Deo nati sunt. (*hic genuflectitur*) ET VERBUM CARO FACTUM EST, et habitávit in nobis: et vídimus glóriam ejus, glóriam quasi Unigéniti a Patre, plenum grátiæ et veritátis.

OFFERTORY. *Ps 88: 12, 15*

Tui sunt cæli et tua est terra: orbem terrárum et plenitúdinem ejus tu fundásti: justítia et judícium præparátio sedis tuæ. ℣. *Magnus et metuéndus super omnes, qui in circúitu ejus sunt: tu domináris potestáti maris, motum autem flúctuum ejus tu mítigas.* ℣. *Misericórdia et véritas praeíbunt ante fáciem tuam: et in beneplácito tuo exaltábitur cornu nostrum.* ℣. *Tu humiliásti sicut vulnerátum supérbum: et in virtúte bráchii tui dispersísti inimícos tuos: firmétur manus tua et exaltétur déxtera tua, Dómine.*

THINE ARE THE HEAVENS, and Thine is the earth: the world and the fullness thereof Thou hast founded: justice and judgment are the preparation of Thy throne. ℣. *Great and terrible above all them that are about Him: Thou rulest the power of the sea: and appeasest the motion of the waves thereof.* ℣. *Mercy and truth shall go before Thy face: and in Thy good pleasure shall our horn be exalted.* ℣. *Thou hast humbled the proud one, as one that is slain: with the strength of Thine arm Thou hast scattered Thine enemies: let Thy hand be strengthened, and Thy right hand exalted, O Lord.*

SECRET.

Obláta, Dómine, múnera, nova Unigéniti tui Nativitáte sanctífica: nosque a peccatórum nostrórũ máculis emúnda. Per eúmdem.

Sanctify our oblations, O Lord, by the new birth of Thy only-begotten Son, and cleanse us from the stains of our sins. Through the same.

The Preface of the Nativity (page 189) follows the Secret.

COMMUNION. *Ps 97: 3*

Vidérunt omnes fines terræ salutáre Dei nostri. (Is 9: 6) ℣. *Puer natus est nobis, et fílius datus est nobis.*
—StDenisMissal|988 • Circa 988AD

ALL THE ENDS OF THE EARTH have seen the salvation of our God. ℣. *For our sakes a child is born, to our race a son is given.*

POSTCOMMUNION.

Præsta, quǽsumus, omnípotens Deus: ut natus hódie Salvátor mundi, sicut divínæ nobis generatiónis est auctor; ita et immortalitátis sit ipse largítor: Qui tecum.

Grant, we beseech Thee, O almighty God, that, as the Savior of the world, born this day, is unto us the author of divine generation, so He may also be the bestower of immortality, Who with Thee.

1962 • Today the Last Gospel is omitted. | *In fine huius Missae non dicitur ultimum evangelium.*

THE LAST GOSPEL • Before 1955, the Last Gospel was not always the opening of St. John's Gospel. Instead, a "Proper Last Gospel" was frequently read; i.e. when certain feasts were commemorated, the gospel ***from the commemorated feast*** became that day's Last Gospel. For the Christmas Daytime Mass, the EPIPHANY GOSPEL was read as a Proper Last Gospel prior to *Cum Nostra Hac Aetate* (23 March 1955). In the 1962 Missal, the only Proper Last Gospel happens on Palm Sunday (a.k.a. "II Sunday of Passiontide") if the ceremonies before Mass are omitted. In 1951, the reformers held the *Maria Laach Conference*, whose 12th resolution called for the total elimination of the Last Gospel, citing the "success" of eliminating the Last Gospel from the experimental Easter Vigil of 1951. The 1961 *Code of Rubrics* (§510) says the Last Gospel is omitted for: (a) Masses where *Benedicámus Dómino* is said (e.g. Holy Thursday in the 1962 version); (b) The Christmas Daytime Mass; (c) Palm Sunday when the ceremonies before Mass do take place; (d) the Mass of the Easter Vigil; (e) Masses for the Dead when absolution over the catafalque follows. Very soon thereafter—on 26 September 1964—INTER OECUMENICI §48j completely eliminated the Last Gospel in all Masses.

STRATEGY • The reformers used this method: (1951) eliminate the Easter Eve Last Gospel; (1955) eliminate Proper Last Gospels; (1961) eliminate the Last Gospel on certain days; (1964) eliminate every Last Gospel.

— *Sunday within the Octave of Christmas* — *II Classis.*

DOMINICA INFRA OCTAVAM NATIVITATIS *This feast is ancient, but has not a station.*

INTROIT. *Wis 18: 14-15*

WHILE ALL THINGS were in quiet silence, and the night was in the midst of her course, Thy almighty word, O Lord, came from heaven, from Thy royal throne. (Ps 92: 1) The Lord hath reigned, He is clothed with beauty: the Lord is clothed with strength, and hath girded Himself. ℣. Glory.

Dum médiũ siléntiũ tenérent ómnia, et nox in suo cursu médium iter habéret, omnípotens Sermo tuus, Dñe, de cælis a regálibus sédibus venit. ℣. Dñs regnávit, decórem indútus est: indútus est Dóminus fortitúdinem, et præcínxit se. ℣. Glória Patri.

The Latin word "MEDIUM" here means "deep." Literally, the phrase means: "While all things possessed deep silence." Translated more freely: "While all things were in the depths of silence."

COLLECT.

O almighty and eternal God, direct our actions in conformity with Thy good pleasure, that in the name of Thy beloved Son we may be worthy to abound in good works. Who with Thee.

Omnípotens sempitérne Deus, dírige actus nostros in beneplácito tuo: ut in nómine dilécti Fílii tui mereámur bonis opéribus abundáre: Qui tecum.

EPISTLE. *Gal 4: 1-7*

BRETHREN, AS LONG AS the heir is a child, he differeth nothing from a servant, though he be lord of all: but is under tutors and governors until the time appointed by the father: so we also, when we were children, were serving under the elements of the world. But when the fullness of the time was come, God sent His Son, made of a woman, made under the law: that He might redeem them who were under the law; that we might receive the adoption of sons. And because you are sons, God hath sent the Spirit of His Son into your hearts, crying: Abba, Father. Therefore now he is not a servant, but a son; and if a son, an heir also through God.

Fratres: Quanto témpore heres párvulus est, nihil differt a servo, cum sit dóminus ómnium: sed sub tutóribus et actóribus est usque ad præfinítum tempus a patre: ita et nos, cum essémus párvuli, sub eleméntis mundi erámus serviéntes. At ubi venit plenitúdo témporis, misit Deus Fílium suum, factum ex mulíere, factum sub lege, ut eos, qui sub lege erant, redímeret, ut adoptiónem filiórum reciperémus. Quóniam autem estis fílii, misit Deus Spíritum Fílii sui in corda vestra, clamántem: Abba, Pater. Itaque jam non est servus, sed fílius: quod si fílius, et heres per Deum.

GRADUAL & ALLELUIA. *Ps 44: 3, 2 & Ps 92: 1*

THOU art beautiful above the sons of men: grace is poured abroad in Thy lips. ℣. My heart hath uttered a good word, I speak my works to the King: my tongue is the pen of a scrivener that writeth swiftly. Alleluia, alleluia. ℣. The Lord hath reigned, He is clothed with beauty: the Lord is clothed with strength, and hath girded Himself with power. Alleluia.

Speciósus forma præ fíliis hóminum: diffúsa est grátia in lábiis tuis. ℣. Eructávit cor meum verbum bonum, dico ego ópera mea Regi: lingua mea cálamus scribæ, velóciter scribéntis.

Allelúja, allelúja. ℣. Dóminus regnávit, decórem índuit: índuit Dóminus fortitúdinem, et præcínxit se virtúte. Allelúja.

GOSPEL. *Luke 2: 33-40*

In illo témpore: Erat Joseph et María Mater Jesu, mirántes super his quæ dicebántur de illo. Et benedíxit illis Símeon, et dixit ad Maríam Matrem ejus: Ecce, pósitus est hic in ruínam et in resurrectiónem multórum in Israël: et in signum, cui contradicétur: et tuam ipsíus ánimam pertransíbit gládius, ut reveléntur ex multis córdibus cogitatiónes.

JOSEPH AND MARY, the mother of Jesus, were wondering at these things which were spoken concerning Him. And Simeon blessed them, and said to Mary His mother: Behold this child is set for the fall, and for the resurrection of many in Israel, and for a sign which shall be contradicted: and thine own soul a sword shall pierce, that out of many hearts thoughts may be revealed.

Et erat Anna prophetíssa, fília Phánuel, de tribu Aser: hæc procésserat in diébus multis, et víxerat cum viro suo annis septem a virginitáte sua. Et hæc vídua usque ad annos octogínta quátuor: quæ non discedébat de templo, jejúniis et obsecratiónibus sérviens nocte ac die. Et hæc, ipsa hora supervéniens, confitebátur Dómino, et loquebátur de illo ómnibus, qui exspectábant redemptiónem Israël. Et ut perfecérunt ómnia secúndum legem Dómini, revérsi sunt in Galilǽam in civitátem suam Názareth. Puer autem crescébat, et confortabátur, plenus sapiéntia: et grátia Dei erat in illo.

And there was one Anna, a prophetess, the daughter of Phanuel, of the tribe of Aser; she was far advanced in years, and had lived with her husband seven years from her virginity. And she was a widow until fourscore and four years; who departed not from the temple, by fastings and prayers serving night and day. Now she at the same hour coming in, confessed to the Lord; and spoke of Him to all that looked for the redemption of Israel. And after they had performed all things according to the law of the Lord, they returned into Galilee, to their city Nazareth. And so the child grew and came to his strength, full of wisdom; and the grace of God rested upon him. CREDO.

OFFERTORY. *Ps 92: 1-2*

Deus enim firmávit orbem terræ, qui non commovébitur: paráta sedes tua, Deus, ex tunc, a sǽculo tu es. ℣. *Dóminus regnávit, decórem índuit: índuit Dóminus fortitúdinem et præcínxit se virtúte.* ℣. *Mirábilis in excélsis Dóminus: testimónia tua credibília facta sunt nimis: domum tuam decent Sancta, Dómine, in longitúdinem diérum.*

* *The word "ENIM" does not occur in the 1962 Missal but is in the Roman Gradual.*

GOD HATH established the world, which shall not be moved: Thy throne, O God, is prepared from of old; Thou art from everlasting. ℣. *The Lord hath reigned, He is clothed with beauty: the Lord is clothed with strength, and hath girded Himself.* ℣. *Wonderful is the Lord on High: How faithful, O Lord, are Thy promises! Holy is Thy house, and must needs be holy until the end of time.*

SECRET.

Concéde, quǽsumus, omnípotens Deus: ut óculis tuæ majestátis munus oblátum, et grátiam nobis piæ devotiónis obtíneat, et efféctum beátæ perennitátis acquírat. Per Dóminum.

Grant, we beseech Thee, O almighty God, that the gift present before the eyes of Thy majesty may both obtain for us the grace of godly devotion and win its effect in a blessed eternity. Through our Lord.

The Preface of the Nativity (page 189) follows the Secret.

COMMUNION. *Matt 2: 20*

TAKE THE CHILD and His mother, and go into the land of Israel: for they are dead that sought the life of the child. ℣. *Firm stood Thy throne ere ever the world began; from all eternity, Thou art.*

Tolle Púerum et Matrem ejus, et vade in terram Ísraël: defúncti sunt enim, qui quærébant ánimam Púeri. (Ps 92: 2) ℣. *Paráta sedes tua ex tunc: a sǽculo tu es.*

—12050CORBIE|853 • Circa 853AD

POSTCOMMUNION.

By the operation of this mystery, O Lord, may our sins be purged, and our just desires fulfilled. Through our Lord.

Per hujus, Dómine, operatiónẽ mystérii, et vítia nostra purgéntur, et justa desidéria compleántur. Per Dóminum.

This Sunday's communion antiphon does not come from a psalm. However, the ancient manuscripts seem to be united that the "extra" verses should come from Psalm 92, which comes from the Introit.

—*Octave Day of Christmas*— *I Classis.*

OCTAVA NATIVITATIS DOMINI *Station at Saint Mary's across the Tiber*

INTROIT. *Is 9: 6*

A CHILD IS BORN TO US, and a Son is given to us: whose government is upon His shoulder: and His name shall be called, the Angel of great counsel. (Ps 97: 1) Sing ye to the Lord a new canticle: because He hath done wonderful things. ℣. Glory.

Puer natus est nobis, et fílius datus est nobis: cujus impérium super húmerum ejus: et vocábitur nomen ejus magni consílii Ángelus. ℣. Cantáte Dómino cánticum novum, quia mirabília fecit. ℣. Glória Patri.

COLLECT.

O God, Who, by the fruitful virginity of blessed Mary, hast bestowed upon mankind the rewards of eternal salvation, grant, we beseech Thee, that we may evermore experience the intercession in our behalf of her through whom we have been found worthy to receive the author of life, Our Lord Jesus Christ, Thy Son, Who with Thee.

Deus, qui salútis ætérnæ, beátæ Maríæ virginitáte fecúnda, humáno géneri prǽmia præstitísti: tríbue, quǽsumus; ut ipsam pro nobis intercédere sentiámus, per quam merúimus auctórem vitæ suscípere, Dóminum nostrum Jesum Christum, Fílium tuum: Qui tecum.

EPISTLE. *Titus 2: 11-15*

DEARLY BELOVED, the grace of God our Savior hath appeared to all men, instructing us, that denying ungodliness and worldly desires, we should live soberly, and justly, and godly in this world, looking for the blessed hope and coming of the glory of

Caríssime: Appáruit grátia Dei Salvatóris nostri ómnibus homínibus, erúdiens nos, ut, abnegántes impietátem et sæculária desidéria, sóbrie et juste et pie vivámus in hoc sǽculo, exspectántes beátam spem et advéntũ glóriæ magni

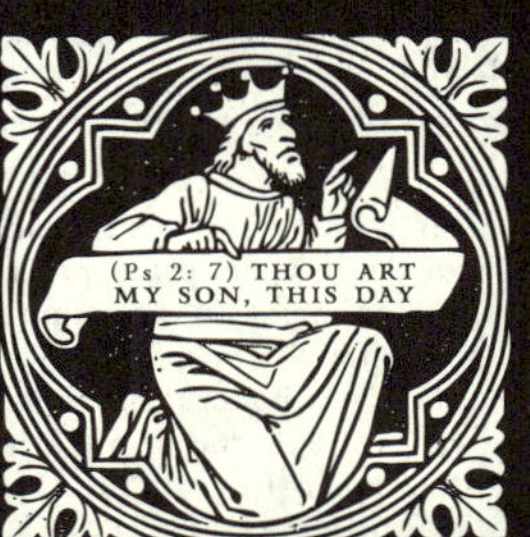

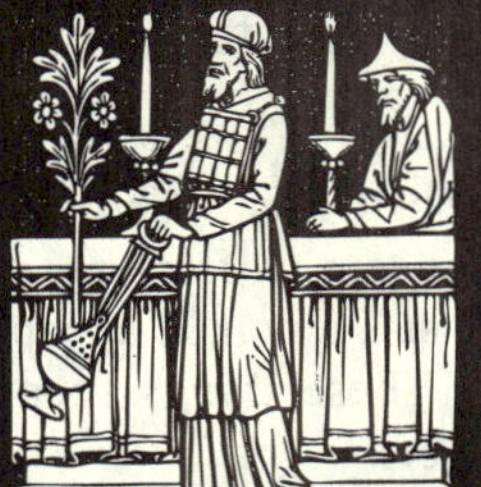

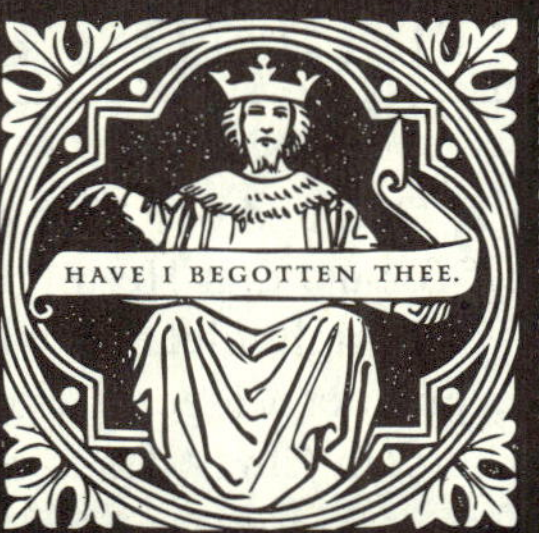

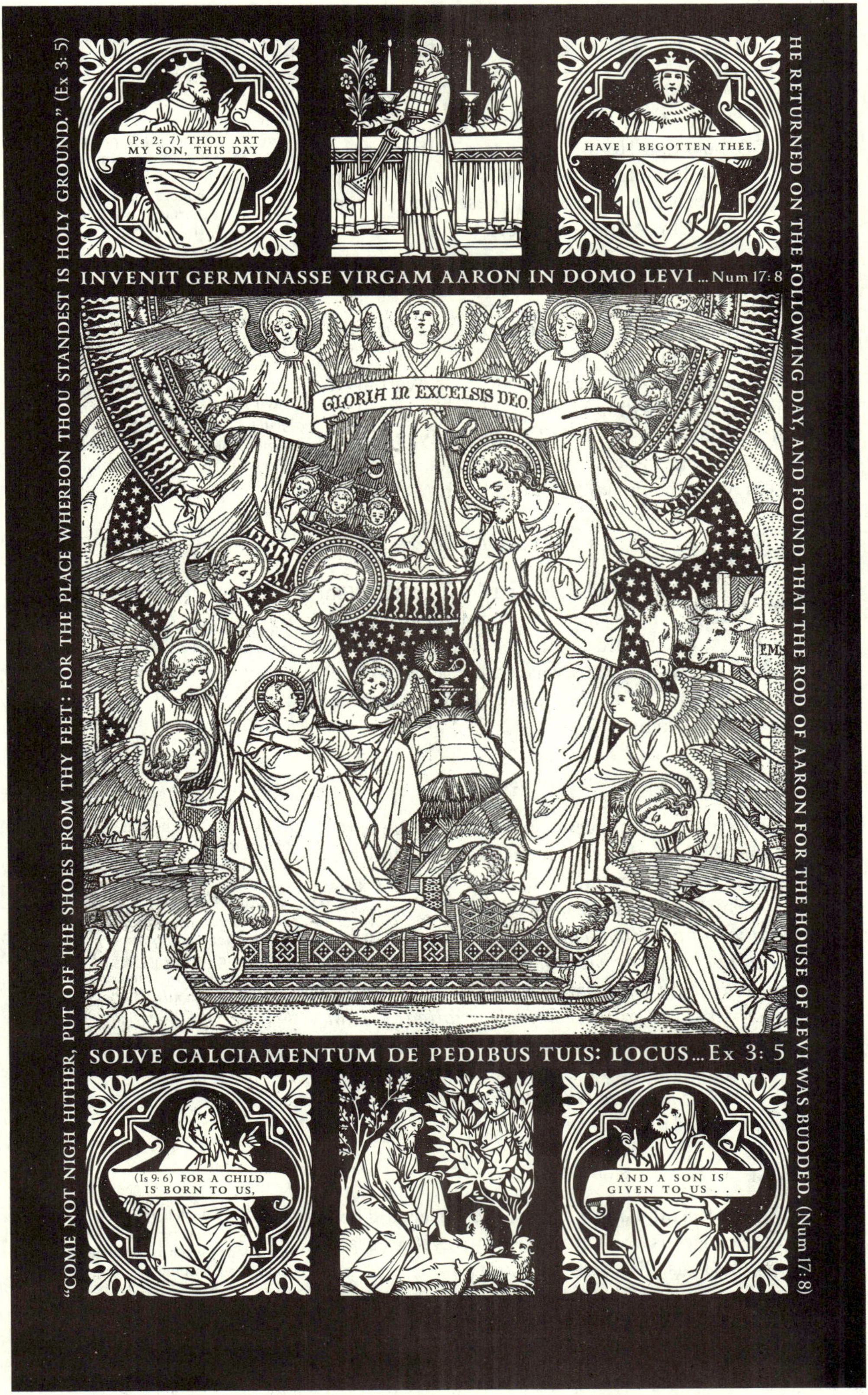
(Ps 2: 7) THOU ART MY SON, THIS DAY
HAVE I BEGOTTEN THEE.
INVENIT GERMINASSE VIRGAM AARON IN DOMO LEVI ... Num 17: 8
GLORIA IN EXCELSIS DEO.
F.M.
SOLVE CALCIAMENTUM DE PEDIBUS TUIS: LOCUS ... Ex 3: 5
(Is 9: 6) FOR A CHILD IS BORN TO US,
AND A SON IS GIVEN TO US . . .
“COME NOT NIGH HITHER, PUT OFF THE SHOES FROM THY FEET: FOR THE PLACE WHEREON THOU STANDEST IS HOLY GROUND.” (Ex 3: 5)
HE RETURNED ON THE FOLLOWING DAY, AND FOUND THAT THE ROD OF AARON FOR THE HOUSE OF LEVI WAS BUDDED. (Num 17:8)

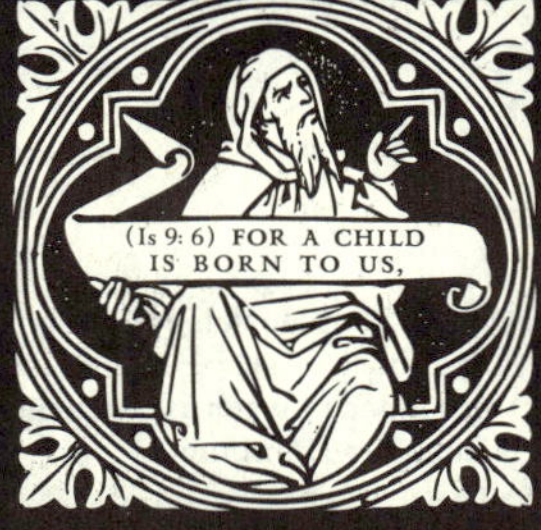

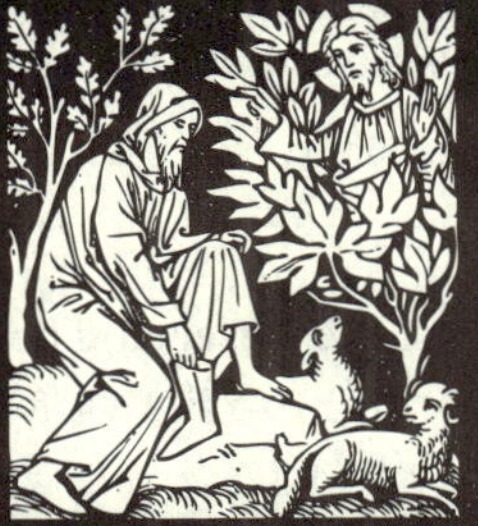

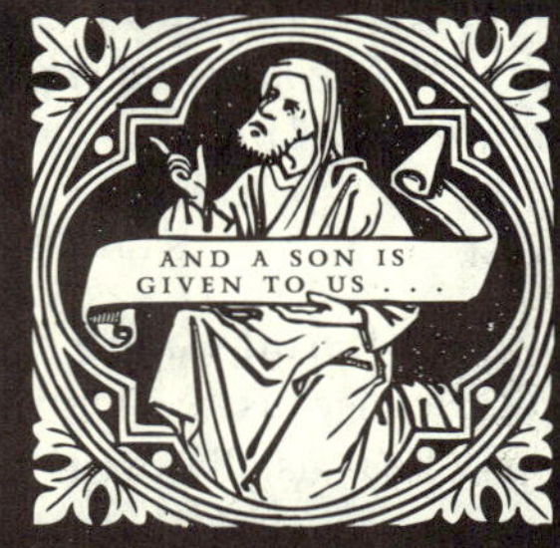

the great God and our Savior Jesus Christ, Who gave Himself for us, that He might redeem us from all iniquity, and might cleanse to Himself a people acceptable, a pursuer of good works. These things speak, and exhort: in Christ Jesus our Lord.

Dei et Salvatóris nostri Jesu Christi: qui dedit semetípsum pro nobis: ut nos redímeret ab omni iniquitáte, et mundáret sibi pópulum acceptábilem, sectatórem bonórum óperum. Hæc lóquere et exhortáre: in Christo Jesu, Dómino nostro.

GRADUAL & ALLELUIA. *Ps 97: 3, 2 & Heb 1: 1-2*

ALL THE ENDS of the earth have seen the salvation of our God: sing joyfully to God all the earth. ℣. The Lord hath made known His salvation: He hath revealed His justice in the sight of the gentiles. Alleluia, alleluia. ℣. God, Who diversely spoke in times past to the fathers by the prophets, last of all in these days hath spoken to us by His Son. Alleluia.

Vidérunt omnes fines terræ salutáre Dei nostri: jubiláte Deo, omnis terra. ℣. Notum fecit Dóminus salutáre suum: ante conspéctum géntium revelávit justítiam suam.

Allelúja, allelúja. ℣. Multifárie olim Deus loquens pátribus in Prophétis, novíssime diébus istis locútus est nobis in Fílio. Allelúja.

GOSPEL. *Luke 2: 21*

AT THAT TIME, after eight days were accomplished that the child should be circumcised, His name was called Jesus, which was called by the angel, before He was conceived in the womb. CREDO.

In illo témpore: Postquã consummáti sunt dies octo, ut circumciderétur Puer: vocátum est nomen ejus Jesus, quod vocátum est ab Ángelo, priúsquã in útero conciperétur.

OFFERTORY. *Ps 88: 12, 15*

THINE are the heavens, and Thine is the earth: the world and the fullness thereof Thou hast founded: justice and judgment are the preparation of Thy throne. ℣. *Great and terrible above all them that are about Him: Thou rulest the power of the sea: and appeasest the motion of the waves thereof.* ℣. *Mercy and truth shall go before Thy face: and in Thy good pleasure shall our horn be exalted.* ℣. *Thou hast humbled the proud one, as one that is slain: with the strength of Thine arm Thou hast scattered Thine enemies: let Thy hand be strengthened, and Thy right hand exalted, O Lord.*

Tui sunt cæli et tua est terra: orbem terrárum et plenitúdinem ejus tu fundásti: justítia et judícium præparátio sedis tuæ. ℣. *Magnus et metuéndus super omnes, qui in circúitu ejus sunt: tu domináris potestáti maris, motum autem flúctuum ejus tu mítigas.* ℣. *Misericórdia et véritas praeibunt ante fáciem tuam: et in beneplácito tuo exaltábitur cornu nostrum.* ℣. *Tu humiliásti sicut vulnerátum supérbum: et in virtúte bráchii tui dispersísti inimícos tuos: firmétur manus tua et exaltétur déxtera tua, Dómine.*

SECRET.

Accept our offerings and prayers, we beseech Thee, O Lord; cleanse us by Thy heavenly mysteries and graciously hear us. Through our Lord.

Munéribus nostris, quæsumus, Dñe, precibúsque suscéptis: et cæléstibus nos munda mystériis, et cleménter exáudi. Per Dóminum.

The Preface of the Nativity (page 189) follows the Secret.

COMMUNION. *Ps 97: 3*

Vidérunt omnes fines terræ salutáre Dei nostri. (Is 9: 6) ℣. *Puer natus est nobis, et fílius datus est nobis.*
—StDenisMissal|988 • Circa 988AD

ALL THE ENDS OF THE EARTH have seen the salvation of our God. ℣. *For our sakes a child is born, to our race a son is given.*

POSTCOMMUNION.

Hæc nos commúnio, Dñe, purget a crímine: et, intercedénte beáta Vírgine Dei Genetríce María, cæléstis remédii fáciat esse consórtes. Per eúmdem.

May this communion, O Lord, cleanse us from sin and, by the intercession of the Blessed Virgin Mary, Mother of God, make us partakers of the heavenly remedy. Through the same.

Feast of the Most Holy Name of Jesus

Same Gospel Twice • The feast of the Holy Name is a modern feast which entered the General Calendar during the 18th century. The Gospel reading—which speaks of the Naming of Our Savior—is identical to that of January 1st, a feast known by the title *In Circumcisione Domini et Octava Nativitatis* ("Circumcision and Christmas Octave Day") until 1962. On 14 February 1969, the feast of the Holy Name was removed "since the imposition of the name of Jesus is already commemorated in the office of the Octave of Christmas." All the Propers for the *Feast of the Holy Name* (1962) are modern adaptations, including the Offertory, which must not be confused with the Offertory for the Fifth Sunday of Lent ("Passion Sunday"). It is easy to tell this is a modern feast; the length and style of the Postcommunion are clues.

When This Feast Occurs • Before 1913, the feast of the Holy Name had replaced a very ancient feast: The Second Sunday after Epiphany. But on 23 October 1913—a few months before his death—Pope Saint Pius X moved the Holy Name to *Dominica a die 2 ad diem 5 Januarii occurrenti vel, si haec defecerit, sie 2 Januarii* ("the Sunday between January 2 and January 5 inclusive or, if no Sunday occurs, January 2"). Another way to express this would be: *Dominica inter Circumcisionem et Epiphaniam vel, si ipsa non occurrat, die 2 Januarii* ("Sunday between Circumcision and Epiphany, and where there is none, 2 January"). The 1961 *Code of Rubrics* (Chapter 3, §17) explains that "normally feasts cannot be permanently fixed on a Sunday" but then lists the exceptions, including the feast of the Holy Name.

Vacant Sunday • The Sunday whereon Pius X placed the Holy Name had previously been *Dominica Vacat* (a "vacant Sunday"). That meant if Sunday occurred on 2 January, it was the *Octave-day of St. Stephen the First Martyr*; if Sunday occurred on 3 January, it was the *Octave-day of St. John the Evangelist*; if Sunday occurred on 4 January, it was the *Octave-day of the Holy Innocents*; if Sunday occurred on 5 January, it was the *Octave-day of St. Thomas of Canterbury*. For this reason, books for the faithful in those times often placed the word "vacant" in parenthesis on this Sunday. Because of the antiquity and splendor of these *Comites Christi* ("Companions of Christ"), replacing the "vacant Sunday" with Neo-Gregorian propers—where the Gospel reading duplicates that of January 1—seems an impoverishment.

Further Changes • The reformers were uncomfortable with feasts having more than one "theme." For instance, the feast Christmas—on its octave day—historically had the Gospel reading of the Circumcision (and Naming of our Savior). The reformers eliminated the octave day of Christmas, although its Gospel reading remained, replacing it with a feast called "Mary, the Mother of God." This was supposedly done "because the *Maternity of Mary* is the most ancient feast known at Rome" {Pristas p65}, but scholars such as Joseph Dyer have said "nothing whatsoever in the ancient sacramentaries or lectionaries give any hint of this," claiming the reformers confused the Roman feast of *Saint Martina* with *Saint Mary*. The feast of the Epiphany likewise had more than one "theme"—specifically, the Magi's Visit, the Miracle at Cana, and the Lord's Baptism. The reformers eliminated the Epiphany's octave day, although its Gospel reading remained, replacing it with a feast called "The Baptism of the Lord." This was first done in 1955—given the title *In Commemoratione Baptismatis Domini Nostri Jesu Christi*—but was not allowed to be on a Sunday. That means when January 13th falls on a Sunday (according to the 1962 calendar), the Baptism of the Lord is neither celebrated nor commemorated, since it is replaced by the Feast of the Holy Family, which is celebrated on the first Sunday after the Epiphany. Some authors believe the Baptism of the Lord was the preëminent "epiphany mystery" of the early church, and this was never fully lost; for instance, a Missal from 1759AD explicitly labels the octave day of the Epiphany as "Baptismus Christi."

— *Most Holy Name of Jesus* — *II Classis.*

DOMINICA INTER OCTAVAM NATIVITATIS ET EPIPHANIAM • SANCTISSIMI NOMINIS JESU

INTROIT. *Philip 2: 10-11*

BEFORE THE NAME of Jesus let every knee bow; of those in heaven, on earth, and under the earth; and let every tongue confess that the Lord Jesus Christ is in the glory of God the Father. (Ps 8: 2) O Lord, our Lord, how wonderful is Thy name in the whole earth! ℣. Glory.

In nómine Jesu omne genu flectátur, cæléstium, terréstrium et infernórum: et omnis lingua confiteátur, quia Dóminus Jesus Christus in glória est Dei Patris. (Ps 8: 2) Dómine, Dóminus noster, quam admirábile est nomen tuum in univérsa terra! ℣. Glória Patri.

COLLECT.

O God, Who didst appoint Thine only-begotten Son to be the Savior of the human race, and didst command that He be called Jesus, mercifully grant that we may enjoy in heaven the vision of Him Whose holy name we venerate on earth. Through the same.

Deus, qui unigénitum Fílium tuũ constituísti humáni géneris Salvatórem, et Jesum vocári jussísti: concéde propítius; ut, cujus sanctum nomen venerámur in terris, ejus quoque aspéctu perfruámur in cælis. Per eúmdem.

EPISTLE. *Acts 4: 8-12*

IN THOSE days, Peter, filled with the Holy Ghost, said, Ye princes of the people and ancients, hear: If we this day are examined concerning the good deed done to the infirm man, by what means he hath been made whole, be it known to you all, and to all the people of Israel, that by the name of Our Lord Jesus Christ of Nazareth, Whom ye crucified, Whom God hath raised from the dead, even by Him this man standeth here before you whole. This is the stone which was rejected by you the builders; which is become the head of the corner: neither is there salvation in any other. For there is no other name under heaven given to men, whereby we must be saved.

In diébus illis: Petrus, replétus Spíritu Sancto, dixit: Príncipes pópuli et senióres, audíte: Si nos hódie dijudicámur in benefácto hóminis infírmi, in quo iste salvus factus est, notum sit ómnibus vobis et omni plebi Ísraël: quia in nómine Dómini nostri Jesu Christi Nazaréni, quem vos crucifixístis, quem Deus suscitávit a mórtuis, in hoc iste astat coram vobis sanus. Hic est lapis, qui reprobátus est a vobis ædificántibus: qui factus est in caput ánguli: et non est in alio áliquo salus. Nec enim aliud nomen est sub cælo datum homínibus, in quo opórteat nos salvos fíeri.

GRADUAL & ALLELUIA. *Ps 105: 47 & Ps 144: 21*

SAVE US, O Lord, our God, and gather us from among the nations: that we may give thanks to Thy holy name, and may glory in Thy praise. (Is 63: 16) Thou, O Lord, art our Father and Redeemer, Thy name is from eternity. | Alleluia, alleluia. ℣. My mouth shall speak the praise of the Lord, and let all flesh bless His holy name. Alleluia.

Salvos fac nos, Dñe, Deus noster, et cóngrega nos de natiónibus: ut confiteámur nómini sancto tuo, et gloriémur in glória tua. (Is 63: 16) Tu, Dñe, Pater noster et Redémptor noster: a sǽculo nomen tuum.

Allelúja, allelúja. ℣. Laudem Dómini loquétur os meum, et benedícat omnis caro nomen sanctum ejus. Allelúja.

GOSPEL. *Luke 2: 21*

In illo témpore: Postquam consummáti sunt dies octo, ut circumciderétur Puer: vocátum est nomen ejus Jesus, quod vocátum est ab Ángelo, priúsquã in útero conciperétur.

WHEN EIGHT DAYS had passed, and the boy must be circumcised, he was called Jesus, the name which the angel had given him before ever he was conceived in the womb. CREDO.

OFFERTORY. *Ps 85: 12, 5*

Confitébor tibi, Dómine, Deus meus, in toto corde meo, et glorificábo nomen tuũ in ætérnum: quóniam tu, Dñe, suávis et mitis es: et multæ misericórdiæ ómnibus invocántibus te, allelúja.

I WILL PRAISE Thee, O Lord my God, with my whole heart, and I will glorify Thy name forever; for Thou, O Lord, art sweet and mild, and plenteous in mercy to all that call upon Thee. Alleluia.

All the PROPRIA MISSAE *for this feast are modern adaptations, and therefore no "extra" verses exist. The first notes and words are identical to the "Passion" Sunday, but that Offertory is from Psalm 110, not Psalm 85.*

SECRET.

Benedíctio tua, clementíssime Deus, qua omnis viget creatúra, sanctíficet, quǽsumus, hoc sacrifícium nostrum, quod ad glóriam nóminis Fílii tui, Dñi nostri Jesu Christi, offérimus tibi: ut majestáti tuæ placére possit ad laudem, et nobis profícere ad salútem. Per eúmdem.

May Thy blessing, O most merciful God, by which the whole creation hath life, sanctify this our sacrifice, which we offer Thee to the glory of the name of Thy Son, Our Lord Jesus Christ, that it may be pleasing to Thy majesty as an act of praise and be profitable to us for our salvation. Through the same.

The Preface of the Nativity (page 189) follows the Secret.

COMMUNION. *Ps 85: 9-10*

Omnes gentes, quascúmque fecísti, vénient et adorábunt coram te, Dñe, et glorificábunt nomen tuum: quóniam magnus es tu et fáciens mirabília: tu es Deus solus, allelúja.

ALL the nations Thou hast made shall come and adore before Thee, O Lord; and they shall glorify Thy name: for Thou art great, and dost wonderful things. Thou art God alone. Alleluia.

POSTCOMMUNION.

Omnípotens ætérnæ Deus, qui creásti et redemísti nos, réspice propítius vota nostra: et sacrifícium salutáris hóstiæ, quod in honórem nóminis Fílii tui, Dñi nostri Jesu Christi, majestáti tuæ obtúlimus, plácido et benígno vultu suscípere dignéris; ut grátia tua nobis infúsa, sub glorióso nómine Jesu, ætérnæ prædestinatiónis título gaudeámus nómina nostra scripta esse in cælis. Per eúmdem.

Almighty, eternal God, Who hast created and redeemed us, graciously regard our desires, and deign to receive with kind and peaceful countenance the sacrifice of the saving victim, which we have offered to Thy majesty, in honor of the name of Thy Son, Our Lord Jesus Christ, that, Thy grace being poured out upon us, we may rejoice in the glorious name of Jesus, the title of eternal predestination, because our names are written in heaven. Through the same.

✠ IBANT MAGI, QUAM VIDERANT, STELLAM SEQUENTES PRAEVIAM: ✠
LUMEN REQUIRUNT LUMINE: DEUM FATENTUR MUNERE.

✠ NOVUM GENUS POTENTIAE: AQUAE RUBESCUNT HYDRIAE: VINUMQUE JUSSA FUNDERE, MUTAVIT UNDA ORIGINEM

THE MAGI WENT, FOLLOWING THE GUIDING STAR
THEY HAD SEEN: BY ITS LIGHT THEY SEEK THE
LIGHT: BY THEIR GIFTS THEY CONFESS THEIR GOD.

A NEW KIND OF MIGHT: THE POTS OF WATER GROW RED: AND BIDDEN TO POUR WINE, THE LIQUID HAS CHANGED ITS SOURCE ✠

The Vespers antiphon for the Epiphany states: "We celebrate a holy-day that three miracles adorn; today the star led the Wise Men to the manger; today wine is made from water at the wedding; today Christ was content to be baptized in the Jordan, that he might save us, alleluia." Other manifestations of Christ's glory and divinity were also celebrated in different localities—*including the Nativity* according to some authors, and this seems solidified by the wording ("in veritáte carnis nostræ visibíliter corporális appáruit") of the Epiphany COMMUNICANTES—but in the early centuries, our Redeemer's BAPTISM AT THE JORDAN was preëminent according to Father Cyril Martindale. Father Fortescue says the three cardinal feasts of the ancient Church were Epiphany, Easter, and Pentecost {*The Mass*, p203}. For this reason, the Sundays which follow the cardinal feasts have a marked character: *Sundays after Epiphany, Sundays after Easter,* and *Sundays after Pentecost.*

I Classis.

—*Epiphany of the Lord*—

IN EPIPHANIA DOMINI *Station at Saint Peter's*

INTROIT. *Mal 3: 1*

Ecce, advénit dominátor Dóminus: et regnum in manu ejus et potéstas et impérium. ℣. Deus, judícium tuum Regi da: et justítiam tuam Fílio Regis. ℣. Glória Patri.

BEHOLD THE LORD the Ruler is come: and a kingdom in His hand, and power and dominion. (Ps 71: 1) Give to the king thy judgment, O God: and to the king's son Thy justice. ℣. Glory.

COLLECT.

Deus, qui hodiérna die Unigénitum tuum géntibus stella duce revelásti: concéde propítius; ut, qui jam te ex fide cognóvimus, usque ad contemplándam spéciem tuæ celsitúdinis perducámur. Per eúmdem.

O God, Who by the guidance of a star didst this day reveal Thine only-begotten Son to the Gentiles, mercifully grant that we, who know Thee now by faith, may be so led as to behold with our eyes the beauty of Thy majesty. Through the same.

EPISTLE. *Is 60: 1-6*

Surge, illumináre, Jerúsalem: quia venit lumen tuum, et glória Dómini super te orta est. Quia ecce, ténebræ opérient terram et calígo pópulos: super te autem oriétur Dóminus, et glória ejus in te vidébitur. Et ambulábunt gentes in lúmine tuo, et reges in splendóre ortus tui. Leva in circúitu óculos tuos, et vide: omnes isti congregáti sunt, venérunt tibi: fílii tui de longe vénient, et fíliæ tuæ de látere surgent. Tunc vidébis et áfflues, mirábitur et dilatábitur cor tuũ, quando convérsa fúerit ad te multitúdo maris, fortitúdo géntium vénerit tibi. Inundátio camelórum opériet te, dromedárii Mádian et Epha: omnes de Saba vénient, aurum et thus deferéntes, et laudem Dómino annuntiántes.

ARISE, be enlightened, O Jerusalem; for thy light is come, and the glory of the Lord is risen upon thee. For behold darkness shall cover the earth, and a mist the people; but the Lord shall arise upon thee, and His glory shall be seen upon thee. And the Gentiles shall walk in thy light, and kings in the brightness of thy rising. Lift up thy eyes round about, and see; all these are gathered together, they are come to thee: thy sons shall come from afar, and thy daughters shall rise up at thy side. Then shalt thou see, and abound, and thy heart shall wonder and be enlarged, when the multitude of the sea shall be converted to thee, the strength of the Gentiles shall come to thee. The multitude of camels shall cover thee, the dromedaries of Madian and Epha; all they from Saba shall come, bringing gold and frankincense, and showing forth praise to the Lord.

GRADUAL & ALLELUIA. *Is 60: 1 & Matt 2: 2*

ALL THEY from Saba shall come, bringing gold and frankincense, and showing forth praise to the Lord. ℣. Arise and be enlightened, O Jerusalem, for the glory of the Lord is risen upon thee.
Alleluia, alleluia. ℣. We have seen His star in the east: and are come with gifts to adore the Lord. Alleluia.

Omnes de Saba vénient, aurum et thus deferéntes, et laudem Dño annuntiántes. ℣. Surge et illumináre, Jerúsalem: quia glória Dómini super te orta est. Allelúja, allelúja. ℣. Vídimus stellam ejus in Oriénte, et vénimus cum munéribus adoráre Dóminum. Allelúja.

GOSPEL. *Matt 2: 1-12*

WHEN JESUS was born in Bethlehem of Juda, in the days of King Herod, behold there came wise men from the east to Jerusalem; saying, Where is He that is born king of the Jews? for we have seen His star in the east, and are come to adore Him. And King Herod, hearing this, was troubled, and all Jerusalem with him. And assembling together all the chief priests and the scribes of the people, he inquired of them where Christ should be born. But they said to him: In Bethlehem of Juda; for so it is written by the prophet: And thou Bethlehem, the land of Juda, art not the least among the princes of Juda; for out of thee shall come forth the ruler that shall rule my people Israel.

Cum natus esset Jesus in Béthlehem Juda in diébus Heródis regis, ecce, Magi ab Oriénte venérunt Jerosólymam, dicéntes: Ubi est, qui natus est rex Judæórum? Vídimus enim stellam ejus in Oriénte, et vénimus adoráre eum. Audiens autem Heródes rex, turbátus est, et omnis Jerosólyma cum illo. Et cóngregans omnes príncipes sacerdótum et scribas pópuli, sciscitabátur ab eis, ubi Christus nascerétur. At illi dixérunt ei: In Béthlehem Judæ: sic enim scriptum est per Prophétam: Et tu, Béthlehem terra Juda, nequáquam mínima es in princípibus Juda; ex te enim éxiet dux, qui regat pópulum meum Israël.

Then Herod privately calling the wise men, learned diligently of them the time of the star which appeared to them; and sending them into Bethlehem, said, Go and diligently inquire after the child, and when you have found Him bring me word again, that I also may come and adore Him. Who having heard the king, went their way; and behold the star which they had seen in the east went before them, until it came and stood over where the child was. And seeing the star, they rejoiced with exceeding great joy. And entering into the house, they found the child with Mary His mother, (*genuflect*) and falling down they adored Him. And opening their treasures, they offered Him gifts: gold, frankincense, and myrrh. And having received an answer in sleep that they should not return to Herod, they went back another way into their own country. CREDO.

Tunc Heródes, clam vocátis Magis, diligénter dídicit ab eis tempus stellæ, quæ appáruit eis: et mittens illos in Béthlehem, dixit: Ite, et interrogáte diligénter de púero: et cum invenéritis, renuntiáte mihi, ut et ego véniens adórem eum. Qui cum audíssent regem, abiérunt. Et ecce, stella, quam víderant in Oriénte, antecedébat eos, usque dũ véniens staret supra, ubi erat Puer. Vidéntes autem stellam, gavísi sunt gáudio magno valde. Et intrántes domum, invenérunt Púerum cum María Matre ejus, (*hic genuflectitur*) ei procidéntes adoravérunt eum. Et, apértis thesáuris suis, obtulérunt ei múnera, aurum, thus et myrrham. Et respónso accépto in somnis, ne redírent ad Heródem, per áliam viam revérsi sunt in regiónem suam.

OFFERTORY. *Ps 71: 10-11*

Reges Tharsis, et ínsulæ múnera ófferent: reges Árabum et Saba dona addúcent: et adorábunt eum omnes reges terræ, omnes gentes sérvient ei. ℣. *Deus judícium tuum Regi da et justítiam tuam Fílio Regis: judicáre pópulum tuum cum justítia et páuperes tuos in judício:* *** omnes gentes sérvient ei.** ℣. *Suscípiant montes pacem pópulo tuo et colles justítiam.* ℣. *Oriétur in diébus ejus justítia et abundántia pacis, donec extollátur luna, et dominábitur a mari usque ad mare.*

THE KINGS of Tharsis and the islands shall offer presents: the kings of the Arabians and of Saba shall bring gifts: and all kings of the earth shall adore Him; all nations shall serve Him. ℣. *Give to the king Thy judgment, O God: and to the king's son Thy justice: To judge Thy people with justice, and Thy poor with judgment.* *** all nations shall serve him.** ℣. *Such be the harvest His subjects shall reap, peace on every mountain, justice on every hill-side.* ℣. *In His days shall justice spring up, and abundance of peace, till the moon be taken away, and He shall rule from sea to sea.*

Sometimes when the Offertory repeats a section—not following the method of the Introit but more like a Responsory—the musical notes are different for the same words; this is one such example (cf. the asterisk).

SECRET.

Ecclésiæ tuæ, quǽsumus, Dñe, dona propítius intuére: quibus non jam aurum, thus et myrrha profértur; sed quod eísdem munéribus declarátur, immolátur et súmitur, Jesus Christus, fílius tuus, Dñs noster: Qui tecum.

Favorably regard the gifts of Thy Church, O Lord, wherein no longer gold is offered, nor frankincense, nor myrrh, but He who by these gifts is signified is become our sacrifice and our food, Jesus Christ, our Lord, Who with Thee.

The Preface of the Epiphany (page 189) follows the Secret.

COMMUNION. *Matt 2: 2*

Vídimus stellam ejus in Oriénte, et vénimus cum munéribus adoráre Dóminum. (Ps 71: 10) ℣. *Reges Tharsis, et ínsulæ múnera ófferent: reges Árabum et Saba dona addúcent.*
—STMAUR|1079 • Circa 1079AD

WE HAVE SEEN His star in the east, and are come with gifts to adore the Lord. ℣. *Gifts shall flow in from the lords of Tharsis and the islanders, tribute from the kings of Arabia and of Saba.*

POSTCOMMUNION.

Præsta, quǽsumus, omnípotens Deus: ut, quæ sollémni celebrámus offício, purificátæ mentis intellegéntia consequámur. Per Dóminum.

Grant, we beseech Thee O almighty God, by the understanding of hearts made pure we may comprehend that which by solemn rite we celebrate. Through Our Lord.

Because the Epiphany communion antiphon does not come from a psalm, the ancient manuscripts indicate sundry options when it comes to the "extra" verses. Some manuscripts—such as 9448PRUM|983; HELMST|1026; and 342SANGALL|933—take the verses from the Introit. Another common practice was to take verses from Psalm 33, "the unvarying Communion-chant which in all Masses accompanied the administration of the Holy Eucharist" for the earliest Catholic liturgies {Wagner p103}.

Feast of the Holy Family

A VERY MODERN FEAST • In the 1962 calendar, the feast of the Holy Family replaces the First Sunday after Epiphany. (It also replaces the Baptism of the Lord when 13 January is a Sunday.) The feast of the Holy Family is a modern feast added to the General Calendar by Pope Benedict XV in 1921.

MISSIONARIES OF NORTH AMERICA • The Jesuit missionaries who came to the United States from France—Father Jean de Brébeuf (d. 1649), Father Isaac Jogues (d. 1646), and companions—had a deep devotion to the Blessed Mother and to Saint Joseph. One of the most important Jesuit missionaries was FATHER JOSEPH CHAUMONOT (d. 1693), who was born in France but died in Quebec. Although he was a Jesuit priest, Père Chaumonot founded the *Congregation of the Holy Family*, which figures extensively in early Canadian history; and the feast of the Holy Family came from Canada.

VARIOUS DAYS • The feast of the Holy Family never had a stable feast day. In Canada during the 1840s, it replaced the Third Sunday after Easter; during the 1870s, it replaced the Second Sunday after Easter. In other localities, it replaced the Third Sunday after Epiphany. In 1921, it was added to the General Calendar (see above) as the First Sunday after Epiphany, replacing a feast of tremendous antiquity—*Missa Dominicae Primae post Epiphaniam*—whose Gregorian propers are extremely beautiful. It seems unfortunate the propers from the ancient feast were not adopted in 1921, especially as the Communion antiphon ("Fili Quid Fecisti") matches perfectly the Gospel reading for the feast of the Holy Family. The propers for the feast of the Holy Family were composed by Abbat Pothier in the nineteenth century, when the feast was still found in the section called *Missae Aliquibus In Locis Celebrandae*. Regarding the texts for the Breviary hymns at Matins, Lauds, and Vespers, those were composed by Pope Leo XIII (d. 1903). In 1969, the feast of the Holy Family was moved to the Sunday within the Octave of Christmas.

—*The Holy Family: Jesus, Mary, & Joseph*— *II Classis.*

DOMINICA I POST EPIPHANIAM • SANCTAE FAMILIAE JESU, MARIAE, JOSEPH

INTROIT. *Prov 23: 24-25*

LET THE FATHER of the Just rejoice greatly; let Thy father and Thy mother be joyful, and let her rejoice that bore Thee. (Ps 82: 2-3) How lovely are Thy tabernacles O Lord of hosts; my soul longeth and fainteth for the courts of the Lord. ℣. Glory.

Exsúltet gáudio pater Justi, gáudeat Pater tuus et Mater tua, et exsúltet quæ génuit te. ℣. Quam diléct a tabernácula tua, Dómine virtútum! concupíscit et déficit ánima mea in átria Dómini. ℣. Glória Patri.

COLLECT.

O Lord Jesus Christ, Who, in the days of Thy subjection to Mary and Joseph, didst consecrate home life by ineffable acts of virtue; by the intercession of Thy holy Mother and of Thy foster Father, make us so to profit by the example they with Thee have set us, that we may be counted members of Thy household for evermore. Who livest.

Dómine Jesu Christe, qui, Maríæ et Joseph súbditus, domésticam vitã ineffabílibus virtútibus consecrásti: fac nos, utriúsque auxílio, Famíliæ sanctæ tuæ exémplis ínstrui; et consórtium cónsequi sempitérnum: Qui vivis.

EPISTLE. *Col 3: 12-17*

BRETHREN, put ye on as the elect of God, holy and beloved, the bowels of mercy, benignity, humility, modesty, patience; bearing with one another,

Fratres: Indúite vos sicut elécti Dei, sancti et dilécti, víscera misericórdiæ, benignitátem, humilitátẽ, modéstiam, patiéntiam: supportántes ínvicem, et donántes vobismetípsis, si quis advérsus áliquem habet querélam: sicut et Dóminus donávit vobis, ita et vos. Super ómnia autem hæc caritátem habéte, quod est vínculum perfectiónis: et pax Christi exsúltet in córdibus vestris, in qua et vocáti estis in uno córpore: et grati estóte. Verbum Christi hábitet in vobis abundánter, in omni sapiéntia, docéntes et commonéntes vosmetípsos psalmis, hymnis et cánticis spirituálibus, in grátia cantántes in córdibus vestris Deo. Omne, quodcúmque fácitis in verbo aut in ópere, ómnia in nómine Dñi Jesu Christi, grátias agéntes Deo et Patri per ipsum.

[*On the Fifth Sunday after Epiphany, the ending is:* "per Jesum Christum Dóminum nostrum."]

and forgiving one another, if any have a complaint against another, even as the Lord hath forgiven you, so you also. But above all these things, have charity, which is the bond of perfection: and let the peace of Christ rejoice in your hearts, wherein also you are called in one body: and be ye thankful. Let the word of Christ dwell in you abundantly, in all wisdom; teaching and admonishing one another, in psalms, hymns, and spiritual canticles, singing in grace in your hearts to God. All whatsoever you do in word or in work, all things do ye in the name of the Lord Jesus Christ, giving thanks to God and the Father through Jesus Christ our Lord.

GRADUAL & ALLELUIA. *Ps 26: 4 & Is 45: 15*

Unam pétii a Dómino, hanc requíram: ut inhábitem in domo Dómini ómnibus diébus vitæ meæ. ℣. Beáti, qui hábitant in domo tua, Dómine: in sǽcula sæculórum laudábunt te.

Allelúja, allelúja. ℣. Vere tu es Rex abscónditus, Deus Ísraël Salvátor. Allelúja.

ONE THING I have asked of the Lord: this will I seek after: that I may dwell in the house of the Lord all the days of my life. (Ps 83: 5) Blessed are they who dwell in Thy house, O Lord; they shall praise Thee for ever and ever.

Alleluia, alleluia. ℣. Truly Thou art a hidden King, the God of Israel, the Savior. Alleluia.

GOSPEL. *Luke 2: 42-52*

Cum factus esset Jesus annórum duódecim, ascendéntibus illis Jerosólymam secúndum consuetúdinem diéi festi, consummatísque diébus, cum redírent, remánsit puer Jesus in Jerúsalem, et non cognovérunt paréntes ejus. Existimántes autem illum esse in comitátu, venérunt iter diéi, et requirébant eum inter cognátos et notos. Et non inveniéntes, regréssi sunt in Jerúsalem, requiréntes eum. Et factum est, post tríduum invenérunt illum in templo sedéntem in médio doctórum, audiéntem illos et interrogántem eos. Stupébant autem omnes, qui eum audiébant, super prudéntia et respónsis ejus. Et vidéntes admiráti sunt.

WHEN JESUS was twelve years old, they going up into Jerusalem according to the custom of the feast, and having fulfilled the days, when they returned, the child Jesus remained in Jerusalem; and His parents knew it not. And thinking that He was in the company, they came a day's journey, and sought Him among their kinsfolk and acquaintance. And not finding Him, they returned into Jerusalem, seeking Him. And it came to pass, that after three days they found Him in the temple sitting in the midst of the doctors, hearing them and asking them questions. And all that heard Him were astonished at His wisdom and His answers. And seeing Him, they wondered.

Et dixit Mater ejus ad illum: Fili, quid fecísti nobis sic? Ecce, pater tuus et ego doléntes quærebámus te. Et ait ad illos: Quid est, quod me quærebátis?

And His mother said to Him, Son, why hast Thou done so to us? Behold Thy father and I have sought Thee sorrowing. And He said to them, How is it that you sought Me? Did you not know that I must be about My Father's business? And they understood not the word that He spoke unto them. And He went down with them, and came to Nazareth; and was subject to them. And His mother kept all these words in her heart. And Jesus advanced in wisdom, and age, and grace with God and man. CREDO.

Nesciebátis, quia in his, quæ Patris mei sunt, opórtet me esse? Et ipsi non intellexérunt verbum, quod locútus est ad eos. Et descéndit cum eis, et venit Názareth: et erat súbditus illis. Et Mater ejus conservábat ómnia verba hæc in corde suo. Et Jesus proficiébat sapiéntia et ætáte et grátia apud Deum et hómines.

OFFERTORY. *Luke 2: 22*

THE PARENTS of Jesus carried Him to the temple, to present Him to the Lord.

Tulérunt Jesum paréntes ejus in Jerúsalem, ut sísterent eum Dómino.

The feast of the Holy Family is a modern feast; therefore, it has no ancient verses. In the nineteenth century, Abbat Pothier adapted this melody to "Laetentur Caeli" (from Christmas Midnight Mass). Before 1908, different localities used different melodies—and even different texts—for the feast of the Holy Family.

SECRET.

To appease Thee, O Lord, we offer the Victim of Salvation, humbly beseeching Thee that, through the prayers of the Virgin Mother of God and of Saint Joseph, Thou wouldst establish our households in Thy peace and favor. Through the same.

Placatiónis hostiam offérimus tibi, Dñe, supplíciter deprecántes: ut, per intercessiónem Deíparæ Vírginis cum beáto Joseph, famílias nostras in pace et grátia tua fírmiter constítuas. Per eúmdem.

The Preface of the Epiphany (page 189) follows the Secret.

COMMUNION. *Luke 2: 51*

JESUS WENT DOWN with them, and came to Nazareth and was subject to them.

Descéndit Jesus cum eis, et venit Názareth, et erat súbditus illis.

This is a modern feast; consequently it lacks "extra" verses for the communion antiphon.

POSTCOMMUNION.

Do Thou, O Lord Jesus, bring us, whom Thou hast refreshed with heavenly mysteries, to imitate the example of Thy holy Family, that at the hour of our death, with the Virgin Mother and blessed Joseph at hand, we may be received by Thee into our everlasting home. Who livest.

Quos cæléstibus réficis sacraméntis, fac, Dñe Jesu, sanctæ Famíliæ tuæ exémpla júgiter imitári: ut in hora mortis nostræ, occurrénte glorιósa Vírgine Matre tua cum beáto Joseph; per te in ætérna tabernácula récipi mereámur: Qui vivis.

II Classis.

— *Second Sunday after Epiphany* —

DOMINICA SECUNDA POST EPIPHANIAM *Station at Saint Eusebius*

INTROIT. *Ps 65: 4*

Omnis terra adóret te, Deus, et psallat tibi: psalmum dicat nómini tuo, Altíssime. ℣. Jubiláte Deo, omnis terra, psalmum dícite nómini ejus: date glóriam laudi ejus. ℣. Glória Patri.

LET ALL THE EARTH adore Thee, O God, and sing to Thee: let it sing a psalm to Thy name, O Thou most high. (Ps 65: 1-2) Shout with joy to God all the earth, sing ye a psalm to His name, give glory to His praise. ℣. Glory.

COLLECT.

Omnípotens sempitérne Deus, qui cæléstia simul et terréna moderáris: supplicatiónes pópuli tui cleménter exáudi; et pacem tuam nostris concéde tempóribus. Per Dóminum.

Almighty, eternal God, Who dost govern all things in heaven and on earth, of Thy mercy hear the supplications of Thy people, and grant Thy peace in our times. Through our Lord.

EPISTLE. *Rom 12: 6-16*

Fratres: Habéntes donatiónes secúndũ grátiam, quæ data est nobis, differéntes: sive prophétiam secúndum ratiónem fídei, sive ministérium in ministrándo, sive qui docet in doctrína, qui exhortátur in exhortándo, qui tríbuit in simplicitáte, qui præest in sollicitúdine, qui miserétur in hilaritáte. Diléctio sine simulatióne. Odiéntes malũ, adhæréntes bono: Caritáte fraternitátis ínvicem diligéntes: Honóre ínvicẽ præveniéntes: Sollicitúdine non pigri: Spíritu fervéntes: Dño serviéntes: Spe gaudéntes: In tribulatióne patiéntes: Oratióni instántes: Necessitátibus sanctórum communicántes: Hospitalitátẽ sectántes. Benedícite persequéntibus vos: benedícite, et nolíte maledícere. Gaudére cum gaudéntibus, flere cum fléntibus: Idípsum ínvicem sentiéntes: Non alta sapiéntes, sed humílibus consentiéntes.

BRETHREN, having different gifts, according to the grace that is given us; either prophecy, to be used according to the rule of faith; or ministry, in ministering; or he that teacheth in doctrine; he that exhorteth in exhorting; he that giveth with simplicity; he that ruleth with carefulness; he that showeth mercy with cheerfulness. Let love be without dissimulation. Hating that which is evil, cleaving to that which is good. Loving one another with the charity of brotherhood, in honor preventing one another. In carefulness, not slothful: in spirit fervent: serving the Lord: rejoicing in hope: patient in tribulation: instant in prayer: communicating to the necessities of the saints; pursuing hospitality. Bless them that persecute you: bless, and curse not. Rejoice with them that rejoice, weep with them that weep. Being of one mind one towards another; not minding high things, but consenting to the humble.

GRADUAL & ALLELUIA. *Ps 106: 20-21 & Ps 148: 2*

Misit Dóminus verbum suum, et sanávit eos: et erípuit eos de intéritu eórum. ℣. Confiteántur Dómino misericórdiæ ejus: et mirabília ejus fíliis hóminũ.

Allelúja, allelúja. ℣. Laudáte Dóminum, omnes Ángeli ejus: laudáte eum, omnes virtútes ejus. Allelúja.

THE LORD sent His word, and healed them: and delivered them out of their distresses. ℣. Let the mercies of the Lord give glory to Him; and His wonderful works to the children of men.

Alleluia, alleluia. ℣. Praise ye the Lord, all His angels: praise ye Him, all His hosts. Alleluia.

GOSPEL. *John 2: 1-11*

THERE WAS A MARRIAGE in Cana of Galilee: and the mother of Jesus was there. And Jesus also was invited, and His disciples, to the marriage. And the wine failing, the mother of Jesus saith to Him, They have no wine. And Jesus saith to her, Woman, what is it to Me and to thee? My hour is not yet come. His mother saith to the waiters, Whatsoever He shall say to you, do ye. Now there were set there six waterpots of stone, according to the manner of the purifying of the Jews, containing two or three measures apiece. Jesus saith to them, Fill the waterpots with water. And they filled them up to the brim. And Jesus saith to them, Draw out now, and carry to the chief steward of the feast: and they carried it. And when the chief steward had tasted the water made wine, and knew not whence it was, but the waiters knew who had drawn the water: the chief steward calleth the bridegroom, and saith to him, Every man at first setteth forth good wine, and when men have well drank, then that which is worse: but thou hast kept the good wine until now. This beginning of miracles did Jesus in Cana of Galilee; and manifested His glory, and His disciples believed in Him. CREDO.

In illo témpore: Núptiæ factæ sunt in Cana Galilǽæ: et erat Mater Jesu ibi. Vocátus est autem et Jesus, et discípuli ejus ad núptias. Et deficiénte vino, dicit Mater Jesu ad eum: Vinum non habent. Et dicit ei Jesus: Quid mihi et tibi est, múlier? nondum venit hora mea. Dicit Mater ejus minístris: Quodcúmque díxerit vobis, fácite. Erant autem ibi lapídeæ hýdriæ sex pósitæ secúndum purificatiónem Judæórum, capiéntes síngulæ metrétas binas vel ternas. Dicit eis Jesus: Impléte hýdrias aqua. Et implevérunt eas usque ad summum. Et dicit eis Jesus: Hauríte nunc, et ferte architriclíno. Et tulérunt. Ut autem gustávit architriclínus aquam vinum fáctam, et non sciébat unde esset, minístri autem sciébant, qui háuserant aquam: vocat sponsum architriclínus, et dicit ei: Omnis homo primum bonum vinum ponit: et cum inebriáti fúerint, tunc id, quod detérius est. Tu autem servásti bonum vinum usque adhuc. Hoc fecit inítium signórũ Jesus in Cana Galilǽæ: et manifestávit glóriam suam, et crediderunt in eum discípuli ejus.

OFFERTORY. *Ps 65: 1-2, 16*

SHOUT WITH JOY to God, all the earth (shout with joy to God, all the earth): sing ye a psalm to His name: come and hear, and I will tell you, all ye that fear God, what great things the Lord hath done for my soul. Alleluia. ℣. *I will pay Thee my vows (I will pay Thee my vows), which my lips have uttered.* ℣. *My mouth hath spoken when I was in trouble (my mouth hath spoken when I was in trouble): Fat burnt-offerings of sheep shall be Thine.*

Identical to the 4th Sunday after Easter:

Jubiláte Deo, univérsa terra: psalmum dícite nómini ejus: veníte et audíte, et narrábo vobis, omnes qui timétis Deum, quanta fecit Dóminus ánimæ meæ, allelúja. ℣. *Reddam tibi vota mea, quae distinxérunt lábia mea.* ℣. *Locútum est os meum in tribulatióne mea: holocáusta medulláta ófferam tibi.*

This Offertory displays a characteristic not uncommon for its genre: the repetition of certain sections for reasons which are not always clear. When the text is repeated in this particular Offertory, the musical notes are (for the most part) different, whereas in other Offertories—such as the 16th Sunday after Pentecost—the same musical phrase and text is repeated verbatim.

SECRET.

Sanctify, O Lord, the gifts we offer, and purify us from the stains of our sins. Through our Lord.

Obláta, Dñe, múnera sanctífica: nosque a peccatórũ nostrórũ máculis emúnda. Per Dóminum.

COMMUNION. *John 2: 7, 8, 9, 10-11*

Dicit Dñs: Impléte hýdrias aqua et ferte architriclíno. Cum gustásset architriclínus aquam vinum factam, dicit sponso: Servásti bonum vinum usque adhuc. Hoc signum fecit Jesus primũ coram discípulis suis. (Ps 65: 5) ℣. *Veníte, et vidéte ópera Dei: terríbilis in consíliis super fílios hóminum.*
—12050CORBIE|853 • Circa 853AD

THE LORD SAITH: Fill the waterpots with water, and carry to the chief steward of the feast. When the chief steward had tasted the water made wine, he saith to the bridegroom: thou hast kept the good wine until now; this first miracle did Jesus before His disciples. ℣. *Come near, and see what God does, how wonderful He is in His dealings with human kind.*

POSTCOMMUNION.

Augeátur in nobis, quǽsumus, Dñe, tuæ virtútis operatio: ut divínis vegetáti sacraméntis, ad eórum promíssa capiénda, tuo múnere præparémur. Per Dóminum.

May the working of Thy power, we beg Thee, O Lord, be increased in us, that, being nourished by divine sacraments, we may by Thy grace be prepared to obtain that which they promise. Through our Lord.

II Classis.

—*Third Sunday after Epiphany*—

DOMINICA TERTIA POST EPIPHANIAM

INTROIT. *Ps 96: 7-8*

Adoráte Deum, omnes Ángeli ejus: audívit, et lætáta est Sion: et exsultavérunt fíliæ Judæ. ℣. Dóminus regnávit, exsúltet terra: lætèntur ínsulæ multæ. ℣. Glória Patri.

ADORE GOD, all you His angels: Sion heard, and was glad; and the daughters of Juda rejoiced. (Ps 96: 1) The Lord hath reigned; let the earth rejoice: let many islands be glad. ℣. Glory.

COLLECT.

Omnípotens sempitérne Deus, infirmitátem nostrã propítius réspice: atque, ad protegéndum nos, déxteram tuæ majestátis exténde. Per Dóminum.

Almighty, eternal God, look with mercy upon our infirmities, and stretch forth the right hand of Thy majesty to protect us. Through our Lord.

EPISTLE. *Rom 12: 16-21*

Fratres: Nolíte esse prudéntes apud vosmetípsos: nulli malum pro malo reddéntes: providéntes bona non tantum coram Deo, sed étiam coram ómnibus homínibus. Si fíeri potest, quod ex vobis est, cum ómnibus homínibus pacem habéntes: Non vosmetípsos defendéntes, caríssimi, sed date locum iræ. Scriptum est enim: Mihi vindícta: ego retríbuam, dicit Dñs. Sed si esuríerit inimícus tuus, ciba il-

BRETHREN, be not wise in your own conceits. To no man rendering evil for evil: providing good things not only in the sight of God, but also in the sight of men. If it be possible, as much as it is in you, having peace with all men. Revenge not yourselves, my dearly beloved; but give place unto wrath, for it is written, Revenge is mine; I will repay, saith the Lord. But if thy enemy be hungry, give him to eat;

if he thirst, give him to drink, for doing this, thou shalt heap coals of fire upon his head. Be not overcome by evil, but overcome evil by good.

lum: si sitit, potum da illi: hoc enim fáciens, carbónes ignis cóngeres super caput ejus. Noli vinci a malo, sed vince in bono malum.

GRADUAL & ALLELUIA. *Ps 101: 16-17 & Ps 96: 1*

THE Gentiles shall fear Thy name, O Lord, and all the kings of the earth Thy glory. ℣. For the Lord hath built up Sion, and He shall be seen in His majesty. | Alleluia, alleluia. ℣. The Lord hath reigned, let the earth rejoice: let many islands be glad. Alleluia.

Timébunt gentes nomen tuum, Dñe, et omnes reges terræ glóriam tuam. ℣. Quóniam ædificávit Dñs Sion, et vidébitur in majestáte sua. | Allelúja, allelúja. ℣. Dñs regnávit, exsúltet terra: læténtur ínsulæ multæ. Allelúja.

GOSPEL. *Matt 8: 1-13*

WHEN JESUS was come down from the mountain, great multitudes followed Him; and behold a leper came and adored Him, saying, Lord, if Thou wilt Thou canst make me clean. And Jesus stretching forth His hand, touched him, saying, I will, be thou made clean: and forthwith his leprosy was cleansed. And Jesus saith to him, See thou tell no man: but go, show thyself to the priest, and offer the gift which Moses commanded for a testimony unto them.

In illo témpore: Cum descendísset Jesus de monte, secútæ sunt eum turbæ multæ: et ecce, leprósus véniens adorábat eum, dicens: Dómine, si vis, potes me mundáre. Et exténdens Jesus manum, tétigit eum, dicens: Volo. Mundáre. Et conféstim mundáta est lepra ejus. Et ait illi Jesus: Vide, némini díxeris: sed vade, osténde te sacerdóti, et offer munus, quod præcépit Móyses, in testimónium illis.

And when He had entered into Capharnaum, there came to Him a centurion beseeching Him, and saying, Lord, my servant lieth at home sick of the palsy, and is grievously tormented. And Jesus saith to him, I will come and heal him. And the centurion making answer, said, Lord, I am not worthy that Thou shouldst enter under my roof: but only say the word, and my servant shall be healed. For I also am a man subject to authority, having under me soldiers: and I say to this man, Go, and he goeth: and to another, Come, and he cometh: and to my servant, Do this, and he doth it. And Jesus hearing this, marvelled; and said to them that followed Him, Amen I say to you, I have not found so great faith in Israel. And I say to you, that many shall come from the east and the west, and shall sit down with Abraham, Isaac, and Jacob in the kingdom of heaven; but the children of the kingdom shall be cast into the exterior darkness: there shall be weeping and gnashing of teeth. And Jesus said to the centurion, Go, and as thou hast believed, so be it done to thee: and the servant was healed at the same hour. CREDO.

Cum autem introísset Caphárnaum, accéssit ad eum centúrio, rogans eum et dicens: Dómine, puer meus jacet in domo paralýticus, et male torquetur. Et ait illi Jesus: Ego véniam, et curábo eum. Et respóndens centúrio, ait: Dñe, non sum dignus, ut intres sub tectum meum: sed tantum dic verbo, et sanábitur puer meus. Nam et ego homo sum sub potestáte constitútus, habens sub me mílites, et dico huic: Vade, et vadit; et álii: Veni, et venit; et servo meo: Fac hoc, et facit. Audiens autem Jesus, mirátus est, et sequéntibus se dixit: Amen, dico vobis, non invéni tantam fidem in Israël. Dico autem vobis, quod multi ab Oriénte et Occidénte vénient, et recúmbent cum Ábraham et Ísaäc et Jacob in regno cælórum: fílii autem regni ejiciéntur in ténebras exterióres: ibi erit fletus et stridor déntium. Et dixit Jesus centurióni: Vade et, sicut credidísti, fiat tibi. Et sanátus est puer in illa hora.

OFFERTORY. *Ps 117: 16, 17*

Identical to Maundy Thursday:

Déxtera Dómini fecit virtútem, déxtera Dómini exaltávit me: non móriar, sed vivam, et narrábo ópera Dómini. ℣. *In tribulatióne invocávi Dóminum et exaudívit me in latitúdine: quia Dñs adjútor meus est.* ℣. *Impúlsus versátus sum, ut cáderem: et Dñs suscépit me: et factus est mihi in salútem.*

THE POWER of the Lord has triumphed, the power of the Lord has brought me to great honor: I am reprieved from death, to live on and proclaim what the Lord has done for me. ℣. *I called on the Lord when trouble beset me, and the Lord listened, and brought me relief, for the Lord is at my side.* ℣. *I reeled under the blow, and had well-nigh fallen, but still the Lord was there to aid me. Who but the Lord has brought me deliverance?*

SECRET.

Hæc hóstia, Dñe, quǽsumus, emúndet nostra delícta: et, ad sacrifícium celebrándum, subditórum tibi córpora mentésque sanctíficet. Per Dóminum.

May this offering, we beseech Thee, O Lord, wipe out our sins, and sanctify the bodies and minds of Thy servants for the celebration of the sacrifice. Through our Lord.

COMMUNION. *Luke 4: 22*

Mirabántur omnes de his, quæ procedébant de ore Dei. (Lk 4: 18) ℣. *Spíritus Dñi super me: propter quod unxit me, evangelizáre paupéribus misit me.*

—4951STEVEN|1128 • Circa 1128AD

THEY ALL wondered at these things, which proceeded from the mouth of God. ℣. *The Spirit of the Lord is upon Me; He has anointed Me, and sent Me out to preach the gospel to the poor, to restore the broken-hearted.*

POSTCOMMUNION.

Quos tantis, Dñe, largíris uti mystériis: quǽsumus; ut effectibus nos eórum veráciter aptáre dignéris. Per Dñm.

O Lord, Who dost give freely the enjoyment of so great mysteries, we beseech Thee that Thou wouldst vouchsafe to render us truly worthy to receive their effects. Through our Lord.

II Classis.

— Fourth Sunday after Epiphany —

DOMINICA QUARTA POST EPIPHANIAM

INTROIT. *Ps 96: 7-8*

Adoráte Deum, omnes Ángeli ejus: audívit, et lætáta est Sion: et exsultavérunt fíliæ Judæ. ℣. Dóminus regnávit, exsúltet terra: læténtur ínsulæ multæ. ℣. Glória Patri.

ADORE GOD, all you His angels: Sion heard, and was glad; and the daughters of Juda rejoiced. (Ps 96: 1) The Lord hath reigned; let the earth rejoice: let many islands be glad. ℣. Glory.

COLLECT.

O God, Who knowest that we are beset by perils so great as to be unendurable because of our human frailty, grant us health of mind and body, so that by Thine assistance we may conquer the things with which we are afflicted because of our sins. Through our Lord.

Deus, qui nos, in tantis perículis constitútos, pro humána scis fragilitáte non posse subsístere: da nobis salútem mentis et córporis; ut ea, quæ pro peccátis nostris pátimur, te adjuvánte vincámus. Per Dóminum.

EPISTLE. *Rom 13: 8-10*

BRETHREN, owe no man any thing, but to love one another; for he that loveth his neighbor hath fulfilled the law. For thou shalt not commit adultery, thou shalt not kill, thou shalt not steal, thou shalt not bear false witness, thou shalt not covet, and if there be any other commandment, it is comprised in this word, thou shalt love thy neighbor as thyself. The love of our neighbor worketh no evil. Love, therefore, is the fulfilling of the law.

Fratres: Némini quidquam debeátis, nisi ut ínvicem diligátis: qui enim díligit próximum, legem implévit. Nam: Non adulterábis, Non occídes, Non furáberis, Non falsum testimónium dices, Non concupísces: et si quod est áliud mandátum, in hoc verbo instaurátur: Díliges próximum tuum sicut teípsum. Diléctio próximi malum non operátur. Plenitúdo ergo legis est diléctio.

GRADUAL & ALLELUIA. *Ps 101: 16-17 & Ps 96: 1*

THE Gentiles shall fear Thy name, O Lord, and all the kings of the earth Thy glory. ℣. For the Lord hath built up Sion, and He shall be seen in His majesty. | Alleluia, alleluia. ℣. The Lord hath reigned, let the earth rejoice: let many islands be glad. Alleluia.

Timébunt gentes nomen tuum, Dñe, et omnes reges terræ glóriam tuam. ℣. Quóniam ædificávit Dñs Sion, et vidébitur in majestáte sua. | Allelúja, allelúja. ℣. Dñs regnávit, exsúltet terra: læténtur ínsulæ multæ. Allelúja.

GOSPEL. *Matt 8: 23-27*

WHEN JESUS ENTERED into the ship, His disciples followed Him. And behold a great tempest arose in the sea, so that the ship was covered with waves, but He was asleep. And they came to Him, and awaked Him, saying, Lord, save us, we perish. And Jesus saith to them, Why are ye fearful, O ye of little faith? Then rising up, He commanded the winds and the sea, and there came a great calm. But the men wondered, saying, What manner of man is this, for the winds and the sea obey Him? CREDO.

In illo témpore: Ascendénte Jesu in navículam, secúti sunt eum discípuli ejus: et ecce, motus magnus factus est in mari, ita ut navícula operirétur flúctibus, ipse vero dormiébat. Et accessérunt ad eũ discípuli ejus, et suscitavérunt eum, dicéntes: Dómine, salva nos, perímus. Et dicit eis Jesus: Quid tímidi estis, módicæ fídei? Tunc surgens, imperávit ventis et mari, et facta est tranquíllitas magna. Porro hómines miráti sunt, dicéntes: Qualis est hic, quia venti et mare obédiunt ei?

OFFERTORY. *Ps 117: 16, 17*

THE POWER of the Lord has triumphed, the power of the Lord has brought me to great honor: I am reprieved from death, to live on and proclaim what the Lord has done for me.

Identical to Maundy Thursday:

Déxtera Dómini fecit virtútem, déxtera Dómini exaltávit me: non móriar, sed vivam, et narrábo ópera Dómini. ℣. *In tribulatióne invocávi Dóminum et exaudívit me in latitúdine: quia Dñs adjútor meus est.* ℣. *Impúlsus versátus sum, ut cáderem: et Dñs suscépit me: et factus est mihi in salútem.*

℣. I called on the Lord when trouble beset me, and the Lord listened, and brought me relief, for the Lord is at my side. ℣. I reeled under the blow, and had well-nigh fallen, but still the Lord was there to aid me. Who but the Lord has brought me deliverance?

SECRET.

Concéde, quǽsumus, omnípotens Deus: ut hujus sacrifícii munus oblátum fragilitátem nostram ab omni malo purget semper et múniat. Per Dóminum.

Grant, we beseech Thee, almighty God, that this sacrifice offered to Thee, may purge us of all evil and fortify our weak nature. Through our Lord.

COMMUNION. *Luke 4: 22*

Mirabántur omnes de his, quæ procedébant de ore Dei. (Lk 4: 18) ℣. *Spíritus Dñi super me: propter quod unxit me, evangelizáre paupéribus misit me.*

THEY ALL wondered at these things, which proceeded from the mouth of God. ℣. *The Spirit of the Lord is upon Me; He has anointed Me, and sent Me out to preach the gospel to the poor, to restore the broken-hearted.*

POSTCOMMUNION.

Múnera tua nos, Deus, a delectatiónibus terrénis expédiant: et cæléstibus semper instáurent aliméntis. Per Dóminum.

May Thy gifts, O God, free us from the allurements of earthly things, and ever restore us with heavenly nourishment. Through our Lord.

II Classis.

— *Fifth Sunday after Epiphany* —

DOMINICA QUINTA POST EPIPHANIAM

INTROIT. *Ps 96: 7-8*

Adoráte Deum, omnes Ángeli ejus: audívit, et lætáta est Sion: et exsultavérunt fíliæ Judæ. ℣. Dóminus regnávit, exsúltet terra: læténtur ínsulæ multæ. ℣. Glória Patri.

ADORE GOD, all you His angels: Sion heard, and was glad; and the daughters of Juda rejoiced. (Ps 96: 1) The Lord hath reigned; let the earth rejoice: let many islands be glad. ℣. Glory.

COLLECT.

Famíliam tuam, quǽsumus, Dómine, contínua pietáte custódi: ut, quæ in sola spe grátiæ cæléstis innítitur, tua semper protectióne muniátur. Per Dóminum.

Keep Thy family, we beseech Thee, O Lord, with Thy continual mercy that, leaning only upon the hope of Thy heavenly grace, it may ever be defended by Thy protection. Through our Lord.

EPISTLE. *Col 3: 12-17*

BRETHREN, put ye on, as the elect of God, holy and beloved, the bowels of mercy, benignity, humility, modesty, patience; bearing with one another, and forgiving one another, if any have a complaint against another, even as the Lord hath forgiven you, so you also. But above all these things, have charity, which is the bond of perfection: and let the peace of Christ rejoice in your hearts, wherein also you are called in one body: and be ye thankful. Let the word of Christ dwell in you abundantly, in all wisdom; teaching and admonishing one another, in psalms, hymns, and spiritual canticles, singing in grace in your hearts to God. All whatsoever you do in word or in work, all things do ye in the name of the Lord Jesus Christ, giving thanks to God and the Father through Jesus Christ our Lord.

Fratres: Indúite vos sicut elécti Dei, sancti et dilecti, víscera misericórdiæ, benignitátem, humilitátem, modéstiam, patiéntiam: supportántes ínvicem, et donántes vobismetípsis, si quis advérsus áliquem habet querélam: sicut et Dóminus donávit vobis, ita et vos. Super ómnia autem hæc caritátem habéte, quod est vínculum perfectionis: et pax Christi exsúltet in córdibus vestris, in qua et vocáti estis in uno córpore: et grati estóte. Verbũ Christi hábitet in vobis abundánter, in omni sapiéntia, docéntes et commonéntes vosmetípsos psalmis, hymnis et cánticis spirituálibus, in grátia cantántes in córdibus vestris Deo. Omne, quodcúmque fácitis in verbo aut in ópere, ómnia in nómine Dómini Jesu Christi, grátias agéntes Deo et Patri per Jesum Christum, Dóminum nostrum.

GRADUAL & ALLELUIA. *Ps 101: 16-17 & Ps 96: 1*

THE Gentiles shall fear Thy name, O Lord, and all the kings of the earth Thy glory. ℣. For the Lord hath built up Sion, and He shall be seen in His majesty. | Alleluia, alleluia. ℣. The Lord hath reigned, let the earth rejoice: let many islands be glad. Alleluia.

Timébunt gentes nomen tuum, Dñe, et omnes reges terræ glóriam tuam. ℣. Quóniam ædificávit Dñs Sion, et vidébitur in majestáte sua. | Allelúja, allelúja. ℣. Dñs regnávit, exsúltet terra: læténtur ínsulæ multæ. Allelúja.

GOSPEL. *Matt 13: 24-30*

JESUS SPOKE this parable to the multitudes: The kingdom of heaven is likened to a man that sowed good seed in his field. But while men were asleep, his enemy came, and oversowed cockle among the wheat, and went his way. And when the blade was sprung up, and had brought forth fruit, then appeared also the cockle. And the servants of the good man of the house coming, said to him, Sir, didst thou not sow good seed in thy field? whence then hath it cockle? And he said to them, An enemy hath done this.

In illo témpore: Dixit Jesus turbis parábolam hanc: Símile factum est regnum cælórum hómini, qui seminávit bonum semen in agro suo. Cum autem dormírent hómines, venit inimícus ejus, et superseminávit zizánia in médio trítici, et ábiit. Cum autem crevísset herba et fructum fecísset, tunc apparuérunt et zizánia. Accedéntes autem servi patrisfamílias, dixérunt ei: Dómine, nonne bonum semen seminásti in agro tuo? Unde ergo habet zizánia? Et ait illis: Inimícus homo hoc fecit.

And the servants said to him, Wilt thou that we go and gather it up? And he said, No: lest perhaps gathering up the cockle you root up the wheat also together with it. Suffer both to grow until the harvest; and in the time of the harvest, I will say to the reapers, Gather up

Servi autem dixérunt ei: Vis, imus, et collígimus ea? Et ait: Non: ne forte colligéntes zizánia eradicétis simul cum eis et tríticum. Sínite útraque créscere usque ad messem, et in témpore messis dicam messóribus: Collígite primum zizánia, et alligáte ea in fascículos ad comburéndum, tríticum autem congregáte in hórreum meum.

first the cockle, and bind it into bundles to burn, but the wheat gather ye into my barn. CREDO.

OFFERTORY. *Ps 117: 16, 17*

Identical to Maundy Thursday:

Déxtera Dómini fecit virtútem, déxtera Dómini exaltávit me: non móriar, sed vivam, et narrábo ópera Dómini. ℣. *In tribulatióne invocávi Dóminum et exaudívit me in latitúdine: quia Dñs adjútor meus est.* ℣. *Impúlsus versátus sum, ut cáderem: et Dñs suscépit me: et factus est mihi in salútem.*

THE POWER of the Lord has triumphed, the power of the Lord has brought me to great honor: I am reprieved from death, to live on and proclaim what the Lord has done for me. ℣. *I called on the Lord when trouble beset me, and the Lord listened, and brought me relief, for the Lord is at my side.* ℣. *I reeled under the blow, and had well-nigh fallen, but still the Lord was there to aid me. Who but the Lord has brought me deliverance?*

SECRET.

Hóstias tibi, Dómine, placatiónis offérimus: ut et delícta nostra miserátus absólvas, et nutántia corda tu dírigas. Per Dóminum.

We offer Thee, O Lord, the sacrifice of reconciliation, that Thou mayest mercifully forgive our sins and direct our wavering hearts. Through our Lord.

COMMUNION. *Luke 4: 22*

Mirabántur omnes de his, quæ procedébant de ore Dei. (Lk 4: 18) ℣. *Spíritus Dñi super me: propter quod unxit me, evangelizáre paupéribus misit me.*

THEY ALL wondered at these things, which proceeded from the mouth of God. ℣. *The Spirit of the Lord is upon Me; He has anointed Me, and sent Me out to preach the gospel to the poor, to restore the broken-hearted.*

POSTCOMMUNION.

Quǽsumus, omnípotens Deus: ut illíus salutáris capiámus efféctum, cujus per hæc mystéria pignus accépimus. Per Dóminum.

We pray Thee, O almighty God, that we may receive the effect of that salvation of which we have received the pledge in these mysteries. Through our Lord.

II Classis.

— *Sixth Sunday after Epiphany* —

DOMINICA SEXTA POST EPIPHANIAM

INTROIT. *Ps 96: 7-8*

Adoráte Deum, omnes Ángeli ejus: audívit, et lætáta est Sion: et exsultavérunt fíliæ Judæ. ℣. Dóminus regnávit, exsúltet terra: læténtur ínsulæ multæ. ℣. Glória Patri.

ADORE GOD, all you His angels: Sion heard, and was glad; and the daughters of Juda rejoiced. (Ps 96: 1) The Lord hath reigned; let the earth rejoice: let many islands be glad. ℣. Glory.

COLLECT.

Grant, we beseech Thee, almighty God, that, ever fixing our thoughts on reasonable things, we may both in word and in deed do what is pleasing to Thee. Through our Lord.

Præsta, quǽsumus, omnípotens Deus: ut, semper rationabília meditántes, quæ tibi sunt plácita, et dictis exsequámur et factis. Per Dóminum.

EPISTLE. *I Thess 1: 2-10*

BRETHREN, we give thanks to God for you all, making a remembrance of you in our prayers without ceasing; being mindful of the work of your faith, and labor, and charity, and of the enduring of the hope of our Lord Jesus Christ before God and our Father: knowing, brethren, beloved of God, your election; for our gospel hath not been unto you in word only, but in power also, and in the Holy Ghost, and in much fullness, as you know what manner of men we have been among you for your sakes. And you became followers of us and of the Lord; receiving the word in much tribulation, with joy of the Holy Ghost: so that you were made a pattern to all that believe, in Macedonia and in Achaia. For from you was spread abroad the word of the Lord, not only in Macedonia and Achaia, but also in every place, your faith which is towards God, is gone forth; so that we need not to speak any thing. For they themselves relate to us, what manner of entering in we had unto you; and how ye turned to God from idols, to serve the living and true God, and to wait for His Son from heaven (whom He raised from the dead), Jesus, Who hath delivered us from the wrath to come.

Fratres: Grátias ágimus Deo semper pro ómnibus vobis, memóriam vestri faciéntes in oratiónibus nostris sine intermissióne, mémores óperis fídei vestræ, et labóris, et caritátis, et sustinéntiæ spei Dñi nostri Jesu Christi, ante Deum et Patrem nostrum: sciéntes, fratres, dilécti a Deo, electiónẽ vestrã: quia Evangéliũ nostrũ non fuit ad vos in sermóne tantum, sed et in virtúte, et in Spíritu Sancto, et in plenitúdine multa, sicut scitis quales fuérimus in vobis propter vos. Et vos imitatóres nostri facti estis, et Dñi, excipiéntes verbũ in tribulatióne multa, cũ gáudio Spíritus Sancti: ita ut facti sitis forma ómnibus credéntibus in Macedónia et in Achája. A vobis enim diffamátus est sermo Dñi, non solum in Macedónia et in Achája, sed et in omni loco fides vestra, quæ est ad Deũ, profécta est, ita ut non sit nobis necésse quidquã loqui. Ipsi enim de nobis annúntiant, qualẽ intróitũ habuérimus ad vos: et quómodo convérsi estis ad Deum a simulácris, servíre Deo vivo et vero, et exspectáre Fílium ejus de cælis (quem suscitávit ex mórtuis) Jesum, qui erípuit nos ab ira ventúra.

GRADUAL & ALLELUIA. *Ps 101: 16-17 & Ps 96: 1*

THE Gentiles shall fear Thy name, O Lord, and all the kings of the earth Thy glory. ℣. For the Lord hath built up Sion, and He shall be seen in His majesty. | Alleluia, alleluia. ℣. The Lord hath reigned, let the earth rejoice: let many islands be glad. Alleluia.

Timébunt gentes nomen tuum, Dñe, et omnes reges terræ glóriam tuam. ℣. Quóniam ædificávit Dñs Sion, et vidébitur in majestáte sua. | Allelúja, allelúja. ℣. Dñs regnávit, exsúltet terra: læténtur ínsulæ multæ. Allelúja.

GOSPEL. *Matt 13: 31-35*

JESUS SPOKE THIS PARABLE to the multitudes: The kingdom of heaven is like to a grain of mustard seed, which a man took and sowed in his field: which is the least indeed of all seeds; but when it is grown up, it is greater than all herbs, and becometh a tree; so that the birds of the air come, and dwell

In illo témpore: Dixit Jesus turbis parábolam hanc: Símile est regnũ cælórum grano sinápis, quod accípiens homo seminávit in agro suo: quod mínimum quidem est ómnibus semínibus: cum autem créverit, majus est ómnibus oléribus, et fit arbor, ita ut vólucres cæli véniant et hábitent in ramis ejus. Áliam parábolã locútus est eis: Símile est regnum cælórum ferménto, quod accéptum múlier abscóndit in farínæ satis tribus, donec fermentátū est totum. Hæc ómnia locútus est Jesus in parábolis ad turbas: et sine parábolis non loquebátur eis: ut implerétur quod dictum erat per Prophétam dicéntem: Apériam in parábolis os meum, eructábo abscóndita a constitutióne mundi.

in the branches thereof. Another parable he spoke to them: The kingdom of heaven is like to leaven, which a woman took and hid in three measures of meal, until the whole was leavened. All these things Jesus spoke in parables to the multitudes, and without parables He did not speak to them; that it might be fulfilled which was spoken by the prophet, saying, I will open my mouth in parables, I will utter things hidden from the foundation of the world. CREDO.

OFFERTORY. *Ps 117: 16, 17*

Identical to Maundy Thursday:

Déxtera Dómini fecit virtútem, déxtera Dómini exaltávit me: non móriar, sed vivam, et narrábo ópera Dómini. ℣. *In tribulatióne invocávi Dóminum et exaudívit me in latitúdine: quia Dn̄s adjútor meus est.* ℣. *Impúlsus versátus sum, ut cáderem: et Dn̄s suscépit me: et factus est mihi in salútem.*

THE POWER of the Lord has triumphed, the power of the Lord has brought me to great honor: I am reprieved from death, to live on and proclaim what the Lord has done for me. ℣. *I called on the Lord when trouble beset me, and the Lord listened, and brought me relief, for the Lord is at my side.* ℣. *I reeled under the blow, and had well-nigh fallen, but still the Lord was there to aid me. Who but the Lord has brought me deliverance?*

SECRET.

Hæc nos oblátio, Deus, mundet, quǽsumus, et rénovet, gubérnet et prótegat. Per Dóminum.

May this oblation, O God, cleanse, renew, govern, and protect us, we beseech Thee. Through our Lord.

COMMUNION. *Luke 4: 22*

Mirabántur omnes de his, quæ procedébant de ore Dei. (Lk 4: 18) ℣. *Spíritus Dn̄i super me: propter quod unxit me, evangelizáre paupéribus misit me.*

—4951STEVEN|1128 • Circa 1128AD

THEY ALL wondered at these things, which proceeded from the mouth of God. ℣. *The Spirit of the Lord is upon Me; He has anointed Me, and sent Me out to preach the gospel to the poor, to restore the broken-hearted.*

POSTCOMMUNION.

Cæléstibus, Dómine, pasti delíciis: quǽsumus; ut semper éadem, per quæ veráciter vívimus, appetámus. Per Dóminum.

Being fed with celestial delights, we beseech Thee, O Lord, that we may ever hunger after those things by which we truly live. Through our Lord.

— *Septuagesima Sunday* — *II Classis.*

DOMINICA IN SEPTUAGESIMA *Station at Saint Lawrence Outside the Walls*

INTROIT. *Ps 17: 5, 6, 7*

THE GROANS OF DEATH surround me, the sorrows of hell encompassed me: and in my affliction I called upon the Lord, and He heard my voice, from His holy temple. (Ps 17: 2-3) I will love Thee, O Lord, my strength: the Lord is my firmament, and my refuge and my deliverer. ℣. Glory.

Circumdedérunt me gémitus mortis, dolóres inférni circumdedérunt me: et in tribulatióne mea invocávi Dñm, et exaudívit de templo sancto suo vocem meam. ℣. Díligam te, Dñe, fortitúdo mea: Dóminus firmaméntum meum, et refúgium meum, et liberátor meus. ℣. Glória Patri.

COLLECT.

Do Thou, we beseech Thee, O Lord, graciously hear the prayers of Thy people, that we, who are justly afflicted for our sins, may be mercifully delivered for the glory of Thy name. Through our Lord.

Preces pópuli tui, quǽsumus, Dñe, cleménter exáudi: ut, qui juste pro peccátis nostris afflígimur, pro tui nóminis glória misericórditer liberémur. Per Dóminum.

EPISTLE. *I Cor 9: 24-27; 10: 1-5*

BRETHREN, KNOW YOU NOT that they that run in the race, all run indeed, but one receiveth the prize? So run, that you may obtain. And every one that striveth for the mastery, refraineth himself from all things: and they indeed that they may receive a corruptible crown, but we an incorruptible one. I therefore so run, not as at an uncertainty; I so fight, not as one beating the air: but I chastise my body, and bring it into subjection: lest perhaps, when I have preached to others, I myself should become a castaway. For I would not have you ignorant, brethren, that our fathers were all under the cloud, and all passed through the sea; and all in Moses were baptized, in the cloud and in the sea; and all did eat the same spiritual food, and all drank the same spiritual drink; (and they drank of the spiritual rock that followed them; and the rock was Christ). But with the most of them God was not well pleased.

Fratres: Nescítis, quod ii, qui in stádio currunt, omnes quidem currunt, sed unus áccipit bravíum? Sic cúrrite, ut comprehendátis. Omnis autem, qui in agóne conténdit, ab ómnibus se ábstinet: et illi quidem, ut corruptíbilem corónam accípiant; nos autẽ incorrúptam. Ego ígitur sic curro, non quasi in incértum: sic pugno, non quasi áërem vérberans: sed castígo corpus meum, et in servitútem rédigo: ne forte, cum áliis prædicáverim, ipse réprobus effíciar. Nolo enim vos ignoráre, fratres, quóniã patres nostri omnes sub nube fuérunt, et omnes mare transiérunt, et omnes in Móyse baptizáti sunt in nube et in mari: et omnes eámdem escam spiritálem manducavérunt, et omnes eúmdem potum spiritálem bibérunt (bibébant autem de spiritáli, consequénte eos, petra: petra autem erat Christus): sed non in plúribus eórum beneplácitum est Deo.

GRADUAL. *Ps 9: 10-11, 19-20*

THE HELPER in due time, in tribulation: let them trust in Thee, who know Thee: for Thou dost not forsake them that seek Thee, O Lord. ℣. For the poor man shall not be forgotten to the end: the patience of

Adjútor in opportunitátibus, in tribulatióne: sperent in te, qui novérunt te: quóniam non derelínquis quæréntes te, Dómine. ℣. Quóniam non in finem oblívio erit páuperis: patiéntia páuperum non períbit in ætérnum: exsúrge, Dómine, non præváleat homo.

the poor shall not perish for ever: arise, O Lord, let not man be strengthened.

TRACT. *Ps 129: 1-4*

De profúndis clamávi ad te, Dómine: Dómine, exáudi vocem meam. ℣. Fiant aures tuæ intendéntes in oratiónẽ servi tui. ℣. Si iniquitátes observáveris, Dómine: Dñe, quis sustinébit? ℣. Quia apud te propitiátio est, et propter legem tuam sustínui te, Dómine.

FROM THE DEPTHS I have cried to Thee, O Lord; Lord, hear my voice. ℣. Let Thine ears be attentive to the prayer of Thy servant. ℣. If Thou shalt observe iniquities, O Lord, Lord, who shall endure it? ℣. For with Thee is propitiation, and by reason of Thy law I have waited for Thee, O Lord.

GOSPEL. *Matt 20: 1-16*

In illo témpore: Dixit Jesus discípulis suis parábolam hanc: Símile est regnum cælórũ hómini patrifamílias, qui éxiit primo mane condúcere operários in víneam suam. Conventióne autem facta cum operáriis ex denário diúrno, misit eos in víneam suam. Et egréssus circa horam tértiam, vidit álios stantes in foro otiósos, et dixit illis: Ite et vos in víneam meam, et quod justum fúerit, dabo vobis. Illi autem abiérunt. Íterum autem éxiit circa sextam et nonam horam: et fecit simíliter. Circa undécimam vero éxiit, et invénit álios stantes, et dicit illis: Quid hic statis tota die otiósi? Dicunt ei: Quia nemo nos condúxit. Dicit illis: Ite et vos in víneam meam. Cum sero autem factum esset, dicit dóminus víneæ procuratóri suo: Voca operários, et redde illis mercédem, incípiens a novíssimis usque ad primos. Cum veníssent ergo qui circa undécimam horam vénerant, accepérunt síngulos denários. Veniéntes autẽ et primi, arbitráti sunt, quod plus essent acceptúri: accepérunt autem et ipsi síngulos denários. Et accipiéntes murmurábant advérsus patremfamílias, dicéntes: Hi novíssimi una hora fecérunt et pares illos nobis fecísti, qui portávimus pondus diéi et æstus. At ille respóndens uni eórum, dixit: Amíce, non facio tibi injúriam: nonne ex denário convenísti mecũ? Tolle quod tuum est, et vade: volo autem et huic novíssimo dare sicut et tibi. Aut non licet mihi, quod volo, fácere? an óculus tuus nequam est, quia ego bonus sum? Sic erunt novíssimi primi, et primi novíssimi. Multi enim sunt vocáti, pauci vero elécti.

JESUS SPOKE to His disciples this parable: The kingdom of heaven is like to a householder, who went out early in the morning to hire laborers into his vineyard. And having agreed with the laborers for a penny a day, he sent them into his vineyard. And going out about the third hour, he saw others standing in the marketplace idle, and he said to them, Go you also into my vineyard, and I will give you what shall be just: and they went their way. And again he went out about the sixth and the ninth hour, and did in like manner. But about the eleventh hour, he went out, and found others standing; and he saith to them, Why stand you here all the day idle? They say to him, Because no man hath hired us. He saith to them, Go you also into my vineyard. And when evening was come, the lord of the vineyard saith to his steward, Call the laborers, and pay them their hire, beginning from the last even to the first. When therefore they were come that came about the eleventh hour, they received every man a penny. But when the first also came, they thought that they should receive more; and they also received every man a penny. And receiving it, they murmured against the master of the house, saying, These last have worked but one hour, and thou hast made them equal to us that have borne the burden of the day and the heat. But he answering, said to one of them, Friend, I do thee no wrong; didst thou not agree with me for a penny? Take what is thine, and go thy way: I will also give to this last even as to thee. Or, is it not lawful for me to do what I will? Is thy eye evil, because I am good? So shall the last be first, and the first last. For many are called, but few are chosen. Credo.

OFFERTORY. *Ps 91: 2*

IT IS GOOD to give praise to the Lord, and to sing to Thy name, O Most High. ℣. *O Lord, how great are Thy works: Thy thoughts are exceeding deep.* ℣. *For behold Thine enemies, O Lord, shall perish and all the workers of iniquity shall be scattered.* ℣. *But my horn shall be exalted like that of the unicorn, and my old age in plentiful mercy: for my eye also hath looked down upon my enemies, and Thine ear shall hear of the malignant that rise against me.*

Bonum est confitéri Dómino, et psállere nómini tuo, Altíssime. ℣. *Quam magnificáta sunt ópera tua Dñe: nimis profúndæ factae sunt cogitatiónes tuae.* ℣. *Ecce inimíci tui Dñe períbunt et dispergéntur omnes, qui operántur iniquitátẽ.* ℣. *Exaltábitur sicut unicórnis cornu meum et senéctus mea in misericórdia úberi: quia respéxit óculus meus inimícos meos et insurgéntes in me malignántes audívit auris tua.*

SECRET.

With our gifts and prayers accepted, we beseech Thee, O Lord, both cleanse us by these heavenly mysteries and graciously hear us. Through our Lord.

Munéribus nostris, quǽsumus, Dñe, precibúsque suscéptis: et cæléstibus nos munda mystériis, et cleménter exáudi. Per Dóminum.

COMMUNION. *Ps 30: 17-18*

MAKE THY FACE to shine upon Thy servant, and save me in Thy mercy: Let me not be confounded, O Lord, for I have called upon thee. ℣. *To Thee, O Lord, I look for refuge, never let me be ashamed of my trust; in Thy faithful care, deliver me.*

Illúmina fáciem tuam super servũ tuũ, et salvum me fac in tua misericórdia: Dñe, non confúndar, quóniam invocávi te. (Ps 30: 2) ℣. *In te, Dómine, sperávi; non confúndar in ætérnum: in justítia tua líbera me.* —342sanGall|933 • Circa 933AD

POSTCOMMUNION.

May Thy faithful, O God, be strengthened by Thy gifts, that receiving them they may still desire them and desiring them may constantly receive them. Through our Lord.

Fidéles tui, Deus, per tua dona firméntur: ut éadem et percipiéndo requírant, et quæréndo sine fine percípiant. Per Dóminum.

— *Sexagesima Sunday* — *II Classis.*

DOMINICA IN SEXAGESIMA *Station at Saint Paul*

INTROIT. *Ps 43: 23-26*

BESTIR THYSELF, O Lord; why dost Thou sleep on? Awake, do not banish us from Thy presence for ever. Why turnest Thou Thy face away, and forgettest our trouble? Our belly hath cleaved to the earth: arise, O Lord, help us and deliver us. (Ps 43: 2) O God, the tale has come to our ears—have not our fathers told it? ℣. Glory.

Exsúrge, quare obdórmis, Dómine? exsúrge, et ne repéllas in finem: quare fáciem tuam avértis, oblivísceris tribulatiónem nostram? adhǽsit in terra venter noster: exsúrge, Dñe, ádjuva nos, et líbera nos. ℣. Deus, áuribus nostris audívimus: patres nostri annuntiavérunt nobis. ℣. Glória Patri.

COLLECT.

Deus, qui cónspicis, quia ex nulla nostra actióne confídimus: concéde propítius; ut, contra advérsa ómnia, Doctóris géntiũ protectióne muniámur. Per Dóminum.

O God, Who seest that we put not our trust in any deed of our own, mercifully grant that by the protection of the Teacher of the gentiles we may be defended against all adversities. Through our Lord.

EPISTLE. *II Cor 11: 19-33; 12: 1-9*

Fratres: Libénter suffértis insipiéntens: cum sitis ipsi sapiéntes. Sustinétis enim, si quis vos in servitútem rédigit, si quis dévorat, si quis áccipit, si quis extóllitur, si quis in fáciem vos cædit. Secúndum ignobilitátem dico, quasi nos infírmi fuérimus in hac parte. In quo quis audet, (in insipiéntia dico) áudeo et ego: Hebrǽi sunt, et ego: Israëlítæ sunt, et ego: Semen Ábrahæ sunt, et ego: Minístri Christi sunt, (ut minus sápiens dico) plus ego: in labóribus plúrimis, in carcéribus abundántius, in plagis supra modum, in mórtibus frequénter. A Judǽis quínquies quadragénas, una minus, accépi. Ter virgis cæsus sum, semel lapidátus sum, ter naufrágium feci, nocte et die in profúndo maris fui: in itinéribus sæpe, perículis flúminum, perículis latrónum, perículis ex génere, perículis ex géntibus, perículis in civitáte, perículis in solitúdine, perículis in mari, perículis in falsis frátribus: in labóre et ærúmna, in vigíliis multis, in fame et siti, in jejúniis multis, in frígore et nuditáte: præter illa, quæ extrínsecus sunt, instántia mea cotidiána, sollicitúdo ómnium Ecclesiárum. Quis infirmátur, et ego non infírmor? quis scandalizátur, et ego non uror? Si gloriári opórtet: quæ infirmitátis meæ sunt, gloriábor. Deus et Pater Dñi nostri Jesu Christi, qui est benedíctus in sǽcula, scit quod non méntior. Damásci præpósitus gentis Arétæ regis, custodiébat civitátem Damascenórũ, ut me comprehénderet: et per fenéstrã in sporta dimíssus sum per murum, et sic effúgi manus ejus. Si gloriári opórtet (non éxpedit quidem), véniam autem ad visiónes et revelatiónes Dñi. Scio hóminem in Christo ante annos quatuórdecim, (sive in córpore néscio, sive extra corpus néscio, Deus scit:) raptum hujúsmodi usque ad tértium cælum. Et scio hujúsmodi hóminem, (sive in córpore, sive extra corpus néscio, Deus scit:) quóniam raptus est in paradisum: et audívit arcána

BRETHREN, you gladly suffer the foolish; whereas yourselves are wise. For you suffer if a man bring you into bondage, if a man devour you, if a man take from you, if a man be lifted up, if a man strike you in the face. I speak according to dishonor, as if we had been weak in this part. Wherein if any man dare (I speak foolishly), I dare also. They are Hebrews; so am I. They are Israelites: so am I. They are the seed of Abraham; so am I. They are the ministers of Christ (I speak as one less wise); I am more: in many more labors, in prisons more frequently, in stripes above measure, in deaths often. Of the Jews five times did I receive forty stripes save one. Thrice was I beaten with rods; once I was stoned; thrice I suffered shipwreck; a night and a day I was in the depth of the sea. In journeying often, in perils of waters, in perils of robbers, in perils from my own nation, in perils from the gentiles, in perils in the city, in perils in the wilderness, in perils in the sea, in perils from false brethren. In labor and painfulness, in much watchings, in hunger and thirst, in fastings often, in cold and nakedness; besides those things which are without, my daily instance, the solicitude for all the churches. Who is weak, and I am not weak? Who is scandalized, and I am not on fire? If I must needs glory, I will glory of the things that concern my infirmity. The God and Father of Our Lord Jesus Christ, Who is blessed for ever, knoweth that I lie not. At Damascus the governor of the nation under Aretas the king, guarded the city of the Damascenes to apprehend me; and through a window in a basket was I let down by the wall, and so escaped his hands. If I must glory (it is not expedient indeed): but I will come to the visions and revelations of the Lord. I know a man in Christ above fourteen years ago (whether in the body, I know not, or out of the body, I know not; God knoweth):

such an one rapt even to the third heaven. And I know such a man (whether in the body, or out of the body, I cannot tell; God knoweth); that he was caught up into paradise; and heard secret words, which it is not granted to man to utter. For such an one I will glory; but for myself I will glory nothing, but in my infirmities. For though I should have a mind to glory, I shall not be foolish; for I will say the truth. But I forbear, lest any man should think of me above that which he seeth in me, or any thing he heareth from me. And lest the greatness of the revelations should exalt me, there was given me a sting of my flesh, an angel of Satan, to buffet me. For which thing thrice I besought the Lord, that it might depart from me. And He said to me, My grace is sufficient for thee; for power is made perfect in infirmity. Gladly therefore will I glory in my infirmities, that the power of Christ may dwell in me.

verba, quæ non licet hómini loqui. Pro hujúsmodi gloriábor: pro me autem nihil gloriábor nisi in infirmitátibus meis. Nam, et si volúero gloriári, non ero insípiens: veritátem enim dicam: parco autem, ne quis me exístimet supra id, quod videt in me, aut áliquid audit ex me. Et ne magnitúdo revelatiónem extóllat me, datus est mihi stímulus carnis meæ ángelus sátanæ, qui me colaphízet. Propter quod ter Dñm rogávi, ut discéderet a me: et dixit mihi: Súfficit tibi grátia mea: nam virtus in infirmitáte perfícitur. Libénter ígitur gloriábor in infirmitátibus meis, ut inhábitet in me virtus Christi.

GRADUAL. *Ps 82: 19, 14*

LET THE GENTILES know that God is Thy name: Thou alone art the Most High over all the earth. ℣. O my God, make them like a wheel, and as stubble before the face of the wind.

Sciant gentes, quóniã nomen tibi Deus: tu solus Altíssimus super omnem terram. ℣. Deus meus, pone illos ut rotam, et sicut stípulam ante fáciem venti.

TRACT. *Ps 59: 4, 6*

THOU HAST moved the earth, O Lord, and hast troubled it. ℣. Heal Thou the breaches thereof, for it hath been moved. ℣. That Thy elect may flee from before the bow: that they may be delivered.

Commovísti, Dómine, terram, et conturbásti eam. ℣. Sana contritiónes ejus, quia mota est. ℣. Ut fúgiant a fácie arcus: ut liberéntur elécti tui.

GOSPEL. *Luke 8: 4-15*

WHEN A VERY great multitude was gathered together and hastened out of the cities unto Him, He spoke by a similitude; The sower went out to sow his seed. And as he sowed, some fell by the wayside; and it was trodden down, and the fowls of the air devoured it. And other some fell upon a rock; and as soon as it was sprung up, it withered away, because it had no moisture. And other some fell among thorns; and the thorns growing up with it, choked it. And other some fell upon good ground; and being sprung up, yielded fruit a hundred fold. Saying these things, He cried out, He that hath ears to hear, let him hear. And His disci-

In illo témpore: Cum turba plúrima convenírent, et de civitátibus properárent ad Jesum, dixit per similitúdinẽ: Éxiit, qui séminat, semináre semen suum: et dum séminat, áliud cécidit secus viam, et conculcátum est, et vólucres cæli comedérunt illud. Et áliud cécidit supra petram: et natum áruit, quia non habébat humórem. Et áliud cécidit inter spinas, et simul exórtæ spinæ suffocavérunt illud. Et áliud cécidit in terram bonam: et ortum fecit fructum céntuplum. Hæc dicens, clamábat: Qui habet aures audiéndi, áudiat. Interrogábant autem eum discípuli ejus, quæ esset hæc parábola. Quibus ipse dixit: Vobis datum est nosse mystérium regni Dei, céteris autem in parábolis: ut vidéntes non videant, et audiéntes non intéllegant. Est autem hæc parábola: Semen est verbum Dei. Qui autem secus viam, hi sunt qui áudiunt: deínde venit diábolus, et tollit verbum de corde eórum, ne credéntes salvi fiant. Nam qui supra petram: qui cum audíerint, cum gáudio suscípiunt verbũ: et hi radíces non habent: qui ad tempus credunt, et in témpore tentatiónis recédunt. Quod autem in spinas cécidit: hi sunt, qui audiérunt, et a sollicitudínibus et divítiis et voluptátibus vitæ eúntes, suffocántur, et non réferunt fructum. Quod autem in bonam terram: hi sunt, qui in corde bono et óptimo audiéntes verbum rétinent, et fructũ ásferunt in patiéntia.

ples asked Him what this parable might be. To whom He said, To you it is given to know the mystery of the kingdom of God, but to the rest in parables; that seeing they may not see, and hearing may not understand. Now the parable is this: The seed is the word of God. And they by the wayside are they that hear; then the devil cometh, and taketh the word out of their heart, lest believing they should be saved. Now they upon the rock are they who when they hear, receive the word with joy; and these have no roots, for they believe for a while, and in time of temptation they fall away. And that which fell among thorns are they who have heard, and going their way, are choked with the cares and riches and pleasures of this life, and yield no fruit. But that on the good ground are they who in a good and very good heart, hearing the word, keep it, and bring forth fruit in patience. CREDO.

OFFERTORY. *Ps 16: 5, 6-7*

Identical to 6th Sunday after Pentecost:

Pérfice gressus meos in sémitis tuis, ut non moveántur vestígia mea: inclína aurem tuam, et exáudi verba mea: mirífica misericórdias tuas, qui salvos facis sperántes in te, Dómine. ℣. *Exáudi, Dómine, justítiam meam, inténde deprecatiónem meam: áuribus pércipe oratiónem meam.* ℣. *Custódi me Dómine ut pupíllam óculi, sub umbra alárum tuárum prótege me: éripe me Dómine ab ímpio.* ℣. *Ego autem cum justítia apparébo in conspéctu tuo: satiábor, dum manifestábitur glória tua.*

MAKE MY STEPS steadfast in Thy paths, that my feet may not falter: incline Thine ear, and hear my words: show forth Thy wonderful mercies, Thou Who savest them that trust in Thee, O Lord. ℣. *Hear, O Lord, my justice: attend to my supplication: give ear unto my prayer.* ℣. *Protect me as Thou wouldst the apple of Thine own eye; hide me under the shelter of Thy wings, save me from the evil-doer.* ℣. *But as for me, I will appear before Thy sight in justice: I shall be satisfied when Thy glory shall appear.*

SECRET.

Oblátum tibi, Dómine, sacrifícium, vivíficet nos semper et múniat. Per Dóminum.

May the sacrifice we offer Thee, O Lord, ever vivify and defend us. Through our Lord.

COMMUNION. *Ps 42: 4*

Introíbo ad altáre Dei, ad Deum, qui lætíficat juventútem meam. (Ps 42: 1) ℣. *Júdica me, Deus, et discérne causam meam de gente non sancta: ab hómine iníquo et dolóso érue me.*
—12050CORBIE|853 • Circa 853AD

I WILL GO in to the altar of God: to God Who giveth joy to my youth. ℣. *Judge me, O God, and distinguish my cause from the nation that is not holy: deliver me from the unjust and deceitful man.*

POSTCOMMUNION.

Súpplices te rogámus, omnípotens Deus: ut, quos tuis réficis sacraméntis, tibi étiam plácitis móribus dignánter deservíre concédas. Per Dóminum.

Grant, we humbly beseech Thee, almighty God, that those whom Thou refreshest with Thy sacraments may serve Thee worthily by a life well pleasing to Thee. Through our Lord.

— *Quinquagesima Sunday* — *II Classis.*

DOMINICA IN QUINQUAGESIMA *Station at Saint Peter*

INTROIT. *Ps 30: 3-4*

BE THOU unto me a God, a protector, and a place of refuge, to save me: for Thou art my strength, and my refuge; and for Thy name's sake Thou wilt be my leader and wilt nourish me. (Ps 30: 2) In Thee, O Lord, have I hoped, let me never be confounded: deliver me in Thy justice, and set me free. ℣. Glory.

Esto mihi in Deum protectórem, et in locum refúgii, ut salvum me fácias: quóniam firmaméntum meum et refúgium meum es tu: et propter nomen tuum dux mihi eris, et enútries me. ℣. In te, Dómine, sperávi, non confúndar in ætérnum: in justítia tua líbera me et éripe me. ℣. Glória Patri.

COLLECT.

Of Thy clemency harken unto our prayers, O Lord, loose us from the bonds of sin, and keep us from all adversity. Through our Lord.

Preces nostras, quǽsumus, Dómine, cleménter exáudi: atque, a peccatórum vínculis absolútos, ab omni nos adversitáte custódi. Per Dóminum.

EPISTLE. *I Cor 13: 1-13*

BRETHREN, if I speak with the tongues of men, and of angels, and have not charity, I am become as sounding brass or a tinkling cymbal. And if I should have prophecy, and know all mysteries, and all knowledge, and if I should have all faith, so that I could remove mountains, and have not charity; I am nothing. And if I should distribute all my goods to feed the poor, and if I should deliver my body to be burned, and have not charity, it profiteth me nothing. Charity is patient, is kind: charity envieth not; dealeth not perversely; is not puffed up; is not ambitious; seeketh not her own; is not provoked to anger; thinketh no evil; rejoiceth not in iniquity, but rejoiceth in the truth; beareth all things, believeth all things, hopeth all things, endureth all things. Charity never falleth away: whether prophecies shall be made void, or tongues shall cease or knowledge shall be destroyed. For we know in part, and we prophesy in part. But when that which is perfect is come, that which is in part shall be done away. When I was a child, I spoke as a child, I understood as a child, I thought as a child: but when I became a man, I put away the things of a child. We see now through a glass in a dark manner; but then face to face. Now

Fratres: Si linguis hóminum loquar et Angelórum, caritátẽ autẽ non hábeam, factus sum velut æs sonans aut cýmbalum tínniens. Et si habúero prophetíam, et nóverim mystéria ómnia et omnẽ sciéntiam: et si habúero omnem fidem, ita ut montes tránsferam, caritátem autem non habúero, nihil sum. Et si distribúero in cibos páuperum omnes facultátes meas, et si tradídero corpus meum, ita ut árdeam, caritátem autem non habúero, nihil mihi prodest. Cáritas patiens est, benígna est: cáritas non æmulátur, non agit pérperam, non inflátur, non est ambitiósa, non quærit quæ sua sunt, non irritátur, non cógitat malum, non gaudet super iniquitáte, congáudet autem veritáti: ómnia suffert, ómnia credit, ómnia sperat, ómnia sústinet. Cáritas numquã éxcidit: sive prophetíæ evacuabúntur, sive linguæ cessábunt, sive sciéntia destruétur. Ex parte enim cognóscimus, et ex parte prophetámus. Cum autem vénerit quod perféctum est, evacuábitur quod ex parte est. Cum essem párvulus, loquébar ut párvulus, sapiébam ut párvulus, cogitábam ut párvulus. Quando autem factus sum vir, evacuávi quæ erant párvuli. Vidémus nunc per spéculum in ænígmate: tunc autem fácie ad fáciem. Nunc cognósco ex parte: tunc autem cognóscam, sicut et cógnitus sum. Nunc autem manent fides, spes, cáritas, tria hæc: major autem horum est cáritas.

I know in part; but then I shall know even as I am known. And now there remain, faith, hope, charity, these three; but the greatest of these is charity.

GRADUAL. *Ps 76: 15, 16*

Tu es Deus qui facis mirabília solus: notam fecísti in géntibus virtútem tuam. ℣. Liberásti in brácchio tuo pópulum tuum, fílios Ísraël et Joseph.

THOU ART the God that alone dost wonders: Thou hast made Thy power known among the nations. ℣. With Thy arm Thou hast redeemed Thy people, the children of Israel and of Joseph.

TRACT. *Ps 99: 1-2*

Jubiláte Deo, omnis terra: servíte Dño in lætítia. ℣. Intráte in conspéctu ejus in exsultatióne: scitóte, quod Dñs ipse est Deus. ℣. Ipse fecit nos, et non ipsi nos: nos autem pópulus ejus, et oves páscuæ ejus.

SING JOYFULLY to God all the earth: serve ye the Lord with gladness. ℣. Come in before His presence with exceeding great joy: know ye that the Lord He is God. ℣. He made us, and not we ourselves: but we are His people, and the sheep of His pasture.

GOSPEL. *Luke 18: 31-43*

In illo témpore: Assúmpsit Jesus duódecim, et ait illis: Ecce, ascéndimus Jerosólymam, et consummabúntur ómnia, quæ scripta sunt per Prophétas de Fílio hominis. Tradétur enim Géntibus, et illudétur, et flagellábitur, et conspuétur: et postquam flagelláverint, occídent eum, et tértia die resúrget. Et ipsi nihil horum intellexérunt, et erat verbum istud abscónditum ab eis, et non intellegébant quæ dicebántur. Factum est autẽ, cum appropinquáret Jéricho, cæcus quidam sedébat secus viam, mendícans. Et cũ audíret turbam prætereúntem, interrogábat, quid hoc esset. Dixérunt autem ei, quod Jesus Nazarénus transíret. Et clamávit, dicens: Jesu, fili David, miserére mei. Et qui præíbant, increpábant eum, ut tacéret. Ipse vero multo magis clamábat: Fili David, miserére mei. Stans autẽ Jesus, jussit illũ addúci ad se. Et cum appropinquásset, interrogávit illum, dicens: Quid tibi vis fáciam? At ille dixit: Dñe, ut vídeam. Et Jesus dixit illi: Réspice, fides tua te salvum fecit. Et conféstim vidit, et sequebátur illũ, magníficans Deum. Et omnis plebs ut vidit, dedit laudem Deo.

TAKING THE TWELVE apostles aside, Jesus warned them: Now we are going up to Jerusalem, and all that has been written by the prophets about the Son of Man is to be accomplished. For He shall be delivered to the gentiles, and shall be mocked, and scourged, and spit upon; and after they have scourged Him, they will put Him to death; and the third day He shall rise again. And they understood none of these things, and this word was hid from them, and they understood not the things that were said. Now it came to pass, when He drew nigh to Jericho, that a certain blind man sat by the wayside, begging. And when he heard the multitude passing by, he asked what this meant. And they told him that Jesus of Nazareth was passing by. And he cried out, saying, Jesus, Son of David, have mercy on me. And they that went before, rebuked him, that he should hold his peace: but he cried out much more, Son of David, have mercy on me. And Jesus standing, commanded him to be brought unto Him: and when he was come near, He asked him, saying, What wilt thou that I do to thee? But he said, Lord, that I may see. And Jesus said to him, Receive thy sight: thy faith hath made thee whole. And immediately he saw, and followed Him, glorifying God: and all the people when they saw it, gave praise to God. CREDO.

OFFERTORY. *Ps 118: 12-13*

BLESSED art Thou, O Lord, teach me Thy will. Blessed art Thou, O Lord, teach me Thy will: with my lips I have pronounced all the judgments of Thy mouth. ℣. *Blessed are the undefiled in the way, who walk in the law of the Lord: blessed are they that search His testimonies, that seek Him with their whole heart. * Remove from Thy people reproach and contempt, for we have not forgotten Thy commandments, O Lord.* ℣. *I have been delighted in the way of Thy testimonies, as in all riches.* ℣. *Remove from me, O Lord, the way of iniquity: remove from me, O Lord, the way of iniquity, and out of Thy law have mercy on me: I have chosen the way of truth: Thy judgments, Thy judgments I have not forgotten. Do but open my heart wide, and easy lies the path Thou hast decreed.*

Benedíctus es, Dómine, doce me justificatiónes tuas. Benedíctus es, Dñe, doce me justificatiónes tuas: in lábiis meis pronuntiávi ómnia judícia oris tui. ℣. *Beáti immaculáti in via, qui ámbulant in lege Dómini: beáti, qui scrutántur testimónia ejus: in toto corde exquirunt eum. * Aufer a plebe tua oppróbrium et contémptum, quia mandáta tua non sumus óbliti, Dómine.* ℣. *In via testimoniórum tuórum delectátus sum sicut in ómnibus divítiis.* ℣. *Viam iniquitátis, Dñe, ámove a me: viam iniquitátis, Dómine, ámove a me et de lege tua miserére mei: viam veritátis elégi: judícia tua, judícia tua non sum oblítus: viam mandatórum tuórum cucúrri, cum dilatáres cor meum.*

Sometimes when the Offertory repeats a section—not following the method of the Introit but more like a Responsory—the musical notes are different for the same words; at other times, the musical notes are identical. This particular Offertory demonstrates both. Because the ancient Offertory chants frequently repeat sections, modify the words of Sacred Scripture, or mix different verses together, some believe it is erroneous to label the Offertory an "antiphon." However, the Missale Romanum (1962), *the* Ordo Cantus Missae (1970), *and the* Graduale Simplex (1967) *explicitly call it "Antiphona ad Offertorium."*

SECRET.

May this offering, we beseech Thee, O Lord, cleanse away our sins, sanctify us in soul and body, and fit us, Thy servants, for the celebration of the sacrifice. Through our Lord.

Hæc hóstia, Dñe, quǽsumus, emúndet nostra delícta: et, ad sacrifícium celebrándũ, subditórum tibi córpora mentésque sanctíficet. Per Dóminum.

COMMUNION. *Ps 77: 29-30*

THEY did eat, and were filled exceedingly, and the Lord gave them their desire: they were not defrauded of that which they craved. ℣. *Attend, O My people, to My law: incline your ears to the words of My mouth.*

Manducavérunt, et saturári sunt nimis, et desidérium eórum áttulit eis Dóminus: non sunt fraudáti a desidério suo. (Ps 77: 1) ℣. *Atténdite, pópule meus, legem meam: inclináte aurem vestram in verba oris mei.*

—Compiegne|862 • Circa 862AD

POSTCOMMUNION.

We beseech Thee, O almighty God, that we, who have partaken of heavenly nourishment, may be fortified by it against all adversities. Through our Lord.

Quǽsumus, omnípotens Deus: ut, qui cæléstia aliménta percépimus, per hæc contra ómnia advérsa muniámur. Per Dóminum.

Ash Wednesday • Blessing of Ashes

The Blessing of Ashes • *De Benedictione Cinerum*

1962 • Before Mass, ashes from olive branches or of the branches of other trees, which were blessed in the preceding year, are blessed in this way: The priest vests in a violet cope—or is vested without the chasuble —and goes together with the ministers (similarly vested) to bless the ashes, which are placed in a vessel upon the Epistle corner of the Altar. First, the choir chants the antiphon "Exaudi nos."

Ante Missam benedicuntur cineres facti de ramis olivarum, sive aliarum arborum, praecedenti anno benedictis, hoc modo: Sacerdos indutus pluviali violaceo vel sine casula, cum ministris similiter indutis, procedit ad benedicendum cineres in vase aliquo super altari positos. Et primo cantatur a choro sequens antiphona:

ANTIPHON. *Ps 68: 17*

Exáudi nos, Dómine, quóniam benígna est misericórdia tua: secúndum multitúdinem miseratiónum tuárũ réspice nos, Dñe. ℣. Salvum me fac, Deus: quóniam intravérunt aquæ usque ad ánimam meam. ℣. Glória Patri. ℟. *Exáudi nos…*

HEAR US, O LORD, for Thy mercy is kind: according to the multitude of Thy mercies have regard to us, O Lord. (Ps 68: 2) Save me, O God, for the waters have reached my soul. ℣. Glory. ℟. Hear us…

1962 • After the antiphon, the Celebrant stands at the Epistle side with his hands joined (he keeps his hands joined during the prayers of all blessings). Without turning to the people, he says the following.

Deinde sacerdos ad latus epistolae, non vertens se ad populum, manibus junctis (quod servatur etiam in orationibus omnium benedictionum quoad manus junctas) dicit:

℣. Dóminus vobíscum.
℟. Et cum spíritu tuo.

℣. The Lord be with you.
℟. And with thy spirit.

[Editor's Note: On 26 September 1964, permission was given to use only one of the following four prayers during the blessing (cf. *Inter Oecumenici* §76), and the same for 2 February (Candlemas) vis-à-vis blessing the candles. On 9 February 1951 (*Dominicae Resurrectionis Vigiliam*), two of the three prayers for "blessing the new fire" on Easter Eve had been eliminated.]

FIRST PRAYER.

Orémus.

Omnípotens sempitérne Deus, parce pæniténtibus, propitiáre supplicántibus: et míttere dignéris sanctum Ángelum tuum de cælis, qui bene ✠ dícat et sancti ✠ ficet hos cíneres, ut sint remédium salúbre ómnibus nomen sanctum tuum humilíter implorántibus, ac semetípsos pro consciéntia delictórum suórum accusántibus, ante conspéctum divínæ cleméntiæ tuæ facínora sua deplorántibus, vel sereníssimam pietátem tuam supplíciter obnixéque flagitántibus: et præsta per invocatiónem sanctíssimi nóminis tui; ut, quicúmque per eos aspérsi fúerint, pro redemptióne peccatórum suórum, córporis sanitátem et ánimæ tutélam percípiant. Per Christum, Dóminum nostrum. ℟. Amen.

Let us pray.

ALMIGHTY, eternal God, spare them that are penitent, be merciful to Thy suppliants, and vouchsafe to send Thy holy angel from heaven to bless ✠ and sanctify ✠ these ashes, that they may be a wholesome remedy to all who humbly call upon Thy holy name, and who, accusing themselves of their sins as their consciences accuse them, deplore their crimes before the face of Thy divine clemency or, eagerly and humbly entreat Thy excellence and goodness; and grant, by the invocation of Thy most holy name, that all who shall be sprinkled with these ashes, for the remission of their sins, may receive health of body and salvation of soul. Through Christ our Lord. ℟. Amen.

SECOND PRAYER.

Let us pray.

O GOD, Who desirest not the death of sinners, but their repentance, most graciously regard the frailty of human nature; and, of Thy loving-kindness, deign to bless ✠ these ashes, which we intend to put upon our heads to express our lowliness and win Thy pardon, that we, who know that we are but ashes and for the guilt of our fall shall return to dust, may be worthy to obtain, through Thy mercy, the forgiveness of all our sins and the rewards promised to the penitent. Through Christ our Lord. ℟. Amen.

Orémus.

Deus, qui non mortem, sed pæniténtiam desíderas peccatórum: fragilitátem condiciónis humánæ benigníssime réspice; et hos cíneres, quos, causa proferéndæ humilitátis atque proferéndæ véniæ, capítibus nostris impóni decérnimus, bene✠dícere pro tua pietáte dignáre: ut, qui nos cínerem esse, et ob pravitátis nostræ demériitum in púlverem reversúros cognóscimus; peccatórum ómnium véniam, et prǽmia pæniténtibus repromíssa, misericórditer cónsequi mereámur. Per Christum, Dñm nostrum. ℟. Amen.

THIRD PRAYER.

Let us pray.

O GOD, Who art moved by humiliation and appeased by penance, incline the ear of Thy goodness to our prayers, and when the heads of Thy servants are touched with these ashes, graciously pour forth the grace of Thy blessing, that Thou mayest fill them with the spirit of compunction and mayest effectually grant what they righteously ask, and ordain that what Thou grantest may remain forever established and unmoved. Through Christ our Lord. ℟. Amen.

Orémus.

Deus, qui humiliatióne flécteris, et satisfactióne placáris: aurem tuæ pietátis inclína précibus nostris; et capítibus servórum tuórum, horum cínerum aspersióne contáctis, effúnde propítius grátiam tuæ benedictiónis: ut eos et spíritu compunctiónis répleas et, quæ juste postuláverint, efficáciter tríbuas; et concéssa perpétuo stabilíta et intácta manére decérnas. Per Christum, Dóminum nostrum. ℟. Amen.

FOURTH PRAYER.

Let us pray.

ALMIGHTY, eternal God, Who didst bestow the healing of Thy pardon upon the Ninivites when they repented in ashes and sackcloth, mercifully grant that we may so imitate them in behavior as to be like them in obtaining pardon. Through our Lord. ℟. Amen.

Orémus.

Omnípotens sempitérne Deus, qui Ninivítis, in cínere et cilício pæniténtibus, indulgéntiæ tuæ remédia præstitísti: concéde propítius; ut sic eos imitémur hábitu, quaténus véniæ prosequámur obténtu. Per Dñm. ℟. Amen.

1962 • Afterwards the Celebrant places incense in the thurible. He then sprinkles the ashes three times with holy water, saying the antiphon "Aspérges Me" without chant and without the psalm. Then he incenses the ashes three times. | *Postea celebrans, imposito incenso in thuribulo, ter aspergit cineres aqua benedicta, dicendo antiphonam "Aspérges Me" sine cantu et sine psalmo, et ter adolet incenso.*

ASH WEDNESDAY • DISTRIBUTION OF ASHES

The Distribution of Ashes • *De Impositione Cinerum*

1962 • The senior priest goes to the Altar and imposes ashes on the Celebrant, who does not kneel. If no other priest is present, the Celebrant himself turns to the Altar and imposes ashes on his own head, saying nothing. The following antiphon is immediately chanted by the choir.

Deinde dignior sacerdos ex clero accedens ad altare, imponit cineres celebranti non genuflexo. Si vera non adsit alius sacerdos, ipsemet celebrans, ad altare conversus, sibi ipsi cineres imponit in capite, nihil dicens, et antiphona cantatur statim a choro.

FIRST ANTIPHON. *Joel 2: 13*

Immutémur hábitu, in cínere et cilício: jejunémus, et plorémus ante Dóminũ: quia multum miséricors est dimíttere peccáta nostra Deus noster.

LET US CHANGE our garments for ashes and sackcloth: let us fast and lament before our Lord: for our God is plenteous in mercy to forgive our sins.

SECOND ANTIPHON. *Joel 2: 17*

Inter vestíbulum et altáre plorábunt sacerdótes minístri Dómini, et dicent: Parce, Dómine, parce pópulo tuo: et ne claudas ora canéntium te, Dñe.

BETWEEN the porch and the altar, the priests, the Lord's ministers, shall weep, and shall say: Spare, O Lord, spare Thy people, and shut not the mouths of them that sing to Thee, O Lord.

1962 • The following Responsory is then sung. | *Sequitur responsorium.*

RESPONSORY. *Esth 13 & Joel 2*

Emendémus in mélius, quæ ignoránter peccávimus: ne, súbito præoccupáti die mortis, quærámus spátium pæniténtiæ, et inveníre non póssimus. * *Atténde, Dómine, et miserére: quia peccávimus tibi.* ℣. Ádjuva nos, Deus, salutáris noster: et propter honórem nóminis tui, Dómine, líbera nos.* *Atténde, Dómine, et miserére: quia peccávimus tibi.* ℣. Glória Patri, et Fílio, et Spirítui Sancto. * *Atténde, Dómine, et miserére: quia peccávimus tibi.*

LET US AMEND AND DO BETTER for those things in which we have sinned through ignorance lest, suddenly prevented by the day of death, we seek time for penance, and be not able to find it.

* Attend, O Lord, and have mercy:
for we have sinned against Thee.

℣. (Ps 78: 9) Help us, O God, our Savior:
and for the honor of Thy name, O Lord, deliver us.

* Attend, O Lord, and have mercy:
for we have sinned against Thee.

℣. Glory be to the Father, and to the Son,
and to the Holy Ghost.

* Attend, O Lord, and have mercy:
for we have sinned against Thee.

1962 • While the antiphons and responsory are sung, the Celebrant, with his head uncovered, first imposes ashes upon the senior priest from whom he has received the ashes, then upon the ministers in vestments, who kneel before the Altar. The Celebrant says the following prayer each time.

Sacerdos vero, dum cantantur antiphonae et responsorium, detecto capite, prima imponit cineres digniori sacerdoti, a quo ipse accepit, deinde ministris paratis, genibus flexis coram altari, dicens:

Genesis 3: 19

REMEMBER, man, that thou are dust, and to dust thou shalt return.

Meménto, homo, quia pulvis es, et in púlverem revertéris.

1962 • Afterwards the others come to the Altar, first the clergy in order, then the people. Kneeling before the Altar, they receive the ashes from the Celebrant one by one—as described above for the ministers—the ashes being imposed in the shape of a cross on each head or forehead. When the distribution of ashes has been completed, the Celebrant returns to the Epistle corner of the Altar and—having washed his hands—prays as follows.

Postea veniunt alii, primo clerus per ordinem, deinde populus: et genibus flexis ante altare, singulatim recipiunt cineres a sacerdote, ut dictum est de ministris. Completa cinerum impositione, sacerdos dicit:

℣. The Lord be with you.
℟. And with thy spirit.

℣. Dóminus vobíscum.
℟. Et cum spíritu tuo.

COLLECT.

Let us pray.

GRANT US, O Lord, to enter upon the duties of our Christian warfare with holy fasts, that, being about to fight against the spirits of wickedness, we may be fortified by the help of self-denial. Through Christ or Lord. ℟. Amen.

Orémus.

Concéde nobis, Dómine, præsídia milítiæ christiánæ sanctis inchoáre jejúniis: ut, contra spiritáles nequítias pugnatúri, continéntiæ muniámur auxíliis. Per Christum, Dóminum nostrum. ℟. Amen.

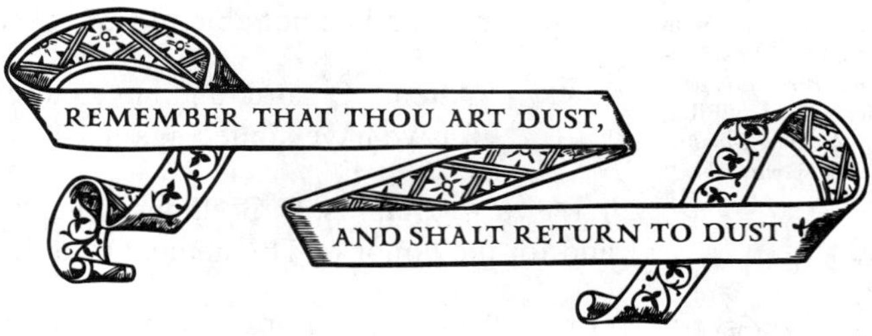

[Editor's Note: The rules regarding omission of the Prayers at the Foot of the Altar may be found in §424 of Rubricae Generales Missalis Romani, conveniently printed at the front of each 1962 Missal. The same document (§426) expands an indult enjoyed by certain countries prior to 1961: *Incensationes quae in Missa solemni fieri debent, fieri possunt etiam in omnibus Missis cantatis* ("The incensations which must be performed in a solemn Mass may be performed also in a Missa Cantata").]

1962 • In the Mass which follows the blessing of ashes, the prayers to be said at the foot of the Altar are omitted, as well as the prayers "Aufer a nobis" and "Orámus te, Dómine." Having taken off the cope and put on the chasuble, the Celebrant immediately goes up the steps and kisses the Altar in the center.

In Missa quae benedictionem cinerum sequitur, omittuntur psalmus "Júdica me, Deus" cum sua antiphona, necnon confessio cum absolutione, versis sequentibus atque orationibus "Aufer a nobis" et "Orámus te, Dómine." Sacerdos igitur cum ad altare accesserit, statim illud ascendit et osculatur in medio.

I Classis. — *Ash Wednesday* —

FERIA QUARTA CINERUM *Station at Saint Sabina*

INTROIT. *Wis 11: 24, 25, 27*

Miseréris ómnium, Dómine, et nihil odísti eórum quæ fecísti, dissímulans peccáta hóminum propter pæniténtiam et parcens illis: quia tu es Dñs, Deus noster. ℣. Miserére mei, Deus, miserére mei: quóniam in te confídit ánima mea. ℣. Glória Patri.

THOU HAST MERCY upon all, O Lord, and hatest none of the things which Thou hast made, winking at the sins of men for the sake of repentance, and sparing them: for Thou art the Lord our God. (Psalm 56: 2) Have mercy on me, O God, have mercy on me: for my soul trusteth in Thee. ℣. Glory.

COLLECT.

Præsta, Dómine, fidélibus tuis: ut jejuniórum veneránda solémnia, et cóngrua pietáte suscípiant, et secúra devotióne percúrrant. Per Dóminum.

Grant to Thy faithful, O Lord, that they may both undertake the venerable solemnities of fasting with piety and carry them through with unwavering devotion. Through our Lord.

EPISTLE. *Joel 2: 12-19*

Hæc dicit Dóminus: Convertímini ad me in toto corde vestro, in jejúnio, et in fletu, et in planctu. Et scíndite corda vestra, et non vestiménta vestra, et convertímini ad Dóminum, Deum vestrum: quia benígnus et misericors est, pátiens, et multæ misericórdiæ, et præstábilis super malítia. Quis scit, si convertátur, et ignóscat, et relínquat post se benedictiónem, sacrifícium et libámen Dómino, Deo vestro? Cánite tuba in Sion, sanctificáte jejúnium, vocáte cœtum, congregáte pópulum, sanctificáte ecclésiã, coadunáte senes, congregáte parvulos et sugéntes úbera: egrediátur sponsus de cubíli suo, et sponsa de thálamo suo. Inter vestíbulum et altáre plorábunt sacerdótes minístri Dñi, et dicent: Parce, Dómine, parce pópulo tuo: et ne des hereditátem tuam in oppróbrium, ut dominéntur eis natiónes. Quare dicunt in pópulis: Ubi est Deus eórum? Zelátus est Dóminus terram suam, et pepércit pópulo suo. Et respóndit Dñs, et dixit populo suo: Ecce, ego mittam

THUS saith the Lord: Be converted to Me with all your heart, in fasting, and in weeping, and in mourning. And rend your hearts and not your garments, and turn to the Lord your God; for He is gracious and merciful, patient and rich in mercy, and ready to repent of the evil. Who knoweth but He will return and forgive and leave a blessing behind Him, sacrifice and libation to the Lord your God? Blow the trumpet in Sion, sanctify a fast, call a solemn assembly, gather together the people, sanctify the Church, assemble the ancients, gather together the little ones and them that suck at the breasts: let the bridegroom go forth from his bed and the bride out of her bride chamber. Between the porch and the altar the priests, the Lord's ministers, shall weep and shall say: Spare, O Lord, spare Thy people; and give not Thine inheritance to reproach, that the heathen should rule over them. Why should they say among the nations:

Where is their God? The Lord hath been zealous for His land, and hath spared His people. And the Lord answered and said to His people: behold I will send you corn and wine and oil, and you shall be filled with them: and I will no more make you a reproach among the nations: saith the Lord almighty.

vobis fruméntum et vinum et óleum, et replebímini eis: et non dabo vos ultra oppróbrium in géntibus: dicit Dóminus omnípotens.

GRADUAL. *Ps 56: 2, 4*

HAVE MERCY on me, O Lord, have mercy on me: for my soul trusteth in Thee. ℣. He hath sent from heaven and delivered me: He hath made them a reproach that trod upon me.

Miserére mei, Deus, miserére mei: quóniam in te confídit ánima mea. ℣. Misit de cælo, et liberávit me, dedit in oppróbrium conculcántes me.

TRACT. *Ps 102: 10*

REPAY US NOT, O Lord, according to the sins we have committed, nor according to our iniquities. ℣. (Ps 78: 8-9) O Lord, remember not our former iniquities, let Thy mercies speedily prevent us: for we are become exceeding poor.

Dómine, non secúndũ peccáta nostra, quæ fécimus nos: neque secúndum iniquitátes nostras retríbuas nobis. ℣. Dómine, ne memíneris iniquitátum nostrárum antiquárum: cito antícipent nos misericórdiæ tuæ, quia páuperes facti sumus nimis.

Traditionally, all present genuflect here:

(*hic genuflectitur*)

℣. Help us, O God, our Savior: and for the glory of Thy Name, O Lord, deliver us: and forgive us our sins for Thy Name's sake.

℣. Ádjuva nos, Deus, salutáris noster: et propter glóriam nóminis tui, Dñe, libera nos: et propítius esto peccátis nostris, propter nomen tuum.

GOSPEL. *Matt 6: 16-21*

WHEN YOU FAST, Jesus said to His disciples, be not as the hypocrites are: sad. For they disfigure their face, that they may appear unto men to fast. Amen I say to you, they have received their reward. But thou, when thou fastest, anoint thy head and wash thy face, that thou appear not to men to fast, but to thy Father who is in secret: and thy Father who seeth in secret will repay Thee. Lay not up to yourselves treasures on earth: where the rust and moth consume, and where thieves break through and steal. But lay up to yourselves treasures in heaven: where neither the rust nor moth doth consume, and where thieves do not break through nor steal. For where thy treasure is, there is thy heart also. CREDO.

In illo témpore: Dixit Jesus discípulis suis: Cum jejunátis, nolíte fíeri, sicut hypócritæ, tristes. Extérminant enim fácies suas, ut appáreant homínibus jejunántes. Amen, dico vobis, quia recepérunt mercédem suam. Tu autem, cum jejúnas, unge caput tuum, et fáciem tuam lava, ne videáris homínibus jejúnans, sed Patri tuo, qui est in abscóndito: et Pater tuus, qui videt in abscóndito, reddet tibi. Nolíte thesaurizáre vobis thesáuros in terra: ubi ærúgo et tínea demolítur: et ubi fures effódiunt et furántur. Thesaurizáte autem vobis thesáuros in cælo: ubi neque ærúgo neque tínea demolítur; et ubi fures non effódiunt nec furántur. Ubi enim est thesáurus tuus, ibi est et cor tuum.

Identical to 11th Sunday after Pentecost:

Exaltábo te, Dómine, quóniam suscepísti me, nec delectásti inimícos meos super me: Dómine, clamávi ad te, et sanásti me. ℣. *Dómine, abstraxísti ab ínferis ánimam meam: salvásti me a descendéntibus in lacum.* ℣. *Ego autem dixi in mea abundántia: Non movébor in ætérnum: Dómine, in voluntáte tua præstitísti decóri meo virtútem.*

OFFERTORY. *Ps 29: 2-3*

I WILL extol Thee, O Lord, for Thou hast upheld me, and hast not made my enemies to rejoice over me: O Lord, I have cried to Thee, and Thou hast healed me. ℣. *O Lord, Thou hast brought forth my soul from hell: Thou hast saved me from them that go down into the pit.* ℣. *And in my abundance I said: I shall never be moved. O Lord, in Thy favor, Thou gavest strength to my beauty.*

SECRET.

Fac nos, quǽsumus, Dómine, his munéribus offeréndis convenienter aptári: quibus ipsíus venerábilis sacraménti celebrámus exórdium. Per Dóminum.

Make us duly fit, we beseech Thee, O Lord, for the offering of these gifts, with which we celebrate the beginning of the august sacrament itself. Through our Lord.

The Preface of Lent (page 189) follows the Secret.

COMMUNION. *Ps 1: 2, 3*

Qui meditábitur in lege Dómini die ac nocte, dabit fructum suum in témpore suo. (Ps 1: 1) ℣. *Beátus vir qui non ábiit in consílio impiórum, et in via peccatórum non stetit, et in cáthedra pestiléntiæ non sedit.*

—4951STEVEN|1128 • Circa 1128AD

HE WHO SHALL meditate upon the law of the Lord, day and night, shall bring forth his fruit in due season. ℣. *Blessed is the man who does not guide his steps by ill counsel, or turn aside where sinners walk, or, where scornful souls gather, sit down to rest.*

POSTCOMMUNION.

Percépta nobis, Dómine, prǽbeant sacraménta subsídium: ut tibi grata sint nostra jejúnia, et nobis profíciant ad medélam. Per Dóminum.

May the sacraments we have received, O Lord, give us help, that our fasts may be pleasing to Thee and profitable to us as a healing remedy. Through our Lord.

PRAYER OVER THE PEOPLE.

Orémus.

Humiliáte cápita vestra Deo.

Inclinántes se, Dñe, majestáti tuæ, propitiátus inténde: ut, qui divíno múnere sunt refécti, cæléstibus semper nutriántur auxíliis. Per Dóminum.

Let us pray.

Bow down your heads before God.

LOOK WITH FAVOR, O Lord, on those who bow before Thy majesty, that they who have been refreshed with the divine gift may ever be strengthened with heavenly aids. Through our Lord.

— *First Sunday of Lent* — *I Classis.*

DOMINICA PRIMA IN QUADRAGESIMA *Station at Saint John Lateran*

INTROIT. *Ps 90: 15, 16*

HE SHALL CALL upon Me, and I will hear him; I will deliver him, and glorify him; I will fill him with length of days. (Ps 90: 1) He that dwelleth in the aid of the Most High, shall abide under the protection of the God of heaven. ℣. Glory.

Invocábit me, et ego exáudiam eum: erípiam eum, et glorificábo eum: longitúdine diérum adimplébo eũ. ℣. Qui hábitat in adjutório Altíssimi, in protectióne Dei cæli commorábitur. ℣. Glória Patri.

COLLECT.

O God, Who dost purify Thy Church with the annual observance of Lent, grant to Thy household that what it strives to obtain from Thee by abstinence it may secure with good works. Through our Lord.

Deus, qui Ecclésiã tuã ánnua quadragesimáli observatióne puríficas: præsta famíliæ tuæ; ut, quod a te obtinére abstinéndo nítitur, hoc bonis opéribus exsequátur. Per Dóminum.

EPISTLE. *II Cor 6: 1-10*

BRETHREN, we exhort you that you receive not the grace of God in vain. For He saith, In an accepted time have I heard thee, and in the day of salvation have I helped thee. Behold now is the acceptable time, behold now is the day of salvation. Giving no offense to any man, that our ministry be not blamed: but in all things let us exhibit ourselves as the ministers of God; in much patience, in tribulations, in necessities, in distresses, in stripes, in prisons, in seditions, in labors, in watchings, in fastings, in chastity, in knowledge, in long-suffering, in sweetness, in the Holy Ghost, in charity unfeigned, in the word of truth, in the power of God; by the armor of justice on the right hand and on the left, by honor and dishonor, by evil report and good report; as deceivers, and yet true; as unknown, and yet known; as dying, and behold we live; as chastised, and not killed; as sorrowful, yet always rejoicing; as needy, yet enriching many; as having nothing, and possessing all things.

Fratres: Exhortámur vos, ne in vácuum grátiam Dei recipiátis. Ait enim: Témpore accépto exaudívi te, et in die salútis adjúvi te. Ecce, nunc tempus acceptábile, ecce, nunc dies salútis. Némini dantes ullam offensiónem, ut non vituperétur ministérium nostrum: sed in ómnibus exhibeámus nosmetípsos sicut Dei minístros, in multa patiéntia, in tribulatiónibus, in necessitátibus, in angústiis, in plagis, in carcéribus, in seditiónibus, in labóribus, in vigíliis, in jejúniis, in castitáte, in sciéntia, in longanimitáte, in suavitáte, in Spíritu Sancto, in caritáte non ficta, in verbo veritátis, in virtúte Dei, per arma justítiæ a dextris et a sinístris: per glóriam et ignobilitátem: per infámiam et bonam famam: ut seductóres et veráces: sicut qui ignóti et cógniti: quasi moriéntes et ecce, vívimus: ut castigáti et non mortificáti: quasi tristes, semper autẽ gaudéntes: sicut egéntes, multos autẽ locupletántes: tamquam nihil habéntes et ómnia possidéntes.

GRADUAL. *Ps 90: 11-12*

GOD hath given His angels charge over thee, to keep thee in all thy ways. ℣. In their hands they shall bear thee up, lest thou dash thy foot against a stone.

Ángelis suis Deus mandávit de te, ut custódiant te in ómnibus viis tuis. ℣. In mánibus portábunt te, ne umquam offéndas ad lápidem pedem tuum.

SCRIPTUM EST, NON IN SOLO PANE VIVIT HOMO. (Mt 4)

AIT JACOB: JURA MIHI. JURAVIT EI ESAU ET VENDIDIT...Gen 25:33

ELEAZARUS COMPELLABATUR CARNEM PORCINAM ... II Machabees 6:18

✠ IT IS WRITTEN, NOT BY BREAD ALONE DOTH MAN LIVE. ✠

JACOB SAID: SWEAR THEREFORE TO ME. ESAU SWORE TO HIM, AND SOLD HIS FIRST BIRTHRIGHT... Gen 25:33

ELEAZAR, ONE OF THE CHIEF SCRIBES, WAS PRESSED TO OPEN HIS MOUTH TO EAT SWINE'S FLESH... II Machabees 6:18

TRACT. *Ps 90: 1-7, 11-16*

HE THAT DWELLETH in the aid of the Most High, shall abide under the protection of the God of heaven. 2. He shall say to the Lord, Thou art my protector and my refuge: my God, in Him will I trust. 3. For He hath delivered me from the snare of the hunters, and from the sharp word. 4. He will overshadow thee with His shoulders, and under His wings thou shalt trust. 5. His truth shall compass thee with a shield: thou shalt not be afraid of the terror of the night. 6. Of the arrow that flieth in the day; of the business that walketh about in the dark: of ruin and the noonday devil. 7. A thousand shall fall at thy side, and ten thousand at thy right hand: but it shall not come nigh to thee. 8. For He hath given His angels charge over thee, to keep thee in all thy ways. 9. In their hands they shall bear thee up, lest thou dash thy foot against a stone. 10. Thou shalt walk upon the asp and the basilisk, and thou shalt trample under foot the lion and the dragon. 11. Because he hath hoped in Me, I will deliver him; I will protect him, because he hath known My name. 12. He shall call upon Me, and I will hear him: I am with him in tribulation. 13. I will deliver him, and I will glorify him; I will fill him with length of days, and I will show him My salvation.

Qui hábitat in adjutório Altíssimi, in protectióne Dei cæli commorábitur. 2. Dicet Dño: Suscéptor meus es tu, et refúgium meum: Deus meus, sperábo in eum. 3. Quóniam ipse liberávit me de láqueo venántium et a verbo áspero. 4. Scápulis suis obumbrábit tibi, et sub pennis ejus sperábis. 5. Scuto circúmdabit te véritas ejus: non timébis a timóre noctúrno. 6. A sagítta volánte per diem, a negótio perambulánte in ténebris, a ruína et dæmónio meridiáno. 7. Cadent a látere tuo mille, et decem míllia a dextris tuis: tibi autem non appropinquábit. 8. Quóniam Ángelis suis mandávit de te, ut custódiant te in ómnibus viis tuis. 9. In mánibus portábunt te, ne umquam offéndas ad lápidẽ pedẽ tuum. 10. Super áspidem et basilíscum ambulábis, et conculcábis leónem et dracónem. 11. Quóniam in me sperávit, liberábo eum: prótegam eum, quóniam cognóvit nomen meum. 12. Invocábit me, et ego exáudiam eum: cum ipso sum in tribulatióne. 13. Erípiam eum et glorificábo eum: longitúdine diérum adimplébo eum, et osténdam illi salutáre meum.

GOSPEL. *Matt 4: 1-11*

JESUS WAS LED by the Spirit into the desert, to be tempted by the devil. And when He had fasted forty days and forty nights, afterwards He was hungry. And the tempter coming said to Him, If Thou be the Son of God, command that these stones be made bread. Who answered and said: It is written, Not in bread alone doth man live, but in every word that proceedeth from the mouth of God. Then the devil took Him up into the holy city, and set Him upon the pinnacle of the temple, and said to Him, If Thou be the Son of God, cast Thyself down: for it is written, That He hath given His angels charge over Thee, and in their hands shall they bear Thee up, lest perhaps Thou dash Thy foot against a stone. Jesus said to Him, It is written again, Thou shalt not tempt the Lord thy God. Again the devil took Him up into a very high mountain: and showed Him all the kingdoms of

In illo témpore: Ductus est Jesus in desértum a Spíritu, ut tentarétur a diábolo. Et cum jejunásset quadragínta diébus et quadragínta nóctibus, póstea esúriit. Et accédens tentátor, dixit ei: Si Fílius Dei es, dic, ut lápides isti panes fiant. Qui respóndens, dixit: Scriptum est: Non in solo pane vivit homo, sed in omni verbo, quod procédit de ore Dei. Tunc assúmpsit eum diábolus in sanctam civitátem, et státuit eum super pinnáculum templi, et dixit ei: Si Fílius Dei es, mitte te deórsum. Scriptum est enim: Quia Ángelis suis mandávit de te, et in mánibus tollent te, ne forte offéndas ad lápidem pedem tuum. Ait illi Jesus: Rursum scriptum est: Non tentábis Dñm, Deum tuum. Íterum assúmpsit eum diábolus in montem excélsum valde: et osténdit ei ómnia regna mundi et glóriam eórum, et dixit ei: Hæc ómnia tibi dabo, si cadens adoráveris me. Tunc dicit ei Jesus: Vade, Sátana; scriptum est enim: Dóminum, Deum tuum, adorábis, et illi soli sérvies. Tunc relíquit eum diábolus: et ecce, Ángeli accessérunt et ministrábant ei.

the world, and the glory of them; and said to Him, All these will I give Thee, if falling down Thou wilt adore me. Then Jesus said to him, Begone, Satan, for it is written, The Lord thy God shalt thou adore, and Him only shalt thou serve. Then the devil left Him; and behold angels came, and ministered to Him. CREDO.

OFFERTORY. *Ps 90: 4-5*

Scápulis suis obumbrábit tibi Dñs, et sub pennis ejus sperábis: scuto circúmdabit te véritas ejus. ℣. *Dicet Dño: Suscéptor meus es, non timébis a timóre noctúrno a sagítta volánte per diem.* ℣. *Quóniam Ángelis suis mandávit de te, ut custódiant te, ne unquam offéndas ad lápidẽ pedẽ tuum.* ℣. *Super áspidem et basilíscum ambulábis: et conculcábis leónẽ et dracónem: quóniam in me sperávit, liberábo eum.*

THE LORD WILL overshadow thee with His shoulders, and under His wings thou shalt trust: His truth shall compass thee with a shield. ℣. *He shall say to the Lord: Thou art my protector; nor shalt thou be afraid of the terror of the night, nor the arrow that flieth in the day.* ℣. *For He hath given His Angels charge over thee, to protect thee, lest thou dash thy foot against a stone.* ℣. *Thou shalt walk upon the asp and the basilisk: and thou shalt trample under-foot the lion and the dragon: because he hath hoped in Me, I will deliver him.*

SECRET.

Sacrifíciũ quadragesimális inítii sollémniter immolámus, te, Dñe, deprecántes: ut, cum epulárum restrictióne carnálium, a noxiis quoque voluptátibus temperémus. Per Dóminum.

We solemnly offer the sacrifice at the beginning of Lent, beseeching Thee, O Lord, that, while we restrict ourselves in the use of bodily food, we may also refrain from indulgence in harmful pleasures. Through our Lord.

The Preface of Lent (page 189) follows the Secret.

COMMUNION. *Ps 90: 4-5*

Scápulis suis obumbrábit tibi, et sub pennis ejus sperábis: scuto circúmdabit te véritas ejus. (Ps 90: 1) ℣. *Qui hábitat in adjutório Altíssimi, in protectióne Dei cæli commorábitur.*

—STMAUR|1079 • Circa 1079AD

HE WILL overshadow thee with His shoulders, and under His wings thou shalt trust: His truth shall compass thee with a shield. ℣. *He that dwelleth in the aid of the most High, shall abide under the protection of the God of heaven.*

POSTCOMMUNION.

Tui nos, Dómine, sacraménti libátio sancta restáuret: et a vetustáte purgátos, in mystérii salutáris fáciat transíre consórtium. Per Dóminum.

May the holy partaking of Thy sacrament strengthen us, O Lord, and purify us from the old life, and make us sharers in the mystery of salvation. Through our Lord.

— *Second Sunday of Lent* — *I Classis.*

DOMINICA SECUNDA IN QUADRAGESIMA *Station at Saint Mary's in Domnica*

INTROIT. *Ps 24: 6, 3, 22*

REMEMBER, O LORD, Thy pity, Thy mercies of long ago, lest at any time our enemies rule over us: deliver us, O God of Israel, from all our tribulations. (Ps 24: 1-2) To Thee, O Lord, have I lifted up my soul: in Thee, O my God, I put my trust; let me not be ashamed. ℣. Glory.

Reminíscere miseratiónum tuárum, Dómine, et misericórdiæ tuæ, quæ a sǽculo sunt: ne umquam domméntur nobis inimíci nostri: líbera nos, Deus Ísraël, ex ómnibus angústiis nostris. ℣. Ad te, Dñe, levávi ánimã meã: Deus meus, in te confído, non erubéscam. ℣. Glória Patri.

COLLECT.

O God, Who seest how we are destitute of all strength, keep us inwardly and outwardly, that in body we may be defended from all adversities, and in mind cleansed of evil thoughts. Through our Lord.

Deus, qui cónspicis omni nos virtúte destítui: intérius exteriúsque custódi; ut ab ómnibus adversitátibus muniámur in córpore, et a pravis cogitatiónibus mundémur in mente. Per Dñm.

EPISTLE. *I Thess 4: 1-7*

BRETHREN, we pray and beseech you in the Lord Jesus, that as you have received of us, how you ought to walk, and to please God, so also you would walk, that you may abound the more. For you know what precepts I have given to you by the Lord Jesus. For this is the will of God, your sanctification; that you should abstain from fornication, that every one of you should know how to possess his vessel in sanctification and honor; not in the passion of lust, like the gentiles that know not God: and that no man overreach, nor deceive his brother in business; because the Lord is the avenger of all these things, as we have told you before, and have testified. For God hath not called us unto uncleanness, but unto sanctification; in Christ Jesus our Lord.

Fratres: Rogámus vos et obsecrámus in Dño Jesu: ut, quemádmodũ accepístis a nobis, quómodo opórteat vos ambuláre et placére Deo, sic et ambulétis, ut abundétis magis. Scitis enim, quæ præcépta déderim vobis per Dñm Jesũ. Hæc est enim volúntas Dei, sanctificátio vestra: ut abstineátis vos a fornicatióne, ut sciat unusquísque vestrũ vas suum possidére in sanctificatióne et honóre; non in passióne desidérii, sicut et gentes, quæ ignórant Deum: et ne quis supergrediátur neque circumvéniat in negótio fratrem suum: quóniam vindex est Dñs de his ómnibus, sicut prædíximus vobis et testificáti sumus. Non enim vocávit nos Deus in immundítiã, sed in sanctificatiónem: in Christo Jesu, Dómino nostro.

GRADUAL. *Ps 24: 17-18*

THE TROUBLES of my heart are multiplied; deliver me from my necessities, O Lord. ℣. See my abjection and my labor, and forgive all my sins.

Tribulatiónes cordis mei dilatátæ sunt: de necessitátibus meis éripe me, Dñe. ℣. Vide humilitátem meam et labórem meum: et dimítte ómnia peccáta mea.

TRACT. *Ps 105: 1-4*

GIVE GLORY to the Lord, for He is good: for His mercy endureth forever. ℣. Who shall declare

Confitémini Dño, quóniam bonus: quóniam in sǽculum misericórdia ejus. ℣. Quis loquétur poténtias Dñi: audítas fáciet omnes laudes ejus? ℣. Beáti, qui custódiunt judícium et fáciunt justítiã in omni témpore. ℣. Meménto nostri, Dñe, in beneplácito pópuli tui: vísita nos in salutári tuo.

the powers of the Lord? Who shall set forth all His praises? ℣. Blessed are they that keep judgment, and do justice at all times. ℣. Remember us, O Lord, in the favor of Thy people: visit us with Thy salvation.

GOSPEL. *Matt 17: 1-9*

In illo témpore: Assúmpsit Jesus Petrũ, et Jacóbum, et Joánnem fratrem ejus, et duxit illos in montem excélsum seórsũ: et transfigurátus est ante eos. Et resplénduit fácies ejus sicut sol: vestiménta autem ejus facta sunt alba sicut nix. Et ecce, apparuérunt illis Móyses et Elías cum eo loquéntes. Respóndens autẽ Petrus, dixit ad Jesum: Dñe, bonum est nos hic esse: si vis, faciámus hic tria tabernácula, tibi unũ, Móysi unum et Elíæ unũ. Adhuc eo loquénte, ecce, nubes lúcida obumbrávit eos. Et ecce vox de nube, dicens: Hic est Fílius meus diléctus, in quo mihi bene complácui: ipsum audíte. Et audiéntes discípuli, cecidérunt in fáciem suam, et timuérunt valde. Et accéssit Jesus, et tétigit eos, dixítque eis: Súrgite, et nolíte timére. Levántes autẽ óculos suos, néminem vidérunt nisi solum Jesum. Et descendéntibus illis de monte, præcépit eis Jesus, dicens: Némini dixéritis visiónem, donec Fílius hóminis a mórtuis resúrgat.

JESUS TOOK PETER and James, and John his brother, and bringeth them up into a high mountain apart: and He was transfigured before them. And His face did shine as the sun, and His garments became white as snow. And behold there appeared to them Moses and Elias talking with Him. And Peter answering, said to Jesus, Lord, it is good for us to be here: if Thou wilt, let us make here three tabernacles, one for Thee, and one for Moses, and one for Elias. And as he was yet speaking, behold a bright cloud overshadowed them; and lo, a voice out of the cloud, saying, This is My beloved Son, in Whom I am well pleased; hear ye Him. And the disciples hearing, fell upon their face and were very much afraid. And Jesus came and touched them, and said to them, Arise and fear not. And they lifting up their eyes saw no one, but only Jesus. And as they came down from the mountain, Jesus charged them, saying, Tell the vision to no man, till the Son of man be risen from the dead. CREDO.

OFFERTORY. *Ps 118: 47, 48*

Meditábor in mandátis tuis, quæ diléxi valde: et levábo manus meas ad mandáta tua, quæ diléxi. ℣. *Pars mea Dñe, dixi custodíre legem tuam: precátus sum vultum tuum in toto corde meo.* ℣. *Miserére mei secúndum elóquium tuum, quia cogitávi vias tuas et convérti pedes meos in testimónia tua.*

I WILL MEDITATE on Thy commandments, which I have loved exceedingly: and I will lift up my hands to Thy commandments, which I have loved. ℣. *O Lord, my portion, I have said, I would keep Thy law: I entreated Thy face with all my heart.* ℣. *Have mercy on me according to Thy word, for I have thought on my ways and turned my feet unto Thy testimonies.*

SECRET.

Sacrifíciis præséntibus, Dñe, quǽsumus, inténde placátus: ut et devotióni nostræ profíciant et salúti. Per Dñm.

Look graciously, we beg, O Lord, upon the sacrifices here before Thee, that they may profit both our devotion and our salvation. Through our Lord.

The Preface of Lent (page 189) follows the Secret.

COMMUNION. *Ps 5: 2-4*

UNDERSTAND my cry: harken to the voice of my prayer, O my King and my God: for to Thee will I pray, O Lord. ℣. *Early in the morning I lay my petition before Thee and await Thy pleasure; no evil thing claims Thy divine assent.*

Intéllige clamórem meum: inténde voci oratiónis meæ, Rex meus et Deus meus: quóniam ad te orábo, Dómine. (Ps 5: 5) ℣. *Mane astábo tibi et vidébo: quóniam non Deus volens iniquitátem tu es.* —RENAUD|965 • Circa 965AD

POSTCOMMUNION.

Grant, we beseech Thee, O almighty God, that we, whom Thou refreshest with Thy sacraments, may also serve Thee worthily with conduct to Thy liking. Through our Lord.

Súpplices te rogámus, omnípotens Deus: ut quos tuis réficis sacraméntis, tibi etiam plácitis móribus dignánter deservíre concédas. Per Dóminum.

—*Third Sunday of Lent*— *I Classis.*

DOMINICA TERTIA IN QUADRAGESIMA *Station at Saint Lawrence Outside the Walls*

INTROIT. *Ps 24: 15-16*

UPON THE LORD I fix mine eyes continually, trusting Him to save my feet from the snare: look Thou upon me, and have mercy on me, for I am alone and poor. (Ps 24: 1-2) To Thee, O Lord, have I lifted up my soul: in Thee, O my God, I put my trust; let me not be ashamed. ℣. Glory.

Óculi mei semper ad Dóminum, quia ipse evéllet de láqueo pedes meos: réspice in me, et miserére mei, quóniam únicus et pauper sum ego. ℣. Ad te, Dómine, levávi ánimam meam: Deus meus, in te confído, non erubéscam. ℣. Glória Patri.

COLLECT.

Have regard to the desires of the lowly, O almighty God, we beseech Thee, and stretch forth the right hand of Thy majesty in our defense. Through our Lord.

Quǽsumus, omnípotens Deus, vota humílium réspice: atque, ad defensiónem nostram, déxteram tuæ majestátis exténde. Per Dóminum.

EPISTLE. *Ephesians 5: 1-9*

BRETHREN, be ye followers of God, as most dear children; and walk in love, as Christ also hath loved us, and hath delivered Himself for us, and oblation and a sacrifice to God, for an odor of sweetness. But fornication, and all uncleanness, or covetousness, let it not so much as be named among you, as becometh saints; nor obscenity, nor foolish talking, nor scurrility, which is to no purpose; but rather giving

Fratres: Estóte imitatóres Dei, sicut fílii caríssimi: et ambuláte in dilectióne, sicut et Christus diléxit nos, et trádidit semetípsum pro nobis oblatiónem, et hóstiam Deo in odórem suavitátis. Fornicátio autem et omnis immundítia aut avarítia nec nominétur in vobis, sicut decet sanctos: aut turpitúdo aut stultilóquium aut scurrílitas, quæ ad rem non pértinet: sed magis gratiárum actio. Hoc enim scitóte intelligéntes, quod omnis fornicátor aut immúndus aut avárus, quod est idolórũ sérvitus, non habet hereditátẽ in regno Christi et Dei. Nemo vos sedúcat inánibus verbis: propter hæc enim venit ira Dei in fílios diffidéntiæ. Nolíte ergo éffici partícipes eórum. Erátis enim aliquándo ténebræ: nunc autem lux in Dómino. Ut fílii lucis ambuláte: fructus enim lucis est in omni bonitáte et justítia et veritáte.

of thanks: for know ye this, and understand, that no fornicator, nor unclean, nor covetous person, which is a serving of idols, hath any inheritance in the kingdom of Christ and of God. Let no man deceive you with vain words; for because of these things cometh the anger of God upon the children of unbelief. Be ye not therefore partakers with them. For you were heretofore darkness; but now light in the Lord. Walk ye as children of the light: for the fruit of the light is in all goodness, and justice, and truth.

GRADUAL. *Ps 9: 20, 4*

Exsúrge, Dñe, non præváleat homo: judicéntur gentes in conspéctu tuo. ℣. In converténdo inimícũ meum retrórsum, infirmabúntur, et períbunt a facie tua.

BESTIR Thyself, Lord, let not human strength prevail; let the heathen stand upon their trial before Thee. ℣. See how my enemies turn back, how they faint and melt away at the sight of Thee!

TRACT. *Ps 122: 1-3*

Ad te levávi óculos meos, qui hábitas in cælis. ℣. Ecce, sicut óculi servórum in mánibus dominórum suórum. ℣. Et sicut óculi ancíllæ in mánibus dóminæ suæ: ita óculi nostri ad Dñm, Deum nostrũ, donec misereátur nostri. ℣. Miserére nobis, Dómine, miserére nobis.

TO THEE have I lifted up my eyes, Who dwellest in heaven. ℣. Behold as the eyes of servants are on the hands of their masters. ℣. And as the eyes of the handmaid are on the hands of her mistress: so are our eyes unto the Lord our God, until He have mercy on us. ℣. Have mercy on us, O Lord, have mercy on us.

GOSPEL. *Luke 11: 14-28*

In illo témpore: Erat Jesus ejíciens dæmónium, et illud erat mutum. Et cum ejecísset dæmóniũ, locútus est mutus, et admirátæ sunt turbæ. Quidam autẽ ex eis dixérunt: In Bëélzebub, príncipe dæmoniórum, éjicit dæmónia. Et álii tentántes, signum de cælo quærébant ab eo. Ipse autem ut vidit cogitatiónes eórum, dixit eis: Omne regnum in seípsum divísum desolábitur, et domus supra domum cadet. Si autem et sátanas in seípsum divísus est, quómodo stabit regnum ejus? quia dícitis, in Bëélzebub me ejícere dæmónia. Si autem ego in Bëélzebub ejício dæmónia: fílii vestri in quo ejíciunt? Ideo ipsi júdices vestri erunt. Porro si in dígito Dei ejício dæmónia: profécto pervénit in vos regnum Dei. Cum fortis armátus custódit átrium suum, in pace sunt ea, quæ póssidet. Si autem fórtior eo supervéniens vícerit eum, univérsa arma ejus áuferet, in quibus confidébat, et spólia ejus distríbuet. Qui non est mecum, contra me est: et qui non cólligit mecum, di-

JESUS WAS casting out a devil, and the same was dumb; and when He had cast out the devil the dumb spoke, and the multitude were in admiration at it, but some of them said, He casteth out devils by Beelzebub the prince of devils. And others tempting, asked of Him a sign from heaven. But He seeing their thoughts, said to them, Every kingdom divided against itself shall be brought to desolation, and house upon house shall fall; and if Satan also be divided against himself, how shall his kingdom stand? Because you say, that through Beelzebub I cast out devils by Beelzebub, by whom do your children cast them out? Therefore they shall be your judges. But if I by the finger of God cast out devils, doubtless the kingdom of God is come upon you. When a strong man armed keepeth his court, those things which he possesseth are in peace: but if a stronger than he come upon him, and overcome him, he will take away all his armor wherein he trusted, and will distribute his spoils. He that is not with Me, is against me: and he that gathereth not with Me, scattereth. When the unclean spirit is gone out of a man, he walketh through places without water, seeking rest: and not finding, he saith, I will return into my house whence I came out: and when he is come, he findeth it swept and garnished. Then he goeth, and taketh with him seven other spirits more wicked than himself, and entering in they dwell there; and the last state of that man becometh worse than the first. And it came to pass, as He spoke these things, that a certain woman from the crowd, lifting up her voice, said to Him, Blessed is the womb that bore Thee, and breasts that gave Thee suck. But He said, Yea, * rather blessed are they who hear the word of God, and keep it. CREDO.

spérgit. Cum immúndus spíritus exíerit de hómine, ámbulat per loca inaquósa, quærens réquiẽ: et non invéniens, dicit: Revértar in domum meam, unde exívi. Et cum vénerit, invénit eam scopis mundátam, et ornátam. Tunc vadit, et assúmit septem álios spíritus secum nequióres se, et ingréssi hábitant ibi. Et fiunt novíssima hóminis illíus pejóra prióribus. Factum est autem, cum hæc díceret: extóllens vocem quædam múlier de turba, dixit illi: Beátus venter, qui te portávit, et úbera, quæ suxísti. At ille dixit: Quinímmo beáti, qui áudiunt verbũ Dei, et custódiunt illud.

* *Note: The word "yea" is pronounced as "yay." The word means "yes," whereas "nay" means "no" in English.*

OFFERTORY. *Ps 18: 9, 10, 11, 12*

THE JUSTICES of the Lord are right, rejoicing hearts, and His judgments are sweeter than honey and the honeycomb; for Thy servant keepeth them. ℣. *The commandment of the Lord is lightsome, enlightening the eyes: the fear of the Lord is holy, enduring for ever and ever: the judgments of the Lord are true.* ℣. *And the words of my mouth shall be such as may please, and the meditation of my heart always in Thy sight.*

Justítiæ Dómini rectæ, lætificántes corda, et judícia ejus dulcióra super mel et favum: nam et servus tuus custódit ea. ℣. *Præcéptum Dómini lúcidum illúminans óculos: timor Dei sanctus pérmanet in sǽculum sǽculi: judícia Dñi vera.* ℣. *Et erunt, ut compláceant elóquia oris mei et meditátio cordis mei in conspéctu tuo semper.*

SECRET.

May this offering, O Lord, we beseech Thee, wipe out our sins, and sanctify the bodies and minds of Thy servants for the celebration of the sacrifice. Through our Lord.

Hæc hóstia, Dñe, quǽsumus, emúndet nostra delícta: et, ad sacrifícium celebrándũ, subditórum tibi córpora mentésque sanctíficet. Per Dóminum.

The Preface of Lent (page 189) follows the Secret.

COMMUNION. *Ps 83: 4-5*

THE SPARROW hath found herself a house, and the turtle a nest, where she may lay her young ones: Thy altars, O Lord of hosts, my King, and my God: Blessed are they that dwell in Thy house, they shall praise Thee forever and ever. ℣. *O Lord of hosts, how I love Thy dwelling-place!*

Passer invénit sibi domũ, et turtur nidũ, ubi repónat pullos suos: altária tua, Dñe virtútum, Rex meus, et Deus meus: beáti, qui hábitant in domo tua, in sǽculũ sǽculi laudábunt te. (Ps 83: 2) ℣. *Quam dilécta tabernácula tua, Dñe virtútũ: concupíscit, et déficit ánima mea in átria Dómini.*

—BLANDIN10144|768 • Circa 768AD

POSTCOMMUNION.

A cunctis nos, quǽsumus, Dñe, reátibus et perículis propitiátus absólve: quos tanti mystérii tríbuis esse partícipes. Per Dóminum.

Be merciful, O Lord, we beseech Thee, and free us from all sins and dangers, as Thou dost grant us to be sharers in this great mystery. Through our Lord.

I Classis. — *Fourth Sunday of Lent* —

DOMINICA QUARTA IN QUADRAGESIMA *Station at the Holy Cross in Jerusalem*

INTROIT. *Is 66: 10, 11*

Lætáre, Jerúsalem: et convéntum fácite, omnes qui dilígitis eam: gaudéte cum lætítia, qui in tristítia fuístis: ut exsultétis, et satiémini ab ubéribus consolatiónis vestræ. ℣. Lætátus sum in his, quæ dicta sunt mihi: in domum Dñi íbimus. ℣. Glória Patri.

REJOICE, O Jerusalem, and come together all you that love her; rejoice with joy, you that have been in sorrow: that you may exult and be filled from the breasts of your consolation. (Ps 121: 1) I rejoiced at the things that were said to me: We shall go into the house of the Lord. ℣. Glory.

COLLECT.

Concéde, quǽsumus, omnípotens Deus: ut, qui ex mérito nostræ actiónis afflígimur, tuæ grátiæ consolatióne respirémus. Per Dóminum.

Grant, we beseech Thee, O almighty God, that we, who justly suffer for our deeds, may be relieved by the consolation of Thy grace. Through our Lord.

EPISTLE. *Gal 4: 22-31*

Fratres: Scriptum est: Quóniam Ábraham duos fílios hábuit: unũ de ancílla, et unum de líbera. Sed qui de ancílla, secúndum carnem natus est: qui autẽ de líbera, per repromissiónem: quæ sunt per allegoríam dicta. Hæc enim sunt duo testaménta. Unum quidem in monte Sina, in servitútem génerans: quæ est Agar: Sina enim mons est in Arábia, qui conjúnctus est ei, quæ nunc est Jerúsalem, et servit cum fíliis suis. Illa autem, quæ sursum est Jerúsalem, líbera est, quæ est mater nostra. Scriptum est enim: Lætáre, stérilis, quæ non paris: erúmpe, et clama, quæ non párturis: quia multi fílii desértæ, magis quam ejus, quæ habet virum. Nos autem, fratres, secúndũ Ísaäc promissiónis fílii sumus. Sed quómodo tunc is, qui secúndum carnem natus fúerat, persequebátur eũ, qui secúndum spíritum: ita et nunc. Sed quid dicit Scriptura? Éjice ancíllam et

BRETHREN: It is written that Abraham had two sons; the one by a bond-woman, and the other by a free-woman. But he who was of the bond-woman was born according to the flesh; but he of the free-woman was by promise. Which things are said by an allegory. For these are the two testaments: the one from Mount Sina, engendering unto bondage, which is Agar: for Sina is a mountain in Arabia, which hath affinity to that Jerusalem which now is, and is in bondage with her children: but that Jerusalem which is above is free, which is our mother. For it is written, Rejoice, thou barren that bearest not; break forth and cry, thou that travailest not; for many are the children of the desolate, more than of her that hath a husband. Now we, brethren, as Isaac was, are the children of promise. But as then he that was born according to the flesh persecuted him that was after the spirit, so also it is now. But what saith the Scripture? Cast out the bond-woman and her son; for the son of the bondwoman shall not be heir with the son of the free-woman. So then, brethren, we are not the children of the bond-woman, but of the free; by the freedom wherewith Christ hath made us free.

fílium ejus: non enim heres erit fílius ancíllæ cũ fílio líberæ. Ítaque, fratres, non sumus ancíllæ fílii, sed líberæ: qua libertáte Christus nos liberávit.

GRADUAL. *Ps 121: 1, 7*

Identical to 18th Sunday after Pentecost:

I REJOICED at the things that were said to me: We shall go into the house of the Lord. ℣. Let peace be in thy strength, and abundance in thy towers.

Lætátus sum in his, quæ dicta sunt mihi: in domum Dñi íbimus. ℣. Fiat pax in virtúte tua: et abundántia in túrribus tuis.

TRACT. *Ps 124: 1-2*

THEY that trust in the Lord shall be as Mount Sion: he shall not be moved forever that dwelleth in Jerusalem. ℣. Mountains are round about it: so the Lord is round about His people, from henceforth now and forever.

Qui confídunt in Dómino, sicut mons Sion: non commovébitur in ætérnum, qui hábitat in Jerúsalem. ℣. Montes in circúitu ejus: et Dñs in circúitu pópuli sui, ex hoc nunc et usque in sǽculum.

GOSPEL. *John 6: 1-15*

JESUS WENT OVER the Sea of Galilee, which is that of Tiberias; and a great multitude followed Him, because they saw the miracles which He did on them that were diseased. Jesus therefore went up into a mountain, and there He sat with His disciples. Now the Pasch, the festival day of the Jews, was near at hand. When Jesus therefore had lifted up his eyes, and seen that a very great multitude cometh to Him, He said to Philip, Whence shall we buy bread that these may eat? And this He said to try him; for He Himself knew what He would do. Philip answered, Two hundred pennyworth of bread is not sufficient for them, that every one may take a little. One of His disciples, Andrew, the brother of Simon Peter, saith to Him, There is a boy here that hath five barley loaves and two fishes; but what are these among so many?

In illo témpore: Ábiit Jesus trans mare Galilǽæ, quod est Tiberíadis: et sequebátur eum multitúdo magna, quia vidébant signa, quæ faciébat super his, qui infirmabántur. Súbiit ergo in montem Jesus: et ibi sedébat cũ discípulis suis. Erat autem próximum Pascha, dies festus Judæórum. Cum sublevásset ergo óculos Jesus et vidísset, quia multitúdo máxima venit ad eũ, dixit ad Philíppum: Unde emémus panes, ut mandúcent hi? Hoc autem dicebat tentans eum: ipse enim sciébat, quid esset factúrus. Respóndit ei Philíppus: Ducentórum denariórum panes non sufficiunt eis, ut unusquísque módicum quid accípiat. Dicit ei unus ex discípulis ejus, Andréas, frater Simónis Petri: Est puer unus hic, qui habet quinque panes hordeáceos et duos pisces: sed hæc quid sunt inter tantos?

Then Jesus said, Make the men sit down. Now there was much grass in the place. The men therefore sat down, in number about five thousand. And Jesus took the loaves; and when He had given thanks, He distributed to them that were set down. In like manner also of the fishes, as much as they would. And when they were filled, He said to His disciples, Gather up the

Dixit ergo Jesus: Fácite hómines discúmbere. Erat autem fœnum multum in loco. Discubuérunt ergo viri, número quasi quinque mília. Accépit ergo Jesus panes, et cum grátias egísset, distríbuit discumbéntibus: simíliter et ex píscibus, quantum volébant. Ut autẽ impléti sunt, dixit discípulis suis: Collígite quæ superavérunt fragménta, ne péreant. Collegérunt ergo, et

THEY BEGAN HOLDING OUT THE JARS FOR HER, WHILE SHE FILLED THEM. BEING TOLD HE HAD NO MORE, THE OIL GAVE OUT (IV KINGS 4:5) ✠ THERE SHALL BE NO LACK OF FLOUR IN THE JAR, NOR SHALL THE OIL WASTE IN THE CRUET, TILL THE LORD SENDS RAIN ON THIS PARCHED EARTH (III KINGS 17:14)

SUMIT UNUS, SUMUNT MILLE: QUANTUM ISTI, TANTUM ILLE...

IN HAC MENSA NOVI REGIS, NOVUM PASCHA NOVAE LEGIS...

KNOWING, THEN, THAT THEY MEANT TO COME AND CARRY HIM OFF—SO AS TO MAKE A KING OF HIM—JESUS WITHDREW ON TO THE HILL-SIDE ALL ALONE.
(JOHN 6: 15)

fragments that remain, lest they be lost. They gathered up therefore, and filled twelve baskets with the fragments of the five barley loaves, which remained over and above to them that had eaten. Now those men, when they had seen what a miracle Jesus had done, said, This is of a truth the prophet that is to come into the world. Jesus therefore, when He knew that they would come to take Him by force and make Him king, fled again into the mountain Himself alone. CREDO.

implevérunt duódecim cóphinos fragmentórum ex quinque pánibus hordeáceis, quæ superfuérunt his, qui manducáverant. Illi ergo hómines cum vidíssent, quod Jesus fécerat signum, dicébant: Quia hic est vere Prophéta, qui ventúrus est in mundum. Jesus ergo cum cognovísset, quia ventúri essent, ut ráperent eum et fácerent eum regem, fugit íterum in montem ipse solus.

OFFERTORY. *Ps 134: 3, 6*

PRAISE YE THE LORD, for He is good: sing ye to His name, for He is sweet: whatsoever He pleased He hath done in heaven and in earth. ℣. *You that stand in the house of the Lord, in the courts of the house of our God: for I have known that the Lord is great, and our God is above all gods.* ℣. *O Lord, Thy name abides for ever; age succeeds age, and Thou art ever unforgotten: the Lord defends His people, takes pity on His servants.* ℣. *You that fear the Lord, bless the Lord: blessèd be the Lord out of Sion, Who dwelleth in Jerusalem.*

Laudáte Dóminum, quia benígnus est: psállite nómini ejus, quóniam suávis est: ómnia, quæcúmque vóluit, fecit in cælo et in terra. ℣. *Qui statis in domo Dñi, in átriis domus Dei nostri: quia ego cognóvi, quod magnus est Dñs et Deus noster præ ómnibus diis.* ℣. *Dómine, nomen tuum in ætérnum et memoriále tuum in sæcula sæculórum: judicábit Dóminus pópulum suum et in servis suis consolábitur.* ℣. *Qui timétis Dóminum benedícite eum: benedíctus Dóminus ex Sion, qui hábitat in Jerúsalem.*

SECRET.

We beseech Thee, O Lord, look favorably upon the sacrifices here before Thee, that they may profit us both for devotion and for salvation. Through our Lord.

Sacrifíciis præséntibus, Dñe, quǽsumus, inténde placátus: ut et devotióni nostræ profíciant et salúti. Per Dñm.

The Preface of Lent (page 189) follows the Secret.

COMMUNION. *Ps 121: 3-4*

JERUSALEM, which is built as a city, which is compact together; for thither did the tribes go up, the tribes of the Lord, to praise Thy name, O Lord. ℣. *I rejoiced at the things that were said to me: We shall go into the house of the Lord.*

Jerúsalem, quæ ædificátur ut cívitas, cujus participátio ejus in idípsum: illuc enim ascendérunt tribus, tribus Dómini, ad confiténdum nómini tuo, Dómine. (Ps 121: 1) ℣. *Lætátus sum in his quæ dicta sunt mihi: in domum Dómini íbimus.* —ALBI|1047 • Circa 1047AD

POSTCOMMUNION.

Grant us, we beseech Thee, O merciful God, that we may treat with unfeigned veneration and ever receive with heartfelt faith Thy holy rites which we constantly celebrate. Through our Lord.

Da nobis, quǽsumus, miséricors Deus: ut sancta tua, quibus incessánter explémur, sincéris tractémus obséquiis, et fidéli semper mente sumámus. Per Dóminum.

PASSIONTIDE • Beginning on Passion Sunday, the "Glória Patri" verse at the ASPERGES, INTROIT, and LAVABO are omitted. Psalm 42 ("Júdica Me") is also omitted—cf. §425 of *Code of Rubrics* (1961)—but not the complete "Prayers at the Foot of the Altar" (*Júdica Me*, *Confíteor* with absolution, *Aufer A Nobis*, and *Orámus Te, Dómine*) which are omitted: on 2 February (after the candles are blessed); on Ash Wednesday (after the ashes are blessed); on Palm Sunday (after the branches are blessed); on the Easter Vigil (after the Litany); and on Rogation Masses (after the Litany). This is easy to remember each year, because the Passion Sunday Introit is "Júdica me, Deus."

VEILING OF IMAGES • Beginning at First Vespers of Passion Sunday, all statues and pictures (including crucifixes) in the church and sacristy are to be covered with an opaque purple veil. The images are not to be uncovered on any pretext—except during the "Creeping to the Cross" on Good Friday—until the veils are removed during the Easter Vigil. But the Stations of the Cross may remain uncovered. This is easy to remember each year, because the Passion Sunday Gospel ends with these words: "They took up stones therefore to cast at Him; but Jesus hid Himself, and went out of the temple." The medieval French bishop Durandus connects the veiling of the statues with the way that Christ veiled His divinity during His Passion.

VEILING ON PALM SUNDAY • Beginning in 1955, some authors refer to Palm Sunday as "Second Passion Sunday." Monsignor McManus claims this new nomenclature was intended to "minimize the significance of the palm branches, in order to restore the solemn procession to its proper position" {McManus p20}. Traditionally, the second Sunday in Passiontide is called PALM SUNDAY. On Palm Sunday, the Processional Cross is not veiled for the 1962 version {McManus p50}, whereas in the 1950 version the Processional Cross is "covered with purple" {Fortescue p272} and—while palm branches are being distributed—a server fastens one to the Processional Cross with a purple ribbon. Notice that the complete "Prayers at the Foot of the Altar" are omitted in 1962, whereas the 1950 version of Palm Sunday omits Psalm 42 only. In the 1962 version of Palm Sunday, the congregation does not hold palm branches during the reading of the Passion (unlike the 1950 version).

I Classis.

— *Fifth Sunday of Lent* —

DOMINICA PRIMA PASSIONIS *Station at Saint Peter*

INTROIT. *Ps 42: 1-2*

Júdica me, Deus, et discérne causam meam de gente non sancta: ab hómine iníquo et dolóso éripe me: quia tu es Deus meus et fortitúdo mea. ℣. Emítte lucem tuam et veritátem tuam: ipsa me deduxérunt et adduxérunt in montem sanctum tuum et in tabernácula tua. ℟. *Júdica me . . .*

JUDGE ME, O GOD, and distinguish my cause from the nation that is not holy: deliver me from the unjust and deceitful man. For Thou art my God and my strength. (Ps 42: 3) Send forth Thy light and Thy truth: they have conducted me, and brought me unto Thy holy hill, and into Thy tabernacles. ℟. *Judge me...*

COLLECT.

Look with favor upon Thy household, we beseech Thee, O almighty God, that, by Thy gift, it may be governed in body and, by Thy preservation, may be guarded in spirit. Through our Lord.

Quæsumus, omnípotens Deus, famíliã tuam propítius réspice: ut, te largiénte, regátur in córpore; et, te servánte, custodiátur in mente. Per Dóminum.

EPISTLE. *Hebrews 9: 11-15*

BRETHREN, Christ being come, a high priest of the good things to come, by a greater and more perfect tabernacle, not made with hands, that is, not of this creation, neither by the blood of goats or of calves, but by His own blood, entered once into the Holies, having obtained eternal redemption. For if the blood of goats and of oxen, and the ashes of an heifer being sprinkled sanctify such as are defiled, to the cleansing of the flesh, how much more shall the blood of Christ, Who, through the Holy Ghost, offered Himself without spot to God, cleanse our conscience from dead works, to serve the living God? And therefore He is the mediator of the New Testament: that by means of His death, for the redemption of those transgressions which were under the former testament; they that are called may receive the promise of eternal inheritance; in Christ Jesus our Lord.

Fratres: Christus assístens Pontifex futurórum bonórum, per ámplius et perféctius tabernáculũ non manufáctum, id est, non hujus creatiónis: neque per sánguinem hircórum aut vitulórum, sed per próprium sánguinem introívit semel in Sancta, ætérna redemptióne invénta. Si enim sanguis hircórum et taurórum, et cinis vítulæ aspérsus, inquinátos sanctíficat ad emundatiónem carnis: quanto magis sanguis Christi, qui per Spíritum Sanctum semetípsum óbtulit immaculátum Deo, emundábit consciéntiam nostram ab opéribus mórtuis, ad serviéndum Deo vivénti? Et ideo novi Testaménti mediátor est: ut, morte intercedénte, in redemptiónem eárum prævaricatiónũ, quæ erant sub prióri Testaménto, repromissiónẽ accípiant, qui vocáti sunt ætérnæ hereditátis, in Christo Jesu, Dómino nostro.

GRADUAL. *Ps 142: 9, 10 & Ps 17: 48-49*

DELIVER ME from my enemies, O Lord, teach me to do Thy will. ℣. My deliverer, O Lord, from the angry nations: Thou wilt lift me up above them that rise up against me: from the unjust man Thou wilt deliver me.

Eripe me, Dómine, de inimícis meis: doce me fácere voluntátem tuam. ℣. Liberátor meus, Dñe, de géntibus iracúndis: ab insurgéntibus in me exaltábis me: a viro iníquo erípies me.

TRACT. *Ps 128: 1-4*

OFTEN have they fought against me from my youth. ℣. Let Israel now say: often have they fought against me from my youth. ℣. But they could not prevail over me: the wicked have wrought upon my back. ℣. They have lengthened their iniquities: the Lord Who is just will cut the necks of sinners.

Sæpe expugnavérunt me a juventúte mea. ℣. Dicat nunc Ísraël: sæpe expugnavérunt me a juventúte mea. ℣. Étenim non potuérunt mihi: supra dorsum meum fabricavérunt peccatóres. ℣. Prolongavérunt iniquitátes suas: Dóminus justus concídit cervíces peccatórum.

OPPOSITE PAGE: The citation for the opening phrase of the Passion Sunday Offertory is unclear. Some authors cite Psalm 137:1a, while others say it is Psalm 118:7a. Addressing the melody itself, Dom Johner reminds us: "From Passion Sunday on, the Missal does not stress the sufferings of Christ so much as does the Breviary in its hymns and antiphons. We never find somber tones exclusively in the Church's mourning. When she thinks of her beloved dead, she does not act like those who have no hope; she sees eternal light rising before them, and asks that this eternal light be theirs. And the most heartfelt sympathy with the sufferings of the Crucified One does not hinder her from singing of Christ's resurrection on Good Friday, and from singing of His cross: *For by the wood the whole world is filled with joy.*"

GOSPEL. *John 8: 46-59*

In illo témpore: Dicébat Jesus turbis Judæórũ: Quis ex vobis árguet me de peccáto? Si veritátem dico vobis, quare non créditis mihi? Qui ex Deo est, verba Dei audit. Proptérea vos non audítis, quia ex Deo non estis. Respondérunt ergo Judǽi et dixérunt ei: Nonne bene dícimus nos, quia Samaritánus es tu, et dæmóniũ habes? Respóndit Jesus: Ego dæmónium non hábeo, sed honoríflco Patrem meum, et vos inhonorástis me. Ego autem non quæro glóriam meam: est, qui quærat et júdicet. Amen, amen, dico vobis: si quis sermónem meum serváverit, mortem non vidébit in ætérnum.

Dixérunt ergo Judǽi: Nunc cognóvimus, quia dæmónium habes. Ábraham mórtuus est et Prophétæ; et tu dicis: Si quis sermónem meum serváverit, non gustábit mortẽ in ætérnum. Numquid tu major es patre nostro Ábraham, qui mórtuus est? et Prophétæ mórtui sunt. Quem teípsum facis? Respóndit Jesus: Si ego glorífico meípsum, glória mea nihil est: est Pater meus, qui gloríficat me, quem vos dícitis, quia Deus vester est, et non cognovístis eum: ego autem novi eum: et si díxero, quia non scio eum, ero símilis vobis, mendax. Sed scio eum et sermónem ejus servo. Ábraham pater vester exsultávit, ut vidéret diem meũ: vidit, et gavísus est. Dixérunt ergo Judǽi ad eum: Quinquagínta annos nondum habes, et Ábraham vidísti? Dixit eis Jesus: Amen, amen, dico vobis, ántequam Ábraham fíeret, ego sum. Tulérunt ergo lápides, ut jácerent in eum: Jesus autem abscóndit se, et exívit de templo.

AT THAT TIME, Jesus said to the multitudes of the Jews, Which of you shall convince Me of sin? If I say the truth to you, why do you not believe Me? He that is of God, heareth the words of God. Therefore you hear them not, because you are not of God. The Jews therefore answered and said to Him, Do not we say well, that Thou art a Samaritan, and hast a devil? Jesus answered, I have not a devil: but I honor My Father, and you have dishonored Me. But I seek not My own glory; there is one that seeketh and judgeth. Amen, amen, I say to you, If any man keep My word, he shall not see death forever.

The Jews therefore said, Now we know that Thou hast a devil. Abraham is dead, and the prophets; and Thou sayest, If any man keep My word, he shall not taste death forever. Art Thou greater than our father Abraham, who is dead? and the prophets are dead. Whom dost Thou make Thyself? Jesus answered, If I glorify Myself, My glory is nothing. It is My Father that glorifieth Me, of Whom you say that He is your God. And you have not known Him; but I know Him. And if I shall say that I know Him not, I shall be like to you, a liar. But I do know Him, and do keep His word. Abraham your father rejoiced that he might see My day: he saw it, and was glad. The Jews therefore said to Him, Thou art not yet fifty years old and hast Thou seen Abraham? Jesus said to them, Amen, amen, I say to you, before Abraham was made, **I AM**. They took up stones therefore to cast at Him; but Jesus hid Himself, and went out of the temple. CREDO.

OFFERTORY. *Ps 118: 17, 107*

Confitébor tibi, Dómine, in toto corde meo: retríbue servo tuo: vivam, et custódiam sermónes tuos: vivífica me secúndum verbum tuum, Dómine. ℣. *Beáti immaculáti in via, qui ámbulant in lege Dómini: beáti, qui scrutántur testimónia ejus, in toto corde exquírunt eum.* ℣. *Viam veritátis elégi, da mihi intelléctum et scrutábor legem tuam: et custódiam illam in toto corde meo: Inclína cor meum in testimónia tua et non in avarítiam: in via tua vivífica me: judícia enim tua jucúnda: Deprecátus sum vultum tuũ in toto corde meo, quia diléxi legem tuã.*

I WILL CONFESS to Thee, O Lord, with my whole heart: render to Thy servant: I shall live and keep Thy words: enliven me according to Thy word, O Lord. ℣. *Blessed are the undefiled in the way, who walk in the law of the Lord: blessed are they that search His testimonies, that seek Him with their whole heart.* ℣. *I have chosen the way of truth, give me understanding, and I will search Thy law, and I will keep it with my whole heart: incline my heart into Thy testimonies and not to covetousness: quicken me in Thy way: for Thy judgments are delightful : I entreated Thy face with all my heart, for I have loved Thy law.*

SECRET.

May these offerings, we pray Thee, O Lord, both loose the bonds of our sins, and win for us the gifts of Thy mercy. Through our Lord.

Hæc múnera, quǽsumus Dñe, ei víncula nostræ pravitátis absólvant, et tuæ nobis misericórdiæ dona concílient. Per Dóminum.

The Preface of the Holy Cross (page 190) follows the Secret.

QUOD IN CENA – *"Christ desired that what He did at the last supper be repeated."* (Lauda Sion 9v)

COMMUNION. *I Cor 11: 24, 25*

THIS is My body which shall be delivered for you: this is the chalice of the New Testament in My blood, saith the Lord: do this, as often as you receive it, in commemoration of Me. ℣. *And while they were still at table, Jesus took bread, and blessed, and broke it, and gave it to his disciples, saying.*

Hoc corpus, quod pro vobis tradétur: hic calix novi Testaménti est in meo sánguine, dicit Dóminus: hoc fácite, quotiescúmque súmitis, in meam commemoratiónem. (Cf. Lk 22:19 & Mt 26:26) ℣. *Cœnántibus autem eis, accépit Jesus panem, et benedíxit, ac fregit, dedítque discípulis suis dicens.*

—4951STEVEN|1128 • Circa 1128AD

—NARBONNE|1033 • Circa 1033AD

Note: Because this communion antiphon is not taken from a psalm, the ancient manuscripts provide sundry "extra" verses. Some manuscripts—such as BAMBERG6LIT|905; 342SANGALL|933; and 121EINSIE|961—take the verses from the Introit. Other manuscripts reference the Last Supper (as shown above).

POSTCOMMUNION.

Draw near to us, O Lord, our God, and with Thy perpetual succor defend those whom Thou hast refreshed with Thy mysteries. Through our Lord.

Adésto nobis, Dómine, Deus noster: et, quos tuis mystériis recreásti, perpétuis defénde subsídiis. Per Dñm.

IF ONLY I AM LIFTED UP FROM THE EARTH, I WILL DRAW ALL MEN TO MYSELF. ✠ Jn 12.32

THE SON OF MAN MUST BE LIFTED UP, AS THE SERPENT WAS LIFTED UP BY MOSES ✠ Jn 3.14

HOLY WEEK

ACCORDING TO THE LITURGICAL BOOKS PRINTED IN 1962

AND WHEN MOSES LIFTED UP HIS HANDS, ISRAEL OVERCAME ... ✠ Exodus 17.11

THE CROWD ANSWERED: "THE LAW SAYS CHRIST IS TO REMAIN UNDISTURBED FOREVER; WHAT DOST THOU MEAN BY SAYING THE SON OF MAN MUST BE LIFTED UP?" Jn 12.34

ET EGO SI EXALTATUS FUERO A TERRA OMNIA TRAHAM AD MEIPSUM. ✠ HOC AUTEM DICEBAT SIGNIFICANS QUA MORTE ESSET MORITURUS.

✠ CUM QUE LEVARET MOYSES MANUS VINCEBAT ISRAEL : SIN AUTEM PAULULUM REMISISSET SUPERABAT AMALEC ... ✠

CHANGES DURING THE 1950s

BEGINNING in the early 1950s and stretching over (approximately) the next decade—until the beginning of Vatican II Council on 11 October 1962—tremendous changes were made to the sacred liturgy with regard to :

(1) The discipline of fasting before Communion [cf. *Sacram Communionem, 1957*];

(2) The permissibility of evening Masses [cf. *Christus Dominus, 1953*];

(3) Eliminating octaves, "proper" Last Gospels, and more [cf. *Cum Nostra Hac Ætate, 1955*];

(4) Rubrical matters, such as whether incense can be used sans Deacon + Subdeacon {Giampietro p314};

(5) Who may proclaim certain readings ("capable reader");

(6) Which prayers the congregation may recite audibly [cf. *De Musica Sacra, 1958*];

(7) The priest quietly "duplicating" readings sung by others (e.g. Epistle and Gospel);

(8) When Holy Communion should be distributed [cf. pages 250 and 510];

(9) The addition of Saint Joseph's name to the Canon (13 November 1962);

(10) Elimination of the pre-Communion Confiteor {Giampietro p314} [cf. *Rubricarum Instructum, 1960*];

(11) An attempt to replace the psalter with the Pius XII version [a.k.a. *"Bea" Psalter*];

(12) Numerous other items, including the addition of new feasts such as *The Queenship of Mary* (31 May) and *Saint Joseph the Craftsman* (1 May).

PIUS XII REFORMS HOLY WEEK • 1951 - 1956

Under Pope Pius XII, the ceremonies of Holy Week were revised. The work was done by the *Commissio Piana*, established in secrecy on 28 May 1948. (Its existence was kept a secret for several years.) Those who served on the *Commissio Piana* were:

(1) Father Ferdinando Antonelli, OFM;

(2) Father Josef Löw, CssR;

(3) Father Augustin Bea, SJ;

(4) Archbishop Alfonso Carinci;

(5) Father Anselmo Albareda, OSB;

(6) Father Annibale Bugnini.

"BATTERING RAM HEAD" • Clemente Cardinal Micara (d. 1965) was president of the *Commissio Piana*, and Father Bugnini was the secretary. Vincentian Father Carlo Braga characterized the Holy Week reforms as "the head of the battering ram which pierced the fortress of our hitherto static liturgy." Father Bugnini agreed, calling the Pius XII Holy Week "a first breach in the walls of a fortress, centuries old, stoutly built, strong and robust, but no longer capable of responding to the spiritual needs of the [contemporary] age, which needed a fresh breath of life."

NOMENCLATURE NOTE • The following pages (see below) present the ceremonies of Holy Week according to the liturgical books of 1962. Needless to say, the 1962 version reflects the changes made by Pope Pius XII during the early 1950s, as well as any changes made after 1955. It bears repeating that 1956 was the first year the complete "Pius XII Holy Week" was used, since MAXIMA REDEMPTIONIS (19 November 1955) was issued late in 1955.

VATICAN II COUNCIL • 1962-1965

The Second Vatican Council mandated—but did not oversee—a reform of the sacred liturgy. Many of the Council fathers had died by the time the 1970 MISSALE ROMANUM was released (more than half a decade after they had voted on *Sacrosanctum Concilium* in December of 1963). While the post-conciliar reformers did not have malice in their hearts, they were deeply influenced by the zeitgeist: the notion that anything "new" was good. Many of the Council fathers ***when they observed the results of their reforms*** would change their opinions. Father Louis Bouyer, someone deeply involved in liturgical reform, would later refer to the reforms as "the pathetic creature we produced," and admitted their goal was impossible: "recasting from top to bottom—*and in a few months!*—an entire liturgy which required twenty centuries to develop." Archbishop Marcel Lefebvre (who would later oppose the liturgical reforms) at first supported them, writing in 1965 that the first part of the Mass "is intended to instruct the faithful"—whereas the traditional understanding stresses ***prayer*** over didactic elements. Archbishop Lefebvre continued:

> "The priest coming nearer to the faithful; communicating with them; praying and singing with them and therefore standing at the pulpit; saying the COLLECT, the EPISTLE, and the GOSPEL in their language; the priest singing in the divine traditional melodies—the *Kyrie*, the *Gloria*, the *Credo*—with the faithful: these are so many good reforms that give back to that part of the Mass its true finality."

SPIRIT OF THE TIMES • The zeitgeist seemingly influenced everyone, including clerics such as Archbishop Fulton J. Sheen, whose "attitudes" (for want of a better term) were well documented since the 1920s. But sometimes men—as they approach their own death—begin to see with a new clarity, and no longer fear the results of speaking the truth. This can be seen in a quote by Father Bouyer (d. 2004), the scholar responsible for creating "Eucharistic Prayer II." [Bouyer was certainly no "traditionalist," as page 4 of his *Liturgical Piety* (Notre Dame Press, 1954) clearly shows.] Father Bouyer wrote as follows in his memoirs (which were revealed a decade after his death):

> "I prefer to say nothing, or so little, of the new calendar, which was the handiwork of a trio of maniacs who suppressed—with no good reason—Septuagesima and the Octave of Pentecost, and who scattered three quarters of the saints higgledy-piddledy, all based on notions of their own!"

UNASSAILABLE SOURCE • Perhaps the most knowledgeable source vis-à-vis the liturgical reforms of the 1950s and 1960s was Cardinal Antonelli, who became a consulter to the SCR in 1930, was one of the six members appointed to the *Commissio Piana*, and was named—on 4 October 1962—Secretary of the Conciliar Commission on the Liturgy. His statement is worth pondering:

> "The CONCILIUM is merely an assembly of people, many of them incompetent, and others well advanced on the road to novelty. The discussions are extremely hurried. Discussions are based on impressions and the voting is chaotic. [...] Many of those who have influenced the reform [...] have no love, and no veneration of that which has been handed down to us. **They begin by despising everything that is actually there."**

EVERY WORD AND EVERY GESTURE • Much has been written (by the reformers themselves) about the great haste which characterized much of their work. In the personal notes of Cardinal Antonelli, however, we see another deep concern of his: viz. the lack of theologians. On 25 July 1968, Antonelli noted {Giampietro p191}:

> "In the CONCILIUM, there are few Bishops with a specifically liturgical expertise, and very few are really theologians. **The most acute deficiency** in the CONCILIUM is the lack of theologians. In fact, it could be said that they had been excluded altogether, which is something dangerous. In the liturgy, every word and every gesture expresses an idea which is always a theological idea. [...] And this has very serious consequences."

In the private diaries of Cardinal Antonelli {Giampietro p196}, he says of Annibale Bugnini:

> "I could say many things about this man. [...] While I would like to be mistaken, I can say that his greatest lacuna was his **lack of any theological training or sensibility.** This was a grave defect and lacuna because in the liturgy, every word and every gesture expresses a theological idea. I have the impression that much has been conceded to the Protestant mentality, especially in matters regarding the sacraments."

LOSS OF SACRED SCRIPTURE • Looking back at the reforms of the 1950s and 1960s—with the advantageous benefit of hindsight—one of the most disturbing trends was the elimination of Sacred Scripture. Consider a few examples of what the reformers did during the 1950s and 1960s:

(1) They eliminated eight readings on Easter Eve, leaving only four readings;

(2) They eliminated various sections of the Passion on Palm Sunday, such as our Blessed Redeemer's institute of the Holy Eucharist;

(3) They eliminated important verses from Sacred Scripture, making sure the faithful would never hear these proclaimed during Mass; e.g. Saint Paul's warning about unworthy reception of the Holy Eucharist (I Corinthians 11:27-29)—which previously had been found each year on Maundy

Thursday and the feast of Corpus Christi—was completely excised from all three liturgical years (ABC) of the reformed Lectionary.

(4) They downgraded the Psalter; the traditional Divine Office prays all 150 psalms ***each week,*** whereas the post-conciliar version cylces through all 150 psalms ***each month.***

(5) They *de facto* quashed what was for centuries the annual time when congregations experienced more Sacred Scripture than at any other time: viz. ***Tenebrae.*** The faithful had attended these when they occurred on the evenings of the SACRED TRIDUUM, before the reformers transferred them to very early in the morning. Even members of the *Commissio Piana* expressed hesitation at such destruction; e.g. Archbishop Carinci noted that *Tenebrae* was "much belovèd by the faithful, and many of them participate in it" {Giampietro p246}.

(6) They *de facto* eliminated the memorable "snippets" of Sacred Scripture for each Mass—Introit, Gradual, Alleluia Verse, Offertory, Communion—which are known as the *Propria Missae* ("Mass Propers"). More than 95% of the *Propria Missae* are direct quotations from Sacred Scripture. The texts and melodies for the *Propria Missae* are more ancient than the *Ordinarium Missae* by many centuries.

(7) Perhaps most significantly of all, the reformers caused grave harm to the faithful's knowledge of Sacred Scripture by imposing a 3-year cycle (ABC) for the Lectionary. The human brain does not easily become familiar with items occuring only ***once every three years.*** Our brains are geared towards annual events: completing a grade in elementary school, birthdays, Spring, Summer, Winter, Autumn, and so forth.

The post-conciliar reformers frequently contradicted—*in quite a flagrant manner*—the explicit mandates of Vatican II, and these contradictions must be corrected. Here are some examples:

GREGORIAN CHANT • Vatican II said that Gregorian Chant must "be given first place in liturgical services" (SC §116) under normal circumstances.

CHOIRS DILIGENTLY PROMOTED • Vatican II said "choirs must be diligently promoted" (SC §114). Moreover, Vatican II specifically recommended polyphony (SC §116) for liturgical celebrations.

DIVINE OFFICE • Vatican II said "the Latin language is to be retained by clerics in the divine office" (SC §101). Dom Anselmo Albareda, one of the six members of the *Commissio Piana*, pointed out that "the unity of language in the liturgy is so great a treasure for the Church that no advantage could compensate for its demise" {Giampietro p249}. On 22 February 1962, Pope John XXIII—who convened the Second Vatican Council on 11 October 1962—published *Veterum Sapientia*, which unequivocally condemns those who would ***downplay or denigrate*** the liturgical use of Latin. (John XXIII had announced his intention to convene Vatican II on 25 January 1959.)

PRESERVED AND FOSTERED • Vatican II said "the treasure of sacred music is to be preserved and fostered with great care" (SC §101).

GREATER THAN ANY OTHER ART • Vatican II said: "The musical tradition of the universal Church is a treasure of inestimable value, greater even than that of any other art" (SC §112).

A COMMAND NOT A SUGGESTION • Vatican II said: "steps should be taken so that the faithful may also be able to say or to sing together in Latin those parts of the Ordinary of the Mass which pertain to them" (SC §54). Moreover, Vatican II said "the use of the Latin language is to be preserved in the Latin rites" (SC §36). The wording of the document makes it clear this was a command, not a suggestion. Father Bouyer reminds us that the language chosen by Jesus for the Last Supper was Hebrew—a "dead" language—not the vernacular.

THE WORD "WHETHER" • Vatican II said the local bishop can "decide whether, and to what extent, the vernacular language is to be used" (SC §36). Notice the document explicitly says the local bishop can decide ***whether*** the vernacular is used. An important document called *Inter Oecumenici* (1964) specifically said: "Missals to be used in the liturgy, however, shall contain besides the vernacular version the Latin text as well."

PIPE ORGAN • Vatican II said: "In the Latin Church the pipe organ is to be held in high esteem, for it is the traditional musical instrument which adds a wonderful splendor to the Church's ceremonies and powerfully lifts up man's mind to God and to higher things" (SC §120).

These things are not forbidden for Catholics! Contrariwise, they were mandated by Vatican II. To "follow the Council's directives" cannot mean forbidding what Vatican II explicitly demanded.

1962 • If there is another church where the blessing of palm branches can conveniently be held, the palms may be blessed there; then follows the procession to the principal church. If no other church is available, the blessing may be held in some suitable place—even outside the church, before some shrine or the processional cross—so long as the procession goes to the church for the Mass.

I Classis.

— *Second Passion Sunday (Palm Sunday)* —

DOMINICA SECUNDA PASSIONIS SEU IN PALMIS

I. BLESSING THE PALM BRANCHES

1962 • The color of the vestments is red. The "Asperges" is omitted. The ceremony begins with the singing of the following Antiphon:

ANTIPHON. *Matt 21: 9*

Hosánna fílio David: benedíctus, qui venit in nómine Dómini. Rex Ísraël: Hosánna in excélsis.

HOSANNA to the Son of David! Blessed is He that cometh in the name of the Lord. O King of Israel: Hosanna in the highest!

1962 • Two alternatives are allowed: (A) The branches are blessed and then distributed to the faithful at the Communion rail; (B) The faithful bring the branches with them into the church—or receive them upon entering the church—and hold them in their hands during the blessing. In either case, the branches must be distributed to the clergy and the servers after the blessing. The branches are prepared on a table which is covered with a white cloth—except for those branches the faithful are holding in their hands (if "Option B" is chosen). The Celebrant stands behind the table, facing the people, and chants without inflection:

℣. Dóminus vobíscum.

℟. Et cum spíritu tuo.

℣. Orémus.

℣. The Lord be with you.

℟. And with thy spirit.

℣. Let us pray.

Béne ✠ dic, quǽsumus, Dómine, hos palmárũ (*seu* "olivárum" *aut* "aliárum árborum") ramos: et præsta; ut, quod pópulus tuus in tui veneratiónẽ hodiérna die corporáliter agit, hoc spirituáliter summa devotióne perfíciat, de hoste victóriam reportándo et opus misericórdiæ summópere diligéndo. Per Dóminum. ℟. Amen.

BLESS ✠, we beseech thee, O Lord, these branches of palms (*or* "olives" *or* "other trees"), and grant that the bodily service with which thy people honor Thee today may be perfected in their souls by deep devotion to God, by victory over the enemy, and by ardent love for works of mercy. Through Christ our Lord. ℟. Amen.

Sprinkled & Censed • The Celebrant sprinkles the branches three times, first those on the table, afterwards—if "Option B" has been chosen—the branches which the faithful hold in their hands. (He sprinkles the branches either at the entrance of the Sanctuary, or, if he prefers, while walking through the body of the church.) Next the Celebrant places incense in the thurible in the usual way and incenses the blessed branches three times. First he incenses those on the table, afterwards—if "Option B" has been chosen—the branches of the faithful, either while he stands at the entrance to the Sanctuary, or while he walks through the body of the church. When "Option B" is used, some choirs prefer to sing the two antiphons (*Púeri Hebræórum*) at this time, rather than having the priest walking up and down the church—sprinkling and incensing—in complete silence.

II. DISTRIBUTION OF PALM BRANCHES

1962 • The distribution of branches then takes place in accordance with local custom. The Celebrant stands at the Altar, facing the people. First he gives the blessed branches to all the clergy in order, next to the servers, and finally, at the edge of the Sanctuary area, to the faithful. When the Celebrant begins to distribute the branches, the antiphons and psalms are chanted:

FIRST ANTIPHON. *John 12: 13 & Mark 11: 9 with Psalm 23*

THE CHILDREN of the Hebrews, carrying olive branches, went forth to meet the Lord, crying aloud and repeating: Hosanna in the highest.

Púeri Hebræórum, portántes ramos olivárum, obviavérunt Dómino, clamántes, et dicéntes: Hosánna in excélsis. [*The following may also be sung using the Pius XII Psalter.*]

1. The earth is the Lord's and the fullness thereof: the world and all they that dwell therein. | 2. For he hath founded it upon the seas; and hath prepared it upon the rivers. ℟. *The children...*

1. Dómini est terra, et plenitúdo ejus: orbis terrárum et univérsi qui hábitant in eo. | 2. Quia ipse super mária fundávit eum: et super flúmina præparávit eum. ℟.

7. Lift up your gates, O ye princes, and be ye lifted up, O eternal gates: and the King of Glory shall enter in. | 8. Who is this King of Glory? the Lord who is strong and mighty: the Lord mighty in battle. ℟. *The children...*

7. Attóllite portas, príncipes, vestras, et elevámini portæ æternáles: et introíbit Rex glóriæ. | 8. Quis est iste Rex glóriæ? Dóminus fortis et potens: Dñs potens in prœlio. ℟.

9. Lift up your gates, O ye princes, and be ye lifted up, O eternal gates: and the King of Glory shall enter in. | 10. Who is this King of Glory? the Lord of hosts, he is the King of Glory. ℟. *The children...*

9. Attóllite portas príncipes vestras, et elevámini portæ æternáles: et introíbit Rex glóriæ. | 10. Quis est iste Rex glóriæ? Dóminus virtútum ipse est Rex glóriæ. ℟.

11. Glory be to the Father, and to the Son, and to the Holy Ghost. | 12. As it was in the beginning, is now, and ever shall be, world without end. Amen. ℟. *The children...*

11. Glória Patri, et Fílio, et Spirítui Sancto. | 12. Sicut erat in princípio, et nunc, et semper, et in sǽcula sæculórum. Amen. ℟.

SECOND ANTIPHON. *Mt 21: 8-9 with Psalm 46*

THE CHILDREN of the Hebrews strewed their garments in the way and cried aloud, repeating: Hosanna to the Son of David: blessed is he that cometh in the name of the Lord.

Púeri Hebræórũ vestiménta prosternébant in via et clamábant, dicéntes: Hosánna fílio David: benedíctus, qui venit in nómine Dómini. [*The following may also be sung using the Pius XII Psalter.*]

1. O clap your hands, all ye nations: shout unto God with the voice of joy. | 2. For the Lord is high, terrible: a great king over all the earth. ℟. *The children...*

1. Omnes Gentes, pláudite mánibus: jubiláte Deo in voce exsultatiónis. 2. Quóniam Dñs excélsus, terríbilis: Rex magnus super omnem terram. ℟.

3. He hath subdued the people under us; and the nations under our feet. | 4. He hath chosen for us his inheritance, the beauty of Jacob which he hath loved. ℟. *The children...*

3. Subjécit pópulos nobis: et Gentes sub pédibus nostris. | 4. Elégit nobis hereditátẽ suã: spéciem Jacob, quam diléxit. ℟.

5. Ascéndit Deus in júbilo: et Dñs in voce tubæ. | 6. Psállite Deo nostro, psállite: psállite Regi nostro, psállite. ℟.

5. God is ascended with jubilee, and the Lord with the sound of trumpet. | 6. Sing praises to our God, sing ye: sing praises to our king, sing ye. ℟. *The children...*

7. Quóniam Rex omnis terræ Deus: psállite sapiénter. | 8. Regnábit Deus super Gentes: Deus sedet super sedem sanctam suam. ℟.

7. For God is the king of all the earth: sing ye wisely. 8. God shall reign over the nations: God sitteth on his holy throne. ℟. *The children...*

9. Príncipes populórum congregáti sunt cũ Deo Ábrahã: quóniam dii fortes terræ veheménter eleváti sunt. ℟.

9. The princes of the people are gathered together, with the God of Abraham: for the strong gods of the earth are exceedingly exalted. ℟. *The children...*

10. Glória Patri, et Fílio, et Spirítui Sancto. | 11. Sicut erat in princípio, et nunc, et semper, et in sæcula sæculórum. Amen. ℟.

10. Glory be to the Father, and to the Son, and to the Holy Ghost. | 11. As it was in the beginning, is now, and ever shall be, world without end. Amen. ℟. *The children...*

1962 • If these psalms be insufficient, let them be repeated until the end of the distribution of the branches. If the distribution is completed first, the psalm is closed with the *Glória Patri*, and the antiphon is repeated.

III. READING OF THE GOSPEL

1962 • After the distribution of the branches has been completed and the table removed, the Celebrant—saying nothing—washes his hands. Then he goes up to the Altar, kisses it in the center, and places incense in the thurible in the usual way. The Deacon brings the EVANGELIARIUM to the Altar and places it there. Everything is done as at Mass when the Gospel is to be chanted. The priest does not quietly duplicate the Gospel reading "since it is to be chanted by the Deacon" {McManus p66}. [The *Code of Rubrics* (1961) says (§473): "In sung Masses, all that the Deacon, or Subdeacon, or Lector sing or read by virtue of their office is omitted by the Celebrant."]

GOSPEL. *Matt 21: 1-9*

In illo témpore: Cum appropinquásset Jesus Jerosólymis, et venísset Béthphage ad montem Olivéti: tunc misit duos discípulos suos, dicens eis: Ite in castéllum, quod contra vos est, et statim inveniétis ásinam alligátam et pullum cum ea: sólvite et addúcite mihi: et si quis vobis áliquid díxerit, dícite, quia Dóminus his opus habet, et conféstim dimíttet eos. Hoc autem totum factum est, ut adimplerétur, quod dictũ est per Prophétã, dicéntẽ: Dícite fíliæ Sion: Ecce, Rex tuus venit tibi mansuétus, sedens super ásinã et pullum, fílium subjugális.

AT THAT TIME, when Jesus drew nigh to Jerusalem, and was come to Bethphage, unto Mount Olivet, then He sent two disciples, saying to them: Go ye into the village that is over against you, and immediately you shall find an ass tied, and a colt with her; loose them and bring them to Me; and if any man shall say anything to you, say ye that the Lord hath need of them; and forthwith he will let them go. Now all this was done that it might be fulfilled which was spoken by the prophet, saying: Tell ye the daughter of Sion: Behold thy King cometh to thee meek, and sitting upon an ass, and a colt the foal of her that is used to the yoke.

Eúntes autem discípuli, fecérunt, sicut præcépit illis Jesus. Et adduxérunt ásinam et pullum: et imposuérunt super eos vestiménta sua, et eum désuper sedére tecérunt. Plúrima autẽ turba stravérunt vestiménta sua in via:

And the disciples going did as Jesus commanded them. And they brought the ass and the colt, and laid their garments upon them, and made Him sit thereon. And a very great multitude spread their garments in the way, and others cut boughs from the trees and strewed them in the way, and the multitudes that went before and that followed cried, saying: Hosanna to the Son of David; Blessèd is He that cometh in the Name of the Lord.

álii autẽ cædébant ramos de arbóribus, et sternébant in via: turbæ autem, quæ præcedébant et quæ sequebántur, clamábant, dicéntes: Hosánna fílio David: benedíctus, qui venit in nómine Dñi.

1962 • After the Gospel the Subdeacon takes the book to the Celebrant who kisses it. The Celebrant is not incensed by the Deacon.

IV. PROCESSION WITH BLESSED PALMS

1962 • The Celebrant places incense in the thurible in the usual way. Then the Deacon, turning to the people, sings "Procedámus in pace" to which all present respond "Amen."

Let us go forth in peace. In the name of Christ. Amen.

1962 • During the procession, all or some of the following antiphons may be sung. Moreover, the 1956 *Ordo Hebdomadae Sanctae Instauratus* says the faithful may chant the hymn "Christus vincit" or other hymns in honor of Christ the King (*Nihil impedit, quominus cantetur a fidelibus hymnus "Christus vincit," vel alius cantus in honorem Christi Regis*). For additional antiphons in Latin, cf. the monastic version of the *Ordo Hebdomadæ Sanctæ* (Desclée, 1961) pages 38-43. For hymns in English to Christ the King, cf. *The Saint Jean de Brébeuf Hymnal* (Sophia Press Institute, 2018).

FIRST ANTIPHON.

THE MULTITUDE goeth forth to meet our Redeemer with flowers and palms, and payeth the homage due to a triumphant conqueror: the Gentiles proclaim the Son of God; and their voices thunder through the skies in praise of Christ: Hosanna!

Occúrrunt turbæ cum flóribus et palmis Redemptóri óbviam: et victóri triumphánti digna dant obséquia: Fílium Dei ore gentes prædicant: et in laudem Christi voces tonant per núbila: Hosánna.

* *The text in the 1950 version includes the words "in excélsis," whereas the ancient manuscripts never do.*

SECOND ANTIPHON.

LET THE FAITHFUL join with the angels and children, singing to the conqueror of death: Hosanna in the highest!

Cum ángelis et púeris fidéles inveniámur, triumphatóri mortis clamántes: Hosánna in excélsis.

THIRD ANTIPHON.

A GREAT MULTITUDE that was met together at the festival cried out to the Lord: Blessèd is He that cometh in the name of the Lord: Hosanna in the highest!

Turba multa, quæ convénerat ad diem festum, clamábat Dómino: Benedíctus, qui venit in nómine Dómini: Hosánna in excélsis.

FOURTH ANTIPHON.

Cœpérunt omnes turbæ descendéntium gaudéntes laudáre Deum voce magna, super ómnibus quas víderant virtútibus, dicéntes: Benedíctus qui venit Rex in nómine Dómini; pax in terra et glória in excélsis.

NEAR THE DESCENT the whole multitude began with joy to praise God with a loud voice for all the mighty works they had seen, saying: Blessèd be the king who cometh in the name of the Lord; peace on earth and glory on high.

HYMN TO CHRIST THE KING. *Saint Theodulf, Bishop of Orleans (d. 821AD)*

℟. Glory, praise, and honor be to You, Christ, king and redeemer. Long ago children in their winning way raised the loving cry "Hosanna."

[*English Translation by Father Joseph Connelly;* Imprimatur 10 December 1954, *Archbishop of Birmingham.*]

All present repeat the refrain:

℟. Glória, laus, et honor, tibi sit Rex Christe Redémptor: Cui pueríle decus prompsit Hosánna pium.

GLORY, PRAISE, AND HONOR be to You, Christ, king and redeemer. Long ago children in their winning way raised the loving cry "Hosanna."

1. Ísraël es tu Rex, Davídis et ínclita proles: Nómine qui in Dómini Rex benedícte venis. ℟. Glória, laus.

1. You are Israel's king and David's glorious son; You come, king most blessed, in the Lord's name.

℟. Glory, praise and honour…

2. Cœtus in excélsis te laudat cælicus omnis, Et mortális homo, et cuncta creáta simul. ℟. Glória, laus.

2. The whole of heaven's assembly on high, mortal man and all created things, united, praise You.

℟. Glory, praise and honour…

3. Plebs Hebrǽa tibi cum palmis óbvia venit: Cum prece, voto, hymnis, ádsumus ecce tibi. ℟. Glória, laus.

3. The Jewish people came to meet You with palm branches; now we are here before You with our prayers and hymns.

℟. Glory, praise and honour…

4. They made their offering of praise to You on the eve of Your passion; we sing our joyful hymn to You now rejoicing in heaven.

℟. Glory, praise and honour...

4. Hi tibi passúro solvébant múnia laudis: Nos tibi regnánti pángimus ecce melos. ℟. Glória, laus.

5. They pleased You then; may our devotion please You now. Good king, merciful king, all that is good pleases You.

℟. Glory, praise and honour...

5. Hi placuére tibi, pláceat devótio nostra: Rex bone, Rex clemens, cui bona cuncta placent. ℟. Glória, laus.

FIFTH ANTIPHON. *With Psalm 147.*

ALL PRAISE Thy name highly and say: Blessèd is He who cometh in the name of the Lord: Hosanna in the highest.

Omnes colláudant nomen tuum et dicunt: Benedíctus qui venit in nómine Dómini: Hosánna in excélsis.

1. Praise the Lord, O Jerusalem: *
praise thy God, O Sion.

1. Lauda, Jerúsalem, Dóminum: *
lauda Deum tuum, Sion.

2. Because He hath strengthened the bolts of thy gates: * He hath blessed thy children within thee.

2. Quod firmávit seras portárum tuárum: * benedíxit fíliis tuis in te.

3. Who hath placed peace in thy borders: *
and filleth thee with the fat of corn.

3. Compósuit fines tuos in pace: *
medúlla trítici sátiat te.

4. Who sendeth forth His speech to the earth: *
His word runneth swiftly.

4. Emíttit elóquiũ suũ in terram: *
velóciter currit verbum ejus.

5. Who giveth snow like wool: *
scattereth frost like ashes.

5. Dat nivem sicut lanam: *
pruínam sicut cínerem spargit.

6. He sendeth his crystal like morsels: *
Who shall stand before the face of his cold?

6. Prójicit gláciẽ suã ut frústula panis:
* coram frígore ejus aquæ rigéscunt.

7. He shall send out his word, and shall melt them: *
His wind shall blow, and the waters shall run.

7. Emíttit verbũ suũ et liquefácit eas:
* flare jubet ventũ suũ et fluunt aquæ.

8. Who declareth his word to Jacob: *
His justices and His judgments to Israel.

8. Annuntiávit verbũ suũ Jacob: *
statúta et præcépta sua Ísraël.

9. He hath not done in like manner to every nation: *
and His judgments He hath not made manifest to them.

9. Non fecit ita ulli natióni: *
præcépta sua non manifestávit eis.

10. Glory be to the Father, and to the Son, *
and to the Holy Ghost.

10. Glória Patri, et Fílio, *
et Spirítui Sancto.

11. As it was in the beginning, is now, and ever shall be, * world without end. Amen.

11. Sicut erat in princípio, et nunc, et semper, * et in sǽcula sæculórum. Amen.

ALL PRAISE Thy name highly and say: Blessèd is He who cometh in the name of the Lord: Hosanna in the highest.

Omnes colláudant nomen tuum et dicunt: Benedíctus qui venit in nómine Dómini: Hosánna in excélsis.

SIXTH ANTIPHON.

Fulgéntibus palmis prostérnimur adveniénti Dómino; huic omnes occurrámus cum hymnis et cánticis, glorificántes et dicéntes: Benedíctus Dñs!

WE ARE STREWN with the shining palms before the Lord as He approacheth; let us all run to meet Him with hymns and songs, glorify Him and say: Blessèd be the Lord!

SEVENTH ANTIPHON.

Ave, Rex noster, Fili David, Redémptor mundi, quem prophétæ prædixérunt Salvatórẽ dómui Ísraël esse ventúrum. Te enim ad salutárẽ víctimam Pater misit in mundũ, quem exspectábant omnes sancti ab orígine mundi, et nunc: Hosánna Fílio David. Benedíctus qui venit in nómine Dómini. Hosánna in excélsis.

HAIL, our King, O Son of David, O world's Redeemer, whom prophets did foretell as the Savior to come of the house of Israel. For the Father sent Thee into the world as victim for salvation; from the beginning of the world all the saints awaited Thee: Hosanna now to the Son of David! Blessèd be He who cometh in the name of the Lord. Hosanna in the highest.

V. UPON ENTERING THE CHURCH

1962 • When the Celebrant passes through the church door, the following Responsory is begun:

RESPONSORY. *cf. John 12*

Ingrediénte Dómino in sanctam civitátem, Hebræórum púeri resurrectiónem vitæ pronuntiántes, * **Cum ramis** palmárum: Hosánna, clamábant, in excélsis. ℣. Cum audísset pópulus, quod Jesus veníret Jerosólymam, exiérunt óbviam ei. * **Cum ramis...**

(*Et non dicitur Glória Patri.*)

WHEN OUR LORD ENTERED the holy city, the Hebrew children, declaring the resurrection of life, * **With palm branches,** cried out: Hosanna in the highest. ℣. When the people heard that Jesus was coming to Jerusalem, they went forth to meet Him: * **With palm branches,** cried out: Hosanna in the highest.

1962 • When the Celebrant comes to the Altar, he makes the required reverence and goes up to the Altar with the sacred ministers. Standing between them and facing the people, the Celebrant chants the prayer to complete the procession, using the ferial tone, with his hands joined.

℣. Dóminus vobíscum.

℟. Et cum spíritu tuo.

℣. The Lord be with you.

℟. And with thy spirit.

Orémus.

Dómine Jesu Christe, Rex ac Redémptor noster, in cujus honórẽ, hos ramos gestántes, solémnes laudes decantávimus: concéde propítius: ut, quocúmque hi rami deportáti fúerint, ibi tuæ benedictiónis grátia descéndat, et, quavis dǽmonũ iniquitáte vel illusióne profligáta, déxtera tua prótegat, quos redémit. Qui vivis.

Let us pray.

O LORD Jesus Christ, our King and Redeemer, in whose honor we have borne these palms and gone on praising Thee with song and solemnity: mercifully grant that whithersoever these palms are taken, there the grace of Thy blessing may descend; may every wickedness and trick of the demons be frustrated; and may Thy right hand protect those it hath redeemed. Who livest.

[Editor's Note: The complete Prayers at the Foot of the Altar are omitted in the 1962 Palm Sunday according to §424c of *Rubricarum Instructum* (25 July 1960), whereas the 1950 version only omits Psalm 42 ("Júdica me"). Also, in the 1962 version of Palm Sunday, the people do not hold palm branches during the Passion.]

VI. THE PALM SUNDAY MASS

Station at Saint John Lateran ("Our Savior's Church")

1962 • The concluding prayer of the procession having been sung, the Celebrant exchanges red vestments for violet. All the prayers to be said at the foot of the Altar are omitted, as well as the prayers "Aufer a nobis" and "Orámus te, Dómine." The Celebrant goes up to the altar immediately, kisses it in the center, and incenses it in the usual way. The Introit begins at once, and the Celebrant will most likely sit at the Sedilia while the "Kýrie Eléison" is being sung.

INTROIT. *Ps 21: 20, 22*

LORD, remove not Thy help to a distance from me, look toward my defense; deliver me from the lion's mouth, and my lowness from the horns of the unicorns. (Ps 21: 2) O God, my God, look upon me: why hast Thou forsaken me? Far from my salvation are the words of my sins. *O Lord, remove not…*

Dómine, ne longe fácias auxílium tuum a me: ad defensiónem meam áspice: líbera me de ore leónis, et a córnibus unicórnium humilitátem meam. ℣. Deus, Deus meus, réspice in me: quare me dereliquísti? longe a salúte mea verba delictórum meórum. *Dómine, ne longe…*

COLLECT.

Almighty and eternal God, Who, in order to give mankind an example of humility, didst will that our Savior should assume our flesh and suffer on the cross; grant in Thy mercy that we be found worthy of the heritage of His patience and the fellowship of His resurrection. Through the same.

Omnípotens sempitérne Deus, qui humáno géneri, ad imitándum humilitátis exémplum, Salvatórem nostrum carnem súmere, et crucem subíre fecísti: concéde propítius; ut et patiéntiæ ipsíus habére documénta, et resurrectiónis consórtia mereámur. Per eúmdem Dóminum nostrum.

EPISTLE. *Phil 2: 5-11*

BRETHREN, Let this mind be in you, which was also in Christ Jesus; Who being in the form of God, thought it not robbery to be equal with God; but made Himself as nothing, taking the form of a servant, being made in the likeness of men, and in habit found as a man. He humbled Himself, becoming obedient unto death, even the death of the cross. For which cause God also hath exalted Him, and hath given Him a name which is above all names: (*Here all genuflect.*) that in the name of Jesus every knee should bow, of those that are in heaven, on earth, and under the earth: and that every tongue should confess that the Lord Jesus Christ is in the glory of God the Father.

Fratres: Hoc enim sentíte in vobis, quod et in Christo Jesu: qui cum in forma Dei esset, non rapínam arbitrátus est esse se æquálem Deo: sed semetípsum exinanívit formam servi accípiens, in similitúdinem hóminum factus, et hábitu invéntus ut homo. Humiliávit semetípsum factus obédiens usque ad mortem, mortem autem crucis. Propter quod et Deus exaltávit illum: et donávit illi nomen, quod est super omne nomen: (*hic genuflectitur*) ut in nómine Jesu omne genu flectátur cæléstium, terréstrium et infernórum, et omnis lingua confiteátur, quia Dóminus Jesus Christus in glória est Dei Patris.

GRADUAL. *Ps 72: 24, 1-3*

Tenuísti manum déxteram meam: et in voluntáte tua deduxísti me: et cum glória assumpsísti me. ℣. Quam bonus Ísraël Deus rectis corde! mei autem pene moti sunt pedes: pene effúsi sunt gressus mei: quia zelávi in peccatóribus, pacem peccatórum videns.

THOU hast held me in Thy right hand, and by Thy will Thou hast conducted me; and with glory Thou hast assumed me. ℣. How good is God to Israel, to them that are of a right heart! But my feet were almost moved, my steps had well nigh slipped; because I had a zeal on occasion of sinners, seeing the peace of sinners.

TRACT. *Ps 21: 2-9, 18, 19, 22, 24, 32*

Deus, Deus meus, réspice in me: quare me dereliquísti? 2. Longe a salúte mea verba delictórum meórum. 3. Deus meus, clamábo per diem, nec exáudies: in nocte, et non ad insipiéntiam mihi. 4. Tu autem in sancto hábitas, laus Ísraël. 5. In te speravérunt patres nostri: speravérunt, et liberásti eos. 6. Ad te clamavérunt, et salvi facti sunt: in te speravérunt, et non sunt confúsi. 7. Ego autem sum vermis, et non homo: oppróbrium hóminum et abjéctio plebis. 8. Omnes, qui vidébant me, aspernabántur me: locúti sunt lábiis et movérunt caput. 9. Sperávit in Dómino, erípiat eum: salvum fáciat eum, quóniam vult eum. 10. Ipsi vero consideravérunt et conspexérunt me: divisérunt sibi vestiménta mea, et super vestem meam misérunt sortem. 11. Líbera me de ore leónis: et a córnibus unicórnium humilitátem meam. 12. Qui timétis Dóminum, laudáte eum: univérsum semen Jacob, magnificáte eum. 13. Annuntiábitur Dómino generátio ventúra: et annuntiábunt cæli justítiam ejus. 14. Pópulo, qui nascétur, quem fecit Dóminus.

O GOD, my God, look upon me: why hast Thou forsaken me? 2 Far from my salvation are the words of my sins. 3 O my God, I shall cry by day, and Thou wilt not hear: and by night, and it shall not be reputed as folly in me. 4 But Thou dwellest in the holy place, the praise of Israel. 5 In Thee have our fathers hoped: they have hoped, and Thou hast delivered them. 6 They cried to Thee, and they were saved: they trusted in Thee, and were not confounded. 7 But I am a worm and no man: the reproach of men, and the outcast of the people. 8 All they that saw Me have laughed Me to scorn: they have spoken with the lips, and wagged the head. 9 He hoped in the Lord, let Him deliver Him: let Him save Him, seeing He delighteth in Him. 10 But they have looked and stared upon Me: they parted My garments amongst them, and upon my vesture they cast lots. 11 Deliver me from the lion's mouth: and my lowness from the horns of the unicorns. 12 Ye that fear the Lord, praise Him: all ye the seed of Jacob, glorify Him. 13 There shall be declared to the Lord a generation to come: and the heavens shall show forth His justice. 14 To a people that shall be born, which the Lord hath made.

Matt 26: 36-75; 27: 1-60

[C] *Chronista;*

[S] *Synagoga;*

✠ *Christus.*

English translation (1950) by Monsignor Ronald Knox.

THE PASSION OF OUR LORD JESUS CHRIST

ACCORDING TO SAINT MATTHEW.

Pássio Dómini nostri Jesu Christi secúndum Matthǽum. In illo témpore:

Jesus came—and they with him—to a plot of land called Gethsemani; and he said
venit Jesus cum illis in villam, quæ dícitur Gethsémani, et dixit

to his disciples: ✠ Sit down here, while I go in there and pray. [C] But he took
discípulis suis: Sedéte hic, donec vadam illuc et orem.

Peter and the sons of Zebedee with him. And now he grew sorrowful and dismayed,
Et assúmpto Petro et duóbus fíliis Zebedǽi, cœpit contristári et mæstus esse.

and said: ✠ My soul is ready to die with sorrow; do you abide here, and watch with
Tunc ait illis: Tristis est ánima mea usque ad mortem: sustinéte hic, et vigiláte mecum.

me. [C] When he had gone a little further, he fell upon his face in prayer, and said,
Et progréssus pusíllum, prócidit in fáciem suam, orans, et dicens:

✠ My Father, if it is possible, let this chalice pass me by; only as thy will is, not
Pater mi, si possíbile est, tránseat a me calix iste. Verúmtamen non sicut ego volo,

as mine is. [C] Then he went back to his disciples, to find them asleep; and he
sed sicut tu. Et venit ad discípulos suos, et invénit eos dormiéntes:

said to Peter, ✠ Had you no strength, then, to watch with me even for an hour?
et dicit Petro: Sic non potuístis una hora vigiláre mecum?

Watch and pray, that you may not enter into temptation; the spirit is willing enough,
Vigiláte, et oráte, ut non intrétis in tentatiónem. Spíritus quidem promptus est,

but the flesh is weak. [C] Then he went back again, and prayed a second time; and
caro autem infírma. Íterum secúndo ábiit et orávit,

his prayer was: ✠ My Father, if this chalice may not pass me by, but I must drink
dicens: Pater mi, si non potest hic calix transíre, nisi bibam illum,

it, then thy will be done. [C] And once more he found his disciples asleep when he
fiat volúntas tua. Et venit íterum, et invénit eos dormiéntes:

came to them, so heavy their eyelids were; this time he went away without disturbing
erant enim óculi eórum graváti. Et relíctis illis, íterum ábiit

them, and made his third prayer, using the same words. After that he returned to his
et orávit tértio, eúndem sermónem dicens. Tunc venit ad discípulos suos,

disciples, and said to them, ✠ Sleep and take your rest hereafter; as I speak, the
et dicit illis: Dormíte jam, et requiéscite:

time draws near when the Son of Man is to be betrayed into the hands of sinners.
ecce, appropinquávit hora, et Fílius hóminis tradétur in manus peccatórum.

Rise up, let us go on our way; already, he that is to betray me is close at hand.
Súrgite, eámus: ecce, appropinquávit, qui me tradet.

Kiss of Betrayal

[C] And all at once, while he was speaking, Judas, who was one of the twelve,
Adhuc eo loquénte, ecce Judas unus de duódecim venit,

came near; with him was a great multitude carrying swords and clubs, who had
et cum eo turba multa cum gládiis et fústibus,

been sent by the chief priests and the elders of the people. The traitor had appointed
missi a princípibus sacerdótum et senióribus pópuli. Qui autem trádidit eum, dedit

them a signal, saying: [S] It is none other than the man whom I shall greet with a
illis signum, dicens: Quemcúmque osculátus fúero, ipse est,

kiss; hold him fast. [C] No sooner, then, had he come near to Jesus than he said:
tenéte eum. Et conféstim accédens ad Jesum, dixit:

[S] Hail, Master, [C] and kissed him. Jesus said to him: ✠ My friend, on what
Ave, Rabbi. Et osculátus est eum. Dixítque illi Jesus: Amíce, ad quid venísti?

errand hast thou come? [C] Then they came forward and laid their hands on Jesus,
Tunc accessérunt, et manus injecérunt in Jesum,

and held him fast. And at that, one of those who were with Jesus lifted a hand
et tenuérunt eum. Et ecce unus ex his, qui erant cum Jesu, exténdens manum,

to draw his sword, and smote one of the high priest's servants with it, cutting
exémit gládium suum, et percútiens servum príncipis sacerdótum, amputávit aurículam ejus.

off his ear. Whereupon Jesus said to him, ✠ Put thy sword back into its place;
Tunc ait illi Jesus: Convérte gládium tuum in locum suum.

all those who take up the sword will perish by the sword. Dost thou doubt that if
Omnes enim, qui accéperint gládium, gládio períbunt. An putas, quia non possum

I call upon my Father, even now, he will send more than twelve legions of angels
rogáre Patrem meum, et exhibébit mihi modo plus quam duódecim legiónes Angelórum?

to my side? But how, were it so, should the scriptures be fulfilled, which have
Quómodo ergo implebúntur Scriptúræ,

prophesied that all must be as it is? [C] And Jesus said to the multitude at that
quia sic opórtet fíeri? In illa hora dixit Jesus turbis:

hour: ✠ You have come out to my arrest with swords and clubs, as if I were a
Tamquam ad latrónem exístis cum gládiis et fústibus comprehéndere me:

robber; and yet I used to sit teaching in the temple close to you, day after day,
quotídie apud vos sedébam docens in templo,

and you never laid hands on me. [C] All this was so ordained, to fulfil what
et non me tenuístis. Hoc autem totum factum est, ut adimpleréntur

was written by the prophets. And now all his disciples abandoned him, and fled.
Scripturæ prophetárum. Tunc discípuli omnes, relícto eo, fugérunt.

Before Caiphas

[C] And those who had arrested Jesus led him away into the presence of the high
At illi tenéntes Jesum, duxérunt ad Cáïpham príncipem sacerdótum,

priest, Caiphas, where the scribes and the elders had assembled. Yet Peter followed
ubi scribæ, et senióres convénerant. Petrus autem sequebátur

him at a long distance, as far as the high priest's palace; where he went in and
eum a longe, usque in átrium príncipis sacerdótum. Et ingréssus intro,

sat among the servants, to see the end. The chief priests and elders and all the
sedébat cum minístris ut vidéret finem. Príncipes autem sacerdótum, et omne concílium,

Council tried to find false testimony against Jesus, such as would compass his
quærébant falsum testimónium contra Jesum, ut eum morti tráderent:

death. But they could find none, although many came forward falsely accusing
et non invenérunt, cum multi falsi testes accessíssent.

him; until at last two false accusers came forward who declared: [S] This man
Novíssime autem venérunt duo falsi testes, et dixérunt: Hic dixit:

said, I have power to destroy the temple of God and raise it again in three days.
Possum destrúere templum Dei, et post tríduum reædificáre illud.

[C] Then the high priest stood up, and asked him: [S] Hast thou no answer
Et surgens princeps sacerdótum, ait illi: Nihil respóndes ad ea,

to make to the accusations these men bring against thee? [C] Jesus was silent;
quæ isti advérsum te testificántur? Jesus autem tacébat.

and the high priest said to him openly: [S] I adjure thee by the living God to tell
Et princeps sacerdótum ait illi: Adjúro te per Deum vivum, ut dicas

us whether thou art the Christ, the Son of God? [C] Jesus answered: ✠ Thy own
nobis, si tu es Christus Fílius Dei. Dicit illi Jesus: Tu dixísti.

lips have said it. And moreover I tell you this; you will see the Son of Man again,
Verúmtamen dico vobis, ámodo vidébitis Fílium hóminis

when he is seated at the right hand of God's power, and comes on the clouds
sedéntem a dextris virtútis Dei, et veniéntem in núbibus cæli.

of heaven. [C] At this, the high priest tore his garments, and said: [S] He has
Tunc princeps sacerdótum scidit vestiménta sua, dicens:

blasphemed; what further need have we of witnesses? Mark well, you have heard
Blasphemávit: quid adhuc egémus téstibus? Ecce nunc audístis blasphémiam:

his blasphemy for yourselves. What is your finding? [C] And they answered:
quid vobis vidétur? At illi respondéntes, dixérunt:

[S] The penalty is death. [C] Then they fell to spitting upon his face and buffeting
Reus est mortis. Tunc exspuérunt in fáciem ejus, et cólaphis eum

him and smiting him on the cheek, saying as they did so: [S] Show thyself a
cecidérunt, álii autem palmas in fáciem ejus dedérunt, dicéntes: Prophetíza nobis,

prophet, Christ; tell us who it is that smote thee.
Christe, quis est qui te percússit?

Saint Peter's Denial

[C] Meanwhile, Peter sat in the court without; and there a maidservant came up
Petrus vero sedébat foris in átrio: et accéssit ad eum una ancílla,

to him, and said: [S] Thou too wast with Jesus the Galilean. [C] Whereupon he
dicens: Et tu cum Jesu Galilǽo eras. At ille

denied it before all the company: [S] I do not know what thou meanest. [C] And
negávit coram ómnibus, dicens: Néscio quid dicis.

he went out into the porch, where a second maidservant saw him, and said, to the
Exeúnte autem illo jánuam, vidit eum ália ancílla, et ait his,

bystanders: [S] This man, too, was with Jesus the Nazarene. [C] And he made
qui erant ibi: Et hic erat cum Jesu Nazaréno.

denial again with an oath: I know nothing of the man. But those who stood there
Et íterum negávit cum juraménto: Quia non novi hóminem.

came up to Peter soon afterwards, and said: [S] It is certain that thou art one of
Et post pusíllum accessérunt qui stabant, et dixérunt Petro: Vere et tu ex illis es:

them; even thy speech betrays thee. [C] And with that he fell to calling down
nam et loquéla tua maniféstum te facit. Tunc cœpit detestári,

curses on himself and swearing he knew nothing of the man; and thereupon the
et juráre quia non novísset hóminem. Et contínuo

cock crew. Then Peter remembered the word of Jesus, how he had said, Before
gallus cantávit. Et recordátus est Petrus verbi Jesu, quod díxerat:

the cock crows, thou wilt thrice disown me; and he went out, and wept bitterly.
Priúsquam gallus cantet, ter me negábis. Et egréssus foras, flevit amáre.

JUDAS HANGS HIMSELF

[C] At day-break, all the chief priests and elders of the people laid their plans
Mane autem facto, consílium iniérunt omnes príncipes sacerdótum et senióres pópuli

for putting Jesus to death, and they led him away in bonds, and gave him up to
advérsus Jesum, ut eum morti tráderent. Et vinctum adduxérunt eum, et tradidérunt

the governor, Pontius Pilate. And now Judas, his betrayer, was full of remorse
Póntio Piláto prǽsidi. Tunc videns Judas, qui eum trádidit, quod damnátus esset, pœniténtia ductus,

at seeing him condemned, so that he brought back to the chief priests and elders
rétulit trigínta argénteos princípibus sacerdótum et senióribus,

their thirty pieces of silver, saying: [S] I have sinned in betraying the blood of an
dicens: Peccávi, tradens sánguinem justum.

innocent man. [C] They answered: [S] What is that to us? It concerns thee only.
At illi dixérunt: Quid ad nos? Tu víderis.

[C] Whereupon he left them, throwing down the pieces of silver there in the temple,
Et projéctis argénteis in templo, recéssit:

and went and hanged himself. The chief priests, thus recovering the money, said:
et ábiens, láqueo se suspéndit. Príncipes autem sacerdótum, accéptis argénteis, dixérunt:

[S] It must not be put in the treasury, since it is the price of blood; [C] and after
Non licet eos míttere in córbonam: quia prétium sánguinis est.

consultation, they used it to buy the potter's field, as a burial place for strangers;
Consílio autem ínito, emérunt ex illis agrum fíguli, in sepultúram peregrinórum.

it is upon that account that the field has been called Haceldama, the field of blood,
Propter hoc vocátus est ager ille Hacéldama, hoc est, ager sánguinis, usque in

to this day. And so the word was fulfilled which was spoken by the prophet Jeremy,
hodiérnum diem. Tunc implétum est, quod dictum est per Jeremíam Prophétam,

when he said, And they took the thirty pieces of silver, the price of one who was
dicéntem: Et accepérunt trigínta argénteos prétium appretiáti,

appraised, for men of the race of Israel appraised him, and bestowed them upon the
quem appretiavérunt a fíliis Ísraël: et dedérunt eos in

potter's field, as the Lord had bidden me.
agrum fíguli, sicut constítuit mihi Dóminus.

BEFORE PONTIUS PILATE

[C] But Jesus stood before the governor. And the governor asked him: [S] Art
Jesus autem stetit ante prǽsidem, et interrogávit eum præses, dicens:

thou the king of the Jews? [C] Jesus told him: ✠ Thy own lips have said it.
Tu es Rex Judæórum? Dicit illi Jesus: Tu dicis.

[C] And when the chief priests and elders brought their accusation against him, he
Et cum accusarétur a princípibus sacerdótum et senióribus,

made no answer. Then Pilate said to him: [S] Dost thou not hear all the testimony
nihil respóndit. Tunc dicit illi Pilátus: Non audis quanta advérsum te dicunt testimónia?

they bring against thee? [C] But Jesus would not answer any of their charges, so
Et non respóndit ei ad ullum verbum,

that the governor was full of astonishment.
ita ut mirarétur præses veheménter.

Pilate Offers A Choice

[C] At the festival, the governor used to grant to the multitude the liberty
Per diem autem solémnem consuéverat præses pópulo dimittere unum vinctum,

of any one prisoner they should choose; and there was one notable prisoner
quem voluissent. Habébat autem tunc vinctum insígnem,

then in custody, whose name was Barabbas; so, when they gathered about him,
qui dicebátur Barábbas. Congregátis ergo illis,

Pilate asked them: [S] Whom shall I release? Barabbas, or Jesus who is called
dixit Pilátus: Quem vultis dimíttam vobis: Barábbam, an Jesum, qui dícitur

Christ? [C] He knew well that they had only given him up out of malice, and
Christus? Sciébat enim quod per invídiam tradidíssent eum.

even as he sat on the judgement seat, his wife had sent him a message: [S] Do
Sedénte autem illo pro tribunáli, misit ad eum uxor ejus, dicens:

not meddle with this innocent man; I dreamed today that I suffered much on his
Nihil tibi et justo illi: multa enim passa sum hódie per visum propter eum.

account. [C] But the chief priests and elders had persuaded the multitude to
Príncipes autem sacerdótum et senióres persuasérunt pópulis,

ask for Barabbas and have Jesus put to death; and so, when the governor openly
ut péterent Barábbam, Jesum vero pérderent. Respóndens autem præses ait illis:

asked them: [S] Which of the two would you have me release? [C] they said:
Quem vultis vobis de duóbus dimítti? At illi dixérunt:

[S] Barabbas. [C] Pilate said to them: [S] What am I to do, then, with Jesus,
Barábbam. Dicit illis Pilátus: Quid ígitur fáciam de Jesu,

who is called Christ? [C] They said: [S] Let him be crucified. [C] And when
qui dícitur Christus? Dicunt omnes: Crucifigátur.

the governor said: [S] Why, what wrong has he done? [C] they cried louder than
Ait illis præses: Quid enim mali fecit? At illi magis clamábant, dicéntes:

ever: [S] Let him be crucified. [C] And so, finding that his good offices went
Crucifigátur. Videns autem Pilátus quia nihil profíceret,

for nothing, and the uproar only became worse, Pilate sent for water and washed
sed magis tumúltus fíeret: accépta aqua, lavit manus

his hands in full sight of the multitude, saying as he did so: [S] I have no part in
coram pópulo, dicens:

the death of this innocent man; it concerns you only. [C] And the whole people
Ínnocens ego sum a sánguine justi hujus: vos vidéritis. Et respóndens univérsus pópulus

answered: [S] His blood be upon us, and upon our children. [C] And with that he
dixit: Sanguis ejus super nos et super fílios nostros.

released Barabbas as they asked; Jesus he scourged, and gave him up to be crucified.
Tunc dimísit illis Barábbam: Jesum autem flagellátum trádidit eis, ut crucifigerétur.

CROWNING WITH THORNS

[C] After this, the governor's soldiers took Jesus into the palace, and gathered the
Tunc mílites prǽsidis suscipiéntes Jesum in prætórium, congregavérunt

whole of their company about him. First they stripped him, and arrayed him in a
ad eum univérsam cohórtem: et exuéntes eum, chlámydem coccíneam circumdedérunt ei,

scarlet cloak; then they put on his head a crown which they had woven out of thorns,
et plecténtes corónam de spinis, posuérunt super caput ejus,

and a rod in his right hand, and mocked him by kneeling down before him, and
et arúndinem in déxtera ejus. Et genu flexo ante eum, illudébant ei,

saying: [S] Hail, king of the Jews. [C] And they spat upon him, and took the rod
dicéntes: Ave Rex Judæórum. Et exspuéntes in eum, accepérunt arúndinem,

from him and beat him over the head with it. At last they had done with mockery;
et percutiébant caput ejus. Et postquam illusérunt ei,

stripping him of the scarlet cloak, they put his own garments on him, and led him
exuérunt eum chlámyde, et induérunt eum vestiméntis ejus, et duxérunt eum

away to be crucified.
ut crucifígerent.

GOLGOTHA, WHERE JESUS IS MOCKED

[C] As for his cross, they forced a man of Cyrene, Simon by name, whom they
Exeúntes autem invenérunt hóminem Cyrenǽum, nómine Simónem: hunc angariavérunt ut tólleret crucem ejus.

met on their way out, to carry it; and so they reached a place called Golgotha, that
Et venérunt in locum, qui dícitur Gólgotha, quod

is, the place named after a skull. Here they offered him wine, mixed with gall,
est Calváriæ locus. Et dedérunt ei vinum bíbere cum felle mixtum.

which he tasted, but would not drink, and then crucified him, dividing his garments
Et cum gustásset, nóluit bíbere. Postquam autem crucifixérunt eum, divisérunt vestiménta

among them by casting lots. The prophecy must be fulfilled: They divide my spoils
ejus, sortem mitténtes: ut implerétur quod dictum est per Prophétam dicéntem: Divisérunt sibi vestiménta mea,

among them, cast lots for my garments. There, then, they sat, keeping guard over
et super vestem meam misérunt sortem. Et sedéntes servábant eum.

him. Over his head they set a written proclamation of his offence, THIS IS JESUS,
Et imposuérunt super caput ejus causam ipsíus scriptam: Hic est Jesus

THE KING OF THE JEWS; and with him they crucified two thieves, one on his right
Rex Judæórum. Tunc crucifíxi sunt cum eo duo latrónes: unus a dextris

and one on his left. The passers-by blasphemed against him, tossing their heads,
et unus a sinístris. Prætereúntes autem blasphemábant eum movéntes cápita sua,

saying: [S] Come now, thou who wouldst destroy the temple and build it up in
et dicéntes: Vah, qui déstruis templum Dei et in tríduo illud reædíficas:

three days, rescue thyself; come down from that cross, if thou art the Son of God.
salva temetípsum: Si Fílius Dei es, descénde de cruce.

[C] The chief priests, with the scribes and elders, mocked him in the same way:
Simíliter et príncipes sacerdótum illudéntes cum Scribis et senióribus dicébant:

[S] He saved others; himself he cannot save. If he is the king of Israel, he has but
Álios salvos fecit, seípsum non potest salvum fácere: si Rex Ísraël est,

to come down from the cross, here and now, and we will believe in him. He trusted
descéndat nunc de cruce, et crédimus ei: confídit

in God; let God, if he favours him, succour him now; he told us, I am the Son of
in Deo: líberet nunc, si vult eum: dixit enim: Quia Fílius Dei sum.

God. [C] Even the thieves who were crucified with him uttered the same taunts.
Idípsum autem et latrónes, qui crucifíxi erant cum eo, improperábant ei.

Christ Dies On The Cross

[C] From the sixth hour onwards there was darkness over all the earth until the
A sexta autem hora ténebræ factæ sunt super univérsam terram usque ad

ninth hour; and about the ninth hour Jesus cried out with a loud voice: ✠ Eli, Eli,
horam nonam. Et circa horam nonam clamávit Jesus voce magna, dicens: Eli, Eli,

lamma sabachthani? [C] that is, ✠ My God, my God, why hast thou forsaken
lamma sabactháni? Hoc est: Deus meus, Deus meus ut quid dereliquísti me?

me? [C] Hearing this, some of those who stood by said: [S] He is calling upon
Quidam autem illic stantes, et audiéntes dicébant: Elíam vocat iste.

Elias: [C] and thereupon one of them ran to fetch a sponge, which he filled
Et contínuo currens unus ex eis accéptam spóngiam implévit acéto

with vinegar and fixed upon a rod, and offered to let him drink; the rest said:
et impósuit arúndini, et dabat ei bíbere. Céteri vero dicébant:

[S] Wait, let us see whether Elias is to come and save him. [C] Then Jesus cried
Sine, videámus an véniat Elías líberans eum. Jesus autem

out again with a loud voice, and yielded up his spirit.
íterum clamans voce magna, emísit spíritum.

Here all kneel, and a short pause is made. [In former days, the faithful would lie prostrate on the ground.]
Hic genuflectitur, et pausatur aliquantulum.

After The Death Of Christ

[C] And all at once, the veil of the temple was torn this way and that from the top
Et ecce velum templi scissum est in duas partes a summo

to the bottom, and the earth shook, and the rocks parted asunder; and the graves
usque deórsum: et terra mota est, et petræ scissæ sunt, et monuménta

were opened, and many bodies arose out of them, bodies of holy men gone to their
apérta sunt: et multa córpora sanctórum, qui dormíerant, surrexérunt.

rest: who, after his rising again, left their graves and went into the holy city, where
Et exeúntes de monuméntis post resurrectiónem ejus, venérunt in sanctam civitátem,

they were seen by many. So that the centurion and those who kept guard over Jesus
et apparuérunt multis. Centúrio autem et qui cum eo erant, custodiéntes Jesum,

with him, when they perceived the earthquake and all that befell, were overcome
viso terræmótu et his, quæ fiébant, timuérunt valde,

with fear, saying: [S] No doubt, but this was the Son of God. [C] Many women
dicéntes: Vere Fílius Dei erat iste.

stood watching from far off; they had followed Jesus from Galilee, to minister
Erant autem ibi mulíeres multæ a longe, quæ secútæ erant Jesum a Galilǽa, ministrántes ei:

to him; among them were Mary Magdalen, and Mary the mother of James and
inter quas erat María Magdaléne, et María Jacóbi, et Joseph mater,

Joseph, and the mother of the sons of Zebedee. And now it was evening, and a
et mater filiórum Zebedǽi. Cum autem sero factum esset,

man came forward, by name Joseph, a rich man from Arimathea, who followed
venit quidam homo dives ab Arimathǽa, nómine Joseph,

Jesus as a disciple like the rest; he it was who approached Pilate, and asked to have
qui et ipse discípulus erat Jesu. Hic accéssit ad Pilátum, et pétiit

the body of Jesus, whereupon Pilate ordered that the body should be given up.
corpus Jesu. Tunc Pilátus jussit reddi corpus.

Joseph took possession of the body, and wrapped it in a clean winding-sheet; then
Et accépto córpore Joseph invólvit illud in síndone munda.

he buried it in a new grave, which he had fashioned for himself out of the rock,
Et pósuit illud in monuménto suo novo, quod excíderat in petra.

and left it there, rolling a great stone against the grave-door. CREDO.
Et advólvit saxum magnum ad óstium monuménti, et ábiit.

1962 • After the Gospel (Saint Matthew's Passion) has been proclaimed, the Celebrant does not kiss the EVANGELIARIUM, he is not incensed, and the response "Laus tibi, Christe" is not made.

[Editor's Note: Traditionally, after the Passion has been sung, the Deacon of the Mass—in an action that some consider the true Palm Sunday Gospel —would sing *Matthew 27.62-66* according the piercingly beautiful "weeping tone." However, the 1955 reform eliminated these verses from Palm Sunday along with *Matthew 27.2-35*, verses which include our Redeemer's institution of the Holy Eucharist. This proposal "to reduce the length of the text by 40 verses" was "advanced by Father Bea" on 21 October 1955, just days before MAXIMA REDEMPTIONIS was issued on 16 November 1955 {Giampietro p287}.]

OFFERTORY. *Ps 68: 21-22*

Impropérium exspectávit Cor meum et misériam: et sustínui, qui simul mecum contristarétur, et non fuit: consolántem me quæsívi, et non invéni: et dedérunt in escam meam fel, et in siti mea potavérunt me acéto. *℣. Salvum me fac, Deus, quóniam intravérunt aquæ usque ad ánimam meam. ℣. Advérsum me exercebántur, qui sedébant in porta, et in me psallébant, qui bibébant vinum. ℣. Ego vero oratiónem meam ad te Dómine: tempus benepláciti, Deus, in multitúdine misericórdiæ tuæ.*

MY HEART hath expected reproach and misery; and I looked for one that would grieve together with Me, and there was none: I sought for one to comfort me, and I found none; and they gave me gall for My food, and in My thirst they gave me vinegar to drink. ℣. *Save me, O God, for the waters are come in even unto my soul. ℣. They that sat in the gate spoke against me: and they that drank wine made me their song. ℣. But as for me, my prayer is to Thee, O Lord; for the time of Thy good pleasure, O God, in the multitude of Thy mercy.*

The Offertory for the feast of the Sacred Heart of Jesus matches the ancient melody for Palm Sunday until the words "et dedérunt in escam meam." The 1962 formulary for the Sacred Heart dates from 29 January 1929.

SECRET.

Grant, we beseech Thee, O Lord, that the gift presented to the eyes of Thy majesty may both obtain for us the grace of devotion and acquire for us the effect of a blessed immortality. Through our Lord.

Concéde, quǽsumus, Dómine: ut óculis tuæ majestátis munus oblátum, et grátiam nobis devotiónis obtíneat, et efféctum beátæ perennitátis acquírat. Per Dóminum.

The Preface of the Holy Cross (page 190) follows the Secret.

COMMUNION. *Matt 26: 42*

FATHER, if this chalice may not pass away, but I must drink it, Thy will be done. ℣. *And so they sang a hymn, and went out to mount Olivet.* ℣. *My God, my God, why hast Thou forsaken me? Loudly I call, but my prayer cannot reach Thee.*

Pater, si non potest hic calix transíre, nisi bibam illum: fiat volúntas tua. (Mt 26: 30) ℣. Et hymno dicto, exiérunt in montem Olivéti. (Ps 21: 2) ℣. Deus, Deus meus, réspice in me: quare me dereliquísti? longe a salúte mea verba delictórum meórum.

—91Angers|944 • Circa 944AD

—StMaur|1079 • Circa 944AD

Palm Sunday demonstrates the variety which existed vis-à-vis non-Psalter communion antiphons. Some manuscripts indicate Psalm 115—doubtless because of its reference to "cálicem salutáris"—whereas others take from Saint Matthew's Gospel or Psalm 21. We have broken, in this instance, our normal rule of only citing a single manuscript.

POSTCOMMUNION.

By the operation of this mystery, O Lord, may our vices be purged away, and our righteous desires have fulfillment. Through our Lord.

Per hujus, Dñe, operatiónem mystérii: et vítia nostra purgéntur, et justa desidéria compleántur. Per Dñm.

1962 • At the end of the Mass the Celebrant gives the blessing as usual but omits the Last Gospel.

Celebrans, in fine Missae, data benedictione more solito, omittit ultimam evangelium, et omnes revertuntur in sacristiam.

But for Masses not preceded by the blessing of palm branches, the Last Gospel is not omitted; in that case, the Celebrant reads the Gospel (Matthew 21: 1-9) that would have been read—had there been a blessing of palm branches—rather than the beginning of Saint John's Gospel.

(Mk 14:33) BUT HE TOOK PETER AND JAMES AND JOHN WITH HIM. AND NOW HE GREW DISMAYED AND DISTRESSED:

"MY SOUL," HE SAID TO THEM, "IS READY TO DIE WITH SORROW; DO YOU ABIDE HERE, AND KEEP WATCH."

1962 • The Solemn Mass of the Lord's Supper is to be celebrated in the evening: **not before 4:00PM nor after 9:00PM;** the official rubrics of the 1962 Missale Romanum say: *Missa solemnis in Cena Domini celebranda est vespere, hora magis opportuna, non autem ante horam quartam post meridiem, nec post horam nonam.* It is not clear why Monsignor McManus contradicts this {McManus p73}. The color of the vestments is white. The Tabernacle—if it be on the High Altar—is to be entirely empty. The Introit may be sung as the Celebrant processes to the Altar, rather than waiting for him to arrive at the Altar. This option is confirmed not only by §27a of *De Musica Sacra* (3 September 1958) but also by an Affirmative Response (29 January 1947) from the Sacred Congregation of Rites when asked: "Whether the Introit may be sung in the ancient manner—that is, additional verses from the Introit's psalm sung with the antiphon interjected between them—covering the entire time it takes the Celebrant to proceed from Sacristy to Altar?"

DE MISSA SOLEMNI VESPERTINA IN CENA DOMINI

I Classis.

— *Holy Thursday* • *Solemn Evening Mass* —

FERIA QUINTA IN CENA DOMINI *Station at Saint John Lateran ("Our Savior's Church")*

INTROIT. *Gal 6: 14 & Ps 66: 2-4*

Nos autem gloriári opórtet in Cruce Dómini nostri Jesu Christi: in quo est salus, vita et resurréctio nostra: per quem salváti et liberáti sumus. (Ps 66: 2) ℣. Deus misereátur nostri, et benedícat nobis: illúminet vultum suum super nos, et misereátur nostri. ℟. *Nos autem...* ℣. Ut cognoscámus in terra viã tuã: in ómnibus géntibus salutáre tuũ. ℟. *Nos autem...* ℣. Confiteántur tibi populi, Deus: confiteántur tibi populi omnes. ℟. *Nos autem...*

BUT IT BEHOOVES us to glory in the cross of our Lord Jesus Christ: in Whom is our salvation, life, and resurrection; by Whom we are saved and delivered. ℣. May God have mercy on us, and bless us: may He cause the light of His countenance to shine upon us; and may He have mercy on us. ℟. *But it...* ℣. That we may know Thy way upon earth, Thy salvation among all nations. ℟. *But it...* ℣. Let the peoples praise Thee, O God; let all the peoples praise Thee. ℟. *But it...*

1962 • *Cum celebrans incipit solemniter "Glória in excélsis Deo," pulsantur campanae et organum, quae, expleto hymno, silent usque ad Vigiliam paschalem.*

The ringing of the bells at the "Gloria" is a sign that from now on they will not be heard again until the first Easter Mass. The Church is accustomed to do a thing solemnly for the last time before it ceases, as we say the "Alleluia" solemnly twice at the end of Vespers before Septuagesima. According to Sir Walter Kirkham Blount ("Office of Holy Week," 1670AD), this silence of the bells is kept "to teach us that the preaching of the Gospel and the voice of those who ought to excite others to follow Christ were silent during this Passion time." Until the first Easter Mass, a "substitute of the bell" may be used, a device called by many names: crotalus, rattle, wooden clapper, and so on. If it is used, it is rattled whenever—on other days—the bell would be rung: at the Sanctus; at the elevation; during the procession; at the Angelus; and so forth.

COLLECT.

Deus, a quo et Judas reátus sui pœnam, et confessiónis suæ latro prǽmium sumpsit, concéde nobis tuæ propitiatiónis efféctum: ut, sicut in passióne sua Jesus Christus Dóminus noster divérsa utrísque íntulit stipéndia meritórum; ita nobis, abláto vetustátis erróre, resurrectiónis suæ grátiam largiátur: Qui tecum.

O God, from Whom Judas received the punishment of his crime, and the thief the reward of his confession, grant us the effect of Thy clemency, that, as Jesus Christ, our Lord, in His passion dealt according to their deserts with the one and the other, so, putting away from us the error of the past, He may bestow upon us the grace of His resurrection. Who with Thee liveth.

EPISTLE. *I Cor 11: 20-32*

BRETHREN: When you come therefore together into one place, it is not now to eat the Lord's supper. For every one taketh, before, his own supper to eat. And one indeed is hungry and another is drunk. What, have you not houses to eat and to drink in? Or despise ye the church of God and put them to shame that have not? What shall I say to you? Do I praise you? In this I praise you not. For I have received of the Lord that which I also delivered unto you, that the Lord Jesus, the same night in which He was betrayed, took bread, and giving thanks, broke and said: Take ye and eat: This is My Body, which shall be delivered for you. This do for the commemoration of Me. In like manner also the chalice, after He had supped, saying: This chalice is the new testament in My Blood. This do ye, as often as you shall drink, for the commemoration of Me. For as often as you shall eat this bread and drink the chalice, you shall show the death of the Lord, until He come. Therefore, whosoever shall eat this bread, or drink the chalice of the Lord unworthily, shall be guilty of the Body and the Blood of the Lord. But let a man prove himself; and so let him eat of that bread and drink of the chalice. For he that eateth and drinketh unworthily, eateth and drinketh judgment to himself, not discerning the Body of the Lord. Therefore are there many infirm and weak among you: and many sleep. But if we would judge ourselves, we should not be judged. But whilst we are judged, we are chastised by the Lord, that we be not condemned with this world.

Fratres: Conveniéntibus vobis in unum, jam non est Domínicam cœnam manducáre. Unusquísque enim suã cœnam præsúmit ad manducándum. Et álius quidem ésurit: álius autem ébrius est. Numquid domos non habétis ad manducándũ et bibéndum? aut ecclésiam Dei contémnitis, et confúnditis eos, qui non habent? Quid dicam vobis? Laudo vos? In hoc non laudo. Ego enim accépi a Dómino quod et trádidi vobis, quóniam Dóminus Jesus, in qua nocte tradebátur, accépit panem, et grátias agens fregit, et dixit: Accípite, et manducáte: hoc est corpus meum, quod pro vobis tradétur: hoc fácite in meam commemoratiónem. Simíliter et cálicem, postquam cenávit, dicens: Hic calix novum testaméntum est in meo sánguine: hoc fácite, quotiescúmque bibétis, in meam commemoratiónem. Quotiescúmque enim manducábitis panem hunc et cálicem bibétis: mortem Dñi annuntiábitis, donec véniat. Ítaque quicúmque manducáverit panem hunc vel bíberit cálicem Dómini indígne, reus erit córporis et sánguinis Dómini. Probet autem seípsum homo: et sic de pane illo edat et de cálice bibat. Qui enim mandúcat et bibit indígne, judícium sibi mandúcat et bibit: non dijúdicans corpus Dómini. Ideo inter vos multi infírmi et imbecílles, et dórmiunt multi. Quod si nosmetípsos dijudicarémus, non útique judicarémur. Dũ judicámur autẽ, a Dño corrípimur, ut non cum hoc mundo damnémur.

GRADUAL. *Phil 2: 8-9*

CHRIST became obedient for us unto death, even the death of the cross. ℣. Wherefore God also hath exalted Him, and hath given Him a name which is above every name.

Christus factus est pro nobis obédiens usque ad mortem, mortem autem crucis. ℣. Propter quod et Deus exaltávit illum: et dedit illi nomen, quod est super omne nomen.

GOSPEL. *John 13: 1-15*

BEFORE THE FESTIVAL-DAY of the Pasch, Jesus knowing that His hour was come, that He should pass out of this world to the Father, having loved His own who were in the world, He loved them unto the end. And when supper was done (the

Ante diem festũ Paschæ, sciens Jesus, quia venit hora ejus, ut tránseat ex hoc mundo ad Patrem: cum dilexísset suos, qui erant in mundo, in finem diléxit eos. Et cena facta, cum diábolus jam misísset in cor, ut tráderet eum Judas Simónis Iscariótæ: sciens, quia ómnia dedit ei Pater in manus, et quia a Deo

HE WENT DOWN, AND WASHED IN THE JORDAN SEVEN TIMES: AND HE WAS MADE CLEAN. (IV KINGS 5: 14)

DESCENDIT ET LAVIT IN JORDANE SEPTIES ... (IV KINGS 5: 14)

LAVABUNT IN EA AARON ET FILII EJUS MANUS ... (EXODUS 30: 19)

WATER BEING PUT INTO IT, AARON AND HIS SONS SHALL WASH THEIR HANDS AND FEET IN IT. (EXODUS 30: 19)

BY THIS SHALL ALL MEN KNOW THAT YE ARE MY DISCIPLES: IF YOU HAVE LOVE ONE FOR ANOTHER. (John 13: 35)

devil having now put into the heart of Judas, the son of Simon the Iscariot, to betray Him), knowing that the Father had given Him all things into His hands and that He came from God and goeth to God: He riseth from supper and layeth aside His garments and, having taken a towel, girded Himself. After that, He putteth water into a basin and began to wash the feet of the disciples and to wipe them with the towel wherewith He was girded.

exívit, et ad Deum vadit: surgit a cena et ponit vestiménta sua: et cum accepísset línteũ, præcínxit se. Deínde mittit aquam in pelvim, et cœpit laváre pedes discipulórũ, et extérgere línteo, quo erat præcínctus.

He cometh therefore to Simon Peter. And Peter saith to Him: Lord, dost Thou wash my feet? Jesus answered and said to him: What I do, thou knowest not now: but thou shalt know hereafter. Peter saith to Him: Thou shalt never wash my feet. Jesus answered him: If I wash thee not, thou shalt have no part with Me. Simon Peter saith to Him: Lord, not only my feet, but also my hands and my head. Jesus saith to him: He that is washed needeth not but to wash his feet, but is clean wholly. And you are clean, but not all.

Venit ergo ad Simónem Petrum. Et dicit ei Petrus: Dómine, tu mihi lavas pedes? Respóndit Jesus et dixit ei: Quod ego fácio, tu nescis modo, scies autem póstea. Dicit ei Petrus: Non lavábis mihi pedes in ætérnum. Respóndit ei Jesus: Si non lávero te, non habébis partem mecum. Dicit ei Simon Petrus: Dómine, non tantum pedes meos, sed et manus et caput. Dicit ei Jesus: Qui lotus est, non índiget nisi ut pedes lavet, sed est mundus totus. Et vos mundi estis, sed non omnes.

For He knew who he was that would betray Him; therefore He said: You are not all clean. Then after He had washed their feet and taken His garments, being set down again, He said to them: Know you what I have done to you? You call Me Master and Lord. And you say well; for so I am. If then I being your Lord and Master, have washed your feet, you also ought to wash one another's feet. For I have given you an example, that as I have done to you, so you do also.

Sciébat enim, quisnam esset, qui tráderet eum: proptérea dixit: Non estis mundi omnes. Postquam ergo lavit pedes eórum et accépit vestiménta sua: cum recubuísset íterum, dixit eis: Scitis, quid fécerim vobis? Vos vocátis me Magíster et Dómine: et bene dícitis: sum étenim. Si ergo ego lavi pedes vestros, Dóminus et Magíster: et vos debétis alter altérius laváre pedes. Exémplum enim dedi vobis, ut, quemádmodum ego feci vobis, ita et vos faciátis.

Unlike the 1950 version, the 1962 Holy Thursday omits the Credo.

1962 • It is very fitting that a brief homily be given after the Gospel to illustrate the principal mysteries which are celebrated in this Mass, namely, the institution of the holy Eucharist and of the Priestly Order, as well as the commandment of the Lord concerning fraternal charity. | *Valde convenit ut post Evangelium habeatur brevis HOMILIA ad illustranda mysteria potissima, quae hac Missa recoluntur, institutio scilicet sacrae Eucharistiae et ordinis sacerdotalis, necnon et mandatum Domini de caritate fraterna.*

DE LOTIONE PEDUM • The washing of feet ("Mandatum" or "Maundy") on Holy Thursday is not of obligation. According to the *Ordo Hebdomadae Sanctae* (1956) the rite takes place at Mass—after the Gospel and Homily—either in the Sanctuary or in the body of the church. Traditionally, the MANDATUM was never performed as part of the Mass; rather, it took place at another time. Even after the reforms of Pope Pius XII "it is still permissible to perform this rite outside of Mass" {McManus p21}. A tendency of the reformers was to attempt to transfer everything inside the Mass—the Sacrament of Marriage, Canonizations, the Sacrament of Baptism, and so forth—whereas traditionally such actions took place outside of Mass. When the MANDATUM was moved inside of Mass, it had unpleasant results probably not foreseen by the reformers, e.g. the duplication of the Communion antiphon. Nothing prevents the congregation from singing during the MANDATUM and when this is done, choirmasters should prepare a booklet for them with the desired melodies. It is probably best to sing the third antiphon to a different melody (or polyphony) rather than duplicating the Communion antiphon.

THE MEN CHOSEN • Regarding the twelve men ("duodecim viris") whose feet are to be washed: "they may be laymen, clerics, or young boys" {McManus p21}. The traditional MANDATUM washed the feet of thirteen men, whereas the 1962 version has twelve men. In the traditional version, the priest kissed the men's feet and gave them coins, but these actions were suppressed {McManus p75} in the 1962 version.

THE WASHING OF THE FEET

1962 • The antiphons should be chanted as soon as Deacon and Subdeacon go to lead the twelve men to their places in the Sanctuary. It is not necessary to sing all the antiphons provided, but the eighth antiphon ("Ubi caritas et amor") must never be omitted {McManus p39}. One antiphon from the 1950 version was eliminated by the reformers: "Benedícta Sit Sancta Trínitas Atque Indivísa Únitas."

FIRST ANTIPHON. *John 13: 34*

Mandátum novum do vobis: ut diligátis ínvicem, sicut diléxi vos, dicit Dñs. (Ps 118: 1) ℣. Beáti immaculáti in via: qui ámbulant in lege Dñi. ℟. *Mandátum novum...*

A NEW COMMANDMENT I give unto you: That you love one another, as I have loved you, saith the Lord. ℣. Blessed are the undefiled in the way: who walk in the law of the Lord. ℟. *A new...*

SECOND ANTIPHON. *John 13: 4, 5, 15*

Postquam surréxit Dóminus a cena, misit aquam in pelvim, et cœpit laváre pedes discipulórum suórum: hoc exémplũ réliquit eis. (Ps 47: 2) ℣. Magnus Dóminus, et laudábilis nimis: in civitáte Dei nostri, in monte sancto ejus. ℟. *Postquam surréxit...*

WHEN THE LORD rose from supper He poured water into a basin and began to wash the feet of His disciples: this was the example He gave unto them. ℣. Great is the Lord and exceedingly to be praised in the city of our God in His holy mountain. ℟. *When the Lord rose...*

THIRD ANTIPHON. *John 13: 12, 13, 15*

Dóminus Jesus, postquam cenávit cum discípulis suis, lavit pedes eórum, et ait illis: Scitis, quid fécerim vobis ego, Dñs et Magíster? Exémplũ dedi vobis, ut et vos ita faciátis. (Ps 84: 2) ℣. Benedixísti, Dómine, terram tuam: avertísti captivitátem Jacob. ℟. *Dóminus Jesus...*

THE LORD JESUS after He had supped with His disciples washed their feet and said to them: Know ye what I your Lord and Master have done to you? I have given you an example that so you do also. ℣. Lord, Thou hast blessed Thy land; Thou hast turned away the captivity of Jacob. ℟. *The Lord Jesus...*

FOURTH ANTIPHON. *John 13: 6-7, 8*

Dómine, tu mihi lavas pedes? Respóndit Jesus et dixit ei: Si non lávero tibi pedes, non habébis partem mecum.

℣. Venit ergo ad Simónem Petrum, et dixit ei Petrus.

℟. *Dómine, tu mihi...*

℣. Quod ego fácio, tu nescis modo: scies autem póstea.

℟. *Dómine, tu mihi...*

LORD, dost Thou wash my feet? Jesus answered and said to him: If I wash not thy feet, thou shalt have no part with Me.

℣. He cometh therefore to Simon Peter, and Peter said to Him: ℟. *Lord, dost Thou wash...*

℣. What I do, thou knowest not now; but thou shalt know hereafter. ℟. *Lord, dost Thou wash...*

FIFTH ANTIPHON. *Cf. John 13: 14*

IF I, BEING YOUR Lord and Master, have washed your feet, how much the more ought you to wash one another's feet? ℣. Hear these things, all ye nations: give ear, all ye inhabitants of the world. ℟. *If I, being your…*

Si ego, Dóminus et Magíster vester, lavi vobis pedes: quanto magis debétis alter altérius laváre pedes? (Ps 48: 2) ℣. Audíte hæc, omnes gentes: áuribus percípite, qui habitátis orbem. ℟. *Si ego, Dóminus…*

SIXTH ANTIPHON. *John 13: 35*

BY THIS SHALL all men know that ye are My disciples, if you have love one for another. ℣. Said Jesus to His disciples. ℟. *By this shall…*

In hoc cognóscent omnes, quia discípuli mei estis, si dilectiónem habuéritis ad ínvicem. ℣. Dixit Jesus discípulis suis. ℟. *In hoc cognóscent…*

SEVENTH ANTIPHON. *I Cor 13: 13*

EVER MAY THERE REMAIN in you, faith, hope, charity, these three things; but the greater of these is charity. ℣. And now there remain faith, hope, and charity, these three; but the greatest of these is charity. ℟. *Ever may…*

Máneant in vobis fides, spes, cáritas, tria hæc: major autem horum est cáritas. ℣. Nunc autem manent fides, spes, cáritas, tria hæc: major horum est cáritas. ℟. *Máneant in vobis…*

1962 • The following antiphon (cf. I John) and its verses are never omitted. It is begun as the Mandatum draws to a close. Some of the preceding antiphons may be omitted.

English Translation by Monsignor Ronald Knox (d. 1957)

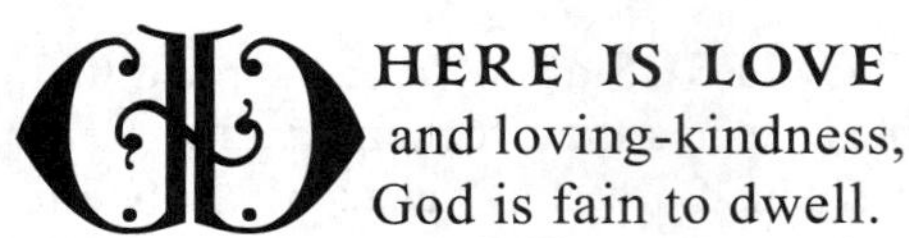

WHERE IS LOVE
and loving-kindness,
God is fain to dwell.

Ubi cáritas et amor, Deus ibi est.

℣. Flock of Christ, who loved us, in one fold contained:
Congregávit nos in unum Christi amor.
℣. Joy and mirth be ours, for mirth and joy he giveth.
Exsultémus et in ipso jucundémur.
℣. Fear we still and love the God who ever liveth:
Timeámus et amémus Deum vivum.
℣. Each to other joined by charity unfeigned.
Et ex corde diligámus nos sincéro.

℟. Where is love and loving-kindness, God is fain to dwell.
Ubi cáritas et amor, Deus ibi est.

℣. Therefore, when we meet, the flock of Christ, so loving:
Simul ergo cum in unum congregámur:

℣. Take we heed lest bitterness be there engendered.
Ne nos mente dividámur, caveámus.

℣. All our spiteful thoughts and quarrels be surrendered:
Cessent júrgia malígna, cessent lites.

℣. Seeing Christ is there, divine among us moving.
Et in médio nostri sit Christus Deus.

A. Where is love and loving-kindness, God is fain to dwell.
Ubi cáritas et amor, Deus ibi est.

℣. So may we be gathered once again, beholding:
Simul quoque cum Beátis videámus.

℣. Glorified the glory, Christ, of thy unveiling:
Gloriánter vultum tuum, Christe Deus:

℣. There, where never ending joys, and never failing:
Gáudium, quod est imménsum atque probum.

℣. Age succeeds to age eternally unfolding.
Sǽcula per infiníta sæculórum.

1962 • When the MANDATUM is finished, the Celebrant washes his hands, saying nothing. All don their maniples and the Celebrant puts on his chasuble. Returning to the middle of the Altar, facing the people, the Celebrant says:

Pater noster, etc. (secreto)	**Pater noster,** etc. (*secretly*)
℣. Et ne nos indúcas in tentatiónem.	℣. And lead us not into temptation.
℟. Sed líbera nos a malo.	℟. But deliver us from evil.
℣. Tu mandásti mandáta tua, Dómine.	℣. Thou, Lord, hast given us Thy commandments.
℟. Custodíri nimis.	℟. To keep them faithfully.
℣. Tu lavásti pedes discipulórum tuórum.	℣. Thou didst wash the feet of the disciples.
℟. Opera mánuum tuárum ne despícias.	℟. Do not scorn the work of Thy hands.
℣. Dómine, exáudi oratiónem meam.	℣. Lord, hear my prayer.
℟. Et clamor meus ad te véniat.	℟. And let my cry come unto Thee.
℣. Dóminus vobíscum.	℣. The Lord be with you.
℟. Et cum spíritu tuo.	℟. And with thy spirit.

Let us pray.

THY BLESSING, LORD, we beseech thee, on this service of duty done! Thou wouldst deign to wash the feet of thy disciples; think no scorn, then, of thy own actions, at thy own bidding perpetuated. Outward stains of us, ourselves can wash away; of inward guilt, none but must look to thee for his cleansing; that mercy, too, deign to grant, who livest and reignest and art God, world without end. ℟. Amen.

Orémus.

Adésto, Dómine, quǽsumus, offício servitútis nostræ: et quia tu discípulis tuis pedes laváre dignátus es, ne despícias ópera mánuum tuárum, quæ nobis retinénda mandásti: ut, sicut hic nobis et a nobis exterióra abluúntur inquinaménta; sic a te ómnium nostrũ interióra lavéntur peccáta. Quod ipse præstáre dignéris, qui vivis et regnas Deus: per ómnia sǽcula sæculórum. ℟. Amen.

English Translation by Monsignor Knox

OFFERTORY. *Ps 117: 16, 17*

THE POWER of the Lord has triumphed, the power of the Lord has brought me to great honor: I am reprieved from death, to live on and proclaim what the Lord has done for me. ℣. *I called on the Lord when trouble beset me, and the Lord listened, and brought me relief, for the Lord is at my side.* ℣. *I reeled under the blow, and had well-nigh fallen, but still the Lord was there to aid me. Who but the Lord has brought me deliverance?*

Identical to 3rd Sunday after Epiphany:

Déxtera Dómini fecit virtútem, déxtera Dómini exaltávit me: non móriar, sed vivam, et narrábo ópera Dómini. ℣. *In tribulatióne invocávi Dóminum et exaudívit me in latitúdine: quia Dñs adjútor meus est.* ℣. *Impúlsus versátus sum, ut cáderem: et Dñs suscépit me: et factus est mihi in salútem.*

SECRET.

We beseech Thee, O holy Lord, almighty Father, eternal God, that He may render our sacrifice acceptable

Ipse tibi, quǽsumus, Dómine sancte, Pater omnípotens, ætérne Deus, sacrifícium nostrum reddat accéptum, qui discípulis suis in sui commemoratiónem hoc fíeri hodiérna traditióne monstrávit, Jesus Christus, Fílius tuus, Dóminus noster: Qui tecum.

to Thee, Who, by giving it to His disciples on this day, taught them that it is done in commemoration of Him, Jesus Christ, Thy Son, our Lord, Who with Thee.

The Preface of the Holy Cross (page 190) follows the Secret.

DURING THE CANON

On certain major feasts, the Communicantes and Hanc Igitur are modified. But Maundy Thursday, as Father Thurston reminds us, "stands absolutely alone among all the feasts of the year" inasmuch as three (3) modifications are made to the Canon.

Communicántes et diem sacratíssimũ celebrántes, quo Dñs noster Jesus Christus pro nobis est tráditus: sed et memóriã venerántes, in primis gloriósæ semper Vírginis Maríæ, Genetrícis ejúsdem Dei et Dómini nostri Jesu Christi: sed et beáti Joseph, ejúsdem Vírginis Sponsi, et beatórum Apostolórum ac Mártyrum tuórum, Petri et Pauli, Andréæ, Jacóbi, Joánnis, Thomæ, Jacóbi, Philíppi, Bartholomæi, Matthæi, Simónis et Thaddæi: Lini, Cleti, Cleméntis, Xysti, Cornélii, Cypriáni, Lauréntii, Chrysógoni, Joánnis et Pauli, Cosmæ et Damiáni: et ómniũ Sanctórum tuórum; quorum méritis precibúsque concédas, ut in ómnibus protectiónis tuæ muniámur auxílio. Per eúmdem Christum, Dñm nostrum. Amen.

HAVING COMMUNION WITH, and celebrating that most sacred day on which our Lord Jesus Christ was for us betrayed; venerating, moreover, the memory, first of all, of the ever glorious Virgin Mary, mother of the same our God and Lord Jesus Christ, also of blessed Joseph, her Spouse; and likewise of Thy blessed apostles and martyrs, Peter and Paul, Andrew, James, John, Thomas, James, Philip, Bartholomew, Matthew, Simon and Thaddeus, of Linus, Cletus, Clement, Xystus, Cornelius, Cyprian, Lawrence, Chrysogonus, John and Paul, Cosmas and Damian, and of all Thy saints; to whose merits and prayers do Thou grant that in all things we may be fortified by the aid of Thy protection. Through the same Christ our Lord. Amen.

With his hands spread over the offerings, the Priest continues the prayer.
Tenens manus expansas super oblata, dicit:

Hanc ígitur oblatiónem servitútis nostræ, sed et cunctæ famíliæ tuæ, quam tibi offérimus ob diem, in qua Dóminus noster Jesus Christus trádidit discípulis suis Córporis et Sánguinis sui mystéria celebránda; quæsumus Dómine, ut placátus accípias: diésque nostros in tua pace dispónas: atque ab ætérna damnatióne nos éripi et in electórum tuórum júbeas grege numerári. Per eúmdem Christum Dóminum nostrum. Amen.

THIS OBLATION, therefore, of our servitude, as also of all Thy household's, which we offer Thee for the day on which our Lord Jesus Christ committed to His disciples the mysteries of His body and blood to celebrate, we beseech Thee, O Lord, graciously to accept, and to dispose our days in Thy peace, and command us to be snatched away from eternal damnation and numbered in the fold of Thine elect. Through Christ our Lord. Amen.

The Priest once again blesses the offerings:

WHICH OBLATION, we beseech, O God, do Thou vouchsafe to make in all ways blessed ✠, ascribed ✠, ratified, reasonable ✠, and acceptable, that it may become unto us the body ✠ and blood ✠ of Thy most beloved Son, our Lord Jesus Christ.

Quam oblatiónem tu Deus in ómnibus, quǽsumus, bene ✠ díctam, adscrí ✠ ptam, ra ✠ tam, rationábilem acceptabilémque fácere dignéris: ut nobis Cor ✠ pus, et San ✠ guis fiat dilectíssimi Fílii tui, Dómini nostri Jesu Christi.

Western rites have "prídie" whereas most Eastern liturgies have "on the *night* He was betrayed."

WHO, ON THE DAY before He suffered for our salvation and the salvation of all, *that is on this day*, took bread into His holy and venerable hands and having lifted up His eyes to heaven, to Thee God, His almighty Father, giving thanks to Thee, blessed it ✠, broke it, and gave it to His disciples, saying, Take ye, and eat ye all of this:

Qui prídie, quam pro nostra omniúmque salúte paterétur, hoc est, hódie, accépit panem in sanctas ac venerábiles manus suas, et elevátis óculis in cælum ad te Deum, Patrem suum omnipoténtem, tibi grátias agens, bene ✠ díxit, fregit, dedítque discípulis suis, dicens: Accípite, et manducáte ex hoc omnes.

FOR THIS IS MY BODY.

HOC EST ENIM CORPUS MEUM.

The rest of the Canon is as normal.
Et reliqua ut in Canone.

In the 1962 version, the third Agnus Dei *is as follows:*
"Agnus Dei, qui tollis peccata mundi: miserere nobis."

1962 • The "Kiss of Peace" is not given; of the three prayers usually said in preparation for Communion, the priest omits the first ("Dómine Jesu Christe, qui dixísti").

Osculum pacis hodie non datur, et omittitur oratio "Dómine Jesu Christe, qui dixisti."

Kiss of Peace • Father Fortescue wrote in 1916: "The Mass of *Maundy Thursday* is a festal Mass, with white vestments and the *Gloria in excelsis*. It is the only case in the year when the Mass of the day and office do not correspond. The office is all mournful. Here the memory which seems most to fill the mind of the Church is the betrayal of Judas." Indeed, the treacherous kiss of Judas is prominent in Matins and Lauds for Holy Thursday. Mediæval liturgists say the kiss of peace ("Pax") is omitted owing to Judas' betrayal, and the reformers agreed {Giampietro p62}.

Reforms of Holy Week • Father Hannibal Bugnini and Father Carlo Braga published a commentary in *Ephemerides Liturgicae* (28 February 1956) explaining the 1955 Holy Week reforms. With regard to why the "Agnus Dei" was changed, they say: *Responsum "miserere nobis" ad tertium "Agnus Dei" suadetur ex omissione osculi pacis; proinde logice non dicitur: "dona nobis pacem." Eadem ratione oratio immediate subsequens, cum sit praeparatio ad osculum pacis, omittitur.* In other words, according to their reasoning, "dona nobis pacem" must not be said because there is no Pax, and the prayer "Dómine Jesu Christe, qui dixísti" must be omitted because that prayer—followed immediately by the Pax—they view as a preparation for the Pax. During the Middle Ages on Maundy Thursday, the Agnus Dei was sung with "miserere nobis" thrice; for speculation as to why this was done, cf. Adrian Fortescue's *A Study of the Roman Liturgy* (London: Longmans and Green, 1912) page 388. The Lateran Basilica in Rome never did sing "dona nobis pacem" {Wagner p102}.

Shadows of The Funeral Mass • The 1962 version of Maundy Thursday (unlike the 1950 version) resembles the Requiem Mass: (1) The *Agnus Dei* is modified; (2) The Pax and prayer before the Pax are omitted; (3) The final blessing is not given. At Masses for the dead and at funerals nothing is ever kissed; not cruets, not the incense spoon, not the book, and so forth. According to the 1962 rubrics, if the Bishop distributes Holy Communion on Holy Thursday "the faithful do not kiss his ring before Communion" {McManus p76}. According to Father Fortescue, kissing of the bishop's ring before reception of Holy Communion "is a remnant of the old kiss of peace before Communion, as the ministers at pontifical High Mass kiss his cheek before receiving" {Fortescue p74}.

COMMUNION. *John 13: 12, 13, 15*

Dóminus Jesus, postquam cœnávit cum discípulis suis, lavit pedes eórum, et ait illis: Scitis quid fécerim vobis ego Dóminus, et Magíster? Exémplum dedi vobis, ut et vos ita faciátis. (Ps 118: 1) ℣. *Beáti immaculáti in via, qui ámbulant in lege Dómini.*

—47CHARTRES|957 • Circa 957AD

THE LORD JESUS, after He had supped with His disciples, washed their feet, and saith to them, Do you know what I, your Lord and Master, have done for you? I have given you an example, that so you do also. ℣. *Blessed are the undefiled in the way, who walk in the law of the Lord.*

Since no organ is allowed, the 1962 *Missale Romanum* (page 162) suggests that Psalm 22, Psalm 71, Psalm 103, and Psalm 150 may also be sung, interspersed with the "Dominus Jesus" communion antiphon.

1962 • After Communion, the Celebrant operates the way he does when the Sanctissimum is exposed, because the ciborium is left on the corporal as the "Solemn Translation & Reservation of the Blessed Sacrament" is to follow.

POSTCOMMUNION.

Reféciti vitálibus aliméntis, quǽsumus Dómine Deus noster: ut quod témpore nostræ mortalitátis exséquimur, immortalitátis tuæ múnere consequámur. Per Dóminum.

Refreshed with life-giving nourishment, we beseech Thee, O Lord, our God, that what we perform in the time of our mortality, we may attain by the gift of Thine immortality. Through our Lord.

In the 1962 version, "Ite, missa est" is replaced by "Benedicámus Dómino." Then the Celebrant says "Placeat tibi, sancta Trinitas" in the usual way. The final blessing and the Last Gospel are omitted.

PROCESSION AFTER MASS

1962 • Now comes the "Solemn Translation and Reservation of the Blessed Sacrament." The Celebrant removes his chasuble and dons a white cope. Kneeling at the foot of the Altar—having placed incense into two thuribles without any blessing—the Celebrant incenses the Sanctissimum three times. Putting on a white humeral veil, he goes up the Altar steps and receives the ciborium from the Deacon: the latter then covers the ciborium with the ends of the humeral veil. The Celebrant comes down from the Altar and goes forward under a canopy: two thurifers (without walking backwards) incense the Sanctissimum continuously until the Place of Repose is reached.

The "Pange Lingua" is on page 518.

During the procession to the Place of Repose (just as in the 1950 version) "the clergy and people carry lighted candles" {McManus p78}. "If the procession is very long, other hymns, psalms, or canticles may be sung" {1961 *Liber Usualis* p685}. The *Pange Lingua* of Saint Thomas Aquinas is never omitted, but its fifth and sixth verses—"Tantum Ergo" and "Genitóri"—are not sung until the Place of Repose is reached and the Celebrant begins to incense the Sanctissimum. If necessary, the hymn is repeated from the second verse.

The Celebrant places the ciborium on the Altar at the Place of Repose, with the assistance of the Deacon if necessary. After genuflecting, the Celebrant puts incense in one of the thuribles again, and incenses the Sanctissimum. Meanwhile the "Tantum Ergo" is chanted (see above). Then the Deacon places the ciborium into the tabernacle. All remain kneeling in silent adoration of the Sanctissimum for a little while. The sign having been given, the Celebrant, ministers, and servers return to the sacristy.

STRIPPING OF THE ALTARS

1962 • The Celebrant and Deacon put on violet stoles. Then the Celebrant and ministers go to the main Altar. They make a reverence to the Altar and, standing, begin the Stripping of the Altar in the following manner. The Celebrant says the following antiphon ("Divisérunt sibi") in a clear tone of voice. In the same voice, the Celebrant says the first words of Psalm 21, which are **"Deus, Deus meus, réspice in me: quare me dereliquísti?"** [Pius XII Psalter: "Deus meus, Deus meus, quare me dereliquísti?"] The rest of the psalm is recited by others, while the Celebrant and the sacred ministers strip all the church altars except the one where the Blessed Sacrament is solemnly adored.

ANTIPHON. *Psalm 21: 19bc*

DIVISÉRUNT sibi vestiménta mea: et super vestem meam misérunt sortem.

They divide my spoils among them, cast lots for my garments.

PSALM XXI. *English Translation by Monsignor Ronald Knox (d. 1957)*

DEUS, DEUS MEUS, RESPICE IN ME:

Quare me dereliquísti? * longe a salúte mea verba delictórum meórum.

1. My God, my God, look upon me: why hast thou forsaken me? Why cannot my sinful words reach thee, who art my salvation?

2. Deus meus, clamábo per diem, et non exáudies: * et nocte, et non ad insipiéntiam mihi.

2. Thou dost not answer, my God, when I cry out to thee day and night, and I am patient still.

3. Tu autem in sancto hábitas: * laus Ísraël.

3. Thou art there none the less, dwelling in thy holy place; Israel's ancient boast.

4. In te speravérunt patres nostri: * speravérunt, et liberásti eos.

4. It was in thee that our fathers trusted, and thou didst reward their trust by delivering them.

5. Ad te clamavérunt, et salvi facti sunt: * in te speravérunt, et non sunt confúsi.

5. They cried to thee, and rescue came; no need to be ashamed of such trust as theirs.

6. Ego autem sum vermis, et non homo: * oppróbrium hóminum, et abjéctio plebis.

6. But I, poor worm, have no manhood left: I am a by-word to all, the laughing-stock of the rabble.

7. Omnes vidéntes me derisérunt me: * locúti sunt lábiis, et movérunt caput.

7. All those who catch sight of me fall to mocking: mouthing out insults, while they toss their heads in scorn.

8. Sperávit in Dómino, erípiat eum: salvum fáciat eum, quóniam vult eum.

8. He committed himself to the Lord, why does not the Lord come to his rescue, and set his favourite free?

9. Quóniam tu es, qui extraxísti me de ventre: * spes mea ab ubéribus matris meæ.

9. What hand but thine drew me out from my mother's womb? Who else was my refuge when I hung at the breast?

10. In te projéctus sum ex útero: †
de ventre matris meæ Deus meus es tu, * ne discésseris a me:

10. From the hour of my birth, thou art my guardian; since I left my mother's womb, thou art my God! Do not leave me now,

11. Quóniam tribulátio próxima est: * quóniam non est qui ádjuvet.

11. when trouble is close at hand; [stand near] when I have none to help me.

12. Circumdedérunt me vítuli multi: * tauri pingues obsedérunt me.

12. My enemies are all about me, packed close as a herd of oxen, hemming me in, strong as bulls.

13. Aperuérunt super me os suum: * sicut leo rápiens et rúgiens.

13. They threaten me with their jaws, as might a lion roaring for its prey.

14. Sicut aqua effúsus sum: * et dispérsa sunt ómnia ossa mea.

14. I am spent as spilt water, all my bones out of joint,

15. Factum est cor meum tamquam cera liquéscens: * in médio ventris mei.

15. my heart turned to molten wax within me;

16. Áruit tamquam testa virtus mea, †
et lingua mea adhǽsit fáucibus meis: * et in púlverem mortis deduxísti me.

16. My strength has shrivelled up like clay in the baking, my tongue sticks fast in my mouth; thou hast laid me in the dust to die.

17. Quóniam circumdedérunt me canes multi: * concílium malignántium obsédit me.

17. Prowling about me like a pack of dogs, their wicked conspiracy hedges me in.

18. Fodérunt manus meas et pedes meos: * dinumeravérunt ómnia ossa mea.

18. They have torn holes in my hands and feet; they mark every bone in my body,

19. Ipsi vero consideravérunt et inspexérunt me: †
divisérunt sibi vestiménta mea, * et super vestem meam misérunt sortem.

19. As they stand there watching me, gazing at me: they divide my spoils among them, cast lots for my garments.

20. Tu autem, Dómine, ne elongáveris auxílium tuum a me: *
ad defensiónem meam cónspice.

20. Then, Lord, do not stand at a distance; if thou wouldst aid me: look to my defence.

21. Erue a frámea, Deus, ánimam meam: * et de manu canis únicam meam.

21. Only life is left me; save that from the sword, from the clutches of these dogs.

22. Salva me ex ore leónis: * et a córnibus unicórnium humilitátem meam.

22. Rescue me from the very mouth of the lion, the very horns of the wild oxen that have brought me thus low.

23. Narrábo nomen tuum frátribus meis: * in médio Ecclésiæ laudábo te.

23. Then I will proclaim thy renown to my brethren: where thy people gather, I will join in singing thy praise,

24. Qui timétis Dóminum, laudáte eum: * univérsum semen Jacob, glorificáte eum.

24. Praise the Lord, all you that are his worshippers; honour to him from the sons of Jacob.

25. Tímeat eum omne semen Ísraël: *
quóniam non sprevit, neque despéxit deprecatiónem páuperis:

25. Reverence to him from Israel's race! He has not scorned or slighted the appeal of the friendless,

26. Nec avértit fáciem suam a me: * et cum clamárem ad eum, exaudívit me.

26. Nor turned his face away from me; my cry for help did not go unheeded.

27. Apud te laus mea in ecclésia magna: * vota mea reddam in conspéctu timéntium eum.

27. Take what I owe thee, my song of praise before a great assembly. I will pay my vows to the Lord in the sight of his worshippers.

28. Edent páuperes, et saturabúntur: † et laudábunt Dóminum qui requírunt eum: * vivent corda eórum in sǽculum sǽculi.

28. The poor shall eat now, and have their fill; those who look for the Lord will give him thanks, their hearts refreshed eternally.

29. Reminiscéntur et converténtur ad Dóminum * univérsi fines terræ:

29. They will bethink themselves of the Lord, and come back to him, the furthest dwellers on earth;

30. Et adorábunt in conspéctu ejus * univérsæ famíliæ géntium.

30. They will worship before him, all the races of the heathen.

31. Quóniam Dómini est regnum:* et ipse dominábitur géntium.

To the Lord royalty belongs, the whole world's homage is his due.

32. Manducavérunt et adoravérunt omnes pingues terræ: * in conspéctu ejus cadent omnes qui descéndunt in terram.

32. The great ones of the earth feast in his presence, and adore: men brought low, even to the dust, bow down at his feet.

33. Et ánima mea illi vivet: * et semen meum sérviet ipsi.

33. I, too, shall live on before him, and beget children to serve him.

34. Annuntiábitur Dómino generátio ventúra: † et annuntiábunt cæli justítiam ejus pópulo qui nascétur, * quem fecit Dóminus.

34. The Lord will claim for his own a generation still to come: heaven itself will make known his faithfulness to a people yet to be born, a people of the Lord's own founding.

1962 • After the altars have been stripped, the Celebrant and sacred ministers return to the main Altar. The Celebrant completes the recitation by repeating the antiphon. Then they return to the sacristy.

ANTIPHON. *Psalm 21: 19bc*

DIVISÉRUNT sibi vestiménta mea: et super vestem meam misérunt sortem.

They divide my spoils among them, cast lots for my garments.

VESPERS ON HOLY THURSDAY (Omitted)

When Pope Pius XII modified holy week in 1955, he changed the traditional times of the ceremonies, moving ceremonies that traditionally took place in the morning to the evening. These changes *de facto* obliterated the ceremonies of TENEBRAE.

For the 1962 version of Holy Thursday, "the Hour of Vespers is omitted" {McManus p79}. This change is not difficult to understand if we remember that Holy Thurday Mass traditionally took place *in the morning*; but Pope Pius XII moved the timing to between **4:00PM** and **9:00PM**. Therefore, there would no longer be a suitable time for Vespers.

Bishops from various countries protested—for pastoral reasons—transferring Holy Thursday to the evening and begged for permission "to permit the celebration of a read Mass and the Communion of the faithful on Holy Thursday morning, or at least the distribution of Holy Communion *extra Missam* to the faithful" {Giampietro p291}.

COMPLINE ON HOLY THURSDAY

The 1962 rubrics say that Compline—the final office which "completes" (*Ad Completorium*) the day—is to be recited on Holy Thursday after the Stripping of the Altars: *Mox in choro dicitur Completorium, candelis exstinctis et absque cantu.* Compline having been recited, the congregation should stay and adore the Blessed Sacrament "at least until midnight" {McManus p79}.

Nothing prevents the congregation from participating in Compline, and this is the traditional way (cf. "Interview with Domenico Cardinal Bartolucci" dated 12 August 2009). Even at a time when women were thought to be excluded from singing during Mass, they were still explicitly encouraged to sing the "Psalms and Hymns of the Divine Office"; cf. "Church Music" in the *American Ecclesiastical Review* (September, 1906). To facilitate this, the faithful should be provided with a booklet containing the Latin text as well as vernacular translations.

FATHER FORTESCUE: HOLY THURSDAY

The following was written by Father Fortescue in 1913. It makes no sense without realizing that before 1955, the Mass on Holy Thursday took place in the morning, often as early as 6:30AM.

AFTER MASS the procession takes the Sanctissimum to the place where It is kept till the next day. This is an example of a real Roman procession, having a definite object. It is usual to call the place to which the Blessed Sacrament is taken the "altar of repose." This is a harmless popular name; but it is not really an altar. No sacrifice is offered on it. At first it seems that nothing more was done than to keep the Sanctissimum reverently in some safe place, often in the sacristy, as It is still reserved in many Eastern Churches. Then people realized that this was the one occasion when they had the Blessed Sacrament in their churches—so they made much of it. They fitted up and adorned a place of honour; they began to watch and pray before the "altar of repose" all the day and all night.

Much of the ideas of such later developments as Exposition of the Blessed Sacrament, of the "Forty Hours," and so on, seems to have begun during this time between Mass on Maundy Thursday and Good Friday. And then—even after it had become usual to reserve the Sanctissimum on the altar of nearly every church all the year round—the old custom of special reverence on this occasion continued. That, too, is nearly always so. *Custom preserves many things in liturgy after their first reason has ceased.* This accounts for the special reverence with which we still treat the Sanctissimum at the "altar of repose," although we have It now in the tabernacle always. And, indeed, on this night of all nights, when our Lord was suffering his bitter torment, it is natural that people should spend part of the time with him in prayer, honouring the gift of that day.

We leave the "altar of repose," come back to the High Altar and say Vespers. This is not really a special feature of these days. On all fast days Vespers are now said in the morning, from the old idea that one does not break one's fast till after Vespers. Easier legislation now allows people to eat at midday on fast days; but the liturgical sequence is preserved; so the meal pushed Vespers back to the morning. The fact that on fast days at the end of Mass the Deacon says not: "Ite missa est," but "Benedicamus Domino," meant once that he did not dismiss the people then, because they were to stay for Vespers. After Vespers the altar is stripped. This ceremony has become to us one of the features of Holy Week; yet it is only one more case of an archaic custom otherwise abolished, but preserved on these days. Once—after Mass on any day—the altar was stripped. Now on Maundy Thursday and Good Friday the stripping of the altar has become a symbol of desolation, or a memory that our Lord was stripped of his garments. ✠

✠ IT WAS I WHO BROUGHT THEE OUT OF EGYPT AND DROWNED PHARAOH IN THE RED SEA: AND THOU HAST BETRAYED ME INTO THE HANDS OF THE CHIEF PRIESTS. ✠ FOR THY SAKE, I STRUCK DOWN THE KINGS OF CANAAN: AND THOU HAST STRUCK MY HEAD WITH A REED. ✠

PILATE SAID: I HAVE EXAMINED HIM IN YOUR PRESENCE, AND COULD FIND NO SUBSTANCE IN ANY OF THE CHARGES YOU BRING AGAINST HIM; NOR COULD HEROD. IT IS PLAIN THAT HE HAS DONE NOTHING WHICH DESERVES DEATH. ✠ Lk 23.14

1962 • *Solemnis Actio liturgica celebranda est horis postmeridianis, et quidem circa horam tertiam; si vera ratio pastoralis id suadeat, inchoari potest inde a meridie, vel tardiori hora, non autem ultra horam nonam serotinam.*

The solemn liturgical service is to be celebrated in the afternoon **about 3:00PM**. If a pastoral reason suggests otherwise, it may begin at noon or at a later hour, but not after **9:00PM** {Giampietro p300}. Some authors say it cannot begin later than **6:00PM** {Goddard p274; McManus p3}—on this, cf. the *Commissio Piana* meeting that took place on 17 Jan 1956 {Giampietro 290}. Whereas previously this ceremony was called "The Morning Office of Good Friday" {Thurston p345}, the reform of Pope Pius XII changed its name to: "Solemn Liturgical Service of the Afternoon of the Passion and Death of the Lord." The opening prayer (added by the reformers) comes from the Gelasian Sacramentary—cf. *Liber Sacramentorum Romanae Ecclesiae* (Clarendon Press, 1894) page 75.

DE SOLEMNI ACTIONE LITURGICA POSTMERIDIANA IN PASSIONE ET MORTE DOMINI

I Classis. —*Good Friday* • *Solemn Afternoon Liturgy*—

FERIA SEXTA IN PASSIONE ET MORTE DOMINI *Station at Holy Cross in Jerusalem*

1962 • *Clerici, ministri, et celebrans, cum ad altare pervenerint, eidem altari reverentiam faciunt: deinde, celebrans et ministri sacri—non vero ministrantes—in faciem procumbunt, reliqui vero adeunt scamna in choro, ibique manent, genibus flexis et profunde inclinati: omnesque in silentio aliquamdiu orant. Signa data, omnes se erigunt, sed genuflexi manent; solus celebrans, stans ante gradus altaris, dicit, manibus junctis et in tono feriali, sequentem orationem:*

The procession moves through the church in silence. The Celebrant and sacred ministers—but not servers—prostrate themselves before the Altar, while everyone else kneels and bows deeply. All pray in silence for a "moderately long time" {McManus p80}. When the sign is given, everyone remains kneeling, but no longer bowed. The Celebrant alone, standing before the steps of the Altar, says the following prayer without inflection, with his hands joined:

Deus, qui peccáti véteris hereditárium mortẽ, in qua posteritátis genus omne succésserat, Christi tui, Dómini nostri, passióne solvísti: da, ut, confórmes eídem facti; sicut imáginem terrénæ natúræ necessitáte portávimus, ita imáginem cæléstis grátiæ sanctificatióne portémus. Per eúmdem Christum Dñm nostrum. ℟. Amen.

O GOD, BY THE PASSION of Christ Thy Son, our Lord, Thou hast banished the inheritance of death due to original sin, which had fallen on all posterity; grant, that being made like to Him, as of necessity we bear the likeness of our human nature, so by being made holy we may manifest the likeness of heavenly grace. Through the same Christ our Lord. ℟. Amen.

FIRST LESSON. *Osee 6: 1-6*

A lector begins these readings without title:

Hæc dicit Dóminus: In tribulatióne sua mane consúrgent ad me: Veníte, et revertámur ad Dóminum: quia ipse cepit, et sanábit nos: percútiet, et curábit nos. Vivificábit nos post duos dies: in die tértia suscitábit nos, et vivémus in conspéctu ejus. Sciémus, sequemúrque, ut cognoscámus Dóminum: quasi dilúculum præparátus est egréssus ejus, et véniet quasi imber nobis temporáneus, et serótinus terræ. Quid fáciam tibi Éphraïm? Quid fáciam tibi Juda? Misericórdia vestra quasi nubes matutína, et quasi ros mane pertránsiens. Propter hoc dolávi in prophétis, occídi eos in verbis oris mei: et judícia tua quasi lux egrediéntur. Quia misericórdiam vólui, et non sacrifícium, et sciéntiam Dei plus quam holocáusta. *("Deo Grátias" is not said.)*

THUS SAITH THE LORD: In their affliction they will rise early to Me: Come, and let us return to the Lord, for He hath taken us, and He will heal us, He will strike, and He will cure us. He will revive us after two days: on the third day He will raise us up and we shall live in His sight. We shall know and we shall follow on, that we may know the Lord. His going forth is prepared as the morning light and He will come to us as the early and the latter rain to the earth. What shall I do to thee, O Ephraim? What shall I do to thee, O Juda? Your mercy is as a morning cloud and as the dew that goeth away in the morning. For this reason have I hewed them by the prophets, I have slain them by the words of my mouth: and thy judgments shall go forth as the light. For I desired mercy and not sacrifice: and the knowledge of God more than holocausts.

FIRST RESPONSORY. *Habacuc 3*

O LORD, I have heard Thy hearing and was afraid: I have considered Thy works and trembled. ℣. In the midst of two animals Thou shalt be made known: when the years shall draw nigh Thou shalt be known: when the time shall come, Thou shalt be manifested. ℣. When my soul shall be in trouble, Thou wilt remember mercy, even in Thy wrath. ℣. God will come from Libanus, and the Holy One from the shady and thickly covered mountain. ℣. His majesty covered the heavens: and the earth is full of His praise.

These were called "tracts" before 1955.

Dómine, audívi audítum tuum, et tímui: considerávi ópera tua, et expávi. ℣. In médio duórũ animáliũ innotescéris: dum appropinquáverint anni, cognoscéris: dũ advénerit tempus, ostendéris. ℣. In eo, dum conturbáta fúerit ánima mea: in ira, misericórdiæ memor eris. ℣. Deus a Líbano véniet, et Sanctus de monte umbróso et condénso. ℣. Opéruit cælos majéstas ejus: et laudis ejus plena est terra.

Let us pray.
℣. Let us kneel.
℟. Arise.

Celebrant: Orémus.
Deacon: ℣. Flectámus génua.
Deacon: ℟. Leváte.

O God, from Whom Judas received the punishment of his crime, and the thief the reward of his confession, grant us the effect of Thy clemency, that, as Jesus Christ, our Lord, in His passion dealt according to their deserts with the one and the other, so, putting away from us the error of the past, He may bestow upon us the grace of His resurrection. Who with Thee.

Deus, a quo et Judas reátus sui pœnam, et confessiónis suæ latro prǽmium sumpsit, concéde nobis tuæ propitiatiónis effectum: ut, sicut in passióne sua Jesus Christus, Dóminus noster, divérsa utrísque íntulit stipéndia meritórum; ita nobis, abláto vetustátis erróre, resurrectiónis suæ grátiam largiátur: Qui tecum.

SECOND LESSON. *Ex 12: 1-11*

Identical to the 9th Prophecy on (1950 version) Holy Saturday:

IN THOSE DAYS, the Lord said to Moses and Aaron in the land of Egypt: This month shall be to you the beginning of months: it shall be the first in the months of the year. Speak ye to the whole assembly of the children of Israel, and say to them: On the tenth day of this month let every man take a lamb by their families and houses. But if the number be less than may suffice to eat the lamb, he shall take unto him his neighbor that joineth to his house, according to the number of souls which may be enough to eat the lamb. And it shall be a lamb without blemish, a male, of one year: according to which rite also you shall take a kid. And you shall keep it until the fourteenth day of this month: and the whole multitude of the children of Israel shall sacrifice it in the evening. And they shall take of blood thereof, and put it upon both the side posts, and on the upper door posts of the houses, wherein they shall eat it. And they shall eat the flesh that night roasted at the fire: and unleavened bread with wild lettuce. You shall not

In diébus illis: Dixit Dóminus ad Móysen et Áäron in terra Ægýpti: Mensis iste vobis princípiũ ménsium primus erit in ménsibus anni. Loquímini ad univérsum cœtum filiórum Ísraël, et dícite eis: Décima die mensis hujus tollat unusquísque agnum per famílias et domos suas. Sin autem minor est númerus, ut suffícere possit ad vescéndum agnum, assúmet vicínum suum, qui junctus est dómui suæ, juxta númerum animárum, quæ sufficere possunt ad esum agni. Erit autem agnus absque mácula, másculus, annículus: juxta quem ritum tollétis et hædum. Et servábitis eum usque ad quartam décimã diem mensis hujus: immolabítque eum univérsa multitúdo filiórum Ísraël ad vésperam. Et sument de sánguine ejus, ac ponent super utrúmque postem et in superlimináribus domórum, in quibus cómedent illum. Et edent carnes nocte illa assas igni, et ázymos panes cum lactúcis agréstibus. Non comedétis ex eo crudum quid nec coctum aqua, sed tantum assum igni: caput cum pédibus ejus et intestínis vorábitis. Nec remanébit quidquam ex eo usque mane. Si quid resíduum fúerit, igne comburétis. Sic autem comedétis illum: Renes vestros accingétis, et calceaménta habébitis in pédibus, tenéntes báculos in mánibus, et comedétis festinánter: est enim Phase (id est tránsitus) Dómini. (*"Deo Grátias" is not said.*)

eat thereof any thing raw, nor boiled in water, but only roasted at the fire. You shall eat the head with the feet and entrails thereof. Neither shall there remain any thing of it until morning. If there be any thing left, you shall burn it with fire. And thus you shall eat it: You shall gird your reins, and you shall have shoes on your feet, holding staves in your hands, and you shall eat in haste; for it is the Phase (that is, the Passage) of the Lord.

SECOND RESPONSORY. *Ps 139: 2-10, 14*

These were called "tracts" before 1955.

Éripe me, Dómine, ab hómine malo: a viro iníquo líbera me. ℣. Qui cogitavérunt malítias in corde: tota die constituébant prœlia. ℣. Acuérunt linguas suas sicut serpéntis: venénum áspidum sub lábiis eórum. ℣. Custódi me, Dómine, de manu peccatóris: et ab homínibus iníquis líbera me. ℣. Qui cogitavérunt supplantáre gressus meos: abscondérunt supérbi láqueum mihi. ℣. Et funes extendérunt in láqueum pédibus meis: juxta iter scándalum posuérunt mihi. ℣. Dixi Dómino: Deus meus es tu: exáudi, Dómine, vocem oratiónis meæ. ℣. Dómine, Dómine, virtus salútis meæ: obúmbra caput meum in die belli. ℣. Ne tradas me a desidério meo peccatóri: cogitavérunt advérsus me: ne derelínquas me, ne umquam exalténtur. ℣. Caput circúitus eórum: labor labiórum ipsórum opériet eos. ℣. Verúmtamen justi confitebúntur nómini tuo: et habitábunt recti cum vultu tuo.

DELIVER ME, O Lord, from the evil man: rescue me from the unjust man. ℣. Who have devised iniquities in their heart: all the day long they designed battles. ℣. They have sharpened their tongues like a serpent; the venom of asps is under their lips. ℣. Keep me, O Lord, from the hand of the wicked: and from unjust men deliver me. ℣. Who have proposed to supplant my steps. The proud have hidden a net for me. ℣. And they have stretched out cords for a snare for my feet; they have laid for me a stumbling-block by the wayside. ℣. I said to the Lord: Thou art my God. Hear, O Lord, the voice of my supplication. ℣. O Lord, Lord, the strength of my salvation: overshadow my head in the day of battle. ℣. Give me not up from my desire to the wicked: they have plotted against me. Do not Thou forsake me, lest at any time they should triumph. ℣. The head of them compassing me about: the labor of their lips shall overwhelm them. ℣. But the just shall give glory to Thy Name: and the upright shall dwell with Thy countenance.

John 18: 1-40; 19: 1-42

[C] *Chronista ;*

[S] *Synagoga ;*

✠ *Christus.*

English translation (1950) by Monsignor Ronald Knox.

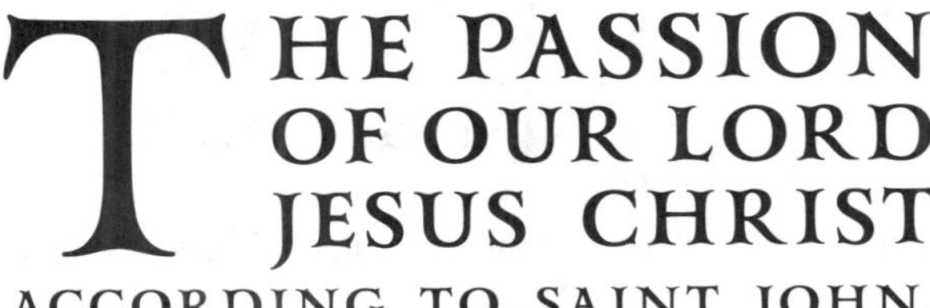

The Passion of Our Lord Jesus Christ according to Saint John. At this time, Jesus,
Pássio Dómini nostri Jesu Christi secúndum Joánnem. In illo témpore:

with his disciples, went out across the Cedron valley. Here there was a garden, into
Egréssus est Jesus cum discípulis suis trans torréntem Cedron, ubi erat hortus,

which he and his disciples went. Judas, his betrayer, knew the place well; Jesus
in quem introívit ipse et discípuli ejus. Sciébat autem et Judas, qui tradébat eum, locum:

and his disciples had often forgathered in it. There, then, Judas came, accompanied
quia frequénter Jesus convénerat illuc cum discípulis suis. Judas ergo cum accepísset cohórtem,

by the guard, and officers sent by the chief priests and Pharisees, with lanterns and
et a pontifícibus et pharisǽis minístros, venit illuc cum latérnis et

torches and weapons. So Jesus, knowing well what was to befall him, went out
fácibus et armis. Jesus ítaque sciens ómnia, quæ ventúra erant super eum, procéssit,

to meet them, and asked: ✠ Who is it you are looking for? [C] They answered:
et dixit eis: Quem quǽritis? Respondérunt ei:

[S] Jesus of Nazareth. [C] And he told them: ✠ I am Jesus of Nazareth. [C] And
Jesum Nazarénum. Dicit eis Jesus: Ego sum.

there was Judas, his betrayer, standing in their company. When he said to them, I am
Stabat autem et Judas, qui tradébat eum, cum ipsis. Ut ergo dixit eis:

Jesus of Nazareth, they all shrank back, and fell to the ground. So, once more, Jesus
Ego sum: abiérunt retrórsum, et cecidérunt in terram. Íterum ergo

asked them: ✠ Who is it you are looking for? [C] and when they said: [S] Jesus
interrogávit eos: Quem quǽritis? Illi autem dixérunt:

of Nazareth, [C] he answered: ✠ I have told you already that I am Jesus. If I am
Jesum Nazarénum. Respóndit Jesus: Dixi vobis, quia ego sum:

the man you are looking for, let these others go free. [C] Thus he would make
si ergo me quǽritis, sínite hos abíre. Ut implerétur sermo,

good the words he had spoken to them, I have not lost any of those whom thou
quem dixit: Quia quos dedísti mihi, non pérdidi ex eis quemquam.

hast entrusted to me. Then Simon Peter, who had a sword, drew it, and struck the
Simon ergo Petrus habens gládium edúxit eum: et percússit

high priest's servant, cutting off his right ear; Malchus was the name of the servant.
pontíficis servum: et abscídit aurículam ejus déxteram. Erat autem nomen servo Malchus.

Whereupon Jesus said to Peter: ✠ Put thy sword back into its sheath. Am I not to
Dixit ergo Jesus Petro: Mitte gládium tuum in vagínam.

drink that cup which my Father himself has appointed for me? [C] And now the
Cálicem, quem dedit mihi Pater, non bibam illum?

guard, with their captain, and the Jewish officers arrested Jesus and pinioned him.
Cohors ergo et tribúnus et minístri Judæórum comprehendérunt Jesum, et ligavérunt eum:

Before the High Priest

They led him off, in the first instance, to Annas, father-in-law of Caiphas, who
et adduxérunt eum ad Annam primum, erat enim socer Cáïphæ,

held the high priesthood in that year. (It was this Caiphas who had given it as
qui erat póntifex anni illíus. Erat autem Cáïphas,

his advice to the Jews, that it was best to put one man to death for the sake of
qui consílium déderat Judǽis: Quia expédit, unum hóminem mori pro pópulo.

the people.) Simon Peter followed Jesus, with another disciple; this disciple was
Sequebátur autem Jesum Simon Petrus et álius discípulus.

acquainted with the high priest, and went into the high priest's court with Jesus,
Discípulus autem ille erat notus pontífici, et introívit cum Jesu in átrium pontíficis.

while Peter stood at the door without. Afterwards the other disciple, who was
Petrus autem stabat ad óstium foris. Exívit ergo discípulus álius,

the high priest's acquaintance, went out and spoke to the door-keeper, and so
qui erat notus pontífici, et dixit ostiáriæ:

brought Peter in. This maid-servant who kept the door asked Peter: [S] Art thou
et introdúxit Petrum. Dicit ergo Petro ancílla ostiária:

another of this man's disciples? [C] And he said: [S] Not I. [C] It was cold,
Numquid et tu ex discípulis es hóminis istíus? Dicit ille: Non sum.

and the servants and officers had made a charcoal fire, and stood there warming
Stabant autem servi et minístri ad prunas, quia frigus erat, et calefaciébant se:

themselves; there Peter stood too, warming himself with the rest. And now the high
erat autem cum eis et Petrus stans et calefáciens se.

priest questioned Jesus about his disciples, and about his teaching. Jesus answered:
Póntifex ergo interrogávit Jesum de discípulis suis et de doctrína ejus. Respóndit ei Jesus:

✠ I have spoken openly before the world; my teaching has been given in the
Ego palam locútus sum mundo: ego semper dócui

synagogue and in the temple, where all the Jews forgather; nothing that I have said
in synagóga et in templo, quo omnes Judǽi convéniunt: et in occúlto locútus sum nihil.

was said in secret. Why dost thou question me? Ask those who listened to me what
Quid me intérrogas? intérroga eos, qui audiérunt,

my words were; they know well enough what I said. [C] When he spoke thus, one
quid locútus sim ipsis: ecce, hi sciunt, quæ díxerim ego. Hæc autem cum dixísset,

of the officers, who was standing by, struck Jesus on the cheek, saying: [S] Is this
unus assístens ministrórum dedit álapam Jesu, dicens:

how thou makest answer to the high priest? [C] Jesus answered: ✠ If there was
Sic respóndes pontífici? Respóndit ei Jesus:

harm in what I said, tell us what was harmful in it; if not, why dost thou strike me?
Si male locútus sum, testimónium pérhibe de malo: si autem bene, quid me cædis?

[C] Annas, you must know, had sent him on, still bound, to the high priest Caiphas.
Et misit eum Annas ligátum ad Cáïpham pontíficem.

Saint Peter's Denial

Meanwhile Simon Peter stood there, and warmed himself. So they asked him:
Erat autem Simon Petrus stans et calefáciens se. Dixérunt ergo ei:

[S] Art thou, too, one of his disciples? [C] And he denied it, saying: [S] Not I.
Numquid et tu ex discípulis ejus es? Negávit ille et dixit: Non sum.

[C] One of the of the high priest's servants, a kinsman of the man whose ear Peter
Dicit ei unus ex servis pontíficis, cognátus ejus, cujus abscídit Petrus aurículam:

had cut off, asked: [S] Did I not see thee with him in the garden? [C] Whereupon
Nonne ego te vidi in horto cum illo?

Peter denied again; and immediately the cock crew.
Íterum ergo negávit Petrus: et statim gallus cantávit.

Before Pontius Pilate

And now they led Jesus away from the house of Caiphas to the governor's palace.
Addúcunt ergo Jesum a Cäïpha in prætórium.

It was morning, and they would not enter the palace themselves; there was the
Erat autem mane: et ipsi non introiérunt in prætórium,

paschal meal to be eaten, and they must not incur defilement. And so Pilate went
ut non contaminaréntur, sed ut manducárent pascha. Exívit ergo Pilátus

to meet them without, and said; [S] What charge do you bring against this man?
ad eos foras et dixit: Quam accusatiónem affértis advérsus hóminem hunc?

[C] They answered; [S] We would not have given him up to thee, if he had not
Respondérunt et dixérunt ei: Si non esset hic malefáctor, non tibi tradidissémus eum.

been a malefactor. [C] Pilate said to them: [S] Take him yourselves and judge
Dixit ergo eis Pilátus: Accípite eum vos,

him according to your own law. [C] Whereupon the Jews said to him: [S] We
et secúndum legem vestram judicáte eum. Dixérunt ergo ei Judǽi:

have no power to put any man to death. [C] This was in fulfilment of the words
Nobis non licet interfícere quemquam. Ut sermo Jesu impleréture,

Jesus had spoken when he prophesied what death he was to die. So Pilate went
quem dixit, signíficans, qua morte esset moritúrus.

back into the palace, and summoned Jesus, and asked him: [S] Art thou the king
Introívit ergo íterum in prætórium Pilátus, et vocávit Jesum et dixit ei: Tu es Rex Judæórum?

of the Jews? [C] Jesus answered: ✠ Dost thou say this of thy own accord, or is
Respóndit Jesus: A temetípso hoc dicis,

it what others have told thee of me? [C] And Pilate answered: [S] Am I a Jew?
an álii dixérunt tibi de me? Respóndit Pilátus: Numquid ego Judǽus sum?

It is thy own nation, and its chief priests, who have given thee up to me. What
Gens tua et pontífices tradidérunt te mihi:

offence hast thou committed? [C] Jesus said: ✠ My kingdom does not belong to
quid fecisti? Respóndit Jesus: Regnum meum non est de hoc mundo.

this world. If my kingdom were one which belonged to this world, my servants
Si ex hoc mundo esset regnum meum,

would be fighting, to prevent my falling into the hands of the Jews; but no, my
minístri mei útique decertárent, ut non tráderer Judǽis:

kingdom does not take its origin here. [C] Pilate asked: [S] Thou art a king, then?
nunc autem regnum meum non est hinc. Dixit ítaque ei Pilátus: Ergo Rex es tu?

[C] And Jesus answered: ✠ It is thy own lips that have called me a king. What I
Respóndit Jesus: Tu dicis, quia Rex sum ego.

was born for, what I came into the world for, is to bear witness of the truth. Whoever
Ego in hoc natus sum et ad hoc veni in mundum, ut testimónium perhíbeam veritáti:

belongs to the truth, listens to my voice. [C] Pilate said to him, [S] What is truth?
omnis, qui est ex veritáte, audit vocem meam. Dicit ei Pilátus: Quid est véritas?

PILATE OFFERS A CHOICE

And with that he went back to the Jews again, and told them: [S] I can find no
Et cum hoc dixísset, íterum exívit ad Judǽos, et dicit eis: Ego nullam invénio
fault in him. You have a custom of demanding that I should release one prisoner at
in eo causam. Est autem consuetúdo vobis, ut unum dimíttam vobis in Pascha:
paschal time; would you have me release the king of the Jews? [C] Whereupon they
vultis ergo dimíttam vobis Regem Judæórum? Clamavérunt ergo
all made a fresh outcry: [S] Barabbas, not this man. [C] Barabbas was a robber.
rursum omnes, dicéntes: Non hunc, sed Barábbam. Erat autem Barábbas latro.

SCOURGED & CROWNED WITH THORNS

Then Pilate took Jesus and scourged him. And the soldiers put on his head a crown
Tunc ergo apprehéndit Pilátus Jesum et flagellávit. Et mílites plecténtes corónam de spinis, imposuérunt cápiti ejus:
which they had woven out of thorns, and dressed him in a scarlet cloak; they would
et veste purpúrea circumdedérunt eum.
come up to him and say: [S] Hail, king of the Jews, [C] and then strike him on the
Et veniébant ad eum, et dicébant: Ave, Rex Judæórum. Et dabant ei álapas.
face. And now Pilate went out again, and said: [S] See, I am bringing him out to
Exívit ergo íterum Pilátus foras et dicit eis: Ecce, addúco vobis eum foras,
you, to show that I cannot find any fault in him. [C] Then, as Jesus came out, still
ut cognoscátis, quia nullam invénio in eo causam. (Exívit ergo Jesus portans corónam
wearing the crown of thorns and the scarlet cloak, he said to them: [S] See, here
spíneam et purpúreum vestiméntum.) Et dicit eis:
is the man.
Ecce homo.

NO KING EXCEPT CAESAR

When the chief priests and their officers saw him, they cried out: [S] Crucify him,
Cum ergo vidíssent eum pontífices et minístri, clamábant, dicéntes: Crucifíge,
crucify him. [C] Pilate said, [S] Take him yourselves and crucify him; I cannot
crucifíge eum. Dicit eis Pilátus: Accípite eum vos et crucifígite: ego enim
find any fault in him. [C] The Jews answered: [S] We have our own law, and
non invénio in eo causam. Respondérunt ei Judǽi: Nos legem habémus,
by our law he ought to die, for pretending to be the Son of God. [C] When Pilate
et secúndum legem debet mori, quia Fílium Dei se fecit. Cum ergo
heard this said, he was more afraid than ever; going back into the palace, he asked
audísset Pilátus hunc sermónem, magis tímuit. Et ingréssus est prætórium íterum: et dixit ad

Jesus: [S] Whence hast thou come? [C] But Jesus gave him no answer. Pilate
Jesum: Unde es tu? Jesus autem respónsum non dedit ei. Dicit ergo

said: [S] Hast thou no word for me? Dost thou not know that I have power to
ei Pilátus: Mihi non lóqueris? nescis, quia potestátem hábeo crucifígere te,

crucify thee, and power to release thee? [C] Jesus answered: ✠ Thou wouldst not
et potestátem hábeo dimíttere te? Respóndit Jesus:

have any power over me at all, if it had not been given thee from above. That is
Non habéres potestátem advérsum me ullam, nisi tibi datum esset désuper.

why the man who gave me up to thee is more guilty yet. [C] After this, Pilate
Proptérea, qui me trádidit tibi, majus peccátum habet. Et exínde quærébat

was for releasing him, but the Jews went on crying out: [S] Thou art no friend
Pilátus dimíttere eum. Judǽi autem clamábant dicéntes:

of Caesar, if thou dost release him; the man who pretends to be a king is Caesar's
Si hunc dimíttis, non es amícus Cǽsaris. Omnis enim, qui se regem facit, contradícit Cǽsari.

rival. [C] When Pilate heard them speak thus, he brought Jesus out, and sat down
Pilátus autem cum audísset hos sermónes, addúxit foras Jesum,

on the judgement seat, in a place which is called Lithostrotos; its Hebrew name is
et sedit pro tribunáli, in loco, qui dícitur Lithóstrotos, hebráice autem

Gabbatha. It was now about the sixth hour, on the eve of the paschal feast. He said
Gábbatha. Erat autem Parascéve Paschæ, hora quasi sexta,

to the Jews: [S] See, here is your king. [C] But they cried out: [S] Away with
et dicit Judǽis: Ecce Rex vester. Illi autem clamábant: Tolle,

him, away with him, crucify him. [C] Pilate said to them: [S] Shall I crucify
tolle, crucífige eum. Dicit eis Pilátus: Regem vestrum crucifígam?

your king? [C] The chief priests answered: [S] We have no king, except Caesar.
Respondérunt pontífices: Non habémus regem nisi Cǽsarem.

Crucified for our Sins

Thereupon he gave Jesus up into their hands, to be crucified: and they, once he
Tunc ergo trádidit eis illum, ut crucifigerétur.

was in their hands, led him away. So Jesus went out, carrying his own cross, to
Suscepérunt autem Jesum et eduxérunt. Et bájulans sibi Crucem, exívit in eum,

the place named after a skull; its Hebrew name is Golgotha. There they crucified
qui dícitur Calváriæ, locum, hebráice autem Gólgotha: ubi crucifixérunt eum,

him, and with him two others, one on each side with Jesus in the midst. And Pilate
et cum eo alios duos, hinc et hinc, médium autem Jesum.

wrote out a proclamation, which he put on the cross; it ran, Jesus of Nazareth,
Scripsit autem et títulum Pilátus: et pósuit super crucem. Erat autem scriptum: Jesus Nazarénus,

the king of the Jews. This proclamation was read by many of the Jews, since the
Rex Judæórum. Hunc ergo títulum multi Judæórum legérunt,

place where Jesus was crucified was close to the city; it was written in Hebrew,
quia prope civitátem erat locus, ubi crucifíxus est Jesus. Et erat scriptum hebráice,

THOU SAYEST I AM A KING. FOR THIS WAS I BORN, AND FOR THIS CAME I INTO THE WORLD; THAT I SHOULD GIVE TESTIMONY OF THE TRUTH. EVERY ONE THAT IS OF THE TRUTH HEARETH MY VOICE.

TU DICIS, QUIA REX SUM EGO. EGO IN HOC NATUS SUM ET AD HOC VENI IN MUNDUM, UT TESTIMONIUM PERHIBEAM VERITATI: OMNIS, QUI EST EX VERITATE, AUDIT VOCEM MEAM.

"CEASE TO COMPLAIN, CONSIDERING MY PASSION."

"THE SON OF MAN MUST SUFFER MANY THINGS."

Greek, and Latin. And the Jewish chief priests said to Pilate: [S] Thou shouldst
græce et latine. Dicébant ergo Piláto pontífices Judæórum:

not write, The king of the Jews; thou shouldst write, This man said, I am the king
Noli scríbere Rex Judæórum, sed quia ipse dixit: Rex sum Judæórum.

of the Jews. [C] Pilate's answer was: [S] What I have written, I have written.
Respóndit Pilátus: Quod scripsi, scripsi.

[C] The soldiers, when they had crucified Jesus, took up his garments, which
Mílites ergo cum crucifixíssent eum, accepérunt vestiménta ejus

they divided into four shares, one share for each soldier. They took up his cloak,
(et fecérunt quátuor partes: unicuíque míliti partem), et túnicam.

too, which was without seam, woven from the top throughout; so they said to
Erat autem túnica inconsútilis, désuper contéxta per totum. Dixérunt ergo

one another: [S] Better not to tear it; let us cast lots to decide whose it shall be.
ad ínvicem: Non scindámus eam, sed sortiámur de illa, cujus sit.

[C] This was in fulfilment of the passage in scripture which says: They divide
Ut Scriptúra impleretúr, dicens: Partíti sunt

my spoils among them; cast lots for my clothing. So it was, then, that the soldiers
vestiménta mea sibi: et in vestem meam misérunt sortem. Et mílites quidem hæc fecérunt.

occupied themselves; and meanwhile his mother, and his mother's sister, Mary the
Stabant autem juxta Crucem Jesu Mater ejus et soror Matris ejus,

wife of Cleophas, and Mary Magdalen, had taken their stand beside the cross of
María Cléophæ, et María Magdaléne.

Jesus. And Jesus, seeing his mother there, and the disciple, too, whom he loved,
Cum vidísset ergo Jesus Matrem et discípulum stantem, quem diligébat,

standing by, said to his mother: ✠ Woman, this is thy son. [C] Then he said to
dicit Matri suæ: Múlier, ecce fílius tuus. Deínde dicit

the disciple: ✠ This is thy mother. [C] And from that hour the disciple took her
discípulo: Ecce mater tua. Et ex illa hora accépit eam discípulus in sua.

into his own keeping. And now Jesus knew well that all was achieved which the
Póstea sciens Jesus, quia ómnia consummáta sunt,

scripture demanded for its accomplishment; and he said: ✠ I am thirsty. [C] There
ut consummarétur Scriptúra, dixit: Sítio.

was a jar there full of vinegar; so they filled a sponge with the vinegar and put it
Vas ergo erat pósitum acéto plenum. Illi autem spóngiam plenam acéto,

on a stick of hyssop, and brought it close to his mouth. Jesus drank the vinegar,
hyssópo circumponéntes, obtulérunt ori ejus. Cum ergo accepísset Jesus acétum,

and said: ✠ It is achieved. [C] Then he bowed his head, and yielded up his spirit.
dixit: Consummátum est. Et inclináte cápite trádidit spíritum.

Here all kneel, and a short pause is made.

[In former days, the faithful would lie prostrate on the ground.]

1962 • *Hic genuflectitur, et pausatur aliquantulum.*

Him Whom They Have Pierced

The Jews would not let the bodies remain crucified on the sabbath, because that
Judǽi ergo (quóniam Parascéve erat), ut non remanérent in cruce córpora sábbato (erat enim

sabbath day was a solemn one; and since it was now the eve, they asked Pilate that
magnus dies ille sábbati), rogavérunt Pilátum, ut

the bodies might have their legs broken, and be taken away. And so the soldiers
frangeréntur eórum crura et tolleréntur. Venérunt ergo mílites:

came and broke the legs both of the one and of the other that were crucified with
et primi quidem fregérunt crura et alteríus, qui crucifíxus est cum eo.

him; but when they came to Jesus, and found him already dead, they did not break
Ad Jesum autem cum venissent, ut vidérunt eum jam mórtuum, non fregérunt ejus crura,

his legs, but one of the soldiers opened his side with a spear; and immediately
sed unus mílitum láncea latus ejus apéruit, et contínuo

blood and water flowed out. He who saw it has borne his witness; and his witness is
exívit sanguis et aqua. Et qui vidit, testimónium perhíbuit: et verum est testimónium ejus.

worthy of trust. He tells what he knows to be the truth, that you, like him, may learn
Et ille scit, quia vera dicit: ut et vos credátis.

to believe. This was so ordained to fulfil what is written: You shall not break a single
Facta sunt enim hæc, ut Scriptúra implerétur: Os non comminuétis ex eo.

bone of his. And again, another passage in scripture says, They will look upon the
Et íterum ália Scriptúra dicit: Vidébunt

man whom they have pierced.
in quem transfixérunt.

1962 • The next section is not read by the "Deacon of the Mass" in the 1962 version; rather, it is connected to the rest of the Saint John Passion without interruption. It can be sung to the normal Passion tone—cf. *Ordo Hebdomadae Sanctae Juxta Ritum Monasticum* (Desclée, 1961) page 282—or the piercingly beautiful "tonus planctus" ("weeping tone") may be used.

Post hæc autem rogávit Pilátum Joseph ab Arimathǽa (eo quod esset discípulus Jesu, occúltus autem propter metum Judæórum), ut tólleret corpus Jesu. Et permísit Pilátus. Venit ergo et tulit corpus Jesu. Venit autẽ et Nicodémus, qui vénerat ad Jesum nocte primum, ferens mixtúram myrrhæ et áloës, quasi libras centum. Accepérunt ergo corpus Jesu, et ligavérunt illud línteis cum aromátibus, sicut mos est Judǽis sepelíre. Erat autem in loco, ubi crucifíxus est, hortus: et in horto monuméntum novum, in quo nondum quisquam pósitus erat. Ibi ergo propter Parascéven Judæórũ, quia juxta erat monuméntum, posuérunt Jesum.

AFTER THIS, Joseph of Arimathea, who was a disciple of Jesus, but in secret, for fear of the Jews, asked Pilate to let him take away the body of Jesus. Pilate gave him leave; so he came and took Jesus' body away; and with him was Nicodemus, the same who made his first visit to Jesus by night; he brought with him a mixture of myrrh and aloes, of about a hundred pounds' weight. They took Jesus' body, then, and wrapped it in winding-cloths with the spices; that is how the Jews prepare a body for burial. In the same quarter where he was crucified there was a garden, with a new tomb in it, one in which no man had ever yet been buried. Here, since the tomb was close at hand, they laid Jesus, because of the Jewish feast on the morrow.

SERMON ELIMINATED • The 1962 version of Good Friday seems to forbid {McManus p82} a sermon—perhaps an attempt to avoid the notion of the *Missa Praesanctificatorum* ("Mass of the Pre-Sanctified")—whereas the 1950 version allows a sermon {Fortescue p304}. In the 1950 Good Friday, the collects are read at the Epistle corner, whereas in the 1962 version the Missal is placed "at the center of the Altar."

VESTMENTS • The Celebrant's vestments in the 1962 version of Good Friday are rather complicated: (1) The Celebrant begins the ceremony wearing only a black Stole; (2) before reading the Solemn Collects, the Celebrant dons a Cope; (3) when the Solemn Collects are finished, the Celebrant removes his Cope, wearing only a black Stole during the Veneration of the Cross; (4) after the Veneration of the Cross, the Celebrant puts on a purple Chasuble. The 1950 version was much simpler, since the Celebrant wore a black Chasuble the entire ceremony—from beginning to end—except during the Creeping to the Cross.

PART II • SOLEMN COLLECTS

1962 • The Celebrant now dons a black cope; the Deacon wears a black dalmatic; the Subdeacon wears a black tunic. The book is placed on the center of the Altar. Whenever the 1962 rubrics have "Flectámus génua," the reforms of Pope Pius XII call for "a brief period of silent prayer" {McManus p82}. The reformers suggest the time required to say one *Pater Noster*—cf. page 101 of *Ordo Hebdomadae Sanctae Instauratus* (Braga & Bugnini, 1956). In the 1950 version, the Subdeacon said "Leváte," but in the 1962 version, the Deacon does that. Having kissed the altar, the Celebrant begins the solemn Collects:

1 of 9 • FOR THE CHURCH. *Pro Sancta Ecclesia*

LET US PRAY, dearly beloved, for the holy Church of God: that our Lord and God may deign to give it peace, keep it in unity, and guard it throughout the world, subjecting to it principalities and powers: and may grant unto us that, leading a peaceful and quiet life, we may glorify God, the Father almighty.

Orémus, dilectíssimi nobis, pro Ecclésia sancta Dei: ut eam Deus et Dóminus noster pacificáre, adunáre, et custodíre dignétur toto orbe terrárum: subjíciens ei principátus, et potestátes: detque nobis quiétam et tranquíllam vitam degéntibus, glorificáre Deum Patrem omnipoténtem.

Let us pray.
℣. Let us kneel.
℟. Arise.

Celebrant: Orémus.
Deacon: ℣. Flectámus génua.
Deacon: ℟. Leváte.

Almighty and everlasting God, Who in Christ hast revealed Thy glory to all nations: guard the works of Thy mercy; that Thy Church, spread over the whole world, may with steadfast faith persevere in the confession of Thy Name. *Through the same Jesus Christ, Thy Son, our Lord, Who liveth and reigneth with Thee in the unity of the Holy Ghost, God, world without end.* (*All respond:* "Amen.")

Omnípotens sempitérne Deus, qui glóriam tuam ómnibus in Christo géntibus revelásti: custódi ópera misericórdiæ tuæ; ut Ecclésia tua toto orbe diffúsa, stábili fide in confessióne tui nóminis persevéret. *Per eúmdem Dñm nostrum Jesum Christum filium tuum, qui tecum vivit et regnat in unitáte Spíritus Sancti, Deus, per ómnia sǽcula sæculórum.* ℟. Amen.

2 of 9 • FOR THE SUPREME PONTIFF. *Pro Summo Pontifice*

LET US PRAY FOR our most holy Father, (*Name of current Pope*); that our Lord and God, Who chose him to the order of the Episcopate, may keep him in health and safety for His holy Church to govern the holy people of God.

Orémus et pro beatíssimo Papa nostro N.: ut Deus et Dóminus noster, qui elégit eum in órdine episcopátus, salvum atque incólumem custódiat Ecclésiæ suæ sanctæ, ad regéndum pópulum sanctum Dei.

Celebrant: Orémus.
Deacon: ℣. Flectámus génua.
Deacon: ℟. Leváte.

Let us pray.
℣. Let us kneel.
℟. Arise.

Omnípotens sempitérne Deus, cujus judício univérsa fundántur: réspice propítius ad preces nostras, et eléctum nobis Antístitem tua pietáte consérva; ut christiána plebs, quæ te gubernátur auctóre, sub tanto Pontífice, credulitátis suæ méritis augeátur. *Per Dñm nostrum Jesum Christum fílium tuum, qui tecum vivit et regnat in unitáte Spíritus Sancti, Deus, per ómnia sǽcula sæculórum.* ℟. Amen.

Almighty and everlasting God, by Whose judgment all things are established, mercifully regard our prayers, and in Thy goodness preserve the Bishop chosen for us: that the Christian people who are ruled by Thine authority, may under so great a Pontiff, be increased in the merits of faith. *Through our Lord Jesus Christ, Thy Son, Who liveth and reigneth with Thee in the unity of the Holy Ghost, God, world without end.*
(*All respond:* "Amen.")

3 of 9 • FOR CLERGY AND FAITHFUL. *Pro Omnibus Ordinibus Gradibusque Fidelium*

Orémus et pro ómnibus Epíscopis, Presbýteris, Diacónibus, Subdiacónibus, Acólythis, Exorcístis, Lectóribus, Ostiáriis, Confessóribus, Virgínibus, Víduis: et pro omni pópulo sancto Dei.

LET US PRAY also for all Bishops, Priests, Deacons, Subdeacons, Acolytes, Exorcists, Readers, Porters, Confessors, Virgins, Widows, and for all the holy people of God.

Celebrant: Orémus.
Deacon: ℣. Flectámus génua.
Deacon: ℟. Leváte.

Let us pray.
℣. Let us kneel.
℟. Arise.

Omnípotens sempitérne Deus, cujus Spíritu totum corpus Ecclésiæ sanctificátur, et régitur: exáudi nos pro univérsis ordínibus supplicántes; ut grátiæ tuæ múnere, ab ómnibus tibi grádibus fidéliter serviátur. *Per Dñm nostrum Jesum Christum fílium tuũ, qui tecum vivit et regnat in unitáte ejúsdem Spíritus Sancti, Deus, per ómnia sǽcula sæculórum.* ℟. Amen.

Almighty and everlasting God, by Whose Spirit the whole body of the Church is sanctified and ruled, hear our humble pleading for all the orders thereof; that by the gift of Thy grace, all in their several degrees may faithfully serve Thee. *Through Jesus Christ, Thy Son, our Lord, Who liveth and reigneth with Thee in the unity of the same Holy Ghost, God, world without end.* (*All respond:* "Amen.")

[Editor's Note: At this point, the 1950 version inserted a "Prayer for the Emperor" beginning with the words: *Orémus et pro Christianissimo Imperatóre...* But Father Fortescue, writing in 1917, says: "The prayer for the Emperor is left out." In place of this prayer, the following was added by Pope Pius XII.]

4 of 9 • FOR THOSE ENGAGED IN PUBLIC AFFAIRS. *Pro Res Publicas Moderantibus*

Orémus et pro ómnibus res públicas moderántibus, eorúmque ministériis et potestátibus: ut Deus et Dóminus noster mentes et corda eórum secúndum voluntátẽ suã dírigat ad nostram perpétuam pacem.

LET US PRAY too for all engaged in affairs of state and for all their ministries and powers; that our God and Lord may guide according to His will their minds and hearts, to our lasting peace.

Celebrant: Orémus.
Deacon: ℣. Flectámus génua.
Deacon: ℟. Leváte.

Let us pray.
℣. Let us kneel.
℟. Arise.

9 of 9 • FOR THE CONVERSION OF UNBELIEVERS. *Pro Conversione Infidelium*

LET US PRAY also for the pagans: that almighty God would remove iniquity from their hearts: that, putting aside their idols, they may be converted to the true and living God, and His only Son, Jesus Christ our God and Lord.

Orémus et pro pagánis: ut Deus omnípotens áuferat iniquitátem a córdibus eórum; ut relíctis idólis suis, convertántur ad Deum vivum et verum, et únicum Fílium ejus Jesum Christum Deum et Dóminum nostrum.

Let us pray.
℣. Let us kneel.
℟. Arise.

Celebrant: Orémus.
Deacon: ℣. Flectámus génua.
Deacon: ℟. Leváte.

Almighty and everlasting God, who ever seekest not the death, but the life of sinners: mercifully hear our prayer, and deliver them from the worship of idols: and join them to Thy holy Church for the praise and glory of Thy Name. *Through our Lord Jesus Christ, Thy Son, Who liveth and reigneth with Thee in the unity of the Holy Ghost, God, world without end.*
(*All respond:* "Amen.")

Omnípotens sempitérne Deus, qui non mortem peccatórum, sed vitam semper inquíris: súscipe propítius oratiónem nostram, et líbera eos ab idolórum cultúra: et ággrega Ecclésiæ tuæ sanctæ, ad laudem et glóriam nóminis tui. *Per Dñm nostrum Jesum Christum fílium tuum, qui tecum vivit et regnat in unitáte Spíritus Sancti, Deus, per ómnia sǽcula sæculórum.* ℟. Amen.

1962 • The Celebrant removes his cope; the sacred ministers likewise remove dalmatic and tunic.

THE LITURGICAL BOOKS often refer to the next ceremony as the "Adoration of the Cross" (*Adoratio Crucis*). Speaking about this ceremony, *The Catholic Encyclopedia* (Imprimatur 1909 by Most Reverend John M. Farley, Archbishop of New York) says:

> The ignorant may allege grave disorder in the act of adoration of the Cross on bended knee. Is not adoration due to God alone? The answer may be found in our smallest catechism. The act in question is not intended as an expression of absolute supreme worship (*latreia*) which, of course, is due to God alone. The essential note of the ceremony is reverence (*proskynesis*) which has a relative character, and which may be best explained in the words of the Pseudo-Alcuin: *Prosternimur corpore ante crucem, mente ante Dominium. Veneramur crucem, per quam redempti sumus, et illum deprecamur, qui redemit* ("While we bend down in body before the cross we bend down in spirit before God. While we reverence the cross as the instrument of our redemption, we pray to Him who redeemed us").

Another Roman Catholic book—*The Office of the Holy Week, According to the Roman Missal and Breviary* (1796AD)—has this to say about the Solemn Veneration of the Cross:

> Next, both Priest and people adore Jesus Christ crucified, expressing their adoration by kneeling thrice before they kiss the sacred wounds represented by the figure on the cross. This ceremony is a great stumbling-block to Protestants, who think us guilty of idolatry by it, especially when the rubric calls it, The Adoration of the Cross, and the Choir at the same time sing, *We adore thy Cross, O Lord, &c.* But we presume they will give us leave to know the meaning of our own words and actions, and believe us, when we tell them, that our genuflexion, and kissing of the cross, are no more than outward expressions of the love and adoration which we bear in our hearts to Jesus Christ crucified; and that the words *adoration* and *adore*, as applied to the Cross, signify only that respect and veneration which is due to things relating to God and his service.

Sir Walter Kirkham Blount published The Roman Catholic Holy Week Book in 1670AD which says: "The Adoration is not terminated in wood of the Cross, but in Iesus-Christ fastened thereon." Page 333 of *The Roman Missal for the Use of the Laity According to the Use of the Holy Roman Church Containing Also the Masses Proper to This Country in Their Respective Places* was published in Birmingham (1845) under the approval of the Roman Catholic bishops, and reads as follows:

> The intention of the church in exposing the cross to our veneration on this day is that we might the more effectually raise up our hearts to **Him** who expired thereon for our redemption. Whenever, therefore, we kneel, or prostrate ourselves before a crucifix, it is **Jesus Christ** only whom we adore, and it is in him alone that our respects terminate.

Some authors believe this ceremony originated at Jerusalem, and cite a description by the Spanish pilgrim Etheria (a.k.a. "Lady Ætheria") when, in 385ad, she visited the holy places.

PART III • UNVEILING OF THE CROSS

1962 • The Deacon brings the Cross in procession with lighted candles. When they reach the Sanctuary, the Celebrant takes the Cross from the hands of the Deacon at the center of the Altar. Bringing the Cross to the Epistle side on floor-level, the Celebrant stands facing the people and uncovers the top of the Cross a little, singing at a low pitch:

All kneel and pray in silence for a few moments, except the Celebrant and candle-bearers.

1962 • The Celebrant then goes up to the Altar and stands on the Epistle side. There he uncovers the right arm of the Crucified. Raising the Cross a little, he sings at a higher pitch than before:

"Ecce lignum Crucis, etc." *and all else repeated as before.*

1962 • Finally the Celebrant goes to the center of the Altar, uncovers the entire Cross, and lifts it up. For the third and last time, in an even higher tone of voice, he sings:

"Ecce lignum Crucis, etc." *and all else repeated as before.*

1962 • Now that he has uncovered the Cross, the Celebrant gives the Cross to two acolytes (who stand on the platform before the center of the Altar, facing the people) supporting the Cross on either side by its arms so that the foot of the Cross stands on the platform. The veneration of the holy Cross then begins, in the following order: first, the Celebrant comes alone, then the ministers, next the clergy, and finally the servers. If it is convenient, all first remove their shoes and, one by one they go to the Cross, making a simple genuflection **three times**, and kiss the feet of the Crucified. Notice that the triple genuflection ("creeping to the Cross") from the 1950 ceremony is retained only for the Celebrant and his retinue {Goddard p182}.

1962 • When their veneration by the Celebrant and retinue has been completed, the holy Cross is carried to the edge of the Sanctuary entrance. There the acolytes hold the Cross in the same way as before, so the faithful—*primum viri, deinde mulieres* ("first the men and then the women")—may kiss the feet of the Crucified with devotion, having first made a simple genuflection.

[*If the Celebrant foresees that the veneration of the holy Cross, as prescribed above, can scarcely be performed without harming good order and devotion—by reason of the large number of people—the veneration by the faithful takes place in this way: the Celebrant takes the Cross from the hands of the servers and stands on the platform of the Altar. With a few words, he invites the congregation to venerate the holy Cross; he then lifts the Cross higher for the faithful to venerate in silence for a brief period.*]

1962 • During the veneration of the holy Cross, the IMPROPERIA ("Reproaches") and other chants are sung by the Schola, divided into two choirs. The Celebrant, the sacred ministers, servers, and all who have completed the veneration of the Cross sit and listen (*sedentes auscultant*)—that is to say, the Celebrant does not "duplicate" these prayers as he did in the 1950 version.

PART IV • VENERATION OF THE CROSS

English translation by Monsignor Ronald Knox (IMPRIMATUR: 24 November 1950).

TELL ME, my own people, what wrong I did thee, how earned thy ill looks. Answer me. ℣. From the land of Egypt I rescued thee; for thy Savior hast thou only a Cross?

(Micheas 6: 3) Pópule meus, quid feci tibi? aut in quo contristávi te? Respónde mihi. ℣. (Mich 6: 4) Quia edúxi te de terra Ægýpti: parásti Crucem Salvatóri tuo.

HOLY GOD IS.
Holy God is.
Holy and strong.
Holy and strong.
Holy thou and immortal, have mercy upon us.
Holy thou and immortal, have mercy upon us.

Hágios o Theós.
Sanctus Deus.
Hágios ischyrós.
Sanctus fortis.
Hágios athánatos, eléison hymás.
Sanctus immortális, miserére nobis.

Forty years through the desert I led thee, with manna fed thee; passing fair was the home I gave thee; for thy Savior, only a Cross? *Holy God is...*

Quia edúxi te per desértum quadragínta annis, et manna cibávi te, et introdúxi te in terram satis bonam: parásti Crucem Salvatóri tuo. *Hágios o Theós...*

What more could I have bestowed, that bestow I did not? Vineyard thou wast of my own planting, how fair to see! Yet bitter the fruit was; thou wouldst quench my thirst with vinegar, and wound with a lance thy Savior's side. *Holy God is...*

Quid ultra débui fácere tibi, et non feci? Ego quidem plantávi te víneam meam speciosíssimam: et tu facta es mihi nimis amára: acéto namque sitim meam potásti: et láncea perforásti latus Salvatóri tuo. *Hágios o Theós...*

* REFRAIN. *The following Refrain (MICHEAS 6: 3) is repeated after each verse:*

℟. TELL ME, my own people,
what wrong I did thee,
how earned thy ill looks. Answer me.

Pópule meus, quid feci tibi? Aut in quo contristávi te? Respónde mihi.

℣. Ego propter te flagellávi Ægýptum cum primogénitis suis: et tu me flagellátum tradidísti.

EGYPT AND EGYPT'S FIRSTBORN for thy sake scourged I; wouldst thou scourge and abandon me?

℣. Ego edúxi te de Ægýpto, deméerso Pharaóne in Mare Rubrum: et tu me tradidísti princípibus sacerdótum.

FROM Egypt I rescued thee,
Pharao and his host I drowned in the Red Sea,
to keep their hands off thee;
into the hands of rulers wouldst thou deliver me?

℣. Ego ante te apérui mare: et tu aperuísti láncea latus meum.

THROUGH the sea
I opened a passage for thee,
and should a lance open my side?

℣. Ego ante te præívi in colúmna nubis: et tu me duxísti ad prætórium Piláti.

IN A COLUMN of cloud
I led thee on thy journey;
wouldst thou lead me off,
and into Pilate's colonnade?

℣. Ego te pavi manna per desértum: et tu me cecidísti álapis et flagéllis.

I FED THEE with manna,
when thou wast fainting in the desert;
must I grow faint with buffets and scourge of thine?

℣. Ego te potávi aqua salútis de petra: et tu me potásti felle et acéto.

WITH WATER from the rock
thy sore need I met;
thou mine with vinegar and gall.

℣. Ego propter te Chananæórum reges percússi: et tu percussísti arúndine caput meum.

CHIEFTAINS of Chanaan
for thy sake smote I;
and must rod of thine smite my head?

℣. Ego dedi tibi sceptrum regále: et tu dedísti cápiti meo spíneam corónam.

A ROYAL SCEPTRE my gift was to thee;
thine to me, a crown of thorns.

℣. Ego te exaltávi magna virtúte: et tu me suspendísti in patíbulo Crucis.

HIGH ABOVE EARTH I exalted thee;
and thou me, but gibbeted on a Cross.

ANTIPHON.

Crucem tuam adorámus, Dómine: et sanctam resurrectiónem tuam laudámus et glorificámus: ecce enim, propter lignum venit gáudium in univérso mundo. (Ps 66: 2) Deus misereátur nostri et benedícat nobis: illúminet vultum suum super nos et misereátur nostri. *Crucem tuam*...

THY CROSS, Lord, we needs must worship, thy holy Resurrection praise and glorify; was it not yonder tree brought the whole world rejoicing? ℣. May God be merciful to us, and bless us. May he smile graciously on us and show us his mercy.
℟. *Thy Cross*...

Crux Fidelis • The following hymn, by Bishop Fortunatus (d. 604), contains these words: *Ipse lignum tunc notávit, damna ligni ut sólveret*—"the Creator Himself then chose the tree that would undo the harm wrought by the former tree." An ancient legend says the Cross of Christ sprang from the bough of a tree in Paradise. (It will be remembered that certain trees can live for thousands of years.) Saint Ambrose has written: "The Cross of Christ has restored Paradise for us. This is the wood which the Lord pointed out to Adam, saying of the Tree of Life which stood in the centre of the garden of Paradise, that its fruit could be eaten, but that of the Tree of Knowledge of Good and Evil was forbidden" (In Ps. 35:3). The response after the 3 May "Third Lesson" (Invention of the Holy Cross) reads: *Hæc est arbor digníssima, in paradísi médio situáta, In qua salútis auctor própria morte mortem ómnium superávit, alleluia*—"This is the noblest of all trees, and is placed in the midst of Paradise: On it, the Author of our salvation vanquished, by his own Death, the death of all men, alleluia." Father Matthew Britt reminds us: "The Tree in Eden [Genesis 3:1-7] was perfidious, but the Tree on Calvary, beautifully described here as *Crux Fidelis*, has become the very symbol of faith. What other tree can ever hope to bear foliage, flowers, and fruit of infinite worth and beauty?" The second antiphon (below) says: "By a tree we were enslaved, and by the holy Cross we are set free." Adam's burial site—according to ancient tradition—was Golgotha, and Adam's skull is often shown underneath the Cross in scenes depicting the Crucifixion.

PASSIONTIDE HYMN. *Venantius Fortunatus, Bishop of Poitiers VI. Cent.*

THREE THINGS cooperated in our fall: a disobedient man, Adam; a proud woman, Eve; and a tree. God takes these elements and uses them as the instruments of victory: the obedient new Adam, Christ; the humble new Eve, Mary; and the tree of the Cross. — *Archbishop Fulton J. Sheen*

O faithful Cross and noble tree above all others; no forest could produce thy equal in foliage, flowers, or fruit; how sweet the wood, sweet the nails, and sweet the burden that hangs thereon.

Kn. Hail, true Cross, of beauty rarest,
King of all the forest trees;
Leaf and flower and fruit thou bearest,
Med(i)cine for a world's disease;
Fairest wood, and iron fairest—
Yet more fair, who hung on these.

O tow'ring Tree! whose branching Head
Like Heav'n is both sublime and spread:
No Citron groves, nor Myrtle Bow'rs
Can boast such Blossoms, Fruits or Flow'rs:
Since Christ's redeeming Arms display'd,
Create the Sweetness of thy Shade.

Crux fidélis is actually the eighth verse, but it is used as a refrain on Good Friday. Because of the poem's great depth, we have provided **three translations**: (1) a literal translation; (2) a version marked with "Kn," by Monsignor Knox; (3) a translation from a *Roman Catholic Primer* printed in 1717AD. The capitalization of each has not been altered.

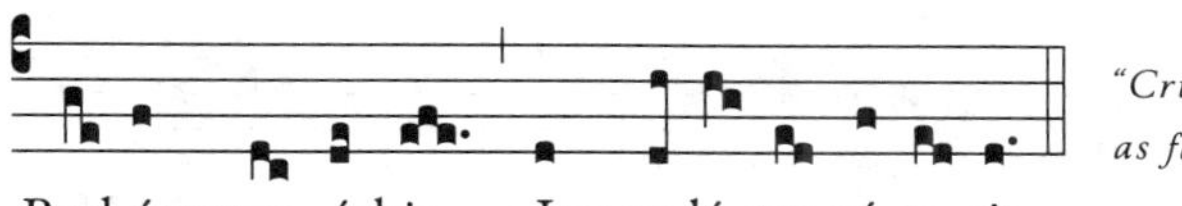

Red-émptor órbis Immo-lá- tus ví-ce- rit.

"Crux fidélis" is repeated as far as "Dulce lignum"

Sing, my tongue, the victory of the glorious battle, sing the triumph of the cross; how the Redeemer of the world being sacrificed yet conquered.

Kn. Sing, my tongue, of warfare ended,
Of the Victor's laurelled crown;
Let the Cross, his trophy splendid,
Be the theme of high renown;
How a broken world was mended—
Life restored by life laid down.

Sing, O my Tongue, the glorious Crown,
Which Christ, the God of Battles won:
How on the Cross thy God on high
Triumphs in Pomp and Victory;
And yields for us his saving Breath
At once to die and vanquish Death.

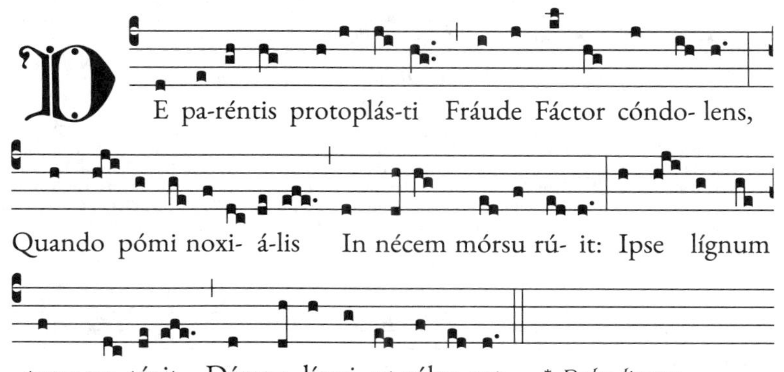

The Creator, pitying Adam's race, when it fell by the taste of the forbidden fruit, then noted the tree; that by a tree the loss from a tree should be repaired.

Kn. God, for man's rebellion grieving,
When the world his hands had made
Perished by a fruit's deceiving,
In that hour his counsel laid,
By a tree the race reprieving
Whom a tree long since betrayed.

A kind Compassion made him take
Such Measures for his Creatures' Sake;
That fatal Wood, where Adam found
Sad Means to give the gen(e)ral Wound;
Should now contribute to restore
Our Life, that caus'd our Death before.

So was the work of our salvation ordered, that art should destroy the art of the deceiver, that healing should come from a tree, as had come the wound.

Kn. Man's eternal health contriving
Wrought he with unfailing art—
Wisdom 'gainst the wisdom striving
Of the tempter's guileful heart;
From that source the balm deriving
Where the foe had steeped his dart.

This Method, Providence decreed
For Christ to crush the Serpent's Head:
Art meets with Art, and countermines
The wily Foe's conceal'd Designs:
Defeats his Bane, and then applies,
Against the Poison, Remedies.

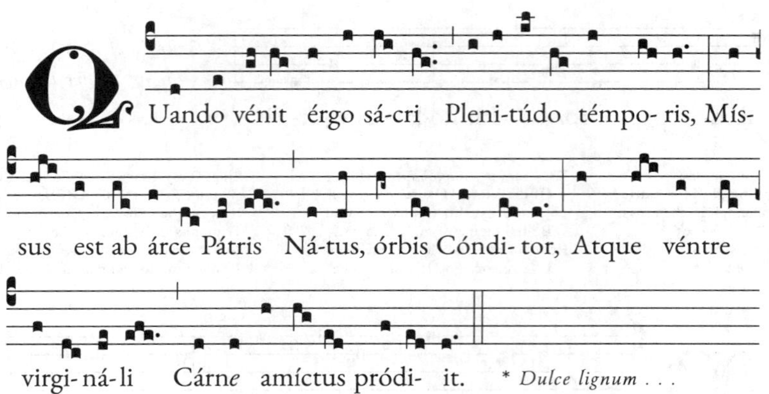

Therefore, in the fulness of the sacred time, the Creator of the world, sent from the Father's home, was born and came forth clothed in flesh from the Virgin's womb.

Kn. Therefore, when that hallow'd hour
Time to its fulfilment brought.
From his Father's heav'nly tower
Came he, who the worlds had wrought,
From his Mother's secret bower,
Clothed in flesh, and welcome sought.

Thus when the sacred Period came,
Behold the World's redeeming Lamb
From God's Paternal Bosom sent,
Came down to human Banishment,
And taking Flesh of Mary's Womb
Stept forth to save the World from Doom.

A child he lay in the narrow cradle and the virgin mother bound his limbs in swaddling clothes; such bands held the hands and feet of God.

Kn. See a helpless Infant crying,
Whom a manger doth enfold;
See his Virgin Mother tying
Rags about him in the cold;
Bound both hand and feet, and lying
'Mid the beasts, your God behold!

Here God and Man an Infant lies,
The narrow Crib augments his Cries:
Those Hands by which the Lightning's hurl'd,
And Arms that grasp the bulky World,
In swathing Bands are wrapt and bound
With Poverty encompass'd round.

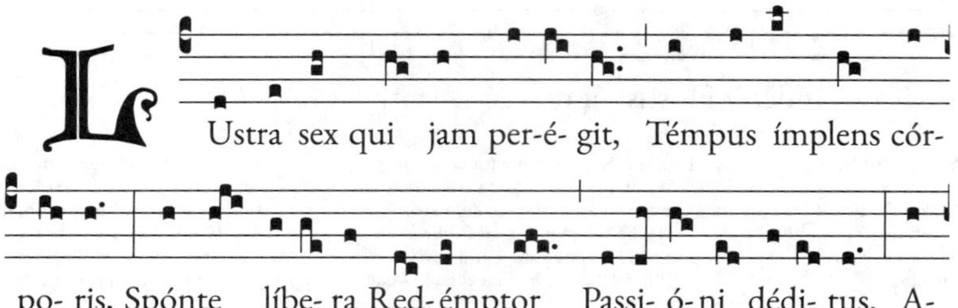

After thirty years amongst us, knowing that the end of his mortal life was near, the Redeemer freely yielded himself to suffering; the Lamb is lifted up on the tree of the Cross to be immolated thereon.

Kn. Now, his years of life perfected,
Our atonement's price to be,
By the doom long since elected,
Bound and nailed to set us free,
Christ, our Victim, hangs rejected
On the Cross of Calvary.

Six Lustra's past, * the Sabbath came
On which the World-redeeming Lamb,
As freely he that Term decreed,
So freely chose for us to bleed,
And on the Cross's Altar laid,
The solemn Expiation made.

* *The 1717 Primer includes a footnote about the word* LUSTRUM, *saying: "A Period Signifying the Revolution of 5 years."*

Submerged in a torrent of bitterness, he languished; the thorns, the nails and the lance transpierced his broken body; water and blood gushed forth, a life-giving torrent wherein are immersed the earth, the sea, the stars, and the entire world!

Kn. Gall he drinks; his strength subduing,
Reed and thorn and nail and spear
Plot his gentle frame's undoing;
Blood and water thence appear,
With their cleansing tide renewing
Earth and sea and starry sphere.

Gall was his Drink: his Flesh they tear
With Thorns and Nails; the bolder Spear
His Side laid ope, and once again
Heav'n's Cataracts were seen to rain
Another Deluge; but the Flood
Was Water mix'd with saving Blood.

O lofty tree, bend thy branches, relax the tension of thy fibres, soften that rigidness—with which nature has endowed thee—and offer a more tender support to the members of thy dying King.

Kn. Bend thy branches down to meet him,
Bend that stubborn heart of thine;
Let thy native force, to greet him,
All its ruggedness resign;
Gently let thy wood entreat him,
Royal suff(e)rer, and divine.

Tall Cedar rais'd to mate the Sky!
Hard as thou art, now mollify,
And teach Men how to treat their God:
Bow gently down beneath thy Load,
That unrelenting Man may learn
To change his Heart and feel Concern.

Thou alone wert found worthy to bear the Victim of the earth; thou, the Ark bringest a shipwrecked world back to safe harbor; thou wert anointed with the Precious Blood, which flowed from the body of the Lamb.

Kn. Victim of our race, he deignèd
  On thy arms to lay his head;
Thou the ark, whose refuge gainèd,
  Sinful man no more may dread;
Ark, whose planks are deeply stainèd
  With the blood the Lamb hath shed.

Thou when the Shipwreck'd World was toss'd
On raging Seas, and Nature lost;
Besprinkled with the Savior's Gore,
Alone wert fit to waft us o'er
To that calm Port of endless Bliss;
Where future Storms and Dangers cease.

1962 • On page 180, the 1962 Missale Romanum says: *Conclusio numquam omittenda*. That means the final stanza ("Sempiterna Sit") is always sung, no matter what other chants have been omitted during the Solemn Veneration of the Cross. (The 1950 rubrics do not contain this injunction.)

Eternal glory be to the blessed Trinity, to the Father and Son; the same honor to the Paraclete. Let all the world praise the name of the one and three.

Kn. Honour, glory, might and merit
  To th'eternal Trinity,
Father, Son, and Holy Spirit,
  Throned in heav'n co-equally;
All that doth the world inherit,
  Praise one God in Persons three.

May all this praise, and honor Thee,
One undivided Trinity,
The Father, and Co-equal Son,
And Holy Spirit, Three in One,
Whose equal Pow'r and goodness claim
One Equal Everlasting Fame.

Further Reading • This magnificent hymn served as the model for the *Pange Lingua* by Saint Thomas Aquinas more than six centuries later. We recommend the following commentaries: Father Joseph Connelly (*Hymns of the Roman Liturgy*, 1957) page 85; Father Aquinas Byrnes (*Hymns of the Dominican Breviary*, 1943) page 92; Father Matthew Britt (*Hymns of the Breviary and Missal*, 1922) page 128. In 1908, Pope Pius X restored the option of singing the ancient versions for all hymns contained in the Missale Romanum, including the *Pange Lingua*, rather than the corrupted versions published under Pope Urban VIII in 1631AD. Additional translations and explanations by Catholic priests and bishops are printed in *The Saint Jean de Brébeuf Hymnal* (2018) starting on page 308.

1962 • The Celebrant removes his black stole, donning a purple chasuble. (The Deacon wears a purple dalmatic; the Subdeacon a purple tunic.) The Cross is placed in the center of the Altar, high enough (assuming the architecture permits it) to be easily seen by the faithful, without inconveniencing the Celebrant in the subsequent ceremonies. The Deacon carries the burse to the Altar and spreads the corporal in the usual way. A vessel of water (with purificator) is placed on the Altar for washing and drying the fingers of the Celebrant after Communion. The book is placed on the Gospel side.

PART V • EUCHARISTIC PROCESSION

1962 • The Blessed Sacrament must be carried from the Place of Repose to the main Altar for Communion. The Deacon (without the Celebrant or Subdeacon) goes to the Place of Repose. Putting on a white humeral veil, the Deacon carries the ciborium—covering it with the ends of the veil—from the Place of Repose to the main Altar. As usual, a small canopy is carried over the Sanctissimum.

Meanwhile the choir sings the following antiphons (added in 1955, and sometimes referred to as "The Pius XII antiphons"), which are in three different modes :

FIRST ANTIPHON.

Adorámus te, Christe, et benedícimus tibi, quia per Crucem tuam redemísti mundum.

WE ADORE THEE, O Christ, and bless Thee: because by Thy cross Thou hast redeemed the world.

SECOND ANTIPHON.

Per lignum servi facti sumus, et per sanctam Crucem liberáti sumus: fructus árboris sedúxit nos, Fílius Dei redémit nos.

BY A TREE we were enslaved, and by the holy Cross we are set free: the fruit of the tree led us astray, but the Son of God has ransomed us.

THIRD ANTIPHON.

Salvátor mundi, salva nos: qui per Crucem et Sánguinẽ tuum redemísti nos, auxiliáre nobis, te deprecámur, Deus noster.

SAVE US, Savior of the world: Thou who by Thy Cross and Blood didst redeem us, help us, we pray Thee, our God.

A Favorite Communion Day • In the 1950 version of Good Friday, the priest alone receives Communion. In the early days of the Church, it seems that the entire congregation received on Good Friday. Indeed, Good Friday was "a favorite Communion day" {Jungmann v2, p409} until near the end of the Middle Ages. In 1955, Pope Pius XII modified the *Missa praesanctificatorum*, allowing the entire congregation to receive. Father Hannibal Bugnini and Father Carlo Braga published a commentary explaining the Holy Week reforms in Ephemerides Liturgicae (28 February 1956) under the title: *Ordo Hebdomadae Sanctae Instauratus: Commentarium*...etc. Pages 105-109 provide extensive documentation, with many sources cited, vis-à-vis Holy Communion on Good Friday. A very important source is the Gelasian Sacramentary—which dates from approximately 734 AD—and here is the relevant citation from folio 66:

Istas orationes supra scriptas expletas, ingrediuntur diaconi in sacrario. Procedunt cum corpore et sanguinis Domini quod ante die remansit: et ponunt super altare. Et venit sacerdos ante altare, adorans crucẽ Dñi et osculans. Et dicit "Orémus." Et sequitur "Præcéptis salutáribus móniti," et oratio Dominica. Inde "Líbera nos Dñe quǽsumus." Haec omnia expleta, ***adorant omnes sanctam crucem et communicant.***

ETSEQUITUR PRAECEPTISSALUTARIB: MONI
TI. ETORATIO DOMINICA INDE LIBERANOS
DNE QUAESUMUS. HAEC OMNIA EXPLETA AD
ORANT OMS SCAM CRUCE ET COMUNICANT

Reception of Holy Communion by the faithful on Good Friday was very much in accordance with I Corinthians 11:26: *Quotiescúmque enim manducábitis panem hunc, et cálicem bibétis, mortem Domini annuntiábitis* ("It is the Lord's death you are heralding, whenever you eat this bread and drink this cup"). Indeed, Father Bugnini and Father Braga specifically cite this verse in their 1956 *Commentarium* (p105), yet the reformers would later carefully excise this verse from the 1970 Missal, whereas in the classical Roman Rite it was read each year on Holy Thursday (Epistle) and Corpus Christi (Communion).

General Communion on Good Friday was a "universal practice that perdured for centuries" {Giampietro p67}. But then a change took place; the priest alone received Holy Communion on Good Friday. This change is first explicitly documented in the 13th century. According to Cardinal Antonelli, this cessation "is easily understood in the context of the general rarification of communion which had reached such a stage by the 13th century that the Ecumenical Lateran Council of 1215 obliged all the faithful to approach the holy table at least once every year" {Giampietro p67}. Nevertheless, until the time of Pope Pius V, some liturgical books still allowed the faithful to receive Holy Communion on Good Friday; e.g. the *Obsequiale Frisingense* of 1493AD (folio 41r), cited by James Monti {Monti p443}. The first document that explicitly forbids reception by the faithful dates from 1622AD {Goddard p277}.

To learn of the great antiquity of the Pater Noster in connection with distribution of Holy Communion, cf. Father Jungmann's *Missarum Sollemnia* (Benziger Brothers, 1950), second volume, page 281. These theories were very much in vogue during the 1950s; e.g. "The priest begins the preparation for the Communion by singing the Our Father" {Solesmes1957 p19}. James Monti discovered several important ceremonies that—in former days—took place at this time in conjunction with the Pater Noster {Monti p442}.

PART VI • HOLY COMMUNION

1962 • The Deacon places the ciborium on the corporal. Then the Celebrant and Subdeacon go to the Altar, genuflect on both knees in adoration, and go up to the Altar. Having genuflected with the Deacon, the Celebrant recites in a clear voice, without chant, the preface of the Lord's Prayer:

Let us pray. Obedient to our Savior's command, and with His teaching for our model, thus we make bold to pray:

Orémus: Præcéptis salutáribus móniti, et divína institutióne formáti, audémus dícere.

Recited Not Sung • Since the "Our Father" is a prayer which prepares for Holy Communion, all those present (both clergy and faithful) recite the entire prayer in Latin together with the Celebrant—in a solemn, grave, distinct manner—with the addition of "Amen." | *Totum vero "Pater Noster," cum sit precatio ad communionem, omnes praesentes, clerici et fideles, una cum celebrante, solemniter, graviter et distincte recitant, lingua latina, addito quoque ab omnibus "Amen."*

Note: This method (introduced in 1955) is different from the normal way of praying the Lord's Prayer, wherein the Celebrant says the first part and the congregation says the other part.

PATER NOSTER, *
qui es in cælis: *
Sanctificétur nomen tuum. *
Advéniat regnum tuum. *
Fiat volúntas tua, sicut in cælo, et in terra. *
Panem nostrum quotidiánum da nobis hódie *
Et dimítte nobis débita nostra, *
sicut et nos dimíttimus debitóribus nostris. *
Et ne nos indúcas in tentatiónem; *
sed líbera nos a malo. * Amen.

The Celebrant alone continues in a clear and distinct voice:

DELIVER US, we beseech Thee, O Lord, from all evils, past, present, and to come; and by the intercession of the blessed and glorious ever Virgin Mary, Mother of God, and of

Líbera nos, quǽsumus, Dómine, ab ómnibus malis, prætéritis, præséntibus, et futúris: et intercedénte beáta, et gloriósa semper Vírgine Dei Genitríce María, cum beátis Apóstolis tuis

Petro et Paulo, atque Andréa, et ómnibus Sanctis, da propítius pacem in diébus nostris: ut, ope misericórdiæ tuæ adjúti, et a peccáto simus semper líberi, et ab omni perturbatióne secúri. Per eúndem Dñm nostrum Jesum Christum, Fílium tuum: Qui tecum vivit et regnat in unitáte Spíritus Sancti Deus, per ómnia sǽcula sæculórum.

the holy Apostles Peter and Paul, and of Andrew, and of all the Saints, mercifully grant peace in our days, that through the assistance of Thy mercy we may be always free from sin, and secure from all disturbance. Through the same Jesus Christ, Thy Son, our Lord, Who with Thee in the unity of the Holy Ghost liveth and reigneth God, world without end.

All present answer: AMEN.

1962 • Next the Celebrant recites the following prayer in a low voice, bowing as usual and with his hands joined and placed upon the Altar:

Percéptio Córporis tui, Dómine Jesu Christe, quod ego indígnus súmere præsúmo, non mihi provéniat in judícium et condemnatiónem: sed pro tua pietáte prosit mihi ad tutaméntum mentis et córporis, et ad medélam percipiéndam: Qui vivis et regnas cum Deo Patre in unitáte Spíritus Sancti Deus, per ómnia sǽcula sæculórum. Amen.

LET NOT the partaking of Thy Body, O Lord Jesus Christ, which I, though unworthy, presume to receive, turn to my judgment and condemnation; but let it, through Thy mercy, become a safeguard and remedy, both for soul and body; Who with God the Father, in the unity of the Holy Ghost, livest and reignest God, for ever and ever. Amen.

1962 • Then he uncovers the ciborium, genuflects, and takes a sacred particle. Holding the particle above the ciborium, bowing and striking his heart with his hand, he says three times in the usual way:

Dómine, non sum dignus, ut intres sub tectum meum: sed tantum dic verbo, et sanábitur ánima mea. (3x)

Lord, I am not worthy that Thou shouldst enter under my roof; but only say the word, and my soul shall be healed. (*Thrice*)

Signing himself with the SANCTISSIMUM, he adds in a low voice:

Corpus Dómini ✠ nostri Jesu Christi custódiat ánimam meam in vitam ætérnam. Amen.

May the Body ✠ of our Lord Jesus Christ preserve my soul unto life everlasting. Amen.

1962 • He then recently receives our Lord in Holy Communion and prays a little while, meditating on the Blessed Sacrament. | *Et sumit Corpus reverenter, ac paululum in meditatione Sacramenti quiescit.*

1962 • The CONFITEOR is now said in the usual way by the Deacon. [Note: the 1965 Missal says here: "The communicants immediately say the CONFITEOR."] | *Et continuo diaconus facit confessionem.*

CONFITEOR DEO omnipoténti, beátæ Maríæ sémper Vírgini, beáto Michäéli Archángelo, beáto Joánni Baptístæ, sánctis Apóstolis Pétro et Páulo, ómnibus sánctis, et tíbi páter, quía peccávi nímis cogitatióne, vérbo et ópere: méa cúlpa, méa cúlpa, méa máxima cúlpa; ídeo précor beátam Maríam sémper Vírginem, beátum Michäélem Archángelum, beátum Joánnem Baptístam, sánctos Apóstolos Pétrum et Páulum, ómnes sánctos, et te páter, oráre pro me ad Dóminum Déum nóstrum.

1962 • Then the Celebrant, genuflecting and turning to the people, says the following in a clear tone of voice, with hands joined. | *Tunc celebrans, facta genuflexione, conversus ad populum, manibus junctis ante pectus, clara voce dicit:*

May almighty God have mercy on you and, having forgiven you your sins, bring you to life everlasting.

All present answer: AMEN.

Misereátur vestri omnípotens Deus, et, dimíssis peccátis vestris, perdúcat vos ad vitam ætérnam.

1962 • The Celebrant continues. | *Celebrans prosequitur.*

May the ✠ almighty and merciful Lord grant us pardon, absolution, and remission of our sins.

All present answer: AMEN.

Indulgéntiam, ✠ absolutiónem et remissiónem peccatórum vestrórum tríbuat vobis omnípotens et miséricors Dóminus.

1962 • The Celebrant turns to the Altar, genuflects, and takes the ciborium. Turned toward the people in the usual way, he says the following in a clear tone of voice. | *Deinde ad altare se convertit, genuflectit, apprehendit pyxidem, et more solito conversus ad populum, in medio altaris, dicit clara voce:*

Behold the Lamb of God, behold Him Who taketh away the sins of the world.

Ecce Agnus Dei, ecce qui tollit peccáta mundi.

LORD, I am not worthy to receive Thee under my roof; my soul will be healed if Thou wilt only speak a word of command. (*Thrice*)

Dómine, non sum dignus, ut intres sub tectum meum: sed tantum dic verbo, et sanábitur ánima mea. (3x)

The Celebrant now distributes Holy Communion. Priests who assist in the distribution wear purple stoles.

During Communion • While Holy Communion is being distributed, the 1962 *Missale Romanum* suggests the singing of Psalm 21 (for texts in English & Latin, see page 114) or else one of the responsories from Good Friday Matins. Singing from the psalter would harken back to a Catholic tradition in which "watchers" would remain in church "reading their psalters continuously" from Good Friday until Easter morning; e.g. an *Ordinarium* (1530AD) from Saale, Germany, "calls for eight priests vested in black copes" to recite the Psalter "night and day" until Easter Lauds {Monti p453}. Traditionally, there would have been nothing sung at this time, since only the Celebrant received Communion—but general Communion was restored in 1955 {Giampietro p250}. Additional options for musical selections (the organ is forbidden on this day):

(1) Silence. A liturgical book from Passau, Germany—printed in 1514AD—says that on Good Friday "all should communicate with the fear of God in silence" {Monti p443}. This was prior to the Council of Trent, when certain churches still allowed general Communion on Good Friday.

(2) Vexilla Regis. The *Vexilla Regis* was traditionally sung on Good Friday, but the reformers eliminated this 6th-century hymn by Bishop Fortunatus—perhaps because its use on Good Friday is not primitive {Goddard p189}. Although it was eliminated, Pope John XXIII famously demanded that it still be included on Good Friday; cf. *Interview with Domenico Cardinal Bartolucci* (Pucci Cipriani, 12 August 2009). Nothing prevents this beautiful hymn from being sung during the distribution of Holy Communion on Good Friday.

[Editor's Note: The reforms to Holy Week during the 1950s—along with the experiment of the "dialogue Mass"—betray a **tendency** which reached its climax in the 1970 *Missale Romanum*: viz. that of "micromanaging" the congregation. The reformers explicitly brag about this tendency {McManus page viii}. Traditionally, the rubrics applied only to the priest, while the congregation was given very few instructions. This was because each member of the congregation is different. Some possess deep theological training, others do not. Some have achieved a high level of education, others have not. Some have a lengthy attention span; others do not. Some Catholics are even "special needs"—from the standpoint of mental capacity. The traditional liturgy took these matters into consideration.]

1962 • When Communion has been completed, the Celebrant washes his fingers in a vessel and dries them with the purificator, saying nothing. Having placed the ciborium in the Tabernacle, he stands in the center of the Altar, with the Missal in front of him. For thanksgiving, he sings the three following prayers in a ferial tone, with his hands joined. All stand and respond "Amen."

Orémus.

Super pópulum tuũ, quǽsumus, Dñe, qui passiónem et mortem Fílii tui devóta mente recóluit, benedíctio copiósa descéndat, indulgéntia véniat, consolátio tribuátur, fides sancta succréscat, redémptio sempitérna firmétur. Per eúmdem Christum Dóminum nostrum. ℟. Amen.

Let us pray.

UPON THY PEOPLE who with devout hearts have recalled the Passion and Death of Thy Son, we beseech Thee, O Lord, may plentiful blessings descend: may gentleness be used with us, and consolation given us, may our faith increase in holiness, our redemption for ever made firm. Through the same Christ our Lord. ℟. Amen.

Orémus.

Omnípotens et miséricors Deus, qui Christi tui beáta passióne et morte nos reparásti: consérva in nobis óperam misericórdiæ tuæ; ut, hujus mystérii participatióne, perpétua devotióne vivámus. Per eúmdem Christum Dñm nostrum. ℟. Amen.

Let us pray.

ALMIGHTY and merciful God, who hast restored us by the Passion and Death of Thy Christ: preserve within us the work of Thy mercy; that by our entering into this mystery we may ever live devoutly. Through the same Christ our Lord. ℟. Amen.

Orémus.

Reminíscere miseratiónum tuárum, Dómine, et fámulos tuos ætérna protectióne sanctífica, pro quibus Christus, Fílius tuus, per suum Cruórem, instítuit paschále mystérium. Per eúmdem Christũ Dñm nostrum. ℟. Amen.

Let us pray.

BE MINDFUL of Thy mercies, O Lord, and hallow with eternal protection us Thy servants, for whom Christ Thy Son established through His Blood this mystery of the Pasch. Through the same Christ our Lord. ℟. Amen.

1962 • The Celebrant and sacred ministers return to the sacristy.

NO VESPERS ON GOOD FRIDAY: When Pope Pius XII modified holy week in 1955, he changed the traditional times of the ceremonies. These changes *de facto* obliterated TENEBRAE and caused many other difficulties. The 1962 rubrics for Good Friday say "the hour of Vespers is omitted" {McManus p89}. Compline is said in choir—without plainsong—and no candles are lighted.

THOU WILT NOT LEAVE MY SOUL IN HELL; NOR ALLOW THY HOLY ONE TO SEE CORRUPTION. (Ps 15: 10)

I HAVE RISEN UP, BECAUSE THE LORD HATH PROTECTED ME. (PSALM 3: 6)

THE THIRD DAY HE WILL RAISE US UP, TO LIVE IN HIS SIGHT. (HOSEA 6: 3)

THE ANGEL CAME AGAIN: AND WAKED ME, AS A MAN THAT IS WAKENED OUT OF HIS SLEEP. (Zachariah 4: 1)

TIMING • The 1962 Missal says: *Solemnis Vigilia paschalis celebranda est hora competenti, ea scilicet, quae permittat Missam solemnem ejusdem vigiliae incipere circa mediam noctem inter sabbatum sanctum et dominicam Resurrectionis. Ubi tamen, ponderatis fidelium et locorum condicionibus, de judicio Ordinarii loci, horam celebrandae Vigiliae anticipari conveniat, haec non inchoetur ante diei crepusculum, aut certe non ante solis occasum.* That is to say "about midnight" between Holy Saturday and Easter Sunday; morevoer the 1962 version "may not begin before twilight and certainly not before sunset."

CONSEQUENCES • The Easter Vigil traditionally took place on Holy Saturday morning. During the 1950s, this tradition—which goes back at least a millennium—was changed, based on what the reformers believed to be a "primitive" practice. This archaeologist change had drastic implications with regard to: (1) the Eucharistic fast; (2) the end of Lenten fast and abstinence; (3) bination, trination, and evening Masses; (4) the Divine Office; and so forth. Cardinal Antonelli explicitly admits {Giampietro p39} the reformers **did not know** the reasons behind the tradition. MAXIMA REDEMPTIONIS (16 nov 1955) said Holy Saturday had been anticipated "for various pertinent reasons." *Dominicae Resurrectionis* (9 feb 1951) had also dodged the question, citing "variisque de causis."

ANTICIPATED MASSES • Msgr. Montini (who would later become Pope Paul VI) requested on 17 January 1956 "that participation at the celebration of Mass at the Solemn Easter Vigil—even if it be held before midnight—should also satisfy the obligation to attend Mass on Easter Sunday," but the *Commissio Piana* rejected his proposal unanimously {Giampietro p290}. The following 1956 interpretation {McManus p9} emphasizes the words *circa mediam noctem* ("approximately midnight"):

> *If, with permission of the local Ordinary, the Vigil service is anticipated so that the Mass takes place before midnight of Holy Saturday, those who are present* ***do not fulfill*** *their obligation of assisting at Mass on Easter Sunday. The obligation of Easter Sunday is fulfilled, of course, by those who assist at the Vigil Mass celebrated* ***about*** *midnight.* [...] *The Mass begins immediately after the second part of the litany, even if it is not yet midnight.*

INDULTS BECOME LAW • Later legislation made such things irrelevant; starting in the 1950s, numerous indults for "anticipated" Masses were granted; e.g. on 10 January 1970 the Vatican granted the request that the faithful "may satisfy the precept of participating in Mass in the afternoon hours of Saturday and the days before holydays of obligation." In 1983, the indults became law (#1248) when the NEW CODE OF CANON LAW was released. The exact time an "anticipated" Mass may begin is not known, but some canonists believe "anticipated" Masses cannot start prior to **4:00PM**; cf. *Evening Masses and Days of Obligation* (Tunink, 2016).

I Classis.

— *Holy Saturday* • *The Paschal Vigil* —

SABBATO SANCTO DE VIGILIA PASCHALI *Station at Saint John Lateran*

1962 • The fire of charcoal or coals is "lighted from flint before the ceremony." The fire itself "should be of sufficient size to permit the prayers to be read by its light" {McManus p60}. The Celebrant, wearing a violet cope, and the sacred ministers, in violet dalmatic and tunic, assemble at the church door for the blessing of the new fire.

I • BLESSING THE NEW FIRE

℣. Dóminus vobíscum.

℟. Et cum spíritu tuo.

℣. The Lord be with you.

℟. And with thy spirit.

Orémus.

Deus, qui per Fílium tuum, anguláren scílicet lápidem, claritátis tuæ ignem fidélibus contulísti: prodúctum e sílice, nostris profutúrum úsibus, novum hanc ignem sanctí✠fica: et concéde nobis, ita per hæc festa paschália cæléstibus desidériis inflammári; ut ad perpétuæ claritátis, puris méntibus, valeámus festa pertíngere. Per eúmdem Christum Dóminum nostrum. ℟. Amen.

Let us pray.

O GOD, WHO THROUGH Thy Son, the cornerstone, hast given to Thy faithful the fire of Thy brightness, sanctify ✠ this new fire, produced out of a flintstone, to be serviceable for our uses; and grant unto us to be so fired with heavenly aspirations through these paschal festivities, that with pure hearts we may be able to attain to the festivities of perpetual brightness. Through the same Christ our Lord. ℟. Amen.

SPRINKLED & CENSED • Then the Celebrant sprinkles the fire three times, saying nothing. One of the servers takes some of the blessed coals and places them in the thurible. The Celebrant places incense in the thurible, blessing it in the usual way, and incenses the fire three times.

II • BLESSING THE PASCHAL CANDLE

1962 • The Celebrant uses a stylus to cut a cross in the wax (and two Greek letters), saying:

CHRIST, yesterday and today, *
The Beginning and End, *
Alpha * et Omega; *

Christus heri et hódie, *
Princípium et Finis, *
Álpha *
et Ómega; *

1962 • Inscribing the four numbers of the current year:

HIS ARE THE TIMES *
and the ages; *
To Him be glory and dominion *
through all ages of eternity. Amen.

Ipsíus sunt témpora *
et sǽcula; *
Ipsi glória et impérium *
per univérsa æternitátis sǽcula.
Amen.

1962 • The Deacon presents the grains of incense to the Celebrant. If they are not yet blessed, the Celebrant thrice sprinkles them with holy water and thrice incenses them, saying nothing. He then fixes the five grains in their holes, saying aloud:

BY HIS HOLY *
and glorious wounds *
may He guard * and keep us, *
Christ the Lord. Amen.

Per sua sancta vúlnera *
gloriósa * custódiat *
et consérvet nos *
Christus Dóminus.
Amen.

1962 • Then the Deacon, lighting a small candle at the new fire, gives it to the Celebrant, who uses it to light the Paschal candle, saying aloud:

MAY THE LIGHT OF CHRIST gloriously rising, * Scatter the darkness of hearts and minds.

Lumen Christi glorióse resurgéntis * Díssipet ténebras cordis et mentis.

INCENSE VS. CANDLE • In the 1950 version, the following prayer blessed the **incense**; on 30 January 1951, *the Commissio Piana* modified this prayer {Giampietro p226} to bless the **candle**. The noun *incensum* has three possible meanings: (1) a lighting; (2) incense; (3) sacrifice. Father Herbert Thurston explains both arguments—admitting both are valid—on pages 422-424 of his *Lent and Holy Week* (1904). The prayer VENIAT in the "experimental" Easter Vigil of 1951 is similar but not identical to the 1950 version; e.g. *super hunc incénsum céreum* vs. *super hoc incénsum* (1950) and *regenerátor inténde* vs. *regenerátor accénde* (1950). Father Thurston is correct that folio 69 (see below) of the Gelasian Sacramentary undeniably uses "incensum" referring to the candle, and the prayer mentions the purity of the candle—which is not made from animal fat or anything contaminated but only from "wax, oil, and papyrus"—as well as the amazing work and purity of the bees. The Gelasian version also uses "inténde."

Yet Cardinal Antonelli explicitly admitted the reformers only knew half the arguement: "All know that in our missals the canticle *Exsultet* is entitled *Benedictio cerei*. Hence liturgists ask how the Deacon can bless the candle. The liturgical historian, however, will know that the true prayer of blessing for the candle is the prayer *Veniat*, which today is used for *Benedictio granorum*. [...] The *Exsultet* is the true *Praeconium paschale* and should revert to having its ancient name, while the Veniat should resume being the *Benedictio cerei*." {Giampietro p43} Please see the editor's note on page 556.

1962 • Without delay, the Celebrant blesses the Paschal candle. (During this prayer, all the lights in the church are extinguished.)

℣. Dóminus vobíscum.

℟. Et cum spíritu tuo.

Orémus.

Véniat, quǽsumus, omnípotens Deus, super hunc incénsum **céreum** larga tuæ bene✠dictiónis infúsio: et hunc noctúrnum splendórem, invisíbilis regenerátor, **inténde**; ut non solum sacrifícium, quod hac nocte litátum est, arcána lúminis tui admixtióne refúlgeat; sed in quocúmque loco ex hujus sanctificatiónis mystério áliquid fúerit deportátum, expúlsa diabólicæ fraudis nequítia, virtus tuæ majestátis assístat. Per Christum Dñm nostrum. ℟. Amen.

℣. The Lord be with you.

℟. And with thy spirit.

Let us pray.

MAY THE ABUNDANT outpouring of Thy ✠ blessing, we beseech Thee, almighty God, descend upon this lighted candle; and do Thou, O invisible Regenerator, lighten this nocturnal brightness, that not only the sacrifice that is offered this night may shine by the secret mixture of Thy light: but also into whatever place anything of this mysterious sanctification shall be brought, there the power of Thy Majesty may be present and all the malicious artifices of Satan may be defeated. Through Christ our Lord. ℟. Amen.

III • LUMEN CHRISTI PROCESSION

1962 • The Deacon, who has exchanged purple vestments for a white dalmatic, carries the lighted candle, and leads the procession into the church. When he enters, he sings at a low pitch:

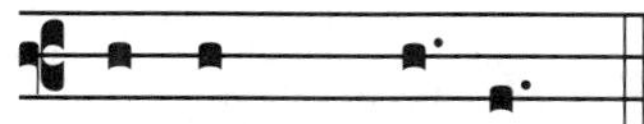

Lumen Chri-sti.

The Light of Christ.

All present (except Subdeacon and thurifer) kneel towards the Paschal candle and answer:

℟. Deo grá-ti- as.

℟. We thank Thee, O God.

1962 • All rise, and the Celebrant lights his own candle from the Paschal candle. The Deacon leads the procession to the middle of the church, and sings at a higher key:

"Lumen Christi. Deo grátias." (*as before*)

1962 • All rise, and the candles of the clergy are lit from the paschal candle. The Deacon now goes in front of the Altar and sings, for the third time, at an even higher key:

"Lumen Christi. Deo grátias." (*as before*)

1962 • At this moment, "the candles of the people are lit from the blessed candle, and the lights of the church as well. Servers may carry candles or tapers lit from the Paschal candle to the people in the church. If the number of the faithful is not too great, some of them may come to light their candles from the Paschal candle, and then return to spread the light from one member of the faithful to another" {McManus p92}. The Deacon places the Paschal candle on a small stand in the middle of the choir.

IV • THE EXSULTET

1962 • The Celebrant goes to his place in choir, at the Epistle side. The Subdeacon stands with the Cross on the Gospel side, opposite the lectern. Once the Celebrant has put incense in the thurible, the Deacon takes the book and asks for a blessing—*Jube, domne, benedícere.* ("Pray you, Sir, ask God's blessing.")—to which the Celebrant responds:

MAY THE LORD be in thy heart and on thy lips, that thou mayest fitly and worthily declare His Easter tidings, in the name of the Father, and of the Son ✠, and of the Holy Ghost. Amen.

Dóminus sit in corde tuo, et in lábiis tuis: ut digne et competénter annúnties suum paschále præcónium: In nómine Patris, et Fílii, ✠ et Spíritus Sancti. Amen.

1962 • The Deacon places the book on the lectern, then incenses both it and the Paschal candle.

ET THE ANGELIC HOST OF HEAVEN NOW EXULT—exult the mysteries divine; and for the victory of so great a King sound the trumpet of salvation. Let earth rejoice, irradiated by such mighty beams, and, being lighted up with the splendor of the eternal King, let her feel the shadows gone from all her sphere.

Holding candles, all stand while the Deacon sings the EXSULTET.

Exsúltet jam Angélica turba cælórum: exsúltent divína mystéria: et pro tanti Regis victória, tuba ínsonet salutáris. Gáudeat et tellus tantis irradiáta fulgóribus: et ætérni Regis splendóre illustráta, totíus orbis se séntiat amisísse calíginem.

LET MOTHER CHURCH ALSO REJOICE, adorned with the effulgence of so great a light; and let this place ring with the voices of many. Wherefore, do ye here present, O most dear brethren, in the wondrous brightness of this holy light, join me, I pray, in invoking the mercy of almighty God, that He, Who, for no merits of mine own, hath deigned to number me among the Levites, may shed upon me the brightness of His light and make me perfectly perform the praise of this candle. Through Our Lord Jesus Christ, His Son, Who with Him liveth and reigneth in the unity of the Holy Spirit, God, forever and ever. ℟. Amen.

Lætétur et mater Ecclésia, tanti lúminis adornáta fulgóribus: et magnis populórum vócibus hæc aula resúltet. Quaprópter adstántes vos, fratres caríssimi, ad tam miram hujus sancti lúminis claritátem, una mecum, quæso, Dei omnipoténtis misericórdiam invocáte. Ut qui me non meis méritis intra Levitárum númerum dignátus est aggregáre: lúminis sui claritátem infúndens, Cérei hujus laudem implére perfíciat. Per Dóminum nostrum Jesum Christum Fílium suum: qui cum eo vivit et regnat in unitáte Spíritus sancti Deus. Per ómnia sǽcula sæculórum. ℟. Amen.

℣. The Lord be with you.
℟. And with thy spirit.
℣. Lift up your hearts.
℟. We have lifted them up to the Lord.
℣. Let us give thanks to the Lord our God.
℟. It is meet and just.

℟. Amen.
℣. Dóminus vobíscum.
℟. Et cum spíritu tuo.
℣. Sursum corda.
℟. Habémus ad Dóminum.
℣. Grátias agámus Dómino Deo nostro.
℟. Dignum et justum est.

Ꝟ ET JUSTUM EST, invisíbilem Deum Patrem omnipoténtem, Filiúmque ejus unigénitum, Dóminum nostrum Jesum Christum, toto cordis ac mentis afféctu, et vocis ministério personáre. Qui pro nobis ætérno Patri, Adæ débitum solvit: et véteris piáculi cautiónem pio cruóre detérsit. Hæc sunt enim festa Paschália, in quibus verus ille Agnus occíditur, cujus sánguine postes fidélium consecrántur.

IT IS TRULY MEET AND JUST, that with all the powers of heart and mind, uplifting, too, our voices, we sing the God invisible, the Father almighty, and His only-begotten Son, Our Lord Jesus Christ; Who hath paid for us unto the eternal Father the debt of Adam, and hath wiped out with His dear blood the reckoning of the ancient offense. For these are the paschal rites wherein the true Lamb is slain with Whose blood the door-posts of the faithful are consecrated.

HÆC NOX EST, in qua primum patres nostros fílios Ísraël edúctos de Ægýpto, Mare rubrum sicco vestígio transíre fecísti. Hæc ígitur nox est, quæ peccatórum ténebras, colúmnæ illuminatióne purgávit. Hæc nox est, quæ hódie per univérsum mundum, in Christo credéntes, a vítiis sæculi, et calígine peccatórum segregátos, reddit grátiæ, sóciat sanctitáti. Hæc nox est, in qua destrúctis vínculis mortis, Christus ab ínferis victor ascéndit.

THIS THE NIGHT on which Thou didst cause our fathers, the children of Israel, to cross dryshod the Red Sea, leading them out of the land of Egypt. This, then, is the night that hath purged away the darkness of sins with the illumination of the pillar of fire. This is the night which now, throughout all the world, doth separate believers in Christ from the iniquities of the world and the gloom of sins, doth restore them unto grace, and join them unto holiness. This is the night on which, bursting the bonds of death, Christ came victorious from the grave.

NIHIL ENIM NOBIS nasci prófuit, nisi rédimi profuísset. O mira circa nos tuæ pietátis dignátio! O inæstimábilis diléctio caritátis: ut servum redímeres, Fílium tradidísti! O certe necessárium Adæ peccátum, quod Christi morte delétum est! O felix culpa, quæ talem ac tantum méruit habére Redemptórem!

FOR IT profited us nothing to be born except that we might be redeemed. O wondrous condescension of Thy great kindness in our regard! O inestimable affection of charity: to redeem the slave, Thou didst give up the Son! O truly necessary sin of Adam, that is wiped out by the death of Christ! O happy fault, that was worthy to have such and so great a redeemer!

O VERE beáta nox, quæ sola méruit scire tempus et horam, in qua Christus ab ínferis resurréxit! Hæc nox est, de qua scriptum est: *Et nox sicut dies illuminábitur: Et nox illuminátio mea in delíciis meis.* (Ps 138: 11-12) Hujus ígitur sanctificátio noctis, fugat scélera, culpas lavat: et reddit innocéntiam lapsis, et mœstis lætítiam. Fugat ódia, concórdiam parat, et curvat impéria.

O TRULY blessèd night, that alone was worthy to know the time and the hour when Christ rose again from the dead. This is the night of which it is written: *And the night shall be enlightened like day; and the night is my enlightening in my pleasures.* The sanctification of this night, therefore, driveth away evil deeds, cleanseth offences, restoring innocence to the fallen and gladness to the mournful. It driveth out hatred, it produceth concord and curbeth tyrannies.

[Editor's Note: In the 1950 version, the Deacon—at this point—walked over to the Paschal candle, inserted five grains of incense, then came back to continue the chant. The *Commissio Piana* changed the vernacular translation from "incense" to "fire" (or other words, depending on the translator), since the incense grains were inserted before the Deacon entered the church in the reformed version. The reformers seemed unaware that in olden times, a small quantity was burned along with incense; e.g. some ancient books instructed the Deacon to remove bits of wax from the Paschal candle and burn them in the thurible "before fixing the grains of incense in their place" {Thurston p424}. In the 1970 Missal, the reformers changed the Latin word ***incénsi*** to ***laudis***.]

IN THANKSGIVING, then, for this night, O holy Father, receive the evening sacrifice of this candle, which most holy Church rendereth to Thee by the hands of her ministers, in this solemn oblation of wax, from the labors of the bees. And now we know the glories of this column which the flickering fire doth kindle in God's honor.

In hujus ígitur noctis grátia, súscipe sancte Pater, incénsi hujus sacrifícium vespertínum: quod tibi in hac Cérei oblatióne solémni, per ministrórum manus de opéribus apum, sacrosáncta reddit Ecclésia. Sed jam colúmnæ hujus præcónia nóvimus, quam in honórem Dei rútilans ignis accéndit.

[Editor's Note: In the 1950 version, the Deacon—at this point—lights the Paschal candle with one of the candles on the Trident, or with a taper from one.]

WHICH FIRE, though it be divided into parts, yet knoweth no diminution of its light. For it is nourished by the fluid wax which the mother bee hath produced for the material of this precious torch.

Qui licet sit divísus in partes, mutuáti tamen lúminis detriménta non novit. Álitur enim liquántibus ceris, quas in substántiam pretiósæ hujus lámpadis, apis mater edúxit.

[Editor's Note: In the 1950 version, "the lamps in the church are relighted" at this point, whereas in the 1962 version the church lights were turned on after the third "Lumen Christi" {McManus p92}. With regard to the following words in brackets ("quae expoliávit...etc.") these were inexplicably deleted by the reformers in 1970.]

O TRULY BLESSED NIGHT that despoiled the Egyptians and enriched the Hebrews! Night in which heavenly are joined with earthly things, divine with human! We beseech Thee, therefore, O Lord, that this wax candle hallowed in honor of Thy Name, may continue to burn to dissipate the darkness of this night. And being accepted as a sweet savor, may be united with the heavenly lights. Let the morning star find its flame alight. That star, I mean, which knows no setting. He Who returning from hell, serenely shone forth upon mankind.

O vere beáta nox, [*quæ exspoliávit Ægýptios, ditávit Hebrǽos! Nox,*] in qua terrénis cæléstia, humánis divína jungúntur. Orámus ergo te, Dómine: ut Céreus iste in honórem tui nóminis consecrátus, ad noctis hujus calíginem destruéndam, indefíciens persevéret. Et in odórem suavitátis accéptus, supérnis lumináribus misceátur. Flammas ejus lúcifer matutínus invéniat. Ille, inquam, lúcifer, qui nescit occásum. Ille, qui regréssus ab ínferis, humáno géneri serénus illúxit.

WE BESEECH THEE therefore, O Lord, that Thou wouldst grant peaceful times during this Paschal Festival, and vouchsafe to rule, govern, and keep with Thy constant protection us Thy servants, and all the clergy, and the devout people, together with our most holy Father, (*Name of Pope*), and our Bishop (*Name of Bishop*).

Precámur ergo te, Dñe: ut nos fámulos tuos, omnémque clerum, et devotíssimum pópulum: una cum beatíssimo Papa nostro [*Name of Pope*] et Antístite nostro [*Name of Bishop*] quiéte témporum concéssa, in his Paschálibus gáudiis, assídua protectióne régere, gubernáre, et conserváre dignéris.

HAVE REGARD also for those who reign over us, and, grant them Thine ineffable kindness and mercy, direct their thoughts in justice and peace, that from their earthy toil, they may come to their heavenly reward with all Thy people. Through the

Réspice étiã ad eos, qui nos in potestáte regunt, et, ineffábili pietátis et misericórdiæ tuæ múnere, dírige cogitatiónes eórum ad justítiam et pacem, ut de terréna operositáte ad cæléstẽ pátriã pervéniant cum omni pópulo tuo.

Per eúmdem Dóminum nostrũ Jesum Christum Fíliũ tuũ: Qui tecum vivit et regnat in unitáte Spíritus Sancti, Deus: Per ómnia sǽcula sæculórũ. ℟. Amen.

same Jesus Christ Thy Son, our Lord, who with Thee liveth and reigneth in the unity of the Holy Ghost, God: World without end. ℟. Amen.

1962 • When the EXSULTET has ended, "both the clergy and people now extinguish their candles" {1953maryland p8}. The 1962 version does not specify whether the church returns to darkness at this point—but customarily the electric lights are turned off (again) until the *Glória In Excélsis* at the Easter Eve Mass.

V • OLD TESTAMENT LESSONS

1962 • The Deacon changes back into his violet vestments and the Lessons are sung by a "capable reader" in surplice {McManus p94}. When it comes to the 1962 version, a "capable reader" is spoken of. On Holy Thursday, this capable reader "wearing a surplice, may read or sing the Epistle while the Celebrant stands at the Altar and listens." On Good Friday, a "capable reader" may sing the Old Testament readings at the beginning. On Holy Saturday, a "capable reader" may read all the Old Testament readings—and even the Epistle. On this, see *Mass & Vespers* (Solesmes, 1957) pages 547, 572, 576, 634, and 639. With the benefit of seventy years' hindsight, our editorial suggestion is that no man should sing the Epistle at any time if he be not ***at a minimum*** tonsured. Regarding the Celebrant "duplicating" readings, MAXIMA REDEMPTIONIS (16 November 1955) declared: "Throughout Holy Week, when Mass—and, on Good Friday, the solemn liturgical service—is celebrated solemnly, the Celebrant omits anything chanted or read (by reason of their own office) by the Deacon, Subdeacon, or lector."

1962 • When it comes to the Collect prayers: (1) All stand up; (2) The Celebrant, standing in the same place, says: *Orémus*; (3) Then the Deacon adds: *Flectámus génua*. (4) All kneel together for a "moderately long period of time" {McManus p80}; (5) In the 1962 version, the Deacon—not the Subdeacon—sings *Leváte*; (6) The Celebrant sings the prayer, with hands joined, "in the ferial tone" {McManus p95}.

English translation by Monsignor Ronald Knox (IMPRIMATUR 1950).

FIRST LESSON. *Genesis 1: 1-31; 2: 1-2*

In princípio creávit Deus cælum et terram. Terra autem erat inánis et vácua, et ténebræ erant super fáciem abýssi: et Spíritus Dei ferebátur super aquas. Dixítque Deus: Fiat lux. Et facta est lux. Et vidit Deus lucem, quod esset bona: et divísit lucem a ténebris. Appellavítque lucem Diem, et ténebras Noctem: factúmque est véspere et mane, dies unus.

OD, AT THE BEGINNING of time, created heaven and earth. Earth was still an empty waste, and darkness hung over the deep; but already, over its waters, brooded the Spirit of God. Then God said: Let there be light; and the light began. God saw the light, and found it good, and he divided the spheres of light and darkness; the light he called Day and the darkness Night. So evening came and morning, and one day passed.

Dixit quoque Deus: Fiat firmaméntum in médio aquárum: et dívidat aquas ab aquis. Et fecit Deus firmaméntum, divisítque aquas, quæ erant sub firmaménto, ab his, quæ erant super firmaméntum. Et factum est ita. Vocavítque Deus firmaméntum, Cælum: et factum est véspere et mane, dies secúndus.

God said, too, Let a solid vault rise amid the waters, to keep these waters apart from those; a vault by which God would separate the waters which were beneath it from the waters above it; and so it was done. This vault God called the Sky. So evening came, and morning, and a second day passed.

Dixit vero Deus: Congregéntur aquæ, quæ sub cælo sunt, in locum unum: et appáreat árida. Et factum est ita. Et vocávit Deus áridam, Terram: congregationésque aquárum appellávit Mária. Et vidit Deus, quod esset bonum.

And now God said, Let the water below the vault collect in one place to make dry land appear. And so it was done; the dry land God called Earth, and the water, where it had collected, he called the Sea. All this God saw, and found it good.

Let the earth, he said, yield grasses that grow and seed; fruit-trees too, each giving fruit of its own kind, and so propagating itself on earth. And so it was done; the earth yielded grasses that grew and seeded, each according to its kind, and trees that bore fruit, each with the power to propagate its own kind. And God saw it, and found it good. So evening came, and morning, and a third day passed. Next, God said, Let there be luminaries in the vault of the sky, to divide the spheres of day and night; let them give portents, and be measures of time, to mark out the day and the year; let them shine in the sky's vault, and shed light on the earth. And so it was done.

Et ait: Gérminet terra herbam viréntem et faciéntem semen, et lignum pomíferum fáciens fructum juxta genus suum, cujus semen in semetípso sit super terram. Et factum est ita. Et prótulit terra herbam viréntem et faciéntem semen juxta genus suum, lignúmque fáciens fructum, et habens unumquódque seméntem secúndum spéciem suam. Et vidit Deus, quod esset bonum. Et factum est véspere et mane, dies tértius. Dixit autem Deus: Fiant luminária in firmaménto cæli, et dívidant diem ac noctem, et sint in signa et témpora et dies et annos: ut lúceant in firmaménto cæli, et illúminent terram. Et factum est ita.

God made the two great luminaries, the greater of them to command the day, and the lesser to command the night; then he made the stars. All these he put in the vault of the sky, to shed their light on the earth, to control day and night, and divide the spheres of light and darkness. And God saw it, and found it good. So evening came, and morning, and a fourth day passed.

Fecítque Deus duo luminária magna: luminare majus, ut præésset diéi: et luminare minus, ut præésset nocti: et stellas. Et pósuit eas in firmaménto cæli, ut lucérent super terram, et præéssent diéi ac nocti, et divíderent lucem ac ténebras. Et vidit Deus, quod esset bonum. Et factum est véspere et mane, dies quartus.

After this, God said, Let the waters produce moving things that have life in them, and winged things that fly above the earth under the sky's vault. Thus God created the huge sea-beasts, and all the different kinds of life and movement that spring from the waters, and all the different kinds of flying things; and God saw it, and found it good.

Dixit étiam Deus: Prodúcant aquæ réptile ánimæ vivéntis, et volátile super terram sub firmaménto cæli. Creavítque Deus cete grándia, et omnem ánimam vivéntem atque motábilem, quam prodúxerant aquæ in spécies suas, et omne volátile secúndum genus suum. Et vidit Deus, quod esset bonum.

He pronounced his blessing on them, Increase and multiply, and fill the waters of the sea; and let there be abundance of flying things on the earth. So evening came, and morning, and a fifth day passed.

Benedixítque eis, dicens: Créscite et multiplicámini, et repléte aquas maris: avésque multiplicéntur super terram. Et factum est véspere et mane, dies quintus.

God said, too, Let the land yield all different kinds of living things, cattle and creeping things and wild beasts of every sort; and so it was done. God made every sort of wild beast, and all the different kinds of cattle and of creeping things; and God saw it, and found it good. And God said: Let us make man, wearing our own image and likeness; let us put him in command of the fishes in the sea, and all that flies through the air, and the cattle, and the whole earth, and all the creeping things that move on earth.

Dixit quoque Deus: Prodúcat terra ánimam vivéntem in génere suo: juménta et reptília, et béstias terræ secúndum spécies suas. Factúmque est ita. Et fecit Deus béstias terræ juxta spécies suas, et juménta, et omne réptile terræ in génere suo. Et vidit Deus, quod esset bonum, et ait: Faciámus hóminem ad imáginem et similitúdinem nostram: et præsit píscibus maris et volatílibus cæli, et béstiis universǽque terræ, omníque réptili, quod movétur in terra.

Et creávit Deus hóminem ad imáginem suam: ad imáginem Dei creávit illum, másculum et féminam creávit eos. Benedixítque illis Deus, et ait: Créscite et multiplicámini, et repléte terram, et subjícite eam, et dominámini píscibus maris et volatílibus cæli, et univérsis animántibus, quæ movéntur super terram.

So God made man in his own image, made him in the image of God. Man and woman both, he created them. And God pronounced his blessing on them, Increase and multiply and fill the earth, and make it yours; take command of the fishes in the sea, and all that flies through the air, and all the living things that move on the earth.

Dixítque Deus: Ecce, dedi vobis omnem herbam afferéntem semen super terram, et univérsa ligna, quæ habent in semetípsis seméntem géneris sui, ut sint vobis in escam: et cunctis animántibus terræ, omníque vólucri cæli, et univérsis, quæ movéntur in terra, et in quibus est ánima vivens, ut hábeant ad vescéndum. Et factum est ita.

Here are all the herbs, God told them, that seed on earth, and all the trees, that carry in them the seeds of their own life, to be your food; food for all beasts on the earth, all that flies in the air, all that creeps along the ground; here all that lives shall find its nourishment. And so it was done.

Vidítque Deus cuncta, quæ fécerat: et erant valde bona. Et factum est véspere et mane, dies sextus. Ígitur perfécti sunt cæli et terra, et omnis ornátus eórum. Complevítque Deus die séptimo opus suum, quod fécerat: et requiévit die séptimo ab univérso ópere, quod patrárat.

And God saw all that he had made, and found it very good. So evening came, and morning, and a sixth day passed. Thus heaven and earth and all the furniture of them were completed. By the seventh day, God had come to an end of making, and rested on the seventh day, with his whole task accomplished.

Celebrant: Orémus.
Deacon: ℣. Flectámus génua.
Deacon: ℟. Leváte.

Let us pray.
℣. Let us kneel.
℟. Arise.

COLLECT AFTER THE FIRST LESSON.

Deus, qui mirabíliter creásti hóminem, et mirabílius redemísti: da nobis, quæsumus, contra oblectaménta peccáti, mentis ratióne persístere; ut mereámur ad ætérna gáudia perveníre. Per Dóminum.

O GOD, Who hast wonderfully created man and more wonderfully redeemed him: grant us, we beseech Thee, to withstand by strength of spirit the allurements of sin, that we may deserve to arrive at everlasting joys. Through our Lord. ℟. Amen.

English translation by Monsignor Ronald Knox (Imprimatur 1950).

SECOND LESSON. *Exodus 14: 24-31; 15: 1*

In diébus illis: Factum est in vigília matutína, et ecce respíciens Dóminus super castra Ægyptiórum per colúmnam ignis et nubis, interfécit exércitum eórum: et subvértit rotas cúrruum, ferebantúrque in profúndum. Dixérunt ergo Ægýptii: Fugiámus Isrælem: Dóminus enim pugnat pro eis contra nos.

IT WAS already the first watch of the morning, when suddenly, through the pillar of fire and mist, the Lord looked down upon the Egyptians, and brought their army to its doom. He turned the wheels of their chariots aside, so that they drove through deep places. And the Egyptians began to say, Back, back! There is no facing Israel; the Lord is fighting on their side against us.

Then the Lord said to Moses, Stretch out thy hand over the sea, so that its waters shall recoil on the Egyptians, on all their chariots and their horsemen. And when Moses stretched out his hand towards the sea, at early dawn, it went back to its bed, so that its waters met the Egyptians in their flight, and the Lord drowned them amid the waters.

Et ait Dóminus ad Móysen: Exténde manum tuam super mare, ut revertántur aquæ ad Ægýptios super currus et équites eórum. Cumque extendísset Móyses manum contra mare, revérsum est primo dilúculo ad priórem locum: fugientibúsque Ægýptiis occurrérunt aquæ, et invólvit eos Dóminus in médiis flúctibus.

Back came the water, overwhelming all the chariots and horsemen of Pharao's army that had entered the sea in their pursuit; not a man escaped. But the sons of Israel made their way through the midst of the sea where it had parted, its waters towering like a wall to right and left. So the Lord rescued Israel that day from the assault of the Egyptians; and when they saw the dead Egyptians washed up on the shore, and the great defeat the Lord had inflicted upon them, the people learned to fear the Lord, putting their trust in him and in his servant Moses. Then Moses and the Israelites sang praises to the Lord, and this was their song :

Reversǽque sunt aquæ, et operuérunt currus, et équites cuncti exércitus Pharaónis, qui sequéntes ingréssi fúerant mare: nec unus quidem supérfuit ex eis. Fílii autem Ísraël perrexérunt per médium sicci maris, et aquæ eis erant quasi pro muro a dextris et a sinístris. Liberavítque Dóminus in die illa Ísraël de manu Ægyptiórum. Et vidérunt Ægýptios mórtuos super litus maris, et manum magnam, quam exercúerat Dóminus contra eos: timuítque pópulus Dóminum, et credidérunt Dómino et Móysi, servo ejus. Tunc cécinit Móyses et fílii Ísraël carmen hoc Dómino, et dixérunt:

CANTICLE AFTER THE SECOND LESSON. *Exodus 15: 1, 2*

LET US SING TO THE LORD, for He is gloriously honored: the horse and the rider He hath thrown into the sea: He has become my Helper and Protector unto salvation. ℣. He is my God, and I will honor Him: the God of my father, and I will extol Him. ℣. He is the Lord that destroys wars: the Lord is His Name.

Cantémus Dómino: glorióse enim honorificátus est: equum, et ascensórem projécit in mare: adjútor, et protéctor factus est mihi in salútẽ. ℣. Hic Deus meus, et honorificábo eum: Deus patris mei, et exaltábo eum. ℣. Dñs cónterens bella: Dóminus nomen est illi.

Let us pray.
℣. Let us kneel.
℟. Arise.

Celebrant: Orémus.
Deacon: ℣. Flectámus génua.
Deacon: ℟. Leváte.

COLLECT AFTER THE SECOND LESSON.

O GOD, Whose ancient miracles we see shining also in our days, whilst by the water of regeneration Thou dost operate for the salvation of the Gentiles, that which by the power of Thy right hand Thou didst confer upon one people, by delivering them from the Egyptian persecution: grant that all the nations of the world may become the children of Abraham, and partake of the dignity of the people of Israel. Through our Lord. ℟. Amen.

Deus, cujus antíqua mirácula étiam nostris sǽculis coruscáre sentímus: dum quod uni pópulo, a persecutióne Ægyptíaca liberándo, déxteræ tuæ poténtia contulísti, id in salútem géntium per aquam regeneratiónis operáris: præsta; ut in Ábrahæ fílios, et in Israëlíticam dignitátem, totíus mundi tránseat plenitúdo. Per Dóminum.

1962 • The 1950 version has twelve prophecies; the 1962 version has four. The reformers call these "lessons," and all came from the 1950 version—except that in the following reading (previously the *Eighth Prophecy*), the first verse was deleted. Father Löw, one of the six members of the *Commissio Piana*, tried to get approval for reading the Holy Saturday prophecies in the vernacular on 13 November 1951, but Dom Anselmo Albareda pushed back, saying "the vernacular might be conceded for the renewal of baptismal promises but never for the readings," and he "warmly emphasized the moral value of a single language in the Church's official worship" {Giampietro p231}. On 2 January 1953, we find Dom Albareda again defending the Church's *lingua sacra*, saying "the unity of language in the liturgy is so great a treasure for the Church that no advantage could compensate for its demise" {Giampietro p249}.

English translation by Monsignor Ronald Knox (IMPRIMATUR 1950).

THIRD LESSON. *Isaias 4: 2-6.*

In die illa erit germen Dñi in magnificéntia, et glória, et fructus terræ sublímis, et exultátio his, qui salváti fúerint de Ísraël. Et erit: Omnis qui relíctus fúerit in Sion, et resíduus in Jerúsalem, sanctus vocábitur, omnis qui scriptus est in vita in Jerúsalem. Si ablúerit Dóminus sordes filiárum Sion, et sánguinem Jerúsalem láverit de médio ejus, in spíritu judícii, et spíritu ardóris. Et creábit Dñs super omnem locum montis Sion, et ubi invocátus est, nubem per diem, et fumum, et splendórẽ ignis flammántis in nocte: super omnẽ enim glóriam protéctio. Et tabernáculum erit in umbráculum diéi ab æstu, et in securitátem, et absconsiónem a túrbine, et a plúvia.

WHEN THAT DAY COMES, bud and fruit there shall be, of the Lord's fostering; burgeoning of glory made manifest, and fruit piled high, the trophy of Israel's gleanings. Set apart for him, all that dwell in Sion now, all that survive the city's purging; none else will be left alive in Jerusalem, when the Lord sweeps away the guilt of Sion's womenfolk, washes Jerusalem clean from the blood that stains her, with the searing breath of his judgement. And all over mount Sion, the shrine of his name, cloud shall hang by day, glowing haze by night, a veil for glory. Canopy they shall have, to shade them from the day's heat, a refuge to give them shelter from storm and rain.

CANTICLE AFTER THE THIRD LESSON. *Isaias 5: 1, 2, 7*

Vínea facta est diléςto in cornu, in loco úberi. ℣. Et macériam circúmdedit, et circumfódit: et plantávit víneam Sorec: et ædificávit turrim in médio ejus. ℣. Et tórcular fodit in ea: vínea enim Dñi Sábaoth, domus Ísraël est.

MY BELOVED had a vineyard on a hill in a fruitful place. ℣. And he enclosed it with a fence, and made a ditch round it, and planted it with the vine of Sorec, and built a tower in the midst thereof. ℣. And he made a winepress in it: for the vineyard of the Lord of hosts is the house of Israel.

Celebrant: Orémus.
Deacon: ℣. Flectámus génua.
Deacon: ℟. Leváte.

Let us pray.
℣. Let us kneel.
℟. Arise.

COLLECT AFTER THE THIRD LESSON.

Deus, qui in ómnibus Ecclésiæ tuæ fíliis, sanctórum prophetárum voce manifestásti, in omni loco dominatiónis tuæ, satórem te bonórum séminum, et electórum pálmitum esse cultórem: tríbue pópulis tuis, qui et vineárum apud te nómine censéntur et ségetum; ut, spinárum et tribulórum squalóre resecáto, digna efficiántur fruge fecúndi. Per Dóminum.

O GOD, Who by the voice of the holy prophets hast declared to all the children of Thy Church that through the whole extent of Thine empire Thou art the Sower of good seed, and the Cultivator of chosen branches: grant to Thy people who are called by Thee, by the name of vines and harvest field, that they may root out all thorns and briars, and produce good fruit in abundance. Through our Lord. ℟. Amen.

FOURTH LESSON. *Deuteronomy 31: 22-30*

English translation by Monsignor Ronald Knox (IMPRIMATUR 1950).

MOSES PUT THE SONG in writing, in those days, and taught it to the men of Israel. The Lord also gave a charge to Josue, the son of Nun: Play the man, and keep thy courage high; it is thy task to settle sons of Israel in the land I have promised to give them, and I will be with thee in the doing of it. And now, when Moses had finished his work of setting forth the terms of this law in a book, he gave orders to the Levites, that carried the ark of the Lord, what they should do with it.

In diébus illis: Scripsit Móyses cánticum, et dócuit fílios Ísraël. Præcepítque Dóminus Jósue, fílio Nun, et ait: Confortáre, et esto robústus: tu enim introdúces fílios Ísraël in terram, quam pollícitus sum, et ego ero tecum. Postquam ergo scripsit Móyses verba legis hujus in volúmine, atque complévit: præcépit Levítis, qui portábant arcam fœderis Dómini, dicens:

Take this book, he said, and lay it up by the side of the ark that bears witness of the Lord's covenant, to vindicate him against you. I know well how rebellious you are, how stiff-necked; even in my life-time, and in spite of my presence among you, you have always been rebelling against the Lord; and when I am dead, worse must follow. Summon the elders and counsellors among all the tribes, and let me say my say in their hearing; let me call upon heaven and earth to bear witness against them.

Tóllite librum istum, et pónite eum in látere arcæ fœderis Dñi, Dei vestri: ut sit ibi contra te in testimónium. Ego enim scio contentiónem tuam et cérvicem tuam duríssimam. Adhuc vivénte me et ingrediénte vobíscum, semper contentióse egístis contra Dóminum: quanto magis, cum mórtuus fúero? Congregáte ad me omnes majóres natu per tribus vestras, atque doctóres, et loquar audiéntibus eis sermónes istos, et invocábo contra eos cælum et terram.

I know well enough that when I am dead you will ruin all, and it will not be long before you stray from the path I have showed you; and I know that when the Lord sees you living amiss, and provoking his anger by your doings, calamity will fall upon you in the end. And so Moses, with the whole assembly of Israel listening to him, pronounced the words of the song which follows, never pausing until it was all finished:

Novi enim, quod post mortem meam iníque agétis et declinábitis cito de via, quam præcépi vobis: et occúrrent vobis mala in extrémo témpore, quando fecéritis malum in conspéctu Dómini, ut irritétis eum per ópera mánuum vestrárum. Locútus est ergo Móyses, audiénte univérso cœtu Ísraël, verba cárminis hujus, et ad finem usque complévit.

CANTICLE AFTER THE FOURTH LESSON. *Deuteronomy 32: 1-4*

ATTEND, O HEAVEN, and I will speak: and let the earth hear the words that come out of my mouth. ℣. Let my speech be expected like the rain: and let my words fall like the dew. ℣. Like the shower upon the grass, and like the snow upon the dry herb, because I will invoke the name of the Lord. ℣. Confess the greatness of our Lord: the works of God are perfect, and all His ways are justice. ℣. God is faithful, in Whom there is no iniquity: the Lord is just and holy.

Atténde, cælum, et loquar: et áudiat terra verba ex ore meo. ℣. Exspectétur sicut plúvia elóquium meum: et descéndant sicut ros verba mea. ℣. Sicut imber super gramen et sicut nix super fœnum: quia nomen Dómini invocábo. ℣. Date magnitúdinem Deo nostro: Deus, vera ópera ejus, et omnes viæ ejus judícia. ℣. Deus fidélis, in quo non est iníquitas: justus et sanctus Dóminus.

Celebrant: Orémus.
Deacon: ℣. Flectámus génua.
Deacon: ℟. Leváte.

Let us pray.
℣. Let us kneel.
℟. Arise.

COLLECT AFTER THE FOURTH LESSON.

Deus, celsitúdo humílium et fortitúdo rectórum, qui per sanctum Móysen púerum tuum, ita erudíre pópulum tuum sacri cárminis tui decantatióne voluísti, ut illa legis iterátio fíeret étiam nostra diréctio: éxcita in omnem justificatárum géntium plenitúdinem poténtiam tuam, et da lætítiam, mitigándo terrórem; ut, ómnium peccátis tua remissióne delétis, quod denuntiátum est in ultiónem, tránseat in salútem. Per Dóminum.

O GOD, the exaltation of the humble, and the strength of the righteous, Who, by Thy holy servant Moses, wast pleased so to instruct Thy people by the singing of Thy sacred canticle, that the renewal of the law should be also our guidance: show forth Thy power to all the multitude of Gentiles justified by Thee, and by mitigating Thy terror grant them joy: that, all sins being blotted out by Thy remission, the threatened vengeance may give way to salvation. Through our Lord. ℟. Amen.

VI • FIRST PART OF THE LITANY

1962 • When the Collect after the fourth Lesson is finished, "two chanters, kneeling in the middle of the Sanctuary, chant the Litanies of the Saints as far as the invocation *Propítius Esto*. All kneel and make the responses. The invocations are not doubled" {McManus p95}. This is called **the beginning of the Litany**. Many choirs often repeat the first invocations ("Kýrie eléison" etc.), but this is not correct according to page 101 of the official *Ordo Hebdomadae Sanctae Instauratus* (Imprimatur 18 January 1956).

LORD, HAVE MERCY.
Christ, have mercy.
Lord, have mercy.
Christ, hear us.
Christ, graciously hear us.

YRIE ELEISON.
Christe eléison.
Kýrie eléison.
Christe, audi nos.
Christe, exáudi nos.

℟. *Have mercy on us.*

℟. *Miserére nobis.*

God the Father of heaven, ℟.
God the Son, Redeemer of the world, ℟.
God the Holy Ghost, ℟.
Holy Trinity, one God, ℟.

Pater de cælis, Deus, ℟.
Fili Redémptor mundi, Deus, ℟.
Spíritus Sancte, Deus, ℟.
Sancta Trínitas, unus Deus, ℟.

* *Pray for us.*

* *Ora pro nobis*

Holy Mary, *
Holy Mother of God, *
Holy Virgin of virgins, *
Saint Michael, *

Sancta María, *
Sancta Dei Génitrix, *
Sancta Virgo vírginum, *
Sancte Míchaël, *

SANCTE Gábriel, * — Saint Gabriel, *
Sancte Ráphaël, * — Saint Raphael, *
Omnes sancti Ángeli et Archángeli, *oráte pro nobis.* — All ye holy Angels and Archangels, *
Omnes sancti beatórum Spiríttuum órdines, *oráte pro nobis.* — All ye holy orders of blessed Spirits, *

SANCTE Joánnes Baptísta, * — Saint John the Baptist, *
Sancte Joseph, * — Saint Joseph, *
Omnes sancti Patriárchæ et Prophétæ, *oráte pro nobis.* — All ye holy Patriarchs and Prophets, *

SANCTE Petre, * — Saint Peter, *
Sancte Paule, * — Saint Paul, *
Sancte Andréa, * — Saint Andrew, *
Sancte Joánnes, * — Saint John, *
Omnes sancti Apóstoli et Evangelístæ, *oráte pro nobis.* — All ye holy Apostles and Evangelists, *
Omnes sancti Discípuli Dómini, *oráte pro nobis.* — All ye holy Disciples of the Lord, *

SANCTE Stéphane, * — Saint Stephen, *
Sancte Lauréntі, * — Saint Lawrence, *
Sancte Vincénti, * — Saint Vincent, *
Omnes sancti Mártyres, *oráte pro nobis.* — All ye holy Martyrs, *

SANCTE Silvéster, * — Saint Sylvester, *
Sancte Gregóri, * — Saint Gregory, *
Sancte Augustíne, * — Saint Augustine, *
Omnes sancti Pontífices et Confessóres, *oráte pro nobis.* — All ye holy Bishops and Confessors, *
Omnes sancti Doctóres, *oráte pro nobis.* — All ye holy Doctors, *

SANCTE Antóni, * — Saint Anthony, *
Sancte Benedícte, * — Saint Benedict, *
Sancte Domínice, * — Saint Dominic, *
Sancte Francísce, * — Saint Francis, *
Omnes sancti Sacerdótes et Levítæ, *oráte pro nobis.* — All ye holy Priests and Levites, *
Omnes sancti Mónachi et Eremítæ, *oráte pro nobis.* — All ye holy Monks and Hermits, *

Saint Mary Magdalene, *

Saint Agnes, *

Saint Cecilia, *

Saint Agatha, *

Saint Anastasia, *

All ye holy Virgins and Widows, *

All ye holy Saints of God, intercede for us.

SANCTA María Magdaléna, *
Sancta Agnes, *
Sancta Cæcília, *
Sancta Ágatha, *
Sancta Anastásia, *
Omnes sanctæ Vírgines et Víduæ,
oráte pro nobis.
Omnes Sancti et Sanctæ Dei,
intercédite pro nobis.

1962 • All rise from their knees, and the cantors return to their places.

VII • BLESSING OF BAPTISMAL WATER

1962 • While the Litany of the Saints is being chanted, the vessel of water to be blessed is prepared in the center of the chancel—toward the Epistle side—in view of the faithful. It is becoming that the vessel of water to be blessed should he suitably ornamented. For the blessing of the baptismal water, the Celebrant stands facing the people, with the vessel of water of water in front of him. The Celebrant says without inflection, with his hands joined:

℣. Dóminus vobíscum.
℟. Et cum spíritu tuo.
Orémus.

℣. The Lord be with you.
℟. And with thy spirit.
Let us pray.

Omnípotens sempitérne Deus, adésto magnæ pietátis tuæ mystériis, adésto sacraméntis: et ad recreándos novos pópulos, quos tibi fons baptísmatis párturit, spíritum adoptiónis emítte; ut quod nostræ humilitátis geréndum est ministério, virtútis tuæ impleátur eféctu. Per Dóminum.

O ALMIGHTY AND EVERLASTING God, be present at these Mysteries, be present at these Sacraments of Thy great loving kindness: and send forth the spirit of adoption to regenerate the new people, whom the font of baptism brings forth; that what is to be done by our humble ministry may be accomplished by the effect of Thy power. Through our Lord.

1962 • He concludes the prayer in the Preface tone: **"World without end."**

Elevans vocem in modum Praefationis, prosequitur junctis manibus: **"Per ómnia sǽcula sæculórum."**

℟. Amen.
℣. Dóminus vobíscum.
℟. Et cum spíritu tuo.
℣. Sursum corda.
℟. Habémus ad Dóminum.
℣. Grátias agámus Dómino Deo nostro.
℟. Dignum et justum est.

℟. Amen.
℣. The Lord be with you.
℟. And with thy spirit.
℣. Lift up your hearts.
℟. We have lifted them up to the Lord.
℣. Let us give thanks to the Lord our God.
℟. It is meet and just.

IT IS TRULY meet and just, right and availing unto salvation, to give Thee thanks always and in all places, O holy Lord, almighty Father, everlasting God, Who by Thine ineffable power dost wonderfully produce the effect of Thy Sacraments: and though we are unworthy to perform such great Mysteries: yet, as Thou dost not abandon the gifts of Thy grace, so Thou inclinest the ears of Thy goodness, even to our prayers. O God, Whose Spirit in the very beginning of the world moved over the waters, that even then the nature of water might receive the virtue of sanctification.

Vere dignum et justum est, æquum et salutáre, nos tibi semper et ubíque grátias ágere, Dómine, sancte Pater, omnípotens ætérne Deus: qui invisíbili poténtia, sacramentórum tuórũ mirabíliter operáris efféctum: et licet nos tantis mystériis exsequéndis simus indígni: tu tamen grátiæ tuæ dona non déserens, étiam ad nostras preces aures tuæ pietátis inclínas. Deus, cujus Spíritus super aquas inter ipsa mundа primórdia ferebátur: ut jam tunc virtútem sanctificatiónis, aquárum natúra concíperet.

O God, Who by water didst wash away the crimes of the guilty world, and by the pouring out of the deluge didst give a figure of regeneration, that one and the same element might in a mystery be the end of vice and the beginning of virtue. Look, O Lord, on the face of Thy Church, and multiply in her Thy regenerations, who by the streams of Thine abundant grace fillest Thy city with joy, and openest the font of Baptism all over the world for the renewal of the Gentiles: that by the command of Thy Majesty she may receive the grace of Thine only Son from the Holy Ghost.

Deus, qui nocéntis mundi crímina per aquas ábluens, regeneratiónis spéciem in ipsa dilúvii effusióne signásti: ut, uníus ejusdémque eleménti mystério, et finis esset vítiis, et orígo virtútibus. Réspice, Dñe, in fáciem Ecclésiæ tuæ, et multíplica in ea regeneratiónes tuas, qui grátiæ tuæ affluéntis ímpetu lætíficas civitátem tuam: fontémque baptísmatis áperis toto orbe terrárum géntibus innovándis: ut, tuæ majestátis império, sumat Unigéniti tui grátiam de Spíritu Sancto.

1962 • At this point the Celebrant divides the water in the form of a cross with his extended hand. He immediately dries his hand with a cloth, and prays as follows.
Hic Celebrans in modum crucis aquam dividit manu extensa, quam statim linteo extergit, dicens:

And may that same holy Spirit, by the hidden virtue of His Godhead, make fruitful this water prepared for the regeneration of men, that a heavenly offspring, conceived in sanctification, may emerge from the immaculate womb of this divine font, reborn to newness of life, and that grace as a mother may bring forth every one, how different so ever in age or gender, into a like spiritual infancy. At Thy bidding, therefore, O Lord, may every unclean spirit depart from hence; far be removed all malice of diabolical deceit. Here let no admixture of the enemy's power have any place; let it not hover in ambush; let it not creep in unperceived; let it not corrupt with infection.

Qui hanc aquam, regenerándis homínibus præparátam, arcána sui núminis admixtióne fecúndet: ut, sanctificatióne concépta, ab immaculáto divíni fontis útero, in novam renáta creatúrã, progénies cæléstis emérgat: et quos aut sexus in córpore, aut ætas discérnit in témpore, omnes in unam páriat grátia mater infántiam. Procul ergo hinc, jubénte te, Dómine, omnis spíritus immúndus abscédat: procul tota nequítia diabólicæ fraudis absístat. Nihil hoc loci hábeat contráriæ virtútis admíxtio: non insidiándo circúmvolet: non laténdo subrépat: non inficiéndo corrúmpat.

1962 • He touches the water with his hand, then dries as before. | *Aquam manu tangit.*

May this holy and innocent creature be free from every assault of the adversary and purged of every flaw of wickedness. May it be a living fountain, a re-

Sit hæc sancta et ínnocens creatúra, líbera ab omni impugnatóris incúrsu, et totíus nequítiæ purgáta discéssu. Sit fons vivus, aqua regénerans, unda purificans: ut omnes hoc lavácro salutífero diluéndi, operánte in eis Spíritu Sancto, perféctæ purgatiónis indulgéntiam consequántur.

generating water, a purifying tide, that all who shall be washed in these waters of salvation may, by the working of the Holy Spirit in them, obtain the favor of perfect cleansing.

1962 • He makes the sign of the Cross three times over the font (without touching the water).
Facit tres cruces super Fontem, dicens:

Unde benedíco te, creatúra aquæ, per Deum ✠ vivum, per Deum ✠ verum, per Deum ✠ sanctum: per Deum, qui te, in princípio, verbo separávit ab árida: cujus Spíritus super te ferebátur.

Wherefore, I bless thee, O creature of water, in the name of the living ✠ God, of the true ✠ God, of the holy ✠ God, of the God Who, in the beginning, by His word divided Thee from the dry land; Whose Spirit was borne upon thee.

1962 • He casts a little water to the four points of the compass, then dries as before. As he sings "Benedíco te" he again signs the cross over the water, not touching it.
Hic manu aquam dividit, et effundit eam versus quatuor mundi partes, dicens:

Qui te paradísi fonte manáre fecit, et in quátuor flumínibus totam terram rigáre præcépit. Qui te in desérto amáram, suavitáte índita, fecit esse potábilem, et sitiénti pópulo de petra prodúxit. Bene✠díco te et per Jesum Christum Fílium ejus únicum, Dóminum nostrum: qui te in Cana Galilǽæ signo admirábili, sua poténtia convértit in vinum. Qui pédibus super te ambulávit: et a Joánne in Jordáne in te baptizátus est. Qui te una cũ sánguine de látere suo prodúxit: et discípulis suis jussit, ut credéntes baptizaréntur in te, dicens: Ite, docéte omnes gentes, baptizántes eos in nómine Patris, et Fílii, et Spíritus Sancti.

HE IT WAS Who bade thee to flow from the fountain of paradise and commanded thee to water all the earth in four rivers. Who, when thou wast bitter in the desert, put sweetness into thee, made thee good to drink, and drew thee from the rock for the thirsty people. I bless ✠ thee also in the name of Jesus Christ, His only Son, our Lord, Who, by a wonderful miracle in Cana of Galilee converted thee into wine, Who with His feet walked upon thee, and was baptized in thee by John in Jordan. Who gave thee forth together with blood from His side, and ordered His disciples that those who believed should be baptized in thee, saying: Go, teach all nations, baptizing them in the name of the Father, and of the Son, and of the Holy Ghost.

1962 • He changes the tone and continues on one note, as when singing a lesson. (Some authors say he continues "in a speaking voice.") | *Mutat vocem, et prosequitur in tono Lectionis.*

Hæc nobis præcépta servántibus tu, Deus omnípotens, clemens adésto: tu benígnus adspíra.

Do Thou, O almighty God, of Thy clemency be with us while we keep these precepts; do Thou benignly inspire us.

1962 • He breathes thrice over the water in the form of a cross.
Halat ter in aquam in modum crucis, dicens:

Tu has símplices aquas tuo ore benedícito: ut præter naturálem emundatiónem, quam lavándis possunt adhibére corpóribus, sint étiam purificándis méntibus efficáces.

THESE PURE waters Thou wilt bless with Thy mouth, that, besides the natural cleansing which they can perform in the washing of bodies, they may also be efficacious for the purifying of souls.

1962 • He takes the Paschal candle from the Deacon (who has taken it from the server). Singing again in the Preface tone, he dips the lower end of the candle a little into the water, as he sings "Descéndat in hanc plenitúdinem fontis, virtus Spíritus sancti." He takes out the candle, dips it again a little deeper, and sings the same words in a higher pitch. He takes out the candle and submerges it deeper still, singing again the third time, still higher.

May the virtue of the Holy Spirit descend upon all the contents of this font.

Descéndat in hanc plenitúdinem fontis virtus Spíritus Sancti.

1962 • Then he blows three times on the water in the form of the Greek letter Psi, and continues:

And may it render the substance of this water fruitful with the quality of regeneration.

Totámque hujus aquæ substántiam, regenerándi fœcúndet effectu.

1962 • He takes the candle out of the water and continues in the Preface tone.

Hic tollitur Cereus de aqua, et prosequitur:

HERE MAY THE STAINS of all sins be washed away; here may nature, created to Thine image, and reformed to the honorable estate of its origin, be cleansed of all the foulness of the past, that every human being, by entering into this sacrament of regeneration, may be born again into a new infancy of true innocence.

Hic ómnium peccatórũ máculæ deleántur: hic natúra ad imáginem tuam cóndita, et ad honórem sui reformáta princípii, cunctis vetustátis squalóribus emundétur: ut omnis homo, sacraméntũ hoc regeneratiónis ingréssus, in veræ innocéntiæ novam infántiam renascátur.

1962 • The Celebrant lowers his voice and sings the following on one note; cf. *The Roman Missal* (1965) page 369. Some authors disagree, and say that this section "is not sung" {McManus p97}

Sequentia dicit legendo.

Through our Lord Jesus Christ Thy Son: Who shall come to judge the living and the dead, and the world by fire. ℟. Amen.

Per Dóminum nostrum Jesum Christum Fílium tuum: qui ventúrus est judicáre vivos et mórtuos, et sǽculum per ignem. ℟. Amen.

1962 • Some of the water is now removed, and stored in the Aspersórium—that is, a vessel—for sprinkling the congregation after the *Renewal of the Baptismal Promises* (see below), and for sprinkling homes and other places at a later time. Then the Celebrant, standing as before, pours a little of the oil of Catechumens into the water in the form of a cross, saying aloud (not singing) the following prayer.

Notice the *Ordo Hebdomadae Sanctae Instauratus* (1956) often erroneously refers to the "font," e.g. *Facit tres cruces super Fontem* (OHSI page 107). Such errors are probably due to the haste with which the ceremonies were assembled by the reformers, as well as the relatively small number of people involved in these modifications.

MAY THIS FONT be sanctified and made fruitful by the Oil of salvation, for those who are born anew therein unto life everlasting. ℟. Amen.

Sanctificétur et fœcundétur fons iste óleo salútis renascéntibus ex eo, in vitam ætérnam. ℟. Amen.

1962 • He pours in chrism in the same way. | *Deinde infundit de Chrismate, modo quo supra, dicens :*

MAY THE INFUSION of the Chrism of our Lord Jesus Christ, and of the Holy Ghost the Comforter, be made in the Name of the Holy Trinity. ℟. Amen.

Infúsio Chrísmatis Dómini nostri Jesu Christi, et Spíritus Sancti Paráclìti, fiat in nómine sanctæ Trinitátis. ℟. Amen.

1962 • He pours both chrism and oil of Catechumens together, making three crosses in the water as he says the last words (where crosses are marked in the Missal). | *Postea accipit ambas ampullas dicti Olei sancti, et Chrismatis, et de utroque simul in modum crucis infundendo, dicit:*

Commíxtio Chrísmatis sanctificatiónis, et ólei unctiónis, et Aquæ baptísmatis, páriter fiat in nómine Pa ✠ tris, et Fí ✠ lii, et Spíritus ✠ Sancti. ℟. Amen.

MAY THIS MIXTURE of the Chrism of sanctification, and of the Oil of unction, and of the water of Baptism, be made to the name of the Fa✠ther, and of the Son ✠, and of the Holy ✠ Ghost. ℟. Amen.

1962 • He then mixes the oil and water together, spreading it all around with the right hand extended. He wipes his hands clean using cotton and bread {McManus p97}.

VIII • SACRAMENT OF BAPTISM

1962 • If there are candidates for baptism present, he baptizes them in the usual way. It is permissible, especially if there are several candidates, to anticipate the ceremonies of the Roman Ritual which precede the conferral of baptism at a convenient hour on the same morning. That is to say, for the baptism of infants up to the words, "Do you believe in God?" (Roman Ritual, tit. II, cap. II, n. 17), and for the baptism of adults up to the words "What is your name?" (Roman Ritual, tit. II, cap. IV, n. 37). To perform the baptisms, the Celebrant must change from violet to white vestments, putting on a white stole and cope. {McManus p97} These vestments he may keep on for the procession to the font; cf. *Liber Usualis* (1961) page 776z.

IX • PROCESSION TO THE FONT

1962 • After the blessing of baptismal water (and any baptisms), the water is carried in procession to the font. During the procession, the canticle "Sicut cervus" is chanted; it is begun while the procession forms to take the baptismal water to the font {McManus p44}. The Paschal candle remains in its place—it is not carried to the Baptistery, as it was in 1950 version.

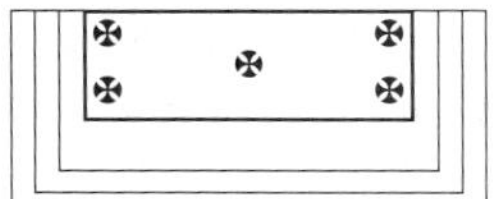

1962 • "Sicut Cervus" is sung after the blessing of the baptismal water, and after the Sacrament of Baptism, while the blessed water is being carried to the font.

CANTICLE. *Ps 41: 2-4*

Sicut cervus desíderat ad fontes aquárum: ita desíderat ánima mea ad te, Deus. ℣. Sitívit ánima mea ad Deum vivum: quando véniam, et apparébo ante fáciem Dei? ℣. Fuérunt mihi lácrimæ meæ panes die ac nocte, dum dícitur mihi per síngulos dies: Ubi est Deus tuus?

AS THE HART panteth after the fountains of water, so my soul panteth after Thee, O God. ℣. My soul hath thirsted for the living God: when shall I come and appear before the face of God? ℣. My tears have been my bread day and night, whilst it is said to me daily: Where is thy God?

1962 • After the blessed water has been poured into the font, the Celebrant chants "Dóminus vobíscum" and the prayer—in the ferial tone—with his hands joined:

℣. The Lord be with you.
℟. And with thy spirit.
Let us pray.

O ALMIGHTY and everlasting God, look mercifully on the devotion of Thy people about to be reborn, who like the hart pant after the fountain of Thy waters: and mercifully grant that the thirst of their faith may, by the Sacrament of Baptism, hallow their souls and bodies. Through our Lord. ℟. Amen.

℣. Dóminus vobíscum.
℟. Et cum spíritu tuo.
Orémus.

Omnípotens sempitérne Deus, réspice propítius ad devotiónem pópuli renascéntis, qui sicut cervus, aquárum tuárum éxpetit fontem: et concéde propítius; ut fídei ipsíus sitis, baptísmatis mystério, ánimam corpúsque sanctíficet. Per Dóminum. ℟. Amen.

The Baptismal Font is incensed.
All then return to the Sanctuary in silence.

X • RENEWAL OF BAPTISMAL PROMISES

1962 • At the *Sedilia*, the Celebrant changes his purple vestments for a white stole and cope; he does not wear a white dalmatic, in spite of what some have claimed {McManus p99}. Meanwhile, the candles of all present are lit from the Paschal candle, which is then incensed by the Celebrant. The Celebrant stands next to the Paschal candle, or at the ambo, or at the pulpit. The Renewal of Baptismal Promises can be done in Latin or the vernacular: *Haec allocutio et renovatio promissionum baptismatis fieri potest, ubique locorum, lingua vernacula; versione tamen ab Ordinaria loci approbata.*

"The people may sit during the allocution, but should stand for the baptismal promises" {McManus p99}.

Facing the congregation, the Celebrant says:

ON THIS MOST SACRED NIGHT, dearly belovèd brethren, Holy Mother Church, recalling the death and burial of our Lord Jesus Christ, returneth His love by keeping vigil; and aboundeth with joy at celebrating His glorious Resurrection. But because, as the Apostle teaches, we are baptized into His death and buried together with Christ: and as Christ rose again from the dead, so we too must walk in newness of life; knowing that our old man hath been crucified together with Christ so that we shall no longer be in servitude to sin. Let us look upon ourselves therefore as dead indeed to sin but living to God in Christ Jesus our Lord.

Therefore, dearly beloved brethren, the Lenten observance now completed, let us renew the promises of Baptism by which formerly we renounced Satan and his works, and the world likewise, the enemy of God; and by which we promised to serve God faithfully in the Holy Catholic Church.

I ask you therefore:

Do you renounce Satan? ℟. **We do renounce him.**

That Thou wouldst vouchsafe to preserve our Apostolic Prelate, and all orders of the Church in holy religion, *

Ut domnum apostólicum et omnes ecclesiásticos órdines in sancta religióne conserváre dignéris, *

That Thou wouldst vouchsafe to humble the enemies of holy Church, *

Ut inimícos sanctæ Ecclésiæ humiliáre dignéris, *

That Thou wouldst vouchsafe to give peace and true concord to Christian kings and princes, *

Ut régibus et princípibus christiánis, pacem et veram concórdiam donáre dignéris, *

That Thou wouldst vouchsafe to confirm and preserve us in Thy holy service, *

Ut nosmetípsos in tuo sancto servítio confortáre et conserváre dignéris, *

That Thou wouldst render eternal blessings to all our benefactors, *

Ut ómnibus benefactóribus nostris sempitérna bona retríbuas, *

That Thou wouldst vouchsafe to give and preserve the fruits of the earth, *

Ut fructus terræ dare et conserváre dignéris, *

That Thou wouldst vouchsafe to grant eternal rest to all the faithful departed, *

Ut ómnibus fidélibus defúnctis réquiem ætérnam donáre dignéris, *

That Thou wouldst vouchsafe graciously to hear us, *

Ut nos exaudíre dignéris, *

Lamb of God, Who takest away the sins of the world, *spare us, O Lord.*

AGNUS Dei, qui tollis peccáta mundi, parce nobis, Dómine.

Lamb of God, Who takest away the sins of the world, *graciously hear us, O Lord.*

Agnus Dei, qui tollis peccáta mundi, exáudi nos, Dómine.

Lamb of God, Who takest away the sins of the world, *have mercy on us.*

Agnus Dei, qui tollis peccáta mundi, miserére nobis.

Christ, hear us.
Christ, graciously hear us.

CHRISTE, audi nos.
Christe, exáudi nos.

At the traditional Mass of Easter Eve (both the 1950 version and the 1962 version):

(1) There is no Vidi Aquam;

(2) There is no Introit;

(3) The (short) Alleluia is followed by a Tract;

(4) There is no Gradual or Greater Alleluia;

(5) There is no Sequence;

(6) There is no Creed;

(7) There is no Offertory Antiphon;

(8) There is no Agnus Dei and the *Kiss of Peace* is omitted;

(9) There is no Communion Antiphon.

For a century, authors have speculated as to why these items are omitted {Thurston p437}. At the traditional (1950) Mass of Easter Eve, the Prayers at the Foot of the Altar and Last Gospel are said—but these items were eliminated by the reform of Pius XII.

XII • MASS OF THE PASCHAL VIGIL

1962 • At the end of the Litany, the cantors solemnly intone Kyrie Eleison, as at Mass. The psalm *Júdica me, Deus*, the *Confíteor*, and all that normally takes place at the beginning of Mass—including the prayers *Aufer a nobis* and *Orámus, te, Dómine*—are omitted. The Celebrant ascends, kisses, and then incenses the Altar. When the choir has finished the Kyrie Eleison, the Celebrant solemnly intones the Gloria in Excelsis. The bells are rung, and the statues and pictures are uncovered.

COLLECT.

GOD, Who dost illuminate this most sacred night with the glory of the Lord's resurrection, preserve in the new offspring of Thy family the spirit which Thou hast given, that, being renewed in body and mind, they may render Thee pure service. Through the same.

Deus, qui hanc sacratíssimam noctem glória Domínicæ Resurrectiónis illústras: consérva in nova famíliæ tuæ progénie adoptiónis spíritum, quem dedísti; ut córpore et mente renováti, puram tibi exhíbeant servitútem. Per eúmdem Dóminum.

EPISTLE. *Col 3: 1-4*

BRETHREN, if you be risen with Christ, seek the things that are above, where Christ is sitting at the right hand of God: mind the things that are above, not the things that are upon the earth. For you are dead, and your life is hid with Christ in God. When Christ shall appear, Who is your life, then you also shall appear with Him in glory.

Fratres: si consurrexístis cum Christo, quæ sursum sunt quǽrite, ubi Christus est in déxtera Dei sedens: quæ sursum sunt sápite, non quæ super terram. Mórtui enim estis, et vita vestra est abscóndita cum Christo in Deo. Cum Christus apparúerit, vita vestra: tunc et vos apparébitis cum ipso in glória.

After the Epistle—all standing—the Celebrant sings the following Alleluja, *each time at a higher pitch, the choir repeating it each time:*

Confitémini Dómino, quóniam bonus: quóniam in sǽculum misericórdia ejus. (Ps 117: 1)

GIVE PRAISE to the Lord for He is good: for His mercy endureth forever. *(The Alleluia is not repeated.)*

TRACT. *Ps 116: 1-2*

Laudáte Dóminum omnes gentes: et collaudáte eum, omnes pópuli. ℣. Quóniam confirmáta est super nos misericórdia ejus: et véritas Dómini manet in ætérnum.

O PRAISE THE LORD, all ye nations, and praise Him, all ye people. ℣. For His mercy is confirmed upon us: and the truth of the Lord remaineth forever.

1962 • Lighted candles are not carried at the Gospel but incense only. The blessing is sought, and everything else is done as usual. | *Ad Evangelium non portantur luminaria, sed tantum incensum: petitur benedictio, et alia fiunt de more.*

GOSPEL. *Matt 28: 1-7*

Véspere autem sábbati, quæ lucéscit in prima sábbati, venit María Magdaléne, et áltera María vidére sepúlchrum. Et ecce terræmótus factus est magnus. Ángelus enim Dómini descéndit de cælo: et accédens revólvit lápidem, et sedébat super eum: erat autem aspéctus ejus sicut fulgur: et vestiméntum ejus sicut nix. Præ timóre autem ejus extérriti sunt custódes, et facti sunt velut mórtui. Respóndens autem Ángelus, dixit muliéribus: Nolíte timére vos: scio enim, quod Jesum, qui crucifíxus est, quǽritis: non est hic: surréxit enim, sicut dixit. Veníte, et vidéte locum, ubi pósitus erat Dóminus. Et cito eúntes, dícite discípulis ejus, quia surréxit: et ecce præcédit vos in Galilǽam: ibi eum vidébitis. Ecce prædíxi vobis.

AND IN THE END of the Sabbath, when it began to dawn towards the first day of the week, came Mary Magdalen and the other Mary to see the sepulchre. And behold there was a great earthquake. For an Angel of the Lord descended from heaven, and coming, rolled back the stone and sat upon it: and his countenance was as lightening and his raiment as snow. And for fear of him the guards were struck with terror and became as dead men. And the Angel answering, said to the women: Fear not you: for I know that you seek Jesus who was crucified: He is not here: for His is risen, as He said. Come and see the place where the Lord was laid. And going quickly, tell ye His disciples that He is risen: and behold He will go before you into Galilee: there you shall see Him. Lo, I have foretold it to you.

1962 • The Creed is not said, but at the end of the Gospel the Celebrant sings *Dóminus vobíscum* and *Orémus* at the Offertory as usual. There is no Offertory antiphon; the organ is played to the beginning of the Preface. At the *Lavábo*, "Glória Patri" is said.

Non dicitur "Credo," sed finito Evangelio Sacerdos dicit. "Dóminus vobíscum," postea: "Orémus." Non dicitur "Offertorium." Ad "Lavábo" dicitur "Glória Patri."

SECRET.

Súscipe, quǽsumus, Dómine, preces pópuli tui, cum oblatiónibus hostiárum: ut paschálibus initiáta mystériis, ad æternitátis nobis medélam, te operánte, profíciant. Per Dóminum.

Accept, we beseech Thee, O Lord, the prayers of Thy people together with the sacrifice they offer: that what has been begun by the Paschal Mysteries, may by Thine arrangement result in our eternal healing. Through our Lord.

The Preface of Easter (page 190) is sung, with the phrase "in hac potissimum nocte."

1962 • In the Canon, the Paschal form of the COMMUNICANTES prayer is said, with the form "noctem sacratissimam celebrantes." The Paschal form of the HANC IGITUR prayer is said. "Pax Dómini sit semper vobíscum" is chanted, but the Kiss of Peace is not given. The *Agnus Dei* is not said.

In the 1950 version, "the Celebrant says the three usual prayers before his Communion" {Fortescue p333}. However, the 1962 version omits the prayer *Dómine Jesu Christi, qui dixísti*—but the other prayers are still said: *Dómine Jesu Christe, Fili Dei vivi* and *Percéptio Córporis tui* {McManus p101}. It should be noticed that the 1951 "experimental" version did not omit that prayer {1953maryland p40}.

A STRANGE RESTORATION • Cardinal Antonelli mentions "the problem of finding a suitable location for the Matins and Lauds of Easter" {Giampietro p42}. It is instructive to read what was said at the time:

> "Much has been written about the restored Paschal Vigil. But now that the novelty is already wearing off, parishes in many areas report dwindling congregations. In many places, also, the Easter Vigil congregation has never approached in numbers that of the Christmas midnight Mass. Nor has the new service always been adopted where we might most have expected to find it. In Westminster Cathedral, for example, it was not in use till 1955. St. Peter's, Rome, has still to abandon the morning service. The early Christian vigils consisted of a night spent in prayer and psalmody, ending with the celebration of Mass. It is a strange restoration which has done away with matins and lauds, so that the one night in the year when not a single psalm of praise crosses the lips of those bound to the recital of the Divine Office, is that which is the central feast of Christendom." —FATHER JOHN J. COYNE (1956)

The reformers abolished Paschal Matins, and Paschal Lauds—while not technically abolished—was severely truncated.

XIII • LAUDS OF EASTER

1962 • There is no Communion Antiphon. After the ablutions, the choir sings the "Allelúja" three times, then Psalm 150 (*Laudáte Dóminum in sanctis ejus*) then "Allelúja" three times.

Post sumptionem Sacramenti, distributio communionis, purificatio et ablutio fiunt more solito; deinde pro LAUDIBUS dominicae Resurrectionis in choro cantatur antiphona:

1. Praise ye the Lord in His holy places: * praise ye Him in the firmament of His power.	1. Laudáte Dóminum in sanctis ejus: * laudáte eum in firmaménto virtútis ejus.
2. Praise ye Him for His mighty acts: * praise ye Him according to the multitude of His greatness.	2. Laudáte eum in virtútibus ejus: * laudáte eum secúndum multitúdinem magnitúdinis ejus.
3. Praise Him with sound of trumpets: * praise Him with psaltery and harp.	3. Laudáte eum in sono tubæ: * laudáte eum in psaltério, et cíthara.
4. Praise Him with timbrel and choir: * praise Him with strings and organs.	4. Laudáte eum in týmpano, et choro: * laudáte eum in chordis, et órgano.
5. Praise Him on high sounding cymbals: † praise Him on cymbals of joy. * Let every spirit praise the Lord.	5. Laudáte eum in cýmbalis benesonántibus: † laudáte eum in cýmbalis jubilatiónis: * omnis spíritus laudet Dóminum.

6. Glória Patri, et Fílio, * et Spirítui Sancto.

6. Glory be to the Father, and to the Son, * and to the Holy Ghost.

7. Sicut erat in princípio, et nunc, et semper, * et in sǽcula sæculórum. Amen.

7. As it was in the beginning, is now, and ever shall be, * world without end. Amen.

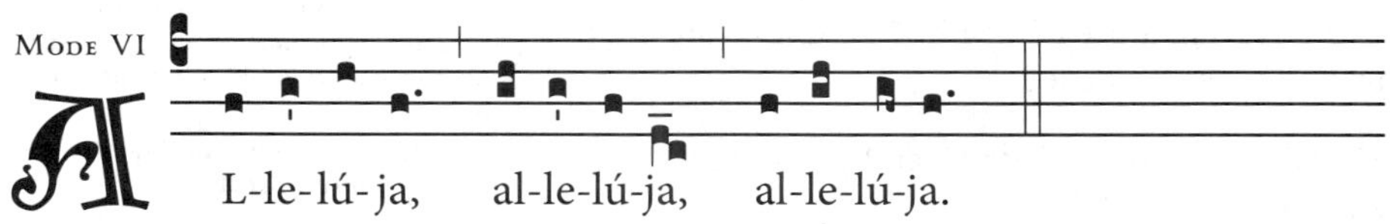

1962 • At once, the Celebrant intones the BENEDICTUS.

CANTICLE OF ZACHARY. *Mark 16: 2 & Luke 1: 68-79*

Et valde mane * una sabbatórum, véniunt ad monuméntum, orto jam sole, allelúja.

AND VERY EARLY in the morning, the first day of the week, they came to the sepulchre, the sun being now risen, alleluia.

1. Benedictus ✠ Dóminus, Deus Israël: * quia visitávit, et fecit redemptiónem plebis suæ:

1. Blessed be the Lord ✠ God of Israel; * because he hath visited and wrought the redemption of his people:

2. Et eréxit cornu salútis nobis: * in omo David, púeri sui.

2. And hath raised up an horn of salvation to us, * in the house of David his servant:

3. Sicut locútus est per os sanctórum, * qui a sæculo sunt, prophetárum ejus:

3. As he spoke by the mouth of his holy Prophets, * who are from the beginning:

4. Salútem ex inimícis nostris, * et de manu ómniũ, qui odérunt nos.

4. Salvation from our enemies, * and from the hand of all that hate us:

5. Ad faciéndam misericórdiam cum pátribus nostris: * et memorári testaménti sui sancti.

5. To perform mercy to our fathers, * and to remember his holy testament,

6. Jusjurándum, quod jurávit ad Ábraham patrem nostrum, * datúrum se nobis:

6. The oath, which he swore to Abraham our father, * that he would grant to us,

7. Ut sine timóre, de manu inimicórum nostrórum liberáti, * serviámus illi.

7. That being delivered from the hand of our enemies, * we may serve him without fear,

8. In sanctitáte, et justítia coram ipso, * ómnibus diébus nostris.

8. In holiness and justice before him, * all our days.

9. Et tu, puer, Prophéta Altíssimi vocáberis: * præíbis enim ante fáciem Dómini, paráre vias ejus:

9. And thou, child, shalt be called the prophet of the Highest: * for thou shalt go before the face of the Lord to prepare his ways:

10. To give knowledge of salvation to his people, * unto the remission of their sins:

10. Ad dandam sciéntiam salútis plebi ejus: * in remissiónem peccatórum eórum:

11. Through the bowels of the mercy of our God, * in which the Orient from on high hath visited us:

11. Per víscera misericórdiæ Dei nostri: * in quibus visitávit nos, óriens ex alto:

12. To enlighten them that sit in darkness, and in the shadow of death: * to direct our feet into the way of peace.

12. Illumináre his, qui in ténebris, et in umbra mortis sedent: * ad dirigéndos pedes nostros in viam pacis.

13. Glory be to the Father, and to the Son, * and to the Holy Ghost.

13. Glória Patri, et Fílio, * et Spirítui Sancto.

14. As it was in the beginning, is now, and ever shall be, * world without end. Amen.

14. Sicut erat in princípio, et nunc, et semper, * et in sǽcula sæculórum. Amen.

The antiphon Et Valde Mane, *is repeated.*

℣. The Lord be with you.
℟. And with thy spirit.
Let us pray.

℣. Dóminus vobíscum.
℟. Et cum spíritu tuo.
Orémus.

POSTCOMMUNION. *Which also serves as the Prayer of Lauds.*

POUR FORTH upon us, O Lord, the spirit of Thy love, to make us of one heart, who, by Thy tender mercy, Thou hast filled with Thy paschal sacrament. Through … in the unity of the same.

Spíritum nobis, Dómine, tuæ caritátis infúnde: ut, quos sacraméntis Paschálibus satiásti tua fácias pietáte concórdes. Per Dñm … in unitáte ejusdem.

1962 • The response at the end of Mass is as follows. The Last Gospel is omitted in the 1962 version.

℟. De-o gra-ti- as, al- le- lú- ia, al- le- lu- ia.

[Editor's Note: In the 1950 version, it is "truncated Vespers" that is sung—not "truncated Lauds." With regard to singing the Divine Office during Holy Saturday's Mass, various practices existed: some placed "truncated Vespers" between the baptisms and Mass, while others sang Vespers during the distribution of Holy Communion {Goddard pages 242 + 246}. During the High Mediæval Period, parts of the Divine Office were often sung while the people received Holy Communion—and not just on Holy Saturday; cf. *Missarum Sollemnia* (Father Joseph A. Jungmann, 1950) volume II, pages 398-399. Where this was customary, we sometimes find a rubric stipulating that "its close would coincide with the *Ite Missa Est* of the Deacon."]

Ordo Missae

Text only • English Translation by Father Francis X. Lasance.

The Priest: In the name ✠ of the Father, and of the Son, and of the Holy Ghost. Amen.

Antiphon: I will go in to the altar of God.

The Servers: ℟. To God, Who giveth joy to my youth.

Psalm 42

P: Judge me, O God, and distinguish my cause from the nation that is not holy; deliver me from the unjust and deceitful man.

S: For Thou art, God, my strength; why hast Thou cast me off? and why do I go sorrowful whilst the enemy afflicteth me?

P: Send forth Thy light and Thy truth: they have conducted me and brought me unto Thy holy hill, and into Thy tabernacles.

S: And I will go in to the altar of God: to God Who giveth joy to my youth.

P: To Thee, O God, my God, I will give praise upon the harp: why art thou sad, O my soul, and why dost thou disquiet me?

S: Hope in God, for I will still give praise to Him, the salvation of my countenance and my God.

P: Glory be to the Father, and to the Son, and to the Holy Ghost.

S: As it was in the beginning, is now, and ever shall be, world without end. Amen.

P: ℣. I will go in to the altar of God.

S: To God, Who giveth joy to my youth.

In Passiontine and in Masses for the Dead, Psalm 42 is omitted (as is the repetition of the Antiphon).

P: Our help ✠ is in the name of the Lord.

S: Who made heaven and earth.

P: I confess to almighty God, to blessed Mary ever virgin, to blessed Michael the archangel, to blessed John the Baptist, to the holy apostles Peter and Paul, to all the saints, and to you, brethren, that I have sinned exceedingly in thought, word, and deed; *(striking his heart three times)* through my fault, through my fault, through my most grievous fault. Therefore I beseech the blessed Mary ever virgin, blessed Michael the archangel, blessed John the Baptist, the holy apostles Peter and Paul, all the saints, and you, brethren, to pray to the Lord our God for me.

S: May almighty God have mercy on thee and, having forgiven thee thy sins, bring thee to life everlasting.

P: Amen.

S: I confess to almighty God, to blessed Mary ever virgin, to blessed Michael the archangel, to blessed John the Baptist, to the holy apostles Peter and Paul, to all the saints, and to thee, Father, that I have sinned exceedingly in thought, word, and deed; *(now strike your heart three times)* through my fault, through my fault, through my most grievous fault. Therefore I beseech the blessed Mary ever virgin, blessed Michael the archangel, blessed John the Baptist, the holy apostles Peter and Paul, all the saints, and thee, Father, to pray to the Lord our God for me.

P: May almighty God have mercy on you and, having forgiven you your sins, bring you to life everlasting. *S:* Amen.

P: May the almighty ✠ and merciful Lord grant us pardon, absolution, and remission of our sins. *S:* Amen.

P: Thou wilt turn again, O God, and quicken us.

S: And Thy people will rejoice in Thee.

P: Show us, O Lord, Thy mercy.

S: And grant us Thy salvation.

P: O Lord, hear my prayer.

S: And let my cry come unto Thee.

P: The Lord be with you.

S: And with thy spirit.

P: Let us pray.

Going up to the Altar, the priest prays silently:

TAKE AWAY from us our iniquities, we beseech Thee, O Lord; that, being made pure in heart we may be worthy to enter into the Holy of Holies. Through Christ our Lord. Amen.

WE BESEECH Thee, O Lord, by the merits of those of Thy saints whose relics are here, and of all the saints, that Thou wouldst vouchsafe to pardon me all my sins. Amen.

■ The Introit (Proper)

Returning to the center, he alternates with the servers:

Lord, have mercy on us. (3x)

Christ, have mercy on us. (3x)

Lord, have mercy on us. (3x)

When the Gloria is to be said or sung, the priest extends his hands, making a slight bow:

GLORY BE to God on high, and on earth peace to men of good will. We praise Thee; we bless Thee; we adore Thee; we glorify Thee. We give Thee thanks for Thy great glory: O Lord God, heavenly King, God the Father almighty. O Lord Jesus Christ, the only-begotten Son. O Lord God, Lamb of God, Son of the Father, Thou, Who takest away the sins of the world, have mercy on us. Thou Who takest away the sins of the world, receive our prayer. Thou Who sittest at the right hand of the Father, have mercy on us. For Thou alone art holy; Thou alone art the Lord; Thou alone, O Jesus Christ, together with the Holy Ghost, art most high ✠ in the glory of God the Father. Amen.

℣. The Lord be with you.

℟. And with thy spirit.

■ The Collect (Proper)

For the various prayer endings, turn to page 200.

■ The Epistle (Proper)

■ The Gradual (Proper)

The "gradual" can refer to all the prayers once said on the steps—Gradual, Tract, Alleluia Verse, Sequence—depending on the liturgical season.

Returning to the center, the priest bows down:

CLEANSE my heart and my lips, O almighty God, Who didst cleanse with a burning coal the lips of the prophet Isaias; and vouchsafe in Thy loving kindness so to purify me that I may be enabled worthily to announce Thy holy Gospel. Through Christ our Lord. Amen. Vouchsafe, O Lord, to bless me. The Lord be in my heart and on my lips, that I may worthily and becomingly announce His gospel, Amen.

■ The Gospel (Proper)

Once the Gospel has been read or sung, the servers quietly respond:

℟. Glory be to Thee, O Lord.

When the priest kisses the book, he says:

May our sins be blotted out by the words of the Gospel.

■ The Homily (Vernacular)

THE CREED

When the homily is finished, the priest returns to the center and says the Creed (on days when it is said):

I BELIEVE IN ONE GOD, the Father almighty, maker of heaven and earth, and of all things visible and invisible. And in one Lord Jesus Christ, the only-begotten Son of God, born of the Father before all ages; God of God, light of light, true God of true God; begotten, not made; consubstantial with the Father, by Whom all things were made. Who for us men, and for our salvation, came down from heaven, and was incarnate by the Holy Ghost of the Virgin Mary, *(here genuflect)* AND WAS MADE MAN. He was crucified also for us, suffered under Pontius Pilate, and was buried. And the third day He arose again, according to the Scriptures, and ascended into heaven. He sitteth at the right hand of the Father: and He shall come again with glory, to judge the living and the dead: and His kingdom shall have no end. And in the Holy Ghost, the Lord and Giver of life, Who proceedeth from the Father and the Son, Who, together with the Father and the Son, is adored and glorified: Who spoke by the prophets. And one holy, catholic, and apostolic Church. I confess one baptism for the remission of sins. ✠ And I expect the resurrection of the dead, and the life of the world to come. Amen.

THE OFFERTORY

The priest kisses the Altar and faces the people:

℣. The Lord be with you.

℟. And with thy spirit.

Let us pray.

■ THE OFFERTORY (PROPER)

RECEIVE, O Holy Father, almighty and eternal God, this spotless host, which I, Thine unworthy servant, offer unto Thee, my living and true God, for my countless sins, trespasses, and omissions; likewise for all here present, and for all faithful Christians, whether living or dead, that it may avail both me and them to salvation, unto life everlasting. Amen.

At the Epistle corner, wine and water are poured:

O GOD, Who in creating man didst exalt his nature very wonderfully and yet more wonderfully didst establish it anew: by the mystery signified in the mingling of this water and wine, grant us to have part in the Godhead of Him Who hath vouchsafed to share our manhood, Jesus Christ, Thy Son, Our Lord, Who liveth and reigneth with Thee in the unity of the Holy Ghost, God; world without end. Amen.

The priest returns to the center of the Altar:

WE offer unto Thee, O Lord, the chalice of salvation, beseeching Thy clemency that it may ascend as a sweet odor before Thy divine majesty, for our own salvation, and for that of the whole world. Amen.

Humbled in mind, and contrite of heart, may we find favor with Thee, O Lord; and may the sacrifice we this day offer up be well pleasing to Thee, Who art our Lord and our God.

COME, Thou, the Sanctifier, God, almighty and everlasting: bless ✠ this sacrifice which is prepared for the glory of Thy holy name.

Returning to the Epistle corner, he washes his fingers while praying Psalm 25:

I WILL WASH my hands among the innocent, and will compass Thine altar, O Lord.

℣. That I may hear the voice of praise, and tell of all Thy wondrous works.

℣. I have loved, O Lord, the beauty of Thy house, and the place where Thy glory dwelleth.

℣. Take not away my soul, O God, with the wicked; nor my life with men of blood.

℣. In whose hands are iniquities: their right hand is filled with gifts.

℣. But as for me, I have walked in my innocence; redeem me, and have mercy on me.

℣. My foot hath stood in the right way; in the churches I will bless Thee, O Lord.

The following two verses are omitted in Masses for the Dead and during Passiontide:

℣. Glory be to the Father, and to the Son, and to the Holy Ghost.

℣. As it was in the beginning, is now, and ever shall be; world without end. Amen.

RECEIVE, O HOLY TRINITY, this oblation offered up by us to Thee in memory of the passion, resurrection, and ascension of Our Lord Jesus Christ and in honor of blessed Mary, ever a virgin, of blessed John the Baptist, of the holy apostles Peter and Paul, of these, and of all the saints, that it may be available to their honor and to our salvation; and may they whose memory we celebrate on earth vouchsafe to intercede for us in heaven. Through the same Christ our Lord. Amen.

Having kissed the Altar, the priest turns to the people:

"Orate Fratres"

BRETHREN, pray that my sacrifice and yours may be well pleasing to God the Father almighty.

℟. May the Lord receive this sacrifice at thy hands, to the praise and glory of His name, to our own benefit, and to that of all His Holy Church.

■ The Secret (Proper)

℣. World without end.

℟. Amen.

℣. The Lord be with you.

℟. And with thy spirit.

℣. Lift up your hearts.

℟. We lift them up to the Lord.

℣. Let us give thanks to the Lord our God.

℟. It is meet and just.

■ The Preface

Please cf. pages 185-197.

HOLY, holy, holy, Lord God of hosts. The heavens and the earth are full of Thy glory. Hosanna in the highest. Blessed ✠ is He Who cometh in the name of the Lord. Hosanna in the highest.

The Canon

WHEREFORE, WE HUMBLY pray and beseech Thee, most merciful Father, through Jesus Christ Thy Son, Our Lord, to receive and to bless these ✠ gifts, these ✠ presents, these ✠ holy unspotted sacrifices, which we offer up to Thee, in the first place, for Thy holy Catholic Church, that it may please Thee to grant her peace, to guard, unite, and guide her, throughout the world: as also for Thy servant *(Name)*, our Pope, and *(Name)*, our Bishop, and for all who are orthodox in belief and who profess the Catholic and apostolic faith.

BE mindful, O Lord, of Thy servants, *(Names)*, and of all here present, whose faith and devotion are known to Thee, for whom we offer, or who offer up to Thee, this sacrifice of praise, for themselves, their families, and their friends, for the salvation of their souls and the health and welfare they hope for, and who now pay their vows to Thee, God eternal, living, and true.

HAVING communion with and venerating the memory, first, of the glorious Mary, ever a virgin, mother of Jesus Christ, our God and our Lord: *of blessed Joseph, spouse of the same virgin*, likewise of Thy blessed apostles and martyrs, Peter and Paul, Andrew, James, John, Thomas, James, Phillip, Bartholomew, Matthew, Simon and Thaddeus; of Linus, Cletus, Clement, Sixtus, Cornelius, Cyprian, Lawrence, Chrysogonus, John and Paul, Cosmas and Damian, and of all Thy saints: for the sake of whose merits and prayers do Thou grant that in all things we may be defended by the help of Thy protection. Through the same Christ, our Lord. Amen.

"Hanc Igitur"

WHEREFORE, we beseech Thee, O Lord, graciously to receive this oblation which we Thy servants, and with us Thy whole family, offer up to Thee: dispose our days in Thy peace; command that we be saved from eternal damnation and numbered among the flock of Thine elect. Through Christ our Lord. Amen.

"Quam Oblationem"

AND DO THOU, O God, vouchsafe in all respects to bless, ✠ consecrate ✠, and approve ✠ this our oblation, to perfect it and render it well-pleasing to Thyself, so that it may become for us the Body ✠ and Blood ✠ of Thy most beloved Son, Jesus Christ our Lord.

WHO, THE DAY before He suffered, took bread into His holy and venerable hands, and having lifted up His eyes to heaven, to Thee, God, His almighty Father, giving thanks to Thee, blessed it ✠, broke it, and gave it to His disciples, saying: Take ye and eat ye all of this: **FOR THIS IS MY BODY.**

IN LIKE MANNER, after He had supped, taking also into His holy and venerable hands this goodly chalice again giving thanks to Thee, He blessed it, and gave it to His disciples, saying: Take ye, and drink ye all of this:

FOR THIS IS THE CHALICE OF MY BLOOD, OF THE NEW AND EVERLASTING TESTAMENT, THE MYSTERY OF FAITH, WHICH FOR YOU AND FOR MANY SHALL BE SHED UNTO THE REMISSION OF SINS.

As often as ye shall do these things, ye shall do them in memory of Me.

WHEREFORE, O Lord, we, Thy servants, as also Thy holy people, calling to mind the blessed passion of the same Christ, Thy Son, our Lord, His resurrection from the grave, and His glorious ascension into heaven, offer up to Thy most excellent majesty of Thine own gifts bestowed upon us, a victim which is pure, a victim which is stainless, the holy bread of life everlasting, and the chalice of eternal salvation.

VOUCHSAFE TO LOOK upon them with a gracious and tranquil countenance, and to accept them, even as Thou wast pleased to accept the offerings of Thy just servant Abel, and the sacrifice of Abraham, our patriarch, and that which Melchisedech, Thy high priest, offered up to Thee, a holy sacrifice, a victim without blemish.

HUMBLY we beseech Thee, almighty God, to command that these our offerings be borne by the hands of Thy holy angel to Thine altar on high in the presence of Thy divine Majesty; that as many of us as shall receive the most sacred Body and Blood of Thy Son by partaking thereof from this altar may be filled with every heavenly blessing and grace: Through the same Christ our Lord. Amen.

BE MINDFUL, also, O Lord, of Thy servants *(Names)*, who have gone before us with the sign of faith and who sleep the sleep of peace.

To these, O Lord, and to all who rest in Christ, grant, we beseech Thee, a place of refreshment, light, and peace. Through the same Christ our Lord. Amen.

"Nobis Quoque"

Striking his heart with his hand, the priest says:

TO US sinners, also, Thy servants, who put our trust in the multitude of Thy mercies, vouchsafe to grant some part and fellowship with Thy holy apostles and martyrs; with John, Stephen, Matthias, Barnabas, Ignatius, Alexander, Marcellinus, Peter, Felicitas, Perpetua, Agatha, Lucy, Agnes, Cecilia, Anastasia, and with all Thy saints. Into their company do Thou, we beseech Thee, admit us, not weighing our merits, but freely pardoning our offenses: through Christ our Lord.

By Whom, O Lord, Thou dost always create, sanctify ✠, quicken ✠, bless ✠, and bestow upon us all these good things.

The Minor Elevation

At one time, the following (Romans 11:36) was the only elevation in the Mass:

THROUGH HIM ✠, and with Him ✠, and in Him ✠, is to Thee, God the Father ✠ almighty, in the unity of the Holy Ghost, *(raises the Sanctissimum)* all honor and glory.

℣. World without end. ℟. Amen.

℣. Let us pray.

Admonished by salutary precepts, and following divine directions, we presume to say:

OUR FATHER, Who art in heaven, hallowed be Thy name; Thy kingdom come; Thy will be done on earth as it is in heaven; give us this day our daily bread; and forgive us our trespasses, as we forgive those who trespass against us, and lead us not into temptation. ℟. But deliver us from evil.

DELIVER US, we beseech Thee, O Lord, from all evils, past, present, and to come: and by the intercession of the blessed and glorious Mary, ever a virgin, Mother of God, and of Thy holy apostles Peter and Paul, of Andrew, and of all the saints, *(he uses the paten to make the sign of the cross)* graciously grant peace in our days, *(he kisses the paten)* that through the help of Thy bountiful mercy we may always be free from sin and secure from all disturbance.

The priest genuflects and then breaks the Host:

THROUGH THE SAME Jesus Christ, Thy Son, our Lord, Who liveth and reigneth with Thee in the unity of the Holy Ghost, God.

℣. World without end.

℟. Amen.

℣. May the peace ✠ of the Lord ✠ be always with ✠ you.

℟. And with thy spirit.

He drops a Particle into the chalice:

May this co-mingling and consecrating of the Body and Blood of Our Lord Jesus Christ avail us who receive it unto life everlasting. Amen.

Bowing down, the priest says:

Lamb of God, Who takest away the sins of the world: have mercy on us. (3x)

At Requiem Masses: *dona eis réquiem (sempitérnam).*

The following prayer is not said at Requiem Masses:

O LORD Jesus Christ, Who didst say to Thine apostles: Peace I leave you, My peace I give you: look not upon my sins, but upon the faith of Thy Church, and vouchsafe to grant her peace and unity according to Thy will: Who livest and reignest God, world without end. Amen.

The "Kiss of Peace" (PAX) is given here at Solemn Mass, but not at Masses for the Dead.

O LORD Jesus Christ, Son of the living God, Who, according to the will of the Father, through the co-operation of the Holy Ghost, hast by Thy death given life to the world: deliver me by this Thy most Sacred Body and Blood from all my iniquities, and from every evil; make me always cleave to Thy commandments, and never suffer me to be separated from Thee, Who with the same God, the Father and the Holy Ghost, livest and reignest God, world without end. Amen.

LET NOT the partaking of Thy Body, O Lord Jesus Christ, which I, all unworthy, presume to receive, turn to my judgement and condemnation; but through Thy loving kindness may it be to me a safeguard and remedy for soul and body; Who, with God the Father, in the unity of the Holy Ghost, livest and reignest, God, world without end. Amen.

AT THE COMMUNION

The priest genuflects, rises, and says:

I WILL take the bread of heaven, and will call upon the name of the Lord.

Striking his heart with his hand three times:

Lord, I am not worthy that Thou shouldst enter under my roof; but only say the word, and my soul shall be healed. (3x)

May the Body of Our Lord Jesus Christ ✠ keep my soul unto life everlasting. Amen.

The priest receives the Body of Our Savior, and after a brief meditation continues:

WHAT shall I render unto the Lord for all the things that He hath rendered unto me? I will take the chalice of salvation and will call upon the name of the Lord. With high praises will I call upon the Lord, and I shall be saved from all mine enemies.

The priest receives the Blood of Our Savior:

May the Blood of Our Lord Jesus Christ ✠ keep my soul unto life everlasting. Amen.

If any of the faithful are to receive Holy Communion, the CONFÍTEOR may be said (according to local custom). Then the priest turns toward the people:

BEHOLD the Lamb of God, behold Him who taketh away the sins of the world.

Lord, I am not worthy that Thou shouldst enter under my roof; but only say the word, and my soul shall be healed. (3x)

To each communicant at the Communion rail:

May the Body of Our Lord Jesus Christ ✠ keep thy soul unto life everlasting. Amen.

After the distribution of Communion, the priest returns to the Altar and receives wine into the chalice.

INTO a pure heart, O Lord, may we receive the heavenly food which has passed our lips; bestowed upon us in time, may it be the healing of our souls for eternity.

At the Epistle side, while the servers pour wine and water over his fingers:

May Thy Body, O Lord, which I have received, and Thy Blood which I have drunk cleave to mine inmost parts: and do Thou grant that no stain of sin remain in me, whom pure and holy mysteries have refreshed: Who livest and reignest world without end. Amen.

Both the Communion Antiphon and Postcommunion are prayed at the Epistle side, but in between, the priest walks to the center for the *Dóminus vobíscum*.

■ THE COMMUNION (PROPER)

■ POSTCOMMUNION (PROPER)

Having kissed the Altar and said the *Dóminus vobíscum*, the priest says or sings the "Ite, Missa est."

℣. Go, it is the dismissal.

℟. Thanks be to God.

At Masses for the Dead, instead of the "Ite, Missa est" it is: ℣. "Requiéscant in pace." ℟. "Amen."

MAY the lowly homage of my service be pleasing to Thee, O most holy Trinity: and do Thou grant that the sacrifice which I, all unworthy, have offered up in the sight of Thy majesty, may be acceptable to Thee, and, because of Thy loving kindness, may avail to atone to Thee for myself and for all those for whom I have offered it up. Through Christ our Lord. Amen.

At Masses for the Dead, the final blessing is omitted:

MAY almighty God, the Father, and the Son ✠ and the Holy Ghost, bless you. ℟. Amen.

THE LAST GOSPEL

℣. The Lord be with you.

℟. And with thy spirit.

℣. The beginning ✠ of the holy Gospel, according to St. John.

℟. Glory be to Thee, O Lord.

IN the beginning was the Word, and the Word was with God, and the Word was God. The same was in the beginning with God. All things were made by Him, and without Him was made nothing that was made. In Him was life, and the life was the light of men: and the light shineth in darkness, and the darkness did not comprehend it. There was a man sent from God, whose name was JOHN. This man came for a witness to give testimony of the light, that all men might believe through him. He was not the light, but was to give testimony of the light. That was the true light which enlighteneth every man that cometh into this world. He was in the world, and the world was made by Him, and the world knew Him not. He came unto His own, and His own received Him not. But as many as received Him, to them He gave great power to become the sons of God: to them that believe in His name: who are born, not of blood, nor of the will of the flesh, nor of the will of man, but of God. *(here genuflect)* **AND THE WORD WAS MADE FLESH,** and dwelt among us, and we saw His glory, the glory as of the only begotten of the Father, full of grace and truth. ℟. Thanks be to God.

LEONINE PRAYERS

After Low Mass, the following may be said:

Hail Mary. (3x) *Hail, Holy Queen.*

℣. Pray for us, O holy Mother of God.
℟. That we may be made worthy of the promises of Christ. *Priest:* Let us pray.

O GOD, our refuge and our strength, look down with favor upon Thy people who cry to Thee; and through the intercession of the glorious and immaculate Virgin Mary, Mother of God, of Saint Joseph, her spouse, of Thy holy Apostles Peter and Paul, and of all the saints, mercifully and graciously hear the prayers which we pour forth to Thee for the conversion of sinners and for the freedom and exaltation of holy mother Church. Through the same Christ Our Lord. ℟. Amen.

Saint Michael the Archangel...etc.

The following is prayed three times:

℣. Most Sacred Heart of Jesus.

℟. Have mercy on us.

PROPER PREFACES

THE EARLY CHURCH • During the first millenium, a substantial number of "proper" prefaces seemed to exist. For example, the LEONINE SACRAMENTARY (from approximately 550AD) contained 267 prefaces, practically one for each Mass. The *Brepols Company*—continuing the work of the Benedictines of Steenbrugge—has a catalogue of ancient prefaces ("Corpus Praefationum") with more than 1,500 entries. Some of ancient prefaces were quite unworthy; e.g. Father Fortescue cites a preface for 28 July in the Leonine Sacramentary containing "a long and violent attack on monks." Others are arresting and treat issues still unresolved today; e.g. Father Fortescue cites a preface from the Ember Day after Pentecost which "defends elaborately the practice of fasting after Pentecost"—cf. *A Study of the Roman Liturgy* (London: Longmans and Green, 1912) page 317.

ELEVEN FROM ELEVENTH • Around the eleventh century, a transition took place. For the next millenium, the Roman Rite consistently had only about eleven prefaces total. For what reason did such a change take place? Father Fortescue suggests that "the preface was considered on the whole too sacred, too near the intangible Canon to be much altered." Practical reasons may also have played a role, since the eleventh century coincided—very generally speaking—with the discovery of accurate pitch notation (as opposed to the previous method of adiastematic notation which gave virtually no indication of pitch), and notating hundreds of prefaces may have been viewed as too burdensome. Diastematic notation takes up much more space.

THE ELEVEN ANCIENT PREFACES • For about a millenium, the following prefaces were all the Roman Rite had. (There were, of course, exceptions such as individual saints' prefaces for religious orders or particular countries.) The preface of the Blessed Virgin Mary seems to have been written—or adapted—by Pope Urban II in 1094AD.

1. PREFACE OF THE NATIVITY (a.k.a. *Christmas*)
2. PREFACE OF THE EPIPHANY
3. PREFACE FOR LENT
4. PREFACE OF THE HOLY CROSS
5. PREFACE FOR EASTER
6. PREFACE OF THE ASCENSION
7. PREFACE OF THE HOLY GHOST (a.k.a. *Pentecost, Whitsun*)
8. PREFACE OF THE HOLY TRINITY (a.k.a. *Sunday Preface*)
9. PREFACE OF THE BLESSED VIRGIN MARY (1094AD)
10. PREFACE OF THE APOSTLES
11. COMMON PREFACE (a.k.a. *Weekday Preface, Daily Preface*)

* The Preface of the Holy Trinity—said on all Sundays of the year, except those that have a proper preface—has been included in the *Ordo Missæ* (page 230).

Four Additional Prefaces • Between 1919 and 1928, four additional prefaces were added. Of these four, the Preface for the Dead is the only one which comes from an existing source (viz. 1738 *Missale Parisiense*) ; all the others were written during the 20th century:

(1919) Preface for the Dead — *Missale Parisiense* (1738)

(1919) Preface for Saint Joseph — Composed in 1919

(1925) Preface for Christ the King — Composed in 1925

(1928) Preface for the Sacred Heart — Composed in 1928

Four "Ad Libitum" Prefaces • Some editions of the 1962 *Missale Romanum*—especially those printed in France or Belgium—include four prefaces sometimes referred to as "Neo-Gallican" (to draw a distinction between the 17th-century Gallican rites and the ancient Gallican rites used before the time of Charlemagne in what we now call France). All four come from the 1738 *Missale Parisiense*. These four were to be used "in certain localities."

1. Preface for Advent — *Missale Parisiense* (1738)
2. Preface of the Blessed Sacrament — *Missale Parisiense* (1738)
3. Preface for Church Dedication — *Missale Parisiense* (1738)
4. Preface of All Saints & Patron Saints — *Missale Parisiense* (1738)

With regard to the "Preface of All Saints & Patron Saints" the rubric says: *Præfatio «de Sanctis» dicitur in festo Omnium Sanctorum, die 1 novembris, in festo Patronorum ac Titularis propriæ ecclesiæ (præterquam Angelorum), et in Missis votivis de iisdem, si præfatione propria carent.* That means: "The Preface of the Saints is said on the Feast of All Saints (November 1st), on the feast of the Patron Saints (and Titular Saints) of a proper church—except angels—and in votive Masses of the same, if they lack a proper preface." A titular is the saint for whom the church is named. A patron is anyone so designated by authority.

Comma Placement • In the 1940s, there was a movement to modify the placement of commas in the beginning to most of the prefaces:

Traditional comma placement :

"Dómine sancte, Pater omnípotens, ætérne Deus"

1940s proposed modification :

"Dómine, sancte Pater, omnípotens ætérne Deus"

The "experimental" holy week (1951) adopted this, as did other publications by the reformers. In their 1973 ICEL translation, the reformers inexplicably deleted the word "holy"—so the question does not seem to be of great signficance :

Vere dignum et justum est, æquum et salutáre,	Father, all-powerful and ever-living God,
nos tibi semper et ubíque grátias ágere:	we do well always and everywhere
Dómine, sancte Pater, omnípotens ætérne Deus:	to give you thanks
per Christum Dóminum nostrum.	through Jesus Christ our Lord.

For many centuries, the Latin languange had no punctuation at all. Indeed, ancient Latin did not place spaces between the words (*scriptio continua*). The editorial committee sees strong arguments in favor of both interpretations.

POPE FRANCIS PREFACES • On the feast of the Annunciation in 2020, the Vatican released *Quo Magis* (dated 22 February 2020), which references seven "new" prefaces for the Extraordinary Form. The document says: "The use or not, in the relevant circumstances, of the newly approved Prefaces remains an *ad libitum* choice." Regarding the three "Neo-Gallican" prefaces—formerly for use "in certain localities"—the *Quo Magis* decree says: "From now on, these may be used wherever Mass is celebrated in the forma extraordinaria." [*The "Neo-Gallican" Advent Preface was excluded.*]

Three come from the "Neo-Gallican" prefaces :

(2020) PREFACE OF THE BLESSED SACRAMENT

"De SS. Sacramento" • *Præfatio de Sanctissimo Sacramento dici potest in festo Sanctissimi Corporis Christi, in Missis votivis de Sanctissimo Sacramento, et in Missis votivis de D.N.I.C. æterno et summo Sacerdote.*

(2020) PREFACE FOR CHURCH DEDICATION

"De Dedicatione Ecclesiae" • *Præfatio de Dedicatione Ecclesiæ dici potest in Missis de Dedicatione ecclesiæ necnon in Missis de anniversario Dedicationis, exceptis Missis in Dedicatione S. Mariæ ad Nives die 5 augusti et in Dedicatione S. Michaëlis Archangeli die 29 septembris.*

(2020) PREFACE OF ALL SAINTS & PATRON SAINTS

"De Omnibus Sanctis et Ss. Patronis" • *Præfatio de Omnibus Sanctis et Ss. Patronis dici potest in Missis festivis et votivis Omnium Sanctorum, et in Missis festivis et votivis Sanctorum Patronorum cum principalium tum secundariorum, necnon Titularis ecclesiæ vel oratorii, modo ne agatur de Angelo vel præfatione propria gaudeant.* (Notice the wording was modified slightly in 2020.)

Four come from the 1970 Missal :

(2020) PREFACE OF THE ANGELS

"De Angelis" — Note: The Vatican version has an error: "décore" should be "decóre."

Præfatio de Angelis dici potest in missis festivis et votivis Angelorum necnon in festo Dedicationis S. Michaëlis Archangeli die 29 septembris.

(2020) PREFACE OF SAINT JOHN THE BAPTIST

"De Sancto Ioanne Baptista" • *Præfatio de Sancto Ioanne Baptista dici potest in Missis festivis et votivis S. Ioannis Baptistæ.*

(2020) PREFACE OF THE MARTYRS

"De Martyribus" • *Præfatio de Martyribus dici potest in Missis festivis et votivis Sanctorum Martyrum, modo ne agatur de S. Ioanne Baptista, vel præfatione propria gaudeant.*

(2020) PREFACE OF THE NUPTIAL MASS (*Wedding Masses*)

"De Nuptiis" — "Pro Sponso et Sponsa" — "De Sponsalibus"

Præfatio de Nuptiis dici potest in Missis votivis "Pro Sponsis."

HISTORICAL NOTE • On 1 July 1960, a majority of the *Commissio Piana* determined "it was necessary to add proper Prefaces" for Advent, the Holy Eucharist, and the Dedication of a Church, but "recognized that such was not possible for the present" because the proposed texts were judged to be "not very satisfactory" by the committee members {Giampietro p314}.

POST-CONCILIAR DEVELOPMENTS • The Second Vatican Council never spoke about adding more prefaces, but did say that "other elements which have suffered injury through accidents of history are now to be restored to the vigor which they had in the days of the holy Fathers" (*Sacrosanctum Concilium* §50b). In 1979, Bishop Rudolf Graber of Regensburg spoke to the INSTITUTUM LITURGICUM of his diocese:

> "At this point, I must address a comment to all liturgists. Apart from the fact that the post-conciliar reform of the liturgy is taking place too quickly and has almost everywhere brought with it changes which cause one to wonder why such changes were necessary, one omission seems particularly regrettable to me: namely, the failure to state what sources the new collects and prefaces, for example, were taken from. How much annoyance among our loyal Catholics could have been avoided if evidence had been provided that various elements had been taken from old sacramentaries and were not more or less arbitrary innovations. I do not know whether this omission can still be made good."

The answer to Bishop Graber's question is partially given by Father Antoine Dumas, who became director of *Coetus 18bis* (responsible for euchological texts) upon the death of Dom Placide Bruylants. In 1971, Dom Dumas published an article ("Les Préfaces du nouveau Missel") in EPHEMERIDES LITUGICAE, explaining that "very few prefaces have been kept in their entirety." The venerable prayers, Dom Dumas admits, were deemed "unsatisfactory" by the reformers, owing to many defects (*insufficances des textes traditionnels*) and so the reformers modified them, making them conform to a "contemporary mindset" (*adaptés à la mentalité contemporaine*). He calls the Preface of the Dead "tiresome" (*fastidieuse*). He labels the ancient Preface for the Apostles—giving no explanation—one of the "false prefaces" (*fausses préfaces*). The traditional Common Preface he refers to as "an empty frame" (*cadre vide*), and finds the traditional preambles and conclusions—loved by so many Catholics—to be "monotonous" (*la monotonie des préambules et des conclusions fixés*). Dom Dumas even says that the authentic prefaces "reproduced in their original form would be intolerable, if not erroneous" (*reproduits clans leur forme originale, eussent été insupportables, sinon fautifs*). As a result, the reformers after Vatican II inserted into the 1970 *Missale Romanum* hundreds of prefaces which were manufactured (in spite of *Sacrosanctum Concilium* §23 and §50). In the United States, there is even a preface for Independence Day on July 4th.

MAGNIFICENT MONOGRAM • More than 1,000 years ago, a very clever monk discovered that the beginning of the preface—**VERE DIGNUM**—forms a monogram. That is to say, if those letters are rotated a certain way, each letter "fits" in the monogram (although several must be rotated 180°). The monogram was often illuminated, covering the entire page with ornate beauty. Below is an excerpt from a manuscript written around the year 988AD, and you will notice the preface for *Missa Dominicæ Primæ post Theophaniam* (First Sunday after Epiphany) indicated by the monogram, which was written in blue ink:

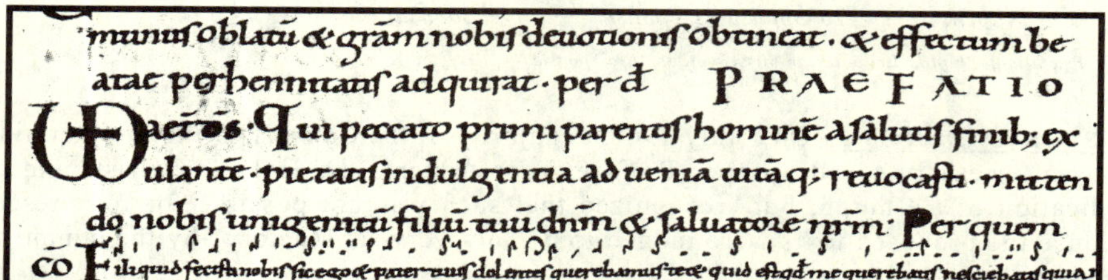

In Nativitate Domini:

VERE DIGNUM et justum est, æquũ et salutáre, nos tibi semper et ubíque grátias ágere: Dñe sancte, Pater omnípotens, ætérne Deus: Quia per incarnáti Verbi mystérium nova mentis nostræ óculis lux tuæ claritátis infúlsit: ut, dum visibíliter Deum cognóscimus, per hunc in invisibílium amórem rapiámur.

Et ídeo cum Ángelis et Archángelis, cum Thronis et Dominatiónibus cumque omni milítia cæléstis exércitus hymnum glóriæ tuæ cánimus, sine fine dicéntes:

PREFACE FOR THE NATIVITY.

WORTHY *and right it is in truth, apt it is and saving, that at all times and places we should thank thee: O holy Lord, Father almighty, eternal God;* because by the mystery of the Word made flesh, from Thy brightness a new light hath risen to shine on the eyes of our souls, in order that, God becoming visible to us, we may be borne upward to the love of things invisible. *And therefore with the angels and archangels, with the thrones and dominations and with all the array of the heavenly host, we sing a hymn to Thy glory and unceasingly repeat:*

In Epiphania Domini:

VERE DIGNUM et justum est, æquũ et salutáre, nos tibi semper et ubíque grátias ágere: Dñe sancte, Pater omnípotens, ætérne Deus: Quia, cum Unigénitus tuus in substántia nostræ mortalitátis appáruit, nova nos immortalitátis suæ luce reparávit.

Et ídeo cum Ángelis et Archángelis, cum Thronis et Dominatiónibus cumque omni milítia cæléstis exércitus hymnum glóriæ tuæ cánimus, sine fine dicéntes:

PREFACE FOR THE EPIPHANY.

WORTHY *and right it is in truth, apt it is and saving, that at all times and places we should thank thee: O holy Lord, Father almighty, eternal God;* because Thine only-begotten Son appearing in our mortal nature hath restored it by the shedding upon us of that new and immortal light which is His very own. *And therefore with the angels and archangels, with the thrones and dominations and with all the array of the heavenly host, we sing a hymn to Thy glory and unceasingly repeat:*

In Quadragesima:

VERE DIGNUM et justum est, æquũ et salutáre, nos tibi semper et ubíque grátias ágere: Dñe sancte, Pater omnípotens, ætérne Deus: Qui corporáli jejúnio vítia cómprimis, mentem élevas, virtútem largíris et prǽmia: per Christũ Dñm nostrũ.

Per quem majestátẽ tuam laudant Ángeli, adórant Dominatiónes, tremunt Potestátes. Cæli cælorúmque Virtútes, ac beáta Seraphim, sócia exsultatióne concélebrant. Cum quibus et nostras voces ut admítti júbeas, deprecámur, súpplici confessióne dicéntes:

PREFACE FOR LENT.

WORTHY *and right it is in truth, apt it is and saving, that at all times and places we should thank thee: O holy Lord, Father almighty, eternal God;* Who on those who chastise their bodies by fasting dost bestow the restraining of evil passions, uplifting of heart, and the enjoying of virtue with its reward; through Christ our Lord.

Through Whom the angels praise, the dominations adore, the powers, trembling with awe, worship Thy majesty: which the heavens, and the forces of heaven, together with the blessed seraphim, joyfully do magnify. And do Thou command that it be permitted to our lowliness to join with them in confessing Thee and unceasingly to repeat:

PREFACE FOR THE HOLY CROSS.

RIGHT IT IS ASSUREDLY and most beseeming, duty of ours and our well-being, to thank thee, holy Lord, almighty Father, eternal God, both always and everywhere. Wood of the cross was thy chosen instrument for the world's salvation; from the fountain-head of death, life should spring anew, and yonder enemy, that by a tree outmatched us, by a tree should be overcome, through Christ our Lord. Ever through him thy greatness is extolled. Angels praising thee, Dominions bowing low, and Powers adread, heaven and all heaven's mighty ones joining with the blessed Seraphim in their song of gladness. O may our voices too with theirs find access, that cry out to thee in humble giving of thanks:

De Sancta Cruce • Translation by Monsignor Knox (Imprimatur 1950)

VERE DIGNUM ET JUSTUM est, æquũ et salutáre, nos tibi semper et ubíque grátias ágere: Dñe sancte, Pater omnípotens, ætérne Deus: Qui salútem humáni géneris in ligno Crucis constituísti: ut, unde mors oriebátur, inde vita resúrgeret: et, qui in ligno vincébat, in ligno quoque vincerétur: per Christũ Dñm nostrum. Per quẽ majestátẽ tuã laudant Ángeli, adórant Dominatiónes, tremunt Potestátes. Cæli cælorúmque Virtútes ac beáta Séraphim sócia exsultatióne concélebrant. Cum quibus et nostras voces ut admítti júbeas, deprecámur, súpplici confessióne dicéntes:

PREFACE FOR EASTER.

RIGHT IT IS assuredly and beseeming, duty of ours and our well-being, of thy praise, Lord, we should ever be the heralds: but most of all and loudest on this day [*] of Christ's offering up, that is our paschal Victim. Paschal Lamb was this indeed, that could take away a whole world's sins, death of ours could overthrow by his dying, and life of ours, that was forfeit, by his rising again restore. Therefore with Angels and Archangels, Thrones and Dominations, and with all the array of heaven's army we sing endlessly of thy glory, after this manner:

In Paschate • Translation by Monsignor Knox (Imprimatur 1950)

VERE DIGNUM ET JUSTUM est, æquũ et salutáre: Te quidem, Dñe, omni témpore, sed [...] gloriósius prædicáre, cum Pascha nostrũ immolátus est Christus. Ipse enĩ verus est Agnus, qui ábstulit peccáta mundi. Qui mortem nostrã moriéndo destrúxit et vitam resurgéndo reparávit.
Et ídeo cum Ángelis et Archángelis, cum Thronis et Dominatiónibus cumque omni milítia cæléstis exércitus hymnum glóriæ tuæ cánimus, sine fine dicéntes:

* During Eastertide, *in hoc potíssimum* ("in this season"); Easter octave, *in hac potíssimum die* ("on this day"); Holy Saturday, *in hac potíssimum nocte* ("on this night").

PREFACE FOR THE ASCENSION.

IT IS TRULY JUST AND RIGHT, *fitting and for our good, always and everywhere to give thanks to Thee, O holy Lord, Father almighty, eternal God;* through Christ our Lord; Who after His resurrection very openly showed Himself to all His disciples, and in their sight was raised up to heaven, in order to give to us to be partakers of His Godhead. *And therefore with the angels and archangels, with the thrones and dominations and with all the array of the heavenly host, we sing a hymn to Thy glory and unceasingly repeat:*

In Ascensione Domini:

VERE DIGNUM ET JUSTUM est, æquũ et salutáre, nos tibi semper et ubíque grátias ágere: Dñe sancte, Pater omnípotens, ætérne Deus, per Christum Dñm nostrum.
Qui post resurrectiónẽ suam ómnibus discípulis suis maniféstus appáruit et, ipsis cernéntibus, est elevátus in cælum, ut nos divinitátis suæ tribúeret esse partícipes.
Et ídeo cum Ángelis et Archángelis, cum Thronis et Dominatiónibus cumque omni milítia cæléstis exércitus hymnum glóriæ tuæ cánimus, sine fine dicéntes:

In Pentecoste :

VERE DIGNUM ET JUSTUM est, æquū et salutáre, nos tibi semper et ubíque grátias ágere: Dñe sancte, Pater omnípotens, ætérne Deus, per Christum Dñm nostrum.
Qui, ascéndens super omnes cælos sedénsque ad déxteram tuam, promíssum Spíritum Sanctum [*hodiérna die*] in fílios adoptiónis effúdit. Quaprópter profúsis gáudiis totus in orbe terrárū mundus exsúltat. Sed et supérnæ Virtútes atque angélicæ Potestátes hymnū glóriæ tuæ cóncinunt, sine fine dicéntes:

* Outside the Pentecost vigil & octave, the words *hodiérna die* are omitted.

PREFACE FOR PENTECOST.

WORTHY *and right it is in truth, apt it is and saving, that at all times and places we should thank thee: O holy Lord, Father almighty, eternal God;* through Christ our Lord; Who, ascending over all the heavens and sitting at Thy right hand, did [*this day*] according to His word, send down the Holy Ghost upon the children of His adoption. Wherefore all peoples upon this earth rejoice with exceeding great joy; the heavenly virtues likewise and the angelic powers sing a hymn to Thy glory and unceasingly repeat:

De Beata Maria Virgine :

VERE DIGNUM ET JUSTUM est, æquū et salutáre, nos tibi semper et ubíque grátias ágere: Dñe sancte, Pater omnípotens, ætérne Deus.
Et te in [......] beátæ Maríæ semper Vírginis collaudáre, benedícere et prædicáre. Quæ et Unigénitū tuū Sancti Spíritus obumbratióne concépit: et, virginitátis glória permanénte, lumen ætérnū mundo effúdit, Jesum Christū, Dóminum nostrum. Per quem majestátem tuam laudant Ángeli, adórant Dominatiónes, tremunt Potestátes. Cæli cælorúmque Virtútes ac beáta Séraphim sócia exsultatióne concélebrant. Cum quibus et nostras voces ut admítti júbeas, deprecámur, súpplici confessióne dicéntes:

PREFACE FOR THE BLESSED VIRGIN MARY.

WORTHY *and right it is in truth, apt it is and saving, that at all times and places we should thank thee: O holy Lord, Father almighty, eternal God;* and on the [......] of the blessed Mary, ever a virgin, should praise and bless and proclaim Thee. For she conceived Thine only-begotten Son by the overshadowing of the Holy Ghost; and losing not the glory of her virginity, gave to the world the everlasting light, Jesus Christ our Lord. Through whom the angels praise Thy majesty, the dominions worship it, and the powers are in awe. The heavens and the heavenly hosts, and the blessed seraphim join together in celebrating their joy. With these we pray Thee join our voices also, while we say with lowly praise:

In Festis Apostolorum :

VERE DIGNUM ET JUSTUM est, æquum et salutáre: Te, Dómine, supplíciter exoráre, ut gregem tuum, Pastor ætérne, non déseras: sed per beátos Apóstolos tuos contínua protectióne custódias. Ut iísdē rectóribus gubernétur, quos óperis tui vicários eídē contulísti præésse pastóres.
Et ídeo cum Ángelis et Archángelis, cum Thronis et Dominatiónibus cumque omni milítia cæléstis exércitus hymnum glóriæ tuæ cánimus, sine fine dicéntes:

PREFACE FOR THE APOSTLES.

IT IS TRULY MEET AND JUST, right and profitable, humbly to beseech Thee, O Lord, to forsake not the flock of which Thou art the eternal shepherd, but through Thy holy apostles ever to guard and keep it, so that it be governed by those rulers whom Thou didst set over it to be its pastors under Thee. *And therefore with the angels and archangels, with the thrones and dominations and with all the array of the heavenly host, we sing a hymn to Thy glory and unceasingly repeat:*

PREFACE FOR THE DEAD.

WORTHY *and right it is in truth, apt it is and saving, that at all times and places we should thank thee: O holy Lord, Father almighty, eternal God;* through Christ our Lord, in Whom the hope of a happy resurrection has shone on us, so that those whom the certain fate of dying renders sad, may be consoled by the promise of future immortality. For with regard to Thy faithful, O Lord, life is changed, not taken away; and the house of their earthly dwelling being destroyed, an eternal dwelling in heaven is obtained. *And therefore with the angels and archangels, with the thrones and dominations and with all the array of the heavenly host, we sing a hymn to Thy glory and unceasingly repeat:*

Praefatio defunctorum :

VERE DIGNUM ET JUSTUM est, æquũ et salutáre, nos tibi semper et ubíque grátias ágere: Dñe sancte, Pater omnípotens, ætérne Deus, per Christum Dóminum nostrum.

In quo nobis spes beátæ resurrectiónis effúlsit, ut, quos contrístat certa moriéndi condício, eósdẽ consolétur futúræ immortalitátis promíssio. Tuis enim fidélibus, Dómine, vita mutátur, non tóllitur: et, dissolúta terréstris hujus incolátus domo, ætérna in cælis habitátio comparátur.

Et ídeo cum Ángelis et Archángelis, cum Thronis et Dominatiónibus cumque omni milítia cæléstis exércitus hymnum glóriæ tuæ cánimus, sine fine dicéntes:

FROM THE PARIS MISSAL (1738)

PREFACE FOR SAINT JOSEPH.

WORTHY *and right it is in truth, apt it is and saving, that at all times and places we should thank thee: O holy Lord, Father almighty, eternal God;* and on the festivity [*veneration*] of Saint Joseph to magnify Thee with due praise, to bless and proclaim Thee. The just man who was given by Thee as a spouse to the Virgin Mother of God, and was placed over Thy Family as a faithful and prudent servant; so that taking the place of the eternal Father, he might guard the only-begotten Son conceived by the shadow of the Holy Ghost, Jesus Christ, Our Lord, through Whom the angels praise Thy majesty, the dominions worship it, the powers are in awe, the heavens and the heavenly hosts and the blessed seraphim join together in celebrating their joy. With these, we pray Thee, join our own voices also, while we sing with lowly praise:

De S. Joseph Sponso B. M. V.

VERE DIGNUM ET JUSTUM est, æquũ et salutáre, nos tibi semper et ubíque grátias ágere: Dñe sancte, Pater omnípotens, ætérne Deus,

Et te in Festivitáte [*Veneratióne*] beáti Joseph débitis magnificáre præcóniis, benedícere et prædicáre. Qui et vir justus, a te Deíparæ Vírgini Sponsus est datus: et fidélis servus ac prudens, super Famíliam tuam est constitútus: ut Unigénitum tuum, Sancti Spíritus obumbratióne concéptum, patérna vice custodíret, Jesum Christum, Dñm nostrum. Per quem majestátem tuam laudant Ángeli, adórant Dominatiónes, tremunt Potestátes. Cæli cælorúmque Virtútes ac beáta Séraphim sócia exsultatióne concélebrant. Cũ quibus et nostras voces ut admítti júbeas, deprecámur, súpplici confessióne dicéntes:

(1919) ADDED BY POPE PIUS XI

PREFACE FOR THE KINGSHIP OF CHRIST.

WORTHY *and right it is in truth, apt it is and saving, that at all times and places we should thank thee: O holy Lord, Father almighty, eternal God;* Who didst anoint with the oil of gladness Thine only-begotten Son, our Lord Jesus

De D. N. Jesu Christo Rege :

VERE DIGNUM ET JUSTUM est, æquũ et salutáre, nos tibi semper et ubíque grátias ágere: Dñe sancte, Pater omnípotens, ætérne Deus.

Qui unigénitũ Fíliũ tuũ, Dñm nostrũ Jesum Christum, Sacerdótem ætérnũ et universórum Regem, óleo exsultatiónis unxísti: ut, seípsum in ara crucis hóstiam immaculátam et pacíficam ófferens, redemptiónis humánæ sacraménta perágeret: et suo subjéctis império ómnibus creatúris, ætérnum et universále regnum, imménsæ tuæ tráderet Majestáti. Regnum veritátis et vitæ: regnũ sanctitátis et grátiæ: regnũ justítiæ, amóris et pacis.

Et ídeo cum Ángelis et Archángelis, cum Thronis et Dominatiónibus cumque omni milítia cæléstis exércitus hymnum glóriæ tuæ cánimus, sine fine dicéntes:

(1925) ADDED BY POPE PIUS XI

Christ, eternal Priest and King of the universe: that, offering Himself as a stainless peace-offering on the altar of the cross, He might fulfill the pledges of man's redemption; and, having all creatures subject to His power, might deliver to Thy sublime majesty an eternal and universal kingdom, a kingdom of truth and life; a kingdom of holiness and grace, a kingdom of justice, love and peace. *And therefore with the angels and archangels, with the thrones and dominations and with all the array of the heavenly host, we sing a hymn to Thy glory and unceasingly repeat:*

De sacratissimo Corde Jesu:

VERE DIGNUM ET JUSTUM est, æquũ et salutáre, nos tibi semper et ubíque grátias ágere: Dñe sancte, Pater omnípotens, ætérne Deus.

Qui Unigénitum tuum, in Cruce pendéntem, láncea mílitis transfígi voluísti: ut apértum Cor, divínæ largitátis sacrárium, torréntes nobis fúnderet miseratiónis et grátiæ: et, quod amóre nostri flagráre numquam déstitit, piis esset réquies et pæniténtibus patéret salútis refúgium.

Et ídeo cum Ángelis et Archángelis, cum Thronis et Dominatiónibus cumque omni milítia cæléstis exércitus hymnum glóriæ tuæ cánimus, sine fine dicéntes:

(1928) ADDED BY POPE PIUS XI

PREFACE FOR THE MOST SACRED HEART.

WORTHY *and right it is in truth, apt it is and saving, that at all times and places we should thank thee: O holy Lord, Father almighty, eternal God;* Who hast willed that Thine only-begotten Son hanging on the cross should be transfixed with a soldier's lance, so that the opened Heart, treasure-place of divine bounty, might flood us with the torrents of compassion and grace, and that that which never ceased to burn with love for us, should be repose for the devout and to the penitent should open the shelter of salvation. *And therefore with the angels and archangels, with the thrones and dominations and with all the array of the heavenly host, we sing a hymn to Thy glory and unceasingly repeat:*

Praefatio communis:

VERE DIGNUM ET JUSTUM est, æquũ et salutáre, nos tibi semper et ubíque grátias ágere: Dñe sancte, Pater omnípotens, ætérne Deus, per Christum Dóminum nostrum.

Per quem majestátẽ tuam laudant Ángeli, adórant Dominatiónes, tremunt Potestátes. Cæli cælorúmque Virtútes, ac beáta Séraphim, sócia exsultatióne concélebrant. Cum quibus et nostras voces ut admítti júbeas, deprecámur, súpplici confessióne dicéntes:

COMMON PREFACE. *Used on weekdays.*

WORTHY *and right it is in truth, apt it is and saving, that at all times and places we should thank thee: O holy Lord, Father almighty, eternal God;* through Christ our Lord. Through Whom the angels praise, the dominations adore, the powers, trembling with awe, worship Thy majesty: Which the heavens, and the forces of heaven, together with the blessed seraphim, joyfully do magnify. And do Thou command that it be permitted to our lowliness to join with them in confessing Thee and unceasingly to repeat:

PREFACE FOR ADVENT. *Ad libitum; for use in certain localities.*

WORTHY and right it is in truth, apt it is and saving, that at all times and places we should thank thee: O Lord, Father holy, God almighty and eternal, through Christ our Lord. | *He it was whom thou in mercy and faithfulness didst promise as Savior to the ravaged race of men: he whose truth would make the unschooled learnèd, his holiness make the ungodly righteous, his power make the unstable steady. So since it is soon he shall come whom thou wilt send, and the day of our deliverance is dawning, with this faith in thy promises in godly joy we revel.* | And so with Angels and Archangels, Thrones and Dominions, with all the soldiery of the heavenly host, we sing a hymn to thy glory, without end declaiming:

ET JUSTUM est, æquũ et salutáre, nos tibi semper et ubíque grátias ágere: Dñe, sancte Pater, omnípotens ætérne Deus, per Christum Dóminum nostrum.

Quem pérdito hóminum géneri Salvatórẽ miséricors et fidélis promisísti: cujus véritas instrúeret ínscios, sánctitas justificáret impios, virtus adjuváret infírmos. Dum ergo prope est ut véniat quem missúrus es, et dies affúlget liberatiónis nostræ, in hac promissiónũ tuárũ fide, piis gáudiis exsultámus.

Et ídeo cum Ángelis et Archángelis, cum Thronis et Dominatiónibus cumque omni milítia cæléstis exércitus hymnum glóriæ tuæ cánimus, sine fine dicéntes:

[Is 14.1, 51.5; Phil 4.5; Ex 4.13]

1962 • *Præfatio "de Adventu" dicitur: (a) tamquam propria in Missis de Tempore a dominica I Adventus usque ad vigiliam Nativitatis Domini inclusive; (b) tamquam de Tempore in ceteris Missis quæ celebrantur eodem tempore, et præfatione propria carent.*

PREFACE FOR THE BLESSED SACRAMENT. *Ad libitum.*

WORTHY and right it is in truth, apt it is and saving, that at all times and places we should thank thee: O Lord, Father holy, God almighty and eternal, through Christ our Lord. | *He, mere shadows in hosts of flesh dispelling, for a sacrifice bequeathed us his own Body and Blood: that a clean offering, the only one to please thee, might be offered to thy name in every place. So in this mystery of unfathomable wisdom, as well as unmeasured charity, that which he accomplished once on the Cross, in wondrous fashion he unfailingly enacts, being himself the one that offers and himself the one that is offered. Ourselves too, made one victim with him, he summons to that sacred banquet where even he is taken as our food, the remembrance of his Passion is refreshed, the mind filled with grace, and a pledge given us of glory to come.* | And so with Angels and Archangels, Thrones and Dominions, with all the soldiery of the heavenly host, we sing a hymn to thy glory, without end declaiming:

ET JUSTUM est, æquũ et salutáre, nos tibi semper et ubíque grátias ágere: Dñe, sancte Pater, omnípotens ætérne Deus, per Christum Dóminum nostrum.

Qui, remótis carnálium victimárum inánibus umbris, Corpus et Sánguinem suum nobis in sacrifícium commendávit: ut in omni loco offerátur nómini tuo, quæ tibi sola complácuit, oblátio munda. In hoc ígitur inscrutábilis sapiéntiæ, et imménsæ caritátis mystério, idípsum quod semel in Cruce perfécit, non cessat mirabíliter operári, ipse ófferens, ipse et oblátio. Et nos, unam secum hóstiam efféctos, ad sacrum invítat convívium, in quo ipse cibus noster súmitur, recólitur memória Passiónis ejus, mens implétur grátia, et futúræ glóriæ nobis pignus datur.

Et ídeo cum Ángelis et Archángelis, cum Thronis et Dominatiónibus cumque omni milítia cæléstis exércitus hymnum glóriæ tuæ cánimus, sine fine dicéntes:

[Mal 1.11; Rom 6.10; Heb 7.27, 9.12, 26, 28, 10.10; 1 Pet 3.18; Rom 12.1]

PREFACE FOR THE DEDICATION OF A CHURCH. *Ad libitum.*

VERE DIGNUM ET JUSTUM est, æquũ et salutáre, nos tibi semper et ubíque grátias ágere: Dñe, sancte Pater, omnípotens ætérne Deus;

Qui hanc oratiónis domum, quam ædificávimus, bonórum ómnium largítor inhábitas, et Ecclésiã, quam ipse fundásti, incessábili operatióne sanctíficas. Hæc est enim vere domus oratiónis, visibílibus ædifíciis adumbráta, templũ habitatiónis glóriæ tuæ, sedes incommutábilis véritatis, sanctuáriũ ætérne caritátis. Hæc est arca, quas nos a mundi erèptos dilúvio, in portum salútis indúcit. Hæc est dilécta et única sponsa, quam acquisívit Christus sánguine suo, quam vivíficat Spíritu suo, cujus in sinu renáti per grátiam tuam, lacte verbi páscimur, pane vitæ roborámur, misericórdiæ tuæ subsídiis confovémur. Hæc fidéliter in terris, sponso adjuvánte, mílitat, et perénniter in cælis, ipso coronánte, triúmphat.

Et ídeo cum Ángelis et Archángelis, cum Thronis et Dominatiónibus cumque omni milítia cæléstis exércitus hymnum glóriæ tuæ cánimus, sine fine dicéntes:

[Is 56.7; 1 Mcc 7.37; Mt 21.13; Mk 11.17; Lk 19.46; Ps 25.8; Jn 6.35, 48]

WORTHY and right it is in truth, apt it is and saving, that at all times and places we should thank thee: O Lord, Father holy, God almighty and eternal, through Christ our Lord. | *Bestower of every good, thou dwellest in this house of prayer which we have built, and by thine unfailing action hallowest the Church that thou hast founded. She indeed is the true house of prayer foreshadowed in our visible buildings, the temple where thy glory abides, the seat of truth unchanging, shrine of charity everlasting. She is the ark that bears us, hauled from the flood of this world, to the harbor of salvation. She is that bride and only beloved whom Christ has claimed with his blood, whom his Spirit enlivens, and in whose heart we, born anew by thy grace, are fed by the milk of the word, braced by the bread of life, tended by thy merciful provision. She fights faithfully on earth with the help of her Spouse and crowned by him in heaven, glories continually in victory.* | And so with Angels and Archangels, Thrones and Dominions, with all the soldiery of the heavenly host, we sing a hymn to thy glory, without end declaiming:

PREFACE OF ALL SAINTS & PATRON SAINTS. *Ad libitum.*

VERE DIGNUM ET JUSTUM est, æquũ et salutáre, nos tibi semper et ubíque grátias ágere: Dñe, sancte Pater, omnípotens ætérne Deus;

Qui glorificáris in concílio Sanctórũ, et eórum coronándo mérita, corónas dona tua: qui nobis in eórum præbes, et conversatióne exémplum, et communióne consórtium, et intercessióne subsídium: ut tantam habéntes impósitam nubem téstiũ, per patiéntiam currámus ad propósitum nobis certámen, et cum eis percipiámus immarcescíbilem glóriae corónã. Per Jesum Christum Dñm nostrum, cujus sánguine ministrátur nobis intróitus in ætérnum regnũ. Per quẽ majestátẽ tuã treméntes adórant Ángeli, et omnes Spiríttuum cæléstium chori sócia exsultatióne concélebrant. Cum quibus et nostras voces, ut admítti júbeas, deprecámur, súpplici confessióne dicentes: [Ps 88.8; Heb 12.1; 1 Pet 5.4; 2 Pet 1.11; Heb 10.19]

WORTHY and right it is in truth, apt it is and saving, that at all times and places we should thank thee: O Lord, Father holy, God almighty and eternal; *Thou art glorified in the assembly of the Saints, and by crowning their merits, crownest thine own gifts: thou dost provide us a pattern in their manner of life, fellowship in their communion, support in their intercession: that having laid upon us so great a cloud of witnesses, in the strife laid before us we shall run steadfastly, and win with them an unfading crown of glory.*

Through Jesus Christ our Lord, through whose blood an entrance is afforded us to an everlasting kingdom. Through him Angels, thrilling with awe, make obeisance to thy majesty, and all the choirs of heavenly Spirits join in keeping festival with kindred revelry. Together with these, we pray, bid thou our utterance also be blended, in humble confession of praise declaiming:

PREFACE OF THE ANGELS. *Ad libitum.*

WORTHY and right it is in truth, apt it is and saving, that at all times and places we should thank thee: O Lord, Father holy, God almighty and eternal; *Nor still our acclamation of thee for thine Archangels and Angels, since it traces back to thy supremacy and glory when the angelic creation thou commendest is honored: and as through lordly splendor it is so worthy, thus thy stature all unmeasured is displayed, thy worthiness all-surpassing, through Christ our Lord.*

Through him throngs of Angels keep the festival of thy majesty, and making obeisance, we unite with their revelry, joining their utterance of praise, proclaiming:

VERE DIGNUM ET JUSTUM est, æquũ et salutáre, nos tibi semper et ubíque grátias ágere: Dñe, sancte Pater, omnípotens ætérne Deus;

Et in Archángelis Angelísque tuis tua præcónia non tacére, quia ad excelléntiam tuam recúrrit et glóriam quod angélica creatúra tibi probábilis honorétur: et, cum illa sit amplo decóre digníssima, tu quam sis imménsus et super ómnia præferéndus osténderis, per Christum Dóminum nostrum. Per quem multitúdo Angelórum tuam célebrat majestátem, quibus adorántes in exsultatióne conjúngimur, una cum eis laudis voce clamántes:

PREFACE OF SAINT JOHN THE BAPTIST. *Ad libitum.*

WORTHY and right it is in truth, apt it is and saving, that at all times and places we should thank thee: O Lord, Father holy, God almighty and eternal, through Christ our Lord. *We join to praise thy grandeur in his Forerunner, blessed John, whom thou didst consecrate with princely honor amid those born of women. He, once conceived, marshaled joys in plenty, he, as yet unborn, leapt with gladness for the coming of man's salvation, and he, alone of all the prophets, displayed the Lamb of our redemption. He, moreover, in streams of water waiting to be hallowed washed the very Author of Baptism, of whom he deserved to bear sovereign witness by shedding of his blood.* And so with Angels and Archangels, Thrones and Dominions, with all the soldiery of the heavenly host, we sing a hymn to thy glory, without end declaiming:

VERE DIGNUM ET JUSTUM est, æquũ et salutáre, nos tibi semper et ubíque grátias ágere: Dñe, sancte Pater, omnípotens ætérne Deus, per Christum Dóminum nostrum.

In cujus Præcursóre beáto Joánne tuam magnificéntiã collaudámus, quem inter natos mulíerum honóre præcípuo consecrásti. Qui cum nascéndo multa gáudia præstitísset, et nondum éditus exsultásset ad humánæ salútis advéntum, ipse solus ómnium prophetárum Agnum redemptiónis osténdit. Sed et sanctificándis étiam aquæ fluéntis ipsum baptísmatis lavit auctórem, et méruit fuso sánguine suprémum illi testimónium exhibére.

Et ídeo cum Ángelis et Archángelis, cum Thronis et Dominatiónibus cumque omni milítia cæléstis exércitus hymnum glóriæ tuæ cánimus, sine fine dicéntes:

[Mt 11.11; Lk 7.28; Jn 1.29, 36]

[Editor's Note: The 2021 decree (*Quo Magis*) adopted this preface from the 1970 Missale Romanum, but kept the traditional ending (above) rather than adopting the 1970 version: *Et ídeo, cum cælórum Virtútibus, in terris te júgiter prædicámus, majestáti tuæ sine fine clamántes.* The same is true for the "Preface of the Martyrs," which kept the traditional ending rather than adopting the 1970 version, which is identical to that of Saint John the Baptist.]

PREFACE OF THE MARTYRS. *Ad libitum.*

WORTHY and right it is in truth, apt it is and saving, that at all times and places we should thank thee: O Lord, Father holy, God almighty and eternal; *For the blood of the blessed Martyrs *, shed in confession of thy name, and following Christ's example, gives testimony of those thy wonders by which thou raisest strength to its height from frailty, and*

VERE DIGNUM ET JUSTUM est, æquũ et salutáre, nos tibi semper et ubíque grátias ágere: Dñe, sancte Pater, omnípotens ætérne Deus;

Quóniam * beatórum mártyrum pro confessióne nóminis tui, ad imitatiónem Christi, sanguis effúsus tua mirabília maniféstat, quibus pérficis in fragilitáte virtútem, et vires infírmas ad testimónium róboras, per Christũ

Dóminum nostrum. [*The following is identical to the Preface for Lent*]

Per quem majestátem tuam laudant Ángeli, adórant Dominatiónes, tremunt Potestátes. Cæli cælorúmque Virtútes, ac beáta Seraphim, sócia exsultatióne concélebrant. Cũ quibus et nostras voces ut admítti júbeas, deprecámur, súpplici confessióne dicéntes: [2 Cor 12.9f, 13.4; 1 Cor 1.25, 27]

scanty force thou bracest to prepare for witness: through Christ our Lord. | *Through him to thy majesty Angels give praise, Dominions make obeisance, where Powers thrill with awe. Heaven and the Virtues of heaven, with the blessed Seraphim, join in keeping festival with kindred revelry. Together with these, we pray, bid thou our utterance also be blended, in humble confession of praise declaiming:*

* or: the blessed Martyr[s] N. [and N].

*Loco verborum * "beatórum mártyrum" dici potest pro opportunitate:*
vel "beáti mártyris N." ("beátæ mártyris N."),
vel "beatórum mártyrum N. et N." ("beatárum mártyrum N. et N.").

PREFACE OF THE NUPTIAL MASS. *Ad libitum.*

VERE DIGNUM ET JUSTUM est, æquũ et salutáre, nos tibi semper et ubíque grátias ágere: Dñe, sancte Pater, omnípotens ætérne Deus; Qui fœdera nuptiárum blando concórdiæ jugo et insolúbili pacis vínculo nexuísti, ut multiplicándis adoptiónũ fíliis sanctórum connubiórum fecúnditas pudíca servíret. Tua enim, Dñe, providéntia, tuáque gratia ineffabílibus modis utrúmque dispénsas, ut, quod generátio ad mundi prodúxit ornátum, regenerátio ad Ecclésiæ perdúcat augméntum, per Christum Dñm nostrum. [*The following is identical to the Preface for Lent*]

Per quem majestátem tuam laudant Ángeli, adórant Dominatiónes, tremunt Potestátes. Cæli cælorúmque Virtútes, ac beáta Seraphim, sócia exsultatióne concélebrant. Cũ quibus et nostras voces ut admítti júbeas, deprecámur, súpplici confessióne dicéntes: [Rm 8.15, 23; Gal 4.5; Eph 1.5]

WORTHY and right it is in truth, apt it is and saving, that at all times and places we should thank thee: O Lord, Father holy, God almighty and eternal; *Thou hast fastened the covenant of marriage with the sweet yoke of harmony and inseverable bond of peace, that the chaste fruitfulness of holy wedlock should serve to increase the children of thine adoption. For in thy providence, O Lord, and thy grace both these thou guidest in soundless ways, that what birth has yielded to adorn this world, new birth may wield to enlarge thy Church, through Christ our Lord.*

Through him to thy majesty Angels give praise, Dominions make obeisance, where Powers thrill with awe. Heaven and the Virtues of heaven, with the blessed Seraphim, join in keeping festival with kindred revelry. Together with these, we pray, bid thou our utterance also be blended, in humble confession of praise declaiming:

INFRA ACTIONEM

DURING THE CANON

COMMUNICANTES FOR CHRISTMAS.

HAVING communion in and celebrating the most sacred day [*night*] on which the stainless virginity of blessed Mary brought forth the Savior of the world, venerating the memory in the first place of the same glorious Mary, ever a virgin, mother of the same Jesus Christ, our God and Lord, likewise of...

Communicántes, et diem sacratíssimum [*noctem sacratíssimam*] celebrántes, quo [*qua*] beátæ Maríæ interneráta virgínitas huic mundo édidit Salvatórem: sed et memóriam venerántes, in primis ejúsdem gloriósæ semper Vírginis Maríæ, Genitrícis ejúsdem Dei et Dñi nostri Jesu Christi: sed et...

COMMUNICANTES FOR THE EPIPHANY.

HAVING communion in and celebrating the most sacred day on which Thine only-begotten Son, co-eternal with Thee in Thy glory, in very truth visibly appeared in our bodily flesh; venerating the memory in the first place of the glorious Mary, ever a virgin, mother of the same Jesus Christ, our God and Lord, likewise of...

Communicántes, et diem sacratíssimum celebrántes, quo Unigénitus tuus, in tua tecum glória coætérnus, in veritáte carnis nostræ visibíliter corporális appáruit: sed et memóriam venerántes, in primis gloriósæ semper Vírginis Maríæ, Genitrícis ejúsdem Dei et Dómini nostri Jesu Christi: sed et...

COMMUNICANTES FOR EASTER.

English Translation by Monsignor Ronald Knox.

HERE MEET WE in fellowship, that holy day [*night*] observing, on which our Lord Jesus Christ, in his human flesh, rose again from the dead; here keep we the memory of her, first of all, the glorious ever-virgin Mary, that is Mother of our Lord and God Jesus Christ; but of others, too, holy apostles and martyrs of thine, Peter and Paul, Andrew, James, John, Thomas, James, Philip, Bartholomew, Matthew, Simon, and Thaddeus; Linus, Cletus, Clement, Sixtus, Cornelius, Cyprian, Laurence, Chrysogonus, John and Paul, Cosmas, and Damian, and all thy saints everywhere. Let their merits, Lord, their intercession avail with thee; shield us with thy protection in every encounter. Through the same Christ our Lord. Amen.

Communicántes, et diem sacratíssimum [*noctem sacratíssimam*] celebrántes Resurrectiónis Dñi nostri Jesu Christi secúndum carnem: sed et memóriam venerántes, in primis gloriósæ semper Vírginis Maríæ, Genitrícis ejúsdem Dei et Dñi nostri Jesu Christi: sed et * beatórũ Apostolórũ ac Mártyrum tuórum, Petri et Pauli, Andréæ, Jacóbi, Joánnis, Thomæ, Jacóbi, Philíppi, Bartholomǽi, Matthǽi, Simónis et Thaddǽi: Lini, Cleti, Cleméntis, Xysti, Cornélii, Cypriáni, Lauréntii, Chrysógoni, Joánnis et Pauli, Cosmæ et Damiáni et ómniũ sanctórũ tuórũ: quorum méritis precibúsque concédas, ut in ómnibus protectiónis tuæ muniámur auxílio. Per eúmdem Christum Dñm nostrum. Amen.

* *On 13 November 1962, five years after the death of Monsignor Knox, Saint Joseph's name was inserted to this prayer.*

HANC IGITUR FOR EASTER. *Translation by Monsignor Ronald Knox.*

Hanc ígitur oblatiónem servitútis nostræ, sed et cunctæ famíliæ tuæ, **quã tibi offérimus pro his quoque, quos regeneráre dignátus es ex aqua, et Spíritu Sancto, tríbuens eis remissiónem ómnium peccatórum,** quǽsumus Dómine, ut placátus accípias, diésque nostros in tua pace dispónas, atque ab ætérna damnatióne nos éripi, et in electórum tuórum júbeas grege numerári. Per Christum Dñm nostrum. Amen.

** Bold text here indicates extra words added to the usual prayer.*

HERE, then, is the offering we make thee, we that are thy ministers, yet in truth it is the offering of all thy household. For these, too, we offer it, to whom thou hast given new birth by water and the Holy Spirit, of all their sins absolving them. We beseech thee. Lord, to grant it favourable acceptance, ordering our days in the peace thou bestowest, from eternal loss delivering us, and in the company of thy elect bidding our names be numbered. Through Christ our Lord. Amen.

COMMUNICANTES FOR THE ASCENSION.

Communicántes, et diẽ sacratíssimum celebrántes, quo Dñs noster, unigénitus Fílius tuus, unítam sibi fragilitátis nostræ substántiam in gloriæ tuæ déxtera collocávit: sed et memóriam venerántes, in primis gloriósæ semper Vírginis Maríæ, Genitrícis ejúsdem Dei et Dómini nostri Jesu Christi: sed et...

HAVING communion in and celebrating the most sacred day on which Our Lord, Thine only-begotten Son, established at Thy right hand in glory that frail nature of ours which He had assumed: venerating the memory in the first place of the glorious Mary, ever a virgin, mother of the same Jesus Christ, our God and Lord, likewise of...

COMMUNICANTES FOR PENTECOST.

Communicántes, et diem sacratíssimum Pentecóstes celebrántes, quo Spíritus sanctus Apóstolis innúmeris linguis appáruit: sed et memóriam venerántes, in primis gloriósæ semper Vírginis Maríæ, Genitrícis Dei et Dñi nostri Jesu Christi: sed et...

HAVING communion in and celebrating the sacred day of Pentecost on which the Holy Ghost appeared to the apostles, betokened by numberless tongues; venerating the memory in the first place of the glorious Mary, ever a virgin, mother of Jesus Christ, our God and Lord, likewise of...

HANC IGITUR FOR PENTECOST.

Identical to that of Easter:

Hanc ígitur oblatiónem servitútis nostræ, sed et cunctæ famíliæ tuæ, **quã tibi offérimus pro his quoque, quos regeneráre dignátus es ex aqua, et Spíritu Sancto, tríbuens eis remissiónem ómnium peccatórum,** quǽsumus Dómine, ut placátus accípias, diésque nostros in tua pace dispónas, atque ab ætérna damnatióne nos éripi, et in electórum tuórum júbeas grege numerári. Per Christum Dñm nostrum. Amen.

** Bold text here indicates extra words added to the usual prayer.*

WHEREFORE, we beseech Thee, O Lord, graciously to receive this oblation which we Thy servants, and with us Thy whole family, make to Thee, offering it up in like manner for those also whom Thou hast been pleased to make to be born again of water and the Holy Ghost. Grant to them the forgiveness of all their sins; do Thou establish our days in Thy peace; nor suffer that we be condemned forever, but rather command that we be numbered in the flock of Thine elect. Through Christ our Lord. Amen.

Prayers addressed to God the Father, without mention of another Person:

Through our Lord.

PER DOMINUM ✠

Per Dóminum nostrum Jesum Christum fílium tuum, qui tecum vivit et regnat in unitáte Spíritus Sancti, Deus, per ómnia sǽcula sæculórum. ℟. Amen.

THROUGH OUR LORD Jesus Christ, Thy Son, Who liveth and reigneth with Thee in the unity of the Holy Ghost, God, world without end. ℟. Amen.

Prayers addressed directly to God the Son:

Who livest.

QUI VIVIS ✠

Qui vivis et regnas, cum Deo Patre in unitáte Spíritus Sancti, Deus, per ómnia sǽcula sæculórum. ℟. Amen.

WHO LIVEST and reignest, with God the Father, in the unity of the Holy Ghost, God, world without end. ℟. Amen.

Prayers to God the Father which mention Jesus at the beginning or in the body:

Through the same.

PER EUMDEM DOMINUM ✠

Per eúmdem Dóminum nostrum Jesum Christum fílium tuum, qui tecum vivit et regnat in unitáte Spíritus Sancti, Deus, per ómnia sǽcula sæculórum. ℟. Amen.

THROUGH THE SAME Jesus Christ, Thy Son, our Lord, Who liveth and reigneth with Thee in the unity of the Holy Ghost, God, world without end. ℟. Amen.

When the final clause refers to Jesus Christ:

Who with Thee.

QUI TECUM ✠

Qui tecum vivit et regnat in unitáte Spíritus Sancti, Deus, per ómnia sǽcula sæculórum. ℟. Amen.

WHO WITH THEE liveth and reigneth in the unity of the Holy Ghost, God, world without end. ℟. Amen.

Prayers to God the Father which mention the Holy Ghost:

Through ... in the unity of the same.

PER DOMINUM ...IN UNITATE EJUSDEM ✠

Per Dóminum nostrum Jesum Christum fílium tuum, qui tecum vivit et regnat in unitáte ejúsdem Spíritus Sancti, Deus, per ómnia sǽcula sæculórum. ℟. Amen.

Through Jesus Christ, Thy Son, our Lord, Who liveth and reigneth with Thee IN THE UNITY OF THE SAME Holy Ghost, God, world without end.

℟. Amen.

Before Mass Begins

1962 • Before the parochial Mass on Sundays comes the sprinkling rite. The Celebrant enters from the sacristy (wearing the Cope) along with a server. Having sprinkled the people, he retires to the sacristy and exchanges Cope for Chasuble—then processes from the back of church along with ministers and servers. It is also lawful for the Celebrant to first process in from the back of the church (wearing the Cope) and then—having sprinkled the people—exchange Cope for Chasuble at the Sedilia. Traditionally, while the sprinkling of the people is taking place, the Celebrant quietly recites the antiphon and "as many verses of the psalm as he can, until he arrives back at the Altar" (Martinucci).

Psalm 50 : 9, 3 • *The following is sung on all Sundays, except during Paschaltide.*

Aspérges me, Dómine, hyssópo, et mundábor: lavábis me, et super nivem dẽalbábor. ℣. Miserére mei, Deus, secúndum magnã misericórdiam tuam. ℣. Glória Patri, et Fílio, et Spirítui Sancto. Sicut erat in princípio, et nunc, et semper, et in sæcula sæculórũ. Amen.

("Glória Patri" is omitted during Passiontide.)

THOU WILT sprinkle me with a wand of hyssop, and I shall be clean; washed, I shall be whiter than snow. ℣. Have mercy on me, O God, as thou art ever rich in mercy. ℣. Glory be to the Father, and to the Son, and to the Holy Ghost. As it was in the beginning, is now, and ever shall be, world without end. Amen. *(The antiphon is repeated.)*

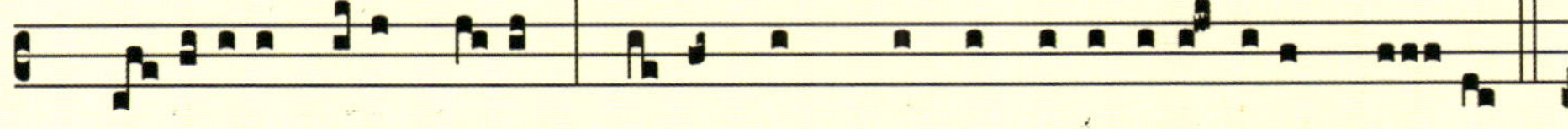

℣. Mi- serére me-i, De- us,* se-cúndum magnã mi-se-ricórdi-am tu- am.

℣. Gló- ri- a Patri, et Fí-li-o, et Spi-rítu-i Sancto:* Si-cut erat in princípi-

o, et nunc, et semper, et in sǽcula sæcu-lórum. A-men.

The antiphon is repeated; then the prayers on the following page are said.

℣. Show us thy mercy, Lord.
℟. And grant us thy deliverance.

℣. O Lord, heed my prayer.
℟. And let my cry come unto thee.

℣. The Lord be with you.
℟. And with you, his minister.

Let us pray.

HOLY LORD, Father almighty, everlasting God, give us audience: graciously send down from heaven some holy angel of thine to keep watch and ward over us, all that dwell in this place to cherish, comfort, and defend: through Christ our Lord. ℟. AMEN.

℣. Osténde nobis, Dñe, misericórdiã tuam. (T.P. *Allẽ*)
℟. Et salutáre tuum da nobis. (T.P. *Allelúja*)

℣. Dómine, exáudi oratiónem meam. (T.P. *Allelúja*)
℟. Et clamor meus ad te véniat. (T.P. *Allelúja*)

℣. Dóminus vobíscum.
℟. Et cum spíritu tuo.

Orémus.

Exáudi nos, Dómine sancte, Pater omnípotens, ætérne Deus, et míttere dignéris sanctum Ángelum tuum de cælis, qui custódiat, fóveat, prótegat, vísitet, atque defendat omnes habitántes in hoc habitáculo. Per Christum Dóminum nostrum. ℟. AMEN.

EZECHIEL 47:1 • *From Easter Sunday through Pentecost Sunday inclusive.*

A VISION I HAD of water that flowed from the temple rightward, alleluia; and never a man that water reached but he won deliverance, and therewith cried aloud, Alleluia, alleluia. (Ps 117:1) ℣. Give thanks to the Lord; the Lord is gracious, his mercy endures for ever. ℣. Glory be to the Father, and to the Son, and to the Holy Ghost. As it was in the beginning, is now, and ever shall be, world without end. Amen. *(The antiphon is repeated.)*

Vidi aquam egrediéntem de templo, a látere déxtro, allelúja: Et omnes ad quos pervénit aqua ista, salvi facti sunt, Et dicent: allelúja, allelúja. ℣. Confitémini Dño quóniam bonus: quóniam in sæculum misericórdia ejus. ℣. Glória Patri, et Fílio, et Spirítui Sancto. Sicut erat in princípio, et nunc, et semper, et in sæcula sæculórum. Amen.

1962 • The antiphon is repeated and concluding prayers (see opposite page) are said. But if the Celebrant has already reached the Altar, the following version—which is less lengthy—may be used :

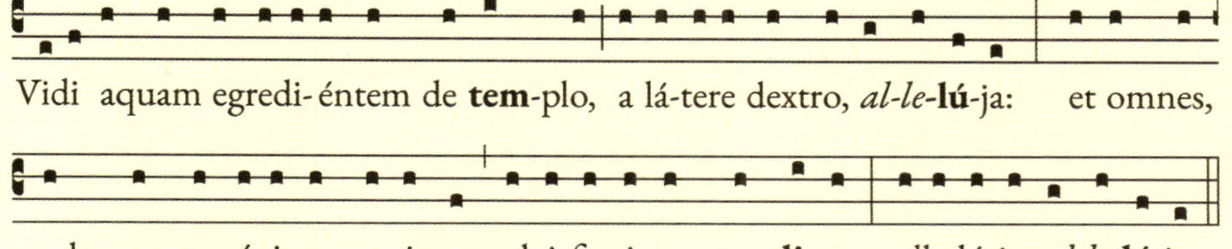

Below is the Vidi Aquam in a manuscript from Soest (Germany) circa 1393AD.
In olden times, the verse was not always Psalm 117; during different sections of Eastertide the verse would change.

IERUSALEM IERUSALEM QUOTIES VOLUI CONGREGARE FILIOS TUOS QUEMADMODUM ... Mt 23:37 ✠ Book of Hours (BELGIUM) circa 1450AD, f.38v

TWO THINGS happen at each Mass: (1) JESUS CHRIST is made present on the Altar; (2) JESUS CHRIST is offered to His Heavenly Father.

A detailed explanation of the Blessed Sacrament by Saint Robert Southwell—an English Jesuit priest martyred in 1595AD—can be found on pages 336-345 of the *Saint Jean de Brébeuf Hymnal* (Sophia Institute Press, 2018); see also the excellent "Introduction to the Mass" (27 pages) in the *Fulton J. Sheen Sunday Missal* (IMPRIMATUR, 4 May 1961). Finally, turn to page 311 of the present volume: viz. the Corpus Christi SEQUENCE by Saint Thomas Aquinas (d. 1274).

Editor's Note: The rubrics provided below are incomplete by design. We shunned overburdening the text, yet attempted to include enough details to allow congregations to follow with ease. On occasion, we provide official rubrics from the 1962 *Missale Romanum*—especially for rubrics which tend to be overlooked or misunderstood. All ministers, servers, and musicians should of course consult the official books.

THE HOLY MASS BEGINS

1962 • The bell is rung as the Celebrant processes to the Altar—except where it is customary to process prior to the sprinkling rite. Organ music or a hymn accompanies this procession; alternately the INTROIT may be sung (especially if it be lengthy). Throughout Solemn Mass, prayers sung by the choir do not necessarily occur at the same moment those same prayers are prayed quietly at the Altar by the Celebrant.

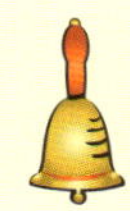

In nómine Patris, ✠ et Fílii, et Spíritus Sancti. Amen.

Normally, the words "Introíbo ad altáre Dei...etc." are said three times: twice as part of an antiphon, and once as verse 4a of Psalm 42 itself. But during Requiem Masses and Passiontide, only the antiphon is said—one time—and Psalm 42 is omitted.

N THE NAME OF THE FATHER, ✠ AND OF THE SON, AND OF THE HOLY GHOST. AMEN.

℣. Introíbo ad altáre Dei.

℣. I will go up to the altar of God.

℟. Ad Deum, qui lætíficat juventútem meam.

℟. To God, the giver of youth and happiness.

℣. Júdica me, Deus, et discérne causã meam de gente non sancta: ab hómine iníquo et dolóso érue me.

℣. O God, sustain my cause; give me redress against a race that knows no piety; save me from a treacherous foe and cruel.

℟. Quia tu es, Deus, fortitudo mea: quare me repulísti, et quare tristis incédo, dum afflígit me inimícus?

℟. Thou, O God, art all my strength, why hast thou cast me out? Why do I go mourning, with enemies pressing me hard?

℣. Emítte lucem tuam et veritátem tuam: ipsa me deduxérunt, et adduxérunt in montem sanctum tuum et in tabernácula tua.

℣. The light of thy presence, the fulfilment of thy promise, let these be my escort, bringing me safe to thy holy mountain, to the tabernacle where thou dwellest.

℟. Et introíbo ad altáre Dei: ad Deum, qui lætíficat juventútem meam.

℟. There I will go up to the altar of God, the giver of youth and happiness.

℣. Confitébor tibi in cíthara, Deus, Deus meus: quare tristis es, ánima mea, et quare contúrbas me?

℣. Thou art my God, with the harp I hymn thy praise. Soul, why art thou downcast, why art thou all lament?

℣. God the almighty, ✠ God the merciful, grant us of all our sins pardon, acquittal and release. ℟. Amen.

Indulgéntiam, ✠ absolutiónem et remissiónẽ peccatórũ nostrórum tríbuat nobis omnípotens et miséricors Dóminus. ℟. Amen.

1962 • They bow slightly when praying the final set of prayers. | *Et inclinatus prosequitur.*

℣. Thou wilt relent, O God, and bring us to life. ℟. And thy people will rejoice in thee.

℣. Deus, tu convérsus vivificábis nos. ℟. Et plebs tua lætábitur in te.

℣. Show us thy mercy, Lord.
℟. And grant us thy salvation.

℣. Osténde nobis, Dómine, misericórdiam tuam. ℟. Et salutáre tuum da nobis.

℣. O Lord, hear my prayer.
℟. And let my cry come unto thee.

℣. Dómine, exáudi oratiónem meam. ℟. Et clamor meus ad te véniat.

℣. The Lord be with you.
℟. And with you, his minister.

℣. Dóminus vobíscum.
℟. Et cum spíritu tuo.

Let us pray.

Orémus.

1962 • Going up to the Altar, the Celebrant prays silently as follows:

RID US OF OUR GUILT, Lord, we pray thee, and give us pure hearts to enter in where all is holiness. Through Christ our Lord. Amen.

Aufer a nobis, quǽsumus, Dómine, iniquitátes nostras: ut ad Sancta sanctórum puris mereámur méntibus introíre. Per Christum Dñm nostrũ. Amen.

1962 • His hands joined, and bowing down over the Altar, the Celebrant says quietly:

ORD, we entreat thee by the merits of thy saints *(kisses the Altar stone)* that are here entombed, and of all thy saints together, pardoned be every fault of mine. Amen.

Orámus te, Dómine, per mérita Sanctórum tuórum, *osculatur altare in medio* quorum relíquiæ hic sunt, et ómnium Sanctórũ: ut indulgére dignéris ómnia peccáta mea. Amen.

1962 • The Altar is censed before the Celebrant reads the INTROIT (unless it be a Requiem Mass, in which case no incense is used until the Offertory). The Deacon first says: *Benedícite, Pater reverénde* ("A blessing, Reverend Father"). Then the Celebrant blesses the incense as follows:

May he bless ✠ thee, in whose honor thou shalt burn. Amen.

Ab illo bene✠dicáris, in cujus honóre cremáberis. Amen.

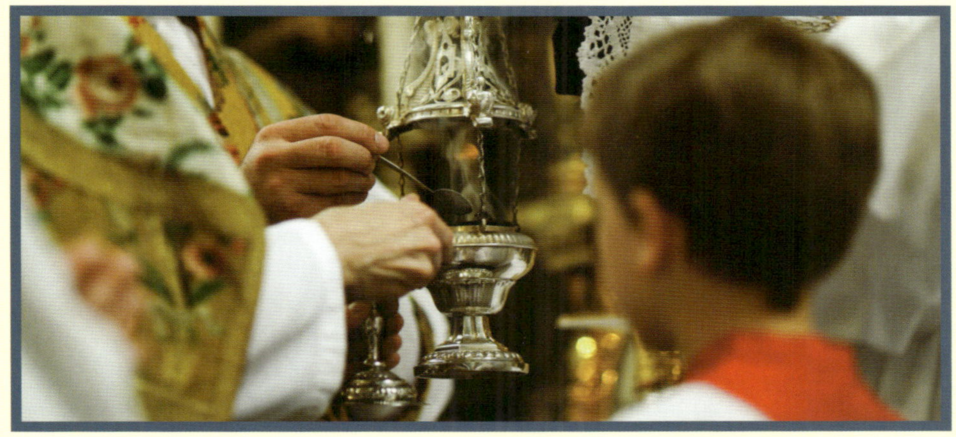

✠ BEFORE THE INTROIT, THE ALTAR IS CENSED

1962 • The Celebrant censes the Altar in silence, and is then censed by the Deacon. Making the sign of the cross—with the ministers standing in a line behind him—he quietly reads the INTROIT.

■ THE INTROIT (PROPER)

NOTE: When you see the "box shape" ■, turn to the *Propria Missae*—i.e. those parts which change depending on the feast being celebrated. Contrariwise, the parts which never change are called the *Ordinarium Missae* ("Mass Ordinary").

SAINT FRANCIS MISSAL • Shown on the right (f. 160v) is an excerpt from an Altar Missal created circa 1177AD. This book is believed to have been touched by Saint Francis of Assisi in the year 1208AD in the *Church of San Nicolò* in Assisi.

Notice how the PRAYERS AT THE BEGINNING OF MASS—starting at **"ante altare"**—require only a small amount of space, because so much was memorized; whereas the prayers on the previous pages (*not shown on the right*) —prayed by the Celebrant as he puts on each vestment—require twice as much space.

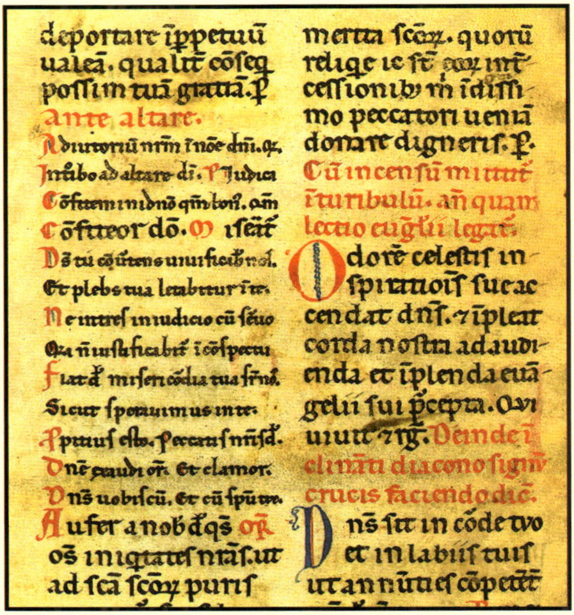

deportare ĩppetuũ
ualeã. qualit̃ cõseq
possim tuã gratiã. P̃
ante altare.
Adiutoriũ nrm̃ ĩ nõe dñi. q̃.
Introibo ad altare di. Judica
Cõfitemini dño qm̃ bon̄. qm̃
Cõfiteor dõ. M isẽat
Ds tu cõuẽtens uiuificab̃ nos.
Et plebs tua letabitur ĩte.
Ne intres in iudicio cũ seruo
Qa n̄ iustificabit̃ ĩ cõspectu
Fiat m̃ misericõdia tua sr̃ns
Sicut sperauimus inte.
Spiritus est. Peccatis nr̃is.
Dn̄e exaudi or̃. Et clamor.
Dn̄s uobiscũ. Et cũ spũ tuo.
Aufer a nob̃ d̃qs or̃
os iniqtates nr̃as. ut
ad scã scõꝝ puris
merita scõꝝ. quorũ
reliq̃e ic st̃ ... int
cessionib; m̃ idigni
mo peccatori uenia
donare digneris. P̃.
Cũ incensũ mittit̃
ĩ turibulũ. añ quam
lectio eũglii legat̃.
Odore celestis in
spirationis suae ac
cendat dn̄s. 7 ĩpleat
corda nostra ad audi-
enda et ĩplenda euã-
gelii sui pcepta. Qui
uiuit 7 rg̃. Deinde i
clinãti diacono signũ
crucis faciendo dic.
Dn̄s sit in cõde tuo
et in labiis tuis
ut annũties cõpetẽt

1962 • After the INTROIT, the Celebrant prays the KYRIE, alternating with the ministers. *Qua finita, junctis manibus, alternatim cum ministris dicit:*

YRIE ELEISON. (3x)

Christe eléison. (3x)

Kýrie eléison. (3x)

℣. Lord, have mercy.
℟. Lord, have mercy.
℣. Lord, have mercy.
℟. Christ, have mercy.
℣. Christ, have mercy.
℟. Christ, have mercy.
℣. Lord, have mercy.
℟. Lord, have mercy.
℣. Lord, have mercy.

PARTICIPATIO ACTUOSA • There is more than one "correct" way to assist at the Holy Mass. Numerous methods are spelled out in *De Musica Sacra* (1958). Pope Pius XII, in MEDIATOR DEI (1947) wrote as follows (§108):

> "Many of the faithful are unable to use the Roman Missal even when it is translated into the vernacular; nor are all capable of understanding correctly the liturgical rites and formulas. So varied and diverse are men's talents and characters that it is impossible for all to be moved and attracted to the same extent by community prayers, hymns, and liturgical services. Moreover, the needs and inclinations of all are not the same, nor are they always constant in the same individual. Who, then, would say—on account of such a prejudice—that all these Christians cannot participate in the Mass, nor share its fruits? On the contrary, ***they can adopt some other method*** which proves easier for certain people; for instance, they can lovingly meditate on the mysteries of Jesus Christ, or perform other exercises of piety, or recite prayers which—though they differ from the sacred rites—are still essentially in harmony with them."

The following is a non-exhaustive list outlining common practices:

SOLEMN MASS • The choir sings everything which is not sung by the Celebrant or sacred ministers; the congregation sings only the responses.

HIGH MASS • The ORDINARIUM MISSAE is sung by the choir in polyphony, while the *Schola Cantorum* sings the PROPRIA MISSAE.

SUNG MASS • The faithful sing the ORDINARIUM while a cantor sings the PROPRIA to simpler melodies (e.g. psalm tones). If a congregation cannot chant everything, "nothing forbids that the more simple of these—such as the *Kýrie*, the *Sanctus*, and the *Agnus Dei*—be chosen for the faithful to chant while the *Glória* and the *Credo* are performed by the choir" (*De Musica Sacra*, 1958, §25b).

DIALOGUE MASS • At a low Mass, the congregation may join in reciting certain parts of the Mass normally reserved to the Altar boy.

LOW MASS WITH HYMNS • In certain localities, it is an immemorial tradition—sanctioned by §14b of *De Musica Sacra* (1958)—to sing hymns in the vernacular while a Low Mass is being offered.

MISSA LECTA • An Altar boy makes all the responses.

*** We have printed the ORDINARIUM MISSAE in such a way that any of the schemata above may be chosen. Moreover, the settings we selected will not strain the average singing voice.**

The Second Vatican Council declared in *Sacrosanctum Concilium* §112: "The musical tradition of the universal Church is a treasure of inestimable value, greater even than that of any other art." Many beautiful plainsong settings of the Ordinarium Missae may be chosen, to say nothing of polyphonic settings by masters such as Giovanni Palestrina (d. 1594), Father Francisco Guerrero (d. 1599), and Father Tomás Luis de Victoria (d. 1611). There are also countless settings which involve the pipe organ.

Kyrie IV

Cunctípotens Génitor Deus

Marvelous Memories • We possess thousands of mediæval manuscripts, and each is approximately 900 pages long. These books contain thousands of intricate pieces of plainsong—and each of them was committed to memory! Saint Isidore of Seville (d. 636AD) wrote: "Unless sounds are held by the memory of man, they perish—for they cannot be written down." Catholic monks eventually figured out a way to ***notate*** ("write down") music, but it required half a millennium. The mediæval manuscripts from approximately 750AD to 1050AD make no sense unless one already knows each melody by heart. It is similar to discovering 200,000 mnemonic devices, which are worthless unless one knows what they stand for. However, an organist named Félix Danjou (d. 1866) discovered the famous "bi-lingual" manuscript—known as Montpellier H. 159—and this "Rosetta Stone" allowed scholars to pierce a hitherto impenetrable world of marvelous Gregorian chant melodies.

Kyrie Tropes • A "melisma" is a syllable upon which one sings many notes. Mediæval choristers had trouble memorizing *melismata* (just as Catholic musicians alive today have trouble). So our ancestors in the faith began to "trope" the Kyrie melodies—that means they wrote poetry for the long *melismata*. After the Council of Trent, tropes were abandoned; but we still call each Gregorian Mass according to the ancient Kyrie trope. That is why the Kyrie shown above (from Mass IV) is known as "Cunctípotens Génitor."

An Example • **Adiastematic notation** is only useful to singers who already know the melody by heart, but **diastematic notation** conveys exact pitches, for those who wish to learn the melody. **Heightened neumes** were an important development—halfway between *adiastematic* and *diastematic*—because the vertical space gave a rough idea of pitch relationships. The example on the right (*heightened neumes*) shows how Kyrie IV "troped" looked around the year 1034AD :

Cunctípotens Génitor Deus omni Creátor, eléison.
All-powerful Begetter, God, Creator to all, have mercy.

Salvíficet píetas tua nos bone rector, eléison.
May thy graciousness bring us to salvation, good Governor, have mercy.

Fons et orígo boni pie luxque perénnis, eléison.
Gracious spring and source of good, and never-failing light, have mercy.

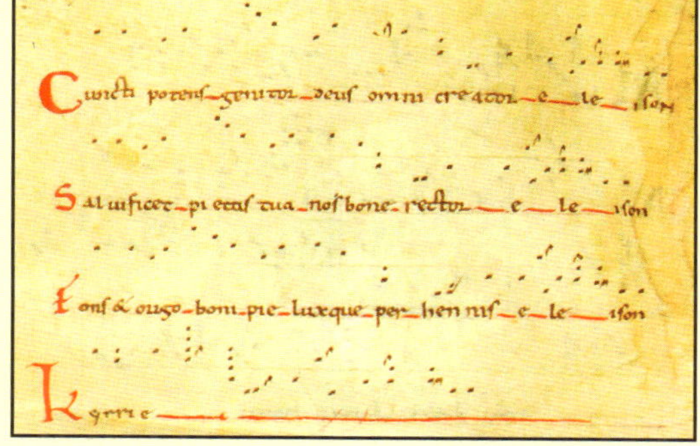

Cantatorium|1034; folio 6v

1962 • After the KYRIE—if it be a day when the GLORIA is said—the Celebrant intones, during which he elevates and joins his hands in a circular motion, bowing his head at the word "Deo." The choir then continues, starting at "Et in terra pax…" The men alternate with the women, switching at each double bar. The GLORIA may be sung in polyphony or with some other setting—including contemporary settings. The following comes from Mass III (*Editio Vaticana*).

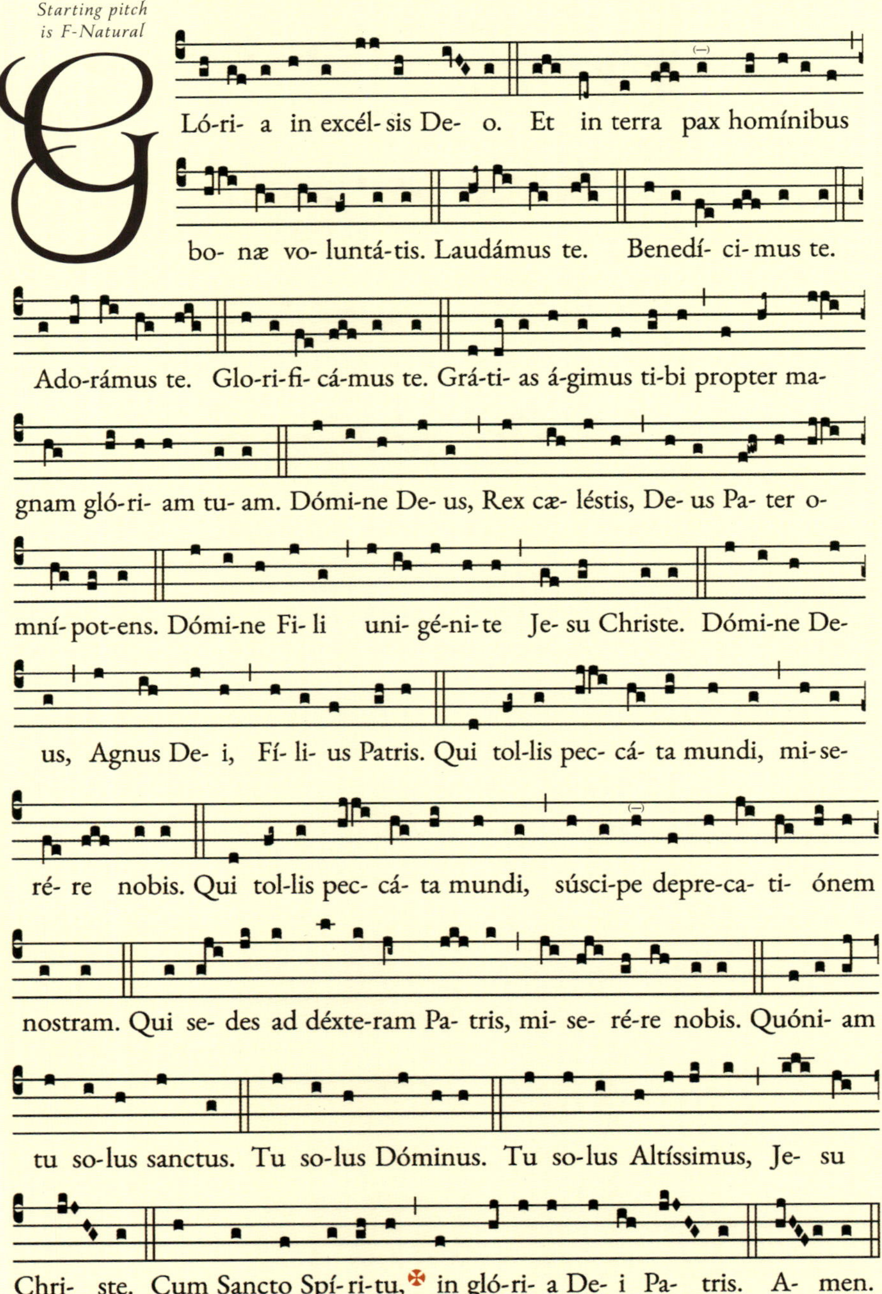

✠ THE CELEBRANT STANDS AT THE CENTER FOR THE GLORIA

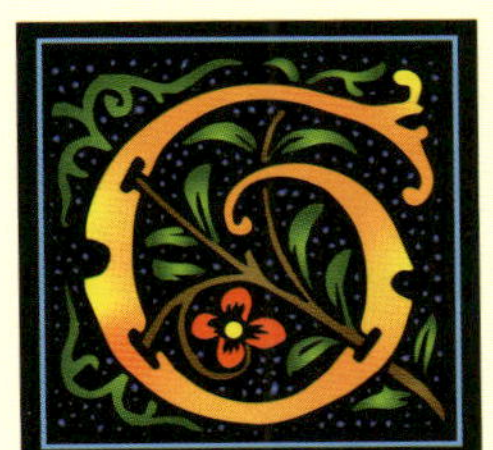

LORY TO GOD IN HIGH HEAVEN, and peace on earth to men that are God's friends. We praise thee, we bless thee, we adore thee, we extol thee, we give thee thanks, such great glory is thine, Lord God, King of heaven, God the Father almighty. O Lord, the only-begotten Son, Jesus Christ, Lord God, Lamb of God, Son of the Father, thou that takest away the sins of the world, have mercy on us. Thou that takest away the sins of the world, to our prayer give welcome. Enthroned at the Father's right hand, have mercy on us. Thou alone art holy, thou alone art Lord, thou alone, Jesus Christ, art raised on high, to share with the ✠ Holy Spirit in the glory of God the Father. Amen.

THE GLORIOUS GLORIA • Some of the greatest masterpieces have been GLORIA settings: by Machaut, Josquin, Lassus, Bach, Mozart, and other masters. Palestrina, for example, took a hymn called *Jam Christus Astra Ascenderat* and combined its tune contrapuntally (in different voice parts) in a staggeringly brilliant way—and Palestrina wrote more than a hundred Mass settings! Composers transformed the CANTUS FIRMUS using different techniques: *Canon, Stretto, Augmentation, Diminution, Ostinato, Inversion*, and so forth. Costanzo Festa (d. 1545) even used retrograde counterpoint. The greatest composers of all—e.g. Morales, Guerrero, and Victoria—were all Catholic priests. On the right is shown the Soprano voice from MISSA AVE MARIS STELLA by Father Cristóbal de Morales (d. 1553). It starts with "Et in terra pax" (since the first four words of the GLORIA are always sung by the Celebrant) and uses the *Ave Maris Stella* tune:

1962 • Having kissed the center of the Altar, the Celebrant faces the people and says:

℣. The Lord be with you.

℟. And with you, his minister.

℣. Dóminus vobíscum.

℟. Et cum spíritu tuo.

1962 • The Celebrant then sings the Collect at the Epistle side of the Altar.

■ COLLECT

1962 • The Subdeacon chants the Epistle and then receives a blessing from the Celebrant.

■ EPISTLE

The response after the Epistle is Deo grátias ("Thanks be to God").

1962 • Then comes the GRADUAL, which refers to everything that was—long ago—sung from the Altar step (*gradus*). That may include the *Gradual Chant*, the *Tract*, the *Alleluia Verse*, and/or the *Sequence*.

■ GRADUAL

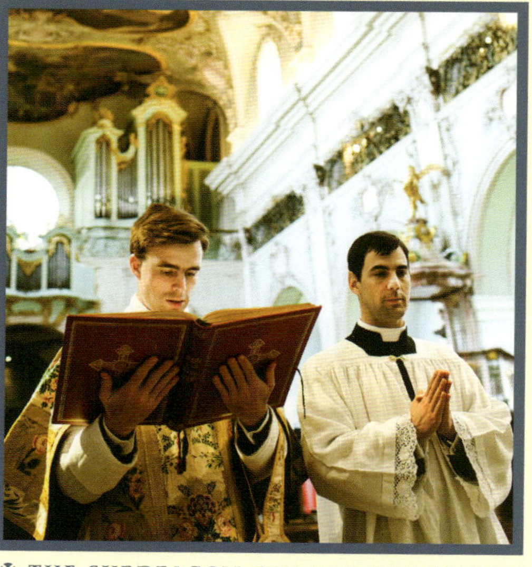

✠ THE SUBDEACON CHANTS THE EPISTLE

1962 • The Deacon places the book of the Gospels ("Evangeliarium") on the middle of the Altar. The Deacon first says: *Benedícite, Pater reverénde* ("A blessing, Reverend Father"). Then the Celebrant blesses the incense as follows.

May he bless ✠ thee, in whose honor thou shalt burn. Amen.

Ab illo bene ✠ dicáris, in cujus honóre cremáberis. Amen.

1962 • Kneeling, the Deacon prays as follows:

CLEANSE THE HEART and lips of me, God almighty, as once thou didst cleanse the lips of the prophet Isaias with a burning coal. So clean a thing let thy loving mercy make of me, that I bring no shame on thy holy gospel by preaching it. Through Christ our Lord. Amen.

Munda cor meum, ac lábia mea, omnípotens Deus, qui lábia Isaíæ Prophétæ cálculo mundásti ignito: ita me tua grata miseratióne dignáre mundáre, ut sanctum Evangéliũ tuũ digne váleam nuntiáre. Per Christum Dñm nostrum. Amen.

✠ THE DEACON RECEIVES A BLESSING FROM THE CELEBRANT

1962 • The Deacon now takes the EVANGELIARIUM and kneels before the Celebrant, receiving a blessing from him :

Jube, Domne, benedícere.	Pray you, Sir, ask God's blessing.

1962 • The Celebrant prays with the following words :

Dóminus sit in corde tuo et in lábiis tuis: ut digne et competénter annúnties Evangéliũ suum: In nómine Patris, ✠ et Fílii, et Spíritus Sancti. Amen.	 **HE LORD** there in your heart, the Lord there on your lips, to make you proclaim his holy gospel well and worthily. In the name of the Father, and of the Son, ✠ and of the Holy Ghost. Amen.

1962 • The Deacon goes in procession—with candles and incense—to the place where the Gospel is to be sung, and then chants:

℣. Dóminus vobíscum.	℣. The Lord be with you.
℟. Et cum spíritu tuo.	℟. And with you, his minister.
℣. Sequéntia sancti Evangélii secúndum N.	℣. A passage from the holy Gospel according to N.
℟. Glória tibi, Dómine.	℟. Glory to thee, Lord.

THE DEACON CENSES THE EVANGELIARIUM BEFORE THE GOSPEL ✠

■ THE GOSPEL (PROPER)

THE GOSPEL READING • The Deacon incenses the EVANGELIARIUM before chanting the Gospel, and he does so using a *lingua sacra* ("sacred language"), not the vernacular. Our Blessed Savior—the SECOND PERSON OF THE DIVINE TRINITY—did not worship in the vernacular, nor did He conduct the Last Supper in the vernacular. Father Louis Bouyer reminds us that Hebrew (the *lingua sacra* our Redeemer used during Temple services and for the Last Supper) was a dead language at that time, just as Latin is dead language in our times. Saint Francis of Assisi never became a priest, but he became a deacon because he desperately wanted to proclaim the Gospel during Mass (using a *lingua sacra*)—and only deacons are allowed this privilege. Father Fortescue has written: "Down to the 7th century silence was commanded before the Gospel. Everyone stood bareheaded, with the attitude of a servant receiving his master's orders. This is described in nearly all early accounts. The Gospel book was at first taken to all present to be kissed, but now only the celebrant and any high prelates present kiss it."

1962 • After the Gospel, the ministers reply: *Laus tibi, Christe* ("Praise be to Thee, O Christ"). The Subdeacon carries the EVANGELIARIUM to the Celebrant, who kisses it and says:

MAY OUR SINS be blotted out by the words of the Gospel.	Per evangélica dicta deleántur nostra delícta.

If there be a homily, it occurs now.

THE PRIEST WHO PREACHES to his people after the Gospel on Sunday morning follows the example of his predecessors in all ages back to the Apostles, and performs what is really an element of the liturgy itself—especially if his sermon explains the lessons, if he "exhorts them to follow these glorious examples." — *Father Adrian Fortescue, 1914.*

THE CELEBRANT PRAYS THE CREED AT THE CENTER OF THE ALTAR ✠

1962 • On days when the Creed is said, the Celebrant intones the first four words, making a circular motion with his hands and bowing at the word "Deum." Older manuscripts often contain *Credimus in unum Deum* ("We believe...etc.") but this plural version began to fade away during the 13th century.

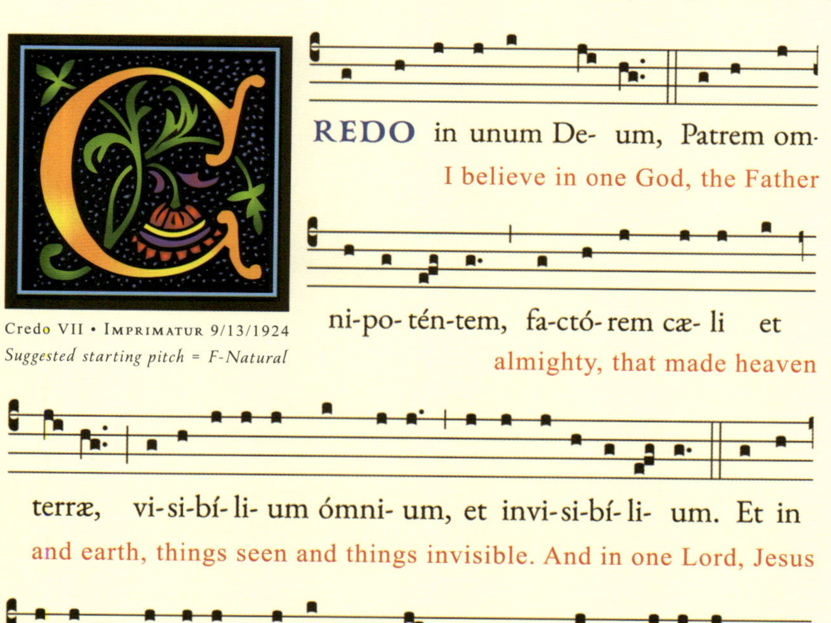

Credo VII • IMPRIMATUR 9/13/1924
Suggested starting pitch = F-Natural

unum Dóminum Je-sum Chris-tum, Fí- li- um De- i uni-gé-

Christ, the only-begotten Son of God, by the Father engendered before

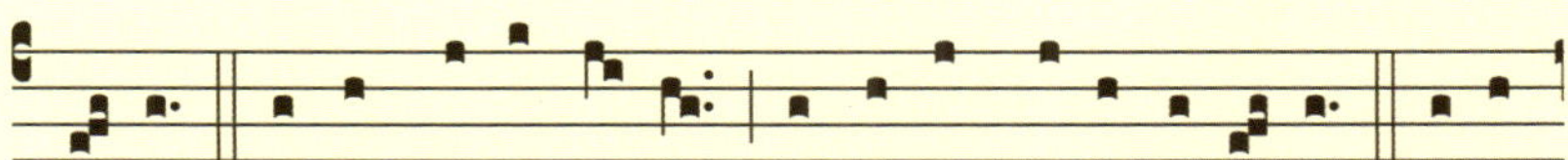

ni- tum. Et ex Patre na- tum ante ómni- a sǽcu- la. De- um

time began; God sprung from God, Light

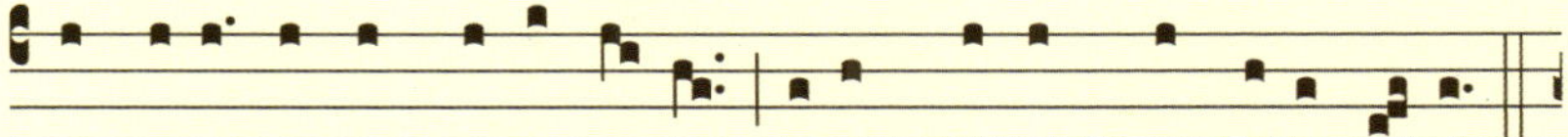

de De- o, lumen de lúmi-ne, De- um ve-rum de De- o ve- ro.

sprung from Light, true God as from true God he came.

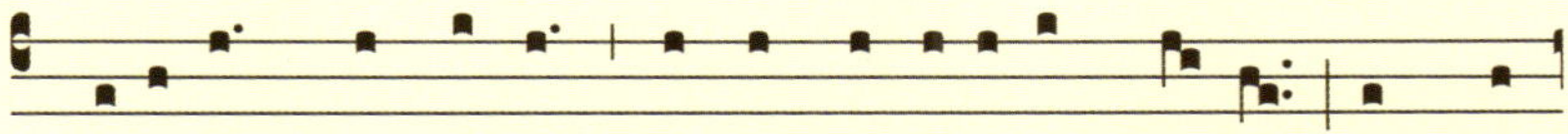

Géni-tum, non factum, consubstanti- á-lem Pa-tri: per quem

Begotten is he, not created, one in substance with the Father

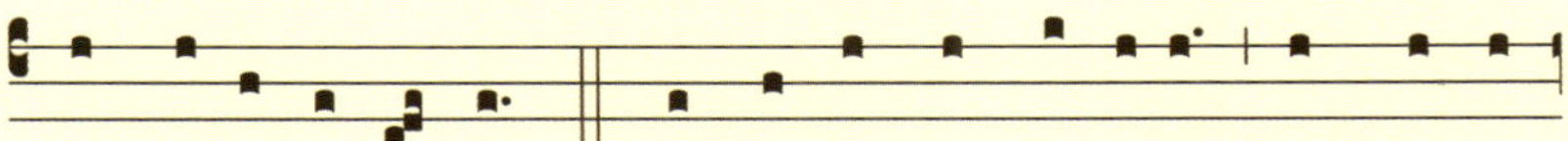

ómni- a facta sunt. Qui propter nos hómines et propter

who created all. Who for love of us men, because he would bring

nostram sa-lú-tem descéndit de cæ- lis. [Et incarná-tus est de

us salvation, came down from heaven, * *Here all genuflect.* by the power of the

Spí-ri- tu Sancto ex Ma-rí- a Vírgi-ne: Et homo factus est.]

Holy Ghost took flesh of the Virgin Mary, and became Man.

Cru-ci- fí-xus ét- i- am pro nobis: sub Pónti- o Pi- lá- to

For love of us, at the bidding of Pontius Pilate he was nailed to a cross,

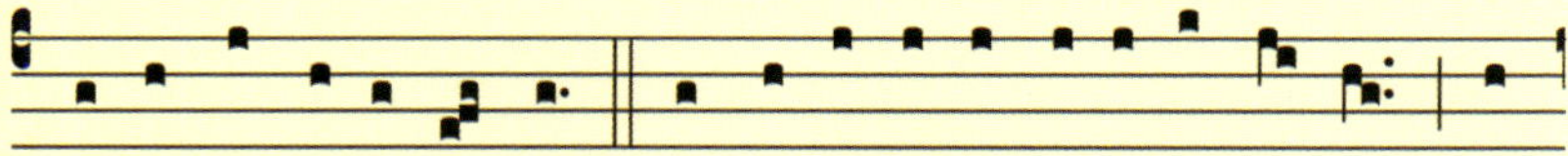

passus, et sepúltus est. Et re-surré-xit térti- a di- e, se-

suffered death & was buried. Then, on the third day—as the scriptures had

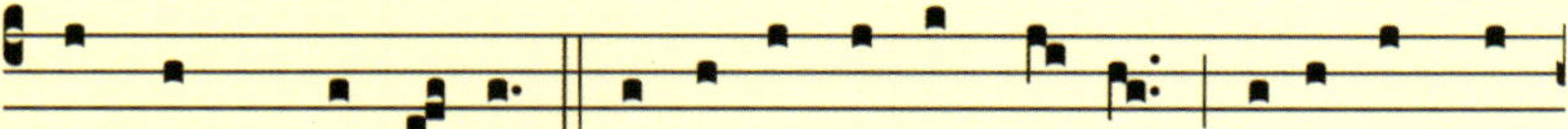

cúndum Scriptú- ras. Et ascéndit in cæ- lum: sedet ad déx-

foretold—he rose from the dead & went up into heaven, where evermore

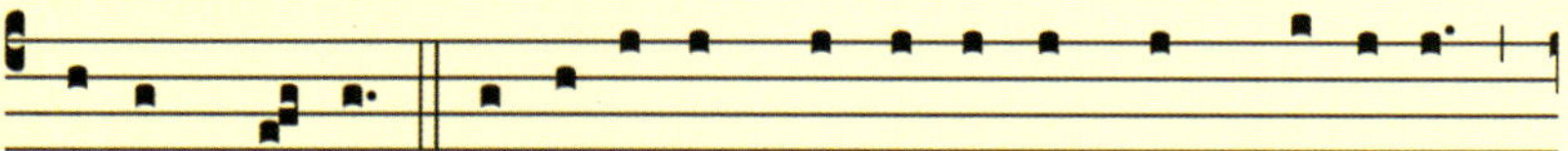

te-ram Pa-tris. Et í-te-rum ventú-rus est cum gló-ri- a,

he sits at the Father's right hand. Thence he shall come again, revealed in

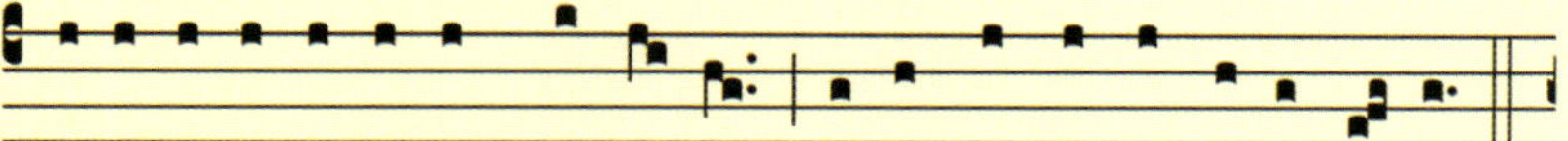

judi-cá-re vi-vos et mórtu- os: cu-jus regni non e-rit fi- nis.

glory, to judge the living and the dead, and of his reigning there shall

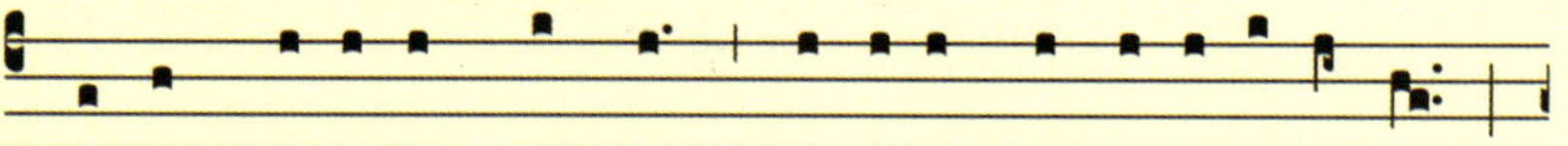

Et in Spí- ri-tum Sanctum, Dóminum, et vi-vi- fi-cántem:

be no end. And in the Holy Ghost, the Lord that gives us life,

qui ex Patre Fi- li- óque pro-cé- dit. Qui cum Patre et Fí- li-

from Father and Son alike proceeding, with Father and Son

o simul ado-rá-tur, et conglo-ri- fi-cá- tur: qui locú-tus est

alike worshipped and glorified, the same that uttered his word

✠ THE DEACON PREPARES THE ALTAR DURING THE CREED

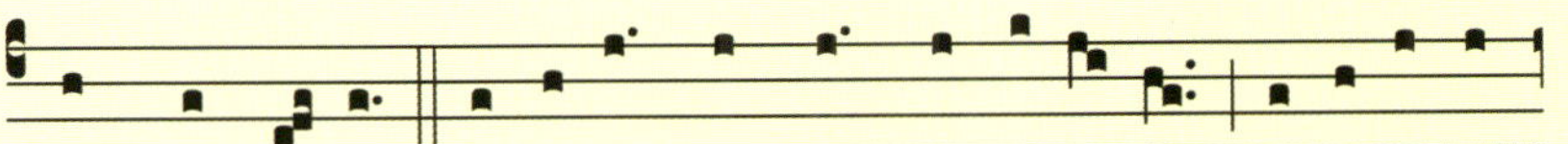

per Prophé- tas. Et unam sanctam cathó-li- cam et apostó-

through the prophets. I believe in one Church, holy, Catholic, and

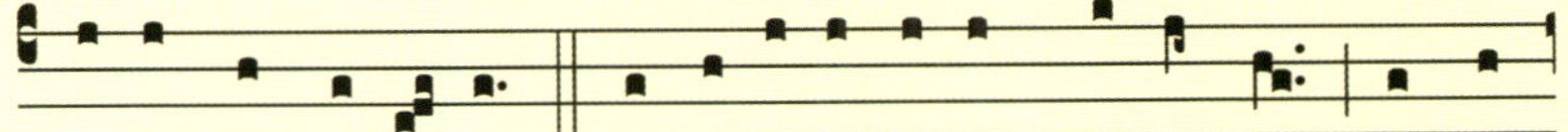

li-cam Ecclé-si- am. Confí-te- or unum baptísma in re-

apostolic; I own but one baptism that avails for the

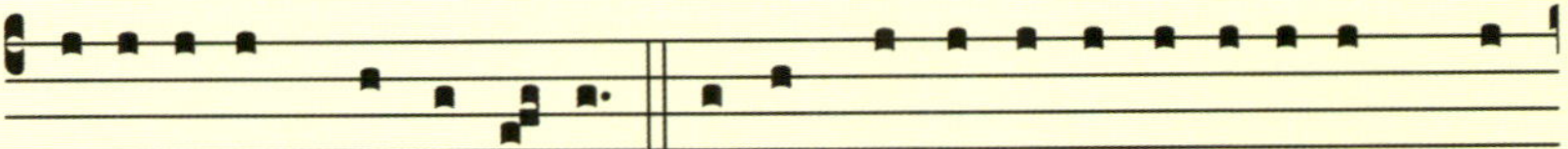

missi- ónem pecca-tó-rum. Et exspécto re-surrecti- ónem mor-

remission of sins; and I hope for the resurrection of the dead,

tu- ó- rum. Et vi- tam ✠ ventú-ri sǽcu- li. A- men.

and the life ✠ that shall be in the world hereafter. Amen.

OFFERING THE BREAD THAT IS TO BE CONSECRATED ✠

1962 • Having kissed the center of the Altar, the Celebrant turns toward the people and sings:

℣. The Lord be with you.
℟. And with you, his minister.
Let us pray.

℣. Dóminus vobíscum.
℟. Et cum spíritu tuo.
Orémus.

THE OFFERTORY ANTIPHON (PROPER)

1962 • The Celebrant takes the paten and offers the bread that will be consecrated:

OLY FATHER, almighty eternal God, here is a victim without spot for thy acceptance; and here is an unworthy slave of thine that dares offer it to thee, who art the true God, the living God. For all my sins I offer it, that are past numbering, for every wrong done, and for every slip of negligence; for all that stand about me here, and for all faithful Christians, living and dead. Salve* let it be for their souls and mine, to bring us eternal life. Amen. ✠

Súscipe, sancte Pater, omnípotens ætérne Deus, hanc immaculátam hóstiam, quam ego indígnus fámulus tuus óffero tibi Deo meo vivo et vero, pro innumerabílibus peccátis, et offensiónibus, et neglegéntiis meis, et pro ómnibus circumstántibus, sed et pro ómnibus fidélibus christiánis vivis atque defúnctis: ut mihi, et illis profíciat ad salútem in vitam ætérnam. Amen. ✠

* *Salve*: "that which soothes, consoles or heals."

1962 • He makes the sign of the cross with the paten over the corporal.

1962 • The Deacon pours wine into the chalice. The Celebrant makes the sign of the cross over the water—unless it be a Requiem Mass—and the Subdeacon pours a few drops of water :

Deus, ✠ qui humánæ substántiæ dignitátẽ mirabíliter condidísti, et mirabílius reformásti: da nobis per hujus aquæ et vini mystérium, ejus divinitátis esse consórtes, qui humanitátis nostræ fíeri dignátus est párticeps, Jesus Christus, Fílius tuus, Dñs noster: Qui tecũ vivit et regnat in unitáte Spíritus Sñcti Deus: per ómnia sǽcula sæculórũ. Amen.

ONDERFULLY, ✠ O God, thou didst go to work in creating the excellent nature of man, and yet more wonderfully in refashioning it. May this water and wine effect what they signify; of his Godhead partake we, who deigned to share our manhood, Jesus Christ, thy Son our Lord, who with thee in the bond of the Holy Spirit lives and reigns and is God, world without end. Amen.

"Deus qui humánæ" • *Salzburg Missal* (1494AD), courtesy of Father Brian Austin, FSSP

fiat Dum miscet aquā cū vio
Deus qui humane substācie
dignitatē et mirabiliter con
didisti et mirabilius reformas
ti da nobis per huius aque et
vini cōmixtionē Hic fundat
aquā in calicē eius divinitatis
esse cōsortes qui humanitatis
nostre fieri dignatus est par
ticeps ihesus xpristus filius t
Hic faciat crucē super calicē
accipiens et stet in medio al
taris calicē manibus tenendo
Offerimus tibi dn̄e ca dicat

THE CELEBRANT OFFERS THE CHALICE THAT IS TO BE CONSECRATED ✠

1962 • The following prayer—in its entirety—is recited by the Celebrant with his eyes lifted toward the Altar Cross, holding the chalice:

HY PITY, LORD, invoking, this cup we offer, that is the pledge of our deliverance. May the fragrance of it find a welcome in thy royal presence, for us and for all mankind winning salvation. Amen. ✠

Offérimus tibi, Dómine, cálicem salutáris, tuã deprecántes cleméntiam: ut in conspéctu divínæ majestátis tuæ, pro nostra et totíus mundi salúte, cum odóre suavitátis ascéndat. Amen. ✠

He makes the sign of the cross with the chalice. He then bows slightly, but only during the following prayer:

LORD, WITH BOWED HEAD * and contrite heart we claim thy audience; such be the offering we make today as shall win thy favor. Lord God.

See note on opposite page.

In spíritu humilitátis et in ánimo contríto suscipiámur a te, Dñe: et sic fiat sacrifícium nostrum in conspéctu tuo hódie, ut pláceat tibi, Dómine Deus.

SANCTIFYING SPIRIT, almighty and everlasting God, come down and bless ✠ this sacrifice we make ready in thy divine honor.

Veni, sanctificátor omnípotens ætérne Deus: *(benedicit oblata, prosequendo)* et béne ✠ dic hoc sacrifíciũ, tuo sancto nómini præparátum.

1962 • The Offertory Incensation now occurs. The Deacon first says: *Benedícite, Pater reverénde* ("A blessing, Reverend Father"). Then the Celebrant blesses the incense:

Per intercessiónẽ beáti Michaélis Archángeli, stantis a dextris altáris incénsi, et ómnium electórum suórum, incénsum istud dignétur Dñs bene✠dícere, et in odórem suavitátis accípere. Per Christum Dóminum nostrum. Amen.

AY THE BLESSÈD archangel Michael, where he stands at the altar's right hand to burn incense, plead for us now; may all the saints plead for us, praying the Lord to bless ✠ this incense, and make it the fragrant offering he would have it be. Through Christ our Lord. Amen.

The following prayer is said as the Celebrant censes the OBLATA (the bread and wine):

Incénsum istud a te benedíctum, ascéndat ad te, Dómine: et descéndat super nos misericórdia tua.

BY THEE BLESSED, to thee, Lord, let our incense rise, and bring down upon us the rain of thy mercy.

* The Subdeacon receives (from the Deacon) the paten and covers it with the Humeral Veil worn over his shoulders. He will hold the paten before his eyes until the Lord's Prayer.

THE SUBDEACON IS CENSED BY THE DEACON ✠

1962 • While censing the Crucifix, relics, and Altar, the Celebrant prays two verses from Psalm 140:

WELCOME AS INCENSE-smoke let my prayer rise up before thee, Lord; when I lift my hands, be it as acceptable as the evening sacrifice. Lord, set a guard on my mouth, a barrier to fence in my lips, lest my heart turn to thoughts of evil, to cover sin with smooth names. *Returning the thurible to the Deacon, the Celebrant prays:* Flame of his love may the Lord kindle in our hearts; may charity burn there undying. Amen.

Dirigátur, Dómine, orátio mea, sicut incénsum, in conspéctu tuo: elevátio mánuũ meárum sacrifícium vespertínũ. Pone, Dómine, custódiam ori meo, et óstium circumstántiæ lábiis meis: ut non declínet cor meum in verba malítiæ, ad excusándas excusatiónes in peccátis. *Dum reddit thuribulum diacono, dicit:* Accéndat in nobis Dñs ignẽ sui amóris, et flámmam ætérnæ caritátis. Amen.

Celebrant, clergy, and congregation are then censed.

1962 • While washing his hands, the Celebrant prays seven verses from Psalm 25. Saint Thomas Aquinas says of this: "We are not wont to handle precious objects except the hands be washed."

(6) **Lavábo** inter innocéntes manus meas: et circúmdabo altáre tuum, Dñe. (7) Ut áudiã vocem laudis, et enárrem univérsa mirabília tua. (8) Dñe, diléxi decórem domus tuæ et locũ habitatiónis glóriæ tuæ. (9) Ne perdas cum ímpiis, Deus, ánimam meam: et cum viris sánguinũ vitã meã. (10) In quorum mánibus iniquitátes sunt: déxtera eórum repléta est munéribus. (11) Ego autem in innocéntia mea ingréssus sum: rédime me et miserére mei. (12) Pes meus stetit in dirécto: in ecclésiis benedícã te, Dñe. Glória Patri, et Fílio, et Spirítui Sancto. Sicut erat in princípio, et nunc, et semper, et in sǽcula saeculórum. Amen. *Passiontide: omit "Gloria Patri."*

SALM XXV

With the pure in heart I will wash my hands clean, and take my place among them at thy altar. (7) Lord, listening there to the sound of thy praises, telling the story of all thy wonderful deeds. (8) How well, Lord, I love thy house in its beauty, the place where thy own glory dwells! (9) Lord, never count this soul for lost with the wicked, this life among the bloodthirsty: (10) hands ever stained with guilt, palms ever itching for a bribe!

(11) Be it mine to guide my steps clear of wrong; deliver me in thy mercy. (12) My feet are set on firm ground; where thy people gather, Lord, I will join in blessing thy name. Glory be to the Father, and to the Son, and to the Holy Ghost. As it was in the beginning, is now, and ever shall be, world without end. Amen.

✠ "LAVABO INTER INNOCENTES MANUS MEAS..."

BOWING SLIGHTLY, THE PRIEST SAYS: "SUSCIPE, SANCTA TRINITAS" ✠

1962 • Bowing slightly, with joined hands on the center of the Altar, the Celebrant continues.
Deinde, aliquantulum inclinatus in medio altaris, junctis manibus super eo, dicit:

HIS OFFERING WE make thee, O holy Trinity, do thou graciously receive. For an abiding token we offer it of our Lord Jesus Christ's passion, resurrection and ascension; in honor, too, of blessèd Mary that is ever a virgin, of blessèd John the Baptist, of the holy apostles Peter and Paul, and of all the saints with them. Honor of theirs and health of ours be the fruit of it; our bedesmen* they in heaven, as we on earth perpetuate their memory. Through the same Christ our Lord. Amen.

Súscipe, sancta Trínitas, hanc oblatiónẽ, quã tibi offérimus ob memóriã passiónis, resurrectiónis, et ascensiónis Jesu Christi, Dómini nostri: et in honórem beátæ Maríæ semper Vírginis, et beáti Joannis Baptistæ, et sanctórum Apostolórum Petri et Pauli, et istórum et ómnium Sanctórum: ut illis profíciat ad honórem, nobis autem ad salútem: et illi pro nobis intercédere dignéntur in cælis, quorum memóriam ágimus in terris. Per eúmdem Christum, Dñm nostrum. Amen.

1962 • Having kissed the Altar, the Celebrant turns toward the people as he says the first two words aloud ("Oráte fratres") extending and then joining his hands—then he faces the Altar.
Postea osculatur altare; et versus ad populum extendens, et jungens manus, voce paululum elevata, elicit:

* Bedesman: a person who prays for another's soul.

Oráte, fratres: ut meum ac vestrum sacrifícium acceptábile fiat apud Deum Patrem omnipoténtem.

PRAY, BRETHREN, that this sacrifice, mine and yours, may find acceptance with God the almighty Father.

1962 • The response is made by the ministers, servers, or all present:

℟. Suscípiat Dóminus sacrifícium de mánibus tuis, ad laudem et glóriam nominis sui, ad utilitátem quoque nostram, totiúsque Ecclésiæ suæ sanctæ. *Sacerdos submissa voce dicit: "Amen."*

℟. May the Lord accept from thy hands this sacrifice; honored be his name and glorified, and we and all his holy Church advantaged. *The Celebrant quietly says "Amen."*

Dark Eyes Missal, circa 1477AD (f.110v)

Greiffenklau Missal, c. 1428AD (f.146v)

FRATRES ET SORORES:

Ancient missals often use the words ***fratres et sorores***—"brothers and sisters"—as is shown by the examples (above and on the left side of the page). However, "fratres" alone is sufficient; it refers to all present.

Missale ad usum ecclesiae Parisiensis cum notis, circa 1415AD (f.121)

St. Francis Missal, circa 1208AD (f.162r)

"IS THERE SUCH A THING AS THE PRIESTHOOD OF THE PEOPLE?"

When Fulton J. Sheen was asked this question, he quoted Pope Pius XI: "Participation in this priesthood and in the office of satisfying and sacrificing, is enjoyed **not only** by those whom our Pontiff, Jesus Christ, employs as ministers to offer up the clean oblation to God's Name in every place from the rising to the setting of the sun; but **the whole Christian people**—rightly called by the Prince of the Apostles, *a chosen generation, a kingly priesthood*—offer sacrifice for sins, both for themselves and for the whole human race." Pope Pius XII wrote: "it must be said that the faithful do also offer the Divine Victim, though in a different way."

1962 • Then, with hands extended, the Celebrant prays the SECRETA ("Secret"). The concluding words—"Per ómnia sǽcula sæculórum"—are said in an audible voice :

THE SECRET ORATION (PROPER)

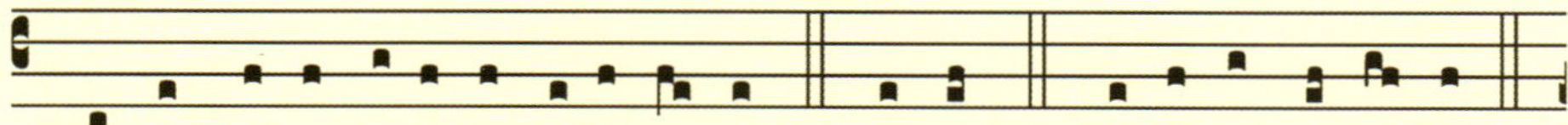

℣. Per ómni- a sǽcu- la sæcu- ló- rum. ℟. Amen. ℣. Dómi-nus vo-bí- scum.
℣. World without end. ℟. Amen. ℣. The Lord be with you.

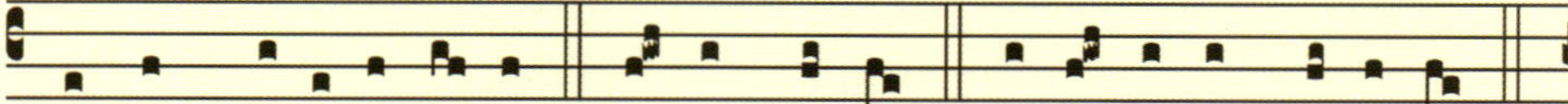

℟. Et cum spí- ri- tu tu- o. ℣. Sur-sum corda. ℟. Ha-bé-mus ad Dómi-num.
℟. And with you, his minister. ℣. Lift up your hearts! ℟. We hold them out to the Lord.

℣. Grá- ti- as a-gámus Dómi-no, De- o nostro. ℟. Dignum et justum est.
℣. Give we thanks to the Lord our God. ℟. Right it is and seemly.

THE PREFACE (PROPER)

1962 • The following Preface ("of the Most Holy Trinity") is used on all Sundays, except during particular seasons and feasts that have a proper Preface. It is printed here for convenience :

ORTHY AND RIGHT IT IS IN TRUTH, apt it is and saving, that at all times and places we should thank thee: O holy Lord, Father almighty, eternal God; who, together with thine only-begotten Son and the Holy Ghost, art one God, one Lord, not in the singleness of one Person, but in the Trinity of one substance. For that which, according to thy revelation, we believe of thy glory, the same we believe of thy Son, the same of the Holy Ghost, without difference or distinction; so that in the confession of one true and eternal Godhead we adore distinctness in persons, oneness in essence, and equality in majesty: Which the angels praise, and the archangels, the cherubim also and the seraphim, who cease not, day by day crying out with one voice, to repeat:

VD ET JUSTUM EST, æquum et salutáre, nos tibi semper et ubíque grátias ágere: Dñe sancte, Pater omnípotens ætérne Deus: Qui cum unigénito Fílio tuo et Spíritu Sancto unus es Deus, unus es Dñs: Non in uníus singularitáte persónæ, sed in uníus Trinitáte substántiæ: Quod enim de tua glória, revelánte te, crédimus, hoc de Fílio tuo, hoc de Spíritu Sñcto, sine differéntia discretiónis sentímus: Ut in confessióne veræ sempiternǽque Deitátis, et in persónis propríetas, et in esséntia únitas, et in majestáte adorétus æquálitas: Quam laudant Ángeli atque Archángeli, Chérubim quoque ac Séraphim, qui non cessant clamáre quotídie, una voce dicéntes:

* *Translation given here is by Fr. Lasance.*

1962 • Then the bell is rung. The Celebrant makes the sign of the cross at the words "Benedíctus qui venit" and does not wait for the choir to finish the Sanctus before starting the Canon.

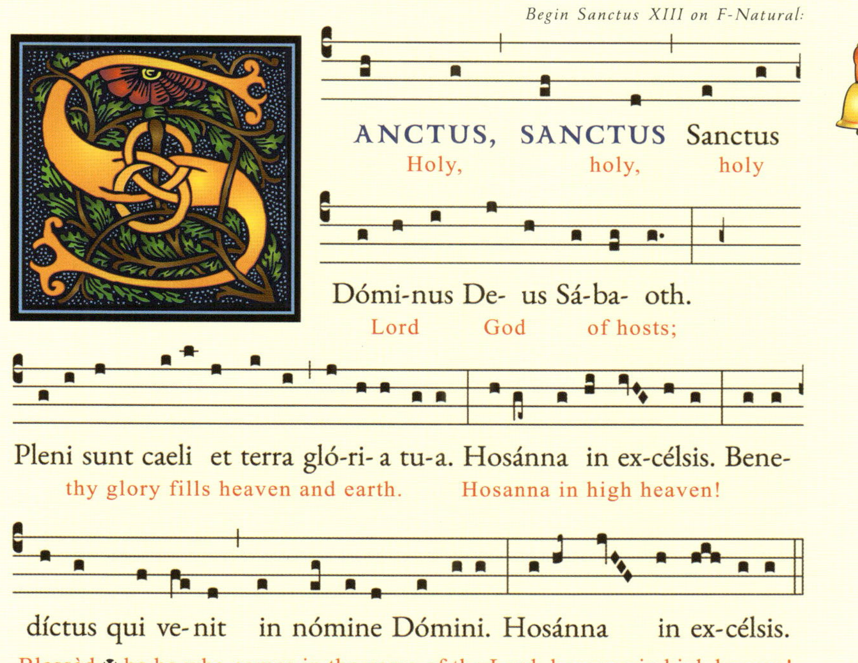

Tonus Ferialis

This version may also be chosen. — Referred to as the "ferial tone," it is often chosen at Masses for the dead.

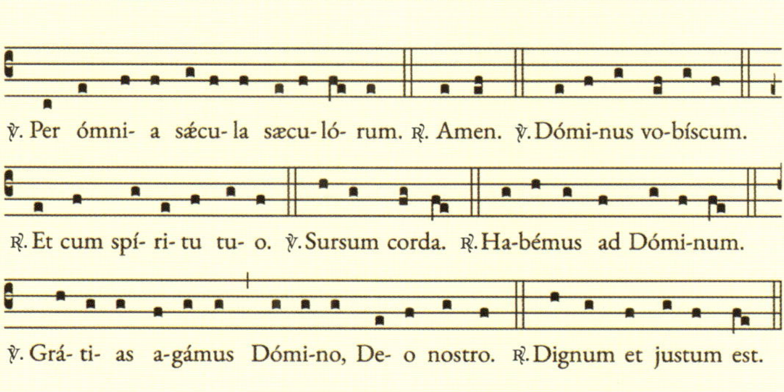

Tonus Solemnior

This version may also be chosen. — It is an even more solemn tone, from the Middle Ages. It is often chosen for high feasts.

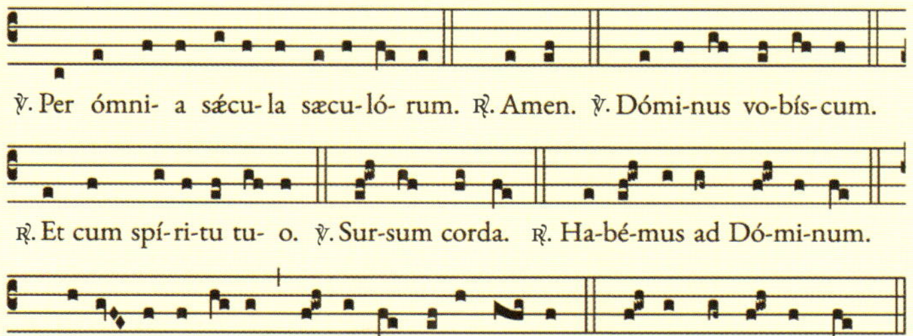

Greiffenklau Missal (NETHERLANDS) circa 1428AD, f.152v

PATER, DIMICTE ILLIS QUIA NESCIUNT QUID FACIUNT.

"Father, forgive them; they know not what they do." — *Luke 23:34*

Canon of the Mass

1962 • The Celebrant first joins his hands, separates, elevates, and rejoins them—in a circular motion—as he lifts his eyes to the Cross, then bows profoundly with joined hands resting on the Altar edge. This entire gesture is made in silence. Only once he is bowed down does he continue:

Te ígitur, clementíssime Pater, per Jesũ Christũ Fílium tuũ Dñm nostrum súpplices rogámus ac pétimus uti accépta hábeas, et benedícas, hæc ✠ dona, hæc ✠ múnera, hæc ✠ sancta sacrifícia illibáta: in primis quæ tibi offérimus pro Ecclésia tua sancta cathólica: quã pacificáre, custodíre, adunáre, et régere dignéris toto orbe terrárum, una cum famulo tuo Papa nostro N. et Antístite nostro N. et ómnibus orthodóxis, atque cathólicæ et apostólicæ fídei cultóribus.

AND SO, MOST MERCIFUL FATHER, IN HUMBLE PRAYER we approach thee; praying thee, for the love of thy Son, our Lord Jesus Christ, this ✠ gift of ours, this ✠ tribute of ours, this ✠ holy sacrifice, virgin-pure, to welcome with thy blessing. And above all else, for thy holy Church universal we offer it; peace and unity grant her, thy guardianship and thy guidance, all the world over. On all alike have mercy, N. our Pope, and N. our bishop, and all right-thinking folk that hold the Catholic and apostolic faith in reverence.

In the following prayer, the Celebrant makes silent mention of those for whom he wishes to pray, and at that moment the Deacon takes a step back.

The Commemoration of the Living

Meménto, Dñe, famulórum famularúmque tuárũ N. et N. ; et ómnium circumstántium, quorum tibi fides cógnita est, et nota devótio: pro quibus tibi offérimus, vel qui tibi ófferunt hoc sacrifíciũ laudis, pro se, suísque ómnibus, pro redemptióne animárum suárum, pro spe salútis et incolumitátis suæ; tibíque reddunt vota sua ætérno Deo, vivo et vero.

REMEMBER, LORD, thy servants and handmaids, N. and N. Remember all who here stand about me; their faith, Lord, thou hast tried, their love thou knowest. For them we do sacrifice in thy honor, and they too offer it for themselves and all they love; for their souls' ransom and their safe-keeping from all harm; they too would pay their vows to thee, who art God eternally, the living and the true God.

On Christmas, Epiphany, Easter, Ascension, and Pentecost, the following prayer is modified; cf. pages 198-199. (Maundy Thursday's modifications are printed in that feast's section.) Saint Joseph was added to the following prayer on 13 November 1962 (effective 8 December 1962).

**ERE MEET WE IN** fellowship, here keep we the memory of her, first of all, the glorious ever-virgin Mary, that is Mother of our Lord and God Jesus Christ; but of others, too — Saint Joseph, her spouse, the holy apostles and martyrs of thine, Peter & Paul, Andrew, James, John, Thomas, James, Philip, Bartholomew, Matthew, Simon, and Thaddeus; Linus, Cletus, Clement, Sixtus, Cornelius, Cyprian, Laurence, Chrysogonus, John and Paul, Cosmas, and Damian, and all thy saints everywhere. Let their merits, Lord, their intercession avail with thee; shield us with thy protection in every encounter. Through the same Christ our Lord. Amen.

Communicántes, et memóriam venerántes, in primis gloriósæ semper Vírginis Maríæ, genitrícis Dei et Dñi nostri Jesu Christi: (1962) *sed et beáti Joseph, ejúsdem Vírginis Sponsi,* et beatórum Apostolórum ac Mártyrum tuórum, Petri et Pauli, Andréæ, Jacóbi, Joánnis, Thomæ, Jacóbi, Philíppi, Bartholomǽi, Matthǽi, Simónis et Thaddǽi, Cleti, Cleméntis, Xysti, Cornélii, Cypriáni, Lauréntii, Chrysógoni, Joánnis et Pauli, Cosmæ et Damiáni et ómnium sanctórũ tuórũ: quorũ méritis precibúsque concédas, ut in ómnibus protectiónis tuæ muniámur auxílio. Per eúmdẽ Christum Dñm nostrum. Amen.

1962 • He extends his hands over the bread and wine and the bell is rung:

HERE, THEN, is the offering we make thee, we that are thy ministers, yet in truth it is the offering of all thy household. We beseech thee, Lord, to grant it favorable acceptance, ordering our days in the peace thou bestowest, from eternal loss delivering us, and in the company of thy elect bidding our names be numbered. Through Christ our Lord. Amen.

Hanc ígitur oblatiónẽ servitútis nostræ, sed et cunctæ famíliæ tuæ, quǽsumus Dñe, ut placátus accípias, diésque nostros in tua pace dispónas, atque ab ætérna damnatióne nos éripi, et in electórum tuórum júbeas grege numerári. Per Christum Dóminum nostrum. Amen.

**N OFFERING** ✠ blessed and ✠ dedicated, a sacrifice ✠ truly done, worthy of our human dignity and thy divine acceptance — this, O God, do thou make of it, body ✠ and blood ✠ that shall be, for our sakes, of thy own well-belovèd Son, our Lord Jesus Christ.

Quam oblatiónem tu, Deus, in ómnibus, quǽsumus, bene✠díctam, adscríp✠tam, ra✠tam, rationábilẽ, acceptabilémque fácere dignéris: ut nobis Cor✠pus et San✠guis fiat dilectíssimi Fílii tui Dñi nostri Jesu Christi.

Hanc igitur
oblacionē
servitutis
nostre. sed et cuncte fa
milie tue quesumus
domine ut placatus
accipias. diesq; nostros
in tua pace disponas
atq; ab eterna damp
nacione nos eripi. et
in electorum tuorum iube
as grege numerari.
Per xpm dnm nostrū.
Amen. Inclinans dic.
Quam oblaci
onem tu de
us in omni
bus quesumus: B e
ne dictam: A scrip
tam: R atam ra
cionabilem acceptabi
lemq; facere digneris
ut nobis. C or pus.
et S an guis. fiat
dilectissimi filij tui do
mini nostri ihu xpi.
Hic elevet hostiam dic.
Qui pridie
quam pate
retur. acce
pit panem in sanctas
ac venerabiles ma
nus suas. et elevatis
oculis in celum ad
te deum patrem suū
omnipotentem tibi
gracias agens. B e
ne dixit. fregit. de
dit discipulis suis di
cens. Accipite et mā
ducate ex hoc omnes.
Hoc est enim corpus

Three Important Prayers • The *Sherborne Missal* (shown above) was created between 1399AD and 1407AD for a monastery in Dorsetshire (England). The capital letters, which show a Catholic priest offering Mass, each begin an important prayer : (1) **Hanc Igitur;** (2) **Quam Oblationem;** (3) **Qui Pridie Quam Pateretur.**

HOC EST ENIM CORPUS MEUM • "FOR THIS IS MY BODY" ✠

ANCIENT WITNESSES • Until the 4th century, the Church was under persecution and kept its liturgical manuscripts secret (*disciplina arcani*). During that century, the Roman Empire began to collapse—and virtually no liturgical manuscripts from that tumultuous period survived. But stability came under the rule of Charlemagne (d. 814AD), and we observe ***in the earliest liturgical records we possess*** that the Canon of the Mass has remained inviolate. Consider the following manuscripts: the first from Paris, the second from Ireland :

Gelasian Sacramentary
CIRCA **725** AD
"**Accipite** et bibite ex [eo] omnes hic est enim calix sanguinis mei novi et æterni testamenti mysterium fidei..."

Stowe Missal
CIRCA **780** AD
"**Accipite** et bibite ex hoc omnes hic est enim calix [sancti] sanguinis mei novi et æterni testamenti misterium fidei..."

QUI prídie quã paterétur *(accipit hostiam)*, accépit panem in sanctas ac venerábiles manus suas, *(elevat oculos ad caelum)* et elevátis óculis in cælum ad te Deum Patrem suum omnipoténtem, *(caput inclinat)* tibi grátias agens, bene ✠ díxit, fregit, dedítque discípulis suis, dicens: Accípite, et manducáte ex hoc omnes.

He speaks the following words of consecration distinctly and attentively over the host.

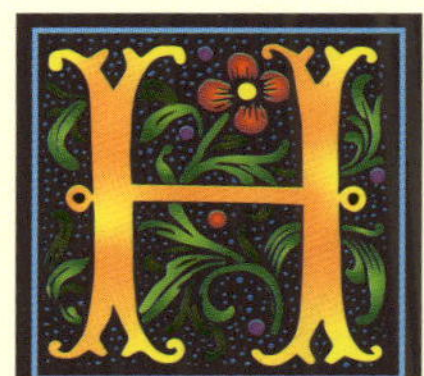

HE, ON THE EVE of his Passion, took bread *(he holds the host)* in those holy, those worshipful hands; to thee, his Father, God omnipotent, *(raises eyes)* lifted his eyes heavenward, *(bows head)* to thee gave thanks, then blessed ✠ and broke, and gave it to his disciples, saying: Take and eat this, all of you:

HOC EST ENIM CORPUS MEUM.

FOR THIS IS MY BODY

1962 • He genuflects and adores the SANCTISSIMUM. He rises, shows It to the people, replaces It upon the corporal, kneels, and adores It again. He does not again separate his thumbs and index fingers, except when he is to touch the host, until the washing of his fingers. He then uncovers the chalice.

Símili modo postquã cœnátũ est *(ambabus manibus accipit calicem)*, accípiens et hunc præclárum Cálicem in sanctas ac venerábiles manus suas, item *(caput inclinat)* tibi grátias agens, bene ✠ díxit, dedítque discípulis suis, dicens: Accípite, et bíbite ex eo omnes:

He speaks the following over the chalice attentively and continuously, lifting it up a little.

SO TOO, WHEN SUPPER was done *(he takes the chalice)*, into his holy and worshipful hands he took this cup all the world holds in honor; once more *(bows head)* he gave thanks to thee, blessed ✠ and gave it to his disciples, saying: Take and drink of this, all of you,

HIC EST ENIM CALIX SÁNGUINIS MEI, NOVI ET ÆTÉRNI TESTAMÉNTI; MYSTÉRIUM FIDEI: QUI PRO VOBIS ET PRO MULTIS EFFUNDÉTUR IN REMISSIÓNEM PECCATÓRUM.

FOR THIS CUP IS THE CUP OF MY BLOOD, THE SEAL OF A NEW AND EVERLASTING COVENANT, FAITH'S COUNTERSIGN; FOR YOU AND FOR MANY BESIDES IT IS TO BE POURED OUT, WINNING PARDON FOR YOUR SINS.

He places the chalice upon the corporal and says:

Hæc quotiescúmque fecéritis, in mei memóriam faciétis.

Do this, whenever you drink it, for a commemoration of me.

1962 • Genuflecting, he adores. He rises, shows the chalice to the people, replaces it upon the corporal, covers it and—genuflecting—again adores.

1962 • Throughout the Canon, the Celebrant joins his hands before making the sign of the cross, and whenever he says "Through (the same) Christ our Lord. Amen."

NFORGOTTEN, Lord, by us thy ministers, by these thy faithful people, how he, thy Son, Christ our Lord, underwent his most blessèd passion; how he rose again from the dead, and ascended into heaven in glory. And still, out of the gifts thou hast bestowed on us, to thy surpassing majesty we offer it, a victim most ✠ pure, a victim most ✠ holy, a victim ✠ without spot; bread so ✠ holy, it brings eternal life, healing ✠ draft * that shall preserve us evermore.

Unde et mémores, Dñe, nos servi tui, sed et plebs tua sancta, ejúsdem Christi Fílii tui Dñi nostri, tam beátæ passiónis, nec non et ab ínferis resurrectiónis, sed et in cælos gloriósæ ascensiónis: offérimus præcláræ majestáti tuæ de tuis donis ac datis, hóstiam ✠ puram, hóstiam ✠ sanctam, hóstiam ✠ immaculátam, Panem ✠ sanctum vitæ ætérnæ, et Cálicem ✠ salútis perpétuæ.

* *Draft*: Monsignor Knox here refers to the contents of the chalice; i.e. that which is drawn out of it.

ON THIS look down, we pray thee, with an eye gracious and content; welcome it, as thou didst welcome the gifts of Abel, thy true servant, and the sacrifice of our father Abraham, and that which thy own high priest Melchisedech brought thee; a sacrifice so holy, free from all spot.

Supra quæ propítio ac seréno vultu respícere dignéris: et accépta habére, sícuti accépta habére dignátus es múnera púeri tui justi Abel, et sacrifícium patriárchæ nostri Ábrahæ, et quod tibi óbtulit summus sacérdos tuus Melchísedech sanctum sacrifíciũ, immaculátam hóstiam.

1962 • Bowing low over the Altar, he prays as follows.
Profunde inclinatus, junctis manibus et super altare positis, dicit:

WE HUMBLY implore thee, O God almighty, bid one of thy holy angels carry up this sacrifice to thy altar high in heaven. There let it plead before thy divine majesty for all who shall partake *(he kisses the Altar)* of this altar on earth. As we receive the most sacred ✠ Body and ✠ Blood of thy Son, may we be filled *(he signs himself)* with every blessing, every grace from above. Through the same Christ our Lord. Amen.

Súpplices te rogámus, omnípotens Deus: jube hæc perférri per manus sancti Ángeli tui in sublíme altáre tuũ, in conspéctu divínæ majestátis tuæ: ut quotquot, *(osculatur altare)* ex hac altáris participatióne, sacrosánctum Fílii tui *(jungit manus, et signat semel super hostiam, et semel super calicem)* Cor✠pus et Sán✠guinem sumpsérimus, *(seipsum signat, dicens)* omni benedictióne cœlésti, et grátia repleámur. *(jungit manus)* Per eúmdem Christum Dóminum nostrum. Amen.

✠ HANDS REST ON THE ALTAR EDGE TO BEGIN: "SUPPLICES TE ROGAMUS"

Below is shown the "Supra Quæ Propítio"—and prayers which precede and follow it:

excvo omnes · Hic est enim calix sanguinis mei noui
& aeterni testamenti mysterium fidei · qui pro uobis
& pro multis effundetur in remissionem peccatorũ ·
Haec quotiescumq: feceritis in mei memoriã facietis ·
Unde & memores dñe nos tui serui sed & plebs tua scã
eiusdem xpi filii tui dñi di nri tam admirabilis na
tiuitatis quam beatae passionis nec non & uenera
bilis ab inferis resurrectionis · sed & in caelos gloriose
ascensionis · Offerimus praeclarae maiestati tuae
de tuis donis ac datis hostiam puram + hostiã scam
+ hostiam inmaculatam + panem scm uitae aeternae
+ & calicem salutis perpetuae ·
Supra quae propitio ac sereno uultu respicere digne
ris & accepta habere sicuti accepta habere dignatus
es munera pueri tui iusti abel · & sacrificium patri
archae nri abrahae · & quod tibi obtulit summus
sacerdos tuus melchisedech scm sacrificium inma
culatam hostiam ·
Supplices te rogamus omnips ds · iube haec perferri per
manus sci angeli tui in sublime altare tuum · in con
spectum diuinae maiestatis tuae · Ut quotquot
ex hac altaris participatione sacrosčm filii tui
+ corpus + & sanguinem sumpserimus · omni bene +
dictione caelesti & gratia repleamur · per eundẽ
xpm dnm nrm · Amen

THEODORIC SACRAMENTARY (f. 15v) • **825**AD

de tuis donis ac datis h + ostiam
puram h + ostiam scam h + ostiã
inmaculatã · P + anem scm uitae
+ aeterne · & calicem salutis ppetuę
Supra quę ppicio ac sereno
uultu respicere digneris & accepta
habere sicuti accepta habere dig
natus es munera pueri tui iusti
abel · & sacrificium patriarche
nri abrahe · & quod tibi obtulit
summus sacerdos tuus melchise
dech scm sacrificiũ inmaculatã
hostiam
Supplices te rogam' omps
ds · iube hec pferri per

FIGEAC SACRAMENTARY (f. 20v) • **1063**AD

MISSALE CISTERCIENSE (Fribourg, Switzerland) f. 143v • **1300AD**

eundem xpistum dominum nostrum.
Nobis quoque peccatoribus famulis tuis de multi
tudine miserationum tuarum sperantibus
partem aliquam et societatem donare digneris. cum
tuis sanctis apostolis et martyribus. cum Iohanne.
Stephano. Mathia. Barnaba. Ignatio. Alex
andro. Marcellino. Petro. Felicitate. Perpetua.
Agatha. Lucia. Agna. Cecilia. Anastasia. et
cum omnibus sanctis tuis. Intra quorum nos con
sortium non estimator meriti. sed venie quesumus

LITURGICAL "MEMORY" • At the beginning of the "Nobis Quoque Peccatóribus," the Celebrant strikes his heart with his hand and raises his voice for the first three words. "The survival of the practice is a typical case of the great endurance of liturgical customs even when the basis for them has long since been removed" {Jungmann p258}.

THE MINOR ELEVATION • Regarding the so-called "minor" elevation: it is minor not because it is of less importance, but because it does not (like its younger sister, the "big" elevation) consist in showing the holy gifts to the people, but only in ***raising them up to God*** as an oblation. {Jungmann p266}.

AT THE MINOR ELEVATION • "OMNIS HONOR ET GLORIA" ✠

The Commemoration of the Dead

Meménto étiam, Dómine, famulórũ famularúmque tuárum **N.** et **N.** qui nos præcessérunt cum signo fídei, et dórmiunt in somno pacis. *Jungit manus, orat aliquantulum pro iis defunctis, pro quibus orare intendit, deinde extensis manibus prosequitur:* Ipsis, Dómine, et ómnibus in Christo quiescéntibus, locum refrigérii, lucis et pacis, ut indúlgeas, deprecámur. Per eúmdẽ Christum Dñm nostrum. Amen.

ND EVER, LORD, be mindful of thy servants and handmaids, **N.** and **N.**, who went before us with the seal of faith upon them, and have fallen asleep now, to rest in peace. *(Here he makes silent mention of those dead for whom he wishes to pray, and—at that moment—the Deacon takes a step back.)* To these, Lord, and to all who lie safe in Christ's keeping, grant a dwelling-place, we beseech thee, where all is refreshment, and light, and repose. Through the same Christ our Lord. Amen.

Nobis quoque peccatóribus, fámulis tuis, de multitúdine miseratiónum tuárum sperántibus, partem áliquam et societátem donáre dignéris, cum tuis sanctis Apóstolis et Martyribus: cum Joánne, Stéphano, Mathía, Bárnaba, Ignátio, Alexándro, Marcellíno, Petro, Felicitáte, Perpétua, Ágatha, Lúcia, Agnéte, Cæcília, Anastásia, et ómnibus sanctis tuis; intra quorũ nos consórtiũ, non æstimátor mériti, sed véniæ, quæsumus, largítor admítte. Per Christum Dóminum nostrum.

AND TO US, that are servants of thine, sinners who yet put their trust in the abundance of thy mercy, grant some portion yet; some fellowship with thy holy apostles and martyrs, John, Stephen, Matthias, Barnabas, Ignatius, Alexander, Marcellinus, Peter, Felicity, Perpetua, Agatha, Lucy, Agnes, Cecilia, Anastasia, and all thy saints. Not weighing our merits, but free pardon bestowing, enroll us, we beseech thee, in their company, through Christ our Lord.

Per quem hæc ómnia, Dómine, semper bona creas, sanctí✠ficas, viví✠ficas, bene✠dícis, et præstas nobis.

THROUGH him, Lord, these gifts of thine thou dost ever create, ever ✠ hallow, ever ✠ quicken, ever ✠ bless, ever confer on us.

He genuflects and makes the sign of the cross three times across the chalice with the Host:

Per ip✠sum, et cum ip✠so, et in ip✠so, est tibi Deo Patri ✠ omnipoténti, in unitáte Spíritus ✠ sancti, *Elevans parum calicem cum hostia, dicit:* omnis honor et glória.

HROUGH ✠ HIM, and together with ✠ him, and in his ✠ name, to thee, Father ✠ Almighty, in the bond of the Holy ✠ Spirit, *(elevates the Sanctissimum)* all honor and praise is given.

The Canon was originally said audibly. Father Fortescue (*Study of the Roman Liturgy*, p326) provides documentation from Emperor Justinian I (d. 565AD) and John Moschos (d. 619AD) suggesting the transition to *submissa voce* began in the 6th century. Even after the Canon became silent, "these final words" (*Per ómnia...*etc.) "were not included in the silence which prevailed throughout the rest of the Canon" so the people could reply "AMEN" {Jungmann p273}. Throughout the Mass, there are several times when the Celebrant says a prayer quietly except for these final words.

1962 • He genuflects, and concludes the prayer aloud :

World without end. ℟. Amen.

LET US PRAY. Obedient to our Savior's command, and with his teaching for our model, thus we make bold to pray:

Per ómnia sǽcula sæculórum. ℟. Amen.

Orémus. Præcéptis salutáribus móniti, et divína institutióne formáti, audémus dícere:

UR FATHER WHO ART IN heaven, hallowed be thy name. Thy kingdom come. Thy will be done, on earth as it is in heaven. Give us this day our daily bread. And forgive us our trespasses, as we forgive them that trespass against us. * And lead us not into temptation:

℟. But deliver us from evil.

The Celebrant says silently: "Amen."

Pater noster, qui es in cælis, sanctificétur nomen tuum: advéniat regnum tuũ: fiat volúntas tua, sicut in cælo et in terra panẽ nostrũ quotidiánũ da nobis hódie; et dímitte nobis débita nostra, sicut et nos dimíttimus debitóribus nostris: * et ne nos indúcas in tentatiónẽ.

℟. Sed líbera nos a malo.

Sacerdos secrete dicit: Amen.

During the next prayer, he will sign himself with the paten and kiss it after the words *da propítius pacem in diébus nostris.*

ROM ALL EVIL, Lord, deliver us, past, present, and to come. So may Mary ever virgin plead for us, that is Mother of God, with the holy apostles Peter and Paul, and Andrew, and all the saints together, as to win us thy favor. ✠ Grant peace in our days; thy grace befriending us, be they ever by sin unhampered, and safe from all alarms. *(He breaks the Sacred Host)* Through the same Jesus Christ, thy Son, our Lord, *(Breaking off a particle of the Sacred Host)* who with thee in the bond of the Holy Spirit lives and reigns and is God:

Líbera nos, quǽsumus Dñe, ab ómnibus malis prætéritis, præséntibus, et futúris, et intercedénte beáta et gloriósa semper Vírgine Dei genitríce María, cũ beátis Apóstolis tuis Petro et Paulo, atque Andréa, et ómnibus sanctis, ✠ da propítius pacem in diébus nostris: ut ope misericórdiæ tuæ adjúti, et a peccáto simus semper líberi, et ab omni perturbatióne secúri. Per eúmdẽ Dñm nostrũ Jesum Christum Fílium tuum, qui tecum vivit et regnat in unitáte Spíritus Sancti Deus.

SACRAMENTARY OF DROGON (f. 20v) • **845AD** This page shows the Lord's Prayer ("Pater Noster").

* During the "Our Father," the Subdeacon ascends the Altar, gives the paten to the Deacon, and removes the Humeral Veil; the Celebrant needs the paten for the next prayer.

CHAPEL MISSAL (Aarau, Switzerland) • **1400AD**

GREIFFENKLAU MISSAL, **1428AD**

MASSES FOR THE DEAD • During a Requiem Mass, instead of "miserére nobis" the Celebrant says "dona eis réquiem." In the Missal shown above (*Greiffenklau Missal*), someone has written the alternate version in red ink.

"AGNUS DEI, QUI TOLLIS PECCATA MUNDI, MISERERE NOBIS." ✠

1962 • Holding the particle over the chalice, the Celebrant sings:

Per ómnia sǽcula sæculórum.
℟. Amen.

World without end. ℟. Amen.

1962 • The Celebrant makes the sign of Cross three times with a particle of the Sacred Host over the chalice, singing:

Pax ✠ Dómini sit ✠ semper vobís ✠ cum.

℟. Et cum spíritu tuo.

BE ✠ IT EVER with ✠ you, that peace ✠ the Lord gives.

℟. And with you, his minister.

1962 • He drops the particle into the chalice and continues silently:

Hæc commíxtio et consecrátio Córporis et Sánguinis Dñi nostri Jesu Christi, fiat accipiéntibus nobis in vitã ætérnam. Amen.

SO MINGLED, so hallowed, may the Body and Blood of our Lord Jesus Christ bring eternal life to us, who partake of it.

1962 • He covers the chalice, genuflects, bows down, and—striking his heart with his hand three times—he says:

Lamb of God, who takest away the sins of the world: **have mercy on us.** (2x)

Lamb of God, who takest away the sins of the world: **grant us peace.**

Note: We omit musical notation for the "Agnus Dei," since the version we recommend (viz. MASS XVIII) has but one note for each syllable and can easily be sung from memory. Conveniently, the melody remains the same for Requiem Masses.

GNUS DEI, QUI TOLLIS PECCATA MUNDI: miserére nobis.

AGNUS DEI, QUI TOLLIS PECCATA MUNDI: miserére nobis.

AGNUS DEI, QUI TOLLIS PECCATA MUNDI: dona nobis pacem.

1962 • In Masses for the dead, the following version is used:

Lamb of God, who takest away the sins of the world: give them rest.

AGNUS DEI, qui tollis peccáta mundi: *dona eis réquiem.*

Lamb of God, who takest away the sins of the world: give them rest.

AGNUS DEI, qui tollis peccáta mundi: *dona eis réquiem.*

Lamb of God, who takest away the sins of the world: give them rest forevermore.

AGNUS DEI, qui tollis peccáta mundi: *dona eis réquiem sempitérnam.*

1962 • In Masses for the dead, the following prayer is not said. Still bowing slightly, the Celebrant prays:

LORD JESUS Christ, who didst tell thy apostles, "Peace is my bequest to you, and the peace which I give you is mine to give," my sins forget, the loyalty of thy Church remember, and make it, as thou wouldst have it be, united and secure: who livest and reignest and art God, world without end. Amen.

Dñe Jesu Christe, qui dixísti Apóstolis tuis: Pacẽ relínquo vobis, pacem meam do vobis: ne respícias peccáta mea, sed fidem Ecclésiæ tuæ: eámque secúndũ voluntátem tuam pacificáre et cöadunáre dignéris. Qui vivis et regnas Deus, per ómnia sæcula sæculórũ. Amen.

1962 • Here, at Solemn Mass, the kiss of peace ("Pax") is given. It is not given at Masses for the dead. The Celebrant and Deacon kiss the Altar (formerly, the priest kissed the SANCTISSIMUM Itself), and those who give the Pax say "Pax tecum" and those who receive it "Et cum spíritu tuo."

ORD JESUS CHRIST, Son of the living God, thou by thy death—such was the Father's will, such aid the Holy Spirit lent thee—didst make a dead world live. Do thou, by this gift of thy most sacred Body and Blood, from all guilt of mine and from every harm deliver me; keep me true to thy commandments, and never let me leave thy side: Who with the same God the Father and Holy Spirit livest and reignest and art God, world without end. Amen.

Dñe Jesu Christe, Fili Dei vivi, qui ex voluntáte Patris, cooperánte Spíritu Sancto, per mortem tuã mundum vivificásti: líbera me per hoc sacrosánctũ Corpus et Sánguinem tuum, ab ómnibus iniquitátibus meis, et univérsis malis, et fac me tuiś semper inhærére mandátis, et a te numquam separári permíttas. Qui cum eódẽ Deo Patre et Spíritu sancto vivis et regnas Deus in sæcula sæculórum. Amen.

ORD JESUS CHRIST, if thy sacred Body I dare, all unworthily, to receive, let not the tasting of it prove my judgment and my undoing; rather in thy mercy let it advantage me, a shield for soul and body, a salve for my infirmities: Who with God the Father, in the bond of the Holy Spirit, livest and reignest and art God, world without end. Amen.

Percéptio Córporis tui, Dñe Jesu Christe, quod ego indígnus súmere præsúmo, non mihi provéniat in judícium et condemnatiónem: sed pro tua pietáte prosit mihi ad tutaméntum mentis et córporis, et ad medélam percipiéndam. Qui vivis et regnas cum Deo Patre in unitáte Spíritus sancti Deus, per ómnia sæcula sæculórum. Amen.

✠ CELEBRANT AND DEACON • THE KISS OF PEACE: "PAX TECUM"

Franciscan Missal (Sion, Switzerland) • **1204**AD —— **"Dómine Jesu Christe..."**

Dñe ihu xpe qui dixisti aplis tuis pacem
meã do uobis. pacem relinquo uobis/ ne
respicias pctã mea/ sed fidem ecclie tue eamqз
sedm uoluntatẽ tuã pacificare et coadunare
digneris/ qui viuis et regnas deus p omnia
scla sclo2 amẽ. Pax tecũ ℟ Et cũ spũ tuo
Domine ihu xpe fili dei uiui qui ex uolũ
tate pris cooperante spũ sco p mortem

Missal of Limoges • **1123**AD —— **"Percéptio Córporis Tui..."**

mentis et corporis· perundem ALIA.
Perceptio corporis et sanguinis tui dñe ihu
xpe. quam ego indignus sumere presumo
nõ michi proueniat ad iudicium neq· ad condemp-
nationem. sed p tua pietate psit michi ad

DEACON AND SUBDEACON • THE KISS OF PEACE: "PAX TECUM" ✠

KISS OF PEACE • The PAX is among the most ancient of liturgical ceremonies—e.g. Tertullian and Saint Augustine make reference to it. In the mediæval period, several formulas were used. A common one had the Celebrant say: *Habéte vínculum caritátis et pacis, ut apti sitis sacrosánctis mystériis* ("May love and peace unite you, and so prepare you for the most holy Sacrament"). The ministers would answer: *Pax Christi et ecclésiae habúndet in córdibus nostris* ("May the peace of Christ and the Church abound in our hearts").

{ cf. Fortescue 371; Ebner 299+356; Jungmann 332 }

"Kiss of Peace" • *Salzburg Missal* (1494AD)

Thieboudi Missal (1439AD)

1962 • Having genuflected, he takes the Sacred Host and paten into his hands, saying:

Panem cæléstem accípiam, et nomen Dómini invocábo.

I WILL take the Bread of Heaven, and will call upon the name of the Lord.

1962 • Bowing a little, he takes both parts of the Host between the thumb and index finger of his left hand (holding the paten underneath the Host between the same index finger and the middle finger of his left hand). Striking his heart three times with his right hand—and raising his voice somewhat—he says the following (devoutly and humbly) three times:

Dómine, non sum dignus, *Et secrete prosequitur:* ut intres sub tectum meũ: sed tantum dic verbo, et sanábitur ánima mea.

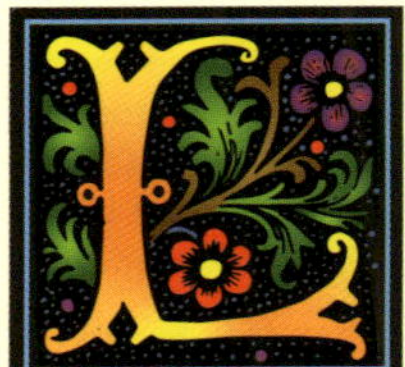

LORD, I am not worthy *(he continues in a low voice)* to receive thee under my roof; my soul will be healed if thou wilt only speak a word of command. (3x)

1962 • The Celebrant crosses himself with the Sacred Host, praying as follows.
Postea dextera se signans cum hostia super patenam, dicit:

Corpus ✠ Dómini nostri Jesu Christi custódiat ánimam meam in vitam ætérnam. Amen.

The Body ✠ of our Lord Jesus Christ bring my soul safely to eternal life. Amen.

1962 • Bowing, the Celebrant reverently receives both parts of the Sacred Host. Placing the paten on the corporal and—with hands joined, no longer bowing—he meditates briefly upon the SANCTISSIMUM. He uncovers the chalice, genuflects, gathers any fragments, and purifies the paten over the chalice, while praying as follows.

Quid retríbuam Dómino pro ómnibus, quæ retríbuit mihi? Cálicem salutáris accípiam, et nomen Dñi invocábo. Laudans invocábo Dóminum, et ab inimícis meis salvus ero.

WHAT RETURN shall I make to the Lord for all that he has given me? I will take the chalice of salvation and invoke the name of the Lord. Praised be the Lord! When I invoke his name I am secure from my enemies.

1962 • Crossing himself with the chalice, he prays as follows.
Accipit calicem manu dextera, et eo se signans, dicit:

Sanguis ✠ Dómini nostri Jesu Christi custódiat ánimam meã in vitam ætérnã. Amen.

The Blood ✠ of our Lord Jesus Christ bring my soul safely to eternal life. Amen.

1962 • Holding the paten in his left hand underneath the chalice, the Celebrant reverently receives all of the Precious Blood together with the particle.
Et sinistra supponens patenam calici, reverenter sumit totum Sanguinem cum particula.

COMMUNION OF THE PEOPLE

BEFORE the middle of the 20th century, it was quite rare for Catholics to receive Holy Communion ***during*** Mass. Except on Holy Thursday, the distribution of Holy Communion normally took place before Mass, after Mass—or even while Mass was taking place (!) but not at Communion time. For further details, please see page 510.

The *Code of Rubrics* (1961) changed the situation, declaring (§502):

> The proper time to distribute Holy Communion to the faithful is during Mass, after the Communion of the Celebrant, who distributes the SANCTISSIMUM himself to those who ask for It (unless it is desirable that he be helped by one or more priests, owing to a large number of communicants). It is altogether unbecoming for another priest to distribute Holy Communion—other than at the proper time for Communion—at the same Altar at which Mass is actually being celebrated. Furthermore, for a reasonable cause it is also permissible to distribute Holy Communion immediately before or after Mass, and indeed outside of Mass.

Page 315 of the *Missale Romanum* (1962) says: *Quo sumpto, si qui sunt communicandi, eos communicet, antequam se purificet.* Translated to English, that means:

> "Having received the Precious Blood, the Celebrant distributes Holy Communion to the members of the congregation—if any will receive—before proceeding to the purification."

This rubric was not "invented" for the 1962 Missal; e.g. it is found on page 38 of the *Ritus Sacri* (1876) as well as page 292 of the *Missale Romanum* (Desclée, 1908). In other words, ***it was always possible in principle*** for the faithful to receive Holy Communion when the Celebrant does. As Father Fortescue wrote in 1917: "On Maundy Thursday there is a distribution of Holy Communion at High Mass. This does not often occur on other days; but any Catholic has normally a right to present himself for Communion at any Mass, on condition that he is in a state of grace."

The *Missale Romanum* (IMPRIMATUR, 11 April 1962) instructs the Celebrant how to distribute Communion to the faithful on page xxxiii: *Quoties sancta Communio infra Missam distributur, celebrans, sumpto sacratissimo Sanguine, omissis confessione et absolutione, dictis tamen Ecce Agnus Dei et ter Dómine, non sum dignus, immediate ad distribtionem sanctæ Eucharistiæ procedit.* Translated to English:

> "Whenever Holy Communion is distributed within the Mass, the Celebrant first consumes the Precious Blood, and then—the CONFITEOR and absolution having been omitted—says the "Ecce Agnus Dei" as well as the "Dómine, non sum dignus" three times. The Celebrant then proceeds immediately to the distribution of the holy Eucharist.

While the "Pre-Communion Confiteor" was suppressed by the 1961 *Code of Rubrics* (§503), it was included in the *Pontificale Romanum* (1962). It was also included on page 182 of the *Missale Romanum* (IMPRIMATUR, 11 April 1962) for Good Friday, along with the absolution. The "Pre-Communion Confiteor" may continue "where the custom exists" according to a letter from the Pontifical Commission *Ecclesia Dei* dated 18 September 2018 (*Prot. N. 39/2011L-ED*).

In Europe, the triple "Dómine, non sum dignus" before Communion is sometimes said in the vernacular. According to Father James O'Kane—cf. page 275 of *Regarding the Sacraments* (1883)—this practice may have force of law; it is based upon ancient tradition {Jungmann p372}.

VERNACULAR HYMNODY • It is sometimes asked whether hymns in the vernacular may be sung during the distribution of Holy Communion at celebrations according to the *Missale Vetustum*. First of all, Pope Pius XII explicitly permitted this practice: cf. *De Musica Sacra* (1958) §14a. Furthermore—as has been explained above—Holy Communion was usually not distributed to the faithful ***during*** Mass (except on Holy Thursday) before the 1960s. Therefore, it does not make sense to seek a "traditional praxis." Those who desire to sing hymns in the vernacular (during the distribution of Holy Communion) should realize that nothing prevents this.

1962 • If the CONFITEOR has been said, the Celebrant says:

Misereátur vestri omnípotens Deus, et, dimíssis peccátis vestris, perdúcat vos ad vitã ætérnam. ℟. Amen.

MAY GOD Almighty be merciful to you, pardon your sins, and bring you to life everlasting. ℟. Amen.

Indulgéntiam, absolutiónem, ✠ et remissiónẽ peccatórum vestrórũ tríbuat vobis omnípotens et miséricors Dóminus. ℟. Amen.

God the almighty, God the merciful, grant us of all our sins ✠ pardon, acquittal, and release. ℟. Amen.

1962 • He turns to the Altar and genuflects. Lifting up the SANCTISSIMUM, he turns toward the people in the usual way and—at the center of the Altar—says the following in a loud voice. | *Deinde ad altare se convertit, genuflectit, apprehendit pyxidem, et more solito conversus ad populum, in medio altaris, dicit clara voce:*

Ecce Agnus Dei, ecce qui tollit peccáta mundi.

Mox subdit:

Dómine, non sum dignus, ut intres sub tectum meum: sed tantum dic verbo, et sanábitur ánima mea; *quod iterum ac tertio repetit.*

BEHOLD the Lamb of God; behold him who takes away the sins of the world.

ORD, I am not worthy to receive thee under my roof; my soul will be healed if thou wilt only speak a word of command.

Said in the same "loud and clear voice," repeated thrice.

1962 • If the number of communicants be great, other priests may distribute Communion, either with the Celebrant at the COMMUNION-RAIL or at some other suitable place; taking care, however, that the good order and devotion of the faithful is not disturbed. | *Si vero multitudo fidelium ad sacram mensam accedentium magna sit, alii quoque sacerdotes, vel una cum celebrante ad cancellos, vel alio loco apto, Communionem distribuere possunt, cauto tamen ut bono ordini ac devotioni fidelium sedulo provideatur.*

THE OLDEST EXTANT EUCHARISTIC HYMN

Sancti Veníte, Christi Corpus Súmite (circa 640AD)

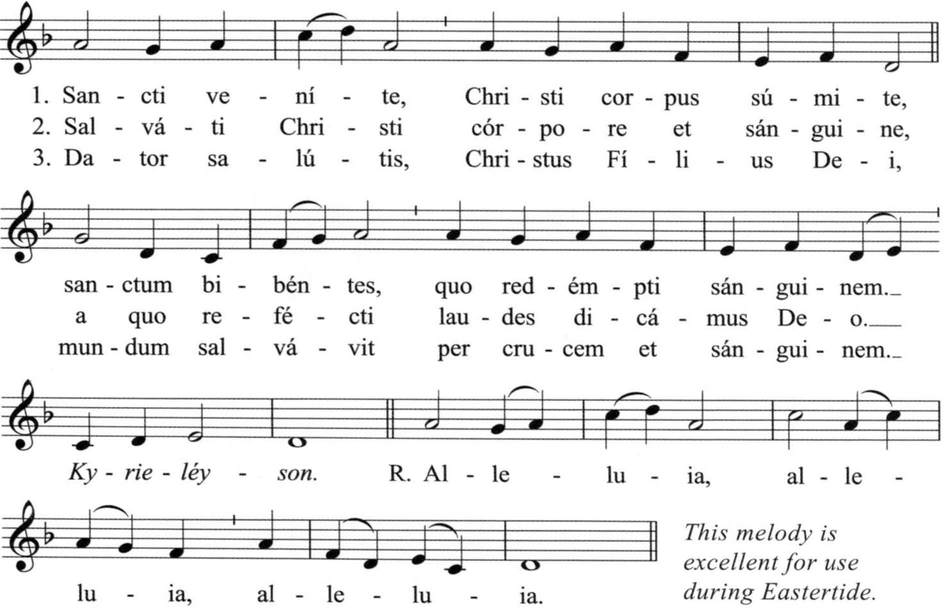

This melody is excellent for use during Eastertide.

4. Pro univérsis | immolátus Dóminus
   ipse sacérdos | exístit et hóstia. *Ky-rie-léy-son.* R.

5. Lege praecéptum | immolári hóstias,
   qua adumbrántur | divína mystéria. *Ky-rie-léy-son.* R.

6. Lucis indúltor | et salvátor ómnium
   praecláram sanctis | largítus est grátiam. *Ky-rie-léy-son.* R.

7. Accédant omnes | pura mente créduli,
   sumant aetérnam | salútis custódiam. *Ky-rie-léy-son.* R.

8. Sanctórum custos, | rector quoque Dóminus
   vitam perénnem | largítur credéntibus. *Ky-rie-léy-son.* R.

9. Caeléstem panem | dat esuriéntibus;
   de fonte vivo | praebet sitiéntibus. *Ky-rie-léy-son.* R.

10. Alph*a* et Ómega | ipse Christus Dóminus
    venit ventúrus | judicáre hómines. *Ky-rie-léy-son.* R.

"Sancti Veníte" is the oldest known Latin Eucharistic Hymn, from the *Bangor Antiphonary*.

ADDITIONAL MELODIES, SATB HARMONIES, LITERAL TRANSLATION, AND ORGAN ACCOMPANIMENTS CAN BE FOUND IN THE *Brébeuf Hymnal*.

THE OLDEST EXTANT EUCHARISTIC HYMN

English Translation: Father Adrian Fortescue (d. 1923)

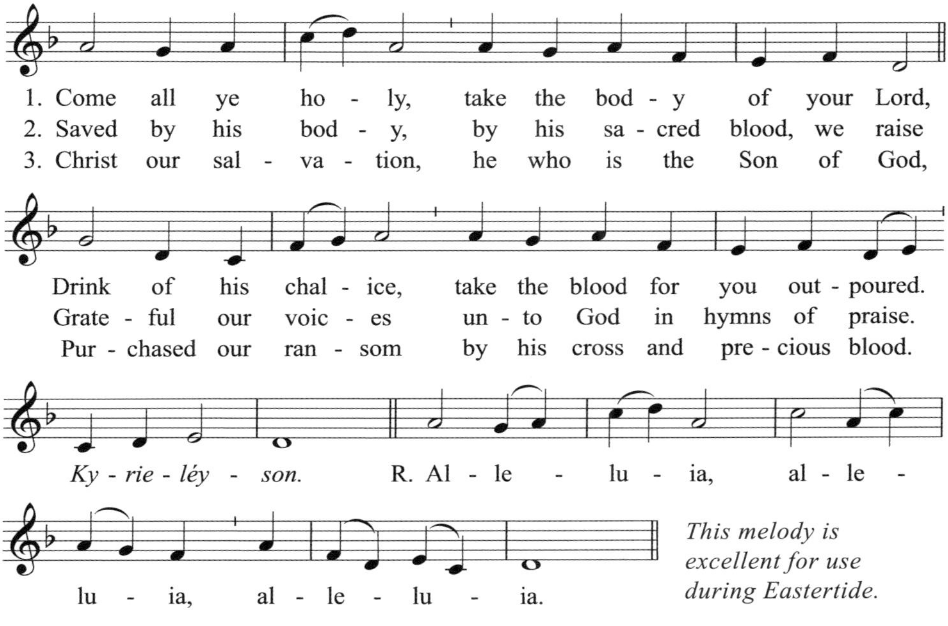

This melody is excellent for use during Eastertide.

4. Dying for all men, | he the Lord prepared this feast,
Offered as victim, | offering himself as priest. *Ky-rie-léy-son.* R.

5. God to our fathers | ordered sacrifice of old;
So he in symbols | Christ the victim true foretold. *Ky-rie-léy-son.* R.

6. Source of all brightness, | sole Redeemer of our race,
He to his holy | servants gives abundant grace. *Ky-rie-léy-son.* R.

7. Come, who with pure hearts | in the Savior's word believe;
Come, and partaking | saving grace from him receive. *Ky-rie-léy-son.* R.

8. God our defender, | guardian sure in this our strife,
Gives to his faithful | after death eternal life. *Ky-rie-léy-son.* R.

9. Bread come from heaven | gives he to the hungering,
As for the thirsty | opens he the living spring. *Ky-rie-léy-son.* R.

10. Christ, source of all things, | who here feeds us sinful men,
When this great day dawns, | judge of all, will come again. *Ky-rie-léy-son.* R.

THE *Saint Jean de Brébeuf Hymnal* (932 pages) contains ancient Latin hymns—translated by Catholic priests, bishops, and cardinals—set to simple-yet-dignified melodies. Unlike other hymnals, it does not mimic or "build upon" Protestant models. Its pew edition contains powerful theological explanations, historical footnotes, and remarkable hymns composed in 1599AD by Catholics under persecution by the heretical Anglican sect.

AVE VIVENS HOSTIA (13th century)

Eucharistic Hymn by Archbishop Pecham of Canturbury (*d.* 1292)

VE, vivens hóstia, | Véritas et vita,
In qua sacrifícia | Cuncta sunt finíta:
Per te Patri glória | Datur infiníta;
Per te stat Ecclésia | Júgiter muníta.

Hail, O living victim, truth and life, in whom all other sacrifices are brought to an end: by thee endless glory is given to the Father; by thee the Church stands constantly protected.

3. Ave, manna cælicum | vérius legáli,
Datum in viáticum | Mísero mortáli,
Medicámen mýsticum | Morbo spiritáli,
Morte dans Cathólicum | Vitæ immortáli.

Hail, O manna more truly from heaven than that received under the Law, given as a wayfaring provision to the wretched and deathbound, mystical remedy for spiritual disease, delivering the Catholic at his death to a life undying.

4. Ave, corpus Dómini | et munus finále,
Corpus junctum Númini, | Nóbile jocále,
Quod relíquit hómini | In memoriále,
Cum fináli término | Mundo dixit vale.

Hail, O body of the Lord and last gift, body united to the Godhead, noble jewel, which he left to man for his remembrance when at his last extremity he bade the world farewell.

7. Hic Jesus veráciter | Duplex est natúra;
Non est partiáliter | Nec solum figúra:
Sed essentiáliter | Caro Christi pura
Latet integráliter | Brevi sub clausúra.

Here in truth is each of Jesus' two natures; nor is Christ's pure flesh present only in part or figuratively: but in its essence it lies hidden in completeness beneath a slight enclosure.

8. Cælo visibíliter | Caro Christi sita:
Forma panis áliter | Latet hic vestíta;
Solus novit quáliter, | Hanc qui ponit ita:
Potest hoc facíliter | Virtus infiníta.

The flesh of Christ is stationed visibly in heaven: here, by contrast, it lies hidden, clothed with the appearance of bread; only he knows how who proposes thus: Boundless power can easily do this.

14. Jesu, vivens hóstia, | Placa majestátem;
Sacraménti grátia | Confer sanitátem;
Paúperum substántia, | Da æternitátem;
Dómini memória, | Fove caritátem.

O Jesus, living victim, appease the divine majesty; through the grace of this sacrament bestow health; O fortune of the poor, grant us everlasting life; O remembrance of the Lord, foster our charity.

This hymn can be sung with any 76 76 D (trochaic) meter, such as SALZBURG E6, HATFIELD, AUS DER TIEFE E6 (*during Lent*), NUN KOMM E4 (*during Advent*), ST KEVIN, TEMPUS ADEST FLORIDUM, JESU LEIDEN PEIN UND TOD, ACH WIE KURZ, AVE VIRGO VIRGINUM, etc.

ADDITIONAL MELODIES, SATB HARMONIES, AND ORGAN ACCOMPANIMENT— as well as the complete hymn (14 verses)—CAN BE FOUND IN THE *Brébeuf Hymnal.*

AVE VIVENS HOSTIA (13th century)

English Translation: Monsignor Ronald A. Knox (d. 1957)

HAIL, true Victim, life and light | Unto sinners lending—
Ev'ry older form and rite | Hath in thee its ending—
Spotless in the Father's sight | Evermore ascending,
Holy church in bitter fight | Evermore befriending.

3. Hail, true Manna from the sky— | Israel never knew thee;
Pilgrims, for the day's supply, | Daily homage do thee;
When our souls in sickness lie, | Yields that sickness to thee;
Christians, when they come to die, | Live immortal through thee.

4. Hail, Christ's Body—gift he made, | His own death foreshowing,
(Godhead under earthly shade | Like a jewel glowing),
Sacred mem'ries, ne'er to fade, | On his Church bestowing,
When to earth farewell he bade, | To his Passion going.

7. Jesus truly in this place | God and Man resideth;
Him no shadow doth replace, | Him no rent divideth,
Very flesh, although his face, | Glorified, he hideth;
Garnered in this little space | All of Christ abideth.

8. Seen in heav'n by blessèd eyes | This his body reigneth;
Form of bread, in other wise, | Here its scope containeth;—
Myst'ry he alone descries | Who the same ordaineth;
Well may he such thing devise | Whom no pow'r restraineth.

14. Plead, true Victim, in our stead | To the Father crying,
Thou, thy children's daily bread, | Daily health supplying;
Banquet for the exile spread, | Grant us life undying;
May our love from thine be fed, | Self and sense denying!

THE *Saint Jean de Brébeuf Hymnal* (932 pages) contains ancient Latin hymns—translated by Catholic priests, bishops, and cardinals—set to simple-yet-dignified melodies. Unlike other hymnals, it does not mimic or "build upon" Protestant models. Its pew edition contains powerful theological explanations, historical footnotes, and remarkable hymns composed in 1599AD by Catholics under persecution by the heretical Anglican sect.

AETERNA CAELI GLORIA (5th century)

English Translation: Robert Campbell of Skerrington (d. 1868)

4. Purest Light, within us dwell,
Never from our souls depart;
Come, the shades of earth dispel,
Fill and purify the heart. (*Alleluia.*)

5. Faith in Him Whose name we bear
In our heart of hearts abound;
Hope, thy brightest torch prepare;
All with holy love be crowned. (*Alleluia.*)

6. Praise the Father, praise the Son,
Spirit blest, to Thee be praise;
To the Godhead Three in One
Glory be through endless days. (*Alleluia.*)

THE *Saint Jean de Brébeuf Hymnal* (932 pages) contains ancient Latin hymns—translated by Catholic priests, bishops, and cardinals—set to simple-yet-dignified melodies. Unlike other hymnals, it does not mimic or "build upon" Protestant models. Its pew edition contains powerful theological explanations, historical footnotes, and remarkable hymns composed in 1599AD by Catholics under persecution by the heretical Anglican sect.

JESU NOSTRA REDEMPTIO (7th century)

English Translation: Father John Fitzpatrick, Oblate of Mary (*d. 1929*)

EDEEMER of our fallen state,
Thou, Jesus, joy of every heart,
Who didst Thy ransomed world create,
Pure light to faithful souls Thou art.

2. What clemency Thy heart o'ercame,
That Thou wouldst bear our load of sin?
And, sinless, die a death of shame,
From death and hell our souls to win?

3. Thou dost the gates of hell withstand,
Its captives from their fetters free,
As victor sit at God's right hand,
And reign with Him triumphantly.

4. Compelled by pity, let Thy grace
Our losses and our ills repair;
And may the vision of Thy face
With us its blessèd radiance share.

5. Our guide to Heaven and the road,
Be Thou the goal to which we tend;
Our joy in this our sad abode,
Our life's reward which ne'er shall end.

---

1. Jesu nostra redémptio,
Amor et desidérium,
Deus Creátor ómnium,
Homo in fine témporum.

2. Quæ te vicit cleméntia,
Ut ferres nostra crímina,
Crudélem mortem pátiens,
Ut nos a morte tólleres?

3. Inférni claustra pénetrans,
Tuos captívos rédimens,
Victor triúmpho nóbili
Ad dextram Patris résidens.

4. Ipsa te cogat píetas
Ut mala nostra súperes
Parcéndo et voti cómpotes
Nos tuo vultu sáties.

5. Tu esto nostrum gáudium,
Qui es futúrus prǽmium,
Sit nostra in te glória,
Per cuncta semper sǽcula.

Title after 1631AD:
Salutis Humanae Sator

ADDITIONAL MELODIES, SATB HARMONIES, LITERAL TRANSLATION, AND ORGAN ACCOMPANIMENTS CAN BE FOUND IN THE *Brébeuf Hymnal*.

This hymn can be sung with any 88 88 meter, such as WINCHESTER NEW, DUGUET, HILDERSTONE, BRESLAU, MELCOMBE, WAREHAM, OLD HUNDREDTH, TRINITY COLLEGE, EISENACH, TALLIS CANON, BRESSANI, LA ROCHELLE, GONFALON ROYAL, etc.

ABLUTIONS WITH WINE AND WATER: "QUOD ORE SUMPSIMUS" ✠

COMMUNION OF THE PEOPLE • Throughout the Church's history, different customs have arisen with regard to how frequently Catholics should receive Holy Communion; even great saints have grappled with this issue. The oldest liturgical book we can consult is the Gelasian Sacramentary, which was written (perhaps) around 725AD. It says: *Post haec communicat sacerdos cum ordinibus sacris cum omni populo.* Those words imply it was not uncommon for the faithful to receive Holy Communion at Mass.

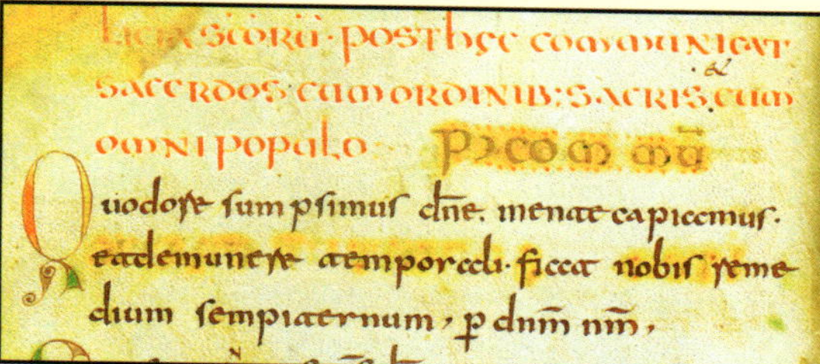

Gellone Sacramentary
CIRCA **785** AD
This is version of the Gelasian Sacramentary. Notice the words in red: *Post haec communicat sacerdos cum ordinibus sacris cum omni populo.*

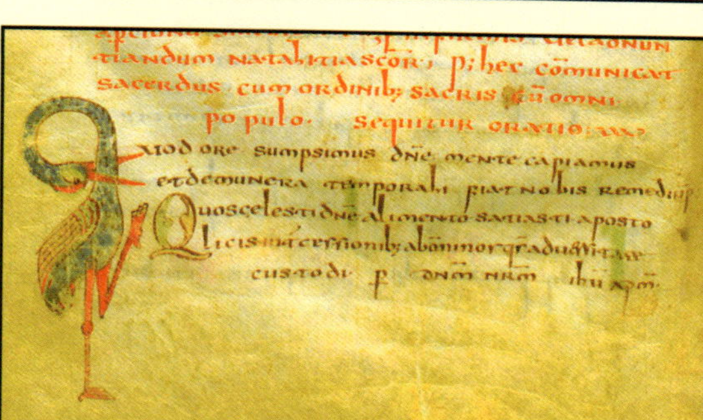

Remedius Sacramentary
CIRCA **800** AD
This is another copy of the Gelasian Sacramentary. It also has those words: *Post haec communicat sacerdos cũ ordinibus sacris cum omni populo.*
The bird standing on one leg is an ornate capital "Q" which starts: **"Quod ore súmpsimus..."**

1962 • Distributing Communion to the people, the Celebrant says:

Corpus Dómini nostri Jesu Christi ✠ custódiat ánimam tuã in vitam ætérnam. Amen.

MAY THE BODY of Our Lord Jesus Christ ✠ keep thy soul unto life everlasting. Amen.

The Communicant does not say: "Amen."

1962 • As the Subdeacon pours wine, the Celebrant says:

Quod ore súmpsimus, Dñe, pura mente capiámus; et de múnere temporáli fiat nobis remédium sempitérnum.

PURE be the soul, Lord, that receives what mouth has eaten; and may thy gift on earth be my health in eternity.

1962 • Then, as wine and water are poured over his fingers, he continues:

Corpus tuum, Dómine, quod sumpsi, et Sanguis quẽ potávi, adhæreat viscéribus meis: et præsta; ut in me non remáneat scélerũ mácula, quem pura et sancta refecérunt sacraménta. Qui vivis et regnas in sǽcula sæculórum. Amen.

ODY OF THINE, Lord, I have tasted, Blood of thine I have drunk, in my soul lodge deep; never a stain of guilt be left in me, revived now by these pure, these holy mysteries: Thou who livest and reignest, world without end. Amen.

1962 • As the Subdeacon attends to the chalice, the Celebrant goes to the Epistle side and quietly reads the Communion Antiphon of the day's Mass:

■ The Communion (Proper)

1962 • Returning to the center, he kisses the Altar. Facing the people, he says :

℣. Dóminus vobíscum.

℟. Et cum spíritu tuo.

℣. The Lord be with you.

℟. And with you, his minister.

1962 • Returning to the the Epistle side, he sings the Postcommunion, which always begins with Orémus ("Let us pray").

■ The Post-Communion (Proper)

1962 • When finished, the Master of Ceremonies closes the Missal. The Celebrant once again goes back to the center, kisses the Altar, turns around, and sings:

℣. Dóminus vobíscum.

℟. Et cum spíritu tuo.

℣. The Lord be with you.

℟. And with you, his minister.

1962 • The Deacon turns to the people and chants:

O, THIS IS the dismissal. ℣. Ite, missa est.

℟. Thanks be to God. ℟. Deo grátias.

1962 • In Masses for the dead, the Deacon sings: *Requiéscant in pace.* ("May they rest in peace") and the response is *Amen.* The final blessing is also omitted.

RESPONSES • "ITE, MISSA EST"

For use at any Mass:

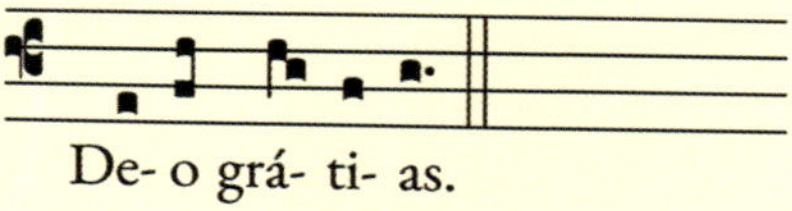

De- o grá- ti- as.

For "Green" Sundays (Mass XI):

De- o grá- ti- as.

For Our Lady (Mass IX and Mass X):

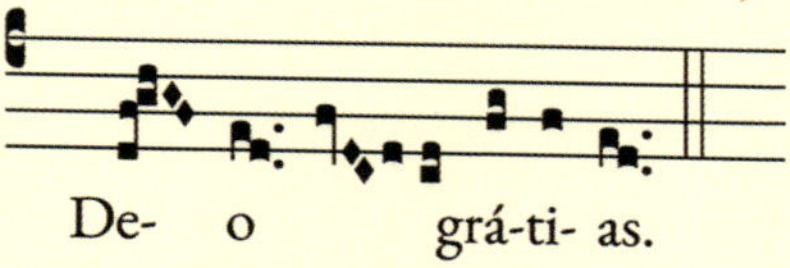

De- o grá-ti- as.

For Advent and Lent (Mass XVII):

De- o grá- ti- as.

A Missa Sabbati Sancti usque ad Sabbatum in Albis inclusive:

De- o grá-ti- as, al-le-lú-ia, alle- lú- ia.

Festive Masses:

De- o grá- ti- as.

Mass II: (*Fons Bonitatis*)

De- o grá- ti- as.

Mass IV: (*Cunctipotens Genitor Deus*)

De- o grá-ti- as.

Mass VIII: (*De Angelis*)

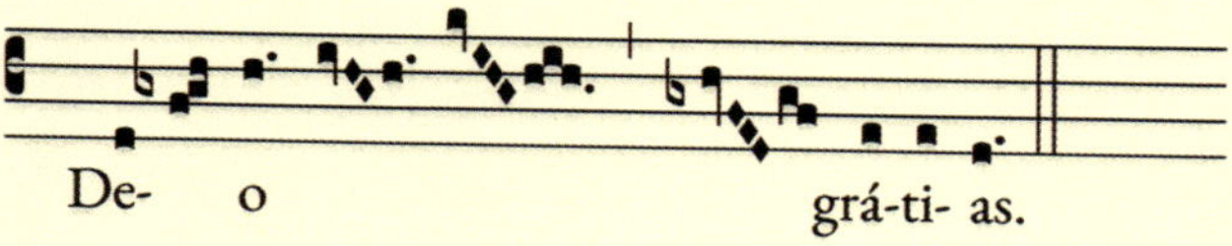

De- o grá-ti- as.

✠ THE DEACON SINGS: "ITE, MISSA EST." • THE PEOPLE REPLY: "DEO GRATIAS."

Ite Missa Est • Shown in a manuscript from Soest (Germany) circa 1393AD.

This excerpt shows what is called "Mass II" in Abbat Pothier's Vatican Edition; notice the heavy use of abbreviation.

The *Sherborne Missal* (circa 1399AD) shows the priest praying the **"Pláceat Tibi."**

THE CELEBRANT PRAYS THE LAST GOSPEL • THE SUBDEACON HOLDS THE CARD. ✠

1962 • Bowing before the Altar with hands folded, the Celebrant prays silently as follows.
Tunc celebrans inclinat se ante medium altaris, et manibus junctis super illud, dicit secrete:

Pláceat tibi, sancta Trínitas, obséquium servitútis meæ: et præsta; ut sacrifícium quod óculis tuæ majestátis indígnus óbtuli, tibi sit acceptábile, mihíque, et ómnibus pro quibus illud óbtuli, sit, te miseránte, propitiábile. Per Christum Dóminum nostrum. Amen.

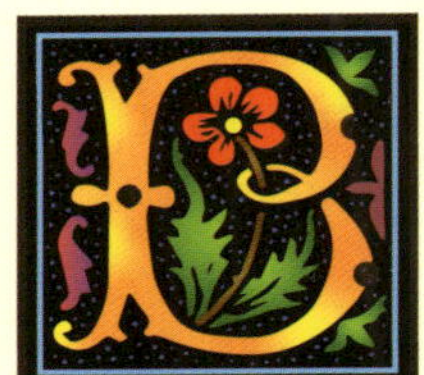

E CONTENT, holy Trinity, with the due performance of my office; may it win acceptance with thee, this sacrifice I have made before thee all unworthily, and for me, and all for whom I offered it, thy pardon. Through Christ our Lord. Amen.

1962 • He kisses the Altar. He briefly looks upward, making a circular gesture with his hands—saying *Benedícat vos omnípotens Deus*—then turns to bless the people: Pater, etc.
Deinde osculatur altare: et elevatis oculis, extendens, elevans, et jungens manus, caputque cruci inclinans, dicit: Benedícat etc. *et versus ad populum, semel tantum benedicens, etiam in Missis solemnibus, prosequitur:* Pater etc.

Benedícat vos omnípotens Deus, Pater, et Fílius, ✠ et Spíritus Sanctus. ℟. Amen.

ALMIGHTY GOD bless you, Father, Son, ✠ and Holy Ghost. ℟. Amen.

THE LAST GOSPEL

1962 • The Celebrant goes to the Gospel corner of the Altar and says:

℣. Dóminus vobíscum.

℣. The Lord be with you.

℟. Et cum spíritu tuo.

℟. And with you, his minister.

Inítium sancti Evangélii secúndum Joánnem.

℣. The beginning of the holy Gospel according to John.

℟. Glória tibi, Dómine.

℟. Glory to thee, Lord.

In princípio erat Verbũ, et Verbum erat apud Deum, et Deus erat Verbum. Hoc erat in princípio apud Deum. Ómnia per ipsum facta sunt, et sine ipso factum est nihil quod factũ est.

T THE BEGINNING of time the Word already was; and God had the Word abiding with him, and the Word was God. He abode, at the beginning of time, with God.

It was through him that all things came into being, and without him came nothing that has come to be. In him there was life, and that life was the light of men. And the light shines in darkness, a darkness which was not able to master it.

In ipso vita erat, et vita erat lux hóminum, et lux in ténebris lucet, et ténebræ eam non comprehendérunt.

A man appeared—sent from God—whose name was John. He came for a witness, to bear witness of the light, so that through him all men might learn to believe. He was not the Light; he was sent to bear witness of the Light. There is one who enlightens every soul born into the world; he was the true Light. He, through whom the world was made, was in the world, and the world treated him as a stranger. He came to what was his own, and they who were his own gave him no welcome. But all those who did welcome him, he empowered to become the children of God, all those who believe in his name; their birth came, not from human stock, not from nature's will or man's, but from God. *(here all genuflect)*

Fuit homo missus a Deo, cui nomen erat Joánnes. Hic venit in testimónium, ut testimónium perhibéret de lúmine, ut omnes créderent per illũ. Non erat ille lux, sed ut testimónium perhibéret de lúmine. Erat lux vera quæ illúminat omnem hóminem veniéntem in hunc mundũ. In mundo erat, et mundus per ipsum factus est, et mundus eum non cognóvit. In própria venit, et sui eum non recepérunt; quotquot autẽ recepérunt eum, dedit eis potestátem fílios Dei fíeri; his qui credunt in nómine ejus, qui non ex sanguínibus, neque ex voluntáte carnis, neque ex voluntáte viri, sed ex Deo nati sunt. *(hic genuflectitur)*

AND THE WORD WAS MADE FLESH, and came to dwell among us, and we had sight of his glory; glory such as belongs to the Father's only-begotten Son, full of grace and truth. ℟. Thanks be to God.

ET VERBUM CARO FACTUM EST, et habitávit in nobis: et vídimus glóriam ejus, glóriã quasi Unigéniti a Patre, plenũ grátiæ et veritátis. ℟. Deo grátias.

SOLEMN HYMN TO THE SON OF GOD

The following hymn is suitable throughout the liturgical year:

F THE FATHER born alone,
Heir co-regent of his throne,
Word he speaks eternally,
Mirror of his majesty: (*Alleluia.*)

2. Man to save, who man became,
Pleased his servile form to claim,
As a blessèd Maiden's child
Earth to heaven reconciled. (*Alleluia.*)

3. Ever God, in time a man,
Limited, whom none may span,
Knowing all, whose wisdom grew,
Paschal Lamb and Shepherd true: (*Alleluia.*)

4. Who by yielding won the strife,
Who by dying garnered life,
Who departed, but to bide
With the Church, your chosen Bride. (*Alleluia.*)

5. Come for men to mediate,
Sovereign Priest and Advocate,
To your own who pledged to send,
For their help, another Friend: (*Alleluia.*)

6. With the Father intercede,
Sinless one, for sinners plead,
That the way of life they tread,
By your grace to glory led. (*Alleluia.*)

7. God almighty, three in one,
Holy Father, holy Son,
With the holy Paraclete,
Let your works your praise repeat: (*Alleluia.*)

8. To your most exalted name
Let unfaltering acclaim
From created things ascend
Now and ever, without end. (*Alleluia.*)

An original text by Father Dominic Popplewell, FSSP. Nine musical settings are included in the *Brébeuf Hymnal*.

This text can be sung with any **77 77 meter**: SAVANNAH, UNIVERSITY COLLEGE, CULBACH, GOTT SEI DANK, ORIENTIS PARTIBUS, LLANFAIR, MONKLAND, etc. It can also be sung with any 77 77 D meter: ACH WIE KURZ 7E, HEUSTIS, PASCHAL LAMB, GROSSER GOTT 7B, SALZBURG, ST GEORGE, etc.

QUEM TERRA, PONTUS (6th century)

English Translation: Father John Fitzpatrick, Oblate of Mary (d. 1929)

HE LORD, whom earth, and sea, and sky
Revere, adore and magnify,
Who o'er this triune system reigns,
To dwell in Mary's cloister deigns!

2. Whom sun, and moon, and all things serve,
Nor ever from this duty swerve,
He makes that womb, which heav'nly grace
Imbues, his virgin lodging-place.

3. A mother blessèd, who can claim
Within the coffer of her frame
To keep her Maker, who has spanned
The whole world with His infant hand!

4. Blessèd by God's own message made,
And fruitful 'neath His spirit's shade
She was, of whom conceived came He,
Whom all the nations longed to see.

5. Jesus the Virgin's only Son,
With Father and with spirit One,
Be praise and glory giv'n to Thee
In time and in eternity.

This hymn can be sung with any 88 88 meter, such as WINCHESTER NEW, DUGUET, HILDERSTONE, BRESLAU, MELCOMBE, WAREHAM, OLD HUNDREDTH, TRINITY COLLEGE, EISENACH, TALLIS CANON, BRESSANI, LA ROCHELLE, GONFALON ROYAL, etc.

SINGING NOTE: Underlined words help singers know how many syllables a word is to receive. For example, radiance would be sung with two (not three) syllables.

1. Quem terra, pontus, æthera,
Colunt, adórant, prædicant,
Trinam regéntem máchinam
Claustrum Maríæ bájulat.

2. Cui luna, sol, et ómnia
Desérviunt per témpora,
Perfúsa cæli grátia,
Gestant Puéllæ víscera.

3. Beáta Mater múnere,
Cujus, supérnus Ártifex,
Mundum pugíllo cóntinens,
Ventris sub arca clausus est.

4. Beáta cæli núntio,
Fecúnda Sancto Spíritu,
Desiderátus Géntibus,
Cujus per alvum fusus est.

5. Glória tibi, Dómine,
Qui natus es de Vírgine,
Cum Patre et Sancto Spíritu,
In sempitérna sæcula.

Title after 1631AD:
Quem Terra, Pontus, Sidera

SALVE REGINA (11th century)

Hermann Contractus, Monk of Reichenau Abbey (d. 1054)

AIL, HOLY QUEEN enthroned above, O Maria!
Hail, Mother of mercy and of love, O Maria! ℟.

2. Our life, our sweetness here below, O Maria!
Our hope in sorrow and in woe, O Maria! ℟.

3. To thee we cry, poor sons of Eve, O Maria!
To thee we sigh, we mourn, we grieve, O Maria! ℟.

4. This earth is but a vale of tears, O Maria!
A place of banishment and fears, O Maria! ℟.

5. Turn, then, most gracious Advocate, O Maria!
Toward us thine eyes compassionate, O Maria! ℟.

6. When this our exile is complete, O Maria!
Show us thy Son, our Jesus sweet, O Maria! ℟.

℟. **TRIUMPH, ALL YE CHERUBIM!** Sing with us ye seraphim!
Heav'n and earth resound the hymn! Salve, salve, salve Regina!

This is a Roman Catholic translation from 1687AD:

This hymn can be sung with any **88 88 meter** — such as WINCHESTER NEW, DUGUET, HILDERSTONE, BRESLAU, MELCOMBE, OLD HUNDREDTH, WAREHAM, TRINITY COLLEGE, EISENACH, BRESSANI, LA ROCHELLE, GONFALON ROYAL, etc.

H**AIL TO THE QUEEN** that reigns above,
Mother of Clemency and Love:
Hail, thou our Hope, Life, Sweetness: We,
Eve's banish'd Children, cry to Thee.

2. We, from this wretched Vale of Tears
Send Sighs and Groans unto thine ears.
O then, sweet Advocate, bestow
A pitying look on us below.

3. After this Exile, let us see
Our Blessèd Jesus, born of Thee,
O merciful, O pious Maid!
O gracious Mary! lend thine Aid.

ADDITIONAL MELODIES, SATB HARMONIES, LITERAL TRANSLATION, AND ORGAN ACCOMPANIMENTS CAN BE FOUND IN THE *Brébeuf Hymnal*.

THE NEW IS IN THE OLD CONCEALED; THE OLD IS BY THE NEW REVEALED.

TYPES • By "types" we mean persons and things in the Old Law prefiguring persons and things in the New. The Old Law itself (and its various sacrifices) were but the types or shadows—not the reality—of future good things promised (cf. Heb 10). Below are some "types" from the Old Testament.

Missale Secundum Usum Ecclesie Parisiensis (f. 342).

PASCHAL LAMB • The Passover feast was the most important Jewish holiday. The Paschal Lamb (Exodus 12) is the most expressive "type" of Christ mentioned in the Old Testament. It was slain the day before the Passover; it was to be without blemish; it was to be offered to God and then eaten; not a bone of it was to be broken; its blood sprinkled on the door-posts preserved the Israelites from temporal death, as the Blood of Christ—the Lamb of God—shed on the Cross preserves us from eternal death. A lamb is remarkable for its gentleness; it submits to unmerited suffering without complaint (Is 53:7); in the Old Law it was slain for sins not its own.

STAFF IN HAND • On Easter Sunday, the Alleluia verse comes from Saint Paul (I Cor 5:7): *Étenim Pascha nostrum immolátus est Christus.* That means: "Has not Christ been sacrificed for us, **our paschal victim?"**

The image shown on the left—which begins the Canon of the Mass (*Te ígitur clementíssime Pater...*)—shows the crucifixion on the top. Underneath is the Last Supper (which was also the feast of the Passover), at which Jesus consecrated the fourth Hallel cup.

The Apostles are shown holding white poles according to the book of Exodus, which says of the Passover: "And this is to be the manner of your eating it; your loins must be girt, your feet ready shod, and **every man's staff in his hand;** all must be done in haste. It is the night of the Pasch."

AZYMES • The azyme-bread was unleavened bread prescribed by the Mosaic Law for the Feast of the Passover. There was also a Feast of the Azymes (Feast of the Unleavened Bread) which continued for seven days. The Azymes and Passover were practically one and the same feast.

SACRIFICE OF ISAAC • Isaac was a "type" of Jesus. God tells Abraham to sacrifice Isaac—Abraham's "only begotten son"—on a mountain. Just as our Lord would carry His cross to Calvary, the wood is placed upon the shoulders of Isaac (Genesis 22:7), and **Isaac carried the wood**. Abraham built an altar, but God intervened before Isaac was sacrificed. Saint Thomas Aquinas, in the Sequence for the feast of Corpus Christi (*Lauda Sion*) wrote as follows:

Ecce panis Angelórum, Factus cibus viatórum: Vere panis filiórum, Non mitténdus cánibus.	Behold, the bread of angels is become the pilgrim's food; truly it is bread for the sons, and is not to be cast to dogs.
In figúris præsignátur, Cum Isaac immolátur: Agnus paschæ deputátur Datur manna pátribus.	It was prefigured in type **when Isaac was brought as an offering,** when a lamb was appointed for the Pasch, and when manna was given to the Jews of old.

SMALL & WHITE MANNA • Manna was the miraculous bread the Israelites survived on during their forty years sojourn in the desert. It came down from heaven every morning, and it was consumed in the morning. It was small and white; and such was its nature that "neither had he more that had gathered more, nor did he find less that had provided less" (Ex 16:18). In the New Testament, Jesus gave a "type" of the Blessed Sacrament when He blessed bread and lifted His eyes to heaven before multiplying the loaves for the multitude. Manna was a "type" of the SANCTISSIMUM (Holy Eucharist).

A suménte non concísus, Non confráctus, non divísus: Integer accípitur. Sumit unus, sumunt mille: Quantum isti, tantum ille: Nec sumptus consúmitur.	The communicant receives the complete Christ: uncut, unbroken, and undivided. Whether one receive or a thousand, the one receives as much as the thousand. Nor is Christ diminished by being received.

MOSES THE LAW-GIVER • Several Old Testament figures and prophets were "types" of Jesus. Moses is certainly one example; and even his birth prefigured that of Christ. Just as the King of Egypt ordered all male children to be killed, King Herod ordered that "all the male children that were in Bethlehem" younger than two years old must be killed (Mt 2:16). But Moses was preserved from death by being placed in a "little basket of reeds" (Ex 2:3), even as Saint Joseph—our Lord's foster father—rescued Him by secretly taking Him to Egypt (Mt 2:14). In other words, in both instances the life of the spiritual leader was attacked at birth by a jealous (temporal) king.

Holy Week • Ancient Manuscripts

Litany of the Saints • Unlike the 1950 version, the 1962 Holy Week splits the litany into two sections, placed "on either side" of the Baptismal ceremonies (viz. *blessing of the font, Sacrament of Baptism, and renewal of baptismal promises*). This was based upon mediæval practice; for example, the Missale Parisiense (**1481ad**) splits the litany, as does the Limoges Missal (**1138ad**). Bishop Durandus (d. 1138ad) also mentions this practice. The image above — Ms. 22049 (f. 108r) — was created circa **1429ad**. It splits the litany exactly as the 1962 version does; notice where the first part of the litany stops, interrupted by the blessing of the font. In mediæval books, the litany of the saints was often lavishly decorated. Consider the following:

Holy Saturday • "Litany of the Saints" — *Greiffenklau Missal* (circa 1428ad)

Benedictio ignis.
Domine san
potens eter

BLESSING THE FIRE

A striking manuscript is the aforementioned Ms. 22049—created circa 1429AD. Throughout the Easter Vigil, splendid miniature pictures are provided, showing what the Celebrant does. Folio 84r (image on the left) shows the blessing of the fire.

DESPERATELY NEEDED • The Holy Week ceremonies are incredibly ancient, and are described in detail by the earliest liturgical books we possess. An encyclopedia juxtaposing the various ancient MSS is needed—but such an endeavor is far beyond the scope of this hand-missal. To provide an example of Holy Week from a very ancient MS, consider the following (below), taken from the LEOFRIC MISSAL (c. **979AD**). At the end of Good Friday, it says *communicent omnes* in red ink, which means the people received. General Communion on Good Friday was a "universal practice that perdured for centuries" {Giampietro p67} but it faded away—and the reasons for this are discussed in great detail on pages 143-144 and 548:

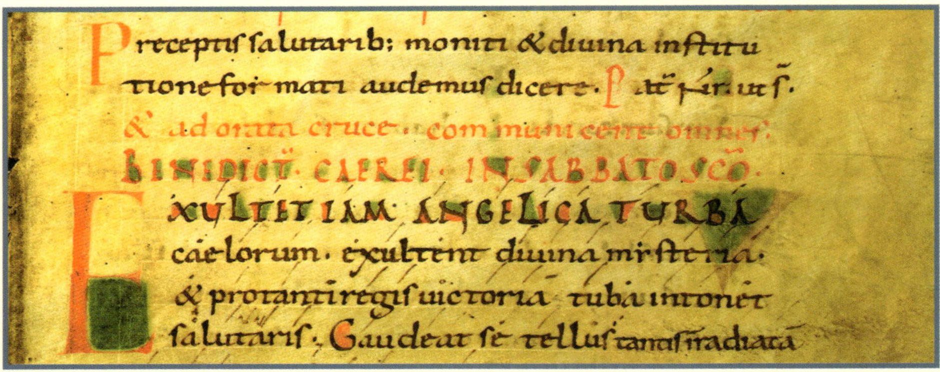
Preceptis salutarib; moniti & diuina institu
tione formati audemus dicere. Pater noster usque finem.
& adorata cruce. communicent omnes.
BENEDICTIO CAEREI. IN SABBATO SCO.
Exultet iam angelica turba
caelorum. exultent diuina mysteria.
& pro tanti regis uictoria tuba intonet
salutaris. Gaudeat se tellus tantis irradiata

O FELIX CULPA • In describing the EXSULTET (cf. pages 558-561), **O felix culpa** ("O happy fault of Adam") was discussed. For centuries, some Catholics rejected this bold language, and the passage is often crossed out in the manuscripts. Indeed, Saint Hugh of Cluny (d. 1109AD) "ordered the words to be effaced in his Missal" {Thurston, p420}, and Ms. 22049 (mentioned above)—which was created circa **1459AD**—omits the entire passage. Yet, we see (below) that the LEOFRIC MISSAL (c. **979AD**) includes the entire passage:

PANGE LINGUA IMITATES • Because our book places such emphasis on Holy Week, consider one more example of how *Hebdomada Major* appeared in ancient MSS. The following page (f. 72r) comes from YRIEIX|1040, created around the year **1040AD**. It shows Good Friday; specifically it shows (below) the "Crux Fidélis"—more properly called "Pange Lingua"—a hymn written by Bishop Venantius Fortunatus (d. 609AD). To give perspective, Fortunatus wrote his hymn 1,000 years before Pope Urban VIII would publish a corrupted version of all the breviary hymns in 1632AD. The manuscript itself (Yrieix|1040) was produced two hundred years before Saint Thomas Aquinas was born in 1225AD. It should be remembered that the "Pange Lingua" of Aquinas imitates the ancient version by Bishop Fortunatus (d. 609AD). Like so many ancient Catholic hymns, the "Pange Lingua" of Fortunatus leads one through Our Redeemer's entire life—not just His passion and death. In the *Saint Jean de Brébeuf Hymnal* (Sophia Press, 2018), numerous settings of both versions of the "Pange Lingua" are provided, translated into English by Catholic priests like Father Ronald Knox, Father Dominic Popplewell, Father Edward Caswall, Father John Fitzpatrick, Father Dylan Schrader, and so forth. Notice (below) how the scribe in 1040AD uses "heightened neumes"—which are not as precise as staff notation, but more helpful than adiastamatic notation:

RUBRICS OF HOLY WEEK • The next page (f. 72v) provides rubrics for Holy Saturday, beginning with *Sabbato sancto paschæ primitus agendum est ut ignis excutiatur de crystallo aut de lapide* ... and so on. The title (below) says: ORDO IN SABBATO SANCTO PASCHAE ["Pasch" = Passover/Easter].

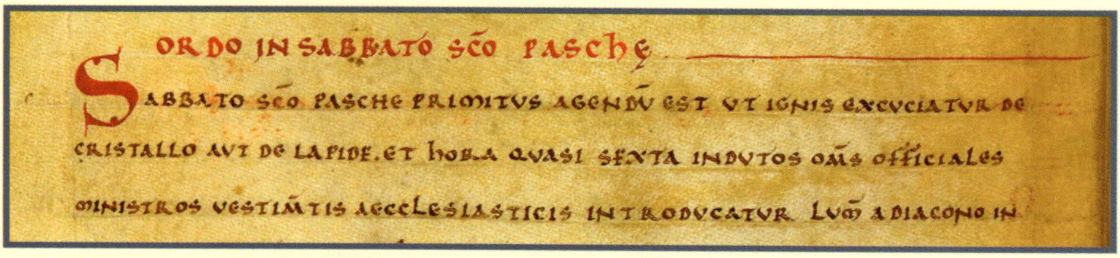

Those rubrics (from **1040AD**) translated into English are as follows:

THE ORDER ON THE HOLY SABBATH [i.e. "Holy Saturday"] OF THE PASCH

On the holy Sabbath of the Pasch, the first thing do be done is that fire be struck from crystal or rock. And about the sixth hour [*hour of sext*]—all the serving ministers wearing church garb—a light is brought into the church by the deacon. And immediately the deacon, wearing a dalmatic, shall proceed to bless the candle, the light being set on a reed held near him. Thus when in blessing he reaches the place where he says: *Sed jam colúmnae hujus praecónia nóvimus* ["But now we know the accolades of this pillar"] he shall light the candle, so when he says: *quam in honóre Dei rútilans ignis accéndit* ["which in God's honor the glowing fire kindles"], already lit, it will begin to shine. Once the candle has been blessed, the deacon shall take off the dalmatic, and put on a chasuble. Then the priest shall say the collect that is found in the sacramentary. And with each collect, when the priest says: *Orémus, Flectámus génua* shall be said, until the litany, because the Roman order so directs. He who reads the lesson shall not say: *Léctio libri Génesis* ["A lesson of the book of Genesis"], but they shall all be started plainly, without any introduction, thus: LESSON I. *In princípio creávit Deus caelum et terram* ["In the beginning God created heaven and earth"] ... ***The rubrics continue.***

"EXTRA" VERSES • OFFERTORY & COMMUNION

THROUGHOUT this book, we have made constant reference to the "extra" verses for Offertory & Communion found in the ancient MSS. Two examples (given below) show what such "extra" verses actually look like in the ancient MSS:

Offertory (Easter Sunday)
...with "extra" verses as found in BAMBERG6LIT|905 (f. 41), circa **905AD**:

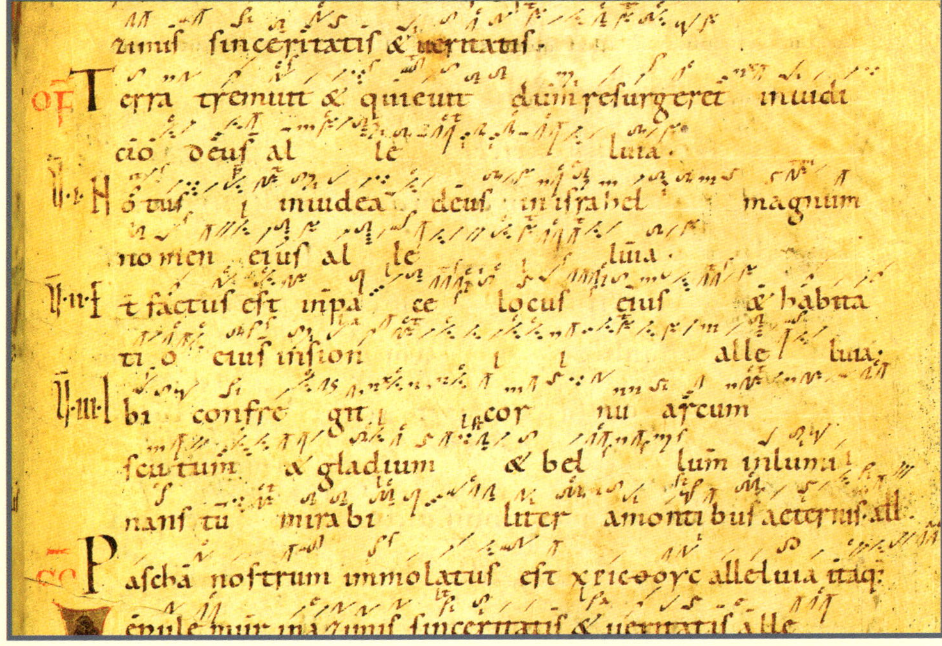

zimis sinceritatis & veritatis.
OF Terra tremuit & quievit dum resurgeret in iudicio deus al le luia.
V. I. Notus in iudea deus in israhel magnum nomen eius al le luia.
V. II. Et factus est in pace locus eius & habitatio eius in sion alle luia.
V. III. Ibi confregit cor nu arcum scutum & gladium & bel lum inluminans tu mirabiliter a montibus aeternis all.
CO Pascha nostrum immolatus est xpictus alleluia itaq: epulemur in azimis sinceritatis & veritatis alle

Communion (Easter Sunday)
...with "extra" verse (Ps 117) as found in STMAUR|1079 (f. 169v), circa **1079AD**:

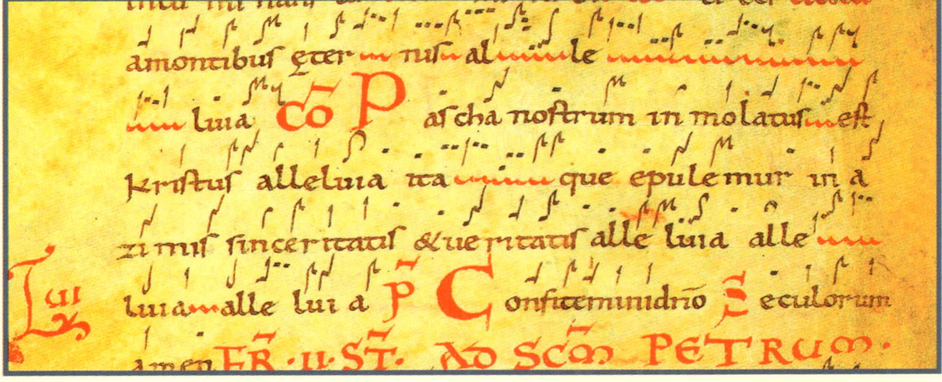

amontibus eter nis al le
luia CO Pascha nostrum in molatus est
xpistus alleluia ita que epulemur in a
zimis sinceritatis & veritatis alle luia alle
luia alle luia PS Confitemini domino Seculorum
amen FR. II. ST. AD SCM PETRUM.

"Te Igitur Clementissime" • Roman Canon

"T" Transformation • The Canon has always begun: *Te ígitur clementissime*. That is to say, with the letter T, lavishly decorated by the early Christians. On the RIGHT is shown the Canon from the *Sacramentary of Drogon* (circa 845AD) which contains three sacrifices—Abel's, Abraham's, and Melchizedek's—drawn right into the letter T.

A certain tension developed vis-à-vis whether to make the T a Crucifix, use it to begin a word, or both. Eventually, the "standard" became to place the Crucifixion on the left page and decorate the first T on the right page. Shown ABOVE is the Canon from an Avignon Missal created circa 1333AD. The artwork is without question beautiful—and yet the Crucifixion seems to distract or "compete with" the decorated T (which encircles a priest saying Mass). The "standard" arrangement, therefore, seems the most aesthetically pleasing, and the large Crucifixion which fills the page is certainly an homage to the most ancient practice.

ALTAR CURTAINS IN THE WEST

ALTAR CURTAINS IN THE WEST

In some Eastern rite churches, a special wall (*iconostasis*) prevents the congregation from viewing the Sanctuary. In the West, a different tradition prevailed: the faithful were allowed to see what the Celebrant was doing—but **curtains** were drawn around the Altar during certain parts of Mass. Those who carefully examine ancient depictions of the Roman Rite will frequently notice a curtain (*parochet*), whose predecessor is the veil of the temple.

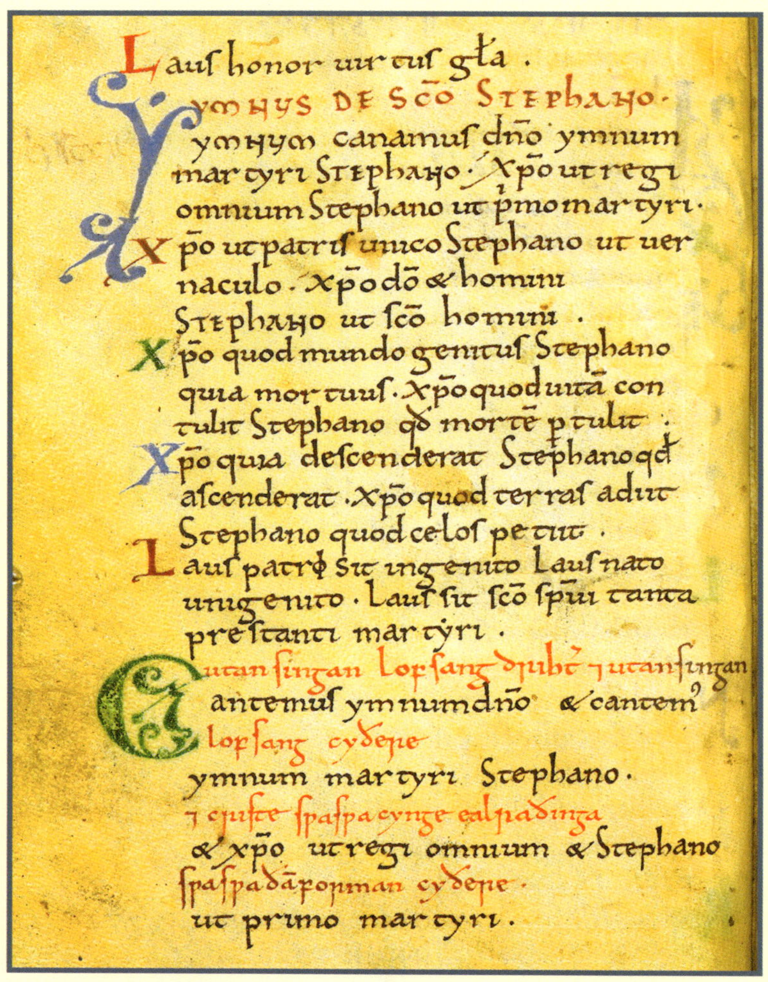
Laus honor uirtus gl̄a.
YMNUS DE SCŌ STEPHANO.
Ymnum canamus dn̄o ymnum
martyri Stephano. Xp̄o ut regi
omnium Stephano ut p̄mo martyri.
Xp̄o ut patris unico Stephano ut uer
naculo. Xp̄o dō & homini
Stephano ut scō homini.
Xp̄o quod mundo genitus Stephano
quia mortuus. Xp̄o quod uitā con
tulit Stephano qd̄ mortē ptulit.
Xp̄o quia descenderat Stephano qđ
ascenderat. Xp̄o quod terras adiit
Stephano quod celos petiit.
Laus patri sit ingenito laus nato
unigenito. Laus sit scō sp̄ui tanta
prestanti martyri.
Utan singan lofsang drihtne 7 utan singan
Cantemus ymnum dn̄o & cantem⁹
lofsang cyðere
ymnum martyri Stephano.
7 criste swaswa cyninge ealra ðinga
& xp̄o ut regi omnium & Stephano
swaswa ðam forman cyðere.
ut primo martyri.

THE CATHOLIC CHURCH AND VERNACULAR HYMNS

In 2018, the release of the *Saint Jean de Brébeuf Hymnal* took the musical world by storm. This 932-page pew book does not mimic or "build upon" Protestant models. The blog of the *Church Music Association of America* (6/10/2019) called it: "hands down, the best Catholic hymnal ever published." The blog went on to proclaim that: "It is such a fantastic hymnal that it deserves to be in the pews of every Catholic church. Its copious selection of hundreds of tunes and texts, including favorites, forgotten gems, and new commissions [...] is not only unparalleled by any other current hymnal, but **well exceeds that of any hymnal from any period."**

The *Saint Jean de Brébeuf Hymnal* translated the great Latin hymns of the Catholic Church into English; and yet this was not really revolutionary. For example, the Roman Catholic manuscript SHOWN ABOVE was created circa 1053AD. It presents the hymns in Latin, then presents them again with Anglo-Saxon ("Old English") in red ink. The excerpt above is a hymn for Saint Stephen, the first martyr (26 December):

HYMNUM canamus Domino, | Hymnum martyri Stephano;
Christo ut Regi omnium, | Stephano ut primo Martyri.

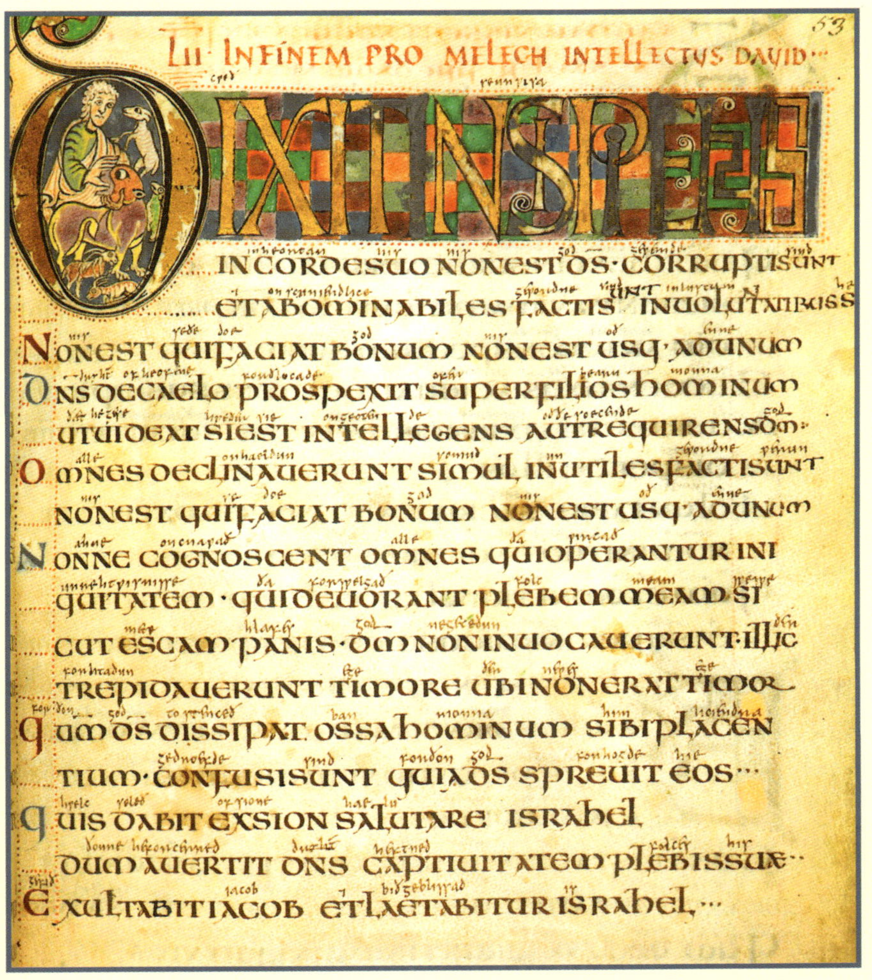
53
LII IN FINEM PRO MELECH INTELLECTUS DAVID
DIXIT INSIPIENS
IN CORDE SUO NON EST DS· CORRUPTI SUNT
ET ABOMINABILES FACTI SUNT IN UOLUNTATIBUS S
NON EST QUI FACIAT BONUM NON EST USQ· AD UNUM
DNS DE CAELO PROSPEXIT SUPER FILIOS HOMINUM
UT UIDEAT SI EST INTELLEGENS AUT REQUIRENS DM·
OMNES DECLINAUERUNT SIMUL INUTILES FACTI SUNT
NON EST QUI FACIAT BONUM NON EST USQ· AD UNUM
NONNE COGNOSCENT OMNES QUI OPERANTUR INI
QUITATEM · QUI DEUORANT PLEBEM MEAM SI
CUT ESCAM PANIS· DM NON INUOCAUERUNT· ILLIC
TREPIDAUERUNT TIMORE UBI NON ERAT TIMOR
QUM DS DISSIPAT OSSA HOMINUM SIBI PLACEN
TIUM· CONFUSI SUNT QUIA DS SPREUIT EOS
QUIS DABIT EX SION SALUTARE ISRAHEL
DUM AUERTIT DNS CAPTIUITATEM PLEBIS SUAE
EXULTABIT IACOB ET LAETABITUR ISRAHEL

THE OLDEST ENGLISH TRANSLATION OF THE BIBLE

In this third edition of the *Saint Edmund Campion Missal*, the Passion of our Lord (proclaimed on Palm Sunday and Good Friday) is typeset in a way that is not common in our age. Our model was the *Vespasian Psalter* **(see above)**, an illuminated psalter produced in southern England circa 735AD. It is the most ancient English translation of any portion of the Bible. The Latin is given in large letters, with the Old English translation in small print.

The page of the *Vespasian Psalter* provided above shows Psalm 13, whose lavishly decorated first verse is as follows:

> DIXIT INSIPIENS in corde suo: Non est Deus.
> Corrupti sunt, et abominabiles facti sunt in studiis suis;
> non est qui faciat bonum, non est usque ad unum.

> THE FOOL HATH SAID in his heart: There is no God.
> They are corrupt, and are become abominable in their ways:
> there is none that doth good, no not one.

UR CATHOLIC FOREFATHERS who sang in church had the complete *Graduale* and *Antiphonale* memorized. In other words, these singers knew hundreds of thousands of notes by memory. Perhaps even more astonishing is that many of these lengthy melodies were ***similar but not identical*** to one another.

On the one hand, much remains unknown (and unknowable) regarding manuscripts written more than a millennium ago. Scholars argue over a manuscript's provenance, what its various signs denote, and under what circumstances a particular manuscript might have been used—and by whom! Some "clues" can be gained by comparing the handwriting of individual manuscripts, looking for pictures of secular rulers or patrons (drawn in the margins), and taking note of individual saints mentioned. On the other hand, the Catholic Church's plainchant is the most ancient music in the galaxy ***that can be known beyond a shadow of a doubt***. The Catholic Church—alone—invented musical notation. At first, Catholics devised a cumbersome method to 'notate' plainsong, using certain intervals from songs already committed to memory. (Needless to say, this difficult method became impossible when those involved knew different versions of a particular song.) Later, the Church moved to *adiastematic* notation—which resembles squiggly lines—but that system was meaningless unless the singer already knew each melody by heart. *Adiastematic* notation is like a mnemonic device; it helps someone remember what he already knows. A slightly better notation soon followed, called *heightened neumes*—but these were still a memory tool. In other words, *heightened neumes* only had meaning for singers who already knew the melody by heart. Eventually, a Benedictine monk named GUIDO D'AREZZO perfected *diastematic notation* ("staff notation"), which made it possible for singers to ***sing music they had never heard before***. This feat was so revolutionary that poor Guido was forced to leave his monastery—due to the jealousy on the part of his fellow monks—but Pope John XIX (d. 1032AD) personally gave Guido his blessing for this valuable musical discovery.

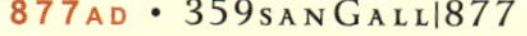

A TRAIL LIKE NONE OTHER • Thanks to this process, which required four centuries to develop, we have an incontrovertible trail—**note by note**—that shows breathtaking correlation between pre-*adiastematic*, then *adiastematic*, then *heightened neumes*, and finally *diastematic notation*. None but a lunatic would deny this astounding correlation, which can be observed in several thousand different chants. Below, we provide the "incontrovertible trail" of a single chant: ALLELUIA from the feast of Saint Stephen, the first martyr (26 December). The dates provided are estimates by expert paleographers.

877AD • 359SANGALL|877

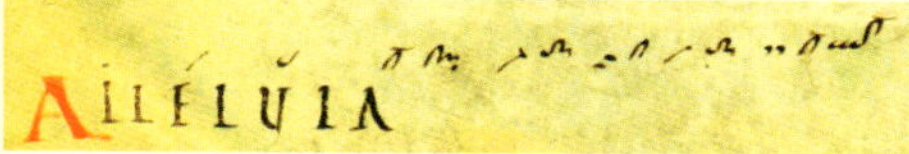

927AD • 239LAON|927

961AD • 121EINSIE|961

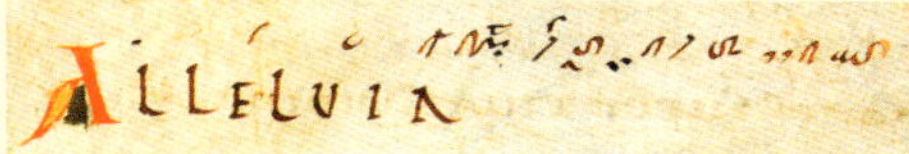

983AD • 9448PRUM|983

989AD • MONTPELLIER H. 159 *Faculté de médecine*

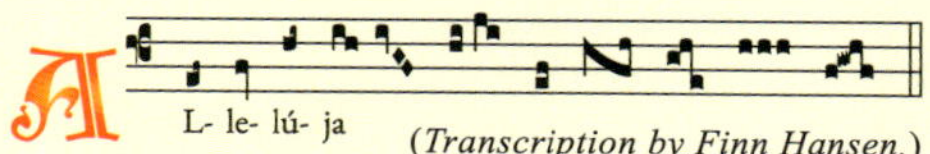

(*Transcription by Finn Hansen.*)

1028AD • 8BAMBERG|1028

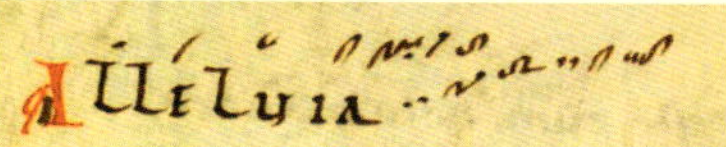

1031AD • 75CAMBRAI|1031

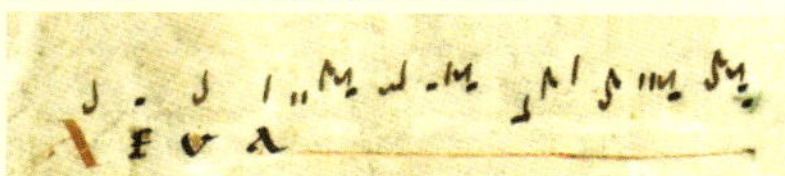

1047AD • ALBI|1047

1052AD • 376SANGALL|1052

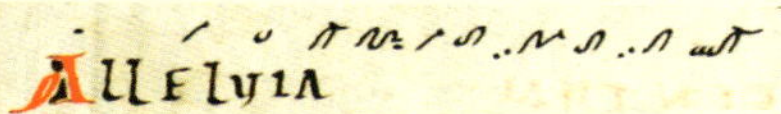

1057AD • NOYON|1057

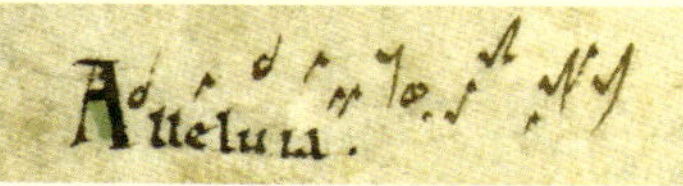

1066AD • 1066nimes|1066

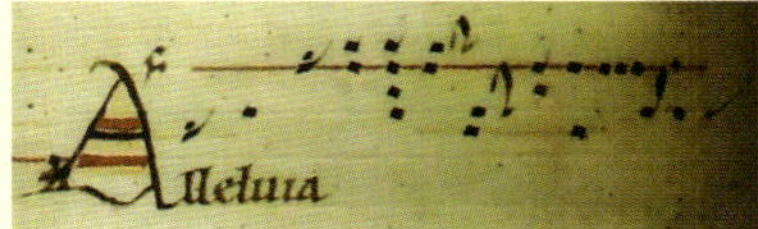

1085AD • 1132limoges|1085

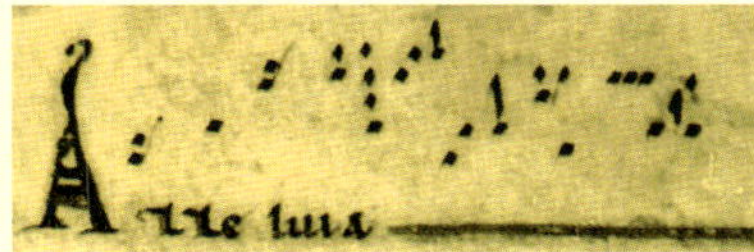

1087AD • Cluniacensem|1087

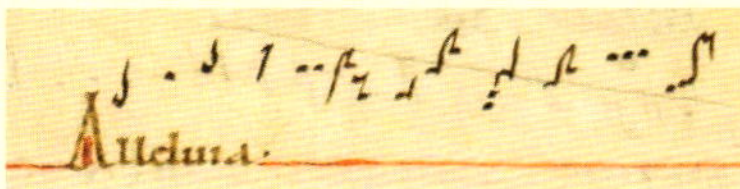

1108AD • 10508normandy|1108

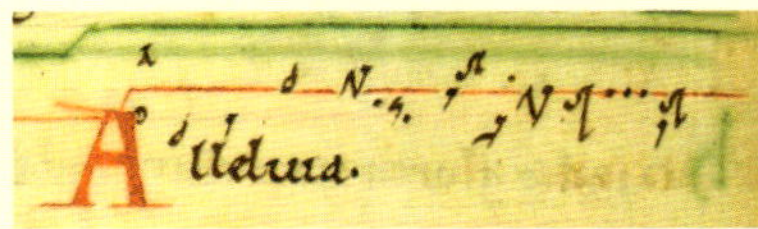

1128AD • 4951steven|1128

1225AD • CistercienseHeidelberg|1225

1233AD • 1112parisiense|1233

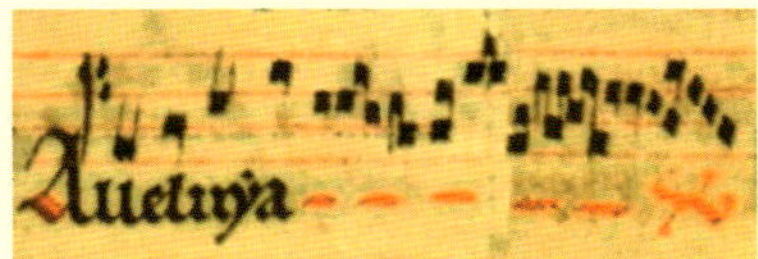

1286AD • Düsseldorf-10a *Hennegau (Belgium)*

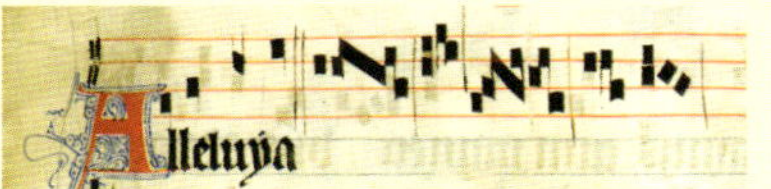

1384AD • 84portugal|1384

1393AD • Düsseldorf-11 *Soest (Germany)*

1461AD • Düsseldorf-19 *Altenberg (Germany)*

1502AD • Düsseldorf-30 *Knights of the Cross*

1513AD • 034braga|1513

1876 • Graduale *Father Hermesdorff (d. 1885)*

1883 • Liber Gradualis *Abbat Pothier (d. 1923)*

1909 • Gradualbuch *Father Weinmann (d. 1929)*

1945 • *Nova organi harm. ad grad. juxta ed. vaticanam*

2012 • Gregorian Missal *(Solesmes Abbey)*

"THE GREATEST TREASURE OF THE CHURCH"

Considering the beauty of the Gregorian melodies, the marvelous artwork often combined with them (*see above*), and the musical treasury ***based upon*** Gregorian chant—such as the masterpieces of Josquin, Guerrero, Victoria, Palestrina, and Duruflé—it should come as no surprise that the Second Vatican Council solemnly declared: "The musical tradition of the universal Church is a treasure of inestimable value, **greater even than that of any other art**" (SC §112).

Indeed, Vatican II said: "the treasure of sacred music is to be ***preserved*** and ***fostered*** with great care" (SC §101). Vatican II said: "choirs must be ***diligently*** promoted" (SC §114). Vatican II said: "Pastors of souls should ***see to it*** that the chief hours, especially Vespers, are celebrated in common in church on Sundays and the more solemn feasts. And the laity, too, are encouraged to recite the divine office, either with the priests, or among themselves, or even individually" (SC §100). How is it possible that church leaders in so many localities are perfectly comfortable contradicting the explicit decrees of the Second Vatican Council? Nevertheless, in spite of any difficulties that may arise, let us remember the adage of Pope Pius IX: *He who does God's work does not do so in vain.*

I Classis. — *Easter Sunday* —

DOMINICA RESURRECTIONIS *Station at Saint Mary Major*

INTROIT. *Ps 138: 18, 5-6*

Resurréxi, et adhuc tecum sum, allelúja: posuísti super me manum tuã, allelúja: mirábilis facta est sciéntia tua, allelúja, allelúja. ℣. Dómine, probásti me et cognovísti me: tu cognovísti sessiónem meam et resurrectiónem meam. ℣. Glória Patri.

I AROSE, and am with Thee still, alleluia: Thou hast laid Thy hand upon Me, alleluia: Thy knowledge is become wonderful, alleluia, alleluia. (Ps 138: 1-2) Lord, Thou hast proved Me, and known Me: Thou hast known My sitting down, and My rising up. ℣. Glory.

COLLECT.

Deus, qui hodiérna die per Unigénitum tuum æternitátis nobis áditum, devícta morte, reserásti: vota nostra, quæ præveniéndo aspíras, étiam adjuvándo poséquere. Per eúmdem Dñm.

O God, Who, this day by Thine only-begotten Son, vanquishing death, hast unlocked for us the gate of eternity, help us to attain the desires to which Thou hast led us by Thine inspirations. Through the same.

EPISTLE. *I Cor 5: 7-8*

Fratres: Expurgáte vetus ferméntum, ut sitis nova conspérsio, sicut estis ázymi. Etenim Pascha nostrum immolátus est Christus. Ítaque epulémur: non in ferménto véteri, neque in ferménto malítiæ et nequítiæ: sed in ázymis sinceritátis et veritátis.

BRETHREN, purge out the old leaven, that you may be a new paste, as you are unleavened: for Christ our pasch is sacrificed. Therefore, let us feast, not with the old leaven, nor with the leaven of malice and wickedness, but with the unleavened bread of sincerity and truth.

GRADUAL & ALLELUIA. *Ps 117: 24, 1 & I Cor 5: 7*

Hæc dies, quam fecit Dóminus: exsultémus et lætémur in ea. ℣. Confitémini Dómino, quóniam bonus: quóniam in sǽculum misericórdia ejus.

Allelúja, allelúja. ℣. Pascha nostrum immolátus est Christus.

THIS IS THE DAY which the Lord hath made: Let us be glad and rejoice therein. ℣. Give praise to the Lord, for He is good: for His mercy endureth forever. | Alleluia, alleluia. ℣. Christ our pasch is sacrificed.

SEQUENCE. *attr. Wipo of Burgundy (d. 1048), chaplain to Emperor Conrad II.*

Translation by Fr. Adrian Fortescue
IMPRIMATUR (28 April 1913)

Sing to Christ your paschal victim,
Christians sing your Easter hymn.

ICTIMAE PASCHALI LAUDES IMMOLENT CHRISTIANI.

AGNUS redémit óves:
Chrístus ínnocens Pátri
reconciliávit peccatóres.

The sinless Lord for sinners,
Christ God's Son for creatures died,
The sheep who strayed,
the Lamb of God redeemed.

MORS et víta duéllo
conflixére mirándo:
dux vítæ mórtuus, régnat vívus.

Then death and life their battle
Wonderfully fought, and now
The King of life, once dead,
for ever lives.

DIC nóbis María,
quid vidísti in vía?

Tell us, Mary, we pray,
What you saw on Easter day?

SEPULCRUM Chrísti vivéntis
et glóriam vídi resurgéntis:

Empty was the grave, and looking
I saw there the glory of his rising.

ANGELICOS téstes,
sudárium, et véstes.

The angel witnesses
I saw, and folded linen.

SURREXIT Chrístus spes méa:
præcédet súos in Galilǽam.

Christ my hope is risen truly
In Galilee he goes before you.

SCIMUS CHRISTUM SURREXISSE
a mórtuis vére:
tu nóbis, víctor Rex, miserére.
Amen. Allelúja.

WE KNOW HE ROSE
FROM DEATH INDEED

And so to him we pray,
Great King and Lord of life,
bless us this day.
Amen. Alleluia.

SEQUENCES • In 1570, Pope Saint Pius V implemented the liturgical reforms called for by the Council of Trent, which had ended in 1563. Only four Sequences were retained—although the *Stabat Mater*, added in 1727, brought the total to five—and these were retained based on their excellence, with the result that some very high feasts, such as Christmas and Epiphany, lost their sequences. While admitting that some fine sequences were lost (e.g. *Salve Festa Dies* by Bishop Fortunatus), Father Fortescue summarized the result: "Without cumbering every Mass with long poems, we have the principle of the sequence and the very best of the old ones." Father Fortescue's 1913 translation of *Victimae Paschali* is remarkable for two reasons: (1) it juxtaposes the paradoxes in a clear way; (2) it fits the plainsong perfectly, and as a result can be sung verbatim.

GOSPEL. *Mark 16: 1-7*

MARY MAGDALEN, and Mary, the mother of James, and Salome bought sweet spices, that coming they might anoint Jesus. And very early in the morning, the first day of the week, they come to the sepulcher, the sun being now risen;

In illo témpore: María Magdaléne et María Jacóbi et Salóme emérunt arómata, ut veniéntes úngerent Jesum. Et valde mane una sabbatórũ, véniunt ad monuméntum, orto jam sole. Et dicébant ad ínvicem: Quis revólvet nobis lápidẽ ab óstio monuménti? Et respiciéntes vidérunt revolútum lápidem. Erat quippe magnus valde. Et introëúntes in monuméntũ vidérunt júvenẽ

GIVE ORDERS, THEN, THAT HIS TOMB SHALL BE SECURELY GUARDED UNTIL THE THIRD DAY. (Mt 27:64)

IN THE SAME QUARTER WHERE HE WAS CRUCIFIED THERE WAS A GARDEN. (Jn 19:41) The word "garden" hinted at Eden and the fall of man, yet suggested through its flowers in the springtime the Resurrection. — *Fulton J. Sheen (d. 1979)*

and they said one to another, Who shall roll back the stone from the door of the sepulcher? And looking, they saw the stone rolled back: for it was very great. And entering into the sepulcher, they saw a young man sitting on the right side, clothed with a white robe, and they were astonished: who saith to them, Be not affrighted; you seek Jesus of Nazareth, Who was crucified: He is risen, He is not here; behold the place where they laid Him: but go, tell His disciples, and Peter, that He goeth before you into Galilee: there you shall see Him, as He told you. Credo.

sedéntem in dextris, coopértum stola cándida, et obstupuérunt. Qui dicit illis: Nolíte expavéscere: Jesũ quǽritis Nazarénũ, crucifíxũ: surréxit, non est hic, ecce locus, ubi posuérunt eũ. Sed ite, dícite discípulis ejus et Petro, quia præcédit vos in Galilǽam: ibi eũ vidébitis, sicut dixit vobis.

OFFERTORY. *Ps 75: 9-10*

The earth trembled and was still, when God arose in judgment. Alleluia. ℣. *In Judea God is known: His name is great in Israel, alleluia.* ℣. *And His place is in peace, and His abode in Sion, alleluia.* ℣. *It was there He broke the archers' volleys, broke shield, and sword, and battle array: how princely was Thy dawning over the everlasting hills, alleluia.*

Terra trémuit, et quiévit, dum resúrgeret in judício Deus, allelúja. ℣. *Notus in Judǽa Deus, in Ísraël magnum nomen ejus, allelúja.* ℣. *Et factus est in pace locus ejus et habitátio ejus in Sion, allelúja.* ℣. *Ibi confrégit cornu, arcum, scutum et gládium et bellum: illúminans tu mirabíliter a móntibus aetérnis, allelúja.*

SECRET.

Receive, we beseech Thee, O Lord, the prayers of Thy people with the offerings of sacrifices, that the things begun in the paschal mysteries may, by Thy operation, avail us for a healing remedy unto life everlasting. Through our Lord.

Súscipe, quǽsumus, Dómine, preces pópuli tui cum oblatiónibus hostiárũ: ut, paschálibus initiáta mystériis, ad æternitátis nobis medélã, te operánte, profíciant. Per Dóminum.

1962 • The Preface of Easter with "on this day" (page 190) follows the Secret. During the Canon, proper Communicantes and Hanc Igitur. These are said until Easter Saturday, inclusively. | *Praefatio paschalis, in qua dicitur: "Te quidem, Dómine...sed in hac potissimum die." Infra actionem "Communicántes" et "Hanc igitur oblatiónem" propria. Et sic dicitur usque ad sabbatum in albis inclusive.*

COMMUNION. *I Cor 5: 7-8*

Christ, our Pasch is immolated, alleluia: therefore let us feast in the unleavened bread of sincerity and truth. Alleluia, alleluia, alleluia. ℣. *It is the Lord's death you are heralding, whenever you drink this chalice, until He comes.*

Pascha nostrũ immolátus est Christus, allelúja: ítaque epulémur in ázymis sinceritátis et veritátis, allelúja, allelúja, allelúja. (I Cor 11: 26) ℣. *Quótiens cálicem hunc bibétis mortem Dñi annuntiábitis donec véniat.*

—Helmst|1026 • Circa 1026AD

POSTCOMMUNION.

Pour upon us, O Lord, the spirit of Thy love, to make us of one mind, whom, by Thy tender mercy, Thou hast filled with the paschal sacrament. Through ... in the unity of the same.

Spíritum nobis, Dómine, tuæ caritátis infúnde: ut, quos sacraméntis paschálibus satiásti, tua fácias pietáte concórdes. Per Dñm ... in unitáte ejusdem.

NOMENCLATURE • "Low Sunday" seems to contrast this feast with Easter itself, the highest feast of all. Its liturgical name is *Dominica in albis depositis* ("Sunday in which the white clothes are put away"), derived from a custom mentioned by Saint Augustine wherein those baptized on Holy Saturday laid aside their white baptismal robes for the first time on this day. A line from the ancient Easter hymn—"et stolis albis cándidi"—is believed to allude to this custom; cf. *Ad Cenam Agni Providi* in the *Saint Jean de Brébeuf Hymnal* (2018). The Introit seems to reference these newly baptized Catholics; Dom P. G. Lefebvre sees the *milk* as representing "faith in Christ," whereas Dom Johner sees the *milk* as representing the Holy Eucharist. Other names include: *Doubting Thomas Sunday; Divine Mercy Sunday; Octava Paschae;* and *Quasimodo Sunday.*

I Classis. — *Low Sunday* —

DOMINICA IN ALBIS IN OCTAVA PASCHAE *Station at Saint Pancras*

INTROIT. *I Pet 2: 2*

Quasi modo géniti infántes, allelúja: rationábile, sine dolo lac concupíscite, allelúja, allelúja allelúja. ℣. Exsultáte Deo, adjutóri nostro: jubiláte Deo Jacob. ℣. Glória Patri.

AS NEWBORN babes, alleluia, desire the rational milk without guile, alleluia, alleluia, alleluia. (Ps 80: 2) Rejoice to God our Helper; sing aloud to the God of Jacob. ℣. Glory.

COLLECT.

Præsta, quǽsumus, omnípotens Deus: ut, qui paschália festa perégimus, hæc, te largiénte, móribus et vita teneámus. Per Dóminum.

Grant, we beseech Thee, O almighty God, that we who have completed the observance of the paschal festival, may keep it, by Thy bounty, in our life and behavior. Through our Lord.

EPISTLE. *I John 5: 4-10*

Caríssimi: Omne, quod natum est ex Deo, vincit mundum: et hæc est victória, quæ vincit mundum, fides nostra. Quis est, qui vincit mundum, nisi qui credit, quóniam Jesus est Fílius Dei? Hic est, qui venit per aquam et sánguinem, Jesus Christus: non in aqua solum, sed in aqua et sánguine. Et Spíritus est, qui testificátur, quóniam Christus est véritas. Quóniã tres sunt, qui testimónium dant in cælo: Pater, Verbum, et Spíritus Sanctus: et hi tres unum sunt. Et tres sunt, qui testimónium dant in terra: Spíritus, et aqua, et sanguis: et hi tres unũ sunt. Si testimónium hóminum accípimus, testimónium Dei majus est: quóniam hoc est testimónium Dei, quod majus est: quóniam testificátus est de Fílio suo. Qui credit in Fílium Dei, habet testimónium Dei in se.

DEARLY BELOVED, Whatsoever is born of God overcometh the world; and this is the victory which overcometh the world, our faith. Who is he that overcometh the world, but he that believeth that Jesus is the Son of God? This is He that came by water and blood, Jesus Christ; water and blood, Jesus Christ; not by water only, but by water and blood. And it is the spirit which testifieth that Christ is the truth. And there are three who give testimony in heaven; the Father, the Word, and the Holy Ghost: and these three are one. And there are three that give testimony on earth; the spirit, the water, and the blood: and these three are one. If we receive the testimony of men, the testimony of God is greater: for this is the testimony of God which is greater, because He hath testified of His Son. He that believeth in the Son of God Hath the testimony of God in himself.

EASTERTIDE ALLELUIA. *Matt 28: 7 & John 20: 26*

ALLELUIA, alleluia. ℣. In the day of My resurrection, saith the Lord, I will go before you into Galilee. | Alleluia. ℣. Eight days after, the doors being shut, Jesus stood in the midst of His disciples and said, Peace be unto you. Alleluia.

Allelúja, allelúja. ℣. In die resurrectiónis meæ, dicit Dóminus, præcédam vos in Galilǽam. Allelúja. ℣. Post dies octo, jánuis clausis, stetit Jesus in médio discipulórum suórum, et dixit: Pax vobis. Allelúja.

GOSPEL. *John 20: 19-31*

WHEN IT WAS LATE that same day, the first of the week, and the doors were shut, where the disciples were gathered together, for fear of the Jews, Jesus came, and stood in the midst, and said to them, Peace be to you. And when He had said this, He showed them His hands and His side. The disciples therefore were glad, when they saw the Lord. He said therefore to them again, Peace be to you : as the Father hath sent Me, I also send you. When He had said this, He breathed on them; and He said to them, Receive ye the Holy Ghost; whose sins you shall forgive, they are forgiven them, and whose sins you shall retain, they are retained. Now Thomas, one of the twelve, who is called Didymus, was not with them, when Jesus came. The other disciples therefore said to him, We have seen the Lord. But he said to them, Except I see in His hands the print of the nails, and put my finger into the place of the nails, and put my hand in to His side, I will not believe.

In illo témpore: Cum sero esset die illo, una sabbatórum, et fores essent clausæ, ubi erant discípuli congregáti propter metum Judæórum: venit Jesus, et stetit in médio, et dixit eis: Pax vobis. Et cum hoc dixísset, osténdit eis manus et latus. Gavísi sunt ergo discípuli, viso Dño. Dixit ergo eis íterum: Pax vobis. Sicut misit me Pater, et ego mitto vos. Hæc cum dixísset, insufflávit, et dixit eis: Accípite Spíritum Sanctum: quorum remiséritis peccáta, remittúntur eis; et quorum retinuéritis, reténta sunt. Thomas autẽ unus ex duódecim, qui dícitur Dídymus, non erat cum eis, quando venit Jesus. Dixérunt ergo ei álii discípuli: Vídimus Dñm. Ille autem dixit eis: Nisi vídero in mánibus ejus fixúram clavórum, et mittam dígitum meũ in locum clavórum, et mittam manum meam in latus ejus, non credam.

And after eight days, again His disciples were within, and Thomas with them. Jesus cometh, the doors being shut, and stood in the midst, and said, Peace be to you. Then He said to Thomas, Put in thy finger hither, and see My hands, and bring hither thy hand, and put it into My side; and be not faithless, but believing. Thomas answered, and said to Him. My Lord, and my God. Jesus saith to him, Because thou hast seen Me, Thomas, thou hast believed: blessed are they that have not seen, and have believed. Many other signs also did Jesus in the sight of His disciples, which are not written in this book. But these are written, that you may believe that Jesus is the Christ the Son of God: and that, believing, you may have life in His name. CREDO.

Et post dies octo, íterum erant discípuli ejus intus, et Thomas cum eis. Venit Jesus, jánuis clausis, et stetit in médio, et dixit: Pax vobis. Deínde dicit Thomæ: Infer dígitum tuum huc et vide manus meas, et affer manũ tuam et mitte in latus meũ: et noli esse incrédulus, sed fidélis. Respóndit Thomas et dixit ei: Dñs meus et Deus meus. Dixit ei Jesus: Quia vidísti me, Thoma, credidísti: beáti, qui non vidérunt, et credidérunt. Multa quidẽ et ália signa fecit Jesus in conspéctu discipulórum suórum, quæ non sunt scripta in libro hoc. Hæc autem scripta sunt, ut credátis, quia Jesus est Christus, Fílius Dei: et ut credéntes vitam habeátis in nómine ejus.

OFFERTORY. *Matt 28: 2, 5, 6*

Ángelus Dómini descéndit de cælo, et dixit muliéribus: Quem quǽritis, surréxit, sicut dixit, allelúja. ℣. *Eúntes dícite discípulis ejus: Ecce praecédet vos in Galilaéam: ibi eum vidébitis, sicut dixit, allelúja. ℣. Jesus stetit in médio eórũ et dixit: Pax vobis! vidéte, quia ego ipse sum.*

AN ANGEL of the Lord descended from heaven, and said to the women: He Whom you seek is risen as He said, alleluia. ℣. *Go, tell ye His disciples: Behold He will go before you into Galilee: there you shall see Him, as He said, alleluia. ℣. Jesus stood in the midst of them and said: Peace be with you! Behold, it is in truth Myself.*

SECRET.

Súscipe múnera, Dómine, quǽsumus, exsultántis Ecclésiæ: et, cui causam tanti gáudii præstitísti, perpétuæ fructum concéde lætítiæ. Per Dñm.

Receive, we pray Thee, O Lord, the gifts of Thine exultant Church, and, as Thou hast afforded her cause for such great joy, grant her the fruit of unending gladness. Through our Lord.

THE PREFACE • The Preface of Easter (page 190) follows the Secret. From now on during Eastertide, the option *in hoc potíssimum* ("in this season") is chosen, whereas during the octave of Easter it had been *in hac potíssimum die* ("on this day") and on Holy Saturday it had been *in hac potíssimum nocte* ("on this night").

1962 • *Praefatio paschalis, in qua dicitur: "in hoc potissimum gloriósius praedicáre."*

COMMUNION. *John 20: 27*

Mitte manum tuam, et cognósce loca clavórum, allelúja: et noli esse incrédulus, sed fidélis, allelúja, allelúja. (Jn 20: 28) ℣. *Respóndit Thomas, et dixit ei: Dóminus meus et Deus meus.*

—ROME|1071 • Circa 1071AD

PUT IN thy hand, and know the place of the nails, alleluia; and be not incredulous but believing, alleluia, alleluia. ℣. *Thomas answered, and said to him: My Lord, and my God.*

POSTCOMMUNION.

Quǽsumus, Dómine, Deus noster: ut sacrosáncta mystéria, quæ pro reparatiónis nostræ munímine contulísti; et præsens nobis remédium esse fácias et futúrum. Per Dóminum.

We beseech, O Lord our God, that Thou make the sacred mysteries which Thou hast given for the bulwark of our redemption, to be unto us a healing both in the present and in the future. Through our Lord.

II Classis.

— *Second Sunday after Easter* —

DOMINICA SECUNDA POST PASCHA *"Good Shepherd Sunday"*

INTROIT. *Ps 32: 5-6*

Misericórdia Dómini plena est terra, allelúja: verbo Dñi cæli firmáti sunt, allelúja, allelúja. ℣. Exsultáte, justi, in Dómino: rectos decet collaudátio. ℣. Glória Patri.

THE EARTH is full of the mercy of the Lord, alleluia: by the word of the Lord the heavens were established, alleluia, alleluia. (Ps 32: 1) Rejoice in the Lord, ye just: praise becometh the upright. ℣. Glory.

COLLECT.

O God, Who by the humility of Thy Son hast lifted up a fallen world, grant that to those whom Thou hast delivered from the misfortunes of eternal death, Thou mayest insure everlasting happiness. Through the same.

Deus, qui in Fílii tui humilitáte jacéntem mundũ erexísti: fidélibus tuis perpétuam concéde lætítiam; ut, quos perpétuæ mortis eripuísti cásibus, gáudiis fácias pérfrui sempitérnis. Per eúmdem Dóminum.

EPISTLE. *I Pet 2: 21-25*

DEARLY beloved, Christ suffered for us, leaving you an example that you should follow His steps. Who did no sin, neither was guile found in His mouth. Who, when He was reviled, did not revile: when He suffered, He threatened not: but delivered Himself to him that judged Him unjustly. Who His own self bore our sins in His body upon the tree: that we, being dead to sins, should live to justice: by Whose stripes you were healed. For you were as sheep going astray; but you are now converted to the shepherd and bishop of your souls.

Caríssimi: Christus passus est pro nobis, vobis relínquens exémplũ, ut sequámini vestígia ejus. Qui peccátum non fecit, nec invéntus est dolus in ore ejus: qui cum maledicerétur, non maledicébat: cũ paterétur, non comminabátur: tradébat autẽ judicánti se injúste: qui peccáta nostra ipse pértulit in córpore suo super lignũ: ut, peccátis mórtui, justítiæ vivámus: cujus livóre sanáti estis. Erátis enim sicut oves errántes, sed convérsi estis nunc ad pastórem et epíscopũ animárũ vestrárum.

EASTERTIDE ALLELUIA. *Lk 24: 35 & Jn 10: 14*

ALLELUIA, alleluia. ℣. The disciples knew the Lord Jesus in the breaking of the bread. | Alleluia. ℣. I am the good shepherd: and I know My sheep, and Mine know Me. Alleluia.

Allelúja, allẽ. ℣. Cognovérunt discípuli Dóminum Jesum in fractióne panis. Allelúja. ℣. Ego sum pastor bonus: et cognósco oves meas, et cognóscunt me meæ. Allelúja.

GOSPEL. *Jn 10: 11-16*

JESUS said to the Pharisees: I am the good shepherd. The good shepherd giveth his life for his sheep. But the hireling, and he that is not the shepherd, whose own the sheep are not, seeth the wolf coming, and leaveth the sheep, and flieth: and the wolf catcheth, and scattereth the sheep: And the hireling flieth, because he is a hireling: and he hath no care for the sheep. I am the good shepherd; and I know Mine, and Mine know Me. As the Father knoweth Me, and I know the Father: and I lay down My life for My sheep. And other sheep I have, that are not of this fold: them also I must bring, and they shall hear My voice, and there shall be one fold and one shepherd. CREDO.

In illo témpore: Dixit Jesus pharisǽis: Ego sum pastor bonus. Bonus pastor ánimam suam dat pro óvibus suis. Mercennárius autem et qui non est pastor, cujus non sunt oves própriæ, videt lupũ veniéntẽ, et dimíttit oves et fugit: et lupus rapit et dispérgit oves: mercennárius autẽ fugit, quia mercennárius est et non pértinet ad eum de óvibus. Ego sum pastor bonus: et cognósco meas et cognóscunt me meæ. Sicut novit me Pater, et ego agnósco Patrem, et ánimã meã pono pro óvibus meis. Et álias oves hábeo, quæ non sunt ex hoc ovíli: et illas opórtet me addúcere, et vocem meam áudient, et fiet unum ovíle et unus pastor.

OFFERTORY. *Ps 62: 2, 5*

O GOD, my God, to Thee do I watch at break of day: and in Thy name I will lift up my hands, alleluia. ℣. *For Thee my soul hath thirsted; for*

Deus, Deus meus, ad te de luce vígilo: et in nómine tuo levábo manus meas, allẽ. ℣. *Sitívit in te ánima mea, quam multiplíciter et caro mea, ut vidérem virtútem tuam et glóriam tuam. ℣. In matutínis meditábor in te, quia factus es adjútor meus: et in velaménto alárum tuárum exsultábo.*

Thee my flesh, O how many ways, to see Thy power and Thy glory. ℣. I will meditate upon Thee in the morning, because Thou hast been my helper: and I will rejoice under the covert of Thy wings.

SECRET.

Benedictiónem nobis, Dñe, cónferat salutárem sacra semper oblátio: ut, quod agit mystério, virtúte perfíciat. Per Dóminum.

May this sacred oblation, O Lord, call down upon us Thine abiding and salutary blessing; may it perfect by its might that which in mystery it brings about. Through our Lord.

The Preface of Easter (page 190) follows the Secret.

COMMUNION. *Jn 10: 14*

Ego sum pastor bonus, allelúja: et cognósco oves meas, et cognóscunt me meæ, allelúja, allẽ. (Ps 32: 12) ℣. *Beáta gens cujus est Dóminus Deus ejus; pópulus quem elégit in hæreditátem sibi.*

I AM the good shepherd, alleluia; and I know My sheep, and Mine know Me, alleluia, alleluia. ℣. *Blessèd is the nation whose God is the Lord: the people whom he hath chosen for his inheritance.*

POSTCOMMUNION.

Præsta nobis, quǽsumus, omnípotens Deus: ut, vivificatiónis tuæ grátiam consequéntes, in tuo semper múnere gloriémur. Per Dóminum.

Grant us, we beseech Thee, O almighty God, that, quickened by Thy grace, we may ever glory in Thy gifts. Through our Lord.

II Classis.

—*Third Sunday after Easter*—

DOMINICA TERTIA POST PASCHA

INTROIT. *Ps 65: 1-2*

Jubiláte Deo, omnis terra, allelúja: psalmũ dícite nómini ejus, allelúja: date glóriam laudi ejus, allelúja, allelúja, allelúja. ℣. Dícite Deo, quam terribília sunt ópera tua, Dñe! in multitúdine virtútis tuæ mentiéntur tibi inimíci tui. ℣. Glória Patri.

SHOUT WITH JOY to God, all the earth, alleluia; sing ye a psalm to His name, alleluia: give glory to His praise. Alleluia, alleluia, alleluia. (Ps 65: 3) Say unto God, how terrible are Thy works, O Lord! In the multitude of Thy strength Thy enemies shall lie to Thee. ℣. Glory.

COLLECT.

Deus, qui errántibus, ut in viam possint redíre justítiæ, veritátis tuæ lumen osténdis: da cunctis, qui christiána professióne censéntur, et illa respúere, quæ huic inimíca sunt nómini; et

O God, Who dost show the light of Thy truth to them that go astray, that they may be able to return to the path of justice, grant unto all who profess themselves and are reckoned Christians, both to reject the things that are opposed to that name and to follow after the things that befit it. Through our Lord.

ea, quæ sunt apta, sectári. Per Dóminum.

EPISTLE. *I Pet 2: 11-19*

DEARLY BELOVED, I beseech you as strangers and pilgrims, to refrain yourselves from carnal desires which war against the soul, having your conversation good among the gentiles: that whereas they speak against you as evil-doers, they may by the good works, which they shall behold in you, glorify God in the day of visitation. Be ye subject therefore to every human creature for God's sake: whether it be to the king as excelling: or to governors as sent by him for the punishment of evildoers, and for the praise of the good: for so is the will of God, that by doing well you may put to silence the ignorance of foolish men. As free, and not as making liberty a cloak for malice, but as the servants of God. Honor all men. Love the brotherhood. Fear God. Honor the king. Servants, be subject to your masters with all fear, not only to the good and gentle, but also to the froward. For this is thankworthy in Christ Jesus our Lord.

Caríssimi: Óbsecro vos tamquam ádvenas et peregrínos abstinére vos a carnálibus desidériis, quæ mílitant advérsus ánimã, conversatiónem vestrã inter gentes habéntes bonam: ut in eo, quod detréctant de vobis tamquam de malefactóribus, ex bonis opéribus vos considerántes, gloríficent Deum in die visitatiónis. Subjécti ígitur estóte omni humánæ creatúræ propter Deum: sive regi, quasi præcellénti: sive dúcibus, tamquam ab eo missis ad vindíctam malefactórum, laudem vero bonórum: quia sic est volúntas Dei, ut benefaciéntes obmutéscere faciátis imprudéntium hóminum ignorántiam: quasi líberi, et non quasi velámen habéntes malítiæ libertátem, sed sicut servi Dei. Omnes honoráte: fraternitátẽ diligite: Deum timéte: regem honorificáte. Servi, súbditi estóte in omni timóre dóminis, non tantum bonis et modéstis, sed étiã dýscolis. Hæc est enim grátia: in Christo Jesu, Dómino nostro.

EASTERTIDE ALLELUIA. *Ps 110: 9 & Lk 24: 46*

ALLELUIA, ALLELUIA. ℣. The Lord hath sent redemption to His people. | Alleluia. ℣. It was necessary for Christ to suffer, and rise from the dead, and so enter into His glory. Alleluia.

Allelúja, allelúja. ℣. Redemptiónem misit Dóminus pópulo suo. Allelúja. ℣. Oportébat pati Christum, et resúrgere a mórtuis: et ita intráre in glóriam suam. Allelúja.

GOSPEL. *Jn 16: 16-22*

TO HIS DISCIPLES, Jesus said: A little while, and now you shall not see Me; and again a little while, and you shall see Me; because I go to the Father. Then some of His disciples said one to another, What is this that He saith to us, A little while, and you shall not see Me; and again a little while, and you shall see Me: and because I go to the Father? They said therefore, What is this that He saith, A little while? We know not what He speaketh. And Jesus knew that they had a mind to ask Him: and He said to them, Of this do you inquire among yourselves because I said, A little while and you shall not see Me;

In illo témpore: Dixit Jesus discípulis suis: Módicũ, et jam non vidébitis me: et íterum módicum, et vidébitis me: quia vado ad Patrem. Dixérunt ergo ex discípulis ejus ad ínvicem: Quid est hoc, quod dicit nobis: Módicum, et non vidébitis me: et íterum módicum, et vidébitis me, et quia vado ad Patrem? Dicébant ergo: Quid est hoc, quod dicit: Módicum? nescímus, quid lóquitur. Cognóvit autem Jesus, quia volébant eum interrogáre, et dixit eis: De hoc quǽritis inter vos, quia dixi: Módicum, et non vidébitis me: et iterũ módicũ, et vidébitis me. Amen, amen, dico vobis: quia plorábitis et flébitis vos, mundus autem gaudébit: vos autẽ contristabímini, sed tristítia vestra vertétur in gáudium. Múlier cum parit, tristítiam habet, quia venit hora ejus: cum autem pepérerit púerum, jam non méminit pressúræ propter gáudium, quia natus est homo in mundum. Et vos ígitur nunc quidem tristítiam habétis, íterum autem vidébo vos, et gaudébit cor vestrũ: et gáudium vestrum nemo tollet a vobis.

and again a little while, and you shall see Me? Amen, amen, I say to you, that you shall lament and Weep, but the world shall rejoice; and you shall be made sorrowful, but your sorrow shall be turned into joy. A woman when she is in labor hath sorrow, because her hour is come; but when she hath brought forth the child, she remembereth no more the anguish, for joy that a man is born into the world. So also you now indeed have sorrow, but I will see you again, and your heart shall rejoice, and your joy no man shall take from you. CREDO.

OFFERTORY. *Ps 145: 2*

Lauda, ánima mea, Dóminum: laudábo Dñm in vita mea: psallam Deo meo, quámdiu ero, allelúja. ℣. *Qui custódit veritátem in sǽculum: fáciet judícium injúriam patiéntibus: dat escam esuriéntibus.* ℣. *Dóminus érigit elísos, Dñs solvit compendítos: custódit Dóminus pupíllum et ádvenam et víduam suscípiet: et viam peccatórũ exterminábit: regnábit Dóminus in aetérnum, Deus tuus, Sion, in sǽculum sǽculi.*

PRAISE THE LORD, O my soul, in my life I will praise the Lord: I will sing to my God as long as I shall be. Alleluia. ℣. *Who keepeth truth for ever: Who executeth judgment for them that suffer wrong: Who giveth food to the hungry.* ℣. *The Lord comforts the burdened, the Lord brings release to the prisoner: the Lord protects the stranger, defends the orphan and widow: and the way of the sinner He will destroy: the Lord shall reign for ever, thy God, O Sion, unto ages of ages.*

SECRET.

His nobis, Dómine, mystériis conferátur, quo, terréna desidéria mitigántes, discámus amáre cæléstia. Per Dñm.

By these mysteries, O Lord, may grace be given us so that, chastening our earthly desires, we may learn to love heavenly things. Through our Lord.

The Preface of Easter (page 190) follows the Secret.

COMMUNION. *Jn 16: 16*

Módicum, et non vidébitis me, allelúja: íterum módicũ, et vidébitis me, quia vado ad Patrem, allelúja, allẽ. (Jn 16: 22) ℣. *Íterũ autem vidébo vos, et gaudébit cor vestrum.* —ALBI|1047 • Circa 1047AD

A LITTLE while, and now you shall not see Me, alleluia: and again a little while, and you shall see Me: because I go to the Father. Alleluia, alleluia. ℣. *But one day I will see you again, and then your hearts will be glad.*

POSTCOMMUNION.

Sacraménta quæ súmpsimus, quǽsumus, Dñe: et spirituálibus nos instáurent aliméntis, et corporálibus tueántur auxíliis. Per Dóminum.

May the sacrament we have received, O Lord, we beseech Thee, both restore us with its spiritual nourishment and protect us with its help for our bodies. Through our Lord.

— *Fourth Sunday after Easter* — *II Classis.*

DOMINICA QUARTA POST PASCHA

INTROIT. *Ps 97: 1-2*

SING YE TO THE LORD a new canticle, alleluia; for the Lord hath done wonderful things, alleluia; He hath revealed His justice in the sight of the gentiles, alleluia, alleluia. (Ps 97: 1) His own right hand, His own holy arm, brought Him victory. ℣. Glory.

Cantáte Dómino cánticum novum, allelúja: quia mirabília fecit Dóminus, allelúja: ante conspéctum géntium revelávit justítiã suã, allelúja, allelúja, allelúja. ℣. Salvávit sibi déxtera ejus: et brácchiũ sanctũ ejus. ℣. Glória Patri.

COLLECT.

O God, Who dost make the minds of the faithful to be of one accord, grant Thy peoples that they may love what Thou commandest and desire what Thou dost promise, so that, amid the changing things of this world, our hearts may be set where true joys abide. Through our Lord.

Deus, qui fidélium mentes unius éfficis voluntátis: da pópulis tuis id amáre quod præcipis, id desideráre quod promíttis; ut inter mundánas varietátes ibi nostra fixa sint corda, ubi vera sunt gáudia. Per Dóminum.

EPISTLE. *James 1: 17-21*

DEARLY BELOVED, Every best gift, and every perfect gift is from above; coming down from the Father of lights, with Whom there is no change, nor shadow of alteration. For of His own will hath He begotten us by the word of truth, that we might be some beginning of His creatures. You know, my dearest brethren; and let every man be swift to hear, but slow to speak, and slow to anger. For the anger of man worketh not the justice of God. Rid yourselves, then, of all defilement, of all the ill-will that remains in you; be patient, and cherish that word implanted in you which can bring salvation to your souls.

Caríssimi: Omne datum óptimum, et omne donum perféctum desúrsum est, descéndens a Patre lúminũ, apud quem non est transmutátio nec vicissitúdinis obumbrátio. Voluntárie enim génuit nos verbo veritátis, ut simus inítium áliquod creatúræ ejus. Scitis, fratres mei dilectíssimi. Sit autẽ omnis homo velox ad audiéndum: tardus autem ad loquéndum et tardus ad iram. Ira enim viri justítiam Dei non operátur. Propter quod abjiciéntes omnem immundítiã et abundántiã malítiæ, in mansuetúdine suscípite ínsitum verbum, quod potest salváre ánimas vestras.

EASTERTIDE ALLELUIA. *Ps 117: 16 & Rom 6: 9*

ALLELUIA, alleluia. ℣. The right hand of the Lord hath wrought power; the right hand of the Lord hath exalted me. | Alleluia. ℣. Christ, rising from the dead, now dieth not; death shall no more have dominion over Him. Alleluia.

Allelúja, allelúja. ℣. Déxtera Dómini fecit virtútem: déxtera Dñi exaltávit me. Allelúja. ℣. Christus resúrgens ex mórtuis jam non móritur: mors illi ultra non dominábitur. Allelúja.

GOSPEL. *John 16: 5-14*

In illo témpore: Dixit Jesus discípulis suis: Vado ad eum, qui misit me: et nemo ex vobis intérrogat me: Quo vadis? Sed quia hæc locútus sum vobis, tristítia implévit cor vestrum. Sed ego veritátem dico vobis: expédit vobis, ut ego vadam: si enim non abíero, Paráclitus non véniet ad vos: si autem abíero, mittam eũ ad vos. Et cum vénerit ille, árguet mundum de peccáto et de justítia et de judício. De peccáto quidem, quia non credidérunt in me: de justítia vero, quia ad Patrem vado, et jam non vidébitis me: de judício autem, quia princeps hujus mundi jam judicátus est. Adhuc multa hábeo vobis dícere: sed non potéstis portáre modo. Cum autẽ vénerit ille Spíritus veritátis, docébit vos omnẽ veritátem. Non enim loquétur a semetípso: sed quæcúmque áudiet, loquétur, et quæ ventúra sunt, annuntiábit vobis. Ille me clarificábit: quia de meo accípiet et annuntiábit vobis.

AT THAT TIME Jesus said to His disciples: I go to Him that sent Me; and none of you asketh Me, Whither goest Thou? But because I have spoken these things to you, sorrow hath filled your heart. But I tell you the truth: it is expedient to you that I go; for if I go not, the Paraclete will not come to you, but if I go, I will send Him to you. And when He is come, He will convince the world of sin, and of justice, and of judgment. Of sin, because they believed not in Me; and of justice, because I go to the Father, and you shall see Me no longer; and of judgment, because the prince of this world is already judged. I have yet many things to say to you, but you cannot bear them now; but when He, the Spirit of truth, is come, He will teach you all truth; for He shall not speak of Himself; but what things soever He shall hear, He shall speak, and the things that are to come He shall show you. He shall glorify Me because He shall receive of Mine, and shall show it to you. CREDO.

OFFERTORY. *Ps 65: 1-2, 16*

Identical to 2nd Sunday after Epiphany:

Jubiláte Deo, univérsa terra: psalmum dícite nómini ejus: veníte et audíte, et narrábo vobis, omnes qui timétis Deum, quanta fecit Dóminus ánimæ meæ, allelúja. ℣. *Reddam tibi vota mea, quae distinxérunt lábia mea.* ℣. *Locútum est os meum in tribulatióne mea: holocáusta medulláta ófferam tibi.*

SHOUT WITH JOY to God, all the earth (shout with joy to God, all the earth): sing ye a psalm to His name: come and hear, and I will tell you, all ye that fear God, what great things the Lord hath done for my soul. Alleluia. ℣. *I will pay Thee my vows (I will pay Thee my vows), which my lips have uttered.* ℣. *My mouth hath spoken when I was in trouble (my mouth hath spoken when I was in trouble): Fat burnt-offerings of sheep shall be Thine.*

This Offertory displays a characteristic not uncommon for its genre: the repetition of certain sections—for reasons which are not always clear. When the text is repeated in this particular Offertory, the musical notes are (for the most part) different, whereas in other Offertories—such as the 16th Sunday after Pentecost—the same musical phrase and text is repeated verbatim.

SECRET.

Deus, qui nos, per hujus sacrifícii veneránda commércia, uníus summæ divinitátis partícipes effecísti: præsta, quǽsumus; ut, sicut tuam cognóscimus veritátem, sic eã dignis móribus assequámur. Per Dóminum.

O God, Who, in this mysterious sacrifice, callest us to have part in that one and most high Godhead which is Thyself: grant us, we beseech Thee, by worthiness of life, more and more to bear witness to the truth which it has pleased Thee to make known to us. Through our Lord.

The Preface of Easter (page 190) follows the Secret.

COMMUNION. *John 16: 8*

WHEN the Paraclete shall come, the Spirit of truth, it will be for Him to prove the world wrong, about sin, and about rightness of heart, and about judging, alleluia, alleluia. ℣. *He Who is to befriend you will not come to you unless I do go, but if only I make My way there, I will send Him to you.*

Dum vénerit Paráclitus Spíritus veritátis, ille árguet mundum de peccáto et de justítia et de judício, allelúja, allelúja. (Jn 16: 7) ℣. *Si enim non abiéro, Paráclitus non véniet ad vos; si autem abiéro, mittam eum ad vos.*

—Albi|1047 • Circa 1047AD

[Editor's Note: The version in the Missal begins: "Cum vénerit..."

POSTCOMMUNION.

Be near us, O Lord, our God, that, through those things which we have faithfully received, we may both be cleansed of sin and rescued from all dangers. Through our Lord.

Adésto nobis, Dómine, Deus noster: ut per hæc, quæ fidéliter súmpsimus, et purgémur a vítiis et a perículis ómnibus eruámur. Per Dóminum.

— *Fifth Sunday after Easter* — *II Classis.*

DOMINICA QUINTA POST PASCHA

INTROIT. *Is 48: 20*

DECLARE the voice of joy, and let it be heard, alleluia: declare it even unto the ends of the earth; the Lord hath delivered His people, alleluia, alleluia. (Ps 65: 1-2) Shout with joy to God all the earth: sing ye a psalm to His name, give glory to His praise. ℣. Glory.

Vocem jucunditátis annuntiáte, et audiátur, allelúja: annuntiáte usque ad extrémũ terræ: liberávit Dñs pópulum suũ, allelúja, allelúja. ℣. Jubiláte Deo, omnis terra, psalmum dícite nómini ejus: date glóriam laudi ejus. ℣. Glória Patri.

COLLECT.

O God, from Whom all good things come, generously grant to us who beseech Thee that we may, by Thy inspiration, think those things which are right and, that we perform them under Thy guidance. Through our Lord.

Deus, a quo bona cuncta procédunt, largíre supplícibus tuis: ut cogitémus, te inspiránte, quæ recta sunt; et, te gubernánte, éadem faciámus. Per Dñm.

EPISTLE. *James 1: 22-27*

DEARLY BELOVED, Be ye doers of the word, and not hearers only, deceiving your own selves. For if a man be a hearer of the word, and not a doer, he shall be compared to a man beholding his own countenance in a glass. For he beheld himself, and went his way, and presently forgot what manner of man he was. But he that hath looked into the perfect law of liberty and hath continued therein, not becoming a

Caríssimi: Estóte factóres verbi, et non auditóres tantum: falléntes vosmetípsos. Quia si quis audítor est verbi et non factor: hic comparábitur viro consideránti vultum nativitátis suæ in spéculo: considerávit enim se et ábiit, et statim oblítus est, qualis fúerit. Qui autem perspéxerit in legẽ perféctam libertátis et permánserit in ea, non audítor obliviósus factus, sed factor óperis: hic beátus in facto suo erit.

Si quis autē putat se religiósum esse, non refrénans linguam suam, sed sedúcens cor suum, hujus vana est relígio. Relígio munda et immaculáta apud Deum et Patrem hæc est: Visitáre pupíllos et víduas in tribulatióne eórum, et immaculátum se custodíre ab hoc sǽculo.

forgetful hearer, but a doer of the work, this man shall be blessed in his deed. And if any man think himself to be religious, not bridling his tongue, but deceiving his own heart, this man's religion is vain. Religion clean and undefiled before God and the Father is this: to visit the fatherless and widows in their tribulation, and to keep one's self unspotted from this world.

EASTERTIDE ALLELUIA. *Trad. & John 16: 28*

Allelúja, allelúja. ℣. Surréxit Christus, et illúxit nobis, quos rédemit sánguine suo. Allelúja. ℣. Exívi a Patre, et veni in mundum: íterū relínquo mundū, et vado ad Patrem. Allelúja.

ALLELUIA, alleluia. ℣. Christ is risen, and hath shone His light upon us whom He hath redeemed with His blood. | Alleluia. ℣. I went out from the Father and came into the world; again, I leave the world and go to the Father. Alleluia.

GOSPEL. *John 16: 23-30*

In illo témpore: Dixit Jesus discípulis suis: Amen, amen, dico vobis: si quid petiéritis Patrem in nómine meo, dabit vobis. Usque modo non petístis quidquam in nómine meo: Pétite, et accipiétis, ut gáudium vestrum sit plenum. Hæc in provérbiis locútus sum vobis. Venit hora, cum jam non in provérbiis loquar vobis, sed palam de Patre annuntiábo vobis. In illo die in nómine meo petétis: et non dico vobis, quia ego rogábo Patrem de vobis: ipse enim Pater amat vos, quia vos me amástis, et credidístis quia ego a Deo exívi. Exívi a Patre et veni in mundum: íterum relínquo mundum et vado ad Patrem. Dicunt ei discípuli ejus: Ecce, nunc palam lóqueris et provérbium nullum dicis. Nunc scimus, quia scis ómnia et non opus est tibi, ut quis te intérroget: in hoc crédimus, quia a Deo exísti.

JESUS SAID to His disciples, Amen, amen I say to you, if you ask the Father anything in My name, He will give it you. Hitherto you have not asked anything in My name: ask and you shall receive, that your joy may be full. These things I have spoken to you in proverbs: the hour cometh when I will no more speak to you in proverbs, but will show you plainly of the Father. In that day, you shall ask in My name; and I say not to you that I will ask the Father for you, for the Father Himself loveth you, because you have loved Me, and have believed that I came out from God. I came forth from the Father, and am come into the world: again I leave the world, and go to the Father. His disciples say to Him, Behold, now Thou speakest plainly, and speakest no proverb. Now we know that Thou knowest all things, and Thou needest not that any man should ask Thee: by this we believe that Thou camest forth from God. CREDO.

OFFERTORY. *Ps 65: 8-9, 20*

Benedícite, gentes, Dóminum, Deum nostrū, et obaudíte vocem laudis ejus: qui pósuit ánimam meam ad vitam, et non dedit commovéri pedes meos: benedíctus Dóminus, qui non amóvit deprecatiónem meam et misericórdiam suam a me, allelúja. ℣. *Jubiláte Deo omnis terra, psalmum dícite nómini ejus: date glóriam laudi ejus.* ℣. *In*

O BLESS the Lord our God, ye gentiles, and make the voice of His praise to be heard: Who hath set my soul to live, and hath not suffered my feet to be moved: blessèd be the Lord, Who hath not turned away my prayer, and His mercy from me, alleluia. ℣. *Shout with joy to God, all the earth, sing ye a psalm to His name: give glory to His praise. ℣. In the multitude of Thy strength Thine enemies shall lie to Thee: let all the earth adore Thee, and sing to Thee, O most high. ℣. Come and see the works of the Lord: how terrible is He in His counsels over the sons of men: to Him I have cried with my mouth, and I extolled Him with my tongue: for the Lord has heard me and was attentive to the voice of my prayer.*

multitúdine virtútis tuæ mentiéntur tibi inimíci tui: omnis terra adóret te et psallat tibi, Altíssime. ℣. Veníte et vidéte ópera Dómini: quam terríbilis in consíliis super fílios hóminum: ad ipsũ ore meo clamávi et exsultávi sub lingua mea: proptérea exaudívit me Deus et inténdit voci oratiónis meæ.

SECRET.

O Lord, we beg Thee to accept the prayers of the faithful, with the sacrifice they offer, that through these acts of filial homage, we may enter into the glory of heaven. Through our Lord.

Súscipe, Dñe, fidélium preces cum oblatiónibus hostiárum: ut, per hæc piæ devotiónis offícia, ad cæléstem glóriam transeámus. Per Dóminum.

The Preface of Easter (page 190) follows the Secret.

COMMUNION. *Ps 95: 2*

SING YE to the Lord, alleluia; sing ye to the Lord, and bless His name; show forth His salvation from day to day, alleluia, alleluia. ℣. *Bring up sacrifices, and come into His courts.*

Cantáte Dómino, allelúja: cantáte Dño et benedícite nomẽ ejus: bene nuntiáte de die in diem salutáre ejus, allelúja, allelúja. (Ps 95: 8) ℣. *Tóllite hóstias, et introíte in átria ejus.*

—COMPIEGNE|862 • Circa 862AD

POSTCOMMUNION.

Grant, O Lord, unto us, who have been regaled with the virtue of the heavenly table, both to desire what is right and to obtain what we desire. Through our Lord.

Tríbue nobis, Dómine, cæléstis mensæ virtúte satiátis: et desideráre, quæ recta sunt, et desideráta percípere. Per Dñm.

—*Ascension Thursday*— *I Classis.*

IN ASCENSIONE DOMINI *Station at Saint Peter*

INTROIT. *Acts 1: 11*

YE MEN OF GALILEE, why wonder you, looking up to heaven? alleluia: He shall so come as you have seen Him going up into heaven, alleluia, alleluia, alleluia. (Ps 46: 2) O clap your hands, all ye nations; shout unto God with the voice of joy. ℣. Glory.

Viri Galilǽi, quid admirámini aspiciéntes in cælum? allelúja: quemádmodum vidístis eum ascendéntem in cælum, ita véniet, allelúja, allelúja, allelúja. ℣. Omnes gentes, pláudite mánibus: jubiláte Deo in voce exsultatiónis. ℣. Glória Patri.

SECRET.

Concéde, quæsumus, omnípotens Deus: ut, qui hodiérna die Unigénitum tuum, Redemptórem nostrũ, ad cælos ascendísse crédimus; ipsi quoque mente in cæléstibus habitémus. Per eúmdẽ Dñm.

Grant, we beseech Thee, O almighty God, that, believing Thine only-begotten, our Redeemer, to have ascended to heaven on this day, we, too, may spiritually dwell in heavenly places. Through the same.

EPISTLE. *Acts 1: 1-11*

Primum quidẽ sermónẽ feci de ómnibus, o Theóphile, quæ cœpit Jesus fácere et docére usque in diem, qua, præcípiens Apóstolis per Spíritũ Sanctum, quos elégit, assúmptus est: quibus et præbuit seípsum vivum post passiónem suam in multas arguméntis, per dies quadragínta appárens eis et loquens de regno Dei. Et convéscens, præcépit eis, ab Jerosólymis ne discéderent, sed exspectárent promissiónẽ Patris, quam audístis (inquit) per os meum: quia Joánnes quidem baptizávit aqua, vos autem baptizabímini Spíritu Sancto non post multos hos dies. Ígitur qui convénerant, interrogábant eum, dicéntes: Dómine, si in témpore hoc restítues regnum Ísraël? Dixit autẽ eis: Non est vestrum nosse témpora vel moménta, quæ Pater pósuit in sua potestáte: sed accipiétis virtútem superveniéntis Spíritus Sancti in vos, et éritis mihi testes in Jerúsalem et in omni Judǽa et Samaría et usque ad últimum terræ. Et cum hæc dixísset, vidéntibus illis, elevátus est, et nubes suscépit eum ab óculis eórũ. Cumque intuerétur in cælum eúntem illum, ecce, duo viri astitérunt juxta illos in véstibus albis, qui et dixérunt: Viri Galilǽi, quid statis aspiciéntes in cælum? Hic Jesus, qui assúmptus est a vobis in cælum, sic véniet, quemádmodũ vidístis eum eúntem in cælum.

THE FORMER TREATISE I made, O Theophilus, of all things which Jesus began to do and to teach, until the day on which, giving commandments by the Holy Ghost to the Apostles whom He had chosen, He was taken up: to whom also He showed Himself alive after His Passion by many proofs, for forty days appearing to them and speaking of the kingdom of God. And eating together with them, He commanded them that they should not depart from Jerusalem, but should wait for the promise of the Father, which you have heard (saith He) by My mouth; for John indeed baptized with water, but you shall be baptized with the Holy Ghost not many days hence. They therefore who were come together asked Him, saying: Lord, wilt Thou at this time restore again the kingdom of Israel? But He said to them: It is not for you to know the times or moments which the Father hath put in His own power: but you shall receive the power of the Holy Ghost coming upon you, and you shall be witnesses unto Me in Jerusalem, and in all Judea and Samaria, and even to the uttermost part of the earth. And when He had said these things, while they looked on, He was raised up: and a cloud received Him out of their sight. And while they were beholding Him going up to heaven, behold two men stood by them in white garments, who also said: Ye men of Galilee, why stand you looking up to heaven? This Jesus, who is taken up from you into heaven, shall so come as you have seen Him going into heaven.

ASCENSIONTIDE ALLELUIA. *Ps 46: 6 & Ps 67: 18-19*

Allelúja, allelúja. ℣. Ascéndit Deus in jubilatióne, et Dóminus in voce tubæ. Allelúja. ℣. Dóminus in Sina in sancto, ascéndens in altum, captívam duxit captivitátem. Allelúja.

ALLELUIA, alleluia. God hath ascended in jubilation, the Lord with the voice of the trumpet. Alleluia. ℣. The Lord is in Sina, in His holy place; ascending on high, He hath led captivity captive. Alleluia.

DUM BENEDICERET ILLIS RECESSIT AB EIS ET FEREBATUR IN CAELUM. (Luke 24:51)
BLESSING THEM, HE DEPARTED FROM THEM, AND WAS CARRIED UP TO HEAVEN.

CUMQUE INTUERENTUR IN CAELUM EUNTE ILLO ECCE DUO VIRI ADSTITERUNT IUXTA ILLOS IN VESTIBUS ALBIS. (Acts 1:10)

WHILE THEY WERE BEHOLDING HIM GOING UP TO HEAVEN, BEHOLD TWO MEN STOOD BY THEM IN WHITE GARMENTS. (Acts 1:10)

THE LORD JESUS, WHEN HE HAD FINISHED SPEAKING TO THEM, WAS TAKEN UP TO HEAVEN, AND IS SEATED NOW AT THE RIGHT HAND OF GOD. (Mark 16:19)

GOSPEL. *Mark 16: 14-20*

In illo témpore: Recumbéntibus úndecim discípulis, appáruit illis Jesus: et exprobrávit incredulitátem eórum et durítiam cordis: quia iis, qui víderant eum resurrexísse, non crediderunt. Et dixit eis: Eúntes in mundum univérsum, prædicáte Evangéliũ omni creatúræ. Qui credíderit et baptizátus fúerit, salvus erit: qui vero non credíderit, condemnábitur. Signa autem eos, qui credíderint, hæc sequéntur: In nómine meo dæmónia ejícient: linguis loquántur novis: serpéntes tollent: et si mortíferum quid bíberint, non eis nocébit: super ægros manus impónent, et bene habébunt. Et Dóminus quidem Jesus, postquam locútus est eis, assúmptus est in cælũ, et sedet a dextris Dei. Illi autem profécti, prædicavérunt ubíque, Dño coöperánte et sermónẽ confirmánte, sequéntibus signis.

WHILE THEY SAT AT TABLE, Jesus appeared to the eleven: and He upbraided them with their incredulity and hardness of heart, because they did not believe them who had seen Him after He was risen again. And He said to them: Go ye into the whole world and preach the Gospel to every creature. He that believeth and is baptized shall be saved: but he that believeth not shall be condemned. And these signs shall follow them that believe: In My Name they shall cast out devils; they shall speak with new tongues; they shall take up serpents; and if they shall drink any deadly thing, it shall not hurt them; they shall lay their hands upon the sick, and they shall recover. And the Lord Jesus, after He had spoken to them, was taken up into Heaven and sitteth on the right hand of God. But they going forth preached everywhere, the Lord working withal, and confirming the word with signs that followed. CREDO.

1962 • After the Gospel, the Paschal candle is extinguished.
Dicto Evangelio, exstinguitur cereus paschalis.

OFFERTORY. *Ps 46: 6*

Ascéndit Deus in jubilatióne, et Dñs in voce tubæ, allelúja. ℣. *Omnes gentes pláudite mánibus: jubiláte Deo in voce exsultatiónis.* ℣. *Quóniam Dñs summus terríbilis: Rex magnus super omnem terram.* ℣. *Subjécit pópulos nobis: et gentes sub pédibus nostris.*

GOD IS ASCENDED in jubilee, and the Lord with the sound of trumpet. Alleluia. ℣. *O clap your hands, all ye nations: acclaim your God with cries of rejoicing.* ℣. *The Lord is high above us, and worthy of dread; He is the sovereign Ruler of all the earth.* ℣. *He has tamed the nations to our will, bowed the Gentiles at our feet.*

[Editor's Note: In the ancient manuscripts, the Offertory for this Sunday was "Viri Galilǽi," which has the same text as the Introit. The 1962 "Ascéndit Deus" Offertory—which has the same text as the first Alleluia—was used for the Sunday after the Ascension. This change seems to have occurred sometime between the 13th century and the 15th century, since liturgical books from the 13th century still contain "Viri Galilǽi" while books in the 16th century have "Ascéndit Deus."]

SECRET.

Súscipe, Dñe, múnera, quæ pro Fílii tui gloriósa Ascensióne deférimus: et concéde propítius; ut a præséntibus perículis liberémur, et ad vitam perveniámus ætérnã. Per eúmdem Dñm.

Receive, O Lord, the offerings which we bring for the glorious ascension of Thy Son, and grant in Thy mercy that we may be delivered from present dangers and may attain unto life everlasting. Through the same.

The Preface of the Ascension (page 190) follows the Secret.

1962 • The proper "Communicantes of the Ascension" (page 199) is said only on the feast day itself.
"Communicantes" vero proprium de Ascensione Domini dicitur tantum in ipso die festo Ascensionis.

COMMUNION. *Ps 67: 33-34*

SING YE TO THE LORD, Who mounteth above the heaven of heavens to the east. Alleluia. ℣. *Let God bestir Himself, needs must His foes be scattered, their malice take flight before His coming.*

Psállite Dómino, qui ascéndit super cælos cælórum ad Oriéntem, allelúja. (Ps 67: 2) ℣. *Exsúrgat Deus, et dissipéntur inimíci ejus; et fúgiant qui odérunt eum a fácie ejus.*

—RENAUD|965 • Circa 965AD

POSTCOMMUNION.

Grant, we beseech Thee, O almighty and merciful God, that what we have received in visible mysteries, we may also obtain in their invisible effect. Through our Lord.

Præsta nobis, quǽsumus, omnípotens et miséricors Deus: ut, quæ visibílibus mystériis suménda percépimus, invisíbili consequámur efféctu. Per Dñm.

— *Sunday after the Ascension* — *II Classis.*

DOMINICA POST ASCENSIONEM DOMINI *This feast is ancient, but has not a station.*

INTROIT. *Ps 26: 7-9*

HEAR, O LORD, my voice with which I have cried to Thee, alleluia: my heart hath said to Thee, I have sought Thy face, Thy face, O Lord, I will seek: turn not away Thy face from me, alleluia, alleluia. (Ps 26: 1) The Lord is my light and my salvation; whom shall I fear? ℣. Glory.

Exáudi, Dómine, vocem meam, qua clamávi ad te, allelúja: tibi dixit cor meum, quæsívi vultum tuum, vultum tuum, Dómine, requíram: ne avértas fáciem tuam a me, allelúja, allelúja. ℣. Dóminus illuminátio mea et salus mea: quem timébo? ℣. Glória Patri.

COLLECT.

Almighty and eternal God, make us ever bear a devout affection toward Thee, and with sincere heart to serve Thy majesty. Through our Lord.

Omnípotens sempitérne Deus: fac nos tibi semper et devótam gérere voluntátem; et majestáti tuæ sincéro corde servíre. Per Dóminum.

EPISTLE. *I Peter 4: 7-11*

DEARLY BELOVED, be prudent, and watch in prayers. But before all things have a constant mutual charity among yourselves; for charity covereth a multitude of sins. Using hospitality one toward another without murmuring. As every man hath received grace, ministering the same one to another; as good stewards of the manifold grace of God. If any man speak, let him speak as the words of God. If any man minister, let him do it as of the power which God administereth; that in all things God may be honored through Jesus Christ, our Lord.

Caríssimi: Estóte prudéntes et vigiláte in oratiónibus. Ante ómnia autẽ mútuã in vobismetípsis caritátem contínuam habéntes: quia cáritas óperit multitúdinem peccatórũ. Hospitáles ínvicem sine murmuratióne: unusquísque, sicut accépit grátiam, in altérutrum illam administrántes, sicut boni dispensatóres multifórmis grátiæ Dei. Si quis lóquitur, quasi sermónes Dei: si quis minístrat, tamquam ex virtúte, quam adminístrat Deus: ut in ómnibus honorificétur Deus per Jesum Christum, Dóminum nostrum.

ASCENSIONTIDE ALLELUIA. *Ps 46: 9 & John 14: 18*

Allelúja, allelúja. ℣. Regnávit Dñs super omnes gentes: Deus sedet super sedem sanctam suã. Allẽ. ℣. Non vos relínquam órphanos: vado, et vénio ad vos, et gaudébit cor vestrum. Allelúja.

ALLELUIA, alleluia. ℣. The Lord hath reigned over all the nations; God sitteth on His holy throne. Alleluia. ℣. I will not leave you orphans; I go and I come to you, and your heart shall rejoice. Alleluia.

GOSPEL. *John 15: 26-27 & 16: 1-4*

In illo témpore: Dixit Jesus discípulis suis: Cum vénerit Paráclitus, quẽ ego mittam vobis a Patre, Spíritũ veritátis, qui a Patre procédit, ille testimónium perhibébit de me: et vos testimónium perhibébitis, quia ab inítio mecũ estis. Hæc locútus sum vobis, ut non scandalizémini. Absque synagógis fácient vos: sed venit hora, ut omnis, qui intérficit vos, arbitrétur obséquium se præstáre Deo. Et hæc fácient vobis, quia non novérunt Patrem neque me. Sed hæc locútus sum vobis: ut, cum vénerit hora eórum, reminiscámini, quia ego dixi vobis.

WHEN THE PARACLETE cometh, Jesus said to His disciples, Whom I will send you from the Father, the Spirit of truth, Who proceedeth from the Father, He shall give testimony of Me: and you shall give testimony, because you are with Me from the beginning. These things have I spoken to you, that you may not be scandalized. They will put you out of the synagogues: yea, the hour cometh, that whosoever killeth you will think that he doth a service to God. And these things will they do to you, because they have not known the Father, nor Me. But these things I have told you, that, when the hour shall come, you may remember that I told you. CREDO.

OFFERTORY. *Ps 46: 6*

Identical to Ascension Thursday:

Ascéndit Deus in jubilatióne, et Dñs in voce tubæ, allelúja. ℣. *Omnes gentes pláudite mánibus: jubiláte Deo in voce exsultatiónis.* ℣. *Quóniam Dñs summus terríbilis: Rex magnus super omnem terram.* ℣. *Subjécit pópulos nobis: et gentes sub pédibus nostris.*

GOD IS ASCENDED in jubilee, and the Lord with the sound of trumpet. Alleluia. ℣. *O clap your hands, all ye nations: acclaim your God with cries of rejoicing.* ℣. *The Lord is high above us, and worthy of dread; He is the sovereign Ruler of all the earth.* ℣. *He has tamed the nations to our will, bowed the Gentiles at our feet.*

SECRET.

Sacrifícia nos, Dómine, immaculáta puríficent: et méntibus nostris supérnæ grátiæ dent vigórem. Per Dñm.

Let this immaculate sacrifice purify us, O Lord, and impart to our souls the vigor of supernal grace. Through our Lord.

The Preface of the Ascension (page 190) follows the Secret.

COMMUNION. *John 17: 12-13, 15*

Pater, cum essem cum eis, ego servábam eos, quos dedísti mihi, allelúja: nunc autem ad te vénio: non rogo, ut tollas eos de mundo, sed ut serves eos

FATHER, while I was with them, I kept them whom Thou gavest Me, alleluia; but now I come to Thee; I pray not that Thou shouldst take them out of the world, but that Thou shouldst keep them from evil, alleluia, alleluia. ℣. *For love of My brethren and My familiar friends, peace is still My prayer for thee.*

a malo, allelúja, allelúja. (Ps 121: 8) ℣. *Propter fratres meos et próximos meos, loquébar pacem de te.*
—12050CORBIE|853 • Circa 853AD

POSTCOMMUNION.

As we have been filled with heavenly gifts, O Lord, grant, we beseech Thee, that we may constantly persevere in thanksgiving. Through our Lord.

Repléti, Dómine, munéribus sacris: da, quǽsumus; ut in gratiárum semper actióne maneámus. Per Dóminum.

THREE CARDINAL FEASTS • The traditional Roman Rite has no "ordinary" time—rather, it has Sundays of a marked character: *Sundays after Epiphany, Sundays after Easter, Sundays after Pentecost.* Some later variations of the Roman Rite—such as the Sarum Use in England—counted "Sundays after Trinity," in spite of the fact that the feast of the Holy Trinity is a recent (non-primitive) feast. Father Fortescue reminds us: "The old sacramentaries count the Sundays after the three Cardinal feasts, EPIPHANY, EASTER, PENTECOST, long before there was a Trinity feast." Over the centuries, great prominence has been placed on Christmas—the feast of *Christ's Birth* (originally commemorated at Epiphany, according to some authors)—whereas the considerable emphasis given to *Christ's Conception* (25 March) by the early Church seemingly has been "transferred" to Christmas. Considering society's attacks on the sanctity of human life, a renewed veneration for the Annunciation might be desirable.

— *Pentecost Sunday* — *I Classis.*

DOMINICA PENTECOSTES *Station at Saint Peter*

INTROIT. *Wis 1: 7*

THE SPIRIT OF THE LORD hath filled the whole earth, alleluia; and that which containeth all things hath knowledge of the voice, alleluia, alleluia, alleluia. (Ps 67: 2) Let God arise, and His enemies be scattered; and let them that hate Him fly before His face. ℣. Glory.

Spíritus Dómini replévit orbem terrárum, allelúja: et hoc quod cóntinet ómnia, sciéntiã habet vocis, allelúja, allelúja, allelúja. ℣. Exsúrgat Deus, et dissipéntur inimíci ejus: et fúgiant, qui odérunt eum, a fácie ejus. ℣. Glória Patri.

COLLECT.

O God, Who on this day didst instruct the hearts of the faithful by the light of the Holy Spirit, grant us, by the same Spirit, to relish what is right and ever to rejoice in His consolation. Through…in the unity of the same.

Deus, qui hodiérna die corda fidélium Sancti Spíritus illustratióne docuísti: da nobis in eódem Spíritu recta sápere; et de ejus semper consolatióne gaudére. Per Dñm . . . in unitáte ejúsdem Spíritus.

EPISTLE. *Acts 2: 1-11*

WHEN THE DAYS of Pentecost were accomplished, they were all together in one place; and suddenly there came a sound from Heaven, as of a mighty wind coming, and it filled the whole house

Cum compleréntur dies Pentecóstes, erant omnes discípuli pariter in eódem loco: et factus est repénte de cælo sonus, tamquã adveniéntis spíritus veheméntis: et replévit totam domum,

✠ JESUS REPLIED: "IT IS NOT FOR YOU TO KNOW THE TIMES AND SEASONS WHICH THE FATHER HAS FIXED BY HIS OWN AUTHORITY. ENOUGH FOR YOU, THAT THE HOLY SPIRIT WILL COME UPON YOU, AND YOU WILL RECEIVE STRENGTH FROM HIM; YOU ARE TO BE MY WITNESSES IN JERUSALEM AND THROUGHOUT JUDAEA, IN SAMARIA, YES, AND TO THE ENDS OF THE EARTH." (Acts 1:7-8) ✠

LIGHT MOST BLESSED, SHINE ON THE HEARTS OF THY FAITHFUL—EVEN INTO THEIR DARKEST CORNERS; FOR WITHOUT THINE AID MAN CAN DO NOTHING GOOD, AND EVERYTHING IS SINFUL.

where they were sitting. And there appeared to them parted tongues as it were of fire, and it sat upon every one of them: and they were all filled with the Holy Ghost, and they began to speak with diverse tongues, according as the Holy Ghost gave them to speak. Now there were dwelling at Jerusalem, Jews, devout men, of every nation under heaven. And when this was noised abroad, the multitude came together, and were confounded in mind, because that every man heard them speak in his own tongue: and they were all amazed, and wondered, saying: Behold, are not all these that speak Galileans? And how have we heard every man our own tongue wherein we were born? Parthians, and Medes, and Elamites, and inhabitants of Mesopotamia, Judea, and Cappadocia, Pontus, and Asia, Phrygia, and Pamphilia, Egypt, and the parts of Lybia about Cyrene, and strangers of Rome, Jews also and Proselytes, Cretes and Arabians: we have heard them speak in our own tongues the wonderful works of God.

ubi erant sedéntes. Et apparuérunt illis dispertítæ linguæ tamquam ignis, sedítque supra síngulos eórũ: et repléti sunt omnes Spíritu Sancto, et cœpérunt loqui váriis linguis, prout Spíritus Sanctus dabat éloqui illis. Erant autẽ in Jerúsalem habitántes Judǽi, viri religiósi ex omni natióne, quæ sub cælo est. Facta autẽ hac voce, convénit multitúdo, et mente confúsa est, quóniam audiébat unusquísque lingua sua illos loquéntes. Stupébant autẽ omnes et mirabántur, dicéntes: Nonne ecce omnes isti, qui loquúntur, Galilǽi sunt? Et quómodo nos audívimus unusquísque linguã nostram, in qua nati sumus? Parthi et Medi et Ælamítæ et qui hábitant Mesopotámiã, Judǽam et Cappadóciam, Pontum et Ásiã, Phrýgiam et Pamphýliam, Ægýptũ et partes Líbyæ, quæ est circa Cyrénen, et ádvenæ Románi, Judǽi quoque et Prosélyti, Cretes et Árabes: audívimus eos loquéntes nostris linguis magnália Dei.

FIRST ALLELUIA. *Ps 103: 30*

ALLELUIA, alleluia. ℣. Send forth Thy Spirit, and they shall be created: and Thou shalt renew the face of the earth.

Allelúja, allelúja. ℣. Emítte Spíritum tuum, et creabúntur, et renovábis fáciem terræ.

SECOND ALLELUIA. *Trad.*

Alleluia. (*Here all kneel*) ℣. Come, O Holy Spirit, fill the hearts of Thy faithful: and kindle in them the fire of Thy love.

Allelúja. (*Hic genuflectitur*) ℣. Veni, Sancte Spíritus, reple tuórum corda fidélium: et tui amóris in eis ignem accénde.

SEQUENCE. *attr. King Robert the Pious of France (d. 1031).*

VENI SANCTE SPIRITUS
Et emítte cǽlitus | Lucis tuae rádium.

English Translation by Father Adrian Fortescue
IMPRIMATUR (28 April 1913)

COME Holy Ghost,
and send down from
heaven the ray of thy light.

VENI pater páuperum,
Veni dator múnerum,
Veni lumen córdium.

COME father of the poor,
come giver of gifts,
come light of hearts.

BEST comforter,
sweet guest of the soul,
sweet refreshment.

Rest in labor,
shade in the heat,
comfort in sorrow.

O MOST blessed light,
fill the depth of the
hearts of thy faithful.

Without thy grace
there is nothing in man,
nothing not harmful.

CLEANSE what is unclean,
water what is dry,
heal what is sick.

Bend what is hard,
warm what is cold,
straighten what is crooked.

GIVE to the faithful
who trust in thee
thy holy sevenfold gift.

Give reward of merit,
give salvation at last,
give eternal joy.

Amen. Allelúia.

CONSOLATOR óptime,
Dulcis hospes ánimae,
Dulce refrigérium.

In labóre réquies,
In aestu tempéries,
In fletu solátium.

O LUX beatíssima,
Reple cordis íntima
Tuórum fidélium.

Sine tuo númine,
Nihil est in hómine,
Nihil est innóxium.

LAVA quod est sórdidum,
Riga quod est áridum,
Sana quod est sáucium.

Flecte quod est rígidum,
Fove quod est frígidum,
Rege quod est dévium.

DA tuis fidélibus,
In te confidéntibus,
Sacrum septenárium.

Da virtútis méritum,
Da salútis éxitum,
Da perénne gáudium.

Amen. Allelúja.

GOSPEL. *John 14: 23-31*

In illo témpore: Dixit Jesus discípulis suis: Si quis díligit me, sermónẽ meum servábit, et Pater meus díliget eum, et ad eum veniémus et mansiónem apud eum faciémus: qui non díligit me, sermónes meos non servat. Et sermónem quem audístis, non est meus: sed ejus, qui misit me, Patris. Hæc locútus sum vobis, apud vos manens. Paráclitus autem Spíritus Sanctus, quẽ mittet Pater in nómine meo, ille vos docébit ómnia et súggeret vobis ómnia, quæcúmque díxero vobis.

IF ANY ONE love Me, Jesus said to His disciples, he will keep My word, and My Father will love him, and We will come to him, and will make our abode with him. He that loveth Me not, keepeth not My words: and the word which you have heard is not Mine, but the Father's, Who sent Me. These things have I spoken to you, abiding with you: but the Paraclete, the Holy Ghost, Whom the Father will send in My name, He will teach you all things, and bring all things to your mind, whatsoever I shall have said to you.

Peace I leave with you, My peace I give unto you: not as the world giveth, do I give unto you. Let not your heart be troubled, nor let it be afraid. You have heard that I said to you, I go away, and I come unto you. If you loved Me, you would indeed be glad, because I go to the Father; for the Father is greater than I. And now I have told you before it came to pass, that when it shall come to pass you may believe. I will not now speak many things with you; for the prince of this world cometh, and in Me he hath not anything. But that the world may know that I love the Father, and as the Father hath given Me commandment, so do I. CREDO.

Pacem relínquo vobis, pacẽ meam do vobis: non quómodo mundus dat, ego do vobis. Non turbétur cor vestrum neque formídet. Audístis, quia ego dixi vobis: Vado et vénio ad vos. Si diligerétis me, gauderétis útique, quia vado ad Patrem: quia Pater major me est. Et nunc dixi vobis, priúsquam fiat: ut, cum factum fúerit, credátis. Jam non multa loquar vobíscũ. Venit enim princeps mundi hujus, et in me non habet quidquam. Sed ut cognóscat mundus, quia díligo Patrem, et sicut mandátum dedit mihi Pater, sic fácio.

OFFERTORY. *Ps 67: 29-30*

CONFIRM THIS, O GOD, which Thou hast wrought in us; from Thy temple, which is in Jerusalem, kings shall offer presents to Thee, alleluia. ℣. *Sing ye to God, sing a psalm to His name, make a way for Him who ascendeth upon the west: the Lord is His name.* ℣. *In the churches bless the Lord God, from the fountains of Israel.* ℣. *Sing ye to God, ye kingdoms of the earth: give praise to the Lord, Who mounteth above the heaven of heavens to the East.*

Confírma hoc, Deus, quod operátus es in nobis: a templo tuo, quod est in Jerúsalẽ, tibi ófferent reges múnera, allelúja. ℣. *Cantáte Dómino: psalmum dícite nómini ejus: iter fácite ei, qui ascéndit super occásum: Dñs nomen est illi.* ℣. *In ecclésiis benedícite Deo Dómino, de fóntibus Ísraël.* ℣. *Regna terræ cantáte Deo: psállite Dño, qui ascéndit cælos cælórum ad Oriéntem.*

SECRET.

Sanctify, we beseech Thee, O Lord, the gifts offered, and cleanse our hearts with the light of the Holy Spirit. Through … in the unity of the same.

Múnera, quǽsumus, Dómine, obláta sanctífica: et corda nostra Sancti Spíritus illustratióne emúnda. Per Dñm … in unitáte ejusdem Spíritus.

The Preface of the Holy Ghost—"Preface of Pentecost" (page 191)—follows the Secret.

1962 • The Preface of the Holy Ghost is said with "on this day" (*hodiérna die*). During the Canon, proper COMMUNICANTES and HANC IGITUR. These are said until the Saturday after Pentecost, inclusively. *Praefatio, Communicántes et Hanc ígitur propria.*

COMMUNION. *Acts 2: 2, 4*

THERE CAME SUDDENLY a sound from heaven as of a mighty wind coming, where they were sitting, alleluia; and they were all filled with the Holy Ghost, speaking the wonderful works of God, alleluia, alleluia. ℣. *Then appeared to them what seemed to be tongues of fire, which parted and came to rest on each of them.*

Factus est repénte de cælo sonus, tamquã adveniéntis spíritus veheméntis, ubi erant sedéntes, allelúja: et repléti sunt omnes Spíritu Sancto, loquéntes magnália Dei, allelúja, allẽ. (Acts 2: 3) ℣. *Et apparuérunt illis dispertítæ linguæ tamquã ignis, seditque supra síngulos eórum.* —NARBONNE|1033 • Circa 1033AD

POSTCOMMUNION.

Sancti Spíritus, Dómine, corda nostra mundet infúsio: et sui roris íntima aspersióne fecúndet. Per Dóminum ... in unitáte ejusdem.

May our hearts be cleansed, O Lord, by the inpouring of the Holy Spirit; may He render them fruitful by watering them with His heavenly dew. Through ... in the unity of the same.

Feast of the Holy Trinity • Regarding the first Sunday after Pentecost, Cardinal Schuster has written: "This Sunday—which followed the night vigil at St Peter's [viz. *Ember Saturday of Pentecost*]—was devoted to rest: *Dominica Vacat.* But about the 8th century, the Roman lists begin to mark an *Octave of Pentecost*, doubtless in imitation of Low Sunday." It was not until 1334 that this feast was extended to the universal Church by Pope John XXII; yet even as late as the sixteenth century, certain dioceses kept this Sunday as the *Octave Day of Pentecost* (celebrating the feast of the Trinity on the following Monday). Father Dominic Johner, cantor of Beuron Abbey, has written: "As early as the eighth century, the Mass formulary had been composed for a votive high Mass in honor of the Holy Trinity. Therefore, in the earliest manuscripts we can find the Gregorian melodies for this feast, but in great part the melodies are borrowed from other sources. The Introit took its melody from the first Sunday of Lent, the Gradual and the Offertory from the feast of SS. Peter and Paul, and the Communion is a free adaptation of the Communion *Feci judícium*." Students of the liturgy will find notice other clues vis-à-vis the late date of this feast; e.g. the *Propria Missae* are superficially unified in a way most earlier feasts are not (each one beginning with the same word). With regard to the Collect, Cardinal Schuster notes that its construction is "not classic in form," lacking in conciseness, and "inharmonious." Dom Johner, similarly, can find little to praise in the Gregorian adaptations, which he finds "particularly unfortunate" with "little regard for the proper phrasing." Yet, all agree that the theology of this Mass formulary is quite profound.

I Classis.

— *Trinity Sunday* —

IN FESTO SANCTISSIMAE TRINITATIS

INTROIT. *Tob 12: 6*

Benedícta sit sancta Trínitas atque indivísa Unitas: confitébimur ei, quia fecit nobíscum misericórdiam suam. ℣. Dómine, Dóminus noster, quam admirábile est nomen tuum in univérsa terra! ℣. Glória Patri.

BLESSED BE the Holy Trinity, and undivided Unity: we will give glory to Him, because He hath shown His mercy to us. (Ps 8: 2) O Lord, our Master, the majesty of Thy name fills all the earth! ℣. Glory.

COLLECT.

Omnípotens sempitérne Deus, qui dedísti fámulis tuis in confessióne veræ fídei, ætérnæ Trinitátis glóriam agnóscere, et in poténtia majestátis adoráre Unitátem: quǽsumus; ut, ejúsdem fídei firmitáte, ab ómnibus semper muniámur advérsis. Per Dñm.

Almighty, eternal God, by Whose gift Thy servants, in the confession of the true faith, acknowledge the glory of the eternal Trinity, and adore the Unity in the power of His majesty, we beseech Thee that in the firmness of the same faith we may ever be defended from all adversities. Through our Lord.

EPISTLE. *Rom 11: 33-36*

O altitúdo divitiárum sapiéntiæ et sciéntiæ Dei: quam incomprehensibília sunt judícia ejus, et investigábiles viæ ejus! Quis enim cognovit sensum Dómini? Aut quis consiliárius ejus fuit? Aut quis prior dedit illi, et retribuétur ei? Quóniam ex ipso et per ipsum et in ipso sunt ómnia: ipsi glória in sǽcula. Amen.

O THE DEPTH of the riches of the wisdom and of the knowledge of God! How incomprehensible are His judgments, and how unsearchable His ways! For who hath known the mind of the Lord? Or who hath been His counsellor? Or who hath first given to Him, and recompense shall be made Him? For of Him, and by Him, and in Him, are all things: to Him be glory for ever. Amen.

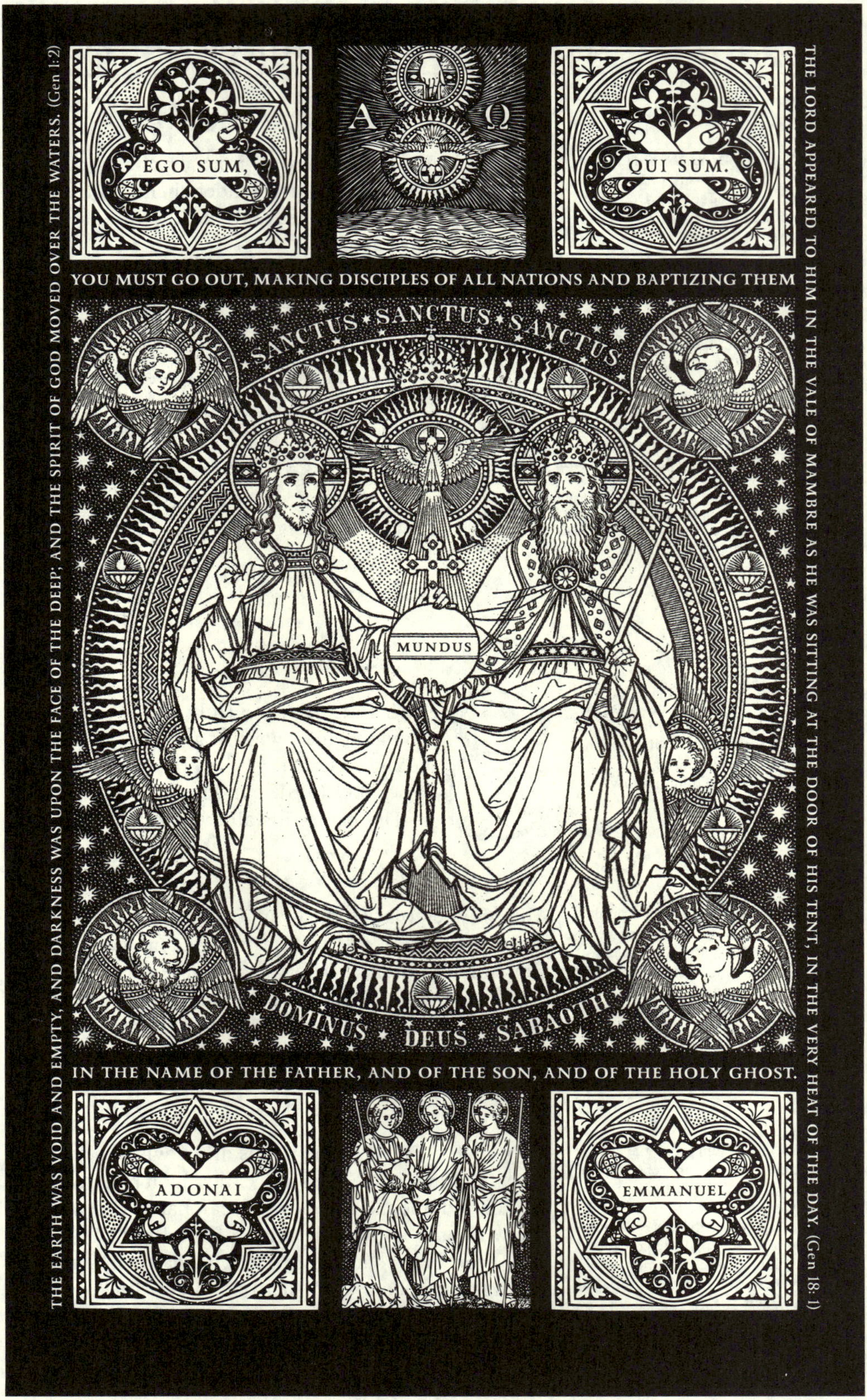
THE EARTH WAS VOID AND EMPTY, AND DARKNESS WAS UPON THE FACE OF THE DEEP; AND THE SPIRIT OF GOD MOVED OVER THE WATERS. (Gen 1:2)
EGO SUM,
A Ω
QUI SUM.
THE LORD APPEARED TO HIM IN THE VALE OF MAMBRE AS HE WAS SITTING AT THE DOOR OF HIS TENT, IN THE VERY HEAT OF THE DAY. (Gen 18: 1)
YOU MUST GO OUT, MAKING DISCIPLES OF ALL NATIONS AND BAPTIZING THEM
SANCTUS SANCTUS SANCTUS
MUNDUS
DOMINUS DEUS SABAOTH
IN THE NAME OF THE FATHER, AND OF THE SON, AND OF THE HOLY GHOST.
ADONAI
EMMANUEL

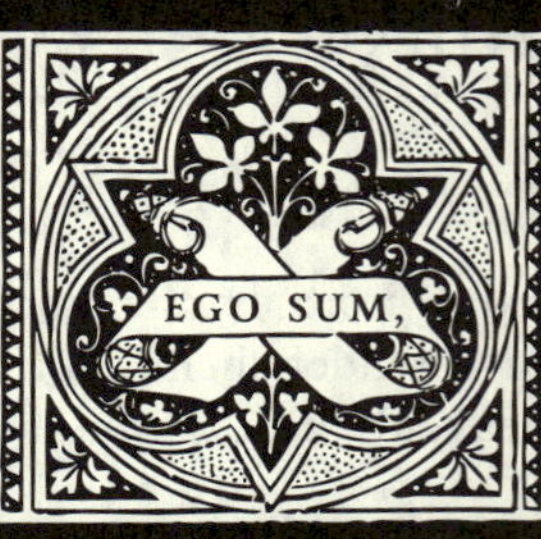

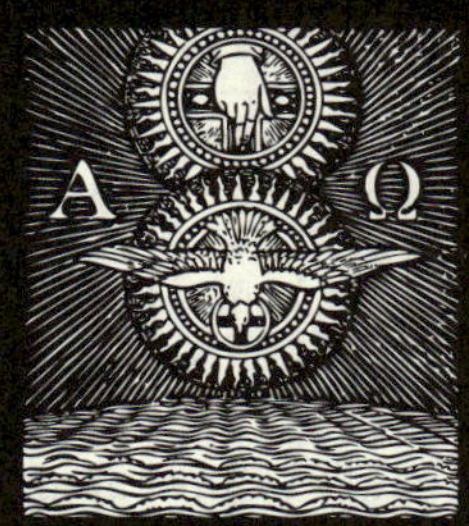

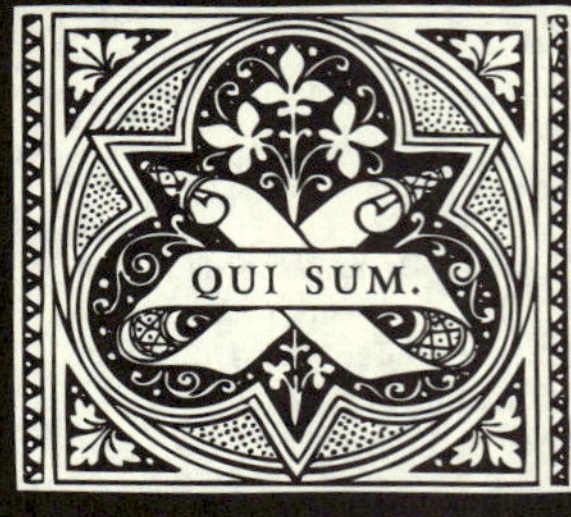

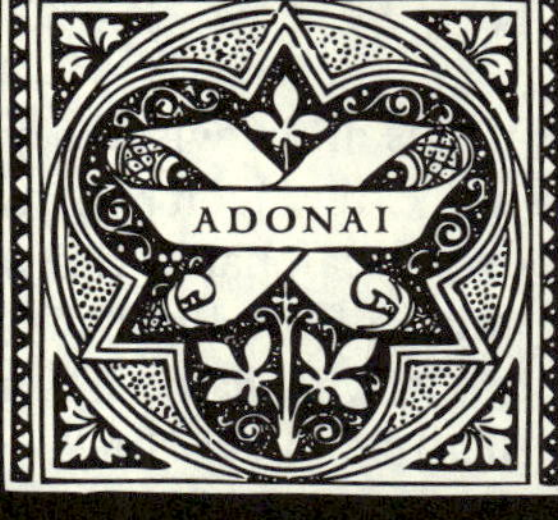

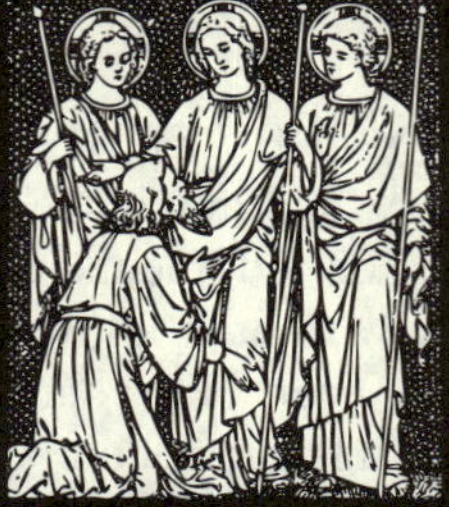

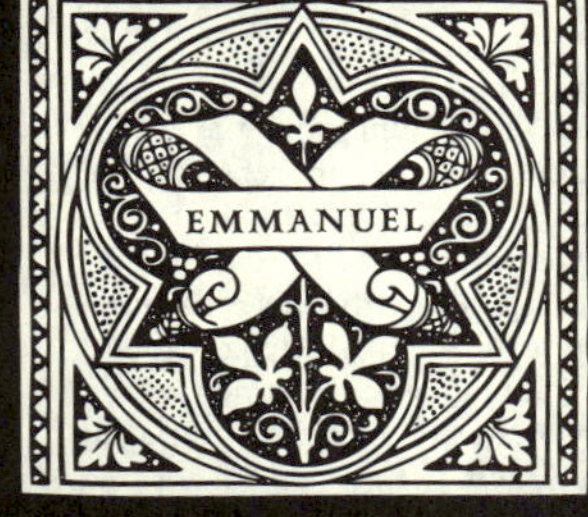

GRADUAL & ALLELUIA. *Dan 3: 55-56 & Dan 3: 52*

Benedíctus es, Dñe, qui intuéris abýssos, et sedes super Chérubim. ℣. Benedíctus es, Dómine, in firmaménto cæli, et laudábilis in sǽcula.

Allelúja, allelúja. ℣. Benedíctus es, Dómine, Deus patrum nostrórum, et laudábilis in sǽcula. Allelúja.

BLESSED ART THOU, O Lord, that beholdest the depths and sittest above the Cherubim. ℣. Blessed art Thou, O Lord, in the firmament of heaven, and worthy of praise forever.

Alleluia, alleluia. ℣. Blessed art Thou, O Lord God of our fathers, and worthy of praise forever. Alleluia.

GOSPEL. *Matt 28: 18-20*

In illo témpore: Dixit Jesus discípulis suis: Data est mihi omnis potéstas in cælo et in terra. Eúntes ergo docéte omnes gentes, baptizántes eos in nómine Patris, et Fílii, et Spíritus Sancti: docéntes eos serváre ómnia, quæcúmque mandávi vobis. Et ecce, ego vobíscum sum ómnibus diébus usque ad consummatiónem sǽculi.

AT THAT TIME, Jesus said to His disciples: All power is given to Me in heaven and in earth. Going, therefore, teach all nations, baptizing them in the name of the Father, and of the Son, and of the Holy Ghost. Teaching them to observe all things whatsoever I have commanded you; and behold I am with you all days, even to the consummation of the world. CREDO.

OFFERTORY. *Tob 12: 6*

Benedíctus sit Deus Pater, unigenitúsque Dei Fílius, Sanctus quoque Spíritus: quia fecit nobíscum misericórdiam suam. ℣. *Benedicámus Patrem et Fílium cum Sancto Spíritu: laudémus et superexaltémus eum in sǽcula.* ℣. *Benedíctus es, qui intuéris abýssos et sedes super Chérubim: et superlaudábilis et superexaltátus in sǽcula.*

BLESSED be God the Father, and the only-begotten Son of God, and also the Holy Spirit; because He hath shown His mercy toward us. ℣. *Let us bless the Father and the Son and the Holy Ghost: let us praise and exalt Him above all for ever.* ℣. *Blessed art Thou, that beholdest the depth, and sittest upon the Cherubim: and worthy to be praised and exalted above all for ever.*

SECRET.

Sanctífica, quǽsumus, Dómine, Deus noster, per tui sancti nóminis invocatiónem, hujus oblatiónis hóstiam: et per eam nosmetípsos tibi pérfice munus ætérnum. Per Dóminum.

By the invocation of Thy holy name, O Lord, our God, sanctify, we beseech Thee, the matter of this oblation, and through it make us ourselves a perfect offering forever. Through our Lord.

COMMUNION. *Tob 12: 6*

Benedícimus Deum cæli et coram ómnibus viventibus confitébimur ei: quia fecit nobíscum misericórdiam suam. (Dan 3:57) ℣. *Benedícite, ómnia ópera Dñi, Dómino: laudáte et superexaltáte eum in sǽcula.*

—HELMST|1026 • Circa 1026AD

WE BLESS the God of heaven, and before all living we will praise Him; because He has shown His mercy to us. ℣. *All ye works of the Lord, bless the Lord: praise and exalt Him above all for ever.*

POSTCOMMUNION.

May the receiving of this sacrament, O Lord, our God, and the confession of our faith in the eternal, holy Trinity and undivided Unity, profit us for the health of body and soul. Through our Lord.

Profíciat nobis ad salútem córporis et ánimæ, Dómine, Deus noster, hujus sacraménti suscéptio: et sempitérnæ sanctæ Trinitátis ejusdémque indivíduæ Unitátis conféssio. Per Dñm.

—*The Feast of Corpus Christi*— *I Classis.*

IN FESTO SANCTISSIMI CORPORIS CHRISTI *Feria quinta post festum Sanctissimae Trinitatis*

INTROIT. *Ps 80: 17*

HE FED THEM with the fat of wheat, alleluia; and filled them with honey out of the rock, alleluia, alleluia, alleluia. (Ps 80: 2) Rejoice to God our helper; sing aloud to the God of Jacob. ℣. Glory.

Cibávit eos ex ádipe fruménti, allelúja: et de petra, melle saturávit eos, allelúja, allelúja, allelúja. ℣. Exsultáte Deo, adjutóri nostro: jubiláte Deo Jacob. ℣. Glória Patri.

COLLECT.

O God, Who in this wonderful sacrament hast left us a memorial of Thy passion, grant us, we beseech Thee, so to venerate the sacred mysteries of Thy body and blood that we may constantly experience in ourselves the fruit of Thy redemption. Who livest.

Deus, qui nobis sub Sacraménto mirábili passiónis tuæ memóriã reliquísti: tríbue, quǽsumus, ita nos Córporis et Sánguinis tui sacra mystéria venerári; ut redemptiónis tuæ fructum in nobis júgiter sentiámus: Qui vivis.

EPISTLE. *I Cor 11: 23-29*

BRETHREN, I have received of the Lord, that which also I delivered to you, that the Lord Jesus, the same night in which He was betrayed, took bread, and giving thanks, broke, and said, Take ye and eat; this is My body which shall be delivered for you; this do for the commemoration of Me. In like manner also the chalice, after He had supped, saying, This chalice is the new testament in My blood; this do ye, as often as you shall drink, for the commemoration of Me. For as often as you shall eat this bread, and drink this chalice, you shall show the death of the Lord until He come. Therefore whosoever shall eat this bread, or drink of the chalice of the Lord unworthily, shall be guilty of the body and of the blood of the Lord. But let a man prove himself; and so let him eat of that bread, and drink of the chalice. For he that eateth and drinketh unworthily, eateth and drinketh judgment to himself, not discerning the body of the Lord.

Fratres: Ego enim accépi a Dño quod et trádidi vobis, quóniã Dñs Jesus, in qua nocte tradebátur, accépit panem, et grátias agens fregit, et dixit: Accípite, et manducáte: hoc est corpus meũ, quod pro vobis tradétur: hoc fácite in meam commemoratiónem. Simíliter et cálicem, postquam cenávit, dicens: Hic calix novum Testaméntum est in meo sánguine. Hoc fácite, quotiescúmque bibétis, in meam commemoratiónem. Quotiescúmque enim manducábitis panem hunc et cálicem bibétis, mortẽ Dñi annuntiábitis, donec véniat. Ítaque quicúmque manducáverit panem hunc vel bíberit cálicem Dñi indígne, reus erit córporis et sánguinis Dñi. Probet autẽ seípsum homo: et sic de pane illo edat et de cálice bibat. Qui enim mandúcat et bibit indígne, judícium sibi mandúcat et bibit: non dijúdicans corpus Dómini.

GRADUAL & ALLELUIA. *Ps 144: 15-16 & John 6: 56-57*

Óculi ómnium in te sperant, Dómine: et tu das illis escam in témpore opportúno. ℣. Áperis tu manum tuam: et imples omne ánimal benedictióne.

Allelúja, allelúja. ℣. Caro mea vere est cibus, et sanguis meus vere est potus: qui mandúcat meam carnem et bibit meum sánguinem, in me manet et ego in eo.

THE EYES of all hope in Thee, O Lord, and Thou givest them meat in due season. ℣. Thou openest Thy hand, and fillest every living creature with Thy blessing.

Alleluia, alleluia. ℣. My flesh is meat indeed, and My blood is drink indeed: He that eateth My flesh and drinketh My blood, abideth in Me, and I in him.

Today's Gradual—also sung on the 20th Sunday after Pentecost—has thirty-five notes on the penult of "áperis," whereas the tonic accent has only one. This is typical of the Gregorian repertoire; one does not compose in order to set every word to music, but in order to translate into music a single idea expressed in a number of words. In a musical phrase, each element is a part of the whole and must take its own place in that whole—for instance the word "coeli" in Sanctus IX, or the word "Domini" in the Benedictus of Mass XI, and so forth. In melismatic chant, the melodic line must be given first place, according to the ancient adage: Musica non subjacet regulis Donati. Gregorian rhythm is inherently musical in nature, and its function is to enhance the expressive power of the holy words. (Dom Joseph Gajard, 1950)

SEQUENCE. *Saint Thomas Aquinas. XIII. cent.*

Translation by Rev. Joseph Connelly
IMPRIMATUR (10 December 1954)
12th century melody by the composer monk, Adam of Saint Victor Abbey (near Paris).

AUDA SION SALVATOREM,
LAUDA DUCEM
ET PASTOREM
IN HYMNIS
ET CANTICIS.
Quantum potes, tantum aude:
Quia major omni laude,
Nec laudáre súfficis.

Sion, praise your Savior. Praise your leader and shepherd in hymns and canticles. ✠ Praise Him as much as you can, for He is beyond all praising and you will never be able to praise Him as He merits.

LAUDIS thema speciális,
Panis vivus et vitális,
Hódie propónitur.
Quem in sacræ mensa cœnæ,
Turbæ fratrum duodénæ
Datum non ambígitur.

But today a theme worthy of particular praise is put before us: the living and life-giving bread ✠ that, without any doubt, was given to the Twelve at table during the holy supper.

SIT LAUS plena, sit sonóra,
Sit jucúnda, sit decóra
Mentis jubilátio.
Dies enim solémnis ágitur,
In qua mensæ prima recólitur
Hujus institútio.

Therefore let our praise be full and resounding and our soul's rejoicing full of delight and beauty, ✠ for this is the festival day to commemorate the first institution of this table.

✠ THE SANCTISSIMUM WAS PREFIGURED IN TYPE WHEN ISAAC WAS BROUGHT AS AN OFFERING, WHEN MELCHIZEDEK THE PRIEST OFFERED BREAD AND WINE, WHEN A LAMB WAS APPOINTED FOR THE PASCH, AND WHEN MANNA WAS GIVEN TO THE JEWS OF OLD. ✠

THE LAW, FORESHADOWING THE DIVINE MYSTERIES, ORDAINED...

THAT SACRIFICES SHOULD BE OFFERED. ✠ "Lege præceptum immolari hostias..."

ON THE CROSS THY GODHEAD WAS HIDDEN;
HERE IS HIDDEN THY MANHOOD, TOO.

At this table of the new King, the new law's new pasch puts an end to the old pasch. ✠ The new displaces the old, reality the shadow, and light the darkness.

IN HAC mensa novi Regis,
Novum Pascha novæ legis,
Phase vetus términat.
Vetustátem nóvitas,
Umbram fugat véritas,
Noctem lux elíminat.

Christ wanted what He did at the supper to be repeated in His memory. ✠ And so we, in accordance with His holy directions, consecrate bread and wine to be salvation's Victim.

QUOD IN cœna Christus gessit,
Faciéndum hoc expréssit
In sui memóriam.
Docti sacris institútis,
Panem, vinum, in salútis
Consecrámus hóstiam.

Christ's followers know by faith that bread is changed into His flesh and wine into His blood. ✠ Man cannot understand this, cannot perceive it; but a lively faith affirms that the change, which is outside the natural course of things, takes place.

DOGMA datur christiánis,
Quod in carnem transit panis,
Et vinum in sánguinem.
Quod non capis, quod non vides,
Animósa firmat fides,
Præter rerum órdinem.

Under the different species, which are now signs only and not their own reality, there lie hid wonderful realities. ✠ His body is our food, His blood our drink. And yet Christ remains entire under each species.

SUB divérsis speciébus,
Signis tantum, et non rebus,
Latent res exímiæ.
Caro cibus, sanguis potus:
Manet tamen Christus totus,
Sub utráque spécie.

The communicant receives the complete Christ: uncut, unbroken, and undivided. ✠ Whether one receive or a thousand, the one receives as much as the thousand. Nor is Christ diminished by being received.

A SUMENTE non concísus,
Non confráctus, non divísus:
Integer accípitur.
Sumit unus, sumunt mille:
Quantum isti, tantum ille:
Nec sumptus consúmitur.

SUMUNT boni, sumunt mali:
Sorte tamen inæquáli,
Vitæ vel intéritus.
Mors est malis, vita bonis:
Vide paris sumptiónis
Quam sit dispar éxitus.

The good and the wicked alike receive Him, but with the unlike destiny of life or death. ✠ To the wicked it is death, but life to the good. See how different is the result, though each receives the same.

FRACTO demum sacraménto,
Ne vacílles, sed meménto,
Tantum esse sub fragménto,
Quantum toto tégitur.

Last of all, if the sacrament is broken, have no doubt. Remember there is as much in a fragment as in an unbroken host.

NULLA rei fit scissúra:
Signi tantum fit fractúra:
Qua nec status nec statúra
Signáti minúitur.

There is no division of the reality, but only a breaking of the sign; nor does the breaking diminish the condition or size of the One hidden under the sign.

ECCE panis Angelórum,
Factus cibus viatórum:
Vere panis filiórum,
Non mitténdus cánibus.

Behold, the bread of angels is become the pilgrim's food; truly it is bread for the sons, and is not to be cast to dogs.

IN figúris præsignátur,
Cum Isaac immolátur:
Agnus paschæ deputátur
Datur manna pátribus.

It was prefigured in type when Isaac was brought as an offering, when a lamb was appointed for the Pasch and when manna was given to the Jews of old.

BONE pastor, panis vere,
Jesu, nostri miserére:
Tu nos pasce, nos tuére:
Tu nos bona fac vidére
In terra vivéntium.

Jesus, good shepherd and true bread, have mercy on us; feed us and guard us. Grant that we find happiness in the land of the living.

TU, qui cuncta scis et vales:
Qui nos pascis hic mortáles:
Tuos ibi commensáles,
Coherédes et sodáles,
Fac sanctórum cívium. Amen. Allelúja.

You know all things, can do all things, and feed us here on earth; make us Your guests in heaven, co-heirs with You and companions of heaven's citizens. Amen. Alleluia.

GOSPEL. *John 6: 56-59*

In illo témpore: Dixit Jesus turbis Judæórum: Caro mea vere est cibus et sanguis meus vere est potus. Qui mandúcat meã carnem et bibit meum sánguinem, in me manet et ego in illo. Sicut misit me vivens Pater, et ego vivo propter Patrem: et qui mandúcat me, et ipse vivet propter me. Hic est panis, qui de cælo descéndit. Non sicut manducavérunt patres vestri manna, et mórtui sunt. Qui mandúcat hunc panem, vivet in ætérnum.

AT THAT TIME, Jesus said to the multitudes of the Jews: My flesh is meat indeed, and My blood is drink indeed. He that eateth My flesh, and drinketh My blood, abideth in Me, and I in him. As the living Father hath sent Me, and I live by the Father, so he that eateth Me, the same also shall live by Me. This is the bread that came down from heaven. Not as your fathers did eat manna and are dead. He that eateth this bread shall live for ever. CREDO.

OFFERTORY. *Lev 21: 6*

Sacerdótes Dñi incénsum et panes ófferunt Deo: et ídeo sancti erunt Deo suo, et non pólluent nomen ejus, allelúja.

THE PRIESTS of the Lord offer incense and loaves to God, and therefore they shall be holy to their God, and shall not defile His name. Alleluia.

SECRET.

Ecclésiæ tuæ, quǽsumus, Dñe, unitátis et pacis propítius dona concéde: quæ sub oblátis munéribus mýstice designántur. Per Dóminum.

Of Thy goodness, we beseech Thee, O Lord, grant to Thy Church the gifts of unity and peace which are mystically represented under the gifts we offer. Through our Lord.

1962 • The *Preface for Weekdays* ("Common Preface") is used for this feast in the 1962 Missal; alternately, the "ad libitum" Preface for the Blessed Sacrament (page 194) may be used. Formerly, however, the *Preface of the Nativity* was used on the feast of Corpus Christi as well as the Transfiguration.

COMMUNION. *I Cor 11: 26-27*

Quotiescúmque manducábitis panem hunc et cálicem bibétis, mortem Dñi annuntiábitis, donec véniat: ítaque quicúmque manducáverit panẽ vel bíberit cálicem Dñi indígne, reus erit córporis et sánguinis Dómini, allelúja.

AS OFTEN as you shall eat this bread, and drink the chalice, you shall show forth the death of the Lord, until He come; therefore whosoever shall eat this bread or drink the chalice of the Lord unworthily, shall be guilty of the body and blood of the Lord. Alleluia.

POSTCOMMUNION.

Fac nos, quǽsumus, Dómine, divinitátis tuæ sempitérna fruitióne repléri: quam pretiósi Córporis et Sánguinis tui temporális percéptio præfigúrat: Qui vivis.

Grant us, we beseech Thee, O Lord, to be filled with the everlasting enjoyment of thy divinity, which the temporal partaking of Thy precious body and blood doth foreshow. Who livest.

[Editor's Note: In 1264, this feast was extended to the universal Church. Owing to its relatively late date, it has "extra" verses for neither Offertory nor Communion. The texts were assembled by Saint Thomas Aquinas (d. 1274), and the melodies borrowed from other places: (1) INTROIT received both text and melody from the Monday after Pentecost; (2) GRADUAL is identical to the 20th Sunday after Pentecost; (3) ALLELUIA took its melody from *Lætábitur Justus*; (4) both OFFERTORY and COMMUNION took their melodies from Pentecost Sunday. The text of the Communion—from I Corinthians about unworthy reception of Communion—was carefully excised by the reformers in 1970 and appears nowhere in the post-conciliar lectionary, whereas in the traditional liturgy it was read each year on the Eucharistic feasts: Holy Thursday and Corpus Christi.]

✠ THE PRIEST THEREFORE GAVE HIM HALLOWED BREAD: FOR THERE WAS NO BREAD THERE, BUT ONLY THE LOAVES OF PROPOSITION. (I Sam 21: 6)

CHRIST'S FOLLOWERS KNOW BY FAITH THAT BREAD IS...

...CHANGED INTO HIS FLESH AND WINE INTO HIS BLOOD.

✠ AND DAVID AND ALL THE HOUSE OF ISRAEL BROUGHT THE ARK OF THE COVENANT OF THE LORD WITH JOYFUL SHOUTING. (II Sam 6: 15)

MAN CANNOT UNDERSTAND THIS, CANNOT PERCEIVE IT; BUT A LIVELY FAITH AFFIRMS THAT THE CHANGE—WHICH IS OUTSIDE THE NATURAL COURSE OF THINGS—TAKES PLACE. ✠ *Saint Thomas Aquinas*

AD PROCESSIONEM

When Pope Pius X formed his Pontifical Commission to create the *Editio Vaticana* (which is still the official edition of the Catholic Church) His Holiness appointed Abbat Josef Pothier as its president. When the *Liber Gradualis* was published in 1908, the world was surprised to see that the authentic Gregorian hymns were provided—in their pristine form—alongside the "mangled versions" by Pope Urban VIII, which were included as options. As Father Fortescue put it: "The Vatican Gradual cheered our hearts by restoring the authentic form of the hymns therein."

The 1908 *Graduale* included (on pages 123-129 of its third section) several hymns for the PROCESSION on the feast of Corpus Christi and one is printed below: viz. JESU NOSTRA REDEMPTIO—the title of which Pope Urban VIII changed to "Salutis Humanæ Sator" in 1632AD.

D-Natural Starting Pitch

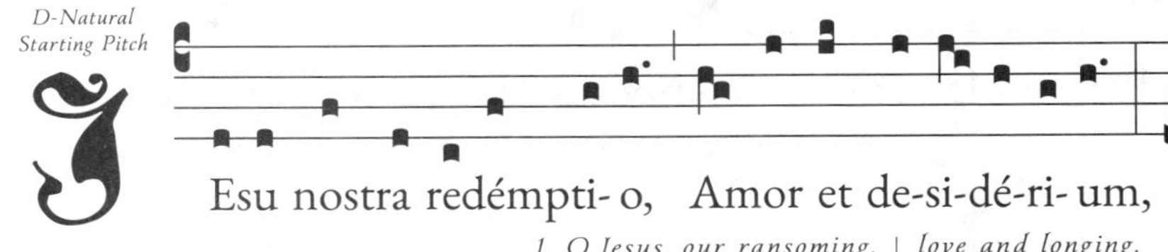

JEsu nostra redémpti- o, Amor et de-si-dé-ri- um,

1. O Jesus, our ransoming, | love and longing,

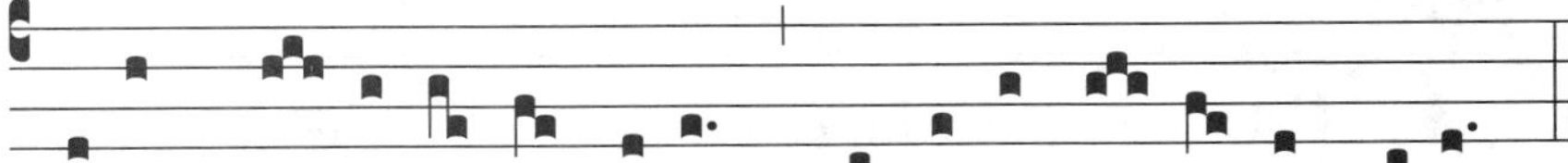

De- us Cre- á-tor ómni- um, Homo in fi- ne témporum.

God, the Creator of all things, | man at the end of time.

VERSE 2

QUæ te vi-cit cleménti- a, Ut ferres nostra crímina,

2. What mercy conquered thee, | so as to bear our misdeeds,

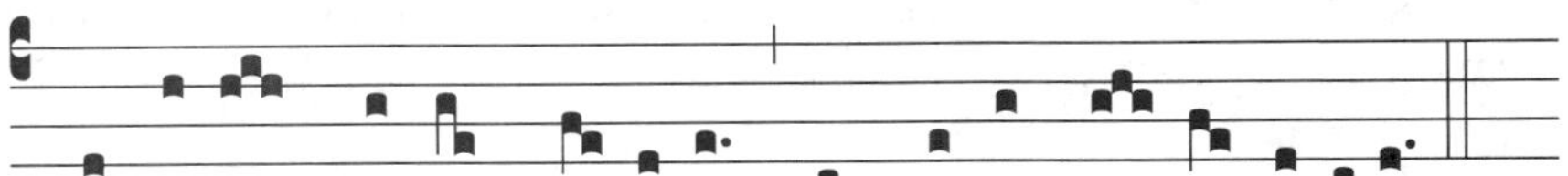

Cru-dé-lem mortem pá- ti- ens, Ut nos a mor- te tólleres?

suffering a cruel death, | so as to lift us from death?

VERSE 3

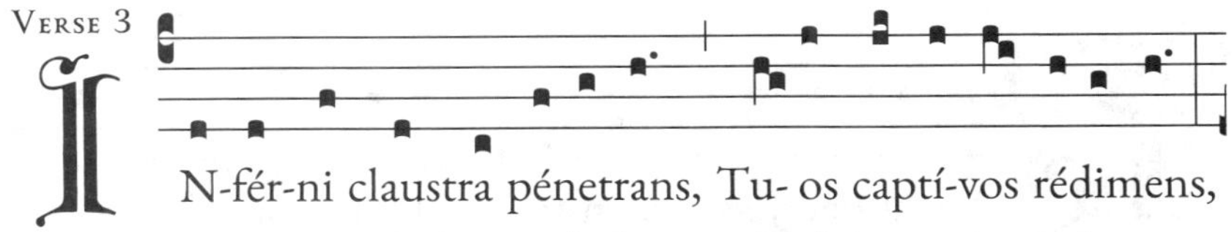

IN-fér-ni claustra pénetrans, Tu- os captí-vos rédimens,

3. Piercing the dungeons of hell, | ransoming thy hostages,

Victor tri- úmpho nó-bi-li Ad dextram Pa- tris ré-si-dens.

conqueror in a famous victory, | enthroned at the Father's right.

Verse 4

in thee be our glory | ever through all the ages.

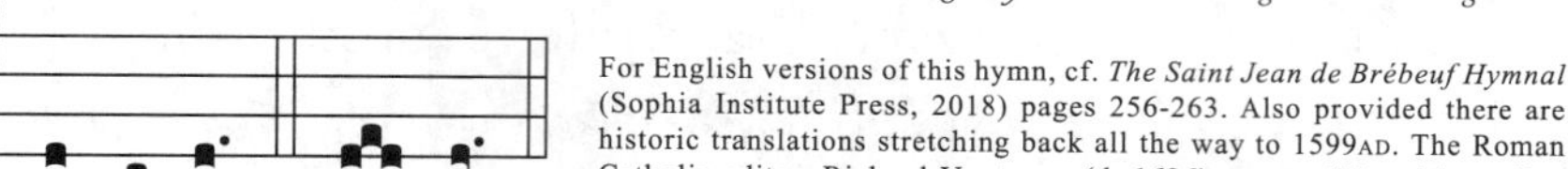

sǽ-cu-la. A-men.

For English versions of this hymn, cf. *The Saint Jean de Brébeuf Hymnal* (Sophia Institute Press, 2018) pages 256-263. Also provided there are historic translations stretching back all the way to 1599AD. The Roman Catholic editor, Richard Verstegan (d. 1636), wrote: "Notwithstanding the difficulty, these hymns have been so turned into English meter that they may be sung unto the same tunes in English that they bear in Latin."

THE SECOND HYMN

A-Natural Starting Pitch

cre- as, Culpæ fu-gas ca- lí-ginem, Et nos reples dul-cé-di-ne.

thou dost banish the darkness of sin and fillest us with thy consolation.

déxteræ, Tu dulce lumen pá-tri- æ, Carnis negátum sénsibus.

hand of the Father; thou, the light that consoles heaven, who cannot be seen by man on earth.

tas, No-bis amó-ris có-pi- am Largí-re per præsénti- am.

bestow on us by thy presence an abundance of love.

Patre et al-mo Spí-ri-tu, In sempi-térna sǽcu-la. A-men.

with the Father and the Holy Ghost, forever and ever.

For more information about this hymn, including an English translation by Cardinal Newman, cf. *The Saint Jean de Brébeuf Hymnal* (Sophia Institute Press, 2018) page 746. An organ accompaniment is also provided—search the tune index for "Jesu Dulcis"—as well as a text-only version which gives melodic flexibility. There are many valid ways to translate the beautiful second verse. A Roman Catholic Primer from 1732 translates it as follows:

> Coheir of God's Paternal Throne,
> Thou sov'reign Bliss to Sense unknown;
> Thrice happy they, who fill'd with Thee
> Possess the Saints' Felicity.

Father John Fitzpatrick, OMI, translates that verse on page 163 (*Breviary & Missal Hymns*, 1931) as follows:

> Happy is he whom, as his guest,
> From God's right hand, Thou visitest:
> Sweet glory of our Father's home,
> Where carnal sense can never come.

THE THIRD HYMN

Many other hymns may be chosen for the procession, including hymns the congregation sings in English. For numerous options in English and Latin, cf. *The Saint Jean de Brébeuf Hymnal* (2018). A hymn often sung during the procession is the PANGE LINGUA by Saint Thomas Aquinas (d. 1274), which for your convenience has been printed on page 518.

In addition, the following hymn by Saint Thomas Aquinas can be sung to many different melodies in the *Brébeuf Hymnal*, including: HILDERSTONE, DUGUET, BRESLAU, MELCOMBE, WAREHAM, OLD HUNDREDTH, MEIN SEEL, TRINITY COLLEGE, EISENACH, ROGERS PARK, BRESSANI, LA ROCHELLE, KEMPEN, BESSEMER, TALLIS CANON, WINCHESTER NEW, and so forth.

VERBUM supérnum pródiens,
Nec Patris linquens déxteram,
Ad opus suum éxiens,
Venit ad vitæ vésperam.

1. The sovereign Word, setting out,
though not leaving the right hand of the Father,
going forth to his work,
came to the evening of his life.

2. In mortem a discípulo
Suis tradéndus ǽmulis,
Prius in vitæ férculo
Se trádidit discípulis.

2. Yet to be delivered to his adversaries
unto death by a disciple,
he delivered himself to the disciples
beforehand in the food of life.

3. Quibus sub bina spécie
Carnem dedit, et sánguinem,
Ut dúplicis substántiæ
Totum cibáret hóminem.

3. Under two appearances
he gave them his flesh and blood,
so as to feed the entire man
of twofold substance.

4. Se nascens dedit sócium,
Convéscens in edúlium,
Se móriens in prétium,
Se regnans dat in praémium.

4. Being born, he gave himself as our ally,
sharing food, as our fare,
dying, as our ransom,
reigning, he gives himself as our recompense.

O SALUTÁRIS Hóstia,
Quæ cæli pandis óstium:
Bella premunt hostília,
Da robur, fer auxílium.

O SAVING VICTIM,
who unfoldest the portal of heaven,
the aggressions of the foe beset us:
give us hardiness, bring us aid.

6. Uni trinóque Dómino
Sit sempitérna glória:
Qui vitam sine término
Nobis donet in pátria.

Amen.

6. To the Lord one and three
be glory everlasting,
and may be grant us life
without limit in the homeland.

The First Sunday after Pentecost is always replaced by Trinity Sunday ("In Festo Sanctissimæ Trinitatis"). However, the Mass formulary—which is incredibly ancient—is used during the following week, so the Mass Propers are often included in liturgical books. This tradition goes back more than a millennium.

II Classis.

—*Second Sunday after Pentecost*—

INTROIT. *Ps 17: 19-20*

Factus est Dóminus protéctor meus, et edúxit me in latitúdinem: salvum me fecit, quóniam vóluit me. ℣. Díligam te, Dómine, virtus mea: Dóminus firmaméntum meum et refúgium meum et liberátor meus. ℣. Glória Patri.

THE LORD became my protector, and He brought me forth into a large place: He saved me, because He was well pleased with me. (Ps 17: 2, 3) I will love Thee, O Lord my strength: the Lord is my firmament, and my refuge, and my deliverer. ℣. Glory.

COLLECT.

Sancti nóminis tui, Dómine, timórem páriter et amórem fac nos habére perpétuum: quia numquam tua gubernatióne destítuis, quos in soliditáte tuæ dilectiónis instítuis. Per Dóminum.

Grant us, O Lord, an abiding fear and love of Thy holy name, for Thou never failest to govern those whom Thou dost firmly establish in Thy love. Through our Lord.

EPISTLE. *I John 3: 13-18*

Caríssimi: Nolíte mirári, si odit vos mundus. Nos scimus, quóniã transláti sumus de morte ad vitam, quóniam dilígimus fratres. Qui non díligit, manet in morte: omnis, qui odit fratrem suũ, homicída est. Et scitis, quóniã omnis homicída non habet vitam ætérnam in semetípso manéntẽ. In hoc cognóvimus caritátem Dei, quóniam ille ánimã suã pro nobis pósuit: et nos debémus pro frátribus ánimas pónere. Qui habúerit substántiam hujus mundi, et víderit fratrem suum necessitátem habére, et cláuserit víscera sua ab eo: quómodo cáritas Dei manet in eo? Filíoli mei, non diligámus verbo neque lingua, sed ópere et veritáte.

DEARLY BELOVED, Wonder not if the world hate you. We know that we have passed from death to life, because we love the brethren. He that loveth not, abideth in death. Whosoever hateth his brother is a murderer: and you know that no murderer hath eternal life abiding in himself. In this we have known the charity of God, because He hath laid down His life for us: and we ought to lay down our lives for the brethren. He that hath the substance of this world, and shall see his brother in need, and shut up his bowels from him, how doth the charity of God abide in him? My little children, let us not love in word nor in tongue, but in deed and in truth.

GRADUAL & ALLELUIA. *Ps 119: 1-2 & Ps 7: 2*

Ad Dóminum, cum tribulárer, clamávi, et exaudívit me. ℣. Dómine, líbera ánimam meam a lábiis iníquis, et a lingua dolósa.

Allelúja, allelúja. ℣. Dómine, Deus meus, in te sperávi: salvum me fac ex ómnibus persequéntibus me et líbera me. Allelúja.

IN MY TROUBLE, I cried to the Lord, and He heard me. ℣. O Lord, deliver my soul from wicked lips and a deceitful tongue.

Alleluia, alleluia. ℣. O Lord my God, in Thee have I put my trust: save me from all them that persecute me, and deliver me. Alleluia.

GOSPEL. *Luke 14: 16-24*

At that time, Jesus spoke to the pharisees this parable:

A CERTAIN MAN made a great supper, and invited many. And he sent his servant, at the hour of supper, to say to them that were invited, that they should come, for now all things are ready. And they began all at once to make excuse. The first said to him, I have bought a farm, and must needs go out, and see it; I pray thee to hold me excused. And another said, I have bought five yoke of oxen, and I go to try them; I pray thee hold me excused. And another said, I have married a wife, and therefore I cannot come. And the servant returning, told these things to his lord.

In illo témpore: Dixit Jesus pharisǽis parábolam hanc: Homo quidam fecit cenam magnam, et vocávit multos. Et misit servum suum hora cenæ dícere invitátis, ut venírent, quia jam paráta sunt ómnia. Et cœpérunt simul omnes excusáre. Primus dixit ei: Villam emi, et necésse hábeo exíre et vidére illam: rogo te, habe me excusátum. Et alter dixit: Juga boum emi quinque et eo probáre illa: rogo te, habe me excusátum. Et álius dixit: Uxórem duxi, et ídeo non possum veníre. Et revérsus servus nuntiávit hæc dómino suo.

Then the master of the house being angry, said to his servant, Go out quickly into the streets and lanes of the city, and bring in hither the poor, and the feeble and the blind, and the lame. And the servant said: Lord, it is done as thou hast commanded, and yet there is room. And the lord said to the servant, Go out into the highways and hedges, and compel them to come in, that my house may be filled. But I say unto you, that none of these men that were invited shall taste of my supper. CREDO.

Tunc irátus paterfamílias, dixit servo suo: Exi cito in pláteas et vicos civitátis: et páuperes ac débiles et cæcos et claudos íntroduc huc. Et ait servus: Dómine, factum est, ut imperásti, et adhuc locus est. Et ait dóminus servo: Exi in vias et sepes: et compélle intráre, ut impleátur domus mea. Dico autem vobis, quod nemo virórum illórum, qui vocáti sunt, gustábit cenam meam.

OFFERTORY. *Ps 6: 5*

TURN to me, O Lord, and deliver my soul, O save me for Thy mercy's sake. ℣. *O Lord, rebuke me not in Thine indignation, nor chastise me in Thy wrath.* ℣. *Have mercy on me, O Lord, for I am weak: heal me, O Lord, for all my bones are troubled.*

Dómine, convértere, et éripe ánimam meam: salvum me fac propter misericórdiam tuam. ℣. *Dómine, ne in ira tua árguas me: neque in furóre tuo corrípias me.* ℣. *Miserére mihi, Dómine, quóniam infírmus sum: sana me, Dómine, quóniam conturbáta sunt ómnia ossa mea.*

SECRET.

Let the oblation about to be offered to Thy holy name, O Lord, purify us and day by day change us to the living of the heavenly life. Through our Lord.

Oblátio nos, Dómine, tuo nómini dicánda puríficet: et de die in diem ad cæléstis vitæ tránsferat actiónem. Per Dóminum.

COMMUNION. *Ps 12: 6*

I WILL sing to the Lord, Who giveth me good things: and I will sing to the name of the Lord the

Cantábo Dómino, qui bona tríbuit mihi: et psallam nómini Dómini altíssimi. (Ps 12: 1) ℣. *Úsquequo, Dómi-*

ne, oblivisceris me in finem? úsquequo avértis fáciem tuam a me?
—StMaur|1079 • Circa 1079AD

most high. ℣. *How long, O Lord, wilt Thou forget me unto the end? How long dost Thou turn away Thy face from me?*

POSTCOMMUNION.

Sumptis munéribus sacris, quǽsumus, Dómine: ut cum frequentatióne mystérii, crescat nostræ salútis efféctus. Per Dóminum.

Having received Thy sacred gifts, we pray, O Lord, that, as we now frequently assist at this mystery so may it cause to increase the grace of our salvation. Through our Lord.

I Classis.

—*Most Sacred Heart of Jesus*—

IN FESTO SACRATISSIMI CORDIS JESU

INTROIT. *Ps 32: 11, 19*

Cogitatiónes Cordis ejus in generatióne et generatiónem: ut éruat a morte ánimas eórum et alat eos in fame. ℣. Exsultáte, justi, in Dómino: rectos decet collaudátio. ℣. Glória Patri.

THE **THOUGHTS** of His Heart to all generations: to deliver their souls from death and feed them in famine. (Ps 32: 1) Rejoice in the Lord, O ye just, praise becometh the upright. ℣. Glory.

COLLECT.

Deus, qui nobis in Corde Fílii tui, nostris vulneráto peccátis, infinítos dilectiónis thesáuros misericórditer largíri dignáris: concéde, quǽsumus; ut, illi devótum pietátis nostræ præstántes obséquium, dignæ quoque satisfactiónis exhibeámus offícium. Per eúmdem Dóminum.

O God, who, in the Heart of Thy Son, wounded by our sins, hast deigned mercifully to bestow infinite treasures of love upon us; grant, we beseech Thee, that as we offer Him the faithful service of our devotion, we may also make worthy reparation. Through the same.

EPISTLE. *Eph 3: 8-12, 14-19*

Fratres: Mihi, ómnium sanctórum mínimo, data est grátia hæc, in géntibus evangelizáre investigábiles divítias Christi, et illumináre omnes, quæ sit dispensátio sacraménti abscónditi a sǽculis in Deo, qui ómnia creávit: ut innotéscat principátibus et potestátibus in cæléstibus per Ecclésiam multifórmis sapiéntia Dei, secúndum præfinitiónem sæculórum, quam fecit in Christo Jesu, Dómino nostro, in quo

BRETHREN: To me, the least of all the saints, is given this grace, to preach among the gentiles the unsearchable riches of Christ; and to enlighten all men, that they may see what is the dispensation of the mystery which hath been hidden from eternity in God, Who created all things: that the manifold wisdom of God may be made known to the principalities and powers in the heavenly places through the Church:

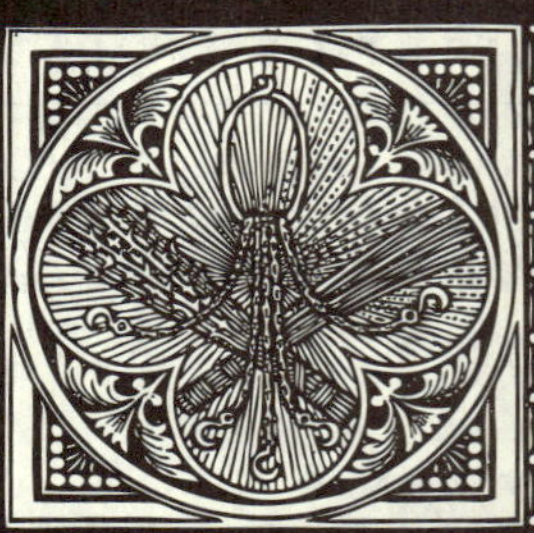

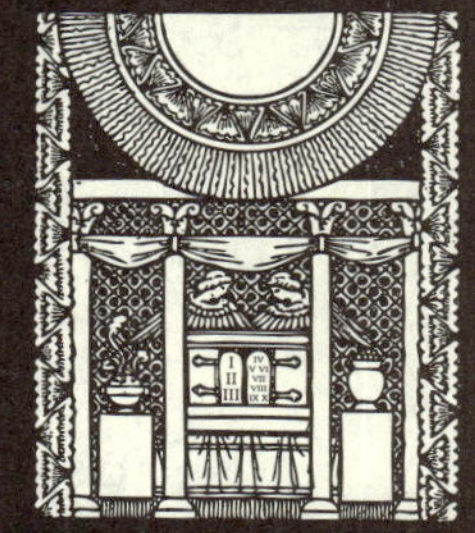

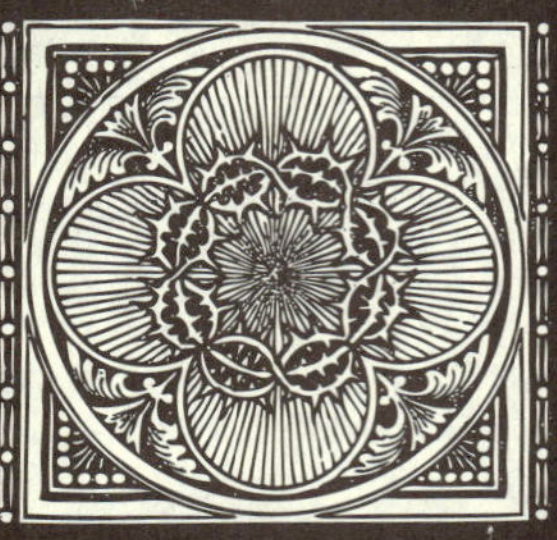

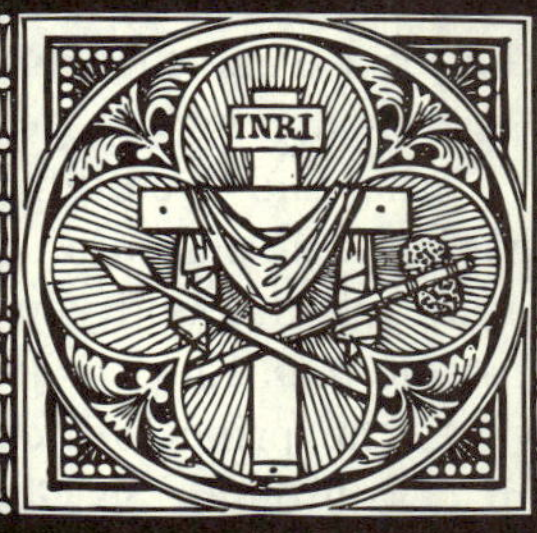

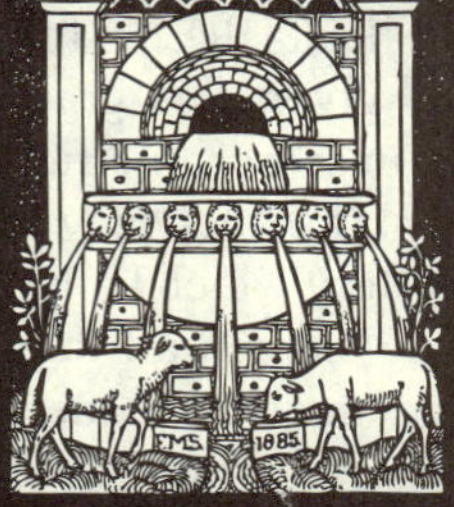

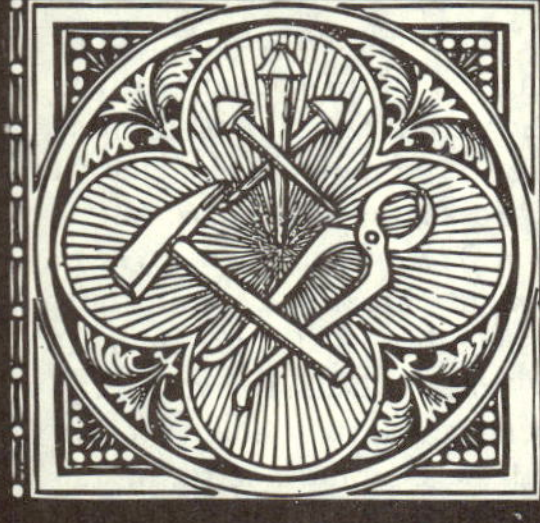

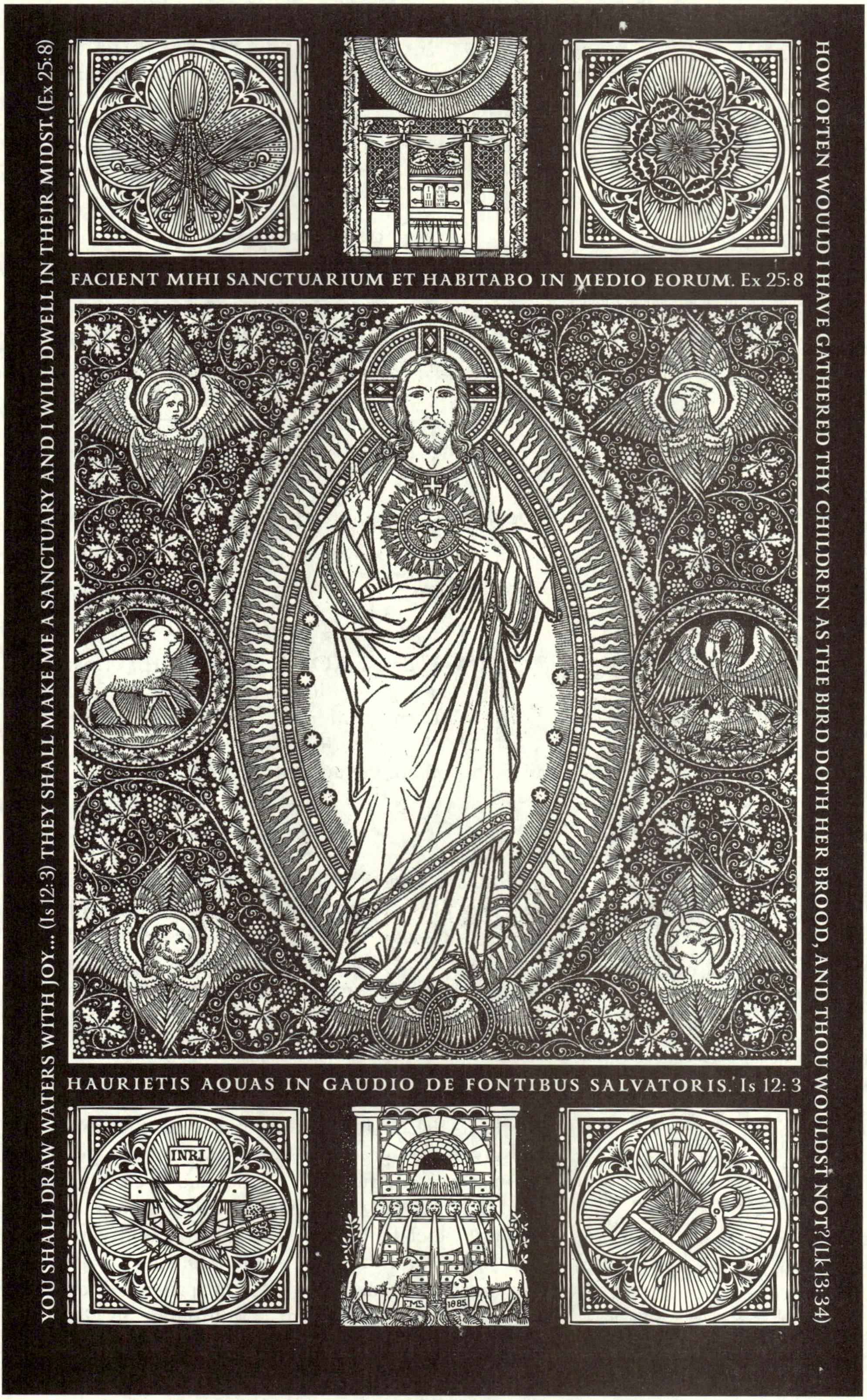
YOU SHALL DRAW WATERS WITH JOY… (Is 12:3) THEY SHALL MAKE ME A SANCTUARY AND I WILL DWELL IN THEIR MIDST. (Ex 25:8)
FACIENT MIHI SANCTUARIUM ET HABITABO IN MEDIO EORUM. Ex 25:8
HOW OFTEN WOULD I HAVE GATHERED THY CHILDREN AS THE BIRD DOTH HER BROOD, AND THOU WOULDST NOT? (Lk 13:34)
HAURIETIS AQUAS IN GAUDIO DE FONTIBUS SALVATORIS. Is 12:3
INRI
FMS
1885

habémus fidúciam et accéssum in confidéntia per fidem ejus. Hujus rei grátia flecto génua mea ad Patrem Dómini nostri Jesu Christi, ex quo omnis patérnitas in cælis ei in terra nominátur, ut det vobis, secúndum divítias glóriæ suæ, virtúte corroborári per Spíritum ejus in interiórem hóminem, Christum habitáre per fidem in córdibus vestris: in caritáte radicáti et fundáti, ut possítis comprehéndere cum ómnibus sanctis, quæ sit latitúdo, et longitúdo, et sublímitas, et profúndum: scire étiam supereminéntem sciéntiæ caritátem Christi, ut impleámini in omnem plenitúdinem Dei.

according to the eternal purpose, which He made in Christ Jesus our Lord, in Whom we have boldness and access with confidence by the faith of Him. For this cause I bow my knees to the Father of our Lord Jesus Christ, of Whom all paternity in heaven and earth is named; that He would grant you, according to the riches of His glory, to be strengthened by His Spirit with might unto the inward man; that Christ may dwell by faith in your hearts; that being rooted and founded in charity, you may be able to comprehend, with all the saints, what is the breadth, and length, and height, and depth: to know also the charity of Christ, which surpasseth all understanding, that you may be filled unto all the fullness of God.

GRADUAL & ALLELUIA. *Ps 24: 8-9 & Matt 11: 29*

Dulcis et rectus Dóminus: propter hoc legem dabit delinquéntibus in via. ℣. Díriget mansúetos in judício, docébit mites vias suas.

Allelúja, allelúja. ℣. Tóllite jugum meum super vos, et díscite a me, quia mitis sum et húmilis Corde, et inveniétis réquiem animábus vestris. Allelúja.

THE LORD is sweet and righteous, therefore He will give a law to sinners in the way. ℣. He will guide the mild in judgment, He will teach the meek His ways.

Alleluia, alleluia. ℣. Take up My yoke upon you and learn of Me, because I am meek and humble of heart, and you shall find rest to your souls. Alleluia.

GOSPEL. *John 19: 31-37*

In illo témpore: Judǽi (quóniam Parascéve erat), ut non remanérent in cruce córpora sábbato (erat enim magnus dies ille sábbati), rogavérunt Pilátum, ut frangeréntur eórum crura, et tolleréntur. Venérunt ergo mílites: et primi quidem fregérunt crura et alteríus, qui crucifíxus est cum eo. Ad Jesum autem cum veníssent, ut vidérunt eum jam mórtuum, non fregérunt ejus crura, sed unus mílitum láncea latus ejus apéruit, et contínuo exívit sanguis et aqua. Et qui vidit, testimónium perhíbuit: et verum est testimónium ejus. Et ille scit quia vera dicit, ut et vos credátis. Facta sunt enim hæc ut Scriptúra implerétur: Os non comminuétis ex eo. Et íterum alia Scriptúra dicit: Vidébunt in quem transfixérunt.

THE JEWS (because it was the Parasceve) that the bodies might not remain upon the cross on the Sabbath-day (for that was a great Sabbath-day) besought Pilate that their legs might be broken, and that they might be taken away. The soldiers therefore came, and they broke the legs of the first, and of the other that was crucified with him. But after they were come to Jesus, when they saw that He was already dead, they did not break His legs, but one of the soldiers with a spear opened His side, and immediately there came out blood and water. And he that saw it hath given testimony; and his testimony is true. And he knoweth that he saith true, that you also may believe. For these things were done that the Scripture might be fulfilled: You shall not break a bone of Him. And again another Scripture saith: They shall look on Him whom they pierced. Credo.

OFFERTORY. *Ps 68: 21*

MY HEART hath expected reproach and misery, and I looked for one that would grieve together with me and there was none; and I sought one that would console me and I found none. [And they gave Me gall for My food, and in My thirst they gave Me vinegar to drink.] ℣. *Save me, O God, for the waters are come in even unto my soul.* ℣. *They that sat in the gate spoke against me: and they that drank wine made me their song.* ℣. *But as for me, my prayer is to Thee, O Lord; for the time of Thy good pleasure, O God, in the multitude of Thy mercy.*

Impropérium exspectávit Cor meum et misériam: et sustínui, qui simul mecum contristarétur, et non fuit: consolántem me quæsívi, et non invéni. [Et dedérunt in escam meam fel, et in siti mea potavérunt me acéto.] ℣. *Salvum me fac, Deus, quóniam intravérunt aquæ usque ad ánimam meam.* ℣. *Advérsum me exercebántur, qui sedébant in porta, et in me psallébant, qui bibébant vinum.* ℣. *Ego vero oratiónem meam ad te Dómine: tempus beneplácíti, Deus, in multitúdine misericórdiæ tuæ.*

SECRET.

O Lord, we beseech Thee, look upon the inconceivable love of the Heart of Thy dear Son: so that our offering may be to Thee an acceptable gift, to us the expiation of sin. Through the same.

Réspice, quǽsumus, Dómine, ad ineffábilem Cordis dilécti Fílii tui caritátem: ut quod offérimus sit tibi munus accéptum et nostrórum expiátio delictórum. Per eúmdem Dóminum.

The Preface of the Most Sacred Heart (page 193) follows the Secret.

COMMUNION. *John 19: 34*

ONE OF THE SOLDIERS with a spear opened His side, and immediately there came out blood and water. ℣. *The mercies of the Lord I will sing for ever: I will show forth Thy truth with my mouth to generation and generation.*

Unus mílitum láncea latus ejus apéruit, et contínuo exívit sanguis et aqua. (Ps 88: 2) ℣. *Misericórdias Dómini in ætérnum cantábo; in generatiónem et generatiónem annuntiábo veritátem tuam in ore meo.*

POSTCOMMUNION.

May Thy holy mysteries, O Lord Jesus, give us holy fervor; that by it perceiving the sweetness of Thy most loving Heart, we may learn to despise earthly things and to love those of heaven. Who livest.

Prǽbeant nobis, Dómine Jesu, divínum tua sancta fervórem: quo dulcíssimi Cordis tui suavitáte percépta; discámus terréna despícere, et amáre cæléstia: Qui vivis.

This particular Mass formulary dates from 29 January 1929. None of the Propers are ancient, but in the case of the Offertory, it matches the ancient melody for Palm Sunday (until the brackets). In the Vatican Edition—published by Abbat Joseph Pothier under Pope Saint Pius X—the Introit was *Egredímini Et Vidéte*; the Gradual was *Dícite Filiæ Sion*; the Alleluia Verse was *Díscite A Me*; the Offertory was *Dómine Deus In Simplicitáte*; and the Communion was *Gustáte Et Vidéte*. The 1908 Vatican Edition also gives an alternate Mass for the Sacred Heart with Introit (*Miserébitur Secúndum*), Gradual (*O Vos Omnes*), Alleluia Verse (*Dícite A Me*), Offertory (*Bénedic Ánima Mea*), and Communion (*Impropérium Expectávit*).

II Classis.

—*Third Sunday after Pentecost*—

INTROIT. *Ps 24: 16, 18*

Réspice in me et miserére mei, Dñe: quóniam únicus et pauper sum ego: vide humilitátem meam et labórem meum: et dimítte ómnia peccáta mea, Deus meus. ℣. Ad te, Dómine, levávi ánimam meam: Deus meus, in te confído, non erubéscam. ℣. Glória Patri.

LOOK THOU upon me, O Lord, and have mercy on me; for I am alone and poor. See my abjection and my labor; and forgive me all my sins, O my God. (Ps 24: 1-2) To Thee, O Lord, have I lifted up my soul: in Thee, my God, I put my trust; let me not be ashamed. ℣. Glory.

COLLECT.

Protéctor in te sperántium, Deus, sine quo nihil est válidum, nihil sanctum: multíplica super nos misericórdiã tuã; ut, te rectóre, te duce, sic transeámus per bona temporália, ut non amittámus ætérna. Per Dóminum.

O God, the protector of all who hope in Thee, without Whom nothing is strong, nothing is holy, multiply Thy mercy upon us, that, with Thee for our ruler and leader, we may so pass through the good things of this life as not to lose those which are eternal. Through our Lord.

EPISTLE. *I Peter 5: 6-11*

Caríssimi: Humiliámini sub poténti manu Dei, ut vos exáltet in témpore visitatiónis: omnem sollicitúdinem vestram projiciéntes in eum, quóniam ipsi cura est de vobis. Sóbrii estóte et vigiláte: quia adversárius vester diábolus tamquam leo rúgiens círcuit, quærens, quem dévoret: cui resístite fortes in fide: sciéntes eándem passiónem ei, quæ in mundo est, vestræ fraternitáti fíeri. Deus autem omnis grátiæ, qui vocávit nos in ætérnam suam glóriam in Christo Jesu, módicum passos ipse perfíciet, confirmábit solidabítque. Ipsi glória et impérium in sǽcula sæculórum. Amen.

DEARLY BELOVED, Be you humbled under the mighty hand of God, that He may exalt you in the time of visitation: casting all your care upon Him, for He hath care of you. Be sober and watch, because your adversary the devil, as a roaring lion, goeth about seeking whom he may devour. Whom resist ye, strong in faith; knowing that the same affliction befalls your brethren who are in the world. But the God of all grace, Who hath called us unto His eternal glory in Christ Jesus, after you have suffered a little, will Himself perfect you, and confirm you, and establish you. To Him be glory and empire for ever and ever. Amen.

GRADUAL & ALLELUIA. *Ps 54: 23, 17, 19 & Ps 7: 12*

Jacta cogitátum tuum in Dómino: et ipse te enútriet. ℣. Dum clamárem ad Dóminum, exaudívit vocem meam ab his, qui appropínquant mihi.
Allelúja, allelúja. ℣. Deus judex justus, fortis et pátiens, numquid iráscitur per síngulos dies? Allelúja.

CAST thy care upon the Lord and He shall sustain thee. ℣. When I cried to the Lord He heard my voice, from them that draw near to me.
Alleluia, alleluia. ℣. God is a just judge, strong and patient; is He angry every day? Alleluia.

GOSPEL. *Luke 15: 1-10*

PUBLICANS and sinners drew near unto Jesus to hear Him: and the pharisees and scribes murmured, saying, This man receiveth sinners and eateth with them. And He spoke to them this parable, saying, What man is there of you that hath a hundred sheep, and if he shall lose one of them, doth he not leave the ninety-nine in the desert, and go after that which was lost, until he find it? And when he hath found it, lay it upon his shoulders rejoicing, and coming home, call together his friends and neighbors, saying to them, Rejoice with me, because I have found my sheep that was lost? I say to you, that even so there shall be joy in heaven upon one sinner that doth penance, more than upon ninety-nine just who need not penance. Or what woman having ten groats, if she lose one groat, doth not light a candle, and sweep the house, and seek diligently until she find it? And when she hath found it, call together her friends and neighbors, saying, Rejoice with me, because I have found the groat which I had lost? So I say to you, there shall be joy before the angels of God upon one sinner doing penance. CREDO.

In illo témpore: Erant appropinquántes ad Jesum publicáni et peccatóres, ut audírent illum. Et murmurábant pharisǽi et scribæ, dicéntes: Quia hic peccatóres récipit et mandúcat cum illis. Et ait ad illos parábolam istam, dicens: Quis ex vobis homo, qui habet centum oves: et si perdíderit unam ex illis, nonne dimíttit nonagínta novem in desérto, et vadit ad illam, quæ períerat, donec invéniat eam? Et cum invénerit eam, impónit in húmeros suos gaudens: et véniens domum, cónvocat amícos et vicínos, dicens illis: Congratulámini mihi, quia invéni ovem meam, quæ períerat? Dico vobis, quod ita gáudium erit in cælo super uno peccatóre pœniténtiam agénte, quam super nonagintanóvem justis, qui non índigent pœniténtia. Aut quæ múlier habens drachmas decem, si perdíderit drachmam unam, nonne accéndit lucérnam, et evérrit domum, et quærit diligénter, donec invéniat? Et cum invénerit, cónvocat amícas et vicínas, dicens: Congratulámini mihi, quia invéni drachmam, quam perdíderam? Ita dico vobis: gáudium erit coram Ángelis Dei super uno peccatóre pœniténtiam agénte.

OFFERTORY. *Ps 9: 11-12, 13*

LET THEM trust in Thee who know Thy name, O Lord: for Thou hast not forsaken them that seek Thee: sing ye to the Lord, Who dwelleth in Sion: for He hath not forgotten the cry of the poor. ℣. *Thou sittest upon the throne, Who judgest in equity: Thou hast rebuked the Gentiles, and the wicked one hath perished: Thou judgest the people in justice: and are become a refuge for the poor.* ℣. *The Lord shall be known when He executeth judgments: the patience of the poor shall not perish for ever. The Lord hath heard the desire of the poor.*

Sperent in te omnes, qui novérunt nomen tuum, Dómine: quóniam non derelínquis quæréntes te: psállite Dómino, qui hábitat in Sion: quóniam non est oblítus oratiónem páuperum. ℣. *Sedes super thronum, qui júdicas æquitátem: increpásti gentes et périit ímpius: judicáre pópulum cum justítia: et factus es refúgium páuperum.* ℣. *Cognoscétur Dóminus judícia fáciens, quóniam patiéntia páuperum non períbit in finem: desidérium páuperum exaudívit Deus.*

SECRET.

Look upon the offerings of Thy suppliant Church, we beseech Thee, O Lord, and grant that, by Thy continual sanctification, they may conduce to the salvation of those who partake of them with faith. Through our Lord.

Réspice, Dómine, múnera supplicántis Ecclésiæ: et salúti credéntium perpétua sanctificatióne suménda concéde. Per Dóminum.

COMMUNION. *Luke 15: 10*

Dico vobis: gáudium est Ángelis Dei super uno peccatóre pœniténtiam agénte. (Luke 15: 7) ℣. *Quam super nonagínta novem justis, qui non índigent pœniténtia.* —YRIEIX|1040 • Circa 1040AD

I SAY TO YOU: there is joy before the angels of God upon one sinner doing penance. ℣. *Than over ninety-nine righteous who are not in need of penance.*

POSTCOMMUNION.

Sancta tua nos, Dómine, sumpta vivíficent: et misericórdiæ sempitérnæ prǽparent expiátos. Per Dóminum.

May Thy holy things which we have received, O Lord, fill us with life, and prepare for Thine everlasting mercies those whom Thou hast purified. Through our Lord.

In certain localities, this communion antiphon was used on the 22nd Sunday after Pentecost. Because it comes from the New Testament, many psalms may be used with it, including psalms 16, 31, 96, and 129.

II Classis.

—*Fourth Sunday after Pentecost*—

INTROIT. *Ps 26: 1, 2*

Dóminus illuminátio mea et salus mea, quem timebo? Dóminus defénsor vitæ meæ, a quo trepidábo? qui tríbulant me inimíci mei, ipsi infirmáti sunt, et cecidérunt. ℣. Si consístant advérsum me castra: non timébit cor meum. ℣. Glória Patri.

THE LORD is my light and my salvation: whom shall I fear? The Lord is the protector of my life: of whom shall I be afraid? My enemies that trouble me have themselves been weakened and have fallen. (Ps 26: 3) If armies in camp should stand together against me, my heart shall not fear. ℣. Glory.

COLLECT.

Da nobis, quǽsumus, Dómine: ut et mundi cursus pacífice nobis tuo órdine dirigátur; et Ecclésia tua tranquílla devotióne lætétur. Per Dóminum.

Grant us, we beseech Thee, O Lord, that the course of the world may be directed for us, and that Thy Church may rejoice in peace. Through our Lord.

EPISTLE. *Rom 8: 18-23*

Fratres: Exístimo, quod non sunt condígnæ passiónes hujus témporis ad futúram glóriam, quæ revelábitur in nobis. Nam exspectátio creatúræ revelatiónem filiórum Dei exspéctat. Vanitáti enim creatúra subjécta est, non volens, sed propter eum, qui subjécit eam in spe: quia et ipsa creatúra liberábitur a servitúte corruptiónis, in libertátem glóriæ filiórum

BRETHREN, I reckon that the sufferings of this time are not worthy to be compared with the glory to come, that shall be revealed in us. For the expectation of the creature waiteth for the revelation of the sons of God. For the creature was made subject to vanity, not willingly, but by reason of him that made it subject in hope; because the creature also itself shall be delivered from the servitude of corruption, into the liberty of the glory of the children of God. For we know that every creature groaneth, and travaileth in pain, even till now; and not only it, but ourselves also, who have the first fruits of the spirit, even we ourselves, groan within ourselves, waiting for the adoption of the sons of God, the redemption of our body; in Christ Jesus our Lord.

Dei. Scimus enim, quod omnis creatúra ingemíscit et párturit usque adhuc. Non solum autem illa, sed et nos ipsi primítias spíritus habéntes: et ipsi intra nos gémimus, adoptiónem filiórum Dei exspectántes, redemptiónem córporis nostri: in Christo Jesu, Dómino nostro.

GRADUAL & ALLELUIA. *Ps 78: 9, 10 & Ps 9: 5, 10*

FORGIVE US our sins, O Lord, lest the gentiles should at any time say, Where is their God? ℣. Help us, O God our Savior; and for the honor of Thy name, O Lord, deliver us.

Alleluia, alleluia. ℣. O God, Who sittest upon the throne, and judgest justice, be Thou the refuge of the poor in tribulation. Alleluia.

Propítius esto, Dómine, peccátis nostris: ne quando dicant gentes: Ubi est Deus eórum? ℣. Ádjuva nos, Deus, salutáris noster: et propter honórem nóminis tui, Dómine, líbera nos.

Allelúja, allelúja. ℣. Deus, qui sedes super thronum, et júdicas æquitátem: esto refúgium páuperum in tribulatióne. Allelúja.

GOSPEL. *Luke 5: 1-11*

WHEN THE MULTITUDE pressed upon Jesus to hear the word of God, He stood by the lake of Genesareth. And He saw two ships standing by the lake; but the fishermen were gone out of them, and were washing their nets; and going up into one of the ships that was Simon's, He desired him to draw back a little from the land: and sitting He taught the multitudes out of the ship. Now when He had ceased to speak, He said to Simon, Launch out into the deep, and let down your nets for a catch. And Simon, answering, said to Him, Master, we have labored all the night, and have taken nothing, but at Thy word I will let down the net. And when they had done this, they enclosed a very great multitude of fishes; and their net broke: and they beckoned to their partners that were in the other ship, that they should come and help them; and they came, and filled both the ships, so that they were almost sinking.

In illo témpore: Cum turbæ irrúerent in Jesum, ut audírent verbum Dei, et ipse stabat secus stagnum Genésareth. Et vidit duas naves stantes secus stagnum: piscatóres autem descénderant et lavábant rétia. Ascéndens autem in unam navim, quæ erat Simónis, rogávit eum a terra redúcere pusíllum. Et sedens docébat de navícula turbas. Ut cessávit autem loqui, dixit ad Simónem: Duc in altum, et laxáte rétia vestra in captúram. Et respóndens Simon, dixit illi: Præcéptor, per totam noctem laborántes, nihil cépimus: in verbo autem tuo laxábo rete. Et cum hoc fecíssent, conclusérunt píscium multitúdinem copiósam: rumpebátur autem rete eórum. Et annuérunt sóciis, qui erant in ália navi, ut venírent et adjuvárent eos. Et venérunt, et implevérunt ambas navículas, ita ut pæne mergeréntur.

Which when Simon Peter saw, he fell down at Jesus' knees, saying, Depart from me, for I am a sinful man, O Lord. For he was wholly astonished, and all that were with him, at the catch of fishes which they had taken: and so were also James and John the sons of Zebedee, who were Simon's partners. And Jesus saith

Quod cum vidéret Simon Petrus, prócidit ad génua Jesu, dicens: Exi a me, quia homo peccátor sum, Dómine. Stupor enim circumdéderat eum et omnes, qui cum illo erant, in captúra píscium, quam céperant: simíliter autem Jacóbum et Joánnem, fílios Zebedæi, qui erant sócii Simónis. Et ait ad Simónem Jesus:

Noli timére: ex hoc jam hómines eris cápiens. Et subdúctis ad terram návibus, relíctis ómnibus, secúti sunt eum.

to Simon, Fear not: from henceforth thou shalt catch men. And having brought their ships to land, leaving all things they followed Him. CREDO.

OFFERTORY. *Ps 12: 4-5*

Illúmina óculos meos, ne umquam obdórmiam in morte: ne quando dicat inimícus meus: Prævălui advérsus eum. ℣. *Úsquequo Dómine oblivíscéris me in finem? Quámdiu ponam consília in ánima mea?* ℣. *Réspice in me et exáudi me: cantábo Dómino, qui bona tríbuit mihi.*

ENLIGHTEN my eyes, that I never sleep in death; lest at any time my enemy say, I have prevailed against him. ℣. *How long, O Lord, wilt Thou forget me unto the end? How long shall I take counsels in my soul?* ℣. *Look upon me, and hear me: I will sing to the Lord, Who giveth me good things.*

SECRET.

Oblatiónibus nostris, quǽsumus, Dómine, placáre suscéptis: et ad te nostras étiam rebélles compélle propítius voluntátes. Per Dóminum.

Receiving our oblations, be appeased, we pray Thee, O Lord, and in Thy kindness constrain our wills toward Thee, even when resisting. Through our Lord.

COMMUNION. *Ps 17: 3*

Dóminus firmaméntum meum, et refúgium meum, et liberátor meus: Deus meus, adjútor meus. (Ps 17: 4, 29) ℣. *Laudans invocábo Dóminum: et ab inimícis meis salvus ero.* ℣. *Quoniam tu illúminas lucérnam meam, Dómine: Deus meus, illúmina ténebras meas.* — HELMST|1026 • Circa 1026AD

THE LORD is my firmament, and my refuge, and my deliverer, my God is my helper. ℣. *Praising I will call upon the Lord: and I shall be saved from my enemies.* ℣. *For Thou lightest my lamp, O Lord: O my God, enlighten my darkness.*

POSTCOMMUNION.

Mystéria nos, Dómine, quǽsumus, sumpta puríficent: et suo múnere tueántur. Per Dóminum.

May the mysteries we have received purify us, we beseech Thee, O Lord, and by their virtue protect us. Through our Lord.

II Classis.

— Fifth Sunday after Pentecost —

INTROIT. *Ps 26: 7, 9*

Exáudi, Dómine, vocem meam, qua clamávi ad te: adjútor meus esto, ne derelínquas me, neque despícias me, Deus, salutáris meus. ℣. Dóminus illuminátio mea et salus mea, quem timébo? ℣. Glória Patri.

HEAR, O Lord, my voice with which I have cried to Thee: be Thou my helper, forsake me not, nor do Thou despise me, O God my Savior. (Ps 26: 1) The Lord is my light, and my salvation: whom shall I fear? ℣. Glory.

COLLECT.

O God, Who hast prepared good things unseen for them that love Thee, pour into our hearts the fervor of Thy love, that, loving Thee in all things and above all things, we may attain Thy promises, which surpass all desire. Through our Lord.

Deus, qui diligéntibus te bona invisibília præparásti: infúnde córdibus nostris tui amóris affèctum; ut te in ómnibus et super ómnia diligéntes, promissiónes tuas, quæ omne desidérium súperant, consequámur. Per Dóminum.

EPISTLE. *I Peter 3: 8-15*

DEARLY beloved, Be ye all of one mind, having compassion one of another, being lovers of the brotherhood, merciful, modest, humble: not rendering evil for evil, nor railing for railing, but contrariwise, blessing: for unto this are you called, that you may inherit a blessing. For he that will love life and see good days, let him refrain his tongue from evil, and his lips that they speak no guile. Let him decline from evil, and do good; let him seek after peace, and pursue it: because the eyes of the Lord are upon the just, and His ears unto their prayers, but the countenance of the Lord upon them that do evil things. And who is he that can hurt you, if you be zealous of good? But if also you suffer anything for justice' sake, blessed are ye. And be not afraid of their fear, and be not troubled: but sanctify the Lord Christ in your hearts.

Caríssimi: Omnes unánimes in oratióne estóte, compatiéntes, fraternitátis amatóres, misericórdes, modésti, húmiles: non reddéntes malum pro malo, nec maledíctum pro maledícto, sed e contrário benedicéntes: quia in hoc vocáti estis, ut benedictiónem hereditáte possideátis. Qui enim vult vitam dilígere et dies vidére bonos, coérceat linguam suam a malo, et lábia ejus ne loquántur dolum. Declínet a malo, et fáciat bonum: inquírat pacem, et sequátur eam. Quia óculi Dómini super justos, et aures ejus in preces eórum: vultus autem Dómini super faciéntes mala. Et quis est, qui vobis nóceat, si boni æmulatóres fuéritis? Sed et si quid patímini propter justítiam, beáti. Timórem autem eórum ne timuéritis: et non conturbémini. Dóminum autem Christum sanctificáte in córdibus vestris.

GRADUAL & ALLELUIA. *Ps 83: 10, 9 & Ps 20: 1*

BEHOLD, O God our protector, and look on Thy servants. ℣. O Lord God of hosts, give ear to the prayers of Thy servants.
Alleluia, alleluia. ℣. In Thy strength, O Lord, the king shall joy; and in Thy salvation he shall rejoice exceedingly. Alleluia.

Protéctor noster, áspice, Deus, et réspice super servos tuos. ℣. Dómine, Deus virtútum, exáudi preces servórum tuórum.
Allelúja, allelúja. ℣. Dómine, in virtúte tua lætábitur rex: et super salutáre tuum exsultábit veheménter. Allelúja.

GOSPEL. *Matt 5: 20-24*

At that time, Jesus said to His disciples:

EXCEPT YOUR JUSTICE abound more than that of the scribes and pharisees, you shall not enter into the kingdom of heaven. You have heard that it was said to them of old: Thou shalt not kill; and whosoever shall kill, shall be in danger of the judgment. But I say to you, that whosoever is angry with his brother, shall be in danger of the judgment;

In illo témpore: Dixit Jesus discípulis suis: Nisi abundáverit justítia vestra plus quam scribárum et pharisæórum, non intrábitis in regnum cælórum. Audístis, quia dictum est antíquis: Non occídes: qui autem occíderit, reus erit judício. Ego autem dico vobis: quia omnis, qui iráscitur fratri suo, reus erit judício. Qui autem díxerit fratri suo, raca: reus erit concílio. Qui autem díxerit, fátue: reus erit gehénnæ ignis. Si ergo offers munus tuum ad altáre, et ibi recordátus fúeris, quia frater tuus habet áliquid advérsum te: relínque ibi munus tuum ante altáre et vade prius reconciliári fratri tuo: et tunc véniens ófferes munus tuum.

and whosoever shall say to his brother, Raca, shall be in danger of the council; and whosoever shall say: Thou fool, shall be in danger of hell fire. If therefore thou offer thy gift at the altar, and there thou remember that thy brother hath anything against thee, leave there thine offering before the altar, and go first to be reconciled to thy brother; and then coming thou shalt offer thy gift. CREDO.

OFFERTORY. *Ps 15: 7, 8*

Benedícam Dóminum, qui tríbuit mihi intelléctum: providébam Deum in conspéctu meo semper: quóniam a dextris est mihi, ne commóvear. ℣. *Consérva me, Dómine, quóniam in te sperávi: ego dixi: Deus meus es tu: Dóminus pars hæreditátis meæ.* ℣. *Notas fecísti mihi vias vitæ, adimplébis me lætítia cum vultu tuo: et delectatiónes in déxtera tua usque in finem.*

I WILL BLESS THE LORD, Who hath given me understanding: I set God always in my sight; for He is at my right hand, that I be not moved. ℣. *Preserve me, O Lord, for I have put my trust in Thee: I have said to the Lord: Thou art my God: the Lord is the portion of my inheritance.* ℣. *Thou hast made known to me the ways of life, Thou shalt fill me with joy with Thy countenance: at Thy right hand are delights even to the end.*

SECRET.

Propitiáre, Dómine, supplicatiónibus nostris: et has oblatiónes famulórum famularúmque tuárum benígnus assúme; ut, quod sínguli obtulérunt ad honórem nóminis tui, cunctis profíciat ad salútem. Per Dóminum.

Be propitiated, O Lord, by our supplications, and graciously accept these oblations of Thy servants and Thy handmaidens, that what each has offered to the honor of Thy name may profit for the salvation of all. Through our Lord.

COMMUNION. *Ps 26: 4*

Unam pétii a Dómino, hanc requíram: ut inhábitem in domo Dómini ómnibus diébus vitæ meæ. (Ps 26: 3b) ℣. *Si exsúrgat advérsum me prælium, in hoc ego sperábo.*

ONE thing I have asked of the Lord, this will I seek after; that I may dwell in the house of the Lord all the days of my life. ℣. *Though an armed onset should threaten me, still I would not lose my confidence.*

POSTCOMMUNION.

Quos cæléstí, Dómine, dono satiásti: præsta, quǽsumus; ut a nostris mundémur occúltis et ab hóstium liberémur insídiis. Per Dóminum.

Grant us, we beseech Thee, O Lord, whom Thou hast filled with the heavenly gift, that we be cleansed of our hidden sins and delivered from the snares of our enemies. Through our Lord.

— *Sixth Sunday after Pentecost* —

II Classis.

INTROIT. *Ps 27: 8-9*

THE LORD is the strength of His people, and the protector of the salvation of His anointed: save, O Lord, Thy people, and bless Thine inheritance, and rule them for ever. (Ps 27: 1) Unto Thee will I cry, O Lord: O my God, be not Thou silent to me, lest if Thou be silent to me, I become like them that go down into the pit. ℣. Glory.

Dóminus fortitúdo plebis suæ, et protéctor salutárium Christi sui est: salvum fac pópulum tuum, Dómine, et bénedic hereditáti tuæ, et rege eos usque in sǽculum. ℣. Ad te, Dómine, clamábo, Deus meus, ne síleas a me: ne quando táceas a me, et assimilábor descendéntibus in lacum. ℣. Glória Patri.

COLLECT.

O God of virtues, to Whom belongeth every excellent thing, implant in our hearts the love of Thy name, and bestow upon us the increase of religion, fostering what things are good, and, by Thy loving care, guarding what Thou hast fostered. Through our Lord.

Deus virtútum, cujus est totum quod est óptimum: ínsere pectóribus nostris amórem tui nóminis, et præsta in nobis religiónis augméntum; ut, quæ sunt bona, nútrias, ac pietátis stúdio, quæ sunt nutríta, custódias. Per Dóminum.

EPISTLE. *Rom 6: 3-11*

BRETHREN, All we who are baptized in Christ Jesus are baptized into His death. For we are buried together with Him by baptism unto death; that as Christ is risen from the dead by the glory of the Father, so we also may walk in newness of life. For if we have been planted together in the likeness of His death, we shall also be in the likeness of His resurrection. Knowing this, that our old man is crucified with Him, that the body of sin may be destroyed, and that we may serve sin no longer. For he that is dead is justified from sin. Now if we be dead with Christ, we believe that we shall live also together with Christ, knowing that Christ, rising again from the dead, dieth now no more, death shall no more have dominion over Him. For in that He died to sin, He died once; but in that He liveth, He liveth unto God. So do you also reckon yourselves to be dead indeed to sin, but alive to God; in Christ Jesus our Lord.

Fratres: Quicúmque baptizáti sumus in Christo Jesu, in morte ipsíus baptizáti sumus. Consepúlti enim sumus cum illo per baptísmum in mortem: ut, quómodo Christus surréxit a mórtuis per glóriam Patris, ita et nos in novitáte vitæ ambulémus. Si enim complantáti facti sumus similitúdini mortis ejus: simul et resurrectiónis érimus. Hoc sciéntes, quia vetus homo noster simul crucifíxus est: ut destruátur corpus peccáti, et ultra non serviámus peccáto. Qui enim mórtuus est, justificátus est a peccáto. Si autem mórtui sumus cum Christo: crédimus, quia simul étiam vivémus cum Christo: sciéntes, quod Christus resúrgens ex mórtuis, jam non móritur, mors illi ultra non dominábitur. Quod enim mórtuus est peccáto, mórtuus est semel: quod autem vivit, vivit Deo. Ita et vos existimáte, vos mórtuos quidem esse peccáto, vivéntes autem Deo, in Christo Jesu, Dómino nostro.

GRADUAL & ALLELUIA. *Ps 89: 13, 1 & Ps 30: 2-3*

RETURN, O Lord, a little; and be entreated in favor of Thy servants. ℣. Lord, Thou hast been our refuge from generation to generation.

Convértere, Dómine, aliquántulum, et deprecáre super servos tuos. ℣. Dómine, refúgium factus es nobis, a generatióne et progénie.

Allelúja, allelúja. ℣. In te, Dómine, sperávi, non confúndar in ætérnum: in justítia tua líbera me et éripe me: inclína ad me aurem tuam, accélera, ut erípias me. Allelúja.

Alleluia, alleluia. ℣. In Thee, O Lord, have I hoped, let me never be confounded: deliver me in Thy justice, and release me: bow down Thine ear to me, make haste to deliver me. Alleluia.

GOSPEL. *Mark 8: 1-9*

In illo témpore: Cum turba multa esset cum Jesu, nec habérent, quod manducárent, convocátis discípulis, ait illis: Miséreor super turbam: quia ecce jam tríduo sústinent me, nec habent quod mandúcent: et si dimísero eos jejúnos in domum suam, deficient in via: quidam enim ex eis de longe venérunt. Et respondérunt ei discípuli sui: Unde illos quis póterit hic saturáre pánibus in solitúdine? Et interrogávit eos: Quot panes habétis? Qui dixérunt: Septem.

WHEN THERE WAS a great multitude with Jesus, and they had nothing to eat, calling His disciples together, He saith to them, I have compassion on the multitude, for behold they have now been with Me three days, and have nothing to eat; and if I shall send them away fasting to their home they will faint in the way: for some of them came from afar off. And His disciples answered Him, From whence can any one fill them here with bread in the wilderness? And He asked them, How many loaves have ye? who said: Seven.

Et præcépit turbæ discúmbere super terram. Et accípiens septem panes, grátias agens fregit, et dabat discípulis suis, ut appónerent, et apposuérunt turbæ. Et habébant piscículos paucos: et ipsos benedíxit, et jussit appóni. Et manducavérunt, et saturáti sunt, et sustulérunt quod superáverat de fragméntis, septem sportas. Erant autem qui manducáverant, quasi quatuor mília: et dimísit eos.

And He commanded the people to sit down on the ground. And taking the seven loaves, giving thanks He broke, and gave to His disciples to set before them; and they set them before the people. And they had a few little fishes, and He blessed them, and commanded them to be set before them. And they did eat, and were filled, and they took up that which was left of the fragments, seven baskets: and they that had eaten were about four thousand: and He sent them away. CREDO.

OFFERTORY. *Ps 16: 5, 6-7*

Identical to Sexagesima Sunday:

Pérfice gressus meos in sémitis tuis, ut non moveántur vestígia mea: inclína aurem tuam, et exáudi verba mea: mirífica misericórdias tuas, qui salvos facis sperántes in te, Dómine. ℣. *Exáudi, Dómine, justítiam meam, inténde deprecatiónem meam: áuribus pércipe oratiónem meam.* ℣. *Custódi me Dómine ut pupíllam óculi, sub umbra alárum tuárum prótege me: éripe me Dómine ab ímpio.* ℣. *Ego autem cum justítia apparébo in conspéctu tuo: satiábor, dum manifestábitur glória tua.*

MAKE MY STEPS steadfast in Thy paths, that my feet may not falter: incline Thine ear, and hear my words: show forth Thy wonderful mercies, Thou Who savest them that trust in Thee, O Lord. ℣. *Hear, O Lord, my justice: attend to my supplication: give ear unto my prayer.* ℣. *Protect me as Thou wouldst the apple of Thine own eye; hide me under the shelter of Thy wings, save me from the evil-doer.* ℣. *But as for me, I will appear before Thy sight in justice: I shall be satisfied when Thy glory shall appear.*

SECRET.

Be propitious to our supplications, O Lord, and graciously accept these offerings of Thy people; and, that the prayer of none may be without effect, the petition of none vain, grant that what we ask in faith we may effectually obtain. Through our Lord.

Propitiáre, Dómine, supplicatiónibus nostris, et has pópuli tui oblatiónes benígnus assúme: et, ut nullíus sit írritum votum, nullíus vácua postulátio, præsta; ut, quod fidéliter pétimus, efficáciter consequámur. Per Dóminum.

COMMUNION. *Ps 26: 6*

I WILL GO ROUND, and offer up in His tabernacle a sacrifice of jubilation; I will sing, and recite a psalm to the Lord. ℣. *The Lord is my light and my salvation, whom shall I fear?* ℣. *The Lord is the protector of my life: of whom shall I be afraid?*

Circuíbo et immolábo in tabernáculo ejus hóstiam jubilatiónis: cantábo et psalmum dicam Dómino. (Ps 26: 1) *Dóminus illuminátio mea, et salus mea: quem timébo?* ℣. *Dóminus protéctor vitæ meæ: a quo trepidábo?* —Bamberg6Lit|905 • Circa 905AD

POSTCOMMUNION.

We have been filled with Thy gifts, O Lord; grant we beseech Thee, that by their effect we may be both cleansed and fortified. Through our Lord.

Repléti sumus, Dómine, munéribus tuis: tríbue, quǽsumus; ut eórum et mundémur efféctu et muniámur auxílio. Per Dóminum.

—*Seventh Sunday after Pentecost*— *II Classis.*

INTROIT. *Ps 46: 2*

O **CLAP YOUR HANDS,** all ye nations: shout unto God with the voice of joy. (Ps 46: 3) For the Lord is most high, He is terrible; He is a great king over all the earth. ℣. Glory.

Omnes gentes, pláudite mánibus: jubiláte Deo in voce exsultatiónis. ℣. Quóniam Dóminus excélsus, terríbilis: Rex magnus super omnem terram. ℣. Glória Patri.

COLLECT.

O God, Whose providence faileth not in setting things in order, we, Thy suppliants, beseech Thee, that Thou wouldst remove from us all things harmful and grant us all that makes for our welfare. Through our Lord.

Deus, cujus providéntia in sui dispositióne non fállitur: te súpplices exorámus; ut nóxia cuncta submóveas, et ómnia nobis profutúra concédas. Per Dóminum.

EPISTLE. *Rom 6: 19-23*

BRETHREN, I speak a human thing, because of the infirmity of your flesh; for as you have yielded your members to serve uncleanness and iniquity unto iniquity, so now yield your members to serve justice, unto sanctification. For when you were the

Fratres: Humánum dico, propter infirmitátem carnis vestræ: sicut enim exhibuístis membra vestra servíre immundítiæ et iniquitáti ad iniquitátem, ita nunc exhibéte membra vestra servíre justítiæ in sanctificatiónem.

Cum enim servi essétis peccáti, líberi fuístis justítiæ. Quem ergo fructum habuístis tunc in illis, in quibus nunc erubéscitis? Nam finis illórum mors est. Nunc vero liberáti a peccáto, servi autem facti Deo, habétis fructum vestrum in sanctificatiónem, finem vero vitam ætérnam. Stipéndia enim peccáti mors. Grátia autem Dei vita ætérna, in Christo Jesu, Dómino nostro.

servants of sin, you were free from justice. What fruit therefore had you then in those things, of which you are now ashamed? For the end of them is death. But now being made free from sin, and become servants to God, you have your fruit unto sanctification, and the end life everlasting. For the wages of sin is death. But the grace of God, life everlasting; in Christ Jesus our Lord.

GRADUAL & ALLELUIA. *Ps 33: 12, 6 & Ps 46: 2*

Veníte, fílii, audíte me: timórem Dómini docébo vos. ℣. Accédite ad eum, et illuminámini: et fácies vestræ non confundéntur.
Allelúja, allelúja. ℣. Omnes gentes, pláudite mánibus: jubiláte Deo in voce exsultatiónis. Allelúja.

COME, children, harken to me; I will teach you the fear of the Lord. ℣. Come ye to Him and be enlightened; and your faces shall not be confounded. Alleluia, alleluia. ℣. O clap your hands, all ye nations: shout unto God with the voice of joy. Alleluia.

GOSPEL. *Matt 7: 15-21*

In illo témpore: Dixit Jesus discípulis suis: Atténdite a falsis prophétis, qui véniunt ad vos in vestiméntis óvium, intrínsecus autem sunt lupi rapáces: a frúctibus eórum cognoscétis eos. Numquid cólligunt de spinis uvas, aut de tríbulis ficus? Sic omnis arbor bona fructus bonos facit: mala autem arbor malos fructus facit. Non potest arbor bona malos fructus fácere: neque arbor mala bonos fructus fácere. Omnis arbor, quæ non facit fructum bonum, excidétur et in ignem mittétur. Ígitur ex frúctibus eórum cognoscétis eos. Non omnis, qui dicit mihi, Dómine, Dómine, intrábit in regnum cælórum: sed qui facit voluntátem Patris mei, qui in cælis est, ipse intrábit in regnum cælórum.

At that time, Jesus said to His disciples...

BEWARE of false prophets, who come to you in the clothing of sheep, but inwardly they are ravening wolves. By their fruits you shall know them. Do men gather grapes of thorns, or figs of thistles? Even so, every good tree bringeth forth good fruit, and the evil tree bringeth forth evil fruit. A good tree cannot bring forth evil fruit, neither can an evil tree bring forth good fruit. Every tree that bringeth not forth good fruit shall be cut down, and shall be cast into the fire. Wherefore by their fruits you shall know them. Not every one that saith to Me, Lord, Lord, shall enter into the kingdom of heaven; but he that doth the will of My Father Who is in heaven, he shall enter into the kingdom of heaven. CREDO.

OFFERTORY. *Dan 3: 40*

Sicut in holocáustis aríetum et taurórum, et sicut in mílibus agnórum pínguium: sic fiat sacrifícium nostrum in conspéctu tuo hódie, ut pláceat tibi: quia non est confúsio confidéntibus in te, Dómine. ℣. *Et nunc séquimur in toto corde et timémus te et quærimus fáciem tuam, Dómine: ne confúndas nos, sed fac nobis juxta mansuetúdinem tuam et secúndum multitúdinem misericórdiæ tuæ.*

AS IN HOLOCAUSTS of rams and bullocks, and as in thousands of fat lambs; so let our sacrifice be made in Thy sight this day, that it may please Thee: for there is no confusion to them that trust in Thee, O Lord. ℣. *And now we follow Thee with all our heart and we fear Thee and seek Thy face, O Lord: put us not to confusion, but deal with us according to Thy meekness, and according to the multitude of Thy mercies.*

SECRET.

O God, Who hast sanctioned the diversity of offerings by the perfection of one sacrifice, receive the sacrifice offered Thee by Thy devoted servants, and sanctify it as Thou didst sanctify the gifts of Abel, that what each one hath offered to the glory of Thy majesty may profit for the salvation of all. Through our Lord.

Deus, qui legálium differéntiam hostiárum uníus sacrifícii perfectióne sanxísti: áccipe sacrifícium a devótis tibi fámulis, et pari benedictióne, sicut múnera Abel, sanctífica; ut, quod sínguli obtulérunt ad majestátis tuæ honórem, cunctis profíciat ad salútem. Per Dóminum.

COMMUNION. *Ps 30: 3*

BOW DOWN THINE EAR, make haste to deliver me. ℣. *In Thee, O Lord, have I hoped, let me never be confounded: deliver me in Thy justice.* ℣. *Be Thou unto me a God, a protector, and a house of refuge, to save me.*

Inclína aurem tuam, accélera, ut erípias me. (Ps 30: 2, 3b) ℣. *In te, Dómine, sperávi, non confúndar in ætérnum; in justítia tua líbera me.* ℣. *Esto mihi in Deum protectórem, et in domum refúgii, ut salvum me fácias.* —StMaur|1079 • Circa 1079AD

POSTCOMMUNION.

May Thy health-giving operation, O Lord, mercifully rid us of our evil inclinations and unto rightful ways strongly lead us. Through our Lord.

Tua nos, Dómine, medicinális operátio, et a nostris perversitátibus cleménter expédiat, et ad ea, quæ sunt recta, perdúcat. Per Dóminum.

—*Eighth Sunday after Pentecost*— *II Classis.*

INTROIT. *Ps 47: 10-11*

WE HAVE RECEIVED Thy mercy, O God, in the midst of Thy temple; according to Thy name, O God, so also is Thy praise unto the ends of the earth: Thy right hand is full of justice. (Ps 47: 2) Great is the Lord and exceedingly to be praised, in the city of our God, in His holy mountain. ℣. Glory.

Identical to 2 February:

Suscépimus, Deus, misericórdiam tuam in médio templi tui: secúndum nomen tuum, Deus, ita et laus tua in fines terræ: justítia plena est déxtera tua. ℣. Magnus Dóminus, et laudábilis nimis: in civitáte Dei nostri, in monte sancto ejus. ℣. Glória Patri.

COLLECT.

Ever graciously bestow upon us in abundance, we beseech Thee, O Lord, the spirit of thinking and doing what things are right, that we, who cannot exist without Thee, may have the strength to live in conformity with Thee. Through our Lord.

Largíre nobis, quǽsumus, Dómine, semper spíritum cogitándi quæ recta sunt, propítius et agéndi: ut, qui sine te esse non póssumus, secúndum te vívere valeámus. Per Dóminum.

EPISTLE. *Rom 8: 12-17*

Fratres: Debitóres sumus non carni, ut secúndum carnem vivámus. Si enim secúndum carnem vixéritis, moriémini: si autem spíritu facta carnis mortificavéritis, vivétis. Quicúmque enim spíritu Dei agúntur, ii sunt fílii Dei. Non enim accepístis spíritum servitútis íterum in timóre, sed accepístis spíritum adoptiónis filiórum, in quo clamámus: Abba (Pater). Ipse enim Spíritus testimónium reddit spirítui nostro, quod sumus fílii Dei. Si autem fílii, et herédes: herédes quidem Dei, coherédes autem Christi.

BRETHREN, we are debtors, not to the flesh, to live according to the flesh; for if you live according to the flesh, you shall die, but if by the spirit you mortify the deeds of the flesh, you shall live. For whosoever are led by the Spirit of God, they are the sons of God. For you have not received the spirit of bondage again in fear, but you have received the spirit of adoption of sons, whereby we cry Abba (Father). For the Spirit Himself giveth testimony to our spirit, that we are the sons of God; and if sons, heirs, also; heirs indeed of God, and joint heirs with Christ.

GRADUAL & ALLELUIA. *Ps 30: 3 & Ps 47: 2*

Esto mihi in Deum protectórem, et in locum refúgii, ut salvum me fácias. ℣. Deus, in te sperávi: Dómine, non confúndar in ætérnum.
Allelúja, allelúja. ℣. Magnus Dóminus, et laudábilis valde, in civitáte Dei nostri, in monte sancto ejus. Allelúja.

BE Thou unto me a God, a protector, and a place of refuge, to save me. (Ps 70: 1) In Thee, O God, have I hoped: O Lord, let me never be confounded.
Alleluia, alleluia. ℣. Great is the Lord, and exceedingly to be praised; in the city of our God, in His holy mountain. Alleluia.

GOSPEL. *Luke 16: 1-9*

In illo témpore: Dixit Jesus discípulis suis parábolam hanc: Homo quidam erat dives, qui habébat víllicum: et hic diffamátus est apud illum, quasi dissipásset bona ipsíus. Et vocávit illum et ait illi: Quid hoc áudio de te? redde ratiónem villicatiónis tuæ: jam enim non póteris villicáre. Ait autem víllicus intra se: Quid fáciam, quia dóminus meus aufert a me villicatiónem? fódere non váleo, mendicáre erubésco. Scio, quid fáciam, ut, cum amótus fúero a villicatióne, recípiant me in domos suas.
Convocátis ítaque síngulis debitóribus dómini sui, dicébat primo: Quantum debes dómino meo? At ille dixit: Centum cados ólei. Dixítque illi: Accipe cautiónem tuam: et sede cito, scribe quinquagínta. Deínde álii dixit: Tu vero quantum debes? Qui ait: Centum coros trítici. Ait illi: Accipe lítteras tuas, et scribe octogínta. Et laudávit dóminus víllicum iniquitátis, quia prudénter fecísset: quia fílii hujus sǽculi prudentióres fíliis lucis in generatióne

At that time, Jesus spoke to His disciples this parable...

THERE WAS A CERTAIN RICH MAN who had a steward; and the same was accused unto him that he had wasted his goods; and he called him, and said to him, How is it that I hear this of thee? give an account of thy stewardship, for now thou canst be steward no longer. And the steward said within himself, What shall I do, because my lord taketh away from me the stewardship? To dig I am not able: to beg I am ashamed. I know what I will do, that when I shall be put out of the stewardship, they may receive me into their houses.

Therefore calling together every one of his lord's debtors, he said to the first, How much dost thou owe my lord? But he said, A hundred barrels of oil. And he said to him, Take thy bill, and sit down quickly and write fifty. Then he said to another, And how much dost thou owe? Who said, A hundred quarters of wheat. He said to him, Take thy bill, and write eighty. And the lord commended the unjust steward, for as much as he had done wisely; for the children of this world are wiser in their generation than the children of light. And I say to you, Make unto you friends of the mammon of iniquity, that when you shall fail, they may receive you into everlasting dwellings. CREDO.

sua sunt. Et ego vobis dico: fácite vobis amicos de mammóna iniquitátis: ut, cum defecéritis, recípiant vos in ætérna tabernácula.

OFFERTORY. *Ps 17: 28, 32*

THOU WILT SAVE the humble people, O Lord, and wilt bring down the eyes of the proud; for Who is God but Thee, O Lord? ℣. *My cry before Him came into His ears.* ℣. *My deliverer from my enemies: Thou wilt lift me up above them that rise up against me.*

Pópulum húmilem salvum fácies, Dómine, et óculos superbórum humiliábis: quóniam quis Deus præter te, Dómine? ℣. *Clamor meus in conspéctu ejus introívit in aures ejus.* ℣. *Liberátor meus de géntibus iracúndis: ab insurgéntibus in me exaltábis me.*

SECRET.

Receive, we beseech Thee, O Lord, the gifts which out of Thine own bounty we bring to Thee, that these most holy mysteries may, by the operation of the power of Thy grace, both sanctify us in the conduct of our present lives and lead us unto everlasting joys. Through our Lord.

Súscipe, quǽsumus, Dómine, múnera, quæ tibi de tua largitáte deférimus: ut hæc sacrosáncta mystéria, grátiæ tuæ operánte virtúte, et præséntis vitæ nos conversatióne sanctíficent, et ad gáudia sempitérna perdúcant. Per Dóminum.

COMMUNION. *Ps 33: 9*

TASTE AND SEE that the Lord is sweet: blessed is the man that hopeth in Him. ℣. *I will bless the Lord at all times: His praise shall be always in my mouth.* ℣. *In the Lord shall my soul be praised: let the meek hear and rejoice.* ℣. *O magnify the Lord with me; and let us extol His name together.*

Gustáte et vidéte, quóniam suávis est Dóminus: beátus vir, qui sperat in eo. (Ps 33: 2-4) ℣. *Benedícam Dóminum in omni témpore: semper laus ejus in ore meo.* ℣. *In Dómino laudábitur ánima mea: áudiant mansuéti, et læténtur.* ℣. *Magnificáte Dóminum mecum: et exaltémus nomen ejus in idípsum.* —239LAON|927 • Circa 927AD

POSTCOMMUNION.

Let the heavenly mystery be to us, O Lord, the restoration of soul and body, that, as we perform its worship, we may experience its effect. Through our Lord.

Sit nobis, Dómine, reparátio mentis et córporis cæléste mystérium: ut, cujus exséquimur cultum, sentiámus efféctum. Per Dóminum.

— *Ninth Sunday after Pentecost* —

II Classis.

INTROIT. *Ps 53: 6-7*

EHOLD, God is my helper, and the Lord is the protector of my soul: turn back the evils upon my enemies,

Ecce, Deus adjuvat me, et Dóminus suscéptor est ánimæ meæ: avérte mala inimícis meis, et in veritáte tua dispérde illos, protéctor meus,

Dómine. ℣. Deus, in nómine tuo salvum me fac: et in virtúte tua líbera me. ℣. Glória Patri.

and cut them off in Thy truth, O Lord, my protector. (Ps 53: 3) Save me, O God, by Thy name, and deliver me in Thy strength. ℣. Glory.

COLLECT.

Páteant aures misericórdiæ tuæ, Dómine, précibus supplicántium: et, ut peténtibus desideráta concédas; fac eos quæ tibi sunt plácita, postuláre. Per Dóminum.

Let the ears of Thy mercy, O Lord, be open to the prayers of Thy suppliants, and that Thou mayest grant their desires to them that seek, make them to ask only for those things that please Thee. Through our Lord.

EPISTLE. *I Cor 10: 6-13*

Fratres: Non simus concupiscéntes malórum, sicut et illi concupiérunt. Neque idolólatræ efficiámini, sicut quidam ex ipsis: quemádmodum scriptum est: Sedit pópulus manducáre et bíbere, et surrexérunt lúdere. Neque fornicémur, sicut quidam ex ipsis fornicáti sunt, et cecidérunt una die vigínti tria mília. Neque tentémus Christum, sicut quidam eórum tentavérunt, et a serpéntibus periérunt. Neque murmuravéritis, sicut quidam eórum murmuravérunt, et periérunt ab exterminatóre. Hæc autem ómnia in figúra contingébant illis: scripta sunt autem ad correptiónem nostram, in quos fines sæculórum devenérunt. Itaque qui se exístimat stare, vídeat ne cadat. Tentátio vos non apprehéndat, nisi humána: fidélis autem Deus est, qui non patiétur vos tentári supra id, quod potéstis, sed fáciet étiam cum tentatióne provéntum, ut possítis sustinére.

BRETHREN, let us not covet evil things, as they also coveted. Neither become ye idolaters, as some of them: as it is written: The people sat down to eat and drink, and rose up to play. Neither let us commit fornication, as some of them committed fornication, and there fell in one day three and twenty thousand. Neither let us tempt Christ, as some of them tempted, and perished by the serpents. Neither do you murmur, as some of them murmured, and were destroyed by the destroyer. Now all these things happened to them in figure, and they are written for our correction, upon whom the ends of the world are come. Wherefore he that thinketh himself to stand, let him take heed lest he fall. Let no temptation take hold on you, but such as is human: and God is faithful, Who will not suffer you to be tempted above that which you are able; but will make also with temptation issue, that you may be able to bear it.

GRADUAL & ALLELUIA. *Ps 8: 2 & Ps 58: 2*

Dómine, Dóminus noster, quam admirábile est nomen tuum in univérsa terra! ℣. Quóniam eleváta est magnificéntia tua super cælos.
Allelúja, allelúja. ℣. Eripe me de inimícis meis, Deus meus: et ab insurgéntibus in me líbera me. Allelúja.

O LORD our Lord, how admirable is Thy name in the whole earth. ℣. For Thy magnificence is elevated above the heavens.
Alleluia, alleluia. ℣. Deliver me from my enemies, O my God: and defend me from them that rise up against me. Alleluia.

GOSPEL. *Lk 19: 4-47*

In illo témpore: Cum appropinquáret Jesus Jerúsalem, videns civitátem, flevit super illam, dicens: Quia si cognovísses et tu, et quidem in hac die tua, quæ ad pacem tibi, nunc autem abscóndita sunt ab óculis tuis.

WHEN JESUS DREW NEAR to Jerusalem, seeing the city, He wept over it saying, If thou also hadst known, and that in this thy day, the things that are to thy peace: but now they are hidden from thine eyes.

For the days shall come upon thee, and thine enemies shall cast a trench about thee, and compass thee round, and straiten thee on every side, and beat thee flat to the ground, and thy children who are in thee; and they shall not leave in thee a stone upon a stone, because thou hast not known the time of thy visitation. And entering into the temple, He began to cast out them that sold therein, and they that bought, saying to them, It is written, My house is the house of prayer, but you have made it a den of thieves. And He was teaching daily in the temple. CREDO.

Quia vénient dies in te: et circúmdabunt te inimíci tui vallo, et circúmdabunt te: et coangustábunt te úndique: et ad terram prostérnent te, et fílios tuos, qui in te sunt, et non relínquent in te lápidem super lápidem: eo quod non cognóveris tempus visitatiónis tuæ. Et ingréssus in templum, cœpit ejícere vendéntes in illo et eméntes, dicens illis: Scriptum est: Quia domus mea domus oratiónis est. Vos autem fecístis illam speluncam latrónum. Et erat docens quotídie in templo.

OFFERTORY. *Ps 18: 9, 10, 11, 12*

THE JUSTICES of the Lord are right, rejoicing hearts, and His judgments are sweeter than honey and the honeycomb; for Thy servant keepeth them. ℣. *The commandment of the Lord is lightsome, enlightening the eyes: the fear of the Lord is holy, enduring for ever and ever: the judgments of the Lord are true.* ℣. *And the words of my mouth shall be such as may please: and the meditation of my heart always in Thy sight.*

Justítiæ Dómini rectæ, lætificántes corda, et judícia ejus dulcióra super mel et favum: nam et servus tuus custódit ea. ℣. *Præcéptum Dómini lúcidum illúminans óculos: timor Dei sanctus pérmanet in sǽculum sǽculi: judícia Dómini vera.* ℣. *Et erunt, ut compláceant elóquia oris mei et meditátio cordis mei in conspéctu tuo semper.*

SECRET.

Grant us, we beseech Thee, O Lord, worthily to frequent these mysteries, for as often as the commemoration of this victim is celebrated, the work of our redemption is performed. Through our Lord.

Concéde nobis, quǽsumus, Dómine, hæc digne frequentáre mystéria: quia, quóties hujus hóstiæ commemorátio celebrátur, opus nostræ redemptiónis exercétur. Per Dóminum.

COMMUNION. *John 6: 57*

HE that eateth My flesh, and drinketh My blood, abideth in Me, and I in him; saith the Lord. ℣. *What is this bread which I am to give? It is My flesh, given for the life of the world.*

Qui mandúcat meam carnem et bibit meum sánguinem, in me manet et ego in eo, dicit Dóminus. (Jn 6: 52) ℣. *Panis quem ego dabo, caro mea est pro mundi vita.* —4951STEVEN|1128 • Circa 1128AD

POSTCOMMUNION.

Let the communion of Thy sacrament, we beseech Thee, O Lord, both cleanse us from sin and make us of one mind and one heart in Thy service. Through our Lord.

Tui nobis, quǽsumus, Dómine, commúnio sacraménti, et purificatiónem cónferat, et tríbuat unitátem. Per Dóminum.

The communion antiphon for this Sunday was used on the 15th Sunday after Pentecost in some ancient books (e.g. RENAUD|965), and is identical to the communion antiphon still used for Thursday in the 2nd week of Lent. Which feast first borrowed from the other is disputed. This communion antiphon is particularly instructive, since it comes, not from the Psalter, but from the New Testament—which means an obvious choice for additional verses is lacking. Some ancient MSS match it with another verse from the New Testament (e.g. 4951STEVEN|1128). Some MSS follow the practice of taking the verses from the Introit—e.g. BAMBERG6LIT|905, 376SANGALL|1052, STMAUR|1079, HELMST|1026, and 47CHARTRES|957—and we observe that they all take from the Thursday in Lent, not the Sunday after Pentecost. Some take directly from the Introit text, others from the Introit's psalm verses, and still others mix both together. Other MSS follow the ancient practice of using Psalm 33 for a communion antiphon which is not derived from a psalm; e.g. RENAUD|965, STDENISMISSAL|988, and 121EINSIE|961. But there are still more options; e.g. 381SANGALL|928 provides a variety of different psalms from which to choose.

II Classis.

—*Tenth Sunday after Pentecost*—

INTROIT. *Ps 54: 17, 18, 20, 23*

Dum clamárem ad Dóminum, exaudívit vocem meam, ab his, qui appropínquant mihi: et humiliávit eos, qui est ante sǽcula et manet in ætérnum: jacta cogitátum tuum in Dómino, et ipse te enútriet. ℣. Exáudi, Deus, oratiónem meam, et ne despéxeris deprecatiónem meam: inténde mihi et exáudi me. ℣. Glória Patri.

WHEN I CRIED to the Lord He heard my voice, from them that draw near to me; and He humbled them, Who is before all ages, and remains for ever; cast thy care upon the Lord, and He shall sustain thee. (Ps 54: 2) Hear, O God, my prayer, and despise not my supplication: be attentive to me and hear me. ℣. Glory.

COLLECT.

Deus, qui omnipoténtiam tuam parcéndo máxime et miserándo manifèstas: multíplica super nos misericórdiam tuam; ut, ad tua promíssa curréntes, cæléstium bonórum fácias esse consórtes. Per Dóminum.

O God, Who dost chiefly manifest Thy power in forbearance and mercy, multiply upon us Thy pity, that, hastening on to Thy promises, we may be made partakers of the blessings of heaven. Through our Lord.

EPISTLE. *I Cor 12: 2-11*

Fratres: Scitis, quóniam, cum gentes essétis, ad simulácra muta prout ducebámini eúntes. Ideo notum vobis fácio, quod nemo in Spíritu Dei loquens, dicit anáthema Jesu. Et nemo potest dícere, Dóminus Jesus, nisi in Spíritu Sancto. Divisiónes vero gratiárum sunt, idem autem Spíritus. Et divisiónes ministratiónum sunt, idem autem Dóminus. Et divisiónes operatiónum sunt, idem vero Deus, qui operátur ómnia in ómnibus. Unicuíque autem datur manifestátio Spíritus ad utilitátem. Álii quidem per Spíritum datur sermo sapiéntiæ, álii autem sermo sciéntiæ secúndum eúmdem Spíritum: álteri fides in eódem Spíritu: álii grátia sanitátum in uno Spíritu: álii operátio virtútum, álii prophetía, álii discrétio spiritũ, álii génera linguárũ, álii interpretátio sermónũ. Hæc autem ómnia operátur

BRETHREN, you know that when you were heathens, you went to dumb idols, according as you were led. Wherefore I give you to understand, that no man speaking by the Spirit of God, saith Anathema to Jesus; and no man can say, The Lord Jesus, but by the Holy Ghost. Now there are diversities of graces, but the same Spirit; and there are diversities of ministries, but the same Lord; and there are diversities of operations, but the same God, Who worketh all in all. And the manifestation of the Spirit is given to every man unto profit. To one indeed, by the Spirit, is given the word of wisdom; and to another, the word of knowledge, according to the same Spirit; to another, faith in the same spirit; to another, the grace of healing in one Spirit: to another, the working of miracles; to another, prophecy; to another, the discerning of spirits; to another, diverse kinds of tongues; to another, interpretation of speeches. But all these things one and the same Spirit worketh, dividing to every one according as He will.

unus atque idem Spíritus, dívidens síngulis, prout vult.

GRADUAL & ALLELUIA. *Ps 16: 8, 2 & Ps 64: 2*

KEEP ME, O LORD, as the apple of Thine eye: protect me under the shadow of Thy wings. ℣. Let my judgment come forth from Thy countenance: let Thine eyes behold the things that are equitable. Alleluia, alleluia. ℣. A hymn, O God, becometh Thee in Sion: and a vow shall be paid to Thee in Jerusalem. Alleluia.

Custódi me, Dómine, ut pupíllam óculi: sub umbra alárum tuárum prótege me. ℣. De vultu tuo judícium meum pródeat: óculi tui vídeant æquitátem.
Allelúja, allelúja. ℣. Te decet hymnus, Deus, in Sion: et tibi reddétur votum in Jerúsalem. Allelúja.

GOSPEL. *Luke 18: 9-14*

JESUS SPOKE this parable to some who trusted in themselves as just, and despised others: Two men went up into the temple to pray; the one was a pharisee, and the other a publican. The pharisee standing prayed thus with himself: O God, I give Thee thanks that I am not as the rest of men, extortioners, unjust, adulterers; as also is this publican. I fast twice in the week; I give tithes of all that I possess. And the publican standing afar off, would not so much as lift up his eyes towards heaven, but struck his breast saying, O God, be merciful to me a sinner. I say to you, this man went down to his house justified rather than the other: because every one that exalteth himself shall be humbled, and he that humbleth himself shall be exalted. CREDO.

In illo témpore: Dixit Jesus ad quosdam, qui in se confidébant tamquam justi et aspernabántur céteros, parábolam istam: Duo hómines ascendérunt in templum, ut orárent: unus pharisǽus, et alter publicánus. Pharisǽus stans, hæc apud se orábat: Deus, grátias ago tibi, quia non sum sicut céteri hóminum: raptóres, injústi, adúlteri: velut étiam hic publicánus. Jejúno bis in sábbato: décimas do ómnium, quæ possídeo. Et publicánus a longe stans nolébat nec óculos ad cælum leváre: sed percutiébat pectus suum, dicens: Deus, propítius esto mihi peccatóri. Dico vobis: descéndit hic justificátus in domum suam ab illo: quia omnis qui se exáltat, humiliábitur: et qui se humíliat, exaltábitur.

OFFERTORY. *Ps 24: 1-3*

TO THEE, O Lord, have I lifted up my soul: in Thee, O my God, I put my trust; let me not be ashamed: neither let my enemies laugh at me: for none of them that wait on Thee shall be confounded. ℣. *Direct me in Thy truth, and teach me; for Thou art God my Savior; and on Thee have I waited all the day long.* ℣. *Look Thou upon me, and have mercy on me, O Lord; Keep Thou my soul, and deliver me: I shall not be confounded, for I have hoped in Thee.*

Identical to the First Sunday of Advent:

Ad te, Dómine, levávi ánimam meam: Deus meus, in te confído, non erubéscam: neque irrídeant me inimíci mei: étenim univérsi, qui te exspéctant, non confundéntur. ℣. *Dírige me in veritáte tua et doce me, quia tu es Deus salutáris meus: et te sustínui tota die.* ℣. *Réspice in me et miserére mei, Dómine, custódi ánimam meam et éripe me, non confúndar, quóniam invocávi te.*

SECRET.

Tibi, Dómine, sacrifícia dicáta reddántur: quæ sic ad honórem nóminis tui deferénda tribuísti, ut éadem remédia fíeri nostra præstáres. Per Dóminum.

Let the sacrifices dedicated to Thee, O Lord, be rendered back, since Thou hast given them to be presented for the honor of Thy name, so that in them Thou mightest afford us a remedy for all our ills. Through our Lord.

COMMUNION. *Ps 50: 21*

Acceptábis sacrifícium justítiæ, oblatiónes et holocáusta, super altáre tuum, Dómine. (Ps 50: 3) ℣. *Miserere mei, Deus, secundum magnam misericordiam tuam.*

—StDenisMissal|988 • Circa 988AD

THOU wilt accept the sacrifice of justice, oblations, and holocausts, upon Thine altar, O Lord. ℣. *Have mercy on me, O God, as Thou art ever rich in mercy.*

POSTCOMMUNION.

Quǽsumus, Dómine, Deus noster: ut, quos divínis reparáre non désinis sacraméntis, tuis non destítuas benígnus auxíliis. Per Dóminum.

O Lord, our God, we pray that in Thy loving-kindness Thou wilt not deprive of Thine assistance those whom Thou ceasest not to restore with divine sacraments. Through our Lord.

II Classis.

—*Eleventh Sunday after Pentecost*—

INTROIT. *Ps 67: 6-7, 36*

Deus in loco sancto suo: Deus qui inhabitáre facit unánimes in domo: ipse dabit virtútem et fortitúdinem plebi suæ. ℣. Exsúrgat Deus, et dissipéntur inimíci ejus: et fúgiant, qui odérunt eum, a fácie ejus. ℣. Glória Patri.

GOD in His holy place; God Who maketh men of one mind to dwell in a house: He shall give power and strength to His people. (Ps 67: 2) Let God arise, and let His enemies be scattered: and let them that hate Him flee from before His face. ℣. Glory.

COLLECT.

Omnípotens sempitérne Deus, qui, abundántia pietátis tuæ, et mérita súpplicum excédis et vota: effúnde super nos misericórdiam tuam; ut dimíttas quæ consciéntia métuit, et adjícias quod orátio non præsúmit. Per Dóminum.

Almighty, eternal God, Who, in the abundance of Thy loving kindness, dost exceed both the deserts and the hopes of Thy suppliants, pour forth Thy mercy upon us, to take away from us those things which our conscience feareth, and to add that which our prayer presumeth not to ask. Through our Lord.

EPISTLE. *I Cor 15: 1-10*

Fratres: Notum vobis fácio Evangélium, quod prædicávi vobis, quod et accepístis, in quo et statis, per quod et salvámini: qua ratióne prædi-

BRETHREN, I make known unto you the gospel which I preached to you, which also you have received, and wherein you stand; by which also you are saved, if you hold fast after what manner I preached unto you, unless you have believed in vain. For I delivered unto you first of all, which I also received, how that Christ died for our sins according to the Scriptures; and that He was buried, and that He rose again the third day according to the Scriptures; and that He was seen by Cephas, and after that by the eleven. Then He was seen by more than five hundred brethren at once; of whom many remain until this present, and some are fallen asleep. After that He was seen by James, then by all the apostles. And last of all He was seen also by me, as by one born out of due time. For I am the least of the apostles, who am not worthy to be called an apostle, because I persecuted the Church of God; but by the grace of God I am what I am; and His grace in me hath not been void.

cáverim vobis, si tenétis, nisi frustra credidístis. Trádidi enim vobis in primis, quod et accépi: quóniã Christus mórtuus est pro peccátis nostris secúndum Scriptúras: et quia sepúltus est, et quia resurréxit tértia die secúndum Scriptúras: et quia visus est Cephæ, et post hoc úndecim. Deínde visus est plus quam quingéntis frátribus simul, ex quibus multi manent usque adhuc, quidam autem dormiérunt. Deínde visus est Jacóbo, deínde Apóstolis ómnibus: novíssime autẽ ómniũ tamquam abortívo, visus est et mihi. Ego enim sum mínimus Apostolórum, qui non sumdignus vocári Apóstolus, quóniã persecútus sum Ecclésiã Dei. Grátia autẽ Dei sum id quod sum, et grátia ejus in me vácua non fuit.

GRADUAL & ALLELUIA. *Ps 27: 7, 1 & Ps 80: 2-3*

IN GOD hath my heart confided, and I have been helped; and my flesh hath flourished again; and with my will I will give praise to Him. ℣. Unto Thee will I cry, O Lord: O my God, be not Thou silent; depart not from me. | Alleluia, alleluia. ℣. Rejoice in God our helper; sing aloud to the God of Jacob: take a pleasant psalm with the harp. Alleluia.

In Deo sperávit cor meum, et adjútus sum: et reflóruit caro mea, et ex voluntáte mea confitébor illi. ℣. Ad te, Dómine, clamávi: Deus meus, ne síleas, ne discédas a me.
Allelúja, allelúja. ℣. Exsultáte Deo, adjutóri nostro, jubiláte Deo Jacob: súmite psalmum jucúndum cum cíthara. Allelúja.

GOSPEL. *Mark 7: 31-37*

GOING OUT of the coast of Tyre, Jesus came by Sidon to the sea of Galilee, through the midst of the coasts of Decapolis. And they bring to Him one deaf and dumb, and they besought Him that He would lay His hand upon him. And taking him from the multitude apart, He put His fingers into his ears, and spitting, He touched his tongue; and looking up to heaven, He groaned and said to him, Ephpheta, that is, Be thou opened: and immediately his ears were opened, and the string of his tongue was loosed, and he spoke right. And He charged them that they should tell no man: but the more He charged them so much the more a great deal did they publish it; and so much the more did they wonder, saying, He hath done all things well; He hath made both the deaf to hear, and the dumb to speak. CREDO.

In illo témpore: Exiens Jesus de fínibus Tyri, venit per Sidónem ad mare Galilǽæ, inter médios fines Decapóleos. Et addúcunt ei surdum et mutum, et deprecabántur eum, ut impónat illi manum. Et apprehéndens eum de turba seórsum, misit dígitos suos in aurículas ejus: et éxspuens, tétigit linguam ejus: et suspíciens in cælum, ingémuit, et ait illi: Ephphetha, quod est adaperíre. Et statim apértæ sunt aures ejus, et solútum est vínculum linguæ ejus, et loquebátur recte. Et præcépit illis, ne cui dícerent. Quanto autem eis præcipiébat, tanto magis plus prædicábant: et eo ámplius admirabántur, dicéntes: Bene ómnia fecit: et surdos fecit audíre et mutos loqui.

OFFERTORY. *Ps 29: 2-3*

Identical to Ash Wednesday:

Exaltábo te, Dómine, quóniam suscepísti me, nec delectásti inimícos meos super me: Dómine, clamávi ad te, et sanásti me. ℣. *Dómine, abstraxísti ab ínferis ánimam meam: salvásti me a descendéntibus in lacum.* ℣. *Ego autem dixi in mea abundántia: Non movébor in ætérnum: Dómine, in voluntáte tua præstitísti decóri meo virtútem.*

I WILL extol Thee, O Lord, for Thou hast upheld me, and hast not made my enemies to rejoice over me: O Lord, I have cried to Thee, and Thou hast healed me. ℣. *O Lord, Thou hast brought forth my soul from hell: Thou hast saved me from them that go down into the pit.* ℣. *And in my abundance I said: I shall never be moved. O Lord, in Thy favor, Thou gavest strength to my beauty.*

SECRET.

Réspice, Dómine, quǽsumus, nostram propítius servitútem: ut, quod offérimus, sit tibi munus accéptum, et sit nostræ fragilitátis subsídium. Per Dóminum.

Look with mercy, we beseech Thee, O Lord, upon our homage, that the gift we offer may be accepted by Thee and be the support of our frailty. Through our Lord.

COMMUNION. *Prov 3: 9-10*

Honóra Dóminum de tua substántia, et de primítiis frugum tuárum: et implebúntur hórrea tua saturitáte, et vino torculária redundábunt. (Ps 36: 1, 16) ℣. *Noli æmulári in malignántibus: neque zeláveris faciéntes iniquitátem.* ℣. *Mélius est módicum justo, super divítias peccatórum multas.*
—Helmst|1026 • Circa 1026ad

HONOR the Lord with thy substance, and with the first of all thy fruits: and thy barns shall be filled with abundance, and thy presses shall run over with wine. ℣. *Be not emulous of evildoers; nor envy them that work iniquity.* ℣. *Better is a little to the just, than the great riches of the wicked.*

POSTCOMMUNION.

Sentiámus, quǽsumus, Dñe, tui perceptióne sacraménti, subsídium mentis et córporis: ut, in utróque salváti, cæléstis remédii plenitúdine gloriémur. Per Dóminum.

By receiving Thy sacrament, we beseech Thee, O Lord, may we experience help in soul and body, that, being saved in both, we may glory in the fullness of our heavenly remedy. Through our Lord.

Because this communion antiphon is not from a psalm, the ancient MSS give various options. Many take the verses from the Introit, whereas others—such as 121Einsie|961*—choose Psalm 111.*

II Classis.

—*Twelfth Sunday after Pentecost*—

INTROIT. *Ps 69: 2-3*

Deus, in adjutórium meum inténde: Dómine, ad adjuvándum me festína: confundántur et revereántur inimíci mei, qui quærunt ánimam meam. ℣. Avertántur retrórsum et erubéscant: qui cógitant mihi mala. ℣. Glória Patri.

INCLINE unto my aid, O God: O Lord, make haste to help me: let my enemies be confounded and ashamed, who seek my soul. (Ps 69: 4) Let them be turned backward and blush for shame, who desire evils to me. ℣. Glory.

COLLECT.

Almighty and eternal God, Whose gift it is that Thy faithful serve Thee worthily and rightly, grant us, we beseech Thee, that we may without offense hasten on to the fulfillment of Thy promises. Through our Lord.

Omnípotens et místericors Deus, de cujus múnere venit, ut tibi a fidélibus tuis digne et laudabíliter serviátur: tríbue, quǽsumus, nobis; ut ad promissiónes tuas sine offensióne currámus. Per Dóminum.

EPISTLE. *II Cor 3: 4-9*

BRETHREN, such confidence we have through Christ toward God. Not that we are sufficient to think anything of ourselves, as of ourselves; but our sufficiency is from God. Who also hath made us fit ministers of the new testament, not in the letter, but in the spirit: for the letter killeth, but the spirit quickeneth. Now if the ministration of death, engraven with letters upon stones, was glorious, so that the children of Israel could not steadfastly behold the face of Moses, for the glory of his countenance; which is made void: how shall not the ministration of the spirit be rather in glory? For if the ministration of condemnation be glory, much more the ministration of justice aboundeth in glory.

Fratres: Fidúciam talem habémus per Christum ad Deum: non quod sufficiéntes simus cogitáre áliquid a nobis, quasi ex nobis: sed sufficiéntia nostra ex Deo est: qui et idóneos nos fecit minístros novi testaménti: non líttera, sed spíritu: líttera enim occídit, spíritus autem vivíficat. Quod si ministrátio mortis, lítteris deformáta in lapídibus, fuit in glória; ita ut non possent inténdere fílii Ísraël in fáciem Móysi, propter glóriam vultus ejus, quæ evacuátur: quómodo non magis ministrátio Spíritus erit in glória? Nam si ministrátio damnatiónis glória est, multo magis abúndat ministérium justítiæ in glória.

GRADUAL & ALLELUIA. *Ps 33: 2-3 & Ps 87: 2*

I WILL BLESS the Lord at all times; His praise shall be ever in my mouth. ℣. In the Lord shall my soul be praised: let the meek hear, and rejoice.
Alleluia, alleluia. ℣. O Lord, the God of my salvation, I have cried in the day, and in the night, before Thee. Alleluia.

Benedícam Dóminum in omni témpore: semper laus ejus in ore meo. ℣. In Dómino laudábitur ánima mea: áudiant mansuéti, et læténtur.
Allelúja, allelúja. ℣. Dómine, Deus salútis meæ, in die clamávi et nocte coram te. Allelúja.

GOSPEL. *Luke 10: 23-37*

At that time, Jesus said to His disciples:

BLESSED ARE THE EYES that see the things which you see. For I say to you, that many prophets and kings have desired to see the things that you see, and have not seen them; and to hear the things that you hear, and have not heard them. And behold a certain lawyer stood up, tempting Him, and saying, Master, what must I do to possess eternal life? But He said to him, What is written in the law? How readest thou? He answering, said, Thou shalt love the Lord thy God with thy whole heart, and

In illo témpore: Dixit Jesus discípulis suis: Beáti óculi, qui vident quæ vos vidétis. Dico enim vobis, quod multi prophétæ et reges voluérunt vidére quæ vos vidétis, et non vidérunt: et audíre quæ audítis, et non audiérunt. Et ecce, quidam legisperítus surréxit, tentans illum, et dicens: Magíster, quid faciéndo vitam ætérnam possidébo? At ille dixit ad eum: In lege quid scriptum est? quómodo legis? Ille respóndens, dixit: Díliges Dóminum, Deum tuum, ex toto corde tuo, et ex tota ánima tua, et ex ómnibus víribus tuis; et ex omni mente tua: et próximum tuum sicut teípsum. Dixítque illi: Recte respondísti: hoc fac, et vives. Ille autem volens justificáre seípsum, dixit ad Jesum: Et quis est meus próximus?

with thy whole soul, and with all thy strength, and with all thy mind; and thy neighbor as thyself. And He said to him, thou hast answered rightly: this do, and thou shalt live. But he, willing to justify himself, said to Jesus, And who is my neighbor?

Suscípiens autem Jesus, dixit: Homo quidam descendébat ab Jerúsalem in Jéricho, et íncidit in latrónes, qui étiam despoliavérunt eum: et plagis impósitis abiérunt, semivívo relícto. Accidit autem, ut sacérdos quidam descénderet eádem via: et viso illo præterívit. Simíliter et levíta, cum esset secus locum et vidéret eum, pertránsiit. Samaritánus autem quidam iter fáciens, venit secus eum: et videns eum, misericórdia motus est. Et appropians, alligávit vúlnera ejus, infúndens óleum et vinum: et impónens illum in juméntum suum, duxit in stábulum, et curam ejus egit. Et áltera die prótulit duos denários et dedit stabulário, et ait: Curam illíus habe: et quodcúmque supererogáveris, ego cum redíero, reddam tibi. Quis horum trium vidétur tibi próximus fuísse illi, qui íncidit in latrónes? At ille dixit: Qui fecit misericórdiam in illum. Et ait illi Jesus: Vade, et tu fac simíliter.

And Jesus answering said, A certain man went down from Jerusalem to Jericho, and fell among robbers, who also stripped him, and having wounded him, went away, leaving him half dead: and it chanced that a certain priest went down the same way, and seeing him, passed by. In like manner also a levite, when he was near the place and saw him, passed by. But a certain Samaritan being on his journey, came near him, and seeing him, was moved with compassion; and going up to him, bound up his wounds, pouring in oil and wine; and, setting him upon his own beast, brought him to an inn, and took care of him: and the next day he took out two pence, and gave to the host, and said, Take care of him, and whatsoever thou shalt spend over and above, I, at my return, will repay thee. Which of these three, in thy opinion, was neighbor to him that fell among robbers? But he said, He that showed mercy to him. And Jesus said to him, Go, and do thou in like manner. CREDO.

OFFERTORY. *Ex 32: 11, 13, 14*

Precátus est Móyses in conspéctu Dómini, Dei sui, et dixit. * Precátus est Móyses in conspéctu Dómini, Dei sui, et dixit: Quare, Dómine, irásceris in pópulo tuo? Parce iræ ánimæ tuæ: meménto Ábraham, Isaac et Jacob, quibus jurásti dare terram fluéntem lac et mel. Et placátus factus est Dóminus de malignitáte, quam dixit fácere pópulo suo. ℣. *Dixit Dóminus ad Móysen: Invenísti grátiam in conspéctu meo et scio te præ ómnibus: et festínans Móyses inclinávit se in terram et adorávit dicens: Scio, quia miséricors es in míllibus, áuferens iniquitátem et peccáta.* ℣. *Dixit Móyses et Áaron, * dixit Moyses et Áaron ad omnem synagógam filiórum Ísraël: Accédite ante Deum: majéstas Dómini appáruit in nube: et exaudívit murmuratiónem vestram in témpore.*

MOSES PRAYED in the sight of the Lord his God, and said. * Moses prayed in the sight of the Lord his God, and said: Why, O Lord, is Thine indignation enkindled against Thy people? Let the anger of Thy mind cease; remember Abraham, Isaac, and Jacob, to whom Thou didst swear to give a land flowing with milk and honey: and the Lord was appeased from doing the evil, which He had spoken of doing against the people. ℣. *The Lord said unto Moses: thou hast found favor in My sight, and I know thee before all others: and Moses hastened to bow down to the earth and adore Him, saying: I know that Thy mercy is unto thousands, taking away iniquity and sin.* ℣. *Moses said, and Aaron, * Moses said, and Aaron to the whole synagogue of the children of Israel: Come before God: the majesty of the Lord appeared in a cloud: and He has heard your murmuring in due time.*

Some believe the repetitions found in the plainsong evoke the speech of Moses, who is said to have stuttered (cf. Exodus 4: 10).

SECRET.

Graciously behold, we pray Thee, O Lord, the sacrifices which we lay upon Thy sacred altars, that, in bringing us plentiful forgiveness, they may give honor to Thy name. Through our Lord.

Hóstias, quǽsumus, Dómine, propítius inténde, quas sacris altáribus exhibémus: ut, nobis indulgéntiam largiéndo, tuo nómini dent honórem. Per Dóminum.

COMMUNION. *Ps 103: 13, 14-15*

THE EARTH shall be filled with the fruit of Thy works, O Lord, that Thou mayest bring bread out of the earth, and that wine may cheer the heart of man; that he may make the face cheerful with oil; and that bread may strengthen man's heart. ℣. *Bless the Lord, O my soul: O Lord my God, Thou art exceedingly great.*

De fructu óperum tuórum, Dómine, satiábitur terra: ut edúcas panem de terra, et vinum lætíficet cor hóminis: ut exhílaret fáciem in óleo, et panis cor hóminis confírmet. (Ps 103: 1) ℣. *Bénedic, ánima mea, Dómino: Dómine Deus meus, magnificátus es veheménter.* —239Laon|927 • Circa 927AD

POSTCOMMUNION.

May the holy partaking of this mystery, we pray Thee, O Lord, vivify us, bringing us at once forgiveness and strengthening. Through our Lord.

Vivíficet nos, quǽsumus, Dómine, hujus participátio sancta mystérii: et páriter nobis expiatiónem tríbuat et munímen. Per Dóminum.

—*Thirteenth Sunday after Pentecost*—

II Classis.

INTROIT. *Ps 73: 20, 19, 23*

HAVE REGARD, O LORD, to Thy covenant, and forsake not to the end the souls of Thy poor: arise, O Lord, and judge Thy cause, and forget not the voices of them that seek Thee. (Ps 73: 1) O God, why hast Thou cast us off unto the end: why is Thy wrath enkindled against the sheep of Thy pasture? ℣. Glory.

Réspice, Dómine, in testaméntum tuum, et ánimas páuperum tuórum ne derelínquas in finem: exsúrge, Dómine, et júdica causam tuam, et ne obliviscáris voces quæréntium te. ℣. Ut quid, Deus, repulísti in finem: irátus est furor tuus super oves páscuæ tuæ? ℣. Glória Patri.

COLLECT.

Almighty, eternal God, grant us the increase of faith, hope, and charity; and that we may deserve to attain what Thou dost promise, make us to love what Thou dost command. Through our Lord.

Omnípotens sempitérne Deus, da nobis fídei, spei et caritátis augméntum: et, ut mereámur ássequi quod promíttis, fac nos amáre quod prǽcipis. Per Dóminum.

EPISTLE. *Gal 3: 16-22*

BRETHREN: To Abraham were the promises made, and to his seed. He saith not, And to his seeds, as of many; but as of one, And to thy seed, which is

Fratres: Ábrahæ dictæ sunt promissiónes, et sémini ejus. Non dicit: Et semínibus, quasi in multis; sed quasi in uno: Et sémini tuo, qui est

Christus. Hoc autem dico: testaméntum confirmátum a Deo, quæ post quadringéntos et trigínta annos facta est lex, non írritum facit ad evacuándam promissiónem. Nam si ex lege heréditas, jam non ex promissióne. Ábrahæ autem per repromissiónem donávit Deus. Quid ígitur lex? Propter transgressiónes pósita est, donec veníret semen, cui promíserat, ordináta per Angelos in manu mediatóris. Mediátor autem unius non est: Deus autem unus est. Lex ergo advérsus promíssa Dei? Absit. Si enim data esset lex, quæ posset vivificáre, vere ex lege esset justítia. Sed conclúsit Scriptúra ómnia sub peccáto, ut promíssio ex fide Jesu Christi darétur credéntibus.

Christ. Now this I say, that the testament which was confirmed by God, the law which was made after four hundred and thirty years, doth not disannul; to make the promise of no effect. For if the inheritance be of the law, it is no more of promise. But God gave it to Abraham by promise. Why then was the law? It was set because of transgressions, until the seed should come, to whom He made the promise: being ordained by angels in the hand of a mediator. Now a mediator is not of one: but God is one. Was the law then against the promises of God? God forbid. For if there had been a law given, which could give life, verily justice should have been by the law. But the Scripture hath concluded all under sin, that the promise by the faith of Jesus Christ might be given to them that believe.

GRADUAL & ALLELUIA. *Ps 73: 20, 19, 22 & Ps 89: 1*

Réspice, Dómine, in testaméntum tuum: et ánimas páuperum tuórum ne obliviscáris in finem. ℣. Exsúrge, Dómine, et júdica causam tuam: memor esto oppróbrii servórum tuórum.

Allelúja, allelúja. ℣. Dómine, refúgium factus es nobis a generatióne et progénie. Allelúja.

HAVE REGARD, O Lord, to Thy covenant, and forsake not to the end the souls of Thy poor. ℣. Arise, O Lord, and judge Thy cause: remember the reproach of Thy servants. | Alleluia, alleluia. ℣. Lord, Thou hast been our refuge, from generation to generation. Alleluia.

GOSPEL. *Luke 17: 11-19*

In illo témpore: Dum iret Jesus in Jerúsalem, transíbat per médiam Samaríam et Galilǽam. Et cum ingrederétur quoddam castéllum, occurrérunt ei decem viri leprósi, qui stetérunt a longe; et levavérunt vocem dicéntes: Jesu præcéptor, miserére nostri. Quos ut vidit, dixit: Ite, osténdite vos sacerdótibus. Et factum est, dum irent, mundáti sunt.

AS JESUS WAS GOING to Jerusalem, He passed through the midst of Samaria and Galilee: and as He entered into a certain town, there met Him ten men that were lepers, who stood afar off, and lifted up their voice, saying, Jesus, master, have mercy on us. Whom when He saw, He said, Go, show yourselves to the priests. And it came to pass, that, as they went, they were made clean.

Unus autem ex illis, ut vidit quia mundátus est, regréssus est, cum magna voce magníficans Deum, et cécidit in fáciem ante pedes ejus, grátias agens: et hic erat Samaritánus. Respóndens autem Jesus, dixit: Nonne decem mundáti sunt? et novem ubi sunt? Non est invéntus, qui redíret et daret glóriam Deo, nisi hic alienígena. Et ait illi: Surge, vade; quia fides tua te salvum fecit.

And one of them, when he saw that he was made clean, went back, with a loud voice, glorifying God: and he fell on his face before His feet, giving thanks: and this was a Samaritan. And Jesus answering, said, Were not ten made clean? And where are the nine? There is no one found to return, and give glory to God, but this stranger. And He said to him, Arise, go thy way; for thy faith hath made thee whole. CREDO.

OFFERTORY. *Ps 30: 15-16*

IN THEE, O Lord, have I hoped: I said, Thou art my God, my times are in Thy hands. ℣. *Make Thy face to shine upon Thy servant, and save me in Thy mercy: O Lord, let me not be confounded, for I have called upon Thee.* ℣. *O how great is the multitude of Thy sweetness, O Lord, which Thou hast hidden for them that fear Thee! Which Thou hast wrought for them that hope in Thee, in the sight of the sons of men.*

In te sperávi, Dómine; dixi: Tu es Deus meus, in mánibus tuis témpora mea. ℣. *Illúmina fáciem tuam super servum tuum et salvum me fac propter misericórdiam tuam: Dómine, non confúndar, quóniam invocávi te.* ℣. *Quam magna multitúdo dulcédinis tuæ, Dómine, quam abscondísti timéntibus te: perfecísti autem sperántibus in te in conspéctu filiórum hóminum.*

SECRET.

Look with favor upon Thy people, O Lord, look with favor upon their gifts; that, being appeased by this oblation, Thou mayest give us pardon and grant us what we ask. Through our Lord.

Propitiáre, Dómine, pópulo tuo, propitiáre munéribus: ut, hac oblatióne placátus, et indulgéntiam nobis tríbuas et postuláta concédas. Per Dóminum.

COMMUNION. *Wis 16: 20*

THOU hast given us, O Lord, bread from heaven, having in it all that is delicious, and the sweetness of every taste. ℣. *And rained down manna for them to eat. The bread of heaven was His gift to them.*

Panem de cælo dedísti nobis, Dómine, habéntem omne delectaméntum et omnem sapórem suavitátis. (Ps 77: 24) ℣. *Et pluit illis manna ad manducándum, et panem cœli dedit eis.*

—RENAUD|965 • Circa 965AD

POSTCOMMUNION.

Having received Thy heavenly sacraments, O Lord, we beseech Thee that we may profit unto the increase of everlasting salvation. Through our Lord.

Sumptis, Dómine, cæléstibus sacraméntis: ad redemptiónis ætérnæ, quǽsumus, proficiámus augméntum. Per Dóminum.

This communion antiphon is from the Book of Wisdom; it does not come from a psalm. Therefore, flexibility existed vis-à-vis the "extra" verses. One custom was to take from the Introit verse, and certain MSS explicitly wrote this out—e.g. STMAUR|1079 and 376SANGALL|1052. Others simply referred the singers to the Introit—e.g. 239LAON|877 and BAMBERG6LIT|905. According to an ancient tradition, Psalm 33 may also be sung. However, several MSS chose Psalm 77 (surely because of its connection to the Holy Eucharist), including HELMST|1026, 121EINSIE|961, and 381SANGALL|928. Still others left no indication at all, except for the "Gloria Patri": ALBI|1047, 4951STEVEN|1128, YRIEIX|1040, and so forth. In those instances, perhaps the singers knew to use the Introit psalm verses.

— *Fourteenth Sunday after Pentecost* —

II Classis.

INTROIT. *Ps 83: 10-11*

BEHOLD, O GOD, our protector, and look on the face of Thy Christ: for better is one day in Thy courts above thousands. (Ps 83: 2-3) How lovely are Thy tabernacles,

Protéctor noster, áspice, Deus, et réspice in fáciem Christi tui: quia mélior est dies una in átriis tuis super mília. ℣. Quam diléꝫta tabernácula tua, Dómine virtútū! concupíscit, et déficit ánima mea in átria Dómini. ℣. Glória Patri.

O Lord of hosts! my soul longeth and fainteth for the courts of the Lord. ℣. Glory.

COLLECT.

Custódi, Dómine, quǽsumus, Ecclésiam tuam propitiatióne perpétua: et quia sine te lábitur humána mortálitas; tuis semper auxíliis et abstrahátur a nóxiis et ad salutária dirigátur. Per Dóminum.

Guard Thy church, we beseech Thee, O Lord, with Thy continual kindness; and because without Thee human frailty falleth, let it, by Thine assistance, ever be both withheld from harm and guided to what is salutary. Through our Lord.

EPISTLE. *Gal 5: 16-24*

Fratres: Spíritu ambuláte, et desidéria carnis non perficiétis. Caro enim concupíscit advérsus spíritum, spíritus autem advérsus carnem: hæc enim sibi ínvicem adversántur, ut non quæcúmque vultis, illa faciátis. Quod si spíritu ducímini, non estis sub lege. Manifésta sunt autem ópera carnis, quæ sunt fornicátio, immundítia, impudicítia, luxúria, idolórum sérvitus, venefícia, inimicítiæ, contentiónes, æmulatiónes, iræ, rixæ, dissensiónes, sectæ, invídiæ, homicídia, ebrietátes, comessatiónes, et his simília: quæ prædíco vobis, sicut prædíxi: quóniam, qui tália agunt, regnum Dei non consequántur. Fructus autem Spíritus est: cáritas, gáudium, pax, patiéntia, benígnitas, bónitas, longanímitas, mansuetúdo, fides, modéstia, continéntia, cástitas. Advérsus hujúsmodi non est lex. Qui autem sunt Christi, carnem suam crucifixérunt cum vítiis et concupiscéntiis.

BRETHREN: Walk in the spirit, and you shall not fulfill the lusts of the flesh: for the flesh lusteth against the spirit, and the spirit against the flesh; for these are contrary one to another; so that you do not the things that you would. But if you are led by the spirit, you are not under the law. Now the works of the flesh are manifest; which are, fornication, uncleanness, immodesty, luxury, idolatry, witchcrafts, enmities, contentions, emulations, wraths, quarrels, dissensions, sects, envies, murders, drunkenness, revellings, and such like; of the which I foretell you, as I have foretold to you, that they who do such things shall not obtain the kingdom of God. But the fruit of the spirit is, charity, joy, peace, patience, benignity, goodness, longanimity, mildness, faith, modesty, continency, chastity. Against such there is no law. And they that are Christ's have crucified their flesh with the vices and concupiscences.

GRADUAL & ALLELUIA. *Ps 117: 8-9 & Ps 94: 1*

Bonum est confídere in Dómino, quam confídere in hómine. ℣. Bonum est speráre in Dómino, quam speráre in princípibus.
Allelúja, allelúja. ℣. Veníte, exsultémus Dómino, jubilémus Deo, salutári nostro. Allelúja.

IT is good to confide in the Lord, rather than to have confidence in man. ℣. It is good to trust in the Lord, rather than to trust in princes. Alleluia, alleluia. ℣. Come, let us praise the Lord with joy; let us joyfully sing to God our Savior. Alleluia.

GOSPEL. *Matt 6: 24-33*

In illo témpore: Dixit Jesus discípulis suis: Nemo potest duóbus dóminis servíre: aut enim unum ódio habébit, et álterum díliget: aut unum sustinébit, et álterum contémnet. Non potéstis Deo servíre et mammónæ. Ideo dico vobis, ne sollíciti sitis ánimæ vestræ, quid manducétis, neque

At that time, Jesus said to His disciples:

NO MAN can serve two masters; for either he will hate the one and love the other, or he will sustain the one and despise the other. You cannot serve God and mammon. Therefore I say to you: Be not solicitous for your life, what you shall eat, nor for your body, what you shall put on. Is not the life more than the meat, and the body more than the raiment?

córpori vestro, quid induámini. Nonne ánima plus est quam esca: et corpus plus quam vestiméntum?

Behold the birds of the air; for they neither sow, nor do they reap, nor gather into barns, and your heavenly Father feedeth them. Are not you of much more value than they? And which of you, by taking thought, can add to his stature one cubit? And for raiment why are you solicitous? Consider the lilies of the field, how they grow; they labor not, neither do they spin; but I say to you, that not even Solomon in all his glory was arrayed as one of these. Now if God so clothe the grass of the field, which is today, and tomorrow is cast into the oven, how much more you, O ye of little faith! Be not solicitous therefore, saying, what shall we eat, or what shall we drink or wherewith shall we be clothed? For after all these things do the heathen seek. For your Father knoweth that you have need of all these things. Seek ye therefore first the kingdom of God, and His justice; and all these things shall be added unto you. CREDO.

Respícite volatília cæli, quóniam non serunt neque metunt neque cóngregant in hórrea: et Pater vester cæléstis pascit illa. Nonne vos magis pluris estis illis? Quis autem vestrum cógitans potest adjícere ad statúram suam cúbitum unum? Et de vestiménto quid sollíciti estis? Consideráte lília agri, quómodo crescunt: non labórant neque nent. Dico autem vobis, quóniam nec Sálomon in omni glória sua coopértus est sicut unum ex istis. Si autem fœnum agri, quod hódie est et cras in clíbanum míttitur, Deus sic vestit: quanto magis vos, módicæ fídei? Nolíte ergo sollíciti esse, dicéntes: Quid manducábimus aut quid bibémus aut quo operiémur? Hæc enim ómnia gentes inquírunt. Scit enim Pater vester, quia his ómnibus indigétis. Quærite ergo primum regnum Dei et justítiam ejus: et hæc ómnia adjiciéntur vobis.

OFFERTORY. *Ps 33: 8-9*

THE ANGEL of the Lord shall encamp round about them that fear Him, and shall deliver them. O taste, and see that the Lord is sweet! ℣. *I will bless the Lord at all times: His praise shall be always in my mouth.* ℣. *In the Lord shall my soul be praised: let the meek hear and rejoice. O magnify the Lord with me; and let us extol His name together.* ℣. *Come ye to Him and be enlightened: and your faces shall not be confounded. This poor man cried, and the Lord heard him: and saved him out of all his troubles.*

Immíttet Ángelus Dómini in circúitu timéntium eum, et erípiet eos: gustáte et vidéte, quóniam suávis est Dóminus. ℣. *Benedícam Dóminum in omni témpore: semper laus ejus in ore meo.* ℣. *In Dómino laudábitur ánima mea: áudiant mansuéti et læténtur: magnificáte Dóminum mecum et exaltémus nomen ejus in ínvicem.* ℣. *Accédite ad eum et illuminámini et vultus vestri non erubéscent. Iste pauper clamávit et Dóminus exaudívit eum et ex ómnibus tribulatiónibus ejus liberávit eum.*

SECRET.

Grant us, we beseech Thee, O Lord, that this saving Victim may become both the cleansing of our sins, and the propitiation of Thy might. Through our Lord.

Concéde nobis, Dómine, quæsumus, ut hæc hóstia salutáris et nostrórum fiat purgátio delictórum, et tuæ propitiátio potestátis. Per Dóminum.

COMMUNION. *Matt 6: 33*

SEEK FIRST the kingdom of God; and all things shall be added unto you, saith the Lord. ℣. *Lord, by the virtue of Thy name deliver me, let Thy sovereign power grant me redress.*

Primum quærite regnum Dei, et ómnia adjiciéntur vobis, dicit Dóminus. (Ps 53: 3) ℣. *Deus, in nomine tuo salvum me fac, et in virtute tua judica me.*

—STMAUR|1079 • Circa 1079AD

POSTCOMMUNION.

Puríficent semper et múniant tua sacraménta nos, Deus: et ad perpétuæ ducant salvatiónis efféctum. Per Dóminum.

May Thy Sacraments, O God, ever purify and fortify us, and bring us to the effect of everlasting salvation. Through our Lord.

In most of the ancient books, this communion antiphon was used on the 9th Sunday after Pentecost: e.g. BAMBERG6LIT|905, 4951STEVEN|1128, HELMST|1026, ALBI|1047, and so forth. This communion antiphon does not come from a psalm, so the additional communion verses come from the Introit (Psalm 53), but—we must remember—the Introit for the 9th Sunday after Pentecost.

II Classis.

—*Fifteenth Sunday after Pentecost*—

INTROIT. *Ps 85: 1, 2-3*

Inclína, Dómine, aurem tuam ad me, et exáudi me: salvum fac servum tuum, Deus meus, sperántem in te: miserére mihi, Dómine, quóniam ad te clamávi tota die. ℣. Lætífica ánimam servi tui: quia ad te, Dómine, ánimam meam levávi. ℣. Glória Patri.

BOW DOWN Thine ear, O Lord, to me, and hear me: save Thy servant, O my God, that trusteth in Thee: have mercy on me, O Lord, for I have cried to Thee all day. (Ps 85: 4) Give joy to the soul of Thy servant; for to Thee, O Lord, have I lifted up my soul. ℣. Glory.

COLLECT.

Ecclésiam tuam, Dómine, miserátio continuáta mundet et múniat: et quia sine te non potest salva consístere; tuo semper múnere gubernétur. Per Dóminum.

Let Thy continual pity, O Lord, cleanse and fortify Thy Church; and, because without Thee it cannot be safely established, let it ever be governed by Thy grace. Through our Lord.

EPISTLE. *Gal 5: 25-26; 6: 1-10*

Fratres: Si spíritu vívimus, spíritu et ambulémus. Non efficiámur inánis glóriæ cúpidi, ínvicem provocántes, ínvicem invidéntes. Fratres, et si præoccupátus fúerit homo in áliquo delícto, vos, qui spirituáles estis, hujúsmodi instrúite in spíritu lenitátis, consíderans teípsum, ne et tu tentéris. Alter altérius ónera portáte, et sic adimplébitis legem Christi. Nam si quis exístimat se áliquid esse, cum nihil sit, ipse se sedúcit. Opus autem suum probet unusquísque, et sic in semetípso tantum glóriam habébit, et non in áltero. Unusquísque enim onus suum portábit. Commúnicet autem is, qui catechizátur verbo, ei, qui se catechízat, in ómnibus bonis. Nolíte erráre: Deus

BRETHREN, if we live in the spirit, let us also walk in the spirit. Let us not be made desirous of vainglory, provoking one another, envying one another. Brethren, and if a man be overtaken in any fault, you, who are spiritual, instruct such a one in the spirit of meekness, considering thyself, lest thou also be tempted. Bear ye one another's burdens, and so you shall fulfill the law of Christ. For if any man think himself to be something, whereas he is nothing, he deceiveth himself. But let every one prove his own work, and so he shall have glory in himself only, and not in another. For every one shall bear his own burden. And let him that is instructed in the word, communicate to him that instructeth him, in all good things. Be not deceived; God is not mocked: for what things a man shall sow, those also shall he reap. For he that soweth in his flesh, of the flesh also shall reap corruption; but he that soweth in the spirit, of the spirit shall reap life everlasting. And in doing good, let us not fail; for in due time we shall reap, not failing. Therefore, whilst we have time, let us work good to all men, but especially to those who are of the household of the Faith.

non irridétur. Quæ enim semináverit homo, hæc et metet. Quóniam qui séminat in carne sua, de carne et metet corruptiónem: qui autem séminat in spíritu, de spíritu metet vitam ætérnam. Bonum autem faciéntes, non deficiámus: témpore enim suo metémus, non deficiéntes. Ergo, dum tempus habémus, operémur bonum ad omnes, máxime autem ad doméstícos fídei.

GRADUAL & ALLELUIA. *Ps 91: 2-3 & Ps 94: 3*

IT IS GOOD to give praise to the Lord; and to sing to Thy name, O most High. ℣. To show forth Thy mercy in the morning, and Thy truth in the night. Alleluia, alleluia. ℣. For the Lord is a great God, and a great king above all the earth. Alleluia.

Bonum est confitéri Dómino: et psállere nómini tuo, Altíssime. ℣. Ad annuntiándum mane misericórdiam tuam, et veritátem tuam per noctem. Allelúja, allelúja. ℣. Quóniam Deus magnus Dóminus, et Rex magnus super omnem terram. Allelúja.

GOSPEL. *Luke 7: 11-16*

JESUS WENT into a city called Naim; and there went with Him His disciples, and a great multitude. And when He came nigh to the city, behold a dead man was carried out, the only son of his mother; and she was a widow, and much people of the city were with her. And when the Lord saw her, He had compassion on her, and said to her, Weep not. And He came near, and touched the bier. And they that carried it stood still. And He said, Young man, I say to thee, Arise: and he that was dead sat up, and began to speak. And He delivered him to his mother. And there came a fear on them all: and they glorified God, saying, A great prophet is risen up amongst us and God hath visited His people. CREDO.

In illo témpore: Ibat Jesus in civitátẽ, quæ vocátur Naïm: et ibant cum eo discípuli ejus et turba copiósa. Cum autẽ appropinquáret portæ civitátis, ecce, defúnctus efferebátur fílius únicus matris suæ: et hæc vídua erat: et turba civitátis multa cum illa. Quam cum vidísset Dñs, misericórdia motus super eam, dixit illi: Noli flere. Et accéssit et tétigit lóculum. (Hi autem, qui portábant, stetérunt.) Et ait: Adoléscens, tibi dico, surge. Et resédit, qui erat mórtuus, et cœpit loqui. Et dedit illum matri suæ. Accépit autem omnes timor: et magnificábant Deũ, dicéntes: Quia prophéta magnus surréxit in nobis: et quia Deus visitávit plebẽ suã.

OFFERTORY. *Ps 39: 2, 3, 4*

PATIENTLY I waited for the Lord's help, and at last He turned His look towards me; and He heard my prayer, and He put a new canticle into my mouth, a song to our God. ℣. *He set my feet upon a rock, and directed my steps.* ℣. *Thou hast multiplied Thy wonderful works, O Lord my God: and in Thy thoughts there is no one like to Thee. And I told the story of Thy just dealings before a great throng.* ℣. *O Lord, God, I have not hid Thy justice within my heart: I have declared Thy truth and Thy salvation. Thou art my helper and my protector.*

Exspéctans exspectávi Dóminum, et respéxit me: et exaudívit deprecatiónem meam: et immísit in os meum cánticum novum, hymnum Deo nostro. ℣. *Státuit supra petram pedes meos et diréxit gressus meos.* ℣. *Multa fecísti tu, Dómine, Deus meus, mirabília tua et cogitatiónibus tuis non est, qui símilis tibi: bene nuntiávi justítiam tuam in ecclésia magna.* ℣. *Dómine, Deus, tu cognovísti justítiam meam: non abscóndi in corde meo veritátem tuam et salutáre tuum dixi: adjútor meus, Dómine, et protéctor meus.*

SECRET.

Tua nos, Dómine, sacraménta custódiant: et contra diabólicos semper tueántur incúrsus. Per Dóminum.

May Thy sacraments, O Lord, keep us and guard us always from the assaults of the devil. Through our Lord.

COMMUNION. *John 6: 52*

Panis, quem ego dédero, caro mea est pro sǽculi vita. (Jn 6: 57) ℣. *Qui mandúcat carnẽ meam et bibit meum sánguinem, in me manet, et ego in illo.*
—4951STEVEN|1128 • Circa 1128AD

THE BREAD that I will give is My flesh for the life of the world. ℣. *He that eateth My flesh, and drinketh My blood, abideth in Me, and I in him.*

POSTCOMMUNION.

Mentes nostras et córpora possídeat, quǽsumus, Dñe, doni cæléstis operátio: ut non noster sensus in nobis, sed júgiter ejus prævéniat efféctus. Per Dóminum.

Let the operation of the heavenly gift, O Lord, possess our souls and bodies, that, its holy grace, not our own impulses, may continually be our guide. Through our Lord.

This communion antiphon does not come from a psalm; therefore, the ancient MSS choose multifarious additional verses.

II Classis.

—*Sixteenth Sunday after Pentecost*—

INTROIT. *Ps 85: 3, 5*

Miserére mihi, Dómine, quóniam ad te clamávi tota die: quia tu, Dómine, suávis ac mitis es, et copiósus in misericórdia ómnibus invocántibus te. ℣. Inclína, Dómine, aurem tuam mihi, et exáudi me: quóniam inops, et pauper sum ego. ℣. Glória Patri.

HAVE MERCY ON ME, O Lord, for I have cried to Thee all the day; for Thou, O Lord, art sweet and mild, and plenteous in mercy to all that call upon Thee. (Ps 85: 1) Bow down Thine ear to me, O Lord, and hear me; for I am needy and poor. ℣. Glory.

COLLECT.

Tua nos, quǽsumus, Dómine, grátia semper et prævéniat et sequátur: ac bonis opéribus júgiter præstet esse inténtos. Per Dóminum.

Let Thy grace, we beseech Thee, O Lord, ever go before us and follow us, and may it make us to be continually zealous in doing good works. Through our Lord.

EPISTLE. *Eph 3: 13-21*

Fratres: Óbsecro vos, ne deficiátis in tribulatiónibus meis pro vobis: quæ est glória vestra. Hujus rei grátia flecto génua mea ad Patrem

BRETHREN, I pray you not to faint at my tribulations for you, which are your glory. For this cause I bow my knees to the Father of our Lord Jesus

Christ, of Whom all paternity, in heaven and earth is named, that He would grant you, according to the riches of His glory, to be strengthened by His Spirit with might unto the inward man. That Christ may dwell by faith in your hearts; that being rooted and founded in charity, you may be able to comprehend with all the saints, what is the breadth, and length, and height, and depth. To know also the charity of Christ, which surpasseth all knowledge; that you may be filled unto all the fullness of God. Now to Him Who is able to do all things more abundantly than we desire or understand, according to the power that worketh in us: to Him be glory in the Church, and in Christ Jesus, unto all generations, world without end. Amen.

Dómini nostri Jesu Christi, ex quo omnis patérnitas in cælis et in terra nominátur, ut det vobis secúndum divítias glóriæ suæ, virtúte corroborári per Spíritum ejus in interiórem hóminem, Christum habitáre per fidem in córdibus vestris: in caritáte radicáti et fundáti, ut possítis comprehéndere cum ómnibus sanctis, quæ sit latitúdo et longitúdo et sublímitas et profúndum: scire etiam supereminéntem sciéntiæ caritátem Christi, ut impleámini in omnem plenitúdinem Dei. Ei autem, qui potens est ómnia fácere superabundánter, quam pétimus aut intellégimus, secúndum virtútem, quæ operátur in nobis: ipsi glória in Ecclésia et in Christo Jesu, in omnes generatiónes sǽculi sæculórum. Amen.

GRADUAL & ALLELUIA. *Ps 101: 16-17 & Ps 97: 1*

THE GENTILES shall fear Thy name, O Lord, and all the kings of the earth Thy glory. ℣. For the Lord hath built up Sion, and He shall be seen in His majesty. | Alleluia, alleluia. ℣. Sing ye to the Lord a new canticle, because the Lord hath done wonderful things. Alleluia.

Timébunt gentes nomen tuum, Dómine, et omnes reges terræ glóriam tuam. ℣. Quóniam ædificávit Dóminus Sion, et vidébitur in majestáte sua.

Allelúja, allelúja. ℣. Cantáte Dómino cánticum novum: quia mirabília fecit Dóminus. Allelúja.

GOSPEL. *Luke 14: 1-11*

WHEN JESUS WENT into the house of one of the chief of the pharisees on the Sabbath-day to eat bread, they watched Him. And behold, there was a certain man before Him that had the dropsy: and Jesus answering, spoke to the lawyers and pharisees, saying, Is it lawful to heal on the Sabbath-day? But they held their peace: but He taking him, healed him, and sent him away. And answering them, He said, Which of you shall have an ass or an ox fall into a pit, and will not immediately draw him out on the Sabbath-day? And they could not answer Him these things. And He spoke a parable also to them that were invited, marking how they chose the first seats at the table, saying to them, When thou art invited to a wedding, sit not down in the first place, lest perhaps one more honorable than thou be invited by him; and he that invited thee and

In illo témpore: Cum intráret Jesus in domum cujúsdam príncipis pharisæórum sábbato manducáre panem, et ipsi observábant eum. Et ecce, homo quidam hydrópicus erat ante illum. Et respóndens Jesus dixit ad legisperítos et pharisǽos, dicens: Si licet sábbato curáre? At illi tacuérunt. Ipse vero apprehénsum sanávit eum ac dimísit. Et respóndens ad illos, dixit: Cujus vestrum ásinus aut bos in púteum cadet, et non contínuo éxtrahet illum die sábbati? Et non póterant ad hæc respóndere illi. Dicébat autem et ad invitátos parábolam, inténdens, quómodo primos accúbitus elígerent, dicens ad illos: Cum invitátus fúeris ad núptias, non discúmbas in primo loco, ne forte honorátior te sit invitátus ab illo, et véniens is, qui te et illum vocávit, dicat tibi: Da huic locum: et tunc incípias cum rubóre novíssimum locum tenére. Sed cum vocátus fúeris, vade, recúmbe in novíssimo loco: ut, cum vénerit, qui te invitávit, dicat tibi: Amíce, ascénde supérius. Tunc erit tibi glória coram simul discumbéntibus: quia omnis, qui se exáltat, humiliábitur: et qui se humíliat, exaltábitur.

him, come and say to thee, Give this man place; and then thou begin with shame to take the lowest place. But when thou art invited, go, sit down in the lowest place: that when he who inviteth thee cometh, he may say to thee, Friend, go up higher: then shalt thou have glory before them that sit at table with thee: because every one that exalteth himself shall be humbled, and he that humbleth himself shall be exalted. CREDO.

OFFERTORY. *Ps 39: 14, 15*

Dómine, in auxílium meum réspice: confundántur et revereántur, qui quærunt ánimam meam, ut áuferant eam: Dómine, in auxílium meum réspice. ℣. *Avertantur retrorsum et erubescant, qui cogitant mihi mala.* ℣. *Exspéctans exspectávi Dóminum et respéxit me: et exaudívit deprecatiónem meam.*

LOOK DOWN, O Lord, to help me; let them be confounded and ashamed that seek after my soul to take it away; look down, O Lord, to help me. ℣. *Let them be turned backward and blush for shame that desire evils to me.* ℣. *Patiently I waited for the Lord's help, and at last He turned His look towards me.*

SECRET.

Munda nos, quǽsumus, Dómine, sacrifícii præséntis efféctu: et pérfice miserátus in nobis; ut ejus mereámur esse partícipes. Per Dóminum.

Cleanse us, we beseech Thee, O Lord, by the effect of the present sacrifice, and in Thy mercy bring to pass in us that we may deserve to be partakers of it. Through our Lord.

COMMUNION. *Ps 70: 16-17, 18*

Dómine, memorábor justítiæ tuæ solíus: Deus, docuísti me a juventúte mea: et usque in senéctam et sénium, Deus, ne derelínquas me. (Ps 70: 1-2a) ℣. *In te, Dómine, sperávi; non confúndar in ætérnum. In justítia tua líbera me, et éripe me.*

—239LAON|927 • Circa 927AD

O LORD, I will be mindful of Thy justice alone: Thou hast taught me, O God, from my youth, and unto old age and gray hairs, O God, forsake me not. ℣. *In Thee, O Lord, I have hoped, let me never be put to confusion: rescue and deliver me, faithful as Thou art.*

POSTCOMMUNION.

Purífica, quǽsumus, Dómine, mentes nostras benígnus, et rénova cæléstibus sacraméntis: ut consequénter et córporum præsens páriter et futúrum capiámus auxílium. Per Dóminum.

In Thy loving-kindness, purify our souls, we beseech Thee, O Lord, and renew them with the heavenly sacrament, that we may receive bodily assistance thereby, both for this life and for the life to come. Through our Lord.

The Offertory verses often do not come directly from Sacred Scripture, in the sense that verses are combined in a singular way. However, this Offertory goes even further, taking its first verse from a completely different psalm, viz. Psalm 69. The words "Dómine, in auxílium meum réspice" are repeated to the exact same musical notes, something worth noting. Dom Johner (d. 1955), Prior of Beuron Abbey, says about this repeat: "It reminds us of the early practice of repeating a part (usually the last) of the antiphon after every verse that was joined to the Offertory."

— *Seventeenth Sunday after Pentecost* —

II Classis.

INTROIT. *Ps 118: 137, 124*

THOU ART JUST, O Lord, and Thy judgment is right; deal with Thy servant according to Thy mercy. (Ps 118: 1) Blessed are the undefiled in the way: who walk in the law of the Lord. ℣. Glory.

Justus es, Dómine, et rectum judícium tuum: fac cum servo tuo secúndum misericórdiam tuam. ℣. Beáti immaculáti in via: qui ámbulant in lege Dómini. ℣. Glória Patri.

COLLECT.

Grant Thy people, we beseech Thee, O Lord, to shun the defilements of the devil, and with pure hearts to follow Thee, the only God. Through our Lord.

Da, quǽsumus, Dómine, pópulo tuo diabólica vitáre contágia: et te solum Deum pura mente sectári. Per Dóminum.

EPISTLE. *Eph 4: 1-6*

BRETHREN, I, a prisoner of the Lord, beseech you that you walk worthy of the vocation in which you are called. With all humility and mildness, with patience, supporting one another in charity, careful to keep the unity of the spirit in the bond of peace. One body and one spirit, as you are called in one hope of your calling. One Lord, one faith, one baptism. One God and Father of all, Who is above all, and through all, and in us all, Who is blessed for ever and ever. Amen.

Fratres: Óbsecro vos ego vinctus in Dómino, ut digne ambulétis vocatióne, qua vocáti estis, cum omni humilitáte et mansuetúdine, cum patiéntia, supportántes ínvicem in caritáte, sollíciti serváre unitátem spíritus in vínculo pacis. Unum corpus et unus spíritus, sicut vocáti estis in una spe vocatiónis vestræ. Unus Dóminus, una fides, unum baptísma. Unus Deus et Pater ómnium, qui est super omnes et per ómnia et in ómnibus nobis. Qui est benedíctus in sǽcula sæculórum. Amen.

GRADUAL & ALLELUIA. *Ps 32: 12, 6 & Ps 101: 2*

BLESSED is the nation whose God is the Lord: the people whom He hath chosen for His inheritance. ℣. By the word of the Lord the heavens were established; and all the power of them by the Spirit of His mouth. | Alleluia, alleluia. ℣. O Lord, hear my prayer: and let my cry come to Thee. Alleluia.

Beáta gens, cujus est Dóminus Deus eórum: pópulus, quem elégit Dóminus in hereditátem sibi. ℣. Verbo Dómini cæli firmáti sunt: et spíritu oris ejus omnis virtus eórum.
Allelúja, allelúja. ℣. Dómine, exáudi oratiónem meam, et clamor meus ad te pervéniat. Allelúja.

GOSPEL. *Matt 22: 34-46*

THE PHARISEES came to Jesus, and one of them, a doctor of the law, asked Him, tempting Him, Master, which is the great commandment of the law? Jesus said to him, Thou shalt love the Lord thy God with thy whole heart, and with thy whole soul, and with

In illo témpore: Accessérunt ad Jesum pharisǽi: et interrogávit eum unus ex eis legis doctor, tentans eum: Magíster, quod est mandátum magnum in lege? Ait illi Jesus: Díliges Dóminum, Deum tuum, ex toto corde tuo et in tota ánima tua et in tota mente tua. Hoc est máximum et primum mandátum. Secúndum autem símile est huic: Díliges próximum tuum sicut teípsum. In his duóbus mandátis univérsa lex pendet et prophétæ. Congregátis autem pharisǽis, interrogávit eos Jesus, dicens: Quid vobis vidétur de Christo? cujus fílius est? Dicunt ei: David. Ait illis: Quómodo ergo David in spíritu vocat eum Dóminum, dicens: Dixit Dóminus Dómino meo, sede a dextris meis, donec ponam inimícos tuos scabéllum pedum tuórum? Si ergo David vocat eum Dóminum, quómodo fílius ejus est? Et nemo póterat ei respóndere verbum: neque ausus fuit quisquam ex illa die eum ámplius interrogáre.

thy whole mind. This is the greatest and the first commandment. And the second is like to this: Thou shalt love thy neighbor as thyself. On these two commandments dependeth the whole law and the prophets. And the pharisees being gathered together, Jesus asked them, saying, What think you of Christ; Whose son is He? They say to Him, David's. He saith to them, How then doth David, in spirit, call Him Lord; saying, The Lord said to My Lord, Sit on My right hand until I make Thine enemies Thy footstool? If David then call Him Lord, how is He his son? And no man was able to answer Him a word; neither durst any man, from that day forth, ask Him any more questions. CREDO.

OFFERTORY. *Dan 9: 17, 18, 19*

Orávi Deum meum ego Dániel, dicens: Exáudi, Dómine, preces servi tui: illúmina fáciem tuam super sanctuárium tuum: et propítius inténde pópulum istum, super quem invocátum est nomen tuum, Deus. ℣. *Adhuc me loquénte et oránte et narránte peccáta mea et delícta pópuli mei Ísraël.* ℣. *Audívi vocem dicéntem mihi: Dániel, intéllege verba, quæ loquor tibi, quia ego missus sum ad te. Nam et Míchaël venit in adjutórium meum.*

I, DANIEL, PRAYED to my God, saying, Hear, O Lord, the prayers of Thy servant; show Thy face upon Thy sanctuary, and favorably look down upon this people upon whom Thy name is invoked, O God. ℣. *I was yet speaking, and praying, and confessing my sins, and the sins of my people Israel.* ℣. *I heard a voice saying unto me : Daniel! understand the words that I speak unto thee; for I am sent unto thee; for Michael likewise cometh to help me.*

SECRET.

Majestátem tuam, Dómine, supplíciter deprecámur: ut hæc sancta, quæ gérimus, et a prætéritis nos delíctis éxuant et futúris. Per Dóminum.

We implore Thy majesty, O Lord, that the holy mysteries which we are celebrating may free us of past and save us from future sins. Through our Lord.

COMMUNION. *Ps 75: 12-13*

Vovéte et réddite Dómino, Deo vestro, omnes, qui in circúitu ejus affértis múnera: terríbili, et ei qui aufert spíritum príncipum: terríbili apud omnes reges terræ.
(Ps 75: 2) ℣. *Notus in Judǽa Deus; in Ísraël magnum nomen ejus.*

VOW YE, and pay to the Lord your God, all you that round about Him bring presents: to Him that is terrible, even to Him Who taketh away the spirit of princes; to the terrible with all the kings of the earth. ℣. *It is in Juda God makes Himself known, in Israel that His name is extolled.*

POSTCOMMUNION.

Sanctificatiónibus tuis, omnípotens Deus, et vítia nostra curéntur, et remédia nobis ætérna provéniant. Per Dóminum.

By Thy grace, O almighty God, let our wicked propensities be cured and everlasting remedies be forthcoming. Through our Lord.

—*Eighteenth Sunday after Pentecost*— *II Classis.*

INTROIT. *Ecclus 36: 18*

GIVE PEACE, O LORD, to them that patiently wait for Thee, that Thy prophets may be found faithful: hear the prayers of Thy servant, and of Thy people Israel. (Ps 121: 1) I rejoiced at the things that were said to me: We shall go into the house of the Lord. ℣. Glory.

Da pacem, Dómine, sustinéntibus te, ut prophétæ tui fidéles inveniántur: exáudi preces servi tui et plebis tuæ Ísraël. ℣. Lætátus sum in his, quæ dicta sunt mihi: in domum Dómini íbimus. ℣. Glória Patri.

COLLECT.

Let the operation of Thy mercy, we beseech Thee, O Lord, direct our hearts, for without Thee we cannot please Thee. Through our Lord.

Dírigat corda nostra, quǽsumus, Dómine, tuæ miseratiónis operátio: quia tibi sine te placére non póssumus. Per Dóminum.

EPISTLE. *I Cor 1: 4-8*

BRETHREN, I give thanks to my God always for you, for the grace of God that is given you in Jesus Christ, that in all things you are made rich in Him, in all utterance and in all knowledge, as the testimony of Christ was confirmed in you, so that nothing is wanting to you in any grace, waiting for the manifestation of our Lord Jesus Christ. Who also will confirm you unto the end without crime, in the day of the coming of our Lord Jesus Christ.

Fratres: Grátias ago Deo meo semper pro vobis in grátia Dei, quæ data est vobis in Christo Jesu: quod in ómnibus dívites facti estis in illo, in omni verbo et in omni sciéntia: sicut testimónium Christi confirmátum est in vobis: ita ut nihil vobis desit in ulla grátia, exspectántibus revelatiónem Dómini nostri Jesu Christi, qui et confirmábit vos usque in finem sine crímine, in die advéntus Dómini nostri Jesu Christi.

GRADUAL & ALLELUIA. *Ps 121: 1, 7 & Ps 101: 16*

I REJOICED at the things that were said to me: We shall go into the house of our Lord. ℣. Let peace be in thy strength, and abundance in thy towers.
Alleluia, alleluia. ℣. The gentiles shall fear Thy name, O Lord: and all the kings of the earth Thy glory. Alleluia.

Lætátus sum in his, quæ dicta sunt mihi: in domum Dñi íbimus. ℣. Fiat pax in virtúte tua: et abundántia in túrribus tuis.
Allelúja, allelúja. ℣. Timébunt gentes nomen tuum, Dómine, et omnes reges terræ glóriam tuam. Allelúja.

GOSPEL. *Matt 9: 1-8*

ENTERING into a ship, Jesus passed over the water and came into His own city. And behold they brought to Him one sick of the palsy lying in a bed; and Jesus seeing their faith, said to the man sick of the palsy, Be of good heart, son, thy sins are forgiven thee. And behold some of the scribes said within themselves, He blasphemeth. And Jesus

In illo témpore: Ascéndens Jesus in navículam, transfretávit et venit in civitátem suam. Et ecce, offerébant ei paralýticum jacéntem in lecto. Et videns Jesus fidem illórum, dixit paralýtico: Confíde, fili, remittúntur tibi peccáta tua. Et ecce, quidam de scribis dixérunt intra se: Hic blasphémat. Et cum vidísset Jesus cogitatiónes eórum, dixit: Ut quid cogitátis mala in córdibus vestris?

Quid est facílius dícere: Dimittúntur tibi peccáta tua; an dícere: Surge et ámbula? Ut autem sciátis, quia Fílius hóminis habet potestátem in terra dimittendi peccáta, tunc ait paralýtico: Surge, tolle lectum tuum, et vade in domum tuam. Et surréxit et ábiit in domum suam. Vidéntes autem turbæ timuérunt, et glorificavérunt Deum, qui dedit potestátẽ talem homínibus.

seeing their thoughts, said, Why do you think evil in your hearts? Whether is it easier to say, Thy sins are forgiven Thee; or to say, Arise and walk? But that you may know that the Son of man hath power on earth to forgive sins (then said He to the man sick of the palsy): Arise, take up thy bed, and go into thy house. And he arose, and went into his house. And the multitude seeing it, feared, and glorified God Who had given such power to men. CREDO.

OFFERTORY. *Ex 24: 4, 5*

Sanctificávit Móyses altáre Dómino, ófferens super illud holocáusta et ímmolans víctimas: * **fecit** sacrifícium vespertínum in odórem suavitátis Dómino Deo, in conspéctu filiórum Ísraël. ℣. *Locútus est Dóminus ad Móysen dicens: Ascénde ad me in montem Sina et statis super cacúmen ejus: Surgens Móyses ascéndit in montem, ubi constítuit ei Deus, et descéndit ad eum Dóminus in nube et ádstitit ante fáciem ejus. Videns Móyses prócidens adorávit dicens: Óbsecro, Dómine, dimítte peccáta pópuli tui. Et dixit ad eum Dóminus: Fáciam secúndum verbum tuum.* [Tunc Móyses * **fecit**...]
℣. *Orávit Móyses Dóminum et dixit: Si invéni grátiam in conspéctu tuo, osténde mihi te ipsum maniféste, ut vídeam te. Et locútus est ad eum Dóminus dicens: Non enim vidébit me homo et vívere potest: sed esto super altitúdinem lápidis et próteget te déxtera mea, donec pertránseam: dum pertransíero, áuferam manum meam et tunc vidébis glóriam meam, fácies autem mea non vidébitur tibi, quia ego sum Deus osténdens mirabília in terra.* [Tunc Móyses * **fecit**...]

MOSES consecrated an altar to the Lord, offering upon it holocausts, and sacrificing victims: he * **made** an evening sacrifice to the Lord God for an odor of sweetness, in the sight of the children of Israel. ℣. *The Lord spoke unto Moses saying: Come up unto Me, upon mount Sinai, and thou shalt stand on the top thereof. Moses rising up, went up the mountain, where the Lord had appointed him: and the Lord came down unto him in a cloud, and stood before his face. Which Moses seeing, fell down and adored, saying: I beseech Thee, O Lord, forgive the sins of Thy people. And the Lord said unto him: I will do according to thy word.* [Then Moses * **made**...]
℣. *Moses prayed to the Lord and said: If I have found favor in Thy sight, show me Thyself openly, that I may see Thee. And the Lord spoke unto him, saying: For man shall not see Me, and live; but be thou on the height of the rock, and my right hand shall protect thee, till I pass: whilst I pass I will take away My hand, and then shalt thou see My glory: but My face shall not be seen by thee; for I am God, showing wonderful things in the earth.* [Then Moses * **made**...]

The Gregorian melodies are rich with text painting. For instance: (a) "Ascénde ad me in montem Sina" rises to the very highest notes; (b) "Osténdens mirabília in terra" has a remarkable treatment of "wonderful things" descending to the earth; (c) "Orávit Móyses" has a pattern of notes that imitates Moses stuttering (cf. Exodus 4:10).

SECRET.

Deus, qui nos, per hujus sacrifícii veneránda commércia, unius summæ divinitátis partícipes éfficis: præsta, quǽsumus; ut, sicut tuam cognóscimus veritátem, sic eam dignis móribus assequámur. Per Dóminum.

O God, Who, through the august communication of this sacrifice, dost make us partakers of the one supreme divinity, grant, we beseech Thee, that, as we know Thy truth, so we may ever follow it with worthy actions. Through our Lord.

COMMUNION. *Ps 95: 8-9*

BRING UP SACRIFICES, and come into His courts: adore ye the Lord in His holy court. ℣. *Sing ye to the Lord a new canticle: sing to the Lord, all the earth.*

Tóllite hóstias, et introíte in átria ejus: adoráte Dóminum in aula sancta ejus. (Ps 95: 1) ℣. *Cantáte Dómino cánticum novum; cantáte Dómino, omnis terra.* —239Laon|927 • Circa 927AD

POSTCOMMUNION.

Strengthened by the sacred gift, we render thanks to Thee, O Lord, beseeching Thy mercy that Thou make us entirely worthy to partake thereof. Through our Lord.

Grátias tibi reférimus, Dómine, sacro múnere vegetáti: tuam misericórdiam deprecántes; ut dignos nos ejus participatióne perfícias. Per Dóminum.

—*Nineteenth Sunday after Pentecost*— *II Classis.*

INTROIT. *Trad.*

I AM THE SALVATION of the people, saith the Lord: in whatever tribulation they shall cry to Me I will hear them; and I will be their Lord for ever. (Ps 77: 1) Attend, O My people, to My law; incline your ears to the words of My mouth. ℣. Glory.

Salus pópuli ego sum, dicit Dóminus: de quacúmque tribulatióne clamáverint ad me, exáudiam eos: et ero illórum Dóminus in perpétuum. ℣. Atténdite, pópule meus, legem meam: inclináte aurem vestram in verba oris mei. ℣. Glória Patri.

COLLECT.

Almighty and merciful God, in Thy loving kindness do Thou keep us from all things that war against us, that, being unhampered alike in soul and in body, we may with free minds perform the works that are Thine. Through our Lord.

Omnípotens et misericors Deus, univérsa nobis adversántia propitiátus exclúde: ut mente et córpore páriter expedíti, quæ tua sunt, líberis méntibus exsequámur. Per Dóminum.

EPISTLE. *Eph 4: 23-28*

BRETHREN, Be ye renewed in the spirit of your mind, and put on the new man, who according to God is created in justice and holiness of truth. Wherefore, putting away lying, speak ye the truth every man with his neighbor, for we are members one of another. Be angry, and sin not. Let not the sun go down upon your anger. Give not place to the devil. He that stole, let him now steal no more; but rather let him labor, working with his hands the thing which is good, that he may have something to give to him that suffereth need.

Fratres: Renovámini spíritu mentis vestræ, et indúite novum hóminem, qui secúndum Deum creátus est in justítia et sanctitáte veritátis. Propter quod deponéntes mendácium, loquímini veritátem unusquísque cum próximo suo: quóniam sumus ínvicem membra. Irascímini, et nolíte peccáre: sol non óccidat super iracúndiam vestram. Nolíte locum dare diábolo: qui furabátur, jam non furétur; magis autem labóret, operándo mánibus suis, quod bonum est, ut hábeat, unde tríbuat necessitátem patiénti.

GRADUAL & ALLELUIA. *Ps 140: 2 & Ps 104: 1*

Dirigátur orátio mea, sicut incénsum in conspéctu tuo, Dómine. ℣. Elevátio mánuum meárum sacrifícium vespertínum. | Allelúja, allelúja. ℣. Confitémini Dño, et invocáte nomen ejus: annuntiáte inter gentes ópera ejus. Allelúja.

LET MY PRAYER be directed as incense in Thy sight, O Lord. ℣. The lifting up of my hands as evening sacrifice. | Alleluia, alleluia. ℣. Give glory to the Lord, and call upon His name: declare His deeds among the gentiles. Alleluia.

GOSPEL. *Matt 22: 1-14*

In illo témpore: Loquebátur Jesus princípibus sacerdótum et pharisǽis in parábolis, dicens: Símile factum est regnum cælórum hómini regi, qui fecit núptias fílio suo. Et misit servos suos vocáre invitátos ad núptias, et nolébant veníre. Íterum misit álios servos, dicens: Dícite invitátis: Ecce, prándium meum parávi, tauri mei et altília occísa sunt, et ómnia paráta: veníte ad núptias.

AT THAT TIME, Jesus spoke to the chief priests and the pharisees in parables, saying, The kingdom of heaven is likened to a king, who made a marriage for his son; and he sent his servants, to call them that were invited to the marriage, and they would not come. Again he sent other servants, saying, Tell them that were invited, Behold, I have prepared my dinner; my beeves and fatlings are killed, and all things are ready; come ye to the marriage.

Illi autem neglexérunt: et abiérunt, álius in villam suam, álius vero ad negotiatiónem suam: réliqui vero tenuérunt servos ejus, et contuméliis afféctos occidérunt. Rex autem cum audísset, irátus est: et, missis exercítibus suis, pérdidit homicídas illos et civitátem illórum succéndit.

But they neglected: and went their ways, one to his farm, and another to his merchandise; and the rest laid hands on his servants, and insulted and killed them. But when the king had heard of it, he was angry; and sending his armies, he destroyed those murderers, and burnt their city.

Tunc ait servis suis: Núptiæ quidem parátæ sunt, sed, qui invitáti erant, non fuérunt digni. Ite ergo ad éxitus viárum et, quoscúmque invenéritis, vocáte ad núptias. Et egréssi servi ejus in vias, congregavérunt omnes, quos invenérunt, malos et bonos: et implétæ sunt núptiæ discumbéntium.

Then he saith to his servants, The marriage indeed is ready, but they that were invited were not worthy. Go ye therefore into the highways, and as many as you shall find, call to the marriage. And his servants going forth into the ways, gathered together all that they found, both bad and good; and the marriage was filled with guests.

Intrávit autem rex, ut vidéret discumbéntes, et vidit ibi hóminem non vestítum veste nuptiáli. Et ait illi: Amíce, quómodo huc intrásti non habens vestem nuptiálem? At ille obmútuit. Tunc dixit rex minístris: Ligátis mánibus et pédibus ejus, míttite eum in ténebras exterióres: ibi erit fletus et stridor déntium. Multi enim sunt vocáti, pauci vero elécti.

And the king went in to see the guests; and he saw there a man who had not on a wedding garment: and he saith to him, Friend, how comest thou in hither, not having on a wedding garment? but he was silent. Then the king said to the waiters, Bind his hands and feet, and cast him into the exterior darkness: there shall be weeping and gnashing of teeth. For many are called, but few are chosen. CREDO.

OFFERTORY. *Ps 137: 7*

IF I SHALL WALK in the midst of tribulation, Thou wilt quicken me, O Lord; and Thou wilt stretch forth Thy hand against the wrath of my enemies: and Thy right hand shall save me. ℣. *In what day soever I shall call upon Thee, hear me: Thou shalt multiply strength in my soul.* ℣. *I bow down in worship towards Thy sanctuary, and I will give glory to Thy name, O Lord, for Thy mercy, and for Thy truth.*

Si ambulávero in médio tribulatiónis, vivificábis me, Dómine: et super iram inimicórum meórum exténdes manum tuam, et salvum me fáciet déxtera tua. ℣. *In quacúmque die invocávero te, exáudi me, Dómine: multiplicábis in ánima mea virtútem tuam.* ℣. *Adorábo ad templum sanctum tuum et confitébor nómini tuo, Dómine, super misericórdia tua et veritáte tua.*

SECRET.

Grant, we beseech Thee, O Lord, that these gifts, which we offer up in the sight of Thy majesty, may be salutary unto us. Through our Lord.

Hæc múnera, quǽsumus, Dómine, quæ óculis tuæ majestátis offérimus, salutária nobis esse concéde. Per Dóminum.

COMMUNION. *Ps 118: 4-5*

THOU hast commanded Thy commandments to be kept most diligently: O that my ways may be directed to keep Thy justifications. ℣. *Blessed are the undefiled in the way, who walk in the law of the Lord.*

Tu mandásti mandáta tua custodíri nimis: útinam dirigántur viæ meæ, ad custodiéndas justificatiónes tuas. (Ps 118: 1) ℣. *Beáti immaculáti in via, qui ámbulant in lege Dómini.*

—239Laon|927 • Circa 927AD

POSTCOMMUNION.

Let Thy healing power, O Lord, in mercy deliver us from our waywardness and cause us ever to cleave to Thy commandments. Through our Lord.

Tua nos, Dómine, medicinális operátio, et a nostris perversitátibus cleménter expédiat, et tuis semper fáciat inhærére mandátis. Per Dóminum.

—*Twentieth Sunday after Pentecost*— *II Classis.*

INTROIT. *Dan 3: 31, 29, 35*

WHATEVER Thou hast done to us, O Lord, Thou hast done by a just judgment; because we have sinned against Thee, and we have not obeyed Thy commandments: but give glory to Thy name, and deal with us according to the multitude of Thy mercy. (Ps 118: 1) Blessed are the undefiled in the way; who walk in the law of the Lord. ℣. Glory.

Omnia, quæ fecísti nobis, Dómine, in vero judício fecísti, quia peccávimus tibi et mandátis tuis non obedívimus: sed da glóriam nómini tuo, et fac nobíscum secúndum multitúdinem misericórdiæ tuæ. ℣. Beáti immaculáti in via: qui ámbulant in lege Dómini. ℣. Glória Patri.

COLLECT.

Being appeased, O Lord, grant to Thy faithful in abundance, we beseech Thee, both forgiveness and

Largíre, quǽsumus, Dómine, fidélibus tuis indulgéntiam placátus et pacem:

ut páriter ab ómnibus mundéntur offénsis, et secúra tibi mente desérviant. Per Dóminum.

peace, that they may both be cleansed from all offenses and with a quiet mind give themselves to Thy service. Through our Lord.

EPISTLE. *Eph 5: 15-21*

Fratres: Vidéte, quómodo caute ambulétis: non quasi insipiéntes, sed ut sapiéntes, rediméntes tempus, quóniam dies mali sunt. Proptérea nolíte fíeri imprudéntes, sed intellegéntes, quæ sit volúntas Dei. Et nolíte inebriári vino, in quo est luxúria: sed implémini Spíritu Sancto, loquéntes vobismetípsis in psalmis et hymnis et cánticis spirituálibus, cantántes et psalléntes in córdibus vestris Dómino: grátias agéntes semper pro ómnibus, in nómine Dómini nostri Jesu Christi, Deo et Patri. Subjécti ínvicem in timóre Christi.

BRETHREN, See how you walk circumspectly, not as unwise, but as wise; redeeming the time, because the days are evil. Wherefore, become not unwise, but understanding what is the will of God. And be not drunk with wine, wherein is luxury: but be ye filled with the holy Spirit, speaking to yourselves in psalms and hymns, and spiritual canticles, singing and making melody in your hearts to the Lord: giving thanks always for all things, in the name of our Lord Jesus Christ, to God and the Father; being subject one to another in the fear of Christ.

GRADUAL & ALLELUIA. *Ps 144: 15-16 & Ps 107: 2*

Óculi ómnium in te sperant, Dómine: et tu das illis escam in témpore opportúno. ℣. Áperis tu manum tuam: et imples omne ánimal benedictióne.

Allelúja, allelúja. ℣. Parátum cor meum, Deus, parátum cor meum: cantábo, et psallam tibi, glória mea. Allelúja.

THE EYES of all hope in Thee, O Lord; and Thou givest them meat in due season. ℣. Thou openest Thy hand, and fillest every living creature with Thy blessing. | Alleluia, alleluia. ℣. My heart is ready, O God, my heart is ready: I will sing, and will give praise to Thee, my glory. Alleluia.

Today's Gradual—also sung on Corpus Christi—has thirty-five notes on the penult of "áperis," whereas the tonic accent has only one. This is typical of the Gregorian repertoire; one does not compose in order to set every word to music, but in order to translate into music a single idea expressed in a number of words. In a musical phrase, each element is a part of the whole and must take its own place in that whole—for instance the word "coeli" in Sanctus IX, or the word "Domini" in the Benedictus of Mass XI, and so forth. In melismatic chant, the melodic line must be given first place, according to the ancient adage: Musica non subjacet regulis Donati. *Gregorian rhythm is inherently musical in nature, and its function is to enhance the expressive power of the holy words. (Dom Joseph Gajard, 1950)*

GOSPEL. *John 4: 46-53*

In illo témpore: Erat quidam régulus, cujus fílius infirmabátur Caphárnaum. Hic cum audísset, quia Jesus adveníret a Judǽa in Galilǽam, ábiit ad eum, et rogábat eum, ut descénderet et sanáret fílium ejus: incipiébat enim mori. Dixit ergo Jesus ad eum: Nisi signa et prodígia vidéritis, non créditis. Dicit ad eum régulus: Dómine, descénde, priúsquam moriátur fílius meus. Dicit ei Jesus: Vade, fílius tuus vivit. Crédidit homo sermóni, quem dixit ei Jesus, et ibat. Jam autem eo descendénte, servi occurrérunt ei et nuntiavérunt, dicéntes, quia fílius ejus víveret. Interrogábat ergo horam ab eis, in qua

THERE WAS a certain ruler whose son was sick at Capharnaum. He having heard that Jesus was come from Judea into Galilee, went to Him, and prayed Him to come down, and heal his son; for he was at the point of death. Jesus therefore said to him, Unless you see signs and wonders, you believe not. The ruler saith to Him, Lord, come down before that my son die. Jesus saith to him, Go thy way, thy son liveth. The man believed the word which Jesus said to him, and went his way. And as he was going down, his servants met him, and they brought word, saying, that his son lived. He asked therefore of them the hour wherein he grew better. And they said to him, yesterday at the seventh hour the fever left him. The father therefore knew that it was at the same hour that Jesus said to him, Thy son liveth; and himself believed, and his whole house. CREDO.

mélius habúerit. Et dixérunt ei: Quia heri hora séptima relíquit eum febris. Cognóvit ergo pater, quia illa hora erat, in qua dixit ei Jesus: Fílius tuus vivit: et crédidit ipse et domus ejus tota.

OFFERTORY. *Ps 136: 1*

UPON THE RIVERS of Babylon, there we sat and wept; when we remembered thee, O Sion. ℣. *For there they that led us into captivity required of us the words of songs, and they that carried us away, said: Sing to us a hymn of the songs of Sion. How shall we sing the song of the Lord in a strange land?* ℣. *If I forget thee, O Jerusalem, let my right hand be forgotten. Let my tongue cleave to my jaws, if I do not remember thee.* * Who **said to us** upon the rivers of Babylon. ℣. *Remember, O Lord, the children of Edom, in the day of Jerusalem.* * Who **said to us** upon the rivers of Babylon.

Super flúmina Babylónis illic sédimus et flévimus: dum recordarémur tui, Sion. ℣. *In salícibus in médio ejus suspéndimus órgana nostra. Quóniam illic interrogavérunt nos, qui captívos duxérunt nos, verba canticórum, et qui abduxérunt nos: Hymnum cantáte nobis de cánticis Sion. Quómodo cantábimus cánticum Dómini in terra aliéna?* ℣. *Si oblítus fúero tui, Jerúsalem, obliviscátur me déxtera mea: adhǽreat lingua mea fáucibus meis, si tui non meminero.* * Qui **dixérunt** super flúmina Babylónis. ℣. *Meménto, Dómine, filiórum Edom in die Jerúsalem.* * Qui **dixérunt** super flúmina Babylónis.

SECRET.

Let these mysteries, we beseech Thee, O Lord, be our heavenly medicine and purge the evil from our hearts. Through our Lord.

Cæléstem nobis præbeant hæc mystéria, quǽsumus, Dómine, medicínam: et vítia nostri cordis expúrgent. Per Dóminum.

COMMUNION. *Ps 118: 49-50*

BE Thou mindful of Thy word to Thy servant, O Lord, in which Thou hast given me hope: this hath comforted me in my humiliation. ℣. *Blessed are the undefiled in the way, who walk in the law of the Lord.*

Meménto verbi tui servo tuo, Dómine, in quo mihi spem dedísti: hæc me consoláta est in humilitáte mea. (Ps 118: 1) ℣. *Beáti immaculáti in via, qui ámbulant in lege Dómini.*
—5319VATICANUS|1105 • Circa 1105AD

POSTCOMMUNION.

That we may be rendered worthy of Thy sacred gifts, O Lord, grant us, we beseech Thee, ever to obey Thy commandments. Through our Lord.

Ut sacris, Dómine, reddámur digni munéribus: fac nos, quǽsumus, tuis semper obedíre mandátis. Per Dóminum.

The universality and supreme antiquity of the Catholic liturgy is demonstrated by the manuscript selected for the communion antiphon, which matches the other manuscripts—from the ninth century on—when it comes to the "extra" verses. The manuscript (5319VATICANUS | 1105) is one of the very few examples of the mysterious "Old Roman Chant."

II Classis.

—*Twenty-first Sunday after Pentecost*—

INTROIT. *Esther 13: 9, 10-11*

In voluntáte tua, Dómine, univérsa sunt pósita, et non est, qui possit resístere voluntáti tuæ: tu enim fecísti ómnia, cælum et terram et univérsa, quæ cæli ámbitu continéntur: Dóminus universórum tu es. ℣. Beáti immaculáti in via: qui ámbulant in lege Dómini. ℣. Glória Patri.

ALL THINGS, O LORD, are at Thy disposal: and there is none that can resist Thy will: for Thou hast made all things, heaven and earth, and all things that are under the cope of heaven: Thou art Lord of all. (Ps 118: 1) Blessed are the undefiled in the way; who walk in the law of the Lord. ℣. Glory.

COLLECT.

Famíliam tuam, quǽsumus, Dómine, contínua pietáte custódi: ut a cunctis adversitátibus, te protegénte, sit líbera, et in bonis áctibus tuo nómini sit devóta. Per Dóminum.

Keep Thy household, we beseech Thee, O Lord, with continual loving-kindness, that by Thy protection it may be free from all adversities and devoted to Thy name in well-doing. Through our Lord.

EPISTLE. *Eph 6: 10-17*

Fratres: Confortámini in Dómino et in poténtia virtútis ejus. Indúite vos armatúram Dei, ut possítis stare advérsus insídias diáboli. Quóniam non est nobis colluctátio advérsus carnem et sánguinem: sed advérsus príncipes et potestátes, advérsus mundi rectóres tenebrárum harum, contra spirituália nequítiæ, in cæléstibus. Proptérea accípite armatúram Dei, ut possítis resístere in die malo et in ómnibus perfécti stare. State ergo succíncti lumbos vestros in veritáte, et indúti lorícam justítiæ, et calceáti pedes in præparatióne Evangélii pacis: in ómnibus suméntes scutum fídei, in quo possítis ómnia tela nequíssimi ígnea exstínguere: et gáleam salútis assúmite: et gládium spíritus, quod est verbum Dei.

BRETHREN, be strengthened in the Lord, and in the might of His power. Put you on the armor of God, that you may be able to stand against the deceits of the devil. For our wrestling is not against flesh and blood, but against principalities and powers, against the rulers of the world of this darkness, against the spirits of wickedness in the high places. Therefore, take unto you the armor of God, that you may be able to resist in the evil day, and to stand in all things perfect. Stand therefore having your loins girt about with truth, and having on the breast plate of justice, and your feet shod with the preparation of the gospel of peace; in all things taking the shield of faith, wherewith you may be able to extinguish all the fiery darts of the most wicked one. And take unto you the helmet of salvation, and the sword of the spirit, which is the word of God.

GRADUAL & ALLELUIA. *Ps 89: 1-2 & Ps 113: 1*

Dómine, refúgium factus es nobis, a generatióne et progénie. ℣. Priúsquam montes fíerent aut formarétur terra et orbis: a sǽculo et usque in sǽculum tu es, Deus.

Allelúja, allelúja. ℣. In éxitu Ísraël de Ægýpto, domus Jacob de pópulo bárbaro. Allelúja.

LORD, Thou hast been our refuge, from generation to generation. ℣. Before the mountains were made, or the earth and the world was formed; from eternity and to eternity Thou art God.

Alleluia, alleluia. ℣. When Israel went out of Egypt, the house of Jacob from a barbarous people. Alleluia.

GOSPEL. *Matt 18: 23-35*

At that time, Jesus spoke to His disciples this parable:

THE KINGDOM OF HEAVEN is likened to a king, who would take an account of his servants. And when he had begun to take the account, one was brought to him that owed him ten thousand talents: and as he had not wherewith to pay it, his lord commanded that he should be sold, and his wife and children, and all that he had, and payment to be made. But that servant falling down, besought him, saying, Have patience with me, and I will pay thee all. And the lord of that servant, being moved with pity, let him go; and forgave him the debt. But when that servant was gone out, he found one of his fellow-servants that owed him a hundred pence: and laying hold of him, he throttled him, saying, Pay what thou owest. And his fellow-servant falling down besought him, saying, Have patience with me, and I will pay thee all. And he would not; but went and cast him into prison till he paid the debt.

In illo tempore: Dixit Jesus discípulis suis parábolam hanc: Assimilátum est regnum cælórum hómini regi, qui vóluit ratiónem pónere cum servis suis. Et cum cœpísset ratiónem pónere, oblátus est ei unus, qui debébat ei decem mília talénta. Cum autem non habéret, unde rédderet, jussit eum dóminus ejus venúmdari et uxórem ejus et fílios et ómnia, quæ habébat, et reddi. Prócidens autem servus ille, orábat eum, dicens: Patiéntiam habe in me, et ómnia reddam tibi. Misértus autem dóminus servi illíus, dimísit eum et débitum dimísit ei. Egréssus autem servus ille, invénit unum de consérvis suis, qui debébat ei centum denários: et tenens suffocábat eum, dicens: Redde, quod debes. Et prócidens consérvus ejus, rogábat eum, dicens: Patiéntiam habe in me, et ómnia reddam tibi. Ille autem nóluit: sed ábiit, et misit eum in cárcerem, donec rédderet débitum.

Now his fellow-servants, seeing what was done, were very much grieved; and they came and told their lord all that was done. Then his lord called him, and saith to him, Thou wicked servant, I forgave thee all the debt, because thou besoughtest me; shouldst not thou then have had compassion also on thy fellow-servant, even as I had compassion on thee? And his lord being angry, delivered him to the torturers until he paid all the debt. So also shall my heavenly Father do to you, if brother does not forgive brother with all his heart. Credo.

Vidéntes autem consérvi ejus, quæ fiébant, contristáti sunt valde: et venérunt et narravérunt dómino suo ómnia, quæ facta fúerant. Tunc vocávit illum dóminus suus: et ait illi: Serve nequam, omne débitum dimísi tibi, quóniam rogásti me: nonne ergo opórtuit et te miseréri consérvi tui, sicut et ego tui misértus sum? Et irátus dóminus ejus, trádidit eum tortóribus, quoadúsque rédderet univérsum débitum. Sic et Pater meus cæléstis fáciet vobis, si non remiséritis unusquísque fratri suo de córdibus vestris.

OFFERTORY. *Job 1*

IN THE LAND of Hus, there was a man called Job; a simple and upright man, fearing God: whom Satan besought that he might tempt: and power was given him from the Lord over his possessions and his flesh; and he destroyed all his substance and his children; and wounded his flesh also with a grievous ulcer. ℣. *Oh! that my sins were weighed in a balance! Oh! that my sins, whereby I have deserved wrath, whereby I have deserved wrath, were weighed in a balance! and the calamity, the calamity that I suffer, it would appear heavier!* ℣. *For what is, for what is, for what is my*

Vir erat in terra Hus, nómine Job: simplex et rectus ac timens Deum: quem Satan pétiit ut tentáret: et data est ei potéstas a Dómino in facultátes et in carnem ejus: perdidítque omnem substántiam ipsíus et fílios: carnem quoque ejus gravi úlcere vulnerávit.

℣. *Útinam appenderéntur peccáta mea: útinam appenderéntur peccáta mea, quibus iram mérui, quibus iram mérui, et calámitas et calámitas et calámitas, quam pátior, et grávior apparéret.* ℣. *Quæ est enim, quæ est enim, quæ est enim fortitúdo mea, ut sustíneam? Aut quis finis meus, ut patiénter agam? ℣. Numquid fortitúdo lápidum est fortitúdo mea? Aut caro mea ǽnea est? Aut caro mea ǽnea est? ℣. Quóniam, quóniam, quóniam non revertétur óculus meus, ut vídeat bona, ut vídeat bona, ut vídeat bona, ut vídeat bona, ut vídeat bona, ut vídeat bona, ut vídeat bona.*

strength, that I can hold out? or what is my end, that I should keep patience? ℣. Is my strength the strength of stones? Or is my flesh of brass? or is my flesh of brass? ℣. For, for, for, mine eye shall not return to see good things, to see good things, to see good things, to see good things, to see good things, to see good things, to see good things, to see good things, to see good things.

Amalarius of Metz (a ninth-century liturgist) says of this Offertory: "In the verses, we have Job himself speaking, his body all humbled, and his soul full of sorrow: the repetition of the same words, their interruptions, their refrain, their broken phrases, vividly represent his panting for breath, and intense suffering."

SECRET.

Súscipe, Dómine, propítius hóstias: quibus et te placári voluísti, et nobis salútem poténti pietáte restítui. Per Dóminum.

Graciously receive, O Lord, the sacrifices with which Thou hast willed that Thou shouldst be appeased and our salvation, by Thy mighty love, restored. Through our Lord.

COMMUNION. *Ps 118: 81, 84, 86*

In salutári tuo ánima mea, et in verbum tuum sperávi: quando fácies de persequéntibus me judícium? iníqui persecúti sunt me, ádjuva me, Dómine, Deus meus. (Ps 118: 87) ℣. *Paulo minus consummavérunt me in terra; ego autem non derelíqui mandáta tua.*
—Renaud|965 • Circa 965AD

MY SOUL hath looked to be saved by Thee, and hath relied on Thy word: when wilt Thou execute judgment on them that persecute me? The wicked ones have long persecuted me: help me, O Lord my God. ℣. *They had almost made an end of me upon earth: but I have not forsaken Thy commandments.*

POSTCOMMUNION.

Immortalitátis alimóniam consecúti, quǽsumus, Dómine: ut, quod ore percépimus, pura mente sectémur. Per Dóminum.

Having obtained the nourishment of immortality, we beseech Thee, O Lord, that what has passed our lips we may embrace with a pure mind. Through our Lord.

II Classis.

—*Twenty-second Sunday after Pentecost*—

INTROIT. *Ps 129: 3-4*

Si iniquitátes observáveris, Dómine: Dómine, quis sustinébit? quia apud te propitiátio est, Deus Ísraël. ℣. De profúndis clamávi ad te, Dómine: Dómine, exáudi vocem meam. ℣. Glória Patri.

SHOULDST THOU, O Lord, observe iniquities, Lord, who shall stand it? for with Thee is propitiation, O God of Israel. (Ps 129: 1-2) From the depths I have cried to Thee, O Lord: Lord, hear my voice. ℣. Glory.

COLLECT.

O God, our refuge and our strength, the very author of piety, be present to the devout supplications of Thy Church, and grant that what we seek in faith we may effectively arrive at. Through our Lord.

Deus, refúgium nostrum et virtus: adésto piis Ecclésiæ tuæ précibus, auctor ipse pietátis, et præsta; ut, quod fidéliter pétimus, efficáciter consequámur. Per Dóminum.

EPISTLE. *Philip 1: 6-11*

BRETHREN, we are confident in the Lord Jesus, that He Who hath begun a good work in you, will perfect it unto the day of Christ Jesus. As it is meet for me to think this for you all, for that I have you in my bands, and in the defense and confirmation of the gospel you are all partakers of my joy. For God is my witness, how I long after you all in the bowels of Jesus Christ. And this I pray, that your charity may more and more abound in knowledge and in all understanding; that you may approve the better things; that you may be sincere and without offence unto the day of Christ; filled with the fruit of justice, through Jesus Christ, unto the glory and praise of God.

Fratres: Confídimus in Dómino Jesu, quia, qui cœpit in vobis opus bonum, perfíciet usque in diem Christi Jesu. Sicut est mihi justum hoc sentíre pro ómnibus vobis: eo quod hábeam vos in corde, et in vínculis meis, et in defensióne, et confirmatióne Evangélii, sócios gáudii mei omnes vos esse. Testis enim mihi est Deus, quómodo cúpiam omnes vos in viscéribus Jesu Christi. Et hoc oro, ut cáritas vestra magis ac magis abúndet in sciéntia et in omni sensu: ut probétis potióra, ut sitis sincéri et sine offénsa in diem Christi, repléti fructu justítiæ per Jesum Christum, in glóriam et laudem Dei.

GRADUAL & ALLELUIA. *Ps 132: 1-2 & Ps 113: 19*

BEHOLD how good and how pleasant it is for brethren to dwell together in unity. ℣. It is like the precious ointment on the head, that ran down upon the beard, the beard of Aaron.
Alleluia, alleluia. ℣. They that fear the Lord, let them hope in Him: He is their helper and protector. Alleluia.

Ecce, quam bonum et quam jucúndum, habitáre fratres in unum ! ℣. Sicut unguéntum in cápite, quod descéndit in barbam, barbam Áäron.

Allelúja, allelúja. ℣. Qui timent Dóminum sperent in eo: adjútor et protéctor eórum est. Allelúja.

GOSPEL. *Matt 22: 15-21*

WITHDRAWING, the pharisees consulted among themselves, how to ensnare Jesus in His speech. And they sent to Him their disciples, with the Herodians, saying, Master, we know that Thou art a true speaker, and teachest the way of God in truth, neither carest Thou for any man, for Thou dost not regard the person of men. Tell us therefore, what dost Thou think? Is it lawful to give tribute to Cæsar, or not? But Jesus knowing their wickedness, said, Why do you tempt me, ye hypocrites? Show Me the coin of the tribute. And they offered Him a penny. And Jesus saith to them, Whose image and superscription is this? They say to Him, Cæsar's.

In illo témpore: Abeúntes pharisǽi consílium iniérunt, ut cáperent Jesum in sermóne. Et mittunt ei discípulos suos cum Herodiánis, dicéntes: Magíster, scimus, quia verax es et viam Dei in veritáte doces, et non est tibi cura de áliquo: non enim réspicis persónam hóminum: dic ergo nobis, quid tibi vidétur, licet censum dare Cæsari, an non? Cógnita autem Jesus nequítia eórum, ait: Quid me tentátis, hypócritæ? Osténdite mihi numísma census. At illi obtulérunt ei denárium. Et ait illis Jesus: Cujus est imágo hæc et superscríptio? Dicunt ei: Cæsaris. Tunc ait illis: Réddite ergo, quæ sunt Cæsaris, Cæsari; et, quæ sunt Dei, Deo.

Then He saith to them, Render therefore to Cæsar, the things that are Cæsar's; and to God, the things that are God's. Credo.

OFFERTORY. *Esther 14: 12, 13*

Recordáre mei, Dómine, omni potentátui dóminans: et da sermónem rectum in os meum, ut pláceant verba mea in conspéctu príncipis. ℣. *Evérte cor ejus in ódium repugnántium nobis et in eos, qui conséntiunt eis: nos autem líbera in manu tua, Deus noster, in ætérnum.* ℣. *Recordáre, quod stéterim in conspéctu tuo, ut lóquerer pro eis bonum et avérterem indignatiónem tuam ab eis.*

REMEMBER me, O Lord, Thou Who rulest above all power; and give a well-ordered speech in my mouth, that my words may be pleasing in the sight of the prince. ℣. *Turn his heart to the hatred of our enemy, and the rest that consent to him: but deliver us by Thy hand, our God, for ever.* ℣. *Remember that I have stood in Thy sight, to speak good for them, and to turn away Thine indignation from them.*

SECRET.

Da, miséricors Deus: ut hæc salutáris oblátio et a própriis nos reátibus indesinénter expédiat, et ab ómnibus tueátur advérsis. Per Dóminum.

Grant, O merciful God, that this saving oblation may forever rid us of our own guilt and defend us from all adversities. Through our Lord.

COMMUNION. *Ps 16: 6*

Ego clamávi, quóniam exaudísti me, Deus: inclína aurem tuam et exáudi verba mea. (Ps 16: 1) ℣. *Exáudi, Dómine, justítiam meam; inténde deprecatiónem meam.*

I HAVE CRIED, for Thou, O God, hast heard me: O incline Thine ear unto me, and hear my words. ℣. *Hear, O Lord, my just complaint: do not spurn my cry for aid.*

POSTCOMMUNION.

Súmpsimus, Dómine, sacri dona mystérii, humíliter deprecántes: ut, quæ in tui commemoratiónem nos fácere præcepísti, in nostræ profíciant infirmitátis auxílium: Qui vivis.

We have taken the gifts of the sacred mystery, O Lord, humbly imploring that what Thou hast bidden us do in commemoration of Thee may avail unto the help of our infirmity. Who livest.

In those years which have only twenty-three Sundays after Pentecost, the following Mass is replaced by "The Last Sunday after Pentecost."

—*Twenty-third Sunday after Pentecost*— *II Classis.*

INTROIT. *Jer 29: 11, 12, 14*

THE LORD saith: I entertain thoughts of peace, not of affliction: you shall call upon Me, and I will hear you; and I will bring back your captive people from all places. (Ps 84: 2) Thou, O Lord, hast blessed Thy land: Thou hast brought back the captive children of Jacob. ℣. Glory.

Dicit Dóminus: Ego cógito cogitatiónes pacis, et non afflictiónis: invocábitis me, et ego exáudiam vos: et redúcam captivitátem vestram de cunctis locis. ℣. Benedixísti, Dómine, terram tuam: avertísti captivitátem Jacob. ℣. Glória Patri.

COLLECT.

Remit, we beseech Thee, O Lord, the sins of Thy people, that by Thy kindness we may be delivered from the trammels of our sins, in which, through our frailty, we have become entangled. Through our Lord.

Absólve, quǽsumus, Dómine, tuórum delícta populórum: ut a peccatórum néxibus, quæ pro nostra fragilitáte contráximus, tua benignitáte liberémur. Per Dóminum.

EPISTLE. *Philip 3: 17-21; 4: 1-3*

BRETHREN, be ye followers of me, and observe them who walk so as you have our model. For many walk, of whom I have told you often (and now tell you weeping) that they are enemies of the cross of Christ; whose end is destruction, whose God is their belly, and whose glory is in their shame; who mind earthly things. But our conversation is in heaven; from whence also we look for the Savior, our Lord Jesus Christ, Who will reform the body of our lowness, made like to the body of His glory, according to the operation whereby also He is able to subdue all things unto Himself. Therefore, my brethren, dearly beloved, and most desired, my joy and my crown: so stand fast in the Lord, my dearly beloved: I beg of Evodia, and I beseech Syntyche to be of one mind in the Lord: and I entreat thee also, my sincere companion, help those women who have labored with me in the gospel with Clement and the rest of my fellow-laborers, whose names are in the book of life.

Fratres: Imitatóres mei estóte, et observáte eos, qui ita ámbulant, sicut habétis formam nostram. Multi enim ámbulant, quos sæpe dicébam vobis (nunc autem et flens dico) inimícos Crucis Christi: quorum finis intéritus: quorum Deus venter est: et glória in confusióne ipsórum, qui terréna sápiunt. Nostra autem conversátio in cælis est: unde étiam Salvatórem exspectámus, Dóminum nostrum Jesum Christum, qui reformábit corpus humilitátis nostræ, configurátum córpori claritátis suæ, secúndum operatiónem, qua étiam possit subjícere sibi ómnia. Itaque, fratres mei caríssimi et desideratíssimi, gáudium meum et coróna mea: sic state in Dómino, caríssimi. Evódiam rogo et Sýntychen déprecor idípsum sápere in Dómino. Etiam rogo et te, germáne compar, ádjuva illas, quæ mecum laboravérunt in Evangélio cum Cleménte et céteris adjutóribus meis, quorum nómina sunt in libro vitæ.

GRADUAL & ALLELUIA. *Ps 43: 8-9 & Ps 129: 1-2*

THOU HAST delivered us, O Lord, from them that afflict us: and hast put them to shame that hate us. ℣. In God we will glory all the day; and in Thy name we will give praise for ever.

Liberásti nos, Dómine, ex affligéntibus nos: et eos, qui nos odérunt, confudísti. ℣. In Deo laudábimur tota die, et in nómine tuo confitébimur in sǽcula.

Allelúja, allelúja. ℣. De profúndis clamávi ad te, Dómine: Dómine, exáudi oratiónem meam. Allelúja.

Alleluia, alleluia. ℣. From the depths I have cried to Thee, O Lord: Lord, hear my prayer. Alleluia.

GOSPEL. *Matt 9: 18-26*

In illo témpore: Loquénte Jesu ad turbas, ecce, princeps unus accéssit et adorábat eum, dicens: Dómine, fília mea modo defúncta est: sed veni, impóne manum tuam super eam, et vivet. Et surgens Jesus sequebátur eum et discípuli ejus. Et ecce múlier, quæ sánguinis fluxum patiebátur duódecim annis, accéssit retro et tétigit fímbriam vestiménti ejus. Dicébat enim intra se: Si tetígero tantum vestiméntum ejus, salva ero. At Jesus convérsus et videns eam, dixit: Confíde, fília, fides tua te salvam fecit. Et salva facta est múlier ex illa hora. Et cum venísset Jesus in domum príncipis, et vidísset tibícines et turbam tumultuántem, dicebat: Recédite: non est enim mórtua puélla, sed dormit. Et deridébant eum. Et cum ejécta esset turba, intrávit et ténuit manum ejus. Et surréxit puélla. Et éxiit fama hæc in univérsam terram illam.

As Jesus was speaking to the multitudes...

BEHOLD A CERTAIN RULER came up, and adored Him, saying, Lord, my daughter is even now dead; but come lay Thy hand upon her, and she shall live. And Jesus, rising up, followed him with His disciples. And behold a woman, who was troubled with an issue of blood twelve years, came behind Him, and touched the hem of His garment. For she said within herself, If I shall touch only His garment, I shall be healed. But Jesus turning and seeing her, said, Be of good heart, daughter, thy faith hath made thee whole. And the woman was made whole from that hour. And when Jesus was come into the house of the ruler, and saw the minstrels and the multitude making a tumult, He said, Give place; for the girl is not dead, but sleepeth. And they laughed Him to scorn. And when the multitude was put forth, He went in, and took her by the hand. And the maid arose. And the fame hereof went abroad into all that country. CREDO.

OFFERTORY. *Ps 129: 1-2*

De profúndis clamávi ad te, Dómine: Dómine, exáudi oratiónem meam: de profúndis clamávi ad te, Dómine. ℣. *Fiant aures tuæ intendéntes in oratiónem servi tui.* ℣. *Si iniquitátes observáveris, Dómine, Dómine, quis sustinébit?*

FROM the depths I have cried out to Thee, O Lord; Lord, hear my prayer: from the depths I have cried out to Thee, O Lord. ℣. *Let Thine ears be attentive to the voice of Thy servant.* ℣. *If Thou, O Lord, wilt keep record of our iniquities, Master, who has strength to bear it?*

SECRET.

Pro nostræ servitútis augménto sacrifícium tibi, Dómine, laudis offérimus: ut, quod imméritis contulísti, propítius exsequáris. Per Dóminum.

We offer Thee, O Lord, the sacrifice of praise for the increase of our service, that Thou mayest graciously complete that which, for no merit of ours, Thou hast granted unto us. Through our Lord.

COMMUNION. *Mark 11: 24*

Amen, dico vobis, quidquid orántes pétitis, crédite, quia accipiétis, et fiet vobis. (Luke 11: 9) ℣. *Pétite, et dábitur vobis; quærite, et inveniétis.*

—ALBI|1047 • Circa 1047AD

AMEN I say to you, whatsoever you ask when you pray, believe that you shall receive, and it shall be done to you. ℣. *Ask, and the gift will come; seek, and you shall find.*

POSTCOMMUNION.

We pray Thee, O almighty God, that Thou wilt not suffer to be overcome by human dangers those to whom Thou grantest participation in things that are divine. Through our Lord.

Quǽsumus, omnípotens Deus: ut, quos divína tríbuis participatióne gaudére, humánis non sinas subjacére perículis. Per Dóminum.

The following Mass is always said on the Last Sunday after Pentecost—that is to say, the final Sunday before the First Sunday of Advent.

—*The Last Sunday after Pentecost*—

II Classis.

INTROIT. *Jer 29: 11, 12, 14*

THE LORD SAITH: I entertain thoughts of peace, not of affliction: you shall call upon Me, and I will hear you; and I will bring back your captive people from all places. (Ps 84: 2) Thou, O Lord, hast blessed Thy land: Thou hast brought back the captive children of Jacob. ℣. Glory.

Dicit Dóminus: Ego cógito cogitatiónes pacis, et non afflictiónis: invocábitis me, et ego exáudiam vos: et redúcam captivitátem vestram de cunctis locis. ℣. Benedixísti, Dómine, terram tuam: avertísti captivitátem Jacob. ℣. Glória Patri.

COLLECT.

Stir up, we beseech Thee, O Lord, the wills of Thy faithful, that, by more earnestly following after the fruit of the divine work, they may the more abundantly partake of Thy mercies. Through our Lord.

Excita, quǽsumus. Dómine, tuórum fidélium voluntátes: ut, divíni óperis fructum propénsius exsequéntes; pietátis tuæ remédia majóra percípiant. Per Dóminum.

EPISTLE. *Col 1: 9-14*

BRETHREN: We cease not to pray for you, and to beg that you may be filled with the knowledge of the will of God, in all wisdom and spiritual understanding; that you may walk worthy of God, in all things pleasing, being fruitful in every good work, and increasing in the knowledge of God; strengthened with all might according to the power of His glory, in all patience and long-suffering with joy; giving thanks to God the Father, Who hath made us worthy to be partakers of the lot of the saints in light; Who hath delivered us from the power of darkness, and hath translated us into the kingdom of the Son of His love, in Whom we have redemption through His blood, the remission of sins.

Fratres: Non cessámus pro vobis orántes et postulántes, ut impleámini agnitióne voluntátis Dei, in omni sapiéntia et intelléctu spiritáli: ut ambulétis digne Deo per ómnia placéntes: in omni ópere bono fructificántes, et crescéntes in sciéntia Dei: in omni virtúte confortáti secúndum poténtiam claritátis ejus in omni patiéntia, et longanimitáte cum gáudio, grátias agentes Deo Patri, qui dignos nos fecit in partem sortis sanctórum in lúmine: qui erípuit nos de potestáte tenebrárum, et tránstulit in regnum Fílii dilectiónis suæ, in quo habémus redemptiónem per sánguinem ejus, remissiónem peccatórum.

GRADUAL & ALLELUIA. *Ps 43: 8-9 & Ps 129: 1-2*

Liberásti nos, Dómine, ex affligéntibus nos: et eos, qui nos odérunt, confudísti. ℣. In Deo laudábimur tota die, et in nómine tuo confitébimur in sǽcula.

Allelúja, allelúja. ℣. De profúndis clamávi ad te, Dómine: Dómine, exáudi oratiónem meam. Allelúja.

THOU HAST delivered us, O Lord, from them that afflict us: and hast put them to shame that hate us. ℣. In God we will glory all the day; and in Thy name we will give praise for ever.

Alleluia, alleluia. ℣. From the depths I have cried to Thee, O Lord: Lord, hear my prayer. Alleluia.

GOSPEL.
Matt 24: 15-35

In illo témpore: Dixit Jesus discípulis suis: Cum vidéritis abominatiónem desolatiónis, quæ dicta est a Daniéle Prophéta, stantem in loco sancto: qui legit, intéllegat: tunc qui in Judǽa sunt, fúgiant ad montes: et qui in tecto, non descéndat tóllere áliquid de domo sua: et qui in agro, non revertátur tóllere túnicam suam. Væ autem prægnántibus et nutriéntibus in illis diébus. Oráte autem, ut non fiat fuga vestra in híeme vel sábbato. Erit enim tunc tribulátio magna, qualis non fuit ab inítio mundi usque modo, neque fiet. Et nisi breviáti fuíssent dies illi, non fíeret salva omnis caro: sed propter eléctos breviabúntur dies illi.

At that time, Jesus said to His disciples:

WHEN you shall see the abomination of desolation, which was spoken of by Daniel the prophet, standing in the holy place; he that readeth, let him understand: then they that are in Judea, let them flee to the mountains; and he that is on the housetop, let him not come down to take anything out of his house; and he that is in the field, let him not go back to take his coat. And woe to them that are with child, and that give suck, in those days. But pray that your flight be not in the winter, or on the sabbath: for there shall be then great tribulation, such as has not been found from the beginning of the world until now, neither shall be: and unless those days had been shortened, no flesh should be saved; but for the sake of the elect, those days shall be shortened.

Tunc si quis vobis díxerit: Ecce, hic est Christus, aut illic: nolíte crédere. Surgent enim pseudochrísti et pseudoprophétæ, et dabunt signa magna et prodígia, ita ut in errórem inducántur (si fíeri potest) étiam elécti. Ecce, prædíxi vobis. Si ergo díxerint vobis: Ecce, in desérto est, nolíte exíre: ecce, in penetrálibus, nolíte crédere. Sicut enim fulgur exit ab Oriénte et paret usque in Occidéntem: ita erit et advéntus Fílii hóminis. Ubicúmque fúerit corpus, illic congregabúntur et áquilæ.

Then if any man shall say to you, Lo, here is Christ, or there; do not believe him: for there shall arise false Christs and false prophets, and shall show great signs and wonders, insomuch as to deceive (if possible) even the elect. Behold, I have told it to you beforehand: if they therefore shall say to you, Behold, He is in the desert, go ye not out; behold, He is in the closets, believe it not. For as lightning cometh out of the east, and appeareth even into the west, so shall also the coming of the Son of man be. Wheresoever the body shall be, there shall the eagles also be gathered together.

Statim autem post tribulatiónem diérum illórum sol obscurábitur, et luna non dabit lumen suum, et stellæ cadent de cælo, et virtútes cælórum commovebúntur: et tunc parébit signum Fílii hóminis in cælo: et tunc plangent omnes tribus terræ: et vidé-

And immediately after the tribulation of those days, the sun shall be darkened, and the moon shall not give her light, and the stars shall fall from heaven, and the powers of heaven shall be moved; and then shall appear the sign of the Son of man in heaven, and then shall all the tribes of the earth mourn; and they shall see the Son of man coming in the clouds of heaven with much power and majesty: and He shall send His angels with a trumpet and a great voice and they shall gather together His elect from the four winds, from the farthest parts of the heavens to the utmost bounds of them. And from the fig-tree learn a parable: when the branch thereof is now tender, and the leaves come forth, you know that summer is nigh. So you also, when you shall see all these things, know ye that it is nigh even at the doors. Amen I say to you, that this generation shall not pass till all these things be done. Heaven and earth shall pass away, but My words shall not pass away. CREDO.

bunt Fílium hominis veniéntem in núbibus cæli cum virtúte multa et majestáte. Et mittet Angelos suos cum tuba et voce magna: et congregábunt electos ejus a quátuor ventis, a summis cælórum usque ad términos eórum. Ab árbore autem fici díscite parábolam: Dum jam ramus ejus tener túerit et fólia nata, scitis, quia prope est æstas: ita et vos cum vidéritis hæc ómnia, scitóte, quia prope est in jánuis. Amen, dico vobis, quia non præteríbit generátio hæc, donec ómnia hæc fiant. Cælum et terra transíbunt, verba autem mea non præteríbunt.

OFFERTORY. *Ps 129: 1-2*

FROM the depths I have cried out to Thee, O Lord; Lord, hear my prayer: from the depths I have cried out to Thee, O Lord. ℣. *Let Thine ears be attentive to the voice of Thy servant.* ℣. *If Thou, O Lord, wilt keep record of our iniquities, Master, who has strength to bear it?*

De profúndis clamávi ad te, Dómine: Dómine, exáudi oratiónem meam: de profúndis clamávi ad te, Dómine. ℣. *Fiant aures tuæ intendéntes in oratiónem servi tui.* ℣. *Si iniquitátes observáveris, Dómine, Dómine, quis sustinébit?*

SECRET.

Be propitious, O Lord, to our supplications, and accept the offerings and prayers of Thy people: turn all our hearts unto Thee, that, being delivered from earthly desires, we may pass on to the enjoyments of heaven. Through our Lord.

Propítius esto, Dómine, supplicatiónibus nostris: et, pópuli tui oblatiónibus precibúsque suscéptis, ómnium nostrum ad te corda convérte; ut, a terrénis cupiditátibus liberáti, ad cæléstia desidéria transeámus. Per Dóminum.

COMMUNION. *Mark 11: 24*

AMEN I say to you, whatsoever you ask when you pray, believe that you shall receive, and it shall be done to you. ℣. *Ask, and the gift will come; seek, and you shall find.*

Amen, dico vobis, quidquid orántes pétitis, crédite, quia accipiétis, et fiet vobis. (Luke 11: 9) ℣. *Pétite, et dábitur vobis; quǽrite, et inveniétis.*
—ALBI|1047 • Circa 1047AD

POSTCOMMUNION.

Grant us, we beseech Thee, O Lord, that, through this sacrament which we have received, whatever is evil in our hearts may be restored by its gift of healing. Through our Lord.

Concéde nobis, quǽsumus, Dómine: ut per hæc sacraménta quæ súmpsimus, quidquid in nostra mente vitiósum est, ipsórum medicatiónis dono curétur. Per Dóminum.

This communion antiphon does not come from a psalm. In such cases, the singers often took additional verses from the Introit, as 239LAON|877 seems to indicate. Another common practice was to take verses from Psalm 33, "the unvarying Communion-chant which in all Masses accompanied the administration of the Holy Eucharist" for the earliest Catholic liturgies {Wagner p103}. However, Psalm 33 was not chosen in this instance. ALBI|1047 chose a verse from the Gospel of Saint Luke. HELMST|1026 gave several possibilities, including the ninth verse of Psalm 60. The most common choice was Psalm 129 (also chosen for the Offertory and Alleluia Verse); cf. 376SANGALL|1052, BAMBERG6LIT|905, 4951STEVEN|1128, and STMAUR|1079.

Year's End Feasts

2021 Anno Domini

24 Oct. • 22nd Sunday after Pentecost
31 Oct. • Feast of Christ the King
— *Replaces the 23rd Sunday after Pentecost*
7 Nov. • Dominica V quæ superfuit Post Epiphaniam
14 Nov. • Dominica VI quæ superfuit Post Epiphaniam
21 Nov. • Last Sunday after Pentecost

2022 Anno Domini

30 Oct. • Feast of Christ the King
— *Replaces the 21st Sunday after Pentecost*
6 Nov. • 22nd Sunday after Pentecost
13 Nov. • 23rd Sunday after Pentecost
20 Nov. • Last Sunday after Pentecost

2023 Anno Domini

29 Oct. • Feast of Christ the King
— *Replaces the 22nd Sunday after Pentecost*
5 Nov. • 23rd Sunday after Pentecost
12 Nov. • Dominica V quæ superfuit Post Epiphaniam
19 Nov. • Dominica VI quæ superfuit Post Epiphaniam
26 Nov. • Last Sunday after Pentecost

2024 Anno Domini

20 Oct. • 22nd Sunday after Pentecost
27 Oct. • Feast of Christ the King
— *Replaces the 23rd Sunday after Pentecost*
3 Nov. • Dominica IV quæ superfuit Post Epiphaniam
10 Nov. • Dominica V quæ superfuit Post Epiphaniam
17 Nov. • Dominica VI quæ superfuit Post Epiphaniam
24 Nov. • Last Sunday after Pentecost

2025 Anno Domini

2 Nov. • 21st Sunday after Pentecost
— *All Souls Day is transferred to Monday*
9 Nov. • Dedic. Our Savior's Basilica (S. John Lateran)
— *Replaces the 22nd Sunday after Pentecost*
16 Nov. • 23rd Sunday after Pentecost
23 Nov. • Last Sunday after Pentecost

2026 Anno Domini

18 Oct. • 21st Sunday after Pentecost
25 Oct. • Feast of Christ the King
— *Replaces the 22nd Sunday after Pentecost*
1 Nov. • Feast of All Saints
— *Replaces the 23rd Sunday after Pentecost*
8 Nov. • Dominica V quæ superfuit Post Epiphaniam
15 Nov. • Dominica VI quæ superfuit Post Epiphaniam
22 Nov. • Last Sunday after Pentecost

2027 Anno Domini

17 Oct. • 22nd Sunday after Pentecost
24 Oct. • 23rd Sunday after Pentecost
31 Oct. • Feast of Christ the King
— *Replaces Dominica IV quæ superfuit Post Epiphaniam*
7 Nov. • Dominica V quæ superfuit Post Epiphaniam
14 Nov. • Dominica VI quæ superfuit Post Epiphaniam
21 Nov. • Last Sunday after Pentecost

2028 Anno Domini

5 Nov. • 22nd Sunday after Pentecost
12 Nov. • 23rd Sunday after Pentecost
19 Nov. • Dominica VI quæ superfuit Post Epiphaniam
26 Nov. • Last Sunday after Pentecost

2029 Anno Domini

21 Oct. • 22nd Sunday after Pentecost
28 Oct. • Feast of Christ the King
— *Replaces the 23rd Sunday after Pentecost*
4 Nov. • Dominica IV quæ superfuit Post Epiphaniam
11 Nov. • Dominica V quæ superfuit Post Epiphaniam
18 Nov. • Dominica VI quæ superfuit Post Epiphaniam
25 Nov. • Last Sunday after Pentecost

2030 Anno Domini

10 Nov. • 22nd Sunday after Pentecost
17 Nov. • 23rd Sunday after Pentecost
24 Nov. • Last Sunday after Pentecost

2031 Anno Domini

26 Oct. • Feast of Christ the King
— *Replaces the 21st Sunday after Pentecost*
2 Nov. • 22nd Sunday after Pentecost
— *All Souls Day is transferred to Monday*
9 Nov. • Dedic. Our Savior's Basilica (S. John Lateran)
— *Replaces the 23rd Sunday after Pentecost*
16 Nov. • Dominica VI quæ superfuit Post Epiphaniam
23 Nov. • Last Sunday after Pentecost

2032 Anno Domini

17 Oct. • 22nd Sunday after Pentecost
24 Oct. • 23rd Sunday after Pentecost
31 Oct. • Feast of Christ the King
— *Replaces Dominica IV quæ superfuit Post Epiphaniam*
7 Nov. • Dominica V quæ superfuit Post Epiphaniam
14 Nov. • Dominica VI quæ superfuit Post Epiphaniam
21 Nov. • Last Sunday after Pentecost

2033 Anno Domini

6 Nov. • 22nd Sunday after Pentecost
13 Nov. • 23rd Sunday after Pentecost
20 Nov. • Last Sunday after Pentecost

2034 Anno Domini

22 Oct. • 21st Sunday after Pentecost
29 Oct. • Feast of Christ the King
— *Replaces the 22nd Sunday after Pentecost*
5 Nov. • 23rd Sunday after Pentecost
12 Nov. • Dominica V quæ superfuit Post Epiphaniam
19 Nov. • Dominica VI quæ superfuit Post Epiphaniam
26 Nov. • Last Sunday after Pentecost

2035 Anno Domini

14 Oct. • 22nd Sunday after Pentecost
21 Oct. • 23rd Sunday after Pentecost
28 Oct. • Feast of Christ the King
— *Replaces Dominica III quæ superfuit Post Epiphaniam*
4 Nov. • Dominica IV quæ superfuit Post Epiphaniam
11 Nov. • Dominica V quæ superfuit Post Epiphaniam
18 Nov. • Dominica VI quæ superfuit Post Epiphaniam
25 Nov. • Last Sunday after Pentecost

This Mass is identical to the Fourth Sunday after Epiphany, except that the Introit, Gradual & Alleluia, Offertory, and Communion come from the Last Sunday after Pentecost.

— *Dominica IV quæ superfuit post Epiphaniam* —

II Classis.

INTROIT. *Jer 29: 11, 12, 14*

THE LORD saith: I entertain thoughts of peace, not of affliction: you shall call upon Me, and I will hear you; and I will bring back your captive people from all places. (Ps 84: 2) Thou, O Lord, hast blessed Thy land: Thou hast brought back the captive children of Jacob. ℣. Glory.

Dicit Dóminus: Ego cógito cogitatiónes pacis, et non afflictiónis: invocábitis me, et ego exáudiam vos: et redúcam captivitátem vestram de cunctis locis. ℣. Benedixísti, Dómine, terram tuam: avertísti captivitátem Jacob. ℣. Glória Patri.

COLLECT.

O God, Who knowest that we are beset by perils so great as to be unendurable because of our human frailty, grant us health of mind and body, so that by Thine assistance we may conquer the things with which we are afflicted because of our sins. Through our Lord.

Deus, qui nos, in tantis perículis constitútos, pro humána scis fragilitáte non posse subsístere: da nobis salútem mentis et córporis; ut ea, quæ pro peccátis nostris pátimur, te adjuvánte vincámus. Per Dóminum.

EPISTLE. *Rom 13: 8-10*

BRETHREN, owe no man any thing, but to love one another; for he that loveth his neighbor hath fulfilled the law. For thou shalt not commit adultery, thou shalt not kill, thou shalt not steal, thou shalt not bear false witness, thou shalt not covet, and if there be any other commandment, it is comprised in this word, thou shalt love thy neighbor as thyself. The love of our neighbor worketh no evil. Love, therefore, is the fulfilling of the law.

Fratres: Némini quidquam debeátis, nisi ut ínvicem diligátis: qui enim díligit próximum, legem implévit. Nam: Non adulterábis, Non occídes, Non furáberis, Non falsum testimónium dices, Non concupísces: et si quod est áliud mandátum, in hoc verbo instaurátur: Díliges próximum tuum sicut teípsum. Diléctio próximi malum non operátur. Plenitúdo ergo legis est diléctio.

GRADUAL & ALLELUIA. *Ps 43: 8-9 & Ps 129: 1-2*

THOU HAST delivered us, O Lord, from them that afflict us: and hast put them to shame that hate us. ℣. In God we will glory all the day; and in Thy name we will give praise for ever.
Alleluia, alleluia. ℣. From the depths I have cried to Thee, O Lord: Lord, hear my prayer. Alleluia.

Liberásti nos, Dómine, ex affligéntibus nos: et eos, qui nos odérunt, confudísti. ℣. In Deo laudábimur tota die, et in nómine tuo confitébimur in sǽcula.

Allelúja, allelúja. ℣. De profúndis clamávi ad te, Dómine: Dómine, exáudi oratiónem meam. Allelúja.

GOSPEL. *Matt 8: 23-27*

In illo témpore: Ascendénte Jesu in navículam, secúti sunt eum discípuli ejus: et ecce, motus magnus factus est in mari, ita ut navícula operirétur flúctibus, ipse vero dormiébat. Et accessérunt ad eum discípuli ejus, et suscitavérunt eum, dicéntes: Dómine, salva nos, perímus. Et dicit eis Jesus: Quid tímidi estis, módicæ fídei? Tunc surgens, imperávit ventis et mari, et facta est tranquíllitas magna. Porro hómines miráti sunt, dicéntes: Qualis est hic, quia venti et mare obédiunt ei?

WHEN JESUS ENTERED into the ship, His disciples followed Him. And behold a great tempest arose in the sea, so that the ship was covered with waves, but He was asleep. And they came to Him, and roused Him, saying, Lord, save us, we perish. And Jesus saith to them, Why are ye fearful, O ye of little faith? Then rising up, He commanded the winds and the sea, and there came a great calm. But the men wondered, saying, What manner of man is this, for the winds and the sea obey Him? CREDO.

OFFERTORY. *Ps 129: 1-2*

De profúndis clamávi ad te, Dómine: Dómine, exáudi oratiónem meam: de profúndis clamávi ad te, Dómine. ℣. *Fiant aures tuæ intendéntes in oratiónem servi tui.* ℣. *Si iniquitátes observáveris, Dómine, Dómine, quis sustinébit?*

FROM the depths I have cried out to Thee, O Lord; Lord, hear my prayer: from the depths I have cried out to Thee, O Lord. ℣. *Let Thine ears be attentive to the voice of Thy servant.* ℣. *If Thou, O Lord, wilt keep record of our iniquities, Master, who has strength to bear it?*

SECRET.

Concéde, quǽsumus, omnípotens Deus: ut hujus sacrifícii munus oblátum fragilitátem nostram ab omni malo purget semper et múniat. Per Dóminum.

Grant, we beseech Thee, almighty God, that this sacrifice offered to Thee, may purge us of all evil and fortify our weak nature. Through our Lord.

COMMUNION. *Mark 11: 24*

Amen, dico vobis, quidquid orántes pétitis, crédite, quia accipiétis, et fiet vobis. (Luke 11: 9) ℣. *Pétite, et dábitur vobis; quǽrite, et inveniétis.*

—ALBI|1047 • Circa 1047AD

AMEN I say to you, whatsoever you ask when you pray, believe that you shall receive, and it shall be done to you. ℣. *Ask, and the gift will come; seek, and you shall find.*

POSTCOMMUNION.

Múnera tua nos, Deus, a delectatiónibus terrénis expédiant: et cæléstibus semper instáurent aliméntis. Per Dóminum.

May Thy gifts, O God, free us from the allurements of earthly things, and ever restore us with heavenly nourishment. Through our Lord.

This Mass is identical to the Fifth Sunday after Epiphany, except that the Introit, Gradual & Alleluia, Offertory, and Communion come from the Last Sunday after Pentecost.

—*Dominica V quæ superfuit post Epiphaniam*— *II Classis.*

INTROIT. *Jer 29: 11, 12, 14*

THE LORD saith: I entertain thoughts of peace, not of affliction: you shall call upon Me, and I will hear you; and I will bring back your captive people from all places. (Ps 84: 2) Thou, O Lord, hast blessed Thy land: Thou hast brought back the captive children of Jacob. ℣. Glory.

Dicit Dóminus: Ego cógito cogitatiónes pacis, et non afflictiónis: invocábitis me, et ego exáudiam vos: et redúcam captivitátem vestram de cunctis locis. ℣. Benedixísti, Dómine, terram tuam: avertísti captivitátem Jacob. ℣. Glória Patri.

COLLECT.

Keep Thy family, we beseech Thee, O Lord, with Thy continual mercy that, leaning only upon the hope of Thy heavenly grace, it may ever be defended by Thy protection. Through our Lord.

Famíliam tuam, quǽsumus, Dómine, contínua pietáte custódi: ut, quæ in sola spe grátiæ cæléstis innítitur, tua semper protectióne muniátur. Per Dóminum.

EPISTLE. *Col 3: 12-17*

BRETHREN, put ye on, as the elect of God, holy and beloved, the bowels of mercy, benignity, humility, modesty, patience; bearing with one another, and forgiving one another, if any have a complaint against another, even as the Lord hath forgiven you, so you also. But above all these things, have charity, which is the bond of perfection: and let the peace of Christ rejoice in your hearts, wherein also you are called in one body: and be ye thankful. Let the word of Christ dwell in you abundantly, in all wisdom; teaching and admonishing one another, in psalms, hymns, and spiritual canticles, singing in grace in your hearts to God. All whatsoever you do in word or in work, all things do ye in the name of the Lord Jesus Christ, giving thanks to God and the Father through Jesus Christ our Lord.

Fratres: Indúite vos sicut elécti Dei, sancti et dilecti, víscera misericórdiæ, benignitátem, humilitátem, modéstiam, patiéntiam: supportántes ínvicem, et donántes vobismetípsis, si quis advérsus áliquem habet querélam: sicut et Dóminus donávit vobis, ita et vos. Super ómnia autem hæc caritátem habéte, quod est vínculum perfectionis: et pax Christi exsúltet in córdibus vestris, in qua et vocáti estis in uno córpore: et grati estóte. Verbũ Christi hábitet in vobis abundánter, in omni sapiéntia, docéntes et commonéntes vosmetípsos psalmis, hymnis et cánticis spirituálibus, in grátia cantántes in córdibus vestris Deo. Omne, quodcúmque fácitis in verbo aut in ópere, ómnia in nómine Dómini Jesu Christi, grátias agéntes Deo et Patri per Jesum Christum, Dóminum nostrum.

GRADUAL & ALLELUIA. *Ps 43: 8-9 & Ps 129: 1-2*

THOU HAST delivered us, O Lord, from them that afflict us: and hast put them to shame that hate us. ℣. In God we will glory all the day; and in Thy name we will give praise for ever.

Liberásti nos, Dómine, ex affligéntibus nos: et eos, qui nos odérunt, confudísti. ℣. In Deo laudábimur tota die, et in nómine tuo confitébimur in sǽcula.

Allelúja, allelúja. ℣. De profúndis clamávi ad te, Dómine: Dómine, exáudi oratiónem meam. Allelúja.

Alleluia, alleluia. ℣. From the depths I have cried to Thee, O Lord: Lord, hear my prayer. Alleluia.

GOSPEL. *Matt 13: 24-30*

In illo témpore: Dixit Jesus turbis parábolam hanc: Símile factum est regnum cælórum hómini, qui seminávit bonum semen in agro suo. Cum autem dormírent hómines, venit inimícus ejus, et superseminávit zizánia in médio trítici, et ábiit. Cum autem crevísset herba et fructum fecísset, tunc apparuérunt et zizánia. Accedéntes autem servi patrisfamílias, dixérunt ei: Dómine, nonne bonum semen seminásti in agro tuo? Unde ergo habet zizánia? Et ait illis: Inimícus homo hoc fecit.

JESUS SPOKE this parable to the multitudes: The kingdom of heaven is likened to a man that sowed good seed in his field. But while men were asleep, his enemy came, and oversowed cockle among the wheat, and went his way. And when the blade was sprung up, and had brought forth fruit, then appeared also the cockle. And the servants of the good man of the house coming, said to him, Sir, didst thou not sow good seed in thy field? whence then hath it cockle? And he said to them, An enemy hath done this.

Servi autem dixérunt ei: Vis, imus, et collígimus ea? Et ait: Non: ne forte colligéntes zizánia eradicétis simul cum eis et tríticum. Sínite útraque créscere usque ad messem, et in témpore messis dicam messóribus: Collígite primum zizánia, et alligáte ea in fascículos ad comburéndum, tríticum autem congregáte in hórreum meum.

And the servants said to him, Wilt thou that we go and gather it up? And he said, No: lest perhaps gathering up the cockle you root up the wheat also together with it. Suffer both to grow until the harvest; and in the time of the harvest, I will say to the reapers, Gather up first the cockle, and bind it into bundles to burn, but the wheat gather ye into my barn. CREDO.

OFFERTORY. *Ps 129: 1-2*

De profúndis clamávi ad te, Dómine: Dómine, exáudi oratiónem meam: de profúndis clamávi ad te, Dómine. ℣. *Fiant aures tuæ intendéntes in oratiónem servi tui.* ℣. *Si iniquitátes observáveris, Dómine, Dómine, quis sustinébit?*

FROM the depths I have cried out to Thee, O Lord; Lord, hear my prayer: from the depths I have cried out to Thee, O Lord. ℣. *Let Thine ears be attentive to the voice of Thy servant.* ℣. *If Thou, O Lord, wilt keep record of our iniquities, Master, who has strength to bear it?*

SECRET.

Hóstias tibi, Dómine, placatiónis offérimus: ut et delícta nostra miserátus absólvas, et nutántia corda tu dírigas. Per Dóminum.

We offer Thee, O Lord, the sacrifice of reconciliation, that Thou mayest mercifully forgive our sins and direct our wavering hearts. Through our Lord.

COMMUNION. *Mark 11: 24*

Amen, dico vobis, quidquid orántes pétitis, crédite, quia accipiétis, et fiet vobis. (Luke 11: 9) ℣. *Pétite, et dábitur vobis; quǽrite, et inveniétis.*

—ALBI|1047 • Circa 1047AD

AMEN I say to you, whatsoever you ask when you pray, believe that you shall receive, and it shall be done to you. ℣. *Ask, and the gift will come; seek, and you shall find.*

POSTCOMMUNION.

We pray Thee, O almighty God, that we may receive the effect of that salvation of which we have received the pledge in these mysteries. Through our Lord.

Quǽsumus, omnípotens Deus: ut illíus salutáris capiámus efféctum, cujus per hæc mystéria pignus accépimus. Per Dóminum.

This Mass is identical to the Sixth Sunday after Epiphany, except that the Introit, Gradual & Alleluia, Offertory, and Communion come from the Last Sunday after Pentecost.

— *Dominica VI quæ superfuit post Epiphaniam* —

II Classis.

INTROIT. *Jer 29: 11, 12, 14*

THE LORD saith: I entertain thoughts of peace, not of affliction: you shall call upon Me, and I will hear you; and I will bring back your captive people from all places. (Ps 84: 2) Thou, O Lord, hast blessed Thy land: Thou hast brought back the captive children of Jacob. ℣. Glory.

Dicit Dóminus: Ego cógito cogitatiónes pacis, et non afflictiónis: invocábitis me, et ego exáudiam vos: et redúcam captivitátem vestram de cunctis locis. ℣. Benedixísti, Dómine, terram tuam: avertísti captivitátem Jacob. ℣. Glória Patri.

COLLECT.

Grant, we beseech Thee, almighty God, that, ever fixing our thoughts on reasonable things, we may both in word and in deed do what is pleasing to Thee. Through our Lord.

Præsta, quǽsumus, omnípotens Deus: ut, semper rationabília meditántes, quæ tibi sunt plácita, et dictis exsequámur et factis. Per Dóminum.

EPISTLE. *I Thess 1: 2-10*

BRETHREN, we give thanks to God for you all, making a remembrance of you in our prayers without ceasing; being mindful of the work of your faith, and labor, and charity, and of the enduring of the hope of our Lord Jesus Christ before God and our Father: knowing, brethren, beloved of God, your election; for our gospel hath not been unto you in word only, but in power also, and in the Holy Ghost, and in much fullness, as you know what manner of men we have been among you for your sakes. And you became followers of us and of the Lord; receiving the word in much tribulation, with joy of the Holy Ghost: so that you were made a pattern to all that believe, in Macedonia and in Achaia. For from you was spread abroad the word of the Lord, not only in Macedonia

Fratres: Grátias ágimus Deo semper pro ómnibus vobis, memóriam vestri faciéntes in oratiónibus nostris sine intermissióne, mémores óperis fídei vestræ, et labóris, et caritátis, et sustinéntiæ spei Dómini nostri Jesu Christi, ante Deum et Patrem nostrum: sciéntes, fratres, diléсti a Deo, electiónem vestram: quia Evangélium nostrum non fuit ad vos in sermóne tantum, sed et in virtúte, et in Spíritu Sancto, et in plenitúdine multa, sicut scitis quales fuérimus in vobis propter vos. Et vos imitatóres nostri facti estis, et Dómini, excipiéntes verbum in tribulatióne multa, cum gáudio Spíritus Sancti: ita ut facti sitis forma ómnibus credéntibus in Macedónia et in Achája. A vobis enim diffamátus est sermo Dómini, non solum in Macedónia et in Achája, sed et in omni loco fides vestra, quæ est ad Deum, profécta est, ita ut non sit nobis necésse quidquam loqui. Ipsi enim de nobis annúntiant, qualem intróitum habuérimus ad vos: et quómodo convérsi estis ad Deum a simulácris, servíre Deo vivo et vero, et exspectáre Fílium ejus de cælis (quem suscitávit ex mórtuis) Jesum, qui erípuit nos ab ira ventúra.

and Achaia, but also in every place, your faith which is towards God, is gone forth; so that we need not to speak any thing. For they themselves relate to us, what manner of entering in we had unto you; and how ye turned to God from idols, to serve the living and true God, and to wait for His Son from heaven (whom He raised from the dead), Jesus, Who hath delivered us from the wrath to come.

GRADUAL & ALLELUIA. *Ps 43: 8-9 & Ps 129: 1-2*

Liberásti nos, Dómine, ex affligéntibus nos: et eos, qui nos odérunt, confudísti. ℣. In Deo laudábimur tota die, et in nómine tuo confitébimur in sǽcula.

Allelúja, allelúja. ℣. De profúndis clamávi ad te, Dómine: Dómine, exáudi oratiónem meam. Allelúja.

THOU HAST delivered us, O Lord, from them that afflict us: and hast put them to shame that hate us. ℣. In God we will glory all the day; and in Thy name we will give praise for ever.
Alleluia, alleluia. ℣. From the depths I have cried to Thee, O Lord: Lord, hear my prayer. Alleluia.

GOSPEL.

Matt 13: 31-35

In illo témpore: Dixit Jesus turbis parábolam hanc: Símile est regnum cælórum grano sinápis, quod accípiens homo seminávit in agro suo: quod mínimum quidem est ómnibus semínibus: cum autem créverit, majus est ómnibus oléribus, et fit arbor, ita ut vólucres cæli véniant et hábitent in ramis ejus.

At that time, Jesus spoke this parable to the multitudes:

THE KINGDOM of heaven is like to a grain of mustard seed, which a man took and sowed in his field: which is the least indeed of all seeds; but when it is grown up, it is greater than all herbs, and becometh a tree; so that the birds of the air come, and dwell in the branches thereof.

Aliam parábolam locútus est eis: Símile est regnum cælórum ferménto, quod accéptum múlier abscóndit in farínæ satis tribus, donec fermentátum est totum. Hæc ómnia locútus est Jesus in parábolis ad turbas: et sine parábolis non loquebátur eis: ut implerétur quod dictum erat per Prophétam dicéntem: Apériam in parábolis os meum, eructábo abscóndita a constitutióne mundi.

Another parable He spoke to them: The kingdom of heaven is like to leaven, which a woman took and hid in three measures of meal, until the whole was leavened. All these things Jesus spoke in parables to the multitudes, and without parables He did not speak to them; that it might be fulfilled which was spoken by the prophet, saying, I will open my mouth in parables, I will utter things hidden from the foundation of the world. CREDO.

OFFERTORY. *Ps 129: 1-2*

De profúndis clamávi ad te, Dómine: Dómine, exáudi oratiónem meam: de profúndis clamávi ad te, Dómine.
℣. *Fiant aures tuæ intendéntes in oratiónem servi tui.* ℣. *Si iniquitátes observáveris, Dómine, Dómine, quis sustinébit?*

FROM the depths I have cried out to Thee, O Lord; Lord, hear my prayer: from the depths I have cried out to Thee, O Lord. ℣. *Let Thine ears be attentive to the voice of Thy servant.* ℣. *If Thou, O Lord, wilt keep record of our iniquities, Master, who has strength to bear it?*

SECRET.

May this oblation, O God, cleanse, renew, govern, and protect us, we beseech Thee. Through our Lord.

Hæc nos oblátio, Deus, mundet, quǽsumus, et rénovet, gubérnet et prótegat. Per Dóminum.

COMMUNION. *Mark 11: 24*

AMEN I say to you, whatsoever you ask when you pray, believe that you shall receive, and it shall be done to you. ℣. *Ask, and the gift will come; seek, and you shall find.*

Amen, dico vobis, quidquid orántes pétitis, crédite, quia accipiétis, et fiet vobis. (Luke 11: 9) ℣. *Pétite, et dábitur vobis; quǽrite, et inveniétis.*

—ALBI|1047 • Circa 1047AD

POSTCOMMUNION.

Being fed with celestial delights, we beseech Thee, O Lord, that we may ever hunger after those things by which we truly live. Through our Lord.

Cæléstibus, Dómine, pasti delíciis: quǽsumus; ut semper éadem, per quæ veráciter vívimus, appetámus. Per Dóminum.

This communion antiphon does not come from a psalm. In such cases, the singers often took additional verses from the Introit, as 239LAON|877 seems to indicate. Another common practice was to take verses from Psalm 33, which was—in the words of Dr. Peter Wagner—"the unvarying Communion-chant which in all Masses accompanied the administration of the Holy Eucharist" for the earliest Catholic liturgies. However, Psalm 33 was not chosen in this instance. ALBI|1047 chose a verse from the Gospel of Saint Luke. HELMST|1026 gave several possibilities, including the ninth verse of Psalm 60. The most common choice was Psalm 129 (also chosen for the Offertory and Alleluia Verse); cf. 376SANGALL|1052, BAMBERG6LIT|905, 4951STEVEN|1128, and STMAUR|1079.

I Classis.

— 8 December, Immaculate Conception —

IN CONCEPTIONE IMMACULATA BEATAE MARIAE VIRGINIS

INTROIT. *Is 61: 10*

Gaudens gaudébo in Dómino, et exsultábit ánima mea in Deo meo: quia índuit me vestiméntis salútis: et induménto justítiæ circúmdedit me, quasi sponsam ornátam monílibus suis. ℣. Exaltábo te, Dómine, quóniam suscepísti me: nec delectásti inimícos meos super me. ℣. Glória Patri.

GREATLY will I rejoice in the Lord, and my soul shall be joyful in my God: for He hath clothed me with the garments of salvation, and with the robe of justice He hath covered me, as a bride adorned with her jewels. (Ps 29: 2) I will extol Thee, O Lord, for Thou hast upheld me: and hast not made my enemies to rejoice over me. ℣. Glory.

COLLECT.

Deus, qui per immaculátam Vírginis Conceptiónem dignum Fílio tuo habitáculum præparásti: quæsumus; ut, qui ex morte ejúsdem Fílii tui prævísa eam ab omni labe præservásti, nos quoque mundos ejus intercessióne ad te perveníre concédas. Per eúmdem Dóminum.

O God, Who, by the Immaculate Conception of the Virgin, didst prepare a worthy dwelling for Thy Son, we beseech Thee that Thou, Who, by the death, foreseen by Thee, of the same Thy Son, didst preserve her from all stain, wilt grant us also, by her intercession, to come to Thee pure in heart. Through the same.

EPISTLE. *Prov 8: 22-35*

Dóminus possédit me in inítio viárum suárum, ántequam quidquam fáceret a princípio. Ab ætérno ordináta sum, et ex antíquis, ántequam terra fíeret. Nondum erant abýssi, et ego jam concépta eram: necdum fontes aquárum erúperant: necdum montes gravi mole constíterant: ante colles ego parturiébar: adhuc terram non fécerat et flúmina et cárdines orbis terræ. Quando præparábat cælos, áderam: quando certa lege et gyro vallábat abýssos: quando ǽthera firmábat sursum et librábat fontes aquárũ: quando circúmdabat mari términum suum et legẽ ponébat aquis, ne transírent fines suos: quando appendébat fundaménta terræ. Cum eo eram cuncta compónens: et delectábar per síngulos dies, ludens coram eo omni témpore: ludens in orbe terrárũ: et delíciæ meæ esse cum fíliis hóminum.

THE LORD possessed me in the beginning of His ways, before He made anything, from the beginning. I was set up from eternity, and of old, before the earth was made. The depths were not as yet, and I was already conceived; neither had the fountains of waters as yet sprung out; the mountains with their huge bulk had not as yet been established: before the hills I was brought forth; He had not yet made the earth, nor the rivers, nor the poles of the world. When He prepared the heavens, I was there; when with a certain law and compass He enclosed the depths; when He established the sky above, and poised the fountains of waters; when He compassed the sea with its bounds, and set a law to the waters that they should not pass their limits; when He balanced the foundations of the earth; I was with Him, forming all things, and was delighted every day, playing before Him at all times, playing in the world: and my delight is to be with the children of men.

Nunc ergo, fílii, audíte me: Beáti, qui custódiunt vias meas. Audíte disciplínam, et estóte sapiéntes, et nolíte abjícere eam. Beátus homo, qui audit

Now therefore, ye children, hear me: blessed are they that keep my ways. Hear instruction, and be wise, and refuse it not. Blessed is the man that heareth me, and

DAVID BROUGHT THE ARK OF GOD FROM THE HOUSE OF OBEDEDOM INTO THE CITY OF DAVID • II Samuel 6:12

SEDES SAPIENTIÆ

ET ADDUXIT ARCAM DEI DE DOMO OBEDEDOM ... (II Samuel 6:12)

TU GLORIA JERUSALEM; TU LAETITIA ISRAEL ... (Judith 15:10)

THEY ALL BLESSED HER, SAYING: THOU ART THE GLORY OF JERUSALEM, THOU ART THE JOY OF ISRAEL • Judith 15:10

TOTA PULCHRA ES MARIA, ET MACULA ORIGINALIS NON EST IN TE ✠

me et qui vígilat ad fores meas cotídie, et obsérvat ad postes óstii mei. Qui me invénerit, invéniet vitam et háuriet salútem a Dómino.

that watcheth daily at my gates, and waiteth at the posts of my doors. He that shall find me, shall find life, and shall have salvation from the Lord.

GRADUAL & ALLELUIA. *Judith 13: 23; 15: 10 & Cant 4: 7*

Benedícta es tu, Virgo María, a Dómino, Deo excélso, præ ómnibus muliéribus super terram. ℣. Tu glória Jerúsalem, tu lætítia Ísraël, tu honorificéntia pópuli nostri.
Allelúja, allelúja. ℣. Tota pulchra es, María: et mácula originális non est in te. Allelúja.

BLESSED art thou, O Virgin Mary, by the Lord, the most high God, above all women, upon the earth. ℣. Thou art the glory of Jerusalem, thou art the joy of Israel, thou art the honor of our people.
Alleluia, alleluia. ℣. Thou art all fair, O Mary, and there is in thee no stain of original sin. Alleluia.

GOSPEL. *Luke 1: 26-28*

In illo témpore: Missus est Ángelus Gábriël a Deo in civitátem Galilǽæ, cui nomen Názareth, ad Vírginem desponsátam viro, cui nomen erat Joseph, de domo David, et nomen Vírginis María. Et ingréssus Ángelus ad eam, dixit: Ave, grátia plena; Dóminus tecum: benedícta tu in muliéribus.

THE ANGEL GABRIEL was sent from God into a city of Galilee, called Nazareth, to a virgin espoused to a man whose name was Joseph, of the house of David: and the virgin's name was Mary. And the angel being come in, said unto her: Hail, full of grace, the Lord is with thee: blessed art thou among women. CREDO.

OFFERTORY. *Luke 1: 28*

Ave, María, grátia plena; Dóminus tecum: benedícta tu in muliéribus, allelúja. ℣. *Quómodo in me fiet hoc, quæ virum non cognósco? Spíritus Dómini supervéniet in te et virtus Altíssimi obumbrábit tibi.* ℣. *Ideóque, quod nascétur ex te Sanctum, vocábitur Fílius Dei.*

HAIL, MARY, full of grace; the Lord is with thee: blessed art thou among women. Alleluia. ℣. *How shall this be done, because I know not man? The Holy Ghost shall come upon thee, and the power of the most High shall overshadow thee.* ℣. *Thus this holy offspring of thine shall be called the Son of God.*

This Offertory is identical to the Offertory for the Fourth Sunday of Advent, except the Offertory for the Fourth Sunday of Advent adds: ET BENEDICTUS FRUCTUS VENTRIS TUI—— *"and blessèd is the fruit of thy womb."*

SECRET.

Salutárem hóstiam, quam in sollemnitáte immaculátæ Conceptiónis beátæ Vírginis Maríæ tibi, Dómine, offérimus, súscipe et præsta: ut, sicut illam tua grátia præveniénte ab omni labe immúnem profitémur; ita ejus intercessióne a culpis ómnibus liberémur. Per Dóminum.

Receive, O Lord, the saving oblation which we offer Thee on the solemnity of the Immaculate Conception of the Blessed Virgin Mary, and grant that, as we confess her to have been preserved, by Thy prevenient grace, from all taint of evil, so, through her intercession, we may be freed from all sin. Through our Lord.

The Preface of the Blessed Virgin Mary (page 191) follows the Secret.

COMMUNION. *Trad.*

GLORIOUS THINGS are spoken of thee, O Mary; for He that is mighty hath done great things unto thee. ℣. *He hath filled the hungry with good things; and the rich He hath sent empty away.*

Gloriósa dicta sunt de te, María: quia fecit tibi magna qui potens est. (Luke 1: 53) ℣. *Esuriéntes implévit bonis: et dívites dimísit inánes.*

POSTCOMMUNION.

May the sacrament which we have received, O Lord, our God, heal in us the wounds of that sin from which, by a singular privilege, Thou didst preserve immaculate the conception of blessed Mary. Through our Lord.

Sacraménta quæ súmpsimus, Dómine, Deus noster: illíus in nobis culpæ vúlnera réparent; a qua immaculátam beátæ Maríæ Conceptiónem singuláriter præservásti. Per Dóminum.

The Feast of the Immaculate Conception

On 8 December 1854, Blessed Pope Pius IX declared that Our Lady "in the first instance of her conception—by a singular privilege and grace granted by God, in view of the merits of Jesus Christ, the Savior of the human race—was preserved exempt from all stain of original sin." Before 1854, the feast had various formularies. A set of Propers assembled by Dom Josef Pothier in 1884 would eventually be adopted for the entire Church (in the *Editio Vaticana* of 1908). The Propers are all Neo-Gregorian. The Introit is based on the melody of *Vocem Jucunditatis* (Fifth Sunday of Easter). The Gradual is based on the melody of *Constitues* (29 June). The Alleluia melody comes from the 12th-century. The Offertory was composed by Dom Fonteinne, who served as choirmaster at Solesmes Abbey before Dom Pothier. The Communion melody is based on *Optimam Partem*, an ancient Communion for the Assumption. After the Second Vatican Council, the Propers for the Immaculate Conception were retained—in spite of the fact that they are Neo-Gregorian—because they had attained "universal use" according to the Praenotanda of the *Ordo Cantus Missae*.

CANDLEMAS • BLESSING OF CANDLES

The feast of the Purification of the Blessed Virgin Mary is celebrated as a feast of the Lord.
Festum Purificationis beatae Mariae Virginis habetur tamquam festum Domini.

[Editor's Note: On 26 September 1964, permission was given to use only one of the following prayers during the blessing (cf. *Inter Oecumenici* §76); similarly, on 9 February 1951 (*Dominicae Resurrectionis Vigiliam*), two of the three prayers for "blessing the new fire" on Holy Saturday had been eliminated.]

The Blessing of Candles • *De Benedictione Candelarum*
The Celebrant vests in a white Cope or without the chasuble, and goes with the ministers who are similarly vested to bless the candles, which are placed in the center before the Altar or on the Epistle side. Standing and facing the Altar, the priest chants without inflection, with his hands joined, the following prayers.
Sacerdos indutus pluviali albo, vel sine casula, cum ministris similiter indutis, procedit ad benedicendas candelas, in medio ante altare, vel ad latus Epistolae positas, et ipse, ibidem stans versus ad altare, dicit manibus iunctis in tono feriali:

℣. Dóminus vobíscum.
℟. Et cum spíritu tuo.
Orémus.

Dómine sancte, Pater omnípotens, ætérne Deus, qui ómnia ex níhilo creásti, et jussu tuo per ópera apum hunc liquórem ad perfectiónem cérei veníre fecísti: et qui hodiérna die petitiónem justi Simeónis implésti: te humíliter deprecámur; ut has candélas ad usus hóminum et sanitátem córporum et animárum, sive in terra sive in aquis, per invocatiónem tui sanctíssimi nóminis et per intercessiónem beátæ Maríæ semper Vírginis, cujus hódie festa devóte celebrántur, et per preces ómnium Sanctórum tuórum, bene✠dícere et sancti✠ficáre dignéris: et hujus plebis tuæ, quæ illas honorífice in mánibus desíderat portare teque cantándo laudáre, exáudias voces de cælo sancto tuo et de sede majestátis tuæ: et propítius sis ómnibus clamántibus ad te, quos redemísti pretióso Sánguine Fílii tui: Qui tecum vivit et regnat in sǽcula sæculórum. ℟. Amen.

℣. The Lord be with you.
℟. And with thy spirit.
Let us pray.

O HOLY LORD, Father almighty, eternal God, Who hast created all things out of nothing, and by Thy word hast caused this liquid through the work of bees to come to the perfection of wax, and Who on this day didst fulfil the petition of just Simeon; deign, we humbly beseech Thee, to bless ✠ and sanctify ✠ these candles for the uses of men, for the health of bodies and of souls, whether on the land or on the waters, by the invocation of Thy most holy name, and by the intercession of the blessed Mary ever virgin, whose festival we this day celebrate, and by the prayers of all Thy saints; and graciously, from Thy holy heaven and the seat of Thy majesty, hear the voices of this Thy people which desireth to carry these candles in their hands, unto Thy honor, and to praise Thee with singing; and be merciful to all who call upon Thee, whom Thou hast redeemed with the most precious blood of Thy Son, Who liveth and reigneth with Thee forever and ever. ℟. Amen.

Orémus.

Omnípotens sempitérne Deus, qui hodiérna die Unigénitum tuum ulnis sancti Simeónis in templo sancto tuo suscipiéndum præsentásti: tuam súpplices deprecámur cleméntiam; ut has candélas, quas nos fámuli tui, in tui nóminis magnificéntiam suscipiéntes, gestáre cúpimus luce accénsas, bene✠dícere et sancti✠ficáre atque lúmine supérnæ benedictiónis accéndere dignéris: quaténus eas tibi Dómino, Deo nostro, offeréndo digni, et sancto igne dulcíssimæ caritátis

Let us pray.

ALMIGHTY, everlasting God, Who on this day didst present Thine only-begotten Son to be taken in holy Simeon's arms in Thy holy temple, we humbly beseech Thy mercy that these candles which we, Thy servants, would take in our hands for the magnifying of Thy name, to carry them lighted, Thou wilt deign to bless ✠ and sanctify ✠ and to kindle with the light of Thy supernal benediction, so that by offering them to

AND WHEN THE DAYS OF HER PURIFICATION ARE EXPIRED, FOR A SON, OR FOR A DAUGHTER, SHE SHALL BRING TO THE DOOR OF THE TABERNACLE … (LEV 12: 6)

(Mal 3: 1) THE LORD SHALL COME TO HIS TEMPLE.

(Ps 47: 10) WE HAVE RECEIVED THY MERCY.

CUMQUE EXPLETI FUERINT DIES PURIFICATIONIS EJUS PRO FILIO … Lev 12: 6

ET IMMOLAVERUNT VITULUM ET OBTULERUNT PUERUM HELI. I Sam 1: 25

(Is 60: 1) THY LIGHT IS COME.

(Ex 13: 2) SANCTIFY UNTO ME EVERY FIRSTBORN.

AND THEY IMMOLATED A CALF, AND OFFERED THE CHILD TO HELI. AND ANNA SAID: I BESEECH THEE, MY LORD, AS THY SOUL LIVETH, MY LORD. (I SAM 1: 25)

tuæ succénsi, in templo sancto glóriæ tuæ repræsentári mereámur. Per eúmdem Dóminum. ℟. Amen.

Thee, our Lord God, we may deserve to be presented worthily, lighted with the holy fire of Thy most dear charity, in the holy temple of Thy glory. Through the same. ℟. Amen.

Orémus.

Dómine Jesu Christe, lux vera, quæ illúminas omnem hóminem veniéntem in hunc mundum: effúnde bene✠dictiónem tuam super hos céreos, et sancti✠fica eos lúmine grátiæ tuæ, et concéde propítius; ut, sicut hæc luminária igne visíbili accénsa noctúrnas depéllunt ténebras; ita corda nostra invisíbili igne, id est, Sancti Spíritus splendóre illustráta, ómnium vitiórum cæcitáte cáreant: ut, purgáto mentis óculo, ea cérnere possímus, quæ tibi sunt plácita et nostræ salúti utília; quaténus post hujus sǽculi caliginósa discrímina ad lucem indeficiéntem pervenire mereámur. Per te, Christe Jesu, Salvátor mundi, qui in Trinitáte perfécta vivis et regnas Deus, per ómnia sǽcula sæculórum. ℟. Amen.

Let us pray.

O **LORD JESUS CHRIST,** the true Light, Who enlightenest every man that cometh into this world, pour forth Thy blessing ✠ upon these waxen candles and sanctify ✠ them with the light of Thy grace; and be pleased to grant that, as these lights, kindled with visible fire, dispel the darkness of night, so our hearts, being enlightened with invisible fire, even the effulgence of the Holy Spirit, may be delivered from the blindness of every vice, that with the eye of the mind purified we may be able to discern those things which are pleasing to Thee and useful for our salvation; whereby, after the dark trials of this world, we may be found worthy to enter into the light that is never obscured; through Thee, Christ Jesus, Savior of the world, Who in perfect Trinity livest and reignest, God, world without end. ℟. Amen.

Orémus.

Omnípotens sempitérne Deus, qui per Móysen fámulum tuum puríssimum ólei liquórem ad luminária ante conspéctum tuum júgiter concinnánda præparári jussísti: bene✠dictiónis tuæ grátiam super hos céreos benígnus infúnde; quaténus sic adminístrent lumen extérius, ut, te donánte, lumen Spíritus tui nostris non desit méntibus intérius. Per Christum Dóminum nostrum. ℟. Amen.

Let us pray.

A**LMIGHTY,** eternal God, Who through Thy servant Moses didst order the purest of oil to be prepared for the continual furnishing of the lamps before Thy presence, graciously pour upon these waxen candles the grace of Thy benediction ✠, whereby they may so serve us for outward light that, by Thy gift, the inward light of the Spirit may not be wanting to our minds. Through Christ our Lord. ℟. Amen.

Orémus.

Dómine Jesu Christe, qui hodiérna die, in nostræ carnis substántia inter hómines appárens, a paréntibus in templo es præsentátus: quem Símeon venerábilis senex, lúmine Spíritus tui irradiátus, agnóvit, suscépit et benedíxit: præsta propítius; ut, ejúsdem Spíritus Sancti grátia illumináti atque edócti, te veráciter agnoscámus et fidéliter diligámus: Qui cum Deo Patre in unitáte ejúsdem Spíritus Sancti vivis et regnas Deus, per ómnia sǽcula sæculórum. ℟. Amen.

Let us pray.

O **LORD** Jesus Christ, Who on this day appearing among men in the substance of flesh wast presented by Thy parents in the temple, and Whom the venerable old man Simeon, being filled with the light of Thy Spirit, recognized, took up, and blessed, be pleased to grant that we, enlightened and taught by the grace of the same Holy Spirit, may know Thee rightly and love Thee faithfully. Who with God the Father livest and reignest in the unity of the same Holy Ghost, God, world without end. ℟. Amen.

After the prayers the Celebrant places incense in the thurible. Then he sprinkles the candles with holy water, saying the antiphon "Thou shalt sprinkle me," without chant and without the psalm. Then he incenses the candles three times.
Finitis orationibus, celebrans ponit incensum in thuribulo: deinde ter aspergit candelas aqua benedicta, dicendo antiphonam "Aspérges me," sine cantu et sine psalmo: et ter adolet incenso.

THOU shalt sprinkle me with hyssop, O Lord, and I shall be cleansed: Thou shalt wash me, and I shall be made whiter than snow.

Aspérges me, Dómine, hyssópo et mundábor: lavábis me, et super nivem dealbábor.

CANDLEMAS • DISTRIBUTION OF CANDLES

Distribution of Candles • *De Distributione Candelarum*
Next the senior cleric goes to the Altar and the Celebrant, without genuflecting, receives a candle from him. Then the Celebrant stands in the center before the Altar, turns toward the people, and distributes the candles, first to the senior cleric from whom he has received the candle, then to the vested Deacon and Subdeacon, and to the other clerics in order, one by one, and last of all to the laity. All kneel with the exception of prelates, if any are present. When the distribution of the candles begins, the choir sings as follows.
Tum dignior ex clero accedit ad altare, et ab eo celebrans accipit candelam, non genuflectens. Postea celebrans stans in medio ante altare, versus ad populum, distribuit candelas, primum digniori, a quo ipse acceperat; deinde diacono et subdiacono paratis, et aliis clericis singulatim per ordinem, ultimo laicis: omnibus genuflectentibus, exceptis Praelatis, si adsint. Et cum inceperit distribuere candelas, a choro cantatur:

ANTIPHON. *Luke 2:32*

℟. A light to the revelation of the gentiles, and the glory of Thy people Israel.

℟. Lumen ad revelatiónem géntium et glóriam plebis tuæ Ísraël.

This antiphon is repeated after each verse:

CANTICLE. *Luke 2: 29-31*

NOW THOU DOST dismiss Thy servant, O Lord, according to Thy word in peace. ℟. A light. —Because my eyes have seen Thy salvation. ℟. A light. —Which Thou hast prepared before the face of all peoples. ℟. A light.

[*The antiphons and canticle are repeated, if necessary, until the end of the distribution, and the conclusion is as follows:*]

—Glory be to the Father, and to the Son, and to the Holy Ghost. ℟. A light. —As it was in the beginning, is now, and ever shall be, world without end. Amen. ℟. A light.

Nunc dimíttis servum tuum, Dómine, secúndum verbum tuum in pace. ℟. Lumen. —Quia vidérunt óculi mei salutáre tuum. ℟. Lumen. —Quod parásti ante fáciem ómnium populorum. ℟. Lumen. [*Quæ si non sufficiant, repetantur quousque distributio finiatur; et clauditur cum:*] —Glória Patri, et Fílio, et Spirítui Sancto. ℟. Lumen. —Sicut erat in princípio, et nunc, et semper, et in sǽcula sæculórum. Amen. ℟. Lumen.

§45b of *Rubricarum Instructum* (25 July 1960) suppressed the antiphon ("Exsúrge Dómine, Ádjuva Nos") and "Flectámus Génua" which formerly took place at this time.

After the distribution of candles, the priest says:
His expletis, sacerdos dicit:

℣. The Lord be with you.
℟. And with thy spirit.

℣. Dóminus vobíscum.
℟. Et cum spíritu tuo.

Orémus.

Exáudi, quǽsumus, Dómine, plebem tuam: et, quæ extrinsécus ánnua tríbuis devotióne venerári, intérius ássequi grátiæ tuæ luce concéde. Per Christum, Dóminum nostrum. ℟. Amen.

Let us pray.

HARKEN to Thy people, we beseech Thee, O Lord; and what Thou dost give us year after year to venerate devoutly, outwardly, grant us to follow it inwardly with the light of Thy grace. Through our Lord. ℟. Amen.

CANDLEMAS • THE PROCESSION WITH CANDLES

The Procession • *De Processione*
First the Celebrant places incense in the thurible, and then the Deacon, turning to the people, says: "Let us set forth in peace." The choir replies: "In the name of Christ. Amen."
Primo celebrans ponit incensum in thuribulum: postea diaconus vertens se ad populum, dicit: "Procedámus in pace." Et chorus respondet: "In nómine Christi. Amen."

℣. Procedámus in pace.
℟. In nómine Christi. Amen.

LET US set forth in peace.
℟. In the name of Christ. Amen.

The thurifer goes first, carrying the thurible, followed by the vested Subdeacon, who carries the Cross between two acolytes with lighted candles, then the clergy in order, finally the Celebrant with the Deacon at his left. All hold lighted candles in their hands. The following antiphons are sung:
Praecedit thuriferarius cum thuribulo fumigante: deinde subdiaconus paratus, deferens crucem, medius inter duos acolythos cum candelabris accensis: sequitur clerus per ordinem, ultimo celebrans cum diacono a sinistris, omnes cum candelis accensis in manibus: et cantantur antiphonae sequentes:

FIRST ANTIPHON.

Adórna thálamum tuum, Sion, et súscipe Regem Christum: ampléctere Maríam, quæ est cæléstis porta: ipsa enim portat Regem glóriæ novi lúminis: subsístit Virgo, addúcens mánibus Fílium ante lucíferum génitum: quem accípiens Símeon in ulnas suas, prædicávit pópulis, Dóminum eum esse vitæ et mortis et Salvatórem mundi.

DECK thy bridal chamber, O Sion, and receive Christ, thy King; embrace Mary, who is the gate of heaven; for she carries the King of glory of the new light; a virgin, she standeth bringing in her hands the Son begotten before the daystar; and receiving Him in his arms, Simeon hath declared to the nations that He is the Lord of life and death, and Savior of the world.

SECOND ANTIPHON. *Luke 2: 26, 27, 28-29*

Respónsum accépit Símeon a Spíritu Sancto, non visúrum se mortem, nisi vidéret Christum Dómini: et cum indúcerent Púerum in templum, accépit eum in ulnas suas, et benedíxit Deum, et dixit: **Nunc dimíttis servum tuum, Dómine, in pace.** ℣. Cum indúcerent púerum Jesum parentes ejus, ut fácerent secúndum consuetúdinem legis pro eo, ipse accépit eum in ulnas suas.

SIMEON received an answer from the Holy Ghost, that he should not see death until he had seen the Christ of the Lord; and when they brought the Child into the temple he took Him in his arms, and blessed God, and said: NOW, O LORD, DOST THOU DISMISS THY SERVANT IN PEACE. ℣. When His parents brought the child Jesus into the temple, to do in His behalf according to the custom of the law, he took Him in his arms.

As the procession enters the church, the following is sung:
Et ingrediendo ecclesiam, cantatur:

RESPONSORY.

THEY OFFERED in His behalf a pair of turtledoves or two young pigeons. As it is written in the law of the Lord. ℣. After Mary's days of purification were fulfilled, according to the law of Moses, they carried Jesus to Jerusalem, to set Him before the Lord. As it is written in the law of the Lord. ℣. Glory be to the Father, and to the Son, and to the Holy Ghost. As it is written in the law of the Lord.

Obtulérunt pro eo Dómino par túrturum, aut duos pullos columbárum: Sicut scriptum est in lege Dómini. ℣. Postquam impléti sunt dies purgatiónis Maríæ, secúndum legem Móysi, tulérunt Jesum in Jerúsalem, ut sísterent eum Dómino. Sicut scriptum est in lege Dómini. ℣. Glória Patri, et Fílio, et Spirítui Sancto. Sicut scriptum est in lege Dómini.

If the blessing of candles and the procession cannot take place in the solemn form, because of the absence of sacred ministers, it is lawful to use the simple form, even without chant, provided that at least three servers assist the Celebrant.
Si candelarum benedictio et processio, ob defectum ministrorum sacrorum, forma solemni fieri nequeat, licet formam simplicem adhibere, etiam absque cantu, dummodo tres saltem ministrantes celebranti inserviant.

When the procession has been completed, the Celebrant and ministers put on the vestments for Mass.

Finita processione, celebrans et ministri accipiunt paramenta pro Missa.

In the Mass which follows the blessing of candles: the "Prayers at the Foot of the Altar" are omitted, as well as the prayers "Aufer a nobis" and "Orámus te, Domine." When the priest comes to the Altar, he immediately goes up to it and kisses it in the center.

In Missa, quae benedictionem candelarum sequitur, omittuntur psalmus "Iudica me, Deus" cum sua antiphona, necnon confessio cum absolutione, versibus sequentibus atque orationibus "Aufer a nobis" et "Orámus te, Dómine." Sacerdos igitur, cum ad altare accesserit, statim illud ascendit et osculatur in medio.

Today, during the Gospel, and also during the Canon, the blessed candle should be held lighted in the hand.

Candelae in manibus tenentur ad Evangelium et toto Canone.

—2 February, Purification of Our Lady—

II Classis.

IN PURIFICATIONE BEATAE MARIAE VIRGINIS

INTROIT. *Ps 47: 10-11*

WE HAVE received Thy mercy, O God, in the midst of Thy temple: according to Thy name, O God, so also is Thy praise unto the ends of the earth: Thy right hand is full of justice. (Ps 47: 2) Great is the Lord, and exceedingly to be praised: in the city of our God, in His holy mountain. ℣. Glory.

Suscépimus, Deus, misericórdiam tuam in médio templi tui: secúndum nomen tuum, Deus, ita et laus tua in fines terræ: justítia plena est déxtera tua. ℣. Magnus Dóminus, et laudábilis nimis: in civitáte Dei nostri, in monte sancto ejus. ℣. Glória Patri.

This Introit is identical to the Introit sung for the 10th Sunday after Pentecost.

COLLECT.

Omnípotens sempitérne Deus, majestátem tuam súpplices exorámus: ut, sicut unigénitus Fílius tuus hodiérna die cum nostræ carnis substántia in templo est præsentátus; ita nos fácias purificátis tibi méntibus præsentári. Per eúmdem Dóminum.

Almighty, eternal God, we humbly beseech Thy majesty that, as Thine only-begotten Son was this day presented in the temple in the substance of our flesh, so Thou mayest cause us to be presented to Thee with minds purified. Through the same.

EPISTLE. *Malachias 3: 1-4*

Hæc dicit Dóminus Deus: Ecce, ego mitto Angelum meum, et præparábit viam ante fáciem meam. Et statim véniet ad templum suum Dominátor, quem vos quǽritis, et Ángelus testaménti, quem vos vultis. Ecce, venit, dicit Dóminus exercítuum: et quis póterit cogitáre diem advéntus ejus, et quis stabit ad vidéndum eum? Ipse enim quasi ignis conflans et quasi herba fullónum: et sedébit conflans et emúndans argéntum, et purgábit fílios Levi et colábit eos quasi aurum et quasi argéntum: et erunt Dómino offeréntes sacrifícia in justítia. Et placébit Dómino sacrifícium Juda et Jerúsalem, sicut dies sǽculi et sicut anni antíqui: dicit Dóminus omnípotens.

THUS saith the Lord God, Behold I send My angel, and he shall prepare the way before My face; and presently the Lord, Whom you seek, and the angel of the testament, whom you desire, shall come to His temple. Behold He cometh, saith the Lord of hosts; and who shall be able to think of the day of His coming? and who shall stand to see Him? for He is like a refining fire, and like the fuller's herb; and He shall sit refining and cleansing the silver, and He shall purify the sons of Levi, and shall refine them as gold, and as silver, and they shall offer sacrifices to the Lord in justice. And the sacrifice of Juda and of Jerusalem shall please the Lord, as in the days of old, and in the ancient years; saith the Lord almighty.

GRADUAL & ALLELUIA. *Ps 47: 10-11, 9 & Saint Augustine (Sermo 13 de Tempore)*

Suscépimus, Deus, misericórdiam tuam in médio templi tui: secúndum nomen tuum, Deus, ita et laus tua in fines terræ. ℣. Sicut audívimus, ita et vídimus in civitáte Dei nostri, in monte sancto ejus.

Allelúja, allelúja. ℣. Senex Púerum portábat: Puer autem senem regébat. Allelúja.

WE HAVE received Thy mercy, O God, in the midst of Thy temple: according to Thy name, O God, so also is Thy praise unto the ends of the earth. ℣. As we have heard, so have we seen, in the city of our God, and in His holy mountain.

Alleluia, alleluia. ℣. The old man carried the child: but the child ruled the old man. Alleluia.

After Septuagesima, the Alleluia is replaced by the following Tract:

TRACT. *Luke 2: 29-32*

Nunc dimíttis servum tuum, Dómine, secúndum verbum tuum in pace. ℣. Quia vidérunt óculi mei salutáre tuum. ℣. Quod parásti ante fáciem ómnium populórum. ℣. Lumen ad revelatiónem géntium et glóriam plebis tuæ Ísraël.

NOW Thou dost dismiss Thy servant, O Lord, according to Thy word in peace. ℣. Because my eyes have seen Thy salvation. ℣. Which Thou hast prepared before the face of all peoples. ℣. A light to the revelation of the gentiles, and the glory of Thy people, Israel.

GOSPEL. *Luke 2: 22-32*

WHEN THE DAY came for Mary to be purified according to the Law of Moses, they carried Jesus to Jerusalem, to present Him to the Lord; as it is written in the law of the Lord, Every male opening the womb shall be called holy to the Lord; and to offer a sacrifice, according as it is written in the law of the Lord, a pair of turtledoves, or two young pigeons. And behold there was a man in Jerusalem named Simeon, and this man was just and devout, waiting for the consolation of Israel, and the Holy Ghost was in him: and he had received an answer from the Holy Ghost, that he should not see death, before he had seen the Christ of the Lord.

In illo témpore: Postquam impléti sunt dies purgatiónis Maríæ, secúndum legem Móysi, tulérunt Jesum in Jerúsalem, ut sísterent eum Dómino, sicut scriptum est in lege Dómini: Quia omne masculínum adapériens vulvam sanctum Dómino vocábitur. Et ut darent hóstiam, secúndum quod dictum est in lege Dómini, par túrturum aut duos pullos columbárum. Et ecce, homo erat in Jerúsalem, cui nomen Símeon, et homo iste justus et timorátus, exspéctans consolatiónem Ísraël, et Spíritus Sanctus erat in eo. Et respónsum accéperat a Spíritu Sancto, non visúrum se mortem, nisi prius vidéret Christum Dómini.

And he came by the Spirit into the temple. And when His parents brought in the child Jesus, to do for Him according to the custom of the law, he also took Him into his arms, and blessed God, and said, Now Thou dost dismiss Thy servant, O Lord, according to Thy word in peace: because my eyes have seen Thy salvation, which Thou hast prepared before the face of all peoples; a light to the revelation of the gentiles, and the glory of Thy people Israel. CREDO.

Et venit in spíritu in templum. Et cum indúcerent púerum Jesum parentes ejus, ut fácerent secúndum consuetúdinem legis pro eo: et ipse accépit eum in ulnas suas, et benedíxit Deum, et dixit: Nunc dimíttis servum tuum, Dómine, secúndum verbum tuum in pace: Quia vidérunt óculi mei salutáre tuum: Quod parásti ante fáciem ómnium populórum: Lumen ad revelatiónem géntium et glóriam plebis tuæ Ísraël.

OFFERTORY. *Ps 44: 3*

GRACE is poured abroad in thy lips: therefore hath God blessed thee for ever, and for ages of ages. ℣. *With thy comeliness and thy beauty set out, proceed prosperously, and reign.*

Diffúsa est grátia in lábiis tuis: proptérea benedíxit te Deus in ætérnum, et in sæculum sæculi. ℣. *Spécie tua et pulchritúdine tua et inténde et próspere procéde et regna.*

SECRET.

Hear our prayers, O Lord, and, in Thy loving-kindness, help us, so that the gifts we offer may be found worthy in the eyes of Thy majesty. Through our Lord.

Exáudi, Dómine, preces nostras: et, ut digna sint múnera, quæ óculis tuæ majestátis offérimus, subsídium nobis tuæ pietátis impénde. Per Dóminum.

The Preface of the Nativity (page 189) follows the Secret.

COMMUNION. *Luke 2: 26*

SIMEON received an answer from the Holy Ghost, that he should not see death until he had seen the Christ of the Lord. ℣. *And he came by the Spirit into*

Respónsum accépit Símeon a Spíritu Sancto, non visúrum se mortem, nisi vidéret Christum Dómini. (Luke 2: 27-28) ℣. *Et venit in spíritu in templum. Et cum indúcerent púerum Jesum paréntes ejus, ut fácerent secúndum consuetúdinem legis pro eo, et ipse accépit eum in ulnas suas.* —NARBONNE|1033 • Circa 1033AD

the temple. And when His parents brought in the child Jesus, to do for Him according to the custom of the law, he also took Him into his arms.

POSTCOMMUNION.

Quæsumus, Dómine, Deus noster: ut sacrosáncta mystéria, quæ pro reparatiónis nostræ munímine contulísti, intercedénte beáta María semper Vírgine, et præsens nobis remédium esse fácias et futúrum. Per Dóminum.

O Lord our God, we beseech Thee, by the intercession of blessed Mary ever virgin, make the sacred mysteries, which Thou hast given for the preservation of our spiritual life, a healing remedy for us, both for the present and for the future. Through our Lord.

I Classis.

— 19 March, Saint Joseph —

Husband of the Blessed Virgin Mary, Confessor and Patron of the Universal Church

S. JOSEPH SPONSI BEATAE MARIAE VIRGINIS CONFESSORIS ET ECCLESIAE UNIVERSAE PATRONI

INTROIT. *Ps 91: 13-14, 2*

Justus ut palma florébit: sicut cedrus Líbani multiplicábitur: plantátus in domo Dómini: in átriis domus Dei nostri. (*T.P. Allelúja, allelúja.*) ℣. Bonum est confitéri Dómino: et psállere nómini tuo, Altíssime. ℣. Glória Patri.

THE JUST MAN shall flourish like the palm-tree; he shall grow up like the cedar of Libanus; planted in the house of the Lord, in the courts of the house of our God. (*P.T. Alleluia, alleluia.*) ℣. It is good to give praise to the Lord; and to sing to Thy name, O Most High. ℣. Glory.

COLLECT.

Sanctíssimæ Genetrícis tuæ Sponsi, quæsumus, Dómine, méritis adjuvémur: ut, quod possibílitas nostra non óbtinet, ejus nobis intercessióne donétur: Qui vivis.

May we be assisted, we beg Thee, O Lord, by the merits of the spouse of Thy most holy Mother, that what our own power obtaineth not may be granted us by his intercession. Who livest.

EPISTLE. *Ecclus 45: 1-6*

Diléctus Deo et homínibus, cujus memória in benedictióne est. Símilem illum fecit in glória sanctórum, et magnificávit eum in timóre inimicórum, et in verbis suis monstra placávit. Glorificávit illum in conspéctu regum, et jussit illi coram pópulo suo, et osténdit illi glóriam suam. In fide et lenitáte ipsíus sanctum fecit illum, et elégit eum ex omni carne. Audívit enim eum et vocem ipsíus, et indúxit illum in nubem. Et dedit illi coram præcépta, et legem vitæ et disciplínæ.

HE WAS BELOVED of God and men, whose memory is in benediction; He made him like the saints in glory, and magnified him in the fear of his enemies; and with his words he made prodigies to cease; He glorified him in the sight of kings, and gave him commandments in the sight of his people, and showed him His glory; He sanctified him in his faith and meekness, and chose him out of all flesh; for He heard him and his voice, and brought him into a cloud; and He gave him commandments before His face, and a law of life and instruction.

MAY THE HOSTS OF HEAVENLY SPIRITS PRAISE THEE, O JOSEPH; MAY ALL THE CHOIRS OF CHRISTENDOM RESOUND WITH THY NAME, THOU WHO, RENOWNED FOR MERITS, WAST UNITED IN CHASTE WEDLOCK TO THE GLORIOUS VIRGIN. WHEN THOU DIDST WONDER AT THY BRIDE GROWN GREAT WITH HER AUGUST CHILD, SORELY WERT THOU AFFLICTED WITH DOUBT; BUT AN ANGEL TAUGHT THEE THAT THE CHILD WAS CONCEIVED BY A BREATH OF THE HOLY SPIRIT.

GRADUAL. *Ps 20: 4-5*

Dómine, prævenísti eum in benedictiónibus dulcédinis: posuísti in cápite ejus corónam de lápide pretióso. ℣. Vitam pétiit a te, et tribuísti ei longitúdinem diérum in sæculum sæculi.

O LORD, Thou hast prevented him with blessings of sweetness: Thou hast set on his head a crown of precious stones. ℣. He asked life of Thee and Thou hast given him length of days for ever and ever.

TRACT. *Ps 111: 1-3*

Beátus vir, qui timet Dñm: in mandátis ejus cupit nimis. ℣. Potens in terra erit semen ejus: generátio rectórum benedicétur. ℣. Glória et divítiæ in domo ejus: et justítia ejus manet in sæculum sæculi.

BLESSED is the man that feareth the Lord: he shall delight exceedingly in His commandments. ℣. His seed shall be mighty upon earth: the generation of the righteous shall be blessed. ℣. Glory and wealth shall be in his house: and his justice remaineth for ever and ever.

In Paschal-time, the Gradual and Tract are replaced by the Greater Alleluia:

GREATER ALLELUIA. *Ecclus 45: 9 & Osee 14: 6*

Allelúja, allelúja. ℣. Amávit eum Dóminus, et ornávit eum: stolam glóriæ índuit eum.

Allelúja. ℣. Justus germinábit sicut lílium: et florébit in ætérnum ante Dóminum. Allelúja.

ALLELUIA, alleluia. ℣. The Lord loved him, and adorned him: He clothed him with a robe of glory.

Alleluia. ℣. The just shall spring as the lily: and shall flourish for ever before the Lord. Alleluia.

GOSPEL. *Matt 1: 18-21*

Cum esset desponsáta Mater Jesu María Joseph, ántequam convenírent, invénta est in útero habens de Spíritu Sancto. Joseph autem, vir ejus, cum esset justus et nollet eam tradúcere, vóluit occúlte dimíttere eam. Hæc autem eo cogitánte, ecce, Ángelus Dómini appáruit in somnis ei, dicens: Joseph, fili David, noli timére accípere Maríam cónjugem tuam: quod enim in ea natum est, de Spíritu Sancto est. Páriet autem fílium, et vocábis nomen ejus Jesum: ipse enim salvum fáciet pópulum suum a peccátis eórum.

WHEN MARY, the mother of Jesus, was espoused to Joseph, before they came together, she was found with child, of the Holy Ghost. Whereupon Joseph her husband, being a just man, and not willing publicly to expose her, was minded to put her away privately. But while he thought on these things, behold the angel of the Lord appeared to him in his sleep, saying: Joseph, son of David, fear not to take unto thee Mary thy wife, for that which is conceived in her is of the Holy Ghost. And she shall bring forth a Son; and thou shalt call His name Jesus. For He shall save His people from their sins. CREDO.

OFFERTORY. *Ps 88: 25*

Véritas mea et misericórdia mea cum ipso: et in nómine meo exaltábitur cornu ejus. (*T.P. Allelúja.*) ℣. *Pósui adjutórium meum super poténtem et exaltávi eléctum de plebe mea.*

MY TRUTH and My mercy are with him: and in My name his horn shall be exalted. (*P.T. Alleluia.*) ℣. *I have laid help upon one that is mighty, and have exalted one chosen out of*

My people. ℣. *My mercy I will not take away from him: and his seat shall be before Me.*

℣. *Misericórdiam meam non dispérgam ab eo: et sedes ejus in conspéctu meo.*

SECRET.

We render unto Thee, O Lord, the debt of our service, and humbly entreat Thee to guard Thy gifts within us, through the intercession of blessed Joseph, the spouse of the mother of Thy Son, Jesus Christ, our Lord, in honor of whose feast we offer unto Thee this sacrifice of praise. Through the same.

Débitum tibi, Dómine, nostræ réddimus servitútis, supplíciter exorántes: ut, suffrágiis beáti Joseph, Sponsi Genetrícis Fílii tui Jesu Christi, Dómini nostri, in nobis tua múnera tueáris, ob cujus venerándam festivitátem laudis tibi hóstias immolámus. Per eúmdem Dóminum.

The Preface of Saint Joseph (page 192) follows the Secret.

COMMUNION. *Matt 1: 20*

JOSEPH, son of David, fear not to take unto thee Mary thy wife: for that which is born in her is of the Holy Ghost. (*P.T. Alleluia.*) ℣. *Blessed is the man that feareth the Lord: he shall delight exceedingly in His commandments.*

Joseph, fili David, noli timére accípere Maríam cónjugem tuam: quod enim in ea natum est, de Spíritu Sancto est. (*T.P. Allelúja.*) (Ps 111: 1) ℣. *Beátus vir, qui timet Dóminum: in mandátis ejus volet nimis.*

POSTCOMMUNION.

Be with us, we beg, O merciful God, and being propitiated by the intercession of blessed Joseph, Thy confessor, watch over the gifts with which Thou hast surrounded us. Through our Lord.

Adésto nobis, quæsumus, miséricors Deus: et, intercedénte pro nobis beáto Joseph Confessóre, tua circa nos propitiátus dona custódi. Per Dóminum.

This feast is from 1847; all the Propers were borrowed from other feast days—at least as far as the melodies are concerned. When "Saint Joseph the Worker" is said as a votive Mass after Septuagesima, the Tract is identical to that given above for 19 March. Some books have altered the Gregorian Chant to utilize the Pius XII Psalter—e.g. "Opes et divítiæ" instead of "Glória et divítiæ"—but either version may be used since they are both Psalm 111: 1-3.

—*25 March, The Annunciation*— *I Classis.*

IN ANNUNTIATIONE BEATAE MARIAE VIRGINIS

INTROIT. *Ps 44: 13, 15, 16, 2*

ALL the rich among the people shall entreat thy countenance; after her shall virgins be brought to the King; her neighbors shall be brought to thee in gladness and rejoicing. (*P.T. Alleluia, alleluia.*) ℣. My heart hath uttered a good word: I speak my works to the King. ℣. Glory.

Vultum tuum deprecabúntur omnes dívites plebis: adducéntur regi vírgines post eam: próximæ ejus adducéntur tibi in lætítia et exsultatióne. (*T.P. Allelúja, allelúja.*) ℣. Eructávit cor meum verbum bonum: dico ego ópera mea Regi. ℣. Glória Patri.

COLLECT.

Deus, qui de beátæ Maríæ Vírginis útero Verbum tuum, Angelo nuntiánte, carnem suscípere voluísti: præsta supplícibus tuis; ut, qui vere eam Genetrícem Dei crédimus, ejus apud te intercessiónibus adjuvémur. Per eúmdem Dóminum.

O God, Who didst will that at the message of an angel Thy word should take flesh in the womb of the Blessed Virgin Mary: grant that we, Thy suppliants, who believe her to be truly the mother of God, may be helped by her intercession with Thee. Through the same.

EPISTLE. *Is 7: 10-15*

In diébus illis: Locútus est Dóminus ad Achaz, dicens: Pete tibi signum a Dómino, Deo tuo, in profúndum inférni, sive in excélsum supra. Et dixit Achaz: Non petam et non tentábo Dóminum. Et dixit: Audíte ergo, domus David: Numquid parum vobis est, moléstos esse homínibus, quia molésti estis et Deo meo? Propter hoc dabit Dóminus ipse vobis signum. Ecce, Virgo concípiet et páriet fílium, et vocábitur nomen ejus Emmánuel. Butýrum et mel cómedet, ut sciat reprobáre malum et elígere bonum.

IN THOSE DAYS, the Lord spoke unto Achaz, saying: Ask thee a sign of the Lord thy God, either unto the depth of hell, or unto the height above. And Achaz said: I will not ask, and I will not tempt the Lord. And He said: Hear ye therefore, O house of David: Is it a small thing for you to be grievous to men, that you are grievous to My God also? Therefore, the Lord Himself shall give you a sign. Behold a virgin shall conceive and bear a son, and his name shall be called Emmanuel. He shall eat butter and honey, that he may know to refuse the evil, and to choose the good.

GRADUAL. *Ps 44: 3, 5*

Diffúsa est grátia in lábiis tuis: proptérea benedíxit te Deus in ætérnum. ℣. Propter veritátem et mansuetúdinem et justítiam: et dedúcet te mirabíliter déxtera tua.

GRACE is poured abroad in thy lips: therefore hath God blessed thee forever. ℣. Because of truth, and meekness, and justice: and thy right hand shall conduct thee wonderfully.

TRACT. *Ps 44: 11, 12, 13, 10, 15, 16*

Audi, fília, et vide, et inclína aurem tuam: quia concupívit Rex speciem tuam. ℣. Vultum tuum deprecabúntur omnes dívites plebis: fíliæ regum in honóre tuo. ℣. Adducéntur regi vírgines post eam: próximæ ejus afferéntur tibi. ℣. Adducéntur in lætítia et exsultatióne: adducéntur in templum Regis.

HARKEN, O daughter, and see, and incline thine ear: for the King hath greatly desired thy beauty. ℣. All the rich among the people shall entreat thy countenance: the daughters of kings in thy honor. ℣. After her shall virgins be brought to the King: her neighbors shall be brought to thee. ℣. They shall be brought with gladness and rejoicing; they shall be brought into the temple of the King.

In Paschal-time, the Gradual and Tract are replaced by the Greater Alleluia:

GREATER ALLELUIA. *Luke 1: 28 & Num 17: 8*

Allelúja, allelúja. ℣. Ave, María, grátia plena; Dóminus tecum: benedícta tu in muliéribus.

ALLELUIA, alleluia. ℣. Hail, Mary, full of grace: the Lord is with thee: Blessed art thou among women.

RECEIVING THAT «AVE» FROM THE MOUTH OF GABRIEL ESTABLISH US IN PEACE, REVERSING THE NAME OF EVE ("EVA").

Allelúja. ℣. Virga Jesse flóruit: Virgo Deum et hóminem génuit: pacem Deus réddidit, in se reconcílians ima summis. Allelúja.

Alleluia. ℣. The rod of Jesse hath blossomed: a virgin hath brought forth One Who was both God and man: God hath given back peace to man, reconciling the lowest with the highest to Himself. Alleluia.

GOSPEL. *Luke 1: 26-38*

In illo témpore: Missus est Ángelus Gábriel a Deo in civitátem Galilǽæ, cui nomen Názareth, ad Vírginem desponsátam viro, cui nomen erat Joseph, de domo David: et nomen Vírginis María. Et ingréssus Ángelus ad eam, dixit: Ave, grátia plena; Dóminus tecum: benedícta tu in muliéribus. Quæ cum audísset, turbáta est in sermóne ejus: et cogitábat, qualis esset ista salutátio. Et ait Ángelus ei: Ne tímeas, María, invenísti enim grátiam apud Deum: ecce, concípies in útero et páries fílium, et vocábis nomen ejus Jesum. Hic erit magnus, et Fílius Altíssimi vocábitur, et dabit illi Dóminus Deus sedem David, patris ejus: et regnábit in domo Jacob in ætérnum, et regni ejus non erit finis.

THE ANGEL GABRIEL was sent from God into a city of Galilee, called Nazareth, to a virgin espoused to a man whose name was Joseph, of the house of David: and the virgin's name was Mary. And the angel being come in, said unto her: Hail, full of grace, the Lord is with thee: blessed art thou among women. Who having heard, was troubled at his saying and thought with herself what manner of salutation this should be. And the angel said to her: Fear not, Mary, for thou hast found grace with God. Behold thou shalt conceive in thy womb and shalt bring forth a Son and thou shalt call His name Jesus. He shall be great and shall be called the Son of the Most High, and the Lord God shall give unto Him the throne of David His father: and He shall reign in the house of Jacob forever, and of His kingdom there shall be no end.

Dixit autem María ad Ángelum: Quómodo fiet istud, quóniam virum non cognósco? Et respóndens Ángelus, dixit ei: Spíritus Sanctus supervéniet in te, et virtus Altíssimi obumbrábit tibi. Ideóque et quod nascétur ex te Sanctum, vocábitur Fílius Dei. Et ecce, Elísabeth, cognáta tua, et ipsa concépit fílium in senectúte sua: et hic mensis sextus est illi, quæ vocátur stérilis: quia non erit impossíbile apud Deum omne verbum. Dixit autem María: Ecce ancílla Dómini, fiat mihi secúndum verbum tuum.

And Mary said to the angel: How shall this be done, because I know not man? And the angel answering, said to her: The Holy Ghost shall come upon thee and the power of the Most High shall overshadow thee. And therefore also the Holy which shall be born of thee shall be called the Son of God. And behold thy cousin Elizabeth, she also hath conceived a son in her old age: and this is the sixth month with her that is called barren; because no word shall be impossible with God. And Mary said, Behold the handmaid of the Lord, be it done to me according to thy word. CREDO.

OFFERTORY. *Luke 1: 28*

Identical to the 4th Sunday of Advent:

Ave, María, grátia plena; Dóminus tecum: benedícta tu in muliéribus, et benedíctus fructus ventris tui. ℣. *Quómodo in me fiet hoc, quæ virum non cognósco? Spíritus Dómini supervéniet in te et virtus Altíssimi obumbrábit tibi.* ℣. *Ideóque, quod nascétur ex te Sanctum, vocábitur Fílius Dei.*

HAIL, Mary, full of grace; the Lord is with thee: blessed art thou among women, and blessed is the fruit of thy womb. ℣. *How shall this be done, because I know not man? The Holy Ghost shall come upon thee, and the power of the most High shall overshadow thee.* ℣. *Thus this holy offspring of thine shall be called the Son of God.*

SECRET.

Confirm, O Lord, in our minds, we beseech Thee, the mysteries of the true faith; that we who confess Him Who was conceived of a virgin to be true God and man, may deserve to arrive at eternal joy, by the power of His saving resurrection. Through the same.

In méntibus nostris, quǽsumus, Dómine, veræ fídei sacraménta confírma: ut, qui concéptum de Vírgine Deum verum et hóminem confitémur; per ejus salutíferæ resurrectiónis poténtiam, ad ætérnam mereámur perveníre lætítiam. Per eúmdem Dóminum.

The Preface of the Blessed Virgin Mary (page 191) follows the Secret.

COMMUNION. *Is 7: 14 with Is 7: 15*

BEHOLD a virgin shall conceive, and bring forth a Son, and His name shall be called Emmanuel. *(P.T. Alleluia.)* ℣. *On butter and honey shall be His thriving, till He is of age to know good from harm.*

Ecce Virgo concípiet et páriet fílium: et vocábitur nomen ejus Emmánuel. *(T.P. Allelúja.)* ℣. *Butýrum et mel comédet, ut sciat reprobáre malum et elígere bonum.* —4951STEVEN|1128 • Circa 1128AD

POSTCOMMUNION.

Pour forth, we beseech Thee O Lord, Thy grace into our hearts, that we, to whom the Incarnation of Christ Thy Son was made known by the message of an angel, may, by His passion and cross, be brought to the glory of His resurrection. Through the same.

Grátiam tuam, quǽsumus, Dómine, méntibus nostris infúnde: ut qui, Ángelo nuntiánte, Christi Fílii tui incarnatiónem cognóvimus; per passiónem ejus et crucem, ad resurrectiónis glóriam perducámur. Per eúmdem Dóminum.

The Annunciation is "one of the most ancient feasts of the Church and can be traced back to the fifth century. Its chants are contained in the oldest manuscripts..." –Dom Johner of Beuron

---

—1 May, Saint Joseph the Worker — *I Classis.*

S. JOSEPH OPIFICIS | SPONSI BEATAE MARIAE VIRGINIS CONFESSORIS

INTROIT. *Wisdom 10: 17*

W**ISDOM** rendered to the just the wages of their labors and conducted them in a wonderful way; and she was to them for a covert by day and for the light of the stars by night; alleluia, alleluia. (Ps 126: 1) Unless the Lord build the house, they labor in vain that build it. ℣. Glory.

Sapiéntia réddidit justis mercédem labórum suórum, et dedúxit illos in via mirábili, et fuit illis in velaménto diéi, et in luce stellárum per noctem, allelúja, allelúja. ℣. Nisi Dóminus ædificáverit domum, in vanum labórant qui ædíficant eam. ℣. Glória Patri.

COLLECT.

O God, Creator of all things, Who didst lay on the human race the law of labor: graciously grant; that by following the example of Saint Joseph and under

Rerum cónditor Deus qui legem labóris humáno géneri statuísti concéde propítius; ut sancti Joseph exémplo et patrocínio, ópera perficiámus quæ præcipis, et præmia consequámur quæ promíttis. Per Dóminum.

his patronage, we may carry out the work Thou dost command, and obtain the reward Thou dost promise. Through our Lord.

EPISTLE. *Col 3: 14-15, 17, 23-24*

Fratres: Caritátem habéte, quod est vínculum perfectiónis, et pax Christi exúltet in córdibus vestris, in qua et vocáti estis in uno córpore, et grati estóte. Omne quodcúmque fácitis in verbo aut in ópere, ómnia in nómine Dómini Jesu Christi, grátias agéntes Deo et Patri per ipsum. Quodcúmque fácitis, ex ánimo operámini, sicut Dómino, et non homínibus, sciéntes quod a Dómino accipiétis retributiónem hereditátis. Dómino Christo servíte.

BRETHREN: Have charity, which is the bond of perfection; and let the peace of Christ rejoice in your hearts, wherein also you are called in one body; and be ye thankful. All whatsoever you do in word or in work, do all in the name of our Lord Jesus Christ, giving thanks to God and the Father by Him. Whatsoever you do, do it from the heart: as to the Lord, and not to men: knowing that you shall receive of the Lord the reward of inheritance. Serve ye the Lord Christ.

GREATER ALLELUIA.

Allelúja, allelúja. ℣. De quacúmque tribulatióne clamáverint ad me, exáudiam eos, et ero protéctor eórum semper.

Allelúja. ℣. Fac nos innócuam, Joseph, decúrrere vitam: sitque tuo semper tuta patrocínio. Allelúja.

ALLELUIA, alleluia. ℣. In whatever tribulation they shall cry to Me, I will hear them and be their protector always.
Alleluia. ℣. Obtain for us, Joseph, grace to lead an innocent life; and may it ever be shielded by thy patronage. Alleluia.

GOSPEL. *Matt 13: 54-58*

In illo témpore: Véniens Jesus in pátriam suam, docébat eos in synagógis eórum, ita ut miraréntur et dícerent: Unde huic sapiéntia hæc et virtútes? Nonne hic est fabri fílius? Nonne mater ejus dícitur María, et fratres ejus Jacóbus et Joseph et Simon et Judas? Et soróres ejus nonne omnes apud nos sunt? Unde ergo huic ómnia ista? Et scandalizabántur in eo. Jesus autem dixit eis: Non est prophéta sine honóre nisi in pátria sua et in domo sua. Et non fecit ibi virtútes multas propter incredulitátem illórum.

WHEN JESUS had come to His own country, He taught them in their synagogues, so that they wondered and said: "How came this man by this wisdom and miracles? Is not this the carpenter's son? Is not His mother named Mary, and His brothers James and Joseph and Simon and Jude? And His sisters, are they not all with us? Whence therefore hath He all these things?" And they were scandalized in His regard. But Jesus said to them, "A prophet is not without honor save in his own country and in his own house." And He wrought not many miracles there because of their unbelief. CREDO.

OFFERTORY. *Ps 89: 17*

Bónitas Dómini Dei nostri sit super nos, et opus mánuum nostrárum secúnda nobis, et opus mánuum nostrárum secúnda. Allelúja.

LET the brightness of the Lord our God be upon us, and direct Thou the works of our hands over us; yea, the work of our hands do Thou direct. Alleluia.

SECRET.

From the work of our hands we offer sacrifice to Thee, O Lord: through the mediation of Saint Joseph may it be a pledge for us of union and peace. Through our Lord.

Quas tibi, Dómine, de opéribus mánuum nostrárum offérimus hóstias, sancti Joseph interpósito suffrágio, pignus fácias nobis unitátis et pacis. Per Dóminum.

The Preface of Saint Joseph (page 192) follows the Secret.

COMMUNION. *Matt 13: 54, 55*

HOW CAME this man by this wisdom and miracles? Is not this the carpenter's son? Is not His mother named Mary? Alleluia. ℣. *Vain is the builder's toil, if the house is not of the Lord's building; vainly the guard keeps watch, if the city has not the Lord for its guardian.*

Unde huic sapiéntia hæc et virtútes? Nonne hic est fabri fílius? Nonne mater ejus dícitur María? Allelúja. (Ps 126: 1) ℣. *Nisi Dóminus ædificáverit domum, in vanum laboravérunt qui ædíficant eam. Nisi Dóminus custodíerit civitátem, frustra vígilat qui custódit eam.*

POSTCOMMUNION.

Grant, O Lord, that what we have received may, by the intercession of blessed Joseph, crown our work and confirm our reward. Through our Lord.

Hæc sancta quæ súmpsimus Dómine: per intercessiónem beáti Joseph; et operatiónem nostram cómpleant, et prǽmia confírment. Per Dóminum.

The feast of "Saint Joseph the Workman" was added to the calendar by Venerable Pope Pius XII in 1955; the Propers were released in 1956. The two Alleluias ("De Quacúmque" and "Fac Nos Innócuam") come from FERIA IV INFRA HEBDOMADAM II POST OCTAVAM PASCHAE « In Solemnitate S. Joseph, Sponsi B.M.V. Confessoris et Ecclesiae Universalis Patroni », *formerly celebrated on the Wednesday before the Third Sunday after Easter. The Offertory is based upon the melody of "Pópulum Húmilem," the ancient Offertory for the 8th Sunday after Pentecost.*

—24 June, Birth of St. John the Baptist— *I Classis.*

IN NATIVITATE SANCTI JOANNIS BAPTISTAE

INTROIT. *Is 49: 1, 2*

THE LORD hath called me by my name from the womb of my mother, and He hath made my mouth like a sharp sword; in the shadow of His hand He hath protected me, and hath made me as a chosen arrow. (Ps 91: 2) It is good to give praise to the Lord, and to sing to Thy name, O Most High. ℣. Glory.

De ventre matris meæ vocávit me Dóminus nómine meo: et pósuit os meum ut gládium acútum: sub teguménto manus suæ protéxit me, et pósuit me quasi sagíttam eléctam. ℣. Bonum est confitéri Dómino: et psállere nómini tuo, Altíssime. ℣. Glória Patri.

COLLECT.

O God, Who hast made this day honorable to us on account of the birth of blessed John, grant Thy people the grace of spiritual joys, and direct the minds

Deus, qui præséntem diem honorábilem nobis in beáti Joánnis nativitáte fecísti: da pópulis tuis spirituálium grátiam gaudiórum; et ómnium

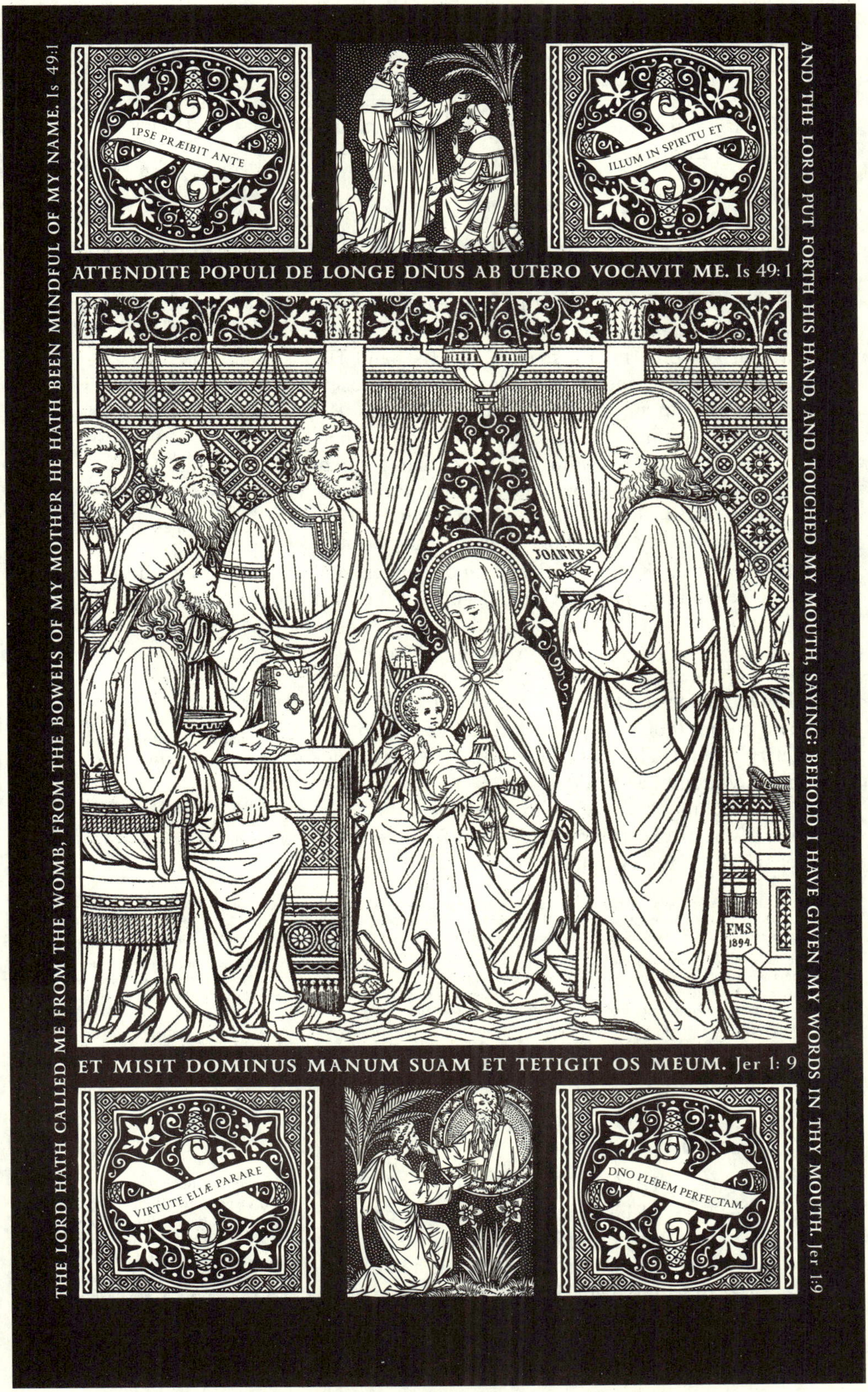
THE LORD HATH CALLED ME FROM THE WOMB, FROM THE BOWELS OF MY MOTHER HE HATH BEEN MINDFUL OF MY NAME. Is 49:1
IPSE PRÆIBIT ANTE
ILLUM IN SPIRITU ET
ATTENDITE POPULI DE LONGE DÑUS AB UTERO VOCAVIT ME. Is 49:1
AND THE LORD PUT FORTH HIS HAND, AND TOUCHED MY MOUTH, SAYING: BEHOLD I HAVE GIVEN MY WORDS IN THY MOUTH. Jer 1:9
F.M.S. 1894.
ET MISIT DOMINUS MANUM SUAM ET TETIGIT OS MEUM. Jer 1: 9
VIRTUTE ELIÆ PARARE
DÑO PLEBEM PERFECTAM.

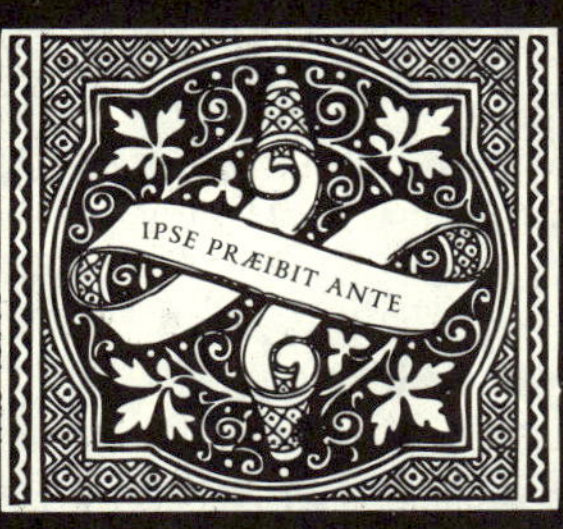

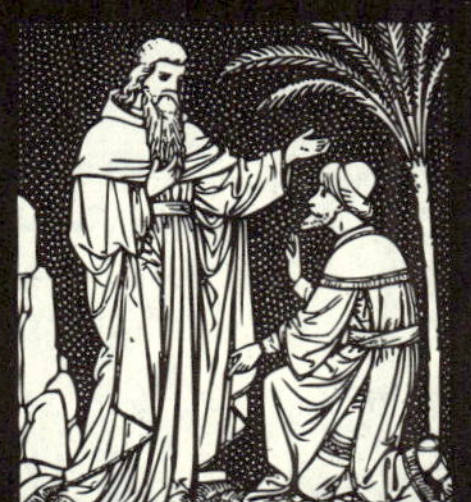

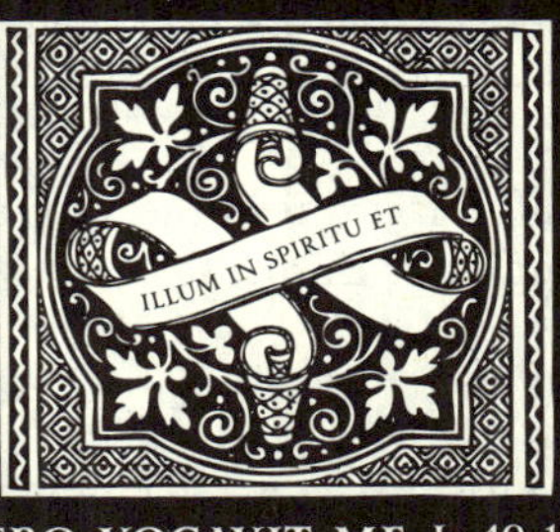

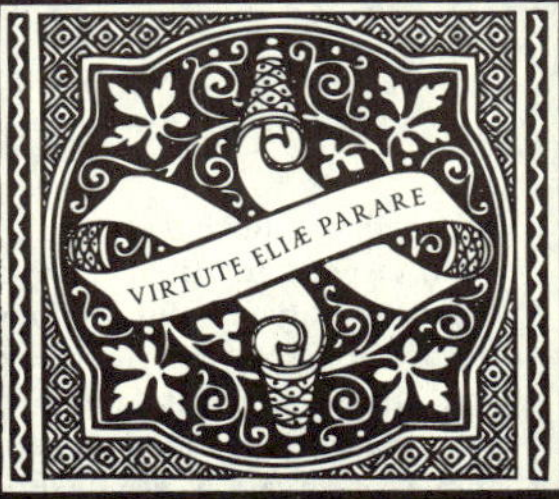

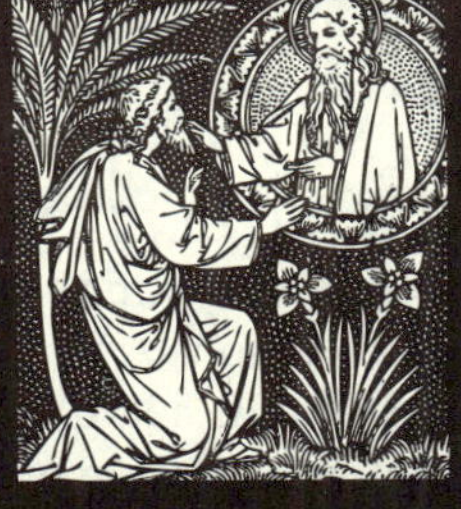

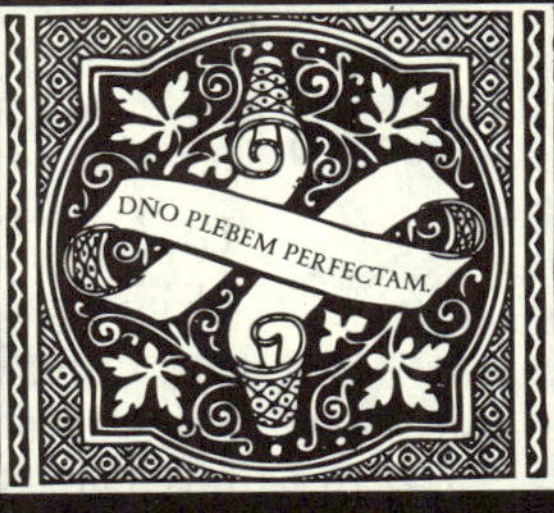

of all the faithful in the way of everlasting salvation. Through our Lord.

fidélium mentes dírige in viam salútis ætérnæ. Per Dóminum.

EPISTLE. *Is 49: 1-3, 5, 6-7*

GIVE EAR, ye islands, and harken, ye people from afar. The Lord hath called me from the womb, from the bowels of my mother He hath been mindful of my name. And He hath made my mouth like a sharp sword; in the shadow of His hand He hath protected me, and hath made me as a chosen arrow; in His quiver He hath hidden me. And He said to me, Thou art My servant Israel, for in thee will I glory. And now saith the Lord that formed me from the womb to be His servant, Behold I have given thee to be the light of the gentiles, that thou mayest be My salvation even to the farthest part of the earth. Kings shall see, and princes shall rise up, and adore for the Lord's sake, and for the Holy One of Israel, Who hath chosen thee.

Audíte, ínsulæ, et atténdite, pópuli, de longe: Dóminus ab útero vocávit me, de ventre matris meæ recordátus est nóminis mei. Et pósuit os meum quasi gládium acútum: in umbra manus suæ protéxit me, et pósuit me sicut sagíttam eléctam: in pháretra sua abscóndit me. Et dixit mihi: Servus meus es tu, Ísraël, quia in te gloriábor. Et nunc dicit Dóminus, formans me ex útero servum sibi: Ecce, dedi te in lucem géntium, ut sis salus mea usque ad extrémum terræ. Reges vidébunt, et consúrgent príncipes, et adorábunt propter Dóminum et sanctum Ísraël, qui elégit te.

GRADUAL & ALLELUIA. *Jer 1: 5, 9 & Luke 1: 76*

BEFORE I formed thee in the womb, I knew thee: and before thou camest forth from the womb did I sanctify thee. ℣. The Lord put forth His hand, and touched my mouth, and said to me: *
Alleluia, alleluia. ℣. Thou, child, shalt be called the Prophet of the Highest; thou shalt go before the Lord to prepare His ways. Alleluia.

Priúsquam te formárem in útero, novi te: et ántequam exíres de ventre, sanctificávi te. ℣. Misit Dóminus manum suam, et tétigit os meum, et dixit mihi.

Allelúja, allelúja. ℣. Tu, puer, Prophéta Altíssimi vocáberis: præíbis ante Dóminum paráre vias ejus. Allelúja.

* The choir always has the option to repeat the Gradual's refrain section—as Abbat Pothier made clear in 1908 when the *Editio Vaticana* was published under Pope Saint Pius X—although this repeat is seldom taken, even in monasteries. For this particular Gradual, taking the repeat is recommended to complete the phrase "and said to me." Section IV in *De Ritibus Servandis in Cantu Missae*:

> When the Epistle or Lesson is finished, the Responsory called the Gradual is begun by one or two singers as far as the asterisk, where the whole chorus—or at least the selected chanters—are instantly to follow on at this point. The verse of the Gradual is sung by two voices, and is completed by the whole choir from the asterisk near the end. Alternatively, the Responsorial mode may be followed when this is more suitable, all the choir then repeating (after the verse has been finished by the solo singer or singers) the first part of the Responsory up to the Verse.
>
> *Finita Epistola aut Lectione, ab uno vel a duobus inchoatur Responsorium, quod dicitur Graduale, usque ad signum* ∗, *et cuncti, aut saltem Cantores designati, prosequuntur debita cum attentione. Duo dicunt Versum Gradualis, quem ab asterisco circa finem totus Chorus absolvit; aut juxta ritum responsorialem, quando magis id videtur opportunum, post versum a solis Cantoribus aut a Cantore expletum, cuncti repetunt primam partem Responsorii usque ad Versum.*

GOSPEL. *Luke 1: 57-68*

ELIZABETH'S FULL TIME of being delivered was come, and she brought forth a son. And her neighbors and kinsfolk heard that the Lord had showed His great mercy towards her, and they congratulated with her. And

Elísabeth implétum est tempus pariéndi, et péperit fílium. Et audiérunt vicíni et cognáti ejus, quia magnificávit Dóminus misericórdiam suam cum illa, et congratulabántur ei. Et factum est in die octávo, venérunt circumcídere púerum, et vocábant eum nómine patris sui Zacharíam. Et respóndens mater ejus, dixit: Nequáquam, sed vocábitur Joánnes. Et dixérunt ad illam: Quia nemo est in cognatióne tua, qui vocátur hoc nómine. Innuébant autem patri ejus, quem vellet vocári eum. Et póstulans pugillárem, scripsit, dicens: Joánnes est nomen ejus. Et miráti sunt univérsi. Apértum est autem íllico os ejus et lingua ejus, et loquebátur benedícens Deum. Et factus est timor super omnes vicínos eórum: et super ómnia montána Judǽæ divulgabántur ómnia verba hæc: et posuérunt omnes, qui audíerant in corde suo, dicéntes: Quis, putas, puer iste erit? Etenim manus Dómini erat cum illo. Et Zacharías, pater ejus, replétus est Spíritu Sancto, et prophetávit, dicens: Benedíctus Dóminus, Deus Ísraël, quia visitávit et fecit redemptiónẽ plebis suæ.

it came to pass, that on the eighth day they came to circumcise the child, and they called him by his father's name, Zachary. And his mother answering, said Not so, but he shall be called John. And they said to her, There is none of thy kindred that is called by that name. And they made signs to his father, how he would have him called. And demanding a writing table, he wrote, saying, John is his name: and they all wondered. And immediately his mouth was opened, and his tongue loosed; and he spoke, blessing God. And fear came upon all their neighbors; and all these things were noised abroad over all the hill country of Judea; and all they that had heard them, laid them up in their heart, saying, What a one, think ye, shall this child be? For the hand of the Lord was with him. And Zachary his father was filled with the Holy Ghost; and he prophesied, saying: Blessèd be the Lord God of Israel; because He hath visited, and wrought the redemption of His people. CREDO.

OFFERTORY. *Ps 91: 13*

Justus ut palma florébit: sicut cedrus, quæ in Líbano est, multiplicábitur. ℣. *Bonum est confitéri Dómino: et psállere nómini tuo Altíssime.* ℣. *Ad annuntiándum mane misericórdiam tuam: et veritátem tuam per noctem.* ℣. *Plantátus in domo Dómini, in átriis domus Dei nostri florébit.*

THE JUST MAN shall flourish like the palm-tree: he shall grow up like the cedar of Libanus. ℣. *It is good to give praise to the Lord: and to sing to Thy name, O most High.* ℣. *To show forth Thy mercy in the morning: and Thy truth in the night.* ℣. *He who is planted in the house of the Lord shall flourish in the courts of the house of our God.*

SECRET.

Tua, Dómine, munéribus altária cumulámus: illíus nativitátem honóre débito celebrántes, qui Salvatórem mundi et cécinit adfutúrum et adésse monstrávit, Dóminum nostrum Jesum Christum, Fílium tuum: Qui tecum.

We heap Thine altars with gifts, O Lord, celebrating with fitting honor the nativity of him who heralded the coming of the Savior, and pointed Him out when He had come, our Lord Jesus Christ, Thy Son. Who with Thee.

* *The "ad libitum" Preface for Saint John the Baptist on page 196 may be used.*

COMMUNION. *Luke 1: 76*

Tu, puer, Prophéta Altíssimi vocáberis: præíbis enim ante fáciem Dómini paráre vias ejus. (Luke 1: 77) ℣. *Ad dandam sciéntiam salútis plebi ejus in remissiónem peccatórum eórum.*

—StMaur|1079 • Circa 1079AD

THOU, child, shalt be called the Prophet of the Highest; for thou shalt go before the face of the Lord, to prepare His ways. ℣. *Thou wilt make known to His people the salvation that is to release them from their sins.*

POSTCOMMUNION.

May Thy Church, O God, be joyful at the birth of blessed John the Baptist, through whom she knew the Author of her regeneration, our Lord Jesus Christ, Thy Son. Who with Thee.

Sumat Ecclésia tua, Deus, beáti Joánnis Baptístæ generatióne lætítiam: per quem suæ regeneratiónis cognóvit auctórem, Dóminum nostrum Jesum Christum, Fílium tuum: Qui tecum vivit.

—*29 June, Holy Apostles, Peter & Paul*— *I Classis.*

SS. PETRI ET PAULI APOSTOLORUM

INTROIT. *Acts 12: 11*

NOW I KNOW in very deed, that the Lord hath sent His angel, and hath delivered me out of the hand of Herod, and from all the expectation of the people of the Jews. (Ps 138: 1-2) Lord, Thou hast proved me, and known me: Thou hast known my sitting down, and my rising up. ℣. Glory.

Nunc scio vere, quia misit Dóminus Ángelum suum: et erípuit me de manu Heródis et de omni exspectatióne plebis Judæórum. ℣. Dómine, probásti me et cognovísti me: tu cognovísti sessiónem meam et resurrectiónem meam. ℣. Glória Patri.

COLLECT.

O God, Who hast consecrated this day to the martyrdom of Thine apostles Peter and Paul, grant to Thy Church in all things to follow their teaching from whom it received the right ordering of religion in the beginning. Through our Lord.

Deus, qui hodiérnam diem Apostolórum tuórum Petri et Pauli martýrio consecrásti: da Ecclésiæ tuæ, eórum in ómnibus sequi præcéptum; per quos religiónis sumpsit exórdium. Per Dóminum.

EPISTLE. *Acts 12: 1-11*

IN THOSE DAYS, Herod the king stretched forth his hands to afflict some of the Church: and he killed James, the brother of John, with the sword; and seeing that it pleased the Jews, he proceeded to take up Peter also. Now it was in the days of the Azymes: and when he had apprehended him, he cast him into prison, delivering him to four files of soldiers to be kept, intending after the pasch to bring him forth to the people. Peter therefore was kept in prison: but prayer was made without ceasing by the Church unto God for him. And when Herod would have brought him forth, the same night Peter was sleeping between two soldiers, bound with two chains; and the keepers before the door kept the prison: and behold an angel

In diébus illis: Misit Heródes rex manus, ut afflígeret quosdam de ecclésia. Occídit autem Jacóbum fratrem Joánnis gládio. Videns autem, quia placéret Judǽis, appósuit, ut apprehénderet et Petrum. Erant autem dies azymórum. Quem cum apprehendísset, misit in cárcerem, tradens quatuor quaterniónibus mílitum custodiéndum, volens post Pascha prodúcere eum pópulo. Et Petrus quidem servabátur in cárcere. Orátio autem fiébat sine intermissióne ab ecclésia ad Deum pro eo. Cum autem productúrus eum esset Heródes, in ipsa nocte erat Petrus dórmiens inter duos mílites, vinctus caténis duábus: et custódes ante óstium custodiébant cárcerem. Et ecce, Ángelus Dómini ástitit: et lumen refúlsit in habitáculo:

HODIE SIMON PETRUS ASCENDIT CRUCIS PATIBULUM. HODIE PAULUS APOSTOLUS, INCLINATO CAPITE, PRO CHRISTI NOMINE MARTYRIO CORONATUS EST. (II VESPERS)

THIS DAY SIMON PETER ASCENDED THE GIBBET OF THE CROSS. THIS DAY THE APOSTLE PAUL, LAYING DOWN HIS HEAD FOR THE NAME OF CHRIST, WAS CROWNED WITH MARTYRDOM.

of the Lord stood by him, and a light shined in the room and he striking Peter on the side, raised him up, saying, Arise quickly; and the chains fell off from his hands: and the angel said to him, Gird thyself and put on thy sandals; and he did so: and he said to him, Cast thy garment about thee and follow me: and going out he followed him: and he knew not that it was true which was done by the angel; but he thought he saw a vision. And passing through the first and the second ward, they came to the iron gate that leadeth to the city, which of itself opened to them; and going out, they passed on through one street, and immediately the angel departed from him. And Peter coming to himself, said, Now I know in very deed that the Lord hath sent His angel, and hath delivered me out of the hand of Herod, and from all the expectation of the people of the Jews.

percussóque látere Petri, excitávit eum, dicens: Surge velóciter. Et cecidérunt caténæ de mánibus ejus. Dixit autem Ángelus ad eum: Præcíngere, et cálcea te cáligas tuas. Et fecit sic. Et dixit illi: Circúmda tibi vestiméntum tuum, et séquere me. Et éxiens sequebátur eum, et nesciébat quia verum est, quod fiébat per Ángelum: existimábat autem se visum vidére. Transeúntes autem primam et secundam custódiam, venérunt ad portam férream, quæ ducit ad civitátem: quæ ultro apérta est eis. Et exeúntes processérunt vicum unum: et contínuo discéssit Ángelus ab eo. Et Petrus ad se revérsus, dixit: Nunc scio vere, quia misit Dóminus Ángelum suum, et erípuit me de manu Heródis et de omni exspectatióne plebis Judæórum.

GRADUAL & ALLELUIA. *Ps 44: 17-18 & Matt 16: 18*

THOU shalt make them princes over all the earth: they shall remember Thy name, O Lord. ℣. Instead of Thy fathers, sons are born to Thee; therefore shall people praise Thee.
Alleluia, alleluia. ℣. Thou art Peter, and upon this rock I will build My Church. Alleluia.

Constítues eos príncipes super omnem terram: mémores erunt nóminis tui, Dómine. ℣. Pro pátribus tuis nati sunt tibi fílii: proptérea pópuli confitebúntur tibi.
Allelúja, allelúja. ℣. Tu es Petrus, et super hanc petram ædificábo Ecclésiam meam. Allelúja.

GOSPEL. *Matt 16: 13-19*

AT THAT TIME, Jesus came into the quarters of Cæsarea Philippi, and He asked His disciples, saying, Whom do men say that the Son of man is? But they said, Some, John the Baptist, and other some, Elias, and others, Jeremias, or one of the prophets. Jesus saith to them, But whom do you say that I am? Simon Peter answered, Thou art Christ, the Son of the living God. And Jesus answering, said to him, Blessed art thou, Simon Bar-Jona, because flesh and blood hath not revealed it to thee, but My Father Who is in Heaven: and I say to thee, that thou art Peter, and upon this rock I will build My church, and the gates of hell shall not prevail against it; and to thee I will give the keys of the kingdom of Heaven; and whatsoever thou shalt bind upon earth, it shall be bound also in Heaven; and whatsoever thou shalt loose on earth, it shall be loosed also in Heaven. CREDO.

In illo témpore: Venit Jesus in partes Cæsaréæ Philíppi, et interrogábat discípulos suos, dicens: Quem dicunt hómines esse Fílium hóminis? At illi dixérunt: Alii Joánnem Baptístam, álii autem Elíam, álii vero Jeremíam aut unum ex Prophétis. Dicit illis Jesus: Vos autem quem me esse dícitis? Respóndens Simon Petrus, dixit: Tu es Christus, Fílius Dei vivi. Respóndens autem Jesus, dixit ei: Beátus es, Simon Bar Jona: quia caro et sanguis non revelávit tibi, sed Pater meus, qui in cælis est. Et ego dico tibi, quia tu es Petrus, et super hanc petram ædificábo Ecclésiam meam, et portæ ínferi non prævalébunt advérsus eam. Et tibi dabo claves regni cælórum. Et quodcúmque ligáveris super terram, erit ligátum et in cælis: et quodcúmque sólveris super terram, erit solútum et in cælis.

OFFERTORY. *Ps 44: 17-18*

Constítues eos príncipes super omnem terram: mémores erunt nóminis tui, Dómine, in omni progénie et generatióne. ℣. *Eructávit cor meum verbum bonum: dico ego ópera mea Regi.* ℣. *Lingua mea cálamus scribæ velóciter scribéntis. Speciósus forma præ fíliis hóminum: diffúsa est grátia in lábiis tuis.* ℣. *Proptérea benedíxit te Deus in ætérnum: accíngere gládio tuo circa femur potentíssime.*

THOU SHALT MAKE them princes over all the earth: they shall remember Thy name, O Lord, throughout all generations. ℣. *My heart hath uttered a good word: I speak my works to the king.* ℣. *My tongue is the pen of a scrivener that writeth swiftly. Thou art beautiful above the sons of men: grace is poured abroad in thy lips.* ℣. *Therefore hath God blessed thee for ever: gird thy sword upon thy thigh, O thou most mighty.*

SECRET.

Hóstias, Dómine, quas nómini tuo sacrándas offérimus, apostólica prosequátur orátio: per quam nos expiári tríbuas et deféndi. Per Dóminum.

May the prayer of Thine apostles, O Lord, accompany the sacrifices which we offer to be consecrated to Thy name, and through it do Thou grant us to be pardoned and defended. Through our Lord.

The Preface of the Apostles (page 191) follows the Secret.

COMMUNION. *Matt 16: 18*

Tu es Petrus, et super hanc petram ædificábo Ecclésiam meam. (Matt 16: 19) ℣. *Et portæ ínferi non prævalébunt advérsum eam. Et tibi dabo claves regni cælórum.* —4951STEVEN|1128 • Circa 1128AD

THOU ART PETER: and upon this rock I will build My Church. ℣. *And I will give to thee the keys of the kingdom of heaven. And the gates of hell shall not prevail against it.*

POSTCOMMUNION.

Quos cælésti, Dómine, aliménto satiásti: apostólicis intercessiónibus ab omni adversitáte custódi. Per Dñm.

Preserve, O Lord from all dangers, by the intercession of Thine apostles, those whom Thou hast filled with heavenly nourishment. Through our Lord.

In the ancient manuscripts, the communion for the vigil of this feast (28 June) was interchanged with the feast day itself (29 June). In other words, 28 June had "Tu Es Petrus" for its communion antiphon, while 29 June had "Simon Johánnis Díligis Me Plus His." It is not known when this change was made, but certain early manuscripts do match our current assignment, e.g. 857NOYON|1057.

—*1 July, The Most Precious Blood*— *I Classis.*

PRETIOSISSIMI SANGUINIS DOMINI NOSTRI JESU CHRISTI

INTROIT. *Apoc 5: 9-10*

THOU hast redeemed us, O Lord, in Thy blood, out of every tribe and tongue, and people, and nation, and hast made us to our God a kingdom. (Ps 88: 2) The mercies of the Lord I will sing forever: I will show forth Thy truth with my mouth to generation and generation. ℣. Glory.

Redemísti nos, Dómine, in sánguine tuo, ex omni tribu et lingua et pópulo et natióne: et fecísti nos Deo nostro regnum. ℣. Misericórdias Dómini in ætérnum cantábo: in generatiónem et generatiónem annuntiábo veritátem tuam in ore meo. ℣. Glória Patri.

COLLECT.

Almighty, eternal God, Who hast appointed Thine only-begotten Son to be the Redeemer of the world, and hast willed to be appeased by His blood, grant us, we beseech Thee, so incessantly to worship the price of our salvation, and to be so defended by its power from the ills of this life on earth, that we may enjoy its everlasting fruit in heaven. Through the same.

Omnípotens sempitérne Deus, qui unigénitum Fílium tuum mundi Redemptórem constituísti, ac ejus Sánguine placári voluísti: concéde, quǽsumus, salútis nostræ prétium solémni cultu ita venerári, atque a præséntis vitæ malis ejus virtúte deféndi in terris; ut fructu perpétuo lætémur in cælis. Per eúmdem Dóminum.

EPISTLE. *Heb 9: 11-15*

BRETHREN, Christ being come, a high priest of the good things to come, by a greater and more perfect tabernacle, not made with hands, that is, not of this creation, neither by the blood of goats or of calves, but by His own blood, entered once into the Holies, having obtained eternal redemption. For if the blood of goats and of oxen, and the ashes of an heifer being sprinkled sanctify such as are defiled, to the cleansing of the flesh, how much more shall the blood of Christ, Who, through the Holy Ghost, offered Himself without spot to God, cleanse our conscience from dead works, to serve the living God? And therefore He is the mediator of the New Testament: that by means of His death, for the redemption of those transgressions which were under the former testament; they that are called may receive the promise of eternal inheritance; in Christ Jesus our Lord.

Fratres: Christus assístens Póntifex futurórum bonórum, per ámplius et perféctius tabernáculum non manufáctum, id est, non hujus creatiónis: neque per sánguinem hircórum aut vitulórum, sed per próprium sánguinem introívit semel in Sancta, ætérna redemptióne invénta. Si enim sanguis hircórum et taurórum et cinis vítulæ aspérsus inquinátos sanctíficat ad emundatiónem carnis: quanto magis sanguis Christi, qui per Spíritum Sanctum semetípsum óbtulit immaculátum Deo, emundábit consciéntiam nostram ab opéribus mórtuis, ad serviéndum Deo vivénti? Et ídeo novi Testaménti mediátor est: ut, morte intercedénte, in redemptiónem eárum prævaricatiónum, quæ erant sub prióri Testaménto, repromissiónem accípiant, qui vocáti sunt ætérnæ hereditátis, in Christo Jesu, Dómino nostro.

GRADUAL & ALLELUIA. *I John 5: 6, 7-8 & I John 5: 9*

THIS is He that came by water and blood, Jesus Christ: not by water only, but by water and blood. ℣. There are three Who give testimony in heaven: the

Hic est, qui venit per aquam et sánguinem, Jesus Christus: non in aqua solum, sed in aqua et sánguine. ℣. Tres sunt, qui testimónium dant in cælo:

WHY THEN IS THY APPAREL RED, AND THY GARMENTS LIKE THEIRS THAT TREAD IN THE WINEPRESS? (Is 63: 2)

HE WAS CLOTHED WITH A GARMENT SPRINKLED WITH BLOOD AND HIS NAME IS CALLED: THE WORD OF GOD. (Rev 19: 13)

I HAVE TRODDEN THE WINEPRESS ALONE, AND OF THE GENTILES THERE IS NOT A MAN WITH ME. (Is 63: 3)

HE WAS OFFERED BECAUSE IT WAS HIS OWN WILL, AND OPENED NOT HIS MOUTH ✠ Is 53.7

Father, the Word, and the Holy Ghost; and these three are one. And there are three that give testimony on earth: the Spirit, the water, and the blood; and these three are one.
Alleluia, alleluia. ℣. If we receive the testimony of men, the testimony of God is greater. Alleluia.

Pater, Verbum et Spíritus Sanctus; et hi tres unum sunt. Et tres sunt, qui testimónium dant in terra: Spíritus, aqua et sanguis: et hi tres unum sunt.

Allelúja, allelúja. ℣. Si testimónium hóminum accípimus, testimónium Dei majus est. Allelúja.

GOSPEL. *John 19: 30-35*

WHEN JESUS had taken the vinegar, He said: It is consummated. And bowing His head He gave up the ghost. Then the Jews (because it was the parasceve), that the bodies might not remain upon the cross on the Sabbath-day (for that was a great Sabbath-day), besought Pilate that their legs might be broken, and that they might be taken away. The soldiers, therefore, came: and they broke the legs of the first and of the other that was crucified with him. But after they were come to Jesus, when they saw that He was already dead, they did not break His legs. But one of the soldiers with a spear opened His side, and immediately there came out blood and water. And he that saw it hath given testimony, and his testimony is true. CREDO.

In illo témpore: Cum accepísset Jesus acétum, dixit: Consummátum est. Et inclináto cápite trádidit spíritum. Judǽi ergo (quóniam Parascéve erat), ut non remanérent in cruce córpora sábbato (erat enim magnus dies ille sábbati), rogavérunt Pilátum, ut frangeréntur eórum crura et tolleréntur. Venérunt ergo mílites: et primi quidem fregérunt crura et altérius, qui crucifíxus est cum eo. Ad Jesum autem cum venissent, ut vidérunt eum jam mórtuum, non fregérunt ejus crura, sed unus mílitum láncea latus ejus apéruit, et contínuo exívit sanguis et aqua. Et qui vidit, testimónium perhíbuit; et verum est testimónium ejus.

OFFERTORY. *I Cor 10: 16*

THE CHALICE of benediction which we bless, is it not the communion of the blood of Christ? And the bread which we break, is it not the partaking of the body of the Lord?

Calix benedictiónis, cui benedícimus, nonne communicátio sánguinis Christi est? et panis, quem frángimus, nonne participátio córporis Dómini est?

Postquam coenatum est is in all rites. It means that the cup our Lord consecrated was the fourth (last) Hallel cup.
—*Dr. Adrian Fortescue (d. 1923)*

SECRET.

Through these divine mysteries, we beseech Thee, may we draw near to Jesus, the mediator of the New Testament, and renew upon Thine altars, O Lord of virtues, the sprinkling of the blood, which speaketh more eloquently than that of Abel. Through the same.

Per hæc divína mystéria, ad novi, quǽsumus, Testaménti mediatórem Jesum accedámus: et super altária tua, Dómine virtútum, aspersiónem sánguinis mélius loquéntem, quam Abel, innovémus. Per eúmdem Dóminum.

The Preface of the Holy Cross (page 190) follows the Secret.

COMMUNION. *Heb 9: 28*

Christus semel oblátus est ad multórum exhauriénda peccáta: secúndo sine peccáto apparébit exspectántibus se in salútem. (Ps 88: 3) ℣. *Quóniam dixísti: In ætérnum misericórdia ædificábitur in cælis; præparábitur véritas tua in eis.*

CHRIST WAS OFFERED once to exhaust the sins of many; the second time He shall appear without sin to them that expect Him, unto salvation. ℣. *For Thou hast said: Mercy shall be built up for ever in the heavens: Thy truth shall be prepared in them.*

POSTCOMMUNION.

Ad sacram, Dómine, mensam admíssi, háusimus aquas in gáudio de fóntibus Salvatóris: sanguis ejus fiat nobis, quǽsumus, fons aquæ in vitam ætérnam saliéntis: Qui tecum.

Admitted to the sacred table, O Lord, we have drawn water in gladness from the fountain of the Savior; may His blood, we beseech Thee, become unto us a well of water springing up unto everlasting life. Who with Thee.

The feast of the Most Precious Blood was added to the universal calendar by Blessed Pope Pius IX in 1849. None of the Propers are ancient, but the formulary—as we have it now—seems to have been identical everywhere. Cf. "Graduel romain à l'usage de la province écclésiastique de Québec" (Quebec, 1896); "Offices de l'Église du matin et du soir suivant le rit romain" (France, 1887); Abbat Pothier's "Liber Gradualis" (Belgium, 1883); Friedrich Pustet's "Graduale de Tempore et de Sanctis" (Ratisbon, 1871); Father Michael Hermesdorff's "Graduale juxta usum Ecclesiæ Cathedralis Trevirensis" (Trier, 1863). The melodies for those texts, however, are diverse.

---

§16a of *Rubricarum Instructum* (25 July 1960): "A feast of the Lord I or II class, falling on a Sunday II class, takes the place of the Sunday with all rights and privileges; accordingly the Sunday is not commemorated." The Transfiguration is a feast of the Lord.

II Classis.

— *6 August, The Transfiguration* —

IN TRANSFIGURATIONE DOMINI NOSTRI JESU CHRISTI

INTROIT. *Ps 76: 19*

Illuxérunt coruscatiónes tuæ orbi terræ: commóta est et contrémuit terra. ℣. Quam dilécta tabernácula tua, Dómine virtútum! concupíscit, et déficit ánima mea in átria Dómini. ℣. Glória Patri.

THY lightnings enlightened the world: the earth shook and trembled. (Ps 83: 2-3) How lovely are Thy tabernacles, O Lord of hosts! my soul longeth and fainteth for the courts of the Lord. ℣. Glory be.

COLLECT.

Deus, qui fídei sacraménta in Unigéniti tui gloriósa Transfiguratióne patrum testimónio roborásti, et adoptiónem filiórum perféctam, voce delápsa in nube lúcida, mirabíliter præsignásti: concéde propítius; ut ipsíus Regis glóriæ nos coherédes effícias, et ejúsdem glóriæ tríbuas esse consórtes. Per eúmdem Dóminum.

O God, Who in the glorious transfiguration of Thine only-begotten Son didst confirm the sacraments of faith by the testimony of the fathers, and Who didst wonderfully foreshow the perfect adoption of Thy children by a voice coming down in a shining cloud, mercifully grant that we be made co-heirs of the King of glory Himself, and grant us to be sharers in that very glory. Through the same.

COLLECT. *Et fit commemoratio Ss. Xisti II Papæ, Felicissimi et Agapiti Martyrum:*

O God, Who dost permit us to celebrate the birthday of Thy holy martyrs, Sixtus, Felicissimus, and Agapitus, grant us to enjoy their companionship in everlasting beatitude. Through our Lord.

Deus, qui nos concédis sanctórum in Mártyrum tuórum Xysti, Felicíssimi, et Agapíti natalítia cólere: da nobis in ætérna beatitúdine de eórum societáte gaudére. Per Dóminum.

EPISTLE. *II Peter 1: 16-19*

DEARLY beloved, We have not followed cunningly devised fables, when we made known to you the power and presence of our Lord Jesus Christ; but having been made eyewitnesses of His majesty. For He received from God the Father honor and glory: this voice coming down to Him from the excellent glory, *This is My beloved Son in Whom I am well pleased, hear ye Him.* And this voice we heard brought from heaven, when we were with Him in the holy mount. And we have the more firm prophetical word, whereunto you do well to attend, as to a light that shineth in a dark place, until the day dawn, and the day-star arise in your hearts.

Caríssimi: Non doctas fábulas secúti notam fécimus vobis Dómini nostri Jesu Christi virtútem et præséntiam sed speculatóres facti illíus magnitúdinis. Accípiens enim a Deo Patre honórem et glóriam, voce delápsa ad eum hujuscémodi a magnífica glória: Hic est Fílius meus diléctus, in quo mihi complácui, ipsum audíte. Et hanc vocem nos audívimus de cælo allátam, cum essémus cum ipso in monte sancto. Et habémus firmiórem prophéticum sermónem: cui bene fácitis attendéntes, quasi lucérnæ lucénti in caliginóso loco, donec dies elucéscat, et lúcifer oriátur in córdibus vestris.

GRADUAL & ALLELUIA. *Ps 44: 3, 2 & Wis 7: 26*

THOU art beautiful above the sons of men: grace is poured abroad in Thy lips. ℣. My heart hath uttered a good word. I speak my works to the King. Alleluia, alleluia. ℣. He is the brightness of eternal light, the unspotted mirror, and the image of His goodness. Alleluia.

Speciósus forma præ fíliis hóminum: diffúsa est grátia in lábiis tuis. ℣. Eructávit cor meum verbum bonum: dico ego ópera mea Regi.

Allelúja, allelúja. ℣. Candor est lucis ætérnæ, spéculum sine mácula, et imágo bonitátis illíus. Allelúja.

GOSPEL. *Matt 17: 1-9*

AT THAT TIME, Jesus took Peter, and James, and John his brother, and bringing them up into a high mountain apart: and He was transfigured before them. And His face did shine as the sun, and His garments became white as snow. And behold, there appeared to them Moses and Elias talking with Him. And Peter answering, said to Jesus, Lord, it is good for us to be here; if Thou wilt, let us make here three tabernacles, one for Thee, and one for Moses, and one for Elias. And as he was yet speaking, behold a bright cloud overshadowed them; and lo, a voice out of the cloud, saying: This is My beloved Son in Whom I am well

In illo témpore: Assúmpsit Jesus Petrum, et Jacóbum, et Joánnem fratrem ejus, et duxit illos in montem excélsum seórsum: et transfigurátus est ante eos. Et resplénduit fácies ejus sicut sol: vestiménta autem ejus facta sunt alba sicut nix. Et ecce, apparuérunt illis Móyses et Elías cum eo loquéntes. Respóndens autem Petrus, dixit ad Jesum: Dómine, bonum est nos hic esse: si vis, faciámus hic tria tabernácula, tibi unum, Móysi unum et Elíæ unum. Adhuc eo loquénte, ecce, nubes lúcida obumbrávit eos. Et ecce vox de nube, dicens: Hic est Fílius meus diléctus, in quo mihi bene complácui: ipsum audíte. Et audiéntes discípuli, cecidérunt in fáciem suam, et timuérunt valde. Et accéssit Jesus, et tétigit eos, dixítque eis: Súrgite, et nolíte timére. Levántes autem óculos suos, néminem vidérunt nisi solum Jesum. Et descendéntibus illis de monte, præcépit eis Jesus, dicens: Némini dixéritis visiónem, donec Fílius hóminis a mórtuis resúrgat.

pleased, hear ye Him. And the disciples hearing, fell upon their face; and were very much afraid: and Jesus came and touched them, and said to them, Arise, and fear not. And they lifting up their eyes saw no one, but only Jesus. And as they came down from the mountain, Jesus charged them, saying, Tell the vision to no man, till the Son of man be risen from the dead. CREDO.

OFFERTORY. *Ps 111: 3*

Glória et divítiæ in domo ejus: et justítia ejus manet in sǽculum sǽculi, allelúja.

GLORY and wealth are in His house: and His justice remaineth forever and ever. Alleluia.

SECRET.

Obláta, quǽsumus, Dómine, múnera gloriósa Unigéniti tui Transfiguratióne sanctífica: nosque a peccatórum máculis, splendóribus ipsíus illustratiónis emúnda. Per eúmdem Dóminum.

Sanctify, we beseech Thee, O Lord, the gifts offered on the glorious transfiguration of Thine only-begotten Son, and by the splendors of that very illumination cleanse us from the stains of our sins. Through the same.

SECRET. *Pro Ss. Martyribus*

Múnera tibi, Dómine, nostræ devotiónis offérimus: quæ et pro tuórum tibi grata sint honóre justórum, et nobis salutária, te miseránte, reddántur. Per Dóminum.

We offer Thee, O Lord, the gifts of our devotion; may they be rendered both pleasing unto Thee, for the honor of Thy just ones, and to us, through Thy mercy, helpful to salvation. Through our Lord.

COMMUNION. *Matt 17: 9*

Visiónem, quam vidístis, némini dixéritis, donec a mórtuis resúrgat Fílius hóminis. (Ps 83: 5) ℣. *Beáti qui hábitant in domo tua, Dómine; in sǽcula sæculórum laudábunt te.*

TELL THE VISION you have seen to no man, till the Son of man be risen from the dead. ℣. *Blessed are they that dwell in Thy house, O Lord: they shall praise Thee for ever and ever.*

POSTCOMMUNION.

Præsta, quǽsumus, omnípotens Deus: ut sacrosáncta Fílii tui Transfiguratiónis mystéria, quæ sollémni celebrámus offício, purificáta mentis intellegéntia consequámur. Per eúmdem Dóminum.

Grant, we beseech Thee, O almighty God, that with the understanding of a purified mind we may follow those sacred mysteries of Thy Son's transfiguration which we celebrate with our solemn office. Through the same.

POSTCOMMUNION. *Pro Ss. Martyribus*

Præsta nobis, quǽsumus, Dómine: intercedéntibus sanctis Martýribus tuis Xysto, Felicíssimo et Agapíto; ut, quod ore contíngimus, pura mente capiámus. Per Dóminum.

Grant us, we beseech Thee; O Lord, by the intercession of Thy holy martyrs, Sixtus, Felicissimus, and Agapitus, that what we touch with our lips we may receive with a pure heart. Through our Lord.

This Mass formulary is relatively recent, circa 1450AD. The Mass Propers were all borrowed from other places. French settings of the Offertory tended to match what we have in the Vatican Edition, whereas German versions set that text to different melodies. The Communion is adapted from an ancient antiphon, changing only one note.

— *15 August, Our Lady's Assumption* — *I Classis.*

IN ASSUMPTIONE BEATAE MARIAE VIRGINIS

INTROIT. *Apocalypse 12: 1*

A GREAT SIGN appeared in heaven: A woman clothed with the sun, and the moon under her feet, and on her head a crown of twelve stars. (Ps 97: 1) Sing ye to the Lord a new canticle: because He hath done wonderful things. ℣. Glory.

Signum magnum appáruit in cælo: múlier amicta sole, et luna sub pédibus ejus, et in cápite ejus coróna stellárum duódecim. ℣. Cantáte Dómino cánticum novum: quia mirabília fecit. ℣. Glória Patri.

COLLECT.

Almighty, everlasting God, who hath taken up the Immaculate Virgin Mary, the Mother of Thy Son, with body and soul into heavenly glory: grant, we beseech Thee, that we may always, intent on higher things, deserve to be partakers of her glory. Through the same.

Omnípotens sempitérne Deus, qui Immaculátam Vírginem Maríam, Fílii tui genitrícem, córpore et ánima ad cæléstem glóriam assumpsísti: concéde, quæsumus; ut, ad supérna semper inténti, ipsíus glóriæ mereámur esse consórtes. Per eúmdem Dóminum.

EPISTLE. *Judith 13: 22-25; 15, 10*

THE LORD hath blessed thee by His power, because by thee He hath brought our enemies to nought. Blessed art thou, O daughter, by the Lord the most high God, above all women upon the earth. Blessèd be the Lord, who made heaven and earth, who hath directed thee to the cutting off the head of the prince of our enemies; because He hath so magnified thy name this day, that thy praise shall not depart out of the mouth of men who shall be mindful of the power of the Lord, forever: for that thou hast not spared thy life, by reason of the distress and tribulation of thy people; but hast prevented our ruin in the presence of our God. Thou art the glory of Jerusalem, thou art the joy of Israel, thou art the honor of our people.

Benedíxit te Dóminus in virtúte sua, quia per te ad níhilum redégit inimícos nostros. Benedícta es tu, fília, a Dómino Deo excélso, præ ómnibus muliéribus super terram. Benedíctus Dóminus, qui creávit cælum et terram, qui te diréxit in vúlnera cápitis príncipis inimicórum nostrórum; quia hódie nomen tuum ita magnificávit, ut non recédat laus tua de ore hóminum, qui mémores fúerint virtútis Dómini in ætérnum, pro quibus non pepercísti ánimæ tuæ propter angústias et tribulatiónem géneris tui, sed subvenísti ruínæ ante conspéctum Dei nostri. Tu glória Jerúsalem, tu lætítia Ísraël, tu honorificéntia pópuli nostri.

GRADUAL & ALLELUIA. *Ps 44: 11-12, 14 & Trad.*

HARKEN O daughter, and see, incline thine ear: and the King shall greatly desire thy beauty. ℣. The daughter of the King comes in, all beautiful: her robes are of golden cloth.
Alleluia, alleluia. ℣. Mary has been taken up into heaven, the choirs of angels rejoice. Alleluia.

Audi, fília, et vide, et inclína aurem tuam, et concupíscit Rex decórem tuum. ℣. Tota decóra ingréditur fília Regis, textúræ áureæ sunt amíctus ejus. | Allelúja, allelúja. ℣. Assúmpta est María in cælum: gaudet exércitus Angelórum. Allelúja.

GAUDEAMUS OMNES IN DOMINO DIEM FESTUM CELEBRANTES SUB HONORE BEATAE MARIAE VIRGINIS: DE CUJUS ASSUMPTIONE GAUDENT ANGELI, ET COLLAUDANT FILIUM DEI. ✠

DIXITQUE DOMINUS: FACIES MEA PRAECEDET TE, ET REQUIEM DABO TIBI. (Ex 33:14)

AND THE LORD SAID: MY FACE SHALL GO BEFORE THEE, AND I WILL GIVE THEE REST.

LET ALL REJOICE IN THE LORD, CELEBRATING A FESTIVAL DAY IN HONOR OF THE BLESSED VIRGIN MARY, FOR WHOSE ASSUMPTION THE ANGELS REJOICE AND GIVE PRAISE TO THE SON OF GOD. ✠

GOSPEL. *Luke 1: 41-50*

ELIZABETH was filled with the Holy Ghost: and she cried out with a loud voice and said: Blessed art thou among women, and blessed is the fruit of thy womb. And whence is this to me, that the mother of my Lord should come to me? For behold, as soon as the voice of thy salutation sounded in my ears, the infant in my womb leaped for joy. And blessed art thou that hast believed, because those things shall be accomplished that were spoken to thee by the Lord. And Mary said, My soul doth magnify the Lord: and my spirit hath rejoiced in God my Savior; because He hath regarded the humility of His handmaid: for behold from henceforth all generations shall call me blessed. Because He that is mighty hath done great things to me, and holy is His name, and His mercy is from generation unto generations, to them that fear Him. CREDO.

In illo témpore: Repléta est Spíritu Sancto Elísabeth et exclamávit voce magna, et dixit: Benedícta tu inter mulíeres, et benedíctus fructus ventris tui. Et unde hoc mihi ut véniat mater Dómini mei ad me? Ecce enim ut facta est vox salutatiónis tuæ in áuribus meis, exsultávit in gáudio infans in útero meo. Et beáta, quæ credidísti, quóniam perficiéntur ea, quæ dicta sunt tibi a Dómino. Et ait María: Magníficat ánima mea Dóminum; et exsultávit spíritus meus in Deo salutári meo; quia respéxit humilitátem ancíllæ suæ, ecce enim ex hoc beátam me dicent omnes generatiónes. Quia fecit mihi magna qui potens est, et sanctum nomen ejus, et misericórdia ejus a progénie in progénies timéntibus eum.

OFFERTORY. *Gen 3: 15*

I WILL PUT enmities between thee and the Woman, and between thy seed and her Seed.

Inimicítias ponam inter te et mulíerem, et semen tuum et semen illíus.

SECRET.

May the offering of our devotion ascend to Thee, O Lord; and through the intercession of the most blessed Virgin Mary, who was taken up into heaven, may our hearts be inflamed with the fire of love, and continually long for Thee. Through our Lord.

Ascéndat ad te, Dómine, nostræ devotiónis oblátio, et, beatíssima Vírgine María in cælum assúmpta intercedénte, corda nostra, caritátis igne succénsa, ad te júgiter áspirent. Per Dóminum.

The Preface of the Blessed Virgin Mary (page 191) follows the Secret.

COMMUNION. *Luke 1: 48-49*

ALL GENERATIONS shall call me blessed, because He that is mighty hath done great things to me. (Luke 1: 46-47) ℣. *My soul magnifies the Lord; my spirit has found joy in God, Who is my Savior.*

Beátam me dicent omnes generatiónes, quia fecit mihi magna qui potens est. ℣. *Magníficat ánima mea Dóminum: et exsultávit spíritus meus in Deo salutári meo.*

POSTCOMMUNION.

Now that we have received, O Lord, the Sacrament of salvation, grant, we beseech Thee, that through the merits and the intercession of the blessed Virgin Mary,

Sumptis, Dómine, salutáribus sacraméntis: da, quǽsumus; ut, méritis et intercessióne beátæ Vírginis Maríæ in cælum assúmptæ, ad resurrectiónis glóriam perducámur. Per Dóminum.

who was taken up into heaven, we may be brought to the glory of the resurrection. Through our Lord.

Our Lady's Assumption was dogmatically defined by Venerable Pope Pius XII on 1 November 1950. At that time, these new Propers (still in an experimental stage) were introduced—and they became universal sometime before 1954. Therefore, all the Propers for this Mass are modern except the Alleluia Verse. The Alleluia Verse is, as Dom Gajard puts it, "of considerable antiquity." The 1950s texts are fitted ("adapted") to ancient melodies. After the Second Vatican Council, several—but not all—of these were kept (in spite of the fact that they are Neo-Gregorian) because they had attained "universal use" according to the PRAENOTANDA *of the "Ordo Cantus Missae."*

II Classis.

—14 September, Exaltation of the Cross—

IN EXALTATIONE SANCTAE CRUCIS

INTROIT. *Gal 6: 14*

Nos autem gloriári opórtet in Cruce Dómini nostri Jesu Christi: in quo est salus, vita et resurréctio nostra: per quem salváti et liberáti sumus. ℣. Deus misereátur nostri, et benedícat nobis: illúminet vultum suum super nos, et misereátur nostri. ℣. Glória Patri.

BUT IT BEHOOVES US to glory in the cross of our Lord Jesus Christ: in Whom is our salvation, life, and resurrection; by Whom we are saved and delivered. (Ps 66: 2) May God have mercy on us, and bless us; may He cause the light of His countenance to shine upon us, and may He have mercy on us. ℣. Glory.

COLLECT.

Deus, qui nos hodiérna die Exaltatiónis sanctæ Crucis ánnua sollemnitáte lætíficas: præsta, quæsumus; ut, cujus mystérium in terra cognóvimus, ejus redemptiónis prǽmia in cælo mereámur. Per eúmdem Dóminum.

O God, Who dost gladden us this day by the annual solemnity of the exaltation of the Holy Cross, grant, we beseech Thee, that, as we have known its mystery on earth, we may deserve in heaven the reward which it had purchased. Through the same.

EPISTLE. *Philipp 2: 5-11*

Fratres: Hoc enim sentíte in vobis, quod et in Christo Jesu: qui, cum in forma Dei esset, non rapínam arbitrátus est esse se æquálem Deo: sed semetípsum exinanívit, formam servi accípiens, in similitúdinem hóminum factus, et hábitu invéntus ut homo. Humiliávit semetípsum, factus obédiens usque ad mortem, mortem autem crucis. Propter quod et Deus exaltávit illum: et donávit illi nomen, quod est super omne nomen:
(*hic genuflectitur*)
ut in nómine Jesu omne genu flectátur cæléstium, terréstrium et infernórum: et omnis lingua confiteátur, quia Dóminus Jesus Christus in glória est Dei Patris.

BRETHREN, Let this mind be in you, which was also in Christ Jesus; Who being in the form of God, thought it not robbery to be equal with God; but made Himself as nothing, taking the form of a servant, being made in the likeness of men, and in habit found as a man. He humbled Himself, becoming obedient unto death, even the death of the cross. For which cause God also hath exalted Him, and hath given Him a name which is above all names: (*genuflect*) that in the name of Jesus every knee should bow, of those that are in heaven, on earth, and under the earth: and that every tongue should confess that the Lord Jesus Christ is in the glory of God the Father.

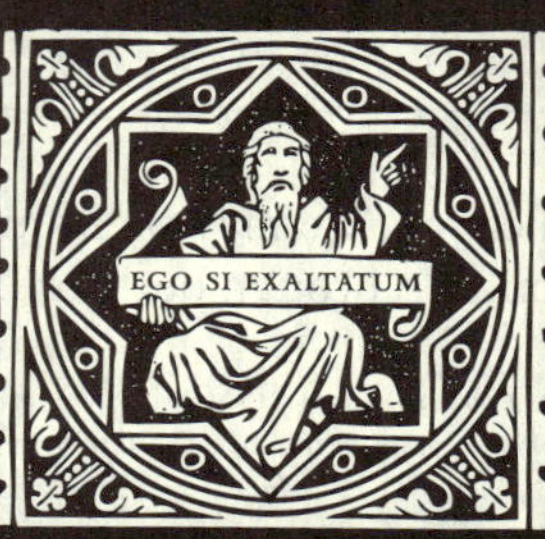

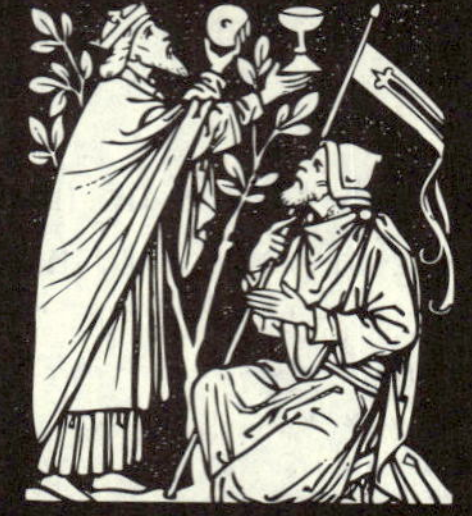

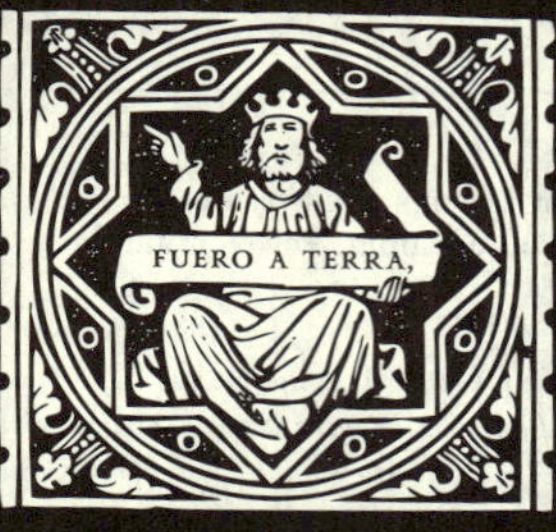

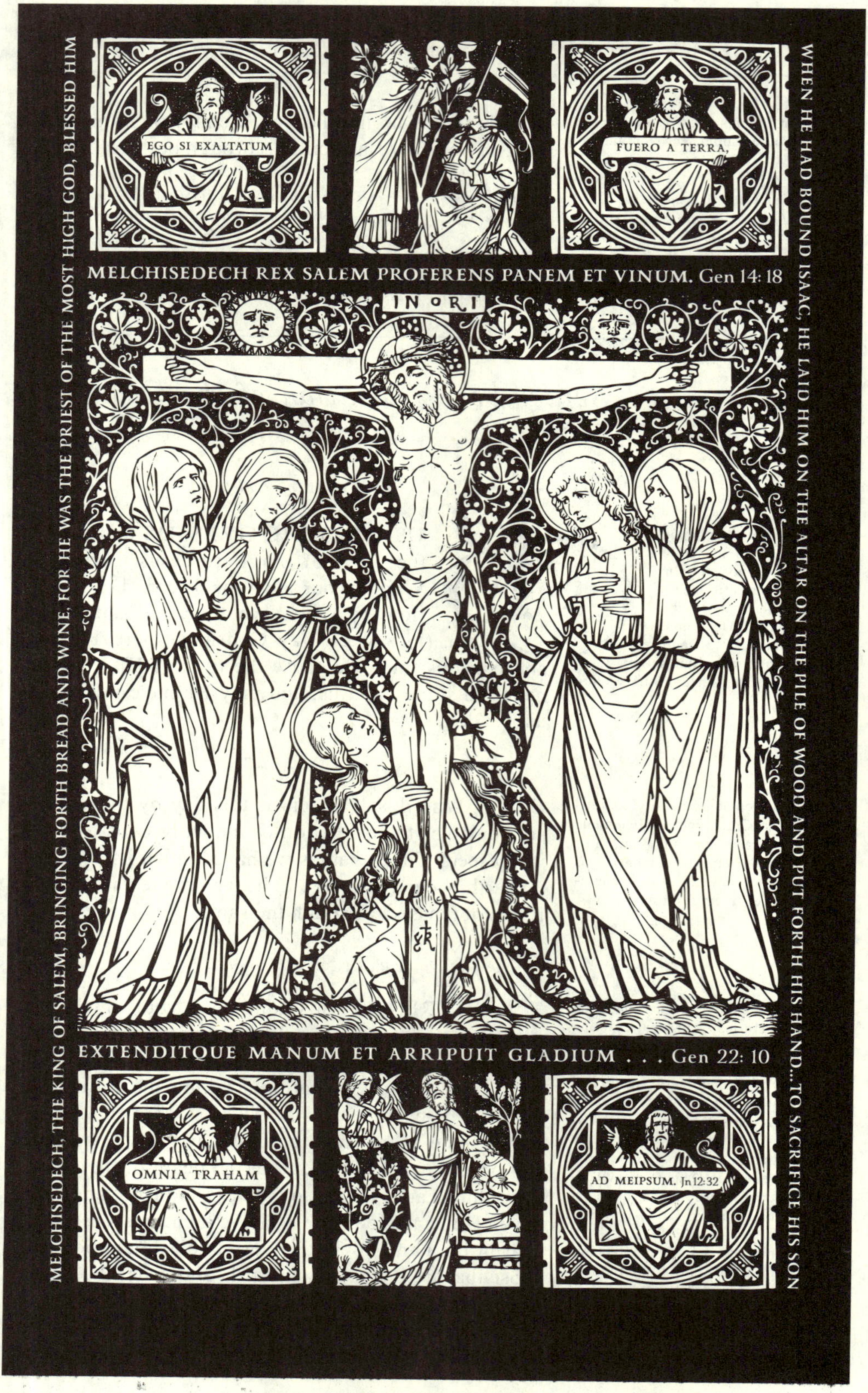
EGO SI EXALTATUM
FUERO A TERRA,
MELCHISEDECH REX SALEM PROFERENS PANEM ET VINUM. Gen 14: 18
INRI
EXTENDITQUE MANUM ET ARRIPUIT GLADIUM . . . Gen 22: 10
OMNIA TRAHAM
AD MEIPSUM. Jn 12:32
MELCHISEDECH, THE KING OF SALEM, BRINGING FORTH BREAD AND WINE, FOR HE WAS THE PRIEST OF THE MOST HIGH GOD, BLESSED HIM
WHEN HE HAD BOUND ISAAC, HE LAID HIM ON THE ALTAR ON THE PILE OF WOOD AND PUT FORTH HIS HAND...TO SACRIFICE HIS SON

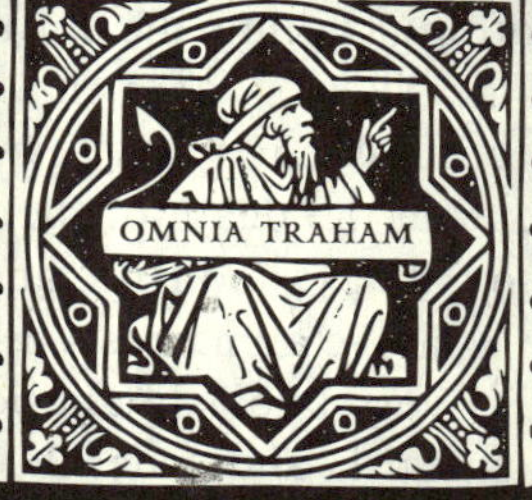

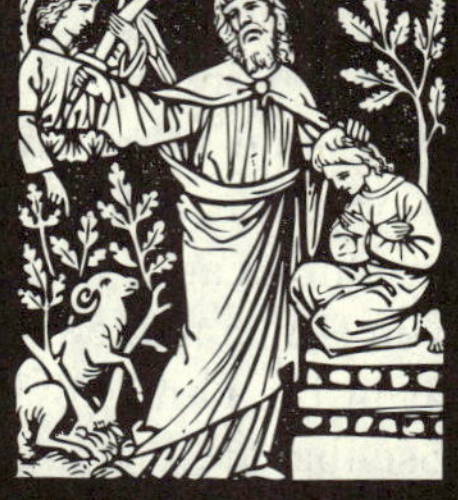

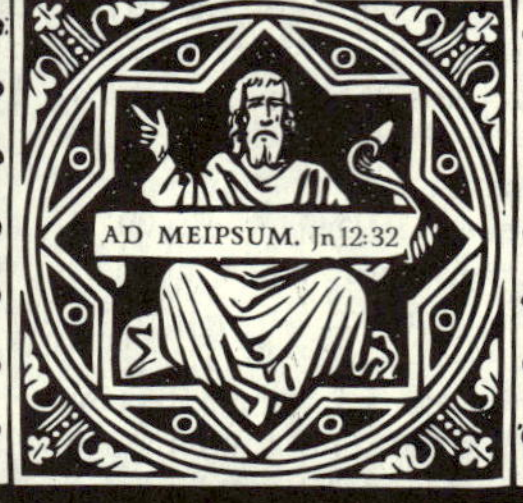

GRADUAL & ALLELUIA. *Phillipp 2: 8, 9 & Trad.*

Christus factus est pro nobis obédiens usque ad mortem, mortem autem crucis. ℣. Propter quod et Deus exaltávit illum, et dedit illi nomen, quod est super omne nomen.

Allelúja, allelúja. ℣. Dulce lignum, dulces clavos, dúlcia ferens póndera: quæ sola fuísti digna sustinére Regem cælórum et Dóminum. Allelúja.

CHRIST BECAME OBEDIENT for us unto death: even the death of the cross. ℣. For which cause also God hath exalted Him and hath given Him a name which is above all names. Alleluia, alleluia. ℣. Sweet the wood, sweet the nails, sweet the load that hangs thereon: to bear up the King and Lord of heaven nought was worthy save thou, O holy cross. Alleluia.

GOSPEL.
John 12: 31-36

In illo témpore: Dixit Jesus turbis Judæórum: Nunc judícium est mundi: nunc princeps hujus mundi ejiciátur foras. Et ego si exaltátum fúero a terra, ómnia traham ad meípsum. (Hoc autem dicébat, signíficans, qua morte esset moritúrus.) Respóndit ei turba; Nos audívimus ex lege, quia Christus manet in ætérnum: et quómodo tu dicis: Opórtet exaltári Fílium hóminis? Quis est iste Fílius hóminis? Dixit ergo eis Jesus: Adhuc módicum lumen in vobis est. Ambuláte, dum lucem habétis, ut non vos ténebræ comprehéndant: et qui ámbulat in ténebris, nescit, quo vadat. Dum lucem habétis, crédite in lucem, ut fílii lucis sitis.

At that time: Jesus said to the multitude of the Jews:

NOW IS THE JUDGMENT of the world: now shall the prince of this world be cast out. And I, if I be lifted up from the earth, will draw all things to Myself. (Now this He said, signifying what death He should die.) The multitude answered Him, We have heard out of the law, that Christ abideth forever: and how sayest Thou, The Son of man must be lifted up? Who is the Son of man? Jesus therefore said to them, Yet a little while, the light is among you. Walk whilst you have the light, that the darkness overtake you not. And he that walketh in darkness knoweth not whither he goeth. Whilst you have the light, believe in the light; that you may be the children of light. CREDO.

OFFERTORY. *Trad.*

Prótege, Dómine, plebem tuam per signum sanctæ Crucis ab ómnibus insídiis inimicórum ómnium: ut tibi gratam exhibeámus servitútem, et acceptábile fiat sacrifícium nostrum, allelúja. ℣. *Te sancta Dei crux humíliter obsecrámus, ut tua virtúte nostrum pectus múnias, ánimas custódias, cogitatiónes sanctífices per Christum Jesum, qui pepéndit in te.* ℣. *Qui pro mundi salúte in ligno crucis ínnocens pependísti, miserére pópulo, quem redemísti: ut sacro signáculo insignítus a perículis ómnibus sit secúrus.* ℣. *Salvátor mundi salva nos omnes et ómnia, quæ ádjuvant, benígnus nobis impénde: et cuncta nocéntia a nobis procul repélle: atque ad protegéndum nos déxteram tuæ majestátis exténde.*

PROTECT Thy people, O Lord, through the sign of the holy cross, from the snares of all enemies, that we may pay Thee a pleasing service, and our sacrifice be acceptable, allelulia. ℣. *Humbly we beg thee, holy cross of God, that through thy power thou mightest strengthen our hearts, guard our souls, hallow our thoughts through Christ Jesus, Who hung from thee.* ℣. *Thou, who wert innocent hanging on the cross for the salvation of the world, have mercy on the people whom Thou hast redeemed: that it, signed with the holy sign, may be safe from all perils.* ℣. *Savior of the world, save all of us and graciously grant us whatever helps us: and remove far from us everything harmful: and stretch out the right hand of Thy majesty to protect us.*

SECRET.

Being about to be fed with the body and blood of Jesus Christ our Lord, through Whom the banner of the cross was sanctified, we beseech Thee O Lord, our God, that, as we have had the grace to adore it, so we may forever enjoy the effect of its salutary glory. Through the same.

Jesu Christi, Dómini nostri, Córpore et Sánguine saginándi, per quem Crucis est sanctificátum vexíllum: quǽsumus, Dómine, Deus noster; ut, sicut illud adoráre merúimus, ita perénniter ejus glóriæ salutáris potiámur efféctu. Per eúmdem Dóminum.

The Preface of the Holy Cross (page 190) follows the Secret.

COMMUNION. *Trad.*

THROUGH the sign of the cross deliver us from our enemies, O our God. ℣. *Shall I not love Thee, Lord, my only defender? The Lord is my firmament, my refuge, and my deliverer.*

Per signum Crucis de inimícis nostris líbera nos, Deus noster. (Ps 17: 2-3) ℣. *Díligam te, Dómine, fortitúdo mea: Dóminus firmaméntum meum, et refúgium meum, et liberátor meus.*

POSTCOMMUNION.

Be Thou with us, O Lord, our God, and as Thou dost make us rejoice in honor of the holy cross, defend us also by its perpetual assistance. Through our Lord.

Adésto nobis, Dómine, Deus noster: et, quos sanctæ Crucis lætári facis honóre, ejus quoque perpétuis deféndе subsídiis. Per Dóminum.

The communion antiphon for 14 September is identical to that of 3 May ("In Inventione S. Crucis"), a feast downgraded in 1961. Both feasts are ancient, yet—bewilderingly—no manuscript assigns extra verses for it. It is difficult to trace the history of this communion antiphon, although it is certainly ancient; e.g. this chant appears in Montpellier H. 159. The melody seems to have been adapted (over a millenium ago) from another communion: "Dilexísti Justítiam," the ancient communion antiphon for the Mass of the Assumption.

PART I • FEAST OF THE EXALTATION OF THE HOLY CROSS

Constantine the Great was sole ruler of the Roman Empire from 324AD until his death in 337AD. He built churches in Rome and "New Rome" (*Constantinople*). His mother, Saint Helena (d. 330AD) razed to the ground idolatrous buildings that pagans had constructed in Jerusalem: a temple to Venus above CALVARY and another to Jupiter above the HOLY SEPULCHER, according to Dom Guéranger. Constantine's mother then discovered what is believed to be the True Cross in 326AD. Emperor Constantine built a basilica above Calvary, and on 14 September 335AD (according to Dom Gaspar Lefebvre) the dedication of this basilica—which we refer to as *The Church of the Holy Sepulcher*—was celebrated with great solemnity by the bishops who that same year assisted at the Council of Tyre, a city in Lebanon about 100 miles north of Jerusalem. Dom Fernand Cabrol (d. 1937) understands a comment by *Ætheria the Pilgrim* (a.k.a. Saint Silvia) to mean that the yearly commemoration of the dedication of this basilica "was on an equal footing with the feasts of Easter and the Epiphany."

Saint Helena divided the True Cross into three sections, according to Dom Lefebvre, sending one section to Rome, another to Constantinople, and the third to Jerusalem. In 614AD, the Persian invaders stole the True Cross from Jerusalem. These events are told by 14 September Matins: cf. Lesson iv ("Chósroas Persárum Rex"), Lesson v ("Quibus Cládibus"), and Lesson vi ("Quod Factum Illústri"). In 629AD, Heraclitus, the great emperor, defeated the Persians and carried the True Cross on his own shoulders into Jerusalem.

PART II • FEAST OF THE EXALTATION OF THE HOLY CROSS

The history of these feasts—both 3 May ("Finding of the Cross") and 14 September ("Exaltation of the Cross")—is shrouded in mystery. It would be a mistake to believe these feasts had a specific and consistent meaning at all times and in all places. The arcane history of both feasts has engendered much confusion. For instance, some claim—on the basis of *Lib. Pontif. I, p. cviii*—that the date on which Saint Helena found the True Cross was 3 May, whereas the *Marian Missal* of 1955 claims it was actually 14 September. Others claim 14 September was the date on which the True Cross was returned by Emperor Heraclitus. Contradicting that, Dom Lefebvre claims the True Cross was returned on 3 May 628AD [sic].

Irrespective of discrepancies, these two feasts have come to denote particular things in our times. The feast of 3 May commemorates the (4th century) finding of the True Cross by Saint Helena. The feast of 14 September commemorates the (7th century) rescue of the True Cross from the Persians by Emperor Heraclitus. While it is true that *Rubricarum Instructum* (25 July 1960) eliminated the 3 May feast from the universal calendar, it was retained in a section marked "Missae Pro Aliquibus Locis." The feast of 14 September has many names: *Triumph of the Cross, Elevation of the Cross, Holy-Rood Day, Uplifting of the Cross,* and so forth, but the word EXALT—which means "to glorify or hold in very high regard"—seems the most fitting of all.

In ancient times, this feast was for all the angels, but owing in large part to the dedication of two churches in Rome to Saint Michael—one on Monte Gargano and the other in the Circus Maximus—the feast came to honor Saint Michael the Archangel specifically, and was celebrated with great fanfare.

—*29 September, Michaelmas*—

I Classis.

IN DEDICATIONE S. MICHAËLIS ARCHANGELI

INTROIT. *Ps 102: 20*

BLESS the Lord, all ye His angels: you that are mighty in strength, and execute His word, harkening to the voice of His orders. (Ps 102: 1) Bless the Lord, O my soul: and let all that is within me bless His holy name. ℣. Glory.

Benedícite Dóminum, omnes Ángeli ejus: poténtes virtúte, qui fácitis verbum ejus, ad audiéndam vocem sermónum ejus. ℣. Bénedic, ánima mea, Dómino: et ómnia, quæ intra me sunt, nómini sancto ejus. ℣. Glória Patri.

COLLECT.

O God, Who dost in wonderful order dispose the ministries of angels and men, mercifully grant that our lives be fortified by those who continually stand in Thy presence and minister before Thee in heaven. Through our Lord.

Deus, qui, miro órdine, Angelórum ministéria hominúmque dispénsas: concéde propítius; ut, a quibus tibi ministrántibus in cælo semper assístitur, ab his in terra vita nostra muniátur. Per Dóminum.

EPISTLE. *Apoc 1: 1-5*

IN THOSE DAYS: God signified the things which must shortly come to pass, sending by His angel to His servant John, who hath given testimony to the word of God, and the testimony of Jesus Christ, what things soever he hath seen. Blessed is he that readeth and heareth the words of this prophecy, and keepeth those things which are written in it; for the time is at hand. John to the seven churches which are in Asia: Grace be unto you and peace from Him that is, and that was, and that is to come; and from the seven spirits which are before His throne; and from Jesus Christ, Who is the faithful witness, the first begotten of the dead, and the prince of the kings of the earth Who hath loved us, and washed us from our sins in His own blood.

In diébus illis: Significávit Deus, quæ opórtet fíeri cito, mittens per Ángelum suum servo suo Joánni, qui testimónium perhíbuit verbo Dei, et testimónium Jesu Christi, quæcúmque vidit. Beátus, qui legit et audit verba prophetíæ hujus: et servat ea, quæ in ea scripta sunt: tempus enim prope est. Joánnes septem ecclésiis, quæ sunt in Asia. Grátia vobis et pax ab eo, qui est et qui erat et qui ventúrus est: et a septem spirítibus, qui in conspéctu throni ejus sunt: et a Jesu Christo, qui est testis fidélis, primogénitus mortuórum et princeps regum terræ, qui diléxit nos et lavit nos a peccátis nostris in sánguine suo.

GRADUAL & ALLELUIA. *Ps 102: 20, 1 & Trad.*

BLESS THE LORD, all ye His angels: you that are mighty in strength, that do His will. ℣. O my soul, bless thou the Lord: and all that is within me praise His holy name.

Benedícite Dóminum, omnes Ángeli ejus: poténtes virtúte, qui fácitis verbum ejus. ℣. Bénedic, ánima mea, Dóminum, et ómnia interióra mea, nomen sanctum ejus.

Allelúja, allelúja. ℣. Sancte Míchaël Archángele, defénde nos in prælio: ut non pereámus in treméndo judício. Allelúja.

℣. Holy archangel Michael, defend us in battle, that we perish not in the dreadful judgment. Alleluia.

GOSPEL. *Matt 18: 1-10*

In illo témpore: Accessérunt discípuli ad Jesum, dicéntes: Quis, putas, major est in regno cælórum? Et ádvocans Jesus párvulum, státuit eum in médio eórum et dixit: Amen, dico vobis, nisi convérsi fuéritis et efficiámini sicut párvuli, non intrábitis in regnum cælórum. Quicúmque ergo humiliáverit se sicut párvulus iste, hic est major in regno cælórum. Et qui suscéperit unum párvulum talem in nómine meo, me súscipit. Qui autem scandalizáverit unum de pusíllis istis, qui in me credunt, expédit ei, ut suspendátur mola asinária in collo ejus, et demergátur in profúndum maris.

THE DISCIPLES CAME to Jesus, saying, Who, thinkest Thou, is the greater in the kingdom of heaven? And Jesus calling unto Him a little child, set him in the midst of them, and said, Amen, I say to you, unless you be converted, and become as little children, you shall not enter into the kingdom of heaven. Whosoever therefore shall humble himself as this little child, he is the greater in the kingdom of heaven: and he that shall receive one such little child in My name, receiveth Me; but he that shall scandalize one of these little ones that believe in Me, it were better for him that a millstone should be hanged about his neck, and that he should be drowned in the depth of the sea.

Væ mundo a scándalis! Necésse est enim, ut véniant scándala: verúmtamen væ hómini illi, per quem scándalum venit! Si autem manus tua vel pes tuus scandalízat te, abscíde eum et prójice abs te: bonum tibi est ad vitam íngredi débilem vel cláudum, quam duas manus vel duos pedes habéntem mitti in ignem ætérnum. Et si óculus tuus scandalízat te, érue eum et prójice abs te: bonum tibi est cum uno óculo in vitam intráre, quam duos óculos habéntem mitti in gehénnam ignis. Vidéte, ne contemnátis unum ex his pusíllis: dico enim vobis, quia Ángeli eórum in cælis semper vident fáciem Patris mei, qui in cælis est.

Woe to the world because of scandals: for it must needs be that scandals come; but nevertheless woe to that man by whom the scandal cometh. And if thy hand, or thy foot, scandalize thee, cut it off, and cast it from thee. It is better for thee to go into life maimed or lame, than having two hands or two feet, to be cast into everlasting fire. And if thine eye scandalize thee, pluck it out, and cast it from thee. It is better for thee having one eye to enter into life, than having two eyes to be cast into hell fire. See that you despise not one of these little ones; for I say to you, that their angels in heaven always see the face of My Father Who is in heaven. CREDO.

OFFERTORY. *Apoc 8: 3, 4*

Stetit Ángelus juxta aram templi, habens thuríbulum áureum in manu sua, et data sunt ei incénsa multa: et ascéndit fumus arómatum in conspéctu Dei, allelúja. ℣. *In conspéctu Angelórum psallam tibi, Dómine: et adorábo ad templum sanctum tuum et confitébor tibi, Dómine.*

AN ANGEL stood near the altar of the temple, having a golden censer in his hand: and there was given to him much incense: and the smoke of the perfumes ascended before God, alleluia. ℣. *I will sing praise to Thee in the sight of Thine angels, O Lord: and I will worship towards Thy holy temple, and I will give glory to Thee, O Lord.*

SECRET.

We offer Thee sacrifices of praise, O Lord, humbly praying that Thou be pleased to receive them, through the angelic intercession in our behalf, and grant that they may avail for our salvation. Through our Lord.

Hóstias tibi, Dñe, laudis offérimus, supplíciter deprecántes: ut eásdẽ, angélico pro nobis interveniénte suffrágio, et placátus accípias, et ad salútẽ nostrã proveníre concédas. Per Dñm.

* *The "ad libitum" Preface for the angels (page 196) may be used.*

COMMUNION. *Dan 3: 58*

ALL YE ANGELS of the Lord, bless the Lord: sing a hymn, and exalt Him above all forever, alleluia. ℣. *Then they cried out upon all things the Lord had made, to bless Him, and praise Him, and extol His name for ever.*

Benedícite, omnes Ángeli Dómini, Dóminum: hymnum dícite et superexaltáte eum in sǽcula. (Dan 3: 57) ℣. *Benedícite, ómnia ópera Dómini, Dómino: laudáte et superexaltáte eum in sǽcula.* —239Laon|927 • Circa 927AD

POSTCOMMUNION.

Relying upon the intercession of blessed Michael, Thine archangel, O Lord, we Thy suppliants pray that what we perform with our lips we may attain with our hearts. Through our Lord.

Beáti Archángeli tui Michäélis intercessióne suffúlti: súpplices te, Dómine, deprecámur; ut, quod ore proséquimur, contingámus et mente. Per Dóminum.

This feast commemorates an important victory that took place against the Turks in 1571. Father Michele Ghislieri—a Dominican priest who ended up becoming Pope Saint Pius V—attributed this victory to the power of the Rosary and instituted this feast, formerly known as "The Feast of Our Lady of Victory." The victory took place on 7 October.

—*7 October, Our Lady of the Rosary*— *II Classis.*

BEATAE MARIAE VIRGINIS A ROSARIO

INTROIT. *Trad.*

LET US ALL rejoice in the Lord, keeping a feastday in honor of the Blessed Virgin Mary, for whose celebration the angels rejoice and unite in praising the Son of God. (Ps 44: 2) My heart hath uttered a good word; I speak my works to the King. ℣. Glory.

Gaudeámus omnes in Dómino, diem festum celebrántes sub honóre beátæ Maríæ Vírginis: de cujus sollemnitáte gaudent Ángeli et colláudant Fílium Dei. ℣. Eructávit cor meum verbum bonum: dico ego ópera mea Regi. ℣. Glória Patri. (*In a Votive Mass, "Salve Sancta Parens" is substituted for this Introit.*)

COLLECT.

O God, Whose only-begotten Son, by His life, death, and resurrection hath purchased for us the rewards of eternal life: grant, we beseech Thee, that, meditating on the mysteries of the most holy Rosary of the Blessed Virgin Mary, we may imitate what they contain and obtain what they promise. Through the same.

Deus, cujus Unigénitus per vitam, mortem et resurrectiónem suam nobis salútis ætérnæ prǽmia comparávit: concéde, quǽsumus; ut, hæc mystéria sacratíssimo beátæ Maríæ Vírginis Rosário recoléntes, et imitémur, quod cóntinent, et quod promíttunt, assequámur. Per eúmdem Dóminum.

VIRGO, DEI GENITRIX, QUEM TOTUS NON CAPIT ORBIS: IN TUA SE CLAUSIT VISCERA FACTUS HOMO.
VIRGIN MOTHER OF GOD, HE WHOM THE WORLD CANNOT CONTAIN WAS ENCLOSED IN THY WOMB, AND WAS MADE MAN.

TE GESTIENTEM GAUDIIS, TE SAUCIAM DOLORIBUS, TE JUGI AMICTAM GLORIA, O VIRGO MATER PANGIMUS.
WE SING THEE O VIRGIN MOTHER AS EXULTING WITH JOY, WOUNDED WITH SORROWS, & ROBED WITH ETERNAL GLORY.

QUOD EVA TRISTIS ABSTULIT, TU REDDIS ALMO GERMINE.
WHAT UNHAPPY EVE LOST, THOU DOST RESTORE BY THY HOLY CHILD.

COLLECT. *Et fit commemoratio S. Marci Papae et Confessoris:*

O Eternal Shepherd, do Thou look favorably upon Thy flock, which we beseech Thee to guard and keep for evermore through the blessed Mark, Supreme Pontiff, whom Thou didst choose to be the chief shepherd of the whole Church. Through our Lord.

Gregem tuum, Pastor ætérne, placátus inténde: et per beátum Marcum Summum Pontíficem perpétua protectióne custódi; quem totíus Ecclésiæ præstitísti esse pastórem. Per Dóminum.

EPISTLE. *Prov 8: 22-24, 32-35*

THE LORD possessed me in the beginning of His ways, before He made anything, from the beginning. I was set up from eternity, and of old, before the earth was made. The depths were not as yet, and I was already conceived. Now therefore, ye children, hear me: Blessed are they that keep my ways. Hear instruction, and be wise, and refuse it not. Blessed is the man that heareth me, and that watcheth daily at my gates; and waiteth at the posts of my doors. He that shall find me, shall find life, and shall have salvation from the Lord.

Dóminus possédit me in inítio viárum suárum, ántequam quidquam fáceret a princípio. Ab ætérno ordináta sum et ex antíquis, ántequam terra fíeret. Nondum erant abýssi, et ego jam concépta eram. Nunc ergo, fílii, audíte me: Beáti, qui custódiunt vias meas. Audíte disciplínam, et estóte sapiéntes, et nolíte abjícere eam. Beátus homo, qui audit me et qui vígilat ad fores meas cotídie et obsérvat ad postes óstii mei. Qui me invénerit, invéniet vitam et háuriet salútem a Dómino.

GRADUAL & ALLELUIA. *Ps 44: 5, 11, 12 & Trad.*

BECAUSE of truth, and meekness, and justice: and thy right hand shall conduct thee wonderfully. ℣. Hear, O daughter, and see, and incline thine ear; for the King hath desired thy beauty.

℣. The solemnity of the glorious Virgin Mary, of the seed of Abraham, sprung from the tribe of Juda, of the noble line of David. Alleluia.

Propter veritátem et mansuetúdinem et justítiam, et dedúcet te mirabíliter déxtera tua. ℣. Audi, fília, et vide, et inclína aurem tuam: quia concupívit Rex spéciem tuam.

Allelúja, allelúja. ℣. Solémnitas gloriósæ Vírginis Maríæ ex sémine Ábrahæ, ortæ de tribu Juda, clara ex stirpe David. Allelúja.

GOSPEL. *Luke 1: 26-38*

THE ANGEL GABRIEL was sent from God into a city of Galilee, called Nazareth, to a virgin espoused to a man whose name was Joseph, of the house of David: and the virgin's name was Mary. And the angel being come in, said unto her: Hail, full of grace, the Lord is with thee: blessed art thou among women. Who having heard, was troubled at his saying and thought with herself what manner of salutation this should be. And the angel said to her: Fear not, Mary, for thou hast found grace with God. Behold thou shalt conceive in thy womb and shalt

In illo témpore: Missus est Ángelus Gábriel a Deo in civitátem Galilǽæ, cui nomen Názareth, ad Vírginem desponsátam viro, cui nomen erat Joseph, de domo David: et nomen Vírginis María. Et ingréssus Ángelus ad eam, dixit: Ave, grátia plena; Dóminus tecum: benedícta tu in muliéribus. Quæ cum audísset, turbáta est in sermóne ejus: et cogitábat, qualis esset ista salutátio. Et ait Ángelus ei: Ne tímeas, María, invenísti enim grátiam apud Deum: ecce, concípies in útero et páries fílium, et vocábis nomen ejus Jesum. Hic erit magnus, et Fílius Altíssimi vocábitur, et dabit illi Dóminus Deus sedem David, patris ejus: et regnábit in domo Jacob in ætérnum, et regni ejus non erit finis.

bring forth a Son; and thou shalt call His name Jesus. He shall be great and shall be called the Son of the Most High, and the Lord God shall give unto Him the throne of David His father: and He shall reign in the house of Jacob forever, and of His kingdom there shall be no end.

Dixit autem María ad Ángelum: Quómodo fiet istud, quóniam virum non cognósco? Et respóndens Ángelus, dixit ei: Spíritus Sanctus supervéniet in te, et virtus Altíssimi obumbrábit tibi. Ideóque et quod nascétur ex te Sanctum, vocábitur Fílius Dei. Et ecce, Elísabeth, cognáta tua, et ipsa concépit fílium in senectúte sua: et hic mensis sextus est illi, quæ vocátur stérilis: quia non erit impossíbile apud Deum omne verbum. Dixit autem María: Ecce ancílla Dómini, fiat mihi secúndum verbum tuum.

And Mary said to the angel, How shall this be done, because I know not man? And the angel answering said to her, The Holy Ghost shall come upon thee, and the power of the Most High shall overshadow thee. And therefore also the Holy which shall be born of thee shall be called the Son of God. And behold thy cousin Elizabeth, she also hath conceived a son in her old age; and this is the sixth month with her that is called barren; because no word shall be impossible with God. And Mary said: Behold the handmaid of the Lord, be it done to me according to thy word. CREDO.

OFFERTORY. *Ecclus 24: 25; 39: 17*

In me grátia omnis viæ et veritátis, in me omnis spes vitæ et virtútis: ego quasi rosa plantáta super rivos aquárum fructificávi.

IN ME IS ALL GRACE of the way and of the truth; in me is all hope of life and of virtue. Like a rose planted on the rivers I have borne fruit.

The melody for this Offertory was adapted from "Diffúsa Est Grátia In Lábiis Tuis," the Offertory for 2 February.

SECRET.

Fac nos, quǽsumus, Dómine, his munéribus offeréndis conveniénter aptári: et per sacratíssimi Rosárii mystéria sic vitam, passiónem et glóriam Unigéniti tui recólere; ut ejus digni promissiónibus efficiámur: Qui tecum.

Grant us, we beseech Thee, O Lord, to be fittingly prepared for the offering of these gifts, and, through the mysteries of the most holy Rosary, so to meditate upon the life, passion, and glory of Thine only-begotten Son, that we may be made worthy of His promises. Who with Thee.

SECRET. *Et fit commemoratio S. Marci Papae et Confessoris:*

Oblátis munéribus, quǽsumus, Dómine, Ecclésiam tuam benígnus illúmina: ut et gregis tui profíciat ubíque succéssus, et grati fiant nómini tuo, te gubernánte, pastóres. Per Dóminum.

In Thy loving kindness we beseech Thee, O Lord, be moved by the offering of our gifts and enlighten Thy Church: that Thy flock may prosper everywhere and the shepherds, under Thy guidance, may be rendered acceptable to Thee. Through our Lord.

The Preface of the Blessed Virgin Mary (page 191) follows the Secret.

COMMUNION. *Ecclus 39: 19*

SEND forth flowers, as the lily, and yield a smell, and bring forth leaves in grace, and praise with canticles, and bless the Lord in His works. ℣. *At thy right hand stands the queen, in Ophir gold arrayed.*

Floréte, flores, quasi lílium, et date odórem, et frondéte in grátiam, collaudáte cánticum, et benedícite Dóminum in opéribus suis. (Ps 44: 10) ℣. *Astítit regína a dextris tuis in vestítu deauráto, circúmdata varietáte.*

POSTCOMMUNION.

May we be assisted, we beseech Thee, O Lord, by the prayers of Thy most holy Mother, whose Rosary we celebrate, that the virtue of the mysteries we adore may be shared and the effect of the sacraments we have received may be obtained. Who livest.

Sacratíssimæ Genitrícis tuæ, cujus Rosárium celebrámus, quǽsumus, Dómine, précibus adjuvémur: ut et mysteriórum, quæ cólimus, virtus percipiátur; et sacramentórum, quæ súmpsimus, obtineátur effféctus: Qui vivis.

POSTCOMMUNION. *Et fit commemoratio S. Marci Papae et Confessoris:*

Since Thy Church has been nourished by the sacred repast, govern her in Thy clemency, we beseech Thee, O Lord, so that under the guidance of Thy mighty rule she may enjoy greater freedom and abiding integrity of religion. Through our Lord.

Refectióne sancta enutrítam gubérna, quǽsumus, Dómine, tuam placátus Ecclésiam: ut, poténti moderatióne dirécta, et increménta libertátis accípiat et in religiónis integritáte persístat. Per Dóminum.

FEAST OF OUR LORD JESUS CHRIST, KING

During the nineteenth century, the Sunday feasts were often replaced by SANCTORALE feasts. It was necessary to consult a *Laity's Directory* to know which feast was being celebrated—quite a "laborious process" as Father Adrian Fortescue noted. Many feasts celebrated on Sunday in those times would strike us as peculiar. For example, the Sunday after Christmas in those days was the *Feast of the Holy Name of Mary* (in many places). The *Feast of the Holy Family* in those days replaced various Sundays after Easter. Particularly confusing were feasts "attached" to a day of the week—such as the first Sunday of the month.

This arrangement was altered by Pope Saint Pius X. With *Divino Afflatu* (1911) and *Abhinc Duos Annos* (1913), he restored the ancient Sunday feasts. Only one "attached" feast remained: *The Feast of the Holy Name.* In 1921, Pope Benedict XV made another exception: *The Feast of the Holy Family.* In 1925, Pope Pius XI made yet another exception: *The Feast of Christ the King.*

An important theme is found in the verses of *Vexilla Christus Inclyta,* a hymn written by Father Vittorio Genovesi (d. 1967) specifically for this feast: "Not by bloodshed did He bring the peoples under His rule, not by force or fear; but by love, as He hung aloft on the cross, did He draw all things to Himself." Another hymn by Father Genovesi, *Te Saeculorum Principem,* makes a connection between the Kingship and the Holy Eucharist: "For this, with arms outstretched, You hung, bleeding, on the cross, and the cruel spear that pierced You showed man a Heart burning with love. For this, You are hidden on our altars—under the form of bread and wine—and pour out upon Your children the grace of salvation from Your pierced side."

The Propers were adapted to ancient melodies. The Introit comes from "Dum Sanctificátus." The Gradual comes from the Epiphany, regarded as the "Kingship Feast" prior to 1925. The Alleluia comes from "Christus Resúrgens Ex Mórtuis." The Offertory comes from "Laeténtur Caeli." The Communion comes from "Ecce Dóminus Véniet."

I Classis.

—*The Feast of Christ the King*—

DOMINI NOSTRI JESU CHRISTI REGIS

INTROIT. *Apocalypse 5: 12; 1: 6*

Dignus est Agnus, qui occísus est, accípere virtútem, et divinitátem, et sapiéntiam, et fortitúdinem, et honórem. Ipsi glória et impérium in sǽcula sæculórum. ℣. Deus, judícium tuum Regi da: et justítiam tuam Fílio Regis. ℣. Glória Patri.

THE LAMB that was slain is worthy to receive power and divinity and wisdom and strength and honor: to Him be glory and empire for ever and ever. (Ps 71: 1) Give to the King Thy judgment, O God, and to the King's Son Thy justice. ℣. Glory.

COLLECT.

Omnípotens sempitérne Deus, qui in dilécto Fílio tuo, universórum Rege, ómnia instauráre voluísti: concéde propítius; ut cunctæ famíliæ géntium, peccáti vúlnere disgregátæ, ejus suavíssimo subdántur império: Qui tecum.

Almighty and eternal God, Who hast wished to restore all things through Thy beloved Son, the King of the universe, graciously grant that all the families of the Gentiles separated by the wound of sin, may be subjected to His most loving dominion, Who with Thee.

EPISTLE. *Col 1: 12-20*

Fratres: Grátias ágimus Deo Patri, qui dignos nos fecit in partem sortis sanctórum in lúmine: qui erípuit nos de potestáte tenebrárum, et tránstulit in regnum Fílii dilectiónis suæ, in quo habémus redemptiónem per sánguinem ejus, remissiónem peccatórum: qui est imágo Dei invisíbilis, primogénitus omnis creatúræ: quóniam in ipso cóndita sunt univérsa in cælis et in terra, visibília et invisibília, sive Throni, sive Dominatiónes, sive Principátus, sive Potestátes: ómnia per ipsum, et in ipso creáta sunt: et ipse est ante omnes, et ómnia in ipso constant. Et ipse est caput córporis Ecclésiæ, qui est princípium, primogénitus ex mórtuis: ut sit in ómnibus ipse primátum tenens; quia in ipso complácuit omnem plenitúdinem inhabitáre; et per eum reconciliáre ómnia in ipsum, pacíficans per sánguinem crucis ejus, sive quæ in terris, sive quæ in cælis sunt, in Christo Jesu Dómino nostro.

BRETHREN, we give thanks to God the Father, Who hath made us worthy to be partakers of the lot of the saints in light: Who hath delivered us from the power of darkness, and hath translated us into the kingdom of the Son of His love. In Whom we have redemption through His blood, the remission of sins; Who is the image of the invisible God, the firstborn of every creature; for in Him were all things created in Heaven and on earth, visible and invisible, whether thrones, or dominations, or principalities, or powers: all things were created by Him and in Him. And He is before all, and by Him all things consist. And He is the head of the body, the Church. Who is the beginning, the firstborn from the dead; that in all things He may hold the primacy: because in Him it hath well pleased the Father that all fullness should dwell; and through Him to reconcile all things unto Himself, making peace through the blood of His cross, both as to the things that are on earth, and the things that are in Heaven, in Christ Jesus our Lord.

GRADUAL & ALLELUIA. *Ps 71: 8, 11 & Dan 7: 14*

HE shall rule from sea to sea, and from the river unto the ends of the earth. ℣. And all kings of the earth shall adore Him: all nations shall serve Him.

℣. His power is an everlasting power that shall not be taken away: and His kingdom that shall not be destroyed. Alleluia.

Dominábitur a mari usque ad mare, et a flúmine usque ad términos orbis terrárum. ℣. Et adorábunt eum omnes reges terræ: omnes gentes sérvient ei.

Allelúja, allelúja. ℣. Potéstas ejus, potéstas ætérna, quæ non auferétur: et regnum ejus, quod non corrumpétur. Allelúja.

GOSPEL. *John 18: 33-37*

PILATE SAID TO JESUS: Art thou the King of the Jews? Jesus answered: Sayest thou this thing of thyself, or have others told it thee of Me? Pilate answered: Am I a Jew? Thine own nation, and the chief priests, have delivered Thee up to me: what hast Thou done? Jesus answered: My kingdom is not of this world. If My kingdom were of this world, My servants would certainly strive that I should not be delivered to the Jews: but now My kingdom is not from hence. Pilate therefore said to Him: Art Thou a king then? Jesus answered: Thou sayest that I am a King. For this was I born, and for this came I into the world; that I should give testimony to the truth. Every one that is of the truth, heareth My voice. CREDO.

In illo témpore: Dixit Pilátus ad Jesum: Tu es Rex Judæórum? Respóndit Jesus: A temetípso hoc dicis, an álii dixérunt tibi de me? Respóndit Pilátus: Numquid ego Judǽus sum? Gens tua et pontífices tradidérunt te mihi: quid fecísti? Respóndit Jesus: Regnum meum non est de hoc mundo. Si ex hoc mundo esset regnum meum, minístri mei útique decertárent, ut non tráderer Judǽis: nunc autem regnum meum non est hinc. Dixit ítaque ei Pilátus: Ergo Rex es tu? Respóndit Jesus: Tu dicis, quia Rex sum ego. Ego in hoc natus sum et ad hoc veni in mundum, ut testimónium perhíbeam veritáti: omnis, qui est ex veritáte, audit vocem meam.

OFFERTORY. *Ps 2: 8*

ASK of Me, and I will give thee the Gentiles for thine inheritance, and the utmost parts of the earth for thy possession.

Póstula a me, et dabo tibi gentes hereditátem tuam, et possessiónem tuam términos terræ.

SECRET.

O Lord, we offer Thee this host for the reconciliation of humanity; grant, we beseech Thee, that Jesus Christ Thy Son our Lord, Whom we immolate in this sacrifice, will bestow on all Gentiles the gifts of unity and peace, Who with Thee liveth.

Hóstiam tibi, Dómine, humánæ reconciliatiónis offérimus: præsta, quǽsumus; ut, quem sacrifíciis præséntibus immolámus, ipse cunctis géntibus unitátis et pacis dona concédat, Jesus Christus Fílius tuus, Dóminus noster: Qui tecum.

The Preface of Christ the King (page 192) follows the Secret.

COMMUNION. *Ps 28: 10, 11*

Sedébit Dóminus Rex in ætérnum: Dóminus benedícet pópulo suo in pace. (Ps 28: 1) ℣. *Afférte Dómino, fílii Dei: afférte Dómino fílios aríetum.*

THE LORD shall sit King forever. The Lord will bless His people with peace. ℣. *Bring to the Lord, O ye children of God: bring to the Lord the offspring of rams.*

POSTCOMMUNION.

Immortalitátis alimóniam consecúti, quǽsumus, Dómine: ut, qui sub Christi Regis vexíllis militáre gloriámur, cum ipso, in cælésti sede, júgiter regnáre possímus: Qui tecum.

Fed with this immortal nourishment, we beseech Thee, O Lord, that we who glory to fight under the standard of Christ the King, may forever reign with Him on the heavenly throne. Who with Thee liveth.

I Classis.

—*1 November, Feast of All Saints*—

IN FESTO OMNIUM SANCTORUM

INTROIT. *Trad.*

Gaudeámus omnes in Dómino, diem festum celebrántes sub honóre Sanctórum ómnium: de quorum sollemnitáte gaudent Ángeli et colláudant Fílium Dei. (Ps 32: 1) Exsultáte, justi, in Dómino: rectos decet collaudátio. ℣. Glória Patri. (*In a Votive Mass, this Introit is replaced.*)

LET US ALL REJOICE in the Lord, celebrating a festival day in honor of all the Saints: at whose solemnity the angels rejoice, and give praise to the Son of God. (Ps 32: 1) Rejoice in the Lord, ye just; praise becometh the upright. ℣. Glory.

COLLECT.

Omnípotens sempitérne Deus, qui nos ómnium Sanctórum tuórum mérita sub una tribuísti celebritáte venerári: quǽsumus; ut desiderátam nobis tuæ propitiatiónis abundántiam, multiplicátis intercessóribus, largiáris. Per Dóminum.

Almighty and everlasting God, Who hast given us in one feast to venerate the merits of all Thy saints; we beseech Thee, through the multitude of intercessors, to grant us the desired abundance of Thy mercy. Through our Lord.

EPISTLE. *Apoc 7: 2-12*

In diébus illis: Ecce, ego Joánnes vidi álterum Angelum ascendéntem ab ortu solis, habéntem signum Dei vivi: et clamávit voce magna quátuor Ángelis, quibus datum est nocére terræ et mari, dicens: Nolíte nocére terræ et mari neque arbóribus, quoadúsque signémus servos Dei nostri in fróntibus eórum. Et audívi númerum signatórum, centum quadragínta quátuor mília signáti, ex omni tribu

IN THOSE DAYS, behold, I, John, saw another angel ascending from the rising of the sun, having the sign of the living God. And he cried with a loud voice to the four angels, to whom it was given to hurt the earth and the sea, saying, Hurt not the earth nor the sea, nor the trees, till we sign the servants of our God in their foreheads. And I heard the number of them that were signed: a hundred and forty-four thousand

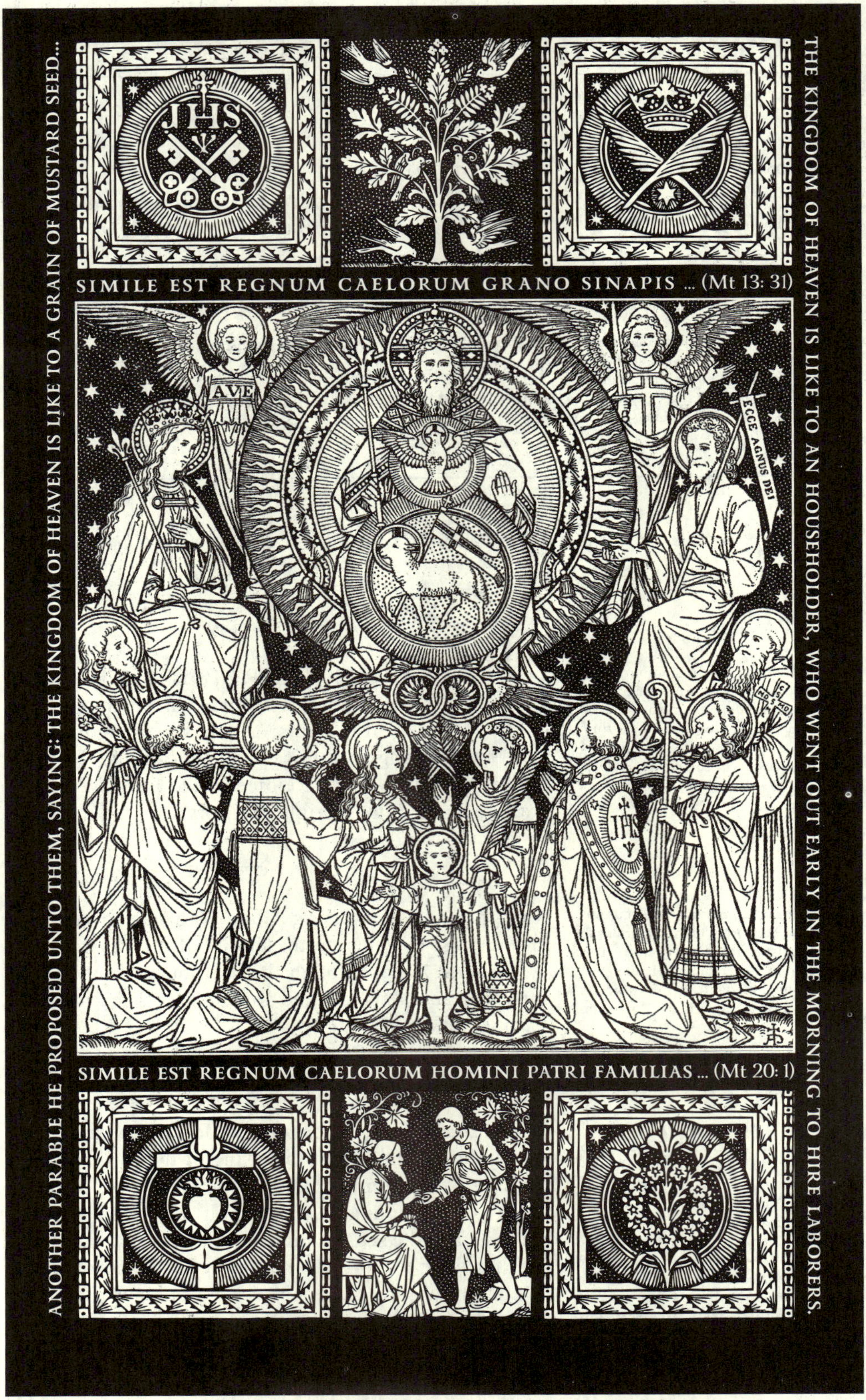
ANOTHER PARABLE HE PROPOSED UNTO THEM, SAYING: THE KINGDOM OF HEAVEN IS LIKE TO A GRAIN OF MUSTARD SEED...
IHS
SIMILE EST REGNUM CAELORUM GRANO SINAPIS ... (Mt 13: 31)
AVE
ECCE AGNUS DEI
IHS
SIMILE EST REGNUM CAELORUM HOMINI PATRI FAMILIAS ... (Mt 20: 1)
THE KINGDOM OF HEAVEN IS LIKE TO AN HOUSEHOLDER, WHO WENT OUT EARLY IN THE MORNING TO HIRE LABORERS.

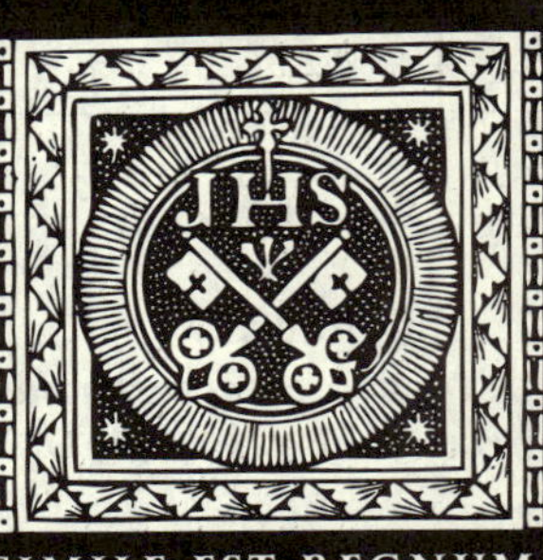

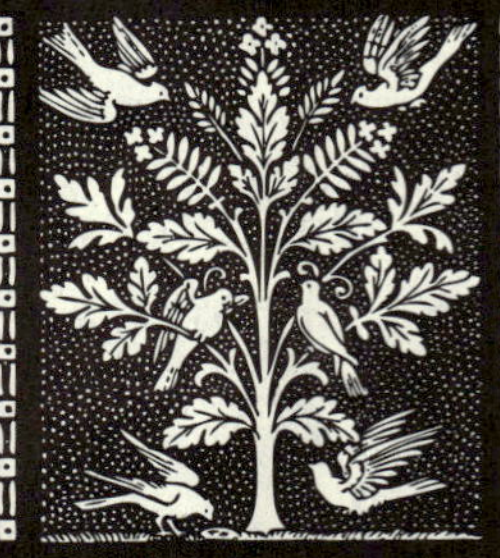

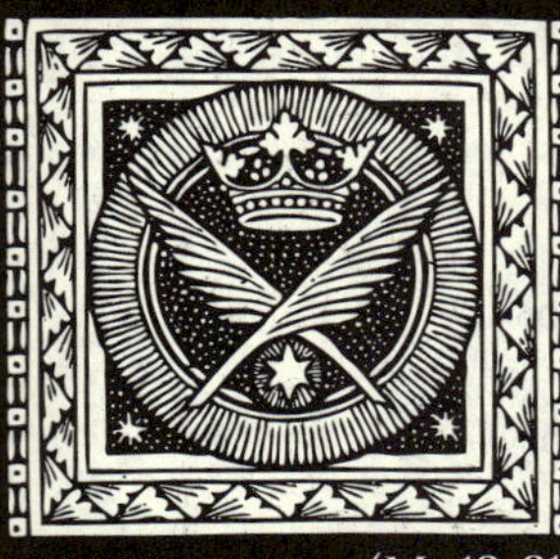

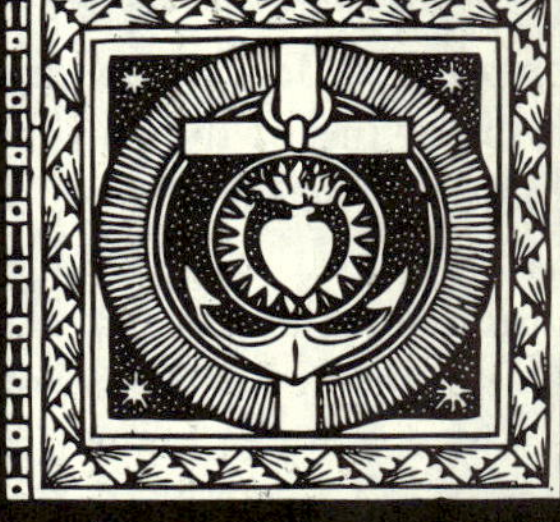

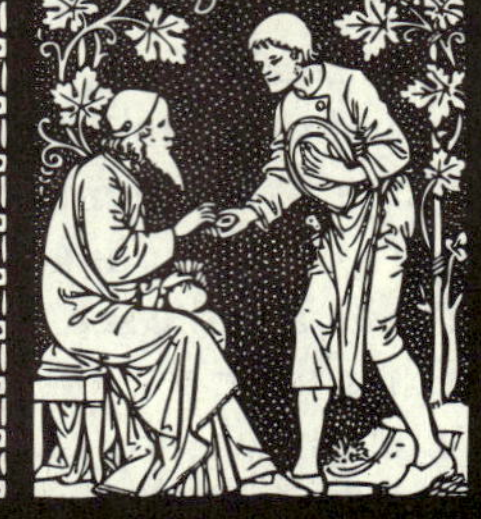

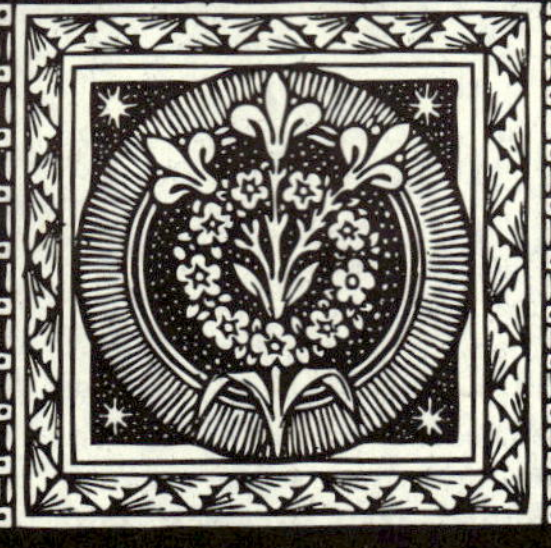

filiórum Ísraël, Ex tribu Juda duódecim mília signáti. Ex tribu Ruben duódecim mília signáti. Ex tribu Gad duódecim mília signáti. Ex tribu Aser duódecim mília signáti. Ex tribu Néphthali duódecim mília signáti. Ex tribu Manásse duódecĩ mília signáti. Ex tribu Símeon duódecĩ mília signáti. Ex tribu Levi duódecim mília signáti. Ex tribu Íssachar duódecĩ mília signáti. Ex tribu Zábulon duódecĩ mília signáti. Ex tribu Joseph duódecim mília signáti. Ex tribu Bénjamin duódecim mília signáti.

were signed out of every tribe of the children of Israel. Of the tribe of Juda were twelve thousand signed: of the tribe of Ruben twelve thousand signed: of the tribe of Gad twelve thousand signed: of the tribe of Aser twelve thousand signed: of the tribe of Nephthali twelve thousand signed: of the tribe of Manasses twelve thousand signed: of the tribe of Simeon twelve thousand signed: of the tribe of Levi twelve thousand signed: of the tribe of Issachar twelve thousand signed: of the tribe of Zabulon twelve thousand signed: of the tribe of Joseph twelve thousand signed: of the tribe of Benjamin twelve thousand signed.

Post hæc vidi turbam magnam, quam dinumeráre nemo póterat, ex ómnibus géntibus et tríbubus et pópulis et linguis: stantes ante thronum et in conspéctu Agni, amícti stolis albis, et palmæ in mánibus eórum: et clamábant voce magna, dicéntes: Salus Deo nostro, qui sedet super thronum, et Agno. Et omnes Ángeli stabant in circúitu throni et seniórum et quatuor animálium: et cecidérunt in conspéctu throni in fácies suas et adoravérunt Deum, dicéntes: Amen. Benedíctio et cláritas et sapiéntia et gratiárum actio, honor et virtus et fortitúdo Deo nostro in sǽcula sæculórum. Amen.

After this, I saw a great multitude which no man could number, of all nations, and tribes, and peoples, and tongues, standing before the throne and in sight of the Lamb, clothed with white robes, and palms in their hands; and they cried with a loud voice saying: Salvation to our God Who sitteth upon the throne, and to the Lamb. And all the angels stood round about the throne, and the ancients, and the four living creatures; and they fell down before the throne upon their faces, and adored God, saying: Amen. Benediction, and glory, and wisdom, and thanksgiving, honor, and power, and strength to our God for ever and ever. Amen.

GRADUAL & ALLELUIA. *Ps 33: 10, 11 & Matt 11: 28*

Timéte Dóminum, omnes Sancti ejus: quóniam nihil deëst timéntibus eum. ℣. Inquiréntes autem Dóminum, non defícient omni bono.
Allelúja, allelúja. ℣. Veníte ad me, omnes, qui laborátis et oneráti estis: et ego refíciam vos. Allelúja.

FEAR the Lord, all ye His saints; for there is no want to them that fear Him. ℣. But they that seek the Lord shall not be deprived of any good.
℣. Come to Me all you that labor and are heavy laden, and I will refresh you. Alleluia.

GOSPEL. *Matt 5: 1-12*

In illo témpore: Videns Jesus turbas, ascéndit in montem, et cum sedísset, accessérunt ad eum discípuli ejus, et apériens os suum, docébat eos, dicens: Beáti páuperes spíritu: quóniam ipsórum est regnum cælórum. Beáti mites: quóniam ipsi possidébunt terram. Beáti, qui lugent: quóniam ipsi consolabúntur. Beáti, qui esúriunt et sítiunt justítiam: quóniam ipsi saturabúntur. Beáti misericórdes: quóniam ipsi misericórdiam consequéntur. Beáti mundo corde: quóniam ipsi Deum vidébunt. Beáti pacífici: quóniam fílii Dei vocabúntur. Beáti, qui

SEEING THE MULTITUDES, Jesus went up into a mountain; and when He was sat down, His disciples came unto Him. And opening His mouth, He taught them, saying: Blessed are the poor in spirit; for theirs is the kingdom of heaven. Blessed are the meek: for they shall possess the land. Blessed are they that mourn; for they shall be comforted. Blessed are they that hunger and thirst after justice; for they shall have their fill. Blessed are the merciful: for they shall obtain mercy. Blessed are the clean of heart; for they shall see God. Blessed are the peace-makers; for they shall be called the children of God. Blessed are they that suffer persecution for justice's sake; for theirs is the kingdom of heaven. Blessed are ye when they shall revile you, and persecute you, and speak all that is evil against you, untruly, for My sake: be glad and rejoice, for your reward is very great in heaven. CREDO.

persecutiónem patiúntur propter justítiam: quóniam ipsórum est regnum cælórum. Beáti estis, cum maledíxerint vobis, et persecúti vos fúerint, et díxerint omne malum advérsum vos, mentiéntes, propter me: gaudéte et exsultáte, quóniam merces vestra copiósa est in cælis.

OFFERTORY. *Wis 3: 1, 2, 3*

THE SOULS OF THE JUST are in the hand of God, and the torment of malice shall not touch them: in the sight of the unwise they seemed to die, but they are in peace. Alleluia. ℣. *And though in the sight of men they suffered torments, their hope is full of immortality.*

Justórum ánimæ in manu Dei sunt, et non tanget illos torméntum malítiæ: visi sunt óculis insipiéntium mori: illi autem sunt in pace, allelúja. ℣. *Et si coram homínibus torménta passi sunt, spes illórum immortalitáte plena est.*

SECRET.

We offer to Thee, O Lord, the gifts of our devotion; may they be pleasing to Thee in honor of all Thy saints; and of Thy mercy let them avail for our salvation. Through our Lord.

Múnera tibi, Dñe, nostræ devotiónis offérimus: quæ et pro cunctórũ tibi grata sint honóre Justórũ, et nobis salutária, te miseránte, reddántur. Per Dñm.

* *The "ad libitum" Preface for All Saints (page 195) may be used.*

COMMUNION. *Matt 5: 8-10*

BLESSED are the clean of heart, for they shall see God: blessed are the peacemakers, for they shall be called the children of God: blessed are they that suffer persecution for justice's sake, for theirs is the kingdom of heaven. ℣. *Rejoice in the Lord, O ye just: praise becometh the upright.*

Beáti mundo corde, quóniam ipsi Deum vidébunt; beáti pacífici, quóniam fílii Dei vocabúntur: beáti, qui persecutiónem patiúntur propter justítiam, quóniam ipsórum est regnum cælórum. (Ps 32: 1) ℣. *Exsultáte, justi, in Dómino: rectos decet collaudátio.*

POSTCOMMUNION.

Grant to Thy faithful people, we beseech Thee, O Lord, ever to rejoice in the veneration of all Thy saints, and to be defended by their unceasing prayers. Through our Lord.

Da, quæsumus, Dómine, fidélibus pópulis ómnium Sanctórum semper veneratióne lætári: et eórum perpétua supplicatióne muníri. Per Dóminum.

Only in the ninth century was this feast definitely introduced into the Church, according to Dom Johner. Some Propers were adapted, while others seem to be original compositions. The Offertory was adapted (in the twelfth century) to the melody of "Stetit Ángelus Juxta" from 29 September. The communion antiphon can be found in many ancient manuscripts—e.g. MONTPELLIER H. 159—yet no manuscript explicitly provides extra verses. Since it is from the New Testament, singers would have known to use the Introit's psalm or Psalm 33. NARBONNE|1033 gives only the Gloria Patri, as does ALBI|1047. It seems that 4951STEVEN|1128 began to specify a verse from the New Testament, but unfortunately that page is torn. Some modern books give Psalm 125.

2 Nov, or (if it falls on a Sunday) 3 Nov • *Die 2 Novembris vel, si in dominicam inciderit, die 3 sequenti*

On this day every priest may celebrate three Masses. For the norms to be followed if a priest celebrates two or three Masses on the same day, see "The Rite To Be Observed In The Celebration Of Mass, Chapter XV." | One who celebrates a single Mass only reads the first Mass formulary ("Ad Primam Missam"). This Mass is also used by one who celebrates a sung Mass, but he may anticipate the second and third Masses. | When one celebrates three Masses without interruption, the Sequence ("Dies Irae") must be said only in the principal Mass, or otherwise in the first Mass; it may be omitted in the other two Masses, unless they are sung Masses. *Hoc die quivis sacerdos tres Missas celebrare potest. De agendis, si sacerdos eodem die duas vel tres Missas celebret, vide "Ritum servandum in celebratione Missae n. 14." | Qui unam dumtaxat Missam celebrat, primam legit; eandem adhibet qui Missam cum cantu celebrat, facta ei potestate anticipandae secundae ac tertiae. | Cum quis tres Missas sine intermissione celebrat, sequentiam dicere debet tantum in Missa principali, secus in prima Missa; in ceteris Missis, nisi sint in cantu, eam omittere potest.*

Feria I Classis.

—*2 November, All Souls' Day*—

IN COMMEMORATIONE OMNIUM FIDELIUM DEFUNCTORUM

INTROIT. *IV Esdr 2: 34, 35*

Réquiem ætérnam dona eis, Dómine: et lux perpétua lúceat eis. ℣. Te decet hymnus, Deus, in Sion, et tibi reddétur votum in Jerúsalem: exáudi oratiónem meam, ad te omnis caro véniet. *Requiem ætérnam…*

GRANT THEM eternal rest, O Lord; and let perpetual light shine upon them. (Ps 64: 2-3) A hymn, O God, becometh Thee in Sion; and a vow shall be paid to Thee in Jerusalem: O Lord, hear my prayer; all flesh shall come to Thee. *Eternal rest…*

COLLECT FOR THE FIRST MASS.

Fidélium, Deus, ómnium Cónditor et Redémptor: animábus famulórum famularúmque tuárum remissiónem cunctórum tríbue peccatórum; ut indulgéntiam, quam semper optavérunt, piis supplicatiónibus consequántur: Qui vivis.

O God, the creator and redeemer of all the faithful, grant to the souls of Thy servants and handmaids the remission of all their sins, that they may obtain by loving prayers the forgiveness which they have always desired. Who livest.

COLLECT FOR THE SECOND MASS.

Deus, indulgentiárum Dómine: da animábus famulórum famularúmque tuárum refrigérii sedem, quiétis beatitúdinem et lúminis claritátem. Per Dóminum.

O God, the Lord of mercies, grant to the souls of Thy servants and handmaids, the anniversary of whose burial we commemorate, an abode of refreshment, the beatitude of rest, and the brightness of light. Through our Lord.

COLLECT FOR THE THIRD MASS.

Deus, véniæ largítor et humánæ salútis amátor: quæsumus cleméntiam tuam; ut ánimas famulórum famularúmque tuárum, quæ ex hoc sæculo transiérunt, beáta María semper Vírgine intercedénte cum ómnibus Sanctis tuis, ad perpétuæ beatitúdinis consórtium perveníre concédas. Per Dóminum.

O God, the bestower of pardon and lover of man's salvation, we beseech Thy clemency, through the intercession of blessed Mary ever a virgin, and all Thy saints, that the brethren, who have passed out of this world may together enjoy everlasting happiness. Through our Lord.

LIBER SCRIPTUS PROFERETUR IN QUO TOTUM CONTINETUR UNDE MUNDUS IUDICETUR. (SEQUENCE)

THEN WILL BE BROUGHT OUT THE BOOK IN WHICH IS WRITTEN THE COMPLETE RECORD THAT WILL DECIDE EACH MAN'S FATE.

EPISTLE FOR THE FIRST MASS. *I Cor 15: 51-57*

Fratres: Ecce, mystérium vobis dico: Omnes quidem resurgémus, sed non omnes immutábimur. In moménto, in ictu óculi, in novíssima tuba: canet enim tuba, et mórtui resúrgent incorrúpti: et nos immutábimur. Opórtet enim corruptíbile hoc indúere incorruptiónem: et mortále hoc indúere immortalitátem. Cum autem mortále hoc indúerit immortalitátem, tunc fiet sermo, qui scriptus est: Absórpta est mors in victória. Ubi est, mors, victória tua? Ubi est, mors, stímulus tuus? Stímulus autem mortis peccátum est: virtus vero peccáti lex. Deo autem grátias, qui dedit nobis victóriam per Dóminum nostrum Jesum Christum.

BRETHREN, Behold, I tell you a mystery: we shall all indeed rise again, but we shall not all be changed. In a moment, in the twinkling of an eye, at the last trumpet; for the trumpet shall sound, and the dead shall rise again incorruptible, and we shall be changed. For this corruptible must put on incorruption, and this mortal must put on immortality. And when this mortal hath put on immortality, then shall come to pass the saying that is written, Death is swallowed up in victory. O death, where is thy victory? O death, where is thy sting? Now the sting of death is sin: and the strength of sin is the law. But thanks be to God, Who hath given us the victory through our Lord Jesus Christ.

EPISTLE FOR THE SECOND MASS. *II Mach 12: 43-46*

In diébus illis: Vir fortíssimus Judas, facta collatióne, duódecim mília drachmas argénti misit Jerosólymam, offérri pro peccátis mortuórum sacrifícium, bene et religióse de resurrectióne cógitans (nisi enim eos, qui cecíderant, resurrectúros speráret, supérfluum viderétur et vanum oráre pro mórtuis): et quia considerábat, quod hi, qui cum pietáte dormitiónem accéperant, óptimam habérent repósitam grátiam. Sancta ergo et salúbris est cogitátio pro defúnctis exoráre, ut a peccátis solvántur.

IN THOSE DAYS, the most valiant man Judas, making a gathering, sent twelve thousand drachmas of silver to Jerusalem for sacrifice to be offered for the sins of the dead, thinking well and religiously concerning the resurrection (for if he had not hoped that they that were slain should rise again, it would have seemed superfluous and vain to pray for the dead); and because he considered that they who had fallen asleep with godliness, had great grace laid up for them. It is therefore a holy and wholesome thought to pray for the dead, that they may be loosed from sins.

EPISTLE FOR THE THIRD MASS. *Apoc 14: 13*

In diébus illis: Audívi vocem de cælo, dicéntem mihi: Scribe: Beáti mórtui, qui in Dómino moriúntur. Ámodo jam dicit Spíritus, ut requiéscant a labóribus suis: ópera enim illórum sequúntur illos.

IN THOSE DAYS I heard a voice from heaven, saying to me, Write, blessed are the dead, who die in the Lord. From henceforth now, saith the Spirit, that they may rest from their labors, for their works follow them.

GRADUAL. *IV Esdr 2: 34, 35*

Réquiem ætérnam dona eis, Dómine: et lux perpétua lúceat eis. ℣. In memória ætérna erit justus: ab auditióne mala non timébit.

ETERNAL rest give to them, O Lord; and let perpetual light shine upon them. (Ps 111: 7) The just shall be in everlasting remembrance; he shall not fear the evil hearing.

The melody of this ancient Gradual seems to have been based upon "Haec Dies," the Easter Sunday Gradual. Its adaptation was completed more than a thousand years ago by an unknown monk. The Tract ("Absólve Dómine") is also ancient, yet belongs to a "later" period—perhaps circa 1350 AD.

TRACT. *Trad.*

O LORD, absolve the souls of all the faithful departed from every bond of sin. ℣. And by the help of Thy grace may they be worthy to escape the sentence of vengeance. ℣. And to enjoy all the beatitude of the light eternal.

Absólve, Dómine, ánimas ómnium fidélium defunctórum ab omni vínculo delictórum. ℣. Et grátia tua illis succurrénte, mereántur evádere judícium ultiónis. ℣. Et lucis ætérnæ beatitúdine pérfrui.

SEQUENCE. *Thomas of Celano, Disciple of Saint Francis Assisi. XIII. cent.*

DIES IRAE,
DIES ILLA,
Sólvet sæclum in favílla:
Téste Dávid cum Sibýlla.

Quántus trémor est futúrus,
Quándo júdex est ventúrus,
Cúncta strícte discussúrus!

Translation by Rev. Joseph Connelly
IMPRIMATUR (10 December 1954)

A day of wrath that day will be. It will dissolve the world into glowing ashes, as David and the Sibyl have testified. ✠ How great a dread there will be when the Judge comes to examine all things in strict justice.

TUBA mírum spárgens sónum
Per sepúlcra regiónum,
Cóget ómnes ánte thrónum.
Mors stupébit, et natúra,
Cum resúrget creatúra,
Judicánti responsúra.

The trumpet's wondrous call will sound in tombs the world over and urge everyone forward to the throne. ✠ Death and nature will stand amazed when creation rises again to give answer to its Judge.

LIBER scríptus proferétur,
In quo tótum continétur,
Únde múndus judicétur.
Júdex érgo cum sedébit,
Quídquid látet, apparébit:
Nil inúltum remanébit.

Then will be brought out the book in which is written the complete record that will decide each man's fate. ✠ And when the Judge is seated, all secret sin will be made known, and no sin will go without its due punishment.

QUID sum míser tunc dictúrus?
Quem patrónum rogatúrus,
Cum vix jústus sit secúrus?
Rex treméndæ majestátis,
Qui salvándos sálvas grátis,
Sálva me, fons pietátis.

In such a plight what can I then plead? Or whom can I ask to plead for me, when the just man will be saved only with difficulty? ✠ King of dread majesty, You give salvation's grace to all that will be saved. Save me, fount of pity.

In Your pity, Jesus, call to mind that I am the reason why You became man. Do not cast me from You on that day. ✠ It was me You were seeking out when, exhausted, You sat by the well; me that You redeemed when You suffered on the cross. Do not allow such toil to have been in vain.

RECORDARE, Jésu píe,
Quod sum cáusa túæ víæ:
Ne me pérdas ílla díe.

Quærens me, sedísti lássus:
Redemísti Crúcem pássus:
Tántus lábor non sit cássus.

Just and avenging Judge, grant me the grace of pardon before that day of reckoning comes. ✠ I groan like one condemned and am red with shame for my sins; spare Your suppliant servant.

JUSTE júdex ultiónis,
Dónum fac remissiónis,
Ánte díem ratiónis.

Ingemísco, támquam réus:
Cúlpa rúbet vúltus méus:
Supplicánti párce, Déus.

You forgave Mary and granted the robber's prayer, and thus gave me hope as well. ✠ Though my prayers do not deserve to be heard, yet in Your goodness graciously bring it about that I do not burn in the unquenchable fire.

QUI Maríam absolvísti,
Et latrónem exaudísti,
Míhi quóque spem dedísti.

Préces méæ non sunt dígnæ:
Sed tu bónus fac benígne,
Ne perénni crémer ígne.

Give me a place among Your sheep, separate me from the goats and set me on Your right hand. ✠ When the accursed have been silenced and sentenced to the acrid flames, call me along with the blessed. ✠ In humility and abasement I make this prayer. My sin is burnt to ashes in the fire of my sorrow. Take care of me when my end is come.

INTER óves lócum præsta,
Et ab hædis me sequéstra,
Státuens in párte déxtra.

Confutátis maledíctis,
Flámmis ácribus addíctis:
Vóca me cum benedíctis.

Óro súpplex et acclínis,
Cor contrítum quási cínis:
Gére cúram méi fínis.

That day when guilty man rises out of the ruins of the world for judgment, will be a day of tears and mourning. Spare him on that day, Lord God. ✠ Jesus, Lord, of Your mercy grant them rest. Amen.

LACRIMOSA díes ílla,
Qua resúrget ex favílla
Judicándus hómo réus:
Húic érgo párce, Déus.

Píe Jésu Dómine,
Dóna éis réquiem.
AMEN.

At that time, Jesus said to the multitudes of the Jews:

GOSPEL FOR THE FIRST MASS. *John 5: 25-29*

AMEN, AMEN, I say unto you, that the hour cometh, and now is, when the dead shall hear the voice of the Son of God; and they that hear shall live. For as the Father hath life in Himself, so He hath given to the Son also to have life in Himself; and He hath given Him power to do judgment, because He is the Son of man. Wonder not at this, for the hour cometh wherein all that are in the graves shall hear the voice of the Son of God; and they that have done good things shall come forth unto the resurrection of life, but they that have done evil, unto the resurrection of judgment.

In illo témpore: Dixit Jesus turbis Judæórum: Amen, amen, dico vobis, quia venit hora, et nunc est, quando mórtui áudient vocem Fílii Dei: et qui audíerint, vivent. Sicut enim Pater habet vitam in semetípso, sic dedit et Fílio habére vitam in semetípso: et potestátem dedit ei judícium fácere, quia Fílius hóminis est. Nolíte mirári hoc, quia venit hora, in qua omnes, qui in monuméntis sunt, áudient vocem Fílii Dei: et procédent, qui bona fecérunt, in resurrectiónem vitæ: qui vero mala egérunt, in resurrectiónem judícii.

(The CREDO is not said in Masses for the Dead; cf. *Ritus Servandus in celebratione Missae*, §13: "De his quae omittuntur in Missa defunctorum.")

At that time, Jesus said to the multitudes of the Jews:

GOSPEL FOR THE SECOND MASS. *John 6: 37-40*

ALL THAT the Father giveth Me shall come to Me; and him that cometh to Me I will not cast out: because I came down from heaven, not to do My own will, but the will of Him Who sent Me. Now this is the will of the Father Who sent Me, that of all that He hath given Me, I should lose nothing, but should raise it up again in the last day; and this is the will of My Father that sent Me, that every one who seeth the Son, and believeth in Him, may have life everlasting; and I will raise him up in the last day.

In illo témpore: Dixit Jesus turbis Judæórum: Omne, quod dat mihi Pater, ad me véniet: et eum, qui venit ad me, non ejíciam foras: quia descéndi de cælo, non ut fáciam voluntátem meam, sed voluntátem ejus, qui misit me. Hæc est autem volúntas ejus, qui misit me, Patris: ut omne, quod dedit mihi, non perdam ex eo, sed resúscitem illud in novíssimo die. Hæc est autem volúntas Patris mei, qui misit me: ut omnis, qui videt Fílium et credit in eum, hábeat vitam ætérnam, et ego resuscitábo eum in novíssimo die.

At that time, Jesus said to the multitudes of the Jews:

GOSPEL FOR THE THIRD MASS. *John 6: 51-55*

I AM THE LIVING BREAD, which came down from heaven. If any man eat of this bread he shall live forever: and the bread that I will give is My flesh for the life of the world. The Jews therefore strove among themselves, saying, How can this man give us His flesh to eat? Then Jesus said to them, Amen, amen, I say unto you, Except you eat the flesh of the Son of man, and drink His blood, you shall not have life in you. He that eateth My flesh, and drinketh My blood, hath everlasting life: and I will raise him up in the last day.

In illo témpore: Dixit Jesus turbis Judæórum: Ego sum panis vivus, qui de cælo descéndi. Si quis manducáverit ex hoc pane, vivet in ætérnũ: et panis, quẽ ego dabo, caro mea est pro mundi vita. Litigábant ergo Judǽi ad ínvicẽ, dicéntes: Quómodo potest hic nobis carnem suam dare ad manducándum? Dixit ergo eis Jesus: Amen, amen, dico vobis: nisi manducavéritis carnẽ Fílii hóminis et bibéritis ejus sánguinem, non habébitis vitã in vobis. Qui mandúcat meam carnem et bibit meũ sánguinem, habet vitam ætérnam: et ego resuscitábo eum in novíssimo die.

OFFERTORY. *Trad.*

Dómine Jesu Christe, Rex glóriæ, líbera ánimas ómnium fidélium defunctórum de pœnis inférni et de profúndo lacu: líbera eas de ore leónis, ne absórbeat eas tártarus, ne cadant in obscúrum: sed sígnifer sanctus Míchaël repræséntet eas in lucem sanctam: * *Quam olim Ábrahæ promisísti et sémini ejus.* ℣. Hóstias et preces tibi, Dómine, laudis offérimus: tu súscipe pro animábus illis, quarum hódie memóriam fácimus: fac eas, Dómine, de morte transíre ad vitam. * *Quam olim Ábrahæ promisísti et sémini ejus.*

O LORD Jesus Christ, King of glory, deliver the souls of all the faithful departed from the pains of hell and from the deep pit; deliver them from the lion's mouth, that hell engulf them not, nor they fall into darkness, but let Michael, the holy standard-bearer, bring them into the holy light * *which Thou once didst promise to Abraham and his seed.* ℣. We offer Thee, O Lord, sacrifices and prayers of praise; do Thou accept them for those souls whom we this day commemorate; grant them, O Lord, to pass from death to the life * *which Thou once didst promise to Abraham and his seed.*

Willi Apel has written: "It was not until the 12th century that the Offertories lost their verses, the only exception being *Dómine Jesu Christe*, which to the present day has retained one verse: *Hóstias Et Preces*." Yet this is not, perhaps, an ideal example of an Offertory "retaining" its verse; originally this verse did not belong to it (cf. Dom Johner). This Offertory is certainly ancient—and is found in manuscripts such as 339sanGall|974, Yrieix|1040, and Helmst|1026—yet does not appear to be extremely ancient.

SECRET FOR THE FIRST MASS.

Hóstias, quǽsumus, Dómine, quas tibi pro animábus famulórum famularúmque tuárum offérimus, propitiátus inténde: ut, quibus fídei christiánæ méritum contulísti, dones et prǽmium. Per Dóminum.

Mercifully look down, we beseech Thee, O Lord, upon the sacrifice which we offer Thee for the souls of Thy servants and handmaids, that, to those on whom Thou didst confer the merit of Christian faith, Thou mayst also grant its reward. Through our Lord.

SECRET FOR THE SECOND MASS.

Propitiáre, Dómine, supplicatiónibus nostris, pro animábus famulórum famularúmque tuárum, pro quibus tibi offérimus sacrifícium laudis; ut eas Sanctórum tuórum consórtio sociáre dignéris. Per Dóminum.

Be propitiated, O Lord, by our supplications for the souls of Thy servants and handmaids, whose anniversary is kept today, for whom we offer Thee the sacrifice of praise, that Thou vouchsafe to join them to the company of Thy saints. Through our Lord.

SECRET FOR THE THIRD MASS.

Deus, cujus misericórdiæ non est númerus, súscipe propítius preces humilitátis nostræ: et animábus fratrum, propinquórum et benefactórum nostrórum, quibus tui nóminis dedísti confessiónem, per hæc sacraménta salútis nostræ, cunctórum remissiónem tríbue peccatórum. Per Dóminum.

O God, Whose mercy is boundless, mercifully receive the prayers of our lowliness, and grant, through these sacraments of our salvation, to the souls of our brethren, kindred, and benefactors, to whom Thou didst grant the confession of Thy name, the remission of all sins. Through our Lord.

The Preface of the Dead *(page 192)* *follows the Secret.*

The Agnus Dei in Masses for the Dead is as follows:

Lamb of God, Who takest away the sins of the world: *give unto them rest.*
Lamb of God, Who takest away the sins of the world: *give unto them rest.*
Lamb of God, Who takest away the sins of the world: *give unto them rest forevermore.*

Agnus Dei, qui tollis peccáta mundi, *dona eis réquiem.*

Agnus Dei, qui tollis peccáta mundi, *dona eis réquiem.*

Agnus Dei, qui tollis peccáta mundi, *dona eis réquiem sempitérnam.*

COMMUNION. *IV Esdr 2: 35, 34*

MAY LIGHT ETERNAL shine upon them, O Lord, * with Thy saints forever, for Thou art kind. ℣. Grant them everlasting rest, O Lord, and let perpetual light shine upon them, * with Thy saints forever, for Thou art kind.

Lux ætérna lúceat eis, Dómine: * Cum Sanctis tuis in ætérnum: quia pius es. ℣. Réquiem ætérnam dona eis, Dómine: et lux perpétua lúceat eis. * Cum Sanctis tuis in ætérnum: quia pius es.

This is the only communion antiphon which retained its "extra" verses—although in this case the extra verse is not from a psalm. Because it is not optional, the extra verse was not placed in Italics. Archbishop Sheen once said: "It is a long established principle of the Church never to completely drop from her public worship any ceremony, object, or prayer which once occupied a place in that worship." The well-known oddities of the Requiem Mass, which hearken back to ancient practices, illustrate this. For example, the *Prayers at the Foot of the Altar* are omitted because they were a later addition. This extra verse is explicit in ancient MSS, whereas most MSS from the later Middle Ages do not include it. Beginning the repeat on "Cum Sanctis" is notated by ALBI|1047, whereas YRIEIX|1040 starts the repeat on "Lúceat Eis." Many modern books use Psalm 129 ("De Profúndis") for the extra verses and replace the "Gloria Patri" with "Réquiem Ætérnam."

POSTCOMMUNION FOR THE FIRST MASS.

May the prayer of Thy suppliants profit the souls of Thy servants and handmaids, we beseech Thee, O Lord, that Thou mayst free them from all sins and make them sharers in Thy redemption. Who livest.

Animábus, quǽsumus, Dómine, famulórum famularúmque tuárum orátio profíciat supplicántium: ut eas et a peccátis ómnibus éxuas, et tuæ redemptiónis fácias esse partícipes: Qui vivis.

POSTCOMMUNION FOR THE SECOND MASS.

Grant, we beseech Thee, O Lord, that the souls of Thy servants and handmaids may be purged by this sacrifice and obtain alike forgiveness and everlasting rest. Through our Lord.

Præsta, quǽsumus, Dómine: ut ánimæ famulórum famularúmque tuárum, his purgátæ sacrifíciis, indulgéntiam páriter et réquiem cápiant sempitérnam. Per Dóminum.

POSTCOMMUNION FOR THE THIRD MASS.

Grant, we beseech Thee, O almighty and merciful God, that the souls of our brethren, kindred, and benefactors, for whom we have offered this sacrifice of praise to Thy majesty, being purified of all sins by the virtue of this sacrament, may, by Thy mercy, receive the beatitude of perpetual light. Through our Lord.

Præsta, quǽsumus, omnípotens et miséricors Deus: ut ánimæ fratrum, propinquórum et benefactórum nostrórum, pro quibus hoc sacrifícium laudis tuæ obtúlimus majestáti; per hujus virtútem sacraménti a peccátis ómnibus expiátæ, lucis perpétuæ, te miseránte, recípiant beatitúdinem. Per Dóminum.

The dismissal in Masses for the Dead is as follows:

℣. Requiéscant in pace.
℟. Amen.

℣. May they rest in peace.
℟. Amen.

---

9 November is the anniversary of the dedication of the Lateran Basilica, the oldest of the four major basilicas in Rome. Saint John Lateran is also called "Cathedral of the Most Holy Savior"—and older hand-missals refer to this feast as: "Dedication of Our Savior's Church." In ancient Rome, this was the church where everyone was baptized. Formerly known as "The Lateran Palace," it was given to Pope Saint Miltiades (d. 314AD) by Emperor Constantine. In 324AD it was consecrated by Pope Saint Sylvester (d. 335AD).

II Classis.

— 9 November, Dedication of Holy Savior —

IN DEDICATIONE ARCHIBASILICAE SANCTISSIMI SALVATORIS

Which uses the Common of the Mass for the Dedication of a Church

INTROIT. *Gen 28: 17 & Ps 83: 2-3*

Terríbilis est locus iste: hic domus Dei est et porta cæli: et vocábitur aula Dei. (*T.P. Allelúja, allelúja.*) ℣. Quam diléćta tabernácula tua, Dómine virtútum! concupíscit, et déficit ánima mea in átria Dómini. ℣. Glória Patri.

TERRIBLE IS THIS PLACE: it is the house of God, and the gate of heaven; and shall be called the court of God. (*P.T.*) How lovely are Thy tabernacles, O Lord of hosts! my soul longeth and fainteth for the courts of the Lord. ℣. Glory.

COLLECT.

Deus, qui nobis per síngulos annos hujus sancti templi tui consecratiónis réparas diem, et sacris semper mystériis represéntas incólumes: exáudi preces pópuli tui, et præsta; ut, quisquis hoc templum benefícia petitúrus ingréditur, cuncta se impetrásse lætétur. Per Dóminum.

O God, Who year by year dost renew the day of the consecration of this Thy holy temple, and dost ever bring us again in safety to the holy mysteries, hear the prayers of Thy people, and grant that whosoever entereth this temple to seek blessings may rejoice to obtain all that he seeketh. Through our Lord.

On the actual day of the dedication, the Collect is as follows:

COLLECT. *In ipso die dedicationis:*

Deus, qui invisibíliter ómnia cóntines, et tamen pro salúte géneris humáni signa tuæ poténtiæ visibíliter osténdis: templum hoc poténtia tuæ inhabitatiónis illústra, et concéde; ut omnes, qui huc deprecatúri convéniunt, ex quacúmque tribulatióne ad te clamáverint, consolatiónis tuæ benefícia consequántur. Per Dóminum.

O God, Who dost invisibly contain all things, and yet dost visibly show the signs of Thy power for the salvation of mankind, illumine this temple by the virtue of Thine indwelling, and grant that all who assemble here to pray, from whatsoever tribulation they shall call upon Thee, may obtain the blessings of Thy consolation. Through our Lord.

COLLECT. *Commemoration of St. Theodore.*

O God, Who dost encompass and protect us with the glorious testimony of blessed Theodore, Thy martyr, grant us to profit by imitating him and to be supported by his prayers. Through our Lord.

Deus, qui nos beáti Theodóri Mártyris tui confessióne gloriósa circúmdas et prótegis: præsta nobis ex ejus imitatióne profícere, et oratióne fulcíri. Per Dóminum.

EPISTLE. *Apoc 21: 2-5*

IN THOSE DAYS, I saw the holy city, the new Jerusalem, coming down out of Heaven, from God, prepared as a bride adorned for her husband. And I heard a great voice from the throne, saying, Behold the tabernacle of God with men; and He will dwell with them: and they shall be His people, and God Himself with them shall be their God: and God shall wipe away all tears from their eyes; and death shall be no more, nor mourning, nor crying, nor sorrow shall be any more, for the former things are passed away. And He that sat on the throne said, Behold, I make all things new.

In diébus illis: Vidi sanctam civitátem Jerúsalem novam descendéntem de cælo a Deo, parátam sicut sponsam ornátam viro suo. Et audívi vocem magnam de throno dicéntem: Ecce tabernáculum Dei cum homínibus, et habitábit cum eis. Et ipsi pópulus ejus erunt, et ipse Deus cum eis erit eórum Deus: et abstérget Deus omnem lácrimam ab óculis eórum: et mors ultra non erit, neque luctus neque clamor neque dolor erit ultra, quia prima abiérunt. Et dixit, qui sedébat in throno: Ecce, nova fácio ómnia.

GRADUAL & ALLELUIA. *Trad. & Ps 137: 2*

THIS PLACE was made by God a priceless mystery, it is without reproof. ℣. O God, before Whom stands the choir of angels, hear the prayers of Thy servants.

℣. I will worship toward Thy holy temple; and I will give glory to Thy name. Alleluia.

Locus iste a Deo factus est inæstimábile sacraméntum, irreprehensíbilis est. ℣. Deus, cui astat Angelórum chorus, exáudi preces servórum tuórum.

Allelúja, allelúja. ℣. Adorábo ad templum sanctum tuum: et confitébor nómini tuo. Allelúja.

After Septuagesima, the Alleluia is replaced by the following Tract:

TRACT. *Ps 124: 1-2*

THEY that trust in the Lord shall be as Mount Sion: He shall not be moved forever that dwelleth in Jerusalem. ℣. Mountains are round about it: so the Lord is round about His people, from henceforth now and forever.

Identical to the 4th Sunday of Lent:

Qui confídunt in Dómino, sicut mons Sion: non commovébitur in ætérnum, qui hábitat in Jerúsalem. ℣. Montes in circúitu ejus, et Dóminus in circúitu pópuli sui, ex hoc nunc, et usque in sæculum.

In Paschal-time, the Gradual and Tract are replaced by the Greater Alleluia:

GREATER ALLELUIA. *Ps 137: 2 & Trad.*

ALLELUIA, alleluia. ℣. I will worship toward Thy holy temple; and I will give glory to Thy name. Alleluia. ℣. The house of the Lord is well founded upon a firm rock. Alleluia.

Allelúja, allelúja. ℣. Adorábo ad templum sanctum tuum: et confitébor nómini tuo.
Allelúja. ℣. Bene fundáta est domus Dómini supra firmam petram. Allelúja.

GOSPEL. *Luke 19: 1-10*

In illo témpore: Ingréssus Jesus perambulábat Jéricho. Et ecce, vir nómine Zachǽus: et hic princeps erat publicanórum, et ipse dives: et quærébat vidére Jesum, quis esset: et non póterat præ turba, quia statúra pusíllus erat. Et præcúrrens ascéndit in árborem sycómorum, ut vidéret eum; quia inde erat transitúrus. Et cum venísset ad locum, suspíciens Jesus vidit illum, et dixit ad eum: Zachǽe, festínans descénde; quia hódie in domo tua opórtet me manére. Et festínans descéndit, et excépit illum gaudens. Et cum vidérent omnes, murmurábant, dicéntes, quod ad hóminem peccatórem divertísset. Stans autem Zachǽus, dixit ad Dóminum: Ecce, dimídium bonórum meórum, Dómine, do paupéribus: et si quid áliquem defraudávi, reddo quádruplum. Ait Jesus ad eum: Quia hódie salus dómui huic facta est: eo quod et ipse fílius sit Ábrahæ. Venit enim Fílius hóminis quǽrere et salvum fácere, quod períerat.

ENTERING IN, Jesus walked through Jericho. And behold there was a man named Zachæus, who was the chief of the publicans, and he was rich; and he sought to see Jesus Who He was, and he could not for the crowd, because he was of low stature. And running before, he climbed up into a sycamore-tree that he might see Him, for He was to pass that way. And when Jesus was come to the place, looking up, He saw him, and said to him: Zachæus, make haste and come down, for this day I must abide in thy house. And he made haste and came down, and received Him with joy. And when all saw it, they murmured, saying that He was gone to be a guest with a man that was a sinner. But Zachæus standing, said to the Lord, Behold, Lord, the half of my goods I give to the poor, and if I have wronged any man of anything, I restore him fourfold. Jesus said to him: This day is salvation come to this house; because he also is a son of Abraham. For the Son of man is come to seek and to save that which was lost. CREDO.

OFFERTORY. *I Paral 29: 17, 18*

Dómine Deus, in simplicitáte cordis mei lætus óbtuli univérsa; et pópulum tuum, qui repértus est, vidi cum ingénti gáudio: * **Deus Ísraël,** custódi hanc voluntátem, allelúja. ℣. *Fecit Sálomon solemnitátem in témpore illo (2x) ; et prosperátus est et appáruit ei Dóminus, Deus Ísraël.* ℣. *Majéstas Dómini ædificávit templum: vidébant omnes fílii Ísraël glóriam Dómini descendéntem super domum et adoravérunt et collaudavérunt Dóminum dicéntes:* * **Deus Ísraël...**

After Septuagesima, the Alleluia in this Offertory is omitted.

O LORD God, in the simplicity of my heart, I have joyfully offered all these things; and I have seen with great joy Thy people, which are present: * **O God of Israel,** keep this will. Alleluia. ℣. *And Solomon kept the solemnity at that time, and Solomon kept the solemnity at that time: and he prospered, and the Lord, the God of Israel, appeared to him.* ℣. *The majesty of the Lord built the temple: all the children of Israel saw the glory of the Lord coming down upon the house, and they adored and praised the Lord, saying:* * **O God of Israel...**

Parenthetical words in the following Secret are said only when the Mass is offered within the very walls of the church, the anniversary of whose dedication is being celebrated:

SECRET. *In anniversario Dedicationis:*

Ánnue, quǽsumus, Dómine, précibus nostris: (*ut, quicúmque intra templi hujus, cujus anniversárium dedicatiónis diem celebrámus, ámbitum continémur, plena tibi atque perfécta córporis et ánimæ devotióne placeámus*) ut, dum hæc vota præséntia réddimus,

Bow down to our prayers, O Lord, we beseech Thee (*that all of us who are within the precincts of this temple, the anniversary of whose dedication we celebrate, may please Thee with full and perfect devotion of body and soul*) that, while we pay our vows here below, we may, by Thine assistance, be worthy to attain unto everlasting rewards. Through our Lord.

ad ætérna prǽmia, te adjuvante, perveníre mereámur. Per Dóminum.

On the actual day of dedication, the following Secret is said:

SECRET. *In ipso die dedicationis:*

O God, Who art the author of the gifts that are to be consecrated to Thee, pour forth Thy blessing upon this house of prayer, that the help of Thy defence may be felt by all who here invoke Thy name. Through our Lord.

Deus, qui sacrandórum tibi auctor es múnerum, effúnde super hanc oratiónis domum benedictiónem tuam: ut ab ómnibus, in ea invocántibus nomen tuum, defensiónis tuæ auxílium sentiátur. Per Dóminum.

SECRET. *Commemoration of St. Theodore.*

Receive, O Lord, the prayers of the faithful with offerings of sacrifices, and, by the intercession of blessed Theodore, Thy martyr, may we pass through these offices of pious devotion to heavenly glory. Through our Lord.

Súscipe, Dómine, fidélium preces cum oblatiónibus hostiárum: et, intercedénte beáto Theodóro Mártyre tuo, per hæc piæ devotiónis offícia ad cæléstem glóriam transeámus. Per Dóminum.

* *The "ad libitum" Preface for the Dedication of a Church (page 195) may be used.*

COMMUNION. *Matt 21: 13 with addition of Luke 11: 9*

MY HOUSE shall be called the house of prayer, saith the Lord: every one that asks therein, receives; and he who seeks, finds; and to him who knocks, it shall be opened. (*P.T. Alleluia.*) ℣. *Ask, and the gift will come; seek, and you shall find.*

Domus mea domus oratiónis vocábitur, dicit Dóminus: in ea omnis, qui petit, áccipit; et qui quærit, invénit; et pulsánti aperiétur. (*T.P. Allelúja.*) ℣. *Pétite, et dábitur vobis; quǽrite, et inveniétis.*

POSTCOMMUNION.

O God, Who from living and chosen stones dost prepare for Thy majesty an eternal dwelling, help Thy people who call upon Thee, so that what is profitable to Thy Church in material growth may be accompanied with an increase of that which is of the spirit. Through our Lord.

Deus, qui de vivis et eléctis lapídibus ætérnum majestáti tuæ prǽparas habitáculum: auxiliáre pópulo tuo supplicánti; ut, quod Ecclésiæ tuæ corporálibus próficit spátiis, spirituálibus amplificétur augméntis. Per Dóminum.

On the actual day of Dedication, the following Postcommunion is used:

POSTCOMMUNION. *In ipso die dedicationis:*

We pray Thee, O almighty God, that in this place, which we, unworthy, have dedicated to Thy name, the ears of Thy loving-kindness may be inclined unto all who make their petitions. Through our Lord.

Quǽsumus, omnípotens Deus: ut in hoc loco, quem nómini tuo indígni dedicávimus, cunctis peténtibus aures tuæ pietátis accómmodes. Per Dóminum.

POSTCOMMUNION. *Commemoration of St. Theodore.*

Præsta nobis, quæsumus, Dómine, intercedénte beáto Theodóro Mártyre tuo; ut, quod ore contíngimus, pura mente capiámus. Per Dóminum.

Grant us, we beseech Thee, O Lord, by the intercession of blessed Theodore, Thy martyr, that what we touch with our lips we may receive with pure hearts. Through our Lord.

THE NOVEMBER 9 OFFERTORY • Willi Apel wrote as follows:

> "The Offertories are in a category all their own. No other type of chant shows so many variants of its basic structure. [...] Not a few Offertories occur in different manuscripts with different numbers of verses or with divergent indications for the repeat of the Antiphon. It is not easy to give a satisfactory explanation for the great amount of structural variability found in these chants."

We have avoided notating the various ways these pieces may be sung—considering it sufficient to provide the Latin and English—but for this particular Offertory we recommend taking the repeat, to avoid ending on "dicéntes." Notice the repetition of *Fecit Sálomon Solemnitátem In Témpore Illo*, which repeats melody and text verbatim. Without question, such ***repeats*** are a characteristic—yet mysterious—feature of Offertories. These repeats are carefully written out in all the ancient manuscripts (a repeat sign is not used), and therefore present a golden opportunity to compare the same adiastematic passage ***written by the same scribe*** twice. The Propers for 9 November are extremely ancient, so naturally this Offertory ("Dómine Deus In Simplicitáte") is found in the most ancient sources we have—121EINSIE|961, STMAUR|1079, 239LAON|877, 75CAMBRAI|1031, 339SANGALL|974, 9448PRUM|983, and so forth—and the repeat is invariably written out, as has been mentioned.

NOTES • THE NUPTIAL MASS (1962 Missal)

According to *Rubricarum Instructum* (25 July 1960), when the special votive Mass of Bride and Bridegroom is allowed, it is celebrated as follows: (A) it may be a sung Mass or a low Mass; (B) the *Gloria* is said; (C) the *Credo* is not said, except during the Octave of Christmas; (D) one commemoration is allowed (only one privileged commemoration if the Mass is sung); (E) privileged commemorations must be made: octave of Christmas, Ember Days in September, ferias of Advent, Lent, and Passiontide, Greater Litanies; subject to the restrictions of letter "D," a commemoration is made of: vigil, feast II and III class. (F) the *oratio imperata* is not said; (G) preface is of the season, if any, otherwise the common preface; (H) the blessing is imparted during the Mass, as in the Missal.

The 1917 Code did not allow Mass in the afternoon or evening—except Christmas Midnight Mass—"without apostolic indult." Those who would receive Holy Communion were to fast from Midnight, taking no food or water, and Holy Communion was often distributed outside of Mass. For example, Holy Communion might be given at 6:15AM on Holy Thursday, with the High Mass beginning at 8:30AM. That is why before the 1950s Catholic weddings (when the Nuptial Mass followed) took place in the morning. Indeed, the traditional *Baltimore Catechism* says: "Catholics should be married in the morning, and with a Nuptial Mass if possible."

This is not to imply Mass after midday never occurred. Numerous documented instances show the Holy See giving such permission: 25 November 1929 in Russia (provided that "a Eucharistic fast of four hours from noon be observed"); in 1946, the Archbishop of Paris received an indult allowing prison chaplains to offer afternoon Masses; in 1942, Cardinal Spellman received permission for the American military forces to have Mass in the afternoon; and so forth. Indeed, Cardinal Pacelli himself—later elected Pope Pius XII—celebrated an evening Mass for 300,000 pilgrims in Lourdes in 1935.

On 6 January 1953, Pope Pius XII issued CHRISTUS DOMINUS, which gave generous allowance for evening Masses with a Eucharistic fast "of three hours from solid food and alcoholic beverages, and of one hour from non-alcoholic beverages." The document's RULE I said: "In the future it shall be a general and common principle for all, both priests and faithful, that natural water does not break the Eucharistic fast." On 19 March 1957, *Sacram Communionem*—a MOTU PROPRIO by Pope Pius XII—provided even more generous permissions for Mass after midday, and essentially eliminated the midnight fast, stating: "Priests and faithful, before Holy Mass or Holy Communion respectively, must abstain for three hours from solid foods and alcoholic liquids, for one hour from non-alcoholic liquids. Water does not break the fast."

Neither of the documents issued by Pope Pius XII in 1953 and 1957 constituted "blanket permission" for Mass after midday or a disrespect for the concept of the Eucharistic fast. Indeed, CHRISTUS DOMINUS stated:

> "The solicitude of the Church for the preservation of the Eucharistic fast may be perceived also from the fact that the Church, in decreeing this fast, imposed serious penalties for its violation. Thus the *Seventh Council of Toledo* in the year 646AD threatened with excommunication anyone who should say Mass after having broken his fast. In the year 672AD, the *Third Council of Braga*, and in the year 685AD the *Second Council of Mâcon* had already pronounced that anyone who incurred this guilt should be deposed from his office and deprived of his honors."

The Holy See insisted that the *Code of Canon Law* (1917) had not been altered, explaining that exceptions had been made. In June of 1957, the Holy Office said the following in a private response: "As a matter of fact, the provision in can. 821 §1 has not been abrogated; consequently, one cannot say that Mass can now be celebrated *by law* in the evening." On this, see Father Shawn P. Tunink's dissertation: *Evening Masses and Days of Obligation* (Catholic University of America, 2016). It cannot be denied that CHRISTUS DOMINUS had encouraged Catholics to keep the Midnight fast ("The law of the Eucharistic fast from midnight continues in force for all of those who do not come under the special conditions which We are going to set forth in this Apostolic Letter") and made clear that evening Masses were intended for those who could not attend Mass in the morning. Nevertheless, the result of these documents—whether intended or not—was universal celebration of Mass at any hour for any reason, as well as annihilation of the Midnight fast.

WEDDING • THE ORDER OF MARRIAGE

The priest, in the presence of the witnesses, begins by putting the following question first to the groom, who stands at the right side of the bride, and then to the bride, addressing each by name.

(*Name of groom*), wilt thou take (*Name of bride*), here present, for thy lawful wife, according to the rite of our holy Mother the Church? ℟. I will.

(*Name of groom*), vis accípere (*Name of bride*), hic præséntem in tuam legítimam uxórem juxta ritum sanctæ matris Ecclésiæ? ℟. Volo.

Then the priest asks the bride:

(*Name of bride*), wilt thou take (*Name of groom*), here present, for thy lawful husband, according to the rite of our holy Mother the Church? ℟. I will.

(*Name of bride*), vis accípere (*Name of groom*) hic præséntem in tuum legítimum marítum juxta ritum sanctæ matris Ecclésiæ? ℟. Volo.

Having obtained their mutual consent, the priest bids the couple join their right hands. Then they pledge themselves each to the other as follows, repeating the words after the priest:

The groom says:

I, (*Name of groom*), take thee, (*Name of bride*), for my lawful wife, to have and to hold, from this day forward, for better, for worse, for richer, for poorer, in sickness and in health, until death do us part.

Then the bride says:

I, (*Name of bride*), take thee, (*Name of groom*), for my lawful husband, to have and to hold, from this day forward, for better, for worse, for richer, for poorer, in sickness and in health, until death do us part.

Ego conjúngo vos in matrimónium. In nómine Patris, et Fílii, ✠ et Spíritus Sancti. ℟. Amen.

(*Priest*) I join you together in marriage, in the Name of the Father, ✠ and of the Son, and of the Holy Ghost. ℟. Amen.

He sprinkles them with holy water. This done, the priest blesses the ring, saying:

℣. Adjutórium nostrum in nómine Dómini.

℟. Qui fecit cælum et terram.

℣. Dómine, exáudi oratiónem meam.

℟. Et clamor meus ad te véniat.

℣. Dóminus vobíscum.

℟. Et cum spíritu tuo.

℣. Our help is in the Name of the Lord.

℟. Who made heaven and earth.

℣. O Lord, hear my prayer.

℟. And let my cry come unto Thee.

℣. The Lord be with you.

℟. And with thy spirit.

Orémus.

Béne✠dic, Dómine, ánulum hunc, quem nos in tuo nómine bene✠dícimus: ut, quæ eum gestáverit, fidelitátem íntegram suo sponso tenens, in pace et voluntáte tua permáneat, atque in mútua caritáte semper vivat. Per Christum Dóminum nostrum. ℟. Amen.

Let us pray.

BLESS, ✠ O Lord, this ring, which we bless ✠ in Thy name, that she who shall wear it, keeping true faith unto her spouse, may abide in Thy peace and in obedience to Thy will, and ever live in mutual love. Through Christ our Lord. ℟. Amen.

Then the priest sprinkles the ring with holy water. The groom, having received the ring from the hand of the priest, places it on the third finger of the left hand of the bride, saying:

Lawful variety exists regarding the ceremonies and prayers used as the ring (or rings) are presented.

WITH this ring I thee wed and I promise unto thee my fidelity.

The priest then says:

In nómine Patris, ✠ et Fílii, et Spíritus Sancti. Amen.

In the name of the Father, ✠ and of the Son and of the Holy Ghost. Amen.

This having been done, the priest adds:

℣. Confirm, O God, that which Thou hast wrought in us.

℟. From Thy holy temple, which is in Jerusalem.

Lord, have mercy.
Christ, have mercy.
Lord, have mercy.

Our Father, etc. (*inaudibly*)

℣. And lead us not into temptation.

℟. But deliver us from evil.

℣. Save Thy servants.

℟. Who hope in Thee, O my God.

℣. Send them help, O Lord, from Thy holy place.

℟. And defend them out of Sion.

℣. Be unto them, Lord, a tower of strength.

℟. From the face of the enemy.

℣. O Lord, hear my prayer.

℟. And let my cry come unto Thee.

℣. The Lord be with you.

℟. And with thy spirit.

Let us pray.

LOOK DOWN with favor, O Lord, we beseech Thee, upon these Thy servants, and graciously protect this, Thine ordinance, whereby Thou hast provided for the propagation of mankind; that they who are joined together by Thy authority may be preserved by Thy help; through Christ our Lord.

℟. Amen.

℣. Confírma hoc, Deus, quod operátus es in nobis.

℟. A templo sancto Tuo quod est in Jerúsalem.

Kýrie eléison.
Christe eléison.
Kýrie eléison.

Pater noster, etc. *secreto usque ad*

℣. Et ne nos indúcas in tentatiónem.

℟. Sed líbera nos a malo.

℣. Salvos fac servos tuos.

℟. Deus meus, sperántes in te.

℣. Mitte eis, Dómine, auxílium de sancto.

℟. Et de Sion tuére eos.

℣. Esto eis, Dómine, turris fortitúdinis.

℟. A fácie inimíci.

℣. Dómine, exáudi oratiónem meam.

℟. Et clamor meus ad te véniat.

℣. Dóminus vobíscum.

℟. Et cum spíritu tuo.

Orémus.

Réspice, quǽsumus, Dómine, super hos fámulos tuos, et institútis tuis, quibus propagatiónem humáni géneris ordinásti, benígnus assíste; ut qui te auctóre jungúntur, te auxiliánte servéntur. Per Christum Dóminum nostrum.

℟. Amen.

The Mass for the Bride and Groom follows. Latin liturgical books call this: "Missa pro Sponso et Sponsa" or "Missa votiva pro sponsis." German books call it: "Votivmesse für Bräutigam und Braut." French books call it: "Messe de Mariage."

NUPTIAL MASS PROPERS • The Nuptial Mass *Propria Missae* are a mixture of old and new. The Mode 6 Communion ("Ecce Sic Benedicétur") can be found in ancient manuscripts such as ALBI|1047 and NARBONNE|1033. However, Abbat Pothier was unaware of this until 1908; previously, both he and Dom Mocquereau had employed a Mode 8 adaptation based on the Palm Sunday Communion ("Pater Si Non Potest"). The Introit is a modern composition with an interesting history. Its text can be found wedded to a melody in 5319VATICANUS|1105—one of the few "Old Roman" manuscripts we have—but Abbat Pothier did not choose that melody. At first, he adapted the text to a Mode 1 melody, perhaps following Father Hermesdorff's 1863 adaptation. For the *Editio Vaticana*, he switched to a Mode 3 melody. Plainsong books from the 19th century show multifarious adaptations in diverse modes for the Nuptial *Propria Missae*.

On 24 June 2019, the Congregation for the Doctrine of the Faith issued a letter—signed by Monsignor Matteo Visioli—stating that the Nuptial Blessing may be chanted in the Extraordinary Form, provided it be sung to the tone found in the 1835 edition of the *Missale Cenomanense* ("Missal of Le Mans, France").

II Classis.

—*Mass for the Bride & Groom*—

MISSA VOTIVA PRO SPONSIS

INTROIT. *Tob 7: 15; 8, 19 and Ps 127: 1*

Deus Ísraël conjúngat vos: et ipse sit vobíscum, qui misértus est duóbus únicis: et nunc, Dómine, fac eos plénius benedícere te. (*T.P. Allelúja, allelúja.*) ℣. Beáti omnes, qui timent Dóminum: qui ámbulant in viis ejus. ℣. Glória Patri.

MAY THE GOD of Israel join you together: and may He be with you, Who was merciful to two only children: and now, O Lord, make them bless Thee more fully. (*P.T. Allē, alleluia.*) ℣. Blessed are all they that fear the Lord; that walk in His ways. ℣. Glory.

COLLECT.

Exáudi nos, omnípotens et miséricors Deus: ut, quod nostro ministrátur offício, tua benedictióne pótius impleátur. Per Dóminum.

Graciously hear us, almighty and merciful God, that what is accomplished by our ministry may be perfected by Thy blessing. Through our Lord.

EPISTLE. *Eph 5: 22-33*

Fratres: Mulíeres viris suis súbditæ sint, sicut Dómino; quóniam vir caput est mulíeris, sicut Christus caput est Ecclésiæ: Ipse, salvátor córporis ejus. Sed sicut Ecclésia subjécta est Christo, ita et mulíeres viris suis in ómnibus. Viri, dilígite uxóres vestras, sicut et Christus diléxit Ecclésiam, et seípsum trádidit pro ea, ut illam sanctificáret, mundans lavácro aquæ in verbo vitæ, ut exhibéret ipse sibi gloriósam Ecclésiam, non habéntem máculam, aut rugam, aut áliquid hujúsmodi, sed ut sit sancta et immaculáta. Ita et viri debent dilígere uxóres suas, ut córpora sua. Qui suam uxórem díligit, seípsum díligit. Nemo enim umquam carnem suam ódio hábuit, sed nutrit, et fovet eam, sicut et Christus Ecclésiam: quia membra sumus córporis ejus, de carne ejus et de óssibus ejus. Propter hoc relínquet homo patrem et matrem suam, et adhærébit uxóri suæ: et erunt duo in carne una. Sacraméntum hoc magnum est, ego autem dico in Christo, et in Ecclésia. Verúmtamen et vos sínguli, unusquísque uxórem suam, sicut seípsum díligat: uxor autem tímeat virum suum.

BRETHREN, let women be subject to their husbands, as to the Lord; because the husband is the head of the wife, as Christ is the head of the Church: He is the savior of His Body. Therefore, as the Church is subject to Christ, so also let the wives be to their husbands in all things. Husbands, love your wives, as Christ also loved the Church, and delivered Himself up for it; that He might sanctify it, cleansing it by the laver of water in the word of life; that He might present it to Himself a glorious Church, not having spot, or wrinkle, nor any such thing, but that it should be holy and without blemish. So also ought men to love their wives as their own bodies. He that loveth his wife, loveth himself: for no man ever hated his own flesh, but nourisheth and cherisheth it; as also Christ doth the Church: for we are members of His body, of His flesh, and of His bones. For this cause shall a man leave his father and mother, and shall cleave to his wife; and they shall be two in one flesh. This is a great sacrament; but I speak in Christ and in the Church. Nevertheless, let every one of you in particular love his wife as himself, and let the wife fear her husband.

GRADUAL & ALLELUIA. *Ps 127: 3 & Ps 19: 3*

THY WIFE shall be as a fruitful vine on the sides of thy house. ℣. Thy children as olive-plants round about thy table.

℣. May the Lord send you help from the sanctuary, and defend you out of Sion. Alleluia.

Uxor tua sicut vitis abúndans in latéribus domus tuæ. ℣. Fílii tui sicut novéllæ olivárum in circúitu mensæ tuæ.

Allelúja, allelúja. ℣. Mittat vobis Dóminus auxílium de sancto: et de Sion tueátur vos. Allelúja.

After Septuagesima, the Alleluia is replaced by the following Tract:

TRACT. *Ps 127: 4-6*

BEHOLD thus shall the man be blessed that feareth the Lord. ℣. May the Lord bless thee out of Sion; and mayest thou see the good things of Jerusalem all the days of thy life. ℣. And mayest thou see thy children's children: peace upon Israel.

Ecce, sic benedicétur omnis homo, qui timet Dóminum. ℣. Benedícat tibi Dóminus ex Sion: et vídeas bona Jerúsalem ómnibus diébus vitæ tuæ. ℣. Et vídeas fílios filiórum tuórum: pax super Ísraël.

In Paschal-time, the Gradual and Tract are replaced by the Greater Alleluia:

GREATER ALLELUIA. *Ps 19: 3 & Ps 133: 3*

ALLELUIA, alleluia. ℣. May the Lord send you help from the sanctuary, and defend you out of Sion. Alleluia. ℣. May the Lord out of Sion bless you; He that made heaven and earth. Alleluia.

Allelúja, allelúja. ℣. Mittat vobis Dóminus auxílium de sancto: et de Sion tueátur vos. Allelúja. ℣. Benedícat vobis Dóminus ex Sion: qui fecit cælum et terram. Allelúja.

GOSPEL. *Matt 19: 3-6*

T**HE PHARISEES** came to Jesus, tempting Him and saying: Is it lawful for a man to put away his wife for every cause? Who answering, said to them, Have ye not read, that He Who made man from the beginning, made them male and female? and He said, For this cause shall a man leave father and mother, and shall cleave to his wife, and they two shall be in one flesh. Therefore now they are not two, but one flesh. What therefore God hath joined together, let no man put asunder.

In illo témpore: Accessérunt ad Jesum pharisǽi, tentántes eum et dicéntes: Si licet hómini dimíttere uxórem suam quacúmque ex causa? Qui respóndens, ait eis: Non legístis, quia qui fecit hóminem ab inítio, másculum et féminam fecit eos? et dixit: Propter hoc dimíttet homo patrem et matrem, et adhærébit uxóri suæ, et erunt duo in carne una. Itaque jam non sunt duo, sed una caro. Quod ergo Deus conjúnxit, homo non séparet.

OFFERTORY. *Ps 30: 15-16*

IN THEE, O Lord, have I hoped: I said, Thou art my God, my times are in Thy hands. ℣. *Make Thy face to shine upon Thy servant, and save me in Thy mercy: O Lord, let me not be confounded, for I have called upon Thee.* ℣. *O how great is the multitude*

Identical to 13th Sunday after Pentecost:

In te sperávi, Dómine; dixi: Tu es Deus meus, in mánibus tuis témpora mea. ℣. *Illúmina fáciem tuam super servum tuum et salvum me fac propter misericórdiam tuam: Dómine, non confúndar, quóniam invocávi te.* ℣. *Quam magna multitúdo dulcédinis tuæ, Dó-*

mine, quam abscondísti timéntibus te: perfecísti autem sperántibus in te in conspéctu filiórum hóminum.

of Thy sweetness, O Lord, which Thou hast hidden for them that fear Thee! Which Thou hast wrought for them that hope in Thee, in the sight of the sons of men.

SECRET.

Súscipe, quǽsumus, Dñe, pro sacra connúbii lege munus oblátũ: et, cujus largítor es óperis, esto dispósitor. Per Dñm.

* *The "ad libitum" Wedding Preface on page 197 may be used.*

Receive, we beseech Thee, O Lord, the offering which we make to Thee on behalf of the sacred bond of wedlock, and be Thou the disposer of the work of which Thou art the author. Through our Lord.

After the PATER NOSTER,—before the priest says "Libera nos, quǽsumus, Dómine"—he stands before the Altar at the Epistle side. Facing the spouses, who kneel, he says the following prayers over them. *Dicto "Pater noster," sacerdos antequam dicat "Libera nos, quǽsumus, Dómine," stans in latere Epistolae versus sponsum et sponsam ante altare genuflexos, dicit super eos sequentes orationes.*

Orémus.

Propitiáre, Dómine, supplicatiónibus nostris, et institútis tuis, quibus propagatiónem humáni géneris ordinásti, benígnus assíste: ut, quod te auctóre júngitur, te auxiliánte servétur. Per Dóminum nostrum.

Let us pray.

MERCIFULLY hear our prayers, O Lord, and graciously protect Thine ordinance, whereby Thou hast provided for the propagation of mankind, that this union made by Thy authority may be preserved by Thy help. Through our Lord.

Orémus.

Deus, qui potestáte virtútis tuæ de níhilo cuncta fecísti: qui dispósitis universitátis exórdiis, hómini, ad imáginem Dei facto, ídeo inseparábile mulíeris adjutórium condidísti, ut femíneo córpori de viríli dares carne princípium, docens, quod ex uno placuísset institui, numquam licére disjúngi: Deus, qui tam excellénti mystério conjugálem cópulam consecrásti, ut Christi et Ecclésiæ sacraméntum præsignáres in fœdere nuptiárum: Deus, per quem múlier júngitur viro, et socíetas principáliter ordináta ea benedictióne donátur, quæ sola nec per originális peccáti pœnam nec per dilúvii est abláta senténtiam: réspice propítius super hanc fámulam tuam, quæ, maritáli jungénda consórtio, tua se éxpetit protectióne muníri: sit in ea jugum dilectiónis et pacis: fidélis et casta nubat in Christo, imitatríxque sanctárum permáneat feminárum: sit amábilis viro suo, ut Rachel: sápiens, ut Rebécca: longǽva et fidélis, ut Sara: nihil in ea ex áctibus suis ille auctor prævaricatiónis usúrpet: nexa fídei mandatísque permáneat: uni thoro juncta, contáctus illícitos fúgiat: múniat infirmitátem suam robóre disciplínæ: sit verecúndia gravis, pudóre venerábilis, doctrínis cæléstibus erudíta: sit fœcúnda in sóbole, sit probáta et ínnocens:

Let us pray.

O GOD, who by Thy mighty power hast made all things out of nothing; Who, in the beginning having set up the world, didst bestow on man, whom Thou hadst created in Thine own likeness, the inseparable help of woman, fashioning her body from his very flesh, and thereby teaching us that it is never lawful to put asunder what it has pleased Thee to make of one substance; O God, Who hast consecrated wedlock by a surpassing mystery, since in the marriage-bond Thou didst foreshow the union of Christ with the Church; O God, by Whom woman is joined to man, and that alliance which Thou didst ordain from the beginning is endowed with a blessing, which alone was not taken away, either in punishment of original sin or by the sentence of the flood, look down in mercy upon this Thy handmaid who, being about to enter upon wedded life, seeks to be strengthened by Thy protection; may the yoke she has to bear be one of love and peace; true and chaste may she marry in Christ, and be a follower of holy women; may she be pleasing to her husband like Rachel; prudent like Rebecca; long-lived and faithful like Sara; may the author of sin have no share in any of her actions; may she remain attached to the faith and commandments, and being joined to one man in wedlock, may she fly all unlawful addresses; may she fortify her weakness by strong discipline; may she be respected for her seriousness and venerated for her modesty; may she be well versed in heavenly lore; may she be fruitful in offspring. May her life be pure and blameless; and may she attain to the rest of the blessed in the kingdom of heaven. May they both see their children's children even to the third and fourth generation and arrive at a happy old age; through our Lord Jesus Christ Thy Son, Who liveth and reigneth with Thee in the unity of the Holy Ghost, one God world without end. Amen.

et ad Beatórum réquiem atque ad cæléstia regna pervéniat: et vídeant ambo fílios filiórum suórum, usque in tértiam et quartam generatiónem, et ad optátam pervéniant senectútem. Per eúmdem Dóminum nostrum Jesum Christum fílium tuum, qui tecum vivit et regnat in unitáte Spíritus Sancti, Deus, per ómnia sæcula sæculórum. Amen.

Then the priest returns to the center of the Altar and says, "Libera nos, quæsumus, Dómine" etc. as usual. After he has received the precious Blood, he gives communion to the spouses, and Mass continues.
Tunc sacerdos reversus ad medium altaris dicat "Libera nos, quæsumus, Dómine," et reliqua more solito; et, postquam sumpserit Sanguinem, communicet sponsos: et prosequatur Missam.

COMMUNION. *Ps 127: 4, 6 with Psalm 127: 1*

BEHOLD, thus shall every man be blessed that feareth the Lord: and mayest thou see thy children's children: peace be upon Israel. (*P.T. Alleluia.*) ℣. Blessed are all they that fear the Lord: that walk in his ways.

Ecce, sic benedicétur omnis homo, qui timet Dóminum: et vídeas fílios filiórum tuórum: pax super Ísraël. (*T.P. Allelúja.*) ℣. *Beáti omnes, qui timent Dóminum: qui ámbulant in viis ejus.* —RENAUD|965 • Circa 965AD

POSTCOMMUNION.

We beseech Thee, almighty God, in Thy great goodness, to show favor to that order of things which Thou Thyself hast established, and to keep in abiding peace those whom Thou hast joined together in lawful union. Through our Lord.

Quæsumus, omnípotens Deus: institúta providéntiæ tuæ pio favóre comitáre; ut, quos legítima societáte connéctis, longæva pace custódias. Per Dóminum.

After the *Ite Missa Est*, before the priest blesses the people, he turns to the spouses and says:
Dicta "Ite, missa est," sacerdos antequam populo benedicat, conversus ad sponsum et sponsam, dicat:

MAY the God of Abraham, the God of Isaac, and the God of Jacob be with you, and may he fulfill his blessing in you: that you may see your children's children even to the third and fourth generation, and may afterwards have life everlasting, by the grace of our Lord Jesus Christ, Who, with the Father and the Holy Ghost, liveth and reigneth God, world without end. ℟. Amen.

Deus Ábraham, Deus Ísaäc et Deus Jacob sit vobíscum: et ipse adímpleat benedictiónem suam in vobis: ut videátis fílios filiórum vestrórum usque ad tértiam et quartam generatiónem, et póstea vitam ætérnam habeátis sine fine: adjuvánte Dómino nostro Jesu Christo, qui cum Patre et Spíritu Sancto vivit et regnat Deus, per ómnia sæcula sæculórum. ℟. Amen.

The priest shall warn them in serious words that, remaining in the fear of God and loving each other, they should keep mutual faith and conjugal chastity, and carefully establish their children in the Catholic religion. Afterwards he sprinkles them with holy water and, having said *"Pláceat tibi, sancta Trínitas,"* he gives the blessing. Then, in the usual way, he begins the Last Gospel.

Moneat eos sacerdos gravi sermone ut, in Dei timore manentes et alterutrum diligentes, mutuam fidem et coniugalem castitatem servent, atque prolem in catholica religione sedulo instituant. Postea eos aspergat aqua benedicta, et dicto "Pláceat tibi, sancta Trínitas," det benedictionem; et legat, ut solitum est, initium Evangelii secundum Ioannem.

— The Sacrament of Confirmation —

RITUS CONFIRMATIONIS E PONTIFICALI ROMANO

1. Come Creator Spirit, visit the souls of thy people, | fill with grace from on high the hearts which thou hast created.

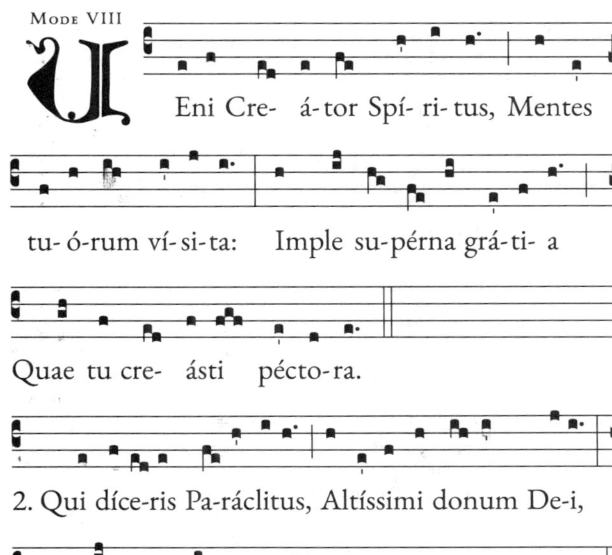

2. Thou who art called the Comforter, gift of the most high God, | living fount, fire, love and unction of souls.

Fons vivus, ignis, cáritas, Et spi-ri-tá-lis úncti-o.

3. Sevenfold in thy gifts, finger of the Father's right hand, | thou promised truly by the Father, giving speech to tongues.

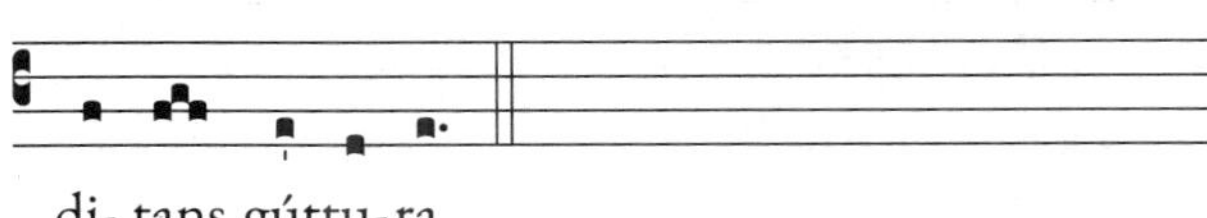

4. Inflame our senses with thy light, pour thy love into our hearts, | strengthen our weak bodies with lasting power.

4. Accénde lumen sénsibus, Infúnd*e* amórem córdi-

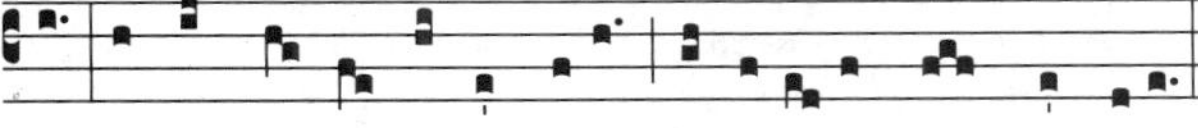

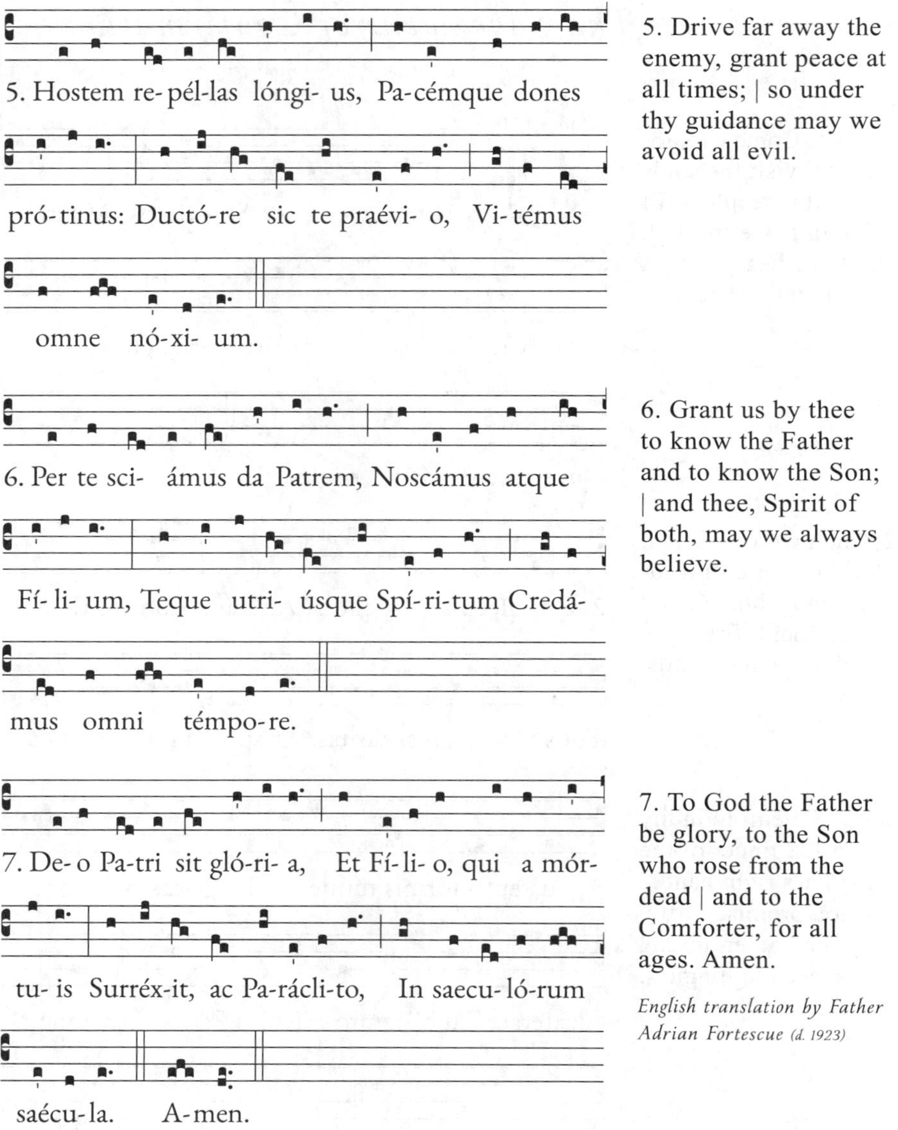

5. Drive far away the enemy, grant peace at all times; | so under thy guidance may we avoid all evil.

6. Grant us by thee to know the Father and to know the Son; | and thee, Spirit of both, may we always believe.

7. To God the Father be glory, to the Son who rose from the dead | and to the Comforter, for all ages. Amen.

English translation by Father Adrian Fortescue (d. 1923)

The "Veni Creátor Spíritus" is frequently sung at the beginning. Nevertheless, the Confirmation ceremony is—as the *New Saint Basil Hymnal* (IMPRIMATUR 14 June 1958) puts it—very much "subject to local custom." There may be a RECEPTION OF THE BISHOP, including the *Ecce Sacérdos Magnus*. The bishop may give an address or even examine the candidates. The Roman Missal (IMPRIMATUR 15 November 1961, by Francis Cardinal Spellman) provides the following rubrics for the beginning of the ceremony:

> The bishop, with amice, stole, and cope of white color over the rochet, with miter and crozier or, if this sacrament should be conferred less solemnly, with white stole and simple miter, approaches the faldstool prepared for him in front of the middle of the Altar, if it is to be in some chapel, or in another suitable place, and while seated addresses those standing by and those to be confirmed with a short sermon. When this has been done, he washes his hands. Then, with his miter removed, he rises and, facing those to be confirmed kneeling before him, says—with hands joined—the following prayers.
>
> *Pontifex supra rochetum, paratus amictu, stola et pluviali albi coloris, cum mitra et baculo pastorali, vel, si hoc Sacramentum minus solemniter conferatur, stola alba et mitra simplici paratus, accedit ad faldistorium ante medium altaris, si sit in aliqua capella, aut in alio convenienti loco sibi paratum et sedens brevi sermone alloquitur adstantes et confirmandos. Quo facto, lavat manus: deinde, deposita mitra, surgit, et versa facie ad confirmandos ante se genuflexos, iunctis manibus dicit…*

Turning toward the candidates, the Bishop says or sings:

Spíritus Sanctus supervéniat in vos, et virtus Altíssimi custódiat vos a peccatis. ℟. Amen.

MAY the Holy Ghost descend upon you, and may the power of the Most High preserve you from sin. ℟. Amen.

℣. Adjutórium nostrum in nómine Dómini.

℟. Qui fecit cælum et terram.

℣. Dómine, exáudi oratiónem meam.

℟. Et clamor meus ad te véniat.

℣. Dóminus vobíscum.

℟. Et cum spíritu tuo.

℣. Our help is in the name of the Lord.

℟. Who hath made heaven and earth.

℣. O Lord, hear my prayer.

℟. And let my cry come unto Thee.

℣. The Lord be with you.

℟. And with thy spirit.

The bishop extends his hands over those to be confirmed, saying:

Orémus.

Omnípotens sempitérne Deus, qui regeneráre dignátus es hos fámulos tuos ex aqua, et Spíritu Sancto; quique dedísti eis remissiónem ómnium peccatórum; emítte in eos septifórmem Spíritum tuum Sanctum Paráclitum de cælis. ℟. Amen.

℣. Spíritum sapiéntiæ, et intelléctus.

℟. Amen.

℣. Spíritum consílii, et fortitúdinis.

℟. Amen.

℣. Spíritum sciéntiæ, et pietátis.

℟. Amen.

Adímple eos Spíritu timóris tui, et consígna eos signo Crucis ✠ Christi, in vitam propitiátus ætérnam. Per eúmdem Dóminum nostrum Jesum Christum Fílium tuum, qui tecum vivit, et regnat in unitáte ejúsdem Spíritus Sancti Deus, per ómnia sǽcula sæculórum. ℟. Amen.

Let us pray.

ALMIGHTY, everlasting God, Who hast vouchsafed to regenerate these Thy servants by water and the Holy Ghost, and hast given them remission of all their sins; send forth upon them from heaven Thy sevenfold Holy Ghost, the Paraclete. ℟. Amen.

℣. The Spirit of wisdom and understanding.

℟. Amen.

℣. The Spirit of counsel and fortitude.

℟. Amen.

℣. The Spirit of knowledge and piety.

℟. Amen.

FILL THEM with the Spirit of Thy holy fear and sign them with the sign of the Cross ✠ of Christ in mercy unto eternal life. Through the same Jesus Christ Thy Son, our Lord, who with Thee liveth and reigneth in the unity of the same Holy Ghost, God, world without end. ℟. Amen.

Each person to be confirmed kneels before the bishop. The sponsor stands behind, placing his right hand on the candidate's shoulder. The bishop addresses each one individually, using the candidate's chosen Confirmation name. Making the sign of the cross on each candidate's forehead with his thumb (which has been dipped in Holy Chrism), the bishop simultaneously extends his fingers over the candidate's head and gives him a triple blessing:

(*Name of candidate*), Signo te signo Cru✠cis et confírmo te Chrísmate salútis: In nómine Pa✠tris, et Fí✠lii, et Spíritus ✠ Sancti.

(*Name of candidate*), I sign thee with the sign of the ✠ Cross, and I confirm thee with the Chrism of salvation. In the name of the Father, ✠ and of the Son, ✠ and of the Holy ✠ Ghost.

— *Everyone confirmed replies:* "Amen."

The bishop then strikes each lightly on the cheek, saying: PAX TECUM, which means, "Peace be with thee." Those being confirmed make no response. If the candidates for Confirmation are numerous, Gregorian chant, hymns, or motets may be sung—especially those in honor of the Holy Ghost or the Blessed Trinity. When all have been confirmed, the bishop washes his hands with lemons and bread (to remove the oils). While the bishop is washing his hands, the following is sung or recited:

Confirm, O God, what Thou hast wrought in us, from Thy holy temple, which is in Jerusalem, alleluia, alleluia.

℣. Glory be to the Father, and to the Son, and the Holy Ghost.

℟. As it was in the beginning, is now, and ever shall be. World without end. Amen.

Confirm, O God . . .

The Antiphon ("Confírma Hoc") is repeated.

When the antiphon has been repeated, the bishop's miter is removed. The bishop rises and—facing the Altar with hands joined—says or sings the following.
Qua repetita, Pontifex, deposita mitra, surgit, et stans versus ad altare, iunctis ante pectus manibus, dicit...

℣. Lord, show us Thy mercy.
℟. And grant us Thy salvation.
℣. O Lord, hear my prayer.
℟. And let my cry come unto Thee.
℣. The Lord be with you.
℟. And with thy spirit.

Let us pray.

O GOD, WHO HAST given Thy Holy Spirit to Thine Apostles, and hast willed that He should be given to the other faithful by them and their successors; regard benignantly the service of our lowliness; and grant that the same Holy Spirit, coming upon those whose foreheads we have anointed with holy chrism and marked with the sign of the

℣. Osténde nobis, Dómine, misericórdiam tuam.
℟. Et salutáre tuum da nobis.
℣. Dómine, exáudi oratiónem meam.
℟. Et clamor meus ad te véniat.
℣. Dóminus vobíscum.
℟. Et cum spíritu tuo.

Orémus.

Deus, qui Apóstolis tuis Sanctum dedísti Spíritum et per eos, eorúmque successóres, céteris fidélibus tradéndum esse voluísti; réspice propítius ad humilitátis nostræ famulátum, et præsta; ut eórum corda, quorum frontem sacro Chrísmate delinívimus, et signo sanctæ Crucis signávimus, idem Spíritus Sanctus in eis supervéniens, templum glóriæ suæ dignánter inhabitándo perfíciat. Qui cum Patre, et Spíritu Sancto vivis, et regnas Deus, in sæcula sæculórum. ℟. Amen.

Cross, may make their hearts a temple of His glory. Who livest and reignest with the Father and the same Holy Spirit, God, world without end. ℟. Amen.

The bishop turns toward the Confirmati, receives the crozier, and blesses them:

Ecce sic benedicétur omnis homo, qui timet Dóminum. Bene✠dícat vos Dóminus ex Sion, ut videátis bona Jerúsalem ómnibus diébus vitæ vestræ, et habeátis vitam ætérnam. ℟. Amen.

Behold, thus shall every man be blessed who fears the Lord: May the Lord bless ✠ you out of Sion, that you may see the good things of Jerusalem all the days of your life, and have life everlasting. ℟. Amen.

The PONTIFICALE suggests that the bishop say a few words of exhortation to the sponsors of the Confirmati. Then he may recite aloud with the Confirmati—in English—the CREED, the OUR FATHER and the HAIL MARY.

Expedita Confirmatione, Pontifex sedens, accepta mitra, patrinis et matrinis annuntiat, quod instruant filios suos bonis moribus, quod fugiant mala et faciant bona, et doceant eos "Credo in Deum," et "Pater Noster," et "Ave Maria," quoniam ad hoc sunt obligati.

The Bishop then imparts to all present the pontifical blessing:

℣. May the Lord's name be blessed.

℟. Now and forevermore.

℣. Our help is in the name of the Lord.

℟. Who made heaven and earth.

℣. May Almighty God bless you: the Father, ✠ the Son, and the Holy Ghost. ℟. Amen.

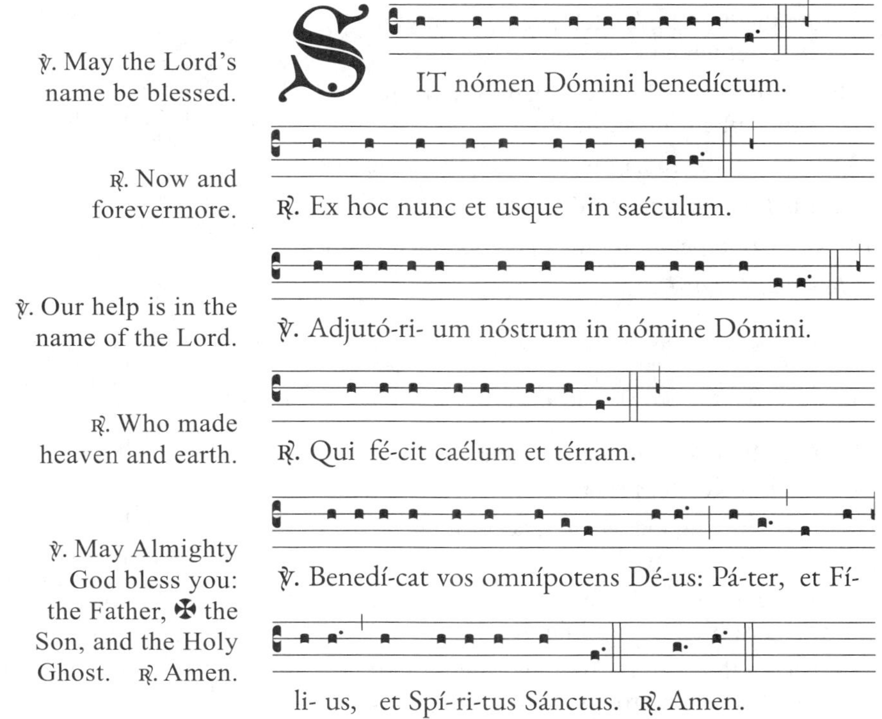

When the procession leaves the church, it is customary in certain localities to sing the "Te Deum" or Psalm 112.

Funeral • On the Day of Death or Burial

At the house of the deceased, the priest sprinkles the body with holy water, and prays this Antiphon with Psalm 129:

IF THOU, O Lord, wilt mark iniquities, Lord, who shall endure it?

1. Out of the depths I have cried to Thee, O Lord! Lord, hear my voice.
2. Let Thine ears be attentive to the voice of my supplication.
3. If Thou, O Lord, shalt observe iniquities, O Lord, who shall endure it?
4. For with Thee there is merciful forgiveness: because of Thy law I wait for Thee, O Lord.
5. My soul hath relied on His word: my soul hath hoped in the Lord.
6. From the morning watch even until night, let Israel hope in the Lord:
7. For with the Lord there is mercy, and with Him is plentiful redemption.
8. And He shall redeem Israel from all his iniquities.
9. Eternal rest grant unto them, O Lord.
10. And let perpetual light shine upon them.

℟. *If Thou, O Lord...*

Si iniquitátes observáveris, Dñe: Dómine, quis sustinébit?

1. De profúndis clamávi ad te, Dómine: Dómine, exáudi vocem meam.
2. Fiant aures tuæ intendéntes: in vocem deprecat iónis meæ.
3. Si iniquitátes observáveris, Dómine: Dómine, quis sustinébit?
4. Quia apud te propitiátio est: et propter legem tuam sustínui te, Dómine.
5. Sustínuit ánima mea in verbo ejus: sperávit ánima mea in Dómino.
6. A custódia matutína usque ad noctem: speret Ísraël in Dómino.
7. Quia apud Dóminum misericórdia: et copiósa apud eum redémptio.
8. Et ipse rédimet Ísraël: ex ómnibus iniquitátibus ejus.
9. Réquiem ætérnam dona eis, Dómine.
10. Et lux perpétua lúceat eis.

℟. *Si iniquitátes...*

On the day of the funeral—"as the body is borne to the church, on leaving the house"—the following Antiphon with Psalm 50 is sung. The priest solemnly intones the antiphon: "Exsultábunt Dómino." Since we no longer live in times when the home of the deceased is usually within walking distance to the church, it may also be sung when the priest and servers leave the sacristy to proceed to the front of the church, to meet the corpse and the family. It is permitted to omit verses, but never verses 21-22.

THE BODY that lies in the dust shall thrill with pride.

1. Have mercy on me, O God, according to Thy great mercy;
2. And according to the multitude of Thy tender mercies, blot out my iniquity.
3. Wash me thoroughly from my offense, and cleanse me from my sin.
4. For I acknowledge my iniquity, and my sin is always before me.
5. Against Thee only have I sinned, and I have done that which is evil in Thy sight, that Thou be found just in Thy sentence, upright in Thy judgment.

Exsultábunt Dómino ossa humiliáta.

1. Miserére mei Deus, secúndum magnam misericórdiam tuam.
2. Et secúndum multitúdinem miseratiónum tuárum, dele iniquitátem meam.
3. Amplius lava me ab iniquitáte mea: et a peccáto meo munda me.
4. Quóniam iniquitátem meam ego cognósco: et peccátum meum contra me est semper.
5. Tibi soli peccávi, et malum coram te feci: ut justificéris in sermónibus tuis, et vincas cum judicáris.

6. Ecce enim in iniquitátibus concéptus sum: et in peccátis concépit me mater mea.

6. For, behold, I was born in iniquities, and in sin did my mother conceive me.

7. Ecce enim veritátem dilexísti: incérta et occúlta sapiéntiæ tuæ manifestásti mihi.

7. For, behold, Thou hast loved truth; the secret and hidden things of Thy wisdom Thou hast made manifest unto me.

8. Aspérges me hyssópo, et mundábor: lavábis me, et super nivem dealbábor.

8. Thou shalt sprinkle me with hyssop, and I shall be cleansed; Thou shalt wash me, and I shall become whiter than snow.

9. Audítui meo dabis gáudium et lætítiam: et exsultábunt ossa humiliáta.

9. Thou shalt make me hear joy and gladness; and the bones that were humbled shall rejoice.

10. Avérte fáciem tuam a peccátis meis: et omnes iniquitátes meas dele.

10. Turn away Thy face from my sins, and blot out all my iniquities.

11. Cor mundum crea in me, Deus: et spíritum rectum ínnova in viscéribus meis.

11. Create in me a pure heart, O God, and renew a steadfast spirit within me.

12. Ne projícias me a fácie tua: et spíritum sanctum tuum ne áuferas a me.

12. Cast me not away from Thy face, and take not Thy Holy Spirit from me.

13. Redde mihi lætítiam salutáris tui: et spíritu principáli confírma me.

13. Restore unto me the joy of Thy salvation, and strengthen me with a noble spirit.

14. Docébo iníquos vias tuas: et ímpii ad te converténtur.

14. I will teach the unjust Thy ways, and the wicked shall be converted to Thee.

15. Líbera me de sanguínibus, Deus, Deus salútis meæ: et exsultábit lingua mea justítiam tuam.

15. Deliver me from sins of blood, O God, Thou God of my salvation: and my tongue shall extol Thy justice.

16. Dómine, lábia mea apéries: et os meum annuntiábit laudem tuam.

16. Thou shalt open my lips, O Lord: and my mouth shall declare Thy praise.

17. Quóniam si voluísses sacrifícium dedíssem útique: holocáustis non delectáberis.

17. For if Thou hadst desired sacrifice, I would surely have given it: with burnt-offerings Thou wilt not be delighted.

18. Sacrifícium Deo spíritus contribulátus: cor contrítum, et humiliátum, Deus non despícies.

18. A sacrifice unto God is a troubled spirit: a contrite and humble heart, O God, Thou wilt not despise.

19. Benígne fac, Dómine, in bona voluntáte tua Sion: ut ædificéntur muri Jerúsalem.

19. Deal favorably, O Lord, in Thy good will with Sion: that the walls of Jerusalem may be built up.

20. Tunc acceptábis sacrifícium justítiæ, oblatiónes, et holocáusta: tunc impónent super altáre tuum vítulos.

20. Then shalt Thou accept the sacrifice of justice, oblations, and whole burnt-offerings: then shall they lay calves upon Thine altar.

21. Réquiem ætérnam dona eis, Domine.

21. Eternal rest grant unto them, O Lord.

22. Et lux perpétua lúceat eis.

22. And let perpetual light shine upon them.

℟. *Exsultábunt Dómino...*

℟. *The body that lies in the dust...*

FUNERAL • ENTRY INTO THE CHURCH

When the corpse enters into the church, the following Responsory ("Subveníte") is sung. The body is placed before the Sanctuary with *the feet* towards the Altar, if a lay person; *the head*, if a priest.

COME to his (*her*) assistance, ye saints of God! Meet him (*her*) ye angels of the Lord. * Receive his (*her*) soul, † offering it in the sight of the Most High.

Subveníte, Sancti Dei, occúrrite, ángeli Dómini; * Suscipiéntes ánimam ejus: † Offeréntes eam in conspéctu Altíssimi.

℣. May Christ who called thee, receive thee; and may the angels lead thee into the bosom of Abraham.

℣. Suscípiat te Christus, qui vocávit te: et in sínum Ábrahæ ángeli dedúcant te:

* Receive his (*her*) soul, † offering it in the sight of the Most High.

* Suscipiéntes ánimam ejus: † Offeréntes eam in conspéctu Altíssimi.

℣. Eternal rest grant to him (*her*), O Lord, and let perpetual light shine upon him (*her*).

℣. Réquiem ætérnam dona ei, Dómine: et lux perpétua lúceat ei.

† offering it in the sight of the Most High.

† Offeréntes eam in conspéctu Altíssimi.

If the Office of the Dead (*Officium Defunctorum*) is to be prayed, it begins now; otherwise the Mass begins as soon as the priest is vested. A Mass for the Dead has many features which distinguish it from others. These are in part reminiscences of (otherwise obsolete) ancient liturgical customs, and are in part suggested by the mournful character of the rite. Thus, incense is not burned at the INTROIT and at the GOSPEL; the psalm "Judica me Deus" is omitted; the kiss of peace is omitted; the Deacon chanting the Gospel is not accompanied by the usual acolytes bearing candles, and no blessing is given.

—*The Funeral Mass ("Requiem Mass")*—

MISSA EXSEQUIALIS | IN DIE OBITUS SEU DEPOSITIONIS DEFUNCTI

INTROIT. *IV Esdr 2: 34, 35*

GRANT THEM eternal rest, O Lord; and let perpetual light shine upon them. (Ps 64: 2-3) A hymn, O God, becometh Thee in Sion; and a vow shall be paid to Thee in Jerusalem: O Lord, hear my prayer; all flesh shall come to Thee. *Eternal rest...*

Réquiem ætérnam dona eis, Dómine: et lux perpétua lúceat eis. ℣. Te decet hymnus, Deus, in Sion, et tibi reddétur votum in Jerúsalem: exáudi oratiónem meam, ad te omnis caro véniet. *Requiem ætérnam...*

COLLECT.

O God, Whose property it is ever to have mercy and to spare, we humbly supplicate Thee for the soul of Thy servant (*Name of the deceased*), which Thou hast this day called out of this world; cast not that soul into the hands of the enemy, nor forget it forever, but command it to be received by the holy angels and taken

Deus, cui próprium est miseréri semper et párcere, te súpplices exorámus pro anima fámuli tui N. (*fámulæ tuæ N.*), quam hódie de hoc sǽculo migráre jussísti: ut non tradas eam in manus inimíci, neque obliviscáris in finem, sed júbeas eam a sanctis Ángelis súscipi, et ad pátriam paradísi perdúci; ut, quia in te sperávit et crédidit, non pœnas inférni sustíneat, sed gáudia ætérna possídeat. Per Dóminum.

to Paradise, its home, so that, since it hath hoped and believed in Thee, it may not bear the pains of hell, but possess everlasting joys. Through our Lord.

EPISTLE. *I Thess 4: 13-18*

Fratres: Nólumus vos ignoráre de dormiéntibus, ut non contristémini, sicut et céteri, qui spem non habent. Si enim crédimus, quod Jesus mórtuus est et resurréxit: ita et Deus eos, qui dormiérunt per Jesum, addúcet cum eo. Hoc enim vobis dícimus in verbo Dómini, quia nos, qui vívimus, qui resídui sumus in advéntum Dómini, non præveniémus eos, qui dormiérunt. Quóniam ipse Dóminus in jussu, et in voce Archángeli, et in tuba Dei descéndet de cælo: et mórtui, qui in Christo sunt, resúrgent primi. Deínde nos, qui vívimus, qui relínquimur, simul rapiémur cum illis in núbibus óbviam Christo in áëra, et sic semper cum Dómino érimus. Itaque consolámini ínvicem in verbis istis.

BRETHREN: We will not have you ignorant concerning them that are asleep, that you be not sorrowful, even as others who have no hope. For if we believe that Jesus died and rose again, even so them who have slept through Jesus will God bring with Him. For this we say unto you in the word of the Lord, that we who are alive, who remain unto the coming of the Lord, shall not prevent them who have slept. For the Lord Himself shall come down from heaven, with commandments, and with the voice of an archangel, and with the trumpet of God; and the dead who are in Christ shall rise first. Then we who are alive, who are left, shall be taken up together with them in the clouds to meet Christ, into the air, and so shall we be always with the Lord. Wherefore comfort ye one another with these words.

GRADUAL. *IV Esdr 2: 34, 35*

Réquiem ætérnam dona eis, Dómine: et lux perpétua lúceat eis. ℣. In memória ætérna erit justus: ab auditióne mala non timébit.

ETERNAL rest give to them, O Lord; and let perpetual light shine upon them. (Ps 111: 7) The just shall be in everlasting remembrance; he shall not fear the evil hearing.

The melody of this ancient Gradual seems to have been based upon "Haec Dies," the Easter Sunday Gradual. Its adaptation was completed more than a thousand years ago by an unknown monk. The Tract ("Absólve Dómine") is also ancient, yet belongs to a "later" period—perhaps circa 1350AD.

TRACT. *Trad.*

Absólve, Dómine, ánimas ómnium fidélium defunctórum ab omni vínculo delictórum. ℣. Et grátia tua illis succurrénte, mereántur evádere judícium ultiónis. ℣. Et lucis ætérnæ beatitúdine pérfrui.

O LORD, absolve the souls of all the faithful departed from every bond of sin. ℣. And by the help of Thy grace may they be worthy to escape the sentence of vengeance. ℣. And to enjoy all the beatitude of the light eternal.

SEQUENCE FOR THE DEAD • Many early liturgical books begin not with the season of Advent, but with Christmas (the birth of our Savior), which is only natural. The end of the book—and therefore, "the end of the liturgical year" to the extent early Christians cared about such things—naturally focused on the Second Coming of Christ. For this reason, the season of Advent still maintains an emphasis on Judgment. The "Dies Irae" was originally composed as a hymn for the First Sunday of Advent. In olden times, it was often sung after the Requiem Mass, as the procession made its way from the church to the cemetery. In the 14th century, the "Dies

Irae" became part of the Requiem Mass, and was universally adopted in the 16th century. In the heyday of the Sequence (12th century and later) practically every Mass had one, but around the time of the Council of Trent they were eliminated except for the best five. Father Fortescue explains: "In nothing does the prudence of the Tridentine reformers so shine as in their treatment of the question of sequences. At that time there was a perfect plethora of these compositions. The great number had little or no value either as poetry or devotional works; the whole idea of the sequence was merely a late farcing, and it lengthened the Mass unduly, making a great interval between the Epistle and Gospel, where already the Gradual and Alleluia were long enough. [...] The commission abolished the vast crowd of inferior ones and kept the very best, just five. Its idea was not to keep the sequences of the chief feasts—Christmas and Epiphany lost theirs—but to keep those that were finest in themselves."

SEQUENCE. *Thomas of Celano, Disciple of Saint Francis Assisi. XIII. cent.*

Translation by Rev. Joseph Connelly
IMPRIMATUR (10 December 1954)

DIES IRAE,
DIES ILLA,
Sólvet sæclum in favílla:
Téste Dávid cum Sibýlla.

Quántus trémor est futúrus,
Quándo júdex est ventúrus,
Cúncta strícte discussúrus!

A day of wrath that day will be. It will dissolve the world into glowing ashes, as David and the Sibyl have testified. ✠ How great a dread there will be when the Judge comes to examine all things in strict justice.

TUBA mírum spárgens sónum
Per sepúlcra regiónum,
Cóget ómnes ánte thrónum.

Mors stupébit, et natúra,
Cum resúrget creatúra,
Judicánti responsúra.

The trumpet's wondrous call will sound in tombs the world over and urge everyone forward to the throne. ✠ Death and nature will stand amazed when creation rises again to give answer to its Judge.

LIBER scríptus proferétur,
In quo tótum continétur,
Únde múndus judicétur.

Júdex érgo cum sedébit,
Quídquid látet, apparébit:
Nil inúltum remanébit.

Then will be brought out the book in which is written the complete record that will decide each man's fate. ✠ And when the Judge is seated, all secret sin will be made known, and no sin will go without its due punishment.

QUID sum míser tunc dictúrus?
Quem patrónum rogatúrus,
Cum vix jústus sit secúrus?

Rex treméndæ majestátis,
Qui salvándos sálvas grátis,
Sálva me, fons pietátis.

In such a plight what can I then plead? Or whom can I ask to plead for me, when the just man will be saved only with difficulty? ✠ King of dread majesty, You give salvation's grace to all that will be saved. Save me, fount of pity.

In Your pity, Jesus, call to mind that I am the reason why You became man. Do not cast me from You on that day. ✠ It was me You were seeking out when, exhausted, You sat by the well; me that You redeemed when You suffered on the cross. Do not allow such toil to have been in vain.

RECORDARE, Jésu píe,
Quod sum cáusa túæ víæ:
Ne me pérdas ílla díe.

Quǽrens me, sedísti lássus:
Redemísti Crúcem pássus:
Tántus lábor non sit cássus.

Just and avenging Judge, grant me the grace of pardon before that day of reckoning comes. ✠ I groan like one condemned and am red with shame for my sins; spare Your suppliant servant.

JUSTE júdex ultiónis,
Dónum fac remissiónis,
Ánte díem ratiónis.

Ingemísco, támquam réus:
Cúlpa rúbet vúltus méus:
Supplicánti párce, Déus.

You forgave Mary and granted the robber's prayer, and thus gave me hope as well. ✠ Though my prayers do not deserve to be heard, yet in Your goodness graciously bring it about that I do not burn in the unquenchable fire.

QUI Maríam absolvísti,
Et latrónem exaudísti,
Míhi quóque spem dedísti.

Préces méæ non sunt dígnæ:
Sed tu bónus fac benígne,
Ne perénni crémer ígne.

Give me a place among Your sheep, separate me from the goats and set me on Your right hand. ✠ When the accursed have been silenced and sentenced to the acrid flames, call me along with the blessed. ✠ In humility and abasement I make this prayer. My sin is burnt to ashes in the fire of my sorrow. Take care of me when my end is come.

INTER óves lócum prǽsta,
Et ab hǽdis me sequéstra,
Státuens in párte déxtra.

Confutátis maledíctis,
Flámmis ácribus addíctis:
Vóca me cum benedíctis.

Óro súpplex et acclínis,
Cor contrítum quási cínis:
Gére cúram méi fínis.

That day when guilty man rises out of the ruins of the world for judgment, will be a day of tears and mourning. Spare him on that day, Lord God. ✠ Jesus, Lord, of Your mercy grant them rest. Amen.

LACRIMOSA díes ílla,
Qua resúrget ex favílla
Judicándus hómo réus:
Húic érgo párce, Déus.

Píe Jésu Dómine,
Dóna éis réquiem.
Amen.

GOSPEL. *John 11: 21-27*

MARTHA SAID TO JESUS, Lord, if Thou hadst been here, my brother had not died: but now also I know that whatsoever Thou wilt ask of God, God will give it Thee. Jesus saith to her, thy brother shall rise again. Martha saith to Him, I know that he shall rise again in the resurrection at the last day. Jesus said to her, I am the resurrection and the life: he that believeth in Me although he be dead, shall live; and every one that liveth, and believeth in Me, shall not die forever. Believest thou this? She saith to Him, Yea, Lord, I have believed that Thou art Christ the Son of the living God, Who art come into this world.

In illo témpore: Dixit Martha ad Jesum: Dómine, si fuísses hic, frater meus non fuísset mórtuus: sed et nunc scio, quia, quæcúmque popósceris a Deo, dabit tibi Deus. Dicit illi Jesus: Resúrget frater tuus. Dicit ei Martha: Scio, quia resúrget in resurrectióne in novíssimo die. Dixit ei Jesus: Ego sum resurréctio et vita: qui credit in me, étiam si mórtuus fúerit, vivet: et omnis, qui vivit et credit in me, non moriétur in ætérnum. Credis hoc? Ait illi: Utique, Dómine, ego crédidi, quia tu es Christus, Fílius Dei vivi, qui in hunc mundum venísti.

OFFERTORY. *Trad.*

O LORD Jesus Christ, King of glory, deliver the souls of all the faithful departed from the pains of hell and from the deep pit; deliver them from the lion's mouth, that hell engulf them not, nor they fall into darkness, but let Michael, the holy standard-bearer, bring them into the holy light * *which Thou once didst promise to Abraham and his seed.* ℣. We offer Thee, O Lord, sacrifices and prayers of praise; do Thou accept them for those souls whom we this day commemorate; grant them, O Lord, to pass from death to the life * *which Thou once didst promise to Abraham and his seed.*

Dómine Jesu Christe, Rex glóriæ, líbera ánimas ómnium fidélium defunctórum de pœnis inférni et de profúndo lacu: líbera eas de ore leónis, ne absórbeat eas tártarus, ne cadant in obscúrum: sed sígnifer sanctus Míchaël repræséntet eas in lucem sanctam: * *Quam olim Ábrahæ promisísti et sémini ejus.* ℣. Hóstias et preces tibi, Dómine, laudis offérimus: tu súscipe pro animábus illis, quarum hódie memóriam fácimus: fac eas, Dómine, de morte transíre ad vitam. * *Quam olim Ábrahæ promisísti et sémini ejus.*

Willi Apel has written: "It was not until the 12th century that the Offertories lost their verses, the only exception being *Dómine Jesu Christe*, which to the present day has retained one verse: *Hóstias Et Preces*." Yet this is not, perhaps, an ideal example of an Offertory "retaining" its verse; originally this verse did not belong to it (cf. Dom Johner). This Offertory is certainly ancient—and is found in manuscripts such as 339sanGall|974, Yrieix|1040, and Helmst|1026—yet does not appear to be extremely ancient.

SECRET.

Be merciful, we beseech Thee, O Lord, to the soul of Thy servant, (*Name of the deceased*), for which we offer to Thee the sacrifice of praise, supplicating Thy majesty that, through these offices of pious propitiation it may be worthy to enter unto everlasting rest. Through our Lord.

Propitiáre, quǽsumus, Dómine, ánimæ fámuli tui N. (*fámulæ tuæ N.*), pro qua hóstiam laudis tibi immolámus, majestátem tuam supplíciter deprecántes: ut, per hæc piæ placatiónis offícia, perveníre mereátur ad réquiem sempitérnam. Per Dóminum.

The Preface of the Dead (page 192) follows the Secret.

The Agnus Dei in Masses for the Dead is as follows:

Agnus Dei, qui tollis peccáta mundi, *dona eis réquiem.*

Agnus Dei, qui tollis peccáta mundi, *dona eis réquiem.*

Agnus Dei, qui tollis peccáta mundi, *dona eis réquiem sempitérnam.*

Lamb of God, Who takest away the sins of the world: *give unto them rest.*

Lamb of God, Who takest away the sins of the world: *give unto them rest.*

Lamb of God, Who takest away the sins of the world: *give unto them rest forevermore.*

COMMUNION. *IV Esdr 2: 35, 34*

Lux ætérna lúceat eis, Dómine: * Cum Sanctis tuis in ætérnum: quia pius es. ℣. Réquiem ætérnam dona eis, Dómine: et lux perpétua lúceat eis. * Cum Sanctis tuis in ætérnum: quia pius es.

MAY LIGHT ETERNAL shine upon them, O Lord, * with Thy saints forever, for Thou art kind. ℣. Grant them everlasting rest, O Lord, and let perpetual light shine upon them, * with Thy saints forever, for Thou art kind.

This is the only communion antiphon which retained its "extra" verses—although in this case the extra verse is not from a psalm. Because it is not optional, the extra verse was not placed in Italics. Archbishop Sheen once said: "It is a long established principle of the Church never to completely drop from her public worship any ceremony, object, or prayer which once occupied a place in that worship." The well-known oddities of the Requiem Mass, which hearken back to ancient practices, illustrate this. For example, the *Prayers at the Foot of the Altar* are omitted because they were a later addition. This extra verse is explicit in ancient MSS, whereas most MSS from the later Middle Ages do not include it. Beginning the repeat on "Cum Sanctis" is notated by ALBI|1047, whereas YRIEIX|1040 starts the repeat on "Lúceat Eis." Many modern books use Psalm 129 ("De Profúndis") for the extra verses and replace the "Gloria Patri" with "Réquiem Ætérnam."

POSTCOMMUNION.

Præsta, quǽsumus, omnípotens Deus: ut ánima fámuli tui N. (*fámulæ tuæ N.*), quæ hódie de hoc sǽculo migrávit, his sacrifíciis purgáta et a peccátis expedíta, indulgéntiam páriter et réquiem cápiat sempitérnam. Per Dóminum.

Grant, we beseech Thee, O almighty God, that the soul of Thy servant, (*Name of the deceased*), which hath today departed this life, being purged by this sacrifice and rid of sins, may obtain alike pardon and everlasting rest. Through our Lord.

The dismissal in Masses for the Dead is as follows:

℣. Requiéscant in pace.

℟. Amen.

℣. May they rest in peace.

℟. Amen.

§510e of *Rubricarum Instructum* (25 July 1960) suppressed the Last Gospel in Requiem Masses which are followed by the absolution. For this reason, the 1962 "Ordo Absolutionis In Exsequiis Praesente Defuncti Corpore" says: *Finita Missa exsequiali, ultimo Evangelio omisso...*

IN YOUR PITY, JESUS, CALL TO MIND THAT I AM THE REASON WHY YOU BECAME MAN....

FUNERAL • ABSOLUTION OF THE CORPSE

The Last Gospel having been omitted, the priest—vested in a black Cope—stands at the foot of the body and says:

ENTER NOT into judgment with Thy servant, O Lord, for in Thy sight shall no man be justified, unless remission of all sins be accorded him by Thee. We beseech Thee, therefore, that Thy judicial sentence weigh not heavily upon him (*her*) who is commended to Thee by the true supplication of the Christian faith, but, with the help of Thy grace, may he (*she*) be worthy to escape the sentence of vengeance, seeing that, while he (*she*) lived, he (*she*) was sealed with the seal of the Holy Trinity. Who livest and reignest world without end. ℟. Amen.

Non intres in judícium cum servo tuo, Dómine, quia nullus apud te justificábitur homo, nisi per te ómnium peccatórum ei tribuátur remíssio. Non ergo eum (*eam*), quæsumus, tua judiciális senténtia premat, quem tibi vera supplicátio fídei christiánæ comméndat: sed grátia tua illi succurrénte, mereátur evádere judícium ultiónis, qui (*quæ*) dum víveret, insignítus (*insignita*) est signáculo sanctæ Trinitátis: Qui vivis et regnas in sǽcula sæculórum. ℟. Amen.

RESPONSORY. *Sung by the Choir or Schola Cantorum*

DELIVER me, O Lord, from eternal death on that dreadful day, * when the heavens and the earth shall be moved, † and Thou shalt come to judge the world by fire.

Líbera me, Dómine, de morte ætérna, in die illa treménda: * Quando cœli movéndi sunt et terra: † Dum véneris judicáre sǽculum per ignem.

℣. I am seized with fear and trembling, when I reflect upon the judgment and the wrath to come.

℣. Tremens factus sum ego, et tímeo, dum discússio vénerit, atque ventúra ira.

* Quando cæli movéndi sunt et terra.

℣. Dies illa, dies iræ, calamitátis et misériæ, dies magna et amára valde.

† Dum véneris judicáre sǽculum per ignem.

℣. Réquiem ætérnam dona ei Dómine, et lux perpétua lúceat ei.

Líbera me, Dómine, de morte ætérna, in die illa treménda: * Quando cœli movéndi sunt et terra: † Dum véneris judicáre sǽculum per ignem.

Towards the end of the Responsory, the priest puts incense into the thurible and blesses it.

* When the heavens, and the earth shall be moved.

℣. That day, a day of wrath, of wasting and of misery, a dreadful and exceeding bitter day.

† When Thou shalt come, to judge the world by fire.

℣. Eternal rest grant unto him (her), O Lord, and let perpetual light shine upon him (her).

DELIVER me, O Lord, from eternal death on that dreadful day, * when the heavens and the earth shall be moved, † and Thou shalt come to judge the world by fire.

When the Responsory has ended, the choir sings:

Lord, have mercy.
Christ, have mercy.
Lord, have mercy.

Kýrie eléison.
Christe eléison.
Kýrie eléison.

The priest sings the first words audibly: "Pater Noster..." *As he continues the prayer in silence, he sprinkles the corpse with holy water and incenses it. Then he resumes:*

℣. Et ne nos indúcas in tentatiónem.
℟. Sed líbera nos a malo.
℣. A porta ínferi.
℟. Erue Dómine ánimam ejus.
℣. Requiéscat in pace.
℟. Amen.
℣. Dómine exáudi oratiónem meam.
℟. Et clamor meus ad te véniat.
℣. Dóminus vobíscum.
℟. Et cum spíritu tuo.

℣. And lead us not into temptation.
℟. But deliver us from evil.
℣. From the gate of hell.
℟. Deliver his (*her*) soul, O Lord.
℣. May he (*she*) rest in peace.
℟. Amen.
℣. O Lord, hear my prayer.
℟. And let my cry come unto Thee.
℣. The Lord be with you.
℟. And with thy spirit.

Orémus.

Deus, cui próprium est miseréri semper et párcere, te súpplices exorámus pro ánima fámuli tui N. (*fámulæ tuæ N.*), quam hódie de hoc sǽculo migráre jussísti: ut non tradas eam in manus inimíci neque obliviscáris in finem, sed júbeas eam a sanctis Ángelis súscipi, et ad pátriam paradísi perdúci; ut, quia in te sperávit et crédidit, non pœnas inférni sustíneat, sed gáudia ætérna possídeat. Per

Let us pray. (If the body is present, this prayer is said.)

O GOD, Whose property is always to have mercy and to spare, we humbly beseech Thee for the soul of Thy servant (*handmaid*), N., which Thou hast this day commanded to depart out of this world: that Thou deliver it not into the hands of the enemy, nor forget it unto the end; but command it to be received by Thy holy angels, and conducted into Paradise, its true country; that, as in Thee it hath hoped and believed, it may not suffer the pains of hell but may take possession of eternal joys. Through Christ our Lord. ℟. Amen.

Christum Dóminum nostrum. ℟. Amen.

Let us pray. (If the body is not present, this prayer is said.)

DELIVER, O Lord, we beseech Thee, the soul of Thy servant (*handmaid*), N., from every bond of his (*her*) sins that in the glory of the resurrection he (*she*) may live anew, being raised up in the fellowship of Thy saints and elect. Through Christ our Lord. ℟. Amen.

Orémus.

Absólve, quǽsumus, Dómine, ánimam fámuli tui N. (*fámulæ tuæ N.*) ab omni vínculo delictórum: ut in resurrectiónis glória, inter Sanctos et eléctos tuos resuscitátus (*resuscitáta*) respíret. Per Christum Dóminum nostrum. ℟. Amen.

℣. Eternal rest grant to him (*her*), O Lord.

℣. Réquiem ætérnam dona ei, Dómine.

℟. And let perpetual light shine upon him (*her*).

℟. Et lux perpétua lúceat ei.

℣. May he (*she*) rest in peace.

℣. Requiéscat in pace.

℟. Amen.

℟. Amen.

℣. May his (*her*) soul and the souls of all the faithful departed, through the mercy of God, rest in peace.

℣. Ánima ejus, et ánimæ ómnium fidélium defunctórum per misericórdiam Dei requiéscant in pace.

℟. Amen.

℟. Amen.

As the body is being carried out of the Church (or as it is being borne to the grave):

MAY the angels lead thee into Paradise; at thy coming may the martyrs receive thee, and bring thee into the holy city, Jerusalem. May the choir of angels receive thee, and with Lazarus, once a beggar, mayest thou have eternal rest.

In paradísum dedúcant te Ángeli; in tuo advéntu suscípiant te Mártyres, et perdúcant te in civitátem sanctam Jerúsalem. Chorus Angelórum te suscípiat, et cum Lázaro quondam páupere ætérnam hábeas réquiem.

HEBDOMADA MAJOR
TRANSLATED INTO ENGLISH BY

MONSIGNOR RONALD KNOX
1888-1957

Nomenclature • The traditional Holy Week is sometimes referred to as the "1954 version"—as opposed to the "1955 version" promulgated by Maxima Redemptionis (16 November 1955). We believe such labels are not particularly helpful, for several reasons:

(a) Priests do not offer Mass according to the "1954 Missal," but many orders do have permission to celebrate Mass according to the liturgical books of 1962;

(b) The Holy Week reforms of Pius XII started in 1951 with *Dominicae Resurrectionis Vigiliam* (9 February 1951), followed by *Instaurata Vigilia Paschalis* (11 January 1952) —they did not begin in 1955;

(c) The official reformed Holy Week took place for the first time in 1956;

(d) the Holy Week reforms did not end in 1955—for example, the *Ritus Simplex Ordinis Hebdomadae Sanctae Instaurati* (5 February 1957) modified what had been promulgated in 1955—and the Ordo Hebdomadae Sanctae Instauratus was not published by the Vatican until 1956. Changes continued to be made: cf. *Rubricarum Instructum* (1960).

For these reasons, our book refers to the 1950 version and the 1962 version. (It goes without saying that the 1962 version incorporates changes made in 1955.)

MANY THERE HAD BEEN PRESENT WHEN JESUS RAISED LAZARUS TO LIFE, AND THESE TOO BORE WITNESS OF HIM. INDEED, THAT WAS WHY THE CROWD WENT OUT TO MEET HIM—BECAUSE THEY HAD HEARD OF HIS PERFORMING THIS MIRACLE. (John 12)

The First Palm Sunday • On the first Palm Sunday, our Lord traveled from Bethany to Jerusalem. People saw a conqueror coming to the place of His triumph—and indeed that was true—but it was not the "political triumph" for which the Jewish leaders had been hoping. Rather, it was a spiritual triumph which began with "catastrophe and defeat" (as Fulton Sheen put it) ending with "the empty tomb and victory." Christ entered Jerusalem "on a day that answered to the 10th day of the moon; when the Jews brought to their houses [*Exodus 12*] the lambs that were to be killed and eaten on the Passover, in memory of their deliverance from the slavery of Egypt, and of their entrance into the land of Promise, by their miraculous passage over the Red Sea."

Origins of the Ceremonies • Nothing is known with certainty vis-à-vis the origins of the special Palm Sunday ceremonies. Sir Walter Kirkham Blount (*The Office of Holy Week*, 1670AD) makes a statement which is terse but absolutely correct: "This ceremony is very ancient." Authors such as Abbat Fernand Cabrol trace the origins to Jerusalem, viz. a fourth century description by Ætheria ("Silvia the Pilgrim"). Father Fortescue has pointed out that "the old, pure Roman rite was nothing if not austerely practical. It contained no ceremonies done for their own sake, no decorative or symbolic features, as do the Eastern rites." For this reason, he finds it difficult to accept that a procession would begin at the Altar and return to the same place where it began. Father Fortescue believes the procession—imitating the journey from Bethany to Jerusalem—originally began at some other church, where an additional Mass may have also been said. Father Herbert Thurston sees the Palm Sunday procession as analogous to processions to Stational Churches—a view shared by Blessed Cardinal Schuster—adding that "the cathedral was in ancient times technically called the ***Jerusalem*** of the diocese." Father Fortescue, continuing to speculate, says: "It was only gradually, as it became difficult to hold a station at another church, that the palms were blessed at the same Altar where the High Mass would be sung; so the earlier Mass, if there was one, was reduced to the fragment we still have." Along with this "fragment"—sometimes referred to as a Dry Mass—is the blessing of the palms, about which Father Thurston says: "It is an almost universal law that the Church employs nothing in her services which she has not previously consecrated in some way or other. The earliest form of blessing palms preserved to us is probably that contained in the pontifical of Egbert, Archbishop of York from 732AD to 766AD."

Folded Chasubles • For the 1950 rites, "folded chasubles" were required for major churches (cathedrals, collegiate churches, and parish churches); they were never mandatory for smaller churches. Their history is quite ancient, and some believe they came about because the Deacon would fold his chasuble—forming a little "puff" in the middle—to avoid handling sacred objects with his bare hands. For certain tasks, the Deacon must fold up his chasuble even more and wear it over his shoulder, but because of the stiff material in certain modern chasubles, it is allowed to substitute a piece of cloth—often called a "broad stole" although it's not a stole—which is worn over the stole. These vestments are not used for the 1962 Holy Week {McManus p50}.

The Branches • Henry John Feasey {pages 54ff} describes the various significances of the branches, far too numerous to enumerate here. Palm Sunday had various names in English history: *Branch Sunday, Olive Sunday, Willow Sunday, Yew Sunday, Fig Sunday*, and so forth. James Monti—in his important work, "Catholic Worship in the Middle Ages" (Ignatius Press, 2012)—points out that: (1) the leafy branches call to mind that Tree, "originally created as a source of sustenance," which was Adam's downfall but the new Adam's remedy (*Ipse lignum tunc notávit, Damna ligni ut sólveret*); (2) the olive branches are "a reminder of the olive branch carried back to the ark of Noah by a dove."

(1950) Palm Sunday • Beginning of the Ceremony

Dominica in Palmis *Ante Missam*

1950 • When Terce has been sung, and the Asperges given in the usual manner, the priest—vested in purple Cope—with his ministers also vested in purple, proceeds to the blessing of the palms, or branches of olive (or of other trees), which are placed in the middle before the Altar, or at the corner of the Epistle side. In the first place, the choir sings the following antiphon. | *Completa Tertia ac facta ante Missam non Pontificalem aspersione aquae, more solito, Sacerdos, indutus Pluviali violaceo, vel sine Casula, cum Ministris similiter indutis, procedit ad benedicendum ramos palmarum, et olivarum, sive aliarum arborum, in medio ante Altare vel ad cornu Epistolae positos. Et primo cantatur a Choro Antiphona...*

The ceremony begins with the Asperges Me *prayed in the normal way except that—just as on Passion Sunday—the "Gloria Patri" is omitted. If a bishop celebrates, there is no sprinkling rite.*

[Editor's Note: The palms are usually placed on a table—covered with a purple or white veil—on the Epistle side {Fortescue p272}. For the 1950 version, the Processional Cross is "covered with purple" {Fortescue p272}, and a palm will be fastened to it—by means of a purple ribbon—while the branches are being distributed to the people. However, the Processional Cross is "not veiled" {McManus p50} in the 1962 version. The 1962 version omits the Asperges.]

Some authors consider the following to be a type of "Missa sicca," with the opening anthem serving as the Introit. The priest reads it in a low voice as the choir sings it. He does not make the sign of the Cross "to remind us that this action preceded the Passion of our Lord Jesus Christ," according to Sir Walter Kirkham Blount ("Office of Holy Week," 1670AD).

(1950) PALM SUNDAY • The Fore-Mass

Dominica in Palmis *Missa Sicca*

ANTHEM. *Matt 21: 9*

HOSANNA for the Son of David! Blessed is he who comes in the name of the Lord. King of Israel! Hosanna in high heaven!

Hosánna fílio David: benedíctus, qui venit in nómine Dómini. Rex Ísraël: Hosánna in excélsis.

1950 • Then the Celebrant—standing at the Epistle side and not turning to the people—with hands joined sings the following in the ferial tone. | *Deinde Sacerdos, stans in cornu Epistolae, non vertens se ad populum, dicit, manibus junctis, in tono Orationis ferialis...*

℣. The Lord be with you.
℟. And with you, his minister.

℣. Dóminus vobíscum.
℟. Et cum spíritu tuo.

Let us pray.

O GOD, whose constant loving is all our right-doing, thy untold graces ever more bounteously bestow; of hope come true by thy Son's death assuring us, of hearts come home by his resurrection: who with thee in the bond of the Holy Spirit lives and reigns and is God, world without end. ℟. Amen.

Orémus.

Deus, quem dilígere et amáre justítia est, ineffábilis grátiæ tuæ in nobis dona multíplica; et, qui fecísti nos in morte Fílii tui speráre quæ crédimus; fac nos eódem resurgénte perveníre quo téndimus: Qui tecum vivit et regnat in unitáte Spíritus Sancti, Deus: per ómnia sǽcula sæculórum. ℟. Amen.

1950 • Then the Subdeacon, standing in the usual place, sings the following Lesson in the tone of the Epistle, and at its close kisses the hand of the Priest. | *Postea Subdiaconus in loco solito cantat sequentem Lectionem in tono Epistolæ, et in fine osculatur manum Sacerdotis.*

[Editor's Note: The rubrics are explicit regarding the *solita oscula* because earlier editions—e.g. that printed for the Catholic King of England, James II, in 1688—had said: "In the end, the Subdeacon does not kiss the hand of the Priest, as at other times."]

LESSON. *Ex 15: 27; 16: 1-7*

AT THIS TIME: The Israelites came to Elim, where they found twelve springs of water and seventy palm-trees, and pitched their tents beside the water. Then, leaving Elim, the Israelite people marched to the desert of Sin, between Elim and Sinai. It was now the fifteenth day of the second

In diébus illis: Venérunt fílii Ísraël in Elim, ubi erant duódecim fontes aquárum et septuagínta palmæ: et castrametáti sunt juxta aquas. Profectíque sunt de Elim, et venit omnis multitúdo filiórum Ísraël in desértum Sin, quod est inter Elim et Sínaï: quintodécimo die mensis secúndi, postquã egréssi sunt de terra Ægýpti. Et murmurávit omnis congregátio filiórum Ísraël contra Móysen et Áäron in solitúdine. Dixerúntque fílii Ísraël ad eos: Útinam mórtui essémus per manum Dómini in terra Ægýpti, quando sedebámus super ollas cárnium, et comedebámus panem in saturitáte: cur eduxístis nos in desértum istud, ut occiderétis omnem multitúdinem fame?

month since they had left Egypt, and the Israelites, one and all, there in the desert, were loud in their complaints against Moses and Aaron. It would have been better, they told them, if the Lord had struck us dead in the land of Egypt, where we sat down to bowls of meat, and had more bread than we needed to content us. Was it well done to bring us out into this desert, and starve our whole company to death?

Dixit autem Dóminus ad Móysen: Ecce, ego pluam vobis panes de cælo: egrediátur pópulus, et cólligat quæ suffíciunt per síngulos dies: ut tentem eum, utrum ámbulet in lege mea an non. Die autem sexto parent quod ínferant: et sit duplum, quam collígere solébant per síngulos dies. Dixerúntque Móyses et Áäron ad omnes fílios Ísraël: Véspere sciétis, quod Dñs edúxerit vos de terra Ægýpti: et mane vidébitis glóriam Dómini.

But the Lord said to Moses, I mean to rain down bread upon you from heaven. It will be for the people to go out and gather enough for their needs day by day; and so I shall have a test, whether they are ready to follow my orders or not. Only when the sixth day comes must they lay in a store twice as large as they gathered on any of the others. So Moses and Aaron told all the people of Israel, This night shall bring proof it was the Lord that rescued you from Egypt, and tomorrow you shall witness his glory.

1950 • Instead of singing a Gradual, the choir chooses one of the following two Responsories to sing.
Deinde cantatur pro Graduali vel aliud Responsorium:

RESPONSORY. *John 11: 47-50, 53*

Collegérunt pontífices et pharisæi concílium, et dixérunt: Quid fácimus, quia hic homo multa signa facit? Si dimíttimus eum sic, omnes credent in eum: ✠ *Et vénient Románi, et tollent nostrum locum et gentem.* ℣. Unus autem ex illis, Caïphas nómine, cum esset póntifex anni illíus, prophetávit dicens: Éxpedit vobis ut unus moriátur homo pro pópulo, et non tota gens péreat. Ab illo ergo die cogitavérunt interfícere eum, dicéntes. ✠ *Et vénient Románi...*

THE CHIEF PRIESTS and Pharisees summoned a council. What are we about? they said. This man is performing many miracles, and if we leave him to his own devices, he will find credit everywhere. ✠ *Then the Romans will come and make an end of our city and our race.* ℣. And one of them, Caiphas, who held the high priesthood that year, said to them in prophecy: It is best for us if one man is put to death for the sake of the people, to save the whole nation from destruction. From that day forward, then, they plotted his death, saying: ✠ *Then the Romans...*

RESPONSORY. *Matthew 26: 39, 41*

In monte Olivéti orávit ad Patrem: Pater, si fíeri potest, tránseat a me calix iste. ✠ *Spíritus quidem promptus est, caro autem infírma: fiat volúntas tua.* ℣. Vigiláte, et oráte, ut non intrétis in tentatiónem. ✠ *Spíritus...*

ON MOUNT OLIVET he prayed to the Father: Father, if it is possible, let this chalice pass me by. ✠ *The spirit is willing enough, but the flesh is weak: thy will be done.* ℣. Watch and pray, that you may not enter into temptation. ✠ *The spirit...*

With all the customary ceremonies at high Mass, the Gospel is now sung by the Deacon.

1950 • *Interim dum cantatur ℟., Diaconus ponit librum Evangeliorum super Altare: et Sacerdos, ministrante Diacono naviculam, ponit incensum in thuribulo. Deinde Diaconus dicit: "Munda cor meum," accipit librum de Altari, petit benedictionem a Sacerdote: postea, Subdiacono librum tenente, medius inter duos Acolythos tenentes candelabra accensa, signat librum, incensat, et cantat Evangelium, ut infra, more consueto: quo finite, Subdiaconus defert librum osculandum Sacerdoti, qui et incensatur a Diacono.*

(1950) Palm Sunday • The Gospel Reading

Dominica in Palmis — *De Lectione Evangelica*

At this time...

WHEN THEY were near Jerusalem, and had reached Bethphage, which is close to mount Olivet, Jesus sent two of his disciples on an errand; Go into the village that faces you, he told them, and the first thing you will find there will be a she-ass tethered, and a foal at her side; untie them and bring them to me. And if anyone speaks to you about it, tell him, The Lord has need of them, and he will let you have them without more ado. All this was so ordained, to fulfil the word spoken by the prophet: Tell the daughter of Sion, Behold, thy king is coming to thee, humbly, riding on an ass, on a colt whose mother has borne the yoke.

GOSPEL. *Matt 21: 1-9*

In illo tėmpore: Cum appropinquásset Jesus Jerosólymis, et venísset Béthphage ad montem Olivéti: tunc misit duos discípulos suos, dicens eis: Ite in castéllum, quod contra vos est, et statim inveniétis ásinam alligátam et pullum cum ea: sólvite et addúcite mihi: et si quis vobis áliquid díxerit, dícite, quia Dóminus his opus habet, et conféstim dimíttet eos. Hoc autem totum factum est, ut adimplerétur, quod dictum est per Prophétam, dicéntem: Dícite fíliæ Sion: Ecce, Rex tuus venit tibi mansuétus, sedens super ásinam et pullum, fílium subjugális.

The disciples went and did as Jesus told them; they brought the she-ass and its colt, and saddled them with their garments, and bade Jesus mount. Most of the multitude spread their garments along the way, while others strewed the way with branches cut down from the trees. And the multitudes that went before him and that followed after him cried aloud, Hosanna for the son of David, blessed is he who comes in the name of the Lord, Hosanna in heaven above!

Eúntes autem discípuli, fecérunt sicut præcépit illis Jesus. Et adduxérunt ásinam et pullum: et imposuérunt super eos vestiménta sua, et eum désuper sedére fecérunt. Plúrima autem turba stravérunt vestiménta sua in via: álii autem cædébant ramos de arbóribus, et sternébant in via: turbæ autem, quæ præcedébant et quæ sequebántur, clamábant, dicéntes: Hosánna fílio David: benedíctus, qui venit in nómine Dómini.

[Editor's Note: For the Gospel that has just been read, the Deacon wears the "broad stole"—unless he wraps his folded chasuble around his shoulder. The Celebrant may read the lesson, one of the responsories, say the "Munda cor meum," and read the Gospel, all at the Epistle side {Fortescue p273}. It will be remembered that in the 1950 rites, the priest quietly recites those readings which are sung audibly by other sacred ministers. After the Gospel, the Celebrant kisses the book and is incensed, as at Mass. The Deacon removes the "broad stole," and the Subdeacon removes the maniple.]

1950 • The palms are then blessed. The priest, still standing at the Epistle corner, sings in the ferial tone.
Post haec benedicuntur rami. Sacerdos stans in eodem cornu Epistolae, dicit in tono Orationis ferialis...

℣. The Lord be with you.
℟. And with you, his minister.

℣. Dóminus vobíscum.
℟. Et cum spíritu tuo.

Orémus.

Auge fidem in te sperántium, Deus, et súpplicum preces cleménter exáudi: véniat super nos múltiplex misericórdia tua: bene ✠ dicántur et hi pálmites palmárum seu olivárum: et sicut in figúra Ecclésiæ multiplicásti Noë egrediéntem de arca, et Móysen exeúntem de Ægýpto cum fíliis Ísraël: ita nos portántes palmas et ramos olivárum, bonis áctibus occurrámus óbviam Christo: et per ipsum in gáudium introëámus ætérnum: Qui tecum vivit et regnat in unitáte Spíritus Sancti Deus:

Let us pray.

O GOD, MAKE US more bold to trust in thee: listen graciously to these humble prayers, and out of all measure thy mercy bestow. To branches of palm or olive grant thy ✠ blessing as of old. Increase thou gavest, when Noe came out of the ark, when Moses left Egypt at the head of Israel's race, and this was but a figure of thy Church. Bear we branches of palm and olive, it is because we would go forth to meet Christ furnished with the deeds of charity, and find through him safe passage into eternal blessedness: who with thee in the bond of the Holy Spirit lives and reigns and is God:

Per omnia sǽcula sæculórum.

℟. Amen.

℣. Dóminus vobíscum.

℟. Et cum spíritu tuo.

℣. Sursum corda.

℟. Habémus ad Dóminum.

℣. Grátias agámus Dómino Deo nostro.

℟. Dignum et justum est.

World without end.

℟. Amen.

℣. The Lord be with you.

℟. And with you, his minister.

℣. Lift up your hearts.

℟. We hold them out to the Lord.

℣. Give we thanks to the Lord our God.

℟. Right it is and seemly.

Vere dignum et justum est, æquum et salutáre, nos tibi semper et ubíque grátias ágere: Dómine sancte, Pater omnípotens, ætérne Deus: Qui gloriáris in consílio sanctórum tuórum. Tibi enim sérviunt creatúræ tuæ: quia te solum auctórem et Deum cognóscunt, et omnis factúra tua te colláudat, et benedícunt te sancti tui. Quia illud magnum Unigéniti tui nomen coram régibus et potestátibus hujus sǽculi líbera voce confiténtur. Cui assístunt Ángeli et Archángeli, Throni et Dominatiónes: cumque omni milítia cæléstis exércitus hymnum glóriæ tuæ cóncinunt, sine fine dicéntes:

RIGHT IT IS ASSUREDLY and most beseeming, duty of ours and our well-being, to thank thee, holy Lord, almighty Father, eternal God, both always and everywhere; such honour thou hast in the assembly of thy holy ones. Nothing thou hast made but renders thee service, owning thee its sole origin and its God; and if the whole chorus of creation so praises thee, shall not thy own saints join in blessing thee, that great name acknowledging, the name of thy only-begotten Son, before kings and rulers of this earth? Angels and Archangels, Thrones and Dominations, wait there in his presence, and with all the array of heaven's army sing endlessly of thy glory, after this manner:

1950 • The Preface finished, the choir sings as follows. | *Finita Praefatione, cantatur a Choro...*

Sanctus, Sanctus, Sanctus Dóminus, Deus Sábaoth. Pleni sunt cæli et terra glória tua. Hosánna in excélsis. Benedíctus qui venit in nómine Dómini. Hosánna in excélsis.

HOLY, HOLY, HOLY Lord God of hosts; thy glory fills heaven and earth. Hosanna in high heaven! Blessed is he who comes in the name of the Lord. Hosanna in high heaven!

1950 • The priest continues. | *Sequitur...*

℣. The Lord be with you.
℟. And with you, his minister.

℣. Dóminus vobíscum.
℟. Et cum spíritu tuo.

[Editor's Note: The "Missa sicca" now gives way to six orations. Sometimes palms are mentioned specifically; at other times mention is made of "branches of the olive and other trees." The first oration, says Cardinal Schuster, "refers exclusively to the branches of olive, without any mention of palms, for these had become very scarce in Europe in the Middle Ages." According to Father Fortescue, the favorite "palms" in the Middle Ages were the willow and the yew; which may explain why these trees were so often planted in churchyards. **Under Pope Pius XII, all the orations except one were suppressed.** The reformers tended to view Palm Sunday as "disproportionatly lengthy" {Goddard p266}. Moreover, the Palm Sunday reforms under Pius XII were intended to "reduce the emphasis on the blessing and distribution of the branches and to enhance the significance of the procession itself" {McManus p17; Giampietro p63}. A theory embraced by many 1950s liturgists said that whenever multiple prayers are found in ancient manuscripts they represent "options"—that is to say, the ancient collator was simply recording all the prayers he knew—and the reformers did explicitly endorse this philosophy vis-à-vis these orations {Giampietro p63}. One difficulty with "ad libitum" theory is explaining why the collator did not indicate them as alternatives by a word like "seu" or "vel." Following the comments of Cardinal Schuster (above) some feel the oration would have been chosen based on the ***specific type of branch*** the Celebrant was blessing. In any event, under Pope Pius XII the fifth prayer (the only one remaining) was modified so that it could reference the specific type of branch being blessed.]

(1950) PALM SUNDAY • Six Orations of Blessing

Dominica in Palmis *Benedictio Palmarum*

FIRST PRAYER • *Let us pray.*

O LORD, HOLY FATHER, eternal God, we beseech thee to ✠ bless and ✠ hallow this thy own handiwork, branches the olive-stem has yielded at thy bidding, of that very wood the dove's mouth brought home to the ark, long ago. May none receive it, but shall win health of mind and body; salve let it be of our frailty, and a pledge of grace. Through our Lord. ℟. Amen.

FIRST PRAYER • *Orémus.*

Pétimus, Dómine sancte, Pater omnípotens, ætérne Deus: ut hanc creatúram olívæ, quam ex ligni matéria prodíre jussísti, quamque colúmba rédiens ad arcam próprio pértulit ore, bene ✠ dícere et sancti ✠ ficáre dignéris: ut, quicúmque ex ea recéperint, accípiant sibi protectiónem ánimæ et córporis: fiátque, Dómine, nostræ salútis remédium, tuæ grátiæ sacraméntum. Per Dóminum. ℟. Amen.

SECOND PRAYER • *Let us pray.*

O GOD, who dost mend what is shattered, and what thou hast mended, ever dost preserve, thou didst bless the chance comers who met Jesus with branches in their hands. Bless ✠ these branches too, of palm or olive, which we take up obediently in honour of thy name; rest they where they will, let them carry thy blessing to all who dwell there. All harm thence banish, and let thy power defend us, in proof that thy Son, Jesus Christ, has redeemed us: who with thee. ℟. Amen.

SECOND PRAYER • *Orémus.*

Deus, qui dispérsa cóngregas, et congregáta consérvas: qui pópulis, óbviam Jesu ramos portántibus, benedixísti: béne ✠ dic étiam hos ramos palmæ et olívæ, quos tui fámuli ad honórem nóminis tui fidéliter suscípiunt; ut, in quemcúmque locum introdúcti fúerint, tuam benedictiónem habitatóres loci illíus consequántur: et, omni adversitáte effugáta, déxtera tua prótegat, quos rédemit Jesus Christus, Fílius tuus, Dóminus noster: Qui tecum. ℟. Amen.

THIRD PRAYER • *Let us pray.*

WONDROUSLY, O God, thou hast dealt with us in thy Providence, imaging forth the order of our salvation even by senseless things! Devoutly may we learn, and to our

THIRD PRAYER • *Orémus.*

Deus, qui miro dispositiónis órdine, ex rebus étiam insensibílibus dispensatiónem nostræ salútis osténdere voluísti: da, quǽsumus, ut devóta tuórum corda fidélium salúbriter intéllegant, quid mýstice desígnet in facto, quod hódie, cælésti lúmine affláta, Redemptóri óbviam procédens, palmárum atque olivárum ramos vestígiis ejus turba substrávit. Palmárum ígitur rami de mortis príncipe triúmphos exspéctant; súrculi vero olivárum spirituálem unctiónem advenísse quodámmodo clamant. Intelléxit enim jam tunc illa hóminum beáta multitúdo præfigurári: quia Redémptor noster, humánis cóndolens miSériis, pro totíus mundi vita cum mortis príncipe esset pugnatúrus ac moriéndo triumphatúrus. Et ídeo tália óbsequens administrávit, quæ in illo et triúmphos victóriæ et misericórdiæ pinguédinem declarárent. Quod nos quoque plena fide, et factum et significátum retinéntes, te, Dómine sancte, Pater omnípotens, ætérne Deus, per eúndem Dóminum nostrum Jesum Christum supplíciter exorámus: ut, in ipso atque per ipsum, cujus nos membra fíeri voluísti, de mortis império victóriam reportántes, ipsíus gloriósæ resurrectiónis partícipes esse mereámur: Qui tecum. ℟. Amen.

comfort, the meaning of all that befell this day, when with palm and olive a great throng of folk, by grace enlightened, strewed the path of their Redeemer. Palm-branches, to foreshow his triumph over the lord of death; olive-shoots, to welcome, as best they could, our spiritual anointing! Such happy foreknowledge was theirs, how this Redeemer, in pity of our mortal lot, for the world's life would do battle with the lord of death, and by death overcome him. Such worship, then, they must do as would honour both the fame of his victory and the rich balm of his mercy. What did they, what meant they, with lively faith we remember; and so, holy Lord, almighty Father, eternal God, we fall to entreating thee, through the same our Lord Jesus Christ. Members of his Body thou hast been pleased to make us; in him then, and through him, over death's dominion triumph we, of his own glorious resurrection be we made partakers: who with thee. ℟. Amen.

FOURTH PRAYER • *Orémus.*

Deus, qui, per olívæ ramum, pacem terris colúmbam nuntiáre jussísti: præsta, quǽsumus; ut hos olívæ, ceterarúmque árborum ramos cælésti bene✠dictióne sanctífices: ut cuncto pópulo tuo profíciant ad salútem. Per Christum Dóminum nostrum. ℟. Amen.

FOURTH PRAYER • *Let us pray.*

O GOD, who didst send the dove with her olive-branch to tell the world of its reprieve, grant our petition. Boughs of olive, and what other wood is here, do thou hallow with thy heavenly ✠ benediction, for the comforting of all Christian people: through Christ our Lord. ℟. Amen.

FIFTH PRAYER • *Orémus.*

Béne✠dic, quǽsumus, Dñe, hos palmárum, seu olivárum ramos: et præsta; ut, quod pópulus tuus in tui veneratiónem hodiérna die corporáliter agit, hoc spirituáliter summa devotióne perfíciat, de hoste victóriam reportándo et opus misericórdiæ summópere diligéndo. Per Dóminum. ℟. Amen.

FIFTH PRAYER • *Let us pray.*

BLESS ✠ Lord, we pray thee, branch of palm, branch of olive; and may thy people with due devotion, inwardly fulfil what they enact outwardly, both triumphing over the foul fiend, and loving above all things thy work of mercy: Through our Lord. ℟. Amen.

1950 • Here the Celebrant puts incense into the thurible and sprinkles the palms with blessed water—praying (not singing) the Antiphon "ASPERGES ME" without the psalm. In silence, he censes the Altar three times. Then he continues as follows.
Hic Celebrans ponit incensum in thuribulum, deinde ter aspergit ramos aqua benedicta, dicendo Antiphonam "Aspérges me" sine cantu, et sine Psalmo: et ter adolet incenso. Postea dicit...

℣. Dóminus vobíscum.
℟. Et cum spíritu tuo.

℣. The Lord be with you.
℟. And with you, his minister.

Sixth Prayer • *Let us pray.*

O GOD, it was for our salvation thou didst send thy Son, our Lord Jesus Christ, into the world; he should bow down to us, and we should come back to thee. In him, as he drew near Jerusalem, the scriptures were fulfilled, when a great throng of believers, all loyal devotion, strewed his way with their garments, and with boughs of palm. Clear be the way our faith spreads for him, never a stone to trip the feet, never a snare to catch them; leaf may we bear abundantly of noble living, and follow worthily in his footsteps: who with thee. ℟. Amen.

Sixth Prayer • *Orémus.*

Deus, qui Fílium tuum Jesum Christum Dóminum nostrum, pro salúte nostra in hunc mundum misísti, ut se humiliáret ad nos, et nos revocáret ad te: cui étiam, dum Jerúsalem veníret, ut adimpléret Scriptúras, credéntium populórum turba, fidelíssima devotióne vestiménta sua cum ramis palmárum in via sternébant: præsta, quǽsumus; ut illi fídei viam præparémus, de qua, remóto lápide offensiónis, et petra scándali, fróndeant apud te ópera nostra justítiæ ramis: ut ejus vestígia sequi mereámur: Qui tecum.
℟. Amen.

(1950) Palm Sunday • Distribution of Palms

Dominica in Palmis *De Distributione Ramorum*

1950 • *Completa benedictione, dignior ex Clero accedit ad Altare, et dat ramum benedictum Celebranti, qui non genuflectit, nec osculatur manum dantis. Postea Celebrans stans ante Altare versus ad populum, distribuit ramos, primum digniori, a quo ipse accepit, deinde Diacono et Subdiacono paratis, et aliis Clericis singulatim per ordinem, ultimo laicis: omnibus genuflectentibus, et ramum ac manum Celebrantis osculantibus, exceptis Praelatis, si adsint.*

English Translation in "Holy Week According To The Roman Missal" (1688AD) by Henry Hills:
The Benediction being ended, the ancientest or chiefest in Ecclesiastical Dignity goes to the Altar, and gives a blest Bough to the Priest, who neither kneels, nor kisses the Ancient's Hand when he receives it, whereas all that he distributes to receive them upon their knees, first kissing his Hand, and then the Bough: Which done, in the middle of the Altar he distributes the Boughs; first of all to the Deacon, next the Subdeacon, then to the Ancient from whom he receiv'd a Bough, and lastly to every one according to Degrees; first to Men, then to the Women.

[Editor's Note: Palm branches may now be given to the people at the Communion rail or entrance of the Sanctuary. The Celebrant does so, having the ministers at his sides, or it may be done by another priest, who will wear a surplice and purple stole. "The Roman books say that women should kiss only the palm, not the hand and that women should kneel separate from men." {Fortescue p275} In contrast to Henry Hills, Dom Cabrol says women kiss first the priest's hand then the palm branch {Cabrol p43}. While the palms are distributed a server ties one to the Processional Cross. According to the 1950 rubrics, both anthems "are repeated as often as is necessary until the end of the distribution of the Palms" (*Quae si non sufficiant, repetantur, quousque ramorum distributio finiatur*). The 1955 revisions by Pope Pius XII added Psalm 23 ("Domini est terra...") and Psalm 46 ("Omnes gentes..."). It would seem advantageous to utilize those psalms during the 1950 distribution; indeed, the 1934 *Liber Usualis* allows this practice, since it added "EUOUAE" to the anthems twenty-one years before the psalms were officially added.]

1950 • While the priest distributes palm branches, the choir sings the following anthems.
Et cum inceperit distribuere, a Choro cantantur sequentes Antiphonae.

Anthem. *John 12: 13*

BOUGHS of olive they took up, the sons of Jewry, and went out to meet the Lord, crying out: Hosanna in high heaven!

Púeri Hebræórum portántes ramos olivárum, obviavérunt Dómino, clamántes, et dicéntes: Hosánna in excélsis.

Another Anthem. *Matthew 21: 8-9*

DOWN in the road they spread their garments, the sons of Jewry, and cried out: Hosanna for the son of David! Blessed is he who comes in the name of the Lord!

Púeri Hebræórum vestiménta prosternébant in via, et clamábant dicéntes: Hosánna fílio David: benedíctus qui venit in nómine Dómini.

1950 • When all have received palm branches, the Celebrant continues. | *Deinde Sacerdos dicit...*

℣. Dóminus vobíscum.

℟. Et cum spíritu tuo.

℣. The Lord be with you.

℟. And with you, his minister.

Orémus.

Omnípotens sempitérne Deus, qui Dóminum nostrum Jesum Christum super pullum ásinæ sedére fecísti, et turbas populórum vestiménta vel ramos árborum in via stérnere, et Hosánna decantáre in laudem ipsíus docuísti: da, quǽsumus; ut illórum innocéntiam imitári possímus, et eórum méritum cónsequi mereámur. Per eúmdem Christum, Dóminum nostrum. ℟. Amen.

Let us pray.

ALMIGHTY, everlasting God, thou who wouldst have our Lord Jesus Christ ride on an ass's colt, and wouldst inspire the sons of Jewry to greet him with hosannas, throwing down their garments, and branches from the trees, in his path: grant us innocence like theirs, and the winning of the crown they won: through the same Jesus Christ our Lord. ℟. Amen.

(1950) PALM SUNDAY • Procession with Palms

Dominica in Palmis *Ad Processionem*

1950 • The Celebrant puts incense into the thurible; then the Deacon, turning to the people, chants as follows, answered by the choir. | *Postea fit Processio. Et primo Celebrans imponit incensum in thuribulum: et Diaconus vertens se ad populum, dicit: "Procedámus in pace." Et Chorus respondet: "In nómine Christi, Amen."*

ro-ce-dámus in pá-ce. ℟. In nómine Chrísti. Amen. *or:* Amen.

Let us go forth in peace. In the name of Christ. Amen.

[Editor's Note: In the procession, everyone holds the palm in the outer hand. Meanwhile the choir sings all or some of the antiphons appointed. During the procession the church bells should be rung, but not the Sanctus bell if Mass is being said at a side Altar {Fortescue p276}. The procession should go outside the church.]

1950 • The thurifer goes first with thurible smoking; then the Subdeacon, carrying the cross, between two acolytes with lighted candles. The clergy follow in order, the Celebrant last with the Deacon on his left, and all with palms in their hands. Some (or all) of the following anthems are sung during the procession. *Praecedit Thuriferarius cum thuribulo fumigante: deinde Subdiaconus paratus, deferens Crucem, medius inter duos Acolythos cum candelabris accensis: sequitur Clerus per ordinem, ultimo Celebrans cum Diacono a sinistris, omnes cum ramis in manibus: et cantantur sequentes Antiphonae, vel omnes, vel aliquae, quousque durat Processio.*

FIRST ANTHEM. *Matthew 21: 1-3, 7, 8-9*

Cum appropinquáret Dóminus Jerosólymam, misit duos ex discípulis suis, dicens: Ite in castéllum, quod contra vos est, et inveniétis pullum ásinæ alligátum, super quem nullus hóminum sedit: sólvite et addúcite mihi. Si quis vos interrogáverit, dícite: Opus Dómino est. Solvéntes adduxérunt ad Jesum: et imposuérunt illi vestiménta sua, et sedit super eum: álii expandébant vestiménta sua in via: álii ramos de arbóribus sternébant:

WHEN the Lord drew near to Jerusalem, he sent two of his disciples on an errand: Go into the village that faces you; and you will find an ass's colt tethered there, one upon which no man has yet ridden; untie it, and bring it to me. If anyone asks you any questions, say: The Lord has need of it. They untied it, and brought it to Jesus, and laid their cloaks upon it: and he seated himself on it. Some spread their cloaks on the way; others strewed branches from the trees; and those who followed kept crying out: Hosanna, blessed is he who comes in the name of the Lord; blessed is the kingdom of our father David; Hosanna in heaven above: son of David, have mercy on us!

et qui sequebántur, clamábant: Hosánna, benedíctus qui venit in nómine Dómini: benedíctum regnum patris nostri David: Hosánna in excélsis: miserére nobis, fili David.

[Editor's Note: These antiphons are extremely difficult, especially during a procession. The best course of action might be to sing the simpler antiphons with appropriate psalms; we find this in the ancient manscripts indicated by "euouae."]

SECOND ANTHEM. *John 12: 12-13*

WHEN the people heard that Jesus was coming into Jerusalem, they took palm-branches with them, and went out to meet him. Children there were that cried out: This is he whose coming was promised, for the restoring of our race; this is our hope of deliverance, Israel's ransom! In what state he comes, with Thrones and Dominations to meet him! Do not be afraid, daughter of Sion; see, thy king is coming to thee, as the scripture foretold, riding on an ass's colt. Welcome to our King, the maker of the world, come down to redeem us!

Cum audísset pópulus, quia Jesus venit Jerosólymam, accepérunt ramos palmárum: et exiérunt ei óbviam, et clamábant púeri, dicéntes: Hic est, qui ventúrus est in salútem pópuli. Hic est salus nostra, et redémptio Ísraël. Quantus est iste, cui Throni, et Dominatiónes occúrrunt! Noli timére, fília Sion: ecce, rex tuus venit tibi, sedens super pullum ásinæ, sicut scriptum est. Salve Rex fabricátor mundi, qui venísti redímere nos.

THIRD ANTHEM.

SIX DAYS before the paschal feast, when the Lord made his way into the city of Jerusalem, there were children that met him with palm-branches in their hands, and cried aloud: Hosanna in high heaven! Blessings on thee, blessings on thy errand so merciful! Hosanna in high heaven!

Ante sex dies solémnis Paschæ, quando venit Dóminus in civitátem Jerúsalem, occurrérunt ei púeri: et in mánibus portábant ramos palmárum, et clamábant voce magna, dicéntes: Hosánna in excélsis: benedíctus qui venísti in multitúdine misericórdiæ tuae: Hosánna in excélsis.

FOURTH ANTHEM.

SEE, what a company goes out with flowers and palm-branches, to meet the Redeemer on his way; worthy homage for the conqueror that comes home in triumph. The whole world acclaims the Son of God, heaven rings with their praises of the Christ; Hosanna in high heaven!

In the 1962 version, this is the first antiphon.

Occúrrunt turbæ cum flóribus et palmis Redemptóri óbviam: et victóri triumphánti digna dant obséquia: Fílium Dei ore gentes prædicant: et in laudem Christi voces tonant per núbila: Hosánna [in excélsis].

* *The text in the Altar Missal includes the words "in excélsis" whereas the ancient manuscripts never do.*

FIFTH ANTHEM.

FAITHFUL would we prove ourselves, with angels and children for our company we must cry aloud to death's conqueror: Hosanna in high heaven!

In the 1962 version, this is the second antiphon.

Cum Ángelis et púeris fidéles inveniámur, triumphatóri mortis clamántes: Hosánna in excélsis.

In the 1962 version, this is the third antiphon.

Turba multa, quæ convénerat ad diem festum, clamábat Dómino: Benedíctus, qui venit in nómine Dómini: Hosánna in excélsis.

SIXTH ANTHEM.

PILGRIMS there were a many that cried to the Lord: Blessed is he who comes in the name of the Lord; Hosanna in high heaven!

(1950) Palm Sunday • At the Church Door

Dominica in Palmis *Ad Vestibulum Ecclesiae*

1950 • At the return of the procession, two or four cantors go into the church ahead of time. They stand, with the doors shut, facing towards the procession, and sing the first stanza of the following hymn. The Celebrant and the others who are outside the church repeat it. The cantors then sing "all or some of the following stanzas as they think best" (cf. *Liber Usualis*, ©1934) and following each verse, those who are outside repeat the refrain: "Glória, laus, et honor, tibi sit Rex Christe Redemptor: Cui puerile decus prompsit Hosánna pium."

In reversione Processionis, duo vel quatuor cantores intrant in ecclesiam, et clauso ostio, stantes versa facie ad Processionem, incipiunt "℣. Glória Laus" et decantant duos primos versus. Sacerdos vero cum aliis extra ecclesiam, repetit eosdem. Deinde qui sunt intus, cantant alios versus sequentes: vel omnes, vel partem, prout videbitur: et qui sunt extra, ad quoslibet duos versus respondent: "Glória Laus," sicut a principio ℣.

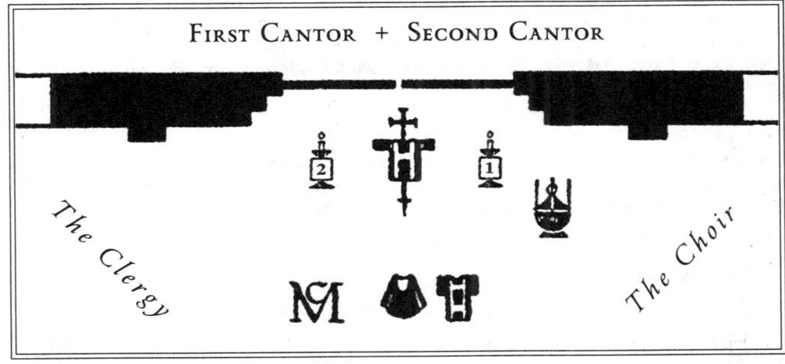

[*English Translation by Father Joseph Connelly;* Imprimatur 10 December 1954, *Archbishop of Birmingham.*]

HYMN. *Saint Theodulf, Bishop of Orleans (d. 821AD)*

℟. Glória, laus, et honor, tibi sit Rex Christe Redémptor: Cui puerile decus prompsit Hosánna pium. (2x)

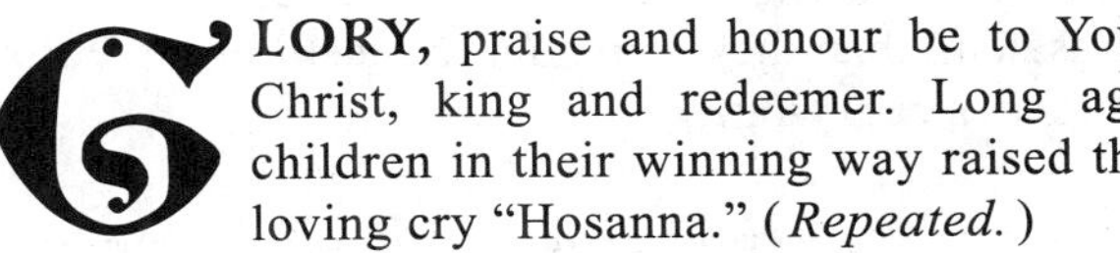

GLORY, praise and honour be to You, Christ, king and redeemer. Long ago children in their winning way raised the loving cry "Hosanna." (*Repeated.*)

1. Ísraël es tu Rex, Davídis et ínclita proles: Nómine qui in Dómini Rex benedícte venis. ℟. Glória, laus.

1. You are Israel's king and David's glorious son; You come, king most blessed, in the Lord's name.

℟. Glory, praise and honour…

2. Cœtus in excélsis te laudat cælicus omnis, Et mortális homo, et cuncta creáta simul. ℟. Glória, laus.

2. The whole of heaven's assembly on high, mortal man and all created things, united, praise You.

℟. Glory, praise and honour…

3. The Jewish people came to meet You with palms; now we are here before You with our prayers and hymns.

℟. Glory, praise and honour...

3. Plebs Hebrǽa tibi cum palmis óbvia venit: Cum prece, voto, hymnis, ádsumus ecce tibi. ℟. Glória, laus.

4. They made their offering of praise to You on the eve of Your passion; we sing our joyful hymn to You now rejoicing in heaven.

℟. Glory, praise and honour...

4. Hi tibi passúro solvébant múnia laudis: Nos tibi regnánti pángimus ecce melos. ℟. Glória, laus.

5. They pleased You then; may our devotion please You now. Good king, merciful king, all that is good pleases You.

℟. Glory, praise and honour...

5. Hi placuére tibi, pláceat devótio nostra: Rex bone, Rex clemens, cui bona cuncta placent. ℟. Glória, laus.

[Editor's Note: In former times, the procession entering the Church was done with "exuberant ceremonial" according to Father Fortescue. In many places, boys (because of "púeri Hebræórum") would sing the hymn by Bishop Theodulf from a very high gallery or platform above the church doors. In many mediæval churches, the Palm Sunday Gallery is a feature of the building, over the main doors. Psalm 23 was often sung: *Attollite portas, principes, vestras, et elevamini, portae aeternales, et introibit rex gloriae* ("Swing back, doors, higher yet ... to let the King enter in triumph"). Regarding the Subdeacon knocking at the door, many authors—e.g. Henry Hills and Sir Walter Kirkham Blount—promote the following symbolism, taken from a Roman Catholic Holy Week guide published in 1688AD: "Then the Subdeacon with the foot of the Cross, knocks at the Church door, which is shut, to signify that, Jesus Christ, through the merit of his Passion, hath open'd Heaven for us, which before was shut, upon the account of our first Parents' transgression." On page 315-348 (*Roman Catholic Worship in the Middle Ages*, 2012), James Monti provides an exhaustive examination of the various rites for the Palm Sunday procession—Spain, England, Rome, etc.—from both a spiritual and historical perspective.]

1950 • Then the Subdeacon knocks at the door with the shaft of the cross; it is opened at once, and the procession enters the church, singing the following responsory. | *Postea Subdiaconus hastili Crucis percutit portam: qua statim aperta, Processio intrat ecclesiam, cantando...*

RESPONSORY. *cf. John 12*

WHEN the Lord made his way into Jerusalem, foretaste of our risen life the children of Jewry gave us, * **palm-branches carrying**, and crying out: Hosanna in high heaven. ℣. No sooner did folk hear, Jesus was near Jerusalem, than they came out to meet him. * **Palm-branches carrying...**

Ingrediénte Dómino in sanctam civitátem, Hebræórum púeri resurrectiónem vitæ pronuntiántes, * **Cum ramis** palmárum: Hosánna, clamábant, in excélsis. ℣. Cum audísset pópulus, quod Jesus veníret Jerosólymam, exiérunt óbviam ei. * **Cum ramis...**

(*Et non dicitur Glória Patri.*)

1950 • Mass is then celebrated. All hold the palms in their hands while the Passion and Gospel are being sung. | *Deinde celebratur Missa, et rami tenentur in manibus dum cantatur Passio et Evangelium tantum.*

[Editor's Note: During *Passiontide* (i.e. the last two weeks before Easter beginning on Passion Sunday), the verse "Gloria Patri" at the ASPERGES, INTROIT, and LAVABO are omitted. Psalm 42 ("Júdica me") is not said during the Prayers at the Foot of the Altar, even on Holy Thursday. This is easy to remember each year, because the Passion Sunday Introit is "Júdica me." Notice that the entire Prayers at the Foot of the Altar are omitted in the 1962 Palm Sunday according to §424c of *Rubricarum Instructum* (25 July 1960), whereas the 1950 version only omits Psalm 42 ("Júdica me"). Notice also that in the 1962 version of Palm Sunday, the people do not hold palm branches during the Passion.]

1950 • After the Palm Sunday procession, the priest must go to the *Sedilia* to change vestments and prepare for Mass, during which time the choir should begin singing the Introit. The 1962 Palm Sunday adds the PRAYER TO COMPLETE THE PROCESSION ("Domine Jesu Christe, Rex ac Redémptor"), but no such prayer exists in the 1950 version.

(1950) PALM SUNDAY • The Holy Mass Begins

Dominica in Palmis *Station at Saint John Lateran ("Our Savior's Church")*

INTROIT. *Ps 21: 20, 22*

Dómine, ne longe fácias auxílium tuum a me: ad defensiónem meam ádspice: líbera me de ore leónis, et a córnibus unicórnium humilitátem meam. ℣. Deus, Deus meus, réspice in me: quare me dereliquísti? longe a salúte mea verba delictórum meórum. *Dómine, ne longe...*

ORD, DO NOT STAND at a distance, if thou wouldst aid me; look to my defence: rescue me from the very mouth of the lion, the very horns of the wild oxen that have brought me thus low. (Ps 21: 2) My God, my God, look upon me: why hast thou forsaken me? Why cannot my sinful words reach thee, who art my salvation? *Lord do not stand...*

Et haec Oratio tantum dicitur.

COLLECT. *No other Collect is said.*

Omnípotens sempitérne Deus, qui humáno géneri, ad imitándum humilitátis exémplum, Salvatórem nostrum carnem súmere, et crucem subíre fecísti: concéde propítius; ut et patiéntiæ ipsíus habére documénta, et resurrectiónis consórtia mereámur. Per eúmdem Dóminum nostrum.

God almighty and eternal, thou wouldst have our Saviour take flesh upon him, and submit to the cross, for mankind's sake; this humility should be their model. Grant us of thy mercy that we may keep the example of his endurance before us, and earn a share in his resurrection: through the same.

The Celebrant—when he reads the Epistle—does not genuflect. When the Subdeacon reads it the Celebrant, Deacon, and all in choir genuflect at the words "Ut in nómine Jesu" to "infernórum." {Fortescue p277}

EPISTLE. *Phil 2: 5-11*

Fratres: Hoc enim sentíte in vobis, quod et in Christo Jesu: qui cum in forma Dei esset, non rapínam arbitrátus est esse se æquálem Deo: sed semetípsum exinanívit formam servi accípiens, in similitúdinem hóminum factus, et hábitu invéntus ut homo. Humiliávit semetípsum factus obédiens usque ad mortem, mortem autem crucis. Propter quod et Deus exaltávit illum: et donávit illi nomen, quod est super omne nomen: (*hic genuflectitur*) ut in nómine Jesu omne genu flectátur cæléstium, terréstrium et infernórum, et omnis lingua confiteátur, quia Dóminus Jesus Christus in glória est Dei Patris.

BRETHREN: yours is to be the same mind which Christ Jesus showed. His nature is, from the first, divine, and yet he did not see, in the rank of Godhead, a prize to be coveted; he dispossessed himself, and took the nature of a slave, fashioned in the likeness of men, and presenting himself to us in human form; and then he lowered his own dignity, accepted an obedience which brought him to death, death on a cross. That is why God has raised him to such a height, given him that name which is greater than any other name; (*Here all genuflect.*) so that everything in heaven and on earth and under the earth must bend the knee before the name of Jesus, and every tongue must confess Jesus Christ as the Lord, dwelling in the glory of God the Father.

GRADUAL. *Ps 72: 24, 1-3*

THOU dost hold me by my right hand: thine to lead me in a way of thy own choosing, thine to take me up to thyself in glory. ℣. What bounty God shows to Israel, to all upright hearts! Yet I came near to losing my foothold, and felt the ground sink under my steps, so indignant was I over the good fortune of the sinners that flout his law.

Tenuísti manum déxteram meam: et in voluntáte tua deduxísti me: et cum glória assumpsísti me. ℣. Quam bonus Ísraël Deus rectis corde! mei autem pene moti sunt pedes: pene effúsi sunt gressus mei: quia zelávi in peccatóribus, pacem peccatórum videns.

TRACT. *Ps 21: 2-9, 18, 19, 22, 24, 32*

MY GOD, MY GOD, look upon me; why hast thou forsaken me? **2** Why cannot my sinful words reach thee, who art my salvation? **3** Thou dost not answer, my God, when I cry out to thee day and night, and I am patient still. **4** Thou art there, none the less, dwelling in the holy place; Israel's ancient boast. **5** It was in thee that our fathers trusted, and thou didst reward their trust by delivering them. **6** They cried to thee, and rescue came; no need to be ashamed of such trust as theirs. **7** But I, poor worm, have no manhood left; I am a by-word to all, the laughing-stock of the rabble. **8** All those who catch sight of me fall to mocking; mouthing out insults, while they toss their heads in scorn. **9** He committed himself to the Lord, why does not the Lord come to his rescue, and set his favourite free? **10** They stand there watching me, gazing at me. They divide my spoils among them, cast lots for my garments. **11** Rescue me from the very mouth of the lion, the very horns of the wild oxen that have brought me thus low. **12** Praise the Lord, all you that are his worshippers; honour to him from the sons of Jacob. **13** The Lord will claim for his own a generation that is still to come; heaven itself will make known his faithfulness. **14** To a people yet to be born, a people of the Lord's own founding.

Deus, Deus meus, réspice in me: quare me dereliquísti? 2. Longe a salúte mea verba delictórum meórum. 3. Deus meus, clamábo per diem, nec exáudies: in nocte, et non ad insipiéntiam mihi. 4. Tu autem in sancto hábitas, laus Ísraël. 5. In te speravérunt patres nostri: speravérunt, et liberásti eos. 6. Ad te clamavérunt, et salvi facti sunt: in te speravérunt, et non sunt confúsi. 7. Ego autem sum vermis, et non homo: oppróbrium hóminum et abjéctio plebis. 8. Omnes, qui vidébant me, aspernabántur me: locúti sunt lábiis et movérunt caput. 9. Sperávit in Dómino, erípiat eum: salvum fáciat eum, quóniam vult eum. 10. Ipsi vero consideravérunt et conspexérunt me: divisérunt sibi vestiménta mea, et super vestem meam misérunt sortem. 11. Líbera me de ore leónis: et a córnibus unicórnium humilitátem meam. 12. Qui timétis Dóminum, laudáte eum: univérsum semen Jacob, magnificáte eum. 13. Annuntiábitur Dómino generátio ventúra: et annuntiábunt cæli justítiam ejus. 14. Pópulo, qui nascétur, quem fecit Dóminus.

1950 • The Passion is read without the ceremonies usual at the Gospel. The "Munda cor meum" is not said, nor is the blessing asked; candles are not used, nor incense; "Dóminus vobíscum" is not said, nor is "Glória tibi Dómine" said after the title. The Celebrant (or Deacon) does not make the sign of the Cross on the book or on himself while reading the title "Pássio Dómini nostri." The same rule is observed for the other days on which the Passion is read. | *Passio Domini incipitur absolute: non dicitur "Munda cor meum," non petitur benedictio, non deferuntur luminaria, nec incensum: non dicitur "Dóminus vobíscum," nec respondetur "Glória tibi Dómine," et Celebrans, seu Diaconus, dum pronuntiat "Pássio Dómini nostri," non signat librum, neque seipsum. Quod et in aliis diebus servatur, quando legitur Passio.*

Singing The Passion (1950 Rubrics) • The Passion is not sung by the Deacon who assists the Celebrant. It is sung by three other Deacons: "the Deacons of the Passion." In case of necessity, the Celebrant himself may sing the *Christus* sections; then there would be but two Deacons of the Passion. It is even allowed—if the cleric acting as Subdeacon is an ordained Deacon—that the ministers of Mass take off their folded chasubles and sing two parts of the

Passion at the usual place, with the Celebrant singing the *Christus* sections at the Altar. Regardless, there must be three ordained Deacons to sing the Passion; otherwise, the Celebrant reads it aloud at the Epistle corner, and the Deacon sings the last part only (*Áltera autem die*).

TURBA SECTIONS (1950 RUBRICS) • Father Fortescue says "the choir may sing the words said by the crowd (the *Turba* sections)" {Fortescue p278}, but fails to specify which "choir" he means. The "choir" can refer to lay Catholics singing at Mass, but the "choir" can also denote a group of clerics and seminarians assisting at Mass seated in the Sanctuary. In the 1962 Palm Sunday, however, lay people are explicitly allowed to sing the *Turba* sections—"but not a choir of nuns" {McManus p69}. If a group of people sing the *Turba* sections, this does not dispense with the *Synagoga* Deacon, though it significantly reduces what he must sing. In such a case, the *Synagoga* Deacon will sing only the words of individuals: Pontius Pilate, Saint Peter, and so forth. The CAEREMONIALE EPISCOPORUM does not suppose that lecterns will be used; instead, it directs the Deacons of the Passion to sing from one book, held by three servers—one standing before each Deacon—who pass it to one another as the parts change.

SIMULTANEOUS READING (1950 RUBRICS) • The "Chronista"—that is to say, the Deacon singing the Narrator's part—begins at once (*Pássio Dómini nostri Jesu Christi secúndum Matthǽum*) and without further ceremony the three Deacons sing the Passion, with hands joined, while everyone else in the church stands, holding palms. Meanwhile, the Celebrant reads the Passion in a low voice—standing at the Epistle corner of the Altar with Deacon and Subdeacon, as at the Introit—stopping before the last part (*Áltera autem die*). When the Celebrant has finished, they turn to face the Deacons of the Passion and stand there holding their palms, supplied to them by the Master of Ceremonies. In the 1962 version, when the Passion is chanted by the three Deacons the Celebrant does not read it. {McManus p69}

During the singing of the Passion according to Saint Matthew, all hold palm branches. Deacons: [C] *Chronista;* [S] *Synagoga;* ✠ *Christus.*

PASSIO DOMINI NOSTRI JESU CHRISTI SECUNDUM MATTHAEUM.

The passion of our Lord Jesus Christ as it is written by Saint Matthew.

At this time: Jesus said to his disciples: ✠ You know that after
In illo témpore: Dixit Jesus discípulis suis: Scitis quid post bíduum

two days the paschal feast is coming; it is then that the Son of
Pascha fiet, et Fílius hóminis tradétur

Man must be given up to be crucified. [C] At this very time, the
ut crucifigátur. Tunc congregáti sunt

chief priests and the elders of the people gathered in the court of
príncipes sacerdótum, et senióres pópuli in átrium príncipis sacerdótum,

the high priest, whose name was Caiphas; and there they plotted to bring Jesus into
qui dicebátur Cáïphas: et consílium fecérunt ut Jesum dolo tenérent,

their power by cunning, and put him to death. Yet they still said: [S] Not on the
et occíderent. Dicébant autem: Non in die

day of the feast, or perhaps there will be an uproar among the people. [C] But then,
festo, ne forte tumúltus fíeret in pópulo. Cum autem

while Jesus was in the house of Simon the leper, at Bethany, a woman came to him,
Jesus esset in Bethánia in domo Simónis leprósi, accéssit ad eum múlier

with a pot of very precious ointment, and poured it over his head as he sat at table.
habens alabástrum unguénti pretiósi, et effúdit super caput ipsíus recumbéntis.

The disciples were indignant when they saw it, and asked: [S] What is the meaning
Vidéntes autem discípuli, indignáti sunt, dicéntes: Ut quid perdítio hæc?

of this waste? It would have been possible to sell this at a great price, and give alms
pótuit enim istud venúmdari multo, et dari

to the poor. [C] This Jesus knew, and said to them, ✠ Why do you vex the woman?
paupéribus. Sciens autem Jesus, ait illis: Quid moléstí estis huic mulíeri?

She did well to treat me so. You have the poor among you always; I am not always
opus enim bonum operáta est in me. Nam semper páuperes habétis vobíscum: me autem non semper

among you. When she poured this ointment over my body, she did it to prepare
habétis. Mittens enim hæc unguéntum hoc in corpus meum, ad sepeliéndum me fecit.

me for my burial; and I promise you, in whatever part of the world this gospel is
Amen, dico vobis, ubicúmque prædicátum fúerit hoc Evangélium in toto mundo,

preached, the story of what she has done shall be told in its place, to preserve her
dicétur et quod hæc fecit, in memóriam ejus.

memory.

Judas Who Was Called Iscariot

[C] And at that, one of the twelve, Judas who was called Iscariot, went to the chief
Tunc ábiit unus de duódecim, qui dicebátur Judas Iscariótes, ad príncipes sacerdótum,

priests and asked them: [S] What will you pay me for handing him over to you?
et ait illis: Quid vultis mihi dare, et ego vobis eum tradam?

[C] Whereupon they laid down thirty pieces of silver. And he, from that time
At illi constituérunt ei trigínta argénteos. Et exínde quærébat

onwards, looked about for an opportunity to betray him. On the first of the days
opportunitátem, ut eum tráderet. Prima autem die

of unleavened bread the disciples came to Jesus and asked, [S] Where wilt
azymórum accessérunt discípuli ad Jesum, dicéntes: Ubi vis

thou have us make ready for thee to eat the paschal meal? [C] And Jesus said,
parémus tibi comédere pascha? At Jesus dixit:

✠ Go into the city, find such a man, and tell him, The Master says, My time is near;
Ite in civitátem ad quemdam, et dícite ei: Magíster dicit: Tempus meum prope est,

I and my disciples must keep the paschal feast at thy house. [C] The disciples did
apud te fácio pascha cum discípulis meis. Et fecérunt discípuli,

as Jesus bade them, and made all ready for the paschal meal there. When evening
sicut constítuit illis Jesus, et paravérunt pascha. Véspere autem

came, he sat down with his twelve disciples, and, while they were at table, he said,
facto, discumbébat cum duódecim discípulis suis. Et edéntibus illis, dixit:

✠ Believe me, one of you is to betray me. [C] They were full of sorrow, and began
Amen, dico vobis, quia unus vestrum me traditúrus est. Et contristáti valde, cœpérunt sínguli dícere:

to say, one after another; [S] Lord, is it I? [C] He answered: ✠ The man who has
Numquid ego sum, Dómine? At ipse respóndens, ait: Qui intíngit mecum

put his hand into the dish with me will betray me. The Son of Man goes on his way,
manum in parópside, hic me tradet. Fílius quidem hóminis vadit,

as the scripture foretells of him; but woe upon that man by whom the Son of Man
sicut scriptum est de illo: væ autem hómini illi, per quem Fílius hóminis

is to be betrayed; better for that man if he had never been born. [C] Then Judas,
tradétur: bonum erat ei, si natus non fuísset homo ille. Respóndens

he who was betraying him, said openly: [S] Master, is it I? [C] Jesus answered:
autem Judas, qui trádidit eum, dixit: Numquid ego sum, Rabbi? Ait illi:

✠ Thy own lips have said it.
Tu dixísti.

HOLY EUCHARIST

[C] And while they were still at table, Jesus took bread, and blessed, and broke
Cenántibus autem eis, accépit Jesus panem, et benedíxit, ac fregit,

it, and gave it to his disciples, saying: ✠ Take, eat, this is my body. [C] Then
dedítque discípulis suis, et ait: Accípite et comédite: hoc est corpus meum. Et

he took a cup, and offered thanks, and gave it to them, saying: ✠ Drink, all of
accípiens cálicem, grátias egit: et dedit illis, dicens: Bíbite ex hoc omnes.

you, of this; for this is my blood, of the new testament, shed for many, to the
Hic est enim sanguis meus novi testaménti, qui pro multis effundétur in

remission of sins. And I tell you this, I shall not drink of this fruit of the vine
remissiónem peccatórum. Dico autem vobis: non bibam ámodo de hoc genímine vitis,

again, until I drink it with you, new wine, in the kingdom of my Father. [C] And
usque in diem illum, cum illud bibam vobíscum novum in regno Patris mei. Et

so they sang a hymn, and went out to mount Olivet. After this, Jesus said to them,
hymno dicto, exiérunt in montem Olivéti. Tunc dicit illis Jesus:

✠ Tonight you will all lose courage over me; for so it has been written, I will
Omnes vos scándalum patiémini in me, in ista nocte. Scriptum est enim:

smite the shepherd, and the sheep of his flock will be scattered. But I will go on
Percútiam pastórem, et dispergéntur oves gregis.

before you into Galilee, when I have risen from the dead. [C] Peter answered
Postquam autem resurréxero præcédam vos in Galilǽam. Respóndens autem Petrus, ait

him: [S] Though all else should lose courage over thee, I will never lose mine.
illi: Et si omnes scandalizáti fúerint in te, ego numquam scandalizábor.

[C] Jesus said to him, ✠ Believe me, this night, before the cock crows, thou wilt
Ait illi Jesus: Amen, dico tibi, quia in hac nocte, ántequam gallus cantet, ter me negábis.

thrice disown me. [C] Peter said to him, [S] I will never disown thee, though I
Ait illi Petrus: Etiam si oportúerit me mori tecum, non te negábo.

must lay down my life with thee. [C] And all the rest of his disciples said the like.
Simíliter et omnes discípuli dixérunt.

GETHSEMANI

[C] So Jesus came, and they with him, to a plot of land called Gethsemani; and he
Tunc venit Jesus cum illis in villam, quæ dícitur Gethsémani,

said to his disciples: ✠ Sit down here, while I go in there and pray. [C] But he took
et dixit discípulis suis: Sedéte hic, donec vadam illuc et orem.

Peter and the sons of Zebedee with him. And now he grew sorrowful and dismayed,
Et assúmpto Petro et duóbus fíliis Zebedǽi, cœpit contristári et mœstus esse.

and said: ✠ My soul is ready to die with sorrow; do you abide here, and watch with
Tunc ait illis: Tristis est ánima mea usque ad mortem: sustinéte hic, et vigiláte mecum.

me. [C] When he had gone a little further, he fell upon his face in prayer, and said,
Et progréssus pusíllum, prócidit in fáciem suam, orans, et dicens:

✠ My Father, if it is possible, let this chalice pass me by; only as thy will is, not
Pater mi, si possíbile est, tránseat a me calix iste. Verúmtamen non sicut ego volo,

as mine is. [C] Then he went back to his disciples, to find them asleep; and he
sed sicut tu. Et venit ad discípulos suos, et invénit eos dormiéntes:

said to Peter, ✠ Had you no strength, then, to watch with me even for an hour?
et dicit Petro: Sic non potuístis una hora vigiláre mecum?

Watch and pray, that you may not enter into temptation; the spirit is willing enough,
Vigiláte, et oráte, ut non intrétis in tentatiónem. Spíritus quidem promptus est,

but the flesh is weak. [C] Then he went back again, and prayed a second time; and
caro autem infírma. Íterum secúndo ábiit et orávit,

his prayer was: ✠ My Father, if this chalice may not pass me by, but I must drink
dicens: Pater mi, si non potest hic calix transíre, nisi bibam illum,

it, then thy will be done. [C] And once more he found his disciples asleep when he
fiat volúntas tua. Et venit íterum, et invénit eos dormiéntes:

came to them, so heavy their eyelids were; this time he went away without disturbing
erant enim óculi eórum graváti. Et relíctis illis, íterum ábiit

them, and made his third prayer, using the same words. After that he returned to his
et orávit tértio, eúndem sermónem dicens. Tunc venit ad discípulos suos,

disciples, and said to them, ✠ Sleep and take your rest hereafter; as I speak, the
et dicit illis: Dormíte jam, et requiéscite:

time draws near when the Son of Man is to be betrayed into the hands of sinners.
ecce, appropinquávit hora, et Fílius hóminis tradétur in manus peccatórum.

Rise up, let us go on our way; already, he that is to betray me is close at hand.
Súrgite, eámus: ecce, appropinquávit, qui me tradet.

Kiss of Betrayal

[C] And all at once, while he was speaking, Judas, who was one of the twelve,
Adhuc eo loquénte, ecce Judas unus de duódecim venit,

came near; with him was a great multitude carrying swords and clubs, who had
et cum eo turba multa cum gládiis et fústibus,

been sent by the chief priests and the elders of the people. The traitor had appointed
missi a princípibus sacerdótum et senióribus pópuli. Qui autem trádidit eum, dedit

them a signal, saying: [S] It is none other than the man whom I shall greet with a
illis signum, dicens: Quemcúmque osculátus fúero, ipse est,

kiss; hold him fast. [C] No sooner, then, had he come near to Jesus than he said:
tenéte eum. Et conféstim accédens ad Jesum, dixit:

[S] Hail, Master, [C] and kissed him. Jesus said to him: ✠ My friend, on what
Ave, Rabbi. Et osculátus est eum. Dixítque illi Jesus: Amíce, ad quid venísti?

errand hast thou come? [C] Then they came forward and laid their hands on Jesus,
Tunc accessérunt, et manus injecérunt in Jesum,

and held him fast. And at that, one of those who were with Jesus lifted a hand
et tenuérunt eum. Et ecce unus ex his, qui erant cum Jesu, exténdens manum,

to draw his sword, and smote one of the high priest's servants with it, cutting
exémit gládium suum, et percútiens servum príncipis sacerdótum, amputávit aurículam ejus.

off his ear. Whereupon Jesus said to him, ✠ Put thy sword back into its place;
Tunc ait illi Jesus: Convérte gládium tuum in locum suum.

all those who take up the sword will perish by the sword. Dost thou doubt that if
Omnes enim, qui accéperint gládium, gládio períbunt. An putas, quia non possum

I call upon my Father, even now, he will send more than twelve legions of angels
rogáre Patrem meum, et exhibébit mihi modo plus quam duódecim legiónes Angelórum?

to my side? But how, were it so, should the scriptures be fulfilled, which have
Quómodo ergo implebúntur Scriptúræ,

prophesied that all must be as it is? [C] And Jesus said to the multitude at that
quia sic opórtet fíeri? In illa hora dixit Jesus turbis:

hour: ✠ You have come out to my arrest with swords and clubs, as if I were a
Tamquam ad latrónem exístis cum gládiis et fústibus comprehéndere me:

robber; and yet I used to sit teaching in the temple close to you, day after day,
quotídie apud vos sedébam docens in templo,

and you never laid hands on me. [C] All this was so ordained, to fulfil what
et non me tenuístis. Hoc autem totum factum est, ut adimpleréntur

was written by the prophets. And now all his disciples abandoned him, and fled.
Scriptúræ prophetárum. Tunc discípuli omnes, relícto eo, fugérunt.

BEFORE CAIPHAS

[C] And those who had arrested Jesus led him away into the presence of the high
At illi tenéntes Jesum, duxérunt ad Cáïpham príncipem sacerdótum,

priest, Caiphas, where the scribes and the elders had assembled. Yet Peter followed
ubi scribæ, et senióres convénerant. Petrus autem sequebátur

him at a long distance, as far as the high priest's palace; where he went in and
eum a longe, usque in átrium príncipis sacerdótum. Et ingréssus intro,

sat among the servants, to see the end. The chief priests and elders and all the
sedébat cum minístris ut vidéret finem. Príncipes autem sacerdótum, et omne concílium,

Council tried to find false testimony against Jesus, such as would compass his
quærébant falsum testimónium contra Jesum, ut eum morti tráderent:

death. But they could find none, although many came forward falsely accusing
et non invenérunt, cum multi falsi testes accessíssent.

him; until at last two false accusers came forward who declared: [S] This man
Novíssime autem venérunt duo falsi testes, et dixérunt: Hic dixit:

said, I have power to destroy the temple of God and raise it again in three days.
Possum destrúere templum Dei, et post tríduum reædificáre illud.

[C] Then the high priest stood up, and asked him: [S] Hast thou no answer
Et surgens princeps sacerdótum, ait illi: Nihil respóndes ad ea,

to make to the accusations these men bring against thee? [C] Jesus was silent;
quæ isti advérsum te testificántur? Jesus autem tacébat.

and the high priest said to him openly: [S] I adjure thee by the living God to tell
Et princeps sacerdótum ait illi: Adjúro te per Deum vivum, ut dicas

us whether thou art the Christ, the Son of God? [C] Jesus answered: ✠ Thy own
nobis, si tu es Christus Filius Dei. Dicit illi Jesus: Tu dixísti.

lips have said it. And moreover I tell you this; you will see the Son of Man again,
Verúmtamen dico vobis, ámodo vidébitis Fílium hóminis

when he is seated at the right hand of God's power, and comes on the clouds
sedéntem a dextris virtútis Dei, et veniéntem in núbibus cœli.

of heaven. [C] At this, the high priest tore his garments, and said: [S] He has
Tunc princeps sacerdótum scidit vestiménta sua, dicens:

blasphemed; what further need have we of witnesses? Mark well, you have heard
Blasphemávit: quid adhuc egémus téstibus? Ecce nunc audístis blasphémiam:

his blasphemy for yourselves. What is your finding? [C] And they answered:
quid vobis vidétur? At illi respondéntes, dixérunt:

[S] The penalty is death. [C] Then they fell to spitting upon his face and buffeting
Reus est mortis. Tunc exspuérunt in fáciem ejus, et cólaphis eum

him and smiting him on the cheek, saying as they did so: [S] Show thyself a
cecidérunt, álii autem palmas in fáciem ejus dedérunt, dicéntes: Prophetíza nobis,

prophet, Christ; tell us who it is that smote thee.
Christe, quis est qui te percússit?

SAINT PETER'S DENIAL

[C] Meanwhile, Peter sat in the court without; and there a maidservant came up
Petrus vero sedébat foris in átrio: et accéssit ad eum una ancílla,

to him, and said: [S] Thou too wast with Jesus the Galilean. [C] Whereupon he
dicens: Et tu cum Jesu Galilǽo eras. At ille

denied it before all the company: [S] I do not know what thou meanest. [C] And
negávit coram ómnibus, dicens: Néscio quid dicis.

he went out into the porch, where a second maidservant saw him, and said, to the
Exeúnte autem illo jánuam, vidit eum ália ancílla, et ait his,

bystanders: [S] This man, too, was with Jesus the Nazarene. [C] And he made
qui erant ibi: Et hic erat cum Jesu Nazaréno.

denial again with an oath: I know nothing of the man. But those who stood there
Et íterum negávit cum juraménto: Quia non novi hóminem.

came up to Peter soon afterwards, and said: [S] It is certain that thou art one of
Et post pusíllum accessérunt qui stabant, et dixérunt Petro: Vere et tu ex illis es:

them; even thy speech betrays thee. [C] And with that he fell to calling down
nam et loquéla tua maniféstum te facit. Tunc cœpit detestári,

curses on himself and swearing he knew nothing of the man; and thereupon the
et juráre quia non novísset hóminem. Et contínuo

cock crew. Then Peter remembered the word of Jesus, how he had said, Before
gallus cantávit. Et recordátus est Petrus verbi Jesu, quod díxerat:

the cock crows, thou wilt thrice disown me; and he went out, and wept bitterly.
Priúsquam gallus cantet, ter me negábis. Et egréssus foras, flevit amáre.

Judas Hangs Himself

[C] At day-break, all the chief priests and elders of the people laid their plans
Mane autem facto, consílium iniérunt omnes príncipes sacerdótum et senióres pópuli

for putting Jesus to death, and they led him away in bonds, and gave him up to
advérsus Jesum, ut eum morti tráderent. Et vinctum adduxérunt eum, et tradidérunt

the governor, Pontius Pilate. And now Judas, his betrayer, was full of remorse
Póntio Piláto prǽsidi. Tunc videns Judas, qui eum trádidit, quod damnátus esset, pœniténtia ductus,

at seeing him condemned, so that he brought back to the chief priests and elders
rétulit trigínta argénteos princípibus sacerdótum et senióribus,

their thirty pieces of silver, saying: [S] I have sinned in betraying the blood of an
dicens: Peccávi, tradens sánguinem justum.

innocent man. [C] They answered: [S] What is that to us? It concerns thee only.
At illi dixérunt: Quid ad nos? Tu víderis.

[C] Whereupon he left them, throwing down the pieces of silver there in the temple,
Et projéctis argénteis in templo, recéssit:

and went and hanged himself. The chief priests, thus recovering the money, said:
et ábiens, láqueo se suspéndit. Príncipes autem sacerdótum, accéptis argénteis, dixérunt:

[S] It must not be put in the treasury, since it is the price of blood; [C] and after
Non licet eos míttere in córbonam: quia prétium sánguinis est.

consultation, they used it to buy the potter's field, as a burial place for strangers;
Consílio autem ínito, emérunt ex illis agrum fíguli, in sepultúram peregrinórum.

it is upon that account that the field has been called Haceldama, the field of blood,
Propter hoc vocátus est ager ille Hacéldama, hoc est, ager sánguinis, usque in

to this day. And so the word was fulfilled which was spoken by the prophet Jeremy,
hodiérnum diem. Tunc implétum est, quod dictum est per Jeremíam Prophétam,

when he said, And they took the thirty pieces of silver, the price of one who was
dicéntem: Et accepérunt trigínta argénteos prétium appretiáti,

appraised, for men of the race of Israel appraised him, and bestowed them upon the
quem appretiavérunt a fíliis Ísraël: et dedérunt eos in

potter's field, as the Lord had bidden me.
agrum fíguli, sicut constítuit mihi Dóminus.

Before Pontius Pilate

[C] But Jesus stood before the governor. And the governor asked him: [S] Art
Jesus autem stetit ante prǽsidem, et interrogávit eum præses, dicens:

thou the king of the Jews? [C] Jesus told him: ✠ Thy own lips have said it.
Tu es Rex Judæórum? Dicit illi Jesus: Tu dicis.

[C] And when the chief priests and elders brought their accusation against him, he
Et cum accusarétur a princípibus sacerdótum et senióribus,

made no answer. Then Pilate said to him: [S] Dost thou not hear all the testimony
nihil respóndit. Tunc dicit illi Pilátus: Non audis quanta advérsum te dicunt testimónia?

they bring against thee? [C] But Jesus would not answer any of their charges, so
Et non respóndit ei ad ullum verbum,

that the governor was full of astonishment.
ita ut mirarétur præses veheménter.

Pilate Offers A Choice

[C] At the festival, the governor used to grant to the multitude the liberty
Per diem autem solémnem consuéverat præses pópulo dimíttere unum vinctum,

of any one prisoner they should choose; and there was one notable prisoner
quem voluissent. Habébat autem tunc vinctum insígnem,

then in custody, whose name was Barabbas; so, when they gathered about him,
qui dicebátur Barábbas. Congregátis ergo illis,

Pilate asked them: [S] Whom shall I release? Barabbas, or Jesus who is called
dixit Pilátus: Quem vultis dimíttam vobis: Barábbam, an Jesum, qui dícitur

Christ? [C] He knew well that they had only given him up out of malice, and
Christus? Sciébat enim quod per invídiam tradidíssent eum.

even as he sat on the judgement seat, his wife had sent him a message: [S] Do
Sedénte autem illo pro tribunáli, misit ad eum uxor ejus, dicens:

not meddle with this innocent man; I dreamed today that I suffered much on his
Nihil tibi et justo illi: multa enim passa sum hódie per visum propter eum.

account. [C] But the chief priests and elders had persuaded the multitude to
Príncipes autem sacerdótum et senióres persuasérunt pópulis,

ask for Barabbas and have Jesus put to death; and so, when the governor openly
ut péterent Barábbam, Jesum vero pérderent. Respóndens autem præses ait illis:

asked them: [S] Which of the two would you have me release? [C] they said:
Quem vultis vobis de duóbus dimítti? At illi dixérunt:

[S] Barabbas. [C] Pilate said to them: [S] What am I to do, then, with Jesus,
Barábbam. Dicit illis Pilátus: Quid ígitur fáciam de Jesu,

who is called Christ? [C] They said: [S] Let him be crucified. [C] And when
qui dícitur Christus? Dicunt omnes: Crucifigátur.

the governor said: [S] Why, what wrong has he done? [C] they cried louder than
Ait illis præses: Quid enim mali fecit? At illi magis clamábant, dicéntes:

ever: [S] Let him be crucified. [C] And so, finding that his good offices went
Crucifigátur. Videns autem Pilátus quia nihil profíceret,

for nothing, and the uproar only became worse, Pilate sent for water and washed
sed magis tumúltus fieret: accépta aqua, lavit manus

his hands in full sight of the multitude, saying as he did so: [S] I have no part in
coram pópulo, dicens:

the death of this innocent man; it concerns you only. [C] And the whole people
Innocens ego sum a sánguine justi hujus: vos vidéritis. Et respóndens univérsus pópulus

answered: [S] His blood be upon us, and upon our children. [C] And with that he
dixit: Sanguis ejus super nos et super fílios nostros.

released Barabbas as they asked; Jesus he scourged, and gave him up to be crucified.
Tunc dimísit illis Barábbam: Jesum autem flagellátum trádidit eis, ut crucifigerétur.

CROWNING WITH THORNS

[C] After this, the governor's soldiers took Jesus into the palace, and gathered the
Tunc mílites prǽsidis suscipiéntes Jesum in prætórium, congregavérunt

whole of their company about him. First they stripped him, and arrayed him in a
ad eum univérsam cohórtem: et exuéntes eum, chlámydem coccíneam circumdedérunt ei,

scarlet cloak; then they put on his head a crown which they had woven out of thorns,
et plecténtes corónam de spinis, posuérunt super caput ejus,

and a rod in his right hand, and mocked him by kneeling down before him, and
et arúndinem in déxtera ejus. Et genu flexo ante eum, illudébant ei,

saying: [S] Hail, king of the Jews. [C] And they spat upon him, and took the rod
dicéntes: Ave Rex Judæórum. Et exspuéntes in eum, accepérunt arúndinem,

from him and beat him over the head with it. At last they had done with mockery;
et percutiébant caput ejus. Et postquam illusérunt ei,

stripping him of the scarlet cloak, they put his own garments on him, and led him
exuérunt eum chlámyde, et induérunt eum vestiméntis ejus, et duxérunt eum

away to be crucified.
ut crucifígerent.

GOLGOTHA, WHERE JESUS IS MOCKED

[C] As for his cross, they forced a man of Cyrene, Simon by name, whom they
Exeúntes autem invenérunt hóminem Cyrenǽum, nómine Simónem: hunc angariavérunt ut tólleret crucem ejus.

met on their way out, to carry it; and so they reached a place called Golgotha, that
Et venérunt in locum, qui dícitur Gólgotha, quod

is, the place named after a skull. Here they offered him wine, mixed with gall,
est Calváriæ locus. Et dedérunt ei vinum bíbere cum felle mixtum.

which he tasted, but would not drink, and then crucified him, dividing his garments
Et cum gustásset, nóluit bíbere. Postquam autem crucifixérunt eum, divisérunt vestiménta

among them by casting lots. The prophecy must be fulfilled: They divide my spoils
ejus, sortem mitténtes: ut implerétur quod dictum est per Prophétam dicéntem: Divisérunt sibi vestiménta mea,

among them, cast lots for my garments. There, then, they sat, keeping guard over
et super vestem meam misérunt sortem. Et sedéntes servábant eum.

him. Over his head they set a written proclamation of his offence, THIS IS JESUS,
Et imposuérunt super caput ejus causam ipsíus scriptam: Hic est Jesus

THE KING OF THE JEWS; and with him they crucified two thieves, one on his right
Rex Judæórum. Tunc crucifíxi sunt cum eo duo latrónes: unus a dextris

and one on his left. The passers-by blasphemed against him, tossing their heads,
et unus a sinístris. Prætereúntes autem blasphemábant eum movéntes cápita sua,

saying: [S] Come now, thou who wouldst destroy the temple and build it up in
et dicéntes: Vah, qui déstruis templum Dei et in tríduo illud reædíficas:

three days, rescue thyself; come down from that cross, if thou art the Son of God.
salva temetípsum: Si Fílius Dei es, descénde de cruce.

[C] The chief priests, with the scribes and elders, mocked him in the same way:
Simíliter et príncipes sacerdótum illudéntes cum Scribis et senióribus dicébant:

[S] He saved others; himself he cannot save. If he is the king of Israel, he has but
Álios salvos fecit, seipsum non potest salvum fácere: si Rex Ísraël est,

to come down from the cross, here and now, and we will believe in him. He trusted
descéndat nunc de cruce, et crédimus ei:

in God; let God, if he favours him, succour him now; he told us, I am the Son of
confídit in Deo: líberet nunc, si vult eum: dixit enim: Quia Fílius Dei sum.

God. [C] Even the thieves who were crucified with him uttered the same taunts.
Idípsum autem et latrónes, qui crucifíxi erant cum eo, improperábant ei.

Christ Dies On The Cross

[C] From the sixth hour onwards there was darkness over all the earth until the
A sexta autem hora ténebræ factæ sunt super univérsam terram usque ad

ninth hour; and about the ninth hour Jesus cried out with a loud voice: ✠ Eli, Eli,
horam nonam. Et circa horam nonam clamávit Jesus voce magna, dicens: Eli, Eli,

lamma sabachthani? [C] that is, ✠ My God, my God, why hast thou forsaken
lamma sabactháni? Hoc est: Deus meus, Deus meus ut quid dereliquísti me?

me? [C] Hearing this, some of those who stood by said: [S] He is calling upon
Quidam autem illic stantes, et audiéntes dicébant: Elíam vocat iste.

Elias: [C] and thereupon one of them ran to fetch a sponge, which he filled
Et contínuo currens unus ex eis accéptam spóngiam implévit acéto

with vinegar and fixed upon a rod, and offered to let him drink; the rest said:
et impósuit arúndini, et dabat ei bíbere. Céteri vero dicébant:

[S] Wait, let us see whether Elias is to come and save him. [C] Then Jesus cried
Sine, videámus an véniat Elías líberans eum. Jesus autem

out again with a loud voice, and yielded up his spirit.
íterum clamans voce magna, emísit spíritum.

Here all kneel, and a short pause is made. [In former days, the faithful would lie prostrate on the ground.]
Hic genuflectitur, et pausatur aliquantulum.

After The Death Of Christ

[C] And all at once, the veil of the temple was torn this way and that from the top
Et ecce velum templi scissum est in duas partes a summo

to the bottom, and the earth shook, and the rocks parted asunder; and the graves
usque deórsum: et terra mota est, et petræ scissæ sunt, et monuménta

were opened, and many bodies arose out of them, bodies of holy men gone to their
apérta sunt: et multa córpora sanctórum, qui dormíerant, surrexérunt.

rest: who, after his rising again, left their graves and went into the holy city, where
Et exeúntes de monuméntis post resurrectiónem ejus, venérunt in sanctam civitátem,

they were seen by many. So that the centurion and those who kept guard over Jesus
et apparuérunt multis. Centúrio autem et qui cum eo erant, custodiéntes Jesum,

with him, when they perceived the earthquake and all that befell, were overcome
viso terræmótu et his, quæ fiébant, timuérunt valde,

with fear, saying: [S] No doubt, but this was the Son of God. [C] Many women
dicéntes: Vere Fílius Dei erat iste.

stood watching from far off; they had followed Jesus from Galilee, to minister
Erant autem ibi mulíeres multæ a longe, quæ secútæ erant Jesum a Galilǽa, ministrántes ei:

to him; among them were Mary Magdalen, and Mary the mother of James and
inter quas erat María Magdaléne, et María Jacóbi, et Joseph mater,

Joseph, and the mother of the sons of Zebedee. And now it was evening, and a
et mater filiórum Zebedǽi. Cum autem sero factum esset,

man came forward, by name Joseph, a rich man from Arimathea, who followed
venit quidam homo dives ab Arimathǽa, nómine Joseph,

Jesus as a disciple like the rest; he it was who approached Pilate, and asked to have
qui et ipse discípulus erat Jesu. Hic accéssit ad Pilátum, et pétiit

the body of Jesus, whereupon Pilate ordered that the body should be given up.
corpus Jesu. Tunc Pilátus jussit reddi corpus.

Joseph took possession of the body, and wrapped it in a clean winding-sheet; then
Et accépto córpore Joseph invólvit illud in síndone munda.

he buried it in a new grave, which he had fashioned for himself out of the rock,
Et pósuit illud in monuménto suo novo, quod excíderat in petra.

and left it there, rolling a great stone against the grave-door. But there were two
Et advólvit saxum magnum ad óstium monuménti, et ábiit.

who sat on there opposite the tomb, Mary Magdalen and the other Mary with her.
Erat autem ibi María Magdaléne et áltera María, sedéntes contra sepúlcrum.

Weeping Tone

The final part of the Passion is sung by the Deacon of the Mass in what is known as the "tonus planctus" or "weeping tone."

When the Passion is finished, the Deacon takes the Celebrant's palm. (This and those of the ministers are given to the Master of Ceremonies to lay on the credence table.) The Subdeacon carries the Missal to the Gospel side. The Celebrant at the middle says the prayer "Munda cor meum," goes to the missal, and reads the end of the Passion in a low voice, neither saying "Dóminus vobíscum" etc. nor making the sign of the cross. At the end, the Subdeacon—who assists him, as at every High Mass—answers "Laus tibi, Christe."

Meanwhile the Deacon of the Mass—wrapping up his folded chasuble and placing it over the shoulder, or else donning the "broad stole"—receives the Evangeliarium and lays it on the Altar. Incense is put on and blessed, the Deacon says "Munda cor meum," receives the Celebrant's blessing, and goes to sing this last part of the Passion, as he sings the Gospel at every High Mass—except he will normally choose the "weeping tone" from the *Editio Vaticana*. (The acolytes do not hold their candles, but they may hold palms.) The book is incensed. The Deacon, without any introduction, begins at once "Áltera autem die." While this is sung, the Celebrant at the Epistle side corner faces the Deacon, holding his palm. All in choir and church stand, holding palms. The Celebrant gives his palm to the Master of Ceremonies when the Deacon has finished. He kisses the book of lessons brought to him by the Subdeacon and is incensed as usual—although in the 1962 Palm Sunday these two actions are omitted. Palm Sunday has no special ceremonies after this.

1950 • *Hic dicitur "Munda cor meum," petitur benedictio, defertur incensum sine luminaribus, et incensatur liber: non dicitur "Dóminus vobíscum," et Celebrans aut Diaconus non signat librum, neque seipsum: et quod sequitur, cantatur in tono Evangelii: in cujus fine Celebrans osculatur librum, et incensatur. Quae omnia et in aliis Passionibus servantur, praeterquam Feria VI in Parasceve.*

NEXT DAY, the next after the day of preparation, the chief priests and the Pharisees gathered in Pilate's presence, and said: Sir, we have recalled it to memory that this deceiver, while he yet lived, said: I am to rise again after three days. Give orders, then, that his tomb shall be securely guarded until the third day; or perhaps his disciples will come and steal him away. If they should then say to the people, He has risen from the dead, this last deceit will be more dangerous than the old. Pilate said to them: You have guards; away with you, make it secure as you best know how. And they went and made the tomb secure, putting a seal on the stone and setting a guard over it. Credo.

Áltera autem die, quæ est post Parascéven, convenérunt príncipes sacerdótum et pharisǽi ad Pilátum, dicéntes: Dómine, recordáti sumus quia sedúctor ille dixit adhuc vivens: Post tres dies resúrgam. Jube ergo custodíri sepúlcrum usque in diem tértium: ne forte véniant discípuli ejus et furéntur eum, et dicant plebi: Surréxit a mórtuis: et erit novíssimus error pejor prióre. Ait illis Pilátus: Habétis custódiam, ite, custodíte, sicut scitis. Illi autem abeúntes, muniérunt sepúlcrum, signántes lápidem, cum custódibus.

OFFERTORY. *Ps 68: 21-22*

NAUGHT else but shame and misery does my heart forbode. I look around for pity, where pity is none; for comfort, where there is no comfort to be found: they gave me gall to eat, and when I was thirsty they gave me vinegar to drink. ℣. *Save me, O God, for the waters are come in even unto my soul.* ℣. *They that sat in the gate spoke against me: and they that drank wine made me their song.* ℣. *But as for me, my prayer is to thee, O Lord; for the time of thy good pleasure, O God, in the multitude of thy mercy.*

Impropérium exspectávit Cor meum et misériam: et sustínui, qui simul mecum contristarétur, et non fuit: consolántem me quæsívi, et non invéni: et dedérunt in escam meam fel, et in siti mea potavérunt me acéto. ℣. *Salvum me fac, Deus, quóniam intravérunt aquæ usque ad ánimam meam.* ℣. *Advérsum me exercebántur, qui sedébant in porta, et in me psallébant, qui bibébant vinum.* ℣. *Ego vero oratiónem meam ad te Dómine: tempus beneplácitì, Deus, in multitúdine misericórdiæ tuæ.*

SECRET.

In thy dread sight, Lord, these gifts we offer; earnest of true devotion may they win for us, and the reward of eternal bliss. Through our Lord.

Concéde, quǽsumus, Dómine: ut óculis tuæ majestátis munus oblátum, et grátiam nobis devotiónis obtíneat, et efféctum beátæ perennitátis acquírat. Per Dóminum.

The Preface of the Holy Cross (page 190) follows the Secret.

COMMUNION. *Matt 26: 42*

FATHER, if this chalice may not pass me by, but I must drink it, then thy will be done. ℣. *And so they sang a hymn, and went out to mount Olivet.* ℣. *My God, my God, why hast thou forsaken me? Loudly I call, but my prayer cannot reach thee.*

Pater, si non potest hic calix transíre, nisi bibam illum: fiat volúntas tua. (Mt 26: 30) ℣. Et hymno dicto, exiérunt in montem Olivéti. (Ps 21: 2) ℣. Deus, Deus meus, réspice in me: quare me dereliquísti? longe a salúte mea verba delictórum meórum.

—91Angers|944 • Circa 944AD

—StMaur|1079 • Circa 1079AD

Palm Sunday demonstrates the variety which existed vis-à-vis non-Psalter communion antiphons. Some manuscripts indicate Psalm 115—doubtless because of its reference to "cálicem salutáris"—whereas others take from Saint Matthew's Gospel or Psalm 21. We have broken, in this instance, our normal rule of only drawing from a single manuscript.

POSTCOMMUNION.

Per hujus, Dómine, operatiónem mystérii: et vítia nostra purgéntur, et justa desidéria compleántur. Per Dóminum.

Such be the potency, Lord, of these mysteries, that guilt of ours may be purged away, and holy hopes accomplished. Through our Lord.

The following is a brief excerpt from *The Imitation of Christ* by Father Thomas à Kempis, who died in 1471AD. (Chapter 12: "The Royal Road of the Holy Cross").

TO MANY, THIS SEEMS a hard saying: "Deny thyself, take up thy cross and follow Me" {Mt 16:24}. But it will be much harder to hear that final word: "Depart from Me, ye cursèd, into everlasting fire" {Mt 25:41}. Behold, in the cross is everything, and upon your dying on the cross everything depends. There is no other way to life and to true inward peace than the way of the holy cross and daily mortification. Go where you will, seek what you will, you will not find a higher way, nor a less exalted but safer way, than the way of the holy cross. Arrange and order everything to suit your will and judgment, and still you will find that some suffering must always be borne, willingly or unwillingly, and thus you will always find the cross.

Either you will experience bodily pain or you will undergo tribulation of spirit in your soul. At times you will be forsaken by God, at times troubled by those about you and—what is worse—you will often grow weary of yourself. You cannot escape, you cannot be relieved by any remedy or comfort but must bear with it as long as God wills. For He wishes you to learn to bear trial without consolation, to submit yourself wholly to Him, that you may become more humble through suffering. No one understands the passion of Christ so heartily as the man whose lot it is to suffer the like himself.

The cross, therefore, is always ready; it awaits you everywhere. No matter where you may go, you cannot escape it—for, wherever you go, you carry yourself with you, and shall always find yourself. Turn where you will—*above, below, without, or within*—you will find a cross in everything, and everywhere you must have patience if you would have peace within and merit an eternal crown.

If you carry the cross willingly, it will carry and lead you to the desired goal where indeed there shall be no more suffering; but here there shall be. If you carry it unwillingly, you create a burden for yourself and increase the load; *and you must bear it nevertheless.* If you cast away one cross, you will find another—and perhaps a heavier one. Do you expect to escape what no mortal man can ever avoid? Which of the saints was without a cross or trial on this earth? Not even Jesus Christ, our Lord, Whose every hour on earth knew the pain of His passion. "It behooveth Christ to suffer, and to rise again from the dead … and so enter into His glory" {Lk 24:46}. How is it that you look for another way than this, the royal way of the holy cross? The whole life of Christ was a cross and a martyrdom—and do you seek rest and enjoyment for yourself? ✠

Maundy Thursday • 1950 vs. 1962

GENERALLY SPEAKING, the Mass of Holy Thursday was hardly modified by the 1955 reforms. The major difference—apart from moving the Mass from the morning to the evening—concerns the MANDATUM ("Washing of the Feet"). The 1955 revision allows the (optional) MANDATUM to take place after the homily "where pastoral reasons recommend this" {McManus p74}, but prior to 1955 the MANDATUM was never part of the Mass. If the MANDATUM was done before 1955, it came immediately after the Stripping of the Altars; or it took place later in the day {Fortescue p296}. Prior to 1955, the MANDATUM was extremely rare outside of monasteries and cathedrals, and therefore—as a matter of prudence—some authors recommended caution before introducing it, lest the faithful find it a strange innovation.

THIRTEEN NOT TWELVE • In the traditonal version, thirteen men's feet were washed {Dale p197; Guéranger p396; Fortescue p290} whereas in the 1962 version it is twelve men's feet {McManus p74}. For the traditional version, "if possible they should be poor men" {Fortescue p296}. The 1962 version understandably omits the Gospel reading at the beginning, since it duplicates the Mass Gospel (read only a few moments earlier). In the 1950 version, coins are given to the men and the priest kisses their feet {Fortescue p297}, but these actions are suppressed in the 1962 version. The Missal does not specify the exact number number of men "but liturgical authorities, following the *Caeremoniale episcoporum* (Lib. II, Cap. xxiv), designate thirteen poor men" {1946 Lallou p69}. It is not known who the thirteenth man represents: some say Saint Matthias, others Saint Paul, and still others Christ Himself. In the 1950 version, the MANDATUM took place "in a side chapel, in the sacristy, or in a hall near the church" {Fortescue p290}, whereas the 1962 version places the MANDATUM "in the center of the Sanctuary, or in the body of the church."

DIFFERENCES • A list of differences between 1950 and 1962 would include the following:

(1) Tabernacle • for the 1962 version, the tabernacle is empty at the beginning of Mass since "only Sacred Hosts consecrated at the solemn evening Mass of Holy Thursday may be distributed" {McManus p73}, a practice allowed but not required in the 1950 version;

(2) Agnus Dei • The third invocation of the AGNUS DEI is modified in the 1962 version;

(3) Vespers • Vespers is omitted in the 1962 version—for those who assist at Mass on Holy Thursday—whereas this was not the case in 1950, a change most likely resulting from the change of time, since 1950 Mass on Holy Thursday was offered in the morning whereas in 1962 the Mass must begin between 4:00pm and 9:00pm;

(4) Incense • Incense cannot be used in the 1950 version without the presence of a Deacon and Subdeacon, but for the 1955 reform—perhaps hinting at "progressive solemnity" of the INSTRUCTION that would come on 5 March 1967—a special exception was made for the Mass of Holy Thursday {McManus p73};

(5) Suppressed • The Last Gospel and final blessing are suppressed. Instead of *Ite, missa est* the Deacon sings *Benedicámus Dómino*. The CONFITEOR before Communion was also suppressed explicitly by the 1955 revision, and would later be suppressed in all Masses by *Rubricarum Instructum*, which took effect on 1 January 1961 (cf. *Rubricae Generales Missalis Romani* §503, "omissis confessione et absolutione");

(6) Credo • The 1962 version omits the Creed, whereas the 1950 version stipulates it (on this, see the sixth resolution of the 1951 Maria Laach *Conference for Liturgical Reform*);

(7) Chalice • Two large hosts are consecrated in the 1950 version—one being preserved (not consumed) for the "Mass of the Pre-Sanctified"—and a second chalice is prepared with paten, pall, veil of white silk, and white silk ribbon—but in the 1962 version none of these actions are done, and the SANCTISSIMUM is carried inside an ordinary ciborium;

(8) Cross & Candlesticks • In the 1962 version, the Cross and candlesticks are removed during the Stripping of the Altar, since the 1962 rubric for the beginning of Good Friday says: "the Altar is to be entirely bare."

(9) Congregational Candles • During the procession to the Place of Repose, in the 1950 version the members of the congregation hold burning candles in their hands {Fortescue p294}. This is supposed to happen in the 1962 version as well {McManus p78}, but is seldom done in practice for reasons that are not known.

The following notes are taken from Father Fortescue, writing in 1917:

MAUNDY THURSDAY • The name "Maundy" is from "Mandatum," the ceremony of washing the feet, whose first antiphon begins: *Mandatum novum do vobis*. It is usual to call a service after the first word of its chants. In the same way we speak of a "Requiem," a "Dirge" (*Dirige* is the beginning of the first antiphon at Matins for the dead), and so on. It is curious that in England the ceremony of washing the feet should have given its name to the whole day. The Mass of Maundy Thursday is a festal Mass, with white vestments and the "Gloria in excelsis." It is the only case in the year when the Mass of the day and office do not correspond. The office is all mournful. Here the memory which seems most to fill the mind of the Church is the betrayal of Judas. (Notice how constantly the kiss of Judas recurs in the office of Maundy Thursday.) But when Mass is said the Church cannot forget—although it is the middle of the week of mourning—that this is the day to which we owe the Holy Eucharist.

PLACE OF REPOSE • The SANCTISSIMUM must be reserved so the priest can receive Holy Communion on Good Friday, a day when no Mass is offered. Nowadays, it would be easy to take the SANCTISSIMUM from the tabernacle; but the ceremonies of Holy Week date from a time when it was by no means the universal custom to reserve the SANCTISSIMUM in every church, so special arrangements had to be made. Therefore, at the Mass of Maundy Thursday, the priest consecrates two hosts. One he receives as usual; the other will be taken to a place prepared (called "Altar of Repose" or "locus aptus" or "sepulchre") where it is kept until his Communion on Good Friday. After Mass, the procession takes the SANCTISSIMUM to the place where it is kept till the next day. This is an example of a real Roman procession, having a definite object. At first it seems nothing more was done than to keep the SANCTISSIMUM reverently in some safe place (often in the sacristry, as is still done in many Eastern Churches). Then people realized that this was the one occasion when they had the Blessed Sacrament in their churches. [Again, quite a different situation exists today.] So they made much of it. They fitted up and adorned a place of honor; they began to watch and pray before the Place of Repose all the day and all night. Later Eucharistic developments (Exposition of the Blessed Sacrament, the "Forty Hours," etc.) seem to have begun during this time between Mass on Maundy Thursday and Good Friday. And then, even after it had become usual to reserve the SANCTISSIMUM in tabernacles all the year round, the old custom of special reverence on this occasion continued. That, too, is nearly always so. Custom preserves many things in liturgy after their first reason has ceased. This accounts for the special reverence with which we still treat the SANCTISSIMUM at the Place of Repose, although we have it now in the tabernacle always. And, indeed, on this night of all nights, when our Lord was suffering his bitter torment, it is natural that people should spend part of the time with Him in prayer, honoring the gift of that day.

STRIPPING OF THE ALTAR • After Vespers the Altar is stripped. This ceremony has become to us one of the features of Holy Week, yet it is only one more case of an archaic custom otherwise abolished but preserved on these days. Once, after Mass on any day, the Altar was stripped. Now on Maundy Thursday and Good Friday the Stripping of the Altar has become a symbol of desolation, or a memory that our Lord was stripped of his garments. For much information about the "denuding of the altars" and the "washing of the altars," see Father Herbert Thurston *Lent and Holy Week* (1904) pages 300-304 and James Monti *Catholic Worship in the Middle Ages* (2012) pages 397-403. Sir William Kirkham Blount, writing in 1670AD, had this to say about the "Uncloathing of the Altars" on Holy Thursday: *This ceremonie is very ancient. For S. Gregorie mentions it in his booke de Sacramentis; and in the Sixteenth and Seaventeenth Councils of Toledo, held in the yeare 693 and 694 in the eight Canon of the former, and in the second of the latter; and likewise in S. Fligius Bishop of Noyon, who lived in the same age, and treats of it in his eigth Homilie.*

Maundy Thursday • Holy Communion

The Council of Trent declared—regarding those in the state of Grace—"the faithful who are present [at Mass] should communicate, not only in spiritual desire, but also by the sacramental participation of the Eucharist" (*Session XXII*, chapter 6). Furthermore, the *Catechism of the Council of Trent*—from the 16th century—says: "Let not the faithful deem it enough to receive the Body of the Lord once a year only; but let them judge that Communion ought to be more frequent; but whether it be more expedient that it should be monthly, weekly, or daily can be decided by no fixed universal rule" (*Part II*, chapter 4, §58). The Fourth Lateran Council, in the 13th century, compelled the faithful under pain of excommunication to receive at least once a year. Indeed, throughout the Church's history many holy men and women encouraged frequent reception of Holy Communion. Others—such as Saint Jerome and Saint Augustine—were hesitant to take a position either for or against the practice. During the Baroque period: "The Communion of the faithful took place as a rule ***after*** the Mass, and ***not*** after the parochial Mass but rather—because of the law of fasting—after one of the early Masses."[1] Even after the time of Pope Saint Pius X ("Pope of the Eucharist"), Communion was seldom distributed to the Faithful ***during*** Mass.

A common practice was to give Holy Communion *before* Mass (very early in the morning), or *after* Mass. Another common practice was to distribute Holy Communion at a side Altar, while Mass at the main Altar was taking place. *The American Ecclesiastical Review* (1955, vol. CXXV, page 66), describes another common practice in which an assistant priest would begin distribution of Holy Communion immediately after the Consecration. The *Code of Rubrics* (1961) declared in §502: "The proper time to distribute Holy Communion to the faithful is during Mass, after the Communion of the Celebrant, who distributes It himself to those who ask for It, unless it is desirable that he be helped by one or more priests, because of the large number of communicants. ***It is altogether unbecoming*** for another priest to distribute Holy Communion—other than at the proper time for Communion—at the same Altar at which Mass is actually being celebrated." Holy Communion before, after, or outside of Mass was permitted "for a reasonable cause"—and Father Henry Dziadosz suggested (15 December 1960) that "relieving the congestion" might justify this.

Prior to the reforms of Pope Pius XII, Holy Communion was distributed to the Faithful ***during*** Mass on Holy Thursday. Father Fortescue wrote in 1917:

> "On Maundy Thursday there is a distribution of Holy Communion at High Mass. This does not often occur on other days; but any Catholic has normally a right to present himself for Communion at any Mass, on condition that he is in a state of grace and fasting from midnight."

Holy Communion was not distributed on Holy Saturday when Father Thurston wrote his book in 1904, and he attributes many of the "missing items" from the Easter Vigil to the fact that traditionally Communion was not distributed at the Easter Vigil Mass {Thurston p434}. However, by the time Father Fortescue wrote his book in 1917, the people were allowed to receive Communion at the Easter Vigil Mass, either during or after the Mass {Fortescue p334}.

Confiteor Before Communion • The Confiteor before Communion was suppressed by the 1961 code of rubrics (§503) yet included in the 1962 *Pontificale Romanum* and the 1962 *Missale Romanum* (on Good Friday). The fact that Holy Communion was distributed so infrequently ***during*** Mass is supremely relevant to this question, which has become a bone of contention. Prior to the Second Vatican Council, Communion was usually distributed *before* Mass, *after* Mass, or *during* Mass—but not *during* Communion time. Even when Communion was supposed to be distributed at Communion time (e.g. on Holy Thursday) it often was not. Saint Agatha's Church in St. Louis was typical of the time: on Holy Thursday (10 April 1941), Communion was distributed at 6:30 AM in the morning and the "High Mass with Procession" began afterwards, at 8:30 AM.

1 The quote reproduces faithfully the original emphases by Father Jungmann; cf. *Missarum Sollemnia* (Benziger Brothers, 1950), first volume, page 148. On the "communion of the people," see also the second volume, pages 347-391.

(1950) MAUNDY THURSDAY • The Holy Mass Begins

Feria quinta in Coena Domini — *Station at Saint John Lateran ("Our Savior's Church")*

[Editor's Note: Psalm 42 ("Júdica me") is not said during the Prayers at the Foot of the Altar. The color of the Divine Office is purple, but the Mass vestments are white. The color of the Altar frontal and tabernacle veil is white. The Altar Cross is veiled in white. Flowers are placed on the High Altar. Covering the liturgical books (Evangeliarium, Epistolarium, and Missal) with colored silk is optional—already in 1917 this was "considered obsolete" {Fortescue p20}.]

INTROIT. *Gal 6: 14*

Nos autem gloriári opórtet in Cruce Dómini nostri Jesu Christi: in quo est salus, vita et resurréctio nostra: per quem salváti et liberáti sumus. (Ps 66: 2) ℣. Deus misereátur nostri, et benedícat nobis: illúminet vultum suum super nos, et misereátur nostri. *Nos autem...*

FOR US, no boasting but in the cross of our Lord Jesus Christ, who is health and life and resurrection to us, by whom we were saved and set free. ℣. May God be merciful unto us and bless us: may he smile graciously on us, and show us his mercy. *For us...*

1950 • *Dicitur "Gloria in excélsis," et tunc pulsantur campanae, et deinceps non amplius usque ad Sabbatum sanctum.*

The ringing of the bells at the "Gloria" is a sign that from now on they will not be heard again until the first Easter Mass. The Church is accustomed to do a thing solemnly for the last time before it ceases, as we say the "Alleluia" solemnly twice at the end of Vespers before Septuagesima. According to Sir Walter Kirkham Blount ("Office of Holy Week," 1670AD), this silence of the bells is kept "to teach us that the preaching of the Gospel and the voice of those who ought to excite others to follow Christ were silent during this Passion time." Until the first Easter Mass, a "substitute of the bell" may be used, a device called by many names: crotalus, rattle, wooden clapper, and so on. If it is used, it is rattled whenever—on other days—the bell would be rung: at the Sanctus; at the elevation; during the procession; at the ANGELUS; and so forth.

COLLECT.

Deus, a quo et Judas reátus sui pœnam, et confessiónis suæ latro præmium sumpsit, concéde nobis tuæ propitiatiónis efféctum: ut, sicut in passióne sua Jesus Christus Dóminus noster divérsa utrísque íntulit stipéndia meritórum; ita nobis, abláto vetustátis erróre, resurrectiónis suæ grátiam largiátur: Qui tecum.

O God, by whom Judas for his guilt was punished, and, for guilt humbly acknowledged, yonder thief was granted his reward, be it ours to profit by thy clemency. To each, in the hour of his Passion, our Lord Jesus Christ gave the recompense each had earned; may he rid us of our old perverse ways, and bestow on us the grace to rise again with him: who with thee.

EPISTLE. *I Cor 11: 20-32*

Fratres: Conveniéntibus vobis in unum, jam non est Domínicam cœnam manducáre. Unusquísque enim suã cœnam præsúmit ad manducándum. Et álius quidem ésurit: álius autem ébrius est. Numquid domos non habétis ad manducándũ et bibéndum? aut ecclésiam Dei contémnitis, et confúnditis eos, qui non habent? Quid dicam vobis? Laudo vos? In hoc non laudo. Ego enim accépi a Dómino quod et trádidi vobis, quóniam Dóminus Jesus, in qua nocte tradebátur, accépit panem, et grátias agens fregit, et dixit:

BRETHREN: When you assemble together, there is no opportunity to eat a supper of the Lord; each comer hastens to eat the supper he has brought for himself, so that one man goes hungry, while another has drunk deep. Have you no homes to eat and drink in, that you should shew contempt to God's church, and shame the poor? Praise you? There is no room for praise here. The tradition which I received from the Lord, and handed on to you, is that the Lord Jesus, on the night when he

BUT MELCHISEDECH, BRINGING FORTH BREAD AND WINE... ✠ Gen 14: 18

TU ES SACERDOS IN AETERNUM SEC. ORDINEM MELCHISEDECH (Ps 109: 4)

PASCHA NOSTRUM IMMOLATUS EST CHRISTUS (I Cor 5: 7)

CHRIST HAS BEEN SACRIFICED FOR US, OUR PASCHAL VICTIM ✠ I Cor 5: 7

THE LORD HATH SWORN AND HE WILL NOT REPENT: THOU ART A PRIEST FOREVER ACC. TO THE ORDER OF MELCHISEDECH. Ps 109: 4

SAY TO THEM: ON THE TENTH DAY OF THIS MONTH LET EVERY MAN TAKE A LAMB BY THEIR FAMILIES AND HOUSES. Ex 12: 3

Accípite, et manducáte: hoc est corpus meum, quod pro vobis tradétur: hoc fácite in meam commemoratiónem. Simíliter et cálicem, postquam cenávit, dicens: Hic calix novum testaméntum est in meo sánguine: hoc fácite, quotiescúmque bibétis, in meam commemoratiónem. Quotiescúmque enim manducábitis panem hunc et cálicem bibétis: mortem Dñi annuntiábitis, donec véniat. Ítaque quicúmque manducáverit panem hunc vel bíberit cálicem Dómini indígne, reus erit córporis et sánguinis Dómini. Probet autem seípsum homo: et sic de pane illo edat et de cálice bibat. Qui enim mandúcat et bibit indígne, judícium sibi mandúcat et bibit: non dijúdicans corpus Dómini. Ideo inter vos multi infírmi et imbecílles, et dórmiunt multi. Quod si nosmetípsos dijudicarémus, non útique judicarémur. Dũ judicámur autẽ, a Dño corrípimur, ut non cum hoc mundo damnémur.

was being betrayed, took bread, and gave thanks, and broke it, and said, Take, eat; this is my body, given up for you. Do this for a commemoration of me. And so with the cup, when supper was ended, This cup, he said, is the new testament, in my blood. Do this, whenever you drink it, for a commemoration of me. So it is the Lord's death that you are heralding, whenever you eat this bread and drink this cup, until he comes. And therefore, if anyone eats this bread or drinks this cup of the Lord unworthily, he will be held to account for the Lord's body and blood. A man must examine himself first, and then eat of that bread and drink of that cup; he is eating and drinking damnation to himself if he eats and drinks unworthily, not recognizing the Lord's body for what it is. That is why many of your number want strength and health, and not a few have died. If we recognized our own fault, we should not incur these judgments; as it is, the Lord judges us and chastises us, so that we may not incur, as this world incurs, damnation.

GRADUAL. *Phil 2: 8-9*

Christus factus est pro nobis obédiens usque ad mortem, mortem autem crucis. ℣. Propter quod et Deus exaltávit illum: et dedit illi nomen, quod est super omne nomen.

CHRIST ACCEPTED an obedience which brought him to death, death on a cross. ℣. That is why God has raised him to such a height and given him that name which is greater than any other name.

GOSPEL. *John 13: 1-15*

Ante diem festum Paschæ, sciens Jesus, quia venit hora ejus, ut tránseat ex hoc mundo ad Patrem: cum dilexísset suos, qui erant in mundo, in finem diléxit eos. Et cena facta, cum diábolus jam misísset in cor, ut tráderet eum Judas Simónis Iscariótæ: sciens, quia ómnia dedit ei Pater in manus, et quia a Deo exívit, et ad Deum vadit: surgit a cena et ponit vestiménta sua: et cum accepísset línteum, præcínxit se. Deínde mittit aquam in pelvim, et cœpit laváre pedes discipulórum, et extérgere línteo, quo erat præcínctus.

BEFORE THE PASCHAL FEAST began, Jesus already knew that the time had come for his passage from this world to the Father. He still loved those who were his own, whom he was leaving in the world, and he would give them the uttermost proof of his love. Supper was over, and the devil had already put it into the heart of Judas, son of Simon, the Iscariot, to betray him. Jesus knew well that the Father had left everything in his hands; knew it was from God that he came, and to God that he went. And now, rising from supper, he laid his garments aside, took a towel, and put it about him; and then he poured water into the basin, and began to wash the feet of his disciples, wiping them with the towel that girded him.

So, when he came to Simon Peter, Peter asked him, Lord, is it for thee to wash my feet? Jesus answered him, It is not for thee to know, now, what I am doing; but thou wilt understand it afterwards. Peter said to him, I will never let thee wash my feet; and Jesus answered him, If I do not wash thee, it means thou hast no companionship with me. Then, Lord, said Peter, wash my hands and my head too, not only my feet. But Jesus told him, A man who has bathed does not need to do more than wash the stains from his feet; he is clean all over. And you are clean now; only, not all of you.

Venit ergo ad Simónem Petrum. Et dicit ei Petrus: Dómine, tu mihi lavas pedes? Respóndit Jesus et dixit ei: Quod ego fácio, tu nescis modo, scies autem póstea. Dicit ei Petrus: Non lavábis mihi pedes in ætérnum. Respóndit ei Jesus: Si non lávero te, non habébis partem mecum. Dicit ei Simon Petrus: Dómine, non tantum pedes meos, sed et manus et caput. Dicit ei Jesus: Qui lotus est, non índiget nisi ut pedes lavet, sed est mundus totus. Et vos mundi estis, sed non omnes.

He knew who his betrayer was; that is why he said, You are not all clean. Then, when he had finished washing their feet and put on his garments, he sat down again, and said to them, Do you understand what it is I have done to you? You hail me as the Master, and the Lord; and you are right, it is what I am. Why then, if I have washed your feet, I who am the Master and the Lord, you in your turn ought to wash each other's feet; I have been setting you an example, which will teach you in your turn to do what I have done for you. Credo.

Sciébat enim, quisnam esset, qui tráderet eum: proptérea dixit: Non estis mundi omnes. Postquam ergo lavit pedes eórum et accépit vestiménta sua: cum recubuísset íterum, dixit eis: Scitis, quid fécerim vobis? Vos vocátis me Magíster et Dómine: et bene dícitis: sum étenim. Si ergo ego lavi pedes vestros, Dóminus et Magíster: et vos debétis alter altérius laváre pedes. Exémplum enim dedi vobis, ut, quemádmodum ego feci vobis, ita et vos faciátis.

Unlike the 1962 version, the 1950 Maundy Thursday has a Credo. If the Mandatum is performed, it does not take place during Mass.

OFFERTORY. *Ps 117: 16, 17*

THE POWER of the Lord has triumphed, the power of the Lord has brought me to great honor: I am reprieved from death, to live on and proclaim what the Lord has done for me. ℣. *I called on the Lord when trouble beset me, and the Lord listened, and brought me relief, for the Lord is at my side.* ℣. *I reeled under the blow, and had well-nigh fallen, but still the Lord was there to aid me. Who but the Lord has brought me deliverance?*

Identical to 3rd Sunday after Epiphany:

Déxtera Dómini fecit virtútem, déxtera Dómini exaltávit me: non móriar, sed vivam, et narrábo ópera Dómini. ℣. *In tribulatióne invocávi Dóminum et exaudívit me in latitúdine: quia Dóminus adjútor meus est.* ℣. *Impúlsus versátus sum, ut cáderem: et Dóminus suscépit me: et factus est mihi in salútem.*

SECRET.

Holy Lord, Father almighty, everlasting God, who shall make this sacrifice of ours acceptable to thee? None but he, that bequeathed to his disciples this day

Ipse tibi, quǽsumus, Dómine sancte, Pater omnípotens, ætérne Deus, sacrifícium nostrum reddat accéptum, qui discípulis suis in sui commemoratiónem hoc fíeri hodiérna traditióne monstrávit, Jesus Christus, Fílius tuus, Dóminus noster: Qui tecum.

the manner of its observance, to be his own commemoration, thy Son, Jesus Christ our Lord: who with thee.

The Preface of the Holy Cross (page 190) follows the Secret.

CHRIST WANTED WHAT HE DID AT THE LAST SUPPER TO BE REPEATED IN HIS MEMORY.

QUOD IN COENA CHRISTUS GESSIT FACIENDUM HOC EXPRESSIT IN SUI MEMORIAM.

— Saint Thomas Aquinas (d. 1274)

(1950) Maundy Thursday • The Canon of the Mass

Feria quinta in Coena Domini *Infra Actionem*

On certain major feasts, the Communicantes and Hanc Igitur are modified. But Maundy Thursday, as Father Thurston reminds us, "stands absolutely alone among all the feasts of the year" inasmuch as three modifications are made to the Canon. Notice the name of Saint Joseph is not mentioned, since that was added on 13 November 1962 (effective 8 December 1962).

Communicántes, et diem sacratíssimum celebrántes, quo Dóminus noster Jesus Christus pro nobis est tráditus: sed et memóriam venerántes, in primis gloriósæ semper Vírginis Maríæ, Genitrícis ejúsdem Dei et Dómini nostri Jesu Christi: sed et beatórum Apostolórum ac Mártyrum tuórum, Petri et Pauli, Andréæ, Jacóbi, Joánnis, Thomæ, Jacóbi, Philíppi, Bartholomǽi, Matthǽi, Simónis et Thaddǽi: Lini, Cleti, Cleméntis, Xysti, Cornélii, Cypriáni, Lauréntii, Chrysógoni,

HERE MEET WE in fellowship, here that holy day we celebrate, on which our Lord Jesus Christ was given up to be our ransom; here keep we the memory of thy saints in honor: first of the glorious ever-virgin Mary, Mother of the same Jesus Christ, our God and Lord, and likewise that of thy blessed apostles and martyrs Peter and Paul, Andrew, James, John, Thomas, James, Philip, Bartholomew, Matthew, Simon, and Thaddeus: of Linus, Cletus, Clement,

Sixtus, Cornelius, Cyprian, Laurence, Chrysogonus, John and Paul, Cosmas and Damian, and all thy saints everywhere. Let their merits, Lord, their intercession, avail with thee; shield us with thy protection in every encounter. Through the same Christ our Lord. Amen.

Joánnis et Pauli, Cosmæ et Damiáni: et ómnium Sanctórum tuórum: quorum méritis precibúsque concédas, ut in ómnibus protectiónis tuæ muniámur auxílio. Per eúmdem Christum, Dóminum nostrum. Amen.

With his hands spread over the offerings, the Priest continues the prayer.
Tenens manus expansas super oblata, dicit:

HERE, THEN, is the offering we make thee, we that are thy ministers, yet in truth it is the offering of all thy household. We make it in this day's honor, the day when our Lord Jesus Christ bequeathed to his disciples that sacrifice of his Body and Blood we still celebrate. We beseech thee, Lord, to grant it favorable acceptance, ordering our days in the peace thou bestowest, from eternal loss delivering us, and in the company of thy elect bidding our names be numbered. Through the same Christ our Lord. Amen.

Hanc ígitur oblatiónem servitútis nostræ, sed et cunctæ famíliæ tuæ, quam tibi offérimus ob diem, in qua Dóminus noster Jesus Christus trádidit discípulis suis Córporis et Sánguinis sui mystéria celebránda; quæsumus Dómine, ut placátus accípias: diésque nostros in tua pace dispónas: atque ab ætérna damnatióne nos éripi et in electórum tuórum júbeas grege numerári. Per eúmdem Christum Dóminum nostrum. Amen.

The Priest once again blesses the offerings:

AN OFFERING ✠ blessed and ✠ dedicated, a sacrifice ✠ truly done, worthy of our human dignity and thy acceptance—this, O God, do thou make of it, Body ✠ and Blood ✠ that shall be, for our sakes, of thy well-beloved Son, our Lord Jesus Christ.

Quam oblatiónem tu Deus in ómnibus, quæsumus, bene ✠ díctam, adscrí ✠ ptam, ra ✠ tam, rationábilem acceptabilémque fácere dignéris: ut nobis Cor ✠ pus, et San ✠ guis fiat dilectíssimi Fílii tui, Dómini nostri Jesu Christi.

The Western rites have "prídie" whereas most Eastern liturgies have "on the *night* He was betrayed."

HE, ON THIS DAY, the very day before he suffered, us and the whole world to ransom, took bread into those holy, those worshipful hands, to thee, his Father, God omnipotent, lifted his eyes heavenward, to thee gave thanks, then ✠ blessed it, and broke, and gave it to his disciples, saying: Take and eat this, all of you,

Qui prídie, quam pro nostra omniúmque salúte paterétur, hoc est, hódie, accépit panem in sanctas ac venerábiles manus suas, et elevátis óculis in cælum ad te Deum, Patrem suum omnipoténtem, tibi grátias agens, bene ✠ díxit, fregit, dedítque discípulis suis, dicens: Accípite, et manducáte ex hoc omnes.

FOR THIS IS MY BODY.

HOC EST ENIM CORPUS MEUM.

The rest of the Canon is as normal.
Et reliqua ut in Canone.

1950 • *"Agnus Dei" dicitur de more, sed pax non datur. Dicuntur tamen tres consuetæ Orationes ante Communionem. Hodie Sacerdos consecrat duas Hostias, quarum unam sumit, alteram reservat pro die sequenti, in quo non conficitur Sacramentum: reservat etiam aliquas particulas consecratas, si opus fuerit pro infirmis: Sanguinem vero totum sumit: et ante ablutionem digitorum ponit Hostiam reservatam in alio Calice, quem Diaconus palla et patena inversa cooperit, et desuper velum expandit, et in medio Altaris collocat. Deinde fit Communio, et completur Missa. Sacerdos autem genuflectit, quandocumque accedit vel recedit a medio Altaris, vel transit ante Sacramentum in calice reservatum: et cum dicere debet "Dóminus vobíscum," non vertit se ad populum in medio Altaris, ne terga vertat Sacramento, sed a latere Evangelii: et in fine ibidem dat benedictionem, et non perficit circulum.*

The AGNUS DEI is said as usual; the kiss of peace is not given, but the three prayers before the Communion are said. According to Father Thurston, many mediæval liturgists say the kiss of peace is omitted "to express detestation for the treachery of Judas."

In 1917, Father Adrian Fortescue wrote as follows: "On Maundy Thursday there is a distribution of Holy Communion at High Mass. This does not often occur on other days; but any Catholic has normally a right to present himself for Communion at any Mass, on condition that he is in a state of grace and fasting from midnight." Sometimes, a white "communion cloth" is placed under the chin of those who receive.

On this day the Celebrant consecrates two large hosts. One of these he receives at the Communion of the Mass, as usual; the second is put into a chalice, which is then veiled, and at the end of Mass is taken in procession to the Place of Repose and there reserved for the Mass of the Presanctified on Good Friday. When the Celebrant has made his communion, the Subdeacon covers the chalice of Mass and sets it aside on the Gospel side, not outside the corporal. The ministers genuflect and again change places. The Deacon uncovers the second chalice and presents it to the Celebrant on the corporal. The Celebrant takes the second Host he has consecrated and places it carefully in this chalice. The Deacon covers the chalice with the pall, then over this he puts the paten, upside down, covers all with the silk veil, and ties the veil around the stem with the ribbon. He places it on the middle of the corporal. The rest of Mass is celebrated according to the rules when the Blessed Sacrament is exposed.

[Editor's Note: Unlike the 1950 Maundy Thursday, the 1962 version: (1) changes the words of the final AGNUS DEI; (2) eliminates the first of the three prayers before Communion (*Dómine Jesu Christe, qui dixísti*); (3) explicitly suppresses the CONFITEOR before Communion {McManus p76}; (4) eliminates the Final Blessing and Last Gospel; (5) changes "Ite, missa est" to "Benedicámus Dómino." During the Middle Ages on Maundy Thursday the AGNUS DEI was sung with "miserere nobis" thrice; for speculation as to why this was done, cf. Adrian Fortescue's *A Study of the Roman Liturgy* (London: Longmans and Green, 1912) page 388.]

COMMUNION. *John 13: 12, 13, 15*

Dóminus Jesus, postquam cœnávit cum discípulis suis, lavit pedes eórum, et ait illis: Scitis quid fécerim vobis ego Dóminus, et Magíster? Exémplum dedi vobis, ut et vos ita faciátis. (Ps 118: 1) ℣. *Beáti immaculáti in via, qui ámbulant in lege Dómini.*

—47CHARTRES|957 • Circa 957AD

THE Lord Jesus, after he had supped with his disciples, washed their feet, and said to them: Do you understand what it is I have done to you, I who am the Lord and Master? I have set you an example, to teach you what to do. ℣. *Blessed are the undefiled in the way, who walk in the law of the Lord.*

POSTCOMMUNION.

Reficti vitálibus aliméntis, quǽsumus Dómine Deus noster: ut quod témpore nostræ mortalitátis exséquimur, immortalitátis tuæ múnere consequámur. Per Dóminum.

O Lord our God, life-giving is the food that has here refreshed us. Here in this mortal life we have done thy bidding; may we find our reward in life eternal: through our Lord.

(1950) MAUNDY THURSDAY • The Procession

Feria quinta in Coena Domini *Ad Processionem*

While the Celebrant reads the Last Gospel, two thurifers bring two thuribles from the sacristy. Candles are given out to the clergy "in choro." Lay people who will take part in the procession may also hold candles {Fortescue p294}. Unlike the 1950 Maundy Thursday, the 1962 version omits the Last Gospel and the Blessing at the end of Mass {McManus p77}. In the 1962 version, "Benedicámus Dómino" replaces the "Ite Missa Est" of 1950—however, in both versions candles are given to those who will walk in the procession.

When Mass has ended, the Celebrant dons a Cope and incenses the Sanctissimum. Once the Deacon has given the chalice to the Celebrant, *Pange Lingua* is intoned by the cantors, and the singers continue it. During the procession, the Celebrant and ministers quietly recite psalms, omitting the *Gloria Patri*. The precise psalms are not specified, but Psalm 115 ("Credidi"), 147 ("Lauda Jerusalem"), 121 ("Laetatus sum"), 112 ("Laudate pueri"), 116 ("Laudate Dominum"), or others from the office of Corpus Christi are suitable.

QUAM LAETUS EST, QUEM VISITAS; CONSORS PATERNAE DEXTERAE,
HAPPY IS HE WHOM THOU VISITEST ; THOU WHO SITTEST AT THE RIGHT HAND OF THE FATHER;

THOU ART THE LIGHT CONSOLING HEAVEN, BUT WHO CANNOT BE SEEN BY MORTAL EYES.
TU DULCE LUMEN PATRIAE, CARNIS NEGATUM SENSIBUS. (LUX ALMA)

The following text was composed by Saint Thomas Aquinas circa 1264AD.
Its inspiration was the "Pange Lingua" composed circa 590AD by Bishop Fortunatus.

MODE 3

Pange, lingua, glo-ri- ó-si Córpo-ris mysté-

Praise, my tongue, the mystery of the glorious Body

ri- um, Sangui-nísque pre-ti- ó-si, Quem in mundi

and of the precious Blood which the king of the nations,

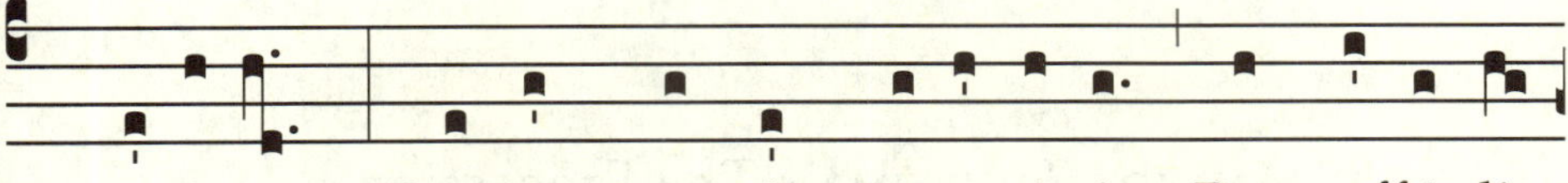

pré-ti- um Fructus ventris gene-ró-si Rex effú-dit

fruit of a royal womb, poured out as the world's ransom.

génti- um. 2. Nobis da-tus, nobis na-tus Ex intácta

2. To us He was given, to us He was born of a pure virgin.

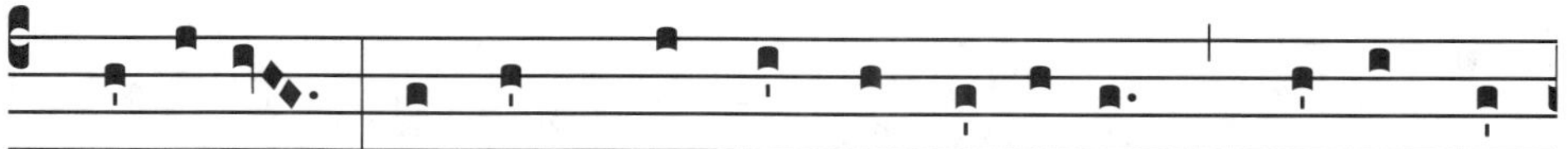

Vírgine, Et in mundo conversá-tus, Sparso ver-

He lived in the world and when He had spread the seed of truth,

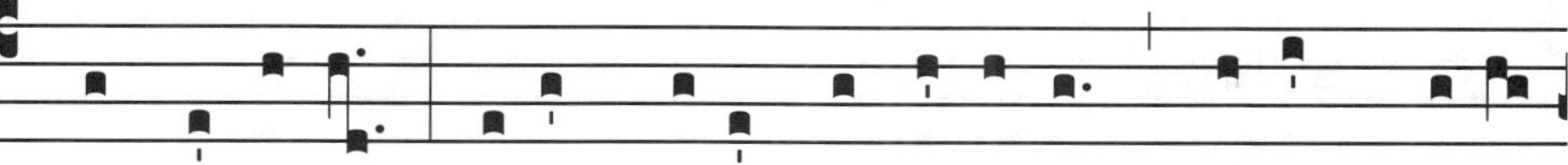

bi sémi-ne, Su- i moras inco-lá-tus Mi-ro clausit

He closed in a wondrous way the period of His sojourn here.

órdine. 3. In suprémæ nocte cenæ Recúmbens

3. As He is reclining with His brethren on the night of the last supper,

cum frátribus, Observá-ta lege plene Ci-bis in

He complies completely with the Law in regard to the legal foods

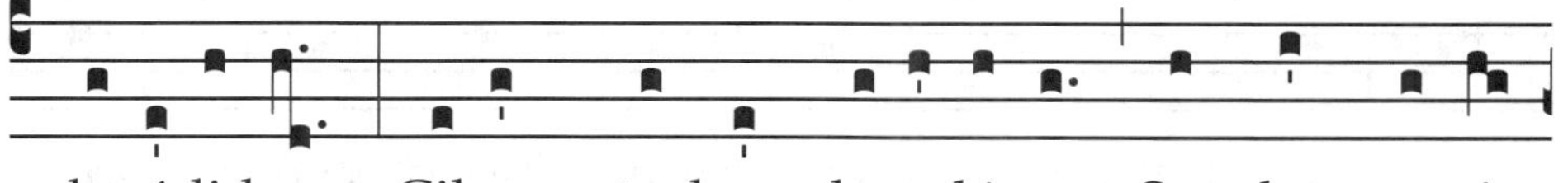

legá-li-bus, Cibum turbæ du-odénæ Se dat su- is

and then gives Himself with His own hands as food to the group of twelve.

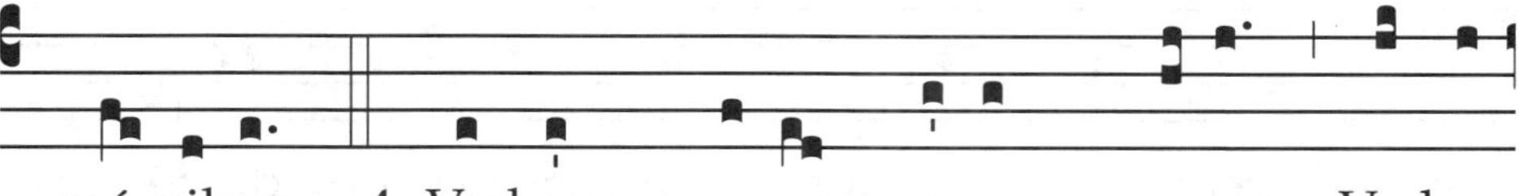

má-nibus. 4. Verbum ca-ro panem verum Verbo

4. The Word made flesh by a word

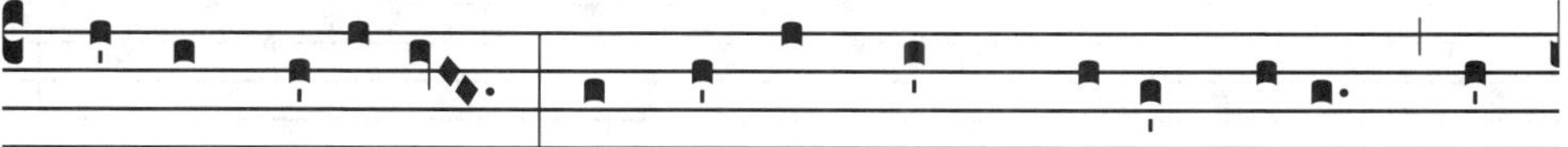

carnem éffi-cit, Fitque sanguis Christi merum, Et,

changes true bread into His flesh, and wine becomes His blood.

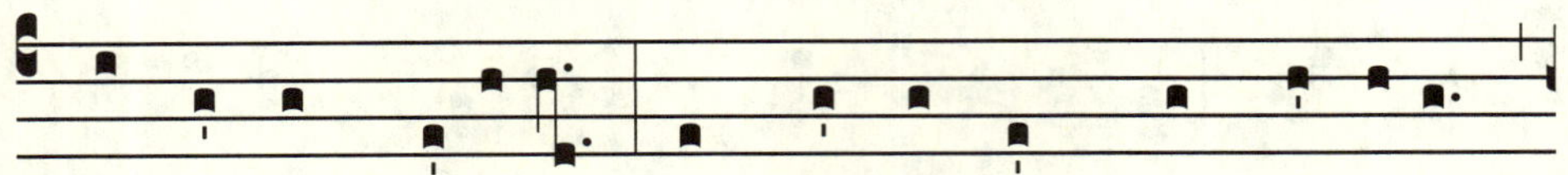

si sensus dé-fi-cit, Ad firmándum cor sincérum

If man cannot perceive this change, faith of itself is enough to

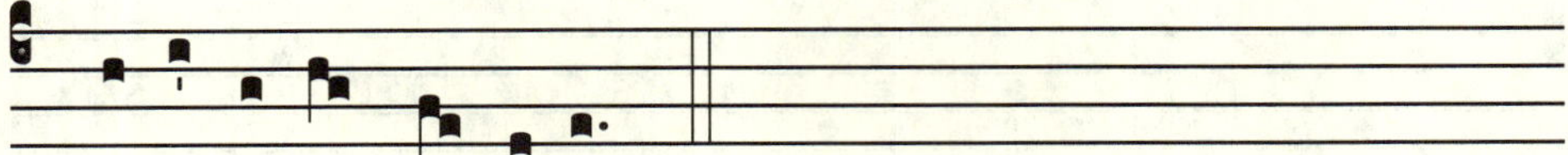

So-la fi-des súf-fi-cit.

convince the well-disposed.

1950 • At the place of repose, the Deacon takes the chalice from the Celebrant and places it in the urn. The "Tantum ergo" is sung. The Celebrant imposes incense (without blessing it) and incenses the Sanctissimum. The Deacon then shuts and locks the urn. The clergy extinguish their candles. The torch-bearers put out their torches and leave them there.

The verse "Tantum ergo" should not be sung before the Celebrant arrives at the place of repose. Until then, other verses of the hymn are repeated.

Tantum ergo sacraméntum Vene-rémur cérnu-

5. Let us therefore humbly reverence so great a sacrament.

i, Et antíquum documéntum Novo cedat rí-tu-

Let the old types depart and give way to the new rite.

i; Præstet fides suppleméntum Sénsu-um de-fé-ctu-

Let faith provide her help where all the senses fail.

i. 6. Geni-tó-ri Geni-tóque Laus et jubi-lá-ti-o,

6. To the Father and the Son be praise, acclamation,

Sa-lus, honor, virtus quoque Sit et benedícti- o;

salvation, honor, might and blessing too.

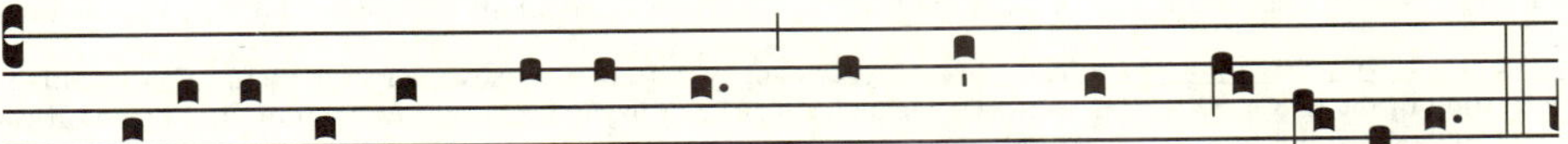

Procedénti ab utróque Compar sit laudá-ti- o.

To the One who proceeds from them both be given equal praise.

English Translation by Rev. Joseph Connelly IMPRIMATUR *(10 December 1954)*

A- men.

(1950) MAUNDY THURSDAY • Vespers

Feria quinta in Coena Domini *Ad Vesperas*

1950 • The Celebrant, ministers, cross-bearer and acolytes remain for a little while at the Place of Repose, while everyone else returns to the place where Vespers will be prayed. Then, the Celebrant and his retinue go to the sacristy, wearing birettas on the way. Meanwhile Vespers is recited. Vespers on Maundy Thursday may also be sung, as the melodies were restored by the "Editio Vaticana" promulgated by Pope Pius X in 1913. The melodies are provided in various books, such as: VESPERALE ROMANUM, (Lethielleux, 1913) page 173; LIBER ANTIPHONARIUS (Solesmes, 1949) page 436; ANTIPHONALE MONASTICUM (Desclée, 1934) page 429; LIBER USUALIS (Desclée, 1934) page 1882. Nothing prevents the Faithful from joining in singing Vespers, and this is the traditional way (cf. "Interview with Domenico Cardinal Bartolucci" dated 12 August 2009). Even at a time when women were thought to be excluded from singing during Mass, they were still explicitly encouraged to sing the "Psalms and Hymns of the Divine Office"; cf. "Church Music" in the *American Ecclesiastical Review* (September, 1906). To facilitate this, the faithful should be provided with a booklet containing the Gregorian melodies as well as vernacular translations.

NOTICE : When Pope Pius XII modified holy week in 1955, he changed the traditional times of the ceremonies. These changes *de facto* obliterated TENEBRAE. Moreover, if the 1950 holy week is offered following the Pius XII times, it will militate against Vespers being prayed after the Mass, for obvious reasons.

(1950) MAUNDY THURSDAY • Stripping of the Altars

Feria quinta in Coena Domini *Ad Denudationem Altarium*

1950 • At the end of Vespers the Celebrant and ministers come back to the Altar, the Celebrant and Deacon wearing purple stoles over the alb. The Celebrant begins the antiphon "Divisérunt sibi," not singing it. The choir continues the antiphon and Psalm 21 ("Deus Deus meus, réspice in me")—cf. page 114. The Celebrant, ministers, and acolytes strip the Altar. They leave only the Cross, covered with purple, and the six candles. They extinguish the candles and Sanctuary lamp. If there be other altars in the church, the Celebrant, ministers, and acolytes go to strip them in the same way. The choir does not recite the antiphon after the psalm until the Celebrant and his retinue return to the High Altar.

(1950) MAUNDY THURSDAY • Washing of the Feet

Feria quinta in Coena Domini *Ad Mandatum*

1950 • Father Fortescue wrote in 1917: "If the MAUNDY—i.e. the washing of thirteen men's feet—is performed, it may follow immediately the stripping of the altars or be done later in the day. This ceremony is generally now performed in cathedrals and religious houses only." (We recall that Mass on Holy Thursday was traditionally offered early in the morning.) If Catholic faithful are present who are accustomed to singing Vespers, Compline, or other parts of the Divine Office, nothing prevents them from singing some—or all—of the MAUNDY antiphons. In such cases, they should be provided with a booklet containing the Gregorian melodies with vernacular translations.

Good Friday • Preliminary Observations

The Friday Called "Good" • Father Herbert Thurston (d. 1939) wrote in 1904: "There are few scenes liturgically more impressive than the appearance of the church at the beginning of the service on Good Friday morning. The bare floor, the dismantled altar, the veiled crucifix, the unlighted candles, and then, when the little procession of the sacred ministers in their black vestments has silently made its way to the Sanctuary, the sudden prostration upon the altar-steps, where they seem to annihilate themselves in the very extremity of self-abandonment—all these are things that can hardly fail to produce an effect upon the most indifferent spectator."

Creeping to the Cross • This ceremony has many different names: Worship of the Cross, Solemn Veneration of the Cross, Adoration of the Cross, and so on. Prior to the Protestant Revolution, in England it was called "The Creeping to the Cross." Father Fortescue says it is not as ancient as the rest of Good Friday, and suggests that this ceremony possibly arose because all the statues were covered during all of Lent—on this, cf. Father Thurston "the Lenten Curtain" [*Lent and Holy Week*, pages 99ff.]—not just during Passiontide. As time went on, it was judged strange not to see the Crucifix on the very day of the Crucifix, so someone uncovered it on this day and a ceremony grew out of this. Father Fortescue believes this may have happened sometime around the 8th century. Naturally, other authors have different theories; e.g. see Cardinal Schuster [*Liber Sacramentorum*, Volume II, page 205]. According to James Monti, the first documented evidence for using a Crucifix, as opposed to a plain wooden Cross, is found in Sigibert's *Customary* (circa 1030AD). To learn about the different forms this ceremony took throughout history, cf. James Monti, *Roman Catholic Worship in the Middle Ages* (Ignatius Press, 2012), pages 409-439. The ceremony was changed in 1955; the congregation no longer "creeps to the Cross" with a triple genuflection—however, the priest and his retinue still do the triple genuflection {Goddard p182}.

Speaking about this ceremony, *The Catholic Encyclopedia* (Imprimatur 1909 by Most Reverend John M. Farley, Archbishop of New York) says: "The ignorant may allege grave disorder in the act of adoration of the Cross on bended knee. Is not adoration due to God alone? The answer may be found in our smallest catechism. The act in question is not intended as an expression of absolute supreme worship (*latreia*) which, of course, is due to God alone. The essential note of the ceremony is reverence (*proskynesis*) which has a relative character, and which may be best explained in the words of the Pseudo-Alcuin: *Prosternimur corpore ante crucem, mente ante Dominium. Veneramur crucem, per quam redempti sumus, et illum deprecamur, qui redemit.*" [Translated to English: "While we bend down in body before the cross we bend down in spirit before God. While we reverence the cross as the instrument of our redemption, we pray to Him who redeemed us."]

Another Roman Catholic book—*The Office of the Holy Week, According to the Roman Missal and Breviary* (1796AD)—has this to say about the Solemn Veneration of the Cross: "Next, both Priest and people adore Jesus Christ crucified, expressing their adoration by kneeling thrice before they kiss the sacred wounds represented by the figure on the cross. This ceremony is a great stumbling-block to Protestants, who think us guilty of idolatry by it, especially when the rubric calls it, The Adoration of the Cross, and the Choir at the same time sing, *We adore thy Cross, O Lord, &c.* But we presume they will give us leave to know the meaning of our own words and actions, and believe us, when we tell them, that our genuflexion, and kissing of the cross, are no more than outward expressions of the love and adoration which we bear in our hearts to Jesus Christ crucified; and that the words *adoration* and *adore*, as applied to the Cross, signify only that respect and veneration which is due to things relating to God and his service." Sir Walter Kirkham Blount published The Roman Catholic Holy Week Book in 1670AD which says: "The Adoration is not terminated in wood of the Cross, but in Iesus-Christ fastened thereon." Page 333 of *The Roman Missal for the Use of the Laity According to the Use of the Holy Roman Church Containing Also the Masses Proper to This Country in Their Respective Places* was published in Birmingham (1845) under the approval of the Roman Catholic bishops, and reads as follows: "The intention of the church in exposing the cross to our veneration on this day is that we might the more effectually raise up our hearts to **Him** who expired thereon for our redemption. Whenever, therefore, we kneel, or prostrate ourselves before a crucifix, it is **Jesus Christ** only whom we adore, and it is in him alone that our respects terminate."

[Editor's Note: The 1962 version has an Opening Prayer ("Deus qui peccáti véteris hereditárium mortem")—sung in front of the Altar, responded to by all present—but no such prayer existed in the 1950 version. In the traditional Good Friday, candlesticks and Crucifix are on the Altar, whereas in the 1962 version the Altar is completely bare. In 1950, the service was called Missa Praesanctificatorum ("Mass of the Presanctified") or simply Good Friday Morning. The 1962 version is called "Solemn Liturgical Action of the Afternoon," and takes place around 3:00pm. In the 1950 version, the priest quietly reads everything (the lessons, the *Improperium*, and so forth) whereas in the 1962 version the priest listens while others sing those. A "lector" is spoken of {Fortescue p303} by the pre-1955 books, but this was assumed to be a man in minor orders. We know this "lector" was not a layman: for instance, an altar server is instructed to "hold the lector's biretta" while he chants the lessons, and no layman at that time would have worn a biretta. In the 1962 version, a "capable reader" is spoken of. On Holy Thursday, this capable reader "wearing a surplice, may read or sing the Epistle while the Celebrant stands at the Altar and listens." On Good Friday, a "capable reader" may sing the Old Testament readings at the beginning. On Holy Saturday, a "capable reader" may read all the Old Testament readings and even the Epistle. On this, see *Mass & Vespers* (Solesmes, 1957) pages 547, 572, 576, 634, and 639. Almost seventy years later, with the benefit of hindsight, our editorial suggestion is that no man should read or sing the Epistle at any time if he be not, at a minimum, tonsured.]

<u>The Usage of Greek</u> • The first liturgical language of the West seems not to have been Latin: it was Greek. Even in Rome itself, Koine Greek was favored by Christians. Throughout the Roman Empire, Greek and Latin coëxisted alongside each other—and both were spoken by all classes. Pope Saint Victor, at the very end of the 2nd century, is said to have transitioned the Western Church from Greek to Latin. Saint Augustine of Hippo, born in 354AD, was the first Western scholar who wrote exclusively in Latin. Scholars agree that the Kyrie Eleyson (from the *Ordo Missae*) is not a "survivor" from the original Greek liturgy—it was imported from the East much later. The Good Friday Hagios o Theos, on the other hand, is a different matter and its provenance is not known. It is very ancient; e.g. it occurs in 239laon|927, from approximately 927AD, as shown here:

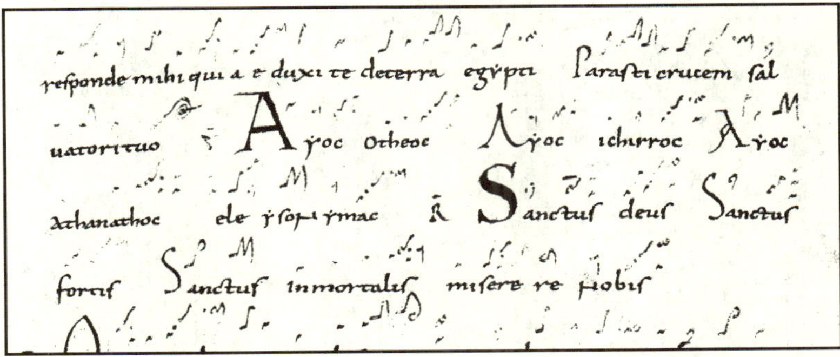

Greek remained in the Latin liturgy for a surprisingly long time. At Easter, it was a custom to proclaim the readings in Latin and Greek. Dr. Peter Wagner (d. 1931) of Fribourg wrote as follows:

> "Manuscripts of non-Roman origin but of the Roman Liturgy confirm the use of Greek chant in the Latin Church. Not infrequently we find the Greek Gloria and Credo (usually written in Latin character); I refer to 381sanGall|928 **[circa 928AD]** and 382sanGall|1030 **[circa 1030AD]**; the MS. 9449 of the National Library at Paris and so forth. Also at S. Blasien in the Black Forest the Gloria was sung both in Latin and Greek. A troper of Montauriol even has the Greek Sanctus and Agnus provided with neums. The above mentioned Paris MS. (it belongs to the 11th century) has a number of chants in the Greek language for the Mass of Pentecost, in addition to which the *Codex 1235 nouv. acquis.* of the same Library, of the 12th century, indicates for the Circumcision the Alleluia verse *Dies sanctificatus* in Greek. [...] The scribes seldom knew Greek, and so these renderings of Greek texts in Latin characters teem with mistakes of every kind. In the Paris MS. 9449 the Introit *Spiritus Domini*, which is provided with rich tropes, is followed by the subjoined text (fol. 49): *Natis thos o theos ke dios corpis this tesan ey extri autu kepye thosan oy me sontes autu a proposo tu autu. Gratias agamus alme Trinitatis semper. Pneupma tu kyrriu. Doxa patri ke yo ke ayo pneumati. Ke nim Kea im ke ystus oco nathon oeo non amen. Pneuma tu kyrriu eplyros empti oygumenu alleluja. Keu thu tbo tho sin craton panta tin nosin akyiphonis alleluia, alleluia, alleluia.*"

Dr. Wagner went on to cite many more examples. Sometimes, an entire chant will be written in Latin except for one word which is written in Greek; e.g. the Maundy Thursday communion antiphon in Bamberg6lit|905.

(1950) Good Friday • Station at Holy Cross in Jerusalem

Feria VI in Parasceve *Statio ad Sanctam Crucem in Jerusalem*

<u>Seven Parts</u>: The morning office of Good Friday consists of seven parts: (1) Lessons; (2) Passion; (3) Collects; (4) Creeping to the Cross; (5) Procession from the Place of Repose; (6) Mass of the Presanctified; (7) Vespers.

1950 • The color of the day is black. The Altar is entirely bare. It has no frontal nor tabernacle veil. The tabernacle is open and empty; the six candles are of unbleached wax and are not lighted till the Mass of the Presanctified. The candlesticks should be, if possible, neither gilt nor of silver, but dark in color. The Altar Cross is covered with either a purple veil or a black veil (both are allowed by the rubrics); but whichever color is used to cover the Altar Cross, all other crosses in the Church—including the Processional Cross—keep the purple veils of Passiontide until they are uncovered.

I OPENED THE SEA BEFORE THEE, AND THOU HAST OPENED MY SIDE WITH A LANCE.

I GAVE THEE WHOLESOME WATER TO DRINK OUT OF THE ROCK, AND THOU HAST BROUGHT ME GALL AND VINEGAR IN MY THIRST.

I LED THEE OUT OF EGYPT, HAVING DROWNED PHARAOH IN THE RED SEA; AND THOU HAST DELIVERED ME UP TO THE CHIEF PRIESTS.

FOR THY SAKE I STRUCK DOWN THE KINGS OF CANAAN: AND THOU HAST STRUCK ME ON THE HEAD WITH A REED. I GAVE THEE A ROYAL SCEPTER, AND THOU HAST GIVEN MY HEAD A CROWN OF THORNS. (Reproaches)

(1950) Good Friday • The Lessons (Part 1 of 7)

Feria VI in Parasceve *In Morte Domini*

1950 • The hour of None—that is to say, the ninth hour (**3:00pm**)—being ended in the choir, the Celebrant, Deacon and Subdeacon (vested in black, and without incense or lights) enter the Sanctuary and fully prostrate themselves, lying on the ground before the Altar in prayer. Meanwhile the acolytes spread a single cloth upon it. This done, the Celebrant ascends the Altar, kisses it in the middle, goes to the Epistle side, and there reads in a low voice the following Prophecy, which is at the same time read aloud in the place where the Epistle is usually chanted.

In Choro, dicta Nona, Sacerdos et ministri induti paramentis nigri coloris, sine luminaribus et incenso, procedunt ad Altare: et ante illud prostrati aliquandiu orant. Interim Acolythi unam tantum tobaleam extendunt super Altare. Sacerdos cum ministris, facta oratione, ascendit ad Altare, et osculatur illud in medio: deinde Lector accedit ad legendum Prophetiam in loco ubi legitur Epistola, et incipit eam sine titulo: quam etiam Sacerdos legit submissa voce apud Altare in cornu Epistolae.

FIRST LESSON. *Osee 6: 1-6*

Hæc dicit Dóminus: In tribulatióne sua mane consúrgent ad me: Veníte, et revertámur ad Dóminum: quia ipse cepit, et sanábit nos: percútiet, et curábit nos. Vivificábit nos post duos dies: in die tértia suscitábit nos, et vivémus in conspéctu ejus. Sciémus, sequemúrque, ut cognoscámus Dóminum: quasi dilúculum præparátus est egréssus ejus, et véniet quasi imber nobis temporáneus, et serótinus terræ. Quid fáciam tibi Éphraïm? Quid fáciam tibi Juda? Misericórdia vestra quasi nubes matutína, et quasi ros mane pertránsiens. Propter hoc dolávi in prophétis, occídi eos in verbis oris mei: et judícia tua quasi lux egrediéntur. Quia misericórdiam vólui, et non sacrifícium, et sciéntiam Dei plus quam holocáusta. (*"Deo Grátias" is not said.*)

HUS says the Lord: Ay, in their distress they will be waiting full early at my door; Back to the Lord! will be their cry; salve he only can bring, that wounded us; hand that smote us shall heal. Dead men today and tomorrow, on the third day he will raise us up again, to live in his presence anew. Acknowledge we, cease we never to acknowledge the Lord, he will reveal himself, sure as the dawn, come back to us, sure as the rains of winter and spring come back to the earth. What way will serve with you, men of Ephraim? Juda, what way will serve? Ruth of yours is but momentary, fades like the early mist, like morning dew. What wonder I should send prophets first, to shape men to my will if they could, and then utter my sentence of ruin? Believe me, this doom of thine shall be clear as daylight. A tender heart wins favour with me, not sacrifice; God's acknowledging, not victim's destroying.

FIRST TRACT. *Habacuc 3*

Dómine, audívi audítum tuum, et tímui: considerávi ópera tua, et expávi. ℣. In médio duórum animálium innotescéris: dum appropinquáverint anni, cognoscéris: dum advénerit tempus, ostendéris. ℣. In eo, dum conturbáta fúerit ánima mea: in ira, misericórdiæ memor eris. ℣. Deus a Líbano véniet, et Sanctus de monte umbróso et condénso. ℣. Opéruit cælos majéstas ejus: et laudis ejus plena est terra.

I HAVE HEARD, LORD, the tale of thy renown, awe-stricken at the divine power thou hast. ℣. There, between the forms of two living creatures, reveal that power; so thou shalt be made known when the years have run their course, so thou wilt appear, when the time comes for thy appearing. ℣. When most my heart is troubled, at the very time when thou art angry, thou wilt bethink thee of thy merciful promise. ℣. He comes from Lebanon, the Lord, the Holy One, from the dark forests on the hills. ℣. Heaven is overspread by his magnificence, earth has no room for his renown.

Let us pray.
℣. To your knees.
℞. Arise.

Celebrant: Orémus.
Deacon: ℣. Flectámus génua.
Subdeacon: ℞. Leváte.

O GOD, by whom Judas for his guilt was punished, and, for guilt humbly acknowledged, yonder thief was granted his reward, be it ours to profit by thy clemency. To each, in the hour of his Passion, our Lord Jesus Christ gave the recompense each had earned; may he rid us of our old perverse ways, and bestow on us the grace to rise again with him; who with thee.

Deus, a quo et Judas reátus sui pœnam, et confessiónis suæ latro præmium sumpsit, concéde nobis tuæ propitiatiónis efféctum: ut, sicut in passióne sua Jesus Christus, Dóminus noster, divérsa utrísque íntulit stipéndia meritórum; ita nobis, abláto vetustátis erróre, resurrectiónis suæ grátiam largiátur: Qui tecum.

SECOND LESSON. *Exodus 12: 1-11*

Identical to the 9th Prophecy on (1950 version) Holy Saturday:

IT WAS WHILE they were still in the land of Egypt that the Lord said to Moses and Aaron, For you, this month is to lead in all the months, to be the first month of the year. Make this proclamation to the whole assembly of Israel: On the tenth day of this month, each family, each household, is to choose out a yearling for its own use. Or, if there are not enough of them to eat a whole lamb, the head of the family must call in some neighbour who lives close by, so that a lamb shall not be too much for their needs. It must be a male yearling lamb, or a male yearling kid, that you choose, with no blemish on it. These victims must be kept ready till the fourteenth day of the month, and on the evening of that day the whole people of Israel must immolate. They must take some of the blood, and sprinkle it on the doorway, jambs and lintel alike, of the house in which the lamb is being eaten. Their meat that night must be roasted over the fire, their bread unleavened; wild herbs must be all their seasoning. No part must be eaten raw, or boiled, it must be roasted over the fire; head, feet, and entrails, all must be consumed, so that nothing remains till next day; whatever is left over, you must put in the fire and burn it. And this is to be the manner of your eating it; your loins must be girt, your feet ready shod, and every man's staff in his hand; all must be done in haste. It is the night of the Pasch, the Lord's passing by.

In diébus illis: Dixit Dóminus ad Móysen et Áäron in terra Ægýpti: Mensis iste vobis princípiũ ménsium primus erit in ménsibus anni. Loquímini ad univérsum cœtum filiórum Ísraël, et dícite eis: Décima die mensis hujus tollat unusquísque agnum per famílias et domos suas. Sin autem minor est númerus, ut suffícere possit ad vescéndum agnum, assúmet vicínum suum, qui junctus est dómui suæ, juxta númerum animárum, quæ suffícere possunt ad esum agni. Erit autem agnus absque mácula, másculus, anníeulus: juxta quem ritum tollétis et hædum. Et servábitis eum usque ad quartam décimã diem mensis hujus: immolabítque eum univérsa multitúdo filiórum Ísraël ad vésperam. Et sument de sánguine ejus, ac ponent super utrúmque postem et in superlimináribus domórum, in quibus cómedent illum. Et edent carnes nocte illa assas igni, et ázymos panes cum lactúcis agréstibus. Non comedétis ex eo crudum quid nec coctum aqua, sed tantum assum igni: caput cum pédibus ejus et intestínis vorábitis. Nec remanébit quidquam ex eo usque mane. Si quid resíduum fúerit, igne comburétis. Sic autem comedétis illum: Renes vestros accingétis, et calceaménta habébitis in pédibus, tenéntes báculos in mánibus, et comedétis festinánter: est enim Phase (id est tránsitus) Dómini. *("Deo Grátias" is not said.)*

SECOND TRACT. *Ps 139: 2-10, 14*

Éripe me, Dómine, ab hómine malo: a viro iníquo líbera me. ℣. Qui cogitavérunt malítias in corde: tota die constituébant prœlia. ℣. Acuérunt linguas suas sicut serpéntis: venénum áspidum sub lábiis eórum. ℣. Custódi me, Dómine, de manu peccatóris: et ab homínibus iníquis líbera me. ℣. Qui cogitavérunt supplantáre gressus meos: abscondérunt supérbi láqueum mihi. ℣. Et funes extendérunt in láqueum pédibus meis: juxta iter scándalum posuérunt mihi. ℣. Dixi Dómino: Deus meus es tu: exáudi, Dómine, vocem oratiónis meæ. ℣. Dómine, Dómine, virtus salútis meæ: obúmbra caput meum in die belli. ℣. Ne tradas me a desidério meo peccatóri: cogitavérunt advérsus me: ne derelínquas me, ne umquam exalténtur. ℣. Caput circúitus eórum: labor labiórum ipsórum opériet eos. ℣. Verúmtamen justi confitebúntur nómini tuo: et habitábunt recti cum vultu tuo.

RESCUE ME, Lord, from human malice, save me from the lovers of oppression, always plotting treachery in their hearts, always intent on strife, tongues sharp as the tongues of serpents, lips that conceal the poison of asps. ℣. Preserve me, Lord, from the power of sinful men, save me from these lovers of oppression who are plotting to trip my feet. What hidden snares they set for me, these tyrants, what nets they spread to catch me, what traps they lay in my path! ℣. To the Lord I make my appeal, Thou art my God, listen to the voice that pleads with thee. ℣. My Lord, my Master, my strong deliverer, it is thou that shieldest my head in the day of battle. ℣. Do not betray my hopes, Lord, into the hands of the wicked; do not forsake me, and let the schemers triumph. ℣. This be the fruit of their conspiracy, that all their busy whispering should recoil upon themselves. ℣. Honest men will yet live to praise thy name; upright hearts enjoy the smile of thy favour.

(1950) Good Friday • The Passion (Part 2 of 7)

Feria VI in Parasceve *Passio Domini Secundum Joannem*

The Passion is begun exactly as on Palm Sunday, except that on Good Friday there are no palms to hold.

Deacons: [C] *Chronista;* [S] *Synagoga;* ✠ *Christus.*

PASSIO DOMINI NOSTRI JESU CHRISTI SECUNDUM JOANNEM.

The passion of our Lord Jesus Christ as it is written by Saint John.

At this time, Jesus, with his disciples, went out across the Cedron
In illo témpore: Egréssus est Jesus cum discípulis suis trans torréntem Cedron,

valley. Here there was a garden, into which he and his disciples went.
ubi erat hortus, in quem introívit ipse et discípuli ejus.

Judas, his betrayer, knew the place well; Jesus and his disciples
Sciébat autem et Judas, qui tradébat eum, locum: quia frequénter Jesus

had often forgathered in it. There, then, Judas came, accompanied
convénerat illuc cum discípulis suis. Judas ergo cum accepísset cohórtem,

by the guard, and officers sent by the chief priests and Pharisees, with lanterns and
et a pontifícibus et pharisǽis minístros, venit illuc cum latérnis et

torches and weapons. So Jesus, knowing well what was to befall him, went out
fácibus et armis. Jesus ítaque sciens ómnia, quæ ventúra erant super eum, procéssit,

to meet them, and asked: ✠ Who is it you are looking for? [C] They answered:
et dixit eis: Quem quǽritis? Respondérunt ei:

[S] Jesus of Nazareth. [C] And he told them: ✠ I am Jesus of Nazareth. [C] And
Jesum Nazarénum. Dicit eis Jesus: Ego sum.

there was Judas, his betrayer, standing in their company. When he said to them, I am
Stabat autem et Judas, qui tradébat eum, cum ipsis. Ut ergo dixit eis:

Jesus of Nazareth, they all shrank back, and fell to the ground. So, once more, Jesus
Ego sum: abiérunt retrórsum, et cecidérunt in terram. Íterum ergo

asked them: ✠ Who is it you are looking for? [C] and when they said: [S] Jesus
interrogávit eos: Quem quǽritis? Illi autem dixérunt:

of Nazareth, [C] he answered: ✠ I have told you already that I am Jesus. If I am
Jesum Nazarénum. Respóndit Jesus: Dixi vobis, quia ego sum:

the man you are looking for, let these others go free. [C] Thus he would make
si ergo me quǽritis, sínite hos abíre. Ut implerétur sermo,

good the words he had spoken to them, I have not lost any of those whom thou
quem dixit: Quia quos dedísti mihi, non pérdidi ex eis quemquam.

hast entrusted to me. Then Simon Peter, who had a sword, drew it, and struck the
Simon ergo Petrus habens gládium edúxit eum: et percússit

high priest's servant, cutting off his right ear; Malchus was the name of the servant.
pontíficis servum: et abscídit aurículam ejus déxteram. Erat autem nomen servo Malchus.

Whereupon Jesus said to Peter: ✠ Put thy sword back into its sheath. Am I not to
Dixit ergo Jesus Petro: Mitte gládium tuum in vagínam.

drink that cup which my Father himself has appointed for me? [C] And now the
Cálicem, quem dedit mihi Pater, non bibam illum?

guard, with their captain, and the Jewish officers arrested Jesus and pinioned him.
Cohors ergo et tribúnus et minístri Judæórum comprehendérunt Jesum, et ligavérunt eum:

BEFORE THE HIGH PRIEST

They led him off, in the first instance, to Annas, father-in-law of Caiphas, who
et adduxérunt eum ad Annam primum, erat enim socer Cáïphæ,

held the high priesthood in that year. (It was this Caiphas who had given it as
qui erat póntifex anni illíus. Erat autem Cáïphas,

his advice to the Jews, that it was best to put one man to death for the sake of
qui consílium déderat Judǽis: Quia expédit, unum hóminem mori pro pópulo.

the people.) Simon Peter followed Jesus, with another disciple; this disciple was
Sequebátur autem Jesum Simon Petrus et álius discípulus.

acquainted with the high priest, and went into the high priest's court with Jesus,
Discípulus autem ille erat notus pontífici, et introívit cum Jesu in átrium pontíficis.

while Peter stood at the door without. Afterwards the other disciple, who was
Petrus autem stabat ad óstium foris. Exívit ergo discípulus álius,

the high priest's acquaintance, went out and spoke to the door-keeper, and so
qui erat notus pontífici, et dixit ostiáriæ:

brought Peter in. This maid-servant who kept the door asked Peter: [S] Art thou
et introdúxit Petrum. Dicit ergo Petro ancílla ostiária:

another of this man's disciples? [C] And he said: [S] Not I. [C] It was cold,
Numquid et tu ex discípulis es hóminis istíus? Dicit ille: Non sum.

and the servants and officers had made a charcoal fire, and stood there warming
Stabant autem servi et minístri ad prunas, quia frigus erat, et calefaciébant se:

themselves; there Peter stood too, warming himself with the rest. And now the high
erat autem cum eis et Petrus stans et calefáciens se.

priest questioned Jesus about his disciples, and about his teaching. Jesus answered:
Póntifex ergo interrogávit Jesum de discípulis suis et de doctrína ejus. Respóndit ei Jesus:

✠ I have spoken openly before the world; my teaching has been given in the
Ego palam locútus sum mundo: ego semper dócui

synagogue and in the temple, where all the Jews forgather; nothing that I have said
in synagóga et in templo, quo omnes Judǽi convéniunt: et in occúlto locútus sum nihil.

was said in secret. Why dost thou question me? Ask those who listened to me what
Quid me intérrogas? intérroga eos, qui audiérunt,

my words were; they know well enough what I said. [C] When he spoke thus, one
quid locútus sim ipsis: ecce, hi sciunt, quæ díxerim ego. Hæc autem cum dixísset,

of the officers, who was standing by, struck Jesus on the cheek, saying: [S] Is this
unus assístens ministrórum dedit álapam Jesu, dicens:

how thou makest answer to the high priest? [C] Jesus answered: ✠ If there was
Sic respóndes pontífici? Respóndit ei Jesus:

harm in what I said, tell us what was harmful in it; if not, why dost thou strike me?
Si male locútus sum, testimónium pérhibe de malo: si autem bene, quid me cædis?

[C] Annas, you must know, had sent him on, still bound, to the high priest Caiphas.
Et misit eum Annas ligátum ad Cáïpham pontíficem.

Saint Peter's Denial

Meanwhile Simon Peter stood there, and warmed himself. So they asked him:
Erat autem Simon Petrus stans et calefáciens se. Dixérunt ergo ei:

[S] Art thou, too, one of his disciples? [C] And he denied it, saying: [S] Not I.
Numquid et tu ex discípulis ejus es? Negávit ille et dixit: Non sum.

[C] One of the of the high priest's servants, a kinsman of the man whose ear Peter
Dicit ei unus ex servis pontíficis, cognátus ejus, cujus abscídit Petrus auriculam:

had cut off, asked: [S] Did I not see thee with him in the garden? [C] Whereupon
Nonne ego te vidi in horto cum illo?

Peter denied again; and immediately the cock crew.
Íterum ergo negávit Petrus: et statim gallus cantávit.

Before Pontius Pilate

And now they led Jesus away from the house of Caiphas to the governor's palace.
Addúcunt ergo Jesum a Cáïpha in prætórium.

It was morning, and they would not enter the palace themselves; there was the
Erat autem mane: et ipsi non introiérunt in prætórium,

paschal meal to be eaten, and they must not incur defilement. And so Pilate went
ut non contaminaréntur, sed ut manducárent pascha. Exívit ergo Pilátus

to meet them without, and said; [S] What charge do you bring against this man?
ad eos foras et dixit: Quam accusatiónem affértis advérsus hóminem hunc?

[C] They answered; [S] We would not have given him up to thee, if he had not
Respondérunt et dixérunt ei: Si non esset hic malefáctor, non tibi tradidissémus eum.

been a malefactor. [C] Pilate said to them: [S] Take him yourselves and judge
Dixit ergo eis Pilátus: Accípite eum vos,

him according to your own law. [C] Whereupon the Jews said to him: [S] We
et secúndum legem vestram judicáte eum. Dixérunt ergo ei Judǽi:

have no power to put any man to death. [C] This was in fulfilment of the words
Nobis non licet interfícere quemquam. Ut sermo Jesu implerétur,

Jesus had spoken when he prophesied what death he was to die. So Pilate went
quem dixit, signíficans, qua morte esset moritúrus.

back into the palace, and summoned Jesus, and asked him: [S] Art thou the king
Introívit ergo íterum in prætórium Pilátus, et vocávit Jesum et dixit ei: Tu es Rex Judæórum?

of the Jews? [C] Jesus answered: ✠ Dost thou say this of thy own accord, or is
Respóndit Jesus: A temetípso hoc dicis,

it what others have told thee of me? [C] And Pilate answered: [S] Am I a Jew?
an álii dixérunt tibi de me? Respóndit Pilátus: Numquid ego Judǽus sum?

It is thy own nation, and its chief priests, who have given thee up to me. What
Gens tua et pontífices tradidérunt te mihi:

offence hast thou committed? [C] Jesus said: ✠ My kingdom does not belong to
quid fecísti? Respóndit Jesus: Regnum meum non est de hoc mundo.

this world. If my kingdom were one which belonged to this world, my servants
Si ex hoc mundo esset regnum meum,

would be fighting, to prevent my falling into the hands of the Jews; but no, my
minístri mei útique decertárent, ut non tráderer Judǽis:

kingdom does not take its origin here. [C] Pilate asked: [S] Thou art a king, then?
nunc autem regnum meum non est hinc. Dixit ítaque ei Pilátus: Ergo Rex es tu?

[C] And Jesus answered: ✠ It is thy own lips that have called me a king. What I
Respóndit Jesus: Tu dicis, quia Rex sum ego.

was born for, what I came into the world for, is to bear witness of the truth. Whoever
Ego in hoc natus sum et ad hoc veni in mundum, ut testimónium perhíbeam veritáti:

belongs to the truth, listens to my voice. [C] Pilate said to him, [S] What is truth?
omnis, qui est ex veritáte, audit vocem meam. Dicit ei Pilátus: Quid est véritas?

PILATE OFFERS A CHOICE

And with that he went back to the Jews again, and told them: [S] I can find no
Et cum hoc dixisset, iterum exivit ad Judǽos, et dicit eis: Ego nullam invénio
fault in him. You have a custom of demanding that I should release one prisoner at
in eo causam. Est autem consuetúdo vobis, ut unum dimíttam vobis in Pascha:
paschal time; would you have me release the king of the Jews? [C] Whereupon they
vultis ergo dimíttam vobis Regem Judæórum? Clamavérunt ergo
all made a fresh outcry: [S] Barabbas, not this man. [C] Barabbas was a robber.
rursum omnes, dicéntes: Non hunc, sed Barábbam. Erat autem Barábbas latro.

SCOURGED & CROWNED WITH THORNS

Then Pilate took Jesus and scourged him. And the soldiers put on his head a crown
Tunc ergo apprehéndit Pilátus Jesum et flagellávit. Et mílites plecténtes corónam de spinis, imposuérunt cápiti ejus:
which they had woven out of thorns, and dressed him in a scarlet cloak; they would
et veste purpúrea circumdedérunt eum.
come up to him and say: [S] Hail, king of the Jews, [C] and then strike him on the
Et veniébant ad eum, et dicébant: Ave, Rex Judæórum. Et dabant ei álapas.
face. And now Pilate went out again, and said: [S] See, I am bringing him out to
Exívit ergo íterum Pilátus foras et dicit eis: Ecce, addúco vobis eum foras,
you, to show that I cannot find any fault in him. [C] Then, as Jesus came out, still
ut cognoscátis, quia nullam invénio in eo causam. (Exívit ergo Jesus portans corónam
wearing the crown of thorns and the scarlet cloak, he said to them: [S] See, here
spíneam et purpúreum vestiméntum.) Et dicit eis:
is the man.
Ecce homo.

NO KING EXCEPT CAESAR

When the chief priests and their officers saw him, they cried out: [S] Crucify him,
Cum ergo vidíssent eum pontífices et minístri, clamábant, dicéntes: Crucifige,
crucify him. [C] Pilate said, [S] Take him yourselves and crucify him; I cannot
crucifíge eum. Dicit eis Pilátus: Accípite eum vos et crucifígite: ego enim
find any fault in him. [C] The Jews answered: [S] We have our own law, and
non invénio in eo causam. Respondérunt ei Judǽi: Nos legem habémus,
by our law he ought to die, for pretending to be the Son of God. [C] When Pilate
et secúndum legem debet mori, quia Fílium Dei se fecit. Cum ergo
heard this said, he was more afraid than ever; going back into the palace, he asked
audísset Pilátus hunc sermónem, magis tímuit. Et ingréssus est prætórium iterum: et dixit ad

EGREDIMINI ET VIDETE FILIAE SION REGEM SALOMONEM IN DIADEMATE. GO FORTH, YE DAUGHTERS OF SION, AND SEE KING SOLOMON IN THE DIADEM, WHEREWITH HIS MOTHER CROWNED HIM... (CANT 3:11)

HEROD WITH HIS ARMY MADE A JEST OF HIM, AND MOCKED HIM, PUT ON HIM A WHITE GARMENT, AND SENT HIM BACK TO PILATE. (Luke 23:11)

ET ILLUDEBANT EI DICENTES: ASCENDE CALVE, ASCENDE CALVE. LITTLE BOYS CAME OUT OF THE CITY AND MOCKED ELISHA, SAYING: GO UP, THOU BALD HEAD; GO UP, THOU BALD HEAD. (IV KINGS 2:23)

Jesus: [S] Whence hast thou come? [C] But Jesus gave him no answer. Pilate
Jesum: Unde es tu? Jesus autem respónsum non dedit ei. Dicit ergo

said: [S] Hast thou no word for me? Dost thou not know that I have power to
ei Pilátus: Mihi non lóqueris? nescis, quia potestátem hábeo crucifígere te,

crucify thee, and power to release thee? [C] Jesus answered: ✠ Thou wouldst not
et potestátem hábeo dimíttere te? Respóndit Jesus:

have any power over me at all, if it had not been given thee from above. That is
Non habéres potestátem advérsum me ullam, nisi tibi datum esset désuper.

why the man who gave me up to thee is more guilty yet. [C] After this, Pilate
Proptérea, qui me trádidit tibi, majus peccátum habet. Et exínde quærébat

was for releasing him, but the Jews went on crying out: [S] Thou art no friend
Pilátus dimíttere eum. Judǽi autem clamábant dicéntes:

of Caesar, if thou dost release him; the man who pretends to be a king is Caesar's
Si hunc dimíttis, non es amícus Cǽsaris. Omnis enim, qui se regem facit, contradícit Cǽsari.

rival. [C] When Pilate heard them speak thus, he brought Jesus out, and sat down
Pilátus autem cum audísset hos sermónes, addúxit foras Jesum,

on the judgement seat, in a place which is called Lithostrotos; its Hebrew name is
et sedit pro tribunáli, in loco, qui dícitur Lithóstrotos, hebráice autem

Gabbatha. It was now about the sixth hour, on the eve of the paschal feast. He said
Gábbatha. Erat autem Parascéve Paschæ, hora quasi sexta,

to the Jews: [S] See, here is your king. [C] But they cried out: [S] Away with
et dicit Judǽis: Ecce Rex vester. Illi autem clamábant: Tolle,

him, away with him, crucify him. [C] Pilate said to them: [S] Shall I crucify
tolle, crucifíge eum. Dicit eis Pilátus: Regem vestrum crucifígam?

your king? [C] The chief priests answered: [S] We have no king, except Caesar.
Respondérunt pontífices: Non habémus regem nisi Cǽsarem.

CRUCIFIED FOR OUR OFFENSES

Thereupon he gave Jesus up into their hands, to be crucified: and they, once he
Tunc ergo trádidit eis illum, ut crucifigerétur.

was in their hands, led him away. So Jesus went out, carrying his own cross, to
Suscepérunt autem Jesum et eduxérunt. Et bájulans sibi Crucem, exívit in eum,

the place named after a skull; its Hebrew name is Golgotha. There they crucified
qui dícitur Calváriæ, locum, hebráice autem Gólgotha: ubi crucifixérunt eum,

him, and with him two others, one on each side with Jesus in the midst. And Pilate
et cum eo álios duos, hinc et hinc, médium autem Jesum.

wrote out a proclamation, which he put on the cross; it ran, Jesus of Nazareth,
Scripsit autem et títulum Pilátus: et pósuit super crucem. Erat autem scriptum: Jesus Nazarénus,

the king of the Jews. This proclamation was read by many of the Jews, since the
Rex Judæórum. Hunc ergo títulum multi Judæórum legérunt,

place where Jesus was crucified was close to the city; it was written in Hebrew,
quia prope civitátem erat locus, ubi crucifíxus est Jesus. Et erat scriptum hebráice,

Greek, and Latin. And the Jewish chief priests said to Pilate: [S] Thou shouldst
græce et latine. Dicébant ergo Piláto pontífices Judæórum:

not write, The king of the Jews; thou shouldst write, This man said, I am the king
Noli scríbere Rex Judæórum, sed quia ipse dixit: Rex sum Judæórum.

of the Jews. [C] Pilate's answer was: [S] What I have written, I have written.
Respóndit Pilátus: Quod scripsi, scripsi.

[C] The soldiers, when they had crucified Jesus, took up his garments, which
Mílites ergo cum crucifixíssent eum, accepérunt vestiménta ejus

they divided into four shares, one share for each soldier. They took up his cloak,
(et fecérunt quátuor partes: unicuíque míliti partem), et túnicam.

too, which was without seam, woven from the top throughout; so they said to
Erat autem túnica inconsútilis, désuper contéxta per totum. Dixérunt ergo

one another: [S] Better not to tear it; let us cast lots to decide whose it shall be.
ad ínvicem: Non scindámus eam, sed sortiámur de illa, cujus sit.

[C] This was in fulfilment of the passage in scripture which says: They divide
Ut Scriptúra impleerétur, dicens: Partíti sunt

my spoils among them; cast lots for my clothing. So it was, then, that the soldiers
vestiménta mea sibi: et in vestem meam misérunt sortem. Et mílites quidem hæc fecérunt.

occupied themselves; and meanwhile his mother, and his mother's sister, Mary the
Stabant autem juxta Crucem Jesu Mater ejus et soror Matris ejus,

wife of Cleophas, and Mary Magdalen, had taken their stand beside the cross of
María Cléophæ, et María Magdaléne.

Jesus. And Jesus, seeing his mother there, and the disciple, too, whom he loved,
Cum vidísset ergo Jesus Matrem et discípulum stantem, quem diligébat,

standing by, said to his mother: ✠ Woman, this is thy son. [C] Then he said to
dicit Matri suæ: Múlier, ecce fílius tuus. Deínde dicit

the disciple: ✠ This is thy mother. [C] And from that hour the disciple took her
discípulo: Ecce mater tua. Et ex illa hora accépit eam discípulus in sua.

into his own keeping. And now Jesus knew well that all was achieved which the
Póstea sciens Jesus, quia ómnia consummáta sunt,

scripture demanded for its accomplishment; and he said: ✠ I am thirsty. [C] There
ut consummarétur Scriptúra, dixit: Sítio.

was a jar there full of vinegar; so they filled a sponge with the vinegar and put it
Vas ergo erat pósitum acéto plenum. Illi autem spóngiam plenam acéto,

on a stick of hyssop, and brought it close to his mouth. Jesus drank the vinegar,
hyssópo circumponéntes, obtulérunt ori ejus. Cum ergo accepísset Jesus acétum,

and said: ✠ It is achieved. [C] Then he bowed his head, and yielded up his spirit.
dixit: Consummátum est. Et inclináte cápite trádidit spíritum.

Here all kneel, and a short pause is made. [In former days, the faithful would lie prostrate on the ground.]
Hic genuflectitur, et pausatur aliquantulum.

Him Whom They Have Pierced

The Jews would not let the bodies remain crucified on the sabbath, because that
Judǽi ergo (quóniam Parascéve erat), ut non remanérent in cruce córpora sábbato (erat enim

sabbath day was a solemn one; and since it was now the eve, they asked Pilate that
magnus dies ille sábbati), rogavérunt Pilátum, ut

the bodies might have their legs broken, and be taken away. And so the soldiers
frangeréntur eórum crura et tolleréntur. Venérunt ergo mílites:

came and broke the legs both of the one and of the other that were crucified with
et primi quidem fregérunt crura et altérius, qui crucifíxus est cum eo.

him; but when they came to Jesus, and found him already dead, they did not break
Ad Jesum autem cum venissent, ut vidérunt eum jam mórtuum, non fregérunt ejus crura,

his legs, but one of the soldiers opened his side with a spear; and immediately
sed unus mílitum láncea latus ejus apéruit, et contínuo

blood and water flowed out. He who saw it has borne his witness; and his witness is
exívit sanguis et aqua. Et qui vidit, testimónium perhíbuit: et verum est testimónium ejus.

worthy of trust. He tells what he knows to be the truth, that you, like him, may learn
Et ille scit, quia vera dicit: ut et vos credátis.

to believe. This was so ordained to fulfil what is written: You shall not break a single
Facta sunt enim hæc, ut Scriptúra implerétur: Os non comminuétis ex eo.

bone of his. And again, another passage in scripture says, They will look upon the
Et íterum ália Scriptúra dicit: Vidébunt

man whom they have pierced.
in quem transfixérunt.

Weeping Tone

The next part—considered analogous to the Gospel at Mass—is sung by the Deacon of the Mass in what is known as the "tonus planctus" or "weeping tone."

At this point, the Deacon of the Mass takes off the folded chasuble and puts on the "broad stole" (unless, of course, he chooses to wrap his folded chasuble and place it over his shoulder, which is more authentic but usually looks less elegant than a "broad stole"). The Deacon wears the "broad stole" from now until after the Celebrant's Communion; then he exchanges it for his folded chasuble. The Deacon brings the book of lessons to the Altar and kneels there, praying "Munda cor meum," but does not ask for the Celebrant's blessing. He sings the last part of the Passion as if it were the Gospel at Mass, except the acolytes stand on either side of the Subdeacon with joined hands, not holding candles. There is no incense, and the Celebrant does not kiss the book afterwards.

1950 • *Quod sequitur, legitur in tono Evangelii: et dicitur "Munda cor meum," sed non petitur benedictio, et non deferuntur luminaria neque incensum, et Celebrans in fine non osculatur librum.*

[Editor's Note: Whenever the Passion is sung—viz. Palm Sunday, Holy Tuesday, Spy Wednesday, and Good Friday—the following rubric is given in the 1950 version: *Tonus Evangelii is seligendus est, qui habeat eundem Tenorem ac tonus Passionis; videlicet tonus, qui primo aut secundo loco ponitur in Cantorino, juxta Editionem typicam Vaticanam; non vero is, qui ibidem "Antiquior" declaratur.* Translated into English: *The Gospel tone to be chosen is that which has the same tenor as the Passion tone; namely, the tone provided in the Cantorinus, according to the typical Vatican edition, in the first or second place; not, however, that which is described in the same book as the "more ancient" tone.* This simply means the "more ancient tone" cannot be chosen since its Tenor (i.e. "reciting tone") does not match the Passion. This is a moot point, since there is no advantage to replacing the Weeping Tone.]

AFTER THIS JOSEPH OF ARIMATHEA, WHO WAS A DISCIPLE OF JESUS, BUT IN SECRET, FOR FEAR OF THE JEWS, ASKED PILATE TO LET HIM TAKE AWAY THE BODY OF JESUS. (John 19.38)

CALL ME NOT NOEMI—BEAUTIFUL—BUT CALL ME MARA—BITTER—FOR THE ALMIGHTY HATH QUITE FILLED ME WITH BITTERNESS. (Ruth 1.20)

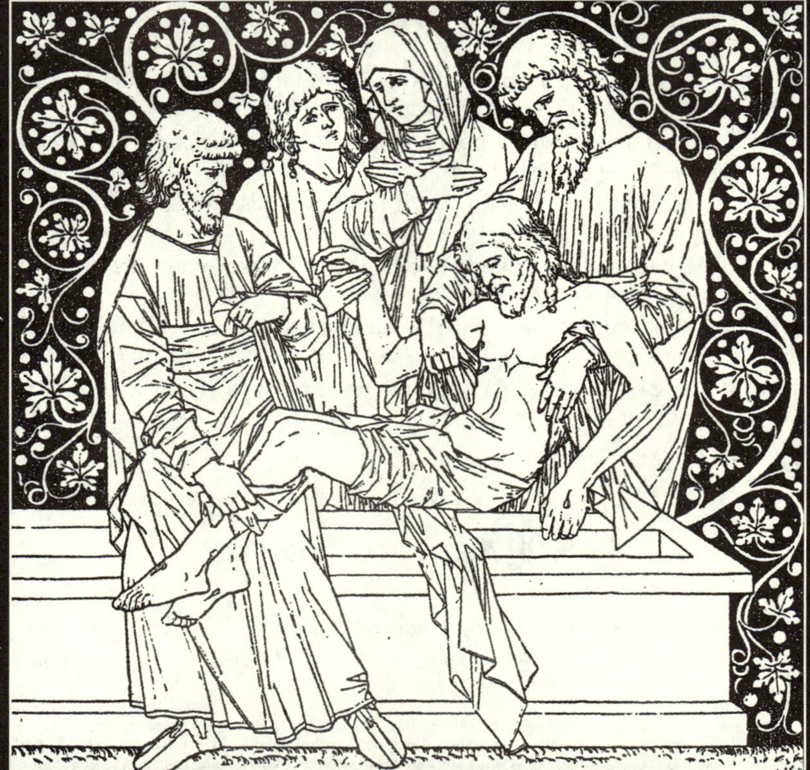

AND CAST HIM INTO AN OLD PIT, WHICH HAD NO WATER. (Gen 37.24)

IN THE SAME QUARTER WHERE HE WAS CRUCIFIED THERE WAS A GARDEN, WITH A NEW TOMB IN IT, ONE IN WHICH NO MAN HAD EVER YET BEEN BURIED. (Jn 19.41)

Post hæc autem rogávit Pilátum Joseph ab Arimathǽa (eo quod esset discípulus Jesu, occúltus autem propter metum Judæórum), ut tólleret corpus Jesu. Et permísit Pilátus. Venit ergo et tulit corpus Jesu. Venit autē et Nicodémus, qui vénerat ad Jesum nocte primum, ferens mixtúram myrrhæ et áloës, quasi libras centum. Accepérunt ergo corpus Jesu, et ligavérunt illud línteis cum aromátibus, sicut mos est Judǽis sepelíre. Erat autem in loco, ubi crucifíxus est, hortus: et in horto monuméntum novum, in quo nondum quisquam pósitus erat. Ibi ergo propter Parascéven Judæórũ, quia juxta erat monuméntum, posuérunt Jesum.

AFTER THIS Joseph of Arimathea, who was a disciple of Jesus, but in secret, for fear of the Jews, asked Pilate to let him take away the body of Jesus. Pilate gave him leave; so he came and took Jesus' body away; and with him was Nicodemus, the same who made his first visit to Jesus by night; he brought with him a mixture of myrrh and aloes, of about a hundred pounds' weight. They took Jesus' body, then, and wrapped it in winding-cloths with the spices; that is how the Jews prepare a body for burial. In the same quarter where he was crucified there was a garden, with a new tomb in it, one in which no man had ever yet been buried. Here, since the tomb was close at hand, they laid Jesus, because of the Jewish feast on the morrow.

If there is to be a sermon it may be preached at this moment.

[Editor's Note: The 1962 version of Good Friday seems not to allow a sermon; cf. McManus p82. The 1950 version allows a sermon; cf. Fortescue p304. In the 1950 Good Friday, the collects are read at the Epistle corner, whereas in the 1962 version the Missal is placed "at the center of the Altar."]

(1950) Good Friday • The Collects (Part 3 of 7)

Feria VI in Parasceve *Orationes Solemnes*

1950 • The priest then, standing at the Epistle side of the Altar, with hands joined, proceeds at once with the following prayers. | *Deinde Sacerdos, stans in cornu Epistolae, incipit absolute, junctis manibus:*

[Editor's Note: The Celebrant's vestments in the 1962 version of Good Friday are rather complicated: (1) The Celebrant begins the ceremony wearing only a black Stole; (2) before reading the Solemn Collects, the Celebrant dons a Cope; (3) when the Solemn Collects are finished, the Celebrant removes his Cope, wearing only a black Stole during the Veneration of the Cross; (4) after the Veneration of the Cross, the Celebrant puts on a purple Chasuble. The 1950 version was much simpler, since the Celebrant wore a black Chasuble the entire ceremony—from beginning to end—except during the Creeping to the Cross.

The 1950 rubric in the Missal says: *Oratio cantatur in tono feriali Orationis Missae, extensis manibus. Et hic modus servatur in subsequentibus.* That means the priest extends his hands whenever he says the prayer which follows "Leváte." Both prayers are sung, although musical notation is never provided for the prayer following "Leváte," which is sung to the Ferial tone. In terms of the melodies, the joining/extending of hands, and the prayers to be sung, there is no difference between the 1950 and 1962 versions—but monasteries often use the solemn tone instead of the ferial; cf. *Ordo Hebdomadae Sanctae* (Solesmes, 1961) page 284.

Regarding these solemn collects, Sir Walter Kirkham Blount (*The Office of Holy Week*, 1670AD) wrote as follows: "Public and solemn prayers are said, not only for the whole Church, and all its members, but also for infidels, and all sorts of people, in imitation of our Savior, Who upon the Cross prayed even for His enemies and executioners: to show that He shed His blood for the whole world."]

FOR THE CHURCH. *Pro Sancta Ecclesia*

Orémus, dilectíssimi nobis, pro Ecclésia sancta Dei: ut eam Deus et Dóminus noster pacificáre, adunáre, et custodíre dignétur toto orbe terrárum: subjíciens ei principátus, et potestátes: detque nobis quiétam et tranquíllam vitam degéntibus, glorificáre Deum Patrem omnipoténtem.

PRAY WE, dearly beloved, for God's holy Church; so may he, our Lord and our God, grant peace to it and make it one and keep it safe all the world over. Princedoms and powers may he quell before it, and ever in quiet and content live we, God the Almighty Father to glorify.

Let us pray.
℣. To your knees.
℟. Stand now erect.

Celebrant: Orémus.
Deacon: ℣. Flectámus génua.
Subdeacon: ℟. Leváte.

Almighty and everlasting God, who hast revealed thy glory to the whole world in Christ, thy merciful design pursue! Wide as the world thy Church is scattered; yet still, with unchanging faith, may it persevere in the confession of thy name. Through the same. ℟. Amen.

Omnípotens sempitérne Deus, qui glóriam tuam ómnibus in Christo géntibus revelásti: custódi ópera misericórdiæ tuæ; ut Ecclésia tua toto orbe diffúsa, stábili fide in confessióne tui nóminis persevéret. Per eúmdem Dóminum. ℟. Amen.

FOR THE SUPREME PONTIFF. *Pro Summo Pontifice*

PRAY WE also for our holy father, Pope (*Name of current Pope*); so may our Lord God, that chose him out for the bishopric, for holy Church's sake preserve him from all harm, of a divine flock the appointed shepherd.

Orémus et pro beatíssimo Papa nostro N.: ut Deus et Dóminus noster, qui elégit eum in órdine episcopátus, salvum atque incólumem custódiat Ecclésiæ suæ sanctæ, ad regéndum pópulum sanctum Dei.

Let us pray.
℣. To your knees.
℟. Stand now erect.

Celebrant: Orémus.
Deacon: ℣. Flectámus génua.
Subdeacon: ℟. Leváte.

Almighty and everlasting God, upon whose decree all things repose, in thy mercy hear us, and in thy love protect the bishop thou hast chosen. Under such governance as his, may the Christian folk, thy subjects, increase evermore in faith's deserving. Through our Lord. ℟. Amen.

Omnípotens sempitérne Deus, cujus judício univérsa fundántur: réspice propítius ad preces nostras, et eléctum nobis Antístitem tua pietáte consérva; ut christiána plebs, quæ te gubernátur auctóre, sub tanto Pontífice, credulitátis suæ méritis augeátur. Per Dóminum. ℟. Amen.

FOR CLERGY & PEOPLE. *Pro Omnibus Ordinibus Gradibusque Fidelium*

PRAY WE also for all bishops, priests, and deacons; for sub-deacon and acolyte, for exorcist, reader and door-keeper; for confessor, virgin and widow and all God's holy people at once.

Orémus et pro ómnibus Epíscopis, Presbýteris, Diacónibus, Subdiacónibus, Acólythis, Exorcístis, Lectóribus, Ostiáriis, Confessóribus, Virgínibus, Víduis: et pro omni pópulo sancto Dei.

Let us pray.
℣. To your knees.
℟. Stand now erect.

Celebrant: Orémus.
Deacon: ℣. Flectámus génua.
Subdeacon: ℟. Leváte.

Almighty and everlasting God, by whose spirit the whole body of thy Church is sanctified and led, listen to our prayer for all estates of men within it. Thy grace for all, that each in his degree may serve thee faithfully! Through the same Jesus Christ, thy Son, our Lord, who with thee in the bond of the same Holy Spirit lives and reigns and is God, world without end. ℟. Amen.

Omnípotens sempitérne Deus, cujus Spíritu totum corpus Ecclésiæ sanctificátur, et régitur: exáudi nos pro univérsis ordínibus supplicántes; ut grátiæ tuæ múnere, ab ómnibus tibi grádibus fidéliter serviátur. Per Dóminum nostrum Jesum Christum fílium tuum, qui tecum vivit et regnat in unitáte ejúsdem Spíritus Sancti, Deus, per ómnia sǽcula sæculórum. ℟. Amen.

[Editor's Note: At this point, many books insert a "Prayer for the Emperor" beginning with the words: *Orémus et pro Christianíssimo Imperatóre*... For example, *Officium Majoris Hebdomadae* (Dessain, 1949) contains this prayer. But Father Fortescue, writing in 1917, says: "The prayer for the Emperor is left out." In place of this prayer, a new prayer was added by Pope Pius XII in his 1955 reform: *Pro Res Publicas Moderantibus* ("For Those Engaged in Public Affairs").]

FOR CATECHUMENS. *Pro Catechumenis*

Orémus et pro catechúmenis nostris: ut Deus et Dóminus noster adapériat aures præcordiórum ipsórum, januámque misericórdiæ; ut per lavácrum regeneratiónis accépta remissióne ómnium peccatórum, et ipsi inveniántur in Christo Jesu Dómino nostro.

PRAY WE also for our catechumens; may our Lord God open their hearts to his word, open to them the gates of his mercy; acquitted of their sins by the cleansing power of the new birth, may these too be numbered with us, in Christ Jesus our Lord.

Celebrant: Orémus.
Deacon: ℣. Flectámus génua.
Subdeacon: ℟. Leváte.

Let us pray.
℣. To your knees.
℟. Stand now erect.

Omnípotens sempitérne Deus, qui Ecclésiam tuam nova semper prole fœcúndas: auge fidem et intelléctũ catechúmenis nostris; ut renáti fonte baptísmatis, adoptiónis tuæ fíliis aggregéntur. Per Dóminum. ℟. Amen.

Almighty and everlasting God, who still dost quicken the womb of thy Church with new offspring, grant our catechumens ever more faith, ever more discernment; in the clear fount of baptism born anew, claim they adoption among thy children. Through our Lord. ℟. Amen.

FOR THE NEEDS OF THE FAITHFUL. *Pro Fidelium Necessitatibus*

Orémus, dilectíssimi nobis, Deum Patrem omnipoténtem, ut cunctis mundum purget erróribus: morbos áuferat: famem depéllat: apériat cárceres: víncula dissólvat: peregrinántibus réditum: infirmántibus sanitátẽ: navigántibus portum salútis indúlgeat.

PRAY WE, dearly beloved, to God the Father almighty, that he would rid mankind of all false doctrine; all sickness drive away, all dearth dispel from us; prisons be opened now, and chains broken; homecoming may he grant to the traveller, health to the sick, and safe harbour to mariners.

Celebrant: Orémus.
Deacon: ℣. Flectámus génua.
Subdeacon: ℟. Leváte.

Let us pray.
℣. To your knees.
℟. Stand now erect.

Omnípotens sempitérne Deus, mæstórum consolátio, laborántium fortitúdo: pervéniant ad te preces de quacúmque tribulatióne clamántium; ut omnes sibi in necessitátibus suis misericórdiam tuam gáudeant affuísse. Per Dóminum. ℟. Amen.

Almighty and everlasting God, comfort, thou, of the mourner, strength of the weary, let there be no cry of distress but reaches thee! Let there be none but tells joyfully, how in his need thy mercy stood beside him. Through our Lord. ℟. Amen.

FOR HERETICS & SCHISMATICS. *Pro Unitate Ecclesiae*

Orémus et pro hæréticis, et schismáticis: ut Deus et Dóminus noster éruat eos ab erróribus univérsis; et ad sanctam matrem Ecclésiam Cathólicam, atque Apostólicam revocáre dignétur.

PRAY WE also for all heretics and schismatics; may our Lord God of all error disabuse them, and graciously bring them back to our holy mother, the Catholic and Apostolic Church.

Let us pray.
℣. To your knees.
℟. Stand now erect.

Celebrant: Orémus.
Deacon: ℣. Flectámus génua.
Subdeacon: ℟. Leváte.

Almighty and everlasting God, Savior of all, whose will is, none should perish, look down in mercy upon souls led astray by the foul fiend. Let such wayward souls think well, and leave their heretical imaginings, and have fellowship with us once again in thy truth. Through our Lord. ℟. Amen.

Omnípotens sempitérne Deus, qui salvas omnes, et néminem vis períre: réspice ad ánimas diabólica fraude decéptas; ut, omni hærética pravitáte depósita, errántium corda resipíscant, et ad veritátis tuæ rédeant unitátem. Per Dóminum. ℟. Amen.

FOR THE JEWS. *6 February 2008 version by Pope Benedict XVI*

PRAY WE also for the Jewish people: May our God and Lord enlighten their hearts, so that they may acknowledge Jesus Christ, savior of all men.

Orémus et pro Judǽis: ut Deus et Dóminus noster illúminet corda eórum, ut agnóscant Jesum Christum salvatórem ómnium hóminum.

Let us pray.
℣. To your knees.
℟. Stand now erect.

Celebrant: Orémus.
Deacon: ℣. Flectámus génua.
Subdeacon: ℟. Leváte.

Almighty and everlasting God, who desirest that all men be saved and come to the knowledge of truth, mercifully grant that, as the fullness of the Gentiles enters into thy Church, all Israel may be saved. Through Christ Our Lord. ℟. Amen.

Omnípotens sempitérne Deus, qui vis ut omnes hómines salvi fiant et ad agnitiónem veritátis véniant, concéde propítius, ut plenitúdine géntium in Ecclésiam tuam intránte omnis Ísraël salvus fiat. Per Christum Dñm nostrũ. ℟. Amen.

1950 *Below is how the prayer appeared in 1950, with a translation by Monsignor Knox. The section in brackets was a footnote from that 1950 publication; presumably Knox wrote it.*

Pray we also for misbelieving Jews; may our Lord God take away the veil from their hearts, that they too may acknowledge our Lord Jesus Christ.

Orémus et pro pérfidis Judǽis: ut Deus et Dóminus noster áuferat velámen de córdibus eórum; ut et ipsi agnóscant Jesum Christum Dóminum nostrum.

[*It is not known why the usual invitation to prayer is omitted at this point. The notion that the Jews are hereby rebuked for their mockery of our Lord, on the first Good Friday, is quite without foundation.*]

Non respondetur "Amen," nec dicitur "Orémus," aut "Flectámus génua," aut "Leváte," sed statim dicitur:

Almighty and everlasting God, who wilt not shut out even the hard hearts of Jewry from thy compassion, listen to the prayer we make for that people in their blindness. The light of Christ, who is thy truth, may these too acknowledge, and lie buried in their darkness no longer. Through the same Lord. ℟. Amen.

Omnípotens sempitérne Deus, qui étiam Judáïcam perfídiam a tua misericórdia non repéllis: exáudi preces nostras, quas pro illíus pópuli obcæcatióne deférimus; ut, ágnita veritátis tuæ luce, quæ Christus est, a suis ténebris eruántur. Per eúmdem Dñm. ℟. Amen.

The Gelasian Sacramentary, which dates from approximately 734 AD, does not omit the genuflection during the "Prayer for the Jews"—rather, it is included in the same manner as every other prayer.

In red and blue ink (not brown ink), we find **"Orémus." Et adnunatiat diaconus: "Flectámus génua." Et post paululum dicit: "Leváte."**

1955 *Pope Pius XII, as part of the 1955 reforms, did not modify the prayer, but he did add the section with "Flectámus génua" — i.e. the genuflection was no longer to be omitted.*

1959 *On 21 March 1959, Pope John XXIII removed the words "pérfidis" and "perfídiam" from the prayer. Those words had sometimes erroneously been translated as "treacherous" whereas the meaning is actually "unbelieving" or "incredulous"* {Giampietro p251}. *Here is how the prayer appears in the* FULTON SHEEN SUNDAY MISSAL (1961):

Orémus et pro Judǽis: ut Deus et Dóminus noster áuferat velámen de córdibus eórum; ut et ipsi agnóscant Jesum Christum Dóminum nostrum.
Orémus. ℣. Flectámus génua. ℟. Leváte.
Omnípotens sempitérne Deus, qui Judǽos étiam a tua misericórdia non repéllis: exáudi preces nostras, quas pro illíus pópuli obcæcatióne deférimus; ut, ágnita veritátis tuæ luce, quæ Christus est, a suis ténebris eruántur. Per eúmdem Dñm. ℟. Amen.

Let us pray also for the Jews, that our God and Lord may remove the veil from their hearts so that they too may acknowledge Jesus Christ our Lord.
Let us pray. ℣. Kneel down. ℟. Arise.
Almighty eternal God, who dost not withhold thy mercy even from the Jews, hear the prayers we offer for that blind people, that they may acknowledge the light of thy truth, which is Christ, and be snatched from their darkness: Through the same Lord. ℟. Amen.

1965 *Piecemeal changes—called for by the Second Vatican Council—began in the early 1960s. The following prayer appeared in the 1965 Missal rather mysteriously, since modification of this prayer had not been authorized by* INTER OECUMENICI *(26 September 1964).*

Orémus et pro Judǽis: ut Deus et Dóminus noster fáciem suam super eos illumináre dignétur; ut et ipsi agnóscant ómnium Redemptórem, Jesum Christum Dóminum nostrum.
Orémus. ℣. Flectámus génua. ℟. Leváte.
Omnípotens sempitérne Deus, qui promissiónes tuas Ábrahæ et sémini ejus contulísti: Ecclésiæ tuæ preces cleménter exáudi; ut pópulus acquisitiónis antíquæ ad Redemptiónis mereámur plenitúdinem perveníre. Per Dóminum. ℟. Amen.

Let us also pray that our God and Lord will look kindly on the Jews, so that they too may acknowledge the Redeemer of all, Jesus Christ our Lord.
Let us pray. ℣. Kneel down. ℟. Arise.
Almighty and eternal God, you made the promises to Abraham and his descendants. In your goodness hear the prayers of your Church so that the people whom from of old you made your own may come to the fullness of redemption. Through our Lord. ℟. Amen.

1970 *When the Novus Ordo Missae was promulgated in 1970, the prayer seems to have been adapted from the 1965 version. Here is the 1970 version:*

Orémus et pro Judǽis, ut, ad quos prius locútus est Dóminus Deus noster, eis tríbuat in sui nóminis amóre et in sui fœderis fidelitáte profícere.
Oratio in silencio. Deinde sacerdos:
Omnípotens sempitérne Deus, qui promissiónes tuas Ábrahæ ejúsque sémini contulísti, Ecclésiæ tuæ preces cleménter exáudi, ut pópulus acquisitiónis prióris ad redemptiónis mereátur plenitúdinem perveníre. ℟. Amen.

Let us pray for the Jewish people, the first to hear the word of God, that they may continue to grow in the love of his name and in faithfulness to his covenant.
Prayer in silence. Then the Priest says:
Almighty and eternal God, long ago you gave your promise to Abraham and his posterity. Listen to your Church as we pray that the people you first made your own may arrive at the fullness of redemption. ℟. Amen.

FOR PAGANS. *Pro Conversione Infidelium*

Orémus et pro pagánis: ut Deus omnípotens áuferat iniquitátem a córdibus eórum; ut relíctis idólis suis, convertántur ad Deum vivum et verum, et únicum Fílium ejus Jesum Christum Deum et Dóminum nostrum.

PRAY WE also for the heathen, that God almighty would assoil their hearts of guilt; may they leave their idols, and return to the living, the true God, and to his only Son, our Lord and God, Jesus Christ.

Let us pray.
℣. To your knees.
℟. Stand now erect.

Celebrant: Orémus.
Deacon: ℣. Flectámus génua.
Subdeacon: ℟. Leváte.

Almighty and everlasting God, whose will is the sinner should find life, not perish eternally, listen in mercy to our prayers for all heathen folk. From the worship of false gods deliver them, and number them with thy holy Church, to the praise and glory of thy name. Through our Lord. ℟. Amen.

Omnípotens sempitérne Deus, qui non mortem peccatórum, sed vitam semper inquíris: súscipe propítius oratiónem nostram, et líbera eos ab idolórum cultúra: et ággrega Ecclésiæ tuæ sanctæ, ad laudem et glóriam nóminis tui. Per Dóminum. ℟. Amen.

(1950) Good Friday • Creeping to the Cross (Part 4 of 7)

Feria VI in Parasceve *Adoratio Crucis in Parasceve*

The Celebrant and ministers go to the Sedilia to remove their chasubles. The Deacon retains his "broad stole," which he had donned before singing the Weeping Tone. (Not until after the Celebrant's Communion will the Deacon exchange it for his folded chasuble.) Coming back to the Altar, the Celebrant stands at the Epistle side, on the ground before the steps, with Subdeacon at his left. Both face the people. The Deacon removes the Cross from the Altar and brings it to the Celebrant, covered with its veil. The Celebrant holds it with the figure of our Lord facing the people. An acolyte brings the missal from the Altar and holds it before the Celebrant. The Deacon stands at the Celebrant's right. The Celebrant unveils the upper part of the Cross and begins the following antiphon, intoning the words "Ecce lignum crucis," and singing the rest with the Deacon and Subdeacon.

1950 • *Completis Orationibus, Sacerdos deposita Casula accedit ad cornu Epistolae, et ibi in posteriori parte anguli Altaris accipit a Diacono Crucem jam in Altari praeparatam: quam, versa facie ad populum, a summitate parum discooperit, incipiens solus Antiphonam "Ecce lignum Crucis," ac deinceps in reliquis juvatur in cantu a ministris usque ad "Veníte, adorémus." Choro autem cantante "Veníte, adorémus," omnes se prosternunt, excepto Celebrante. Deinde procedit ad anteriorem partem anguli ejusdem cornu Epistolae: et discooperiens brachium dextrum Crucis, elevansque eam paulisper, altius quam primo incipit: "Ecce lignum Crucis," aliis cantantibus, et adorantibus, ut supra. Deinde Sacerdos procedit ad medium Altaris: et discooperiens Crucem totaliter, ac elevans eam, tertio altius incipit: "Ecce lignum Crucis," aliis cantantibus et adorantibus, ut supra.*

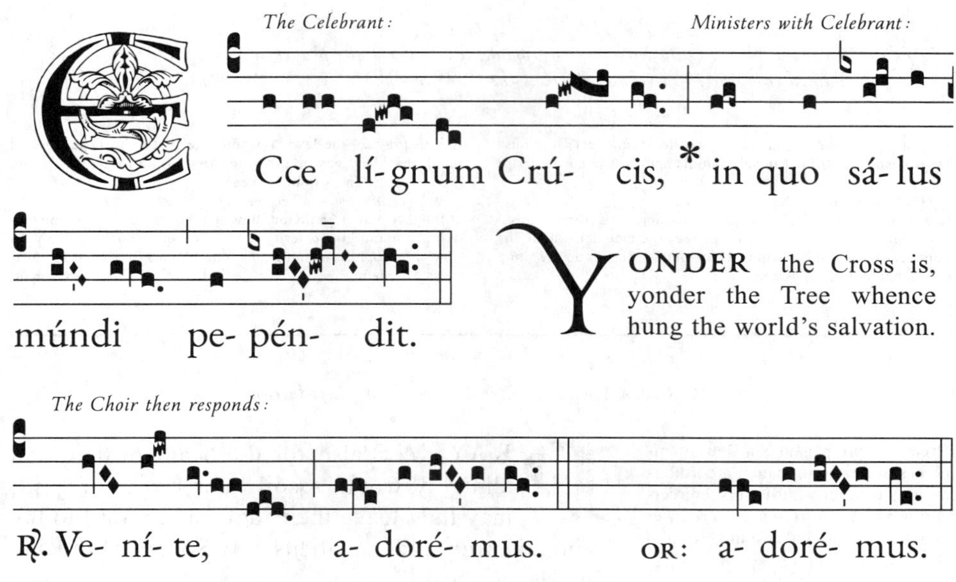

YONDER the Cross is, yonder the Tree whence hung the world's salvation.

℟. Come, let us worship.

When the choir answers "Veníte, adorémus" everyone kneels except the Celebrant. All rise. Then the Celebrant goes to stand on the foot-pace at the Epistle corner, facing the people between the ministers, as before. He uncovers the right arm of the Cross (as well as the head of the figure of Christ, according to some books), sings as before except at a higher pitch. All kneel during the answer. The third time he goes to the middle of the Altar, uncovers the whole Cross, and sings again in a still higher pitch. When the answer is sung all remain kneeling. The Celebrant carries the Cross to the middle of the Sanctuary, kneels there, and lays it so that the upper part rests on the cushion. He rises and genuflects to the Cross; all rise at the same moment. He goes to the SEDILIA, where the ministers meet him. As soon as the Celebrant has completely uncovered the Altar Cross, servers unveil the Processional Cross and all others in the church.

The Celebrant, having laid aside his Maniple and shoes, goes first to worship the Cross. He makes a prostration ("double genuflection") at the end of the carpet on which the Cross rests, rises, makes another prostration about half way up the carpet, then a third immediately before the Cross. This third time he bends and kisses the feet of the crucifix. Going back to the SEDELIA, the Celebrant puts on his shoes, Maniple, and folded Chasuble, washing his hands if desired. Having removed their shoes, the Ministers, the clergy, and the servers worship the Cross in the same way the Celebrant did. **NOTICE:** When mention is made of a "prostration," this does not denote the special prostration made by the Celebrant at the beginning of Good Friday, or during the litany on Holy Saturday. It denotes what is sometimes called a "double genuflection"—viz. kneeling on both knees and bowing the head and shoulders slightly {Fortescue p21}.

The Cross is then carried to a place outside the Sanctuary, for veneration by the laity. A server may kneel by the Cross and wipe the feet of the figure each time when they have been kissed. Another way, also allowed, is that a priest in surplice and black stole take a crucifix (either the one that has served hitherto or a smaller one) to the Communion rails and there let the people kiss it. They come up as they do when going to Communion. He may wipe the feet with a cloth each time.

The Creeping to the Cross should be accomplished in an orderly way; there should be at least three pairs before the crucifix all the time. As the first pair kneel to kiss the Cross, the second pair make their second prostration in the middle of the carpet, and the third pair at the same time make their first at the end of the carpet. All rise, the first pair genuflect to the Cross, and then return to their places; the second pair now becomes the first. Meanwhile a new pair has come to the end of the carpet.

After the last "Veníte, adorémus" the choir begins to sing the "Reproaches" (IMPROPERIA) and the hymn "Pange Lingua" with the verse "Crux Fidélis" repeated, as in the GRADUALE ROMANUM. They may sing all or part of this, according to the time occupied by the worship of the Cross. While the Creeping to the Cross proceeds, the Celebrant and ministers read the Reproaches, sitting at the SEDILIA with head covered. An acolyte fetches the Missal from the Altar, holding it before them. They read the text alternately, with Celebrant saying the verses, the ministers answering each time "Ágios o Theós," "Pópule meus," "Crux Fidélis," and so on.

1950 • *Postea Sacerdos solus portat Crucem ad locum ante Altare praeparatum, et genuflexus ibidem eam locat: mox depositis calceamentis, accedit ad adorandam Crucem, ter genua flectens antequam eam deosculetur. Hoc facto revertitur, et accipit calceamenta, et Casulam. Postmodum Ministri Altaris, deinde alii Clerici, et laici, bini et bini, ter genibus flexis, ut dictum est, Crucem adorant. Interim, dum fit adoratio Crucis, cantantur Improperia, et alia quae sequuntur, vel omnia, vel pars eorum, prout multitudo adorantium vel paucitas requirit: quae etiam Sacerdos sedens ad scamnum legit cum Ministris, ut infra:*

(Micheas 6: 3) Pópule meus, quid feci tibi? aut in quo contristávi te? Respónde mihi. ℣. (Mich 6: 4) Quia edúxi te de terra Ægýpti: parásti Crucem Salvatóri tuo.

TELL ME, my own people, what wrong I did thee, how earned thy ill looks. Answer me. ℣. From the land of Egypt I rescued thee; for thy Savior hast thou only a Cross?

Hágios o Theós.
Sanctus Deus.
Hágios ischyrós.
Sanctus fortis.
Hágios athánatos, eléison hymás.
Sanctus immortális, miserére nobis.

HOLY GOD IS.
Holy God is.
Holy and strong.
Holy and strong.
Holy thou and immortal, have mercy upon us.
Holy thou and immortal, have mercy upon us.

Quia edúxi te per desértum quadragínta annis, et manna cibávi te, et introdúxi te in terram satis bonam: parásti Crucem Salvatóri tuo. *Hágios o Theós…*

Forty years through the desert I led thee, with manna fed thee; passing fair was the home I gave thee; for thy Savior, only a Cross? *Holy God is…*

Quid ultra débui fácere tibi, et non feci? Ego quidem plantávi te víneam meam speciosíssimam: et tu facta es mihi nimis amára: acéto namque sitim meam potásti: et láncea perforásti latus Salvatóri tuo. *Hágios o Theós…*

What more could I have bestowed, that bestow I did not? Vineyard thou wast of my own planting, how fair to see! Yet bitter the fruit was; thou wouldst quench my thirst with vinegar, and wound with a lance thy Savior's side. *Holy God is…*

℣. Egypt and Egypt's firstborn for thy sake scourged I;
wouldst thou scourge and abandon me?

℣. Ego propter te flagellávi Ægýptum cum primogénitis suis: et tu me flagellátum tradidísti.

REFRAIN. *The following Refrain* (Micheas 6: 3) *is repeated after each verse:*

TELL ME, my own people, what wrong I did thee, how earned thy ill looks. Answer me.

Pópule meus, quid feci tibi? Aut in quo contristávi te? Respónde mihi.

℣. From Egypt I rescued thee,
Pharao and his host I drowned in the Red Sea,
to keep their hands off thee;
into the hands of rulers
wouldst thou deliver me?

℣. Ego edúxi te de Ægýpto, demérso Pharaóne in Mare Rubrum: et tu me tradidísti princípibus sacerdótum.

℣. Through the sea
I opened a passage for thee,
and should a lance open my side?

℣. Ego ante te apérui mare: et tu aperuísti láncea latus meum.

℣. In a column of cloud
I led thee on thy journey;
wouldst thou lead me off,
and into Pilate's colonnade?

℣. Ego ante te præívi in colúmna nubis: et tu me duxísti ad prætórium Piláti.

℣. I fed thee with manna,
when thou wast fainting in the desert;
must I grow faint
with buffets and scourge of thine?

℣. Ego te pavi manna per desértum: et tu me cecidísti álapis et flagéllis.

℣. With water from the rock
thy sore need I met;
thou mine with vinegar and gall.

℣. Ego te potávi aqua salútis de petra: et tu me potásti felle et acéto.

℣. Chieftains of Chanaan
for thy sake smote I;
and must rod of thine smite my head?

℣. Ego propter te Chananæórum reges percússi: et tu percussísti arúndine caput meum.

℣. A royal sceptre my gift was to thee;
thine to me, a crown of thorns.

℣. Ego dedi tibi sceptrum regále: et tu dedísti cápiti meo spíneam corónam.

℣. High above earth I exalted thee;
and thou me, but gibbeted on a Cross.

℣. Ego te exaltávi magna virtúte: et tu me suspendísti in patíbulo Crucis.

A Note on Greek • In 1906, a non-Catholic described hearing the Good Friday Hagios o Theos: "So, as in delirium a man talks in a long-forgotten tongue, now—when her heart is rent—the Catholic Church drops twenty centuries without an effort, and speaks as she spoke underground in Rome, and in Paul's hired house, and in Crete and Alexandria and Jerusalem."

ANTIPHON.

Crucem tuam adorámus, Dómine: et sanctam resurrectiónem tuam laudámus et glorificámus: ecce enim, propter lignum venit gáudium in univérso mundo. (Ps 66: 2) Deus misereátur nostri et benedícat nobis: illúminet vultum suum super nos et misereátur nostri. *Crucem tuam...*

THY CROSS, Lord, we needs must worship, thy holy Resurrection praise and glorify; was it not yonder tree brought the whole world rejoicing? ℣. May God be merciful to us, and bless us. May he smile graciously on us and show us his mercy. *Thy Cross...*

HYMNUS.

THREE THINGS cooperated in our fall: a disobedient man, Adam; a proud woman, Eve; and a tree. God took these elements and used them as the instruments of victory: the obedient new Adam, Christ; the humble new Eve, Mary; and the tree of the Cross. — *Archbishop Fulton J. Sheen*

Some consider this 6th-century poem by Venantius Fortunatus, Bishop of Poitiers, to be the crown jewel of Latin hymnody. We recommend the following commentaries: Father Joseph Connelly (*Hymns of the Roman Liturgy*, 1957) page 85; Father Aquinas Byrnes (*Hymns of the Dominican Breviary*, 1943) page 92; Father Matthew Britt (*Hymns of the Breviary and Missal*, 1922) page 128; and *The Saint Jean de Brébeuf Hymnal* (2018), page 308. In 1908, Pope Pius X restored the option of singing the ancient versions for all hymns contained in the Roman Missal, rather than the modified versions published in 1631AD under Pope Urban VIII. Nevertheless, the Urbanite version remained quite popular—and fully licit—so we have reproduced it below, with a literal translation by Father Joseph Connelly (Imprimatur: 10 December 1954 by Most Rev'd Francis Grimshaw, Archbishop of Birmingham).

℟. Crux fidélis, inter omnes arbor una nóbilis: nulla silva talem profert fronde, flore, gérmine. * Dulce lignum, dulces clavos, dulce pondus sústinet.

FAITHFUL CROSS, tree that is alone in its glory among all other trees; no forest ever yielded its equal in leaf, flower and fruit. * Loving nails and loving wood bear a loving burden.

When *Crux fidélis* is repeated [CR] it stops at **Dulce lignum*. But sometimes [DU] only the **Dulce* section is repeated.

Pange, lingua, gloriósi láuream certáminis, et super Crucis trophǽo dic triúmphum nóbilem: quáliter Redémptor orbis immolátus vícerit. CR

TELL, MY TONGUE, of the victory gained in glorious conflict, and sing a triumphal song about the trophy of the Cross, telling how man's redeemer offered His life and thus won the day. CR

De paréntis protoplásti fraude Factor cóndolens, quando pomi noxiális in necem morsu ruit: ipse lignum tunc notávit, damna ligni ut sólveret. DU

THE CREATOR in grief at the harm done to the first man when, by eating of the fatal apple, he fell headlong to death, Himself at that moment marked a tree to undo the harm done by a tree. DU

Hoc opus nostræ salútis ordo depopóscerat: multifórmis proditóris ars ut artem fálleret: et medélam ferret inde, hostis unde lǽserat. CR

THE PLAN of our salvation had demanded this work so that God's wisdom might outwit the craftiness of the betrayer and his many disguises and find a remedy in a tree just as the enemy had done hurt to man through a tree. CR

For musical notation and more English translations, please see page 138.

WHEN THEREFORE the time appointed by God came, the Son, the world's creator, was sent from heaven and, clothed in man's flesh, was born of a Virgin. Du

Quando venit ergo sacri plenitúdo témporis, missus est ab arce Patris Natus, orbis Cónditor: atque ventre virgináli carne amíctus pródiit. Du

THE INFANT cries as He lies in the narrow crib; the Virgin Mother wraps and envelops Him in the swaddling clothes, and a tight-drawn band fastens together the hands and feet of God. Cr

Vagit Infans inter arcta cónditus præsépia: membra pannis involúta Virgo Mater álligat: et Dei manus pedésque stricta cingit fáscia. Cr

THE REDEEMER had now completed thirty years and had come to the end of His earthly life, and then of His own free will He gave Himself up to the Passion. The Lamb was lifted up on to the tree of the Cross to be sacrificed. Du

Lustra sex qui jam perégit, tempus implens córporis, sponte líbera Redémptor passióni déditus, Agnus in Crucis levátur immolándus stípite. Du

HE TASTES the gall; He swoons; the thorns, nails and lance pierce His tender body; water and blood flow out. In this stream the whole world, earth, sea and sky are purified. Cr

Felle potus ecce languet: spina, clavi, láncea mite corpus perforárunt, unda manat et cruor: terra, pontus, astra, mundus, quo lavántur flúmine! Cr

SOFTEN your branches, noble tree, relax your taut fibres and let your natural hardness give way to yielding suppleness, and so offer yourself as a gentle support for the body of the King of heaven. Du

Flecte ramos, arbor alta, tensa laxa víscera, et rigor lentéscat ille, quem dedit natívitas: et supérni membra Regis tende miti stípite. Du

YOU ALONE were worthy to bear the victim of the world and, like the ark, to give a shelter to a shipwrecked world—an ark which the sacred blood, poured out from the body of the Lamb, has anointed. Cr

Sola digna tu fuísti ferre mundi víctimam: atque portum præparáre arca mundo náufrago: quam sacer cruor perúnxit, fusus Agni córpore. Cr

The 1962 version of Good Friday contains the following injunction: "Conclusio numquam omittenda." That means the final stanza ("Sempiterna Sit") is always sung, no matter what other chants have been omitted during the Solemn Veneration of the Cross. The 1950 rubrics do not contain this rule.

ETERNAL GLORY to the blessed Trinity; equal glory to the Father, the Son and the Paraclete. Let the whole world praise the name of the one God in three Persons. Du

Sempitérna sit beátæ Trinitáti glória: æqua Patri Filióque; par decus Paráclito: Unius Triníque nomen laudet univérsitas. Amen. Du

Towards the end of the Creeping to the Cross, an acolyte lights the six candles on the Altar and those of the acolytes. The Deacon spreads the corporal on the Altar, laying the Purificator near it on the Epistle side. When the Creeping to the Cross is ended, the Deacon returns the Cross to the Altar—in its usual place—where, as already stated, the candles have been lit as for solemn Mass. As the Deacon kneels to take up the Cross, all in the Sanctuary kneel too, including the Celebrant and Subdeacon. They remain on their knees until the Cross is placed on the Altar. The acolytes take away the cushion and carpet. The Procession to the place of repose follows.

Two thurifers go to prepare the thuribles, then carry them straight to the place of repose and wait there. Other servers go to the place of repose and light the liturgical torches, which will be carried on the way back to the High Altar. The men who hold the canopy also wait there.

(1950) Good Friday • The Procession (Part 5 of 7)

Feria VI in Parasceve *Dum defertur Sanctissimum ad Altare*

The procession forms in the Sanctuary and goes by the shortest way—in total silence—to the place of repose. When they arrive, the Celebrant kneels on the lowest step; all kneel along with him. They wait here a short time, while the servers prepare certain items. When all is ready, the Deacon goes up to the "Capsula" (in practice, many Churches use an additional Tabernacle rather than a special "Capsula"), opens it, and comes back to his place.

The Celebrant incenses the Sanctissimum as usual. Donning a white humeral veil, the Celebrant ascends to the place of repose, kneeling on the edge of the foot-pace. The Deacon rises, takes the chalice from the Capsula (leaving it open and empty), and hands it to the Celebrant. The Celebrant rises and turns to the people. The cantors intone the hymn Vexilla Regis, and the choir continues. Father Fortescue says the Crotalus may be rattled during the procession—the operative word being "may"—but such a choice seems deleterious to the singing. In some places, the first stanza ("Vexílla etc.") was used as a refrain; cf. the various editions of the *Missale Parisiense*. The rubrics suggest that choristers will take part in the procession, holding lighted candles. Regardless of which parties hold lighted candles during the procession, such candles are not extinguished until the Celebrant's Communion {Fortescue p309}. In the reform of 1955, Pope Pius XII eliminated the Vexilla Regis, replacing it with three antiphons—*Adorámus Te*, *Per Lignum*, and *Salvátor Mundi*—which are regrettably in three different modes.

As explained above, the hymns of the Roman Gradual were restored in 1908, when Pope Pius X allowed the ancient versions to be used instead of the "Urbanite" versions published in 1631AD. The official *Graduale Romanum* (Vatican Press, 1908) published the ancient version of Vexilla Regis, although the Urbanite version always remained an option. Similar to the "Pange Lingua" by Bishop Fortunatus, both versions—ancient and Urbanite—coëxisted alongside each other for decades. Even as late as 1961, the Solesmes Abbey *Graduale* printed both versions, as did the 1953 Schwann *Graduale* (edited by Abbat Urbanus Bomm, Karl Gustav Fellerer, and Monsignor Johannes Overath). The Urbanite version is provided below, without prejudice, since that version seems more common for hand-missals. A translation of the ancient version can be found on page 527 in *The Saint Jean de Brébeuf Hymnal* (2018), while pages 548-549 provide a side-by-side comparison of both versions.

Vexilla Regis Prodeunt

Vexílla Regis pródeunt: Fulget Crucis mystérium, Qua vita mortem pértulit Et morte vitam prótulit.	THE BANNERS of the King go forth, the mystery of the cross shines, by which our Life bore death and by death gave us life.
Quæ vulneráta lánceæ Mucróne diro, críminum Ut nos laváret sórdibus, Manávit unda et sánguine.	TO wash us from the stain of sin he was pierced by the sharp point of the lance and shed water and blood.
Impléta sunt quæ cóncinit David fidéli cármine, Dicendo natiónibus: Regnávit a ligno Deus.	WHAT David in his true hymn told to the nations is now fulfilled: God reigns from the tree.
Arbor decóra et fúlgida, Ornáta Regis púrpura, Elécta digno stípite Tam sancta membra tángere.	FAIR and radiant tree, with royal purple adorned, chosen to touch so sacred limbs with thy boughs.

BLESSED CROSS, on whose arms
the redemption of the world is borne;
thou, from whom his body hangs,
dost snatch from hell its prey.

Beáta, cujus bráchiis
Prétium pepéndit sǽculi,
Statéra facta córporis,
Tulítque prædam tártari.

O CROSS hail, our only hope!
At this passion-tide increase grace
to the good and take sin from the wicked.

O Crux, ave, spes única,
Hoc Passiónis témpore
Piis adáuge grátiam,
Reísque dele crímina.

THEE, holy Trinity fount of salvation,
let every spirit praise.
To whom thou givest the victory of the cross,
to them give also its prize. AMEN.

Te, fons salútis Trínitas,
Colláudet omnis spíritus:
Quibus Crucis victóriam
Largíris, adde prǽmium.
AMEN.

(1950) GOOD FRIDAY • Mass of the Presanctified (Part 6 of 7)

Feria VI in Parasceve *Ad Missam Praesanctificatorum*

"The Blessed Sacrament having been placed on the altar, there followed, in accordance with the *Ordines Romani*, the *Pater Noster* and the Holy Communion; later, for greater reverence, other prayers were added, which gave this rite of the presanctified the appearance of a Mass." —Cardinal Schuster [*Liber Sacramentorum*, Volume II, page 220]

[Editor's Note: Abbat Fernand Cabrol described the special COMMIXTIO rite, which was observed for many centuries in the East and West. This is when "ordinary wine was added to the consecrated wine, and a particle of the Sacred Host dissolved in unconsecrated wine, as though to sanctify them" {Cabrol p270}. Writing in 1926, Abbat Cabrol continued: "A remainder of this rite still survives in the Mass of Good Friday. The Deacon pours wine and the Subdeacon water into the Chalice, and the priest after having elevated the Sacred Host divides it into three particles, one of which is placed in the wine and consumed, after the priest has communicated with the other two particles. The contact of the Sacred Host does indeed sanctify the wine, but it is erroneous to believe that it changes it into the most precious Blood, as was once incorrectly held. The consecration of the bread and wine can be brought about only by the words of consecration—and we repeat that there is no consecration in the Mass of the Presanctified. It has been asked recently whether the faithful might be admitted to Holy Communion on Good Friday. The general custom is not in favor of this plea, but there seems to be no valid reason against it, considering that originally the Mass of the Presanctified was instituted solely to this end. This is a question of discipline which still remains to be pronounced upon by the Church. The rubric in the Missal foresees that the priest may have to consecrate several additional hosts on Maundy Thursday, to be reserved for the sick." On page 443 (*Catholic Worship in the Middle Ages*, 2012), James Monti writes: "Early mediæval texts, including the seventh-century Gelasian Sacramentary of Rome, speak of a general Communion of all the faithful at the Good Friday liturgy, a practice that persisted in some places to the end of the Middle Ages." With regard to when Holy Communion stopped being given to the faithful on Good Friday, cf. page 250 of Father Giampietro's *Development of the Liturgical Reform* (2009).]

1950 • When the procession reaches the High Altar, the Deacon takes the Chalice (which contains the SANCTISSIMUM) from the Celebrant and places it on the Altar. He unties the veil over the chalice, but leaves it covered. The humeral veil is removed from the Celebrant's shoulders and taken away. Incense is put into the thurible, but not blessed. Sir Walter Kirkham Blount (*The Office of Holy Week*, 1670AD) says this is "to signify that the Author of all blessing is dead." The SANCTISSIMUM is incensed.

The Celebrant ascends the High Altar. Holding the paten over the corporal, the Celebrant lets the SANCTISSIMUM slip from the Chalice onto the paten. The rubrics say: "Si tetigerit Sacramentum, digitos abluat in aliquo vase." Henry Hills (*Holy Week According To The Roman Missal*, 1688AD) translates this as: "If by chance he has touched the Host, he must wash his fingers in some Vessel, and dry them upon the Purificator." Then the Celebrant takes the paten and lets the SANCTISSIMUM slip from it on to the corporal, not making the sign of the cross with the paten. Wine and water are put into the Chalice. The Celebrant does not bless the water, or recite the customary prayer ("Deus qui humánae substántiae").

The Deacon covers the Chalice with a pall. Then the Celebrant puts incense into the thurible without blessing it, and censes the offerings and Altar in the usual way, genuflecting before and after and whenever he passes before the Blessed Sacrament. Today, we notice the "oblata" being incensed is a Host which was already consecrated on (Holy Thursday). It is already—as the older books say—"the blessed body of our Lord."

1950 • When censing the offerings ("oblata"), he prays as follows:
Cum incensat oblata, dicit:

Incénsum istud, a te benedíctum, ascéndat ad te, Dómine: et descéndat super nos misericórdia tua.

BY THEE BLESSED, to thee, Lord, let our incense rise, and bring down upon us the rain of thy mercy.

1950 • While censing the Altar he prays Psalm 140: 2-4.
Cum incensat Altare, dicit:

Dirigátur, Dómine, orátio mea, sicut incénsum in conspéctu tuo: elevátio mánuum meárum sacrifícium vespertínum. Pone Dómine custódiam ori meo, et óstium circumstántiæ lábiis meis: ut non declínet cor meum in verba malítiæ, ad excusándas excusatiónes in peccátis.

WELCOME as incense-smoke let my prayer rise up before thee, Lord; when I lift up my hands, be it as acceptable as the evening sacrifice. Lord, set a guard on my mouth, a barrier to fence in my lips. Do not turn my heart towards thoughts of evil, to cover sin with smooth names.

1950 • As he returns the thurible to the Deacon he says:
Quando reddit thuribulum Diacono, dicit:

Accéndat in nobis, Dóminus ignem sui amóris, et flammam ætérnæ caritátis. Amen.

Flame of his love may the Lord kindle in our hearts; may charity burn there undying. Amen.

1950 • The Celebrant is not censed. He washes his hands a little way from the altar at the Epistle corner in silence; then, bowing at the middle of the altar, he prays as follows.

Et ipse non incensatur. Postea aliquantulum extra Altare in cornu Epistolae lavat manus, nihil dicens: deinde in medio Altaris inclinatur, junctis manibus, dicit:

In spíritu humilitátis, et in ánimo contríto suscipiámur a te, Dómine: et sic fiat sacrifícium nostrum in conspéctu tuo hódie, ut pláceat tibi, Dómine Deus.

LORD, WITH BOWED HEAD and contrite heart, we claim thy audience; such be the offering we make today as shall win thy favor, Lord God.

1950 • Then he turns at the Gospel corner towards the people, and—in the usual way—prays as follows.

Deinde versus ad populum in cornu Evangelii, dicit more solito:

Oráte, fratres, ut meum ac vestrum sacrifícium acceptábile fiat apud Deum Patrem omnipoténtem.

Pray, brethren, that this sacrifice, mine and yours, may find acceptance with God the almighty Father.

1950 • No answer is made. Then, facing the altar, the Celebrant immediately continues as follows.

Et per eamdem viam revertitur, non perficiens circulum: et consequenter, omissis aliis, dicit:

Orémus: Præcéptis salutáribus móniti, et divína institutióne formáti, audémus dícere.

Let us pray. Obedient to our Savior's command, and with his teaching for our model, thus we make bold to pray:

OUR FATHER, who art in heaven, hallowed be thy name; thy kingdom come; thy will be done on earth as it is in heaven. Give us this day our daily bread; and forgive us our trespasses, as we forgive them that trespass against us; and lead us not into temptation:

The choir answers: But deliver us from evil.

The Celebrant silently: Amen.

Pater noster, qui es in cælis: Sanctificétur nomen tuum: Advéniat regnum tuum: Fiat volúntas tua, sicut in cælo, et in terra. Panem nostrum quotidiánum da nobis hódie: Et dimítte nobis débita nostra, sicut et nos dimíttimus debitóribus nostris. Et ne nos indúcas in tentatiónem:

The choir: Sed líbera nos a malo.

Sub silentio: Amen.

1950 • The Celebrant sings "Líbera Nos Dómine" in the ferial tone, that is, without any inflection of the voice. During this prayer he extends the hands. He does not take the paten nor make the sign of the cross.

FROM ALL EVIL, Lord, deliver us, past, present, and to come. So may Mary ever plead for us, that is Mother of God, with the holy apostles Peter and Paul, and Andrew, and all the saints together, as to win us thy favor. Grant peace in our days; thy grace befriending us, be they ever by sin unhampered, and safe from all alarms: through the same Jesus Christ, thy Son, our Lord: who is God, living and reigning with thee in the unity of the Holy Spirit, world without end.

The choir answers: Amen.

Líbera nos, quæsumus, Dómine, ab ómnibus malis, prætéritis, præséntibus, et futúris: et intercedénte beáta, et gloriósa semper Vírgine Dei Genitríce María, cum beátis Apóstolis tuis Petro et Paulo, atque Andréa, et ómnibus Sanctis, da propítius pacem in diébus nostris: ut, ope misericórdiæ tuæ adjúti, et a peccáto simus semper líberi, et ab omni perturbatióne secúri. Per eúndem Dóminum nostrum Jesum Christum, Fílium tuum: Qui tecum vivit et regnat in unitáte Spíritus Sancti Deus, per ómnia sæcula sæculórum.

The choir: Amen.

1950 • The Celebrant puts the paten under the Sacred Host, which he raises up, so that it may be seen by the people (but he does not lift the paten); and he immediately breaks it over the Chalice into three parts, the last of which he puts in the Chalice in the usual manner, but in silence. The "Pax Dómini" is not said, nor the "Agnus Dei." The kiss of peace is not given. Of the three Prayers before Holy Communion, only the last is prayed—as follows—with the Celebrant bowing over the Altar.

Tunc Celebrans, facta reverentia usque ad terram, supponit patenam Sacramento, quod in dextera accipiens, elevat, ut videri possit a populo: et statim supra Calicem dividit in tres partes, quarum ultimam mittit in Calicem more solito, nihil dicens. "Pax Dómini" non dicitur, nec "Agnus Dei," neque pacis osculum datur. Postmodum, praetermissis duabus primis Orationibus, dicit tantum sequentem:

LORD JESUS CHRIST, if thy Sacred Body I dare, all unworthily, to receive, let not the tasting of it prove my judgement and undoing; rather in thy mercy let it advantage me, a shield for soul and body, a salve for my infirmities: who with God the Father in the bond of the Holy Spirit, livest and reignest and art God, world without end. Amen.

Percéptio Córporis tui, Dómine Jesu Christe, quod ego indígnus súmere præsúmo, non mihi provéniat in judícium et condemnatiónem: sed pro tua pietáte prosit mihi ad tutaméntum mentis et córporis, et ad medélam percipiéndam: Qui vivis et regnas cum Deo Patre in unitáte Spíritus Sancti Deus, per ómnia sæcula sæculórum. Amen.

1950 • Then he genuflects and takes up the paten with the Body of Christ, and—with the greatest humility and reverence—says the following prayer. | *Tunc genuflectit, et accipit patenam cum Corpore Christi: et maxima humilitate ac reverentia dicit:*

I will take the Bread of Heaven and will call upon the name of the Lord.

Panem cæléstem accípiam, et nomen Dómini invocábo.

1950 • Striking his heart with his hand, he prays three times:
Percutit pectus suum, ter dicens:

Dómine, non sum dignus, ut intres sub tectum meum: sed tantum dic verbo, et sanábitur ánima mea.

LORD, I am not worthy to receive thee under my roof; my soul will be healed if thou wilt only speak a word of command.

1950 • Next, he signs himself with the Blessed Sacrament as usual, and adds:
Postea signat se Sacramento, dicens:

Corpus Dómini ✠ nostri Jesu Christi custódiat ánimam meam in vitam ætérnam. Amen.

The Body of our Lord Jesus Christ ✠ bring my soul safely to eternal life. Amen.

1950 • And he reverently receives the Body. Then—omitting all that is usually said before receiving the Precious Blood—he receives the particle of the Host with the wine from the Chalice. Having washed his fingers in the usual way and taken the ablution bowing at the middle of the Altar, he prays as follows.

Et sumit Corpus reverenter. Deinde, omissis omnibus, quæ dici solent ante sumptionem Sanguinis, immediate particulam Hostiæ cum vino reverenter sumit de calice. Et more solito facta ablutione digitorum, et sumpta purificatione, in medio Altaris inclinatus, manibus junctis, dicit:

Quod ore súmpsimus Dómine, pura mente capiámus: et de múnere temporáli fiat nobis remédium sempitérnum.

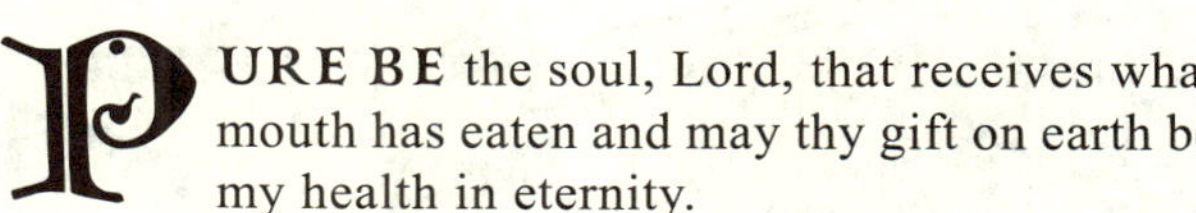

PURE BE the soul, Lord, that receives what mouth has eaten and may thy gift on earth be my health in eternity.

[Editor's Note: All holding candles extinguish them after the Celebrant's Communion. As the rubrics say, the Subdeacon pours wine and water into the chalice over the Celebrant's fingers—which the Celebrant drinks as usual—but the normal first pouring of wine alone into the chalice is omitted today. The Deacon goes to the credence table, takes off the "broad stole," and puts on his folded chasuble.]

1950 • All the other customary prayers are omitted. No blessing is given. The Celebrant and his retinue depart in silence. | *Non dicitur "Corpus tuum, Dómine," nec Postcommunio, nec "Pláceat tibi," nec datur benedictio; sed facta reverentia Altari, Sacerdos cum Ministris discedit: et dicuntur Vesperae sine cantu: et denudatur Altare.*

(1950) Good Friday • Vespers (Part 7 of 7)

Feria VI in Parasceve *Ad Vesperas*

1950 • When the Celebrant and ministers have left the church, the choir recites Vespers. Meanwhile two servers take from the Altar the missal and Altar cloth, leaving only the cross and six candles alight. After Vespers the candles are put out. Vespers on Good Friday is identical to Holy Thursday, except the Magnificat antiphon is *Cum Accepisset Acétum* ("Jesus drank the vinegar") instead of *Cœnántibus Autem Illis* ("While they were still at table"). In spite of the rubric above—"dicuntur Vesperae sine cantu"—Vespers on Good Friday may be sung. The melodies were restored in the *Editio Vaticana* (1913) promulgated by Pope Pius X. The melodies are provided in various books, such as: Vesperale Romanum, (Lethielleux, 1913) page 173; Liber Antiphonarius (Solesmes, 1949) page 436; Antiphonale Monasticum (Desclée, 1934) page 429; and the Liber Usualis (Desclée, 1934) page 1,882.

Nothing prevents the Faithful from joining in singing Vespers, and this is the traditional way. Even at a time when women were thought to be excluded from singing during Mass, they were still explicitly encouraged to sing the "Psalms and Hymns of the Divine Office." On this subject, see "Church Music" in the *American Ecclesiastical Review* (September, 1906) and the Interview with Cardinal Domenico Cardinal Bartolucci dated 12 August 2009. To facilitate this, the faithful should be provided with a booklet containing the Gregorian melodies as well as vernacular translations.

Notice: When Pope Pius XII modified holy week in 1955, he changed the traditional times of the ceremonies. These changes *de facto* obliterated Tenebrae. Moreover, if the 1950 holy week is offered following the Pius XII times, it might militate against Vespers being prayed after Good Friday's *Missa Praesanctificatorum*.

✠ GREAT NEED WAS THERE OF ADAM'S TRANSGRESSION, THAT CHRIST MIGHT DIE FOR ITS ATONING; HAPPY FAULT, THAT WON SO HOLY AND SO HIGH A REDEEMER! ✠ THIS IS THE NIGHT FORETOLD IN PROPHECY: NIGHT SHINES CLEAR AS THE DAY ITSELF, NIGHT SHALL BE THE ONLY WITNESS OF MY PLEASURES. (Exsultet)

The Easter Vigil of Holy Saturday morning—a long and complicated ceremony full of ancient mysteries—should not be unduly weighed down with explanations. Therefore, the lengthy explanations (which focus on the changes made during the 1950s) will be found at the end, rather than at the beginning. Nevertheless, we believe the following notes on the TRIPLE CANDLE *(a.k.a. "Reed") and* EXSULTET *(a.k.a. "Praeconium Paschale") will be found apposite:*

THE TRIPLE CANDLE • The 1950 books make use of a TRIDENT: a reed with three candles. According to some authors, this three-branched candlestick should be "decorated with flowers"—cf. page 173 of *Die Sonn- und Festtagslieder des vatikanischen Graduale* (Prior Johner, 1928)—but in some localities the handle resembles a serpent. Many theological explanations have been given for the Trident, which "did not figure in the original ceremony" {Cabrol p301}, and Father Thurston calls the Trident "a comparatively late importation" {Thurston p415}. Some believe it is merely a substitute for the Paschal candle, which in some churches was absolutely massive in size—too large to be transported from the church porch {Monti p472}—although interestingly, the traditional rubrics demand it be carried to the Baptismal font later on. This was certainly the view accepted by the reformers, and stated explicitly on page 128 of *Ordo Hebdomadae Sanctae Instauratus* (Braga & Bugnini, 1956): "Moles tamen et altitudo cerei, pluribus in ecclesiis tanta effecta est ut per hastam tantum accendi, et nullo modo in processione a diacono deferri potuerit." Father Thurston believes the Trident—with its multiple candles—came into existence for a very practical reason, citing a Sarum book from around 1210AD: "Let the candle upon the reed be lighted, and let another candle be lighted at the same time, so that the candle upon the reed can be rekindled if it should chance to be blown out" {Thurston p416}. Cardinal Bernard of Porto, in his *Ordo Officiorum* (circa 1140AD) agrees with this "backup candle" theory, and "expressly states this as the reason for multiple lights on the candle staff" {Monti p473}. Father Fortescue also agrees—at least tentatively—with this "backup candle" theory, and notes that in early times sometimes two (not three) candles were lit {*Holy Week Book*, p32}. Whatever the "true" origin may be, the Trident fits beautifully with the triple "Lumen Christi" rite. Our current rubrics have the Trident move forward in silence, whereas the Sarum rubrics prescribed a very beautiful hymn (*Inventor rutili*) to be sung during the "Lumen Christi" procession.

The Deacon uses the Trident's fire to light the Paschal candle immediately before he sings: *qui licet sit divísus in partes, mutuáti tamen lúminis detriménta non novit* ("which fire, though it be divided into parts, yet knoweth no diminution of its light") and quickly thereafter all the lamps in the church are lit. Does this "division" refer to the Trident, to the various lights in the church, the Paschal candle itself, or all of the above? Abbat Cabrol reminds us the Paschal candle was so large that its wick "was made of three or more strands." At an earlier time, (as mentioned above) instead of the Trident, it seems the Paschal candle itself was "brought to the threshold of the Church during the blessing of the new fire" and "lighted during the procession" {Cabrol p301}. "The practice of carrying the Paschal candle itself (whether lit or unlit) in procession to the Sanctuary is found in a number of early documents" {Goddard p280}.

THE EXSULTET • Both Saint Jerome and Saint Augustine provide testimony that composing the "Praeconium Paschale" was the duty of the Deacon. Over the centuries, the "Exsultent" became stable and universal, and certainly no Deacon today would dream of replacing or editing what Abbat Cabrol calls "the most beautiful lyric in the Roman liturgy." Even one of the most radical liturgical reformers—Father Augustin Bea, S.J.—declared in the years immediately before the Second Vatican Council: "No concession should ever be made for the singing of the Exultet, in whole or in part, in the vernacular." Certain passages were not—in the end—adopted by the Church, such as a "euology in the style of Virgil" which gives first place to the bee among all other living creatures {Cabrol 301}. One passage that was ultimately accepted by the Church famously spoke of "Adam's happy fault." For centuries, some Catholics did not accept this bold language, and the passage (*O certe necessárium Adae peccátum, O felix culpa, quae talem ac tantum méruit habére Redemptórem*) is often crossed out in the manuscripts. Indeed, Saint Hugh of Cluny "ordered the words to be effaced in his Missal" {Thurston, p420}, and a BENEDICTIONAL (MS 22049) created circa 1459AD omits the entire passage. Rockstro, the famous student of Mendelssohn, said of the musical setting for the Exsultet: "this composition is universally acknowledged to be the finest specimen of plainsong we possess."

Eight Parts • The Holy Saturday service—referred to in pre-1955 books as "Holy Saturday Morning"—is the longest of any usually celebrated in a Catholic church. In addition to the Sacrament of Baptism, Confirmations are sometimes added to this service, and—in certain localities—the conferral of Sacred Orders {McManus p100}. The entire ceremony consists of eight parts :

(1) Blessing of the New Fire;

(2) "Lumen Christi" Procession;

(3) Blessing of the Candle;

(4) Prophecies;

(5) Blessing of the Font;

(6) Litany of the Saints;

(7) Mass of Easter Eve;

(8) Truncated Vespers.

The "truncated" Vespers is also known as *pro vesperis* — "that which substitutes for Vespers."

(1950) Holy Saturday • Station at Saint John Lateran

Sabbato Sancto *Statio ad Sanctum Joannem in Laterano*

1950 • The color of the "Praeconium Paschale" and Easter Vigil Mass is white, but purple for all the rest. For this reason, the High Altar is vested in the best white frontal covered with a purple one. Moreover, in front of the Altar, the carpet used on high feasts is spread, but covered with a purple one. The tabernacle is open and empty. There are six altar candles of bleached wax (not lit) and a Missal at the Epistle corner.

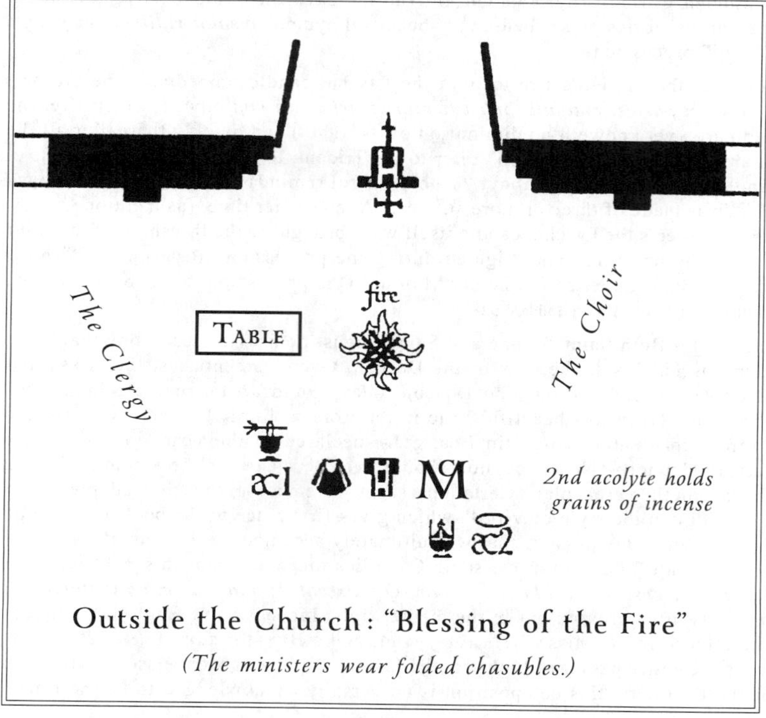

Outside the Church: "Blessing of the Fire"

(The ministers wear folded chasubles.)

1950 • At the church entrance, the Celebrant—wearing a violet Cope—blesses the new fire, previously kindled outside by means of flint and steel. Inside the Church, near the Altar on the Gospel side is the Paschal candle, unlit inside its candlestick. By its side—turned in the direction in which the Gospel is sung—is a lectern covered with white or gold. A stand which will hold the "Trident" is at hand.

(1950) Holy Saturday • Blessing of the New Fire

Sabbato Sancto — *Benedictio Novi Ignis*

1950 • The Celebrant sings the three collects in the ferial tone, and the choir answers "Amen" after each. The 1962 version omits all but one of these collects, adding numerous short prayers not found in the traditional version: *Christus heri et hódie* ; *Ipsius sunt témpora* ; and so forth.

℣. Dóminus vobíscum.

℟. Et cum spíritu tuo.

℣. The Lord be with you.

℟. And with you, his minister.

Orémus.

Deus, qui per Fílium tuum, angulárem scílicet lápidem, claritátis tuæ ignem fidélibus contulísti: prodúctũ e sílice, nostris profutúrum úsibus, novum hanc ignem sanctí✠fica: et concéde nobis, ita per hæc festa paschália cæléstibus desidériis inflammári; ut ad perpétuæ claritátis, puris méntibus, valeámus festa pertíngere. Per eúmdem Christum Dóminum nostrum. ℟. Amen.

Let us pray.

CORNER-STONE, O God, thy Son is, and to all his faithful the Source of Light; and here is fire, newly struck from the flint, to be ✠ hallowed, if thou wilt, for our daily using. O may this Easter rejoicing with such heavenly desires enkindle us, to that feast we may come hereafter, where is light perpetual: through the same Christ our Lord. ℟. Amen.

Orémus.

Dómine Deus, Pater omnípotens, lumen indeficiens, qui es cónditor ómnium lúminum: béne✠dic hoc lumen, quod a te sanctificátum, atque benedíctum est, qui illumináṡti omnem mundum: ut ab eo lúmine accendámur, atque illuminémur igne claritátis tuæ: et sicut illumináṡti Móysen exeúntem de Ægýpto, ita illúmines corda et sensus nostros; ut ad vitam, et lucem ætérnam perveníre mereámur. Per Christum, Dóminum nostrum. ℟. Amen.

Let us pray.

LORD GOD, Father almighty, Light that fails not, and Author of all lights that are; thy ✠ blessing on this light, already by thee blessed and sanctified, when thou didst illumine the whole world! May we, too, catch fire, with thy clear shining all ablaze, mind and heart of us fully enlightened, as by yonder cloud that led Moses out of Egypt, till at last we find our way to life and light eternal: through Christ our Lord. ℟. Amen.

Orémus.

Dómine sancte, Pater omnípotens, ætérne Deus: benedicéntibus nobis hunc ignem in nómine tuo, et unigéniti Fílii tui Dei ac Dómini nostri Jesu Christi, et Spíritus Sancti, coöperári dignéris; et ádjuva nos contra igníta tela inimíci, et illústra grátia cæléṡti: Qui vivis et regnas cum eódem Unigénito tuo, et Spíritu Sancto, Deus: per ómnia sǽcula sæculórum. ℟. Amen.

Let us pray.

HOLY LORD, Father almighty, everlasting God, in thy name, in the name of thy only-begotten Son, our Lord and God Jesus Christ, in the name of the Holy Spirit, this fire we bless. Make our work thine; against the fiend's fiery arrows protect us still, and with thy heavenly grace enlighten us: who with the same, thy only-begotten Son, and with the Holy Spirit, livest and reignest, and art God, for ever and ever. ℟. Amen.

[Editor's Note: Unlike the 1962 version, the Celebrant says neither "Dóminus vobíscum" nor "Orémus" at this point. Notice the Deacon will not insert those incense grains until the Exsultet is almost finished being sung, specifically when he reaches the words "curvat impéria." The following prayer is similar but not identical to the 1962 version; e.g. *super hunc incénsum céreum* (1962) vs. *super hoc incénsum* (1950) and *regenerátor inténde* (1962) vs. *regenerátor accénde* (1950). For insight as to why these changes may have been made, see Father Herbert Thurston's *Lent and Holy Week* (1904) pages 422-424 and Father Steuart's *Development of Christian Worship* (1953) page 275.]

1950 • Then he blesses five grains of incense—which will later be inserted into the Paschal candle—saying the following prayer. (The acolyte who holds the grains of incense stands with them before the Celebrant.)

Deinde benedicit quinque grana incensi ponenda in Cereo, dicens absolute hanc Orationem.

ON THIS INCENSE, we pray thee, Almighty God, may thy ✠ blessing fall abundantly; this glow in midnight darkness do thou kindle, and all unseen renew. Bathed be the sacrifice we offer this night with the unseen influence of thy light-giving; and if aught be carried away hence that is hallowed by the touch of these mysteries, there where it rests may the foul fiend's malice be quite driven away, and thy august power be present: through Christ our Lord. ℟. Amen.

Véniat, quǽsumus, omnípotens Deus, super hoc incénsum larga tuæ bene✠dictiónis infúsio: et hunc noctúrnum splendórem invisíbilis regenerátor accénde; ut non solum sacrifícium, quod hac nocte litátum est, arcána lúminis tui admixtióne refúlgeat; sed in quocúmque loco ex hujus sanctificatiónis mystério áliquid fúerit deportátum, expúlsa diabólicæ fraudis nequítia, virtus tuæ majestátis assístat. Per Christum Dóminum nostrum. ℟. Amen.

(1950) Holy Saturday • "Lumen Christi" Procession

Sabbato Sancto *Ad Processionem*

1950 • During this prayer, an acolyte puts some coals from the blessed fire into a thurible. After the prayer is ended, the Celebrant puts incense into the thurible, blessing it in the usual way. He then sprinkles three times with holy water the five grains of incense and the fire, speaking (not singing) "Aspérges me, etc.," without its usual psalm verse. He incenses the fire with three double swings; then he incenses the grains of incense in the same way, saying nothing.

Meanwhile, all the lights in the church have been extinguished, so that they may be lighted from the newly-blessed fire. The Celebrant again puts incense into the thurible and blesses it, as usual. [Editor's Note: In the 1962 version, incense is not placed into the thurible until the procession has ended.] Then the Deacon, having exchanged his purple folded chasuble for a white dalmatic, joins the procession, carrying the Trident. The procession—consisting of all present, led by the thurifer and the acolyte holding the plate of incense grains—moves through the church doors.

As soon as the Celebrant is inside the church, the procession pauses. The Deacon lights one of the three wicks on the Trident by means of a taper—which was lit from the new fire. (He lowers the Trident to do so.) Then he holds the reed upright and genuflects, and all present genuflect with him—except the Subdeacon who has the Cross. At a very low pitch, the Deacon intones "Lumen Christi" as follows.

Dum benedicit grana incensi, Acolythus assumens de carbonibus benedictis ponit in thuribulo: et finita Oratione supradicta, Sacerdos de navicula ponit incensum in thuribulo, benedicens illud more solito: deinde praedicta grana incensi, et ignem ter aspergit aqua benedicta, dicens: "Aspérges me, Dómine," sine cantu et sine Psalmo, et ter adolet incenso. Interim omnia luminaria Ecclesiae exstinguuntur, ut de igne benedicto postmodum accendantur. Tum Diaconus indutus dalmatica albi coloris, accipit arundinem cum tribus candelis in summitate illius, triangulo distinctis. Praecedit Thuriferarius cum Acolytho deferente in vase quinque grana incensi: sequitur Subdiaconus cum Cruce, et Clerus per ordinem: deinde Diaconus cum arundine, post eum Celebrans. Cum Diaconus ingressus est Ecclesiam, inclinat arundinem, et Acolythus deferens candelam accensam de novo igne, accendit unam ex illis tribus candelis desuper positis: et Diaconus elevans arundinem, genuflectit, similiter et omnes alii cum eo, praeter Subdiaconum Crucem ferentem, et cantat solus:

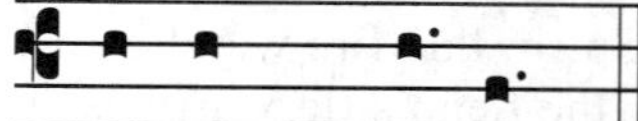

Lumen Chri-sti.

Christ's light behold we!

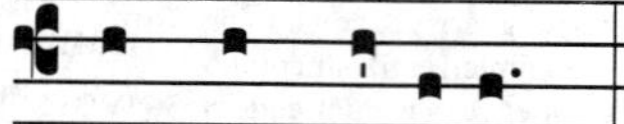

℟. Deo grá-ti- as.

℟. Thanks be to God.

1950 • At the middle of the church the same ceremony is repeated; the Deacon lights the second wick and sings at a higher pitch the following. | *Et procedens ad medium Ecclesiae, ibi accenditur alia candela: et iterum genuflexus, ut supra, altius cantat:*

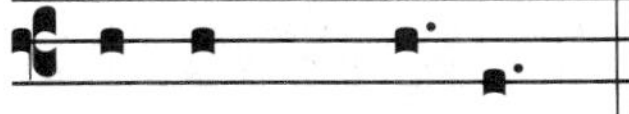

Lumen Chri-sti.

Christ's light behold we!

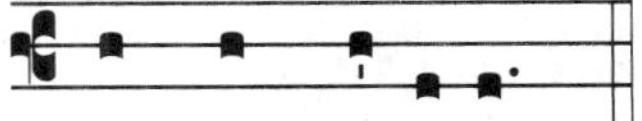

℟. Deo grá-ti- as.

℟. Thanks be to God.

1950 • The Deacon goes forward into the Sanctuary, in front of the Altar, and—again genuflecting as before—lights the third wick and sings in a still higher key as follows. | *Tertio procedit ante Altare, ubi accenditur tertia candela: et rursum genuflexus, ut prius, adhuc altius dicit:*

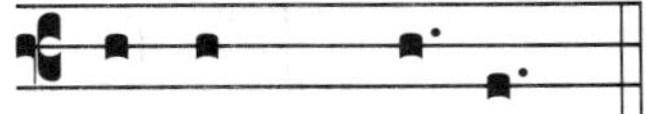

Lumen Chri-sti.

Christ's light behold we!

℟. Deo grá-ti- as.

℟. Thanks be to God.

(1950) Holy Saturday • Blessing of the Candle

Sabbato Sancto *Benedictio Cerei*

1950 • Having kissed the Altar, the Celebrant proceeds to the Epistle side—although some liturgists say he stays in the center. The Deacon takes the book containing the Exsultet, kneels before the Celebrant, and asks his blessing ("Jube, domne, benedícere.") as for the Gospel. The Celebrant prays as follows. *Deinde Celebrans ascendit ad Altare in cornu Epistolae, et Diaconus dat arundinem uni Acolytho: et accipiens librum, petit a Celebrante benedictionem, ut fit ad Evangelium, Sacerdote dicente:*

Dóminus sit in corde tuo, et in lábiis tuis: ut digne et competénter annúnties suum Paschále præcónium: In nómine Patris, et Fílii, ✠ et Spíritus Sancti. Amen.

THE LORD be in your heart and on your lips, so that you may fitly and worthily proclaim his Easter tidings: in the name of the Father, and of the Son, ✠ and of the Holy Ghost. Amen.

[Editor's note: The Exsultet has many names: *Praeconium Paschale* ("Paschal Praise"), *Eucharistia Lucernaris*, Easter Laud, Easter Praeconium, Blessing of the Paschal Candle, Sanctification of the Candle, and so on. In the Middle Ages, it was called *Benedictio Cerei* ("Blessing of the Candle"). Cardinal Schuster (d. 1954), a Benedictine who became Archbishop of Milan, wrote as follows: "This composition of the Deacon has a very special character, and liturgical tradition demanded that it should be read from a parchment scroll, which the Deacon, standing in the ambo, gradually unrolled. It was usually illustrated, but the pictures were painted upside down, so that the people should be able to see them as the scroll was unfolded." The Exsultet had various forms through the centuries; in particular, although no longer found in the Missal, it often praised "the purity and diligence of bees" {Schuster p295}. Some versions compared the purity of the bee to that of Our Lady; see James Monti *Catholic Worship in the Middle Ages* (Ignatius Press, 2012), page 482.]

1950 • Then the Deacon goes to the lectern, puts the book on it, opens it, and incenses it as at the Gospel. Meanwhile the Celebrant has gone to the Epistle side (unless he moved there earlier) and faces the Deacon. The Subdeacon turns the Cross, so that it faces the Celebrant. On the Deacon's left are acolytes: one holding the Trident, the other holding the grains of incense which are to be fixed in the Paschal candle. The Deacon begins to sing the Exsultet with hands joined, and all present stand. The Celebrant does not quietly read; he stands and listens to the Deacon singing. | *Postea vadit ad pulpitum, et ponit super eo librum, et incensat. A dextris Diaconi stent Subdiaconus cum Cruce, et Thuriferarius: a sinistris duo Acolythi, ille qui tenet arundinem, et alius tenens in vase quinque grana incensi benedicti figenda in Cereo. Tunc, surgentibus omnibus, et stantibus, ut fit ad Evangelium, Diaconus cantat:*

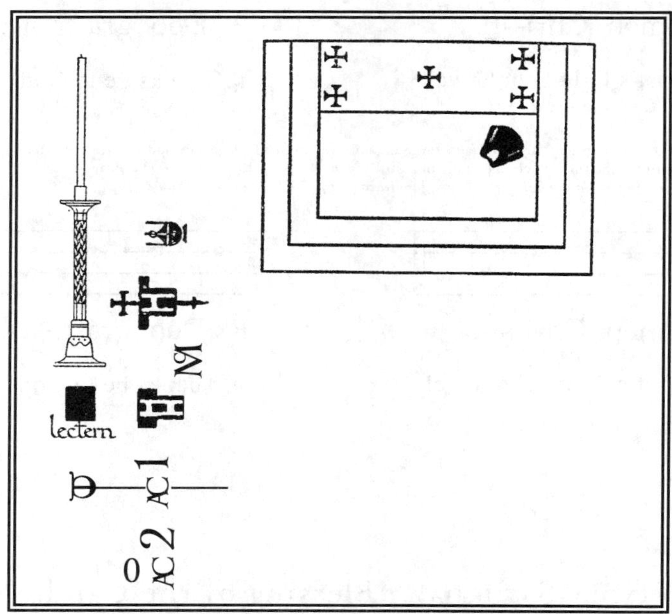

Father Fortescue: "Everyone standing, he begins that magnificent chant, the Exsultet. Perhaps nowhere in our rite have we so splendid an example of emotional poetry as this. Its music, too, first herald of the Easter joy, is unequalled. Competent musicians have described this as the most beautiful plainsong melody of all. The Exsultet, strikingly unlike our usual liturgical texts, is full of emotion about Spring, the bees, and even about the Deacon who sings it. Plainly it is not originally Roman. It is certainly very old; we can trace it from the fourth century."

OY FOR ALL HEAVEN'S angel citizens, joy in the secret council-chambers of God! In praise of this royal Conqueror, let the trumpet sound deliverance. Bathed in that bright sunshine, let earth too rejoice; splendors of the eternal King all about her, nothing of her orb but feels the shadows gone.

Exsúltet jam Angélica turba cælórum: exsúltent divína mystéria: et pro tanti Regis victória, tuba ínsonet salutáris. Gáudeat et tellus tantis irradiáta fulgóribus: et ætérni Regis splendóre illustráta, totíus orbis se séntiat amisísse calíginem.

Lætétur et mater Ecclésia, tanti lúminis adornáta fulgóribus: et magnis populórum vócibus hæc aula resúltet. Quaprópter adstántes vos, fratres caríssimi, ad tam miram hujus sancti lúminis claritátem, una mecum, quæso, Dei omnipoténtis misericórdiam invocáte. Ut qui me non meis méritis intra Levitárum númerum dignátus est aggregáre: lúminis sui claritátem infúndens, Cérei hujus laudem impléré perfíciat. Per Dóminum nostrum Jesum Christum Fílium suum: qui cum eo vivit et regnat in unitáte Spíritus sancti Deus. Per ómnia sǽcula sæculórum.

JOY, TOO, FOR THE CHURCH, that has yonder flashing rays for her jewels; with the loud acclaim of worshippers let these courts ring again! Brethren well-belovèd, by the strange glow of this holy light drawn together, pray you, in my company cry to Almighty God for mercy. His choice, not worth of mine, it was that enrolled me for his minister; may the outpouring of his own light enable me, the high mystery of yonder candle while I set forth. Through his Son Jesus Christ our Lord, who with him, in the bond of the Holy Spirit, lives and reigns and is God: World without end.

℟. Amen.

℣. Dóminus vobíscum.

℟. Et cum spíritu tuo.

℣. Sursum corda.

℟. Habémus ad Dóminum.

℣. Grátias agámus Dómino Deo nostro.

℟. Dignum et justum est.

℟. Amen.

℣. The Lord be with you.

℟. And with you, his minister.

℣. Lift up your hearts!

℟. We hold them out to the Lord.

℣. Give we thanks to the Lord our God.

℟. Right it is and seemly.

Vere dignum et justum est, invisíbilem Deum Patrem omnipoténtem, Filiúmque ejus unigénitum, Dñm nostrum Jesum Christum, toto cordis ac mentis afféctu, et vocis ministério personáre. Qui pro nobis ætérno Patri, Adæ débitum solvit: et véteris piáculi cautiónem pio cruóre detérsit. Hæc sunt enim festa Paschália, in quibus verus ille Agnus occíditur, cujus sánguine postes fidélium consecrántur.

RIGHT IT IS ASSUREDLY and most beseeming, not the whole love of heart and mind only, but tongue should perform its office, praising God aloud; God the Father, invisible and almighty, and with him his only Son, Jesus Christ our Lord. He, in our name, paid to the eternal Father the whole debt of Adam, blotting out the bond that still held us forfeit, with his dear Blood. Paschal feast is this; here the Lamb is slain, with whose Blood the doors of his faithful people are hallowed.

Hæc nox est, in qua primum patres nostros fílios Ísraël edúctos de Ægýpto, Mare rubrum sicco vestígio transíre fecísti. Hæc ígitur nox est, quæ peccatórum ténebras, colúmnæ illuminatióne purgávit. Hæc nox est, quæ hódie per univérsum mundum, in Christo credéntes, a vítiis sǽculi, et calígine peccatórum segregátos, reddit grátiæ, sóciat sanctitáti. Hæc nox est, in qua destrúctis vínculis mortis, Christus ab ínferis victor ascéndit.

THIS NIGHT, LONG AGO, thou didst rescue the sons of Israel, our fathers, out of Egypt, over the Red Sea bidding them pass dryshod; none but this [night], with pillar of cloud to enlighten it, shadow of man's sin could purge away. This same night in our time the whole world knows of; Christ's believers, from this ill world and sin's darkness estranging, it restores to grace, to holiness weds them. On this night death's bonds were riven, and from the grave, its Conqueror, Christ arose.

MAN'S BIRTH WERE BANE, save for boon of man's redemption; what strange lavishing of mercy was this, what untold excess of love, when thou, for a slave's ransom, wouldst barter thy own Son! Great need was there of Adam's transgression, that Christ might die for its atoning; happy fault, that won so holy and so high a Redeemer!

Nihil enim nobis nasci prófuit, nisi rédimi profuísset. O mira circa nos tuæ pietátis dignátio! O inæstimábilis diléctio caritátis: ut servum redímeres, Fílium tradidísti! O certe necessárium Adæ peccátum, quod Christi morte delétum est! O felix culpa, quæ talem ac tantum méruit habére Redemptórem!

NEVER WAS NIGHT so blessèd as this; the very time, the very hour, of Christ's rising from the dead who else might witness? This is the night foretold in prophecy: *Night shines clear as the day itself, night shall be the only witness of my pleasures.* A night sanctified, our misdeeds banishing, our guilt assoiling *, of sinners the pardon, of mourners the consolation. Now feuds are forgotten, now friendships are a-fashioning, now is the pride of tyrants brought low.

O vere beáta nox, quæ sola méruit scire tempus et horam, in qua Christus ab ínferis resurréxit! Hæc nox est, de qua scriptum est: *Et nox sicut dies illuminábitur: Et nox illuminátio mea in delíciis meis.* (Ps 138: 11-12) Hujus ígitur sanctificátio noctis, fugat scélera, culpas lavat: et reddit innocéntiam lapsis, et mœstis lætítiam. Fugat ódia, concórdiam parat, et curvat impéria.

1950 • Here the Deacon fixes the five grains of blessed incense in the candle in the form of a cross. He comes back to the lectern and continues the chant. | *Hic Diaconus infigit quinque grana incensi benedicti in Cereo in modum crucis, hoc ordine:*

	1	
4	2	5
	3	

O THEN, in thy night of pardon, accept, holy Father, this our evening sacrifice; incense thy holy Church offers thee, and wax of the bee's making, year by year through her ministers. Such tidings they be, yonder pillar makes known to us, that now to God's glory the bright fire enkindles:

In hujus ígitur noctis grátia, súscipe sancte Pater, incénsi hujus sacrifícium vespertínum: quod tibi in hac Cérei oblatióne solémni, per ministrórum manus de opéribus apum, sacrosáncta reddit Ecclésia. Sed jam colúmnæ hujus præcónia nóvimus, quam in honórem Dei rútilans ignis accéndit.

1950 • The Deacon lights the Paschal candle with one of the candles on the Trident, or with a taper from one. (It may be necessary for the Master of Ceremonies to take down the Paschal candle to light it.)

Hic Diaconus accendit Cereum cum una e tribus candelis in arundine positis.

FIRE THAT INTO MANY FLAMES is parted, yet diminishes never; so bravely it melts, wax of the bee's gendering, life of this holy candle to nourish.

Qui licet sit divísus in partes, mutuáti tamen lúminis detriménta non novit. Álitur enim liquántibus ceris, quas in substántiam pretiósæ hujus lámpadis, apis mater edúxit.

1950 • Here the lamps in the church are relighted. | *Hic accenduntur lampades.*

[Editor's Note: When the Deacon has sung "apis mater eduxit" he pauses; an acolyte uses the triple candle to light a candle on a pole, then goes to light all the lamps in the church, beginning with those before the High Altar (but not the candles on the Altar, which will not be lit until just before Mass). Meanwhile the choir and clergy may sit, rising again as soon as the Deacon continues. When the lamp or lamps before the High Altar are lit, the Deacon continues and sings to the end. Some authors—such as Bishop Bartholomew Eustace—say the church lamps are lit from the Paschal candle, not the triple candle.]

* *Assoiling* • from the Latin word "absolvere" (to absolve); Knox seems to be making a play on words. The Latin has *culpas lavat* ("washes guilts") whereas *assoil* reminds us of "soiled" or tarnished.

O vere beáta nox, quæ exspoliávit Ægýptios, ditávit Hebræos! Nox, in qua terrénis cæléstia, humánis divína jungúntur. Orámus ergo te, Dómine: ut Céreus iste in honórem tui nóminis consecrátus, ad noctis hujus calíginem destruéndam, indeficiens persevéret. Et in odórem suavitátis accéptus, supérnis luminaribus misceátur. Flammas ejus lúcifer matutínus invéniat. Ille, inquam, lúcifer, qui nescit occásum. Ille, qui regréssus ab ínferis, humáno géneri serénus illúxit.

O NIGHT of happy augury, that laid Egypt bare, the Hebrews endowing! Of earth and heaven, of things divine and things human, one night the meeting-place! Such a light be this candle of ours, Lord, we beseech thee, to thy glory devoted, as will overcome our darkness, burning on undiminished. Be it accepted, Lord, like incense before thee, with all the lights of heaven to bear it company; dawn of the Day-star find it still unextinguished, that only Day-star which knows no setting, Christ the sunshine of the world, from death arisen.

Precámur ergo te, Dñe: ut nos fámulos tuos, omnémque clerum, et devotíssimum pópulum: una cum beatíssimo Papa nostro [*Name of Pope*] et Antístite nostro [*Name of Bishop*] quiéte témporum concéssa, in his Paschálibus gáudiis, assídua protectióne régere, gubernáre, et conserváre dignéris. ✠ *See note below.*

FOR OURSELVES, LORD, and for all thy ministers; for thy people that devoutly serve thee; for the most holy father [*Name of Pope*] our Pope, and for our Bishop [*Name of Bishop*], we make intercession; in this time of Paschal holiday may we dwell at peace, preserved, controlled, and guided by thy care unremitting. ✠ *See note below.*

Per eúmdem Dóminum nostrum Jesum Christum Fílium tuum: Qui tecum vivit et regnat in unitáte Spíritus Sancti, Deus: Per ómnia sǽcula sæculórũ. ℟. Amen.

Through the same Lord Jesus Christ, thy Son, who with thee in the bond of the Holy Spirit, lives and reigns and is God: for ever and ever. ℟. Amen.

✠ During the nineteenth century, the section of the Exsultet praying for the emperor (or king) began to be omitted. For instance, *The Complete Office of Holy Week*—with 1875 Imprimatur by Most Rev'd John McCloskey, Archbishop of New York—omits this section, as does the popular hand-missal by Father Francis Xavier Lasance (d. 1946). Father Adrian Fortescue, writing in 1918, says this clause is "always omitted." Abbat Guéranger says this clause—like the prayer for the Emperor on Good Friday—was only said "in countries subject to the German Emperor." Nonetheless, some editions of the *Missale Romanum* do include it:

Réspice étiam ad devotíssimum Imperatórem nostrum *N.*, cujus tu, Deus, desidérii vota prænóscens, ineffábili pietátis et misericórdiæ tuæ múnere, tranquíllum perpétuæ pacis accómmoda: et cæléstem victóriam cum omni pópulo suo.

Regard likewise our king, *N.*, and knowing the desires of his heart grant O God by the ineffable grace of thy bounty and mercy that he may enjoy a tranquility of perpetual peace and together with his people a heavenly victory.

In 1955, Venerable Pope Pius XII revised Holy Week. As part of this reform, the section in the Exsultet about the emporer—which had been omitted for almost a century—was replaced by a clause written in 1951 (cf. *Dominicae Resurrectionis Vigiliam,* §13). Those who use the 1962 Missal will use it:

Réspice étiam ad eos, qui nos in potestáte regunt, et, ineffábili pietátis et misericórdiæ tuæ múnere, dírige cogitatiónes eórum ad justítiam et pacem, ut de terréna operositáte ad cæléstem pátriam pervéniant cum omni pópulo tuo.

Direct thy gaze also on those who are our political rulers, and with thy tenderness and mercy, gifts too sublime for words, guide their thoughts towards justice and peace. In this way, their earthly labor done, in company with all thy people, they may reach their heavenly fatherland.

OMITTING PROPHECIES? Father Fortescue wrote in 1918: "It is forbidden to leave out the prophecies; all must be sung entire. It is forbidden for the lector to sing only a part of each, stopping when the Celebrant has read the whole. If there are not twelve lectors, the same person may sing several prophecies. It is better that he should not sing two consecutively. The lectors follow in order of rank, beginning with those of lower rank."

LECTORS IN 1950: In the middle of the choir, lectors sing the twelve prophecies, with hands resting on the lectern or book, as the Celebrant reads each prophecy quietly at the Altar. The "lector" spoken of by the pre-1955 books was assumed to be a man in minor orders. We know this "lector" was not a layman: for instance, an altar server is instructed to "hold the lector's biretta" while he chants the lessons, and no layman at that time would have worn a biretta.

LECTORS IN 1962: In the 1962 version, a "capable reader" is spoken of. On Holy Thursday, this capable reader "wearing a surplice, may read or sing the Epistle while the Celebrant stands at the Altar and listens." On Good Friday, a "capable reader" may sing the Old Testament readings at the beginning. On Holy Saturday, a "capable reader" may read all the Old Testament readings and even the Epistle. On this, see *Mass & Vespers* (Solesmes, 1957) pages 547, 572, 576, 634, and 639. Almost seventy years later, with the benefit of hindsight, our editorial suggestion is that no man should read or sing the Epistle at any time if he be not, at a minimum, tonsured.

1950 • As soon as the *Praeconium Paschale* is ended, all present sit. The Deacon closes the book and leaves it on the lectern. The Celebrant and ministers return to the Sedilia, where the Celebrant exchanges his purple Cope for a purple Chasuble. The Deacon takes off his white Dalmatic and dons a purple folded chasuble. All three sacred ministers now, for the first time, put on purple maniples.

(1950) HOLY SATURDAY • The Prophecies

Sabbato Sancto *Prophetiae*

1950 • During the reading of the lessons, the catechumens may be catechized and otherwise prepared for Baptism. Some authors say this "final instruction" should take place on the church porch; cf. Monsignor William J. Lallou's *Prophecies on Holy Saturday* (Catholic Biblical Association, 1944) page 300.

While the Prophecies are chanted, the Celebrant reads them quietly. The Celebrant and ministers stand in a line at the Epistle corner, as at the Introit. When the Celebrant has finished reading in a quiet voice, he may sit at the Sedilia with the ministers until the lector concludes his sung version. They are called "Prophecies" although not all belong to the prophetical books—yet each has some indirect reference at least to the coming Messiah. They are read without any heading or introduction.

Completa benedictione Cerei, Diaconus, depositis albis, sumit violacea paramenta, et vadit ad Celebrantem: qui exuitur pluviali, et sumit manipulum et casulam violacei coloris. Postea leguntur Prophetiae sine titulo, nec in earum fine respondetur "Deo grátias," et Celebrans legit eas submissa voce ad Altare in cornu Epistolae. In fine Prophetiarum dicuntur Orationes modo subscripto. Ante, vel interim dum Prophetiae leguntur, Presbyteri catechizent catechumenos baptizandos, et praeparent ad baptismum.

FIRST PROPHECY. *Genesis 1: 1-31; 2: 1-2*

OD, AT THE BEGINNING of time, created heaven and earth. Earth was still an empty waste, and darkness hung over the deep; but already, over its waters, brooded the Spirit of God. Then God said: Let there be light; and the light began. God saw the light, and found it good, and he divided the spheres of light and darkness; the light he called Day and the darkness Night. So evening came and morning, and one day passed.

In princípio creávit Deus cælum et terram. Terra autem erat inánis et vácua, et ténebræ erant super fáciem abýssi: et Spíritus Dei ferebátur super aquas. Dixítque Deus: Fiat lux. Et facta est lux. Et vidit Deus lucem, quod esset bona: et divísit lucem a ténebris. Appellavítque lucem Diem, et ténebras Noctem: factúmque est véspere et mane, dies unus.

Dixit quoque Deus: Fiat firmaméntum in médio aquárum: et dívidat aquas ab aquis. Et fecit Deus firmaméntum, divisítque aquas, quæ erant sub firmaménto, ab his, quæ erant super firmaméntum. Et factum est ita. Vocavítque Deus firmaméntum, Cælum: et factum est véspere et mane, dies secúndus.

God said, too, Let a solid vault rise amid the waters, to keep these waters apart from those; a vault by which God would separate the waters which were beneath it from the waters above it; and so it was done. This vault God called the Sky. So evening came, and morning, and a second day passed.

Dixit vero Deus: Congregéntur aquæ, quæ sub cælo sunt, in locum unum: et appáreat árida. Et factum est ita. Et vocávit Deus áridam, Terram: congregationésque aquárum appellávit Mária. Et vidit Deus, quod esset bonum.

And now God said, Let the water below the vault collect in one place to make dry land appear. And so it was done; the dry land God called Earth, and the water, where it had collected, he called the Sea. All this God saw, and found it good.

Et ait: Gérminet terra herbam viréntem et faciéntem semen, et lignum pomíferum fáciens fructum juxta genus suum, cujus semen in semetípso sit super terram. Et factum est ita. Et prótulit terra herbam viréntem et faciéntem semen juxta genus suum, lignúmque fáciens fructum, et habens unumquódque seméntem secúndum spéciem suam. Et vidit Deus, quod esset bonum. Et factum est véspere et mane, dies tértius.

Let the earth, he said, yield grasses that grow and seed; fruit-trees too, each giving fruit of its own kind, and so propagating itself on earth. And so it was done; the earth yielded grasses that grew and seeded, each according to its kind, and trees that bore fruit, each with the power to propagate its own kind. And God saw it, and found it good. So evening came, and morning, and a third day passed.

Dixit autem Deus: Fiant luminária in firmaménto cæli, et dívidant diem ac noctem, et sint in signa et témpora et dies et annos: ut lúceant in firmaménto cæli, et illúminent terram. Et factum est ita.

Next, God said, Let there be luminaries in the vault of the sky, to divide the spheres of day and night; let them give portents, and be measures of time, to mark out the day and the year; let them shine in the sky's vault, and shed light on the earth. And so it was done.

Fecítque Deus duo luminária magna: lumináre majus, ut præésset diéi: et lumináre minus, ut præésset nocti: et stellas. Et pósuit eas in firmaménto cæli, ut lucérent super terram, et præéssent diéi ac nocti, et divíderent lucem ac ténebras. Et vidit Deus, quod esset bonum. Et factum est véspere et mane, dies quartus.

God made the two great luminaries, the greater of them to command the day, and the lesser to command the night; then he made the stars. All these he put in the vault of the sky, to shed their light on the earth, to control day and night, and divide the spheres of light and darkness. And God saw it, and found it good. So evening came, and morning, and a fourth day passed.

Dixit étiam Deus: Prodúcant aquæ réptile ánimæ vivéntis, et volátile super terram sub firmaménto cæli. Creavítque Deus cete grándia, et omnẽ ánimã vivéntẽ atque motábilem, quam prodúxerant aquæ in spécies suas, et omne volátile secúndũ genus suum. Et vidit Deus, quod esset bonum.

After this, God said, Let the waters produce moving things that have life in them, and winged things that fly above the earth under the sky's vault. Thus God created the huge sea-beasts, and all the different kinds of life and movement that spring from the waters, and all the different kinds of flying things; and God saw it, and found it good.

He pronounced his blessing on them, Increase and multiply, and fill the waters of the sea; and let there be abundance of flying things on the earth. So evening came, and morning, and a fifth day passed.

Benedixítque eis, dicens: Créscite et multiplicámini, et repléte aquas maris: avésque multiplicéntur super terrã. Et factum est véspere et mane, dies quintus.

God said, too, Let the land yield all different kinds of living things, cattle and creeping things and wild beasts of every sort; and so it was done. God made every sort of wild beast, and all the different kinds of cattle and of creeping things; and God saw it, and found it good. And God said:

Dixit quoque Deus: Prodúcat terra ánimam vivéntẽ in génere suo: juménta et reptília, et béstias terræ secúndum spécies suas. Factúmque est ita. Et fecit Deus béstias terræ juxta spécies suas, et juménta, et omne réptile terræ in génere suo. Et vidit Deus, quod esset bonum, et ait:

Let us make man, wearing our own image and likeness; let us put him in command of the fishes in the sea, and all that flies through the air, and the cattle, and the whole earth, and all the creeping things that move on earth.

Faciámus hóminem ad imáginem et similitúdinem nostrã: et præsit píscibus maris et volatílibus cæli, et béstiis universǽque terræ, omníque réptili, quod movétur in terra.

So God made man in his own image, made him in the image of God. Man and woman both, he created them. And God pronounced his blessing on them, Increase and multiply and fill the earth, and make it yours; take command of the fishes in the sea, and all that flies through the air, and all the living things that move on the earth.

Et creávit Deus hóminem ad imáginem suam: ad imáginem Dei creávit illum, másculum et féminam creávit eos. Benedixítque illis Deus, et ait: Créscite et multiplicámini, et repléte terram, et subjícite eam, et dominámini píscibus maris et volatílibus cæli, et univérsis animántibus, quæ movéntur super terram.

Here are all the herbs, God told them, that seed on earth, and all the trees, that carry in them the seeds of their own life, to be your food; food for all beasts on the earth, all that flies in the air, all that creeps along the ground; here all that lives shall find its nourishment. And so it was done.

Dixítque Deus: Ecce, dedi vobis omnem herbam afferéntem semen super terram, et univérsa ligna, quæ habent in semetípsis seméntem géneris sui, ut sint vobis in escam: et cunctis animántibus terræ, omníque vólucri cæli, et univérsis, quæ movéntur in terra, et in quibus est ánima vivens, ut hábeant ad vescéndum. Et factum est ita.

And God saw all that he had made, and found it very good. So evening came, and morning, and a sixth day passed. Thus heaven and earth and all the furniture of them were completed. By the seventh day, God had come to an end of making, and rested on the seventh day, with his whole task accomplished.

Vidítque Deus cuncta, quæ fécerat: et erant valde bona. Et factum est véspere et mane, dies sextus. Ígitur perfécti sunt cæli et terra, et omnis ornátus eórum. Complevítque Deus die séptimo opus suum, quod fécerat: et requiévit die séptimo ab univérso ópere, quod patrárat.

1950 • Each of the twelve prophecies is sung in the same way, although after the fourth, eighth, and eleventh the choir adds a Tract in mode VIII. All in the church sit during the prophecies and chanting, but stand as soon as the ministers are in line behind the Celebrant, genuflect at "Flectamus genua," and stand during the collects. At the conclusion of each collect, all present respond: "Amen."

Celebrant: Orémus.
Deacon: ℣. Flectámus génua.
Subdeacon: ℟. Leváte.

Let us pray.
℣. To your knees.
℟. Stand now erect.

COLLECT AFTER THE FIRST PROPHECY.

Deus, qui mirabíliter creásti hóminem, et mirabílius redemísti: da nobis, quǽsumus, contra oblectaménta peccáti, mentis ratióne persístere; ut mereámur ad ætérna gáudia perveníre. Per Dóminum.

WONDROUS, Lord, was thy making of us, and yet more wondrous our redeeming! May reason, we pray thee, keep its sovereignty in our hearts, proof against the allurements of sin; so be it ours to win eternal happiness. Through our Lord.

SECOND PROPHECY. *Gen. 5:31 — 8:21*

Noë vero cum quingentórum esset annórum, génuit Sem, Cham et Japheth. Cumque cœpíssent hómines multiplicári super terram, et fílias procreássent, vidéntes fílii Dei fílias hóminum quod essent pulchræ, accepérunt sibi uxóres ex ómnibus, quas elégerant.

AND NOE WAS five hundred years old when he became the father of Sem, Cham, and Japheth. Time passed, and the race of men began to spread over the face of earth, they and the daughters that were born to them. And now the sons of God saw how beautiful were these daughters of men, and took them as wives, choosing where they would.

Dixítque Deus: Non permanébit spíritus meus in hómine in ætérnum, quia caro est: erúntque dies illíus centum vigínti annórum. Gigántes autem erant super terram in diébus illis. Postquam enim ingréssi sunt fílii Dei ad fílias hóminum illǽque genuérunt, isti sunt poténtes a sǽculo viri famósi. Videns autem Deus, quod multa malítia hóminum esset in terra, et cuncta cogitátio cordis inténta esset ad malum omni témpore, pœnítuit eum quod hóminem fecísset in terra.

But God said, This spirit of mine shall not endure in man for ever, he is but mortal clay; his life-time shall be a hundred and twenty years. Those were the days when the giants lived on earth; whenever the sons of God had commerce with the daughters of men and they bore children, these were the heroes whose fame has come down to us from long ago. And now God found that earth was full of men's iniquities, and that the whole frame of their thought was set continually on evil; and he repented of having made men on the earth at all.

Et tactus dolóre cordis intrínsecus: Delébo, inquit, hóminem, quem creávi, a fácie terræ, ab hómine usque ad animántia, a réptili usque ad vólucres cæli; pœnitet enim me fecísse eos. Noë vero invénit grátiam coram Dómino.

So, smitten with indignation to the depths of his heart, he said, I will blot out mankind, my creature, from the face of the earth, and with mankind all the beasts and the creeping things and all that flies through the air; I repent of having made them. Only on Noe did God look with favor.

And these were the children of Noe, the man who was accepted as faultless in such a generation, the close friend of God: Noe begot three sons, Sem, Cham, and Japheth. There lay the world, corrupt in God's sight, full of oppression; and God, seeing the world so corrupt (no creature on earth but had lost its true direction), said to Noe, The time has come for me to make an end of all mankind; their coming has filled the earth with oppression; I mean to destroy them, and earth with them.

Hæc sunt generatiónes Noë: Noë vir justus atque perféctus fuit in generatiónibus suis, cum Deo ambulávit. Et génuit tres filios, Sem, Cham et Japheth. Corrúpta est autem terra coram Deo et repléta est iniquitáte. Cumque vidísset Deus terram esse corrúptam (omnis quippe caro corrúperat viam suam super terram), dixit ad Noë: Finis univérsæ carnis venit coram me: repléta est terra iniquitáte a fácie eórum, et ego dispérdam eos cum terra.

Make thyself an ark from planks of wood; in that ark make cabins, and give it a coat of pitch within and without. These are to be the measurements: four hundred and fifty feet of length, seventy-five feet of breadth, and forty-five feet of height. The ark is to have a course of windows, which thou wilt make a foot and a half in height; and thou wilt make a door in its side; and it is to have a hold, and a lower and upper deck.

Fac tibi arcam de lignis lævigátis: mansiúnculas in arca fácies, et bitúmine línies intrínsecus, et extrínsecus. Et sic fácies eam: Trecentórum cubitórum erit longitúdo arcæ, quinquagínta cubitórum latitúdo, et trigínta cubitórum altitúdo illíus. Fenéstram in arca fácies, et in cúbito consummábis summitátem ejus: óstium autem arcæ pones ex látere: deórsum cœnácula et trístega fácies in ea.

Thou must know that I mean to bring a flood of water over the earth, and destroy every creature that lives and breathes under heaven; all that earth holds must perish. But with thee this covenant of mine shall stand; thou shalt take refuge in the ark, thou and thy sons, and thy wife, and thy sons' wives with thee. And take with thee into the ark, to preserve them, a pair of each kind of living creature, male and female, all the different birds, all the different beasts, all the different creeping things of earth; two of each shall go with thee, so that all may survive.

Ecce ego addúcam aquas dilúvii super terram, ut interfíciam omnem carnem, in qua spíritus vitæ est subter cælum. Univérsa quæ in terra sunt, consuméntur. Ponámque fœdus meum tecum: et ingrediéris arcam tu et fílii tui, uxor tua, et uxóres filiórum tuórum tecum. Et ex cunctis animántibus univérsæ carnis bina indúces in arcam, ut vivant tecum: masculíni sexus et feminíni. De volúcribus juxta genus suum, et de juméntis in génere suo, et ex omni réptili terræ secúndum genus suum: bina de ómnibus ingrediéntur tecum, ut possint vívere.

And it is for thee to provide thyself with all that is eaten as food, and store it up, so that thou and they may have food to eat. All this Noe did, at God's bidding. He was six hundred years old when the waters of the flood covered the earth. All the springs of the great depth beneath broke through, and the flood-gates of heaven were opened; and it rained for forty days and forty nights on the earth. That very day Noe and his sons, Sem, Cham, and Japheth, his wife and the three wives of his sons took refuge in the ark; and with them all the different kinds of wild beasts, of cattle, of the creeping things of earth, and of things that fly. But still the ark rode safe on the waters.

Tolles ígitur tecum ex ómnibus escis, quæ mandi possunt, et comportábis apud te: et erunt tam tibi, quam illis in cibum. Fecit ígitur Noë ómnia, quæ præcéperat illi Deus. Erátque sexcentórum annórum quando dilúvii aquæ inundavérunt super terram. Rupti sunt omnes fontes abýssi magnæ, et cataráctæ cæli apértæ sunt: et facta est plúvia super terram quadragínta diébus et quadragínta nóctibus. In artículo diéi illíus ingréssus est Noë, et Sem, et Cham et Japheth fílii ejus: uxor illíus, et tres uxóres filiórum ejus cum eis in arcam: ipsi et omne ánimal secúndum genus suum, univérsaque juménta in génere suo, et omne quod movétur super terram in génere suo, cunctúmque volátile secúndum genus suum. Porro arca ferebátur super aquas.

Et aquæ prævaluérunt nimis super terram: opertíque sunt omnes montes excélsi sub univérso cælo. Quíndecim cúbitis áltior fuit aqua super montes, quos operúerat. Consúmptaque est omnis caro quæ movebátur super terram, vólucrum, animántium, bestiárum, omniúmque reptílium, quæ reptant super terram. Remánsit autem solus Noë, et qui cum eo erant in arca. Obtinuerúntque aquæ terram centum quinquagínta diébus. Recordátus autem Deus Noë, cunctorúmque animántium et ómnium jumentórum, quæ erant cum eo in arca, addúxit spíritum super terram, et imminútæ sunt aquæ. Et clausi sunt fontes abýssi, et cataráctæ cæli: et prohíbitæ sunt plúviæ de cælo. Reversǽque sunt aquæ de terra eúntes et redeúntes: et cœpérunt mínui post centum quinquagínta dies. Cumque transíssent quadragínta dies, apériens Noë fenéstram arcæ, quam fécerat, dimísit corvum: qui egrediebátur, et non revertebátur, donec siccaréntur aquæ super terram. Emísit quoque colúmbam post eum, ut vidéret si jam cessássent aquæ super fáciem terræ. Quæ cum non invenísset ubi requiésceret pes ejus, revérsa est ad eum in arcam: aquæ enim erant super univérsam terram: extendítque manum, et apprehénsam íntulit in arcam. Exspectátis autem ultra septem diébus áliis, rursum dimísit colúmbam ex arca. At illa venit ad eum ad vésperam, portans ramum olívæ viréntibus fóliis in ore suo. Intelléxit ergo Noë quod cessássent aquæ super terram. Exspectavítque nihilóminus septem álios dies: et emísit colúmbam, quæ non est revérsa ultra ad eum.

Higher and higher the waters rose above the ground, till all the high mountains under heaven disappeared; the flood stood fifteen cubits higher than the mountains it covered. All mortal things that moved on earth were drowned, birds and cattle and wild beasts, and all the creeping things of earth. Only Noe and his companions in the ark were left. And the waters held their own over the land for a hundred and fifty days. Then God bethought him of Noe, and of all the wild beasts and the cattle that went with him in the ark; so he made his spirit pass over the earth, and with that, the waters abated. The springs of the great depth closed up again; so, too, did the flood-gates of heaven, and rain fell from heaven no longer; more and more the waters receded from the land, beginning to abate, now that the hundred and fifty days were over. Noe let forty days pass, and then undid the opening he had made in the ark, and sent out one of the ravens, which went this way and that, and had not come back to him when the waters dried up over the earth. Then, to make sure whether the waters had become shallow over all the surface of the ground, he sent out one of the doves. The dove could find no resting-place to perch on, so it came back to the ark and its master; and he put out his hand to catch it, and took it back into the ark. Seven days more he waited, and then sent the dove out from the ark again; this time, it came back to him at nightfall, with a twig of olive in its mouth, the leaves still green on it; and then Noe made sure that the waters had become shallow all over the ground. But still he waited another seven days, and now, when he sent it out, it came back no more.

Locútus est autem Deus ad Noë, dicens: Egrédere de arca, tu et uxor tua, fílii tui et uxóres filiórum tuórum tecum. Cuncta animántia, quæ sunt apud te, ex omni carne, tam in volatílibus quam in béstiis et univérsis reptílibus, quæ reptant super terram, educ tecum, et ingredímini super terram: créscite et multiplicámini super eam. Egréssus est ergo Noë, et fílii ejus: uxor illíus, et uxóres filiórum ejus cum eo. Sed et ómnia animántia, juménta, et reptília quæ reptant super terram secúndum genus suum, egréssa sunt de arca. Ædificávit autem Noë altáre Dómino: et tollens de cunctis pecóribus et volúcribus mundis, óbtulit holocáusta super altáre. Odoratúsque est Dóminus odórem suavitátis.

Then God's word came to Noe, telling him, Come out of the ark, with thy wife and thy sons and their wives. Bring out with thee all the living creatures thou hast there, of all kinds, birds and beasts and creeping things that creep on the earth; occupy this earth, increase and multiply upon it. So Noe came out, and his sons and his wife and his sons' wives with him; and the living creatures came out of the ark, beasts and all creeping things that roam on the earth, in all their various kinds. Thereupon Noe built an altar to the Lord, and chose out beasts that were clean and birds that were clean and made burnt-offerings there. And the Lord smelt a fragrant perfume.

Let us pray.
℣. To your knees.
℟. Stand now erect.

Celebrant: Orémus.
Deacon: ℣. Flectámus génua.
Subdeacon: ℟. Leváte.

COLLECT AFTER THE SECOND PROPHECY.

O GOD, WHO ART Force unwearying and Light unfailing, look down in mercy on thy own wondrous design, the universal Church; and by the ordering of thy Providence, the work of man's salvation ever silently pursue. Let the whole world prove, with its own eyes for witness, how the fallen is yet raised up, and old things made new, and all things return to health at last, through him only, from whom they had their being: our Lord Jesus Christ, thy Son; who with thee.

Deus, incommutábilis virtus, et lumen ætérnum: réspice propítius ad totíus Ecclésiæ tuæ mirábile sacraméntum, et opus salútis humánæ, perpétuæ dispositiónis effectu tranquíllius operáre; totúsque mundus experiátur et vídeat, dejécta érigi, inveteráta renovári, et per ipsum redíre ómnia in íntegrum, a quo sumpsére princípium: Dóminum nostrum Jesum Christum, Fílium tuum: Qui tecum.

THIRD PROPHECY. *Genesis 22: 1-19*

AFTER THIS, GOD would put Abraham to the test. So he called to him, Abraham, Abraham; and when he said, I am here, at thy command, God told him, Take thy only son, thy beloved son Isaac, with thee, to the land of Clear Vision, and there offer him to me in burnt sacrifice on a mountain which I will show thee. Rising, therefore, at dawn, Abraham saddled his ass, bidding two of the men-servants and his son Isaac follow him; he cut the wood needed for the burnt sacrifice, and then set out for the place of which God had spoken to him.

In diébus illis: Tentávit Deus Ábraham, et dixit ad eum: Ábraham, Ábraham. At ille respóndit: Adsum. Ait illi: Tolle fílium tuum unigénitum, quem díligis, Ísaäc, et vade in terram visiónis: atque ibi ófferes eum in holocáustum super unum móntium, quem monstrávero tibi. Ígitur Ábraham de nocte consúrgens, stravit ásinum suum: ducens secum duos júvenes, et Ísaäc fílium suum. Cumque concidísset ligna in holocáustum, ábiit ad locum quem præcéperat ei Deus.

It was two days later when he looked up and saw it, still far off; and now he said to his servants, Wait here with the ass, while I and my son make our way yonder; we will come back to you, when we have offered worship there. Then he took the wood for the sacrifice, and gave it to his son Isaac to carry; he himself carried the brazier and the knife.

Die autem tértio, elevátis óculis, vidit locum procul: dixítque ad púeros suos: Exspectáte hic cum ásino: ego et puer illuc usque properántes, postquam adoravérimus, revertémur ad vos. Tulit quoque ligna holocáusti, et impósuit super Ísaäc fílium suum: ipse vero portábat in mánibus ignem et gládium.

As they walked along together Isaac said to him, Father. What is it, my son? he asked. Why, said he, we have the fire here and the wood; where is the victim we are to sacrifice? My son, said Abraham, God will see to it that he has a victim. So they went on together till they reached the place God had shown him.

Cumque duo pérgerent simul, dixit Ísaäc patri suo: Pater mi. At ille respóndit: Quid vis fili? Ecce, inquit, ignis et ligna: ubi est víctima holocáusti? Dixit autem Ábraham: Deus providébit sibi víctimam holocáusti, fili mi. Pergébant ergo páriter: et venérunt ad locum quem osténderat ei Deus, in quo ædificávit altáre, et désuper ligna compósuit: cumque alligásset Ísaäc fílium suum, pósuit eum in altáre super struem lignórum. Extendítque manum, et arrípuit gládium, ut immoláret fílium suum. Et ecce Ángelus Dómini de cælo clamávit, dicens: Ábraham, Ábraham. Qui respóndit: Adsum. Dixítque ei: Non exténdas manum tuam super púerum, neque fácias illi quidquam: nunc cognóvi, quod times Deum, et non pepercísti unigénito fílio tuo propter me.

And here he built an altar, and set the wood in order on it; then he bound his son Isaac and laid him down there on the altar, above the pile of wood. And he reached out, and took up the knife, to slay his son. But now, from heaven, an angel of the Lord called to him, Abraham, Abraham. And when he answered, Here am I, at thy command, the angel said, Do the lad no hurt, let him alone. I know now that thou fearest God; for my sake thou wast ready to give up thy only son.

Levávit Ábraham óculos suos, vidítque post tergum aríetem inter vepres hæréntem córnibus, quem assúmens óbtulit holocáustum pro fílio. Appellavítque nomen loci illíus, Dóminus videt. Unde usque hódie dícitur: In monte Dóminus vidébit.

And Abraham, looking about him, saw behind him a ram caught by the horns in a thicket; this he took, and offered it as a burnt sacrifice, instead of his son. So Abraham called that spot, The Lord will see to it; and the saying goes to this day, On the mountain top, the Lord will see to it.

Vocávit autem Ángelus Dómini Ábraham secúndo de cælo, dicens: Per memetípsum jurávi, dicit Dóminus: quia fecísti hanc rem, et non pepercísti fílio tuo unigénito propter me: benedícam tibi, et multiplicábo semen tuum sicut stellas cæli et velut arénam quæ est in líttore maris: possidébit semen tuum portas inimicórum suórum, et benedicéntur in sémine tuo omnes gentes terræ, quia obedísti voci meæ. Revérsus est Ábraham ad púeros suos, abierúntque Bersabée simul, et habitávit ibi.

Once more the angel of the Lord called to Abraham out of heaven, and he said, This message the Lord has for thee: I have taken an oath by my own name to reward thee for this act of thine, when thou wast ready to give up thy only son for my sake. More and more will I bless thee, more and more will I give increase to thy posterity, till they are countless as the stars in heaven, or the sand by the seashore; thy children shall storm the gates of their enemies; all the races of the world shall find a blessing through thy posterity, for this readiness of thine to do my bidding. Then Abraham went back to his servants, and took them with him to Bersabee; it was at Bersabee that Abraham made his dwelling.

Celebrant: Orémus.
Deacon: ℣. Flectámus génua.
Subdeacon: ℟. Leváte.

Let us pray.
℣. To your knees.
℟. Stand now erect.

COLLECT AFTER THE THIRD PROPHECY.

Deus, fidélium Pater summe, qui in toto orbe terrárum, promissiónis tuæ fílios diffúsa adoptiónis grátia multíplicas: et per Paschále sacraméntum, Ábraham púerum tuum universárum, sicut jurásti, géntium éfficis patrem; da pópulis tuis digne ad grátiam tuæ vocatiónis introíre. Per Dóminum.

O GOD, OF FAITHFUL SOULS the true Father, ever spreading through the world the grace of adoption, and making fresh heirs of thy promises! Father of all nations thy servant Abraham might not be, save through thy Paschal covenant. Thy people now, may they be worthy of the grace that called them. Through our Lord.

FOURTH PROPHECY. *Exodus 14: 24-31; 15: 1*

IT WAS ALREADY the first watch of the morning, when suddenly, through the pillar of fire and mist, the Lord looked down upon the Egyptians, and brought their army to its doom. He turned the wheels of their chariots aside, so that they drove through deep places. And the Egyptians began to say, Back, back! There is no facing Israel; the Lord is fighting on their side against us.

In diébus illis: Factum est in vigília matutína, et ecce respíciens Dóminus super castra Ægyptiórum per colúmnam ignis et nubis, interfécit exércitum eórum: et subvértit rotas cúrruum, ferebantúrque in profúndum. Dixérunt ergo Ægýptii: Fugiámus Isrælem: Dóminus enim pugnat pro eis contra nos.

Then the Lord said to Moses, Stretch out thy hand over the sea, so that its waters shall recoil on the Egyptians, on all their chariots and their horsemen. And when Moses stretched out his hand towards the sea, at early dawn, it went back to its bed, so that its waters met the Egyptians in their flight, and the Lord drowned them amid the waters.

Et ait Dóminus ad Móysen: Exténde manum tuam super mare, ut revertántur aquæ ad Ægýptios super currus et équites eórum. Cumque extendísset Móyses manum contra mare, revérsum est primo dilúculo ad priórem locum: fugientibúsque Ægýptiis occurrérunt aquæ, et invólvit eos Dóminus in médiis flúctibus.

Back came the water, overwhelming all the chariots and horsemen of Pharao's army that had entered the sea in their pursuit; not a man escaped. But the sons of Israel made their way through the midst of the sea where it had parted, its waters towering like a wall to right and left. So the Lord rescued Israel that day from the assault of the Egyptians; and when they saw the dead Egyptians washed up on the shore, and the great defeat the Lord had inflicted upon them, the people learned to fear the Lord, putting their trust in him and in his servant Moses. Then Moses and the Israelites sang praises to the Lord, and this was their song:

Reversǽque sunt aquæ, et operuérunt currus, et équites cuncti exércitus Pharaónis, qui sequéntes ingréssi fúerant mare: nec unus quidem supérfuit ex eis. Fílii autem Ísraël perrexérunt per médium sicci maris, et aquæ eis erant quasi pro muro a dextris et a sinístris. Liberavítque Dóminus in die illa Ísraël de manu Ægyptiórum. Et vidérunt Ægýptios mórtuos super litus maris, et manum magnam, quam exercúerat Dóminus contra eos: timuítque pópulus Dóminum, et credidérunt Dómino et Móysi, servo ejus. Tunc cécinit Móyses et fílii Ísraël carmen hoc Dómino, et dixérunt:

TRACT AFTER THE FOURTH PROPHECY. *Exodus 15: 1, 2*

A PSALM FOR THE LORD, so great is he and so glorious; horse and rider hurled into the sea! He is my helper and protector and has brought me deliverance. ℣. Shall I not praise him, my own God; shall I not extol him, the God of my father before me? ℣. He is the Lord that destroys wars: the Lord is his name.

Cantémus Dómino: gloriόse enim honorificátus est: equum, et ascensórem projécit in mare: adjútor, et protéctor factus est mihi in salútem. ℣. Hic Deus meus, et honorificábo eum: Deus patris mei, et exaltábo eum. ℣. Dóminus cónterens bella: Dóminus nomen est illi.

Celebrant: Orémus.
Deacon: ℣. Flectámus génua.
Subdeacon: ℟. Leváte.

Let us pray.
℣. To your knees.
℟. Stand now erect.

COLLECT AFTER THE FOURTH PROPHECY.

Deus, cujus antíqua mirácula étiam nostris sǽculis coruscáre sentímus: dum quod uni pópulo, a persecutióne Ægyptíaca liberándo, déxteræ tuæ poténtia contulísti, id in salútem géntium per aquam regeneratiónis operáris: præsta; ut in Ábrahæ fílios, et in Israëlíticam dignitátem, totíus mundi tránseat plenitúdo. Per Dóminum.

O GOD, IN OUR TIME thy ancient marvels have not lost their splendor. Long since, thy constraining power rescued one people from its bondage in Egypt; now, through the waters of new birth, it brings all mankind salvation. Might but the whole world change its allegiance, Abraham's children and citizens of the true Israel now! Through our Lord.

FIFTH PROPHECY. *Isaias 54: 17; 55: 1-11*

Hæc est heréditas servórum Dómini: et justítia eórum apud me, dicit Dóminus. Omnes sitiéntes veníte ad aquas: et qui non habétis argéntum, properáte, émite et comédite: veníte, émite absque argénto et absque ulla commutatióne vinum et lac. Quare appénditis argéntum non in pánibus, et labórem vestrum non in saturitáte? Audíte audiéntes me, et comédite bonum, et delectábitur in crassitúdine ánima vestra.

SUCH THEIR LOT SHALL BE that are the Lord's servants; such protection shall they have of me, says the Lord. So many athirst, and will you not come to the water? So many destitute; who will come and get him food, get wine and milk free, no price to be paid? What, always spending, and no bread to eat, always toiling, and never a full belly? Do but listen, here you shall find content; here are dainties shall ravish your hearts.

Inclináte aurem vestram, et veníte ad me: audíte, et vivet ánima vestra, et fériam vobíscum pactum sempitérnum, misericórdias David fidéles. Ecce testem pópulis dedi eum, ducem ac præceptórem géntibus. Ecce gentem, quam nesciébas, vocábis: et gentes, quæ te non cognovérunt, ad te current propter Dóminum, Deum tuum, et sanctum Ísraël, quia glorificávit te. Quǽrite Dóminum, dum inveníri potest: invocáte eum, dum prope est. Derelínquat ímpius viam suam et vir iníquus cogitatiónes suas, et revertátur ad Dóminum, et miserébitur ejus, et ad Deum nostrum: quóniam multus est ad ignoscéndum.

To my summons give heed and hearing; so your spirits shall revive; a fresh covenant awaits you, this time eternal; gracious promise of mine to David shall be ratified now. Before all the world my witness thou, a prince and a ruler among the nations! Summons of thine shall go out to a nation thou never knowest; peoples that had never heard of thee shall hasten to thy call, such glory has thy God, the Holy One of Israel, bestowed on thee. To the Lord betake you while he may yet be found; cry out while he is close at hand to hear. Leave rebel his ill-doing, sinner his guilty thoughts, and come back to the Lord, sure of his mercy, our God, rich in pardon.

Not mine, the Lord says, to think as you think, deal as you deal; by the full height of heaven above earth, my dealings are higher than your dealings, my thoughts than your thoughts. Once fallen from the sky, does rain or snow return to it? Nay, it refreshes the earth, soaking into it and making it fruitful, till it provides the sower with fresh seed, and hungry mouths with bread. So it is with the word by these lips of mine once uttered; it will not come back, an empty echo, the way it went; all my will it carries out, speeds on its errand; says the Lord, the Almighty.

Non enim cogitatiónes meæ cogitatiónes vestræ: neque viæ vestræ viæ meæ, dicit Dóminus. Quia sicut exaltántur cæli a terra, sic exaltátæ sunt viæ meæ a viis vestris, et cogitatiónes meæ a cogitatiónibus vestris. Et quómodo descéndit imber et nix de cælo, et illuc ultra non revértitur, sed inébriat terram, et infúndit eam, et germináre eam facit, et dat semen serénti et panem comedénti: sic erit verbum meum, quod egrediátur de ore meo: non revertátur ad me vácuum, sed fáciet, quæcúmque vólui, et prosperábitur in his, ad quæ misi illud: dicit Dóminus omnípotens.

Let us pray.
℣. To your knees.
℟. Stand now erect.

Celebrant: Orémus.
Deacon: ℣. Flectámus génua.
Subdeacon: ℟. Leváte.

COLLECT AFTER THE FIFTH PROPHECY.

GOD ALMIGHTY AND ETERNAL, of thy own renown bethink thee; beyond all our fathers hoped for, thy pledge redeem! Fresh heirs to thy promises let thy sacred adoption engender, till thy Church sees it abundantly rewarded, that faith of holy men long ago. Through our Lord.

Omnípotens sempitérne Deus, multíplica in honórem nóminis tui, quod patrum fídei spopondísti: et promissiónis fílios sacra adoptióne diláta; ut, quod prióres sancti non dubitavérunt futúrum, Ecclésia tua magna jam ex parte cognóscat implétum. Per Dóminum.

SIXTH PROPHECY. *Baruch 3: 9-38*

LISTEN, ISRAEL, to the warnings that shall bring thee life; give attentive audience, if thou wouldst learn to be wise. What means it, Israel, that thou findest thyself in the enemy's land, grown old in exile, unclean as a dead body, no more taken into account than men who have gone down to their graves? It is because thou hast forsaken the fountain whence all wisdom comes. If thou hadst but followed the path God showed thee, thou mightest have lived in peace eternally.

Audi, Ísraël, mandáta vitæ: áuribus pércipe, ut scias prudéntiam. Quid est Ísraël quod in terra inimicórum es? inveterásti in terra aliéna, coinquinátus es cum mórtuis: deputátus es cum descendéntibus in inférnum. Dereliquísti fontem sapiéntiæ. Nam si in via Dei ambulásses, habitásses útique in pace sempitérna.

Learn where to find wisdom, and strength, and discernment; so thou wilt find length of years, too, and true life, and cheerfulness, and peace. Who can tell where wisdom dwells, who has made his way into her storehouse?

Disce ubi sit prudéntia, ubi sit virtus, ubi sit intelléctus: ut scias simul ubi sit longitúrnitas vitæ et victus, ubi sit lumen oculórum, et pax. Quis invénit locum ejus? et quis intrávit in thesáuros ejus?

Ubi sunt príncipes géntium, et qui dominántur super béstias, quæ sunt super terram? qui in ávibus cæli ludunt, qui argéntum thesaurízant, et aurum, in quo confídunt hómines, et non est finis acquisitiónis eórum? qui argéntum fábricant, et sollíciti sunt, nec est invéntio óperum illórum?

What has become of those heathen princes, who gained mastery of the beasts that roam the earth, tamed the birds for their pastime; heaping up silver and gold, man's confidence, man's interminable quest? How anxiously they toiled for wealth! And now these devices of theirs are beyond our tracing.

Extermináti sunt, et ad ínferos descendérunt, et álii loco eórum surrexérunt. Júvenes vidérunt lumen, et habitavérunt super terram: viam autem disciplínæ ignoravérunt, neque intellexérunt sémitas ejus, neque fílii eórum suscepérunt eam, a fácie ipsórum longe facta est: non est audíta in terra Chánaän, neque visa est in Theman. Fílii quoque Agar, qui exquírunt prudéntiam, quæ de terra est, negotiatóres Merrhæ et Theman, et fabulatóres, et exquisitóres prudéntiæ et intellegéntias: viam autem sapiéntiæ nesciérunt, neque commemoráti sunt sémitas ejus.

They disappeared, went to their graves, and others succeeded them; a younger generation saw the light and peopled the earth in its turn; but still they could not find their way to the true wisdom, the path to it was hidden still. Their children, too, clutched at it in vain; it was as far as ever from their reach. In Chanaan, none had heard tell of it, in Theman none had caught sight of it; even the sons of Agar, so well schooled in earthly wisdom, even the merchants of Merrha and Theman, with all their lore of legend, their skill and cunning laboriously gained, never found the track of true wisdom, or told us what its haunts were.

O Ísraël, quam magna est domus Dei et ingens locus possessiónis ejus! Magnus est et non habet finem: excélsus et imménsus. Ibi fuérunt gigántes nomináti illi, qui ab inítio fuérunt, statúra magna, sciéntes bellum. Non hos elegit Dóminus, neque viam disciplínæ invenérunt: proptérea periérunt. Et quóniam non habuérunt sapiéntiam, interiérunt propter suam insipiéntiam. Quis ascéndit in cælum, et accépit eam et edúxit eam de núbibus? Quis transfretávit mare, et invénit illam? et áttulit illam super aurum eléctum? Non est, qui possit scire vias ejus neque qui exquírat sémitas ejus:

Israel, how wide is God's house, how spacious is his domain, large beyond all bound, high beyond all measure! The heroes of old were nurtured there, men whose fame comes down to us from the beginning of time, huge in stature, great warriors; but it was not these God had chosen; they died without ever attaining true knowledge. Not for them was the possession of wisdom, and in their folly they perished. What man ever scaled heaven, and gained wisdom there, brought it back from the clouds? What man ever crossed the sea, and found it there, brought it back like a cargo of pure gold? The path to it none may know, the clue of it none may find.

sed qui scit univérsa, novit eam et adinvénit eam prudéntia sua: qui præparávit terram in ætérno témpore, et replévit eam pecúdibus et quadrupédibus: qui emíttit lumen, et vadit: et vocávit illud, et obédit illi in tremóre. Stellæ autem dedérunt lumen in custódiis suis, et lætátæ sunt: vocátæ sunt, et dixérunt: Ádsumus: et luxérunt ei cum jucunditáte, qui fecit illas. Hic est Deus noster, et non æstimábitur álius advérsus eum. Hic adinvénit omnem viam disciplínæ, et trádidit illam Jacob púero suo et Ísraël diléсto suo. Post hæc in terris visus est, et cum homínibus conversátus est.

Only he who knows all things possesses it, only his mind conceives it. He it is who framed the abiding earth, and filled it with cattle and four-footed beasts of every kind. It is on his errand that the light goes forth, his summons that it obeys with awe; joyfully the stars shine out, keeping the watches he has appointed, answer when he calls their muster-roll, and offer their glad radiance to him who fashioned them. Such a God is ours; what rival will be compared to him? He it is who has the key to all knowledge, and he has given it to his servant Jacob, to the well-loved race of Israel; not till then would he reveal himself on earth, and hold converse with mortal men.

Let us pray.
℣. To your knees.
℟. Stand now erect.

Celebrant: Orémus.
Deacon: ℣. Flectámus génua.
Subdeacon: ℟. Leváte.

COLLECT AFTER THE SIXTH PROPHECY.

O GOD, WHOSE CALLING of the nations bids thy Church in every age increase, to all whom thou dost cleanse in these waters of baptism let thy mercy evermore grant protection. Through our Lord.

Deus, qui Ecclésiam tuam semper géntium vocatióne multíplicas: concéde propítius; ut quos aqua baptísmatis ábluis, contínua protectióne tueáris. Per Dóminum.

SEVENTH PROPHECY. *Ezechiel 37: 1-14*

AT THIS TIME: The Lord's power laid hold of me, and by the spirit of the Lord I was carried away and set down in the midst of the plain, which was covered with bones. Round the whole extent of them he took me, heaped up high on the plain, and all of them parched quite dry. Son of man, he said, can life return to these bones? Lord God, said I, thou knowest.

In diébus illis: Facta est super me manus Dómini, et edúxit me in spíritu Dómini: et dimísit me in médio campi, qui erat plenus óssibus: et circumdúxit me per ea in gyro: erant autem multa valde super fáciem campi síccaque veheménter. Et dixit ad me: Fili hóminis, putásne vivent ossa ista? Et dixi: Dómine Deus, tu nosti.

Then he bade me utter a prophecy over the bones: Listen, dry bones, to the word of the Lord. A message to these bones from the Lord; I mean to send my spirit into you, and restore you to life. Sinews shall be given you, flesh shall grow on you, and skin cover you; and I will give you breath to bring you to life again; will you doubt, then, the Lord's power? So I prophesied as he had bidden me, and as I prophesied a sound came, and I felt a stirring, and the bones came together, each at its proper joint; under my eyes the sinews and the flesh clothed them, and the skin covered them, but there was no breath in them even now.

Et dixit ad me: Vaticináre de óssibus istis: et dices eis: Ossa árida, audíte verbum Dómini. Hæc dicit Dóminus Deus óssibus his: Ecce, ego intromíttam in vos spíritum, et vivétis. Et dabo super vos nervos, et succréscere fáciam super vos carnes, et superexténdam in vobis cutem: et dabo vobis spíritum, et vivétis, et sciétis, quia ego Dóminus. Et prophetávi, sicut præcéperat mihi: factus est autem sónitus prophetánte me, et ecce commótio: et accessérunt ossa ad ossa, unumquódque ad junctúram suam. Et vidi, et ecce, super ea nervi et carnes ascendérunt: et exténta est in eis cutis désuper, et spíritum non habébant.

Son of man, he said, prophesy now to the breath of life; give the breath of life itself this message from the Lord God: Come, breath of life, from the four winds, and breathe on these slain men to make them live. So I prophesied as he had bidden me, and the breath of life came into them, so that they lived again; and all rose to their feet, host upon host of them.

Et dixit ad me: Vaticináre ad spíritum, vaticináre, fili hóminis, et dices ad spíritum: Hæc dicit Dóminus Deus: A quátuor ventis veni spíritus, et insúffla super interféctos istos, et revivíscant. Et prophetávi sicut præcéperat mihi: et ingréssus est in ea spíritus, et vixérunt: steterúntque super pedes suos exércitus grandis nimis valde.

Then he told me, Son of man, in these bones here thou seest the whole race of Israel. They are complaining

Et dixit ad me: Fili hóminis, ossa hæc univérsa, domus Ísraël est: ipsi dicunt:

Aruérunt ossa nostra, et périit spes nostra, et abscíssi sumus. Proptérea vaticináre, et dices ad eos: Hæc dicit Dóminus Deus: Ecce ego apériam túmulos vestros, et edúcam vos de sepúlcris vestris pópulus meus: et indúcam vos in terram Ísraël. Et sciétis, quia ego Dóminus, cum aperúero sepúlcra vestra, et edúxero vos de túmulis vestris, pópule meus: et dédero spíritum meum in vobis, et vixéritis, et requiéscere vos fáciam super humum vestram: dicit Dóminus omnípotens.

that their very bones have withered away, that all hope is lost, they are dead men. It is for thee to prophesy, giving them this message from the Lord God: I mean to open your graves and revive you, my people; I mean to bring you home to the land of Israel. Will you doubt, then, my people, the Lord's power, when I open your graves and revive you? When I breathe my spirit into you, to give you life again, and bid you dwell at peace in your own land? says the Lord, the Almighty.

Celebrant: Orémus.
Deacon: ℣. Flectámus génua.
Subdeacon: ℟. Leváte.

Let us pray.
℣. To your knees.
℟. Stand now erect.

COLLECT AFTER THE SEVENTH PROPHECY.

Deus, qui nos ad celebrándum Paschále sacraméntum, utriúsque testaménti páginis ínstruis: da nobis intellígere misericórdiam tuam; ut ex perceptióne præséntium múnerum, firma sit exspectátio futurórum. Per Dóminum.

O GOD, FOR THE KEEPING of this thy Paschal solemnity, good warrant we find in either Testament. O make us understand thy mercy better, and learn from thy blessings here sure confidence in those which shall be ours hereafter. Through our Lord.

EIGHTH PROPHECY. *Isaias 4: 1-6.*

Apprehéndent septem mulíeres virum unum in die illa, dicéntes: Panem nostrum comedémus, et vestiméntis nostris operiémur: tantúmmodo invocétur nomen tuum super nos, aufer oppróbrium nostrum. [Editor's Note: *In 1955, this reading was retained, but the first verse was eliminated; the revised version begins at* "In die illa."] In die illa erit germen Dómini in magnificéntia, et glória, et fructus terræ sublímis, et exultátio his, qui salváti fúerint de Ísraël.

Et erit: Omnis qui relíctus fúerit in Sion, et resíduus in Jerúsalem, sanctus vocábitur, omnis qui scriptus est in vita in Jerúsalem. Si ablúerit Dóminus sordes filiárum Sion, et sánguinem Jerúsalem láverit de médio ejus, in spíritu judícii, et spíritu ardóris. Et creábit Dóminus super omnem locum montis Sion, et ubi invocátus est, nubem per diem, et fumum, et splendórem ignis flammántis in nocte: super omnem enim glóriam protéctio. Et tabernáculum erit in umbráculum diéi ab æstu, et in securitátem, et absconsiónem a túrbine, et a plúvia.

DAY OF DESOLATION! Here are seven women catching hold of one man, and promising: We will earn our bread, find ourselves in clothing; only let us bear thy name, and be saved from the reproach of barrenness! When that day comes, bud and fruit there shall be, of the Lord's fostering; burgeoning of glory made manifest, and fruit piled high, the trophy of Israel's gleanings.

Set apart for him, all that dwell in Sion now, all that survive the city's purging; none else will be left alive in Jerusalem, when the Lord sweeps away the guilt of Sion's womenfolk, washes Jerusalem clean from the blood that stains her, with the searing breath of his judgement. And all over mount Sion, the shrine of his name, cloud shall hang by day, glowing haze by night, a veil for glory. Canopy they shall have, to shade them from the day's heat, a refuge to give them shelter from storm and rain.

TRACT AFTER THE EIGHTH PROPHECY. *Isaias 5: 1, 2, 7*

A FRIEND I LOVE WELL had a vineyard in a corner of his ground, that was all fruitfulness. ℣. He fenced it in, and dug round about it, and he planted a vine of Sorec, and he built a tower in the middle. ℣. And he set up a wine-press in it: for the vineyard of the Lord of Hosts is the house of Israel.

Vínea facta est dilécto in cornu, in loco úberi. ℣. Et macériam circúmdedit, et circumfódit: et plantávit víneam Sorec: et ædificávit turrim in médio ejus. ℣. Et tórcular fodit in ea: vínea enim Dómini Sábaoth, domus Ísraël est.

Let us pray.
℣. To your knees.
℟. Stand now erect.

Celebrant: Orémus.
Deacon: ℣. Flectámus génua.
Subdeacon: ℟. Leváte.

COLLECT AFTER THE EIGHTH PROPHECY.

THIS, O GOD, thou hast revealed to us by thy prophets, that in all thy domain, wherever the Church's children are, thou alone sowest the good seed, thou alone trainest the branch that will surely thrive. What should we ask for thy people, vineyard and harvest of thine, but that ill growths of thorn and brier be cut away, and every plant repay thy care? Through our Lord.

Deus, qui in ómnibus Ecclésiæ tuæ fíliis, sanctórum prophetárum voce manifestásti, in omni loco dominatiónis tuæ, satórem te bonórum séminum, et electórum pálmitum esse cultórem: tríbue pópulis tuis, qui et vineárum apud te nómine censéntur et ségetum; ut, spinárum et tribulórum squalóre resecáto, digna efficiántur fruge fecúndi. Per Dóminum.

NINTH PROPHECY. *Exodus 12: 1-11*

IT WAS WHILE they were still in the land of Egypt that the Lord said to Moses and Aaron, For you, this month is to lead in all the months, to be the first month of the year. Make this proclamation to the whole assembly of Israel: On the tenth day of this month, each family, each household, is to choose out a yearling for its own use. Or, if there are not enough of them to eat a whole lamb, the head of the family must call in some neighbour who lives close by, so that a lamb shall not be too much for their needs. It must be a male yearling lamb, or a male yearling kid, that you choose, with no blemish on it. These victims must be kept ready till the fourteenth day of the month, and on the evening of that day the whole people of Israel must immolate. They must take some of the blood, and sprinkle it on the doorway, jambs and lintel alike, of the house in which the lamb is

Identical to the second reading on Good Friday:

In diébus illis: Dixit Dóminus ad Móysen et Áaron in terra Ægýpti: Mensis iste vobis princípium ménsium primus erit in ménsibus anni. Loquímini ad univérsum cœtum filiórum Ísraël, et dícite eis: Décima die mensis hujus tollat unusquísque agnum per famílias et domos suas. Sin autem minor est número, ut sufficere possit ad vescéndum agnum, assúmet vicínum suum, qui junctus est dómui suæ, juxta númerum animárum, quæ sufficere possunt ad esum agni. Erit autem agnus absque mácula, másculus, anniculus: juxta quem ritum tollétis et hædum. Et servábitis eum usque ad quartam décimam diem mensis hujus: immolabítque eum univérsa multitúdo filiórum Ísraël ad vésperam. Et sument de sánguine ejus, ac ponent super utrúmque postem et in superlimináribus domórum, in quibus cómedent illum. Et edent carnes nocte illa assas igni, et ázymos panes cum lactúcis agréstibus. Non comedétis ex eo crudum quid nec coctum aqua, sed tantum assum igni: caput cum pédibus ejus et intestínis vorábitis. Nec remanébit quidquam ex eo usque mane. Si quid resíduum fúerit, igne comburétis. Sic autem comedétis illum: Renes vestros accingétis, et calceaménta habébitis in pédibus, tenéntes báculos in mánibus, et comedétis festinánter: est enim Phase (id est tránsitus) Dómini.

being eaten. Their meat that night must be roasted over the fire, their bread unleavened; wild herbs must be all their seasoning. No part must be eaten raw, or boiled, it must be roasted over the fire; head, feet, and entrails, all must be consumed, so that nothing remains till next day; whatever is left over, you must put in the fire and burn it. And this is to be the manner of your eating it; your loins must be girt, your feet ready shod, and every man's staff in his hand; all must be done in haste. It is the night of the Pasch, the Lord's passing by.

Celebrant: Orémus.
Deacon: ℣. Flectámus génua.
Subdeacon: ℟. Leváte.

Let us pray.
℣. To your knees.
℟. Stand now erect.

COLLECT AFTER THE NINTH PROPHECY.

Omnípotens sempitérne Deus, qui in ómnium óperum tuórum dispensatióne mirábilis es: intélligant redémpti tui, non fuísse excelléntius, quod inítio factus est mundus, quam quod in fine sæculórum Pascha nostrum immolátus est Christus: Qui tecum.

ALMIGHTY AND EVERLASTING God, in all the ordering of thy Providence most wonderful; confess we ever, souls thou hast redeemed, the world's first making was no greater thing than Christ's offering, after long years, of this paschal sacrifice. Who with thee.

TENTH PROPHECY. *Jonas 3: 1-10*

In diébus illis: Factum est verbum Dómini ad Jonam prophétam secúndo, dicens: Surge, et vade in Níniven civitátem magnam: et prædica in ea prædicatiónem, quam ego loquor ad te. Et surréxit Jonas, et ábiit in Níniven juxta verbum Dómini: et Nínive erat cívitas magna itínere diérum trium.

ONCE AGAIN, at this time, the Lord's voice came to Jonas: Up, and to the great city of Nineve make thy way; there preach what preach I bid thee. That voice he obeyed; rose up and took the road for Nineve, a great city indeed, three days' journey from end to end.

Et cœpit Jonas introíre in civitátem itínere diéi uníus: et clamávit, et dixit: Adhuc quadragínta dies, et Nínive subvertétur. Et credidérunt viri Ninivítæ in Deum: et prædicavérunt jejúnium, et vestíti sunt saccis a majóre usque ad minórem. Et pervénit verbum ad regem Nínive: et surréxit de sólio suo, et abjécit vestiméntum suum a se, et indútus est sacco, et sedit in cínere.

And when he had advanced into it as far as one day's journey would carry him, he began crying out: In forty days Nineve will be overthrown. With that, the Ninevites showed faith in God, rich and poor alike, proclaiming a fast and putting on sackcloth; nay, the king of Nineve himself, when word of it reached him, came down from his throne, put on sackcloth, and sat down humbly in the dust.

And a cry was raised in Nineve, at the bidding of the king and his nobles: A fast for man and beast, for herd and flock; no food is to be eaten, no water drunk; let man and beast go covered with sackcloth; cry out lustily to the Lord, and forsake, each of you, his sinful life, his wrongful deeds! God may yet relent and pardon, forgo his avenging anger and spare our lives. Thus God saw them amending their lives in good earnest, and the Lord our God had mercy on his people.

Et clamávit, et dixit in Nínive ex ore regis et príncipum ejus, dicens: Hómines, et juménta, et boves, et pécora non gustent quidquam: nec pascántur, et aquam non bibant. Et operiántur saccis hómines, et juménta, et clament ad Dóminum in fortitúdine, et convertátur vir a via sua mala, et ab iniquitáte, quæ est in mánibus eórum. Quis scit si convertátur, et ignóscat Deus: et revertátur a furóre iræ suæ, et non períbimus? Et vidit Deus ópera eórum, quia convérsi sunt de via sua mala: et misértus est pópulo suo Dóminus, Deus noster.

Let us pray.
℣. To your knees.
℟. Stand now erect.

Celebrant: Orémus.
Deacon: ℣. Flectámus génua.
Subdeacon: ℟. Leváte.

COLLECT AFTER THE TENTH PROPHECY.

O GOD, WHO HAST MADE all nations one in the confession of thy name, will and power grant us to do thy bidding; so, called to an eternal destiny, one may thy people be in truth of thought, in holiness of action. Through our Lord.

Deus, qui diversitátem géntium in confessióne tui nóminis adunásti: da nobis, et velle, et posse quæ præcipis; ut pópulo ad æternitátem vocáto, una sit fides méntium, et píetas actiónum. Per Dóminum.

ELEVENTH PROPHECY. *Deuteronomy 31: 22-30*

MOSES PUT THE SONG in writing, in those days, and taught it to the men of Israel. The Lord also gave a charge to Josue, the son of Nun: Play the man, and keep thy courage high; it is thy task to settle sons of Israel in the land I have promised to give them, and I will be with thee in the doing of it. And now, when Moses had finished his work of setting forth the terms of this law in a book, he gave orders to the Levites, that carried the ark of the Lord, what they should do with it.

In diébus illis: Scripsit Móyses cánticum, et dócuit fílios Ísraël. Præcepítque Dóminus Jósue, fílio Nun, et ait: Confortáre, et esto robústus: tu enim introdúces fílios Ísraël in terram, quam pollícitus sum, et ego ero tecum. Postquã ergo scripsit Móyses verba legis hujus in volúmine, atque complévit: præcépit Levítis, qui portábant arcam fœderis Dómini, dicens:

Take this book, he said, and lay it up by the side of the ark that bears witness of the Lord's covenant, to vindicate him against you. I know well how rebellious you are, how stiff-necked; even in my life-time, and in spite of my presence among you, you have always been rebelling against the Lord; and when

Tóllite librum istum, et pónite eum in látere arcæ fœderis Dñi, Dei vestri: ut sit ibi contra te in testimónium. Ego enim scio contentiónem tuam et cérvicem tuam duríssimam. Adhuc vivénte me et ingrediénte vobíscum, semper contentióse egístis contra Dóminum: quanto magis, cum mórtuus fúero? Congregáte ad me omnes majóres natu per tribus vestras, atque doctóres, et loquar audiéntibus eis sermónes istos, et invocábo contra eos cælum et terram.

I am dead, worse must follow. Summon the elders and counsellors among all the tribes, and let me say my say in their hearing; let me call upon heaven and earth to bear witness against them.

Novi enim, quod post mortem meam iníque agétis et declinábitis cito de via, quam præcépi vobis: et occúrrent vobis mala in extrémo témpore, quando fecéritis malum in conspéctu Dómini, ut irritétis eum per ópera mánuum vestrárum. Locútus est ergo Móyses, audiénte univérso cœtu Ísraël, verba cárminis hujus, et ad finem usque complévit.

I know well enough that when I am dead you will ruin all, and it will not be long before you stray from the path I have showed you; and I know that when the Lord sees you living amiss, and provoking his anger by your doings, calamity will fall upon you in the end. And so Moses, with the whole assembly of Israel listening to him, pronounced the words of the song which follows, never pausing until it was all finished:

TRACT AFTER THE ELEVENTH PROPHECY. *Deuteronomy 32: 1-4*

Atténde, cælum, et loquar: et áudiat terra verba ex ore meo. ℣. Exspectétur sicut plúvia elóquium meum: et descéndant sicut ros verba mea. ℣. Sicut imber super gramen et sicut nix super fœnum: quia nomen Dómini invocábo. ℣. Date magnitúdinem Deo nostro: Deus, vera ópera ejus, et omnes viæ ejus judícia. ℣. Deus fidélis, in quo non est iníquitas: justus et sanctus Dóminus.

LISTEN, YOU HEAVENS, while I have my say; earth, be attentive to the words I utter. ℣. Here is teaching fulsome with import as the rain, here are warnings that must soak in like the dew. ℣. Wholesome as showers are to the grass, as moisture to the growing crops: the renown of the Lord shall be my theme. ℣. To our God belongs majesty; the God who shelters us, how perfect is all he does, how right are all his dealings! ℣. God, faithful and unerring, God, holy and just.

Celebrant: Orémus.
Deacon: ℣. Flectámus génua.
Subdeacon: ℟. Leváte.

Let us pray.
℣. To your knees.
℟. Stand now erect.

COLLECT AFTER THE ELEVENTH PROPHECY.

Deus, celsitúdo humílium et fortitúdo rectórum, qui per sanctum Móysen púerum tuum, ita erudíre pópulum tuum sacri cárminis tui decantatióne voluísti, ut illa legis iterátio fíeret étiam nostra diréctio: éxcita in omnem justificatárum géntium plenitúdinem poténtiam tuam, et da lætítiam, mitigándo terrórem; ut, ómnium peccátis tua remissióne delétis, quod denuntiátum est in ultiónem, tránseat in salútem. Per Dóminum.

O GOD, OF HUMBLED SOULS the uplifting, of upright souls the strength, not for nothing wouldst thou have thy servant Moses sing his holy admonition; for his own people a reminder of the law they knew, for us, in our turn, a warning. Up, Lord, and over a ransomed world exert thy sway; our hearts comfort, our fears dispel! What were thy threats of vengeance but the means to save us, if pardon of thine our sins assoil? Through our Lord.

TWELFTH PROPHECY. *Daniel 3: 1-24*

KING NABUCHODONOSOR, in those days, made a golden image sixty cubits high and six cubits broad, which he set up on the plain of Dura, in the province of Babylon; and word went out from king Nabuchodonosor summoning all the governors, magistrates, judges, chieftains, rulers, prefects, and leading men from every part of his dominion to be present at the dedication of the image king Nabuchodonosor had set up.

In diébus illis: Nabuchodónosor rex fecit státuam áuream altitúdine cubitórum sexagínta, latitúdine cubitórum sex, et státuit eam in campo Dura provínciæ Babylónis. Ítaque Nabuchodónosor rex misit ad congregándos sátrapas, magistrátus, et júdices, duces, et tyránnos, et præféctos, omnésque príncipes regiónum, ut convenírent ad dedicatiónem státuæ, quam eréxerat Nabuchodónosor rex.

So they gathered there, governors, magistrates, judges, chieftains, rulers, noblemen in high office, and leading men from every part, for the dedication of king Nabuchodonosor's image. And, as they stood before the image he had set up, a herald cried lustily to men of all people, nations, and languages: As soon as you hear the sound of horn, flute, harp, zither, dulcimer, pipe, and other instruments of music, you are to fall down and worship the image of gold which king Nabuchodonosor has set up. Whoever does not fall down in worship, will be thrown, there and then, into the heart of a raging furnace.

Tunc congregáti sunt sátrapæ, magistrátus, et júdices, duces, et tyránni, et optimátes, qui erant in potestátibus constitúti, et univérsi príncipes regiónum, ut convenírent ad dedicatiónem státuæ, quam eréxerat Nabuchodónosor rex. Stabant autem in conspéctu státuæ, quam posúerat Nabuchodónosor rex, et præco clamábat valénter: Vobis dícitur pópulis, tríbubus, et linguis: In hora, qua audiéritis sónitum tubæ, et fístulæ, et cítharæ, sambúcæ, et psaltérii, et symphóniæ, et univérsi géneris musicórum, cadéntes adoráte státuam áuream, quam constítuit Nabuchodónosor rex. Si quis autem non prostrátus adoráverit, eádem hora mittétur in fornácem ignis ardéntis.

No sooner, then, did the sound of horn, flute, harp, zither, dulcimer, pipe, and the rest reach the assembly, than all of them, whatever their people, tribe, or language, fell down in worship of king Nabuchodonosor's image. It was then that certain Chaldeans came forward with malicious accusations against the Jews. They wished long life to king Nabuchodonosor, and said, Lord King, thy command was that all men, at the sound of horn, flute, harp, zither, dulcimer, pipe, and the rest, should fall down and worship the golden image, on pain of being thrown into a raging furnace. And here are certain Jews, entrusted by thee with the affairs of Babylon province, called Sidrach, Misach, and Abdenago, who have set the royal command at defiance, and will not reverence thy gods, or worship the golden image thou hast set up.

Post hæc ígitur statim ut audiérunt omnes pópuli sónitum tubæ, fístulæ, et cítharæ, sambúcæ, et psaltérii, et symphóniæ, et omnis géneris musicórum, cadéntes omnes pópuli, tribus et linguæ adoravérunt státuam auream, quam constitúerat Nabuchodónosor rex. Statímque in ipso témpore accedéntes viri Chaldǽi accusavérunt Judǽos, dixerúntque Nabuchodónosor regi: Rex, in ætérnum vive: tu, rex, posuísti decrétum, ut omnis homo, qui audiérit sónitum tubæ, fístulæ, et cítharæ, sambúcæ, et psaltérii, et symphóniæ, et univérsi géneris musicórum, prostérnat se et adóret státuam áuream: si quis autem non prócidens adoráverit, mittátur in fornácem ignis ardéntis. Sunt ergo viri Judǽi, quos constituísti super ópera regiónis Babylónis, Sidrach, Misach, et Abdénago: viri isti contempsérunt, rex, decrétum tuum: deos tuos non colunt, et státuam áuream, quam erexísti, non adórant.

Upon this, Nabuchodonosor sent for Sidrach, Misach, and Abdenago, in a transport of rage; and when they were brought, without delay, into his presence, this was the threat king Nabuchodonosor uttered: So Sidrach, Misach, and Abdenago will not reverence

Tunc Nabuchodónosor in furóre et in ira præcépit, ut adduceréntur Sidrach, Misach, et Abdénago: qui conféstim addúcti sunt in conspéctu regis. Pronuntiánsque Nabuchodónosor rex, ait eis: Veréne, Sidrach, Misach et Abdénago, deos meos non cólitis, et státuam áuream, quam constítui, non adorátis? Nunc ergo si estis paráti, quacúmque hora audiéritis sónitum tubæ, fístulæ, cítharæ, sambúcæ, et psaltérii, et symphóniæ, omnísque géneris musicórum, prostérnite vos et adoráte státuam, quam feci: quod si non adoravéritis, eádem hora mittémini in fornácem ignis ardéntis; et quis est Deus, qui erípiet vos de manu mea?

my gods, or worship this golden image of mine? Here is your choice, then; either you will fall down and worship this image of mine when the sound of horn, flute, harp, zither, dulcimer, pipe and the other music reaches you, or you will then and there be thrown into a raging furnace. You are in my power; what God can deliver you?

Respondéntes Sidrach, Misach, et Abdénago, dixérunt regi Nabuchodónosor: Non opórtet nos de hac re respóndere tibi. Ecce enim, Deus noster, quem cólimus, potest erípere nos de camíno ignis ardéntis, et de mánibus tuis, o rex, liberáre. Quod si nolúerit, notum sit tibi, rex, quia deos tuos non cólimus et státuam áuream, quam erexísti, non adorámus.

Then Sidrach, Misach, and Abdenago said to king Nabuchodonosor, There is no need for any answer of ours to that question; thou wilt see for thyself whether the God we worship is able to rescue us from the raging furnace, and from thy royal power. But whether he rescues us or no, be assured, sir king, here are men who do not reverence thy gods, or worship any image of thine.

Tunc Nabuchodónosor replétus est furóre, et adspéctus faciéi illíus immutátus est super Sidrach, Misach, et Abdénago, et præcépit, ut succenderétur fornax séptuplum quam succéndi consuéverat. Et viris fortíssimis de exércitu suo jussit ut ligátis pédibus Sidrach, Misach, et Abdénago, mítterent eos in fornácem ignis ardéntis. Et conféstim viri illi vincti, cum braccis suis, et tiáris, et calceaméntis, et véstibus, missi sunt in médium fornácis ignis ardéntis. Nam jússio regis urgébat: fornax autem succénsa erat nimis. Porro viros illos, qui míserant Sidrach, Misach et Abdénago, interfécit flamma ignis. Viri autem hi tres, id est, Sidrach, Misach, et Abdénago, cecidérunt in médio camíno ignis ardéntis, colligáti. Et ambulábant in médio flammæ laudántes Deum, et benedicéntes Dómino.

At this, Nabuchodonosor fell into a rage; his features, as he glared at Sidrach, Misach, and Abdenago, were distoned with fury. He would have the furnace heated seven times hotter than its wont; and into this raging furnace he bade his chosen bodyguard throw Sidrach, Misach, and Abdenago with their feet shackled. So they were bound just as they were, in breeches and turban, shoes and coat, and thrown into the heart of the raging furnace; the king's order admitted no delay. So fiercely was the furnace heated that those who threw them in were burned to death. Meanwhile these three, Sidrach, Misach, and Abdenago, fell fast-bound into the heart of the fires that raged in it; and there, in the hottest of the flames, they walked to and fro, singing to God their praises, blessing the Lord.

1950 • After the twelfth prophecy, "Flectamus genua" is not said and no one genuflects.
Hic non dicitur "Flectámus génua," sed tantum:

COLLECT AFTER THE TWELFTH PROPHECY.

Orémus.

Omnípotens sempitérne Deus, spes única mundi, qui prophetárum tuórum præcónio, præséntium témporum declarásti mystéria: auge pópuli tui vota placátus; quia in nullo fidélium, nisi ex tua inspiratióne, provéniunt quarúmlibet increménta virtútum. Per Dóminum.

Let us pray.

ALMIGHTY and everlasting God, the world's only hope, by the utterance of thy ancient prophets thou didst signify the means of grace we now enjoy. And now, Lord, make our prayers more fruitful; never yet was there growth of holiness among thy faithful, but it came from thy inspiring. Through our Lord.

1950 • If the church has no font, the whole of this part is omitted. In that case, the Celebrant removes his chasuble (and the ministers their folded chasubles), prostrates himself at the Altar, and the chanting of the litany is begun.

1950 • If there are children to be baptized, the first part of the baptism rite should be carried out before the font is blessed. In this case, another priest or deacon may do so during the prophecies {Fortescue p327}.

(1950) HOLY SATURDAY • Blessing of the Font

Sabbato Sancto — *Benedictio Fontis*

1950 • Towards the end of the twelfth prophecy, the acolytes light their candles. An altar server removes the Paschal candle from its candlestick. The Celebrant and ministers go to the Sedilia and remove their maniples. The Celebrant exchanges his chasuble for a purple Cope, but the ministers retain their purple folded chasubles. The procession goes to the baptistery. The server who carries the Paschal candle is in front. On the way to the font the tract "Sicut Cervus" is sung.

His expletis, si Ecclesia habuerit fontem baptismalem, Sacerdos benedicturus fontem, accipit pluviale violaceum, et praecedente Cruce, cum candelabris, et Cereo benedicto accenso, descendit cum Clero et ministris paratis ad fontem: et interim cantatur sequens:

TRACT. *Ps 41: 2-4*

O GOD, MY WHOLE SOUL longs for thee, as a deer for running water. ℣. My whole soul thirsts for the living God: shall I never again make my pilgrimage into God's presence? ℣. Morning and evening, I have known no other food than tears; daily must I listen to the taunt, Where is thy God now.

Sicut cervus desíderat ad fontes aquárum: ita desíderat ánima mea ad te, Deus. ℣. Sitívit ánima mea ad Deum vivum: quando véniam, et apparébo ante fáciem Dei? ℣. Fuérunt mihi lácrimæ meæ panes die ac nocte, dum dícitur mihi per síngulos dies: Ubi est Deus tuus?

1950 • Before entering the baptistery for the blessing of the water, the Celebrant first says the following near the font. | *Deinde Sacerdos, antequam intret ad benedictionem fontis, dicit hanc Orationem juxta fontem.*

℣. The Lord be with you.
℟. And with you, his minister.

℣. Dóminus vobíscum.
℟. Et cum spíritu tuo.

Let us pray.

ALMIGHTY and everlasting God, look down in mercy upon souls that are coming to new birth, eager as the deer that longs for running water; slaked by baptismal grace, may that thirst bring them hallowing both of soul and body. Through our Lord. ℟. Amen.

Orémus.

Omnípotens sempitérne Deus, réspice propítius ad devotiónem pópuli renascéntis, qui sicut cervus, aquárum tuárum éxpetit fontem: et concéde propítius; ut fídei ipsíus sitis, baptísmatis mystério, ánimam corpúsque sanctíficet. Per Dóminum. ℟. Amen.

1950 • Then he goes to bless the font, praying as follows.
Postea procedit ad benedictionem fontis, dicens:

℣. The Lord be with you.
℟. And with you, his minister.

℣. Dóminus vobíscum.
℟. Et cum spíritu tuo.

Orémus.

Omnípotens sempitérne Deus, adésto magnæ pietátis tuæ mystériis, adésto sacraméntis: et ad recreándos novos pópulos, quos tibi fons baptísmatis párturit, spíritum adoptiónis emítte; ut quod nostræ humilitátis geréndum est ministério, virtútis tuæ impleátur efféctu. Per Dóminum.

Let us pray.

ALMIGHTY and everlasting God, sacrament and means of grace with thou hast instituted, be here to ratify. Pour out the spirit of adoption, to fashion anew that new race which baptism shall here engender. To us, creatures of earth, thy ministry is committed, but effect is none save what thy power accomplishes. Through our Lord.

1950 • He concludes the prayer in the Preface tone: **"World without end."**

Elevans vocem in modum Praefationis, prosequitur junctis manibus: **"Per ómnia sǽcula sæculórum."**

℟. Amen.

℣. Dóminus vobíscum.

℟. Et cum spíritu tuo.

℣. Sursum corda.

℟. Habémus ad Dóminum.

℣. Grátias agámus Dómino Deo nostro.

℟. Dignum et justum est.

℟. Amen.

℣. The Lord be with you.

℟. And with you, his minister.

℣. Lift up your hearts!

℟. We hold them out to the Lord.

℣. Give we thanks to the Lord our God.

℟. Right it is and seemly.

Vere dignum et justum est, ǽquum et salutáre, nos tibi semper et ubíque grátias ágere, Dómine, sancte Pater, omnípotens ætérne Deus: qui invisíbili poténtia, sacramentórum tuórũ mirabíliter operáris efféctum: et licet nos tantis mystériis exsequéndis simus indígni: tu tamen grátiæ tuæ dona non déserens, étiam ad nostras preces aures tuæ pietátis inclínas. Deus, cujus Spíritus super aquas inter ipsa munda primórdia ferebátur: ut jam tunc virtútem sanctificatiónis, aquárum natúra concíperet.

RIGHT IT IS ASSUREDLY and most beseeming, duty of ours and our well-being, to thank thee, holy Lord, almighty Father, eternal God, both always and everywhere. Outward sacraments thy invisible power makes effectual, that gracious gift never revoking; even to us, unworthy of these thy mysteries, a merciful ear thou still inclinest. Over water thy spirit moved, when all things thou madest; so soon, pregnant it needs must be with power to sanctify.

Deus, qui nocéntis mundi crímina per aquas ábluens, regeneratiónis spéciem in ipsa dilúvii effusióne signásti: ut, uníus ejusdémque eleménti mystério, et finis esset vítiis, et orígo virtútibus. Réspice, Dñe, in fáciem Ecclésiæ tuæ, et multíplica in ea regeneratiónes tuas, qui grátiæ tuæ affluéntis ímpetu lætíficas civitátem tuam: fontémque baptísmatis áperis toto orbe terrárum géntibus innovándis: ut, tuæ majestátis império, sumat Unigéniti tui grátiam de Spíritu Sancto.

THE FLOOD ITSELF, by water purging man's guilt, new birth betokened; strange element, at once the tomb of our vileness, the womb of holiness! Of thy Church's prayer, Lord, take cognisance; lavishly on her children bestow the gift of new birth. Who with grace abounding thy city refreshest, in all the whole world renewing mankind by baptism; such is thy royal will, grace of thy only-begotten Son from the Spirit receive we.

1950 • After the words "grátiam de Spíriti sancto" the Celebrant holds the right hand stretched out, with fingers joined, and traces a cross in the water. The Deacon hands him a towel with which to dry his hand.

Hic Sacerdos manu extensa dividit aquam in modum crucis, et eam statim linteo extergit, dicens:

FOR OUR REGENERATION, let his power secretly infused grant this water fecundity; from the pure womb of the font, conceived in holiness, new-created let man come forth, a heavenly offspring; young be they or old, man or woman, all to one state of childhood grace here engenders. At thy command, Lord, banished be every spirit of evil, far removed be every snare of the foul fiend. Here be no room for Satan's encroachment, ambush, or stealthy approach, or brewing of poison.

Qui hanc aquam, regenerándis homínibus præparátam, arcána sui núminis admixtióne fecúndet: ut, sanctificatióne concépta, ab immaculáto divíni fontis útero, in novam renáta creatúrã, progénies cæléstis emérgat: et quos aut sexus in córpore, aut ætas discérnit in témpore, omnes in unam páriat grátia mater infántiam. Procul ergo hinc, jubénte te, Dómine, omnis spíritus immúndus abscédat: procul tota nequítia diabólicæ fraudis absístat. Nihil hoc loci hábeat contráriæ virtútis admíxtio: non insidiándo circúmvolet: non laténdo subrépat: non inficiéndo corrúmpat.

1950 • He touches the water with his hand, then dries as before. | *Aquam manu tangit.*

Holy and spotless, Lord, be this thy handiwork, from the enemy's assault shielded, from all his craft delivered. Fresh spring let it be, water of life, a cleansing fountain; in this health-giving stream may none be washed, but he shall feel the work of thy Spirit within him, purified and pardoned.

Sit hæc sancta et ínnocens creatúra, líbera ab omni impugnatóris incúrsu, et totíus nequítiæ purgáta discéssu. Sit fons vivus, aqua regénerans, unda puríficans: ut omnes hoc lavácro salutífero diluéndi, operánte in eis Spíritu Sancto, perféctæ purgatiónis indulgéntiam consequántur.

1950 • He makes the sign of the Cross three times over the font (without touching the water).

Facit tres cruces super fontem, dicens:

Substance of water, I bless thee by God ✠ ever-living, God ✠ ever true, God ✠ ever holy; he it was, at the beginning of the world, from dry land parted thee, his Spirit brooded over thee.

Unde benedíco te, creatúra aquæ, per Deum ✠ vivum, per Deum ✠ verum, per Deum ✠ sanctum: per Deum, qui te, in princípio, verbo separávit ab árida: cujus Spíritus super te ferebátur.

1950 • He casts a little water to the four points of the compass, then dries as before. As he sings "Benedíco te" he again signs the cross over the water, not touching it.

Hic manu aquam dividit, et effundit eam versus quatuor mundi partes, dicens:

HE IT WAS BADE THEE FLOW from that fountain in Paradise, in four streams dividing thee to water the whole world. He it was, in the desert, bitter found thee and wholesome drink left thee; ay, and brought thee out of the rock for his people that thirstèd. I ✠ bless thee by his Son, Jesus Christ our Lord, that into wine, at Cana of Galilee, wondrously transformed thee.

Qui te paradísi fonte manáre fecit, et in quátuor flumínibus totam terram rigáre præcépit. Qui te in desérto amáram, suavitáte índita, fecit esse potábilem, et sitiénti pópulo de petra prodúxit. Bene✠díco te et per Jesum Christum Fílium ejus únicum, Dóminum nostrum: qui te in Cana Galilǽæ signo admirábili, sua poténtia convértit in vinum.

Qui pédibus super te ambulávit: et a Joánne in Jordáne in te baptizátus est. Qui te una cum sánguine de látere suo prodúxit: et discípulis suis jussit, ut credéntes baptizaréntur in te, dicens: Ite, docéte omnes gentes, baptizántes eos in nómine Patris, et Fílii, et Spíritus Sancti.

FEET OF HIS have trodden thee; with thee, in Jordan river, the Christ was christened. From his side thou didst flow, with his Blood mingling; with thee, his disciples should bring faith to the whole world, in the name of the Father and Son and Holy Ghost baptizing.

1950 • He changes the tone and continues on one note, as when singing a lesson. (Some authors say he continues "in a speaking voice.") | *Mutat vocem, et prosequitur in tono Lectionis.*

Hæc nobis præcépta servántibus tu, Deus omnípotens, clemens adésto: tu benígnus adspíra.

THESE thy own commandments observing, thy merciful help, God almighty, we claim, thy gracious influence.

1950 • He breathes thrice over the water in the form of a cross.
Halat ter in aquam in modum crucis, dicens:

Tu has símplices aquas tuo ore benedícito: ut præter naturálem emundatiónem, quam lavándis possunt adhibére corpóribus, sint étiam purificándis méntibus efficáces.

WATER, that is but water, may thy breath hallow, its native power to cleanse so wondrously enlarging, not body of man but soul it shall purify.

1950 • He takes the Paschal candle from the Deacon (who has taken it from the server). Singing again in the Preface tone, he dips the lower end of the candle a little into the water, as he sings "Descéndat in hanc plenitúdinem fontis, virtus Spíritus sancti." He takes out the candle, dips it again a little deeper, and sings the same words in a higher pitch. He takes out the candle and submerges it deeper still, singing again the third time, still higher.

Descéndat in hanc plenitúdinem fontis virtus Spíritus Sancti.

ON THIS FONT, and all it holds, virtue come down of the Holy Spirit.

1950 • Then he blows three times on the water in the form of the Greek letter Psi, and continues:

Totámque hujus aquæ substántiam, regenerándi fœcúndet efféctu.

PREGNANT BE the whole substance of this water with power to regenerate.

1950 • He takes the candle out of the water and continues in the Preface tone.
Hic tollitur Cereus de aqua, et prosequitur:

Hic ómnium peccatórũ máculæ deleántur: hic natúra ad imáginem tuam cóndita, et ad honórem sui reformáta princípii, cunctis vetustátis squalóribus emundétur: ut omnis homo, sacraméntũ hoc regeneratiónis ingréssus, in veræ innocéntiæ novam infántiam renascátur.

HERE BE THE STAIN of guilt washed away altogether; here, in thy image fashioned, and restored to its first beauty, be man's nature assoiled from defilement inveterate. This sacrament of regeneration whoever approaches, into the very innocence of childhood be he born again.

1950 • He lowers his voice and sings the following on one note; the choir answers "Amen" on the same note {Fortescue p329}. (Other authors say "in a speaking voice.") In the 1962 version, this section "is not sung" {McManus p97}. | *Sequentia dicit legendo.*

THROUGH THY SON, Jesus Christ our Lord, who comes to judge both the living and the dead, for the whole world's assaying. ℟. Amen.

Per Dóminum nostrum Jesum Christum Fílium tuum: qui ventúrus est judicáre vivos et mórtuos, et sǽculum per ignem. ℟. Amen.

1950 • A server fills the portable holy water stoup ("Aspersorium") with water from the font. Another priest in a purple stole—or the Celebrant himself—now goes around the church sprinkling the congregation with the baptismal water. While the people are sprinkled, a server takes from the font some of the water in a vessel and from this fills the holy water stoups in the church. Some is also reserved for the blessing of houses and other places. The Celebrant, standing at the font as before, pours a little of the oil of Catechumens into the water in the form of a cross, saying aloud (not singing) the following prayer. | *His peractis, Sacerdos qui benedicit fontem, infundit de oleo Catechumenorum in aquam in modum crucis, intelligibili voce dicens:*

BY THIS OIL, that is sin's salve, be yonder font sanctified and made fruitful, for all such as would be born anew to eternal life. ℟. Amen.

Sanctificétur et fœcundétur fons iste óleo salútis renascéntibus ex eo, in vitam ætérnam. ℟. Amen.

1950 • He pours in chrism in the same way. | *Deinde infundit de Chrismate, modo quo supra, dicens :*

CHRISM of our Lord Jesus Christ, chrism of the Holy Spirit, in the name of the Blessed Trinity be here poured forth. ℟. Amen.

Infúsio Chrísmatis Dómini nostri Jesu Christi, et Spíritus Sancti Paráclіti, fiat in nómine sanctæ Trinitátis. ℟. Amen.

1950 • He pours both chrism and oil of Catechumens together, making three crosses in the water as he says the last words (where crosses are marked in the Missal). | *Postea accipit ambas ampullas dicti olei sancti, et Chrismatis, et de utroque simul in modum crucis infundendo, dicit:*

CHRISM'S HALLOWING, and oil's anointing, and water's baptizing, here be mingled together, in the name of the ✠ Father, and of the ✠ Son, and of the Holy ✠ Ghost. ℟. Amen.

Commíxtio Chrísmatis sanctificatiónis, et ólei unctiónis, et Aquæ baptísmatis, páriter fiat in nómine Pa ✠ tris, et Fí ✠ lii, et Spíritus ✠ Sancti. ℟. Amen.

1950 • He then mixes the oil and water together, spreading it all around with the right hand extended. He wipes his hand on cotton wool, and then on the towel held for him by the Deacon.

Tunc miscet ipsum oleum cum aqua, et spargit manu sua per omnem fontem.

(1950) Holy Saturday • Sacrament of Baptism

Sabbato Sancto *De Sacramento Baptismi*

1950 • If the Sacrament of Baptism is to be administered, it follows now, administered in every way as usual except that the sacred ministers assist on either side, handing to the Celebrant what is wanted.

[Editor's Note: If the ministers have worn folded chasubles they do not remove them during the baptism, even though the Celebrant will change into white Stole and Cope. The candle given after baptism is lit from the Paschal candle. In the Middle Ages, when baptism after birth became almost universal, Easter Vigil baptisms vastly declined—yet "even toward the end of the mediæval era, some liturgical books still provided for cases of vigil baptisms" {Monti p488}. After baptizing, the Celebrant puts on the purple vestments again—the ministers never removed their purple vestments—but it is not required for the the Celebrant to again put on the purple Cope, since he will be going straight into the litany. For the litany, the Cope is removed.]

1950 • While the font is being blessed, a server lays three purple cushions before the Altar. The litany should begin while the procession returns to the Altar, sung by two cantors wearing surplices who take part in the procession immediately behind the Cross. The litany is sung "under the double rite," that is to say, the entire invocation and its response must be repeated each time by the choir and/or congregation {Dale p227; Fortescue p331}. Curiously, in the 1962 version the litany is not doubled {Löw p15; McManus p95}, yet when the (non-doubled) litany fails to correspond with the reformed ceremonies, the congregation is told to repeat the litany {1953maryland p24}. On arriving in the Sanctuary the Celebrant, Deacon, and Subdeacon prostrate themselves before the Altar. [Editor's Note: In the 1962 version, the Celebrant and ministers do not prostrate themselves before the Altar; instead, they kneel {McManus p95}.]

(1950) HOLY SATURDAY • Litany of the Saints

Sabbato Sancto *Litaniae Sanctorum*

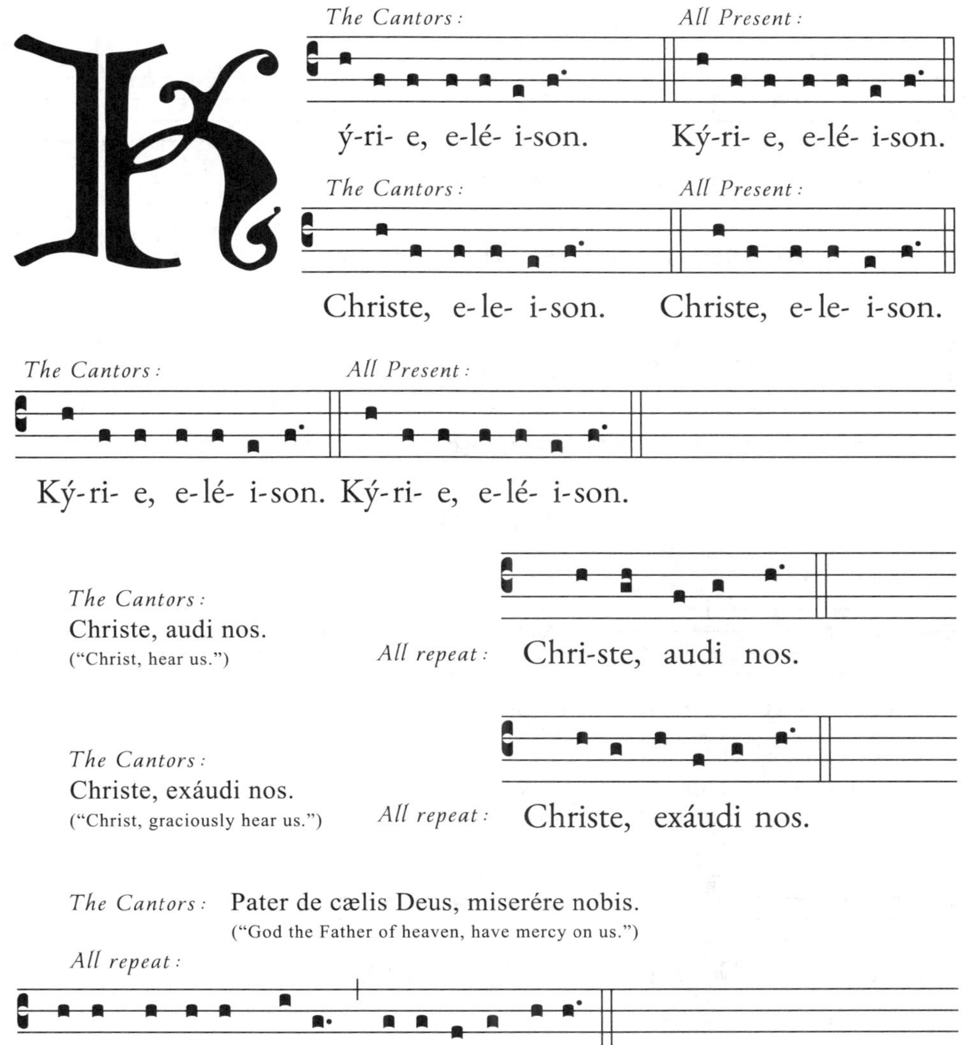

The Cantors: Pater de cælis Deus, miserére nobis.
("God the Father of heaven, have mercy on us.")

All repeat:

Pa-ter de cæ-lis **De**- us, mi-se-ré-re nobis.

The Cantors: Fili Redémptor mundi Deus, miserére nobis.
("God the Son, Redeemer of the world, have mercy on us.")

All repeat:

Fi- li Redémptor mundi **De**- us, mi-se-ré-re nobis.

The Cantors: Spíritus Sancte Deus, miserére nobis.
("God the Holy Ghost, have mercy on us.")

All repeat:

Spí- ri-tus Sancte **De**- us, mi-se-ré-re nobis.

The Cantors: Sancta Trínitas unus Deus, miserére nobis.
("Holy Trinity, one God, have mercy on us.")

All repeat:

Sancta Tríni-tas, unus **De**- us, mi-se-ré-re nobis.

The Cantors: Sancta María, ora pro nobis.
("Holy Mary, pray for us.")

All repeat:

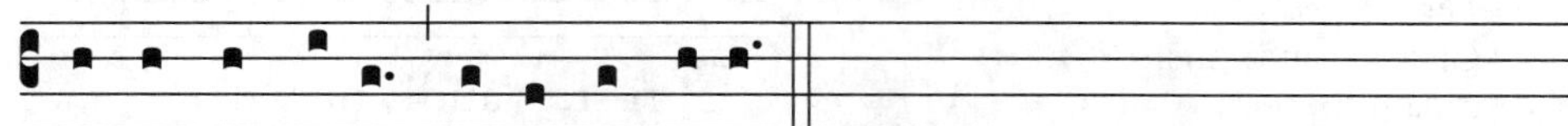

Sancta Ma- **rí**- a, o- ra pro nobis.

The Cantors: Sancta Dei Génitrix, ora pro nobis.
("Holy Mother of God, pray for us.")

All repeat:

Sancta De- i **Gé**-ni-trix, o- ra pro no-bis.

The Cantors: Sancta Virgo vírginum, ora pro nobis.
("Holy Virgin of virgins, pray for us.")

All repeat:

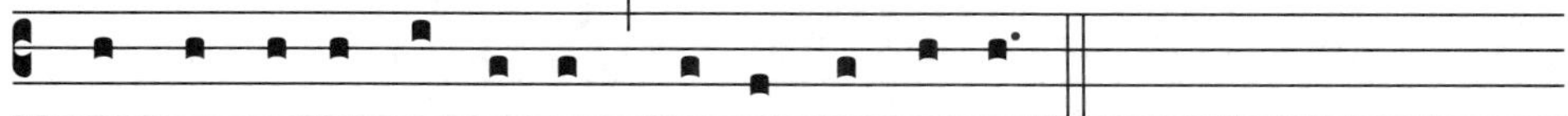

Sancta Virgo **vír**-gi-num, o- ra pro no-bis.

The Cantors: Sancte Míchaël, ora pro nobis.
("Saint Michael, pray for us.")

All repeat:

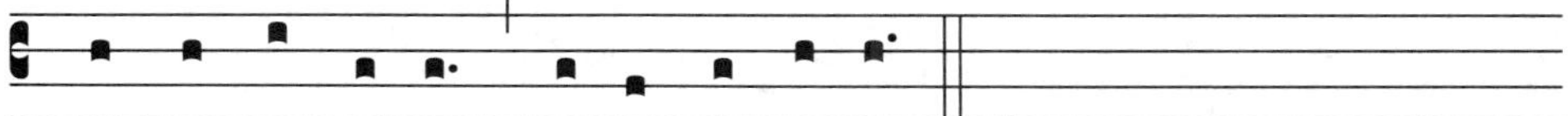

Sancte **Mí**-cha- ël, o- ra pro no-bis.

The Cantors: Sancte Gábriel, ora pro nobis.
("Saint Gabriel, pray for us.")

All repeat:

Sancte **Gá**-bri- el, o-ra pro nobis.

The Cantors: Sancte Ráphaël, ora pro nobis.
("Saint Raphael, pray for us.")

All repeat:

Sancte **Rá**-pha- ël o-ra pro nobis.

The Cantors: Omnes sancti Ángeli et Archángeli, oráte pro nobis.
("All holy Angels and Archangels, pray for us.")

All repeat:

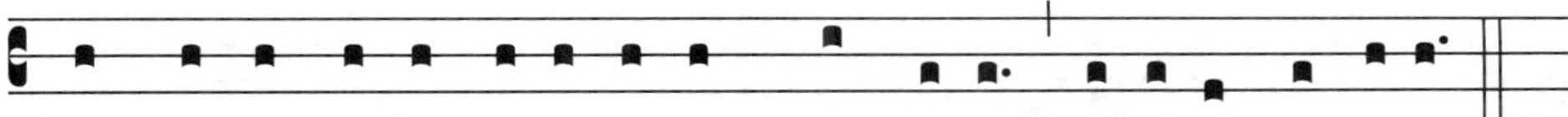

Omnes sancti Ánge- li et Arch- **án**-ge- li, o-rá-te pro nobis.

The Cantors: Omnes sancti beatórum Spiríituum órdines, oráte pro nobis.
("All holy orders of blessed spirits, pray for us.")

All repeat:

Omnes sancti be- a-tó-rum Spi-rí-tu- um **ór**-di-nes, o-rá-te pro nobis.

The Cantors: Sancte Joánnes Baptísta, ora pro nobis.
("Saint John the Baptist, pray for us.")

All repeat:

Sancte Jo- ánnes Ba- **ptí**-sta, o-ra pro nobis.

The Cantors: Sancte Joseph, ora pro nobis.
("Saint Joseph, pray for us.")

All repeat:

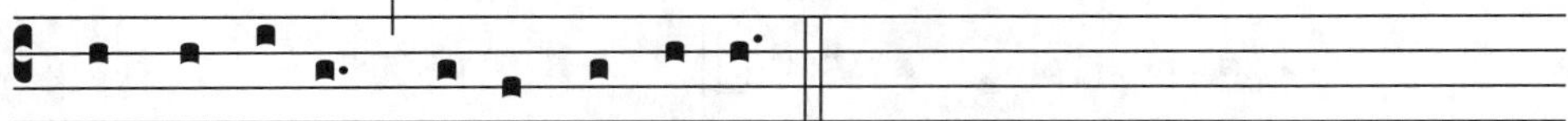

Sancte **Jo**-seph, o- ra pro no-bis.

The Cantors: Omnes sancti Patriárchæ et Prophétæ, oráte pro nobis.
("All holy Patriarchs and Prophets, pray for us.")

All repeat:

Omnes sancti Patri- árchæ et Pro- **phé**-tæ, o-rá-te pro nobis.

The Cantors: Sancte Petre, ora pro nobis.
("Saint Peter, pray for us.")

All repeat:

Sancte **Pe**-tre, o- ra pro no-bis.

SANCTE Paule, ora pro nobis. ("Saint Paul, pray for us.")
Sancte Pau-le, ora pro nobis.

SANCTE Andréa, ora pro nobis. ("Saint Andrew, pray for us.")
Sancte An-dré-a, ora pro nobis.

SANCTE Joánnes, ora pro nobis. ("Saint John, pray for us.")
Sancte Jo-án-nes, ora pro nobis.

OMNES sancti Apóstoli et Evangelístæ, oráte pro nobis.
Omnes sancti Apóstoli et Evange-lí-stæ, oráte pro nobis.
("All holy Apostles and Evangelists, pray for us.")

OMNES sancti Discípuli Dómini, oráte pro nobis.
Omnes sancti Discípuli Dó-mini, oráte pro nobis.
("All holy Disciples of the Lord, pray for us.")

SANCTE Stéphane, ora pro nobis. ("Saint Stephen, pray for us.")
Sancte Sté-phane, ora pro nobis.

SANCTE Lauréntі, ora pro nobis. ("Saint Laurence, pray for us.")
Sancte Lau-rén-ti, ora pro nobis.

SANCTE Vincénti, ora pro nobis. ("Saint Vincent, pray for us.")
Sancte Vin-cén-ti, ora pro nobis.

OMNES sancti Mártyres, oráte pro nobis.
Omnes sancti Már-tyres, oráte pro nobis.
("All holy Martyrs, pray for us.")

SANCTE Silvéster, ora pro nobis. ("Saint Silvester, pray for us.")
Sancte Sil-vé-ster, ora pro nobis.

SANCTE Gregóri, ora pro nobis. ("Saint Gregory, pray for us.")
Sancte Gre-gó-ri, ora pro nobis.

SANCTE Augustíne, ora pro nobis. ("Saint Augustine, pray for us.")
Sancte Augu-stí-ne, ora pro nobis.

OMNES sancti Pontífices et Confessóres, oráte pro nobis.
Omnes sancti Pontífices et Confes-só-res, oráte pro nobis.
("All holy Bishops and Confessors, pray for us.")

OMNES sancti Doctóres, oráte pro nobis.
Omnes sancti Do-ctó-res, oráte pro nobis.
("All holy Doctors, pray for us.")

SANCTE Antóni, ora pro nobis. ("Saint Anthony, pray for us.")
Sancte An-tó-ni, ora pro nobis.

SANCTE Benedícte, ora pro nobis. ("Saint Benedict, pray for us.")
Sancte Bene-dí-cte, ora pro nobis.

SANCTE Domínice, ora pro nobis. ("Saint Dominic, pray for us.")
Sancte Do-mí-nice, ora pro nobis.

SANCTE Francísce, ora pro nobis. ("Saint Francis, pray for us.")
Sancte Fran-cí-sce, ora pro nobis.

OMNES sancti Sacerdótes et Levítæ, oráte pro nobis.
Omnes sancti Sacerdótes et Le-ví-tæ, oráte pro nobis.
("All holy Priests and Levites, pray for us.")

OMNES sancti Mónachi et Eremítæ, oráte pro nobis.
Omnes sancti Mónachi et Ere-mí-tæ, oráte pro nobis.
("All holy Monks and Hermits, pray for us.")

SANCTA María Magdaléna, ora pro nobis. ("Saint Mary Magdalen, pray for us.")
Sancta María Magda-lé-na, ora pro nobis.

SANCTA Agnes, ora pro nobis. ("Saint Agnes, pray for us.")
Sancta A-gnes, ora pro nobis.

SANCTA Cæcília, ora pro nobis. ("Saint Cecilia, pray for us.")
Sancta Cæ-cí-lia, ora pro nobis.

SANCTA Ágatha, ora pro nobis. ("Saint Agatha, pray for us.")
Sancta Á-gatha, ora pro nobis.

SANCTA Anastásia, ora pro nobis. ("Saint Anastasia, pray for us.")
Sancta Ana-stá-sia, ora pro nobis.

OMNES sancti Apóstoli et Evangelístæ, oráte pro nobis.
Omnes sancti Apóstoli et Evange-lí-stæ, oráte pro nobis.
("All holy Apostles and Evangelists, pray for us.")

OMNES sanctæ Vírgines et Víduæ, oráte pro nobis.
Omnes sanctæ Vírgines et Ví-duæ, oráte pro nobis.
("All holy Virgins and Widows, pray for us.")

The Cantors: Omnes Sancti et Sanctæ Dei, intercédite pro nobis.
("All holy men and women, Saints of God, pray for us.")

All repeat:

Omnes Sancti et Sanctæ **De**- i, intercé-di- te pro no-bis.

The Cantors: Propítius esto, parce nobis, Dómine.
("Be merciful, spare us, O Lord.")

All repeat:

Pro-pí- ti- us **e**-sto, par-ce no-bis, Dó-mi-ne.

The Cantors: Propítius esto, exáudi nos, Dómine.
("Be merciful, graciously hear us, O Lord.")

All repeat:

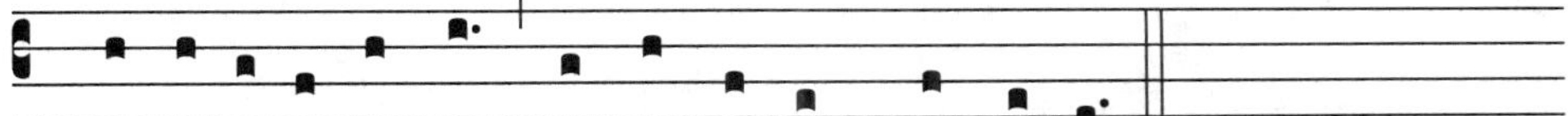

Pro-pí- ti- us **e**-sto, ex-áu-di nos, Dó-mi-ne.

The Cantors: Ab omni malo, líbera nos, Dómine.
("From all evil, deliver us, O Lord.")

All repeat:

Ab *o-mni* **ma**-lo, lí-be-ra nos, Dó-mi-ne.

The Cantors: Ab omni peccáto, líbera nos, Dómine.
("From all sin, deliver us, O Lord.")

All repeat:

Ab o-*mni pec*-**cá**-to, lí-be-ra nos, Dó-mi-ne.

The Cantors: A morte perpétua, líbera nos, Dómine.
("From everlasting death, deliver us, O Lord.")

All repeat:

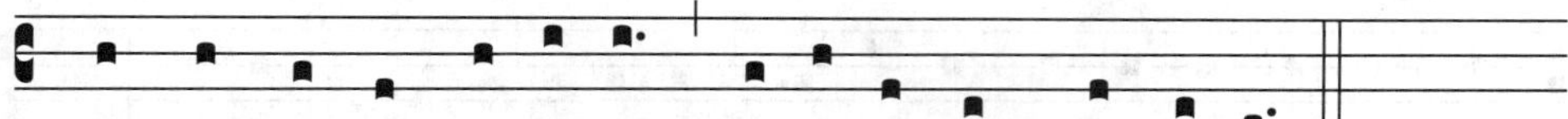

A mor-*te per*-**pé**-tu-a, lí-be-ra nos, Dó-mi-ne.

PER mystérium sanctæ Incarnatiónis tuæ, líbera nos, Dómine.
Per mystérium sanctæ Incarnati-*ó-nis* **tu**-æ, líbera nos, Dómine.
("Through the mystery of thy holy Incarnation, deliver us, O Lord.")

PER Advéntum tuum, líbera nos, Dómine.
Per Ad-*vén-tum* **tu**-um, líbera nos, Dómine.
("Through thy Coming, deliver us, O Lord.")

PER Nativitátem tuam, líbera nos, Dómine.
Per Nativi-*tá-tem* **tu**-am, líbera nos, Dómine.
("Through thy Nativity, deliver us, O Lord.")

PER Baptísmum et sanctum Jejúnium tuum, líbera nos, Dómine.
Per Baptísmum et sanctum Jejú-*ni-um* **tu**-um, líbera nos, Dómine.
("Through thy Baptism and holy Fasting, deliver us, O Lord.")

PER Crucem et Passiónem tuam, líbera nos, Dómine.
Per Crucem et Passi-*ó-nem* **tu**-am, líbera nos, Dómine.
("Through thy Cross and Passion, deliver us, O Lord.")

PER Mortem et Sepultúram tuam, líbera nos, Dómine.
Per Mortem et Sepul-*tú-ram* **tu**-am, líbera nos, Dómine.
("Through thy Death and Burial, deliver us, O Lord.")

PER sanctam Resurrectiónem tuam, líbera nos, Dómine.
Per sanctam Resurrecti-*ó-nem* **tu**-am, líbera nos, Dómine.
("Through thy holy Resurrection, deliver us, O Lord.")

PER admirábilem Ascensiónem tuam, líbera nos, Dómine.
Per admirábilem Ascensi-*ó-nem* **tu**-am, líbera nos, Dómine.
("Through thy wonderful Ascension, deliver us, O Lord.")

PER advéntum Spíritus Sancti Parácliti, líbera nos, Dómine.
Per advéntum Spíritus San-*cti Pa*-**rá**-cliti, líbera nos, Dómine.
("Through the coming of the Holy Ghost, the Paraclete, deliver us, O Lord.")

IN die judícii, líbera nos, Dómine.
In di-*e ju*-**dí**-cii, líbera nos, Dómine.
("In the day of judgment, deliver us, O Lord.")

The Cantors: Peccatóres, te rogámus, audi nos.
("We sinners beseech thee to hear us.")

All repeat:

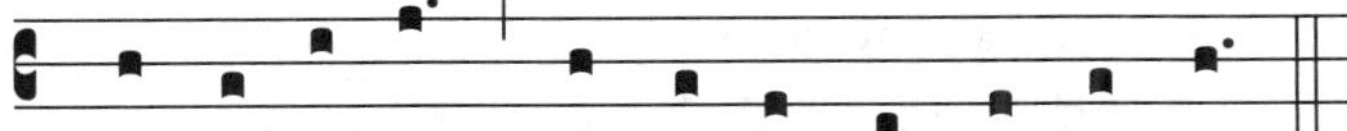

Pec-*ca*-**tó**-res, te ro-gá-mus, au-di nos.

The Cantors: Ut nobis parcas, te rogámus, audi nos.
("That thou wouldst spare us, we beseech thee, hear us.")

All repeat:

Ut no-*bis* **par**-cas, te ro-gámus, audi nos.

The Cantors:

Ut Ecclésiam tuam sanctam ’ régere et conserváre dignéris, te rogámus, audi nos.

("That it may please thee to be the guide and guardian of thy holy Church, we beseech thee, hear us.")

All repeat:

Ut Eccle-si- am tu- am sanctam régere et conserváre *di*-**gné**-ris,

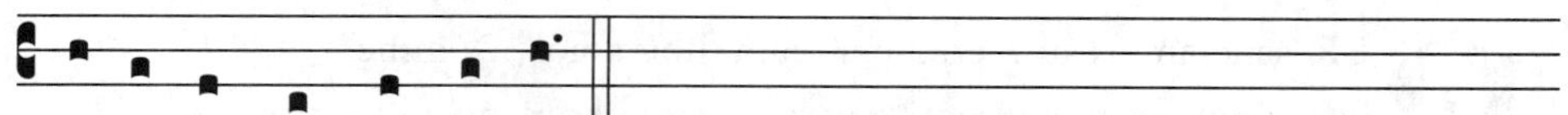

te ro-gá-mus, au-di nos.

UT DOMNUM apostólicum et omnes ecclesiásticos órdines ’ in sancta religióne conserváre dignéris, te rogámus, audi nos.

Ut domnum apostólicum et omnes ecclesiásticos órdines ’ in sancta religióne conserváre *di*-**gné**-ris, te rogámus, audi nos.

("That it may please thee to preserve in rightness of living our holy Father the Pope, and all of every degree, thy ministers, we beseech thee, hear us.")

UT INIMÍCOS sanctæ Ecclésiæ ’ humiliáre dignéris, te rogámus, audi nos.

Ut inimícos sanctæ Ecclésiæ ’ humiliáre *di*-**gné**-ris, te rogámus, audi nos.

("That it may please thee to humble the enemies of holy Church, we beseech thee, hear us.")

UT RÉGIBUS et princípibus christiánis ’ pacem et veram concórdiam donáre dignéris, te rogámus, audi nos.

Ut régibus et princípibus christiánis ’ pacem et veram concórdiam donáre *di*-**gné**-ris, te rogámus, audi nos.

("That it may please thee to give peace and true concord to Christian kings and princes, we beseech thee, hear us.")

UT NOSMETÍPSOS in tuo sancto servítio ’ confortáre et conserváre dignéris, te rogámus, audi nos.

Ut nosmetípsos in tuo sancto servítio ’ confortáre et conserváre *di*-**gné**-ris, te rogámus, audi nos.

("That it may please thee to confirm and preserve us in thy holy service, we beseech thee, hear us.")

UT ÓMNIBUS benefactóribus nostris ’
sempitérna bona retríbuas, te rogámus, audi nos.

Ut ómnibus benefactóribus nostris ’
sempitérna bona *re*-**trí**-buas, te rogámus, audi nos.

("That thou wouldst reward all our benefactors with eternal blessings, we beseech thee, hear us.")

UT FRUCTUS terræ ’ dare et conserváre
dignéris, te rogámus, audi nos.

Ut fructus terræ ’ dare et conserváre
di-**gné**-ris, te rogámus, audi nos.

("That it may please thee to grant us the fruits of earth, and keep them undiminished, we beseech thee, hear us.")

UT ÓMNIBUS fidélibus defúnctis ’ réquiem ætérnam
donáre dignéris, te rogámus, audi nos.

Ut ómnibus fidélibus defúnctis ’ réquiem ætérnam
donáre *di*-**gné**-ris, te rogámus, audi nos.

("That it may please thee to grant eternal rest to all the faithful departed, we beseech thee, hear us.")

UT NOS exaudíre dignéris, te rogámus, audi nos.

Ut nos exaudíre *di*-**gné**-ris, te rogámus, audi nos.

("That it may please thee graciously to hear us, we beseech thee, hear us.")

Agnus De- i, qui tollis peccá- ta mundi: parce nobis, Dómine.

("Lamb of God, who takest away the sins of the world, spare us, O Lord."

Agnus De- i, qui tollis peccá- ta mundi: exáudi nos, Dómine.

("Lamb of God, who takest away the sins of the world, graciously hear us, O Lord.")

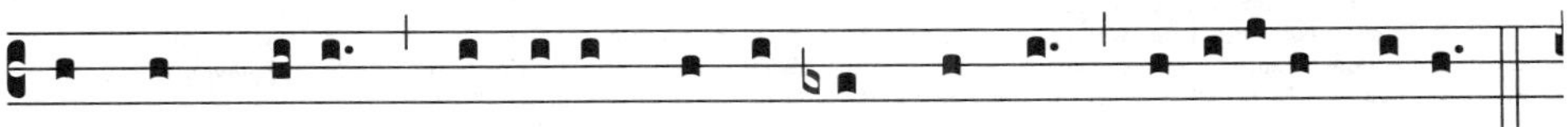

Agnus De- i, qui tollis peccá- ta mundi: mi-serére nobis.

("Lamb of God, who takest away the sins of the world, have mercy on us.")

Christe, audi nos. Christe, ex-áudi nos.

("Christ, hear us. Christ, graciously hear us.")

At the traditional Mass of Easter Eve (and also the 1962 version):

(1) There is no Vidi Aquam;

(2) There is no Introit;

(3) The (short) Alleluia is followed by a Tract;

(4) There is no Gradual or Greater Alleluia;

(5) There is no Sequence;

(6) There is no Creed;

(7) There is no Offertory Antiphon;

(8) There is no Agnus Dei and the *Kiss of Peace* is omitted;

(9) There is no Communion Antiphon.

For a century, authors have speculated as to why these items are omitted {Thurston p437}.

At the traditional (1950) Mass of Easter Eve, the Prayers at the Foot of the Altar and Last Gospel are said, but these items were eliminated by the reform of Pius XII.

(1950) Holy Saturday • The First Easter Mass

Sabbato Sancto — *De Missa Solemni Vigiliae Paschalis*

1950 • When the cantors intone the invocation *Peccatóres, te rogámus, audi nos* ("We sinners beseech thee to hear us") the Celebrant and sacred ministers rise and return to the sacristy where they lay aside their purple vestments to don the richer ones of white appointed for Easter.

According to Father Lasance: "They return before the Altar at such time as will enable them to recite the Psalm—*Júdica Me* with *Glória Patri*—and Confíteor while the choir is closing the litany with the chant of the *Kýrie Eléison.*" However, Father Fortescue says the procession comes from the sacristy "as the cantors sing the petition *Agnus Dei*" arriving at the Altar right before the *Kýrie Eléison* is sung {Fortescue p332}. Father Dale says the cantors, at the *Peccatóres*, should "sing slower, in order to give time conveniently to prepare the things necessary for Mass." {Dale p222}.

Some liturgists insist that the *Kýrie Eléison* be started only after the Celebrant has arrived in the Sanctuary, because they consider the *Kýrie Eléison* as "standing in lieu of the Introit for the Mass of this day" {Dale p223}, and a decree of the Sacred Congregation of Rites (14 April 1753) said the Introit must not begin until the Celebrant reaches the Altar. But even if one accepts this theory, it was invalid by 1950, as the following question was sent Sacred Congregation of Rites in 1947: "The question is asked whether it is allowed to sing the Introit at Sung Masses—whether solemn or pontifical—in the ancient manner, that is, that many verses of the psalm of the Introit are sung, in such a way that the antiphon of the Introit is interjected between them? In this procedure, the chant of the Introit is extended to the whole time that the Celebrant takes to proceed from the Sacristy or Sacrario to the altar?" The response by the Sacred Congregation of Rites was dated 29 January 1947: "An affirmative response is given, provided that all is done according to the prudent judgment of the Bishop." Indeed, the rubrics of the *Graduale Romanum* (Vatican Press, 1908) allow this practice; cf. "De Ritibus Servandis in Cantu Missae" §1.

[Editor's Note: The reform of Pope Pius XII eliminated Psalm 42 and the *Confíteor* {McManus p100} but said nothing about the other prayers at the beginning of Mass: *Deus tu convérsus*; the *Aufer a nobis*; *Orámus te Dómine*; and so forth. On this, see *Dominicae Resurrectionis Vigiliam* (1951) Titulus III §1. The assumption in 1951 was that the Celebrant would skip everything, ascend the steps, kiss the Altar, and begin the *Kýrie Eléison*. The *Code of Rubrics* (1961) clarified matters: "*Psalmus Júdica me, Deus*, cum sua antiphona, et confessio cum absolutione dicuntur, ante gradus altaris, in qualibet Missa sive in cantu sive lecta; omittuntur autem una cum sequentibus versibus et orationibus *Aufer a nobis* et *Orámus te, Dómine*. However, in *Requiem* Masses and Passiontide, only Psalm 42 was traditionally omitted.]

Versatile Litany • In former times, the Litany was often split into two sections, because whether the community is processing to a baptismal church {Dobszay p38}, baptismal chapel, or baptismal font, a litany by its very nature can be "adjusted" to fit the correct timing: on the way there (first half) and on the way back (second half). For instance, a Benedictional (ms 22049) created circa 1429ad splits the *Litany of the Saints*, placing the Blessing of the Font in the middle, just as the 1951 "experimental" version did. Many other traditions also existed; for example, a Spanish Missal from 1568ad has the litany being sung only after the Celebrant has reached the baptismal font {Monti p484}. Many traditions of Holy Saturday have not survived, such as the splendid (and ancient) rite of "Accendite"—when the the High Altar candles were lit before the Easter Eve Mass.

End and Beginning • The ending of the Litany becomes the beginning of the Easter Eve Mass; that is, the final repetions of *Kýrie Eléison* double as the opening *Kýrie Eléison* of the Easter Eve Mass, which has no Introit. The rubrics assume that Mass would be sung by those *in choro* (i.e. by clerics sitting in the chancel). For this reason, the two cantors who were kneeling in the middle of the chancel leading the Litany are told to "go back to their place" after they intone the *Kýrie Eléison*. However, these instructions should not be interpreted as discouraging other settings of the *Kýrie*—such as Renaissance polyphony.

While in the Sacristy • While the Celebrant is in the sacristy exchanging his purple vestments for white ones, the following actions take place: the High Altar candles are lit; flowers are placed upon the Altar; the purple Altar frontal is removed (revealing the white frontal underneath it); the cushions and purple carpet are removed; a carpet adorned for the greatest feast of the year is brought out; the Missal (covered with white) and Altar cards are placed on the Altar. During this time, according to Father Lasance, "the pictures and statues in the church are unveiled" but Fortescue and Thurston say this uncovering not does not take place until the *Glória in excélsis* has been intoned. [Editor's Note: In the 1962 version, the images are uncovered during the *Glória*.]

The Gloria on Holy Saturday • Having said the Prayers at the Foot of the Altar, the Celebrant ascends the Altar—kissing it—and incenses the Altar as at every High Mass. Having quietly read the *Kýrie Eléison*, he solemnly intones the *Glória in excélsis*. This has long been an important moment; according to Father Fortescue, "the Ordo of Saint-Amand [circa 850ad] limits the *Glória in Excelsis* (for priests) to Easter Eve and the day of their ordination." For as long as the priest is quietly saying the *Glória*, the organ is played {Fortescue p333} and the bells are rung—a custom traceable to the 8th century {Monti p491}. It is allowed for the Church bells to continue ringing while the choir sings the *Glória*.

1950 • *Hic Cantores solemniter incipiunt: "Kýrie eléison. etc." Interim Sacerdos cum Ministris in paramentis albis accedit ad Altare: et dicto Psalmo "Júdica me, Deus," cum "Glória Patri," facit Confessionem, ut moris est, in loco consueto: deinde ascendens, osculatur Altare, incensat more solito, et finitis a Choro "Kýrie, eléison," incipit solemniter "Glória in excélsis," et pulsantur campanae.*

Turning on the Lights • In the 1950 version as well as the 1962 version, the church lights are supposed to be turned on toward the beginning of the ceremony: in 1950 during the *Exsultet*; in 1962 after the 3rd *Lumen Christi*. (In neither version are the Altar candles lit until the Mass.) Nevertheless, in some places it is customary to keep the entire Church dark until *Glória*. (Needless to say, such an action would be inconsequential if the Easter Vigil takes place in broad daylight.) This custom is justified inasmuch as the rubrics "are silent on the question of electric lights." At the beginning of the ceremony, the 1950 version said: *Hic accenduntur lampades* ("here the lamps in the church are relighted"). The Pius XII version says: *Et accenduntur candelae populi de cereo benedicto, et luminaria ecclesiae* ("the people's candles are lit from the Paschal candle, and the lights of the church are lighted"). It seems an acceptable practice would be lighting all the "lamps" at the time appointed by the rubrics, while keeping electric lights off until the *Glória*. This is consonant with the spirit of the liturgy, as historically the Glória was a moment of great jubilation. For example, a Spanish Missal from 1568ad speaks of a large veil which covered the entire Altar being removed at the *Glória* on Easter Eve. Another widespread custom was for all present to kneel (or lie prostrate) during the Easter Eve *Glória* {Monti p492}.

COLLECT.

Deus, qui hanc sacratíssimam noctem glória Domínicæ Resurrectiónis illústras: consérva in nova famíliæ tuæ progénie adoptiónis spíritum, quem dedísti; ut córpore et mente renováti, puram tibi exhíbeant servitútem. Per eúmdem Dóminum.

O GOD, BY THE SPLENDOR of our Lord's resurrection thou turnest this holy night into day! Keep safe, in these new children of thy family, the spirit of adoption thou hast here bestowed; soul and body regenerate, may they ever do thee service unblemished. Through the same.

EPISTLE. *Col 3: 1-4*

Fratres: si consurrexístis cum Christo, quæ sursum sunt quǽrite, ubi Christus est in déxtera Dei sedens: quæ sursum sunt sápite, non quæ super terram. Mórtui enim estis, et vita vestra est abscóndita cum Christo in Deo. Cum Christus apparúerit, vita vestra: tunc et vos apparébitis cum ipso in glória.

BRETHREN: Risen, then, with Christ, you must lift your thoughts above, where Christ now sits at the right hand of God. You must be heavenly-minded, not earthly-minded; you have undergone death, and your life is hidden away now with Christ in God. Christ is your life, and when he is made manifest, you too will be made manifest in glory with him.

1950 • When the Celebrant has read the Epistle (quietly), he does not go on at once to read the Gradual. He waits until he has blessed the Subdeacon after the chanted Epistle. Then, at the Epistle corner, he sings "Alleluia" thrice—with hands joined—raising the pitch each time. The choir answers, repeating Alleluia at the same pitch.

Finita Epistola, Celebrans incipit "Allelúja" et totum decantat ter, elevando vocem gradatim: et Chorus post quamlibet vicem, in eodem tono repetit illud idem.

1950 • The Celebrant reads (while the choir sings) the following psalms. | *Postea Chorus prosequitur:*

Give thanks to the Lord; the Lord is gracious, his mercy endures for ever. *(The Alleluia is not repeated.)*

Confitémini Dómino, quóniam bonus: quóniam in sæculum misericórdia ejus. (Ps 117: 1)

TRACT. *Ps 116: 1-2*

PRAISE the Lord, all you nations: let all the peoples of the world do him honor. ℣. Abundant has his mercy been towards us; the Lord remains true to his word for ever.

Laudáte Dóminum omnes gentes: et collaudáte eum, omnes pópuli.℣. Quóniam confirmáta est super nos misericórdia ejus: et véritas Dómini manet in ætérnum.

1950 • The priest quietly reads the Gospel before it is chanted by the Deacon. At the Gospel lights are not carried, but only incense: a blessing is asked, and the rest is done as usual. Sir William Blount wrote in 1670AD: "No Tapers are Carried, when the Gospell is read; to note unto us, that Christ's Resurrection (who is the Tru light of the world) was not, as yet, manifested to men. But incense is used to represent the perfumes prepared by the Three Maries, to anoynt our Saviour's bodie."

Ad Evangelium non portantur luminaria, sed tantum incensum: petitur benedictio, et alia fiunt de more.

GOSPEL. *Matt 28: 1-7*

ON THE NIGHT after the sabbath, at the hour when dawn broke on the first day of the week, Mary Magdalen and the other Mary came near to contemplate the tomb. And suddenly there was a great trembling of the earth, because an angel of the Lord came to the place, descending from heaven, and rolled away the stone and sat over it; his face shone like lightning, and his garments were white as snow; so that the guards trembled for fear of him, and were like dead men. But the angel said openly to the women, You need not be afraid; I know well that you have come to look for Jesus of Nazareth, the man who was crucified. He is not here; he has risen, as he told you. Come and see the place where the Lord was buried. You must go in haste, and tell his disciples that he has risen from the dead; and now he is going on before you into Galilee, where you shall have sight of him. That is my message to you.

Véspere autem sábbati, quæ lucéscit in prima sábbati, venit María Magdaléne, et áltera María vidére sepúlchrum. Et ecce terræmótus factus est magnus. Ángelus enim Dómini descéndit de cælo: et accédens revólvit lápidem, et sedébat super eum: erat autem aspéctus ejus sicut fulgur: et vestiméntum ejus sicut nix. Præ timóre autem ejus extérriti sunt custódes, et facti sunt velut mórtui. Respóndens autem Ángelus, dixit muliéribus: Nolíte timére vos: scio enim, quod Jesum, qui crucifíxus est, quǽritis: non est hic: surréxit enim, sicut dixit. Veníte, et vidéte locum, ubi pósitus erat Dóminus. Et cito eúntes, dícite discípulis ejus, quia surréxit: et ecce præcédit vos in Galilǽam: ibi eum vidébitis. Ecce prædíxi vobis.

1950 • There is no Creed. The Celebrant sings *Dóminus vobíscum* and *Orémus* at the Offertory as usual, but the Offertory antiphon is not sung. The organ is played to the beginning of the Preface.

Non dicitur "Credo," sed finito Evangelio Sacerdos dicit: "Dóminus vobíscum," postea: "Orémus." Non dicitur "Offertorium." Ad "Lavábo" dicitur "Glória Patri."

SECRET.

Súscipe, quǽsumus, Dómine, preces pópuli tui, cum oblatiónibus hostiárum: ut paschálibus initiáta mystériis, ad æternitátis nobis medélam, te operánte, profíciant. Per Dóminum.

ACCEPT, LORD, the prayers of thy people, that come to do thee sacrifice. May the new life these paschal mysteries have wrought in us be a sovereign remedy of thine for our eternal well-being. Through our Lord.

1950 • The Preface of Easter is sung, with the phrase "in hac potissimum nocte." In the Canon, the Paschal form of the COMMUNICANTES prayer is said, again with the form "noctem sacratissimam celebrantes." The Paschal form of the HANC IGITUR prayer is said. "Pax Dómini sit semper vobíscum" is chanted, but the Kiss of Peace is not given. The *Agnus Dei* is not said, but the usual three prayers before Communion are said in the 1950; however, the 1962 version omits the prayer "Dómine Jesu Christi, qui dixísti."

(1950) HOLY SATURDAY • Vespers

Sabbato Sancto *Ad Vesperas*

1950 • There is no Communion Antiphon. After the ablutions, the choir sings the "Allelúja" three times, then Psalm 116 (*Laudáte Dóminum omnes gentes*) then "Allelúja" three times. [Editor's Note: In the 1962 version, Psalm 150 (*Laudáte Dóminum in sanctis ejus*) replaces Psalm 116.]

Post sumptionem Sacramenti, pro Vesperis in Choro cantatur:

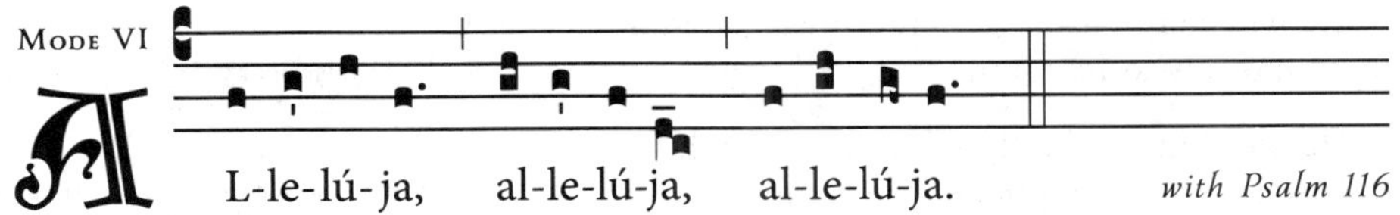

℣. Laudáte Dóminum, omnes gentes: * laudáte eum, omnes pópuli.

℣. Praise the Lord, all you nations; let all the peoples of the world do him honor.

℣. Quóniam confirmáta est super nos misericórdia ejus, * et véritas Dómini manet in ætérnum.

℣. Abundant has his mercy been towards us; the Lord remains true to his word for ever.

℣. Glória Patri, et Fílio, * et Spirítui Sancto:

℣. Glory be the Father, and to the Son, and to the Holy Ghost.

℣. Sicut erat in princípio, et nunc, et semper, * et in sǽcula sæculórum. Amen.

℣. As it was in the beginning, is now, and ever shall be, world without end. Amen.

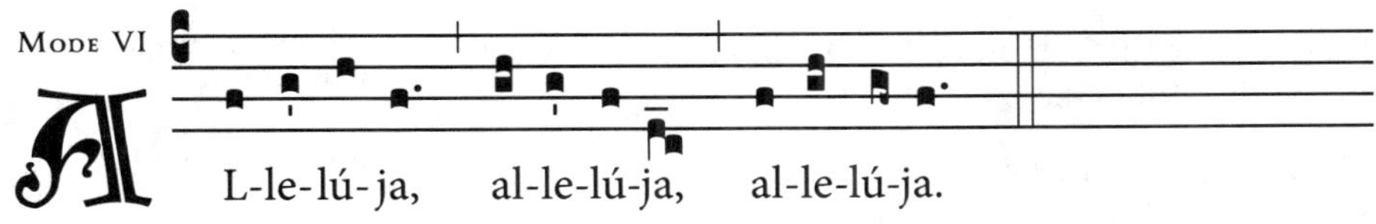

1950 • While the choir sings the psalm, the Celebrant—at the Epistle corner—says it quietly, with the antiphon, alternately with the ministers. They stand as at the Introit. With joined hands, the Celebrant then intones the antiphon "Véspere autem Sábbati" and the choir continues it while the Celebrant and ministers recite it in a low voice. Then two cantors intone the Magnificat. The Celebrant makes the sign of the cross and goes to the middle and, having blessed the incense as usual, the Altar is incensed. While he incenses, the Celebrant quietly recites the Magnificat alternately with the ministers.

Capitulum, Hymnus et Versus non dicuntur, sed statim Celebrans in cantu incipit Antiphonam ad "Magníficat" quam Chorus prosequitur.

MAGNIFICAT ANTIPHON.

ON THE NIGHT after the Sabbath. * At the hour when dawn broke on the first day of the week, Mary Magdalen and the other Mary came near to contemplate the tomb, alleluia.

Véspere autem Sábbati. * Quæ lucéscit in prima sábbati: venit María Magdaléne, et áltera María, vidére sepúlchrum, alleluja.

OUR LADY'S OWN HYMN. *Luke 1: 46-55*

1. My soul magnifies * the Lord.

1. Magníficat * ánima mea Dóminum.

2. My spirit has found joy * in God, who is my Savior.

2. Et exsultávit spíritus meus: * in Deo salutári meo.

3. Because he has looked graciously upon the lowliness of his handmaid: * behold, from this day forward all generations will count me blessed.

3. Quia respéxit humilitátem ancíllæ suæ: * ecce enim ex hoc beátam me dicent omnes generatiónes.

4. Because he who is mighty has wrought for me his wonders, * he whose name is holy.

4. Quia fecit mihi magna qui potens est: * et sanctum nomen ejus.

5. He has mercy, from generation to generation, * upon those who fear him.

5. Et misericórdia ejus a progénie in progénies, * timéntibus eum.

6. He has done valiantly with the strength of his arm: * driving the proud astray in the imagination of their hearts.

6. Fecit poténtiam in brácchio suo * dispérsit supérbos mente cordis sui.

7. He has put down the mighty from their seat, * and exalted the lowly.

7. Depósuit poténtes de sede, * et exaltávit húmiles.

8. He has filled the hungry with good things, * and sent the rich away empty-handed.

8. Esuriéntes implévit bonis: * et dívites dimísit inánes.

9. He has protected his servant Israel, * keeping his merciful design in remembrance:

9. Suscépit Ísraël púerum suum: * recordátus misericórdiæ suæ.

10. According to the promise which he made to our forefathers, * Abraham and his posterity for evermore.

10. Sicut locútus est ad patres nostros, * Ábraham, et sémini ejus in sǽcula.

11. Glory be the Father, and to the Son, * and to the Holy Ghost.

11. Glória Patri, et Fílio, * et Spirítui Sancto.

12. As it was in the beginning, is now, * and ever shall be, world without end. Amen.

12. Sicut erat in princípio, et nunc, et semper, * et in sǽcula sæculórum. Amen.

Véspere autem Sábbati. * Quæ lucéscit in prima sábbati: venit María Magdaléne, et áltera María, vidére sepúlchrum, alleluja.

ON THE NIGHT after the Sabbath, at the hour when dawn broke on the first day of the week, Mary Magdalen and the other Mary came near to contemplate the tomb, alleluia.

℣. Dóminus vobíscum.

℟. Et cum spíritu tuo.

℣. The Lord be with you.

℟. And with you, his minister.

POSTCOMMUNION. *Which also serves as the Collect of Vespers.*

Spíritum nobis, Dómine, tuæ caritátis infúnde: ut, quos sacraméntis Paschálibus satiásti tua fácias pietáte concórdes. Per Dóminum . . . in unitáte ejusdem.

LORD, we beseech thee, pour out thy Spirit into our hearts; thou hast made us free of thy paschal sacrament, and now, by thy grace, live we in love together. Through our Lord … in the bond of the same Holy Spirit.

1950 • The response at the end of Mass is as follows :

℟. De-o gra-ti- as, al- le- lú- ia, al- le- lu- ia.

Divine Office During Mass • The "abbreviated" Vespers (a.k.a. *pro vesperis*) during the Mass of Easter Eve did not always occur at the place indicated by the 1950 rubrics. For example, during the 9th century, various practices existed in different localities: some placed the "abbreviated" Vespers between the baptisms and Mass, while others sang Vespers during the distribution of Holy Communion {Goddard p246}. Indeed, during the High Mediæval Period, parts of the Divine Office were often sung while the people received Holy Communion—and not just on Holy Saturday; for sundry examples, please refer to pages 398-399 of Father Jungmann's *Missarum Sollemnia.* According to John of Avranches (d. 1097) Vespers was to be inserted on Holy Thursday during the Communion. Wherever such a practice was customary, we sometimes find a rubric stipulating that "its close would coincide with the *Ite Missa Est* of the Deacon." The reformers desperately sought a logical approach to the "pro vesperis" (or "pro laudibus") after they modified the traditional timing of the Easter Vigil, and discussed the matter on 30 January 1951 {Giampietro p227}. Throughout Church history, many customs arose vis-à-vis music during the distribution of Holy Communion, including songs in the vernacular; e.g. Bishop Urban Sagstetter (d. 1573) mandated communion songs in the vernacular in his diocese {Jungmann p399}. An extremely popular and ancient communion song often sung on Easter was "Venite populi ad sacrum et immortale mysterium." Father Jungmann has pointed out that "the insertion of a canonical hour after Communion [...] was not unheard of"—and such a tradition seems worthy of revival.

More Than One Way • Variety existed vis-à-vis how the Easter Vigil was celebrated. In the Gelasian Sacramentary—from approximately 725AD—Mass did not begin immediately after the baptisms. Rather, the priests waited in the Sacristy and began Mass "only when the first stars appear in the sky"—and we are not told whether the congregation remained in the church during the intervening gap, during which (according to some ancient books) Vespers was sung or extra litanies were added {Goddard p242}.

✠ HE THREW HIS ARMS ROUND BENJAMIN'S NECK, IN TEARS; BENJAMIN TOO WEPT AS HE CLUNG TO HIM. Gen 45:14

THE DISCIPLES WENT BACK HOME; BUT MARY STOOD BEFORE THE TOMB, WEEPING. (Jn 20)

TO THEIR MINDS THE STORY SEEMED MADNESS, AND THEY COULD NOT BELIEVE IT. (Lk 24)

✠ AND RECEIVING HIM KISSED HIM—AS DID ALSO HIS WIFE—AND THEY BEGAN TO WEEP FOR JOY. Tobias 11:11

ONLY PURITY AND SINLESSNESS COULD WELCOME THE ALL HOLY SON OF GOD INTO THE WORLD—AND HENCE MARY IMMACULATE MET HIM AT THE DOOR OF EARTH—BUT ONLY A REPENTANT SINNER COULD FITTINGLY UNDERSTAND THE TRIUMPH OVER SIN. IN THIS CONTRAST IS HIDDEN THE GREAT TRUTH OF EASTER DAY: THE RESURRECTION IS FOR SINNERS. (Fulton J. Sheen)

Notes on the Easter Vigil of Holy Saturday

Experimental Vigil • Pope Pius XII reformed Holy Week on 16 November 1955 by means of *Maxima Redemptionis*, a decree which took effect on 25 March 1956. However, the Easter Vigil had already been modified "on an experimental basis." The experimental vigil was announced on 9 February 1951 (just 43 days before it was to take effect) by means of an article in Acta Apostolicae Sedis, the Holy See's journal. This announcement—commonly referred to as *Dominicae Resurrectionis Vigiliam*—also included eight pages of rubrics, explaining the elements being modified: e.g. the "Renewal of Baptismal Promises" is given in chapter 7 (in Latin). About nine months later, on 11 January 1952, the Vatican published a slightly revised version of the rubrics—this time approximately 14 pages in length—again in the Acta Apostolicae Sedis. Based on these decrees, a little booklet was produced: *Ordo Sabbati Sancti Quando Vigilia Paschalis Instaurata Peragitur*. This booklet was more convenient than celebrating the experimental vigil from journal articles. Generally speaking, the differences between the 1951 Acta article and the 1955 official version (used in "the liturgical books of 1962") are insignificant, with one exception: the 1955 truncated Lauds ceremony—towards the end of Mass—uses Psalm 150 (*Laudáte Dóminum in sanctis ejus*) whereas the 1951 "experimental" version (and the traditional version) had Psalm 116 (*Laudáte Dóminum omnes gentes*).

> **Conclusion:** Generally speaking, the 1951, 1952, 1955, and 1962 versions of the Easter Vigil are identical, except for extreme minutiae such as *accénde* (1951) vs. *inténde* (1952) in the "Véniat quǽsumus" prayer.

Beginning Buoy • The 1951 "experimental" Easter Vigil was without question the "buoy" marking the beginning of massive liturgical changes—reaching their final conclusion in 1970—although such changes were often arrived at by subtle and circuitous routes. To examine these changes is far beyond the scope of these notes, but something which must not be ignored is the haste with which they were made, which resulted in carelessness and confusion. Consider one example: high on the liturgical progressives' list of desiderata was the elimination of "duplication" by the priest. The 1951 "experimental" Vigil achieved this, when the Celebrant—during the reading of the prophecies—is told to "sit and listen to them being sung" instead of quietly reading them at the Altar (*Celebrans et ministri, clerus et populus, sedentes auscultant*). On 16 November 1955, this practice was extended to all of holy week:

Per totam hebdomadã sanctã, id est a dominica II Passionis seu in palmis usque ad missam vigiliæ paschalis inclusive, in missa (et feria VI in solemni actione liturgica), si solemniter celebratur, scilicet cum ministris sacris, ea omnia, quæ diaconus vel subdiaconus aut lector, vi proprii officii cantant vel legunt, **a celebrante omittuntur.**	During the entire Holy Week—that is from the second Sunday in Passiontide or Palm Sunday up to the Mass of the Easter vigil inclusive, in the Mass (and on Friday in the solemn liturgical service)—whenever the function is solemn—that is, performed with sacred ministers—**the Celebrant is to omit** whatever the Deacon, the Subdeacon, or the lector sing or read in the performance of their own part of the ceremony.

However, that practice was not extended to items sung by the choir; that would not occur until 1970. Yet, there was confusion. For example, in 1953, Father Benedict Steuart wrote as follows regarding the experimental Easter Vigil Mass: "When the cantors have finished chanting the *Kyries*, the Celebrant at once intones the *Gloria in excelsis*, during which the bells are rung. The rubric says nothing about any private recitation of either *Kyries* or *Gloria* by Celebrant and ministers, and the same is true with regard to the Epistle and Gospel. The Celebrant then (it seems) may sit down immediately with his ministers at the sedilia until the collect. But the Celebrant himself still intones the *Alleluia* three times, after the Epistle has been chanted by the Subdeacon."

COMPARISON : 1950 vs. 1962

LIGHTING THE FIRE • In spite of what is sometimes claimed, the Pius XII revisions did not modify how the fire is started. In the traditional version, the fire is started "before the ceremony" {Dale p216}. Father Fortescue agrees, saying the fire is lit "just before the ceremony begins, with a spark struck from a flint" {Fortescue p319}. In the 1962 version, "a fire is struck from flint" before the ceremony {McManus p89}. Philip Goddard {pages 205-207} cites numerous eighth-century witnesses saying the Holy Saturday fire was lit "from the light which was hidden away on Good Friday." In other places, the fire for Holy Saturday was "reserved on Maundy Thursday."

LIGHTS IN THE CHURCH • Archbishop Fulton J. Sheen famously said: "Fire has two great qualities: Light and Heat." Our Blessed Lord said (Jn 8:12): "I am the light of the world. He that followeth me walketh not in darkness, but shall have the light of life." Incandescent light bulbs became popular circa 1890, which—in a small way—blurred or weakened the symbolism. Abbat Guéranger (d. 1875) wrote: "All the Lamps in the Church have been extinguished; formerly, the Faithful used to put out the fires in their houses before going to the Church: they lighted them, on their return, with light taken from the blessed Fire, which they received as a symbol of our Lord's Resurrection. Let us not here omit to notice that the putting out of all the lights in the Church is a symbol of the abrogation of the Old Law, which ended with the rending of the Veil of the Temple; and that the new Fire represents the preaching of the New Law, whereby our Lord Jesus Christ, the Light of the World, fulfilled all the figures of the ancient Covenant." Father Dale says: "The lamps of the church should be so prepared that they may easily be lighted at the proper time" {Dale p214}.

In the traditional version, the church remains dark until the *Exsultet* nears its conclusion—to be precise, at the words *apis mater eduxit*—where the prayer speaks of a "a flame divided but undimmed" {Fortescue p326}. An acolyte uses the Triple Candle to light a candle on a pole; then he lights all the lamps in the church. As mentioned above, most churches these days use electric lights.

✠ *But the 1962 version is different:* In the 1962 version, while the blessing of the New Fire is taking place "all the lights in the church have been extinguished, so that they may be lighted from the newly-blessed fire" {1953maryland p3}. In the 1962 version, the people hold candles, and this "participation by the people" was considered very important by the reformers. After the third (and final) *Lumen Christi*—instead of towards the end of the *Exsultet*—"the candles of the people are lighted from the blessed candle, and the lights of the church as well. Servers may carry candles or tapers lighted from the Paschal candle to the people in the church. If the number of the faithful is not too great, some of them may come to light their candles from the Paschal candle, and then return to spread the light from one member of the faithful to another" {McManus p92}. When the *Exsultet* has ended, "clergy and people now extinguish their candles" {1953maryland p8}. The 1962 version does not specify whether the church returns to darkness at this point, but customarily the lights are again turned off until the *Gloria In Excelsis* at the Easter Vigil Mass.

CANDLES HELD BY THE PEOPLE • At the beginning of the "Renewal of Baptismal Promises," the people are instructed to light their candles, which they extinguished at the end of the *Exsultet*, but this seems inconvenient unless each parishioner brought matches with them; they are never told how they should re-light their candles {1953maryland p24}. When the *Baptismal Renewal* has ended, they are told to extinguish their candles {1953maryland p25}. As mentioned, this "participation by the people" was considered very important by the reformers, but it should be noted that the Traditional Holy Week also had the congregation hold candles (on Holy Thursday).

BLESSING OF THE NEW FIRE • In the 1950 version, three (3) prayers bless the New Fire. The reformers eliminated all but the first. The other prayers may have been "options"—because sometimes ancient compilers simply recorded all the variants they knew {Goddard p278; Giampietro p63}.

EXSULTET MODIFIED • A prayer for the Emperor in the *Exsultet* had fallen into disuse, but the reformers restored it—adjusting the text slightly to correspond to the circumstances of that time. The replacement clause was first published in the ACTA APOSTOLICAE SEDIS on 9 February 1951 (cf. *Dominicae Resurrectionis Vigiliam*, §13).

DISPLACEMENT OF ACTIONS WITH PASCHAL CANDLE • In the traditional version, a *Trident* ("triple candle") is used to carry the New Fire to the Paschal candle. In the 1962 version, the Paschal candle is lit directly from the New Fire and no *Trident* is used. Moreover, during the singing of the *Exsultet* in the traditional version, the Deacon speaks of "a flame divided but undimmed"—at which point the church lamps are lit from the New Fire. In the 1962 version, however, the church lamps were already lit before the *Exsultet* began (at the third "Lumen Christi"). In the traditional version, the Deacon places incense grains into the Paschal candle in the middle of the *Exsultet*. In the 1962, these grains of incense were placed by the Celebrant towards the beginning of the ceremony, with some special prayers (e.g. *Christus heri et hódie*) and the tracing of Greek letters Alpha and Ómega. In the traditional version, the Deacon lights the Paschal candle itself while singing the Exsultet—after the words *rútilans ignis ascéndit*—but in the 1962 version, the Paschal candle was lit at the very beginning of the ceremony.

CANDLE BLESSING TO "OFFICIAL EASTER SONG" • Traditionally, the *Exsultet* had been a blessing of the Paschal candle by the Deacon ("Benedictio Cerei") and the various physical actions eliminated by the reformers had been part of that blessing. "As shown by its form (*Præfatio*), the *Exsultet* was originally more than a mere verbal action (*præconium paschale*, i.e. the announcement of Easter); it was the frame and the means for the *consecration* and offering of the candle" {Dobszay p39}. The reformers had the Celebrant (not the Deacon) bless the Paschal candle, yet hesitated to eliminate the *Exsultet*—on account of its renown and beauty—so they used different nomenclature: *Easter Eve* (1952) called it "Hymn of Praise of the Paschal Candle"; Father Diekmann (1953) calls it "The Easter Song"; the *Saint Andrew Bible Missal* (1966 IMPRIMATUR) calls it "Proclamation of the Easter Message"; the booklet by the *Daughters of Saint Paul* (1964 IMPRIMATUR by Cardinal Cushing of Boston) calls it "the official Easter song"; and so forth.

INCENSE BLESSING MODIFIED • A change was made {Giampietro p226} to the prayer "Véniat Quǽsumus" in an attempt to clarify what Father Thurston suggests might have been a "one thousand year old blunder." On this, see Father Thurston's *Lent and Holy Week* (1904) pages 422-424, Abbat Cabrol's *Holy Week* (1926) page 301, and Father Steuart's *Development of Christian Worship* (1953) page 275. The reformed version unambiguously blesses the candle by means of a change in 1951 (*hunc incénsum céreum* vs. *hoc incénsum*) and a change in 1952 (*regenerátor inténde* vs. *regenerátor accénde*). Before the reforms of Pope Pius XII, this prayer blessed the grains of incense. For centuries, there has been debate over this question. The noun **incensum** has three possible meanings: a lighting, incense, and sacrifice. Moreover, in ancient times, a certain quantity of wax was used to burn the incense. Essentially, the prayers could be referring to: (a) grains of incense; (b) a candle; (c) a sacrifice; or all three at once. The reformers believed it should mean "candle," so in 1951 they added the word *cereum* (see above). Finally, in 1970, they changed the word *incénsi* to *laudis* in the Exsultet, whereas even as late as 1965 it had remained inviolate:

1950 • In hujus ígitur noctis grátia, súscipe sancte Pater, **incénsi** hujus sacrifícium vespertínum: quod tibi in hac Cérei oblatióne solémni, per ministrórum manus de opéribus apum, sacrosáncta reddit Ecclésia.

1970 • In hujus ígitur noctis grátia, súscipe, sancte Pater, **laudis** huius sacrifícium vespertínum, quod tibi in hac cérei oblatióne sollémni, per ministrórum manus de opéribus apum, sacrosáncta reddit Ecclésia.

Notice how the translation of the Latin was changed in 1951, although the Latin remained the same until 1970:

> **1670** (Sir Walter Kirkham Blount) • Receive then O Holy father from us on this happy night the *evening sacrifice of this incense* which thy holy Church by its ministers renders unto thee in the solemne oblation of this waxe candle made of the worke of bees...
>
> **1925** (Father Lefevbre) • Therefore, in the grace of this night, receive, O holy Father, the *evening sacrifice of this incense*, which the holy Church presents to thee in the solemn offering of this wax candle, the work of bees, by the hands of thy ministers.
>
> **1937** (Father Lasance) • In thanksgiving, then, for this night, O holy Father, receive the *evening sacrifice of this incense*, which most holy Church rendereth to Thee by the hands of her ministers, in this solemn oblation of wax, from the labors of the bees.
>
> **1950** (Monsignor Knox) • O then, in thy night of pardon, accept, holy Father, this our evening sacrifice; *incense* thy holy Church offers thee, *and wax* of the bee's making, year by year through her ministers.

1952 (*Easter Eve*) • Therefore, on this sacred night, receive, O holy Father, *the flame of this evening sacrifice*, which holy Church presents to Thee by the hands of Thy ministers in the solemn offering of this Candle of wax, the work of bees.

1953 (Father Diekmann) • Wherefore, in this night of grace, receive, O holy Father, this *evening sacrifice of burning light*; holy Church, by the hands of her servants, offers it to thee in the solemn oblation of this Candle wrought by the labor of bees.

1953 (Maryland) • O then, in thy night of pardon, accept, holy Father, the *evening sacrifice of this lighted candle,* wax of the bee's making holy Church offers thee year by year through her ministers. [Notice how they bowdlerize the work of Monsignor Knox.]

1965 (United States Bishops' Conference) • Therefore, O holy Father, accept on this night the *evening sacrifice of fire* which your holy Church presents to you by the hands of her ministers in the solemn offering of this candle of wax made by bees.

Some publishers—such as Father Perotti's *Easter Vigil* (1954)—held to the traditional translation. Another example would be *Holy Week Masses* (1956 IMPRIMATUR by Cardinal Stritch of Chicago):

1956 (*Holy Week Masses*) • In thanksgiving for this night, then, holy Father, receive the *evening sacrifice of this incense*, which Holy Church, by the hands of her ministers, renders to Thee in the solemn offering of this wax candle wrought by bees.

In addition to changing *incénsi* to *laudis*, the reformers deleted other parts of the *Exsultet* in 1970 (see below). In retrospect, these alterations appear pointless, since the official 1973 ICEL translation—mandated until 2011—skipped over huge swaths of this ancient prayer. The following table gives the 1973 "long form," but one could be forgiven for erroneously thinking it is the "short form" (*Præconii paschalis forma brevior*), since it inexplicably omits massive sections:

THE EXSULTET	1973 ICEL TRANSL.	LITERAL TRANSLATION
In hujus ígitur noctis grátia, súscipe, sancte Pater, **incénsi** hujus sacrifícium vespertínum, quod tibi in hac Cérei oblatióne solémni, per ministrórum manus de opéribus apum, sacrosáncta reddit Ecclésia.	Therefore, heavenly Father, in the joy of this night, receive our evening sacrifice of praise, your Church's solemn offering.	In thanksgiving, then, for this night, O holy Father, receive the evening sacrifice of this incense, which most holy Church rendereth to Thee by the hands of her ministers, in this solemn oblation of wax, from the labors of the bees.
Sed jam colúmnæ hujus præcónia nóvimus, quam in honórem Dei rútilans ignis accéndit. Qui, licet sit divísus in partes, mutuáti tamen lúminis detriménta non novit. Álitur enim liquántibus ceris, quas in sub stántiam pretiósæ hujus lámpadis apis mater edúxit.	Accept this Easter Candle, a flame divided but undimmed, a pillar of fire that glows to the honor of God!	And now we know the glories of this column which the flickering fire doth kindle in God's honor. Which fire, though it be divided into parts, yet knoweth no diminution of its light. For it is nourished by the fluid wax which the mother bee hath produced for the material of this precious torch.
O vere beáta nox, *{these words were deleted in 1970}* **quæ exspoliávit Ægýptios,** **ditávit Hebræos!** **Nox,** in qua terrénis cæléstia, humánis divína jungúntur!	* *Inexplicably, the ICEL "long form" (©1973) ignores and skips over entire sentences.*	O truly blessed night *{these words were deleted in 1970}* **that laid Egypt bare,** **the Hebrews endowing!** **Night** in which heavenly are joined with earthly things, divine with human!
Orámus ergo te, Dómine: ut Céreus...	Let it mingle with the lights...	We therefore pray Thee, O Lord, that this candle...

PASCHAL CANDLE PLACEMENT • The Paschal candle is placed on the Gospel side in the traditional version, but the 1962 version places it in the center of the Sanctuary. In the traditional version, the *Exsultet* begins with the Paschal candle unlit, whereas in the 1962 version, the Paschal candle was lit towards the beginning of the service, before the procession into the church.

INCENSING THE PASCHAL CANDLE • In the 1962 version, immediately before singing the *Exsultet*, the Deacon incenses the Paschal candle, walking around it. This does not occur in the traditional version.

DUPLICATION BY THE CELEBRANT • In the 1951 "experimental" version, the priest is instructed to sit and listen to the prophecies, rather than quietly reciting them at the Altar while they are being chanted. By 1962, the priest will be told to "omit what is proclaimed by the sacred ministers or by a lector" (*omittit ea quae a ministris sacris vel a lectore proferuntur*).

Every vestige of this traditional practice would eventually be swept away, when priests were told in 1970 to listen to everything sung—*Gloria, Credo, Introit, Offertory*, etc.—rather than read these items quietly at the Altar. The Pius XII reform eliminated the traditional "doubling" of the litany (see below), yet introduced a new type of duplication, instructing the singers to repeat the first part of the litany over and over again (cf. *Instaurata Vigilia Paschalis* §23). Furthermore, the 1962 *Baptismal Renewal* introduces a duplicated *Our Father*, in spite of the fact that this same prayer will occur at Mass in a few minutes.

Silent Prayer • At the "flectamus genua" sections, the 1962 version insists that "all, including the Celebrant himself, kneel for a brief period in silent prayer" {McManus p94; 1953maryland p11}. Previously, the Subdeacon had immediately answered "leváte." But the 1962 rubrics specifically say: *omnes, flexis genibus, per aliquod temporis spatium in silentio orant* ("all pray **for a certain length of time** on bended knees").

Subdeacon Demoted • At the "flectamus genua" sections, the Subdeacon was the one who replied "Leváte" {Fortescue p327}. However, starting in 1952, the Deacon is the one who responds "Leváte" {McManus p94}. [Incidentally, *Dominicae Resurrectionis Vigiliam* (1951) still had the Subdeacon respond; cf. Tit. II Cap. IV §16: *dicto a subdiacono "Leváte."* This minor discrepancy is just another example of the "experimental" nature of the 1951 decree.]

Litany Not Doubled • In the traditional version, the Litany of the Saints is sung "under the double rite; that is to say, that from the commencement to the end, the clergy repeat the same invocations as the Cantors" {Dale p227}. The reformed version eliminated the doubling: "This litany is not doubled" {Löw p15} and again: "The invocations are not doubled" {McManus p95}. The doubling seems to have been first eliminated in 1952— "quin tamen duplicentur" (Tit. II Cap. V §18)—not in 1951. Some of the ancient liturgical books instruct the singers to repeat the invocations three, five, or even seven times—e.g. folios 70r + 73v of **9438limoges|1138**, created circa 1138AD—apparently for practical reasons {Thurston p434; Dobszay p38}. As has been noted, *Instaurata Vigilia Paschalis* §23 introduced a new type of "doubling" by instructing the singers to repeat the first part of the litany over and over again to fill up space.

Litany Cut in Half • In the traditional version, the Litany of the Saints is sung straight through, but the 1962 version divides it into two sections: cf. *Dominicae Resurrectionis Vigiliam* (1951) Tit. II Cap. VIII §27. Father Stefano Carusi, of the Institute of the Good Shepherd, wrote that splitting the Litany demonstrates "no liturgical sense whatsoever" and says "this innovation is incoherent and incomprehensible" {*La Riforma Della Settimana Santa*, 28 March 2010}. Moreover, Father Carusi makes the following assertion: "Never was it known that an impetratory prayer was split into two parts. The introduction of the baptismal rites in the middle is of an even greater incoherence."

Father Carusi is incorrect; this is no innovation. It corresponds to mediæval practice, at least in certain localities. For instance, a Benedictional (MS 22049) created circa 1429AD — four centuries before Annibale Bugnini was born—splits the Litany of the Saints exactly as the 1962 version does. The Missale Parisiense (1481AD) also splits the Litany; as does the Limoges Missal (c. 1138AD). Sometimes multiple litanies were sung {Monti p 485}; indeed, the Gelasian Sacramentary—created circa 725AD—stipulates three litanies {Goddard 242}. Ferdinando Cardinal Antonelli served on the *Commissio Piana* and was later named Secretary of the Conciliar Commission on the Liturgy. His personal notes {Giampietro p39} have the following vis-à-vis splitting the litany:

> "Originally, the litanies served the supplemental function of occupying the laity in the absence of the clergy and those being baptized [*since they went to the Baptistery*], and they were sometimes repeated as many as seven times. When the Baptism of adults ceased, the litanies remained as a transitional element between the blessing of the font and the Mass. Since the Kyrie flowed into the Mass it could not be omitted. In the Middle Ages, however, as Durandus (d. 1296) mentions in the *Pontificale*, the practice had developed of splitting the litany, having one part before the blessing of the font, and the other part after. This usage was revived."

ADDITION OF NEW PRAYERS • Pope Pius XII added the "Renewal of Baptismal Promises" to the Easter Vigil. This formula was something "completely new" {Giampietro p227}—and was bragged about as a "startling innovation" {1953maryland page iii}—which contradicts Archbishop Bugnini, who, on page 314 of his *Reform of the Liturgy* (1990), declared that the 1951 reform "restored the Easter Vigil to its original splendor." Some authors believe the reformers based these prayers on folio 67 of the GELASIAN SACRAMENTARY, a book which seemed to be favored heavily by the reformers. The prayers were revealed in the ACTA APOSTOLICAE SEDIS on 9 February 1951.

THE VERNACULAR • Significantly, the *Renewal of Baptismal Promises* was allowed to be done in the vernacular. It is true that the use of the vernacular for Sacraments was not unheard of before that time; in the United States, it had been employed at weddings and baptisms. Indeed, as early as 1787, Most Rev'd John Carroll, Archbishop of Baltimore, had written a communiqué asking for a wider use of the vernacular during the Holy Mass, claiming that "in this country either for want of books or inability to read, the great part of our congregations must be utterly ignorant of the meaning and sense of the publick offices of the Church." Nevertheless, this introduction of vernacular in 1951 was still a radical departure, especially in that it demanded a vocal dialogue between priest & congregation in the middle of a church ceremony. [cf. Giampietro page 227]

OMISSION OF THE COMMUNION PRAYER • In the traditional version, "the Celebrant says the three usual prayers before his Communion" {Fortescue p333}. However, in the 1955 version, the prayer *Dómine Jesu Christi, qui dixísti* is omitted, but the other prayers are said: *Dómine Jesu Christe, Fili Dei vivi* and *Percéptio Córporis tui* {McManus p101}. It should be noticed that the 1951 "experimental" version did not omit that prayer {1953maryland p40}.

PRAYERS AT THE FOOT + LAST GOSPEL • The 1962 version eliminates *Júdica Me* and the *Confíteor* at the beginning {McManus p100} whereas the traditional version contains the normal Prayers at the Foot {Fortescue p333} including the verses *Glória Patri* and *Sicut Erat* during Psalm 42. In the 1962 version, the Last Gospel is suppressed {1953maryland p44} whereas the traditional version ends as usual. The total elimination of these two items—from every Mass—would be accomplished in 1964; cf. the first and twelfth goals of the 1951 *Maria Laach Conference*, treated in Scott Alcuin Reid's *The Nature of the Liturgical Movement* (King's College, London: 2002) pages 173-176.

BEFORE POSTCOMMUNION • In the traditional version—before the Postcommunion—a very brief Vespers ceremony with *Magnificat* is sung, and the "Spíritum nobis, Dómine" serves as the Postcommunion. In the 1962 version, there is a very brief Lauds ceremony with the *Canticle of Zachary*, and the "Spíritum nobis, Dómine" likewise serves as the Postcommunion.

ELIMINATION OF PROPHECIES • The traditional Holy Saturday had twelve prophecies. In ancient times, it had been four (4) prophecies, but "around the year 1000" the system of twelve (12) such readings "became the standard for almost a thousand years" {Goddard p230}. The 1962 version eliminated eight, leaving four. The readings retained by the 1962 version are in bold typefont:

(1) Genesis 1:1-31; 2:1-2
(2) Genesis 5:32—8:21
(3) Genesis 22:1-19
(4) Exodus 14:24-31; 15:1a
. . . *followed by a canticle: "Cantémus Dómino"*
(5) Isaias 54:17; 55:1-11
(6) Baruch 3:9-38
(7) Ezechiel 37:1-14
(8) Isa 4:1-6 * — * *Notice: the 1962 version deleted the first verse.*
. . . *followed by a canticle: "Vínea Facta Est"*
(9) Exodus 12:1-11 * — * *Identical to the second reading on Good Friday.*
(10) Jonas 3:1-10
(11) Deuteronomy 31:22-30
. . . *followed by a canticle: "Atténde Caelum"*
(12) Daniel 3:1-24

More on the Prophecies • In the 13th century, Durandus says the number of lessons in the Holy Saturday services varied in different places (cf. *Rationale*, VI, 81). There were instances of as few as four—or as many as fourteen—of these prophecies. Another tradition was **twenty-four**: twelve in Latin, twelve in Greek. The *Gelasian Sacramentary* mentions ten prophecies. [See also Monsignor Lallou's *Prophecies on Holy Saturday* (1944) page 305.] Cardinal Antonelli—one of the six clerics who served on the *Commissio Piana* which modified Holy Saturday—wrote: "For many centuries the Roman liturgy in particular used a much smaller number of prophecies, for example, at the time of Saint Gregory the Great there were only four" {Giampietro p43}. In some of the derived monastic rites, as in those of the Carthusians and Dominicans, there are only four prophecies. The first three prophecies in the 1962 version match the traditional Dominican books; cf. *Triduo Ante Pascha et Dominica Resurrectionis* (1927) page 268. Some mediæval books—which only have four prophecies—end with Isaias 54-55 (the fifth prophecy in the 1950 version) rather than Deuteronomy 31, and that is also the traditional Dominican practice. Owing to the great variety that existed over the centuries, it is difficult to understand why some assert that the reduction of prophecies from twelve to four caused "irreparable damage" to the Roman Rite. One can recognize this reality without venturing an opinion for or against; what is crucial is to ***understand*** what actually occurred. A well-known Catholic columnist, failing to realize that Pius XII eliminated eight prohecies and the Last Gospel, recently wrote as follows:

> "I believe that the restoration of the Easter Vigil and the renewal of the Paschal Triduum by Pius XII were impressive developments of the Roman Rite, as I think the richer menu of biblical readings available at Mass today was another important achievement of the mid-20th century liturgical movement."

Why does this author say the ***elimination*** of biblical readings is "impressive" then immediately declare the ***addition*** of a "richer menu of biblical readings" to be an achievement? Such bewildering statements will continue until the realities of the reform are made known.

For Catholics who attend the 1950 Easter Vigil, it will be helpful to recall the words of Father John Parsons (November 2001) regarding the twelve prophecies:

> "They are not twelve readings in a row, but rather three nocturns of four readings each. Each nocturn has a theme summed up in the sung responsory that marked its end. The first four—*the Creation, the Flood, the Sacrifice of Isaac, and the Crossing of the Red Sea*—are about God's creation of a Chosen People; the second four are about the increasing inadequacy of that people's response to God's Call; while the last nocturn is about God's solution of this conundrum through the sending of the Messiah, who is foreshadowed in three readings as respectively Priest, Prophet, and King."

The catechumens are given their final instruction on the church porch while these prophecies are being chanted, and Father Thurston reminds us: "That these prophecies had no essential connection with the instruction of the catechumens—but were simply intended to open the minds and hearts of the whole assembly to the new creation typified in the Easter mystery—may fairly be inferred from the fact that this portion of the service is still retained even in churches which have no baptismal font." Yet Father Thurston seems to draw here an unnecessary conflict; there is no reason these twelve prophecies could not have been based upon readings which—in the judgment of the early Church—were considered very appropriate and helpful when instructing converts. László Dobszay summarized them as follows {Dobszay p41}:

> "The Old Testament readings with their 'prefigurative' meaning are meant to help the catechumens and all the faithful who will receive the renewed grace of Baptism."

A Comma Issue • In the late 1940s, some liturgists objected to the comma placement in: *Dómine sancte, Pater omnípotens, ætérne Deus* ("Holy Lord, almighty Father, eternal God"). They felt it should be: *Dómine, sancte Pater, omnípotens ætérne Deus* ("O Lord, holy Father, almighty and eternal God"). Starting in 1951, the reformers began changing the phrase; and in the 1962 and 1965 editions of the *Missale Romanum* the new comma placement was used. However, in 1973 the ICEL translations eliminated the word *sancte* ("holy")—so the effort was worthless:

Vere dignum et justum est, æquum et salutáre,	Father, all-powerful and ever-living God,
nos tibi semper et ubíque grátias ágere:	we do well always and everywhere
Dómine, sancte Pater, omnípotens ætérne Deus:	to give you thanks
per Christum Dóminum nostrum.	through Jesus Christ our Lord.

QUESTION • How did the Easter Vigil end up being moved from the ***evening before*** Easter to the ***morning of*** Holy Saturday—and then (starting in 1951) back to the evening?

SETTING THE STAGE • It is difficult for Catholics today to accept that the Easter Vigil was celebrated in the early morning of Holy Saturday. Nevertheless, it was—often as early as 6:30AM. That being said, our current situation of "anticipated" Masses—which fulfill the Sunday obligation yet take place on Saturday afternoon—would have been **unthinkable** to our grandparents. It is not within the scope of these notes to examine this complicated subject exhaustively; nevertheless, it is crucial to bear in mind that radical liturgical changes were made during the 1950s: (1) vis-à-vis fasting regulations; and (2) regarding permission for Masses to be said in the afternoon or evening. With regard to "vigil Masses" and "anticipated Masses," an excellent source is *Evening Masses and Days of Obligation*, a 2016 dissertation by Father Shawn Tunink. An excellent starting place with respect to changes in the Eucharistic fast would be: *Christus Dominus: Concerning The Discipline To Be Observed With Respect To The Eucharistic Fast* (6 January 1953).

THE ORIGINAL VIGIL • We have scant information about how the liturgy was conducted in the early church. While we do possess sermons of Saint Augustine given during the Easter Vigil circa 410AD, when it comes to *precise and detailed information* regarding how the ceremonies took place we have very little. All scholars agree the Easter Vigil originally lasted all night. For instance, Abbat Cabrol: "The office now celebrated in the morning is in reality the one which formerly began on Saturday evening, was prolonged all through the night and ended at daybreak with Mass at the very hour at which the Resurrection took place." James Monti provides clues that support—at least vaguely—Abbat Cabrol's statement, going back all the way to the year 150AD {Monti 458ff}. Father Thurston said that "in primitive times it would seem that the service was later still, and lasted almost until dawn on Easter Sunday." The reformers believed the "authentic" vigil service would ***begin*** at midnight {Giampietro p42}. Pope Pius XII declared on 9 February 1951:

> "The celebration of this Vigil took place during the night which precedes the Lord's Resurrection. In the course of time because of various reasons, this celebration was advanced, at first to the evening, then to the afternoon, and finally to the morning of Holy Saturday, and at the same time diverse changes were introduced, not without injury to the original symbolism."

Abbat Guéranger put it this way: "In the West, dating from the 11th century, the Mass of the Resurrection Hour has been gradually anticipated, until it has been brought even to the morning of Holy Saturday. Durandus of Menda—who wrote his *Rationale of the Divine Offices* towards the close of the 13th century—tells us that in his time there were very few Churches which observed the primitive custom" {Guéranger p551}.

PUSHED BACK IN TIME • We observe the same tendency with certain sections of the Divine Office, which tended to be gradually pushed back in time; e.g. clerics may "anticipate" *Matins* (the morning prayers) the day before it happens—as early as 2:00pm. Father Fortescue put it this way:

> "The first thing to understand about the service of Holy Saturday morning is that it was all composed to be held during the night between Saturday and Sunday. This is the most conspicuous case of the way services so often are pushed back in time. Gradual development first drove it back to the evening before, then to the afternoon, and now finally we keep it on Saturday morning. […] In the West, it must soon have seemed strange to sing Mass in the afternoon; so, once the original hour was changed, the time would soon become the morning rather than the evening of Saturday."

VARIOUS CAUSES • This gradual "pushing back" seems to result from human nature: the desire of people to get their religious obligations out of the way. In our age, we observe many elderly people attending Mass on Saturday afternoon—rather than Sunday morning—to get their obligation "over with." Monsignor Lallou presumably agreed with this general impression when he wrote: "Reasons of convenience dictated the anticipation of these ceremonies, until they have reached their present time of performance resulting in the incongrous celebration of the Easter Mass a good twenty hours before, in strict chronology, it is due" {Lallou p299}.

Father Henri Leclercq (d. 1945), a monk of Solesmes Abbey, suggested a different reason: "This meeting of people in the darkness of the night often occasioned abuses which the clergy felt powerless to prevent by active supervision unless by so anticipating the ceremonies that all of them could take place in daylight." As alluded to earlier, Lenten fasting laws also contributed to this gradual "pushing back" {Monti p467}. Father Thurston points to something which suggests not all liturgists were pleased by these developments: "Even as late as the 9th or 10th century it is expressly stipulated by liturgical writers that the *Gloria in excelsis* should not be sung until the stars had begun to appear..." {Thurston p405}.

James Monti cites examples where the Easter Vigil did take place in the evening, but says there was also "the belief, traceable to the sixth century, that Mass—as the re-presentation of the sacrifice of Calvary—should take place in the daytime insofar as the crucifixion took place in the daytime" {Monti p467}.

A PRICELESS WITNESS • An effort to restore the Easter Vigil to the evening was undertaken by Saint John Gualbert (d. 1073AD), founder of the Vallombrosan Order—a Benedictine congregation of Italy—as related by his biographer Blessed Andrew of Strumi (d. 1097AD):

> "Who in Tuscany other than he moved from the day to the night the annual and renowned office to be done on the night of the holy Resurrection? For with stealthy negligence and gathering gluttony this office was performed at *None* [Editor's Note: the ninth hour, **3:00PM**] on Saturday, that is now rightly and worthily done in the holy night, this our father John beginning and establishing in our times."

Thus the Easter Vigil rubrics of the 12th-century *Customary of Vallombrosa* direct that the blessing of the Easter Fire—with which the vigil commences—is to start only when "the dusk of night shall have begun to appear" {Monti p467}. Cardinal Antonelli admits not understanding why the Easter Vigil was moved to the morning, but agrees that Saint John Gualbert's witness is priceless {Giampietro p39}, writing on 14 March 1951:

> "Neither is it known what grave reason suggested moving this rite to earlier in the day. It is enough, however, to make reference to the contemporary biography of San Giovanni Gualberto (d. 1073AD), who restored the nocturnal celebration in Tuscany, because after 3:00PM people were given to revelry."

During the 9th, 10th, and 11th centuries, the general preference was to start to start the vigil around 3:00PM, but many localities in those days also celebrated the vigil early on Holy Saturday morning, meaning the Resurrection "was celebrated by way of anticipation even before the official end of Lent, at midday" {Goddard p246}.

AFTER NONE • A traditional time to begin the Easter Vigil was "after *None* has been prayed"—that is to say, the ninth hour, normally about **3:00PM** in the afternoon—yet we must remember the Divine Office has been prayed at various times of day throughout history. In 1939, for example, Westminster Cathedral (Roman Catholic) sang *None* at **8:45AM.** It seems that in the era of Dom Guéranger this afternoon celebration of the Easter Vigil was observed in certain localities {Guéranger p553}, although such a celebration would be in conflict with the 1917 *Code of Canon Law*—issued 42 years after Guéranger's death—which says: "The beginning of the celebration of Mass shall not occur earlier than one hour before first light or later than **1:00PM**" (although an exception was always made for Christmas Midnight Mass). It is worth repeating that a reason often cited for the morning celebration of the Easter Vigil Mass was the precept that anyone receiving Holy Communion must be fasting from food ***and all liquids*** since midnight, and the Easter Vigil is very demanding on priests both mentally and physically—but the Celebrant must receive Communion.

POPE SAINT PIUS V • On 29 March 1566—in a decree called "Revocation of the Privilege Conceded to Anyone of Celebrating Masses in the Evening Time"—Pope Saint Pius V withdrew permission for celebrating Mass in the evening, "thereby making the celebration on Holy Saturday morning obligatory and universal" {Monti p468}. Hand-missals often referred to the ceremonies preceding Mass as "Office Before Mass On Holy Saturday Morning." *The Roman Missal for the Use of the Laity* (London, 1806) mentions that—in the earliest centuries—the Easter Eve Mass took place about midnight, adding: "in order to perpetuate the remembrance of the fervent piety of her first children, the Church still retains the word *night* in the Office of *this day*."

Conclusions & Further Questions

Conclusions on Timing • From the evidence presented, it should be clear that throughout history, the Easter Vigil was celebrated ***at different times***, in various localities, for different reasons. It is folly to pretend someone can discover the "correct" time at which the Easter Vigil should take place. Indeed, the primary error—which must be overcome—is an erroneous belief that the "correct" time for the Easter Vigil can be discovered. Catholics must reject absurd statements such as the following, made in *Holy Week Masses* (1956 Imprimatur by Cardinal Stritch):

> "During the Middle Ages, these religious services were, for various reasons, transferred to the morning hours. *Torn from their proper time-setting, they lost their original meaning."*

Consider this excellent summary by Goddard {p246}:

> "It was already the practice at the time of the *Old Gelasian Sacramentary* (7th to 8th century) for the Vigil to begin in the early afternoon. [...] In *Ordo Romanus 16*, from the 8th century, it is given as the ninth hour, or around **3:00pm**, and this is still the time mentioned in *Ordo Romanus 28*, of about 800AD. But in *Ordo Romanus 30B*, around a century later, it has become the eighth hour (**2:00pm**), and in the Romano-German Pontifical of about 950AD it is the seventh (**1:00pm**). In the Pontifical of the Roman Curia the time has crept back to the sixth hour (**Noon**), and this is also the time of Durandus. [...] The Ponticial of the 12th century prescribed either the fifth (**11:00am**) or the sixth hour (**Noon**)."

The manuscript Yrieix|1040 —from approximately 1040AD—says vis-à-vis the beginning of the Easter Vigil: *Et hora quasi sexta...* ("And about the sixth hour..."); that is to say, **Noon**.

Contradictions • Many authors have stuggled to come to terms with what Abbat Guéranger calls the "apparent contradiction" of the Easter Vigil {Guéranger p551}. For instance, Guéranger says: "The great object of the whole of today's Service, and the center to which every one of the ceremonies converges, is the Baptism of the Catechumens. The Faithful must keep this incessantly before them, or they will be at a loss how to understand or profit by the Liturgy of today." Cardinal Antonelli agrees: "The principle element of the Vigil consisted of the rites of Baptism" {Giampietro p37}. Others strongly disagree, such as Abbat Bernard Capelle (d. 1961) who said the Easter Vigil "was not primarily a commemoration of baptism" {Reid p162}. Other authors consider the Mass of the Resurrection as "the great object" of the Service. László Dobszay pointed out that the Easter Vigil "is not an exceptional form of the Mass but an autonomous rite built up according to its own logic, different from any other celebration" {Dobszay p41}.

First Mass of Easter? • The old liturgical books explicitly call the Mass on Holy Saturday "the first Mass of Easter" {Fortescue p332}. Father Steuart, a strong supporter of the reformers, says the Mass of Easter Eve "really is the first Mass of Easter Day" {Steuart p273}. Catholics, therefore, must have been confused by a decree from the *Sacred Congregation of Rites* (11 January 1952) which said Catholics fulfill their Sunday obligation if the Easter Vigil Mass starts around Midnight whereas Catholics ***do not fulfill their Sunday obligation*** if the Easter Vigil began at a slightly earlier time such as 8:00pm {1953maryland p45}.

Some modern liturgists say in no uncertain terms that the Easter Vigil Mass "is not the First Mass of Easter." Speaking about the Easter Vigil Mass (as celebrated prior to the reforms of Pius XII), they have put forward the idea that it "awaits but does not celebrate" Easter, and say "Paschal Matins and Lauds"—which constitute the "true night service of Easter"—constitute "the beginning of the celebration of the Resurrection." Perhaps the biggest obstacle such liturgists must overcome—if they desire to obtain acceptance for this "await but not celebrate" thesis—are the special words of the Canon said during Mass of Easter Eve (*noctem sacratíssimum celebrántes*):

> "observing ***that holy night,*** on which our Lord Jesus Christ,
> in his human flesh, rose again from the dead..."

Foretaste of Easter • Traditionally, liturgical authors have placed the Easter Vigil in a category all its own. While they admit that much of the ceremony is penitential, they explain "contradictory" items such as the white vestments for the *Exsultet*, the Alleluia at the Mass, or the *Gloria* with bells ringing at the Mass—to say nothing of mediæval ceremonies such as the *Accendite*—by saying that the Church "has thought proper to give her children a foretaste of the joys of Easter" {Guéranger p551}. The reality is that the Easter Vigil is complex and mysterious: it is neither "happy" nor "sad." As Dobszay reminds us:

> "The reformers ought to have admitted that certain celebrations and feasts may have their own logic of content and form and, as a result, their own emotional, psychological and dramatic implications, and that these *exceptions* are useful not only in respect to the representation of liturgical ideas but are of pastoral benefit as well. Unification, the emergence of stereotypical forms is not the highest asset to the liturgy."

The modern "await but not celebrate" theory appears to be a "solution in search of a problem."

AN EXAMPLE • Perhaps an example will demonstrate the open mind one must cultivate when approaching complex liturgical celebrations. In the 1499 Missal of Jaén, "the rubrics direct that after the blessing of the baptismal font concludes, the celebrating priest and those ministering to him withdraw into the sacristy to remove their 'Lenten Vestments' and take in their place white vestments" {Monti p489}. Honorius of Autun sees these white vestments "as a symbol of the catechumens' reception of their baptismal robes." However, the Celebrant in the 1950 version does not put on white vestments immediately after blessing the font. Rather, he dons a purple stole and lies prostrate during the Litany. This tiny example is meant to remind us of something which should be borne in mind: there was not an "invariable and correct way" in which Holy Saturday was celebrated. Different localities had their own customs and traditions. Certain actions—such as when the Paschal candle should be lit—have been argued over for hundreds of years, and without a doubt scholars will continue to argue these questions.[1]

NOT IDENTICAL TO EASTER SUNDAY • Some modern authors, eager to denigrate the reforms of Pius XII, have asserted that "the pre-1955 Easter Vigil is the crown jewel of the Tridentine rite." But the crown jewel for Catholics can only be the Mass—wherein the Second Person of the Blessed Trinity becomes present on our Altars and is offered to the Heavenly Father—yet the Mass of Easter Eve has less music than any other Mass! *Even a ferial Mass has more music than the Easter Vigil Mass*. At the traditional Mass of Easter Eve :

(1) There is no VIDI AQUAM ;

(2) There is no INTROIT ;

(3) The (short) ALLELUIA is followed by a TRACT (!) ;

(4) There is no GRADUAL or GREATER ALLELUIA ;

(5) There is no SEQUENCE ;

(6) There is no CREED ;

(7) There is no OFFERTORY ANTIPHON ;

(8) There is no AGNUS DEI and the *Kiss of Peace* is omitted ;

(9) There is no COMMUNION ANTIPHON.

We must emphasize[2] that none of these omissions were the result of changes made by Pius XII. As mentioned above, the Easter Vigil is unique, and such omissions are examples of its "many curious special features" (as Father Fortescue describes it). The reasons behind these omissions are not known with certainty.[3]

---

1 "Much, for instance, might have been said about the practice of lighting the candle at the words *rutilans ignis accendit*—a rubric which has originated simply in a misunderstanding of the words. All the most venerable service-books represent the candle as lighted at the very beginning, and the illuminations in many of the Exsultet-rolls quite confirm this idea" {Thurston p438}.

2 On page 163 of *The Nature of the Liturgical Movement* (King's College, London: 2002), Scott Alcuin Reid says that Pope Pius XII eliminated the AGNUS DEI and CREDO from the Mass of Easter Eve in the 1951 reform. He is incorrect; they were never part of the Mass of Easter Eve.

3 For speculation on why these items were omitted, see Father Fortescue, page 36 (*The Holy Week Book*, 1913) and Father Thurston, page 437 (*Lent and Holy Week*, 1904). Some of the "curious special features" are of surprising antiquity. For instance, servers without candles at the Gospel goes back more than 1,200 years {Monti p493}. The truncated Vespers goes back to at least the 10th century {Monti p494}.

Advantages of an Earlier Time

Advantages of Tradition • Those who seek to modify Church praxis without understanding how such praxis came about risk falling into what Pope Pius XII called "exaggerated and senseless antiquarianism" (cf. *Mediator Dei*, §64). Cardinal Antonelli—named "Secretary of the Conciliar Commission on the Liturgy" on 4 October 1962—had this to say about his fellow reformers:

> "The Consilium is merely an assembly of people, many of them incompetent, and others well advanced on the road to novelty. The discussions are extremely hurried. Discussions are based on impressions and the voting is chaotic. [...] Many of those who have influenced the reform [...] have no love, and no veneration of that which has been handed down to us. They begin by despising everything that is actually there."

With the benefit of hindsight, let us consider the benefits and disadvantages of moving the Easter Vigil from Saturday morning to Saturday evening, as was done during the 1950s.

Easter Sunday Mass • The main celebration at parishes should be on Easter Sunday, supported by its joyful and magnificent music: the beautiful Sequence (*Victimae Paschali Laudes*), the ancient "Pascha Nostra" Alleluia, the Creed, the Introit, the Offertory antiphon, the Agnus Dei, the Communion antiphon, and so on. The experience of seventy years has shown that when the Easter Vigil is celebrated with maximum solemnity (lasting until approximately 2:30am on Easter Sunday morning), the Easter Sunday Masses suffer. Contrariwise, when the Easter Vigil was celebrated on Holy Saturday—during the morning, afternoon, or even early evening—there was ample time for the ceremonies on both days to be well prepared, as well as an opportunity for rest, something appropriate and important for priests of an advanced age.

School on Saturday? • A constant assertion made by the reformers to justify moving the Easter Vigil to the middle of the night is that Catholics—we are told—are just too busy to attend Mass on Holy Saturday morning. Indeed, *Maxima Redemptionis* (1955) claims attendance was low because "the services had long been moved back to the morning hours when schools, factories, and public business of every kind are usually open and functioning." But are schools really open on Saturday mornings? Was it really true that Catholics could never—not even once a year—give up a few hours on a Saturday morning?

Missing the Point • Writing in 1953, Father Josef Löw tried to defend moving the Easter Vigil to the middle of the night as follows {Löw p5} :

> "The new order need not prove an additional burden to the priest; his burden will simply be transferred to another time of day; the whole morning will be free."

But Father Löw completely misses the point. It isn't a question of leaving Holy Saturday morning "free"—the difficulty is ending what Abbat Guéranger calls "the longest and most trying Service of the Latin Liturgy" around 2:30am. By the time the church is fully closed (with items put in their place) the priest might get to bed by 4:00am. The Easter Sunday Masses—the high point of the liturgical year—will begin in just a few hours! Unless the priest stays up all night, will there be even a moment to prepare mentally, emotionally, and prayerfully? And what about the preparations required for the solemn Masses of Easter to be carried out properly?

Danger of Fainting • In those days, a priest who offered the midnight Vigil Mass was not allowed to eat before offering the Easter Sunday Mass—although a concession was made that he "may take liquid nourishment up to one hour before the next Mass." Would it not have been better to make sure priests—especially those of an advanced age—are alert for the Easter Sunday Masses, since offering Mass properly requires great concentration? (Here we are speaking of internal concentration on prayer, not whether he can physically go through the motions.) Father Löw tried to defend placing a burden on Catholics by the night ceremony as follows:

> "Our times, unfortunately, have become strangely unwilling to make sacrifices; but perhaps chiefly when there is question of the Church, or of the Lord. Let a major event be advertised, a boxing match between two well-known fighters, let us say, and it is remarkable how we are willing without batting an eye to sacrifice time, money, comfort and a lot of other things. [...] But if we are asked, once a year, to make a sacrifice for the Lord God, for the benefit and well-being of our own soul, is that too much?"

Father Löw desires the Faithful to "make sacrifices," and no one will argue that Christians should make sacrifices for the Lord. Yet, the reformers eliminated much of the traditional Easter Vigil—such as reducing twelve prophecies to four—***precisely to avoid*** asking the Faithful to make sacrifices. Father Löw's argument is blatantly contradictory.

UNREALISTIC EXPECTATIONS • The reformers—apparently having no insight into the lives of families with small children—insisted that, when it comes to those attending the midnight Easter Vigil "the majority will return for another Mass on Easter Day itself" {Löw p16}. Indeed, when Msgr. Montini (who would later become Pope Paul VI) requested on 17 January 1956 "that participation at the celebration of Mass at the Solemn Easter Vigil—even if it be held before midnight—should also satisfy the obligation to attend Mass on Easter Sunday," the *Commissio Piana* rejected his proposal unanimously {Giampietro p290}. It must be remembered that (in those days) if the Faithful received Holy Communion at the midnight Easter Vigil Mass, "they may not receive again" at any Easter Sunday Mass {Löw p15}. Indeed, it is possible the reformers knew the midnight Easter Vigil Mass was untraditional (as explained above, a more traditional time would have been early evening on Holy Saturday) but used the Midnight Mass scenario as a type of "back door," since Christmas Midnight Mass was such a familiar reality.

HOPELESSLY THWARTED? • The reformers, in their eagerness to promote the reformed version, sometimes made cockamamie statements. For example, Monsignor McManus wrote in 1956: "If the faithful should come only to the Vigil Mass, the papal restoration of the sacred Easter Eve would be ***hopelessly thwarted***." McManus also made the following absurd statement: "All the rites of the Vigil, including the blessing of baptismal water, need take no longer than an hour and a half." (The *Commissio Piana* estimated 3 hours.) Those years seem the heyday of the fantasist. Archbishop Bugnini claimed that the restoration of the Easter Vigil in 1951 "elicited an explosion of joy throughout the Church." But did allowing the Faithful to hold candles * and getting rid of eight out of twelve readings from Sacred Scripture really elicit an explosion of joy?

On the other hand, those who defend the traditional rites often overcompensate. An example would be a 28 March 2010 article by Father Stefano Carusi—widely circulated in spite of egregious errors. For instance, Father Carusi wrote as follows regarding the elimination of the *Trident*:

> "When this reform came into effect all the Paschal candlesticks in Christendom were rendered useless for Holy Saturday itself, even though some dated back to the dawn of Christianity. Under the pretext of returning to the sources, such liturgical masterpieces from antiquity became unusable museum pieces."

Father Carusi's (flawed) argument is as follows: Because the 1951 version requires the Paschal candle to be carried by the Deacon, some ancient candles—which are gargantuan in size—cannot be used. In his desperation to attack the reform of Pius XII, Father Carusi fails to realize that the 1950 rubrics say the Paschal candle is carried to the font by an Altar server {Fortescue p327}. Therefore, Father Carusi's quarrel is with the traditional Holy Week, not the 1951 revision. In fact, where the Paschal candle was massive in size, solutions were available. For instance, a "Sarum rubric directs that not the Paschal candle itself, ***but some other in its place***, should be taken to the font" {Thurston p438}. Throughout Europe, Paschal candles were sometimes 27 feet high, and certain customs—such as inscribing the date onto the Paschal candle—go back at least to the sixth century.

COLLATERAL DAMAGE • A very ancient and powerful tradition called TENEBRAE was virtually destroyed when the Holy Week ceremonies were moved to the evening. Other devotions—such as the "Seven Last Words"—were also harmed. Catholics are not slaves to a false literalism. For instance, Catholics know Mass can be "authentic" without taking place in the evening (even though the Last Supper took place in the evening). Going down that path would lead us to celebrate Mass lying down, because in the time of Jesus people ate reclining. When Our Lord offered Mass for the first time at the Last Supper, He did so in *anticipation* of the Sacrifice of Calvary, which would occur the following day. Catholics realize God is outside of time.

---

* The reformers touted their improvements to the Easter Vigil, such as allowing the congregation to hold candles in their hands (as the traditional Holy Week already did on Maundy Thursday)—thus allowing people to "participate." Yet these same reformers eliminated other "opportunities to participate," such as the congregation holding branches in their hands during the singing of the Passion on Palm Sunday.

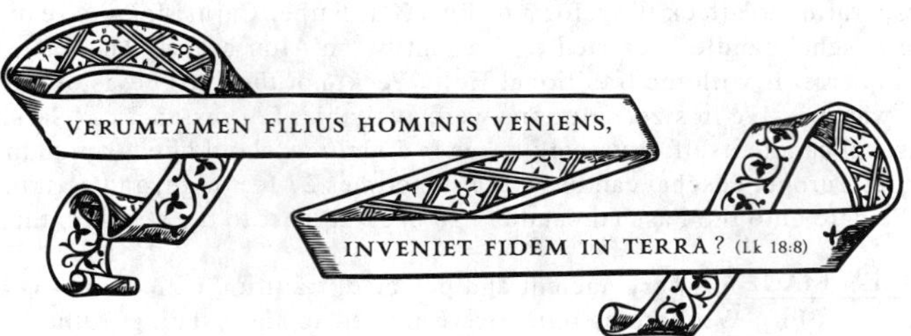
VERUMTAMEN FILIUS HOMINIS VENIENS,
INVENIET FIDEM IN TERRA? (Lk 18:8)

BLESSING OF THE FONT • 1950 vs. 1962

Saint Edmund Campion Missal, Third Edition

There is, of course, the traditional version of the *Blessing of the Font*, as found in the 1950 liturgical books; but the revisions that took place under Pope Pius XII offer two more versions. To clear up all confusion, we offer the following explanations (see below).

The reformers had initially intended to eliminate the *Blessing of the Font*: "It was proposed to introduce a new element **which would take the place of both the rite of Baptism and of the blessing of the font.** This would take the form of a solemn renewal of baptismal promises by all the faithful who were present" {Giampietro p43}.

HOLY SATURDAY 1950
BAPTISMAL RITES COMPARED

1950 • Towards the end of the twelfth prophecy, the acolytes light their candles. An altar server removes the Paschal candle from its candlestick. The Celebrant and ministers go to the Sedilia and remove their maniples. The Celebrant exchanges his chasuble for a purple Cope, but the ministers retain their purple folded chasubles. The procession goes to the baptistery. The server who carries the Paschal candle is in front. On the way to the font the tract "Sicut Cervus" is sung.

1950 • On the way to the Baptistery, "Sicut Cervus" is sung.

Towards the end of the blessing of the font, another priest in a purple stole—or the Celebrant himself—goes around the church sprinkling the congregation with the baptismal water {Fortescue p330}.

[Suggestion: No music is prescribed for that sprinkling, and the pipe organ cannot be played; nevertheless, a short anthem—sung by the choir during that sprinkling—would seem preferable to silence.]

[Editor's Note: If there are children to be baptized, the first part of the Baptism rite may be carried out before the font is blessed. "In this case, another priest or deacon may do so during the prophecies, wearing a surplice and purple stole" {Fortescue p327}. At the Baptistery, he begins the baptism rite up to the end of the anointing with oil of Catechumens, to the moment where he would change the stole from purple to white. Alternately, the Celebrant himself may do this—that is, the first part of the Baptism rite—before he proceeds to bless the font, after the prayer at the entrance of the Baptistery.]

1950 • After blessing of font, the Sacrament of Baptism is administered (and sometimes the Sacrament of Confirmation). The candidates for Baptism meet the Celebrant at the font. Such Baptisms are done "with the usual ceremonies" {Dale p227}. The candle given after baptism is lit at the Paschal candle. As the procession returns to the Altar, the litany of the saints is begun by two cantors in surplices, walking immediately behind the Cross.

1950 • "The litany should begin while the procession returns to the Altar" {Fortescue p331}.

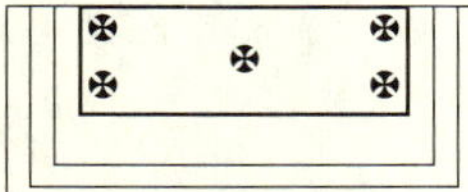

HOLY SATURDAY "Version A" 1962
BAPTISMAL RITES COMPARED

1962 A • After the prophecies, "two chanters, kneeling in the middle of the Sanctuary, chant the Litanies of the Saints as far as the invocation *Propitius esto*. All kneel and make the responses. The invocations are not doubled" {McManus p95}. This is called "the beginning of the Litany."

1962 A • After the beginning of the Litany, the rite of blessing the baptismal water takes place, "if the church has a baptismal font; otherwise the rite continues with the renewal of baptismal promises" {McManus p95}. While the first part of the Litany of the Saints is being chanted, the vessel of water to be blessed ("a large vessel for baptismal water, distinct from the font") is prepared in the center of the Sanctuary, toward the Epistle side, in view of the faithful.

[Editor's Note: Many authors who favored the reform of Pius XII were thrilled about this "large vessel." For example: "The blessing of the baptismal water follows the old rite, but is carried out with full dramatic effect, in plain view of the faithful..." {1953maryland page iii}. On 8 September 1960, Father Joseph A. Owens echoed the excitement: "If Pius X is considered the Pope of Holy Communion, we might well call Pius XII the Pope of Baptism for he brought the font out into the center of the ceremonies in his *Restored Order of Holy Week Services*." But often the vessel was a cheaply constructed vase, or even a plastic container—even though MAXIMA REDEMPTIONIS said it "should be decorated in a fitting manner." It is difficult to understand what is so "dramatic" about any of this.]

1962 A • In blessing the baptismal water, the Celebrant stands facing the people. "This vessel, which may be decorated, and all other requisites are put before the Paschal candle, in the sight of the Faithful" {*Easter Eve* (1952), p27}. The blessing of the baptismal water ends as usual: viz. the mixing of oil, with the prayer "Commíxtio Chrísmatis."

1962 A • "If there are any to be baptized, Baptism is conferred according to the *Rituale*, but in the Sanctuary itself" {*Easter Eve* (1952), p34}. The first ceremonies—which take place outside the Baptistery—may be done before the Paschal vigil, "especially if several are to be baptized" {Solesmes1957 p639m}. That is to say, "the preliminary rites of Baptism (prior to the final questions) may be performed on Holy Saturday morning for those to be baptized at the Vigil" {McManus p3}. In this case, the Celebrant begins the baptismal rite with the question "Credis?" (*in the Baptism of infants*) or "Quis vocaris?" (*in the Baptism of adults*), and continues from this point.

1962 A • After the blessing (and Baptism), the baptismal water is carried in procession to the font. During the procession, the canticle "Sicut cervus" is chanted; it is begun while the procession forms to take the baptismal water to the font {McManus p44}. The prayer "Omnípotens sempitérne Deus, réspice propítius ad devotiónem" is said after the "Sicut cervus" has been sung. The displacement of these two prayers—which say "my whole soul longs for thee, as a deer for running water" and "souls that are coming to new birth, eager as the deer that longs for running water"—seem to do violence to the rite because the blessing and Baptism(s) have already happened.

1962 • "Sicut Cervus" is sung after the blessing of the baptismal water, and after the Sacrament of Baptism, when the blessed water is being carried to the font.

1962 A • As stated, after the blessed water has been poured into the font, the Celebrant says a prayer ("Omnípotens sempitérne Deus, réspice propítius ad devotiónem"). In the traditional version, that prayer was said before entering the Baptistery for the blessing of the water.

1962 A • Finally the Celebrant incenses the font and all return in silence to the Sanctuary for the Renewal of Baptismal Promises.

1962 • After the blessed water has been poured into the font, the procession returns in silence.

1962 A • The people are supposed to light their candles during the Renewal of Baptismal Promises, but the rubrics nowhere explain how this is to be done. When they arrive at the Sanctuary, the Celebrant exchanges his purple vestments for a white Dalmatic, incenses the Paschal candle, *then stands in front of it* (or in the ambo or pulpit) and faces the people for the Renewal of Baptismal Promises {*Easter Eve* (1952), p35}. Other authors say the priest stands next to the Paschal candle, or behind the lectern used for the blessing of the holy water {McManus p99}.

1962 A • Unlike the traditional blessing of the font, in which the congregation is sprinkled toward the end of the blessing of the font—to be specific, immediately before the prayer "Sanctificétur et fœcundétur"—the revised version has the congregation being sprinkled after the Renewal of Baptismal Promises. "This sprinkling of the people (and the clergy) is done in the same way as at the Sunday Asperges" {McManus p99}.

1962 A • After the Renewal of Baptismal Promises, the chanters begin the second part of the Litany. The Celebrant and ministers, however, go to the sacristy to put on white vestments for the celebration of solemn Mass. The Altar is prepared for solemn Mass, with lighted candles and flowers. Meanwhile, the Paschal candle is placed in its large candlestick, on the Gospel side; whereas the small candlestick (in which the Paschal candle has been kept until this time) is removed, as well as the violet frontal on the Altar {McManus p100}.

HOLY SATURDAY "Version B" 1962
BAPTISMAL RITES COMPARED

"Version B" • The 1962 version of Holy Saturday allows the holy water to be blessed in a more traditional place: viz. the BAPTISTERY instead of the Sanctuary. The following are the official (1955) rubrics—similar but not identical to the rubrics in the 1951 "experimental" version (cf. *Ordo Sabbati Sancti Quando Vigilia Paschalis Instaurata*, page 37)—which explain:

Sicubi vero baptisterium exstat ab ecclesia separatum, et praeferatur benedictionem aquae baptismalis in ipso baptisterio fieri, post invocationem "Sancta Trínitas, unus Deus, miserére nobis," descenditur ad fontem hoc modo: praecedit clericus cum cereo benedicto, sequitur alius subdiaconus cum cruce, vel crucifer, medius inter acolythos cum candelabris accensis, deinde clerus per ordinem, demum celebrans cum ministris sacris. Cantores vero et populus remanent in locis suis, et prosequuntur cantum Litaniarum, repetitis, si opus est, invocationibus inde a *Sancta María, ora pro nobis*.

Benedictio aquae baptismalis fit ut supra, his tantum mutatis: dum pergitur ad fontem, cantatur canticum "Sicut cervus," et celebrans, antequam intret ad benedictionem fontis, dicit orationem *Omnípotens sempitérne Deus, réspice propítius ad devotiónem*, ut supra; postea procedit ad benedictionem fontis.

Benedictione peracta, omnes redeunt in silentio in ecclesiam, et datur initium renovationi promissionum Baptismatis.

In places where there is a Baptistery distinct from the church, and it is preferred to bless the baptismal water in the Baptistery itself, after the invocation "Sancta Trínitas, unus Deus, miserére nobis," the procession to the font takes place in this way: a cleric with the blessed candle goes first, followed by a second subdeacon with the cross, or a crossbearer, who walks between acolytes carrying lighted candles, then the clergy in order, and finally the Celebrant with the sacred ministers. The chanters and the people remain in their places and continue the singing of the litany, repeating, if necessary, the invocation beginning with "Sancta María, ora pro nobis."

The blessing of the baptismal water takes place as above, with these changes only: during the procession to the font, the canticle "Sicut cervus" is sung and the Celebrant, before he enters to bless the font, says the prayer: "Omnípotens sempitérne Deus, réspice propítius ad devotiónem." After this, he proceeds with the blessing of the font.

When the blessing has been completed, all return in silence to the church, and the renewal of baptismal promises begins.

1962 B • After the prophecies, "two chanters, kneeling in the middle of the Sanctuary, chant the Litanies of the Saints as far as the invocation *Propitius esto*. All kneel and make the responses. The invocations are not doubled" {McManus p95}. This is called "the beginning of the Litany."

1962 B • There is no "large vessel" in this version. The people and cantors are told to "remain in their places and continue the [first part of the] Litany" {Solesmes1957 p639Q} while the Celebrant goes to the Baptistery. Without question, the people will finish the first part of the Litany before the Celebrant has finished his blessing in the Baptistery; in this case, they are told to keep repeating the first part of the Litany over and over again, beginning with "Sancta María, ora pro nobis."

[Editor's Note: While the people are singing the first part of the Litany, the canticle "Sicut cervus" is supposed to be sung—while the Celebrant is processing to the font—yet it is unclear who sings this, since "the chanters and people" were instructed to remain "in their places" (*cantores vero et populus remanent in locis suis*). Regardless of who sings "Sicut cervus," it should not be intoned until the procession has left; otherwise cacophony would result, since the people are singing the first part of the Litany over and over. The 1951 "experimental" version said nothing about where to insert the "Sicut cervus"—or the prayer "Omnípotens sempitérne Deus, réspice propítius ad devotiónem." On this, please see page 37 of *Ordo Sabbati Sancti Quando Vigilia Paschalis Instaurata*.]

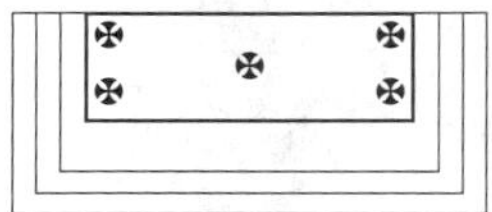

1962 B • "Sicut Cervus" is sung while the people are still in the Church singing the first part of the Litany over and over, on the way to the Baptistery.

1962 B • Before entering to bless the font, the Celebrant says "Omnípotens sempitérne Deus, réspice propítius ad devotiónem," just as he did in the traditional version (before entering the Baptistery).

[Editor's Note: It should be noted that the official 1955 rubrics still speak of the "blessing of the font" (*et celebrans, antequam intret ad benedictionem fontis*) as opposed to the blessing of the water. This was most likely due to oversight.]

1962 B • When the font has been blessed, the Celebrant returns to the Altar for the RENEWAL OF BAPTISMAL PROMISES. The procession is undertaken in silence.

1962 B • After the font has been blessed, the procession returns in silence; then comes the RENEWAL OF BAPTISMAL PROMISES.

1962 B • Neither the 1951 "experimental" version nor the 1955 official version indicates where the Sacrament of Baptism is to be administered. Perhaps it takes place in the Baptistery, after the font has been blessed. Perhaps it takes place in the Sanctuary, before the Renewal of Baptismal Promises.

YOU KNOW WELL ENOUGH THAT WE WHO WERE TAKEN UP INTO CHRIST BY BAPTISM HAVE BEEN TAKEN UP, ALL OF US, INTO HIS DEATH.

The Very Reverend Ronald Knox
(1888-1957)

(1950) • The Text Of The Holy Week Offices With A New Translation By Ronald A. Knox. • Burns, Oates and Washbourne.

+ Imprimatur: 24 November 1950 by the Archdiocese of Westminster (Britain)

Monsignor Ronald Arbuthnott Knox (d. 1957) : Catholic priest; Radio broadcaster (BBC); Author of crime novels; Renowned theologian and scholar; Translator of the Bible. At a young age, Knox distinguished himself as a brilliant classicist, winning awards for Latin and Greek compositions, and at Oxford he "won almost every attainable honor." During the Great War, he served in military intelligence. When Knox converted to Catholicism in

1917, his father—the Anglican Bishop of Manchester—cut him out of his will, although Knox had previously been the favorite son.

In 1939, the English hierarchy commissioned Knox to translate the Bible single-handedly. Venerable Pope Pius XII sent a note, shortly before Monsignor Knox died, calling this translation "a praiseworthy achievement ... a monument of many years of patient study and toil." A fabulous achievement, for which Knox has received very little credit, are the forty-seven (47) rhymed translations of the ancient breviary hymns composed for the *New Westminster Hymnal*. These hymn translations are noteworthy for their unique style and their faithfulness to the Latin. Indeed, they often incorporate the pre-Urbanite versions in a subtle and remarkable way.

This incredibly rare 1950 translation of Holy Week does not "copy-paste" the Knox translation of the Bible for the Scripture readings. Monsignor Knox made revisions—sometimes drastic ones—perhaps because Knox did not consider liturgical translation to be identical to Scripture translation. In a few places, the publisher inexplicably neglected to indicate translations not by Knox; e.g. the Holy Thursday "Pange Lingua" is actually by Walter Hayward Shewring (d. 1990), a Classics professor at Ampleforth College who had converted to Catholicism while a student at Oxford. Knox's liturgical translations are bold, majestic, and stirring; in particular, his versions of the Reproaches, the Exsultet, Collects, and Canon are dazzling. The fact that Monsignor Knox was able to publish so much in the immediate aftermath of the Second World War—the entire Bible, close to fifty hymns, the Holy Week Book, articles, books, and so forth—beggars the imagination. Knox lived long enough to see Pius XII reform Holy Week, and believed this curtailment was an "impoverishment" according to Evelyn Waugh's 1959 biography.

In liturgical books, the word *office* also refers to the Holy Mass; and an equally good translation is "Holy Week Services." This book begins with a wonderful introduction by Fortescue (reprinted from the 1916 edition of the *Holy Week Book*). Knox seems to have met Fortescue (d. 1923) at Saint Edmund's College, Ware—at that time, the Seminary for the Westminster Archdiocese—which is just north of London. In 1923, Fortescue was a professor of church history there, while Knox taught there from 1919 to 1926 (Scripture and Greek, among other subjects). From 1923 to 1925, Fulton Sheen was also teaching there, and became friends with Knox.

In his famous *Life of Christ* (1958), Archbishop Fulton J. Sheen wrote:

> "Of the many translations of Scripture, we have chosen the Knox translation as the best, using the Rheims Douay version only in a very few texts."

This rare 1950 book came to us courtesy of Mr. Andrew Coyne.

DIFFERENCES BETWEEN THE KNOX BIBLE AND THIS BOOK

Evelyn Waugh, a longtime friend of Monsignor Knox, wrote that these Holy Week translations were made "for Messrs Burns, Oates, and Washbourne, a version designed to be read alongside the Latin, not be sung in its stead." Waugh notes how different these translations are from the 1911 versions Knox had created forty years earlier. We have already mentioned the magnificent versions done from scratch: the Exsultet, the Reproaches, the Collects, and so on.

The Scripture readings generally match those of the Knox Bible—yet there are many discrepancies. Who made these changes? One would assume it was Knox himself. What was the motivation for these changes? Some have suggested they were made to "match" the Pope Pius XII Psalter—which had been released in 1945, and was increasingly being added to liturgical books—but there are difficulties with such a theory.

Some differences are striking, such as Psalm 139 on Good Friday:

KNOX BIBLE (1949)	KNOX HOLY WEEK (1950)
3. always plotting treachery in their hearts, always at their quarrelling…	3. always plotting treachery in their hearts, always **intent on strife…**
4. lips that hide the poison of adders.	4. lips that conceal the poison of **asps.**
9. Lord, do not let malice have its way with me, do not prosper its evil designs.	9. **Do not betray my hopes, Lord, into the hands of the wicked; do not forsake me, and let the schemers triumph.**
10. They carry their heads high as they close in around me; let their conspiracy prove its own undoing;	10. **This be the fruit of their conspiracy, that all their busy whispering should recoil upon themselves.**

Below are examples of subtle differences:

KNOX BIBLE (1949)	KNOX HOLY WEEK (1950)
Exodus 13:27 — "and the Lord drowned them amid the waves."	Exodus 13:27 — "and the Lord drowned them amid the **waters**."
Genesis 1:2 — "Earth was still an empty waste, and darkness hung over the deep; but already, over its waters, stirred the breath of God."	Genesis 1:2 — "Earth was still an empty waste, and darkness hung over the deep; but already, over its waters, **brooded the Spirit of God**."
Isaias 55:7 — "sure of his mercy, our God, so rich in pardon."	Isaias 55:7 "sure of his mercy, our God, [...] rich in pardon."

Psalm 116 — "Praise the Lord, all you Gentiles ... the Lord remains faithful to his word for ever."	Psalm 116 — "Praise the Lord, all you **nations** ... the Lord remains **true** to his word for ever."
Luke 1:51 — "driving the proud astray in the conceit of their hearts."	Luke 1:51 — "driving the proud astray in the **imagination** of their hearts."

Several verses from Psalm 21—from Good Friday—demonstrate both subtle and drastic modifications:

KNOX BIBLE (1949)	KNOX HOLY WEEK (1950)
1. My God, my God: why hast thou forsaken me? Loudly I call, but my prayer cannot reach thee.	1. My God, my God, **look upon me:** why hast thou forsaken me? **Why cannot my sinful words reach thee, who art my salvation?**
2. Thou dost not answer, my God, when I cry out to thee day and night, thou dost not heed.	2. Thou dost not answer, my God, when I cry out to thee day and night, **and I am patient still.**
12. My enemies ring me round, packed close as a herd of oxen, strong as bulls from Basan;	12. My enemies **are all about me,** packed close as a herd of oxen, **hemming me in, strong as bulls.**
16. parched is my throat, like clay in the baking, and my tongue sticks fast in my mouth; thou hast laid me in the dust, to die.	**16. My strength has shrivelled up** like clay in the baking, **[...]** my tongue sticks fast in my mouth; thou hast laid me in the dust to die.
18. they have torn holes in my hands and feet; I can count my bones one by one;	18. They have torn holes in my hands and feet; **they mark every bone in my body,**
20. Then, Lord, do not stand at a distance; if thou wouldst aid me, come speedily to my side.	20. Then, Lord, do not stand at a distance; if thou wouldst aid me: **look to my defence.**
21. Only life is left me; save that from the sword, from the power of these dogs;	21. Only life is left me; save that from the sword, from the **clutches** of these dogs.
28. the poor shall eat now, and have their fill; those who look for the Lord will cry out in praise of him, Refreshed be your hearts eternally!	28. The poor shall eat now, and have their fill; those who look for the Lord will **give him thanks, their hearts refreshed eternally.**
32. Him shall they worship, him only, that are laid to rest in the earth, even from their dust they shall adore.	**32. The great ones of the earth feast in his presence, and adore: men brought low, even to the dust, bow down at his feet.**
33. I, too, shall live on in his presence, and beget children to serve him;	33. I, too, shall live on **before him,** and beget children to serve him.

34. these to a later age shall speak of the Lord's name; these to a race that must yet be born shall tell the story of his faithfulness, Hear what the Lord did.	**34. The Lord will claim for his own a generation still to come: heaven itself will make known his faithfulness to a people yet to be born, a people of the Lord's own founding.**

A few more examples, both stark and modest, will suffice:

KNOX BIBLE (1949)	KNOX HOLY WEEK (1950)
John 1:8 — He was not the Light; he was sent to bear witness to the light.	John 1:8 — He was not the Light; he was sent to bear witness **of the Light.**
Psalm 42:2 — Thou, O God, art all my strength; why hast thou cast me off? Must I go mourning, with enemies pressing me hard?	Psalm 42:2 — Thou, O God, art all my strength, why hast thou cast me **out? Why do** I go mourning, with enemies pressing me hard?
Psalm 42:4 — There I will go up to the altar of God, the giver of triumphant happiness; thou art my own God, with the harp I hymn thy praise.	Psalm 42:4 — There I will go up to the altar of God, the giver of **youth and happiness.** Thou art my [...] God, with the harp I hymn thy praise.
Psalm 42:5 — Soul, art thou still downcast? Wilt thou never be at peace?	Psalm 42:5 — Soul, why art thou [...] downcast, **why art thou all lament?**
Psalm 138:12,11 — With thee the night shines clear as day itself; night should surround me, friendlier than day.	Psalm 138:12,11 — [...] Night shines clear as **the** day itself; **night shall be the only witness of my pleasures.**

HEBREW ACROSTICS • Monsignor Knox was a master of many languages, including Hebrew, Latin, Aramaic, and Greek. When he noticed alphabetical acrostics in the Bible, his English translations meet the challenge. There are too many examples to cite, but a few might be mentioned: Proverbs 31; Psalm 144; Psalm 33; Psalm 36; Psalm 111, and so forth. We strongly encourage all to examine what Monsignor Knox did with Psalm 118 (a long alphabetical acrostic), especially the difficult letters such as "V." We will present his translation of Psalm 24 as an example:

ALL MY HEART goes out to thee,
O Lord my God.

BELIE NOT the trust I have in thee,
let not my enemies boast of my downfall.

CAN ANY that trust in thee be disappointed,
as they are disappointed who lightly break their troth?

DIRECT my way, Lord, as thou wilt,
teach me thy own paths.

EVER LET thy truth guide and teach me,
O God my deliverer, my abiding hope.

FORGET NOT, Lord, thy pity,
thy mercies of long ago.

GIVE HEED no more to the sins and frailties of my youth,
but think mercifully of me, as thou, Lord, art ever gracious.

HOW GRACIOUS is the Lord, how faithful,
guiding our strayed feet back to the path!

IN HIS OWN LAWS he will train the humble,
in his own paths the humble he will guide.

JEALOUS BE thy keeping of covenant and ordinance,
and the Lord's dealings will be ever gracious, ever faithful with thee.

KINDLY BE thy judgement of my sin,
for thy own honour's sake, my grievous sin.

LET A MAN but fear the Lord,
what path to choose he doubts no longer.

MUCH JOY he shall have of his lands
and to his heirs leave them.

NO STRANGER the Lord is, no secret his covenant,
to his true worshippers.

ON THE LORD I fix my eyes continually,
trusting him to save my feet from the snare.

PITY ME, Lord, as thou seest me
friendless and forlorn.

QUIT MY HEART of its burden,
deliver me from my distress.

RESTLESS and forlorn, I claim thy pity,
to my sins be merciful.

SEE how many are my foes,
and how bitter is the grudge they bear me.

TAKE MY SOUL into thy keeping; come to my rescue,
do not let me be disappointed of my trust in thee.

UPRIGHTNESS and purity be my shield,
as I wait patiently, Lord, for thy help.

WHEN wilt thou deliver Israel, my God,
from all his troubles?

Regarding the Missale Vetustum

HOLINESS VS INFALLIBILITY • The holiness and piety of a cleric does not guarantee his liturgical views will be correct. Consider *Medicæa* decrees issued by Pius IX and Leo XIII. Both popes were virtuous and holy, but their liturgical documents were erroneous—and later had to be withdrawn. Specifically, Pope Pius IX declared a corrupt and mutilated plainsong version (*Editio Medicæa*) to be "the ***true*** Gregorian chant" (20 Jan 1871), falsely claiming that "this edition contains the Gregorian chant which the Roman Catholic Church has always kept, and therefore—by reason of tradition—may be held to be more in agreement with what Pope Gregory the Great introduced into the sacred liturgy" (14 Aug 1871). A few years later, it was again "approved and declared authentic" (14 Apr 1877). Pope Leo XIII also "approved and declared authentic" (15 Nov 1878) this corrupt edition, and later published *Romanorum Pontificum*, which proclaimed it to be "the only music now accepted and approved by the Holy See, as representing the ***genuine*** chant of the Roman Churches" (27 Apr 1883). Dom André Mocquereau—at the 1920 GREGORIAN CONGRESS—called these errors "blunders" and "regrettable mistakes," pointing out that the Sacred Congregation of Rites "recalled this decree some years later, as soon as it realized the facts upon which it was based were false."

ANOTHER EXAMPLE • Another example of a saintly pope who made a ghastly liturgical error—later condemned and rescinded—is Pope Urban VIII, who destroyed all the ancient hymns. In the words of Father Adrian Fortescue, Pope Urban VIII "with a patient care that one cannot help admiring, set to work to destroy every hymn in the office." Not a single authority has ever defended what Pope Urban VIII did. Father Father Clemens Blume called it a "death blow." Father Fortescue called it "the crushing blow which destroyed the beauty of all Breviary hymns." Father Jules Baudot, quoting Chevalier, says the urbanite reform "spoiled the work of Christian antiquity." More than 300 years would elapse before the Church would finally quash the corrupted versions by Urban VIII.

THE SOLE EXPRESSION • Recently, the Vatican issued a document declaring the *Missale Recens* to be "the sole expression of the Roman Rite." Innumerable difficulties result from such an assertion, and this decree—like *Romanorum Pontificum* of 1883—will have to be withdrawn at some point in the future. Even those responsible for the liturgical reforms of the 1960s would not agree that the *Missale Recens* is the "sole expression" of the Roman Rite. Consider the following:

(1) Giacomo Cardinal Lercaro—not at all "traditionalist"—was in charge of all the liturgical reforms. On 2 March 1965, Lercaro published an article in *l'Avennire d'Italia* in which he strongly condemned liturgical abuses, giving concrete examples of practices he considered "fanciful" and "deplorable" {Chiron p119}. What were these deplorable abuses? (a) Communion in the hand; (b) a Celebrant reciting the Canon in an audible voice. Moreover, in a letter (25 January 1966) to the bishops' conferences, Cardinal Lercaro also called female altar servers "a grave infraction."

(2) Franjo Cardinal Seper—appointed in 1968 by Paul VI as Prefect for the Vatican's *Congregation for the Doctrine of the Faith*—made clear his appraisal of the ambiguity {Chiron p169} of Eucharistic Prayer No. 2: "Me? I'll never adopt that Canon." Did Cardinal Seper thereby reject the "sole expression" of the Roman Rite?

(3) Pope Saint Paul VI himself—on 22 January 1967—attempted to intervene, to save the Last Gospel {Chiron p134}. His intervention was unsuccessful, however, and the Last Gospel was eliminated.

(4) Pope Saint John XXIII—he who convened the Second Vatican Council (which began on 11 October 1962)—published a forceful and unambiguous defense of Latin called Veterum Sapientia on 22 February 1962. John XXIII summarized:

> "Impelled by the weightiest of reasons, We are fully determined to restore this language to its position of honor, and to do all We can to promote its study and use [...] to ensure that the ancient and uninterrupted use of Latin be maintained and, where necessary, restored."

John XXIII went on to say that bishops "must be on their guard lest anyone under their jurisdiction, eager for revolutionary changes, writes against the use of Latin in the teaching of the higher sacred studies or in the Liturgy, or through prejudice makes light of the Holy See's will in this regard or interprets it falsely."

(5) Anselmo Cardinal Albareda—deeply involved in the 1960s reforms as well as the clandestine *Commissio Piana*—spoke in no uncertain terms about liturgical Latin: "The unity of language in the liturgy is so great a treasure for the Church that no advantage could compensate for its demise" {Giampietro p249}. Moreover, Augustin Cardinal Bea—deeply involved in liturgical reform going back to the 1940s—said something similar: "No concession should ever be made for the singing of the Exsultet, in whole or in part, in the vernacular."

(6) Father Louis Bouyer was one of the chief liturgical reformers. It was Father Bouyer who—with assistance from Father Bernard Botte—composed Eucharistic Prayer No. 2 {Bouyer p221}. Bouyer was certainly no "traditionalist," as page 4 of his *Liturgical Piety* (Notre Dame Press, 1954) demonstrates, but when he saw the results of the liturgical reforms, he was deeply disturbed. Indeed, he referred to the post-conciliar reforms as "the pathetic creature we created." He called the reformed calendar "insane" {Bouyer p223} and "the handiwork of a trio of maniacs." Father Bouyer admits that the reformers had no chance of success, since their goal was "recasting from top to bottom—***and in a few months!***—an entire liturgy which had required twenty centuries to develop" {Bouyer p219}.

(7) Ferdinando Cardinal Antonelli—a franciscan—had been named "Secretary of the Conciliar Commission on the Liturgy" on 4 October 1962 (the date having been chosen to correspond with the feast of Saint Francis of Assisi). His words have quoted extensively throughout this volume, and it would be inappropriate to duplicate them here. Therefore, one quote will have to represent them all:

> "In the Concilium, there are few Bishops with a specifically liturgical expertise, and very few are really theologians. The most acute deficiency in the Concilium is the lack of theologians. In fact, it could be said that they had been excluded altogether, which is something dangerous. In the liturgy, every word and every gesture expresses an idea which is always a theological idea. [...] And this has very serious consequences."

Conclusion • We have not been quoting "traditionalists" above. Nor have we cited from Vatican II itself—while it could easily be demonstrated the *Missale Recens* contradicts the explicit mandates of the Council, such as Sacrosanctum Concilium §36, §54, §89a, §100, §101, §112, §114, and §116. Rather, we have cited the words of the reformers themselves: **those who actually created** the *Missale Recens*. To claim the *Missale Recens* is the "sole expression" of the Roman Rite, one must condemn those responsible for its creation—such as Cardinal Lercaro, who said reading the Canon audibly was a "fanciful" and "deplorable" practice. One must likewise condemn the fathers of Vatican II. One must also repudiate much post-conciliar legislation: 5 nov 1971; 2 jul 1988; 7 jul 2007; 4 nov 2009; 8 april 2011; 22 feb 2020. In other words, Church leaders must realize the impossibility of appealing to "post-conciliar" legislation, which condemns the very things it demands: female altar servers, audible Canon, hand-communion, women lectors inside the sanctuary, exclusion of Latin, exclusion of plainsong, and so forth. It follows that—for anyone capable of rational thought—the *Missale Vetustum* cannot be forbidden or denounced by appealing to post-conciliar legislation.

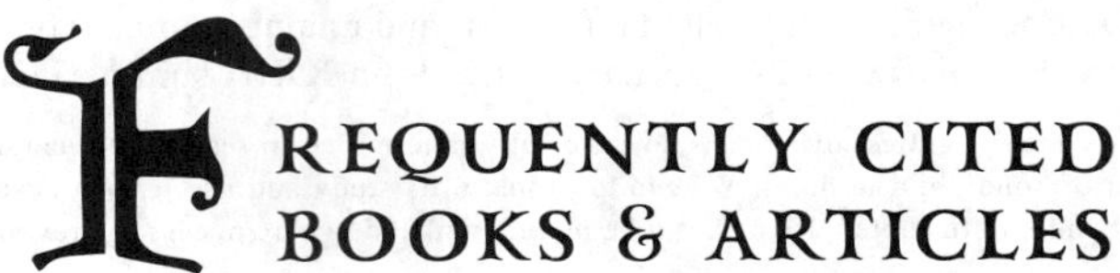

Frequently Cited Books & Articles

1886 • **Guéranger,** Prosper Louis Pascal. *The Liturgical Year (Passiontide and Holy Week); Translated from the French by Dom Laurence Shepherd.* Worcestershire: Stanbrook Abbey, 1886.

Dom Guéranger was a Canon of the cathedral chapter of Tours, but in 1831 he raised funds to purchase an old building which—in former days—had been a *priory* (a small religious house) and transformed it into a monastery. In 1837, Pope Gregory XVI, himself a Benedictine, raised the Priory of Solesmes to an Abbey and constituted it as the head of the French Benedictines. Two months later, Guéranger was appointed as Abbat.

1897 • **Feasey,** Henry John. *Ancient English Holy Week Ceremonial.* London: Thomas Baker, 1897.

In some ways, this tome might be considered a "predecessor" of the book by Monti, except that it focuses primarily on the traditions of English Catholics.

1904 • **Thurston,** Herbert. *Lent and Holy Week; Chapters on Catholic Observance and Ritual.* London: John Griffin, 1904.

+ Imprimatur: 15 February 1904 by Cardinal Bourne (d. 1935), Archbishop of Westminster (Britain)

1918 • **Fortescue,** Adrian. *The Ceremonies of the Roman Rite Described.* London: Burns & Oates, 1918.

Father Fortescue (d. 1923): Artist; Calligrapher; Polyglot; Photographer; Byzantine scholar; Pastor of the Church of Saint Hugh (Letchworth); contributed numerous articles to the Catholic Encyclopedia. Between 1899 and 1905 Fortescue passed doctoral examinations in moral theology, dogma, ecclesiastical history, canon law, Arabic, and biblical science—passing the examination in Semitic languages with great distinction—and on 10 June 1905 was awarded a triple doctorate. Emperor Franz Joseph personally awarded him the degree. This book is clear and eminently meticulous.

+ Imprimatur: 6 September 1917 by the Archdiocese of Westminster (Britain)

1927 • **Cabrol,** Fernand. *The Complete Offices of Holy Week in Latin and English.* London: B. Herder Book Company, 1927.

Dom Cabrol (d. 1937): Prior of Solesmes Abbey; Abbat of Farnborough; honored by the British Empire for services to the Red Cross during the Great War; contributed numerous articles to the *Catholic Encyclopedia.*

+ Imprimatur: August 1927 by Most Rev'd William Timothy Cotter (d. 1940), Bishop of Portsmouth

1952 • **Vatican Press.** *Ordo Sabbati Sancti Quando Vigilia Paschalis Instaurata.* Rome: Typis Polyglottis Vaticanis, 11 January 1952.

What this booklet is—and how it came to be—has already been explained in the notes above. Generally speaking, it follows *Dominicae Resurrectionis Vigiliam,* which was printed on 9 February 1951 in Acta Apostolicae Sedis (the Holy See's journal) just 43 days before it was to take effect, and included eight pages of rubrics explaining how things were to be done. On 11 January 1952, the Vatican published a slightly revised version of the rubrics—this time approximately 14 pages in length—again in the Holy See's journal. This booklet is based on that revision. An example demonstrating how the revision is not identical would be the baptistery option: The 1951 version said "wherever ancient custom calls for the water to be blessed in the separate baptistery, it takes place there," whereas the 1952 version said "the water may be blessed in the separate baptistery if there is a preference to do so."

1952 • { **Easter Eve 1952** } . *Easter Eve; A Manual for the Faithful attending the New Service of the Paschal Vigil.* London: Catholic Truth Society, 1952.

On the back cover of this book, it says: "The Text of this Paschal Vigil service has been added as a supplement to the new revised Large edition of the Saint Andrew Daily Missal." It appears to have been produced by "The Liturgical Apostolate" at the Abbey of Saint André in Belgium. It is 59 pages long and contains both English and Latin, yet uses English only for the Ordinary of the Mass.

+ Cum permissu Superiorum

1953 • { **1953maryland** } . *Order for the Restored Vigil of Easter in Latin and English.* Maryland: The Newman Press, 1953.

This is a confusing book. It was supposedly published in ***Westminster, Maryland***; that is, in the United States. Yet, its Imprimatur comes from the Archdiocese of Westminster *in England.* To make matters worse, the English translation in this book was stolen—without any acknowledgment—from Monsignor Knox. In some cases, his translation was bowdlerized by them; e.g. the *Exsultet* starting at "Fugat ódia, concórdiam parat..." Knox's English translation also has an Imprimatur from Westminster (Britain), by Monsignor Eustace Anthony Morrogh Bernard (d. 1972), at that time Vicar-General of the Archdiocese of Westminster. The Latin, too, was lifted from the Knox version, and they made no attempt to disguise this theft. Indeed, the unique abbreviations in the Knox version (e.g. Dñs for Dóminus) are copied verbatim by the Maryland company, in identical places. The Maryland company has corrected a few typos, such as the misplaced accent in the Knox version on "insónet" [sic] of the *Exsultet.*

1956 • **McManus**, Frederick. *The Rites of Holy Week.* Paterson, New Jersey: Saint Anthony Guild Press, 1956.

Monsignor Frederick Richard McManus (d. 2005) was the leader of the "progressive" school of liturgy in the United States for four decades. However, one could not wish for a better guide to the revised Holy Week than this clear and detailed manual.

+ Imprimatur: 16 February 1956 by Richard Cardinal Cushing (d. 1970) Archbishop of Boston

1956 • **Bugnini**, Annibale. "Ordo Hebdomadae Sanctae Instauratus: Commentarium ad S.R.C. Decretum *Maxima Redemptionis Nostrae Mysteria* diei 16 novembris 1955 et ad *Ordinem Hebdomadae Sanctae Instauratum.*" Ephemerides Liturgicae (28 February 1956).

Printed in Rome. In this document—176 pages in length—Father Annibale Bugnini and Father Carlo Braga explain why the changes were made to Holy Week in the early 1950s.

1957 • **Solesmes Abbey**. *Mass and Vespers with Gregorian Chant for Sundays and Holy Days—Latin and English Text—edited by the Benedictines of the Solesmes Congregation.* Tournai: Desclée & Co, 1957.

+ Imprimatur: 22 August 1957

2003 • **Dobszay**, László. *The Bugnini-Liturgy and the Reform of the Reform.* Hungary: Catholic Church Music Associates, 2003.

2012 • **Monti**, James. *A Sense of the Sacred: Roman Catholic Worship in the Middle Ages.* San Francisco: Ignatius Press, 2012.

Monti provides exhaustive details about the different ceremonies of Holy Week during the Middle Ages, with special emphasis on ancient Spanish liturgical books; a masterful and definitive study.

+ Imprimatur: 27 November 2012 by the Archdiocese of New York

2009 • **Giampietro**, Nicola. *The Development of the Liturgical Reform as seen by Cardinal Ferdinando Antonelli.* Colorado: Roman Catholic Books, 2009.

Essential reading for anyone attempting to understand the liturgical reforms of the 20th century.

WORKS CITED INFREQUENTLY

We condemn the deplorable practice in which some authors—*in an effort to impress the reader*—list all the books and articles they have ever encountered on a given subject. Nevertheless, we feel obliged to include at a minimum all the works cited:

1670 • **Blount**, Walter. *The office of the Holy week according to the Missall and Roman Breviary; translated out of French with a new explication taken out of the Holy Fathers, of the mysteries, ceremonies, Gospels, lessons, psalms, and of all that belongs to this office. Enricht with many figures.* Paris: Sir Walter Kirkham Blount, 1670.

Sir Walter Kirkham Blount (pronounced "Blunt") was born on 7 March 1646, in Worcestershire, England and died on 12 May 1717 in Ghent (Belgium). This book contains a full English translation alongside the Latin, with copious explanations—indeed, many thousands of words. For example, the following is approximately 1/6 of Blount's complete "notes" before the Gospel on Palm Sunday: "He goes to the place appointed for reading the Gospell with the Subdeacon, Thurifer, and two Acolyts, who carry two tapers lighted before him, to signify the joy which the faithfull ought to have for this great blessing of the light of faith. He turns towards the people that they may heare the Gospell, the Subdeacon holding the booke open before him, to testify that what he reads to the people is only what the priest ordered him."

1688 • **Hills,** Henry. *The Office of the Holy Week: According to the Roman Missal and Breviary.* London: Henry Hills, 1688.

Printed by Henry Hills, Printer to the King's Most Excellent Majesty for his Household and Chappel; And are to be sold at his Printing-house on the Ditch-side in Black-Fryers. This translation was allowed to be printed in London since it appeared during the reign of James II of England, a Catholic. He had converted from Anglicanism secretly in 1667, and refused to take a mandatory oath (1673 "Test Act") denouncing the doctrine of Transubstantiation, instead choosing to relinquish the post of Lord High Admiral. A devout man, he once said: "If occasion were, I hope God would give me his grace to suffer death for the true Catholic religion as well as banishment." His brother—who reigned as King Charles II of England until 1685—became a Catholic on his deathbed.

1853 • **Dale**, Hilarius. *Ceremonial according to the Roman Rite; Translated from the Italian of Joseph Baldeschi, Master of Ceremonies of the Basilica of Saint Peter at Rome.* London: Charles Dolman, 1853.

+ Imprimatur: 1 July 1873 by Cardinal Manning (d. 1892), Archbishop of Westminster (Britain)

1860 • **Bouvry**, Ghislain. *Expositio Rubricarum Breviarii, Missalis et Titualis Romani.* Regensburg: Charles Meyer, 1860.

The rubrics for Holy week begin on page 440.

1875 • *The Complete Office of Holy Week According to the Roman Missal and Breviary, in Latin and English.* New York: Benziger Brothers, 1875.

+ Imprimatur: 1875 by Most Rev'd John McCloskey (d. 1885), Archbishop of New York

1896 • **Ebner**, Adalbert. *Quellen und Forschungen zur Geschichte und Kunstgeschichte des Missale Romanum im Mittelalter.* Freiburg: Herder, 1896.

Father Ebner's tome is one the most fascinating and important liturgical books ever published; Father Josef Andreas Jungmann (d. 1975) relied upon it heavily.

1901 • **Wagner**, Peter. *Introduction to the Gregorian Melodies; A Handbook of Plainsong.* London: Plainsong & Mediæval Music Society, 1901.

This book was later reprinted verbatim by Monsignor Francis P. Schmitt in *Caecilia Magazine* (1957). Dr. Peter Wagner (d. 1931) was the director of the Gregorian Academy—at the University of Freiburg (Switzerland)—where he taught Karl Gustav Fellerer (d. 1984) and others.

1906 • **McGovern**, James. *The Manual of the Holy Catholic Church.* Chicago: Catholic Art and Publication office, 1906.

Pages 47-64 contains valuable information about celebrating Holy Week in small churches.

+ Imprimatur: 1906 by Most Rev'd James Edward Quigley (d. 1915), Archbishop of Chicago

1913 • *The Holy Week Book; Compiled by authority from the Roman Missal and Breviary as Reformed by order of Pope Pius X; With an Introduction by Adrian Fortescue.* London: Burns, Oates, and Washbourne, 1913.

This book is the direct predecessor of the 1950 *Holy Week Book* translated by Monsignor Ronald Knox. The magnificent *Introduction* by Father Fortescue is identical, as is the rest of the book: the Stations of the Cross, the Appendix with the Blessing of the Oils, and so forth. Needless to say, the English translation is not identical, because Monsignor Knox would not create until 37 years later. The translation of the rubrics was modified in 1950, even in such minor details as "violet" vs. "purple."

+ Imprimatur: 27 January 1913 by the Archdiocese of Westminster (Britain)

1914 • **Fortescue**, Adrian. *The Mass: A Study of the Roman Liturgy.* New York: Longmans and Green, 1914.

+ Imprimatur: 28 March 1912 by Canon Edmund Surmont,
Vicar General for the Archdiocese of Westminster (Britain)

1923 • *Officium Majoris Hebdomadæ et Octavæ Paschæ Cum Cantu.* Ratisbon: Pustet, 1923.

+ Imprimatur: 11 December 1922

1925 • **Schuster**, Ildefonso. *The Sacramentary* ("Liber Sacramentorum") *Volume II; Historical & Liturgical Notes on the Roman Missal.* London: Burns, Oates, & Washbourne, 1925.

Alfredo Ildefonso Schuster (d. 1954) was a Cardinal and formerly a Benedictine Abbat. As Archbishop of Milan, he visited every parish of the diocese five times. His body is incorrupt. Volume II of his massive Liber Sacramentorum contains Septuagesima through Pentecost.

+ Imprimatur: 1 October 1925

1925 • **Lefebvre**, Gaspar. *The Daily Missal with Vespers for Sundays.* Saint Andrew's Abbey, 1925.

Dom Pierre Gaspar Lefebvre (d. 1966) founded a publication in 1919 called *The Parish Liturgical Bulletin*, designed for priests, Mass servers, sacristans, and cantors. Dom Lefebvre published many articles and books on the sacred liturgy; the most famous was *The Saint Andrew Missal.*

+ Imprimatur: 13 May 1925 by Archbishop Daniel Austin Dowling (d. 1930) of Minnesota

1936 • **Lasance**, Francis. *The New Roman Missal.* Benziger Brothers, 1936.

Very little is known about the publication of this Missal. It seems to have been produced during the 1930s and underwent various editions—some with Latin and English, others with English only—until the death of Father Francis Xavier Lasance in 1946. His Missal was posthumously "updated" (e.g. the new feast of the Assumption on 15 August). Father Lasance was trained by the Society of Jesus (classics and philosophy) at Xavier College in Cincinnati, studied theology at Saint Meinrad, and was ordained for the Archdiocese of Cincinnati. It was during the last half of his life that he wrote the many prayer books, hand-missals, and *devotionalia* which were so widely used. The *New Roman Missal* was produced with the help of Benedictine Father Augustine Walsh, a monk of Saint Anselm's Priory.

1944 • **Lallou**, William. "The Prophecies on Holy Saturday" *The Catholic Biblical Quarterly,* vol. 6, no. 3, (1944), pp. 299–305.

Monsignor William J. Lallou (d. 1973) was a professor at St. Charles Seminary and CUA.

1946 • **Lallou**, William. "Should We Revive The Mandatum?" *The American Ecclesiastical Review,* vol. CXV, (1946), pp. 69-68.

1946 • **Eustace**, Bartholomew. *Ritual for small churches; A Translation of the "Memoriale Rituum."* New York: Joseph F. Wagner, 1946.

Three years after writing this book, Father Bartholomew Joseph Eustace (d. 1956) was consecrated the Bishop of Camden (New Jersey). This book is based on the *Memoriale Rituum*, which is basically a 100-page instruction manual for celebrating Holy Week in small churches.

+ Imprimatur: 12 February 1935 by Patrick Cardinal Hayes (d. 1938), Archbishop of New York

1949 • *Officium Majoris Hebdomadae et octavae Paschae; a Vesperis Sabbati ante Dominicam in Palmis usque ad Missam Sabbati in Albis; cum cantu; juxta ordinem Breviarii, Missalis et Pontificalis Romani.* Mechelen: H. Dessain, 1949.

+ Imprimatur: 14 March 1949

1949 • **Knox**, Ronald. *Trials of a Translator.* New York: Sheed & Ward, 1949.

+ Imprimatur: 26 February 1949 by the Archdiocese of Westminster (Britain)

1950 • **Jungmann**, Joseph. *Missarum Sollemnia; The Mass of the Roman Rite: Its Origins and Development.* New York: Benziger Brothers, 1950.

This book was reprinted by "Christian Classics, Inc." located in Westminster, Maryland. It was translated from German into English by Father Francis Brunner (d. 1965), a Redemptorist priest who edited the *Caecilia Magazine*, dedicated to Sacred Music. Because of the magnificent and meticulous footnotes by Father Jungmann, it would be difficult to overstate the value of this work. **If no volume is indicated by our Missal, that means we refer to "Volume II."**

+ Imprimatur: 22 September 1950 by Francis Cardinal Spellman (d. 1967), Archbishop of New York

1953 • **Steuart**, Benedict. *The development of Christian Worship; an outline of liturgical history.* London: Longmans & Green, 1953.

+ Imprimatur: 11 July 1953 by the Archdiocese of Westminster (Britain)

1953 • **Diekmann**, Godfrey. *The Easter Vigil; Arranged for Use in Parishes.* Collegeville, Minnesota: The Liturgical Press, 1953.

+ Imprimatur: 13 December 1952 by Bishop Peter William Bartholome (d. 1982)

1953 • **Löw**, Josef. "We Must Celebrate the Easter Night" *Worship XXVII,* March (1953) pp. 161-171.

Father Josef Löw was Vice-Relator of the Historical Section for the Sacred Congregation of Rites.

1954 • **Perotti**, Leonard David. *The Easter Vigil: The Restored Rite in English.* Paterson, New Jersey: St. Anthony Guild Press, 1954.

Father Leonard David Perotti (d. 1987) served in many locations, including the Lateran in Rome. At the time this book was published, Father Perotti was novice master at Saint Bonaventure's Monastery in Paterson, New Jersey. The booklet is 47 pages long and compares unfavorably to booklets which print both English and Latin, such as the 1952 "Easter Eve" booklet produced in Belgium .

+ Imprimatur: 19 January 1954 by Most Rev'd James A. McNulty (Bishop of Paterson).

1956 • *Holy Week Masses; Complete English Text of all the Masses & Ceremonies of Holy Week for Congregational Use.* Chicago: J. S. Paluch, 1956.

+ Imprimatur: 17 February 1956 Samuel Cardinal Stritch (d. 1958), Archbishop of Chicago

1956 • **McGarry**, J. G. "Holy Week 1956." *The Furrow*, vol. 7, no. 6, (1956), pp. 323–332.

Canon J. G. McGarry taught homiletics at St. Patrick's College, Maynooth. This 11-page article contains interesting information about the liturgical life of Ireland, with special emphasis on Holy Week.

1958 • **Apel**, Willi. *Gregorian Chant.* Indiana University Press, 1958.

1989 • **Dyer**, Joseph. *The Singing of Psalms in the Early-Medieval Office.* Medieval Academy of America, 1989.

1993 • **Hiley**, David. *Western Plainchant: A Handbook.* Oxford University Press, 1993.

2002 • **Reid**, Scott Alcuin. *The nature of the Liturgical Movement and the principles of liturgical reform.* London: King's College, 2002.

2010 • **McFarland**, Jason. *Cantus Ad Introitum: The Entrance Song in Roman Catholic Worship.* Catholic University of America, 2010.

2010 • **Malloy**, Rebecca. *Inside the Offertory: Aspects of Chronology and Transmission.* Oxford University Press, 2010.

2011 • **Goddard**, Philip. *Festa Paschalia.* Herefordshire: Gracewing, 2011.

Those who seek a careful comparison between the traditional rites and the reform under Pius XII will be disappointed, and readers should understand that this book contains numerous errors. For example, on page 189 Goddard erroneously describes the 1955 Good Friday procession to the High Altar as a "silent procession," whereas Pope Pius XII added three antiphons to be sung during this procession. On page 184, he describes Venantius Fortunatus as a "5th century" bishop, whereas Fortunatus lived in the late 6th century and died in the early 7th century. On the other hand, Goddard's book does contain valuable references to Holy Week as recorded in the ancient liturgical books. Goddard relies heavily on the *Ordo Hebdomadae Sanctae Instauratus*—a 1956 commentary by Annibale Bugnini and Carlo Braga on the 1955 reforms—which he refers to as "OHS." The OHS is currently available online as a PDF file, but only in Latin.

2013 • **Pristas**, Lauren. *Collects of the Roman Missals:A Comparative Study of the Sundays in Proper Seasons before and after the Second Vatican Council.* London: Bloomsbury Academic, 2013.

2015 • **Bouyer**, Louis. *The Memoirs of Louis Bouyer: From Youth and Conversion to Vatican II, the Liturgical Reform, and After.* Ohio: Angelico Press, 2015.

This book was first published (in French) in 2014. The English Translation is by Dr. John Pepino.

2018 • **Chiron**, Yves. *Annibale Bugnini: Reformer of the Liturgy.* Brooklyn: Angelico Press, 2018.

This book was first published (in French) in 2016. The English Translation is by Dr. John Pepino.

2017 • **Stingl**, Anton. *Versus Ad Communionem.* Regensburg: Editions Sankt Ottilien: 2017.

This book is valuable, but not without typos. For example, for the Communion *Panem De Caelo*, Stingl indicates that what he calls "A"—that is to say, ALBI|1047—has a *repetendum* on 128v, line 11. But consulting the manuscript, one sees there is no *repetendum*. On page 109, Mr. Stingl spells the words "sáeculum sáeculi" instead of "saéculum saéculi"—which can cause problems since the Latin language has words like "áeris" (different than "aéris").

NORTH AMERICAN PATRON SAINTS

Saint Edmund Campion Missal, Third Edition

ETIAM SI OCCIDERIT ME, SPERABO IN IPSO (Job 13:15) • *Though He slay me, yet will I trust in him.*

PATRON SAINTS OF NORTH AMERICA

Sancti Patróni Américae Septentrionális

Father Gabriel Lalemant († 17 mar 1649)

His martyrdom was longer and more brutal than any of the others, although he was the weakest and most frail of all. He is depicted holding hot coals and an awl.

Father Antoine Daniel († 4 jul 1648)

He is shown wearing vestments, as he had just finished celebrating Mass when he died. His right hand clutches a pistol, because he was killed by a bullet.

Saint René Goupil († 29 sep 1642)

Killed for making the sign of the cross over a child, Goupil was a *donné*, not a priest. But shortly before his martyrdom, Jogues accepted his vows as a Jesuit.

Saint Jean de Lalande († 19 oct 1646)

Lalande was not a priest; he was a *donné* like Goupil and Couture. He assisted Father Jogues.

Father Isaac Jogues († 18 oct 1646)

His fingers were mutilated by the Iroquois, but the pope gave him a special dispensation to offer Mass. Killed by a tomahawk, his head is depicted bleeding.

Father Jean de Brébeuf († 16 mar 1649)

Holding pen and book, owing to his translation work, Brébeuf carries—under the book—a flaming ax, with which he was cruelly burned during his martyrdom.

Father Charles Garnier († 7 dec 1649)

Shown clasping a lily, since he was killed on the eve of the Immaculate Conception, which—although not yet formally defined—he had taken a vow to uphold.

Father Noël Chabanel († 8 dec 1649)

He was a poet and teacher of rhetoric; for this reason, he is shown holding a small book of poems.

In the United States, the name of Father Jogues is mentioned first in the feast's title and prayers; in other localities, the name of Father Brébeuf comes first. In the United States, no commemoration is made.

— 26 September, The North American Martyrs —

SS. JOANNIS DE BRÉBEUF, ISAACI JOGUES ET SOCIORUM, MARTYRUM

INTROIT. *Apoc 7: 14*

Hi sunt qui venérunt de tribulatióne magna, et lavérunt stolas suas, et dealbavérunt eas in sánguine Agni. ℣. Laudáte Dñm, omnes gentes; laudáte eum omnes pópuli. ℣. Glória Patri.

THESE ARE THEY who are come out of great tribulation, and have washed their robes, and have made them white in the blood of the Lamb. (Ps 11: 1) O praise the Lord, all ye nations; praise Him, all ye people. ℣. Glory.

COLLECT.

Deus, qui primítias fídei in amplíssimis Boreális Américæ regiónibus sanctórum Mártyrum tuórum Joánnis, Isaáci eorúmque Sociórum prædictióne et sánguine consecrásti: concéde propítius: ut, eórũ intercessióne, flórida christianórum seges ubíque in dies augeátur. Per Dóminum.

O God, Who didst consecrate the first-fruits of the faith in the northern regions of America by the preaching and blood of Thy blessed Martyrs John, Isaac, and their Companions: vouchsafe unto us, we beseech Thee, that through their intercession the fruitful harvest of Christians may everywhere daily receive an increase. Through our Lord.

COLLECT. *Commemoration of Sts. Cyprian & Justina.*

Beatórum Mártyrum Cypriáni et Justínæ nos, Dómine, fóveant continuáta præsídia: quia non désinis propítius intuéri, quos tálibus auxíliis concésseris adjuvári. Per Dominum.

May the continual protection of the blessed martyrs, Cyprian and Justina, comfort us, O Lord; for Thou dost not cease to behold with favor those whom Thou hast granted the grace of such assistance. Through our Lord.

EPISTLE. *II Cor. 12: 11-15*

BRETHREN; I ought to have been commended by you: for I have no way come short of them that are above measure apostles, although I be nothing. Yet the signs of my apostleship have been wrought on you, in all patience, in signs, in wonders, and mighty deeds. For what is there that you have had less than the other churches, but that I myself was not burdensome to you? Pardon me this injury. Behold now the third time I am ready to come to you; and I will not be burdensome unto you. For I seek not the things that are yours, but you. For neither ought the children to lay up for the parents, but the parents for the children. But I most gladly will spend and be spent myself for your souls; although loving you more, I be loved less.

Fratres: Ego a vobis débui commendári: nihil enim minus fui ab iis qui sunt supra modum Apóstoli, tamétsi nihil sum. Signa tamen apostolátus mei facta sunt super vos, in omni patiéntia, in signis et prodígiis et virtútibus. Quid est enim quod minus habuístis præ céteris ecclésiis, nisi quod ipse non graváví vos? Donáte mihi hanc injúriam. Ecce tértio hoc parátus sum veníre ad vos; et non ero gravis vobis. Non enim quæro quæ vestra sunt, sed vos; nec enim debent fílii paréntibus thesaurizáre, sed paréntes fíliis. Ego autem libénter impéndam et superimpéndar ipse pro animábus vestris: licet plus vos díligens, minus díligar.

GRADUAL & ALLELUIA. *Ps 123: 7-8 & II Cor. 1: 5*

OUR SOUL hath been delivered, as a sparrow, out of the snare of the fowlers. ℣. The snare is broken, and we are delivered: our help is in the name of the Lord, Who made Heaven and earth.
Alleluia, alleluia. ℣. As the sufferings of Christ abound in us, so also by Christ doth our comfort abound. Alleluia.

Ánima nostra sicut passer erépta est de láqueo venántium. ℣. Láqueus contrítus est et nos liberáti sumus: adjutórium nostrum in nómine Dómini, qui fecit cælum et terram.

Allelúja, allelúja. ℣. Sicut abúndant passiónes Christi in nobis, ita et per Christum abúndat consolátio nostra. Allelúja.

After Septuagesima, the Alleluia is replaced by the following Tract:

TRACT. *Ps 125: 5-6*

THEY that sow in tears shall reap in joy. ℣. Going they went and wept, casting their seeds. ℣. But coming they shall come with joyfulness, carrying their sheaves.

Qui séminant in lácrimis, in gáudio metent. ℣. Eúntes ibant et flebant, mitténtes sémina sua. ℣. Veniéntes autem vénient cum exsultatióne, portántes manípulos suos.

In Paschal-time, the Gradual and Tract are replaced by the Greater Alleluia:

GREATER ALLELUIA. *II Cor. 1: 5 & Ex 15: 11*

ALLELUIA, alleluia. ℣. As the sufferings of Christ abound in us, so also by Christ doth our comfort abound. Alleluia. ℣. Glorious is God in His saints: marvelous in majesty, doing wonderful things. Alleluia.

Allelúja, allelúja. ℣. Sicut abúndant passiónes Christi in nobis, ita et per Christum abúndat consolátio nostra. Allelúja. ℣. Gloriósus Deus in Sanctis suis: mirábilis in majestáte, fáciens prodígia. Allelúja.

GOSPEL. *Lk 6: 17-23* *At that time...*

In illo témpore: Descéndens Jesus de monte, stetit in loco campéstri, et turba discipulórum ejus, et multitúdo copiósa plebis ab omni Judǽa, et Jerúsalem, et marítima, et Tyri, et Sidónis, qui vénerant, ut audírent eum, et sanaréntur a languóribus suis. Et qui vexabántur a spirítibus immúndis curabántur. Et omnis turba quærébat eum tángere: quia virtus de illo exíbat, et sanábat omnes. Et ipse, elevátis óculis in discípulos suos, dicébat: Beáti páuperes: quia vestrum est regnum Dei. Beáti, qui nunc esurítis: quia saturabímini. Beáti, qui nunc fletis: quia ridébitis. Beáti éritis, cum vos óderint hómines, et cum separáverint vos, et exprobráverint, et ejécerint nomen vestrum tamquam malum, propter Fílium hóminis. Gaudéte in illa die, et exsultáte: ecce enim merces vestra multa est in cælo.

OMING DOWN from the mountain, Jesus stood on a level place; a multitude of His disciples was there, and a great gathering of the people from all Judaea, and Jerusalem, and the sea-coast of Tyre and Sidon. These had come there to listen to Him, and to be healed of their diseases; and those who were troubled by unclean spirits were also cured; so that all the multitude was eager to touch Him, because power went out from Him, and healed them all. And He, lifting up his eyes on His disciples, said, Blessed are ye poor, for yours is the kingdom of God. Blessed are ye that hunger now, for you shall be filled. Blessed are ye that weep now, for you shall laugh. Blessed shall you be when men shall hate you, and when they shall separate you, and shall reproach you, and cast out your name as evil, for the Son of man's sake: be glad in that day and rejoice, for behold, your reward is great in Heaven.

OFFERTORY. *Wis 3: 6*

Tamquam aurum in fornáce probávit illos Dóminus, et quasi holocáusti hóstiam accépit illos.

AS GOLD IN THE FURNACE the Lord hath proved them, and as a victim of a holocaust He hath received them.

SECRET.

Immaculátam Hóstiam fac nos, Dómine, méntibus tibi puris offérre, quam sanctis Martýribus tuis illibátus vitæ candor et juge mortificatiónis stúdium dapem suavíssimam efficiébant. Per Dominum.

O Lord, grant that we may offer to Thee with pure minds the immaculate Host which a spotless purity of life and continual desire for mortification rendered to Thy blessed Martyrs a most delightful banquet. Through our Lord.

SECRET. *Commemoration of Sts. Cyprian & Justina.*

Múnera tibi, Dómine, nostræ devotiónis offérimus: quæ et pro tuórum tibi grata sint honóre justórum, et nobis salutária, te miseránte, reddántur. Per Dominum.

We offer Thee, O Lord, the gifts of our devotion; may they, through Thy mercy, be rendered both pleasing unto Thee, for the honor of Thy just ones, and profitable for our salvation. Through our Lord.

℣. Per ómnia sǽcula sæculórum.

℟. Amen.

℣. World without end.

℟. Amen.

℣. The Lord be with you.
℟. And with thy spirit.
℣. Lift up your hearts.
℟. We have lifted them up unto the Lord.
℣. Let us give thanks to the Lord our God.
℟. It is meet and just.

℣. Dóminus vobíscum.
℟. Et cum spíritu tuo.
℣. Sursum corda.
℟. Habémus ad Dóminum.
℣. Grátias agámus Dño Deo nostro.
℟. Dignum et justum est.

COMMON PREFACE.

WORTHY and right it is in truth, apt it is and saving, that at all times and places we should thank thee: O holy Lord, Father almighty, eternal God; through Christ our Lord. Through Whom the angels praise, the dominations adore, the powers, trembling with awe, worship Thy majesty: Which the heavens, and the forces of heaven, together with the blessed seraphim, joyfully do magnify. And do Thou command that it be permitted to our lowliness to join with them in confessing Thee and unceasingly to repeat:

VERE DIGNUM ET JUSTUM est, æquũ et salutáre, nos tibi semper et ubíque grátias ágere: Dñe sancte, Pater omnípotens, ætérne Deus, per Christũ Dñm nostrũ. Per quẽ majestátẽ tuã laudant Ángeli, adórant Dominatiónes, tremunt Potestátes. Cæli cælorúmque Virtútes, ac beáta Séraphim, sócia exsultatióne concélebrant. Cũ quibus et nostras voces ut admítti júbeas, deprecámur, súpplici confessióne dicéntes:

The following may also be used — cf. QUO MAGIS (22 feb 2020).

PREFACE OF THE MARTYRS. *Ad libitum.*

WORTHY and right it is in truth, apt it is and saving, that at all times and places we should thank thee: O Lord, Father holy, God almighty and eternal; For the blood of the blessed Martyrs—***John, Isaac, and their companions***—shed in confession of thy name, and following Christ's example, gives testimony of those thy wonders by which thou raisest strength to its height from frailty, and scanty force thou bracest to prepare for witness: through Christ our Lord. Through him to thy majesty Angels give praise, Dominions make obeisance, where Powers thrill with awe. Heaven and the Virtues of heaven, with the blessed Seraphim, join in keeping festival with kindred revelry. Together with these, we pray, bid thou our utterance also be blended, in humble confession of praise declaiming:

VERE DIGNUM ET JUSTUM est, æquũ et salutáre, nos tibi semper et ubíque grátias ágere: Dñe, sancte Pater, omnípotens ætérne Deus; Quóniam beatórum mártyrum ***Joánnis Isaáci eorúmque sociórum*** pro confessióne nóminis tui, ad imitatiónẽ Christi, sanguis effúsus tua mirabília maniféstat, quibus pérficis in fragilitáte virtútẽ, et vires infírmas ad testimóniũ róboras, per Christũ Dñm nostrũ. Per quẽ majestátẽ tuã laudant Ángeli, adórant Dominatiónes, tremunt Potestátes. Cæli cælorúmque Virtútes, ac beáta Seraphĩ, sócia exsultatióne concélebrant. Cum quibus et nostras voces ut admítti júbeas, deprecámur, súpplici confessióne dicéntes:

SANCTUS, SANCTUS, SANCTUS, etc.

COMMUNION. *Philip 1: 20-21*

Magnificábitur Christus in córpore meo, sive per vitam sive per mortem: mihi enim vívere Christus est et mori lucrum. (Job 13: 15a, 16) ℣. Étiam si occíderit me, in ipso sperábo. Et ipse erit Salvátor meus: non enim véniet in conspéctu ejus omnis hypócrita.

CHRIST shall be magnified in my body, whether it be by life or by death: for to me, to live is Christ, and to die is gain. ℣. *Though He slay me, yet will I trust in Him. And He shall be my Savior: for no hypocrite shall come before His presence.*

POSTCOMMUNION.

Fórtium pane reféctis tríbue nobis, omnípotens Deus: ut, sicut sancti Mártyres tui Joánnes, Isaácus eorúmque Sócii, eódem roboráti, ánimam suam pro frátribus pónere non dubitárunt; ita nos, alter altérius ónera portántes, próximos nostros ópere et veritáte diligámus. Per Dominum.

O almighty God, we are refreshed by the Food of the valiant. When Thy holy martyrs John, Isaac, and their companions were strengthened by this same Bread, they did not hesitate to lay down their own lives for their brethren; may we also bear one another's burdens and love our neighbors with an effective and sincere charity. Through our Lord.

POSTCOMMUNION. *Commemoration of Sts. Cyprian & Justina.*

Præsta nobis, quæsumus, Dómine: intercedéntibus sanctis Martýribus tuis Cypriáno et Justína; ut, quod ore contíngimus, pura mente capiámus. Per Dominum.

Grant us, we beseech Thee, O Lord, by the intercession of Thy holy martyrs, Cyprian and Justina, that what we touch with our lips we may receive with a pure heart. Through our Lord.

ETIAM SI OCCIDERIT ME,
SPERABO IN IPSO
(Job 13:15)

✠

HYMNS FOR THE TRADITIONAL MASS

ONE WITH HERSELF • Pope Benedict XVI said the continued use of the *Missale Vetustum* is important because the Catholic Church must be "one with herself inwardly, one with her own past." Those who study Church history discover that sacred music—while always valued highly—was not always utilized the same way. For instance, in past centuries the pipe organ would sometimes "replace" the singers (*alternatim*). At Low Mass in certain localities, organists played throughout the entire Mass, even during the Consecration. In the missions of North America, the various tribes were allowed to sing the *Ordinarium Missae* in the vernacular: Mohawk, Huron, Algonquin, and so on.

THE DISTANT PAST • Well over two centuries ago, the Preface to *Hymns for the Use of the Catholic Church in the United States of America* (Baltimore, 1807) spoke about the importance of "singing of the praises of God and of the Lamb." Specifically, that book—most likely the work of Archbishop John Carroll (d. 1815)—declared: "It cannot be doubted but that the most proper time for this holy exercise [*singing*] is when the faithful meet together in Church; and especially when the Lamb that was slain on the cross for the redemption of the world, comes down on our altars, and there continues to offer himself for us to his heavenly Father." Going back another two centuries, in a *Roman Catholic Primer* (1599AD) published in Antwerp, we discover a remarkable statement by the Catholic publisher (Richard Verstegan): "Notwithstanding the difficulty, these hymns have been so turned into English meter that they may be sung unto the same tunes in English that they bear in Latin." Going back five centuries earlier still, we have seen (cf. page 276) how the ancient hymns were translated into the vernacular (Anglo-Saxon) circa 1053AD.

THE MORE RECENT PAST • Before the Second Vatican Council, hymns were regularly sung during Low Mass. The *Christ the King Hymnal* (1954 IMPRIMATUR) provides English songs for the Ordinary of the Mass and explains when each should be sung. During the *Glória in excélsis*, it provides "Let Glory In The Highest." During the *Credo in unum Deum*, it provides "My God, I Believe." It provides songs to be sung during the Introit, Offertory, Sanctus, Elevation, and so forth. Nor was this an American phenomenon. For example, the *Crown of Jesus Roman Catholic Hymnal* (London, 1864) provides songs to be sung throughout the Mass: during the Introit, during the *Confiteor*, during the Canon, and so forth. Further examples of Roman Catholic hymnals which explicitly instruct the congregation to sing the Ordinary of the Mass in the vernacular include: *Mass Hymns by Father Thomas Seed* (1906); *Catholic Hymnal* by Father Gregory Ould (1910); *Holy Cross Hymnal* by Cardinal O'Connell of Boston (1915); *New Saint Basil Hymnal* (1958).

Bad Traditions • Much of what is found in these books will strike "traditional" Catholics as grotesque. For example, Father Ould calls the Creed a "hymn" and replaces it with a *recto tono* recitation of the Apostles' Creed. (He does the same thing for the *Pater Noster*.) Father Seed replaces the *Aspérges Me* with a metrical hymn in English. There are even "hymns" to be sung during the Sign of the Cross and Final Blessing. *Caecilia Magazine of Catholic Church Music* (1937) explained as follows: "During a Low Mass, there is usually time for four hymns—one from the beginning of Mass up to (or through) the Gospel, but certainly to be finished by (or before) the end of the Gospel Reading, so as not to interfere with (or delay) the making of announcements or the preaching of the sermon. A second hymn can be started at the *Credo*; another after the Elevation, and the last one during Communion, to end with the last Gospel for the prayers after Mass."

In Our Own Times • Different countries have different customs vis-à-vis vernacular hymnody. Speaking in general, processional and recessional hymns sung in the vernacular are always allowed everywhere. At Low Mass, especially for school children, vernacular hymns are sometimes sung during Offertory and Communion. When it comes to High Mass, the usual custom is for no vernacular to be used (except before and after Mass). On the other hand, Pope Pius XII specifically allowed vernacular hymns at the High Mass—cf. §14a of *De Musica Sacra* (1958). It must be remembered that ***it is impossible to return fully*** to the preconciliar practice because until 1961 Holy Communion was usually not distributed during Mass (although such a thing was always possible *theoretically*). In an effort to quash the practice of distributing Communion outside of Mass—or while Mass was going on!—the 1961 *Code of Rubrics* (§502) declared "the proper time to distribute Communion" to be after the Celebrant receives, and stipulated that it was "altogether unbecoming" for another priest to distribute Communion "at the same Altar at which Mass is actually being celebrated." To summarize: nothing forbids the singing of vernacular hymnody during a High Mass. Our editorial committee believes that singing dignified hymns towards the end of Communion (the antiphon having been sung in Latin) is a praiseworthy practice which assists the faithful in their worship of Almighty God. Indeed, Bishop Urban Sagstetter issued a decree in 1565AD saying "a hymn or psalm should be sung in the vernacular" after Communion to help the devotion of the faithful.

Latin Mass Hymnals • Parishes seeking a hymnal for the Extraordinary Form should consider *The Saint Jean de Brébeuf Hymnal*. Named in honor of one of the greatest saints of North America, this Catholic hymnal stands alone—compared to other Catholic hymnals—***since it does not mimic*** or "build upon" Protestant models. The last time anything comparable was brought to fruition was eighty years ago, when the *New Westminster Hymnal* was created by Monsignor Ronald Knox, Dom Gregory Murray, and several other experts. But the *Brébeuf Hymnal* is much more expansive, elegant, and user-friendly than that book (whose creation was interrupted by World War II). The Brébeuf pew edition is 932 pages; the organist edition fills three volumes; and the choral supplement—which for the first time in history notates each verse for the singer—is 1,292 pages. Moreover, about 800 videos have been created (with hundreds more forthcoming), available online for free, which teach volunteer choir members the SATB parts to these marvelous hymns.

WISDOM FROM FORTESCUE • In 1913, Father Adrian Fortescue wrote the following with regard to the ancient Latin hymns of the Catholic Church:

> Our old Latin hymns are immeasurably more beautiful than any others ever composed. Other religious bodies take all their best hymns in translations from us. It would be a disgrace if we Catholics were the only people who did not appreciate what is our property. And, from every point of view, we of the old Church cannot do better than sing to God as our fathers sang to him during all the long ages behind us. Nor shall we find a better expression of Catholic piety than these words, hallowed by centuries of Catholic use, fragrant with the memory of the saints who wrote them in that golden age when practically all Christendom was Catholic.

The *Saint Jean de Brébeuf Hymnal* (2018) provides superb English translations—paired with dignified, memorable, robust melodies congregations love to sing—for precisely the hymns praised by Father Fortescue in that 1913 quotation. These English translations were created by ***Catholic priests and bishops*** such as Caswall, Fitzpatrick, Popplewell, Knox, Fortescue, Husenbeth, Wallace, Schrader, Hopkins, Bagshawe, Aylward, Henry, and Southwell. A partial list of the ancient hymns included in the *Brébeuf Hymnal* would include:

> *Christe Redemptor Omnium; Salve Regina; Salve Caput Cruentatum; Adeste Fideles; Die Parente Temporum; Ex More Docti Mystico; Vexilla Regis Prodeunt; Tantum Ergo; Aeterne Rex Altissime; Auctor Beate Saeculi; Lavacra Puri Gurgitis; Aurora Caelum Purpurat; Anima Christi; Clarum Decus Jejunii; O Filii Et Filiae; Veni Creator Spiritus; Audi Benigne Conditor; Hymnum Canamus Gloriae; Qui Procedis Ab Utroque; Mater Facta Sed Intacta; Adoro Te Devote Latens Deitas; O Gloriosa Virginum; De Profundis Exclamantes; Summi Largitor Praemii; O Amor Quam Ecstaticus; Consors Paterni Luminis; Rebus Creatis Nil Egens; Corde Natus Ex Parentis; Regina Caeli Laetare; O Sola Magnarum Urbium; Regina Caeli Jubila; Non Abluunt Lymphae Deum; Urbs Jerusalem Beata; Nunc Sancte Nobis Spiritus; O Salutaris Hostia; O Sanctissima; Quicumque Certum Quaeritis; Pendens In Crucis Cornibus; O Sol Salutis Intimis; Rex Gloriose Martyrum; O Splendor Aeterni Patris; Omni Die Dic Mariae; Panis Angelicus; Per Te Mundus Laetabundus; Placare Christe Servulis; Quem Terra Pontus Sidera; Quicumque Christum Quaeritis; Rex Sempiterne Caelitum; Salutis Humanae Sator; Salve Mundi Domina; Aeterna Caeli Gloria; Agnoscat Omne Saeculum; Alto Ex Olympi Vertice; Amor Jesu Dulcissime; Salve Regina Caelitum; Sancti Venite; Urbs Sion Aurea Patria Lactea; Splendor Paternae Gloriae; Stabat Mater Dolorosa; Summi Parentis Filio; Surrexit Christus Hodie; Te Deum Laudamus; Te Gestientem Gaudiis; Te Saeculorum Principem; Veni Sancte Spiritus; Veni Veni Emmanuel; Ad Cenam Agni Providi; Crudelis Herodes Deum; Ad Preces Nostras Deitatis; Creator Alme Siderum; Verbum Supernum Prodiens; Victimae Paschali Laudes; Victis Sibi Cognomina; Vita Sanctorum Decus Angelorum; Vox Clara Ecce Intonat; Gloria Laus; Hoste Dum Victo Triumphans; Gloriosi Salvatoris; En Clara Vox Redarguit; Hostis Herodes Impie; In Dulci Jubilo; Instantis Adventum Dei; Jam Desinant Suspiria; Jesu Nostra Redemptio; Jesu Redemptor Omnium; Adesto Pater Domine; Jordanis Oras Praevia; O Pater Sancte Mitis Atque Pie; Jam Christe Sol Justitiae; Aurora Lucis Rutilat; Ave Vivens Hostia; Veni Redemptor Gentium; Mundus Effusis Redemptus; Puer Natus Est Nobis; Laudes Creaturarum; A Solis Ortus Cardine; Lux Alma Jesu Mentium; Ad Regias Agni Dapes; Caelestis Urbs Jerusalem; Conditor Alme Siderum; O Esca Viatorum; Angularis Fundamentum; Ave Maris Stella; Pange Lingua Gloriosi.*